FUNDAMENTAL RIGHTS IN EUROPE

FUNDAMENTAL RIGHTS IN EUROPE

The European Convention on Human Rights and its Member States, 1950–2000

edited by
Professor Robert Blackburn
Professor of Constitutional Law, King's College, University of London
and
Dr Jörg Polakiewicz
Legal Advice Department and Treaty Office, Council of Europe

OXFORD
UNIVERSITY PRESS

Great Clarendon Street, Oxford OX2 6DP

Oxford University Press is a department of the University of Oxford.
It furthers the University's objective of excellence in research, scholarship,
and education by publishing worldwide in

Oxford New York

Athens Auckland Bangkok Bogotá Buenos Aires Cape Town
Chennai Dar es Salaam Delhi Florence Hong Kong Istanbul Karachi
Kolkata Kuala Lumpur Madrid Melbourne Mexico City Mumbai Nairobi
Paris São Paulo Shanghai Singapore Taipei Tokyo Toronto Warsaw

with associated companies in Berlin Ibadan

Published in the United States
by Oxford University Press Inc., New York

First published 2001

British Library Cataloguing in Publication Data
Data available

Library of Congress Cataloging in Publication Data
Fundamental rights in Europe: the European Convention on Human Rights and its member
states, 1950–2000 / edited by Robert Blackburn and Jörg Polakiewicz.
p. cm.
Includes bibliographical references and index.
1. Convention for the Protection of Human Rights and Fundamental Freedoms (1950).
2. Human rights—Europe. I. Blackburn, Robert, 1952– . II. Polakiewicz, Jörg.
KJC5132.F86 2001 341.4′81′094—dc21 2001036818

ISBN 0–19–924348–4

1 3 5 7 9 10 8 6 4 2

Typeset by Hope Services (Abingdon) Ltd
Printed in Great Britain
on acid-free paper by
Biddles Ltd., Guildford and King's Lynn

CONTENTS

Preface by the Editors ix
Foreword by the President of the European Court of Human Rights xiv
The Contributing Authors xvi
Table of ECHR Cases xxv
Table of Legislation and Treaties xxxvii

PART I—Introductory: International and Comparative Aspects of the ECHR and its Member States

1 The Institutions and Processes of the Convention 3
Robert Blackburn
2 The Status of the Convention in National Law 31
Jörg Polakiewicz
3 The Execution of Judgments of the European Court of Human Rights 55
Jörg Polakiewicz
4 Current Developments, Assessment, and Prospects 77
Robert Blackburn

PART II—The Effect of the ECHR on the Legal and Political Systems of Member States

5 AUSTRIA 103
Hannes Tretter
6 BELGIUM 167
Silvio Marcus-Helmons and Philippe Marcus-Helmons
7 BULGARIA 191
Alexander Arabadjiev
8 CYPRUS 217
Andreas Nicolas Loizou
9 CZECH REPUBLIC 241
Dalibor Jílek and Mahulena Hofmann
10 DENMARK 259
Peter Germer
11 ESTONIA 277
Rait Maruste
12 FINLAND 289
Allan Rosas

13 FRANCE 313
Catherine Dupré
14 GERMANY 335
Andreas Zimmermann
15 GREECE 355
Krateros Ioannou
16 HUNGARY 383
Hanna Bokor-Szegö and Mónika Weller
17 ICELAND 399
Gudrun Gauksdóttir
18 IRELAND 423
Donncha O'Connell
19 ITALY 475
Enzo Meriggiola
20 LITHUANIA 503
Vilenas Vadapalas
21 LUXEMBOURG 531
Dean Spielmann
22 MALTA 559
Joseph Said Pullicino
23 NETHERLANDS 595
Leo F. Zwaak
24 NORWAY 625
Erik Møse
25 POLAND 657
Andrew Drzemczewski and Marek Antoni Nowicki
26 PORTUGAL 681
João Madureira
27 ROMANIA 711
Renate Weber
28 RUSSIA 731
Maxim Ferschtman
29 SLOVAKIA 755
Milan Blaško
30 SLOVENIA 781
Arne Mavčič
31 SPAIN 809
Guillermo Escobar Roca
32 SWEDEN 833
Iain Cameron

33 SWITZERLAND 855
Marco Borghi
34 TURKEY 879
Yasemin Özdek and Emine Karacaoğlu
35 UKRAINE 915
Victor Potapenko and Pavlo Pushkar
36 THE UNITED KINGDOM 935
Robert Blackburn

Appendices
a) Speech by the Secretary General at the Commemorative Ceremony for the 50th Anniversary of the European Convention on Human Rights 1009
b) Resolutions and Declaration for the Future at the European Ministerial Conference, 4 November 2000 1012

Select Bibliography 1020
Index 1039

PREFACE

On 4 November 2000 the Council of Europe celebrated the half-centenary of its Convention for the Protection of Human Rights and Freedoms. Few would have believed it possible on the day the Convention was signed in Rome by the foreign ministers of its founding member states[1] that by the turn of the century the Convention would have become the most effective and influential international human rights instrument in the world. Over the last twenty-five years especially, the Convention has emerged as 'a benchmark for the democratic states of Europe . . . providing a basis for a European public law'.[2] Few, too, could have dared hope after the horrors of the Second World War and the partition of Europe which immediately followed that by 2000 the scale of the Council of Europe's activities would have grown to embrace forty-one European member states containing 800 million people, all of whom are guaranteed in law the protection of the fundamental rights and freedoms set out in the Convention. Sir Winston Churchill's dream is now close to the point of reality:

> this Council when created must eventually embrace the whole of Europe, and all the main branches of the European family must someday be partners in it.[3]

This book chronicles the huge achievements of the Council of Europe and its human rights work conducted through the European Convention on Human Rights over the past fifty years. The primary purpose of the book is to provide a detailed study of the practical effect of the Convention upon and within the domestic legal and governmental systems of thirty-two of its member countries.[4] In the book's introductory section, the editors discuss the international and comparative aspects of the Convention's work, giving: an account of the institutions and processes of the Convention and its enforcement machinery in Strasbourg; a comparative analysis of the status of the Convention in the domestic law of member states; an explanation of how the judgments of the

[1] Belgium, Denmark, France, Germany, Iceland, Ireland, Italy, Luxembourg, the Netherlands, Norway, Turkey, and the United Kingdom were the first states to sign the ECHR on 4 November 1950, followed by Greece and Sweden on 28 November. A full list of member states together with the dates of their signature and ratification of the ECHR is given in chapter 1 below at page 12.

[2] F. G. Jacobs, 'Human Rights in Europe', Paul Sieghart Memorial Lecture 1992, British Institute of Human Rights.

[3] Speech to Royal Institute of International Affairs, 15 February 1950.

[4] Countries not included in the book are either small populations with little human rights case-law or recently joined members with limited Convention experience, except where the member state is of special importance or topical interest.

Court of Human Rights are executed; and an assessment and commentary on current developments and future prospects, such as the future interrelationship of the Convention with the European Union (all of whose members are parties to the Convention). There follow thirty-two chapters each dealing with an individual member state belonging to the Council of Europe, focusing on the impact of the Convention within its domestic national affairs over the period since the country's signature and ratification of the Convention. With one exception,[5] each of the thirty-two contributors is a national of the member state about which he or she is writing, as well as being a distinguished legal practitioner, jurisconsult, or judicial office-holder in their country.

The chapters in the book follow a broadly common structure suggested by the editors. (1) In the chapters' opening sections the national context in which their country's membership of the Convention was entered into is explained, together with any special features of their traditional legal and political ideas or practices with respect to the protection of civil liberties and human rights. (2) The precise status of the Convention within the member state is explained and discussed, especially the extent to which the Convention and jurisprudence of the Strasbourg court has been regarded as a source of law or authority, its relationship with the constitutional law of the state, and, where applicable, the method by which domestic incorporation of the Convention has taken place.[6] (3) Major parliamentary or administrative developments with regard to scrutiny or enforcement procedures connected to the Convention are identified and discussed. (4) A selection of leading human rights cases is discussed, starting from the individual grievance and exhaustion of domestic remedies through to its resolution in Strasbourg and (where a violation has been held by the Court of Human Rights to exist) the positive remedial action taken by the government or legislative body of the member state concerned. (5) Finally, contributors offer some reflections on the overall effect of the Convention within their country and consider likely future developments. This suggested formula for the chapters was intended to be treated flexibly, and has been adapted by each contributing author in a manner appropriate to his or her country's conditions or experience of the Convention. For, as is much in evidence in the book, the manner and degree of the Convention's influence within the thirty-two countries has varied substantially depending on a number of factors, such as: whether the country

[5] The author of the chapter on Sweden, Dr Iain Cameron, is a UK citizen but holds a permanent teaching post in Sweden as Professor of International Law at the University of Uppsala.

[6] As at 1 March 2000, the Convention has been or is about to be incorporated into the national legal system of all member states. The United Kingdom was a notable latecomer to incorporation: see chapter 36. Ireland is currently in the process of incorporating the Convention into domestic law, though (unlike the UK) it has its own constitutional bill of rights which was largely drafted on the basis of the Convention's articles: see chapter 18.

concerned already possessed a code of fundamental rights and freedoms in its constitutional law prior to ratification of the Convention; the extent to which international treaties to which a member state is a party, and thus the Convention itself, are given direct internal recognition and effect in the country's domestic administrative and legal affairs; and the length of time since the Convention was ratified by the member state and the right of individual petition granted to its citizens and persons within its borders.

Taken together, the substance of these chapters and their detailed accounts are a powerful testimony to the great success of the European Convention on Human Rights and the machinery in the Council of Europe which supports it. The fiftieth anniversary of the Convention represents a real milestone in its history, taking place as it does against the recent background of major expansion in its membership[7] and a dramatically increased workload, whilst the new full-time Court of Human Rights at Strasbourg enters its third year of business following Protocol No. 11's entry into force on 1 November 1998.[8] The early years of the new millennium will see developments in European human rights law gathering even greater momentum, with little room for mere consolidation or for the enforcement bodies and Court of Human Rights being allowed to rest upon their past success. More than ever, the Convention is being looked to as a major cohesive force for carrying forward the international efforts to help extend and develop democracy and human rights throughout the continent, particularly among the newer member states joining from the former Soviet Communist bloc.

This book has been a long time in the making. Its genesis occurred at two plenary meetings of the National Correspondents (national legal consultants) of the Council of Europe's Directorate of Human Rights held in Strasbourg in 1993 and 1995, both of which events were chaired by Professor Robert Blackburn, the United Kingdom National Correspondent since 1982.[9] This network of National Correspondents or human rights specialists, one drawn from each member state, has been commissioned by the Council of Europe

[7] Membership has almost doubled in just ten years. Ratifications to the Convention since 1990 include Albania (1996), Andorra (1996), Bulgaria (1992), Croatia (1997), the Czech Republic (1992), Estonia (1996), Georgia (1999), Hungary (1992), Latvia (1997), Lithuania (1995), Macedonia (1997), Moldova (1997), Poland (1993), Romania (1993), Russia (1998), Slovakia (1993), Slovenia (1994), and Ukraine (1996). (The formal description adopted by the Council of Europe of 'The Former Yugoslav Republic of' Macedonia is sometimes shortened in this book to Macedonia for reasons of convenience; it is not intended to imply any position on the difference over the name.)

[8] On the changes brought about by Protocol No. 11, see chapter 1 below; and on the sharp increase in the workload of the new Court of Human Rights, see chapter 4 below.

[9] Until 1986 Professor Blackburn acted as United Kingdom National Correspondent in collaboration with the late Anthony McNulty CBE, the former Secretary of the European Commission of Human Rights.

every year since 1982 to prepare reports on the influence of the Convention within their country.[10] These plenary meetings, organized by the Human Rights Information Centre to compare the findings and methodologies of the National Correspondents, appeared to Professor Blackburn to provide an opportunity for a unique collaborative project involving as many as possible of the Council of Europe's member states. Thus, many of the National Correspondents are contributing authors to the book, and most others either work in Strasbourg or are associated in some way with the work of the Council of Europe. This has proved especially advantageous since research and writing about foreign affairs is not easy to arrange from a position within any individual country, both because of the more limited expertise available on matters affecting foreign jurisdictions and legal systems, and because of the practical difficulties inherent in forging a large number of working relationships with persons working abroad.

In 1998 Professor Blackburn invited Dr Jörg Polakiewicz to join him as co-editor, to assist with some of the organizational problems inherent in producing such a large collection, not least with regard to maintaining contact and communication with authors from all around Europe and in matters of translation into English, and also to commission some additional chapters. Their period of editorial work together has been enjoyable and rewarding. The editors warmly thank all the contributors to this book for their helpful and willing co-operation throughout the project and, in the case of the more prompt contributors, their patience in awaiting publication. The editors are indebted to James Lawson, the Director of the Council of Europe's Human Rights Information Centre, for his continuing support throughout this project, and gratefully acknowledge his and his colleagues' help in supplying up-to-date statistics and information as well as permission to reproduce or adapt Council of Europe materials in the tables and illustrations set out in chapter 1. Sir Basil Hall, formerly a member of the European Commission of Human Rights, and Sir Nicolas Bratza, a judge of the European Court of Human Rights, kindly read and offered comments on earlier drafts of chapters 1, 4, and 36. Special thanks are due also to Amy Baker, Barrister of the Middle Temple (England and Wales), for her editorial assistance during 1998–99, particularly in matters of liaison between the numerous participants to the project; and to our publishers at Oxford University Press, especially John Louth and Michael Watson.

[10] The areas for report are: legislation on subject-matter similar to the articles of the Convention; judicial decisions applying or referring to the Convention or of major human rights significance; parliamentary debates or other events concerning the Convention; and bibliographical details of new legal writing (doctrine) on human rights.

The book aims to state the situation as at 1 March 2000, with some later events being taken into account at proof stage. Each of the contributing authors on the member states considers the influence of the Convention since the dates of signature and ratification by their national government. The length of time covered by the individual chapters therefore varies considerably, and this is reflected in the varying length of chapters. So too, the lengthy preparation of the book means that some original versions of chapters were written much earlier than others. In these cases, chapters have been updated within the body of the text or by way of footnotes or postscripts, depending on the structure of the original draft and/or the extent and importance of the new or current development in the member state concerned.

Any views expressed in the book are personal and are not in any way the responsibility of the Council of Europe or the official or non-governmental bodies of which the editors or contributing authors may be members or office-holders.

R.B.
J.P.
London and Strasbourg

FOREWORD

As the European Convention on Human Rights enters its fifty-first year, just two years after the entry into force of a major reform of the Convention mechanism, the European Court of Human Rights, now the sole component of the Convention enforcement machinery, finds itself entrusted with the role of final arbiter in the application and interpretation of an instrument whose reach covers a geographical area stretching from Reykjavik to Vladivostok, from the Atlantic to the Pacific, an area with a population of some 800 million. At the same time the Convention's importance has never been greater, as the cornerstone in the programme of consolidation of democracy and the rule of law throughout the greater Europe. The reinforcement of the judicial character of the system, with the entry into force of Protocol No. 11 to the Convention which removed the hitherto optional character of the right of individual petition and the jurisdiction of the Court, reflected the recognition by the Contracting States of the role of international judicial protection.

The subsidiary nature of the Convention was acknowledged in the Court's earliest judgments. Since then the Court has consistently stressed that primary responsibility for the protection of human rights falls on the national authorities. This subsidiarity finds its source in both the Convention and the case-law. The requirement of exhaustion of domestic remedies (Article 35), the obligation to provide an effective remedy (Article 13) in the Convention, the doctrine of the margin of appreciation, and the fourth-instance rule in the case-law establish its parameters.

With the extension of the Convention community subsidiarity has acquired even greater significance. The effectiveness of the protection of fundamental rights at domestic level will ultimately determine whether the Convention can rise to the challenges of the new century. There are two sides to this. In Strasbourg the Court must continue to respect the principle of subsidiarity by applying the rule of exhaustion strictly, by concentrating its efforts on its quasi-constitutional role of consolidating the body of Convention law and those cases which contribute to it. In the Contracting States it is the application of the Convention standards by in particular the national courts which gives proper effect to the principle. When national courts not only address Convention issues directly but also apply the Strasbourg case-law, then we can say that the subsidiary system is functioning to its fullest extent and that the Court can fulfil its task as a court, not of last instance, but of last resort.

Academics and practitioners have traditionally played an important role in the understanding of the Convention and its application at national level.

This important volume, with its learned editors and eminent contributors, will add to that tradition. Its specific significance is to focus attention on the relationship between the Convention and the domestic systems, notably the form of incorporation and the impact of the Convention on national law in terms of its application by the national courts and the influence of Strasbourg judgments. The book shows the extent to which the Convention has taken root in the European legal system.

Professor Blackburn and Dr Polakiewicz, and their authors, are to be congratulated, and on behalf of the Court over which I have the honour to preside, thanked for this contribution to the effective operation of the Convention system and therefore to human rights protection throughout the greater Europe.

Luzius Wildhaber
President of the European Court of Human Rights
4 November 2000

THE CONTRIBUTING AUTHORS

Alexander Arabadjiev is a Judge of the Constitutional Court of Bulgaria, having served in that position since the establishment of the Constitutional Court in 1991. He is a former Member of the European Commission of Human Rights.

Robert Blackburn is Professor of Constitutional Law at King's College London. Among his published works are *The Electoral System in Britain* (1995), *The Crown and the Royal Family* (Halsbury's Laws of England, 1998), *Constitutional Reform: The Labour Government's Constitutional Reform Agenda* (co-editor with Raymond Plant, 1999) and *Towards a Constitutional Bill of Rights for the UK* (1999). He is a Governor of the British Institute of Human Rights, and during 1996–2000 founded and directed the Human Rights Incorporation Project at King's College producing specialist research and advice on incorporation of the ECHR into UK domestic law. He has conducted extensive research on the domestic impact of the ECHR on the legislation, judicial decision-making, and parliamentary affairs of member states, and since 1982 has been the UK National Correspondent of the Council of Europe Directorate of Human Rights. He is a Fellow of the Royal Historical Society and a Solicitor of the Supreme Court of England and Wales.

Milan Blaško is a lawyer at the Registry of the European Court of Human Rights and a former Member of the Secretariat of the European Commission of Human Rights.

Hanna Bokor-Szegö is Professor of International Law at the University of Economic Sciences in Budapest (Department of International Relations). She is Scientific Director of the Hungarian Centre for Human Rights Public Foundation and a former President of the Hungarian Branch of the International Law Association. She has published widely on Hungarian and international law, including *New States and International Law* (which won a prize awarded by the Academy of Sciences in 1972) and *The Role of the United Nations in International Legislation* (1978). Between 1964 and 1976 she was a Member of the United Nations Commission on the Status of Women, serving as its President in 1969. She has been a Hungarian delegate at several UNESCO conferences and the Vienna Conferences on the law of treaties, and in 1977–1978 headed the Hungarian delegation to the United Nations Conference on State Succession in matters of treaties. She has been the

Hungarian National Correspondent of the Council of Europe Directorate of Human Rights since 1991.

Marco Borghi is Professor of Constitutional Law at the University of Fribourg (Switzerland) where he directs the Institut Interdisciplinaire d'Ethique et des Droits de l'Homme. He is also Professor at the Universita della Svizzera Italiana, Faculty of Economics, Lugano.

Iain Cameron is Professor in Public International Law at the University of Uppsala. He has published extensively in the fields of international law and constitutional law, particularly on human rights issues. He has acted as Expert Adviser to several Swedish government commissions of inquiry proposing legislation or action in the field of international law. His most recent book is *National Security and the European Convention on Human Rights* (2000).

Andrew Drzemczewski has worked at the Council of Europe since 1985, and is currently Head of the Monitoring Unit of the Directorate of Strategic Planning. He is a graduate of the London School of Economics, the University of California (Berkeley), and the International Institute of Human Rights (Strasbourg). Dr Drzemczewski is a Barrister-at-Law and Member of the Honourable Society of the Middle Temple, London. He is the author of *European Human Rights Convention in Domestic Law: A Comparative Study* (1983, reprinted 1997) and over a hundred articles and case-notes on international and human rights law subjects. He is a legal correspondent for *The Times* newspaper in London, having written over 150 of its Human Rights Law Reports.

Catherine Dupré graduated in 1994 from the University of Montpellier (DEA de Droit Public Français). She obtained her PhD from the European University Institute (Florence) in 1998 for a thesis entitled '*L'importation juridique et la cour constitutionnelle hongroise: L'exemple du droit à la dignité humaine, 1990–1996*'. She is currently a lecturer in law at the University of Birmingham, where she teaches civil liberties and British constitutional law. Her research interests include comparative constitutional law, especially post-Communist transition, human rights, and fundamental rights in the context of constitutional adjudication.

Maxim Ferschtman is a practising lawyer who formerly worked at the Registry of the European Court of Human Rights and in the Council of Europe's monitoring unit.

Gudrun Gauksdóttir has been a lecturer in public international law and human rights at the University of Iceland. She has also delivered lectures at the University of Lund, Sweden, where she is a doctoral candidate in the Faculty of Law.

Peter Germer is Professor of Constitutional Law at Aarhus University. He studied at the University of Copenhagen 1958–1964, where he received a gold medal for a thesis on the law of the European Communites in 1963, and the Candidatus Juris in 1964, after which he graduated at Harvard Law School as Master of Laws in 1969 and Doctor in Laws in 1969. He has been President of the Human Rights Chamber of Bosnia and Herzegovina since 1996, and was formerly Visiting Professor at the Council of Europe in 1973, Danish National Correspondent of the Council of Europe Directorate of Human Rights 1983–1993, Legal Adviser to the Nepal Law Reform Commission 1990–1991, and Legal Adviser to the Estonian Foreign Ministry, 1991–1992. He is the author of several books and numerous articles, including *The Essence of Free Speech* (1973), *Danish Constitutional Law* (2nd edn, 1995), and *An Introduction to International Law* (2nd edn, 1996).

Mahulena Hofmann is Senior Research Fellow at the Max Planck Institute of Comparative Public Law and International Law in Heidelberg, Germany. She is a graduate of Charles University, Prague, where she now teaches international and constitutional law, and in 1984 she successfully defended her doctoral thesis before the Czechoslovak Academy of Sciences. In 1990 she was awarded an Alexander von Humboldt Foundation Scholarship to conduct research at the Max Planck Institute, and between 1997 and 1999 she was a member of the Steering Committee of the research project at the European University, Florence, on 'Eastern Enlargement of the European Union: The Case of the Czech Republic and Slovakia'. She has written widely on aspects of the EU enlargement process and on the constitutional law systems of eastern and central European countries, and is co-author with G. Brunner and P. Hollander of *Verfassungsgerichtsbarkeit in der Tschechischen Republik* (2001).

Krateros Ioannou was a Judge of the Court of Justice of the European Communities until his death in 1999. He was formerly Professor of International Law at the University of Thrace, the Director of the Centre of International and European Economic Law at Thessaloniki, and Honorary Legal Adviser to the Greek Ministry of Foreign Affairs.

Dalibor Jílek is Associate Professor of International Law at Masaryk University in Brno, where he was Vice-Dean for international relations, research, and science 1991–1997, and is now Head of the International and European Law Department. He has also been Head of Department of International Humanitarian Law and National Legal Branches at the

Military University of Ground Forces in Vyškov since 1996. He has been a member of the Permanent Court of Arbitration of the Hague since 1994, a member of the Advisory Committee to the 1995 Framework Convention for the Protection of National Minorities since 1998, and is the Czech Republic National Correspondent of the Council of Europe Directorate of Human Rights. He became Chairman of the Appellate Commission of the Minister of the Interior of the Czech Republic for the Asylum Procedure in 1999. His books (published in Czech) include *Problems of International Responsibility of International Organizations* (1991), *An Introduction to Law of the European Communities* (1992), *The Response of International Law to Mass Refugeehood* (1996), and *Asylum and Refugeehood in International Law* (1997).

Emine Karacaoğlu is a Research Associate of the Faculty of Law, University of Dicle, Diyarbakır, where she lectures on constitutional law. She is currently completing her doctorate on international humanitarian law at the University of İstanbul, having previously graduated with an LLM degree from the University of Nottingham (UK), and BA and MA degrees from the University of Dicle.

Andreas Nicolas Loizou was a Judge at the European Court of Human Rights between 1990 and 1998, and was formerly President of the Supreme Court of Cyprus.

João Madureira is a Legal Adviser in the Office of Documentation and Comparative Law, Attorney-General's Office, Lisbon.

Philippe Marcus-Helmons is a Barrister-at-Law in Brussels, and was formerly Legal Adviser to the Belgian High Commissioner for Refugees between 1992 and 1994.

Silvio Marcus-Helmons is Professor of Law at the Université Catholique de Louvain (Belgium), where he lectures on Public International Law and Human Rights and in 1968 founded the Centre for Human Rights. He is a Docteur en Droit (Université Catholique de Louvain, 1958), a Master of Comparative Jurisprudence (New York University, 1961), and a graduate of the Institute for International Graduate Studies (Geneva, 1963). He has been a Special Adviser to the Belgian Minister of Justice (1965–1968), and a representative of Belgium and of The Holy See at several international conferences. He has been a Visiting Professor at universities in various countries, and has published numerous works, mainly in the field of human rights.

Rait Maruste is a Judge at the European Court of Human Rights, elected in 1998. Formerly he was Chief Justice of the Supreme Court of Estonia between 1992 and 1998, and a Lecturer and Assistant Professor of Law at Tartu University between 1978 and 1992.

Arne Mavčič is Senior Adviser and Head of the Legal Information Centre at the Constitutional Court of the Republic of Slovenia. He is a Visiting Professor of the Maribor Law School, Slovenia, and President of the Board of State Examinations in Justice. He is the Liaison Officer for Slovenia to the European Commission for Democracy through Law (Venice Commission), and is National President of the World Jurist Association for Slovenia. He has written over 140 articles on constitutional law, and his recent books include *Slovenian Constitutional Review: Its Position in the World and its Role in the Transition to a New Democratic System* (1995), *Constitutional Law of Slovenia* (1998), and *The Constitutional Court of the Republic of Slovenia* (1999).

Enzo Meriggiola is President of the Third Civil Chamber of the Italian Supreme Court.

Erik Møse is Vice-President of the International Criminal Tribunal for Rwanda. He was formerly a Judge in the Court of Appeals in Oslo, prior to which he practised as a Supreme Court Barrister, and was the Head of Division in the Ministry of Justice. He participated in the drafting of Protocols Nos. 6 to 11 of the European Convention on Human Rights, and has served as Chairman of several international committees, including the Committee of Experts which drafted the European Torture Convention (1984–1985) and the Council of Europe's Steering Committee for Human Rights (1993–1994). He was chairman of the Committee which in 1993 submitted proposals for the incorporation into Norwegian law of human rights conventions. He is a Lecturer at the University of Oslo and Fellow at the University of Essex, and has published extensively in the field of human rights law.

Marek Antoni Nowicki is a former Member of the European Commission of Human Rights and since July 2000 has been Ombudsperson in Kosovo. He has written widely on issues of European human rights law and its application in Poland.

Donncha O'Connell is the Director of the Irish Council for Civil Liberties, an independent non-governmental organization founded in 1976 which campaigns to promote and defend human rights and civil liberties. He is also a Member of the Faculty of Law at the National University of Ireland, Galway (currently on leave of absence). He continues to teach Human Rights and Equality Law on a part-time basis at Trinity College, Dublin and University

College, Dublin. While based at NUI, Galway he was a Visiting Lecturer at l'Université de Poitiers, France and a Visiting Scholar at Boston College, USA. He writes extensively on human rights issues and occasionally contributes to judicial education programmes organized by the Council of Europe in association with the International Helsinki Federation in Central and Eastern Europe.

Yasemin Özdek is Associate Professor of General Public Law at the Public Administration Institute of Turkey and the Middle East, Ankara, and lectures in the field of human rights law. She has BA, MA, and PhD degrees from the Faculty of Law, University of Ankara, and holds an MA degree from the Deutsche Hochschule für Verwaltungswissenschaften Speyer (Germany). Her most recent book is *International Politics and Human Rights* (Ankara, Öteki Pub., 2000).

Jörg Polakiewicz has worked at the Council of Europe since 1993. After a period spent with the Secretariat of the European Commission for Democracy through Law (Venice Commission), he currently holds the post of Deputy Head of the Council of Europe's Legal Advice Department and Treaty Office. He is a visiting Lecturer at the Europa-Institut of the University of the Saarland in Saarbrücken. From 1986 to 1993 he worked as a Research Fellow at the Max Planck Institute for Comparative Public and International Law in Heidelberg. In addition to numerous articles on public international, European, and constitutional law, he is the author of *Treaty-making in the Council of Europe* (1999) and *The Obligations of States arising from the Judgments of the European Court of Human Rights* (published in German, 1993).

Victor Potapenko is Head of the Department of International Legal Co-operation at the Supreme Court of Ukraine, where he has worked for over fifteen years. He has written widely on human rights issues, and participated in the work of numerous conferences and study sessions on the reform of the system of justice of Ukraine.

Joseph Said Pullicino has been Chief Justice and President of the Constitutional Court, Malta, since 1995. He is Malta's representative on the Council of Europe's Venice Commission for Democracy Through Law. On various occasions he has been appointed by the Venice Commission as rapporteur and has submitted reports and opinions, among which are: *Law of Ukraine: On the Judicial System* (1999), *Control of Internal Security Services* (1998), *Affirmative Action: The Constitutional Court Conference on Equality* (South Africa, 1998), *Constitutional Jurisprudence in the Area of Freedom of Religion and Beliefs* (Warsaw, 1999), *The High Council of Justice under the*

Albanian Constitution (1998), and *Comment on the Bulgarian Judicial System Act as Amended* (1999).

Pavlo Pushkar is a practising lawyer in Kiev. He is an LLM graduate in international law from the University of Nottingham and is currently writing a doctoral thesis at the Kiev Taras Shevchenko University. He also worked as a Head of Division in the Department of International Legal Co-operation, Supreme Court of Ukraine. He has written widely on issues of European human rights law and its application in Ukraine and is a regular participant at seminars and conferences on the subject.

Guillermo Escobar Roca is Professor of Constitutional Law at the University of Alcalá, Madrid. He has been Professor at the University of León and Visitor at the Max Planck Institute for Comparative Public and International Law in Heidelberg. He has published widely in fields of public law, especially in fundamental rights, environmental law, and telecommunications and media law. His books include *La objeción de conciencia en la Constitución española* (1993), *La ordenación constitucional del medio ambiente* (1995), *El estatuto de los periodistas* (2001), and (with Jose Maria Chillon) *La Comisión del Mercado de las Telecomunicaciones* (2001).

Allan Rosas is the Deputy Director General of the Legal Service of the European Commission at Brussels, and was formerly Professor of Law at Abo Akademi University, Finland.

Dean Spielmann is a practising lawyer in Luxembourg, and a member of the Luxembourg Advisory Commission of Human Rights. He holds a *licence en droit* of the Catholic University of Louvain and a Master of Law degree from the University of Cambridge. He is a lecturer at the Centre Universitaire de Luxembourg, and a visiting lecturer at the Université Nancy 2. He has written widely in the fields of human rights, criminal law and procedure, and administrative law. He is Co-Editor of *Annales du droit luxembourgeois* and a Member of the Editorial Boards of *Revue trimestrielle des droits de l'homme* and *Bulletin des droits de l'homme*.

Hannes Tretter is Director of the Ludwig Boltzmann Institute for Human Rights in Vienna, and Assistant Professor at the Institute of State and Administrative Law at the University of Vienna. He is Deputy Director of one of the Human Rights Commissions of the Austrian Human Rights Advisory Council, and Co-Director of the Austrian RAXEN National Focal Point on Racism and Xenophobia. He is Defence Counsel at the Court of Appeal in Vienna and has acted as a Legal Adviser and Counsel in cases brought before the European Court of Human Rights. His main interests are

European human rights protection systems, the guarantee of human rights in Austria, and human rights violations and protection in the Balkans. He is author and editor of many human rights articles and books, including *Die Grundrechte in Österreich* (1998), and 'The implementation of Judgments of the European Court of Human Rights in Austria', in Barkhuysen *et al.* (eds), *The Execution of Strasbourg and Geneva Human Rights Decisions in the National Legal Order* (1999).

Vilenas Vadapalas is Professor of Law and Chairman of the Department of International and Comparative Law at Vilnius University, Sauletekio. He has worked as a lawyer in the secretariat of the European Court of Human Rights, and is Legal Adviser to the Ministry of Foreign Affairs regarding Lithuania's preparations for accession to the European Union.

Renate Weber is Attorney-at-Law at the Bucharest Bar, and an *ad hoc* Judge at the European Court of Human Rights. She is Lecturer in International Human Rights Law at the National School for Political Studies and Administration in Bucharest, and the chair of the Open Society Foundation in Romania. She was formerly co-chair of the Romanian Helsinki Committee 1994–1999, Executive Director of the Centre for Human Rights (Bucharest) 1993–1999, and Vice-President of the International Helsinki Federation for Human Rights 1994–1996. She is Editor of the journals *International Studies* and *The Romanian Review for Human Rights* and has written widely on the Romanian legal system, the implementation of international human rights by the Romanian courts, and the protection of minorities and human rights in Romanian law.

Mónika Weller is Legal Adviser in the Ministry of Justice, Office of Agent for the Hungarian government. She has worked for the Hungarian Centre for Human Rights since 1990, and is currently completing her doctorate on European human rights law. She was a Research Fellow in the Institute for Legal and Administrative Sciences of the Hungarian Academy of Sciences until 1997.

Andreas Zimmermann, Privatdozent, Dr jur (Heidelberg), LLM (Harvard) is a Research Fellow at the Max Planck Institute for Comparative Public and Public International Law (Heidelberg) and Privatdozent at the Law Faculty of the University of Heidelberg. He is currently a Visiting Professor at the University of Hannover. He was a Member of and Legal Adviser to the German delegation during the negotiations leading to the adoption of the Rome Statute of the International Criminal Court. His publications include *Das neue Grundrecht auf Asyl* (1994), 'The Right to a Fair Trial in Situations of Emergency and the Question of Emergency Courts', in D. Weissbrodt and

R. Wolfrum (eds), *The Right to a Fair Trial* (1997), 'The Creation of a Permanent International Criminal Court', *Max-Planck-Yearbook of United Nations Law* (1998), *Staatennachfolge in Verträge* (2000), and *Dispute Settlement: Texts and Materials* (2nd edn, 2001).

Leo Zwaak is a Lecturer at Utrecht University and Senior Researcher at the Netherlands Institute of Human Rights (SIM). He has written extensively on European human rights law and the legal protection of human rights in the Netherlands, and his many publications include *Digest of Strasbourg Case-Law relating to the European Convention on Human Rights*, *International Human Rights Procedures: Petitioning the ECHR, CCPR and CERD* (1991), *Law and Practice of the European Convention on Human Rights and the European Social Charter* (with Donna Gomien and David Harris, 1996) and *Theory and Practice of the European Convention on Human Rights* (with P. van Dijk and G. van Hoof *et al.*, 3rd edn, 1998).

TABLE OF ECHR CASES

A v United Kingdom (1980) 984
A and Others v Denmark (1996) 271, 272–3, 274
Abdoella v Netherlands (1992) 612
Abdulaziz, Cabales and Balkandali v United Kingdom (1985) 33, 286, 348, 972, 1002
Acquaviva v France (1995) 325
Adolf v Austria (1982) 140, 142
Aerts v Belgium (1998) 184
Ahmed v Austria (1996) 119, 129, 378–9
Ahmet Sadık v Greece 1653 ....35, 52
Ahmut v Netherlands (1996) 123, 616–17
Airey v Ireland (1979) 426, 437, 449, 466
Akdivar and Others v Turkey (1997) 57, 60, 732
Albert and Le Compte v Belgium (1983) 181, 817
Allenet de Ribemont (1996) 65
Andreassen v Norway (1995) 651, 653
Andronicou and Constantinou v Cyprus (1997) 235–6
Anne-Marie Andersson v Sweden (1997) 848
Artico v Italy (1980) 499, 690, 795
Artner v Austria (1992) 145
Asch v Austria (1991) 112, 145
Assenov and Others v Bulgaria (1998) 209, 210, 211, 212
Austria v Italy (1961) 498
Autronic v Switzerland (1990) 873, 875
Aydin v Turkey (1997) 33, 732

B v Austria (1990) 72, 131, 133, 797, 798
B v France (1992) 328
B v UK (1983) 644
Baader, Meinhof, Grundmann v FRG (1975) 349
Baraona v Portugal (1987) 695
Barbera, Messegue and Jabardo v Spain (1988) 52, 68–9, 824
Barford v Denmark (1989) 82
Barfuss v Czech Republic (2000) 258
Beaumartin v France (1994) 327, 555
Beer and Regan v Germany (1999) 351
Beldjoudi v France (1992) 328–9

Belgian Linguistic v Belgium (1968) 57, 453, 542
Belilos v Denmark (1988) 267, 861, 862, 865, 872
Bellet v France (1995) 328
Bendenoun v France (1994) 326
Benham v United Kingdom (1996) 71
Benkessiouer v France (1998) 326
Benthem v Netherlands (1985) 607, 621
Berrehab v Netherlands (1988) 286, 603, 616
Bloch v France (1997) 326
Boddaert v Belgium (1992) 185
Bonisch v Austria (1985) 61, 141
Botten v Norway (1996) 651, 653
Bouamar v Belgium (1988) 187, 817
Bouchelkia v France (1997) 329
Boughanemi v France (1996) 329
Boyle and Rice v United Kingdom (1988) 981
Brandstetter v Austria (1991) 112, 141, 143
Brannigan and McBride (1993) 983
Brežný and Brežný v Slovakia (1996) 759, 773
Bricmont v Belgium (1989) 183, 793
British American Tobacco Company Ltd v Netherlands (1995) 610
Brogan v United Kingdom (1988) 623, 645, 732, 972, 975, 982
Brozicek v Italy (1989) 56, 491, 500–1
Brumarescu v Romania (1999) 724
Bulut v Austria (1996) 135, 138
Bunkate v Netherlands (1993) 612

C v Belgium (1996) 185
C v Ireland (1961) 445
C v Ireland (1979) 447
Campbell and Cosans v United Kingdom (1992) 72, 972, 976, 977
Campbell and Fell v United Kingdom (1984) 33, 981
Can v Austria (1985) 112, 891
Casado Coca v Spain (1994) 823
Castillo Algar v Spain (1998) 57
Cazenave de la Roche (1998) 325
CDI Holding AG v Slovakia (1996) 777
Ceský v Czech Republic (2000) 257
Chorherr v Austria (1993) 81, 121, 130
Christian Association Jehovah's Witnesses v Bulgaria (1998) 206, 212
Chrysostomos and Others v Turkey (1990) 34, 231

Clooth v Belgium (1991) 57, 60, 62, 183
Colozza v Italy (1985) 488–9, 549
Connie Zammit v Malta (1991) 591
Cooke v Austria (2000) 144
Corigliano v Italy (1982) 499
Costello-Roberts v United Kingdom (1993) 970, 977
Couez v France (1998) 326
Croke v Ireland (2000) 471
Cruz Varas and Others v Sweden (1991) 51, 852
Cyprus v United Kingdom (1956) 367
Cyprus v United Kingdom (1957) 367
Cyprus v Turkey (1979) 896

Dalban v Romania (1999) 725
De Becker v Belgium (1962) 6, 58, 180, 186, 888
De Cubber v Belgium (1984) 68, 73, 173, 182, 185, 688, 860
De Haan v Netherlands (1997) 613, 622
De Haes and Gijsels v Belgium (1997) 184
De Jong, Baljet and van den Brink v The Netherlands (1984) 605
De Moor v Belgium (1994) 183
De Wilde, Ooms and Versyp v Belgium (1971) 62, 253, 816
Debled v Belgium (1994) 185
Delcourt v Belgium (1970) 180
Demai v France (1994) 328
Demicoli v Malta (1991) 588–9, 593
Deumeland v Germany (1986) 850
Deweer v Austria (1981) 181, 187, 795
Djeroud v France (1991) 328
Dobbertin v France (1993) 327
Dombo Beheer v Netherlands (1993) 613, 622, 795
Doorson v Netherlands (1996) 614–15
Dorin Lupulet v Romania (1996) 523
Drozd and Janousek v Spain (1992) 823
Dudgeon v United Kingdom (1981) 58, 230, 430, 457, 720, 972, 978–9
Duinhof and Duiif v The Netherlands (1984) 605

E v Norway (1990) 650–1, 652
Eckle v Germany (1982) 61
Editions Periscope v France (1992) 554, 555
Efstratiou v Greece (1996) 835
Ekbatani v Finland (1988) 293, 847

Elsholz v Germany (2000)....................352
Engel and Others v Netherlands (1976)..........60, 108, 589, 605, 620, 793, 859
Ensslin, Baader, Raspe v FRG (1978)....................349
Erdagoz v Turkey (1997)....................233, 901, 902
Ergi v Turkey (1998)....................33
Eriksen v Norway (1997)....................652
Eriksson v Sweden (1989)....................58
Erkner and Hofauer v Austria (1987)....................133, 156
Erkalo v Netherlands (1998)....................607
Ettl and Others v Austria (1987)....................136, 138

FE v France (1998)....................328
Feldbrugge v Netherlands (1986)....................611, 621, 850
Fey v Austria (1993)....................139
Findlay v United Kingdom (1997)....................989
Fischer v Austria (1995)....................135, 138
Foti v Italy (1982)....................499
Fressoz and Roire v France (1999)....................8
Funke v France (1993)....................427–8, 647, 820, 1002
FXM v Ireland (1985)....................448

Garcia Alva v Germany (2001)....................351
Gasus Dosier- und Fordertechnik GmbH v Netherlands (1995)....................619
Gaulieder v Slovakia (2000)....................776
Gaygusuz v Austria (1979)....................116, 128, 158–9
Gea Catalan v Spain (1995)....................823
Gillow v United Kingdom (1986)....................458
Golder, Silver, Campbell and Fell v United Kingdom (1975)29, 51, 450, 891, 946, 972, 980
Gradinger v Austria (1995)....................121, 122, 136, 161, 163
Greece v United Kingdom (1956)....................6, 25
Groppera v Switzerland (1990)....................874
Guerra and Others v Italy (1998)....................836
Guincho v Portugal (1984)....................693–4, 704
Gul v Switzerland (1996)....................123
Gussenbauer v Austria (1974)....................111

H v Belgium (1987)....................182
H v France (1990)....................327
H v Ireland (1983)....................455
H v Ireland (1994)....................465

Haas and Haasová (1998) 774–5
Hadjianastasiou v Greece (1992)....................372
Hamer v France (1996) 325
Handyside v United Kingdom (1976) 25, 537, 578
Harman v United Kingdom (1982) 974
Hasan and Chaush v Bulgaria (2000) 211–12
Hauschildt v Denmark (1989)....................56, 265, 271, 273, 604, 646, 688
Hazar v Turkey (1993) 901
Heaney v Ireland (1994 427
Helle v Finland (1997) 308
Henra and Leterme v France (1998) 328
Hentrich v France (1994) 60
Herczegfalvy v Austria (1992)....................130
Hoffman v Austria (1993) 146
Hokkanen v Finland (1994)....................305–6, 309, 310, 388
Holm v Sweden Series (1993) 848
Holy Monasteries v Greece (1994) 377
Hood v United Kingdom (2000) 71
Hornsby v Greece (1997) 379
Hozee v Netherlands (1998) 612
Huber v France (1998) 326
Huber v Switzerland (1990) 871

Ignaccolo-Zenide v Romania (2000) 726
Informationsverein Lentia 2000 and Others v Austria (1993) 115, 148, 149
Inze v Austria (1987)....................116, 159, 542
Ireland v United Kingdom (1978) 6, 32, 34, 59, 64, 253, 424, 816, 972, 982
IS v Slovakia (1997) 769

Jacubowski v Germany (1994) 352
James and Others v United Kingdom (1986) 33, 390, 521
Janusz Podbielski v Poland (1998) 673
Jersild v Denmark (1994) 68, 201, 269, 271
JJ v Netherlands (1998) 615–16
Johansen v Norway (1985)....................650
Johnston v Ireland (1978) 454, 457, 467
Jon Kristinsson v Iceland (1990) 405–6, 418, 420
Juozas Jecius v Lithuania (1997)....................512, 522–3

K v Ireland (1982)....................451

K v Ireland (1984) 455
Kalashnikov v Russia (2001) 751
Kamasinski v Austria (1989) 112, 132, 142, 143, 145–6
Karakaya v France (1994) 328
Katikaridis and Others v Greece (1996) 379
Kavanagh v Government of Ireland and Others (1996) 435
KDS v The Netherlands (1986) 615–16
Keegan v Ireland (1994) 426, 468
Kefalas and Others v Greece (1995) 371
Kerojarvi v Finland (1995) 307
Keus v Netherlands (1990) 607
Khan v United Kingdom (2000) 1001
Kjeldsen, Busk Madsen and Pedersen v Denmark (1976) 262, 390
Klass v Germany (1993) 350, 352, 952
Koendjibihari v Netherlands (1990) 606
Kokkinakis v Greece (1993) 82, 374
Kolompar v Belgium (1992) 185
Konig v FRG (1978) 449
Kopecký v Slovakia (2001) 775
Koster v The Netherlands (1991) 605
Kostovski v The Netherlands (1989) 614, 621, 645
Kremzow v Austria (1993) 142–4, 162
Kroon and Others v Netherlands (1994) 617–18, 622
Kruslin and Huvig v France (1990) 328
Kurt Nielsen v Denmark (2000) 271, 273

L and L v Ireland (1980) 448
Ladislav and Aurel Brezny v Slovak Republik (1996) 523
Lala v Netherlands (1994) 615
Lamy v Belgium (1989) 182
Langborger v Sweden (1989) 848
Larissis and Others v Greece (1999) 375
Lauko v Slovakia (1998) 771
Lawless v Ireland (No 1) (1960) 6, 16, 185, 444, 466
Le Compte, Van Leuven and De Meyere v Belgium (1981) . 72, 181, 187, 201, 391, 783
Leander v Sweden (1987) 848
Lechner and Hess v Austria (1987) 132–3
Leitzow v Germany (2001) 351
Letellier v France (1991) 60, 268, 798
Leutscher v Netherlands (1996) 610

Lingens v Austria Series A No 103 (1986) 82, 148
Lithgow and Others v United Kingdom (1986) 33, 127, 458, 521
Lobo Machado v Portugal (1996) 688, 701
Loizidou v Turkey (1995) 34, 58, 75, 232, 234, 817, 901
Longinu Aquilina v Malta (1999) 590
Lopez Ostra v Spain (1994) 825–6
Loukanov v Bulgaria (1997) 7, 207
Luberti v Italy (1984) 500
Ludi v Swtizerland (1992) 872
Luedicke, Belkacem and Koc v Germany (1978) 60, 64, 353, 491, 686
Lukáčová-Kurucová v Slovakia (1995) 769
Lustig-Prean and Beckett v United Kingdom (1999) 973, 979
Lutz v Germany (1987) 802

M v Ireland (1981) 450
McCann and Others v United Kingdom (1995) 236, 237, 973, 982
McGonnell v United Kingdom (2000) 988
Maillard v France (1998) 326
Májaric v Slovenia (2000) 806
Malige v France (1998) 326
Malone v United Kingdom (1984) 437, 972, 977
Manoussakis and Others v Greece (1996) 378
Mansur v Turkey (1994) 901
Marckx v Belgium (1979) . 57, 58, 59, 61, 63, 116, 176, 181, 186, 450, 540, 602
Markt intern v Germany (1989) 352
Martins Moreira v Portugal (1988) 694, 697, 699, 704, 706
Masson and Van Zon (1995) 610
Mathieu-Mohin and Clerfayt v Belgium (1987) 184, 463
Matos e Silva v Portugal (1996) 702
Matter v Slovakia (1997) 775
Matthews v United Kingdom (1999) 37
Matznetter v Austria (1969) 132, 133
Mauer v Austria (1997) 137
Mavronichis v Cyprus (1998) 237
Mentes and Others v Turkey (1998) 57, 60
Megyeri v Germany (1992) 350
Mellacher and Others v Austria (1989) 160
Minelli v Switzerland (1983) 47, 869–70
Mitap and Muftuoglu v Turkey (1998) 903
Modinos v Cyprus (1993) 230
Monnet v France (1997) 327

Moreira de Azevedo v Portugal (1990)....72, 698–9, 706
Moustaquim v Belgium (1991)....183, 187
MS v Slovakia (1997)....768
MS v Sweden (1997)....848
Muller v Switzerland (1988)....874
Muyldermans v Belgium (1991)....184

Neigel v France (1997)....238
Neumeister v Austria (No 1) (1968)....58, 60, 132, 133, 798
Neves and Silva v Portugal (1989)....554, 696, 698
News Verlags GmbH & CoKG v Austria (2000)....153–4
Nielsen v Denmark (1988)....223, 451
Niemitz v Germany (1992)....352
Nikishina v Russia (2000)....751
Nikolova v Bulgaria (2000)....210
Norris v Ireland (1988)....57, 59, 230, 456–7, 467, 720
Nortier v Netherlands (1993)....613
Nsona v Netherlands (1996)....617

Obermeier v Austria (1990)....133, 137
Oberschlick I v Austria (1991)....126, 148, 149, 152, 162
Oberschlick II v Austria (1997)....152–3, 162
Observer and Guardian v United Kingdom (1991)....33, 987
O'C v Ireland (1986)....457–8
Oerlemans v Netherlands (1991)....608, 610
O'H v Ireland (1994)....464–5
Olsson v Sweden (No 1) (1988)....58, 457
Open Door and Others v Ireland (1992)....460–1, 467–8
Ortenberg v Austria (1994)....138
Osman v United Kingdom (1998)....985
Otelo Saraiva de Carvalho v Portugal (1994)....700
Otto-Preminger-Institut v Austria (1994)....157
Öztürk v Germany (1984)....121, 353, 802

Pakelli v Germany (1983)....56, 351
Palaoro v Austria (1995)....122, 136
Papamichalopoulos and Others v Greece (1995)....57, 60, 61, 62, 373
Pauger v Austria (1997)....134–5
Pauwels v Belgium (1988)....182
Pelladoah v Netherlands (1994)....615
Pentidis and Others v Greece (1997)....72, 378

Peschke v Austria (1981) 112
Petra v Romania (1998) 725
Petrovic v Austria (1998) 147
Pfarrmeier v Austria (1995) 122, 136
Pfeifer and Plankl v Austria (1992) 138
Philis v Greece (1991) 372
Piermont v France (1996) 836
Pitevich v Russia (2001) 752
Piersack v Belgium (1984) 60, 68, 182
Pine Valley Developments and Others v Ireland (1991) 459–60, 467
Platform 'Arzte fur das Leben' v Austria (1988) 127, 158
Poiss v Austria (1987) 134
Pramstaller v Austria (1995) 122, 136
Preložnik v Slovakia (1997) 769
Pressos Compania Naviera SA *et al.* v Belgium (1995) 183
Pretto v Italy (1983) 499–500
Prinz v Austria (2000) 144
Proccola v Luxembourg (1995) 331, 553, 556, 557, 621
Protsch v Austria (1996) 160
Punzelt v Czech Republic (2000) 258
Purcell and Others v Ireland (1991) 462
Putz v Austria (1996) 140

Quaranta v Switzerland (1991) 871–2
Quinn v Ireland (2000) 471

Raninen v Finland (1997) 308
Rasmussen v Denmark (1984) 25
Rebitzer v Austria (1967) 111
Rees v United Kingdom (1986) 25
Rehbock v Slovenia (2000) 806
Remšíková v Slovakia (2000) 770
Ribitsch v Austria (1995) 123
Richard and Pailot v France (1998) 328
Ringeisen v Austria (Nos 2 & 3) (1972) 65, 109, 132, 133
Rotaru v Romania (2000) 722
Ruiz Mateos v Spain (1993) 824, 825
Ruiz Torija v Spain (1994) 825
Rushiti v Austria (2000) 136, 139

S v Switzerland (1991) 872

Sabeur Ben Ali v Italy (2000) 590
Salvador Torres v Spain (1995) 823
Sanchez-Reisse v Switzerland (1986) 871
Schmautzer v Austria (1995) 122, 136
Schonberger and Durmaz v Switzerland (1988) 871
Schops v Germany (2001) 351
Schouten and Meldrum v Netherlands (1994) 612
Schuler-Zgraggen v Switzerland (1995) 60, 68
Scozzari and Giunta v Italy (2000) 58
Sekanina v Austria (1993) 142, 648
Selmouni v France (1999) 65
Sheffield and Horsham v United Kingdom (1998) 218–19
Sidiropoulos and Others v Greece (1998) 380
Sigurdur Sigurjonsson v Iceland (1993) 406, 419–20
Silva Rocha v Portugal (1996) 702
Silva Pontes v Portugal (1994) 694, 696
Silver and Others v United Kingdom (1983) 33, 972, 981
Socialist Party and Others v Turkey (1998) 70, 732
Société Periscope v France (1992) 325
Société Stenuit v France (1992) 326
Soering v United Kingdom (1989) 428, 945, 985
Spisak v Slovakia (2000) 776
Sporrong and Lönnroth v Sweden (1982) 72, 458, 837, 847–8
Sramek v Austria (1984) 139, 585
Stallinger and Kuso v Austria (1997) 135, 139
Stamoulakatos v Greece (1993) 371
Stan Greek Refineries v Greece (1994) 74, 375
Steen Bille Frederiksen and Others v Denmark (1988) 262
Stjerna v Finland (1994) 306
Stögmuller v Austria (1969) 132, 224, 816
Sunday Times v United Kingdom (1979) 578, 770, 972, 987
Swedish Engine Drivers' Union v Sweden (1976) 33
Syrkin v Russia (1999) 751
Szczepan Styranowski (1998) 673
Szucs v Austria (1997) 136, 139

Taykov v Russia (2000) 752
TC v Slovakia (1996) 769
Teixeira de Castro v Portugal (1998) 52, 704
Telesystem Radio ABC v Austria (1997) 149
Terra Woningen BV v Netherlands (1996) 611–12

Thorgeir Thorgeirsson v Iceland (1992) 406, 418–19
Tolstoy Miloslavsky v United Kingdom (1995) 57
Tomasi v France (1992) 325, 350
Tonio Vella v Malta (1994) 592
Torgny Gustafsson v Sweden (1998) 849
Toth v Austria (1991) 60, 112, 131
Treholt v Norway (1991) 650
Tumilovich v Russia (1999) 750
TW v Malta (1999) 589
Tyrer v United Kingdom (1978) 29, 975–6

Umlauft v Austria (1995) 122, 136
Union Alimentaria Sanders v Spain (1989) 825
Unterpertinger v Austria (1986) 68, 112, 144, 645

Valenzuela Contreras v Spain (1998) 73
Vallee v France (1994) 327–8
Valsamis v Greece (1996) 379, 835
Van de Hurk v The Netherlands (1994) 555, 609, 610
Van de Mussele v Belgium (1982) 184
Van der Leer v Netherlands (1990) 606
Van der Sluijs, Zuiderveld and Klappe v The Netherlands (1984) 605
Van der Tang v Spain (1995) 823
Van Droogenbroeck v Belgium (1982) 182, 514
Van Mechelen v Netherlands (1997) 615
Van Oosterwyck v Belgium (1980) 184
Van Raalte v Netherlands (1997) 618
Varbanov v Bulgaria (2000) 21
Vasilescu v Romania (1998) 724, 727
Velikova v Bulgaria (2000) 211
Vereinigung Demokratischer Soldaten Osterreichs and Gubi v
Netherlands (1994) 150–2, 619
Vermeire v Belgium (1991) 59, 176, 183
Vermeulen v Belgium (1996) 181
Vernillo v France (1991) 327
Vidal v Belgium (1992) 183, 793
Vogt v Germany (1996) 352

W and W v Ireland (1983) 447
Wabl v Austria (2000) 155
Waite and Kennedy v Germany (1999) 351

Wassink v Netherlands (1990) 71, 606
Weber v Switzerland (1990) 972
Weisinger v Austria (1991)..133
Wemhoff v Germany (1968)...798, 816, 1003
Werner v Austria (1997)...135, 136, 139
Windisch v Austria (1990) 68, 112, 145
Winterwerp v The Netherlands (1979) 605–6, 644, 816
Worm v Austria (1997) 153

X v Belgium (1965) 223
X v France (1992) 327
X v France (1997) 329
X v Ireland (1971) 445, 463
X v United Kingdom (1975) 360, 644, 984
X and Y v Netherlands (1985) 616, 621, 820

Y. v United Kingdom (1980) 984
Yağsı and Sargın v Turkey (1991)...901, 902, 903
Young, James and Webster v United Kingdom (1981).......................262, 986

Z v Finland (1997) 58, 68, 307–8
Zimmermann and Steiner v Switzerland (1983)....................73, 109, 870, 874
Zumtobel v Austria (1993) 135–6

TABLE OF LEGISLATION AND TREATIES

A. Treaties and Conventions

EC Treaty 1957
Art 6 ... 37
(1) ... 91
(2) ... 90
Art 220 ... 91
European Convention for the Protection of Human Rights and Fundamental Freedoms 1950 ... 6, 167, 241, 259, 278
Art 1 ... 28, 32, 227, 481
Art 2 ... 9, 108, 117–18, 173, 210, 214, 227, 345, 461
(2) ... 345
Art 3 ... 9, 108, 118–19, 129–30, 163, 173, 200, 227, 231, 308, 341, 346–7, 350, 370, 394, 452, 617, 869, 976, 982, 984, 985
Art 4 ... 9, 227, 513
(2) ... 347
Art 5 ... 9, 58, 60, 104, 108–9, 119–20, 123, 130–2, 163, 164, 169, 200, 207, 227, 310, 347–8, 350, 366, 394, 439, 444, 449, 513, 607, 652, 671, 712, 740, 743, 751, 757, 786, 797, 803, 810, 859, 920
(1) ... 71, 182, 184, 231, 232, 529, 606, 797
(b) ... 650
(c) ... 169, 172, 224, 286, 445, 512, 523, 528
(e) ... 702
(2) ... 524, 527
(3) ... 169, 172, 182, 209, 210, 340, 344, 445, 490, 514, 524, 528, 563, 589, 590, 603, 605, 645, 740, 751, 824, 860, 871, 875, 922
(4) ... 169, 172, 174, 181, 182, 209, 210, 298, 465, 500, 514, 605, 606, 607, 651, 702, 984
(5) ... 286, 923
Art 6 ... 9, 25, 51, 71, 74, 104, 109–13, 121–3, 132–46, 163, 164, 172, 177, 204, 207, 227, 265, 307, 310, 348, 351, 370, 405, 408, 410, 414, 418, 444, 449, 452, 484, 485, 488, 489, 501, 536, 545, 547, 550, 566, 609, 641, 648, 671, 686, 689, 696–702, 704, 740, 743, 757, 786, 810, 822, 888, 981, 988, 1002
(1) ... 38, 61, 69, 70, 92, 154, 169, 173, 174, 175, 178, 179, 182, 183, 184, 185, 187, 223, 225, 237–8, 266, 267, 270–1, 272, 273, 275, 286, 299, 323–4, 325, 345, 366, 391, 392, 394, 415, 416, 449, 450, 500, 526, 528, 543, 544, 547, 554, 555, 605, 606, 608, 610–14, 619, 621, 646, 651, 673, 686, 688, 689, 693, 697, 704, 724, 751, 769, 772, 802, 817, 818, 825, 829, 862, 865, 866, 870, 872, 902, 980, 986

European Convention for the Protection of Human Rights and Fundamental Freedoms 1950 (*cont.*):
Art 6 (*cont.*):
(2) ... 171, 345, 465, 498, 611, 647, 648
(3) ... 183, 340, 491, 498, 501, 703, 870
(a) ... 223
(b) ... 388, 690
(c) ... 223, 615, 646, 690, 771
(d) ... 222, 614, 641, 772, 873
(e) ... 412, 686
Art 7 ... 9, 58, 374, 445
(1) ... 554
(2) ... 335
Art 8 ... 9, 25, 35, 113–15, 123–5, 129, 146–7, 158, 163, 164, 177, 178, 224, 227, 232, 235, 302, 303, 305, 307, 308, 322–3, 328–9, 348, 352, 395, 408, 416, 418, 449, 452, 454, 456, 529, 536, 540, 541, 542, 572, 573, 602, 603, 616, 618, 751, 775, 803, 805, 848, 922, 955, 971, 977, 980, 981
(1) ... 92, 176, 303
(2) ... 93, 125, 185, 551, 573, 979
Art 9 ... 9, 25, 70, 146, 178, 204, 211, 348, 374, 601, 626, 751, 977
(1) ... 177, 303
(2) ... 194, 196, 205, 516
(4) ... 299
Art 10 ... 9, 25, 58, 70, 83, 93, 115–16, 125–6, 129, 148–54, 163, 180, 196, 204, 205, 225, 269, 314, 352, 374, 406, 419, 461, 462, 463, 467, 536, 537, 538, 551, 619, 652, 671, 787, 822, 874, 885, 890, 895, 977, 987
(2) ... 272, 539, 551, 821
Art 11 ... 9, 25, 70, 116, 126–7, 129, 158, 163, 184, 186, 204, 264, 406, 419, 420, 447, 692, 752, 783, 977
(1) ... 446
(2) ... 541, 893
(3) ... 540
Art 12 ... 9, 177, 366, 454, 564, 603, 981
Art 13 ... 9, 32, 33, 158, 204, 209, 211, 227, 231, 306, 308, 310, 372, 394, 449, 452, 459, 460, 507, 536, 598, 648, 724, 751, 848, 925, 952, 981
Art 14 ... 9, 10, 59, 70, 147, 176, 179, 180, 218, 227, 302, 318, 350, 449, 452, 455, 457, 459, 460, 513, 517, 540, 564, 574, 604, 618, 619, 719, 774, 814, 822, 976, 979
(1) ... 366
(3) ... 501
Art 15 ... 25, 335, 356, 364, 368, 445, 887, 899
(1) ... 983
Art 17 ... 227, 444, 870, 893

Art 18 .... 70, 177
Art 21
(2) 18
(3) 18
Art 22 783
Art 24 .... 18, 226, 227, 228, 895
Art 25 .... 233, 234, 239, 246, 305, 313, 325, 335, 399, 459, 462, 464, 627, 783, 810, 855, 879, 898, 900, 928
(1) 210
(4) 627
Art 26 .... 52, 93, 192, 462, 567, 694–5, 707, 708, 768, 913
Art 28 .... 17, 270, 896
(1) 777
Art 29 17
Art 30 17
Art 31 229
Art 32 .... 17, 227, 232, 705
Art 33 11
Art 34 967
Art 35 28
(1) 58, 750
Art 38 .... 17, 21
Art 39 .... 17, 21
Art 41 .... 55, 56, 61, 62
Art 43 18
Art 44 .... 55, 66
Art 45 55
Art 46 .... 19, 55, 57, 64, 161, 192, 234, 239, 246, 313, 335, 782, 879, 913, 928
(1) 56, 57, 66, 69, 72, 73
(2) 63
Art 48 233
(b) 232
Art 50 .... 56, 183, 184, 212, 235, 235, 651, 706
Art 53 .... 52, 64, 105, 343, 706
(2) 100
Art 54 63
Art 56 596
Art 63 314
Art 64 .... 286, 627, 757, 810, 900
First Protocol 1952 6
Art 1 .... 9, 58, 70, 75, 116, 127–8, 129, 158–61, 163, 178, 183, 227, 234, 235, 366, 374, 376, 394, 407, 452, 457, 458, 459, 463, 529, 536, 555, 581, 619, 702, 724, 726, 752, 773–5, 847
Art 2 .... 9, 180, 712, 976

European Convention for the Protection of Human Rights and Fundamental Freedoms 1950 (*cont.*):
First Protocol 1952 (*cont.*):
Art 3 ....9, 70, 289, 340, 693, 776
Third Protocol 1970 8
Fourth Protocol 1963 6
Art 1 9
Art 2 ....9, 513, 517, 518, 732, 739, 740, 748
(1) 529
(2) 341
Art 3 9
Art 4 9
Fifth Protocol 1971 8
Sixth Protocol 1983 ....6, 9, 128, 389, 599
Art 1 ....200, 985
Art 2 200
Seventh Protocol 1984 ....9, 173, 819
Art 1 10
Art 2 ....9, 548, 557, 640, 783
Art 3 9
Art 4 ....10, 161
Art 5 ....10, 306, 314, 388
Eighth Protocol 1990 8
Ninth Protocol 1990 ....6, 16, 17, 846
Tenth Protocol 8, 706
Eleventh Protocol 1994 ....6, 15–16, 19, 20, 34, 56–7, 207, 228, 239, 552, 938
Twelfth Protocol 2000 8

European Social Charter 1961 10

General Act of Arbitration 1928 56

International Convention on the Elimination of all forms of Racial Discrimination 1966 290
International Convention on the Elimination of all forms of Discrimination Against Women 1979 ....290, 575, 892
International Convention against Torture and Other Cruel, Inhuman or Degrading Treatment or Punishment 1984 290
International Labour Organization Convention 1948 ....
Art 3 447

North Atlantic Treaty Organization 1949 4

Single European Act 1986 ....90, 945

Statute of the Council of Europe
Art 3 .... 192–3, 248, 733
Art 4 248

Treaty of Friendship, Co-operation and Mutual Assistance 1948 290
Treaty of Lausanne 1925 217
Treaty of Peace 1947 290

UN Covenant on Civil and Political Rights 1966 .... 489, 492, 516, 538, 711, 936
Art 9 490
Art 12 641
Art 14 .... 667, 746
(5) 640
Art 22(3) 447
Art 26 719
UN Covenant on Economic, Social and Cultural Rights 1966 .... 10, 711, 936
Art 2 59
(2) 719
Art 3 669
UN Declaration of Human Rights 1948 .... 5, 167, 242, 658, 936
Art 10 667
Art 11 427

Vienna Convention on the Law of Treaties 1969 .... 858, 919
Art 15 250
Art 16 251
Art 21(1) 220
Art 27 32
Art 31 .... 29, 51
Art 32 51
Art 33 51

B. National Legislation

Austria

Aliens Act 1997 .... 108, 123
Para 5 128
Armed Forces Act 151
Assembly Act 1953 126
Association's Act 116
Asylum Act 1997 115
Basic Law 1867
Art 5 .... 127, 128, 151

Basic Law 1867 (*cont.*):
Art 10a 115
Art 11 126
Art 13 ....125, 151
Chemical Substances Act 1996 114
Civil Code
s 1330 156
Code of Administrative Procedure 1990 110
Code of Criminal Procedure 1962
s 33(2) 68
s 363a 67, 162
Code of Criminal Procedure Adaptation Act 1974 112
Code of Criminal Procedure Amendment Act 1962 111
Copyright Act
s 78 155
Criminal Code Amendment Act 1971 111
Criminal Code Amendment Act 1983 112
Criminal Code Amendment Act 1987 112
Criminal Code Amendment Act 1993 112–13
Criminal Code Compensation Act 1969 ....111, 136
Federal Constitution 1920 103
Art 44(3) 123
Art 85 128
Art 144 38
Food Act 1975 141
Gun Use Act 1969 108
Law of Data Protection 1978 113
Law on the Protection of Personal Liberty 1988 ....108, 120
Law on Reproductive Medicine
Para 3 125
Legal Aid Act 111
National Socialist Party Prohibition Act 1945 149
Penal Code
Art 80 136
Art 209 124–5
Penal Code Amendment Act 1996 113
Private Radio Act 116
Regional Planning Act 123
Rent Act 1981 160
Security Police Act 108
State Treaty of Vienna 1955 104
Water Law Act 123

Belgium
Civil Code 59, 61
Commercial Code
Art 442 177
Constitution 1831...167
Criminal Code
Art 2..171
Art 123.6 186
Law of 13 May 1955 170
Law of 2 August 1963 180
Law of 20 December 1970..186
Law of 6 August 1971 186
Law of 6 July 1983 187
Law of 24 December 1993..171
Preventive Custody Act 1970 174
Remand in Custody Act 1990 187
Vagrancy Act 1891...181
Youth Protection Act 182

Bulgaria
Alternative Service Act 212
Civil Servants Act 1999 204
Code of Criminal Procedure 210
Constitution 1991 ....192, 194
Art 5(4) 41, 193, 195, 197
Art 37(2)...196
Arts 39–41 205
Art 44(2)...196
Art 56...204
Art 85(3)...196
Art 117 (1)..193
Art 150(1)...202
Judiciary Act 1998 215
Ministry of the Interior Act
Art 80...214

Cyprus
Administration of Justice (Miscellaneous Provisions) Law 1964.............222
Constitution
Art 10
(2)...224
(3)...224

Constitution 1991 (*cont.*):
Art 11(1)(f) ... 218
Art 12(5) ... 222
(a) ... 223
Art 15 ... 224, 230
Art 17 ... 224
Art 19 ... 225
Art 28 ... 218
(1) ... 218
Art 30
(2) ... 223, 225
(3) ... 222
(b) ... 223
(d) ... 223
Art 32 ... 219
Art 137 ... 221
Art 144 ... 222
Art 169(3) ... 220
Criminal Code
s 171 ... 238
s 173 ... 238
Law No 39 of 1962 ... 219
Fugitive Offenders Act 1881
s 5 ... 222
Public Service Law 1967 ... 224

Czech Republic
Constitution
Art 10 ... 41, 254, 255–6, 258
Art 39(4) ... 257, 258
Art 49(2) ... 248, 258
Art 87 ... 257
Constitutional Act No 143/1968
Art 61 (1)(a) ... 244
Constitutional Act No 23/1991 ... 241, 243
s 2 ... 243, 244, 253, 256
Constitutional Act No 542/1992 ... 245

Denmark
Administration of Justice Act
s 962(2) ... 261, 263
Act No 285 of 9 June 1982 ... 264

Act No 347 of 29 May 1990 264
Act No A 285 of 29 April 1992 .... 44, 260, 261, 264
s 1 260
Act No 750 of 19 October 1998 260
Constitution
s 59 267

Estonia
Constitution 1992 278
Art 3 .... 280, 281
Art 15 281
(1) 283
(2) 283
Art 78
(6) 279
Art 102 285
Art 121 279
Art 123 .... 41, 280–1
Art 149(3) 281
Art 152 281
Constitutional Review Court Procedure Act
Art 4(1)(5) 281
Art 6(1)(2) 281
Legal Chancellor Act
Art 13 281
Art 15 281
Ratification Act 1996 279

Finland
Act No 450/1987 292
Act No 361/1990 293
Act No 438/1990 293
Act No 696/1990 299
Act of 4 May 1990 .... `45
Act No 463/1991 293
Act No 843/1991 293
Aliens Act 1982 298
Constitution Act 1919 .... 289, 295
s 1 294
s 2 294
s 33 294
Military Discipline Act (No 331/1983) 298

Military Injuries Act (No 404/1948) 307
Parliament Act 1928 289
Paternity Act 1975 301

France
Act of 10 June 1983 (community service) 320
Act No 91-646 of 10 July 1991 330
Act of 8 February 1995 (judicial organization) 330
Code of Criminal Procedure
  Art 626-1 67
  Art 626-7 67
Constitution 1958
  Art 55 .... 315, 317

Georgia
Constitution
  Art 6(2) 41

Germany
Aliens Law 1990 ....
  s 53(4) 341
Basic Law 1949
  Art 2(1) 47, 342
  Art 3(1) 47
  Art 16(a) 342
  Art 25 339
  Art 31 338
  Art 59(2) 47, 338
  Art 103(2) 335
Code of Criminal Procedure
  s 32 345
  s 33a 344
  s 359 6
    (6) 343
Constitution
  Art 93(1) 342
Traffic Code
  s 25a 346

Greece
Constitution 1952 355

Constitution 1975 .... 358, 361
Art 16(5) 360
Art 28(1) 358, 359
Art 36(1) 358
Law 1363/1938 378
s 4 374
Law 1672/1939 378
Law 2329/1953 .... 355, 356
Law 653/1977 379
Law 1700/1987 377
Law 1701/1987 376
Law 1705/1987 359
Legislative Decree 53/1974 357
Legislative Decree 196/74 357

Hungary
Act No I of 1968 ....
s 71/A 392
Act No XI of 1987 384
Act No LXXVI of 1993 387
Art No LXXXV of 1993 387
Act No XXXIV of 1994 387
Code of Criminal Procedure 391
Constitution
Art 7
(1) 41, 49, 383, 384
(2) 384
Art 8(2) 384
Law-Decree No 27 of 1982 ....
s 16(1) 384

Iceland
Act No 19 of 1940 (Penal Code) 412
Art 108 419
Act No 44 of 1944 402
Act No 13 of 1987 406
Act No 48 of 1988 ....
Art 26 406
Act No 92 of 1989 .... 406, 414, 420
Art 6 415
Act No 3 of 1991 406
Act No 62 of 1994 (incorporation) 44, 400, 402, 407, 421

Act No 62 of 1994 (incorporation) (*cont.*):
Art 1 402
Art 2 ....402, 404
Art 3 402
Act No 69 of 1994 415
Act No 61 of 1995 421
Act No 80 of 1995 415
Act No 25 of 1998 402
Children's Act No 20 of 1992 406
Code of Criminal Procedure No 74 of 1974 412
Art 19(2) 413
Code of Criminal Procedure No 19 of 1991 406
Constitution
Art 2 408
Art 61 408
Art 66 408
Art 67 415
Art 70 ....416, 417
Art 72 412
Art 73 ....409, 417

Ireland
Adoption Act 1998 468
Bail Act 1997 436
Broadcasting Authority Act 1960 ....
s 31 461
Children Act 1987 466–7
Civil Legal Aid Act 1995 466
Constitution 1937 438
Art 15.2 ....425, 432, 433, 434
Art 26 467
Art 29
.3 432–5
.6 ....45, 425, 432–5
Art 34 448
.3.2 439
Art 38 427
.3 448
Art 40
.3.2 441
.3.3 438
.6.1 428
Art 45 442
Art 46 439

Art 47 ... 439
Criminal Assets Bureau Act 1996 ... 438
Criminal Justice Act 1964 ...
s 2 ... 465
Criminal Justice Act 1984
s 18 ... 427
s 19 ... 427
Criminal Justice (Drug Trafficking) Act 1996 ... 438
Criminal Law (Amendment) Act 1885
s 11 ... 456
Criminal Law (Sexual Offences) Act 1993 ... 467
Domicile and Recognition of Foreign Divorces Act 1986 ... 454
Explosive Substances Act 1883 ...
s 4 ... 465
Local Government (Planning and Development) Act 1982 ... 459
Mental Treatment Act 1945 ... 432
Offences Against the Person Act 1861
s 61 ... 456
s 62 ... 456
Offences Against the State Act 1939 ...
s 52 ... 471
Offences Against the State (Amendment) Act 1940 ... 426, 438, 444
Proceeds of Crime Act 1996 ... 438

Italy
Constitution
Art 2 ... 43, 480
Art 10 ... 480
Art 13 ... 515
Art 24 ... 486
Art 27 ... 486
Criminal Code
Art 143 ... 501
Art 175 ... 501
Disciplinary Procedure Act 1946 ... 484
Law No 848 of 4 August 1955 ... 475

Lithuania
Code of Civil Procedure
Art 371 ... 509–10
Code of Criminal Procedure
Art 50-I ... 523, 528

Code of Criminal Procedure (*cont.*):
Art 372 525
Art 457 510
Constitution 1992
Art 18 503
Art 20 515
Art 25 520
Art 26 516
Art 29 516–17
Art 30 525
Art 32 .....517, 518
Art 48 513
Art 105 513
Art 106 .....513, 526
Art 135 504
Art 138 .....45, 504, 506, 507, 515
Art 212-I 528
Art 226(6) 526
Law of 21 May 1991 507
Law on Compensation
Art 9 527
Law on the Courts
Art 38(2) 509
Law on International Treaties of the Republic of Lithuania of 1991
Art 12 506
Law on Civil Servants with the Constitution .....
Art 16 520
Statute of the Seimas .....
Art 140(5–1) 510
Art 141 511
Art 144(5) 510
Art 148 511

Luxembourg
Act of 26 November 1982 .....536, 551, 553
Act of 16 June 1989 .....
Art 64–1 545
Constitution
Art 37(1) 531
Civil Code
Art 349 541
Art 354 540
Art 375 541

Art 380 541
Art 756 540
Art 832 542
Art 1382 ....538, 551
Art 1383 ....538, 551
Criminal Code of Procedure
s 116(6) 546
s 215 548
s 443 533
(5) 67
s 444 533
s 445 533
s 446 533
s 447 533

Macedonia
Constitution
Art 118 41

Malta
Act X 577
Act XI of 1983 577
Act XXXVII of 1986 591
Act XIV of 1987 ....564, 566, 570, 581
s 2 ....562, 563, 566
s 3 566
s 6 564
Act XXIX of 1989 592
Act XIX of 1991 561
Act XXIV of 1995 ....592, 593
European Convention Act 1987 ....67, 562
s 3(2) 565
s 6 67
Code of Organization and Civil Procedure
Art 79 586
(2) 592
Art 115(3) 571
Art 242 570
Art 307 580
Colonial Laws Validity Act 1865 560
Constitution 1961 560
Art 5 560

Constitution 1961 (*cont.*):
Art 34(3)....563
Art 35(1)....564
Art 37....579, 580
(1)....579–81
Art 38....570, 572, 580
Art 39
(1)....584
(2)....584
Art 40....576
Art 41....574
Art 44(4)(c)....575
Art 45....564, 574, 576
Art 46(2)....567
Art 95(6)....568
Controlled Companies (Procedure for Liquidation) Act....584
Criminal Code
Art 136....573
Art 454(4)....583
Art 517....578
Art 575....592
Art 636(b)....578
Art 686....579
Dangerous Drugs Ordinance
Art 27....590
Devolution of Certain Church Property Act 1983....577
Independence Act 1964....560
Professional Secrecy Act 1994
Art 3....594
Ratification of Treaties Act 1983....562

Moldova
Constitution
Art 4(2)....41, 48

Netherlands
Civil Code....602
Art 959....602
Constitution 1983
Art 1....618
Art 73....600
Art 93....37, 598

Art 94 37
Art 120 599
General Child Benefits Act 622
s 25(2) 618
Industrial Appeals Act
Art 74 609–10

Norway
Aliens Act 1988 ....
s 4 632
Code of Civil Procedure 632
s 407 653
(7) 67
Code of Criminal Procedure
s 4 632
s 172 646
s 108 646
s 391 653
(2) 67
Constitution 638
Art 2 638
Art 100c 40
Art 110c 634–5, 636, 638, 639
Incorporation Act 635
s 1 636
s 2 636
s 3 636–7
s 4 632

Poland
Aliens Act 1963 663
Code of Administrative Proceedings
Art 196 667
Code of Criminal Procedure
s 540(3) 67
Constitution 1997 49
Art 9 660
Art 86 660
Art 87(1) 663
Art 88 42
Art 90 660
Art 188 ....42, 660, 668

Constitutional Tribunal Act 1985 668

Portugal
Code of Civil Procedure 687
  Art 501 696
  Art 771 708
Code of Criminal Procedures
  Art 92 ....684, 686
  Art 93 703
  Art 108 ....685, 707
  Art 109 ....685, 707
  Art 365 701
  Art 443 689
  Art 449 708
  Art 469 690
  Art 664 687
Constitution 1974 681
  Art 8(2) 682
  Art 16 39
    (2) 685
  Art 28 515
  Art 32 689
  Art 294 682
Law 65/78 of 13 October
  Art 2 681
  Art 4 681
Law 12/87 of 7 April 682

Romania
Constitution 1991
  Art 11 ....714, 715, 716
    (2) 714
  Art 16 719
  Art 20 ....41, 714, 715, 716
    (1) 714
  Art 21 719
  Art 51 714
  Art 144 720
  Art 145 720–1
Penal Code
  Art 149(3) 720
  Art 200(1) 720

Art 275 724
Art 504 720

Russia
Code of Criminal Procedure 1960 ....733, 738
Art 11 741
Art 47 743
Art 89 741
Art 90 741
Art 92 741
Art 96 741
Art 97 ....741, 742
Art 101 741
Art 122 741
Art 325 746
Art 335(2) 747
Constitution 1993 733
Art 15(4) 41, 735
Art 17(1) 736
Art 27 ....739, 748
Art 46(3) 737
Art 55 743
Art 125(6) 736
Presidential Decree 1226 of 14 June 1994 733

Slovakia
Armed Forces Service Act 1959
s 17 758
Code of Civil Procedure
s 250f 772, 777
Constitution 1992 755
Art 11 ....756, 760
Art 17(2) 756
Art 23(4) 766
Art 25 756
Art 26 768
Art 34 756
Art 125 757
(e) 761
Art 127 ....762, 763
Art 130
(1) 761
(3) 763, 764, 766, 768, 769, 770

Constitution 1992 (*cont.*):
Art 132 762
Art 144 761
Art 152 758
Art 153 758
Constitutional Law No 23/1991 760
Art 2 760
Constitutional Law No 542/1992 755
Extrajudicial Rehabilitation Act 1991 773
Judicial Rehabilitation Act 1990 773
Land Ownership Act 1991 773
Minor Offences Act
s 83(1) 776
Substitute Civilian Service Act 1992 765

Slovenia
Basic Property Relations Act
Art 73 802
Constitution 1991 781
Art 8 ....784, 785
Art 19 798
Art 23 ....786, 800
Art 25 803
Art 27 792
Art 33 797
Art 153 785
Art 156(1) 789
Art 160 ....784, 785
(1) 789, 807
Art 162 807
Constitutional Court Act
Art 1 789
Art 12 785
Art 13 785
Art 21(3) 789
Art 23(1) 789
Art 43 785
Art 50(2) 791
Art 70 784
Art 80(2) 785
Art 112 786
Art 113 786

Criminal Procedure Act 1977
Art 16 ... 793
Art 167(2) ... 793
Art 177 ... 793, 795
Art 200 ... 799
Art 397 ... 799
Ombudsman Act
Art 2 ... 790
Art 3 ... 790
Art 4 ... 790
Art 6 ... 790
Art 7 ... 790
Art 9 ... 790
Art 25 ... 790
Art 31 ... 790
Art 34 ... 791
Art 36 ... 791
Art 39 ... 791
Art 42 ... 790
Art 43 ... 791
Art 45 ... 790

Spain
Civil Code
Art 1(5) ... 809
Art 2(1) ... 811
Constitution 1978
Art 10(2) ... 39, 48, 813, 814, 815, 828
Art 16(1) ... 821
Art 17 ... 515
Art 18(10 ... 821
Art 24(2) ... 818, 819, 828
Art 28 ... 810
Art 33 ... 811
Art 55 ... 810
Art 93 ... 809, 811
Art 94(1) ... 809, 812
Art 95(1) ... 812
Art 96(1) ... 809, 811, 828
Art 116 ... 810
Art 164(1) ... 815

Sweden
Constitution ... 44
Expropriation Act 1988 ... 852
Freedom of Expression Act 1991 ... 833
Freedom of the Press Act 1949 ... 833
Housing Court (Amendment) Act 1991 ... 852
Instrument of Government 1974 ... 833
  Chapter 2 ... 834–5
Law (1994:1219) of 5 May 1994 ... 44
Protection of Security Act 1996 ... 852

Switzerland
Constitution
  Art 4 ... 868
  Art 5(4) ... 877
  Art 51 ... 859
  Art 52 ... 859
  Art 58 ... 868
  Art 89 ... 856
  Art 113(3) ... 857–8, 865, 877
  Art 114 ... 877
  Art 190 ... 877
Federal Criminal Procedure Act
  Art 43(2) ... 863
  Art 47 ... 860
  Art 66 ... 860
  Art 68 ... 863
  Art 73 ... 860
  Art 84 ... 863
Federal Judicature Act
  s 139a ... 67, 72, 876

Turkey
Civil Code
  Art 159 ... 892
  Art 292 ... 892
Constitution 1924
  Art 26 ... 881
Constitution 1961
  Art 22 ... 885
  Art 31 ... 887
  Art 57 ... 886
  Art 97 ... 882

Constitution 1982
Art 13 ... 887
Art 14 ... 889
Art 15 ... 884, 889, 904
Art 16 ... 884
Art 17 ... 889
Art 19 ... 886, 889
Art 33(2) ... 886
Art 38 ... 889
Art 42 ... 884
Art 90 ... 882, 906
Art 104 ... 882
Arts 119–122 ... 899
Penal Code
Art 125 ... 904
Art 141(1) ... 893
Art 142(2) ... 893

Ukraine
Civil Procedure Code 1963
Art 428 ... 918
Constitution 1996 ... 917
Art 1 ... 917, 919
Art 6 ... 930
Art 9 ... 45, 917
Art 27 ... 920
Art 29 ... 922
Art 30 ... 928
Art 31 ... 928
Art 55 ... 925, 926, 927
Art 56 ... 923
Art 57 ... 919
Art 59 ... 928
Art 62 ... 923, 928
Art 64 ... 926
Art 92 ... 924
Art 124 ... 921, 926, 930
Art 125 ... 921, 930
Criminal Procedure Code
Art 43 ... 921
(1) ... 921
Art 53(1) ... 923
Art 142 ... 921

Criminal Procedure Code (*cont.*):
Art 190 922
Art 263 921
Art 303 921

United Kingdom
Air Forces Act 1955 940
Appellate Jurisdiction Act 1876 989
Army Act 1955 940
Contempt of Court Act 1981 987
Crime and Disorder Act 1998 .....
s 36 940
Criminal Justice and Public Order Act 1994 1003
Education Act 1996 977
Employment Act 1982 986
Government of Wales Act 1998 1005–6
s 107 1006
House of Lords Act 1999 997
Human Rights Act 1998 .....42, 472, 935, 939, 960
s 2 .....473, 964, 1003
(2) 965
s 3 .....962–3, 969
s 4 .....963, 964, 966
s 5(1) 965
s 6 .....968, 969, 970
(1) 966
(2) 966
s 7(5) 966
s 9 966
s 12 970
(2) 971
(4) 971
s 13(1) 971
s 15 939
s 17 939
s 20(2) 965
s 21(5) 940
Interception of Communications Act 1985 978
Marriage Act 1983 981
Married Women's Property Act 1964
s 1 940
Mental Health Act 1983 984
Murder (Abolition of Death Penalty) Act 1965 939

Northern Ireland Act 1972 59
Prevention of Terrorism (Temporary Provisions) Act 1983
School Standards and Framework Act 1998
  s 131 977
Scotland Act 1998 990
  s 29(2)(d) 1005
  s 57(2) 1005
Summary Jurisdiction Act 1960 (Isle of Man) 975
Treaty of Union 1707 947

PART I

Introductory: International and Comparative Aspects of the ECHR and its Member States

1

The Institutions and Processes of the Convention

ROBERT BLACKBURN

A. The founding aims of the Council of Europe
B. The Convention's articles of human rights
C. The enforcement machinery of the Convention
D. Winning popular confidence and sustaining governmental support
E. The legal method of the Court of Human Rights

A. THE FOUNDING AIMS OF THE COUNCIL OF EUROPE

The origins of the Council of Europe lay in the political initiatives that followed the Second World War designed to promote closer formal associations between the sovereign states of Europe.[1] The overriding wish in the European international community was to adopt new measures that would do everything possible to help avoid future wars such as those which had ravaged Europe in 1939–45 and earlier in 1914–18. Many conferences and agreements on European unity took place in the years immediately following the cessation of the War, the most important of which for the future of European human rights was the Congress of Europe held in The Hague on 8–10 May 1948, organized by the International Committee of Movements for European Unity. The resolution adopted at that meeting, which comprised 713 delegates from sixteen countries, with Britain's Winston Churchill as President of Honour and three Chairmen drawn from France, Belgium, and Spain, declared:

[1] See A. H. Robertson, *The Council of Europe* (Manchester University Press, 2nd edn 1961) and A. H. Robertson and J. G. Merrills, *Human Rights in Europe: A Study of the European Convention on Human Rights* (Manchester University Press, 3rd edn 1993), ch. 1.

We desire a united Europe, throughout whose area the free movement of persons, ideas and goods is restored; We desire a Charter of Human Rights guaranteeing liberty of thought, assembly and expression as well as the right to form a political opposition; We desire a Court of Justice with adequate sanctions for implementation of this Charter.

The Statute of the Council of Europe was signed on 5 May 1949 at St James's Palace, London, by its ten founding members, being Belgium, Denmark, France, Ireland, Italy, Luxembourg, the Netherlands, Norway, Sweden, and the United Kingdom. The first chapter of the Statute declared that:

The aim of the Council of Europe is to achieve a greater unity between its Members for the purpose of safeguarding and realising the ideals and principles which are their common heritage and facilitating their economic and social progress; [and that] this aim shall be pursued through the organs of the Council of Europe by discussion of questions of common concern and by agreements and common action in economic, social, cultural, scientific, legal and administrative matters and in the maintenance and further realisation of human rights and fundamental freedoms.

The Preamble to the Statute further stated that member states were:

convinced that the pursuit of peace based upon justice and international co-operation is vital for the preservation of human society and civilisation, [and reaffirmed] their devotion to the spiritual and moral values which are the common heritage of their people and the true source of individual freedom, political liberty and the rule of law, principles which form the basis of all genuine democracy.

Human rights from the outset formed the central focus and preoccupation of the Council's work. Other major functions of inter-governmental co-operation, notably with respect to industrial co-operation and in the field of defence, were not to form part of the special role the Council sought to define for itself or the task it set itself to achieve: European-wide forms of industrial and economic association would be dealt with by the European Communities established in 1951–58; and the North Atlantic Treaty Organization signed in 1949 would deal with military affairs. A major impetus behind the Council's concern with human rights came from a belief in the need to promote democratic ideals and practices as a means of pre-empting the emergence of totalitarianism within any individual member states. Recent experience had strongly suggested that government suppression of the rights and freedoms of individuals soon led to political dictatorship and international armed conflict. Similarly, the Council's emphasis on human rights was directly influenced by the post-War threat perceived from the Soviet bloc countries in eastern Europe.

This overriding concern was manifested in the European Convention on Human Rights, which was signed during the sixth session of the Committee of Ministers held in Rome during November 1950.[2] Afterwards, Robert Schuman remarked that the Convention 'provides foundations on which to base the defence of human personality against all tyrannies and against all forms of totalitarianism'. From the inception of the Council of Europe to today, democracy and human rights have rightly been perceived as forming two sides of the same coin upon which a peaceful association of European states depends. This is spelt out emphatically in the Preamble to the Convention, declaring:

> profound belief in those fundamental freedoms which are the foundation of justice and peace in the world and are best maintained on the one hand by an effective political democracy and on the other by a common understanding and observance of the human rights upon which they depend.

The Convention emerged from the wider international human rights movement that had led to the General Assembly of the United Nations adopting its Universal Declaration of Human Rights on 10 December 1948, and the Convention was described by its founding members two years later as 'the first steps for the collective enforcement of certain of the rights stated in the Universal Declaration'. To appreciate the scale and nature of the Convention's achievements in its subsequent 50-year history, it is necessary to see the precise ways in which its organization has been moulded and often to look behind its theoretical structure as laid down in the articles of the Convention at the attitudes and methods adopted by those working within its central institutions: the Commission of Human Rights (until 1999), the Court of Human Rights, the Committee of Ministers, and the Council's Secretariat. Historically, a number of specific factors have played a leading role in shaping the actual work and level of influence of the Convention, among them being: the importance of establishing the compulsory jurisdiction of the Court[3] and the right of individual petition by citizens of member states; the conciliatory approach adopted by the Commission of Human Rights towards the governments of member states;[4] the development by the Court of Human Rights of interpretation rules fostering a European law system whilst respecting a degree

[2] For the background negotiations and preparation of the EHCR, see ibid. The role played by individual national governments in the process is referred to in the chapters below on countries which were founding members.

[3] Compulsory jurisdiction of the Court was controversial in 1949–50, with reservations being expressed particularly strongly by the UK government: generally see A. H. Robertson, 'The European Convention for the Protection of Human Rights', 27 *British Yearbook of International Law* (1950) 145. A compromise was reached by making the Court's jurisdiction over a member state only compulsory on the state's declaration to that effect under Article 46 (as it was before Protocol No. 11).

[4] See page 21 below.

of national difference;[5] and the inter-relationship between the Convention and the law of the European Union which has served to magnify the legal and political processes of human rights in Europe.[6]

Historical Landmarks for the ECHR and its Member States, 1950–2000[7]

04.11.1950	Signing in Rome of the Council of Europe Convention for the Protection of Human Rights and Fundamental Freedoms (ECHR), the first international legal instrument to guarantee the protection of human rights.
20.03.1952	Signing of the First Protocol to the ECHR, extending the rights that are protected: the right to peaceful enjoyment of one's possessions, to education, and to free elections by secret ballot (enters into force 18.05.1954).
03.09.1953	The ECHR enters into force.
12.07.1954	The European Commission of Human Rights is established. Its first President: Sir Humphrey Waldock (British).
09.06.1958	First case declared admissible by the Commission: *De Becker v Belgium.*
01.01.1959	First inter-state case declared admissible by the Commission: *Greece v United Kingdom,* concerning exceptional decrees and regulations issued in Cyprus by the United Kingdom.
23.02.1959	First session of the European Court of Human Rights. First President: Lord Arnold Duncan McNair (British), first Vice-President: René Cassin (French).
01.07.1961	First judgment by the Court. In the case of *Lawless v Ireland,* concerning administrative detention, the Court ruled that there had been no violation of the Convention.
16.09.1963	Signing of Protocol No. 4 to the Convention, on deprivation of liberty, choice of residence, and expulsion from a state (enters into force 02.05.1968).
18.01.1978	First judgment by the Court in an inter-state case: *Ireland v United Kingdom.*

[5] Such as the doctrine of margin of appreciation: see page 25 below.

[6] For a discussion of the European Union's Charter of Fundamental Rights and Freedoms and the proposal for EU accession to the ECHR as a contracting party, see chapter 4 below.

[7] This is an adapted version of a Council of Europe Directorate of Human Rights chart prepared for the Council's 50th anniversary ceremony in Rome.

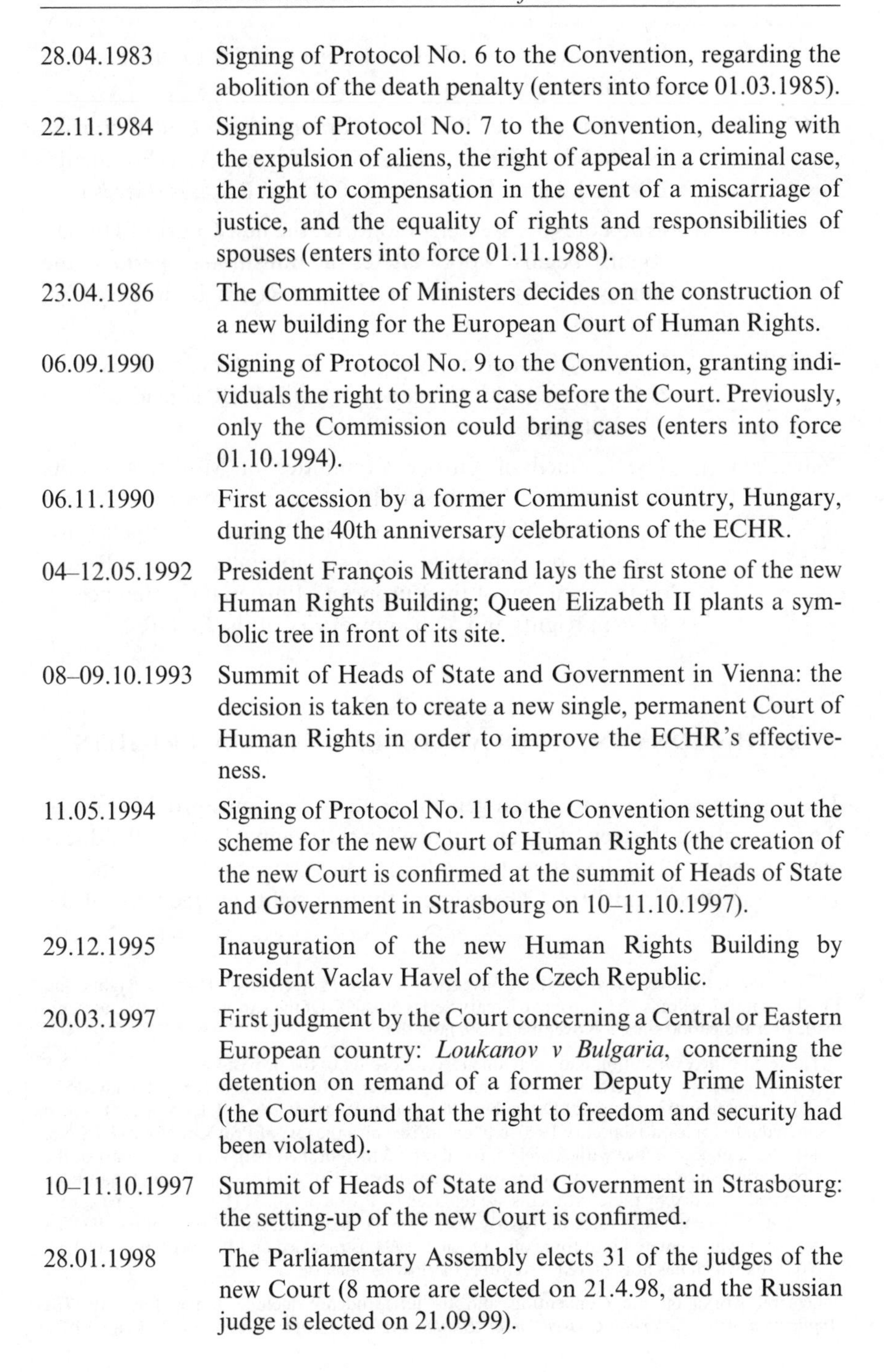

28.04.1983	Signing of Protocol No. 6 to the Convention, regarding the abolition of the death penalty (enters into force 01.03.1985).
22.11.1984	Signing of Protocol No. 7 to the Convention, dealing with the expulsion of aliens, the right of appeal in a criminal case, the right to compensation in the event of a miscarriage of justice, and the equality of rights and responsibilities of spouses (enters into force 01.11.1988).
23.04.1986	The Committee of Ministers decides on the construction of a new building for the European Court of Human Rights.
06.09.1990	Signing of Protocol No. 9 to the Convention, granting individuals the right to bring a case before the Court. Previously, only the Commission could bring cases (enters into force 01.10.1994).
06.11.1990	First accession by a former Communist country, Hungary, during the 40th anniversary celebrations of the ECHR.
04–12.05.1992	President François Mitterand lays the first stone of the new Human Rights Building; Queen Elizabeth II plants a symbolic tree in front of its site.
08–09.10.1993	Summit of Heads of State and Government in Vienna: the decision is taken to create a new single, permanent Court of Human Rights in order to improve the ECHR's effectiveness.
11.05.1994	Signing of Protocol No. 11 to the Convention setting out the scheme for the new Court of Human Rights (the creation of the new Court is confirmed at the summit of Heads of State and Government in Strasbourg on 10–11.10.1997).
29.12.1995	Inauguration of the new Human Rights Building by President Vaclav Havel of the Czech Republic.
20.03.1997	First judgment by the Court concerning a Central or Eastern European country: *Loukanov v Bulgaria*, concerning the detention on remand of a former Deputy Prime Minister (the Court found that the right to freedom and security had been violated).
10–11.10.1997	Summit of Heads of State and Government in Strasbourg: the setting-up of the new Court is confirmed.
28.01.1998	The Parliamentary Assembly elects 31 of the judges of the new Court (8 more are elected on 21.4.98, and the Russian judge is elected on 21.09.99).

05.05.1998	Russia ratifies the ECHR (the last country to do so before the 50th anniversary).
24.07.1998	Election of the President for the new Court: Luzius Wildhaber (Swiss). Election of the Vice-Presidents: Elisabeth Palm (Swedish) and Christos Rozakis (Greek).
01–03.11.1998	Protocol No. 11 enters into force: the new Court of Human Rights begins work. (After a transitional period, the European Commission of Human Rights is dissolved on 01.11.99).
21.01.1999	First judgment given by the new Court: *Fressoz and Roire v France* (in which a violation of the ECHR is held to have taken place).
26.06.2000	The Council of Europe Committee of Ministers adopts Protocol No. 12 to the ECHR, which provides for a general prohibition of discrimination. The Protocol was opened for signature by member States on 4 November 2000 in Rome, on the occasion of the European Ministerial Conference on Human Rights and 50th anniversary of the ECHR.

B. THE CONVENTION'S ARTICLES OF HUMAN RIGHTS

There are presently twenty-seven general rights or freedoms provided for in the Convention, thirteen of them contained in the original body of the document signed in 1950, the others later added in successive protocols signed in 1952, 1963, 1983, and 1984.[8] The original thirteen rights or freedoms of the

[8] For the full current text of the Convention for the Protection of Human Rights and Fundamental Freedoms, see European Treaty Series No. 005. Of the various treaty amendments made over the period since 4 November 1950, note that

> The text of the Convention had been amended according to the provisions of Protocol No. 3 (ETS No. 45), which entered into force on 21 September 1970, of Protocol No. 5 (ETS No. 55), which entered into force on 20 December 1971 and of Protocol No. 8 (ETS No. 118), which entered into force on 1 January 1990, and comprised also the text of Protocol No. 2 (ETS No. 44) which, in accordance with Article 5, paragraph 3 thereof, had been an integral part of the Convention since its entry into force on 21 September 1970. All provisions which had been amended or added by these Protocols are replaced by Protocol No. 11 (ETS No. 155), as from the date of its entry into force on 1 November 1998. As from that date, Protocol No. 9 (ETS No. 140), which entered into force on 1 October 1994, is repealed and Protocol No. 10 (ETS No. 146), which has not entered into force, has lost its purpose.

General works on the Convention and its jurisprudence include James Fawcett, *The Application of the European Convention on Human Rights* (Oxford: Clarendon, 2nd edn 1987);

Convention, contained in Articles 2 to 14, drew heavily upon the Universal Declaration of Human Rights adopted by the General Assembly of the United Nations on 10 December 1948, both in subject-matter and in terminological drafting.[9]

These thirteen articles in the main body of the Convention relate to the most basic rights of individuals, uppermost in the minds of western Europe in the aftermath of the horrors committed prior to and during the Second World War and also in response to totalitarian practices evident, or becoming so, in some eastern European countries at the time. They seek to guarantee: the right to life (Article 2), the prohibition of torture (Article 3), the prohibition of slavery and forced labour (Article 4),the right to liberty and security (Article 5), the right to a fair trial (Article 6), no punishment without law (Article 7), the right to respect for private and family life (Article 8), freedom of thought, conscience, and religion (Article 9), freedom of expression (Article 10), freedom of assembly and association (Article 11), the right to marry and have children (Article 12), the right to an effective remedy (Article 13) and the prohibition of discrimination in the enjoyment of Convention rights (Article 14).

The Protocols later added to the Convention were optional and require separate ratification. The First Protocol in 1952 provided for protection of property (Article 1), the right to education (Article 2), and the right to free elections (Article 3). Protocol No. 4 in 1963 prohibited three forms of conduct by government, being imprisonment for debt (Article 1), the expulsion of nationals (Article 3) and collective expulsion of aliens (Article 4), and required everyone lawfully within the territory of a state to have freedom of movement (Article 2). Protocol No. 6 in 1983 provided for the abolition of the death penalty; and Protocol No. 7 the following year required a right of appeal in criminal matters (Article 2), compensation for wrongful conviction (Article 3), and the right not to be tried or punished for the same offence twice

P. van Dijk and G. van Hoof, *Theory and Practice of the European Convention on Human Rights* (The Hague: Kluwer, 3rd edn 1998); F. G. Jacobs and R. White, *The European Convention on Human Rights* (Oxford: Clarendon, 2nd edn 1995); Donna Gomien, David Harris, and Leo Zwaak, *Law and Practice of the European Convention on Human Rights and the European Social Charter* (Council of Europe publishing, 1996); L. E. Pettiti, E. Decaux, and P-H. Imbert (eds), *La Convention Européenne des Droits de l'Homme: Commentaire article par article* (Paris: Economica, 2nd edn 1999); D. Harris, M. O'Boyle, and C. Warbrick, *Law of the European Convention on Human Rights* (London: Butterworths, 1995); M. Janis, R. Kay, and A. Bradley, *European Human Rights Law* (Oxford University Press, 2nd edn 2000); R. Ergec, *La Convention Européenne des Droits de l'Homme* (Brussels: Bruylant, 1990); J. A. Frowein and W. Peukert, *Europäische Menschenrechtskonvention: EMRK Kommentar* (Kehr: Engel, 2nd edn 1996).

[9] For the most part the articles drafted for the Convention in 1950 took the brief principles of the Universal Declaration as their starting point and added further elaboration. The later UN International Covenant on Civil and Political Rights 1966 (which came into effect in 1976) is a much fuller document.

(Article 4). Protocol No. 7 provided also for procedural safeguards relating to expulsion of aliens (Article 1) and for equality between spouses (Article 5).

These human rights, particularly in the body of the Convention signed in 1950, are therefore principally of a civil and political nature. This was always intended to be the case, and both the United Nations (UN) and the Council of Europe later covered the protection of social and economic rights in separate international instruments, respectively the Covenant on Economic, Social, and Cultural Rights (1966) and the European Social Charter signed in Turin on 18 October 1961 and entering into force 26 February 1965.[10] The property and education rights included in the First Protocol to the European Convention on Human Rights may be seen to have a different nature from the rest of the document. However, its net effect has been considerably to widen the important civil right of freedom from discrimination in the Convention (Article 14), which in 1950 was drafted not as a general right but as limited to the enjoyment of the other rights and freedoms set out in the Convention.[11] When draft Protocol No. 12 comes into effect, the non-discrimination provisions of the Convention will again be substantially enlarged, by providing that no-one can be discriminated against by any public authority on any ground.[12]

[10] On the Social Charter see Donna Gomien, David Harris, Leo Zwaak, *Law and Practice of the European Convention on Human Rights and the European Social Charter* (Council of Europe publishing, 1996); Paul O'Higgins, 'The European Social Charter' in Robert Blackburn and John Taylor (eds), *Human Rights for the 1990s* (London: Mansell, 1991).

[11] For non-discrimination in state provision of education, see for example the *Belgian Linguistics Case (No. 2)*, Judgment of 23 July 1968, Series A No. 6. Article 14 of the ECHR reads:

> *The enjoyment of the rights and freedoms set forth in this Convention* [editor's italics] shall be secured without discrimination on any ground such as sex, race, colour, language, religion, political or other opinion, national or social origin, association with a national minority, property, birth or other status.

[12] The Protocol became open for signature and ratification on 4 November 2000. 25 member states immediately signed the Protocol which will come into force when 10 of the states have ratified it within their own countries. This new non-discrimination provision set out in Protocol No. 12, Article 1 (General prohibition of discrimination) is:

> 1: The enjoyment of any right set forth by law shall be secured without discrimination on any ground such as sex, race, colour, language, religion, political or other opinion, national or social origin, association with a national minority, property, birth or other status. 2: No one shall be discriminated against by any public authority on any ground such as those mentioned in paragraph 1.

C. THE ENFORCEMENT MACHINERY OF THE CONVENTION: STANDING; THE FORMER COMMISSION OF HUMAN RIGHTS; THE COURT OF HUMAN RIGHTS

The founding principles on which the Council of Europe was constructed placed great importance on the need for enforcement proceedings against member states for human rights violations committed within their borders. The 1949 Statute declared in Article 3 that:

> every member of the Council of Europe must accept the principles of the rule of law and of the enjoyment by all persons within its jurisdiction of human rights and fundamental freedoms.

It stipulated at Article 8 that serious violations of human rights would be grounds for expelling or suspending a member state from the Council. After a member state has completed ratification of the 1950 Human Rights Convention, it undertakes that its domestic law and administrative practices conform to the Convention's articles and, where any violation of human rights is held to exist by the Strasbourg organs, that it will take positive action to remedy the breach, if necessary by introducing corrective legislation in its national Parliament.[13]

Inter-state applications are provided for by Article 33 of the Convention.[14] A feature of this process has always been that neither a complainant state, nor one of its citizens, must have been a victim to obtain standing to bring the case before the Court. To this extent member states serve as vigilant and objective observers of one another, though in practice most of the few inter-state cases which have been brought have involved political differences between the two parties, sometimes of an overtly hostile nature.[15]

The most novel and striking feature of the enforcement machinery agreed in 1950, after much discussion and some disagreement between the ten founding members,[16] was to allow private individuals to bring applications to the Strasbourg enforcement machinery alleging a human rights violation of

[13] Generally on domestic implementation and effects of membership of the Convention, see Andrew Drzemczewski, *European Human Rights Convention in Domestic Law* (Oxford: Clarendon Press, 1983); C. A. Gearty (ed), *European Civil Liberties and the European Convention on Human Rights* (The Hague: Kluwer, 1997); E. A. Alkema, A. Drzemczewski, and J. Schokkenbroek (eds), 'The Domestic Implementation of the European Convention on Human Rights in Eastern and Western Europe', in *All-European Human Rights Yearbook*, vol. 2, 1992 (Kehl: Engel, 1993).

[14] Formerly Article 24 in the 1950 version.

[15] Such as the three complaints brought against Turkey by Cyprus in 1974–78 following the invasion of Cyprus by Turkey.

[16] See note 3 above.

Table 1.1. Signatures and Ratifications of the Convention and its Protocols, 1950–2000[17]

	ECHR		*Protocol No. 1*		*Protocol No. 4*		*Protocol No. 6*		*Protocol No. 7*	
Member States	*Signed*	*Ratified*	*Signed*	*Ratified*	*Signed*	*Ratified*	*Signed*	*Ratified*	*Signed*	*Ratified*
Albania	13/07/95	02/10/96	02/10/96	02/10/96	02/10/96	02/10/96	04/04/00	21/09/00	02/10/96	02/10/96
Andorra	10/11/94	22/01/96	—	—	—	—	22/01/96	22/01/96	—	—
Austria	13/12/57	03/09/58	13/12/57	03/09/58	16/09/63	18/09/69	28/04/83	05/01/84	19/03/85	14/05/86
Belgium	04/11/50	14/06/55	20/03/52	14/06/55	16/09/63	21/09/70	28/04/83	10/12/98	03/11/93	—
Bulgaria	07/05/92	07/09/92	07/05/92	07/09/92	03/11/93	04/11/00	07/05/99	29/09/99	03/11/93	04/11/00
Croatia	06/11/96	05/11/97	06/11/96	05/11/97	06/11/96	05/11/97	06/11/96	05/11/97	06/11/96	05/11/97
Cyprus	16/12/61	06/10/62	16/12/61	06/10/62	06/10/88	03/10/89	07/05/99	19/01/00	02/12/99	15/09/00
Czech Republic	21/02/91	18/03/92	21/02/91	18/03/92	21/02/91	18/03/92	21/02/91	18/03/92	21/02/91	18/03/92
Denmark	04/11/50	13/04/53	20/03/52	13/04/53	16/09/63	30/09/64	28/04/83	01/12/83	22/11/84	18/08/88
Estonia	14/05/93	16/04/96	14/05/93	16/04/96	14/05/93	16/04/96	14/05/93	17/04/98	14/05/93	16/04/96
Finland	05/05/89	10/05/90	05/05/89	10/05/90	05/05/89	10/05/90	05/05/89	10/05/90	05/05/89	10/05/90
France	04/11/50	03/05/74	20/03/52	03/05/74	22/10/73	03/05/74	28/04/83	17/02/86	22/11/84	17/02/86
Georgia	27/04/99	20/05/99	17/06/99	—	17/06/99	13/04/00	17/06/99	13/04/00	17/06/99	13/04/00
Germany	04/11/50	05/12/52	20/03/52	13/02/57	16/09/63	01/06/68	28/04/83	05/07/89	19/03/85	—
Greece	28/11/50	28/03/53	20/03/52	28/11/74	—	—	02/05/83	08/09/98	22/11/84	29/10/87
Hungary	06/11/90	05/11/92	06/11/90	05/11/92	06/11/90	05/11/92	06/11/90	05/11/92	06/11/90	05/11/92
Iceland	04/11/50	29/06/53	20/03/52	29/06/53	16/11/67	16/11/67	24/04/85	22/05/87	19/03/85	22/05/87
Ireland	04/11/50	25/02/53	20/03/52	25/02/53	16/09/63	29/10/68	24/06/94	24/06/94	11/12/84	—
Italy	04/11/50	26/10/55	20/03/52	26/10/55	16/09/63	27/05/82	21/10/83	29/12/88	22/11/84	07/11/91
Latvia	10/02/95	27/06/97	21/03/97	27/06/97	21/03/97	27/06/97	26/06/98	07/05/99	21/03/97	27/06/97

Liechtenstein	23/11/78	08/09/82	07/05/87	14/11/95	—	—	15/11/90	15/11/90	—	—
Lithuania	14/05/93	20/06/95	14/05/93	24/05/96	14/05/93	20/06/95	18/01/99	08/07/99	14/05/93	20/06/95
Luxembourg	04/11/50	03/09/53	20/03/52	03/09/53	16/09/63	02/05/68	28/04/83	19/02/85	22/11/84	19/04/89
Macedonia	09/11/95	10/04/97	14/06/96	10/04/97	14/06/96	10/04/97	14/06/96	10/04/97	14/06/96	10/04/97
Malta	12/12/66	23/01/67	12/12/66	23/01/67	—	—	26/03/91	26/03/91	—	—
Moldova	13/07/95	12/09/97	02/05/96	12/09/97	02/05/96	12/09/97	02/05/96	12/09/97	02/05/96	12/09/97
Netherlands	04/11/50	31/08/54	20/03/52	31/08/54	15/11/63	23/06/82	28/04/83	25/04/86	22/11/84	—
Norway	04/11/50	15/01/52	20/03/52	18/12/52	16/09/63	12/06/64	28/04/83	25/10/88	22/11/84	25/10/88
Poland	26/11/91	19/01/93	14/09/92	10/10/94	14/09/92	10/10/94	18/11/99	30/10/00	14/09/92	—
Portugal	22/09/76	09/11/78	22/09/76	09/11/78	27/04/78	/09/11/78	28/04/83	02/10/86	22/11/84	—
Romania	07/10/93	20/06/94	04/11/93	20/06/94	04/11/93	20/06/94	15/12/93	20/06/94	04/11/93	20/06/94
Russia	28/02/96	05/05/98	28/02/96	05/05/98	28/02/96	05/05/98	16/04/97	—	28/02/96	05/05/98
San Marino	16/11/88	22/03/89	01/03/89	22/03/89	01/03/89	22/03/89	01/03/89	22/03/89	01/03/89	22/03/89
Slovakia	21/02/91	18/03/92	21/02/91	18/03/92	21/02/91	18/03/92	21/02/91	18/03/92	21/02/91	18/03/92
Slovenia	14/05/93	28/06/94	14/05/93	28/06/94	14/05/93	28/06/94	14/05/93	28/06/94	14/05/93	28/06/94
Spain	24/11/77	04/10/79	23/02/78	27/11/90	23/02/78	—	28/04/83	14/01/85	22/11/84	—
Sweden	28/11/50	04/02/52	20/03/52	22/06/53	16/09/63	13/06/64	28/04/83	09/02/84	22/11/84	08/11/85
Switzerland	21/12/72	28/11/74	19/05/76	—	—	—	28/04/83	13/10/87	28/02/86	24/02/88
Turkey	04/11/50	18/05/54	20/03/52	18/05/54	19/10/92	—	—	—	14/03/85	—
Ukraine	09/11/95	11/09/97	19/12/96	11/09/97	19/12/96	11/09/97	05/05/97	04/04/00	19/12/96	11/09/97
United Kingdom	04/11/50	08/03/51	20/03/52	03/11/52	16/09/63	—	27/01/99	20/05/99	—	—

[17] As at 4 November 2000.

which they had been the victim. Individual applications have constituted by far the major part of the workload of the Commission and Court, providing the driving force behind the sophisticated body of human rights jurisprudence built up by the Court on a case-by-case basis. The fact that all contracting states to the Convention eventually ratified the optional right of individual petition, and that since Protocol No. 11 it has become compulsory for new members to do so, has also given tangible manifestation to the hugely important post-Second World War concept that today's international human rights law is about ensuring justice for individual citizens regardless of frontiers, and is not, as international law had previously been understood, simply a matter of relationships between governments.

The coming into effect of Protocol No. 11 on 1 November 1998 revolutionized the supervisory and enforcement machinery of the Convention. This major organizational reform, agreed on 11 May 1994, was initiated principally to increase the Strasbourg machinery's capacity to deal with the influx of new member states and the huge upturn in the number of individual applications received alleging human rights violations. Andrew Drzemczewski and Jens Meyer-Ladewig observed at the time of the agreement on Protocol No. 11 that:

> Pressure for reform of the system came from three main sources: firstly, the increase in the number and complexity of cases that are being brought; secondly, the full participation of an ever-increasing number of Central and Eastern European countries; and thirdly . . . the movement of the European Community (Union) towards a single market and political union with increased awareness of the legal and political importance of human rights protection as a component part of the European Union's concerns.[18]

The principal changes put into effect by Protocol No. 11 are that:

- The pre-existing part-time institutions of the European Commission of Human Rights and the European Court of Human Rights are now superseded by a single new full-time European Court of Human Rights.
- All applications under the Convention now go directly to the Court.
- The right of individual petition becomes mandatory for all member states.

As discussed below, many of the working practices and procedures of the new Court are a continuation of those originally adopted and developed by the Commission and part-time Court. Their substitution by the new full-time Court is best described and understood as a 'merger' between the two bodies,

[18] *Human Rights Law Journal* (1994) 84.

intended to streamline its work, avoid duplication, shorten procedures, and render its overall processing of applications more effective.[19]

Under the system operating until 1998 all applications were dealt with initially by the European Commission of Human Rights. The Commission performed the great majority of the work of legal review under the Convention, with only a relatively small number of cases being referred to the Court. The Commission began work in July 1954 and in its first forty years to 31 December 1994 it registered a total of 26,058 individual applications. Of these 2,027 were declared admissible by the Commission, with 211 leading to a friendly settlement. By comparison, the Court commenced work in 1959, in the calendar year 1960 receiving its first two references and delivering its first judgment in the case of *Lawless v Ireland*,[20] and by the end of 1994 it had received 506 referred cases and delivered a total of 498 judgments.

The approach of the Commission was first to conduct an examination into the admissibility of the case, striking out applications that were manifestly ill founded. A preliminary examination was undertaken by a member of the Commission acting as rapporteur, following which the question of admissibility would be referred as appropriate to a committee of three members, a Chamber of the Commission comprising at least seven of its members, or the plenary Commission to decide. Depending on the level of seriousness or the complexity of the case, the Commission would communicate the complaint to the government concerned and request its written observations. It might also hold a hearing at which both parties could make oral submissions. Secondly, if a case was found admissible, the Commission or a Chamber would consider the case in depth with the assistance of the parties, where necessary holding its own investigation into the facts. A friendly settlement of the dispute would be promoted by way of the Commission putting itself at the disposal of the parties for attempts at conciliation between them. If no settlement was forthcoming, however, the Commission produced its Report. Within three months, the Commission or government could refer the case to the Court; after 1994 (where the member state had ratified Protocol No. 9) the individual applicant also had the right to do so. The former part-time Court regularly sat in plenary session until 1994, though a Chamber composed of nine judges was authorized to do so.[21] Protocol No. 9 conferred new rights on individual applicants to bring cases before the Court and established a new

[19] Generally see 'Merger of the European Commission and European Court of Human Rights' in *Human Rights Law Journal* (1987) 1; and special issue on Protocol No. 11 in *Human Rights Law Journal* (1994) 81. See also Andrew Drzemczewski, 'The European Human Rights Convention: A New Court of Human Rights in Strasbourg as of 1st November 1998', paper delivered to Conference on 'The Future of International Human Rights' at Lexington, Virginia, 26–27 March 1998.

[20] Judgment of 14 November 1960, Series A No. 1.

[21] Under former Article 43.

filtering system of committees of three judges who would determine whether the case should go forward to a Chamber or not.

The formal structure and operation of the post-1998 permanent Court of Human Rights is set out in the articles of the Convention as revised by Protocol No. 11. Under Article 32 the jurisdiction of the Court extends to all matters concerning the interpretation and application of the Convention and the Protocols, and in the event of dispute as to whether the Court possesses jurisdiction, the Court itself determines the issue. To consider cases brought before it, the Court is structured into Committees of three judges, Chambers of seven judges, and a Grand Chamber of seventeen judges. Under Article 28 a Committee may by unanimous vote declare individual cases inadmissible, but if no such decision is taken then under Article 29 a Chamber will proceed to decide the admissibility and merits of individual applications. Inter-state cases go direct to a Chamber of the Court.[22] Under Article 35, laying down admissibility criteria, the court may only accept a case after the applicant has exhausted all domestic remedies and within a period of six months from the date on which the final domestic decision was taken.

The pre-existing working practices of the Commission and the Court are reflected in the revised articles governing the Court today, and they include broadly similar wording from the earlier articles and/or the Rules of Court. This is so, for example, with respect to the manner of examination of a case and friendly settlement proceedings under Article 38 (based on former Article 28); and of the successful conclusion of friendly settlements under Article 39 (modelled on former Rule of Court no. 49), involving the Court striking the case from its lists and publishing a decision confined to a brief statement of the facts and solution reached. The presumption in favour of public oral hearings and public access to written documents at the trial is set down in Article 40 (which is modelled on former Rules of Court nos. 18 and 56). Article 45 (modelled on former Article 51) lays down the general rule that all judgments and most other decisions of the Court must be reasoned, whether they deal with the merits of the case, the award of just satisfaction, or questions relating to jurisdiction or procedure.

The authority of the Court is at its greatest when it sits as a Grand Chamber of seventeen judges. Under Article 30, a Chamber may relinquish jurisdiction of a case in favour of the Grand Chamber where the case raises a serious question affecting the interpretation of the Convention or where the resolution of a question before the Chamber might reach a result inconsistent with a previously delivered judgment of the Court. Contrary to the former Rules of Court, Article 30 does not oblige a Chamber to relinquish jurisdiction,

[22] Article 29(2).

instead conferring a discretion.[23] Where a case raises a serious question affecting the interpretation or application of the Convention and its Protocols or a serious issue of general importance, Article 43 provides that either or both of the parties to the case may refer a decision of the Chamber within three months to the Grand Chamber. However, a rehearing of the case in this way is only possible in exceptional circumstances, and the requirement for a serious issue to be at stake is to be construed restrictively.[24] A referral will be particularly appropriate when an important precedent is likely to be set, when future development of the Court's case-law is at stake, or a substantial political or policy issue is involved.

The total number of judges of the Court of Human Rights is equal to that of member states, currently forty-one.[25] Each member state is responsible for nominating a new judge, by forwarding the names of three candidates to the Parliamentary Assembly which makes the final selection and formal appointment. However, nominations are not limited to persons who are nationals of the state putting their names forward and there is no numerical limitation upon judges of the same nationality, though in practice it is agreed that no more than two judges of the same nationality should be appointed to the Court.[26] In 1998 Mr Lucius Caflisch, a Swiss national, was appointed a judge following his nomination by the government of Liechtenstein, and Mr Luzius Wildhaber, another Swiss national, was nominated and appointed in respect of Switzerland itself. Similarly, Mr Luigi Ferrari Bravo, an Italian national, was appointed in respect of San Marino in addition to Mr Benedetto Conforti, another Italian national, appointed from the Italian government's nominees. Individuals appointed are either professionally qualified for serving in judicial office or distinguished University professors ('jurisconsultants of recognized competence') and they serve six-year terms of office with security of tenure.[27] Half the membership of the Court is to fall vacant every three years, providing for some continuity (with the appointments of half the initial appointees in 1998 lapsing in 2001); and on reaching the end of their term of office members may be re-elected, subject to their compulsory retirement on reaching the age of 70 years. Article 21(2–3) stipulates the important requirement that all judges sit in their individual capacity, not as representatives of

[23] See Rule 51 of the former Rules of Court, paragraph 1, second sentence.

[24] Explanatory Report to Protocol No. 11, paragraphs 99–102.

[25] See Articles 20–24; for further discussion with recommendations on the procedures for appointing judges of the Court of Human Rights see Chapter 4 below.

[26] According to the Explanatory Report to Protocol No. 11, paragraph 59.

[27] Judges are removable only upon a two-thirds majority vote of the plenary Court that the judge in question has ceased to fulfill the required conditions, one of which is high moral character: Article 24.

their state governments, and they are prohibited from undertaking any activity which is incompatible with their independence or impartiality.[28]

The plenary Court is required to appoint from among its members various office-holders. Together with those persons appointed to serve for three-year terms when Protocol No. 11 came into force on 1 November 1998, these are the President of the Court (Mr Luzius Wildhaber, Swiss), two Vice-Presidents (Ms Elisabeth Palm, Swedish; Mr Christos Rozakis, Greek) and two Section Presidents. The total membership of the Court is divided into four Sections, all of which aim to be balanced in terms of geography, gender, and legal tradition, and each of which provides the membership on a rolling basis for one of the Court Chambers.

The competence of the Committee of Ministers[29] to determine the merits of a case has been removed altogether by Protocol No. 11, and its role in the human rights machinery is now to supervise the enforcement of the Court's judgments.[30] Previously, under the then Article 32, where a case had not been referred to the Court within the three-month period, the Committee of Ministers could proceed to act in a judicial capacity and determine whether a human rights violation had taken place. To many this role was inappropriate for a political body, composed as it is of Ministers for Foreign Affairs from member states. In the early history of the Convention, however, the Committee had a significant role to play as an alternative route for resolving allegations of human rights violations, particularly concerning member states who had not yet accepted the jurisdiction of the Court of Human Rights under the then Article 46. The Committee's judicial role became increasingly anomalous once acceptance of the jurisdiction of the Court became a condition for membership of the Council.

Though Protocol No. 11 represents a marked change in the organizational history of the Convention's enforcement machinery, the new Court will be

[28] The constitution of the former part-time Court and the Commission before Protocol no. 11 had been different in a few respects. Both of these bodies contained as many members as there were states parties to the Council of Europe (in the case of the Commission the member state concerned must have ratified the Convention) but unlike today there was a prohibition on any two or more members of either the Commission or the Court being nationals of the same country. A member state could nominate one foreign national, however: after joining the Council of Europe, Liechtenstein put forward a Canadian as its first nominee who was then duly appointed a judge of the Court. Until 1998, judges served nine-year terms of office and Commissioners six years. Judges were appointed by the Parliamentary Assembly from names submitted by member states; Commissioners were appointed by the Committee of Ministers from a list of names prepared by the Bureau of the President of the Assembly, drawn from nominations of the parliamentary representatives of member states in the Assembly.

[29] The Committee is the policy-making and executive organ of the Council of Europe. On its human rights work between 1953–98, see Adam Tomkins, 'The Committee of Ministers: Its Roles under the European Convention on Human Rights', *European Human Rights Law Review*, Launch Issue (1995) 49.

[30] See page 63 below.

Table 1.2. *Development in the number of individual applications lodged with the Court (formerly the Commission), 1955–2000*

	Provisional files	*Applications registered*	*Decisions taken*	*Applications declared inadmissible or struck off the list*	*Applications declared admissible*	*Decisions to reject in the course of the examination of the merits*	*Judgments delivered by the Court*
1955–1983	25 308	10 709	9 984	9 658	326	8	76
1984	3 007	586	582	528	54	0	18
1985	2 831	596	582	512	70	0	11
1986	2 869	706	511	469	42	0	17
1987	3 675	860	590	559	31	0	32
1988	4 108	1 009	654	602	52	0	26
1989	4 900	1 445	1 338	1 243	95	0	25
1990	4 942	1 657	1 216	1 065	151	0	30
1991	5 550	1 648	1 659	1 441	217	1	72
1992	5 875	1 861	1 704	1 515	189	0	81
1993	9 323	2 037	1 765	1 547	218	1	60
1994	9 968	2 944	2 372	1 789	582	1	50
1995	10 201	3 481	2 990	2 182	807	0	56
1996	12 143	4 758	3 400	2 776	624	0	72
1997	12 469	4 750	3 777	3 073	703	1	106
1998	16 353	5 981	4 420	3 658	762	0	105
1999	20 399	8 396	4 250	3 519	731	0	177
2000	26 398	10 486	7 852	6 769	1 082	0	695
Total	180 319	63 910	49 646	42 905	6 736	12	1 709

carrying forward and building upon most of the positive aspects of the forms and patterns of work pioneered and established by the former Commission and Court. Future historians will view the foundations of our European human rights legal heritage as having been laid in the formative period to 1 November 1998, between the Convention's original enforcement machinery entering into force and Protocol No. 11 coming into effect.

D. WINNING POPULAR CONFIDENCE AND SUSTAINING GOVERNMENTAL SUPPORT

Vital to the success of the Convention throughout its existence has been the steady accumulation of popular support which the right of individual access to the Commission and Court has brought to the Convention over the past fifty years. For ordinary people it has been almost universally regarded as a benevolent force and a body of last resort where justice might be obtained whenever domestic remedies are lacking. Despite occasional predictable outbursts of hostile comment from government politicians following adverse rulings against them on sensitive issues, the Commission and Court have also successfully managed to work with, and carry along the confidence of, officials of member states. This achievement in gaining the confidence of public and governments alike, avoiding institutional bias—or the appearance of one—in favour of one or the other, has been crucial to the successful development of the Convention. It owes a great deal to the special procedures for friendly settlements under Articles 38 and 39,[31] whereby if the Court (formerly the Commission) declares the application admissible, a senior official will seek to facilitate an out-of-court settlement between the parties acceptable to both, conducting if necessary an investigation into the facts surrounding the grievance, and acting as a broker between the two. This

[31] Article 38 reads:

Examination of the case and friendly settlement proceedings—1. If the Court declares the application admissible, it shall (a) pursue the examination of the case, together with the representatives of the parties, and if need be, undertake an investigation, for the effective conduct of which the States concerned shall furnish all necessary facilities; (b) place itself at the disposal of the parties concerned with a view to securing a friendly settlement of the matter on the basis of resepct for human rights as defined in the Convention and the protocols thereto. 2. Proceedings conducted under paragraph 1(b) shall be confidential.

Article 39 then reads:

Finding of a friendly settlement—If a friendly settlement is effected, the Court shall strike the case out of its list by means of a decision which shall be confined to a brief statement of the facts and of the solution reached.

involves considerable skill, combining a proactive peacemaking role with a non-confrontational manner. As a former Secretary to the Commission, Anthony McNulty, described the situation in 1971 (having himself been involved in many friendly settlement initiatives):

It is a reasonable deduction that the Commission has substantially established itself in the confidence both of the public and of the parties to the Convention. It is particularly this basis for co-operation between the Commission and Government, rather than a relationship of prosecutor and accused, which has brought this about and generally made the Convention workable.[32]

So far as maintaining the confidence and continuing membership of governments has been concerned over these fifty years, the Council of Europe has been sensitive to political realities and the differing paces at which individual states are prepared to accept the necessary invasiveness into domestic legal and political systems. The growing scope of the Convention, as many new rights and freedoms are added, has been implemented by protocols that are optional, allowing member states to determine when they choose to participate through a separate system of ratifications. The Court can also be seen to have operated in a diplomatically astute manner, seeking a common denominator of morally accepted standards and procedures across Europe whilst countenancing a certain elasticity for national governments to determine sensitive or controversial questions.[33] As van Dijk and van Hoof have put it:

The success or failure of international instruments, including those like the European Convention, in the end depends on the political will of the states involved. Legal arguments, however cogent they may be, in the final analysis seldom override political considerations when states feel that their vital interests are at stake.[34]

Alongside the beneficially proactive role adopted in individual application cases, carried out by the Strasbourg organs where a friendly settlement with governments might be reached, at the more general supervisory level the Council's human rights secretariat can be seen as having followed a softer, tactful line of approach, designed not to upset prickly government politicians who from time to time have harboured resentments about foreign or international controls upon their national freedom of action. The Convention contains no mandatory requirements for national governments to report to the Secretariat annually on human rights developments in its jurisdiction.[35]

[32] Quoted in R. Beddard, *Human Rights and Europe* (Cambridge: Grotius, 3rd edn. 1993) 5.

[33] Notably the 'margin of appreciation' doctrine, on which see below.

[34] *Theory and Practice of the European Convention on Human Rights* (The Hague: Kluwer, 2nd edn, 1990) 618.

[35] Contrast the periodic reporting requirements under the UN International Covenant on Civil and Political Rights, Article 40.

Table 1.3. *ECHR Control Mechanisms before and after Protocol No. 11, 1998*[36]

A: FORMER CONTROL MECHANISM (1953–98)

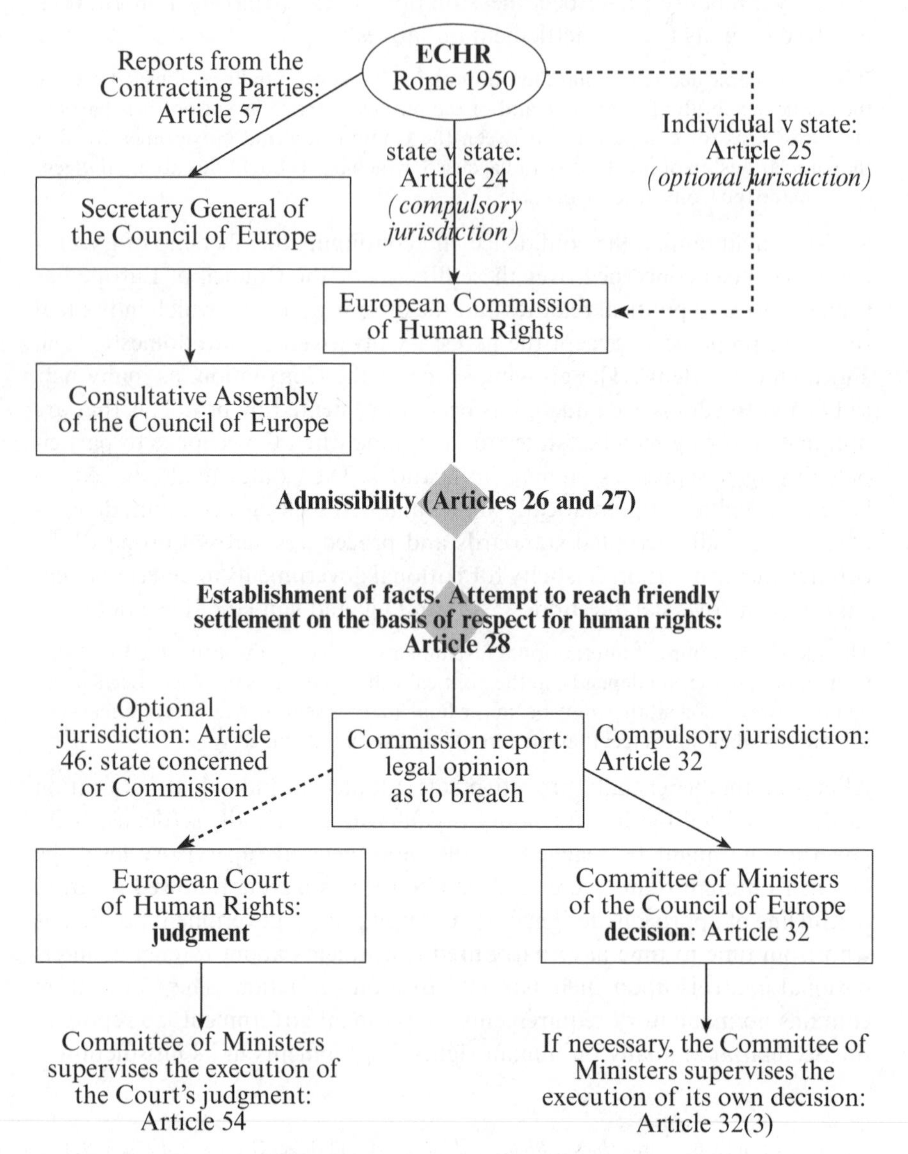

[36] Council of Europe, 2000.

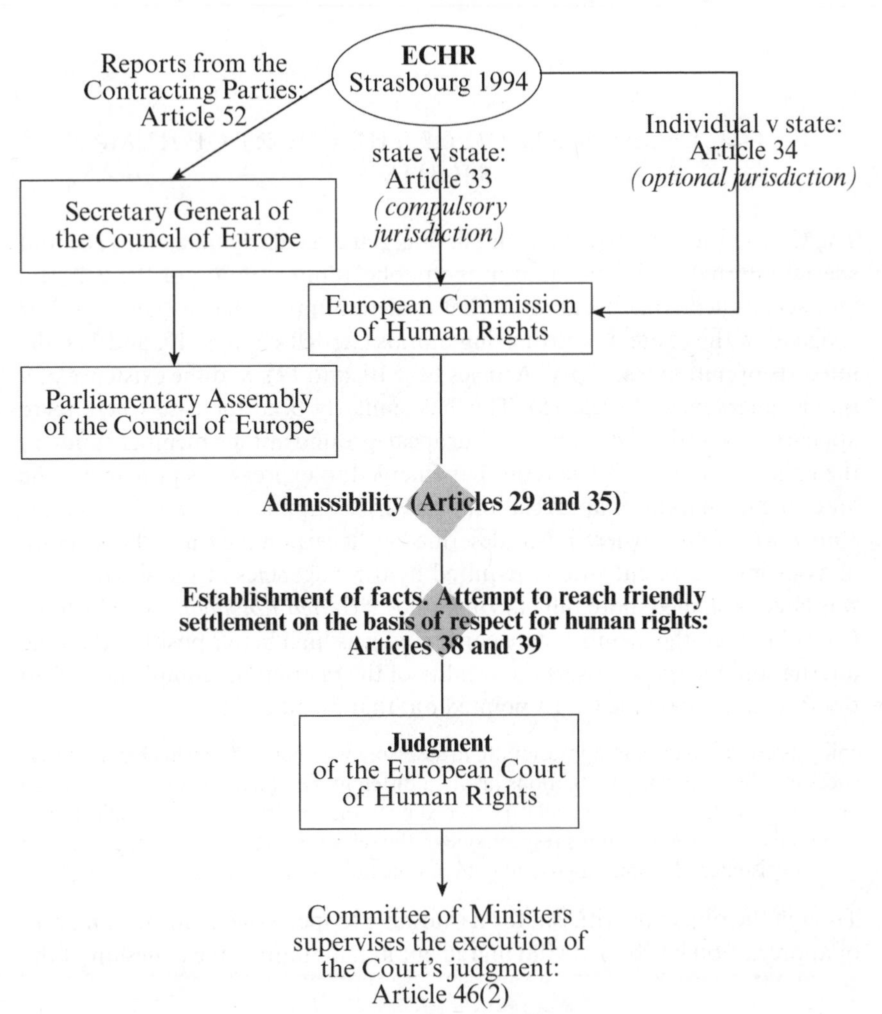

The Secretary General does possess the power under Article 52 of the Convention to require a member state to furnish an explanation to him or her of the manner in which its internal law ensures the effective implementation of any of the provisions of the Convention. But this procedure, which might offend the sensibilities of a recipient government already self-conscious over the particular matter of concern (and give the Council's secretariat the aura of prosecutor) has only ever been exercised five times; and in each case it has tactfully been addressed to member states generally, never at an individual state.

E. THE LEGAL METHOD OF THE COURT OF HUMAN RIGHTS

The Court, and formerly the Commission, have regularly taken into account special internal problems faced in the public administration of the country, and sanctioned some local discretion in determining what is 'necessary' or 'exigent' in the context of protecting morals (Articles 6, 8, 9, 10, and 11), the interests of national security (Articles 6, 8, 10, and 11), and the existence of a public emergency (Article 15). This has similarly been the case where there appears to be little or no common European ground among member states on the issue in question.[37] The term that emerged to express this principle is the 'doctrine of margin of appreciation'. Its earliest application was in *Greece v United Kingdom,*[38] where it was described as 'a certain measure of discretion in assessing the extent strictly required by the exigencies of the situation'. It was later explained more fully in *Handyside v United Kingdom*,[39] in which the Court believed the member state concerned was 'in a better position than the international judge' to assess the validity of the restrictions complained of. In the *Rasmussen* case the Court pointed out that member states:

> enjoy a certain 'margin of appreciation' in assessing whether and to what extent differences in otherwise similar situations justify a different treatment in law . . . The scope of the margin of appreciation will vary according to the circumstances, the subject-matter and its background; in this respect, one of the relevant factors may be the existence or non-existence of common ground between the laws of the contracting parties.[40]

Though the object of criticism for its variable scope,[41] the doctrine of margin of appreciation has been a vital ingredient in maintaining the cohesion of the

[37] See for example *Rasmussen v Denmark*, Judgment of 28 November 1984, Series A No. 87, para. 40 concerning the rights of fathers; and *Rees v United Kingdom*, 17 October 1986, Series A No. 106, para. 37 on the rights of transsexuals.

[38] Application 176/57, (1958–59) 2 Yearbook 174, 176.

[39] Judgment of 7 December 1976, Series A No. 24, paras. 48–49. Generally see P. van Dijk and G. J. H. van Hoof, *Theory and Practice of the European Convention on Human Rights* (The Hague: Kluwer, 3rd edn 1998) 82f.

[40] Note 3 above.

[41] For example 'the margin of appreciation is reduced almost to vanishing point in certain areas': D. J. Harris, M. O'Boyle, C. Warbrick, *Law of the European Convention on Human Rights* (London: Butterworths, 1995) 14. See further comments page 81 below.

Convention, and particularly over the past ten years the doctrine has become more clearly developed in the categories and situations in which it might apply.[42]

The work of the European Court of Human Rights and its jurisprudence has been reactive to the particular events and applications which have been presented to it. The method of the Court has been to adopt an essentially common law approach, allowing it to elaborate upon the meaning and application of the human rights articles in the Convention on a case-by-case basis, regarding itself as bound by the doctrine of *stare decisis* (precedent). There are no provisions in the Convention for the Court to issue general statements akin to the General Comments made by the Human Rights Committee established by the International Covenant on Civil and Political Rights. The Court has operated within clearly perceived perameters of its purpose, by reference to the fundamental aims of the Council of Europe. These include, first, that the Convention and its decision-making should operate as a common denominator among member states, representing a standard below which European human rights must not fall. In other words, as the legal writers Donna Gomien, David Harris, and Leo Zwaak have put it, the Convention, like other international human rights instruments, serves to 'delineate thresholds for state compliance and not ceilings'[43] and within member states it is to be hoped that standards of rights and freedoms are enlarged through national legislation, whether of a constitutional nature or otherwise.

Secondly, the Court has regularly emphasized the subsidiary nature of the Convention. Before any individual application can be presented to the European Court of Human Rights, and formerly the Commission, the applicant must show that he or she has pursued all possible avenues for redressing his or her grievance within the domestic legal and administrative systems of the state concerned. Article 35 specifically restricts the jurisdiction of the Court to cases where all domestic remedies have been exhausted. As the former president of the Court, Rolv Ryssdal, commented:

> The machinery set up by the Convention is of a subsidiary nature: in other words, it falls in the first place to the national authorities and in particular the national courts to ensure that the rights and freedoms of the individual are protected. It is thus essential that the domestic legal system makes provision for appeals and remedies

[42] See van P. Dijk and G. J. H. van Hoof, *Theory and Practice of the European Convention on Human Rights* (The Hague: Kluwer, 3rd edn 1998), chapter II:3 who nonetheless conclude that 'no hard and fast rules governing the scope of the margin of appreciation can be identified'. See page 81 below.

[43] *Law and Practice of the European Convention on Human Rights and the European Social Charter* (Council of Europe, 1996) 17.

Table 1.4. *Violations by Member States found by the European Court of Human Rights and the Committee of Ministers, 1960–2000*

State Party	*Population*	*Number of violations* Court of Human Rights (to 31.12.00)	*Committee of Ministers (to 31.12.99)*	*Date of acceptance of right of individual petition (former Article 25)*
Albania	3,731,000	0	0	2.10.96
Andorra	65,877	0	0	22.1.96
Austria	8,072,000	70	79	3.9.58
Belgium	10,188,000	27	16	5.7.55
Bulgaria	8,306,000	6	4	7.9.92
Croatia	4,498,000	0	0	6.11.96
Cyprus	766,000	6	1	1.1.89
Czech Republic	10,304,000	4	0	18.3.92
Denmark	5,284,000	4	1	13.1.53
Estonia	1,453,844	0	0	16.4.96
Finland	5,140,000	9	2	10.5.90
France	58,607,000	128	229	2.10.81
Georgia	5,411,000	0	0	20.5.99
Germany	82,071,000	20	12	5.7.55
Greece	10,522,000	47	14	10.11.85
Hungary	10,153,000	1	4	5.11.92
Iceland	278,702	2	0	29.3.55
Ireland	3,626,087	8	2	25.2.53
Italy	57,523,000	378	1951	1.8.73
Latvia	2,474,000	0	0	27.6.97
Liechtenstein	32,015	1	0	8.9.82
Lithuania	3,701,300	4	0	20.6.95
Luxembourg	417,000	2	0	28.4.58
Macedonia	2,190,000	0	0	10.4.97
Malta	378,518	4	0	1.5.87
Moldova	4,335,000	0	0	12.9.97
Netherlands	15,604,000	33	27	28.6.60
Norway	4,445,460	6	1	10.12.55
Poland	38,650,000	16	3	1.5.93
Portugal	9,920,760	30	65	9.11.78
Romania	22,520,000	7	1	20.6.94
Russia	145,400,000	0	0	5.5.98
San Marino	26,000	3	0	22.3.89
Slovakia	5,383,000	4	4	18.3.92
Slovenia	1,987,000	2	0	20.6.94

State Party	*Population*	*Number of violations* Court of Human Rights (to 31.12.00)	Committee of Ministers (to 31.12.99)	*Date of acceptance of right of individual petition (former Article 25)*
Spain	39,270,000	13	4	1.7.81
Sweden	8,846,000	22	20	4.2.52
Switzerland	7,114,600	26	8	28.11.74
Turkey	63,745,000	65	10	28.1.87
Ukraine	50,500,000	0	0	11.9.97
United Kingdom	56,467,000	82	55	14.1.66

appropriate to prevent, and if necessary, to redress and compensate the violation of the rights and freedoms guaranteed.[44]

Though historically the Court has refrained from construing Article 1 of the Convention ('the High Contracting Parties shall secure to everyone within their jurisdiction the rights and freedoms defined in . . . the Convention') as an actual requirement for member states to incorporate the Convention's human rights articles into its domestic law,[45] the strong prevailing opinion at Strasbourg has always been that the most effective way of both enforcing the Convention's principles and minimizing the work of the Court of Human Rights is through incorporation. It may well have been the Court's inherent diplomacy and sensitivity in seeking to avoid confrontation over an issue that might well have put continued membership of some states who doggedly refused to incorporate the Convention at risk which explains, at least in part, its interpretation of Article 1.[46]

Thirdly, the Court has viewed its role as facilitating an organic process and dialogue between national systems and the Strasbourg machinery towards establishing a common European law on human rights. This has involved the Court paying close attention to the distinctive legal traditions and cultures of member states and welcoming the positive contributions that national judicial systems of member states can make in articulating and developing theory and practice on human rights, which in turn serves to influence the

[44] Cour (90) 318.

[45] See page 32 below.

[46] See for example the United Kingdom government's clearly expressed public determination that it would not incorporate the Convention throughout the administrations of Margaret Thatcher 1979–90 and John Major 1990–97: chapter 36 below.

developing jurisprudence of the Court of Human Rights. The Commission and Court has not sought the uniformity or harmonization of laws and procedures relating to civil liberties and human rights for their own sake or simply in order to impose what it believes would be a better standard of human rights. This organic process clearly works best where the member state's judicial system may apply the human rights articles of the Convention, through incorporation of the Convention in its domestic law, or of its own bill of rights where similar or analogous provisions exists. This, in the words of former judge Rolv Ryssdal:

> gives the European organs an opportunity to discover the views of the national courts regarding the interpretation of the Convention and its application to a specific set of circumstances. The dialogue which thus develops between those who are called upon to apply the Convention on the domestic level and those who must do so on the European level is crucial for an effective protection of the rights guaranteed under the Convention.[47]

These characteristics of the jurisprudence of the Court as they have emerged over the past fifty years are reflected in the judgments and dicta of the Court on its own rules by which it proceeds to interpret the Convention. These take as their starting point Article 31 of the Vienna Convention on the Law of Treaties, which states that:

> a treaty shall be interpreted in good faith in accordance with the ordinary meaning to be given to the terms of the treaty in their context and in the light of its object and purpose.

As with all international human rights treaties, the fundamental purpose of the Convention is to protect the rights of the individual and not to lay down mutual obligations between states which are to be restrictively interpreted.[48] Another important principle repeatedly stressed by the Court is that interpretations and meanings of terms in the human rights articles of the Convention are evolutionary or 'dynamic': they are to be understood and applied according to changing Europe-wide social and political values and attitudes. Thus, as expressed in the *Tyrer* case, the Convention is to be regarded as a 'living instrument . . . which must be interpreted in the light of present-day conditions'.[49] The Court's whole approach to these interpretative issues, then, were ably summed up by Judge Bernhardt as follows:

> The general rules of treaty interpretation are in principle also applicable to human rights treaties, but the object and purpose of these treaties are different and, therefore, the traditional rules need some adjustment. The notions contained in human rights

[47] Cour (90) 318.
[48] See *Commission Report, Golder v United Kingdom*, 1 June 1973, Series B No. 16, 40.
[49] *Tyrer v United Kingdom*, Judgment of 25 April 1978, Series A No. 26, page 15.

conventions have an autonomous international meaning; however, such meaning must be determined by a comparative analysis of the legal situation in the participating states. To the extent that this analysis shows considerable differences and disparities among the states, a national 'margin of appreciation' is and must be recognised. Human rights treaties must be interpreted in an objective and dynamic manner, by taking into account social conditions and developments; the ideas and conditions prevailing at the time when the treaties were drafted retain hardly any continuing validity. Nevertheless, treaty interpretation must not amount to treaty revision. Interpretation must therefore respect the text of the treaty concerned.[50]

[50] Judge R. Bernhardt, 'Thoughts on the interpretation of human-rights treaties', in F. Matscher and H. Petzold, *Protecting Human Rights: The European Dimension* (Köln, 1988) 70–71, quoted in Francis G. Jacobs and Robin C. A. White, *The European Convention on Human Rights* (Oxford University Press, 2nd edn 1996) 38.

2

The Status of the Convention in National Law

JÖRG POLAKIEWICZ

A. The Convention as a treaty under international law and the issue of incorporation
B. The status of the Convention in the member states of the Council of Europe (an overview)
C. The position of the Convention with regard to the fundamental rights and freedoms of national constitutions
D. Application of the rights and freedoms of the Convention in domestic law

A. THE CONVENTION AS A TREATY UNDER INTERNATIONAL LAW AND THE ISSUE OF INCORPORATION[1]

1. The traditional view: the Convention as a treaty under international law which does not entail any obligation to incorporate its provisions into domestic law

The discussion on whether the Convention contains an obligation to incorporate its provisions into domestic law starts traditionally from the premiss that the Convention is a treaty concluded under the rules of international law. It follows that, at least on the international level, the Convention is superior

[1] See J. P. Gardner (ed), *Aspects of Incorporation of the European Convention on Human Rights* (British Institute of International and Comparative Law/British Institute of Human Rights, 1993); R. Bernhardt, 'The Convention and Domestic Law', in: R. St-J. Macdonald/F. Matscher/H. Petzold (eds) *The European System for the Protection of Human Rights* (Köln: Heymanns, 1993) 25–40.

to any national law. No state can refer to its domestic law in order to escape obligations derived from the Convention.[2]

The implementation of international law within domestic legal systems is one of the classical subjects of international law which is often discussed with reference to the theories of monism and dualism.[3] At least in theory, two different situations have to be distinguished. In states with a monist tradition, the rights and freedoms of a treaty can be applied by the courts immediately after ratification of the treaty. In States favouring a dualist approach to international law, the substantive norms of a treaty must be 'transformed' or 'adopted' in order to become applicable in domestic law.[4]

With regard to the internal application of the Convention's rights and freedoms, this difference appears not to be decisive. Irrespective of whether a country follows a monist or dualist tradition, a parliamentary act is usually required in order to give direct effect to the Convention's provisions. This act can either be the act of ratification, ie the law approving the treaty and authorizing the deposit of an instrument of ratification in Strasbourg, or a separate enabling act, as is the case particularly in countries with a common law tradition.

In the past it had been suggested that the Convention, and in particular its articles 1 and 13, created a legal obligation to make its provisions internally applicable.[5] The treaties establishing the European Communities were referred to as examples of treaties under public international law creating such an obligation.

Back in 1978, in the case of *Ireland v United Kingdom*, the Strasbourg Court showed a clear preference for incorporation. It stressed that the intention of the Convention's drafters found 'a particularly faithful reflection' in those instances where its provisions had been incorporated into domestic law.[6] However, in subsequent cases, the Commission and the Court have consistently held that neither articles 1 or 13 of the ECHR nor the Convention in

[2] See art 27 of the 1969 Vienna Convention on the Law of Treaties as well as numerous judgments of the Permanent Court of International Justice and the International Court of Justice, eg *Wimbledon* case (1923), P.C.I.J., Series A no. 1, 19; *Fisheries* case, I.C.J. Reports 1951, 116 (132); *Nottebohm* case, I.C.J. Reports 1955, 4 (20–1).

[3] See I. Brownlie, *Principles of Public International Law* (4th edn, 1990), 32–5; T. Buergenthal, 'Self-Executing and Non-Self-Executing Treaties in National and International Law', *Recueil des cours* 235 (1992–IV), 304 (341–67); A. Cassese, 'Modern Constitutions and International Law', *Recueil des cours* 192 (1985–III), 192 et seq.

[4] The problem whether international treaties can be incorporated in domestic law without losing their character as international law, which may have consequences for their interpretation, has been extensively discussed. Opinions vary from country to country.

[5] T. Buergenthal, 'The Effect of the European Convention on Human Rights on the Internal Law of Member States', I.C.L.Q., Supplementary Publication No. 11 (1965), 79 (80–83); P. Pescatore, 'L'application judiciaire des traités internationaux dans la Communauté européenne et dans ses Etats membres', *Mélanges P.-H. Teitgen* (1984), 355 et seq.

[6] Judgment of 18.1.1978, Series A no. 25, § 239.

general lay down any given manner for ensuring within domestic law the effective implementation of any of the provisions of the Convention.[7]

The question of incorporation has primarily been addressed with reference to article 13 of the ECHR which guarantees to everyone whose rights and freedoms are violated 'an effective remedy before a national authority'. According to the Court, instead of imposing an obligation to give direct effect to the substantive provisions of the Convention, article 13 of the ECHR only guarantees the availability at the national level of an effective remedy to enforce the substance of the Convention rights and freedoms in whatever form they may happen to be secured. If the Convention's rights and freedoms cannot be directly invoked before national judicial or administrative authorities, it is sufficient to provide a domestic remedy to deal with the substance of the relevant Convention complaint and to grant appropriate relief, it being understood that states enjoy some discretion as to the manner in which they conform to their obligations under this provision.[8] Nevertheless, the remedy required by article 13 of the ECHR must be effective in practice as well as in law, in particular in the sense that its exercise must not be unjustifiably hindered by acts or omissions of the responsible state authorities.[9] A state that does not make the Convention rights enforceable is especially at risk of being in breach of article 13.[10]

It is therefore generally accepted that states are in principle free to choose the means which suit them best for ensuring the effective enjoyment of the rights and freedoms set forth in the Convention, be it incorporation or not. Like other rules of international law, the Convention requires that the parties guarantee a certain result—the conformity of their domestic law and practice with the conventional duties—but it leaves the manner in which this result is achieved to the discretion of the Parties.[11]

2. The special features of the Convention and their impact on domestic implementation

The Convention has certain features which transcend the traditional barrier between the individual and the international order and which distinguish it

[7] See eg *Observer and Guardian v UK*, judgment of 26.11.1991, Series A no. 216, § 76; *Silver and Others*, judgment of 25.3.1983, Series A no. 61, § 113; *Swedish Engine Drivers' Union* judgment of 6.2.1976, Series A no. 20, § 50.

[8] *James and Others*, judgment of 21.2.1986, Series A no. 98, § 84; *Lithgow and Others*, judgment of 8.7.1986, Series A no. 102, § 205; *Ergi v Turkey*, judgment of 28.7.1998, *Reports of Judgments and Decisions* 1998–IV, 1781 (§ 96).

[9] *Aydin* v *Turkey*, judgment of 25.9.1997, *Reports of Judgments and Decisions* 1997–VI, 1895–96 (§ 103); *Salman v Turkey*, application no. 21986/93, judgment of 27.6.2000, § 121.

[10] See eg *Abdulaziz, Cabales, and Balkandali*, judgment of 28.5.1985, Series A no. 94, § 93; *Campbell and Fell*, judgment of 28.6.1984, Series A no. 80, § 127; *Silver and Others*, judgment of 25.3.1983, Series A no. 61, §§ 118–19.

[11] Bernhardt, *supra* note 1, 25–6.

from other international treaties. It is designed to protect individuals against improper actions by their own national authorities. In this sense, the Convention has the same function as constitutional fundamental rights guarantees. It has granted subjective rights and freedoms which, in the words of the Convention's Preamble, benefit from a collective enforcement through the international supervision exercised by the European Court of Human Rights which may be addressed directly by anyone who is under the jurisdiction of one of the states parties. Since the entry into force of Protocol No. 11 to the ECHR on 1 November 1998, the Court sits permanently in Strasbourg.[12]

With reference to its special features, the Strasbourg Court held that the Convention 'creates over and above a network of mutual, bilateral undertakings, objective obligations'.[13] Recognizing that the Convention combines elements of international and constitutional law, both the Court and the Commission have characterized it as 'a constitutional instrument of European public order (*ordre public*)' in the field of human rights.[14] In this sense, the practice of the European Court and the Commission of Human Rights has contributed substantially to the development of a truly European constitutional jurisprudence.[15] Decisions often find incompatibilities between domestic law and practice on one side and the Convention guarantees on the other requiring immediate changes in domestic law or practice.[16]

The thesis that all national authorities are required to secure the enforcement of the Convention, including the Court's judgments, leads necessarily to a reappraisal of the Convention's status in domestic law. In states in which its rights and freedoms have not been incorporated with precedence over domestic legislation, national authorities may often not be in a position to secure effective compliance with the requirements of the Convention.[17]

[12] Protocol No. 11 to the Convention for the Protection of Human Rights and Fundamental Freedoms, Restructuring the Control Machinery Established Thereby (ETS 155, 1994). See A. Drzemczewski/J. Meyer-Ladewig, 'Principal characteristics of the new ECHR control mechanism, as established by Protocol No. 11, signed on 11 May 1994', H.R.L.J. 14 (1994), 81–115; A. Drzemczewski, 'A major overhaul of the European Human Rights Convention control mechanism: Protocol No. 11', in: *Collected Courses of the Academy of European Law* 1995, vol. IV (1997), 121–244.

[13] *Ireland v United Kingdom*, judgment of 18.1.1978, Series A no. 25, § 239.

[14] *Loizidou v Turkey* (Preliminary Objections), judgment of 23.3.1995, Series A no. 310, § 75; Admissibility decision of the Commission, applications nos. 15299, 15300, and 15318/89—*Chrysostomos and Others v Turkey* (4.3.1991), H.R.L.J. 12 (1990) 113 (121).

[15] See B. Simma, 'From Bilateralism to Community Interests in International Law', *Recueil des Cours* 250 (1994–VI), 373 et seq.; J. A. Frowein, 'Die Herausbildung europäischer Verfassungsprinzipien', in: *Rechtsstaat und Menschenwürde, Festschrift für W. Maihofer zum 70. Geburtstag* (Frankfurt, Klostermann, 1988), 149–58.

[16] See Ch 3 below.

[17] J. Polakiewicz, *Die Verpflichtungen der Staaten aus den Urteilen des Europäischen Gerichtshofs für Menschenrechte* [The obligations of States arising from the judgments of the European Court of Human Rights] (Berlin, Springer, 1992), 237–41.

The limits of statutory interpretation are reached in cases of a clear-cut conflict between the domestic law and the requirements of the Convention. Even if a judge is convinced that domestic law is contrary to the European Convention on Human Rights, he or she must apply it. Lord Denning described this dilemma in his characteristic style in *Taylor v Co-operative Retail Services*:

Mr Taylor was subjected to a degree of compulsion which was contrary to the freedom guaranteed by the European Convention on Human Rights. He was dismissed by his employers because he refused to join a trade union which operated the 'closed shop'. He cannot recover any compensation from his employer under English law because, under the Acts of 1974 and 1976, his dismissal is to be regarded as fair. But those Acts themselves are inconsistent with the freedom guaranteed by the European Convention. The United Kingdom government is responsible for passing those Acts and should pay him compensation. He can recover it by applying to the European Commission and thence to the European Court of Human Rights . . . This means that the appeal must be dismissed. He cannot recover any compensation in these courts. But, if he applies to the European Court of Human Rights, he may in the long run—and I am afraid it may be a long run—obtain compensation there. So in the end justice may be done. But not here.[18]

The well-known rule whereby it is presumed that national legislation has been enacted in conformity with the country's international obligations is again no remedy when statutory provisions are completely lacking. In the absence of any legislation, English courts were unable to create, solely by judicial construction, a regime for telephone tapping that would satisfy the requirements of article 8 of the ECHR.[19]

Incorporation is the most faithful way of implementing the Convention into domestic law. It gives national authorities the opportunity to afford redress in cases of human rights violations before the case is taken to Strasbourg. Protracted proceedings in a forum that is both remote from and unfamiliar to the claimant can thus be spared. The settlement of litigation on the national level, saving both time and money, always remains the preferable solution. International control, as carried out by the Court in Strasbourg, is and should be only subsidiary in nature.[20] Only incorporation of the Convention with precedence over conflicting domestic legislation will enable national authorities to comply fully with the Court's judgments. It follows that an obligation to incorporate the Convention's substantive provisions can

[18] [1982] Industrial Cases Reports 600 (610).

[19] *Malone v Commissioner of Police of the Metropolis* [1979] 2 All E.R. 620.

[20] *Ahmet Sadık v Greece*, judgment of 15.11.1996, *Reports of Judgments and Decisions* 1996–V, 1653 (§ 30). In the *Eckle v Germany* judgment of 15.7.1982 (Series A no. 51) the Court declared that the subsidiary character of the conventional machinery of protection is 'all the more pronounced' in states where the Convention's provisions are directly applicable (31).

be derived from the special character of the Convention and in particular from its articles 1, 41, and 46.

B. THE STATUS OF THE CONVENTION IN THE MEMBER STATES OF THE COUNCIL OF EUROPE (AN OVERVIEW)[21]

On 4 November 2000 all member states of the Council of Europe had ratified the Convention. Following the entry into force of *United Kingdom's* Human Rights Act 1998 and similar legislation in *Ireland* its rights and freedoms will soon be directly applicable in all states parties.[22] Under the Dayton Peace Agreements the Convention has even become applicable in a state which has not ratified it. According to article II.2 of the Constitution of *Bosnia and Herzegovina*, contained in Annex 4 to the Peace Agreements, the Convention has to be applied throughout the territory of Bosnia and Herzegovina.[23]

The status of the Convention in the hierarchy of domestic legal norms varies considerably from one country to another. In some cases, national solutions are based directly on constitutional provisions (eg *Austria, Bulgaria, the Czech Republic, Estonia, France, Georgia, Greece, Latvia, Lithuania, Moldova, the Netherlands, Macedonia,*[24] *Romania, Russia, Slovakia, Slovenia, Spain*, and *Ukraine*) while in others they have emerged from practice and in particular from the case-law of the higher courts (eg *Belgium, Italy, Germany, Lithuania*, and *Switzerland*).

As far as the member states of the European Union are concerned, the status of the European Convention on Human Rights is also influenced by

[21] Andrew Drzemczewski, *European Human Rights Convention in Domestic Law* (Oxford University Press, 1983); C. A. Gearty (ed), *European Civil Liberties and the European Convention on Human Rights* (The Hague: Kluwer, 1997); J. Polakiewicz, 'The Application of the European Convention on Human Rights in Domestic Law', *Human Rights Law Journal* (1997), 405–11; *id*, 'The Implementation of the European Convention on Human Rights in Western Europe: A Survey of National Law and Practice', *All-European Human Rights Yearbook*, vol. 2 (1992), 11–52; *id*, 'The Implementation of the European Convention on Human Rights in Western Europe: An Evaluation', ibid, 147–71; J. Polakiewicz/V. Jacob-Foltzer, 'The European Human Rights Convention in Domestic Law: The Impact of Strasbourg Case-law in States where Direct Effect is given to the Convention', H.R.L.J. 12 (1991), 65–85 (first part) and 125–42 (second part).

[22] Armenia and Azerbaijan signed the Convention on 25 January 2001 when they acceded to the Council of Europe. See the information available at the Council of Europe's treaty web site at <http://conventions.coe.int>.

[23] See European Commission for Democracy through Law, 'Opinion on the constitutional situation in Bosnia and Herzegovina with particular regard to human rights protection mechanisms', H.R.L.J. 1997, 297–307.

[24] The term 'Macedonia' is used for convenience, and is not intended to imply any position on the difference over the name.

Community law. Article 6 of the Treaty on European Union provides as follows:

The Union shall respect fundamental rights, as guaranteed by the European Convention for the Protection of Human Rights and Fundamental Freedoms signed in Rome on 4 November 1950 and as they result from the constitutional traditions common to the Member States, as general principles of Community law.

National authorities in the member states of the European Union are under an obligation to respect the Convention whenever they are acting in areas falling within the competence of the European Union. As the Strasbourg Court recalled in *Matthews v United Kingdom*:

[t]he Convention does not exclude the transfer of competences to international organisations provided that the Convention rights continue to be 'secured'.[25]

When implementing EU legislation, member states' compliance with the Convention's principles will also be controlled by the Court of Justice of the European Communities in Luxembourg which has developed an important body of case-law relating to the Convention.[26]

1. The Convention as directly applicable international law with superiority over the whole domestic legal order

According to the *Dutch* Constitution of 1983, the provisions of treaties and decisions of international institutions, whose contents are binding on everyone, shall have binding effect as from the time of their publication (article 93) and precedence over domestic law (article 94).[27] Dutch courts give precedence to the self-executing provisions of the Convention over domestic law that is not in conformity therewith, be it antecedent or posterior, statutory or constitutional. The Supreme Court even affirmed the priority of the Convention

[25] Judgment of 18 Feb 1999, application no. 24833/94, § 32.

[26] See among many others I. Persaud, 'The reconstruction of human rights in the European legal order', in Gearty, *op. cit. supra* note 21, 347 (364–85); P. Alston/J. H. H. Weiler, *An 'Ever Closer Union' in Need of a Human Rights Policy: The European Union and Human Rights* (under point 8.B), available on the Internet at <http://www.law.harvard.edu/Programs/JeanMonnet/>; J. H. H. Weiler/N. J. S. Lockhart, 'Taking rights seriously' seriously: The European Court and its fundamental rights jurisprudence', Common Market Law Review 32 (1995), 51–94 and 579–627; F. Mancini/V. Di Bucci, 'Le développement des droits fondamentaux en tant que partie du droit communautaire', in *Collected Courses of the Academy of European Law* 1990, vol. I, 27–52.

[27] Although the wording of art 94 only refers to 'statutory regulations', it was not intended to put the supremacy of treaties over all other legal provisions, including the constitution, into question. This supremacy had already been introduced in the Constitution of the Netherlands in 1953, see H. Schermers, 'Netherlands', in: F. G. Jacobs/S. Roberts (eds), *The Effect of Treaties in Domestic Law* (1987), 109 et seq.; E. A. Alkema, 'Foreign Relations in the Netherlands Constitution of 1983', Netherlands International Law Review 31 (1984), 307 (325–7).

and Protocol No. 6 thereto over conflicting treaty provisions, when it refused to allow an American serviceman to be handed over to the US authorities on the grounds that he would face capital punishment.[28]

2. The Convention as part of the Constitution

Austria ratified the European Convention on Human Rights on 3 September 1958. The Amendment to the Federal Constitution of 4 March 1964 raised it to the level of constitutional law with retroactive effect. Since then all rights contained in the Convention have the same legal status as the traditional Austrian Bill of Rights, ie possessing the rank of constitutional law and, as such, they take precedence over prior or later statute law.[29] Consequently, all judicial and administrative remedies for the protection of fundamental rights and freedoms including the individual appeal against administrative acts and decisions to the Constitutional Court (article 144 of the Federal Constitution) apply equally to the rights included in the Convention.[30]

The rather broad interpretation of the concept of 'civil rights and obligations' in article 6 § 1 of the ECHR proved to be a serious challenge for the Austrian system of administration with its comprehensive, but limited review by a single court, the Administrative Court (*Verwaltungsgerichtshof*). In a decision of 14 October 1987, the Austrian Constitutional Court noted that such far-reaching consequences for the judicial organization were neither intended nor foreseeable when Austria became a Party to the Convention.[31] The Court even raised the question whether:

> the transfer of constitutional law-making to an international organ would not constitute a total revision of the Federal Constitution within the meaning of article 44 § 3 of the Federal Constitution which requires a plebiscite of the whole population.

However, Austria eventually decided to reform its system of administrative justice and introduced first-instance administrative courts.

[28] Supreme Court, judgment of 30.3.1990, I.L.M. 1990, 1388 [abbreviated English translation].

[29] Austrian Constitutional Court, case no. G 28164, judgment of 14 Oct 1966, Österreichische Juristenzeitung 21 (1966), 248 = Yearbook of the ECHR 1966, 734 [abbreviated English translation].

[30] See M. Nowak, 'The Implementation of the ECHR in Austria', in: *The Implementation in National Law of the ECHR, Proceedings of The Fourth Copenhagen Conference on Human Rights*, 28 and 29 Oct 1988 (1989), 32 et seq.

[31] Collection of decisions of the Constitutional Court (*Sammlung der Erkenntnisse und wichtigsten Beschlüsse des Verfassungsgerichtshofs*) no. 11500/1987, *Miltner*.

3. The Convention as directly applicable law with superiority over domestic legislation

In the great majority of states parties to the Convention, treaties in general and the Convention in particular possess a higher rank than normal legislation, but remain inferior to the national constitution. One typical example is article 55 of the *French* Constitution which provides that:

> . . . treaties or agreements properly ratified or approved shall, upon their publication, have an authority superior to legislation, provided always that the relevant agreement or treaty is applied by the other Party.

The constitutions of *Cyprus* and *Greece* also contain more or less explicit provisions which give precedence to international treaty law.[32] *Portugal* and *Spain* adopted new constitutions in 1974 and 1978 which stipulate that international human rights guarantees should be used to interpret national fundamental rights.[33] The primacy of international treaties over conflicting domestic legislation is generally recognized. It is therefore not surprising that the practice of the Strasbourg Court plays an important role in the case-law of the Cypriot Supreme Court and the Spanish Constitutional Court.[34] Faced with a less explicit constitutional regulation, the Portuguese Constitutional Court decided only in 1991 that the binding force of an international treaty cannot be affected by municipal legislation, be it prior or subsequent to the treaty's ratification.[35]

In *Belgium* and *Luxembourg*, the pre-eminence of international law was confirmed by the respective Courts of Cassation.[36] National courts generally give precedence to the provisions of the European Convention and refrain from applying national legislation which is in conflict with the Convention. In *Switzerland*, which ratified the Convention in 1974, it was mainly through the case-law of the Federal Court that the internal rank of the Convention was determined. Emphasizing the constitutional character of the rights and

[32] Art 169 § 3 of the Cypriot Constitution; art 28 § 1 of the Greek Constitution of 1975 (*comp. Ahmet Sadik v Greece*, judgment of 15.11.1996, *Reports of Judgments and Decisions* 1996–V, 1654 (§ 31)); art 96 § 1 of the Spanish Constitution of 1978; art 8 § 2 of the Portuguese Constitution of 1974.

[33] Art 16 of the Portuguese Constitution; art 10 § 2 of the Spanish Constitution.

[34] E. Garcia de Enterria, 'Valeur de la jurisprudence de la Cour européenne des droits de l'homme en droit espagnol', in: *Protecting Human Rights: The European Dimension, Studies in honour of G. J. Wiarda* (Köln, Heymanns, 1988), 221 et seq.

[35] Acórdão 371/91 of 10.10.1991, Diário da República, II Série, No. 284, 10.12.1991.

[36] Cass., judgment of 8.6.1950, Pasicrisie luxembourgeoise, vol. 15, 41; Cass., judgment of 14.7.1954, Pasicrisie luxembourgeoise, vol. 16, 151 = Journal des Tribunaux 1954, 694 for Luxembourg; Cass., judgment of 27.5.1971, Journal des Tribunaux 1971, 460 = Common Market Law Reports 1972, 330 for Belgium.

freedoms enshrined therein,[37] the Federal Court declared already in 1985 in an *obiter dictum* that the Convention derogated from prior and under certain circumstances even from subsequent statutes.[38] In a judgment of 1 November 1996, it recognized the Convention's precedence not only over domestic legislation, but also over bilateral treaties.[39] In order to protect his family life (article 8 of the ECHR) the Court refused the extradition of an Italian citizen which had been requested by Germany on the basis of two extradition treaties concluded in 1967 and 1977 respectively.

Malta follows the common law tradition and requires incorporation of international treaties through an act of Parliament. Although it had ratified the Convention in 1967, the substantive provisions of the Convention (articles 2 to 18) and its Protocol (articles 1 to 3) were only made enforceable by the European Convention Act of 19 August 1987. This Act grants precedence to these provisions over ordinary legislation, whether prior or subsequent to the Convention's incorporation.

In 1994, *Norway* introduced a new provision into the Constitution according to which state authorities must respect and ensure human rights (article 110c). Formal legislation incorporating the European Convention and its Protocols Nos. 1, 4, 6, and 7 ('the Human Rights Law') along with the two UN Covenants, entered into force on 21 May 1999. The law declares that the treaties are to be given priority if there is a conflict between the international standards and a domestic statute.[40]

The far-reaching process of constitutional reform in the countries of *Central and Eastern Europe*[41] may be seen as further evidence for the emergence of a common European conviction that the rights and freedoms of the Convention should be applied with precedence over domestic legislation in order to guarantee their effective observance. All countries of Central and Eastern Europe which have ratified the Convention since 1989 have, without exception, incorporated it into their domestic law. The legal systems of these countries are characterized by a dualistic approach to international law which would normally preclude an international treaty's direct enforceability before the courts. It is therefore noteworthy that direct effect and the precedence of international human rights treaties over conflicting national legislation have

[37] Federal Court, judgment of 19.3.1975, ATF 101 Ia 67.

[38] Federal Court, judgment of 29.5.1985, ATF 111 Ib 68 (71).

[39] Federal Court, judgment of 1.11.1996, ATF 122 II 485.

[40] See E. Møse, Ch 20 below, pp. 635 et seq.

[41] E. Stein, 'International Law in Internal Law: Toward Internationalization of Central-Eastern European Constitutions?', A.J.I.L. 88 (1994), 427–50; E. Konstantinov, 'Die osteuropäischen Länder und der Rechtsschutz durch die Europäische Menschenrechtskonvention', Recht in Ost und West 42 (1998), 21–6; J. Schokkenbroek/I. Ziemele, 'The European Convention on Human Rights and the Central and Eastern European Member States of the Council of Europe: An Overview', 75 Nederlands Juristenblad (2000), 1914–1920.

been enshrined in a number of constitutional instruments of the new democracies in Eastern and Central Europe. This is the case in *Bulgaria* (article 5 § 4 of the Constitution),[42] the *Czech Republic* (article 10 of the Constitution),[43] *Romania* (article 20 of the Constitution),[44] *Slovakia* (article 11 of the Constitution),[45] *Moldova* (article 4 § 2 of the Constitution),[46] *Macedonia* (article 118 of the Constitution),[47] the *Russian Federation* (article 15 § 4 of the Constitution),[48] and *Georgia* (article 6 § 2 of the Constitution).[49] The *Hungarian* Constitution simply declares that 'the legal system of the Republic of Hungary shall ensure harmony between the assumed international law obligations and domestic law' (article 7 § 1).

Estonia's Constitution of 24 February 1918, which is again applied following the country's independence in 1991, establishes that international treaties are superior in force to national legislation (article 123 of the Constitution).[50]

[42] 'Any international instruments which have been ratified by the constitutionally established procedure, promulgated and in force with respect to the Republic of Bulgaria, shall be considered part of the domestic legislation of the country. They shall supersede any domestic legislation stipulating otherwise'.

[43] 'The ratified and promulgated international treaties on human rights and fundamental freedoms, by which the Czech Republic is bound, shall be applicable as directly binding regulations having priority before the law'.

[44] '1. Constitutional provisions concerning the citizens' rights and liberties shall be interpreted and enforced in conformity with the Universal Declaration of Human Rights, with covenants and other treaties Romania is a Party to.

2. Where any inconsistencies exist between the covenants and treaties on fundamental rights Romania is a Party to, and international laws, the international regulations shall take precedence.'

[45] 'International instruments on human rights and freedoms ratified by the Slovak Republic and promulgated under statutory requirements shall take precedence over national laws provided that the international treaties and agreements guarantee greater constitutional rights and freedoms.' See now Article 7 § 5 of the amended Constitution.

[46] 'Wherever disagreements appear between conventions and treaties signed by the Republic of Moldova and her own national laws, priority shall be given to international regulations.'

[47] 'The international agreements ratified in accordance with the Constitution are part of the internal legal order and cannot be changed by law.'

[48] 'Universally recognised principles and norms of international law and the international treaties of the Russian Federation are a constituent part of its legal system. If an international treaty of the Russian Federation establishes rules other than those provided by a law, the rules of the international treaty apply.' See also art 5 § 2 of the Federal Law on International Treaties, I.L.M. 34 (1995), 1370 (1375).

[49] 'The legislation of Georgia corresponds with universally recognised norms and principles of international law. International treaties or agreements concluded with and by Georgia, if they are not in contradiction to the Constitution of Georgia, have prior legal force over internal normative acts.'

[50] 'The Republic of Estonia shall not conclude foreign treaties which contradict the Constitution. If Estonian laws or other acts contradict foreign treaties ratified by the *Riigikogu* [Parliament], the provisions of the foreign treaty shall be applied.' See R. Maruste, 'Status of the European Convention on Human Rights in the Estonian legal system', in: P. Mahoney/F. Matscher/H. Petzold/L. Wildhaber (eds), *Protecting Human Rights: The European Perspective* (2000), 873 (877); B. Sejane (ed), *Latvia on the Way to EU: Legal Dimension* [publication prepared by a working group of the Ministry of Justice] (1998), 4; A. Neljas, 'Estonia', in: M. Scheinin (ed), *International Human Rights Norms in the Nordic and Baltic Countries* (1996), 27 et seq.

In a judgment of 11 June 1997 concerning the adoption of disciplinary sanctions against a police prefect, the Supreme Court held that in a case of conflict between a law and the Convention, the Convention as an international treaty ratified by the *Riigikogu* [Parliament] shall apply.[51] The new *Polish Constitution* which was adopted by the National Assembly on 2 April 1997 also appears to give precedence to international treaty law.[52]

The *United Kingdom* constitutes a special case. According to long-standing constitutional practice, treaties can be ratified without the need for legislative approval, but they acquire the status of domestic law only by means of an act of Parliament.[53] Although the United Kingdom was the first state to ratify the Convention as early as 1951, it was not incorporated until the Human Rights Act 1998.[54] The Act instructs all courts and tribunals to take Convention rights into account. Legislation must be read and given effect in a way which is compatible with the Convention. A victim of an unlawful act, ie an act by a public authority which is incompatible with a Convention right, may either bring proceedings against this authority under the Human Rights Act or may rely on the Convention right(s) concerned in any other legal proceeding. The court which finds an act of a public authority unlawful may grant appropriate relief or remedy, or under certain circumstances award damages. In a concession to parliamentary sovereignty, it was provided that legislation incompatible with Convention rights remains formally valid. In such cases, certain superior courts may make a declaration of incompatibility. Although the declaration as such does not affect the validity of the provision, the Human Rights Act foresees in such cases the introduction of amending legislation by the competent Minister or the Crown.

4. The Convention with the rank of statutory law

In several other states which traditionally follow a dualistic approach to international law the Convention (like other international treaties) is part of domestic law with the same rank and status as normal legislation (*Denmark, Finland, Germany, Iceland, Italy, Liechtenstein, Lithuania, Sweden*, and possi-

[51] Supreme Court (Constitutional Review Chamber), judgment of 11.6.1997, *Riigi Teataja* [State Gazette] 1997, no. 50, 821 [English translation and full text available in the CODICES database of the European Commission for Democracy Through Law (Venice Commission), see <http://codices.coe.int>.

[52] See arts 88 and 188 of the Constitution. The latter provision authorizes the Constitutional Tribunal to adjudicate upon the 'conformity of a statute with ratified international agreements whose ratification required prior consent granted by statute'.

[53] R. Higgins, 'United Kingdom', in F. G. Jacobs/S. Roberts (eds), *The Effect of Treaties in Domestic Law* (1987), 123 et seq.

[54] The Human Rights Act 1998 entered into force fully on 2 Oct 2000. See generally J. Wadham/H. Mountfield, *The Human Rights Act 1998* (Blackstone, 1999); Robert Blackburn, *Towards a Constitutional Bill of Rights for the United Kingdom* (Pinter, 1999).

bly *Ukraine*). The question whether treaties are 'transformed' into domestic law or incorporated without losing their nature as an international treaty appears to be of minor importance for the practical application of the Convention.

In theory, the Convention has in these states the same rank as other legislation. This means that the *lex posterior* rule would in principle apply, in the sense and with the consequence that the Convention would supersede older statutes, but later statutes would prevail over Convention provisions. This theoretical position does not appear to have much practical importance, since other principles come into play: the principle *lex specialis derogat leges generales* (by which the treaty rule can be considered to be the special law) and the widely recognized rule of presumption (according to which statutes should be construed in such a way as to bring them into conformity with the international obligations incurred by the state). Finally, in countries which have a catalogue of fundamental rights in their constitution, the Convention rights may be used as a complementary source in order to determine the scope and content of national constitutional guarantees which, in their turn, take precedence over conflicting legislation. The theoretical possibility that a later statute may be given precedence over the Convention thus appears not to have any real significance.

In *Germany,* where the Convention was incorporated with the rank and status of a federal statute, the Federal Constitutional Court expressly held that priority must be given to the Convention even over statutes enacted later, because it cannot be assumed that the legislature, without clearly stating so, wanted to deviate from Germany's obligations under public international law.[55]

In *Italy*, the Convention has been incorporated with the force and status of an ordinary law.[56] Although Strasbourg case-law has highlighted structural deficiencies of the Italian judicial system, the Convention has had for a long time only little influence on domestic case-law. Some Italian courts applied the principle *lex posterior* and declined to recognize the self-executing character of the Convention's substantive provisions.[57] The Constitutional Court recognized only in 1993 that the rights and freedoms of the Convention constitute 'inviolable human rights' in the sense of article 2 of the Italian

[55] Decision of 26.3.1987, BVerfGE 74, 358 (370) = Eu.G.R.Z. 1987, 203 (206) [English translation in *Decisions of the Bundesverfassungsgericht*, vol. 1/Part II: International Law and Law of the European Communities 1952–1989, 634].

[56] Corte costituzionale, judgment no. 188/1980 of 22.12.1980, Giur. cost. 1980, I, 1612; judgment no. 91/1986 of 14.4.1986, Giur. cost. 1986, I, 518.

[57] See Polakiewicz, *All-European Human Rights Yearbook*, 2 (Kehl, Engel, 1992), 28–9; D. Leonardi, 'Italy', in Gearty, *op. cit. supra* note 21, 307 (312–24).

Constitution.[58] This means that, being derived from a 'source related to an atypical competence', they are not susceptible to being abrogated by subsequent ordinary legislation.

The *Nordic countries* (with the exception of *Norway*) incorporated the Convention by granting it the rank and status of a domestic statute. *Denmark*, *Sweden*, and *Iceland* had ratified the Convention already during the 1950s, but incorporated it only recently.[59] In *Denmark*, the Convention and its Protocols Nos. 1 to 8 were made part of municipal law as from 1 July 1992.[60] *Iceland* and *Sweden* decided to incorporate its provisions in 1994 and 1995 respectively.[61] By giving direct effect to the provisions of the Convention, the already existing practice of national courts to use the Convention in the application of domestic legislation was formally acknowledged. Although the Swedish Supreme Court had already resorted to the Convention in order to interpret the Constitution,[62] the Convention was incorporated with the rank and status of an ordinary law only. However, at the same time, a new provision was added to the Swedish Constitution (chapter 2, article 23, of the Instrument of Government) according to which 'a law or other regulation may not be issued in conflict with [the Convention]'.[63] Without conferring a constitutional status on the Convention, this provision obliges courts and administrative authorities to disregard legislative or other enactments which manifestly conflict with the Convention. It seems to follow that laws which conflict with the Convention but do not manifestly contradict it should be applied.[64] *Finland*

[58] Corte costituzionale, judgment no. 10/1993 of 19.1.1993, Rivista di Diritto Internazionale 1993, 255, concerning art 6 § 3 litt. a of the ECHR. Art 2 of the Italian Constitution reads as follows: 'The Republic recognises and guarantees the inviolable rights of man, as an individual, and in the social groups where he expresses his personality, and demands the fulfilment of the intransgressible duties of political, economic and social solidarity.'

[59] See Scheinin, *op. cit. supra* note 50; F. Sundberg, 'La question de l'effet direct de la Convention. La situation dans les pays scandinaves', in: P. Tavernier (ed), *Quelle Europe pour les droits de l'homme? La Cour de Strasbourg et la réalisation d'une 'union plus étroite' (35 ans de jurisprudence: 1959–1994)* (1996), 109–124; S. Stenderup Jensen, 'The Application of the ECHR in Domestic Scandinavian Law', Scandinavean Studies in Law 35 (1991), 57 et seq.

[60] Law No. A 285 of 29 Apr 1992; see R. Hofmann, 'Das dänische Gesetz vom 29. April 1992 zur innerstaatlichen Anwendbarkeit der EMRK', Eu.G.R.Z. 1992, 253–6.

[61] Law No. 62/1994 of 19 May 1994 [Iceland] and Law (1994:1219) of 5 May 1994 which entered into force on 1 Jan 1995 [Sweden]. In its judgment of 29.2.1996 (UÖ 33/96, *Ny Juridiskt Arkiv* 1996, 14), the Swedish Supreme Court held that the revision of the provision concerning property rights in chapter 2, art 18 § 1, of the Instrument of Government of 1973 (due to the incorporation of the European Convention on Human Rights) did not have a restrictive effect on the application of the Land Parcelling Act of 1970.

[62] *Högsta Domstolen*, judgment of 22.3.1989, N.J.A. 1989, 131 = Nordisk Doms Samling 1990, 155.

[63] I. Cameron/M. K. Eriksson, *An Introduction to the European Convention on Human Rights* (2nd edn, 1995), 130–2 [translation by the authors].

[64] Cameron/Eriksson refer to the *travaux préparatoires* which indicate that, in general, the more vaguely the superior rule is formulated, the less likely it is that the conflict with an inferior rule will be manifest: ibid, p. 131 note 21.

only joined the Council of Europe in 1989. The substantive provisions of the Convention were immediately incorporated into domestic law by an Act of 4 May 1990 which entered into force on 10 May 1990.[65]

In *Lithuania*, the system of co-ordination of international and national law is based on the idea that international treaty provisions are subject to transformation, only thereby acquiring direct effect in domestic law. Article 138 of the Constitution provides that

> international treaties which are ratified by the *Seimas* [Parliament] of the Republic of Lithuania shall be a constituent part of the legal system of the Republic of Lithuania.

On 24 January 1995, the Constitutional Court of Lithuania gave an opinion on the relationship between the Constitution and the European Convention on Human Rights.[66] The Court held that:

> the Convention, when ratified and in force in Lithuania, will form a constituent part of the legal system of the Republic of Lithuania and should be implemented as the law of the Republic of Lithuania. Its provisions correspond to the level of laws in the system of sources of law of the Republic of Lithuania, since article 12 of the Law on International Treaties of the Republic of Lithuania stipulates that 'the international treaties of the Republic of Lithuania shall have the force of law on the territory of the Republic of Lithuania'.[67]

The new *Ukrainian Constitution* which was adopted on 28 June 1996 contains similar wording. Article 9 provides that '[i]nternational treaties that are in force . . . are part of the national legislation of Ukraine'.

5. *The Convention without formal internal legal validity*

Ireland possesses a constitutional bill of rights which matches Convention rights in many respects. According to article 29 § 6 of the Irish Constitution 'no international agreement shall be part of the domestic law of the State save as may be determined by the *Oireachtas* [Parliament]'. Irish courts had thus been effectively barred from applying the Convention. In *Re O Laighléis*, the Supreme Court held that:

[65] Only the entry into force of the provisions of Protocols Nos. 6 and 7 was deferred until 1 June and 1 Aug 1990 respectively.

[66] Opinion 22/94 [English translation and full text available in the CODICES database, *supra* note 51]. See V. Vadapalas, 'Opinion of the Constitutional Court of Lithuania in the Case Concerning the Conformity of the European Convention on Human Rights with the Constitution of Lithuania', Z.a.ö.R.V. 55 (1995), 1077 et seq. See also Case No. 8/95 of 17.10.1995, East European Case Reporter of Constitutional Law 4 (1997), 250, concerning the Law on International Treaties.

[67] The English translation was provided by Vadapalas (see previous note) p. 1085. The Court acknowledged, however, that the Civil Code (article 606) and the Code of Civil Procedure (article 482) give precedence to international treaties.

> the *Oireachtas* has not determined that the Convention . . . is to be part of the domestic law of the State, and accordingly this Court cannot give effect to the Convention if it be contrary to domestic law or purports to grant rights or impose obligations additional to those of domestic law.[68]

In the past, there have only been sporadic references to the Convention by Irish courts.[69]

However, in the Northern Ireland peace agreements concluded on 10 April 1998, Ireland committed itself to examining further the question of the incorporation of the European Convention on Human Rights into domestic law. Any measures to be taken must result in 'at least an equivalent level of protection of human rights as will pertain in Northern Ireland' where the Convention has been incorporated by the United Kingdom. Incorporation legislation is currently being prepared and is expected to be adopted in the near future.

C. THE POSITION OF THE CONVENTION WITH REGARD TO THE FUNDAMENTAL RIGHTS AND FREEDOMS OF NATIONAL CONSTITUTIONS

In most European countries, the Convention rights and freedoms are applied in parallel with the fundamental rights and freedoms guaranteed by the national constitution. This is the case in *Belgium, Germany, France, Italy, Portugal, Spain, Switzerland*, and increasingly in the countries of *Central and Eastern Europe*. Due to their common experience of totalitarian power, human rights violations, and disrespect for fundamental due process guarantees, most of the countries of the former Eastern bloc introduced detailed catalogues of fundamental rights and freedoms in their new constitutions, often inspired by the Universal Declaration of Human Rights and the European Convention on Human Rights.

The significance of the European Convention on Human Rights tends to be diminished in the presence of a detailed catalogue of 'national' fundamental rights and freedoms. Especially if the existence of such guarantees is coupled with a strong tradition of judicial protection of political and civil rights, as in *Italy* and *Germany*, 'influence' from Strasbourg tends to be of less importance. However, the examples of *Germany* and *Spain* show that even under these conditions the practice of the European Court of Human Rights can

[68] [1960] Irish Reports 93.

[69] P. Dillon-Malone, 'Individual Remedies and the Strasbourg System in an Irish Context', in: L. Heffernan (ed), *Human Rights—A European Perspective* (1994), 48 (49).

become relevant for the interpretation and application of national fundamental rights if the national constitutional court is willing to modify its purely domestic view. It is no exaggeration to speak of the beginning of a true dialogue between national jurisdictions and the European Court in Strasbourg.[70]

In *Germany* incorporation by federal statute (*Zustimmungsgesetz*) according to article 59 § 2 of the Basic Law assigned to the Convention only the rank and status of a federal law. The Federal Constitutional Court has therefore repeatedly held that an individual constitutional complaint cannot be based *directly* on an alleged violation of the European Convention.[71] The rights contained in the Convention are nevertheless taken into account by the Court. According to its consistent case-law, a constitutional complaint may be based on the allegation that the act or omission complained of violated the plaintiff's fundamental right to equality under article 3 § 1 of the Basic Law by an arbitrary misapplication or arbitrary non-application of the Convention.[72]

The Convention has also become directly relevant for the application of the constitution's fundamental rights. In a landmark ruling of 26 March 1987[73] the Federal Constitutional Court was faced with an alleged violation of the principle of presumption of innocence. Referring *inter alia* to the *Minelli* case,[74] the Court found a violation of article 2 § 1 of the Basic Law read together with the rule-of-law principle which are seen as the legal basis for the presumption of innocence under domestic law. In this context, the Court made the following declaration:

> In interpreting the Basic Law, the content and state of development of the European Convention on Human Rights are also to be taken into consideration insofar as this does not lead to a restriction or derogation of basic rights protection under the Basic Law, an effect that even the Convention itself seeks to rule out (article 60). For this reason, the case-law of the European Court of Human Rights also serves in this regard

[70] M.-A. Eissen, 'L'interaction des jurisprudences constitutionnelles nationales et de la jurisprudence de la Cour européenne des Droits de l'Homme', in: D. Rousseau/F. Sudre (eds), *Conseil constitutionnel et Cour européenne des Droits de l'Homme* (Paris, STH, 1990), 137 (153).

[71] Decisions of 14.1.1960, BVerfGE 10, 271 (274); 14.3.1973, BVerfGE 34, 384 (395); 13.1.1976, BVerfGE 41, 126 (149); 17.5.1983, BVerfGE 64, 135 (157); 13.1.1987, BVerfGE 74, 102 (128).

[72] Decisions of 17.5.1983, BVerfGE 64, 135 (157); 13.1.1987, BVerfGE 74, 102 (128). Art 3 § 1 ('All men shall be equal before the law') is interpreted as a fundamental right protecting against unreasonable (arbitrary) distinctions. The Court has brought arbitrary misapplication of law by courts under this constitutional provision.

[73] BVerfGE 74, 358 [English translation in *Decisions of the Bundesverfassungsgericht*, vol. 1/Part II: International Law and Law of the European Communities 1952–1989, 634].

[74] Judgment of 25.3.1983, Series A no. 62.

as an interpretational aid in defining the content and reach of the Basic Law's basic and principles of rule by law.[75]

Article 10 § 2 of the *Spanish* Constitution requires that constitutional provisions concerning fundamental rights and freedoms are to be interpreted in accordance with the Universal Declaration of Human Rights and other international human rights instruments ratified by Spain.[76] When the Constitutional Court cites the Convention, which is the human rights instrument most frequently referred to under this provision, it regularly refers to judgments by the Strasbourg Court interpreting the Convention provision at issue. In this way the case-law of the Strasbourg Court has become directly relevant to the interpretation of the Spanish Constitution.[77] This approach had been suggested by legal doctrine, according to which Article 10 § 2 of the Constitution required Spanish courts to consider as binding not only the Convention's provisions, but also their interpretation which had been developed by the Strasbourg Court.[78]

The *Swiss Federal Court* regularly applies the rights and freedoms of the Convention, sometimes in parallel with the fundamental rights of the constitution, sometimes on their own.[79] The *Portuguese* Constitutional Court which refers less frequently to the Convention has nevertheless acknowledged that its principles should be taken into account as 'auxiliary elements clarifying the sense and scope of constitutional norms and principles'.[80] There are

[75] BVerfGE 74, 358 (370); confirmed by BVerfGE 83, 119 (128); 88, 103 (112). The Saxon Constitutional Court applied the same principles with regard to the Constitution of the Land of Saxony, judgment of 14 May 1996, Eu.G.R.Z. 1996, 437.

[76] Article 4 § 1 of the Constitution of Moldova contains a similar provision: 'Constitutional provisions for human rights and freedoms shall be understood and implemented in accordance with the Universal Declaration of Human Rights and with other conventions and treaties endorsed by the Republic of Moldova'.

[77] See surveys by E. García de Enterría, 'Valeur de la jurisprudence de la Cour européenne des Droits de l'Homme en droit espagnol', in: *Protecting Human Rights: The European Dimension, Studies in honour of G. J. Wiarda* (1988), 221 (233 et seq.); J. Delgado Barrio, 'Proyección de las decisiones del Tribunal Europeo de Derechos Humanos en la jurisprudencia española', *Revista de Administración Pública* No. 119 (1989), 233 et seq. See, for example, Constitutional Court, judgment of 23.2.1995, Boletín Oficial del Estado (Official State Bulletin) no. 77 of 31/03/1995; judgment of 17.3.1995, Boletín Oficial del Estado no. 98 of 25/04/1995; judgment of 6.2.1995, Boletín Oficial del Estado no. 59 of 10/03/1995.

[78] E. Linde in: E. García de Enterría (ed), *El sistema europeo de protección de los derechos humanos* (1979), 154 speaks of an 'autovinculación de la Constitución española a la interpretación practicada por el Tribunal Europeo de los Derechos Humanos'.

[79] See J. P. Müller, 'Wandel des Souveränitätsbegriffs im Lichte der Grundrechte—dargestellt am Beispiel von Einwirkungen des internationalen Menschenrechtsschutzes auf die schweizerische Rechtsordnung', in: R. Rhinow/S. Breitenmoser/B. Ehrenzeller, *Fragen des internationalen und nationalen Menschenrechtsschutzes* (1997), 45–66; M. E. Villiger, *Handbuch der Europäischen Menschenrechtskonvention (EMRK) unter besonderer Berücksichtigung der schweizerischen Rechtslage* (1993), 33 et seq.

[80] Acórdão 124/90 of 19.4.1990, Diário da Républica 1991, série II, 8.2.1991; Acórdão 186/92 of 20.5.1992, Diário da Républica, série II, 18.9.1992; see J. M. Cardoso da Costa, 'Le Tribunal

also some judgments by the *Turkish* Constitutional Court which applied the Convention and recognized its value for the interpretation of constitutional law.[81]

The new Constitutional Courts of *Hungary* and *Poland* are taking a similar position. Under article 7 § 1 of the Constitution, the Hungarian Constitutional Court is required to ensure harmony between international and domestic law when evaluating a statute's constitutionality.[82] International human rights law is regularly taken into account when interpreting national statutes.[83] Even before the adoption of a new Constitution in 1997, the Polish Constitutional Tribunal used the principle that 'Poland is a democratic State governed by the rule of law and enforcing the principles of social justice' in order to take advantage of international human rights treaties for the interpretation and application of domestic statutes.[84] In its resolution of 2 March 1994, the Tribunal ruled that certain provisions of the Law on Radio and Television had to be interpreted in the light of the Polish Constitution. It added that:

> the freedom of expression is affirmed in international human rights treaties, in particular Article 10 of the ECHR. Poland's ratification of this Convention signifies that all State organs are tied by commitments found therein.[85]

D. APPLICATION OF THE RIGHTS AND FREEDOMS OF THE CONVENTION IN DOMESTIC LAW

The main responsibility for ensuring the observance of the Convention in domestic law lies with the legislature and the judiciary. In the first place, it is for the legislature to ensure that national legislation is in conformity with the

constitutionnel portugais et les juridictions européens', in: P. Mahoney/F. Matscher/H. Petzold/L. Wildhaber (eds), *Protecting Human Rights: The European Perspective* (2000) 193 (209).

[81] See Ch 30 below.

[82] Decision 53/1993 of 13.10.1993, *1956 War Crimes Case*, available in the CODICES database, *supra* note 51.

[83] See, for example, Decision 2/1994 of 14.1.1994; Decision 58/1995 of 15.9.1995, both available in the CODICES database, *supra* note 51.

[84] *See* A. Drzemczewski/M. Nowicki, 'The Impact of the ECHR in Poland: a Stock-taking after Three Years', E.H.R.L.R. 1996, 261 (269–73) and the examples given in the report of the Polish Constitutional Tribunal delegation in *Protection constitutionnelle et protection internationale des droits de l'homme: concurrence ou complémentarité?* [Proceedings of the Ninth Conference of European Constitutional Courts, Paris, May 10–13, 1993, published by the French Constitutional Council], vol. I (1994), 442 (449–50).

[85] Sygn. akt. W 3/93 OTK 1994/I, item 17—the translation is taken from Drzemczewski/Nowicki (previous note) 272.

rules of the Convention. In the past, conformity between national legislation and the Convention was often presumed. Even today, the Convention is only referred to sporadically during parliamentary debates, mainly in order to confirm that proposed legislation is in full harmony with its requirements.

The impact of the European Convention on Human Rights has been strongest on the new member states which have acceded to the Council of Europe since 1989. With assistance from the Council of Europe, the new member states have carried out studies with a view to examining the compatibility of their legislation with the requirements of the European Convention on Human Rights.[86] In the candidate countries, inter-ministerial committees or working groups were set up in order to analyse and assess the domestic legislation and its compatibility with the Convention. In this way, the necessary legislative reforms could often be implemented before the Convention became binding on the states concerned.

However, even when such an exercise has taken place, it remains important to follow the developing Strasbourg case-law. Incorporation should not be a pretext for passivity by the legislature such that the responsibility for ensuring that the Convention is effectively observed rests solely with the judiciary. It is recommended to follow the example of those countries (eg the Netherlands) which have established special procedures to examine the compatibility of draft legislation with the Convention.

The role of municipal courts in ensuring effective protection of the rights and freedoms contained in the Convention can hardly be overestimated.[87] Since the Convention rights are directly applicable in practically all member states of the Council of Europe, it is primarily before these courts that its guarantees will be invoked. The possibility of submitting an application to the European Court of Human Rights and of having the case eventually decided remains a time-consuming exercise which can only be envisaged as a last resort.

In the past, direct application of the Convention by a national judge was sometimes objected to on the basis that the rights and freedoms contained therein were too abstract and vague to be of any help for a national judge or lawyer. The following statement made by Lord Denning in 1976 was characteristic of the understanding of the Convention in many countries:

> The Convention is drafted in a style very different from the way which we are used to in legislation. It contains wide general statements of principle. They are apt to lead to

[86] See Council of Europe doc. H (96)12, prepared by P. Titiun and A. Drzemczewski, 'Ensuring Compatibility of Domestic Law with the ECHR prior to Ratification: the Hungarian Model', reproduced in H.R.L.J. 16 (1995) 241–60.

[87] S. K. Martens, 'Incorporating the European Convention: The Role of the Judiciary', *European Human Rights Law Review* 1 (1998) 5–14.

much difficulty in application because they give rise to much uncertainty. They are not the sort of thing which we can easily digest. Article 8 is an example. It is so wide as to be incapable of practical application. So it is much better for us to stick to our own statutes and principles, and only to look to the Convention for guidance in case of doubt.[88]

Today, such reasoning must appear anachronistic. The Convention and its Protocols are not merely a catalogue of basic fundamental rights and freedoms. They constitute a body of law which has been tested, developed, and applied by the Court and the Commission for more than forty years. In their case-law, the supervisory bodies have addressed many of today's critical human rights problems, such as torture and inhuman and degrading treatment, the use of firearms by the police, fair trial guarantees, immigration, child care, access to personal data, and the rights of illegitimate children, homosexuals, and transsexuals. Although the Court and the Commission have in principle acknowledged that the Convention's provisions are to be construed using the traditional rules of interpretation contained in the 1969 Vienna Convention on the Law of Treaties (articles 31 to 33)[89] they have deliberately chosen a dynamic approach to interpretation in order to adapt the Convention to the changing social, moral, and economic realities of the member states of the Council of Europe.[90] The true significance of many of the Convention's provisions can therefore only be properly understood when the practices of the Strasbourg Court and Commission are taken into account.

The increasing importance of Strasbourg case-law influences the application of the Convention by national judges. Whereas in the past vague references to particular Convention provisions were made, national courts now regularly take into account the concrete application of these provisions by the Strasbourg Court. The fair trial guarantees or the independence and impartiality of a judge, for example, are not determined by a mere reference to article 6 of the ECHR. National courts refer to the specific criteria for the appreciation of these qualities in the context of different proceedings which have been developed in a series of cases.[91] It is therefore important that the Court develops its case-law consistently and logically, not limiting its rulings

[88] *R v Chief Immigration Officer, ex parte Salamat Bibi* [1976] 3 All E.R. 843, 847.

[89] *Golder*, judgment of 21.2.1975, Series A no. 18, § 29; *Cruz Varas & Others*, judgment of 20.3.1991, Series A no. 201, § 100.

[90] R. Bernhardt, 'Thoughts on Interpretation of Human Rights Treaties', in: *Protecting Human Rights: The European Dimension, Studies in honour of G. J. Wiarda* (1988), 65–71.

[91] See D. Harris/M. O'Boyle/C. Warbrick, *Law of the European Convention on Human Rights* (Butterworths, London, 1995), 202 et seq. with extensive references to the relevant case-law.

to the mere determination of a violation but having regard to the often complex circumstances of the case taken as whole.[92]

A national judge will of course rarely apply the Convention in isolation. In the first place, any decision will be determined in accordance with the applicable domestic law. The Convention becomes only relevant when human rights issues are at stake. In such cases, however, the Convention should be taken into account even if the applicant did not invoke it directly. In the *Ahmet Sadık v Greece* case, when discussing the exhaustion of domestic remedies (article 26 of the ECHR), Judge Martens rightly observed that:

> in those cases where domestic courts, under their national law, are in a position to apply the Convention *ex officio*, those courts *must* do so under the Convention.[93]

The judge's examination will usually be twofold: first, the judge must examine whether the applicable legislation as such is in conformity with the Convention. Secondly, it must be determined whether the application of the law in the concrete case meets the requirements of the Convention. Administrative or judicial discretion will have to be exercised having regard to the provisions of the Convention as a relevant consideration in the application of national statutes and regulations. Often conflicting rights will have to be weighed against each other (eg freedom of expression and protection of honour; right to private or family life and rights of others or compelling reasons of public policy).

National courts all over Europe now refer regularly to the Convention and its interpretation by the Convention organs, trying to avoid conflicts between the Convention and national law. There is a growing convergence as far as the techniques of interpretation and control are concerned.

The growing influence of Strasbourg case-law all over Europe should, however, not lead to the false impression that the Court decides all human rights questions authoritatively for the whole continent. Contrary to European Union law, the law of the Convention does not require a strictly uniform application throughout Europe.[94] The Convention remains a minimum standard (article 53 of the ECHR) which allows for 'margins of appreciation', obliging the national judge to have due regard to the peculiar considerations

[92] Eg *Barberà, Messegué, and Jabardo*, judgment of 6.12.1988, Series A no. 146, § 89; *Teixeira de Castro v Portugal*, judgment of 9.6.1998, *Reports of Judgments and Decisions* 1998–IV, §§ 37–9. See also the dissenting opinion by Judge van Dijk in *Van Mechelen and Others v the Netherlands*, judgment of 23 Apr 1997, *Reports of Judgments and Decisions* 1997–III, 718.

[93] Partly dissenting opinion of Judge Martens, joined by Judge Foighel, *Ahmet Sadik v Greece* case, judgment of 15.11.1996, *Reports of Judgments and Decisions* 1996–V, 1660 (§ 11). In this context he referred to the EC Court of Justice, judgment of 14.12.1995, joint cases C-430/93 and C-431/93, Rec. 1995 I, 4705 et seq.

[94] R. Ryssdal, 'Address to the Conference of Presidents and Attorney Generals of the Supreme Courts of the EEC' (Council of Europe, 18 May 1992), §§ 11 et seq.

of law and policy in his or her own country.[95] Mere knowledge of the Court's case-law is not enough. What really counts is the understanding of legal mechanisms in the national context and a certain sensitivity for human rights issues which allow a creative use of the precedents from Strasbourg.

[95] See the various contributions in *The Doctrine of the Margin of Appreciation under the European Convention on Human Rights: Its Legitimacy in Theory and Application in Practice*, H.R.L.J. 1998, 1–36.

3

The Execution of Judgments of the European Court of Human Rights[1]

JÖRG POLAKIEWICZ

A. Introduction
B. Cessation of a continuing violation
*C. Reparation (*restitutio in integrum*)*
D. Revision of domestic legislation and administrative practices and the role of the Committee of Ministers under Article 46(2) of the ECHR
E. The payment of just satisfaction awarded by the Strasbourg Court
F. Enforceability of judgments before domestic courts
G. The precedent value of the judgments
H. Evaluation of compliance by the states

A. INTRODUCTION

The provisions of articles 41, 44, 45, and 46 of the ECHR are based on the traditional dualist understanding of the effects of judgments of international

[1] See J. Polakiewicz, *Die Verpflichtungen der Staaten aus den Urteilen des Europäischen Gerichtshofs für Menschenrechte* [The obligations of States arising from the judgments of the European Court of Human Rights] (Berlin: Springer, 1992); G. Ress, 'The Effects of Judgments and Decisions in Domestic Law', in: R. St-J. Macdonald/F. Matscher/H. Petzold (eds) *The European System for the Protection of Human Rights* (Dordrecht: Nijhoff, 1993) 801–51; *id*, 'The ECHR and State Parties: The Legal Effect of the Judgments of the European Court of Human Rights on the Internal Law and before Domestic Courts of the Contracting States', in I. Maier (ed), *Protection of Human Rights in Europe* (Heidelberg: Müller, 1982) 209–69; A. Drzemczewski/P. Tavernier, 'L'exécution des "décisions" des instances internationales de contrôle dans le domaine des droits de l'homme', in Société française de droit international, *La protection des droits de l'homme et l'évolution du droit international* (Paris: Pedone, 1998) 197 (in particular 215–70); J. Velu, 'Report on "Responsibilities for States Parties to the European Convention"', in *Proceedings of the Sixth International Colloquy about the ECHR*, Seville 1985 (Strasbourg: Council of Europe, 1988) 532–705.

tribunals. According to this view, such judgments were supposed to have no direct effect on domestic law and national authorities unless the domestic law itself requires or at least permits national authorities to apply or to execute them.[2] The Convention contains no provision similar to article 68 § 2 of the American Convention on Human Rights[3] which would confer an immediate legal effect upon the judgments of the Court in domestic law. As the Strasbourg Court itself has repeatedly held, it has no competence to annul, repeal, or modify statutory provisions or individual decisions taken by administrative, judicial, or other national authorities.[4]

The respondent state is nevertheless under an international obligation, resulting from article 46 § 1 of the ECHR,[5] to comply with all the consequences of the judgment. In this respect, is has to be observed that, in addition to decisions on purely procedural grounds, the Strasbourg Court delivers two types of judgments (cf article 41 of the ECHR). First, there are *declaratory judgments* as to whether a certain state action is in conflict with the provisions of the Convention. Secondly, the Court may award '*just satisfaction*' to the applicant, which usually takes the form of pecuniary compensation for material and moral damages as well as for costs and expenses incurred before the Convention institutions.

The legal consequences of the declaratory part of a judgment finding a violation of the Convention are sometimes difficult to determine with precision. The finding of a violation by the Court amounts to the determination of an internationally wrongful act. The Convention's *travaux préparatoires* bear witness to the drafters' intention that general principles of state responsibility should be applied in order to determine the obligations of a state found in violation of the Convention.[6] The wording of former article 50 of the Convention which prescribed the duty of reparation was clearly influenced by similar clauses in previously concluded international arbitration treaties, such as the 1928 General Act of Arbitration[7] and other bilateral treaties. Protocol

[2] H. Mosler, 'Judgments of International Courts and Tribunals', in: *Encyclopedia of Public International Law*, Instalment 1 (1981) 111 (116).

[3] 'That part of a judgment that stipulates compensatory damages may be executed in the country concerned in accordance with domestic procedure governing the execution of judgments against the state.'

[4] See eg *Pakelli*, judgment of 25.4.1983, Series A no. 64, § 45; *Hauschildt*, judgment of 24.5.1989, Series A no. 154, § 54; *Brozicek*, judgment of 19.12.1989, Series A no. 167, § 47.

[5] 'The High Contracting Parties undertake to abide by the final judgment of the Court in any case to which they are parties.'

[6] Report of the Committee of Experts of 16.3.1950, *Collected Edition of the 'Travaux Préparatoires'*, vol. IV, 45.

[7] L.N.T.S., vol. 93, 343.

No. 11 to the ECHR slightly simplified this wording but without introducing any substantial changes.[8]

In the case of *Papamichalopoulos v Greece*, the Strasbourg Court defined the obligations which result from the finding of a violation as follows:

> . . . a judgment in which the Court finds a breach of the Convention imposes on the respondent state a legal obligation to put an end to the breach and make reparation for its consequences in such a way as to restore as far as possible the situation existing before the breach.[9]

The obligations following from the judgments of the European Court of Human Rights are 'obligations of result'.[10] States parties enjoy a certain freedom of choice as to the means of fulfilling their obligations under article 46 § 1 of the Convention.[11] Arguing that it falls to the Committee of Ministers to supervise the execution of its judgments, the Strasbourg Court has always refrained from making any consequential orders or declaratory statements.[12]

B. CESSATION OF A CONTINUING VIOLATION

When the Strasbourg Court finds a violation of the Convention, the respondent state is under an obligation immediately to discontinue the wrongful

[8] Art 46 of the ECHR as amended by Protocol No. 11 combines the provisions of former arts 50 and 54 and reads as follows:
'*Binding force and execution of judgment*
1. The High Contracting Parties undertake to abide by the final judgment of the Court in any case which they are parties.
2. The final judgment of the Court shall be transmitted to the Committee of Ministers, which shall supervise its execution.'

[9] *Papamichalopoulos and Others v Greece*, judgment (art 50) of 31.10.1995, Series A no. 330–B, § 34. See also *Clooth v Belgium*, judgment (art 50) of 5.3.1998, *Reports of Judgments and Decisions* 1998–I, 491 (§ 14); *Akdivar and Others v Turkey*, judgment (art 50) of 1.4.1998, *Reports of Judgments and Decisions* 1998–II, 723–724 (§ 47); *Menteş and Others v Turkey*, judgment (art 50) of 24.7.1998, *Reports of Judgments and Decisions* 1998–IV, 1695 (§ 24); *Castillo Algar v Spain*, judgment of 28.10.1998, *Reports of Judgments and Decisions* 1998–VIII, 3118–3119 (§ 60); *Scozzari and Giunta v Italy*, judgment of 13.7.2000, *infra* note 16.

[10] Compare the draft rules on state responsibility: *Yearbook of the I.L.C.* 1980, vol. II (Part 2), 31.

[11] *Belgian Linguistic*, judgment of 23.7.1968, Series A no. 6, 34–35; *Marckx*, judgment of 13.6.1979, Series A no. 31, § 58; *Norris*, judgment of 26.10.1988, Series A no. 142, § 50; *Vermeire*, judgment of 29.11.1991, Series A no. 214–C, § 26; *Papamichalopoulos and Others v Greece*, judgment (art 50) of 31.10.1995, Series A no. 330–B, § 34; *Menteş and Others v Turkey*, judgment (art 50) of 24.7.1998, *Reports of Judgments and Decisions* 1998–IV, 1695 (§ 24); *Castillo Algar v Spain*, judgment of 28.10.1998, *Reports of Judgments and Decisions* 1998–VIII, 3118–3119 (§ 60).

[12] *Tolstoy Miloslavsky v UK*, judgment of 13.7.1995, Series A no. 316–A, §§ 69–72; *Akdivar and Others v Turkey*, judgment (art 50) of 1.4.1998, *Reports of Judgments and Decisions* 1998–II, 724 (§ 47); *Menteş and Others v Turkey*, judgment (art 50) of 24.7.1998, *Reports of Judgments and Decisions* 1998–IV, 1695 (§ 24); *Castillo Algar v Spain*, judgment of 28.10.1998, *Reports of Judgments and Decisions* 1998–VIII, 3118–3119 (§ 60).

action. The practical consequences of this obligation should not be overestimated. Given the fact that the Strasbourg Court usually decides only after local remedies have been exhausted (article 35 § 1 of the ECHR) and an attempt to reach a friendly settlement has failed (article 38 of the ECHR) it is rare that the violation is still continuing when the Court delivers its judgment.

Cessation becomes relevant if the declared violation has a continuing character. Taking into account the criteria which the European Court and Commission of Human Rights have developed in order to distinguish between 'continuing violations' and 'instantaneous acts producing continuing effects', the following cases may be cited as examples of continuing violations:[13]

- the act of maintaining in force and applying a law which has been declared incompatible with the Convention;[14]
- continuing detention in violation of article 5 of the ECHR;[15]
- the execution of a judgment which is based on penal legislation found to be incompatible with the Convention (eg retroactive legislation incompatible with article 7 of the ECHR) or which is based on an improper application of penal legislation (eg punishing statements which constitute a legitimate exercise of the freedom of expression guaranteed by article 10 of the ECHR);
- continuing interference with private or family life in violation of article 8 of the European Convention on Human Rights (for example by denying access to children who have been removed from care and custody of their parents[16] or by making confidential data accessible to the public);[17]
- continuing denial of access to property in violation of article 1 of Protocol No. 1 to the ECHR.[18]

The obligation of cessation is of particular importance with regard to cases where statutory provisions are found to infringe the rights and freedoms of

[13] Polakiewicz, *supra* note 1, 63–91.

[14] Application no. 214/56, *De Becker v Belgium* (9.6.1958) *Yearbook of the ECHR*, vol. 2 (1958/1959), 214 (233 et seq.); *Marckx*, judgment of 13.6.1979, Series A no. 31. As for general international law, see R. Ago, 'Fifth Report on State Responsibility', *Yearbook of the I.L.C.* 1976, vol. II, Part 1, 3 (§ 62); American Law Institute, *Restatement of the Law: The Foreign Relations Law of the United States*, vol. 2 (St. Paul, American Law Institute, 1987), § 901 (p. 341).

[15] *Neumeister*, judgment of 27.6.1968, Series A no. 8, 38.

[16] See, for example, *Scozzari and Giunta v Italy*, applications nos. 39221/98 and 41963/98, judgment of 13 July 2000; *Olsson*, judgment of 24.3.1988, Series A no. 130; *Eriksson*, judgment of 22.6.1989, Series A no. 156. These are very delicate situations where the child's best interests should take precedence.

[17] *Z v Finland*, judgment of 25.2.1997, *Reports of Judgments and Decisions* 1997–I, 352–353 (§§ 112–113).

[18] *Loizidou v Turkey (Merits)*, judgment of 18.12.1996, *Reports of Judgments and Decisions* 1996–VI, 2236–2238 (§§ 57–64).

the Convention. The Commission and the Court addressed this question in the *Vermeire* case.[19] The applicant, who had been born out of wedlock, complained of having been excluded from inheritance rights to her paternal grandparents' estates in spite of the *Marckx* judgment by the European Court which had declared the relevant provisions of the Belgian Civil Code to be in violation of article 8 in conjunction with article 14 of the ECHR.[20]

In its judgment of 29 November 1991, the Court again found a violation of article 14 in conjunction with article 8 of the Convention, arguing that the Belgian courts should have complied with the *Marckx* judgment which had been neither imprecise nor incomplete about the rule prohibiting discrimination of illegitimate children. The Belgian government had pointed to the difficulties which a thorough revision of the legal status of children born out of wedlock posed. The Court rejected this argument and held that:

> the freedom of choice allowed to a atate as to the means of fulfilling its obligations under article 46 § 1 cannot allow it to suspend the application of the Convention while waiting for such a reform to be completed.[21]

The immediate abrogation or suspension of a statute may often raise difficult constitutional problems for the respondent state. In principle, it will be sufficient that the statutory provisions are no longer applied. An exception will have to be allowed for provisions of penal legislation which are in direct contradiction with the Convention. The effect that certain human conduct which enjoys protection under the Convention is deemed unlawful cannot be offset by the mere non-application of statutory provisions. In such cases, the maintenance in force of the impugned legislation constitutes a continuing interference with Convention rights.[22]

Setting aside legislative provisions which are contrary to the Convention but have not yet been formally abrogated should not pose particular problems in countries where the Convention takes precedence over domestic legislation. In other countries, state authorities may be directed on a case-by-case basis to respect the Court's judgments. In the case of *Ireland v United Kingdom*, the British Attorney-General guaranteed before the Commission that certain retroactive provisions of the Northern Ireland Act 1972 would no longer be applied.[23] Following the judgment in the *Luedicke, Belkacem, and*

[19] *Vermeire*, judgment of 29.11.1991, Series A no. 214–C. See J. Polakiewicz, 'Die innerstaatliche Durchsetzung der Urteile des Europäischen Gerichtshofs für Menschenrechte. Gleichzeitig eine Anmerkung zum Vermeire-Urteil des Europäischen Gerichtshofs für Menschenrechte', Z.a.ö.R.V. 52 (1992), 149–90.

[20] *Marckx*, judgment of 13.6.1979, Series A no. 31.

[21] *Vermeire*, *supra* note 19, § 26.

[22] *Dudgeon*, judgment of 22.10.1981, Series A no. 45, § 41; *Norris*, judgment of 26.10.1988, Series A no. 142, § 38.

[23] *Ireland v UK*, report by the Commission, *Yearbook of the E.C.H.R.*, vol. 15 (1971) 80 (237).

Koç case, the German judicial authorities were ordered not to levy any costs for translation and interpretation in criminal proceedings although the respective statute was amended a few years later.[24]

C. REPARATION (*RESTITUTIO IN INTEGRUM*)

According to the famous dictum by the Permanent Court of International Justice in the *Chorzów* case, full reparation for an internationally wrongful act:

> must, as far as possible, wipe out all consequences of the illegal act and re-establish the situation which would, in all probability, have existed if that act had not been committed.[25]

Applied to the findings of the Strasbourg Court this means that the respondent state is in principle obliged to wipe out all legal and factual consequences of a Convention violation and to reinstate the applicant in the position in which he or she would have been without the violation.[26]

The scope of the *restitutio in integrum* is dependent on the concrete circumstances of the case and it has to be granted only as far as possible. In its practice, the Strasbourg Court has identified certain measures which may bring about at least a partial *restitutio in integrum*:

- the restitution of property taken in violation of article 1 of the Protocol;[27]
- the reopening of proceedings which were flawed by procedural errors;[28]
- the taking into account of the duration of an unlawful detention (violation of article 5 of the ECHR)[29] or of excessively lengthy proceedings

[24] Ress, in: *Protection of Human Rights*, *supra* note 1, 264.

[25] *Factory at Chorzów (Claim for indemnity) (The Merits)*, P.C.I.J., Series A no. 17 (13.9.1928) 47.

[26] *Papamichalopoulos and Others v Greece*, judgment (art 50) of 31.10.1995, Series A no. 330–B, § 34; *Clooth v Belgium*, judgment (art 50) of 5.3.1998, *Reports of Judgments and Decisions* 1998–I, 491 (§ 14); *Akdivar and Others v Turkey*, judgment (art 50) of 1.4.1998, *Reports of Judgments and Decisions* 1998–II, 723–724 (§ 47); *Menteş and Others v Turkey*, judgment (art 50) of 24.7.1998, *Reports of Judgments and Decisions* 1998–IV, 1695 (§ 24); Ress, in: *The European System*, *supra* note 1, 803.

[27] *Hentrich v France*, judgment of 22.9.1994, Series A no. 296–A, § 71; *Papamichalopoulos v Greece*, judgment (art 50) of 31.10.1995, Series A no. 330–B, §§ 35–8. In the latter case, the reasoning of the Court suggests that restitution would not be the adequate remedy for 'an expropriation that would have been legitimate but for the failure to pay fair compensation', *ibid*, § 35.

[28] *Piersack*, judgment (art 50) of 26.10.1984, Series A no. 85, § 11; *Schuler-Zgraggen v Switzerland*, judgment (art 50) of 31.1.1995, Series A no. 305–A, §§ 14–15.

[29] *Neumeister*, judgment (art 50) of 7.5.1974, Series A no.17, § 40; *Engel and Others*, judgment (art 50) of 23.11.1976, Series A no. 22, § 10 [art 5.1]; *Letellier*, judgment of 26.6.1991, Series A no. 207, § 62 [art 5.3]; *Toth*, judgment of 12.12.1991, Series A no. 224, § 91 [art 5.3].

(violation of article 6.1 of the ECHR)[30] in the determination of the penalty; and
- the pardoning of a convicted person and the consequential deletion of the conviction from the criminal records.[31]

If the principle of *restitutio in integrum* were to be applied unfettered, the respondent state would be obliged to abrogate legal provisions with retroactive effect and to repeal all individual acts based on them in the past.[32] Such potentially far-reaching effects of the Court's judgments would easily collide with other considerations, in particular the interests of legal certainty. In the *Marckx* case, in which whole chapters of the Belgian Civil Code were held to be in violation of the Convention, the Court acknowledged this fact and limited the potentially retroactive effects of its findings. Invoking reasons of legal certainty and referring to a similar practice of the Court of Justice in Luxembourg and certain national constitutional courts, the Court declared that the Belgian state was exempted from reopening legal acts or situations that antedated the delivery of the judgment.[33]

Article 41 of the ECHR shows that *restitutio in integrum* is only required insofar as it is possible under the municipal law of the respondent state.[34] It is the object and purpose of this provision to avoid the unsatisfactory situation that a state would be bound internationally to repeal or modify domestic decisions which have acquired the force of *res judicata* and cannot be repealed under domestic law.[35] Although it is highly recommended to introduce proceedings which permit the review or reopening of proceedings following an adverse finding by the Court, there is no obligation to do so under the Convention.[36] The binding force of court decisions, the interests of legal certainty, the *bona fide* confidence of third parties, as well as statutory terms of preclusion or prescription are all legitimate grounds which may, under the applicable municipal law, prevent the elimination of all the consequences of a declared violation. In such cases, applicants must content themselves with monetary compensation.

The alternative of monetary compensation should be applied if the national law of the respondent state does not allow full reparation, or if

[30] *Eckle*, judgment (art 50) of 21.6.1983, Series A no. 65, § 24.

[31] *Bönisch*, judgment (art 50) of 2.6.1986, Series A no. 103, §§ 11–12.

[32] See P.-H. Teitgen, 'The Temporal Effect of the Judgments of the European Court of Human Rights and the Court of Justice of the European Communities', H.R.L.J. 1 (1980) 36 (38 et seq.).

[33] *Marckx*, judgment of 13.6.1979, Series A no. 31, § 58.

[34] Cf *Papamichalopoulos and Others v Greece*, judgment (art 50) of 31.10.1995, Series A no. 330–B, § 34.

[35] J. A. Frowein/W. Peukert, in: J. A. Frowein/W. Peukert, *EMRK-Kommentar* (Kehl, Engel, 1996), Artikel 53, marginal note 3.

[36] See *infra* notes 61 et seq.

restitutio in integrum is impossible due to the nature of the violation found.[37] It is for example materially impossible to wipe out all the consequences of unlawful detention.[38] If national law does not allow—or allows only partial—reparation to be made for the consequences of the breach, article 41 of the European Convention on Human Rights empowers the Court to afford the injured party such satisfaction as appears to it appropriate.[39]

D. REVISION OF DOMESTIC LEGISLATION AND ADMINISTRATIVE PRACTICES AND THE ROLE OF THE COMMITTEE OF MINISTERS UNDER ARTICLE 46 § 2 OF THE ECHR

Legislative provisions of domestic law found to be incompatible with the Convention must be amended.[40] Numerous judgments by the Strasbourg Court have prompted or accelerated legislative or administrative reforms in the respondent[41] and sometimes even in third states.[42] In accordance with article 41 of the ECHR, the respondent state is normally not required to amend the relevant legislation retroactively.

From a theoretical point of view, legislative amendments adopted following an adverse finding in Strasbourg can be seen either as a measure of *restitutio* (in particular when the law as such has been found to be incompatible with the Convention) or as a safeguard against future violations. In individual applications, the Court usually does not examine the compatibility of legislative pro-

[37] *Papamichalopoulos and Others v Greece*, judgment (art 50) of 31.10.1995, Series A no. 330–B, § 34.

[38] *De Wilde, Ooms, and Versyp* ('Vagrancy' cases), judgment (art 50) of 10.3.1972, Series A no. 14, § 20; *Guzzardi*, judgment of 6.11.1980, Series A no. 39, § 113.

[39] *Papamichalopoulos and Others v Greece, supra* note 37, § 34; *Clooth v Belgium*, judgment (art 50) of 5.3.1998, *Reports of Judgments and Decisions* 1998–I, 491 (§ 14).

[40] W. Ganshof van der Meersch, 'European Court of Human Rights', in *Encyclopedia of Public International Law*, Instalment 8 (1985), 192 (204–205); Velu, *supra* note 1, 572 et seq.; J. A. Frowein/M. Villiger, 'Constitutional Jurisdiction in the Context of State Powers; Modalities, Contents and Effects of the Decisions on the Constitutionality of Legal Regulations'; Report of the European Commission, H.R.L.J. 9 (1988), 23 (50ff.); J. Velu/R. Ergec, *La Convention européenne des droits de l'homme* (Bruxelles, Bruylant, 1990) 1052 et seq.

[41] See the impressive survey given in European Court of Human Rights, *Survey of Activities 1959–1998* (Strasbourg, Heymanns, 1999) 86–133.

[42] Eg the Dutch law on illegitimate children was changed in view of the *Marckx* judgment rendered against Belgium (*Wet van 27 oktober 1982, houdende wijziging van enige bepalingen in het Burgerlijk Wetboek tot wegneming van het onderscheid tussen wettige en natuurlijke afstamming in het erfrecht*, Staatsblad van het Koninkrijk der Nederlanden 1982, No. 608). The Danish law on so-called closed shops in industrial relations was changed in view of *the Young, James, and Webster* judgment rendered against the United Kingdom (Law No. 285 vom 9.6.1982, *Lov om beskyttelse mod afskedigelse på grund af foreningsforhold*).

visions or administrative practices as such with the Convention.[43] The Court deals with individual cases and does not undertake an *in abstracto* review of national legislation or practices. However, even when individual measures of implementation constitute the main object of an application, the Court's judgments often reveal inconsistencies or lacunae in the underlying legislation or practices which provoked the human rights violation in the individual case. In such cases legislative or administrative reforms are called for as a measure to prevent similar future breaches of the Convention.[44]

Acting under article 46 § 2 of the Convention (formerly article 54), the Committee of Ministers of the Council of Europe supervises the execution of the Court's judgments.[45] In 1976, it adopted rules for the application of article 54 of the ECHR.[46] All new judgments are automatically put on its agenda and, at intervals of not more than six months, the measures taken by the respondent state in order to abide by the judgment are examined. This supervision takes place, in principle, at the regular human rights meeting of the Committee of Ministers.

The Committee does not only ensure that the applicant receives the payment of financial compensation ordered by the Court. Depending on the circumstances which gave rise to the violation of the Convention, states also submit information on general or individual measures, usually in the form of legislative, administrative, or regulatory amendments, designed to avoid similar violations in the future. Such information is particularly important where the Court's judgments highlight structural inadequacies in the organization and functioning of the respondent state's administrative or judicial system. A reference to the adopted measures is regularly published in an appendix to the Committee of Minister resolution declaring that it has exercised its functions under the Convention.[47]

[43] Exceptions are applications brought directly against statutory provisions (for example *Marckx*, judgment of 13.6.1979, Series A no. 31; *Dudgeon*, judgment of 22.10.1981, Series A no. 45) or judgments which reveal an absence of adequate fair trial guarantees in domestic proceedings (in particular violations of arts 5 and 6 of the ECHR).

[44] Polakiewicz, *supra* note 1, 149 et seq.

[45] A. Tomkins, 'The Committee of Ministers: Its Roles under the European Convention on Human Rights', European Human Rights Law Review 1 (1995), 49–62; P. Leuprecht, 'The Execution of Judgments and Decisions', in: R. St-J. Macdonald/F. Matscher/H. Petzold (eds), *The European System for the Protection of Human Rights* (1993), 791 (796–800); J.-F. Flauss, 'La pratique du Comité des Ministres du Conseil de l'Europe au titre de l'article 54 de la Convention européenne des Droits de l'Homme (1985–1988)' A.F.D.I. 34 (1988) 408 et seq.

[46] 'Rules adopted by the Committee of Ministers for the application of Article 54 of the ECHR', approved by the Committee of Ministers at the 254th meeting of the Ministers' Deputies in Feb 1976. New 'Rules for the application of Article 46 § 2 of the ECHR' were adopted by the Committee of Ministers on 10 January 2001, at the 736th meeting of Ministers' Deputies.

[47] See also the 'Reply by the Committee of Ministers to a written question concerning the execution of certain cases pending before the Committee of Ministers, Written Question No. 378 by

It is interesting to note that states submit information on general measures even in cases where the Court had refrained from ruling expressly on the conformity of statutory or regulatory provisions with the Convention. The highly formalistic view, according to which the obligations resulting from article 46 (formerly articles 53 and 54) of the Convention apply only to the individual case before the Court,[48] ignores the fact that, in addition to providing a remedy for individual applicants, the proceedings before the Court denote certain objective features. Transcending the person and the interests of the applicant,[49] they are instrumental for the prevention of further violations and the clarification of the nature and scope of the obligations under the Convention.

E. THE PAYMENT OF JUST SATISFACTION AWARDED BY THE STRASBOURG COURT

According to the Court's case-law, 'just satisfaction' in the sense of article 41 of the ECHR comprises monetary compensation for moral and pecuniary damages as well as reimbursement of costs and expenses.[50] The part of the judgment in which the Strasbourg Court awards just satisfaction obliges the respondent state to pay the specified sum of money to the applicant. In its early case-law, the Court did not make any specific orders concerning the payment of interest.[51] Nowadays, the Court automatically awards default interest for the time between the judgment and the actual payment of the specified sum. Interest has become an integral part of just satisfaction. The rate of interest usually corresponds to the statutory rate of interest applicable in the respondent state.

Mrs Ragnarsdóttir, MM. Clerfayt, Hagård and Jurgens', adopted by the Committee of Ministers at their 646th meeting on 22 Oct 1998.

[48] See H. Golsong, 'The European Court of Human Rights and the national law-maker: Some general reflections', in: *Protecting Human Rights: The European Dimension, Studies in honour of G. J. Wiarda* (1988), 239 (241–2).

[49] *Deweer*, judgment of 27.2.1980, Series A no. 35, §38; *Luedicke, Belkacem, and Koç*, judgment of 28.11.1978, Series A no. 29, § 36; *Ireland v United Kingdom*, judgment of 18.1.1978, Series A no. 25, § 154.

[50] C. Tomuschat, 'Just satisfaction under Article 50 of the European Convention on Human Rights', in P. Mahoney/F. Matscher/H. Petzold/L. Wildhaber (eds), *Protecting Human Rights: The European Perspective* (2000) 1409 (1413).

[51] In the *Sunday Times* case, the Court even refused to award interest arguing that 'it must be assumed the United Kingdom will comply promptly with the obligation incumbent on it under Article 53 of the Convention', judgment (art 50) of 6.11.1980, § 44.

Following the judgments in the *Ringeisen* case,[52] it was argued that monetary compensation awarded by the Court for personal non-pecuniary damages should be exempt from any seizure or attachment by creditors of the applicant.[53] However, in the *Allenet de Ribemont* case, the Court declared that whether a sum awarded by the Court under article 50 of the ECHR (now article 41) was exempt from attachment was a question for the national authorities acting under the relevant domestic law.[54] The Court confirmed this finding in *Selmouni v France*, but added that:

> it would be incongruous to award the applicant an amount in compensation for, *inter alia*, ill treatment constituting a violation of article 3 of the Convention and costs and expenses incurred in securing that finding if the state itself were then to be both the debtor and creditor in respect of that amount.[55]

The Court's reasoning seems to imply that, in the absence of explicit provisions in the applicable domestic law, the sums awarded by the Court are not free from attachment or seizure by creditors of the applicant.

The Court's hesitations in this respect are difficult to understand. Why should the execution of a judgment in which the applicant was awarded 'just satisfaction' be subject to different legislations in different countries? Other international courts clearly recognized that competence to award compensation as a consequence of an internationally wrongful act entails competence to make consequential orders regarding the form and modalities of payment.[56] At least insofar as the compensation covers non-pecuniary damages suffered personally by the applicant, the payment should in principle be exempt from seizure or attachment by his or her creditors. An exception could perhaps be allowed for attachments made with a view to satisfying maintenance payments owed to close relatives.

[52] Judgments of 22.6.1972 and 23.6.1973, Series A nos. 15 and 16.

[53] Polakiewicz, *supra* note 1, 190–2; W. Peukert, in: Frowein/Peukert, *supra* note 35, Artikel 50, marginal note 67.

[54] Judgment (interpretation of the judgment of 10 Feb 1995) of 7.8.1996, *Reports of Judgments and Decisions* 1996–III, 910 (§ 19). The Court probably missed an opportunity in this case to clarify the status of its judgments in domestic law: see the Dissenting Opinion of Judge De Meyer, *ibid*, 913.

[55] *Selmouni v France*, application no. 25803/94, judgment of 28 July 1999, § 133.

[56] Permanent Court of International Justice, *Case concerning the Factory at Chorzów (Claim for indemnity) (Jurisdiction)*, P.C.I.J. Series A no.9, 32 (26.7.1927); *Case concerning the Factory at Chorzów (Claim for indemnity) (The Merits)*, P.C.I.J., Series A no.17, 61 (13.9.1928); Inter-american Court of Human Rights, *Velásquez Rodriguez*, judgment of 21.7.1989, H.R.L.J. 1990, 127 (§§ 53 et seq.)

F. ENFORCEABILITY OF JUDGMENTS BEFORE DOMESTIC COURTS[57]

In line with the traditional understanding of international law, neither the Convention itself nor the respective national acts through which it has been incorporated or transformed into domestic law confer any immediate legal effect on the judgments of the Strasbourg Court. However, the obligations of cessation and reparation which follow from the finding of a violation are binding on all authorities of the respondent state. Within the ambit of their respective competences, national courts and administrative authorities are therefore required to provide redress for victims of ongoing violations and, as far as possible, reparation for past violations.

In 1985, a chamber of the *German* Federal Constitutional Court held that, according to former articles 52 and 53 (now articles 44 and 46 § 1) of the Convention, all German courts were under an obligation to respect the *res judicata* of Strasbourg judgments within their respective personal, material, and temporal limits.[58] Similar decisions have been given by supreme and constitutional courts in the *Netherlands*,[59] *Spain*,[60] and *Switzerland*.[61]

Immediate redress is required in the rare cases of violations which continue even after the judgment in Strasbourg. In such cases article 41 of the ECHR, which effectively shields the domestic legal order from direct effects resulting from the rulings by the Strasbourg Court, cannot be invoked.[62] States parties to the Convention are under an obligation to stop violations which have been established with binding force (article 46 § 1 of the ECHR) even where the national legislature or judiciary are responsible for the violations. Domestic rules as to the division of powers between constitutional authorities cannot be invoked in order to escape the international responsibility following from the Court's judgment.[63]

[57] See in particular Ress, in: *The European System*, *supra* note 1, 801 et seq.; Polakiewicz, *supra* note 1, 215 et seq.

[58] *Pakelli* decision of 11.10.1985, Eu.G.R.Z. 1985, 654 = Z.a.ö.R.V. 46 (1986), 289 with note by J. A. Frowein.

[59] Judgment of the Supreme Court (*Hoge Raad*) of 1.2.1991, N.J.C.M. Bulletin 1991, 325; see Polakiewicz, *supra* note 1, 236–7.

[60] See the practice of Spanish courts following the *Barberà* judgment and especially the decision (*Auto 312/90*) of the Spanish Constitutional Court of 18.7.1990, summarized in Polakiewicz, *supra* note 1, 88 et seq.

[61] Swiss Federal Insurance Court, judgment of 24.3.1994, Eu.G.R.Z. 1996, 619.

[62] Polakiewicz, *supra* note 1, 91–7; E. Klein, 'Should the binding effect of the judgments of the European Court of Human Rights be extended?' in: P. Mahoney/F. Matscher/H. Petzold/L. Wildhaber (eds), *Protecting Human Rights: The European Perspective* (2000) 705 (708).

[63] See, for a similar reasoning as far as Community law is concerned, Court of Justice of the European Communities, judgment of 5.3.1996, C-46/93, C-48/93, C-46/93, C-48/93 *Brasserie du*

As regards reparation, the Convention recognizes that it will often be impossible for the respondent state to wipe out all the consequences of a judicial decision which has acquired the force of *res judicata*. In January 2000, the Committee of Ministers invited the parties to the Convention to examine their national legal systems with a view to ensuring that there exist adequate possibilities of re-examination of the case, including reopening of proceedings, in instances where the Court has found a violation of the Convention.[64] Various states have already adopted special legislation which expressly allows for the possibility of reopening proceedings in the wake of an adverse finding in Strasbourg.[65] *Malta*'s European Convention Act 1987 introduced a special procedure whereby the Constitutional Court is charged to enforce Strasbourg judgments internally.[66] *Austria*,[67] *Luxembourg*,[68] *Germany*,[69] *Hungary* (see p. 397), *France*,[70] *Norway*,[71] *Poland*,[72] and *Switzerland*[73] have introduced

Pêcheur SA v Bundesrepublik Deutschland and *R v Secretary of State for Transport, ex parte Factortame Ltd and Others*.

[64] Recommendation No. R (2000) 2 on the re-examination or reopening of certain cases at domestic level following judgments of the European Court of Human Rights, adopted by the Committee of Ministers on 19 Jan 2000, at the 694th meeting of Ministers' Deputies.

[65] See Drzemczewski, *supra* note 1, 243–8; 'Study of the Committee of Experts for the Improvement of Procedures for the Protection of Human Rights (DH-PR), Institution of Review Proceedings at the National Level to Facilitate Compliance with Strasbourg Decisions', H.R.L.J. 13 (1992) 71 et seq.

[66] Section 6 of the *European Convention Act 1987* (Act No. XIV) reads as follows:
'(1) Any judgment of the European Court of Human Rights to which a declaration made by the Government of Malta in accordance with Article 46 of the Convention applies, may be enforced by the Constitutional Court in Malta, in the same manner as judgments delivered by that court and enforceable by it, upon an application filed in the Constitutional Court and served on the Attorney General containing a demand that the enforcement of such judgement be ordered.
(2) Before adjudging upon [sic] any such demand the Constitutional Court shall examine if the judgment of the European Court of Human Rights sought to be enforced is one to which a declaration as referred to in subsection (1) of this section applies.
(3) The Constitutional Court shall order the enforcement of a judgment referred to in this section if it finds such judgment is one to which a declaration referred to in subsection (2) of this section applies'. See J. Cremona, 'The European Convention on Human Rights as Part of Maltese Law', in: *Judicial Protection of Human Rights at the National and International Level*, vol. II (1991) 565 (571–2).

[67] Section 363a of the Code of Criminal Procedure, introduced in 1996.

[68] Section 443 § 5 of the Code of Criminal Procedure.

[69] § 359 No. 6 of the Code of Criminal Procedure, introduced by a Law of 9 July 1998 (*Bundesgesetzblatt* 1998 I, 1802), allows the reopening of proceedings in favour of the convicted person 'in the event the European Court of Human Rights found a violation of the European Convention for the Protection of Human Rights and Fundamental Freedoms or its Protocols and the judgment is based on this violation'.

[70] Section 89 of Law no. 2000–516 of 15 June 2000, La Semaine juridique 2000, 1277, introduced arts 626–1 to 626–7 into the French Code of Criminal Procedure.

[71] Section 391 § 2 of the Code of Criminal Procedure. Norway included a similar provision (Section 407 § 7) in its Code of Civil Procedure.

[72] Section 540 § 3 of the new Code of Criminal Procedure, which entered into force on 1 Sep 1998.

[73] Section 139a of the Federal Judicature Act (*Bundesgesetz über die Organisation der Bundesrechtspflege*); similar legislative provisions are in force in some Swiss cantons, see

special review procedures allowing criminal proceedings to be reopened following a judgment of the European Court of Human Rights. In other countries, existing legislation may be used to this effect (for example in *Denmark* and *Finland*). In addition to the proceedings which may be initiated by the applicant, in some countries the General Prosecutor's Office may also start proceedings to annul convictions based on a violation or incorrect application of the law, including the internally applicable Convention (for example in *Austria* and *Belgium*).[74]

There are numerous examples of domestic proceedings having been reopened following a judgment by the Strasbourg Court (*inter alia* the *Piersack*,[75] *Unterpertinger*,[76] *Windisch*,[77] *Schuler-Zgraggen*,[78] *Jersild*,[79] and *Z v Finland*[80] cases). According to the Strasbourg Court such proceedings bear witness to the 'commitment to the Convention and the Court's case-law'[81] and brought about 'a result as close to *restitutio in integrum* as was possible in the nature of things'.[82]

Some of the problems related to the reopening of domestic proceedings were highlighted by the *Barberà* case. The applicants had been convicted and sentenced to long prison sentences for their participation in the assassination

S. Trechsel, 'Der Einfluß der Europäischen Menschenrechtskonvention auf das Strafrecht und Strafverfahrensrecht der Schweiz', Zeitschrift für die gesamte Strafrechtswissenschaft 100 (1988) 667 (679).

[74] See section 441 of the Belgian *Code d'instruction criminelle*; section 33 § 2 of the Austrian Code of Criminal Procedure.

[75] Court of cassation, judgment of 18.5.1983, Pasicrisie belge 1983 I, 1046; see also *Piersack*, judgment (art 50) of 26.10.1984, Series A no. 85. Following the new proceedings, the applicant was again convicted. However, in the *De Cubber* case (judgment by the European Court of Human Rights of 26.10.1984, Series A no. 86) the Court of cassation refused to reopen the proceedings, arguing that the request was based purely on points of law already ruled upon before the application was lodged with the Convention organs (judgment by the Court of cassation of 27.1.1987, Journal des Tribunaux 1987, 440); see Polakiewicz, *supra* note 1, 125–8.

[76] *Unterpertinger*, judgment of 24.11.1986, Series A no. 110. Following the new proceedings, the applicant was acquitted.

[77] *Windisch*, judgment of 27.9.1990, Series A no. 186. The judgment of the Austrian Supreme Court of 23.8.1990 (12 Os 95/90–5) was rendered before the judgment of the Strasbourg Court because the proceedings had already been started on the basis of the Commission's report.

[78] Swiss Federal Insurance Court, judgment of 24.3.1994, Eu.G.R.Z. 1996, 619, given after the *Schuler-Zgraggen* judgment of 24.6.1993, Series A no. 263; see *Schuler-Zgraggen*, judgment (art 50) of 31.1.1995, Series A no. 305–A.

[79] *Jersild v Denmark*, judgment of 23.9.1994, Series A no. 298. The competent Danish court dealing with the matter held that the judgment of the Strasbourg Court was a special circumstance indicating that some evidence had not been correctly assessed.

[80] *Z v Finland*, judgment of 25.2.1997, *Reports of Judgments and Decisions* 1997–I, 323. Following this judgment, the Chancellor of Justice intervened before the Supreme Court arguing that the impugned decision constituted an error in the application of the law (chapter 31, section 8 § 4 of the Code of Judicial Procedure). The Supreme Court acceded to the request and decided to extend the period of confidentiality for the medical data in question.

[81] *Schuler-Zgraggen*, judgment (art 50) of 31.1.1995, Series A no. 305–A, § 14.

[82] *Piersack*, judgment (art 50) of 26.10.1984, Series A no. 85, § 11.

of a Catalan businessman, Mr. Bultó, in 1977. In its judgment of 6 December 1988, the European Court found several procedural flaws amounting to a violation of article 6 § 1 of the ECHR. The Court held that:

> [h]aving regard to the belated transfer of the applicants from Barcelona to Madrid, the unexpected change in the court's membership immediately before the hearing opened, the brevity of the trial, and above all the fact that the very important pieces of evidence were not adequately adduced and discussed in the applicants' presence and under the watchful eye of the public, the . . . proceedings in question, taken as a whole, did not satisfy the requirements of a fair and public hearing.[83]

Following the Strasbourg judgment, the applicants' prison sentences were suspended. In its judgment of 16 December 1991, the Spanish Constitutional Court quashed the criminal convictions and ordered a retrial.[84] Although it rejected the arguments derived from the binding force of the Strasbourg Court's judgments, it held the prison sentences to be incompatible with Spanish constitutional law. According to the Court, the declared violation of article 6 § 1 of the ECHR constituted an infringement of the applicants' fundamental rights under the Spanish Constitution. The execution of the sentences would lead to the perpetuation of a situation which had been held to be in breach of fundamental rights and would also violate the right of personal liberty. In the absence of an adequate procedure to reopen the case through the ordinary courts, the constitutional complaints procedure (*Amparo*) was held to be the only means to set aside the binding force of the initial convictions. As a result of the new proceedings, the applicants were acquitted.

The further execution of domestic judgments which the Strasbourg Court finds to be in breach of the Convention may constitute a violation of article 46 § 1 of the ECHR. Such a situation arises in particular when the substantive law on which criminal convictions were based is incompatible with the Convention (eg retroactive penal legislation) or when the legislation as such is wholly legitimate, but its application in the applicant's case violated Convention rights.[85]

An interesting example is the case of Mr Perinçek, the former Chairman of Turkey's Socialist Party. In 1992 the Turkish Constitutional Court ordered

[83] *Barberà, Messegué, and Jabardo*, judgment of 6.12.1988, Series A no. 146, § 89.

[84] STC 245/91, Suplemento del Boletín del Estado no. 13 of 15.1.1992. See Committee of Ministers, Resolution DH (94) 84 of 16.11.1994; J. Polakiewicz, 'Die Aufhebung konventionswidriger Gerichtsentscheidungen nach einem Urteil des EGMR. Anmerkung zu dem Urteil des spanischen Verfassungsgerichts vom 16. Dezember 1991 im Fall Barberà', Z.a.ö.R.V. 52 (1992), 804–27.

[85] These problems are discussed in the above-mentioned *Pakelli* decision of the German Federal Constitutional Court (11.10.1985) Eu.G.R.Z. 1985, 654 = Z.a.ö.R.V. 46 (1986) 289 with note by J. A. Frowein.

the dissolution of the Socialist Party because, according to the Court, its objectives encouraged separatism and incited a socially integrated community to fight for the creation of an independent federated state. This evaluation was based *inter alia* on public declarations concerning Kurdish national and cultural rights which Mr Perinçek, then chairman of the Party, had made in 1991 during an electoral campaign. In its judgment of 25 May 1998, the European Court of Human Rights came to the conclusion that these statements:

> though critical and full of demands, did not appear . . . to call into question the need for compliance with democratic principles and rules.[86]

Accordingly, the Court found a violation of article 11 of the Convention. On the basis of the same statements Mr Perinçek had been sentenced by the State Security Court of Ankara on 15 October 1996 to a fourteen-month prison sentence and banned from further political activities. The State Security Court stated that the sanction of dissolution of the party also carried with it personal criminal responsibility. The conviction was confirmed by the Court of Cassation on 8 July 1998, one month and a half after the judgment of the European Court.

When considering the execution of the Court's judgment in the case of the *Socialist Party and Others v Turkey*, the Committee of Ministers adopted Interim Resolution DH (99) 245 which called on Turkey to comply with the judgment and:

> to erase, without delay, through action by the competent Turkish authorities, all the consequences resulting from the applicant's criminal conviction on 8 July 1998.[87]

In the operative part of the Court's judgment of 25 May 1998, its *res judicata* seems to extend only to the dissolution of the Socialist Party as such which, according to the Court, constituted a violation of article 11 of the ECHR.[88] However, several parts of the Court's judgment clearly show that the issues under articles 10 and 11 were inseparable.[89] The dissolution of the Party cannot be dissociated from criminal convictions based on the very same public

[86] *Socialist Party and Others v Turkey*, judgment of 25.5.1998, *Reports of Judgments and Decisions* 1998–III, 1258 (§ 52).

[87] Adopted on 4 Mar 1999, at the 662nd meeting of Ministers' Deputies. On 28 July 1999, at the 677th *bis* meeting of the Ministers' Deputies, Interim Resolution DH(99)529 was adopted urging Turkey 'without further delay, to take all the necessary action to remedy the situation of the former Chairman of the Socialist Party, Mr Perinçek'.

[88] As in most cases, the operative part of the Court's judgment simply states '[f]or these reasons, the Court unanimously holds that there has been a violation of article 11 of the Convention, holds that it is unnecessary to determine whether there has been a violation of Articles 6 § 1, 9, 10, 14, and 18 of the Convention and articles 1 and 3 of Protocol No. 1 . . .': *Socialist Party and Others v Turkey*, judgment of 25.5.1998, *Reports of Judgments and Decisions* 1998–III, 1262.

[89] See in particular §§ 41, 48, and 52 of the judgment.

statements. It could be argued that Mr Perinçek, as one of the applicants before the Strasbourg Court, even had an individual right to have the judgment fully executed. On 8 August 1999 Mr Perinçek was finally released from prison.

Another situation arises when the fair trial guarantees of the Convention (in particular article 6) have been violated. Since it is not the final judgment that constitutes the violation found by the Strasbourg Court, its mere execution is not necessarily contrary to the requirements of the Convention. However, in certain cases such execution may violate article 5 § 1 of the ECHR. According to the Strasbourg Court's case-law, the lawfulness of a detention has to be determined in the light not only of domestic law, but also of the text of the Convention, the general principles embodied therein, and the aim of the restrictions permitted by article 5 § 1 of the ECHR, namely to protect the individual against arbitrariness.[90] Criminal convictions resulting in a *lawful* deprivation of liberty under the Convention must have been pronounced on the basis of fair and public hearings. Criminal procedure and its substantive outcome cannot be completely separated.[91] In cases where a causal link between the procedural irregularities and the final conviction can be established, judgments of the European Court may entail a prohibition of any further execution of a national sentence.[92] In the absence of specific enforcement procedures, such a prohibition can only be enforced under the general rules governing judicial proceedings in each country.

In other cases, the reopening of proceedings may not constitute an appropriate remedy. If the Strasbourg Court finds only procedural errors which did not influence the final outcome of the proceedings (such as excessively lengthy

[90] Eg *Wassink*, judgment of 27.9.1990, Series A no. 185–A, § 24; *Benham v United Kingdom*, judgment of 10.6.1996, *Reports of Judgments and Decisions* 1996–III, 752–753 (§ 40); see also D. Harris/M. O'Boyle/C. Warbrick, *Law of the European Convention on Human Rights* (London, Butterworths, 1995) 107–12. The Commission discussed these problems in the *Kremzow* case, application no. 23888/94, decision as to admissibility of 18.10.1995. This case was also referred to the Court of Justice of the European Communities in Luxembourg, judgment of 29.5.1997, Case C-299/95, H.R.L.J. 1997, 236.

[91] See the partly dissenting Opinion of Judge Zupančič in the cases of *Hood v United Kingdom* and *Cable and Others v United Kingdom*, judgments of 18.2.1999, who declared that the Court's judgments 'should at least imply that the national legislation ought to provide for a retrial of cases in which the proceedings have been found not to comply with essential procedural requirements'.

[92] See Supreme Court of the Netherlands, judgment of 1.2.1991, N.J.C.M. Bulletin 1991, 325 with a note by J. van der Velde. Following the *Van Mechelen* judgment of 23.4.1997, *Reports of Judgments and Decisions* 1997–III, 691, the applicants were released, see *Van Mechelen v the Netherlands*, judgment (art 50) of 30.10.1997, *ibid*, 2429 (§ 6). In the principal judgment, the Court had found a violation of art 6 § 1 taken together with art 6 § 3 (d) of the ECHR in that the conviction of the applicants had been based to a decisive extent on the evidence of police officers of whose identity the defence was unaware and whose demeanour under direct questioning they had been prevented from observing.

proceedings) reopening the case will not be justified. *Switzerland* therefore opted for a review procedure which is subsidiary in nature (section 139a of the Federal Judicature Act). It should be applied in cases where reparation for a Convention breach can only be obtained by reopening the proceedings. However, if pecuniary interests alone are at stake and full reparation can be provided by monetary compensation, a reopening of proceedings will not be granted.[93] Finally, review proceedings should not be instituted against the will of the applicant. Such proceedings do not necessarily lead to a more favourable decision. After protracted proceedings in Strasbourg, the applicant will have to consider carefully whether it is really worth returning before the national courts.

G. THE PRECEDENT VALUE OF THE JUDGMENTS

Under the Convention, only the parties to a dispute are bound by a judgment of the Court (article 46 § 1 of the ECHR). However, the binding force of the judgments (*res judicata*) has to be distinguished from their potential precedent value for similar cases.

When deciding on the merits of a case, the Strasbourg Court seeks to clarify the nature and extent of the obligations resulting from the rather broadly framed rights and freedoms. This purpose of the Court's judgments has been explicitly acknowledged by states when referring cases to the Court under article 48 of the original Convention.[94] In *Ireland v United Kingdom*, the Strasbourg Court declared that its judgments:

> in fact serve not only to decide those cases brought before the Court but, more generally, to elucidate, safeguard and develop the rules instituted by the Convention, thereby contributing to the observance by the states of the engagements undertaken by them as contracting states.[95]

In other judgments, the Court has stated that its previous case-law had clarified the nature and extent of the Parties' obligations under the Convention.[96]

[93] Federal Court, judgment of 20.10.1997 *Walter Stürm v Public Prosecutor's Office and Cantonal Court of the Canton of Valais*, ATF 123 I 283.

[94] See, for example, *König*, Series B no. 25, 162 [Germany]; *Winterwerp*, Series B no. 31, 54 [Netherlands]; *Schiesser*, Series B no. 32, 10 [Switzerland]; *Le Compte et al.*, Series B no. 38, 65 [Belgium]; *Campbell and Cosans*, Series B no. 42, 61 [United Kingdom]; *Droogenbroek*, Series B no. 44, 39 [Belgium]; *Sporrong and Lönnroth*, Series B no. 46, 10 [Sweden].

[95] Judgment of 18.1.1978, Series A no. 25, § 154.

[96] See, for example, *Pentidis and Others v Greece*, judgment of 9.6.1997, *Reports of Judgments and Decisions* 1997–III, 990 (§ 19); *Moreira de Azevedo*, judgment of 23.10.1990, Series A no. 189, § 73; *B v Austria*, judgment of 28.3.1990, Series A no. 175, § 54; *Martins Moreira*, judgment of

State practice and the case-law of national courts clearly show that findings by the Strasbourg organs enjoy a highly persuasive authority. Even before formal incorporation of the Convention, there were examples of British courts referring to judgments by the Strasbourg Court as binding precedents for the determination of the nature and scope of Convention rights.[97] It may indeed be argued that the interpretation of a provision which the Strasbourg Court has developed in a series of individual applications, and which transcends the particular facts of these cases, becomes an integral part of that provision and thereby acquires its binding force.[98] The Court seems to imply that any conditions developed in its case-law stem from the Convention itself and should not be considered as judge-made law.[99] National judicial and administrative authorities are therefore well advised to take the Strasbourg case-law into account whenever applying the Convention. However, disregard of even a consistent pattern of interpretation given by the Strasbourg Court will not constitute an independent violation of the *res judicata* of the Court's judgments (article 46 § 1 of the ECHR). But, there is a high probability that it will lead to new violations of the applicable substantive provisions of the Convention.

H. EVALUATION OF COMPLIANCE BY THE STATES

On the whole, compliance with judgments of the Strasbourg Court has remained satisfactory over the last forty years. The effective implementation

26.10.1988, Series A no. 143, § 60; *De Cubber*, judgment (art 50) of 14.9.1987, Series A no. 124–B, § 21; *Lingens*, judgment of 8.7.1986, Series A no. 103, § 46; *Guincho*, judgment of 10.7.1984, Series A no. 81, § 38; *Zimmermann and Steiner*, judgment of 13.7.1983, Series A no. 66, § 32.

[97] See *inter alia United Kingdom Association of Professional Engineers v Advisory, Conciliation, and Arbitration Service (H.L.)* [1980] 2 W.L.R. 254 (266 *per* Lord Scarman)—'[a]nd if it be a possible interpretation of the European Convention, I shall not adopt it unless and until the European Court of Human Rights declares that it is correct'; *A.G. v Guardian Newspapers Ltd (No. 2) (Ch.D.)* [1988] 3 All E.R. 545 (582 per Scott J) '[b]ut if it is right to take into account the government's Convention obligations under art 10, the article must, in my view, be given a meaning and effect consistent with the rulings of the court established by the convention to supervise its application'; High Court of the Isle of Man, judgment of 6.10.1981, *O'Callaghan v Teare*, [1981–83] Manx Law Reports 103 (109) '[i]n our view a decision of the European Court of Human Rights is binding on us in respect of the question as to whether or not a particular act is a breach of that Convention or not'.

[98] See L. Wildhaber, 'Erfahrungen mit der Europäischen Menschenrechtskonvention', Revue de droit suisse, 98 (1979) II, 329 (355); Ress, in: *The European System*, *supra* note 1, 811–12; R. Bernhardt, 'The Convention and Domestic Law', in: R. St-J. Macdonald/F. Matscher/H. Petzold (eds) *The European System for the Protection of Human Rights* (Dordrecht, Nijhoff, 1993) 25 (39); P. Leuprecht, 'The Execution of Judgments and Decisions', *ibid*, 791 (792–3).

[99] *Valenzuela Contreras v Spain*, judgment of 30.7.1998, *Reports of Judgments and Decisions* 1998–V, 1928 (§ 60) (concerning telephone tapping).

of general measures such as administrative or legislative reforms has admittedly sometimes been slow because of practical or budgetary reasons or because of the sheer scale of the reforms required.[100] Following the *Marckx* case,[101] for example, substantial reforms regarding parentage and patrimonial rights had to be carried out by Belgium which took more than ten years. The respondent states have also usually complied with the awards of just satisfaction, even where substantial sums of money were involved.[102]

It is only recently that the execution of some judgments has given rise to considerable problems which threaten to undermine the credibility of the whole system. One example is the excessive length of court proceedings in Italy which has become endemic over the years. More than 1,500 violations of article 6 of the ECHR have been found since the first judgment indicating the existence of this problem. In spite of several structural and legislative reforms, the trend in the number of new cases referred to Strasbourg has so far not changed.[103]

In its judgment in *Ferrari v Italy* of 28 July 1999, the Grand Chamber of the Strasbourg Court unanimously held as follows:

> The Court notes at the outset that Article 6 § 1 of the Convention imposes on the Contracting States the duty to organise their judicial systems in such a way that their courts can meet the requirements of this provision. . . . It wishes to reaffirm the importance of administering justice without delays which might jeopardise its effectiveness and credibility (*Katte Klitsche de la Grange v Italy* judgment of 27 October 1994, Series A no. 293–B, p. 39, § 61). It points out, moreover, that the Committee of Ministers of the Council of Europe, in its Resolution DH (97) 336 of 11 July 1997 (Length of civil proceedings in Italy: supplementary measures of a general character) considered that 'excessive delays in the administration of justice constitute an important danger, in particular for the respect of the rule of law'.
>
> The Court next draws attention to the fact that since 25 June 1987, the date of the *Capuano v Italy* judgment (Series A no. 119) it has already delivered sixty-five judgments in which it has found violations of Article 6 § 1 in proceedings exceeding a 'reasonable time' in the civil courts of the various regions of Italy. Similarly, under former Articles 31 and 32 of the Convention, more than 1,400 reports of the Commission resulted in resolutions by the Committee of Ministers finding Italy in breach of Article 6 of the Convention for the same reason.

[100] See E. Jurgens, 'Execution of judgments of the European Court of Human Rights', (Parliamentary Assembly document 8808, July 2000).

[101] *Marckx*, judgment of 13.6.1979, Series A no. 31.

[102] Concerning *Stan Greek Refineries* (judgment of 9.12.1994, Series A no. 301–B), see Committee of Ministers' Resolution DH (97) 184 of 20.3.1997. See also 'Reply from the Committee of Ministers to Written Question No. 362 on non-payment of compensation awarded by way of just satisfaction by the European Court of Human Rights', Parliamentary Assembly Doc. 7457 (17.1.1995).

[103] 'Reply from the Committee of Ministers to Written Question No. 384 by Mr Clerfayt', adopted at the 708th meeting of the Ministers' Deputies on 3 May 2000.

The frequency with which violations are found shows that there is an accumulation of identical breaches which are sufficiently numerous to amount not merely to isolated incidents. Such breaches reflect a continuing situation that has not yet been remedied and in respect of which litigants have no domestic remedy.[104]

In another judgment against Italy delivered on the same day, the Court described the delays as 'a practice that is incompatible with the Convention'.[105] These judgments effectively shift the burden of proof. Taking into account the 'continuing situation', the Court starts its examination of new applications from the premiss that the reasonable time requirement has not been met and it will be up to the Italian government to advance special circumstances to prove the opposite.

The Committee of Ministers has also put pressure on Italy. Following a series of resolutions, it has decided that all the Italian cases concerning the length of proceedings will be kept on the agenda of its human rights meetings pending the adoption and implementation of satisfactory measures. The Committee indicated that it will take all appropriate measures, including:

periodic stock-takings leading to possible further interim resolutions or other decisions indicating the progress in the effective implementation of measures to alleviate the burden of Italian courts and expedite proceedings.[106]

A particularly delicate situation developed in the *Loizidou* case, where Turkey was held responsible for the fact that the applicant had lost all control over her property in Northern Cyprus following the events of summer 1974. The Court found that the denial of access to her property constituted a violation of article 1 of Protocol No. 1 to the ECHR[107] and awarded the applicant pecuniary damages.[108] The just satisfaction awarded by the Court is still outstanding. Turkey took the view that the execution of the judgment cannot be considered in isolation, but should be part of a global solution of the Cyprus problem.[109]

The Committee of Ministers rejected the political arguments advanced by Turkey in its Interim Resolution DH (99) 680:

Considering that the Government of Turkey has indicated that the sums awarded by the European Court could only be paid to the applicant in the context of a global settlement of all property cases in Cyprus and concluding that the conditions of payment

[104] Application no. 33440/96, § 21.

[105] *Di Mauro v Italy*, application no. 34256/96, judgment of 28 July 1999, § 23.

[106] 'Reply from the Committee of Ministers', *supra* note 103.

[107] *Loizidou v Turkey (Merits)*, judgment of 18.12.1996, *Reports of Judgments and Decisions* 1996–VI, 2236–2238 (§§ 57–64).

[108] Judgment (art 50) of 28.7.1998, *Reports of Judgments and Decisions* 1998–IV, 1807.

[109] See reply by Mr Martonyi, Minister of Foreign Affairs of Hungary and Chairman-in-Office of the Committee of Ministers, Parliamentary Assembly, 1999 Ordinary Session (Second Part), Report, Eleventh sitting, 27 Apr 1999.

envisaged by the Government of Turkey cannot be considered to be in conformity with the obligations flowing from the Court's judgment;
deploring the fact that Turkey has not yet complied with the judgment by paying to the applicant the sums awarded by the Court;
stressing the obligation undertaken by all contracting States to abide by the judgments of the Court, in accordance with Article 53 of the European Convention on Human Rights;
strongly urges Turkey to review its position and to pay the just satisfaction awarded in this case in accordance with the conditions set out by the European Court of Human Rights so as to ensure that Turkey, as a High Contracting Party, meets its obligations under the Convention.[110]

Situations like these nevertheless show the limits of supervision by the Committee of Ministers which, in the absence of effective sanctions for non-compliance, has to rely on the co-operation of member states. Only in extreme cases can the application of article 8 in conjunction with article 3 of the Statute of the Council of Europe concerning suspension and withdrawal of membership be envisaged. For these reasons, it could be appropriate to strengthen the supervisory mechanism of the Convention by introducing a system of *astreintes* (daily fines for a delay in performance of a legal obligation) to be imposed on states which persistently fail to execute a Court judgment.[111]

[110] Adopted at the 682nd meeting of Ministers' Deputies on 6 Oct 1999. See also Interim Resolution DH (2000) 105 adopted on 25 July 2000.

[111] Such a proposal is included in Recommendation 1477 (2000) 'Execution of Judgments of the European Court of Human Rights', adopted by the Parliamentary Assembly on 28 September 2000 (30th Sitting).

4

Current Developments, Assessment, and Prospects

ROBERT BLACKBURN

A. Current developments and issues
1. The non-judicial human rights work of the Council of Europe
2. The human rights and freedoms protected by the Convention
3. Consistency in the jurisprudence of the Court of Human Rights
B. The appointment of judges to the Court of Human Rights
C. The European Convention on Human Rights and the European Union

Most of the major developments now affecting the Convention, and those likely to do so in the foreseeable future, are or will be themselves driven by the immense new challenges and opportunities presented by the enlargement of the Council of Europe. Great care by the Directorate and Court of Human Rights in its administrative and judicial work needs to be supported by a strong commitment from member state governments in order to continue to establish and make successful the substantial organizational changes brought in by Protocol No. 11, for there are clearly some inherent problems. Above all, there is increasing pressure on the Court with the number of applications being brought before it increasing sharply over the past two years and set to rise even faster. The total number of judgments of the Court in its entire history to 1998 was 903, yet in the first nine months of 1999 alone the figure was 108. A press release issued by the Court Registrar on 26 June 1999, entitled 'Steep Rise in Workload for European Court of Human Rights', reported that the Court had before it 10,000 registered applications and more than 47,000 provisional files, as well as around 700 letters and more than 200 overseas telephone calls a day. The President of the Court, Mr Luzius Wildhaber, responded by saying:

> The volume of work is daunting, but it is set to become more challenging still, especially as applications come in from countries which ratified the European Convention on Human Rights in the late 1990s. What can be done? There can be no doubt that the

Council of Europe's member states have a vital role to play. To reduce the Court's workload, firm political commitment is needed to ensure the Convention is respected at national level. Government, legislators and the judiciary in member states need to work together to enforce the Convention and all its articles and protocols.

A. CURRENT DEVELOPMENTS AND ISSUES

1. The non-judicial human rights work of the Council of Europe

Alongside the judicial and enforcement machinery of the ECHR stands the wide range of non-judicial Council of Europe organizational activities with respect to human rights, some of which directly complement the subject-matter the ECHR, such as the Convention for the Prevention of Torture and Inhuman or Degrading Treatment or Punishment and the Commission against Racism and Intolerance.[1] Special emphases of the Council of Europe's efforts in the field of human rights generally have been, and remain, the promotion of greater public awareness of the importance of human rights, fostering public education and a better understanding of the ECHR and the values it espouses, and identifying and studying new threats or problem areas.

One of the most valuable current initiatives aimed at facilitating the Council of Europe's pursuit of these aims, particularly in eastern Europe, is the recent creation of a new post of Council of Europe Commissioner for Human Rights. The decision to establish this position was taken at the Council of Europe's summit on 10–11 October 1997, and on 21 September 1999 Mr Alvaro Gil-Robles was elected the first office-holder by the Parliamentary Assembly, taking up the post on 15 October. As set out in the articles of the official Resolution of the Committee of Ministers,[2] the Commissioner shall be:

> a non-judicial institution to promote education in, awareness of and respect for human rights, as embodied in the human rights instruments of the Council of Europe.

Article 1(2) makes it clear that it is not the role of the Commissioner to involve himself with individual complaints, and his functions must not overlap with the work of the Court of Human Rights and the supervisory bodies existing under the various human rights instruments of the Council of

[1] In addition to the reports and literature produced by these and other bodies of the Council of Europe concerned with promoting human rights (which are available through the Human Rights Information Centre at Strasbourg), for a description of their work see *Human Rights: A Continuing Challenge for the Council of Europe* (1995) and the periodical *Human Rights Information Bulletin*.

[2] Resolution (99) 50.

Europe. The particular types of work in which the Commissioner will involve himself are set out in Article 3 of the Resolution, and they represent some important new directions for the Council of Europe's work in addition to buttressing its existing efforts in the fields of information and education.

Taken together, the collective functions required of the Commissioner for Human Rights signal a far more proactive approach to the protection of human rights, whereas most of the existing human rights institutions at the Council of Europe are reactive. Some of the Commissioner's work will be designed to help prevent poor human rights practice developing, or being allowed to continue, in order to pre-empt violations of the ECHR and complaints to Strasbourg. Thus the Commissioner is required to involve himself in facilitating the activities of national ombudsmen or similar institutions in the field of human rights. He should co-operate with existing human rights structures in member countries, and where they do not exist he should 'encourage their establishment'. The Commissioner should seek to identify shortcomings in the law and practice of member states with regard to European human rights standards, and he should promote and assist member states' implementation of these standards. In the course of his work, any specific matters of concern requiring major action by the Council of Europe may be detailed in a Report submitted by him to the Committee of Ministers or the Parliamentary Assembly.

Generally therefore the Commissioner will help raise the political profile of human rights internationally and increase pressure on governments and other national agencies to prioritize their efforts to maintain and raise standards within their borders. His first official mission was a 5-day visit to Russia starting on 29 November 1999 to speak with members of the Russian government, parliamentarians, and non-governmental organization representatives to discuss certain aspects of the situation in Chechnya. Speaking at Strasbourg on 10 December 1999, the last international Human Rights Day before 2000, Mr Gil-Robles said:

> Over 41 European countries have now signed up to the European Convention on Human Rights and almost all of them have used it as the basis of their own domestic human rights law. Those promises must be backed up with action. The European Human Rights Convention was drafted after the Second World War to put a stop to inhumanity and cruelty. Yet at the beginning of the new century we are still seeing deplorable crimes committed in Europe in violation of human rights treaties. If we are to create a world where respect for human rights is a core value, we must act now. Governments must transfer human rights standards from paper to practice.

2. The human rights and freedoms protected by the Convention

Whilst the Court of Human Rights goes through a major process of change with its internal reorganization after Protocol No. 11, and faces the challenges of enlargement and a greatly increased workload, the context within which it carries out its work is also changing and there are several suggestions for change or modification to the ECHR on the agenda. The rights set out in the Convention are themselves continuing to come under close review. A new Protocol (No. 12) on non-discrimination was prepared by the Steering Committee for Human Rights in 1999, which (as referred to above[3]) seeks to extend the prohibition of discrimination to cover the enjoyment of 'any rights set forth by law', replacing the earlier provision in Article 14 which is limited to the protection of Convention rights. The wording of Protocol No. 12, which became open for signature at the meeting of Council of Europe member states in Rome in November 2000, was criticized earlier in that year in an Opinion of the Parliament Assembly[4] for 'not fully meeting expectations'. This was on the basis that it fails to add 'sexual orientation' to the list of grounds for which discrimination is prohibited[5] and because it makes no reference to the principle of equal rights for women and men. An alternative drafting of the new Protocol was recommended by the Parliamentary Assembly to rectify the defects of which it complained.[6]

The Convention is frequently criticized, particularly by those opposed to its incorporation into the domestic law of their own country, on the ground that its articles reflect the civil and political agenda of the 1950s and are today inadequate as a modern charter of fundamental rights and freedoms for citizens. However, such sentiments too readily overlook political realities, chief among them being the practical requirement of securing and maintaining common consent among a wide body of European political and legal opinion on what such rights should be. The Council of Europe has adopted a conventional selection of human rights for the ECHR, ensuring that their enforcement can be made effective through the judicial process, and seeking the widest common denominator of agreement across the vast terrain covered by Council of Europe membership. To some extent the Court has managed to extend the original understanding of the scope of the rights agreed in 1950, by treating it as a 'living instrument' and interpreting the articles in a creative way to reflect developing moral values. Where gaps have emerged or particular articles need reinforcing, the response of the Council of Europe has often been to initiate separate non-judicial conventions or commissions on the subject, such as, with regard to the limited scope of Article 8 protecting privacy

[3] Page 10 above.

[4] Opinion No. 216 (2000) adopted on 26 January 2000.

[5] The list of grounds in Article 14 is non-exhaustive but the view of the Assembly was that forms of discrimination which are regarded as 'being especially odious' should be spelt out in the Convention.

[6] Pressure for further revisions of the non-discrimination provisions in the Convention are therefore likely to continue.

in the light of new technologies, the convention on the protection of individuals with regard to automatic processing of personal data,[7] and with regard to equality, the work of the Steering Committee for Equality between Women and Men and the European Commission against Racism and Intolerance.

The Council of Europe has updated the Convention and extended the rights and freedoms which it seeks to guarantee through the process of negotiating with member states the addition of optional protocols. These have brought many new rights to the Convention, for example in relation to education, property ownership, free elections, and freedom of movement. The Council's consensual approach to the content of the ECHR, setting down minimum standards and encouraging individual states to adopt their own system of human rights law and practice at a higher level more attuned to their own domestic traditions and culture, has been extraordinarily successful. This is true not only in general terms but in the case of some individual rights, notably abolition of the death penalty which has now been accepted by 40 of the member states of the Council of Europe,[8] which is a genuinely major achievement.

3. Consistency in the jurisprudence of the Court of Human Rights

Regarding the methods of the Court, its doctrine of the margin of appreciation, discussed above,[9] has sometimes been perceived as allowing individual states to evade the standards of human rights practice shared elsewhere in Europe. For this reason, as well as for the inconsistency with which the doctrine has occasionally been applied, it has been the subject of criticism and proposals for refinement. A leading work on the Convention by P. van Dijk and G. J. H. van Hoof[10] has criticized the Court's application of the doctrine on three grounds. First, those authors state, the Court has been 'very sparse in substantiating its approach'. In some cases there has been negligible explanation as to precisely why the restrictive national measures in dispute were held to be compatible with the complainant's rights and freedoms guaranteed by the Convention. In the case of *Chorherr v Austria* (1993) for example, no reasoning was given at all.[11] Secondly, the case-law of the Court in some respects appears to be unclear or contradictory on the application of the

[7] See its 1981 report, published in the UK as Cmnd. 8341.

[8] As at 4 November 2000 the only state which has not yet signed Protocol No. 6 abolishing the death penalty is Turkey (and Russia has not as yet ratified its agreement).

[9] See page 25 above.

[10] *Theory and Practice of the European Convention on Human Rights* (The Hague: Kluwer, 4th edn 1998) 92–95.

[11] Judgment of 25 August 1993, Series A No. 266–B.

doctrine. So, for example, two cases concerning criminal defamation by journalists, *Barfod v Denmark* (1989)[12] and *Lingens v Austria* (1986),[13] display divergent attitudes over the doctrine with respect to freedom of the press under Article 10. To remedy this, van Dijk and van Hoof believe that:

> the consistency and transparency of the Court's reasoning would be improved if more emphasis were given to the principles and factors that govern the field of application as well as the scope of the margin of appreciation and the level of scrutiny.

Thirdly, a looser test appears to be emerging in the Court when applying the doctrine of margin of appreciation to the interpretation of the provisos to Articles 8–11 on what is 'necessary in a democratic society'. A stricter test which was previously applied by the Court, emphasizing necessity and pressing social needs, has in some cases given way to wider tests involving reasonableness and balance. This was evident, for example, in the case of *Kokkinakis v Greece*[14] where the criterion was said to be what was 'justifiable in principle and proportionate'. Most commentators on this subject, including van Dijk and van Hoof, have called for a consistent application of the earlier more narrowly drawn necessity criteria, particularly as the numbers of cases involving the doctrine, especially from eastern Europe, looks set to rise.

The broader issue of how best to promote consistency in all the Court's approaches to its methods and jurisprudence raises questions about the internal structure of the Court. Concomitant with the increase in member states has been the increase in the number of judges of the Court to 41. This strengthens the Court in terms of its manpower but at the same time widens its diversity in terms of national legal cultures and characteristics. As has been seen,[15] the work of the Court now takes place in four or more separate Chambers operating simultaneously. These new developments could increase the danger of inconsistencies emerging between the various Chambers' interpretations of the human rights articles of the Convention, a problem which could be magnified by the national differences of approach brought by the new member states.

The Grand Chamber is in theory responsible for promoting consistency of approach and ensuring a similar application of principles across the Court's division into Chambers and sub-division into Committees. In practice, one would expect the number of cases going to the Grand Chamber to be small. Under article 30 Chambers have a discretion rather than an obligation to relinquish problematic cases to the Grand Chamber; and under Article 43 referrals to the Grand Chamber by a party to the proceedings are limited to

[12] Judgment of 22 February 1989, Series A No. 149.
[13] Judgment of 8 July 1986, Series A No. 103.
[14] Judgment of 25 May 1993, Series A No. 260–A.
[15] See page 17 above.

exceptional cases. There are also obvious resource pressures against utilizing a bench of seventeen judges except where absolutely necessary. Nonetheless, the early working of the Grand Chamber managed to establish itself as a well oiled machine, because under transitional arrangements for implementing Protocol No. 11 the Grand Chamber was required to hear all outstanding cases referred to the Court by the former Commission. Thus between January and October 1999, out of a total of 108 cases before the Court, fifty-seven of them were dealt with by the Grand Chamber. In future the Court will need to balance its division of function and workload with the requirement of maintaining a coherent application of the principles. Only through such a consistent approach can the Convention strengthen and further develop its common European human rights jurisprudence, whose operation maintains the confidence of all member states and their citizens. Consideration may need to be given in the future to the creation of a fully fledged appellate forum at the Court.

Of even more fundamental significance to the future of the ECHR are two questions which are considered separately below. One is the authority and composition of the Court of Human Rights itself. As the work of the Court expands, both territorially and in the number of cases (the more so if the EU accedes to the ECHR) it is vital that the membership and judgments of the Court command universal respect by being of the highest quality and integrity. The procedures presently laid down and followed by member states and the Council itself for selecting and appointing judges of the Court of Human Rights are widely believed to be in need of re-evaluation and improvement. The second issue concerns the future relations between the ECHR and the European Community/Union, in the light of proposals within the EU regarding its own Charter of Fundamental Rights and Freedoms and that it accede to the European Convention on Human Rights as a contracting party, thereby guaranteeing that all EC/EU legal and administrative measures conform with the human rights standards of the Convention. This has very large implications for the ECHR, given the powerful infrastructure of the EU and its own sophisticated legal system. If the practical complexities can be resolved, and clarity achieved on the harmonization of the work of the European Court of Human Rights in Strasbourg and that of the European Court of Justice in Luxembourg, EU accession to the Convention could prove a major asset in strengthening and underpinning the influence of the ECHR across the wider continent of Europe.

B. THE APPOINTMENT OF JUDGES TO THE COURT OF HUMAN RIGHTS

It is a matter of the utmost importance to the authority of the European Court of Human Rights that the people who are appointed as its judges are of the highest judicial calibre and ability. In its fifty-year history the Convention has been fortunate to have had many distinguished judges and members serving on the Court and Commission,[16] and it is these men and women who through their intelligence, sensitivity, and vision have successfully moulded the unifying foundations of the European human rights legal system and jurisprudence that we now possess.

At the turn of the new century, the responsibilities resting on the shoulders of the judiciary of the Court of Human Rights are greater than ever before. For not only do the individual members of the Court require considerable skill in the international dimension of their collaboration, but the significance and consequences of their decision-making have reached an unprecedented degree of importance and influence. The Court has become the most famous international tribunal across wider Europe. Virtually all member states have now incorporated the Convention into their own domestic law, thereby giving the rulings and opinions of the Court direct legal authority within each of the national legal systems of member states. Just as the number of cases coming before the Court has increased, so too has there been a greater frequency of the Court finding a violation of the Convention rights, requiring national governments to take positive action to amend their domestic legislation or administrative practice to bring it into conformity with the Court's ruling. Finally, the standards and values of the Convention as elaborated in detail by the rulings and judgments of the Court of Human Rights, are being relied upon as crucial to the liberalization of recent member states in Eastern Europe. The Court is an architect of the fledgling democracies of Europe (as well as to further countries aspiring to join the Council) by providing authoritative frameworks within which they can develop their own national systems of constitutional law, judicial procedure, and administrative practice.

The procedures by which judicial appointments to the Court are nominated and approved are therefore crucial to the continuing success of the Convention. For each judicial vacancy that arises in respect of a particular country, the process has been that, first, a nomination of three candidates is

[16] A list of the judges of the European Court of Human Rights from its beginning until the adoption of Protocol No. 11 in 1998 is published in *European Court of Human Rights, Survey: Forty Years of Activity 1959–1998* (Koln, Heymanns, 1999), 138–44. A list of the current judges of the Court is available on the Council of Europe's internet site: www.echr.coe.int.

made by the member state, ranked in order of preference; then the final choice of the nominees is made by the Parliamentary Assembly. Until 1997 this choice was in practice always dictated by the government of the member state concerned. This was because when a member state's list of nominations was presented to the Assembly to vote upon, it was not accompanied by any information about the candidates for Assembly members, who thus had no basis on which to form an opinion. In these circumstances, unsurprising, the first choice on each list was simply rubber-stamped. These arrangements gave rise to widespread dissatisfaction within the Assembly.[17] This eventually prompted a new procedure being adopted in 1998 when the membership of the entire new Court came up for selection as a result of the organizational changes under Protocol No. 11.

This change in procedure involved the Parliamentary Assembly setting up a sub-committee of its Committee on Legal Affairs and Human Rights to examine candidates nominated by member states and to submit a Report to the Assembly with its recommendations. A standard form of curriculum vitae was required to be completed by all persons nominated by member states,[18] and they were to be invited for a personal interview before the sub-committee. This, then, for the first time genuinely involved the Parliamentary Assembly in the selection process, an important step away from the Court's composition being determined as an inter-governmental matter and towards a more collective European form of decision-making. The constitutional role of the Assembly with respect to the Court must be to protect the integrity and high quality of its judges as a collective body, a task of great importance given the great judicial, indeed quasi-legislative power which the Court now possesses to alter the domestic law of 41 member states across the continent of Europe. Furthermore, the Assembly's participation is an ultimate safeguard against an individual member state sending an insufficiently qualified person to the Court, influenced perhaps by reasons of insular national or political self-interest.

[17] One United Kingdom member of the Assembly for over 20 years, Lord Hardy, recently commented that throughout his tenure of office to 1997:

> I and other British members were incensed and dissatisfied at the way in which the Council of Europe elected judges . . . We would be presented with the names of three people. We would be told to vote for one of them, but usually, no one told us anything about the three people. One could sometimes obtain a little information from the delegation of the country whose judge we were about to select. However, sometimes we would have been better off sticking a pin in the piece of paper to determine our choice of vote. Indeed, on a number of occasions I flatly refused to exercise the vote because I knew nothing about the candidates (House of Lords debate, 13 July 1998, col. 81).

[18] These curricula vitae were published: Council of Europe Parliamentary Assembly, Election of Members of the new European Court of Human Rights, Doc. 7985, 15 January 1998.

Further refinement of the new procedures governing the Assembly's involvement in judicial appointments to the Court of Human Rights is still necessary, however, in order to focus and further strengthen the work of the Assembly, and respond to valid criticisms made following the 1998 selection process.[19] In all legal systems, national or international, there is a sensitive balance to be struck in the appointment of top judicial office-holders, particularly with respect to the relative degree of influence over the process by the legal establishment and governing politicians. Within the 41 member states of the Council of Europe widely diverse methods are employed for making internal senior judicial appointments, reflecting different national traditions and ideas on how this balance is best reconciled within its own constitutional system.[20] In some countries the minister of justice exercises sole control over the matter; in others there are formal parliamentary procedures for approving senior judicial appointments; yet others have career judiciaries which have the effect of limiting the choice of nominees.[21] To some extent these national

[19] See for example H. G. Schermers, 'Election of Judges to the European Court of Human Rights', 23 *European Law Review* (1998) 568. In a United Kingdom parliamentary debate on the European Court of Human Rights, Lord Lester QC, a senior human rights lawyer, referred to:

> the seriously defective nature of the procedures adopted and carried out by the Parliamentary Assembly for the first elections to the new court . . . the procedures were opaque and unfair (House of Lords debate, 13 July 1998, col. 76).

What prompted Lord Lester's critical comments was the episode in which the Council of Europe Parliamentary Assembly sub-committee's recommendation had departed from the first choice of the UK government (Sir Nicolas Bratza QC) and recommended instead its third choice, a Scottish lawyer (Mr Robert Reed QC). This recommendation was strongly criticized by Lord Lester and others (see David Pannick QC's 1998 article in *Times*, and protestations by MPs in the House of Commons in summer 1998) on the grounds that, first, the UK government had gone through a scrupulously fair selection process at home; and secondly, no reasons for departing from the UK government's first choice were given by the sub-committee to the Assembly.

In the event, the Assembly rejected the sub-committee's report by 89 votes to 79, and appointed the first choice of the UK government. It is pertinent to add that the lobbying in support of the UK government's first choice was by ordinary members of the Assembly. The UK Lord Chancellor (minister of justice) Lord Irvine QC assured the House of Lords in the parliamentary debate initiated by Lord Lester on the subject on 13 July 1998 that:

> government officials did not lobby on behalf of any of the candidates for election to the European Court of Human Rights [and that] officials did, however, make clear to officials of the secretariat and of other member states of the Council of Europe, that the government continued to support the candidates in the order proposed, but that the selection process was for the Parliamentary Assembly. It is, of course, the duty of officials to communicate the views of Ministers in precisely this way (col. 99).

[20] For a comparative study of judicial appointments, see Eleni Skordaki, *Judicial Appointments: An International Review of Existing Models* (London: Law Society Research Study No. 5, 1991).

[21] Similarly there is considerable divergence in the quality and meaning of 'judicial independence' particularly in terms of separation from the executive and legislature: thus in some Eastern European countries judges are still largely appointed as instruments of the state; and in the United Kingdom judges of the highest appellate body in the country are appointed life members of the state legislature.

differences are manifested in the present practice of the member states' nominations to the European Court of Human Rights. More worrying is the suggestion, made by Lord Kirkhill, Chairman of the Parliamentary Assembly's sub-committee of the Committee on Legal Affairs and Human Rights, that 'the majority of the nations in membership elect their judges in a quite straightforward political fashion'.[22]

This suggests that future developments at the Council of Europe might involve three considerations. First, the Assembly should prepare a framework of common principles and procedures to guide member states in selecting and ranking their nominees to the Court.[23] This framework should be regarded as mandatory whilst allowing for a degree of subsidiarity over points of detail according to legitimate national differences concerning the country's own judiciary. These guidelines should stress the seniority and importance of the judicial work involved, requiring nominations of persons with distinguished legal careers and reputations. The guidelines should stipulate that nomination should be founded upon judicial or juristic criteria alone. Any national practice whereby the major political parties alternate in nominating a candidate of their choice should cease.[24] The domestic selection procedures should encourage a wide field of well qualified candidates by advertizing or otherwise as appropriate by submitting their names for consideration; and an independent appointments body should conduct a thorough scrutiny of applicants, including consultation across the judiciary and personal interviews. The administration of the national selection process should be carried out impartially under the responsibility of the member state's minister of justice.

Secondly, the role of the Parliamentary Assembly in the selection of appointments to the Court of Human Rights should be more tightly defined. Its express principal purpose should be to supervise the integrity of the process by which each member state selects and ranks its nominees to the Council of Europe. This will require the existing sub-committee of the Assembly's Committee on Legal Affairs and Human Rights to continue its work of conducting inquiries of the persons nominated by member states and to extend

[22] UK House of Lords debate on the European Court of Human Rights, 13 July 1998, col. 87.

[23] As a possible prelude to such a step the Parliamentary Assembly on 23 September 1999 agreed a Resolution that

> it recommends that the Committee of Ministers invite the governments of the member states to apply common criteria when drawing up lists of candidates for the office of judge in the European Court of Human Rights and to consult their national parliaments on this matter so as to ensure the transparency of the national selection procedure (Recommendation 1429 (1999) and Resolution 1200 (1999)).

[24] See the comments on this practice at the European Court of Justice by Lord Slynn of Hadley (a former advocate general and judge of that court): UK House of Lords debate, 13 July 1998, col. 90.

the perameters of its work. Its scrutiny procedures might usefully be extended, for example, by obtaining blind references from authoritative sources from within the country concerned confirming the qualifications and reputation of the candidate. The interviews held with candidates will need to become more searching and sophisticated than the brief 15-minute sessions conducted in 1998. The sub-committee should contain senior figures in the Assembly who are themselves highly qualified in legal and/or judicial work.[25] Where the sub-committee believes it right or appropriate to advise the Parliamentary Assembly to overturn a member state's preferred nominee and instead select one of the other two candidates, such a recommendation should be accompanied by written reasons, for example a material defect in the member state's domestic selection process.

Thirdly, it is fundamental that member states should respect the jurisdiction of Parliamentary Assembly to make the final selection of whom to appoint as a judge to the Court of Human Rights. Once the member state has submitted its list of three nominations, it should cease to play any active role in the judicial appointment process unless called upon for further information or details. In no circumstances should a state government's officials lobby the Assembly for its preferred candidate, whether prior to or during the proceedings of the Assembly, especially when the sub-committee has recommended a candidate other than the state's first preference. The Assembly may choose to reject its sub-committee's advice and appoint the member state's first choice,[26] and it is important that the Assembly has the power to reject all the names submitted to it and request the government of the member state concerned to re-open its selection process and present a new list of three candidates.[27]

[25] The chairman of the sub-committee in its 1998 work was Lord Kirkhill, a former UK Home Office Minister of State.

[26] As in the case of the United Kingdom in 1998 (see note 19 above).

[27] In the present circumstances a proposal to remove the ranking of the three nominees is unlikely to meet with widespread agreement. However, if in the forthcoming decades the Parliamentary Assembly is strengthened in its composition and representative nature, allowing its decision-making in appointments to become more proactive, such a step could benefit the Court of Human Rights. It would in effect empower the Assembly to formulate a European view on which candidate would best serve the overall collective interests of the Court taking into account any special present needs and requirements.

C. THE EUROPEAN CONVENTION ON HUMAN RIGHTS AND THE EUROPEAN UNION

The ECHR has been a growing source of influence on the legal and political affairs of the European Community/European Union.[28] Ever since the European Community's foundation in the 1950s all its member states have also been members of the Council of Europe and parties to the Convention. Indeed in the 1990s this became a condition for new EC/EU membership. A communal reference point for human rights standards has therefore co-existed alongside the work of the EC/EU which interacts with each of its member states.[29] The utility of this framework of human rights values started to be accepted in the case-law of the European Court of Justice in the 1960s and 1970s, when the work of the Convention and Court of Human Rights began seriously to gather momentum in Europe, and also when the United Nations adopted its International Covenants on Civil and Political Rights and on Economic, Social, and Cultural Rights. The proposition that 'fundamental rights were enshrined in the general principles of Community law and protected by the Court' was first declared by the European Court of Justice in its judgment in the *Stauder* case in 1969.[30] This was shortly followed by the *Nold* case in 1974 where specific reference was made to the common human rights standards of member states and the authority of the human rights treaties to which they belonged:[31]

> The Court is bound to draw inspiration from constitutional traditions common to the member states, and it cannot therefore uphold measures which are incompatible with fundamental rights recognised and protected by the Constitutions of those states . . . Similarly, international treaties for the protection of human rights, on which the member states have collaborated or of which they are signatories, can supply guidelines which should be followed within the framework of Community law.

[28] See Henry Schermers, 'The European Communities bound by Fundamental Human Rights', (1990) 27 *CMLRev.* 249; A. Clapham, *Human Rights and the European Community: A Critical Overview* (1991); A. Cassese, A. Clapham, and J. Weiler (eds), *Human Rights and the European Community: Methods of Protection* (1991); P. Twomey, 'The European Union: Three Pillars without a Human Rights Foundation', in D. O'Keeffe and P. Twomey (eds), *Legal Issues of the Maastricht Treaty* (1994); F. G. Jacobs, 'European Community Law and the European Convention on Human Rights', in D. Curtin and T. Heukels, *Institutional Dynamics of European Integration: Essays in Honour of Henry G. Schermers* (1994); Noreen Burrows, 'The European Union and the European Convention', in Brice Dickson (ed), *Human Rights and the European Convention* (1997); Philip Alston (ed), *The EU and Human Rights* (1999).

[29] The EU/Council of Europe overlapping membership as at 1 March 2000 comprises Belgium, Denmark, Germany, Greece, Spain, France, Ireland, Italy, Luxembourg, the Netherlands, Austria, Portugal, Finland, Sweden, and the United Kingdom.

[30] Case 29/69, *Stauder v Ulm* [1969] ECR 419.

[31] Case 4/73, *Nold v Commission* [1974] ECR 491 at 507.

Since then there has been a line of cases before the European Court of Justice in which the European Convention on Human Rights has been employed as an aid to the interpretation of the EC/EU Treaties and the legislative and administrative acts of the Community institutions.[32] Furthermore, the human rights principles of the Convention have been applied by the European Court of Justice to limit the actions of national authorities when they have been purporting to implement a Community law. Since Community law has supremacy over national law, insofar as the Convention's principles are deemed part of the general law of the Community, where one or more of the Convention's human rights articles are relevant and applicable the national action can be challenged within the terms of the Convention itself. Thus in the *Kirk* case in 1984 the European Court of Justice applied the principle of no punishment without law contained in Article 7 of the Convention. The Court declared that the prohibition of retroactive penal provisions was a fundamental human right and the regulation in question (the United Kingdom's Sea Fish Order 1982 which restricted fishing by other member nations):

> may not . . . have the effect of validating *ex post facto* national measures of a penal nature which impose penalties for an act which, in fact, was not punishable at the time at which it was committed.[33]

In the 1980s and 1990s the political institutions of the European Communities became increasingly keen to incorporate some form of declaration or charter of common fundamental rights into their work. This is reflected in the progressively greater prominence given to human rights in the EC/EU treaties. The Treaty of Rome in 1957 made no direct reference to human rights, being essentially concerned with economic matters, although it did affirm the member states' shared objectives of safeguarding peace and freedom. However, the Single European Act of 1986 specifically referred in its Preamble to the European Convention on Human Rights, pledging:

> to work together to promote democracy on the basis of the fundamental rights recognised in the constitutions and laws of the member states, in the Convention for the Protection of Human Rights and Fundamental Freedoms and the European Social Charter, notably freedom, equality and social justice.

Subsequently the Treaty on European Union (TEU) signed in 1992 made further reference to the Convention (in its Article F.2, since 1997 in Article 6.2), providing that:

[32] For studies of the case-law see especially N. Grief and L. Betten, *EC Law and Human Rights* (1998) and Philip Alston (ed), *The EU and Human Rights* (1999).

[33] Case 63/83, *R v Kirk* [1984] ECR 2689.

The Union shall respect fundamental rights, as guaranteed by the European Convention for the Protection of Human Rights and Fundamental Freedoms signed in Rome on 4 November 1950 and as they result from the constitutional traditions common to the member states, as general principles of Community law.

In 1997 some significant amendments were made to the TEU by the Treaty of Amsterdam, which modified and strengthened this commitment. Article 6.1 (ex Article F) of the TEU contains the declaration that:

the Union is founded on the principles of liberty, democracy, respect for human rights and fundamental freedoms, and the rule of law, principles which are common to the member states.

A further amendment widened the existing duty upon the European Court of Justice to ensure respect for the law in the interpretation and application of the Treaty by extending its scope to Article 6.

Two political declarations on fundamental rights with accompanying references to the European Convention on Human Rights were made by the European Parliament in 1977 and 1989. The declaration on 5 April 1977 was made jointly by the European Parliament with the European Council and European Commission. Its Preamble, which pointed to the fact that all member states were parties to the European Convention on Human Rights, stated that the treaties establishing the EC were based on the 'principle of respect for the law', and gave moral backing for the approach of the European Court of Justice in defining the scope of 'that law' as including (over and above the rules embodied in the Treaties and secondary Community legislation) the general principles of law and in particular the fundamental rights, principles and rights on which the constitutional law of member states is based.[34] The text of the declaration continued:

(1) The European Parliament, the Council and the Commission stress the prime importance they attach to the protection of fundamental rights, as derived in particular from the constitutions of Member States and the European Convention on Human Rights and Fundamental Freedoms. (2) In the exercise of their powers and in pursuance of the aims of the European Communities they respect and will continue to respect these rights.

The Resolution and Declaration of the European Parliament made on 12 April 1989 was longer and more elaborate.[35] As with the 1977 declaration, it was non-legal and of political authority alone. The Resolution made reference to numerous human rights sources, among them the Council of Europe's

[34] See above on the Court's human rights approach. Article 220 (formerly Article 164) of the EC Treaty requires the Court to ensure that the law is observed in the interpretation and application of the Treaty.

[35] Doc. A2–3/89.

Convention on Human Rights and its Social Charter and the United Nations' Covenants on Civil and Political Rights and on Economic, Social, and Cultural Rights, and heavily emphasized the link between democracy and human rights:

> [it is] essential to promote democracy on the basis of fundamental rights . . . respect for fundamental rights is indispensable for the legitimacy of the Community.

It also referred to the the strength of the Community and the shared sense of citizenship among its peoples:

> the identity of the Community makes it essential to give expression to the shared values of the citizens of Europe . . . there can be no European citizenship unless every citizen enjoys equal protection of his rights and freedoms.

The Preamble to the Declaration reaffirmed the existence of a common legal tradition based on respect for human dignity and fundamental rights and that these rights derived from the constitutional traditions common to member states of the EC and the European Convention on Human Rights. The Preamble made two further interesting references (of some significance to issues discussed below), one of which was to the wider European order, rather than just the EC: 'continuing and reviving the democratic unification of Europe, having regard to the creation of an internal area without frontiers'; the other was a reference to 'the particular responsibility of the European Parliament with regard to the well-being of men and women'. The Declaration set out a list of fundamental rights in 28 articles, covering dignity, the right to life, equality before the law, freedom of thought, opinion, and information, privacy, protection of the family, freedom of movement, the right of ownership, freedom of assembly and of association, freedom to choose an occupation, working conditions, collective social rights, social welfare, the right to education, the principle of democracy, the right of access to information, access to the courts, *non bis in idem*, non-retroactivity, the death penalty, and environmental and consumer protection. These articles emphasized a selection of particular rights, distinct from (though overlapping with[36]) the European

[36] Compare for example the rights to freedom of expression in the Declaration (Article 5(1) Everyone shall have the right to freedom of expression. This right shall include freedom of opinion and the freedom to receive and impart information and ideas, particularly philosophical, political and religious. (2) Art, science and research shall be free of constraint. Academic freedom shall be respected) with the wording of the ECHR (Article 10(1) Everyone has the right to freedom of expression. This right shall include freedom to hold opinions and to receive and impart information and ideas without interference by public authority and regardless of frontiers . . .); or concerning the right to privacy as expressed in the Declaration (Article 6(1) Everyone shall have the right to respect and protection for their identity. (2) Respect for privacy and family life, reputation, the home and private correspondence shall be guaranteed) with the wording in the ECHR (Article 8(1) Everyone has the right to respect for his private and family life, his home and his correspondence).

Convention on Human Rights, and were accompanied by little or no detail on what legitimate restrictions might be placed upon them.[37]

However, the purely political nature of the European Parliament's 1989 Declaration of Fundamental Rights and Freedoms (as with all declaratory political bills of rights) renders it less important for the articles to be precise about what in legal cases is the crucially important practical matter of what restrictions may be legitimately imposed by public authorities (or others) upon the rights in question. The references to rights in the European Parliament's Declaration are in essence statements of policy objectives.[38] Yet such non-legal declarations have real practical significance not only as guidelines for internal institutional purposes, and symbolically in the context of EC citizenship, but also for the EU/EC's standing in the wider world and in its dealings with individual foreign states. The protection of human rights has come to play a leading role in international relations and is directly relevant to the work conducted under the EU pillar of foreign and defence affairs. It is highly advantageous, therefore, for the EU to possess its own document on human rights standards, agreed to by all its member states, to facilitate the closer integration of all its foreign policy work. If it insists upon a particular

[37] A broad general limitation was stated in Article 26:

> The rights and freedoms set out in this Declaration may be restricted within reasonable limits necessary in a democratic society only by a law which must at all events respect the substance of such right and freedoms.

So for example no particular restriction was stated in the article on freedom of expression, whereas in ECHR Article 10 a restriction reads:

> (2) The exercise of these freedoms, since it carries with it duties and responsibilities, may be subject to such formalities, conditions, restrictions or penalties as are prescribed by law and are necessary in a democratic society, in the interests of national security, territorial integrity or public safety, for the prevention of disorder or crime, for the protection of health or morals, for the protection of the reputation or rights of others, for preventing the disclosure of information received in confidence, or for maintaining the authority and impartiality of the judiciary.

Similarly no special restriction on the right to privacy was expressed in the Declaration, whereas there is in ECHR Article 8(2):

> There shall be no interference by a public authority with the exercise of this right except such as is in accordance with the law and is necessary in a democratic society in the interests of national security, public safety or the economic well-being of the country, for the prevention of disorder or crime, for the protection of health or morals, or for the protection of the rights and freedoms of others.

See and compare the general limitation clause for the later EU Charter on Fundamental Rights in December 2000, which is considerably more sophisticated than that in the 1989 Declaration: below page 100.

[38] Insofar as the Declaration provides a right to complain to the European Parliament (in Article 23) about alleged violations of the rights in the document, this is a mechanism for drawing Parliament's attention to a problem with a view to resolving it politically or through administrative channels rather than through a formal process of adjudication.

set of moral standards for other countries, without which it will refuse to conduct or allow normal relations, then the EU must very clearly show its own commitment to those same standards.[39] Thus consistency between the internal and the external human rights policies of the EU underpins all its work.

All these factors which affect the inter-relationship between human rights as recognized and enforced across the wider region of Europe under the ECHR, and the evolving nature and work of the EU, gave rise in 1999–2000 to serious proposals and preparatory work towards, first, the EU adopting a Charter of Fundamental Rights of the European Union; and secondly, the EC (or the Union, if it acquires legal personality) acceding to the ECHR. The political decision to launch a major initiative to draft a Charter of Fundamental Rights was taken at the meeting of Heads of State or Government at the Cologne European Council on 3 and 4 June 1999. The official announcement of the decision said that the protection of fundamental rights was 'a founding principle of the Union and an indispensable prerequisite for her legitimacy' and stressed the role which an EU charter of such rights could play in making 'their overriding importance and relevance more visible to the Union's citizens'. In setting out the guiding principles for determining the content of this charter, the European Council first reiterated the pre-existing basis for human rights in the EC/EU, namely that it should contain the rights and freedoms as well as the basic procedural rights guaranteed in the ECHR and in the common constitutional traditions of member states 'as general principles of Community law'. Secondly, it directed that the charter should also include 'the fundamental rights that pertain only to the Union's citizens'. Thirdly, the European Council said that in drawing up the charter account should be taken of economic and social rights as contained in the European Social Charter and in the Community Charter of the Fundamental Social Rights of Workers.[40] Two distinctive features of the new Charter of Fundamental Rights for the EU, therefore, were to be that it is distinctive to the EU and its citizens, and that it covers a wider range of fundamental rights than those contained in the ECHR.

The work of the *ad hoc* body, or convention, established to draw up the draft Charter was impressive and attracted an immense amount of interest and debate in legal and political circles. Some basic yet complex issues remained to be decided, among them the question whether the charter should be a legal instrument (as opposed to a declaration, similar in status to the 1989

[39] The same standards expected of foreign states with whom the EU collectively or individually carries on relations is also expected of and between its own member states. An EU Charter of Fundamental Rights should make it clearer when and how member states whose domestic affairs have fallen below accepted EU standards should be dealt with.

[40] Article 135, Treaty of European Union.

Declaration of the European Parliament) and if so to what extent social and economic rights should feature in the charter, particularly when such rights have traditionally been regarded as difficult or impossible to enforce through a judicial process. The precise wording of each fundamental right is also an important issue (especially if the charter is to be legally enforceable through the European Court of Justice) including the level of detail which each article should contain, especially on the legitimate restrictions which can be imposed on such rights. Above all, however, there is the crucial question of the inter-relationships between this EU Charter and the ECHR and between the European Court of Justice in Luxembourg and the European Court of Human Rights in Strasbourg.

A subsequent meeting of the European Council at Tampere on 15 and 16 October 1999 settled the detail for the composition, method of work, and practical arrangements for the *ad hoc* convention responsible for preparing the draft Charter. The Council wished it to be widely representative of the EU's various constituent components, rather than dominated by the European Commission, and settled upon a membership of 62 persons, comprising 15 heads of state or government of member states, one representative of the President of the European Commission, 16 members of the European Parliament (selected from among its members), and 30 members of national Parliaments (two from each national Parliament, selected from their members). An unusual element in this inter-governmental initiative, therefore (particularly as its implementation necessitates a Treaty amendment) has been the Council permitting the large involvement of parliamentarians. The convention elected Mr Roman Herzog, former President of the Federal Republic of Germany, to serve as its president for the whole duration of its work. The largest component in the convention is made up of members of the European Parliament which has backed the idea of a charter for several decades and is now 'very excited by the prospect of drafting a charter'.[41] At the time of writing, the convention has held several meetings and has involved official observers, including two representatives from the European Court of Justice and two from the Council of Europe including one from the Court of Human Rights.[42]

It is essential that nothing resulting from this laudable initiative for a Charter of Fundamental Rights for the European Union serves to destabilize

[41] Andrew Duff MEP, giving oral evidence to the House of Lords European Union Scrutiny Sub-Committee E, 1 March 2000.

[42] 1 March 2000. The two members are Mr H. C. Krüger, the Deputy Secretary-General of the Council of Europe, and Mr Marc Fischbach, a Judge of the Court of Human Rights (Luxembourg). The convention has consulted widely across EU and national official agencies and committees, and invited evidence from 'civil society' particularly from non-governmental organizations. Much of the documentation generated is published on the convention's website.

the difficult work of the ECHR and Court of Human Rights at this critical juncture in its development, with its sharply increased membership and workload. There are clearly some major problems to resolve and dangers to be avoided in formulating an effective working Charter: above all, there must be no possibility of creating two rival European systems of human rights protection, involving the Luxembourg and Strasbourg Courts operating in competing jurisdictions with separate and potentially conflicting bodies of European human rights jurisprudence. This could only weaken the protection of fundamental rights for people across the EU since it would permit unscrupulous state agencies to distinguish between the alternative articles, choosing whichever standard better suited their purpose and thereby justifying what would otherwise be a violation of human rights. From a wider perspective, it would be immensely harmful to the fledgling democracies of eastern Europe if the Council of Europe's human rights work across 41 states were perceived as secondary to that of the EU Charter. That would diminish the authority and influence of the ECHR over the continuing development and construction of new legal and administrative safeguards for human rights in those countries. Consequently, the narrowing of human rights differences between all states across the continent of Europe, which is a precondition of moving closer towards a more closely integrated European social order, would suffer.

The solution to most of these problems is for the European Union to acquire legal personality and accede to the ECHR as a contracting party. This step has been supported in the majority view of the European Commission since the early 1980s (and intermittently even before then). Accession to the ECHR was first proposed to the European Council by the Commission in a memorandum of 4 April 1979.[43] After a decade of further reflection the proposal was renewed in a further memorandum of 19 November 1990 which argued that a conspicuous gap in the Community legal system could be filled through EC accession to the ECHR.[44] In giving evidence to a UK parliamentary committee inquiry on the subject in 1992, the Commission's lawyer Dr J. Pipkorn summarized the position of the Commission:

> It makes the position of the Community in the field of human rights more coherent and fills a gap in the protection of human rights as regards Community legal acts.[45]

The European Council responded by requesting the Court of Justice for its opinion as to whether the existing treaty provisions would allow Community

[43] Bulletin of the European Communities, supplement 2/79.

[44] Communication on Community Accession to the European Convention for the Protection of Human Rights and Fundamental Freedoms, 19 November 1990 (Cons. doc. 10555/90, 4 December 1990).

[45] Quoted in HL Deb., 26 November 1992, col. 1106.

accession to the ECHR, to which the Court answered in the negative,[46] thereby clarifying that formal treaty amendments at an inter-governmental conference would become necessary once the policy had been confirmed by the agreement of member states.

The effect of EU accession to the ECHR would be that all decisions, laws, and actions by Community and Union bodies would become subject to review by the European Court of Human Rights for their compatibility with the ECHR. This would include the decisions of the European Court of Justice. Whilst there might be some resistance to the perceived subordination of EU institutions and its Court to the jurisprudence of Strasbourg, based upon misconceived assertions about the superior quality of human rights and legal traditions within the EU, in substance these bear little difference to the misunderstandings and empty controversies that in the past surrounded some individual nations' debates about whether or not to incorporate the ECHR into their domestic legal system.[47] It is inevitable that the relationships between the respective legal orders will be viewed by some in hierarchical terms, but to do so is unhelpful in this context since the issue is one of reconciliation between the different systems, and clearly some unifying supranational scheme of arbitration is necessary to achieve this. Three further points on this matter should be borne in mind. First, as already discussed, the principle of subsidiarity is strongly emphasized in the methods of the EHCR. Before any petition can be presented to the Court of Human Rights all local remedies must have been exhausted and, following EU accession, this will include all possible avenues for complaint within the structure of the EU and before the European Court of Justice. Furthermore, if any difficult administrative idiosyncrasies arise from the special nature of the EU as a contracting party because of its international structure, it is likely that the Strasbourg Court's doctrine of the margin of appreciation would provide the necessary flexibility.[48]

Secondly, the fundamental rights protected by the Court of Human Rights are specifically designed to be universal in nature. In other words, they are to be understood as a minimum standard below which no contracting party should permit its laws and administrative practice to fall. The intention behind the ECHR is that most, or all, contracting parties should adopt higher standards of their own, being more detailed and attuned to their particular traditions and society. This will be equally applicable to the EU, and is the reason why there need be no inconsistency or conflict between the

[46] Opinion 2/94 of the Court, 28 March 1996.

[47] See for example the arguments about statutory incorporation of the ECHR in the UK prior to its final adoption in 1998: chapter 36, pp. 956–7 and references cited therein.

[48] See page 25 above.

Luxembourg and Strasbourg Courts if the EU adopts its own Charter of Fundamental Rights, so long as it simultaneously accedes to the ECHR (and, as is necessary, accepts the compulsory jurisdiction of the Court of Human Rights). Similarly, the EU Charter could certainly be a legal instrument and remain compatible with the jurisdiction of the Strasbourg Court so long as there is accession to the ECHR. From the point of view of the ECHR's enforcement machinery, there is every advantage in the EU Charter of Fundamental Rights adopting more detailed legal protections of its own and including additional rights which do not exist in the present form of the ECHR. For example, no right of access to information is expressly included in Article 10 of the ECHR (though an interpretation of the wording in that Article might reasonably be extended to cover such a right[49]), and the creation of a such a right within the EU, whether contained in the Charter or elsewhere, would be entirely welcome and consistent with the minimum standards laid down in the ECHR. There can be no objection to the EU Charter going beyond what is contained in the ECHR; the important point is that the laws and standards of the EU (as with all member parties) must not fall below the requirements of the ECHR.

Thirdly, an important feature of the European Court of Human Rights is that its rulings do not have direct legal effect. In other words, following the EU's accession to the ECHR, the effect of an adverse ruling by the Court of Human Rights would not be to repeal or amend a provision of EC/EU law directly, but to impose an obligation upon the Commission and Council to bring forward legislation of their own, or to change their administrative practice, in order to satisfy the requirements of the European Court of Human Rights' judgment. This is different to the position of the European Court of Justice with respect to the application of EU laws to the legal provisions and administrative practices of its member states where the Court's judgments do indeed have direct effect and are applied accordingly by courts operating within the national legal systems.[50] The jurisprudence of the Court of Human Rights will nonetheless become more strongly persuasive and influential than at present in assisting the European Court of Justice in its interpretation of Community laws, acts, and obligations (and of course where a precedent for a particular situation exists, the Luxembourg Court would be bound to apply the Strasbourg Court's earlier ruling).

[49] Such an opinion was expressed by the Council of Europe's Deputy Secretary General, Mr H. C. Krüger, in oral evidence to the UK House of Lords European Scrutiny Sub-committee E, 22 March 2000.

[50] Generally see T. C. Hartley, *The Foundations of European Community Law* (Oxford University Press, 4th edn 1998); L. Neville Brown and Tom Kennedy, *The Court of Justice of the European Communities* (4th edn 1994).

This raises the question of what amendments would be necessary or desirable to the EC/EU treaties and to the ECHR itself in order to enable the EU's accession to the ECHR. The Treaty on European Union would have to confer legal personality (which only the EC has at present) upon the EU, to allow it to become an international contracting party.[51] Some amendments would be required to the European Community Treaty to the effect that the Court of Justice is the final arbiter of Community law and excluding other forms of judicial settlement between member states.[52] It would also be desirable to create a special procedure within the terms of the EU/EC treaties and the ECHR which empowered the European Court of Justice in appropriate or difficult cases to refer points of law relating to the interpretation of the ECHR to the Court of Human Rights for a preliminary ruling. This would help minimize the number of instances in which the European Court of Human Rights reverses or contradicts the legal reasoning and judgments of the European Court of Justice, and would promote a better working relationship between the two courts by removing a possible source of rivalry or tension. It is likely that a new separate protocol to the ECHR would be needed, dealing specifically with EU–ECHR relations, due to the unusual position of the EU as a international contracting party.

At the time of writing the final outcome of the 1999–2000 EU initiative for a Charter of Fundamental Rights remains speculative. The indications are that a code of succinctly worded rights will emerge as the form of the Charter to be presented by the convention to the European Council, and that its subject-matter will range across political, civil, social, and economic issues, with a general limitation clause, as in the form of the European Parliament's Declaration in 1989, discussed above. Assuming that a guiding purpose of the Charter is to make a statement about EU citizenship, then a short code of this nature would have the advantage of intelligibility to ordinary people who wish to read and learn about their rights as citizens of the EU,[53] whereas the more elaborate text of the ECHR is much more in the nature of a lawyer's document. Present indications also suggest that there is widespread support for EU accession to the ECHR, both from within the institutions of the EU and from various national agencies and non-governmental organizations,[54]

[51] Unless the EC alone were to become the contracting party, but this would narrow the scope of EU citizenship.

[52] See F. G. Jacobs and R. C. White, *The European Convention on Human Rights* (1996) for a brief discussion of these implications of accession.

[53] To a short general list of fundamental rights there can of course separately be added more specific detailed rights, procedures, and restrictions by way of further measures of EU/EC primary or secondary legislation.

[54] See the large volume of evidence submitted to the convention preparing the charter, available at http://ue.eu.int/df. See also generally Report of the House of Lords Select Committee on the European Union, *EU Charter of Fundamental Rights*, HL [1999–2000] 67 (London: Stationery Office 2000).

and that this step of major importance to the future of both the ECHR and the EU may receive inter-governmental endorsement in principle fairly soon, though its actual implementation would necessarily be delayed for a longer period while the practical details are negotiated and the formal application to the Council of Europe submitted and approved.[55]

[55] While this book was in press the Convention completed its final version of the Charter on 2 October 2000. It contains 57 Articles covering a very wide range of citizens' rights and freedoms, including those of political, civil, social, economic, administrative, and consumer subject-matter, subject to a general limitation clause at Article 52(1) that:

> any limitation on the exercise of the rights and freedoms recognised by this Charter must be provided for by law and respect the essence of those rights and freedoms. Subject to the principle of proportionality, limitations may be made only if they are necessary and genuinely meet objectives of general interest recognised by the Union or the need to protect the rights and freedoms of others.

Of the Charter's relationship with the ECHR, Article 52(2) states:

> Insofar as this Charter contains rights which correspond to rights guaranteed by the Convention for the Protection of Human Rights and Fundamental Freedoms, the meaning and scope of those rights shall be the same as those laid down by the said Convention. This provision shall not prevent Union law providing more extensive protection.

The European Council examined the draft Charter at its meeting (attended by the three Vice-Presidents of the Convention) on Saturday 14 October 2000, following which President Chirac announced:

> This morning we gave the unanimous agreement of the Heads of State or Government to the draft Charter of Fundamental Rights of the European Union. The Charter can therefore be declared at the Nice European Council [scheduled for December 2000], following agreement by all the institutions concerned.

Accordingly, the Charter was duly 'solemnly proclaimed' on 7 December 2000 by the European Parliament, the Council of Ministers, and the European Commission during the EU summit held at Nice, and the text of the Charter was published in the Official Journal of the EC (C364 of 18 December 2000).

The question of whether any formal legal status should be conferred upon the Charter proved contentious at the Nice summit, with some members including the UK strongly opposing such a move, preferring the Charter to remain purely symbolic and declaratory. The matter was deferred for further consideration at a later date, but meanwhile at the very least the European Court of Justice can be expected to integrate the Charter's articles straightaway into its own definitional standards of the common fundamental rights whose protection it is the Court's function to uphold. The other important question of EC accession to the ECHR, which was formally proposed by Finland during the intergovernmental conference preceding the Nice summit, also proved contentious and was similarly deferred. Both these issues now await further intergovernmental deliberations before any possible future action is taken at the next EU summit to be held in 2004.

See further H. C. Krüger and J. Polakiewicz, 'Proposals for a Coherent Human Rights Protection System in Europe', *Human Rights Law Journal*, vol. 22 (2001), No. 1-2.

PART II

The Effect of the ECHR on the Legal and Political Systems of Member States

5

Austria

HANNES TRETTER[1]

A. INTRODUCTION

1. Domestic fundamental rights and their protection

Before Austria ratified the ECHR (below: Convention) in 1958, fundamental rights and freedoms were only guaranteed by the Austrian 'bill of rights', the Basic Law of 1867 on the General Rights of Nationals (*Staatsgrundgesetz über die allgemeinen Rechte der Staatsbürger 1867—StGG 1867*, below: Basic Law 1867) which as a law of the Austrian-Hungarian Monarchy was incorporated into the constitutional legal order of the new democratic Republic of Austria in 1920. Amended several times, it is still in force. This Basic Law contained (and still contains) a core of civil and political rights symbolizing the legal achievements of the Austrian bourgeoisie and constitutionalism *vis-à-vis* the police state of the nineteenth century. In 1867 a high court, the *Reichsgericht*, was appointed to decide on applications asserting the rights and freedoms guaranteed to the people.

In the course of drawing up the Austrian Constitution of 1920 (*Bundes-Verfassungsgesetz 1920*, below: *B-VG*) the proposed new and integral bill of rights including civil, political, cultural, and social rights fell through because of a disagreement between the main political parties. That is why the Basic Law of 1867 as a minimum consensus became part of the new Austrian Constitution which remained in force until 1933 when the Corporative State (*Ständestaat*) and then the Nazi regime took over power in Austria. In 1945, after the collapse of the Third Reich, the Austrian Constitution, and with it the Basic Law of 1867, was set in force again. Based on the Constitution of 1920, a new high court, the Constitutional Court (*Verfassungsgerichtshof*)

[1] The author would like to thank Lukas Gehrke, Tina Gewis, Susanne Kovacs, Karin Lukas, Nikolaus Marschik, and Tanja Vospernik, all employees at the Ludwig Boltzmann Institute of Human Rights, for their valuable contributions to this report. I also wish to express my sincere gratitude to Gerhard Auinger and Leopold Stollwitzer for their review work on the English text.

was established. One of its fields of jurisdiction was (and is) to dispense justice on compliance with the rights and freedoms guaranteed by the Basic Law of 1867.

2. *Ratification of the Convention and its Protocols*

After Austria regained its full sovereignty by the State Treaty of Vienna in 1955, it became a member of the Council of Europe in 1956 and ratified the Convention and its first Additional Protocol of 1952 (1st Protocol) in 1958. The following Additional Protocols on substantive rights were not ratified very quickly: 1969 (4th Protocol of 1963), 1984 (6th Protocol of 1983) and 1986 (7th Protocol of 1984). By contrast, all procedural Additional Protocols were quickly ratified.

3. *Reservations*

Austria made some reservations and declarations regarding the Convention and its Protocols:

The Convention was ratified with the reservation that the provisions of article 5 shall be so applied that there shall be no interference with the measures for the deprivation of liberty prescribed in the laws on administrative procedure,[2] subject to review by the Administrative Court or the Constitutional Court as provided for in the Austrian Federal Constitution. Furthermore the provisions of article 6 shall be so applied that there shall be no prejudice to the principles governing public court hearings laid down in article 90 of the Federal Constitution Law.

Desirous of avoiding any uncertainty concerning the application of article 1 of the 1st Protocol in connection with the State Treaty of 15 May 1955 for the Restoration of an Independent and Democratic Austria, Austria ratified the Protocol with the reservation that there shall be no interference with the provisions of Parts IV 'Claims arising out of the War' and V 'Property, Rights and Interests' of the above-mentioned State Treaty.

The 4th Protocol was signed with the reservation that article 3 shall not apply to the provisions of the Law of 3 April 1919, StGBl. No. 209 concerning the banishment of the House of Habsburg-Lorraine and the confiscation of their property, as set out in the Federal Constitutional Law.

In connection with the 7th Protocol Austria declared that higher tribunals within the meaning of article 2 para. 1 include the Administrative Court and the Constitutional Court and that articles 3 and 4 exclusively relate to crimi-

[2] BGBl. No. 172/1950.

nal proceedings within the meaning of the Austrian Code of Criminal procedure.[3]

To date, Austria has not withdrawn its reservation.

4. *Individual complaints*

Together with the ratification of the Convention and the 1st Protocol in 1958 Austria has since accepted (at three-year intervals) without interruption, the competence of the European Commission of Human Rights (below: Commission) to deal with individual complaints as well as the jurisdiction of the European Court of Human Rights (below: Court).

B. THE STATUS OF THE CONVENTION IN NATIONAL LAW

After its ratification, the Convention was officially published in the Austrian Federal Law Gazette without any comment on its legal status. Since a major controversy arose very soon afterwards as to whether the Convention formed part of constitutional law, so an amendment to the Constitution in 1964 finally clarified its status as constitutional law, from which it derived its direct applicability. Austria was the first state which fully incorporated the Convention into its constitutional legal order. The Convention was therefore granted the same legal status as the domestic bill of rights. Therefore, on one hand, legislation has to observe and give effect to the rights and freedoms of the Convention; on the other hand, all courts and administrative authorities are obliged to apply the Convention within their jurisdiction, which means that they have to interpret the law in a manner which does not infringe the rights of the Convention. Some problems were caused by the parallelism of national fundamental rights and freedoms and the Convention. Initially, the Constitutional Court held that the Convention rights had not altered the protection of fundamental rights, ie that parallel rights were identical with regard to their contents. It was only later, under the influence of Strasbourg case-law, that the Court developed a more differentiated view. In particular, it has become common practice for the Court to examine which right is more beneficial for the person affected, although it is not assumed that one right should derogate from the other. Where a domestic fundamental right is more favourable, article 53 is applied; if a Convention right is better, the

[3] This 'declaration' was seen as a reservation by the Court's judgement in the *Case of Gradinger*, Series A 328–C. As a reservation it was not accepted as admissible due to the fact that the government failed to enclose the texts of the relevant laws (see also E/9 below).

Convention is given priority in line with the principle of *pro libertate*, which is derived from the rule of law. This result is also suggested by the fact that it is not only the Convention which has domestic effect, but also that Austria is obliged under international law to guarantee the rights and freedoms of the Convention.

In this context the jurisdiction of the Constitutional Court is of the utmost importance. It has the competence to review *ex parte* final decisions of administrative authorities (but not of judicial authorities[4]) to examine whether they violate the fundamental rights and freedoms guaranteed on the constitutional level, and to overturn them if they do. The Constitutional Court is also competent to review laws *ex parte* and *ex officio* to decide if they are constitutional and to abolish them if they are not. Based on this competence the Constitutional Court has since 1958 developed a rich jurisdiction regarding the rights and freedoms of the Convention and has quashed a considerable number of administrative decisions and laws which infringed rights and freedoms granted by the Convention. Doing so, the Constitutional Court has influenced jurisdiction as well as legislation, giving the rights and freedoms of the Convention more effect within national law. This positive influence is dimmed by the fact that the Constitutional Court in many cases is only reacting to findings against Austria by the Strasbourg Court, rather than reviewing the national legal order, according to the requirements of the Convention, on its own initiative. It must also be noted that the Constitutional Court in many cases starts from the premiss that a Convention right cannot go further than the parallel national fundamental right without examining or justifying this assumption in detail. Thus, the pressure of a Court judgment is sometimes required to improve the incorporation of the Convention in substantive terms.

Since it entered into force, legal science has dealt intensively with the Convention and related case-law. It is not possible here to give a full account of the entire Austrian literature on the Convention. Two books have systematically addressed the Convention and highlighted its influence on the Austrian legal system: the Handbook *Die Europäische Menschenrechtskonvention in der Rechtsprechung der österreichischen Höchstgerichte*,[5] published in 1983 by Felix Ermacora, Manfred Nowak, and Hannes Tretter, and the three-volume edition of *Grund- und Menschenrechte in Österreich* by Rudolf Machacek, Willibald Pahr, and Gerhard Stadler in 1991, 1992, and 1997.[6]

[4] The review of decisions by judicial authorities is a matter for the Supreme Court.
[5] Publisher: Braumüller, Vienna.
[6] Publisher: Engel, Kehl am Rhein—Strasbourg—Arlington.

C. THE STATUS OF THE CONVENTION IN PARLIAMENTARY PROCEEDINGS

1. Introduction

The Austrian legislation has continuously been influenced by the Convention itself and by the case-law of the Strasbourg organs in different fields, although it cannot be said that it has been 'profoundly influenced'.[7] For that too little readiness to observe and fulfil the Convention obligations on the part of government and parliament was and is prevailing. Often only the minimum was done to observe the obligations arising from the Convention with regard to the relevant jurisdiction, rather than amending the questionable legislation thoroughly.

The following describes the principal cases in which Austrian law has been amended or set into force as a consequence of decisions and judgments issued by the Strasbourg organs or by national courts, mainly the Constitutional Court, in respect of the rights and freedoms of the Convention and—in a few cases—as a consequence of the Convention itself without the pressure of jurisdiction.[8]

The legislator frequently refers to the Convention expressly either in the relevant law itself or in parliamentary explanatory reports. In several instances Convention rights and restrictive clauses were partly or wholly quoted in legal provisions, although it is unclear what the purpose of such an approach may be. The reiteration of constitutional provisions in ordinary law guarantees that the authorities enforcing the law are obliged also to use the Convention provisions cited therein as a basis for their decisions. However, this is already required because the authorities are obliged to interpret ordinary law provisions in conformity with the Constitution anyway, and therefore not much is to be gained in terms of normative function from a repetition of Convention provisions. It would be more useful to focus in more detail on the provisions of the Convention in ordinary law—where necessary, by reference to the Convention right concerned.

Although it is less suggested by the wording than by the content, the Convention and the pertinent case-law have further influenced the national

[7] See Polakiewicz/Jacob-Foltzer, *The European Human Rights Convention in Domestic Law*, HRLJ Vol. 12 (1991), No. 3, 65 (67).

[8] See a summary by Okresek, *Die Auswirkungen der Judikatur der Straßburger Menschenrechtsorgane auf die österreichische Rechtsordnung*, in: Neisser (ed), *Menschenrechte als politischer Auftrag, Verlag Medien und Recht*, Vienna 1993; and Okresek, *Der Einfluß der EMRK und der Judikatur der Straßburger Konventionsorgane auf die österreichische Rechtsordnung*, in: Österreichisches Institut für Menschenrechte, Newsletter 1997/3a, 144.

legislation, both in reaction to findings against Austria by the Strasbourg Court and as a result of decisions which, while affecting other countries, raised objections under the Convention against Austrian laws.

In the following, an overview is given of laws which were put into force or amended for reasons related to the Convention.

2. *Articles 2 and 3*

The Aliens Act (*Fremdengesetz*[9]) implements the case-law established in respect of article 3, prohibiting the deportation of foreigners to countries where they risk being subjected to inhuman or degrading treatment, punishment, or the death penalty. Although the law does not explicitly refer to the Convention, a reference to article 3 and article 2 in conjunction with the 6th Protocol is found in the Explanatory Report.

The Gun Use Act of 1969 (*Waffengebrauchsgesetz 1969*[10]) reflected Convention considerations on articles 2 and 3 at a very early time, especially in addressing the principle of proportionality in connection with the use of service guns.

The Security Police Act (*Sicherheitspolizeigesetz*[11]) regulates the tasks and powers of the security police. Some provisions relating to the use of necessary violence were included, which may be traced back to article 3 and the pertinent case-law (in particular, rulings of the Constitutional Court regarding human dignity derived from article 3). Thus, the law regulated in detail, on the basis of proportionality, the way in which human rights may be interfered with, giving the protection of life and limb priority over the protection of other rights. These rules were further specified by the Guideline Ordinance (*Richtlinien-Verordnung*[12]), to the observance of which everyone has a valid claim.

3. *Article 5*

Referring to the *Engel Case* in 1985,[13] the former Federal Army Disciplinary Act (*Heeresdisziplinargesetz*) was amended in view of the requirement that restrictions of personal freedom based on disciplinary law fall within the scope of article 5.

In 1988 the Federal Constitutional Law on the Protection of Personal Liberty (*Bundesverfassungsgesetz über den Schutz der persönlichen Freiheit*[14])

[9] BGBl. No. I 1997/75, last amended by BGBl. No. I 1998/158.
[10] BGBl. No. 1969/149, last amended by BGBl. No. 1974/422.
[11] BGBl. No. 1991/566, last amended by BGBl. No. 1998/158.
[12] BGBl. No. 1993/266.
[13] *Engel and others v the Netherlands*, judgment of the Court of 8 June 1976, Series A 22.
[14] BGBl. No. 1988/864, last amended by BGBl. No. 1993/35.

was passed to combine the various legal requirements on the protection of personal freedom in the meaning of article 5 and to guarantee their contents at the constitutional level. The codification of this law was also meant to help withdraw the Austrian reservation in respect of article 5.[15] Regarding this, the pertinent Explanatory Report of the Government Bill emphasizes the relevant case-law of the Commission and the Court.[16]

To enable criminal decisions to be reviewed by the Supreme Court according to article 5 the Law on Fundamental Rights Applications (*Grundrechtsbeschwerdegesetz*) was set in force in 1992.[17] In defining the right to personal liberty, the Law refers, *inter alia*, to article 5 and establishes a 'proportionality test' within the meaning of the Strasbourg case-law.

4. *Article 6*

4.1. *Legal protection in administrative law*

Establishment of administrative authorities with judicial character

In reaction to the judgment of the Strasbourg Court in the *Ringeisen Case*[18] and several subsequent judgments of the Constitutional Court having regard to the Strasbourg decision, administrative authorities of a judicial character (*Verwaltungsbehörden mit richterlichem Einschlag*) were established to fulfil the requirements of article 6 concerning the independence and impartiality of tribunals and to substitute hierarchically subordinate administrative authorities.[19] The relevant explanatory materials always refer to the Strasbourg jurisprudence, particularly the judgment in the case of *Ringeisen*.

Acceleration of proceedings before courts of public law

In 1984, a constitutional amendment to reduce the burden on the Constitutional and Administrative Courts was adopted. One reason for the amendment was the judgment of the Court in the case of *Zimmermann and Steiner v Switzerland*, in which it found that the right to a fair trial was violated by unreasonably lengthy proceedings before the Swiss Federal Court. Given that member states are obliged to take the necessary measures to avoid excessive lengthy proceedings, and that in Austria both the Constitutional Court and the Administrative Court must decide on civil rights and criminal charges within the meaning of article 6 para. 1, measures to speed up pro-

[15] This reservation could not be withdrawn in respect of the provision of the 7th Protocol, which requires that everyone convicted of a criminal offence by a tribunal shall have the right to have his conviction or sentence reviewed by a higher tribunal, and according to the judgment of the Court in the *Gradinger Case* (see D/4, E/4.4, and 9 below).

[16] RV. 134 d.B. St. Prot. NR. XVII. GP.

[17] BGBl. No. 1992/864 as amended by BGBl. No. 1993/35.

[18] Judgment of the Court of 16 July 1971, Series A 13.

[19] See above all VfSlg. 6995/1973 and 7099/1973.

ceedings before these courts were adopted. The decision enabling the courts of public law to refuse to deal with an appeal if it had no prospect of success or did not relate to a fundamental question proved most useful in practice.

Oral hearing before the Administrative Court
The judgment in the *Fischer* case[20] caused the legislators to amend the Administrative Court Act (*Verwaltungsgerichtshofgesetz*) in order to show that an oral hearing must in any event be held before the Administrative Court where this results from article 6.

Establishment of independent administrative tribunals
To escape the problems raised by the jurisdiction of the Strasbourg organs concerning the validity of article 6 of the Convention in Austrian[21] administrative law, Independent Administrative Tribunals (*Unabhängige Verwaltungssenate—UVS*) were established in 1988.[22] They are organized as independent and impartial tribunals within the meaning of article 6 of the Convention.[23] Establishing these tribunals was intended as a move to withdraw the Austrian reservation in respect of article 5, which under the Austrian case-law has been extended to article 6 and all administrative penal proceedings leading to deprivation of personal liberty. The establishment of these tribunals also became necessary due to the case-law of the Court[24] that the terms 'civil rights and obligations' must be understood in a broad sense to include traditional administrative matters which were not to be decided by independent authorities.[25]

Along with the creation of these tribunals, a comprehensive amendment of the Code of Administrative Procedure was adopted in 1990.[26] The aim was to organize proceedings before the tribunals in conformity with articles 5 and 6 (including full cognition with regard to questions of fact and law, publicity, and publication of decisions).

[20] *Fischer v Austria*, judgment of 26 April 1995, Series A 312.

[21] See the Explanatory Report to the legal draft RV. 668 d.B. St.Prot. NR. XVII GP.

[22] BGBl. No. 1988/685.

[23] Recently the Constitutional Court stated that certain members of the Viennese Independent Adminsitrative Tribunal lacked impartiality in the meaning of art 6 para. 1 because they—as former officials of the Regional Government—shall return in their former department; see the judgment of the Constitutional Court of 2 Oct 1997, B 2434/95.

[24] See above all the judgments in the cases of *Ringeisen v Austria*, *König v Germany*, and *Bentham v The Netherlands*.

[25] Against VfSlg. 11500/1987 (*Miltner* case), after what those matters do not belong to the heart of 'civil rights and obligations'; in those cases the legal control by the Constitutional Court and the Administrative Court are sufficient to fulfil the obligations arising from art 6. See also D/5.2 below.

[26] See BGBl. No. 1990/356–358.

4.2. Criminal proceedings

Code of Criminal Procedure Amendment Act 1962 (equality of arms in appeal proceedings)
An amendment to the Code of Criminal Procedure of 1962[27] was adopted in reaction to complaints raised in Strasbourg of violations of the right to equality of arms in criminal proceedings. The amendment provided for a public appeal hearing to which defendants must be summoned if not detained, and brought before the court if detained. In addition, a federal law on the renewal of appeals in criminal proceedings provided that trials in regard to which the Commission had accepted an application under the previous law at the time of submission had to be reopened.

Criminal Code Compensation Act
Following a decision of the Commission,[28] the Criminal Code Compensation Act[29] was enacted, which provides that persons who have suffered a material damage due to a criminal conviction or detention are entitled to assert their claims before an independent and impartial court based on law. Such claims may also be asserted by persons who are unable to refute the suspicion of having committed a criminally punishable offence.

Criminal Code Amendment Act 1971 (detention on remand and application for release from detention)
The Criminal Code Amendment Act 1971[30] was Austria's reaction to several complaints which had led to findings against it because of the length of detention on remand.

Legal Aid Act
In the light of article 6, a Legal Aid Act was passed which provided for the defendant's right to counsel free of charge where this was in the interest of the law, and above all, the right to have an adequate defence. This law was the result of a complaint brought by a lawyer against Austria on the ground that the obligation to work as legal aid counsel amounted to forced or compulsory labour within the meaning of article 4 para. 2.[31]

[27] BGBl. No. 1962/229.
[28] Case of *Rebitzer v Austria*, Decision of 24 May 1971, Appl. No. 3245/1967.
[29] BGBl. No. 1969/70; the explanatory notes on the government bill have explicit regard to art 6 para. 1 of the Convention.
[30] BGBl. No. 1971/273.
[31] *Gussenbauer v Austria*, Appl. No. 4897/1971, and Appl. No. 5219/1971 (Collection of Decision 42, pp. 41 and 94).

Code of Criminal Procedure Adaptation Act 1974 (public hearing before investigating judge)

The Code of Criminal Procedure Adaptation Act 1974[32] was designed to ensure—in reaction to several complaints[33]—that the parties to criminal proceedings are given the opportunity to hear witnesses.

Criminal Code Amendment Act 1983 (personal attendance of the defendant at the appeal hearing)

Following a friendly settlement in a human rights case,[34] a provision was included in the Criminal Code Amendment Act 1983[35] that a detained defendant was to be allowed to attend a hearing before the appeal court if he so requests or where this is in the interest of justice.

Criminal Code Amendment Act 1987 (surveillance of conversation with counsel)

In the wake of a human rights application which resulted in a friendly settlement before the Court[36] the Criminal Code Amendment Act 1987[37] was adopted to amend a provision of the Code of Criminal Procedure.[38] In the proceedings, during which the Commission found a violation of article 6 para. 3, the applicant complained about the surveillance of conversations with his defence counsel during the first three months of his detention on remand. The provision of the Code of Criminal Procedure in question was changed so that the investigating judge, as a rule, is now only permitted (with a few justified and precisely specified exceptions) to be present at meetings between an accused and his defence counsel during the first two weeks of detention.

New provisions of the Criminal Code Amendment Act 1993

This amendment to the Code of Criminal Procedure[39] includes a number of new provisions which became necessary as a result of several judgments given by the Strasbourg Court. The Explanatory Reports contain numerous references to all the relevant judgments, not only those issued against Austria.[40] The new provisions related specifically to the enhancement of the controversial nature of criminal proceedings and to such issues as equality of arms, grounds for the exclusion of judges in retrials, witness protection programmes, extending the scope of applicability of witness testimonies, observance of basic law provisions in nullity proceedings before the Supreme Court

[32] BGBl. No. 1974/423.

[33] Appl. No. 5049/1971.

[34] *Peschke v Austria*, Appl. No. 8289/1978.

[35] BGBl. No. 1983/168.

[36] *Can v Austria*, Appl. No. 9300/1981.

[37] BGBl. No. 1987/605.

[38] Para. 45 StPO.

[39] BGBl. No. 1993/526.

[40] Cases concerning Austria: *Brandstetter*, *Toth*, *Kamasinski*, *Unterpertinger*, *Windisch*, and *Asch*.

(*Oberster Gerichtshof*) as well as translation assistance and reimbursement of interpretation costs. It must be noted that this amendment expressly specified infringements of article 6 as a ground for nullity.[41]

Penal Code Amendment Act 1996 (equality of arms)
The judgment in the *Bulut* case was the reason for an amendment to the Code of Criminal Procedure,[42] with a view to ensuring that statements by the Public Prosecutor must in any case be transmitted to the accused, previously not the case.

Code of Criminal Procedure Amendment Act 2000 (sufficient time to prepare a plea of nullity)
In a recent decision (VfGH of 16 March 2000, G 151/99) the Constitutional Court found that four weeks was not long enough to prepare a plea of nullity before the Supreme Court after the decision of a criminal court. The fact that the fixed legal time limit of four weeks could not be extended, even in exceptional circumstances as in the current case, led the Constitutional Court to abolish the relevant provisions in the Code of Criminal Procedure as being a breach of the right to have adequate time for the preparation of a defence against the prosecution case, as laid down in article 6 para. 3(b) of the European Convention on Human Rights. Thus, para. 285 of the Code of Criminal Procedure was amended to ensure adequate preparation time (of more than four weeks) in cases of complexity, ie in cases with particularly lengthy hearings, detailed protocols, or other court documentation.

4.3. Proceedings under the Code of Financial Offences In its decision of 1984[43] the Constitutional Court annulled provisions of the Code of Financial Offences governing confiscation for non-compliance with article 6, because there was no independent tribunal which decided on this interference with a civil right. This decision led to an amendment of the above Code. At the same time, provisions relating to the assumption of innocence and legal aid were also included in the amendment.

5. Article 8

5.1. Right to data protection This basic right was introduced into the Austrian system of basic rights[44] to protect the personal sphere of the individual human being in connection with modern information technologies and to afford him legal protection against unjustified investigation, processing, and use of his personal data. As explained by the Report of the Constitutional

[41] Paras. 281 and 345 StPO. [42] BGBl. No. 1996/762. [43] VfSlg. 10291/1984.
[44] Para. 1 of the Law of Data Protection 1978 (*Datenschutzgesetz 1978*), BGBl. No. 1978//565, as last amended by BGBl. No. 1994/632.

Committee of the Parliament, the idea was to carry forward the principles contained in article 8 of the Convention and to create a form of individual protection independent of the technical method of interference with the personal sphere. The constitutional provision of article 1 para. 2 of the Act explicitly states that restrictions of the right to data protection must only be applied to protect the valid interests of others or on the basis of laws which are necessary to achieve the aims listed in article 8 para. 2. The draft version of the new Data Protection Act[45] also explicitly refers to article 8 para. 2.

The Chemical Substances Act (*Chemikaliengesetz 1996*[46]) obliges enterprises to inform the authorities on the production, storage, and transport of dangerous chemicals. With reference to article 8, the law entitles the companies to qualify certain types of information as trade secrets. In such a case, the authorities must handle such information confidentially except where conflicting interests within the meaning of article 8 para. 2 are predominant.

The law on international co-operation in police matters (*Polizeikooperationsgesetz*[47]) provides that personal data must not be transmitted for legal assistance purposes, *inter alia*, if it is to be assumed that the foreign authority requesting such data does not guarantee the necessary protection of the private sphere of the person affected within the meaning of article 8 or fails to meet the explicit data protection requirements of the Austrian authority.

5.2. Personality protection for victims of punishable offences, witnesses, suspects, and convicted persons Without being preceded by human rights proceedings before the Strasbourg organs, provisions for the protection of witness were included in the Code of Criminal Procedure because of article8 with the Criminal Code Amendment Act 1987.[48] Provisions for the protection of the private sphere of victims of punishable offences and of suspects and convicted persons were written into an amendment to the Media Act in 1992.

5.3. Respect for the private and family life of foreigners in regard to residence-terminating measures and family reunion Earlier regulations of the Aliens Act had to be amended in the light of the case-law of the Strasbourg institutions and the Constitutional Court in respect of article 8, making it mandatory for the authorities to take decisions on expulsion or extradition in observance of the private and family life of the persons concerned and to review decisions in terms of their proportionality.[49]

[45] *Regierungsvorlage des Datenschutzgesetzes* 2000, 1613 d.B. St.Prot. NR. XX. GP.

[46] BGBl. No. 1997/53. [47] BGBl. No. 1997/104. [48] BGBl. No. 1987/605.

[49] See the judgment of the Constitutional Court VfSlg. 10737/1985 cancelling a provision of the Foreign Police Act (*Fremdenpolizeigesetz*) which allowed the expelling of foreigners for certain reasons but did not oblige the authority to take into consideration the personal and family situation of the person concerned.

The explanatory notes of the government bill for the current Aliens Act 1997 (*Fremdengesetz 1997*)[50] contain several references to article 8 of the Convention, especially in connection with the right of legal aliens or new immigrants staying in Austria to have their families reunited. The law excludes, however, the protection of fake marriages under article 8, which corresponds to the concept of family life as developed by the Convention organs. Expulsions must take place only in compliance with the admissible aims stated in article 8 para. 2, with a weighing of the different interests being generally required (except in those cases where foreigners try to cross the border illegally or are caught shortly after having unlawfully entered Austrian territory; special rules apply to EU citizens or persons of comparable status).

The Asylum Act 1997 (*Asylgesetz 1997*)[51] provides for the concept of 'safe third countries', to which a person may be deported who could already have obtained protection from persecution within the meaning of the Geneva Refugee Convention in that country. The requirements for a country to be qualified as a safe third country are ratification of the Geneva Refugee Convention plus the establishment of a corresponding asylum procedure, and ratification of the European Convention on Human Rights. The Act expressly provides for the right to prolongation of asylum if the person concerned is unable to continue a family life within the meaning of article 8 in another country.

6. *Article 10*

6.1. Protection of telecommunication secrecy In 1974 a special provision was included in the Basic Law of 1867 (article 10a) to protect telecommunication secrecy.[52] The reason for this amendment was a decision by the Supreme Court (which is responsible for civil and criminal matters) that the scope of protection under article 8 of the Convention also covered court-ordered surveillance of telephone conversations.[53]

6.2. Abolition of the monopoly of the Austrian Broadcasting Corporation In reaction to the application and the report of the Commission in the case of *Informationsverein Lentia 2000 and others*,[54] shortly before the judgment of the Court was delivered the Austrian Parliament abolished the broadcasting monopoly of the Austrian Broadcasting Corporation (*Österreichischer Rundfunk—ORF*), which the Court held to be a violation of article 10, and

[50] BGBl. No. I 1997/75, last amended by BGBl. No. I 1998/86.
[51] BGBl. No. I 1997/76, last amended by BGBl. No. 1998/106.
[52] BGBl. No. 1974/8.
[53] See 960 d.B. St. Prot. NR. XIII GP.
[54] *Case of Informationsverein Lentia 2000 and others*, judgment of 24 Nov 1993, Series A 276.

passed the Private Radio Act (*Regionalradiogesetz*) which provided for a small number of private broadcasting licences, albeit only for radio and on a regional level. The restrictive and indefinite character of this law led to several appeals to the Constitutional Court which abolished the relevant norm on the ground that it lacked sufficient legal determination. The amended law grants broadcasting licences to a suitable number of local and regional private radio enterprises. However, a law on private television licences is still lacking.

7. Article 11

Regard to article 11 is being had by an amendment to the Association's Act (*Vereinsgesetz*) 1951 adopted in 1987.[55] Under that amendment, the establishment of an association, which would be unlawful in respect of its aim, name or organization, must only be prohibited if the requirements of article 11 para. 2 are fulfilled. A similar reference to the Convention in the case of its dissolution has not been provided for unknown reasons.

8. Article 1 of the 1st Protocol

The 1987 decision in the case of *Inze against Austria*, which found a violation of the discrimination ban in connection with the right to respect of property in a case of unequal treatment of legitimate and illegitimate children under the farm inheritance law was found, caused the Austrian legislators, who had explicit regard to that decision and to the decision in the case of *Marckx against Belgium*,[56] to amend the law.

In accordance with the Strasbourg Court's ruling in the case of *Gaygusuz v Austria* and in two subsequent decisions of the Constitutional Court abolishing various provisions of the Unemployment Insurance Act (*Arbeitslosenversicherungsgesetz*) the Parliament finally created a new legal situation which guaranteed general and equal access to emergency assistance, which is now in conformity with article 1 of the First Protocol of the Convention. (See sections D9 and E8 below.)

[55] BGBl. No. 1951/233, last amended by BGBl. No. 1993/257.
[56] Judgment of the Court of 13 June 1979, Series A 31.

D. LEADING HUMAN RIGHTS CASES DECIDED BY THE NATIONAL COURTS

1. Introduction

The Austrian case-law relating to the Convention is so comprehensive that it is impossible to provide an all-encompassing summary.[57] Domestic courts and administrative authorities have ruled on nearly every right or freedom enshrined in the Convention. This is rooted in the fact that the Convention has constitutional significance and must therefore be directly enforced by every authority in its respective jurisdiction. Due to its competence to approve legislative and administrative acts the Constitutional Court has developed the most extensive case-law with regard to the Convention, particularly if compared to the other Austrian high courts—the Administrative Court and the Supreme Court.[58] Thus, it appears legitimate to present a synopsis of key human rights cases and issues decided by the Constitutional Court, and to provide some examples of relevant case-law adopted by the other two courts. Insofar as the case-law of the high courts has influenced legislation, the amendments are discussed in section C above (particularly the case-law concerning article 6 of the Convention).

2. Article 2

2.1. Admissibility of abortion In only a few cases has the Constitutional Court had to make rulings concerning article 2. Like other constitutional courts, the Austrian Constitutional Court had to decide whether the admissibility of abortion was compatible with article 2.[59] It held the Austrian law allowing the termination of a pregnancy within the first three months (*Fristenlösung*) to be compatible with article 2. The Constitutional Court stated that the wording of the first sentence of article 2 leaves it open whether the right to life extends to unborn life. But regarding article 2 as a whole, there is every reason to believe that the right to life is not granted to an unborn child. Since the Convention allows exceptions to the right to life of already born in exceptional cases, it would not be consistent if all interference with an unborn child was excluded by the Convention. Therefore, the Constitutional Court concluded, legal abortion is compatible with the right to life of unborn children.

[57] Comprehensively and systematically the jurisprudence is described in the books mentioned in B, above.

[58] See B, above.

[59] VfSlg. 7400/1974.

2.2. Life-threatening use of weapons In two decisions, the Constitutional Court had to deal with the life-threatening use of weapons. In both cases shots were aimed at two persons fleeing in order to prevent them from escaping, not to kill them. In the first case[60] the Court stated that the use of a weapon was no violation of article 2 if there was a strong suspicion of a criminal act, whereas in the second case[61] the Constitutional Court found that the use of the weapon was a breach of the right to life due to a lack of proportionality between the force used and the interest pursued, namely to arrest an illegal immigrant. Moreover, in this finding the Court pointed out that every shot aimed constitutes a danger to life and must therefore be examined in the light of article 2.

3. Article 3

3.1. Introduction Compared to the Strasbourg case-law, the Constitutional Court has established a more autonomous and extensive jurisdiction. In line with its consistent practice, the sphere of application of article 3 has been related to measures by police authorities and in connection with the termination of residence under the Aliens Act. Like the Strasbourg Court, the Constitutional Court has not taken a standardized dogmatic approach to article 3 of the Convention, but decides each case following some rules and consideration of whether there is a violation of the provision or not. The absolute and unrestricted wording of article 3 has not led the Court to give a general definition of what is to be subsumed under the provision. Rather, it examines if a measure can be qualified as a violation as being 'an interference with the dignity of man as a human being of a particularly serious nature'. Thus, a measure may be qualified as a violation of article 3 but, on the other hand, it can also be seen as necessary and justified in order to reach legally accepted objectives. In other words, the Constitutional Court—like the Strasbourg Court—relies heavily upon the principle of proportionality, on which basis it has developed a jurisdiction based on case-law. Up to now, the Court has only had to deal with the question of whether treatment was 'degrading' or 'inhuman' within the meaning of article 3. The question has not yet arisen of whether a measure was 'torture'.

3.2. Measures regarding police forces As regards police and security forces, the Constitutional Court was, *inter alia*, asked to rule on the following cases based on article 3: use of weapons,[62] use of physical force,[63] use of a rubber truncheon,[64] use of handcuffs,[65] pulling by the hair,[66] slapping the face,[67]

[60] VfSlg. 8082/1977.
[61] VfSlg. 15046/1997.
[62] VfSlg. 8082/1977, 10427/1985.
[63] VfSlg. 9298/1981.
[64] VfSlg. 11230/1987.
[65] VfSlg. 9196/1981 and 12271/1990.
[66] VfSlg. 8146/1977, 1687/1988.
[67] VfSlg. 8296/1978, 10052/1984.

chaining to a tree,[68] beating with fists and feet,[69] exposing the body,[70] pushing down a slope,[71] strangling,[72] use of a police dog,[73] pushing through a window,[74] etc. The Constitutional Court has only examined conditions of detention, detention centres, and the medical treatment of prisoners on the basis of article 3 with regard to measures taken by police and security forces.

3.3. Measures terminating residence Although the Constitutional Court has not yet considered referring to the case-law of the Strasbourg organs as regards police and security forces, it did refer to the institutions of the Convention on article 3 with regard to measures terminating residence. In accordance with the Strasbourg Court, the Constitutional Court argues that a state may be responsible under article 3 in cases of expulsion or extradition. This is relevant in cases where there is a valid and legitimate fear that the non-national in question may be confronted with the actual threat of torture or of inhuman or degrading treatment or punishment in the country to which he or she is to be expelled.[75] The existence of these actual threats must be examined individually and on a case-by-case basis. In doing so, a given state must do more than examine the information published by the state from which the threats allegedly originate. However, according to the Constitutional Court, the protection of the principle of non-refoulement as postulated by article 3 does not apply during the procedural process for the granting of asylum, nor with regard to the issuance of a residence ban; instead, it only applies after a decision on the expulsion of the non-national has been made.[76]

With reference to the judgment of the Strasbourg Court in the *Ahmed* case[77] and the political situation in Somalia, the Constitutional Court agreed in one case with the Strasbourg Court's view that state persecution as well as non-state persecution must be considered in the light of article 3.[78]

4. Article 5

Like the Commission and the Court, the Austrian high courts, especially the Constitutional Court, have developed extensive case-law concerning article 5. But, as far as administrative law is concerned, this case-law is profoundly influenced by Austria's reservation in respect of article 5. This reservation stipulates that the provisions of article 5 shall be applied so as not to interfere with the measures for the deprivation of liberty prescribed in the laws on

[68] VfSlg. 9231/1981. [69] VfSlg. 10250/1984 and 11687/1988.
[70] VfSlg. 10661/1965, 10848/1986, and 12258/1990. [71] VfSlg. 8155/1977, 11228/1987.
[72] VfSlg. 11328/1987. [73] VfSlg. 12190/1989. [74] VfSlg. 12623/1991.
[75] VfSlg. 13897/1994.
[76] See VfSlg. 11044/1986 and 13314/1992.
[77] *Case of Ahmed*, judgment of 17 December 1996, Reports 1996–IV.
[78] VfSlg. 14998/1997.

administrative procedure, subject to review by the Administrative Court and Constitutional Court, as provided for in the Austrian Federal Constitution.[79] For a long time the reservation was applied not only to those administrative penalties already in force when the Convention was ratified, but also to all subsequent penalties which were similar to the earlier ones or based on them. As a consequence the Constitutional Court's case-law on article 5 could hardly develop into an autonomous regime. The Constitutional Court interpreted article 5—more or less in accordance with the Strasbourg case-law—along the lines of the rulings relating to the domestic right to liberty. It stressed repeatedly the similarity of the protection granted by article 5 of the Convention and article 8 of the Basic Law of 1867 together with the former Basic Law on the Protection of Personal Freedom of 1867, although the scope of protection of article 5 goes well beyond that of article 8 and the Basic Law on the Protection of Personal Freedom of 1867, particularly in that the admissibility of deprivation of liberty has to be examined from the substantive requirements of article 5. When a violation of the right to personal freedom was found, which was rare, it was said to be a violation of article 8 of the Basic Law of 1867 and the Basic Law on the Protection of Personal Freedom of 1867; no breach of article 5 was (expressly) found.

The extensive new codification of the right to liberty as laid down in the Federal Constitutional Law on the Protection of Personal Freedom (*Bundesverfassungsgesetz über den Schutz der persönlichen Freiheit*) in 1988[80] brought about a fundamental change of the legal environment. This new law replaced article 8 of the Basic Law of 1867 and the Basic Law on the Protection of Personal Freedom of 1867, but had no impact on the legal dimensions of article 5. The Federal Constitutional Law on the Protection of Personal Freedom largely follows article 5 with regard to language and structure. Nonetheless, it would be inappropriate simply to apply the results of article 5 commentary to the above-mentioned Constitutional Law, which does not consist of mere repetitions or summaries of article 5 alone. The objective of the amendment was not only to preserve the present status of constitutional protection of the right to liberty, but also to establish the higher level of legal protection which already existed in ordinary law in constitutional law itself. Nonetheless, it must be examined on a case-by-case basis which norm is the most favourable one with regard the protection of the right to liberty and security of a person. Every interference with the right to liberty has to be judged cumulatively with a view to both provisions. The interference is inadmissible if it is prohibited under one of these rules only.

[79] See also chapters D/5 and E/3.

[80] BGBl. No. 1988/684

5. *Article 6*

5.1. Administrative criminal proceedings As with article 5, the case-law of the Austrian Constitutional Court in respect of article 6 with regard to administrative law is extensive and has significantly influenced the Austrian legislation.

Its reservation to article 5 states that the provisions of this right shall be applied so as not to interfere with the measures for the deprivation of liberty prescribed in the laws on administrative procedure.[81] The Constitutional Court has extended this reservation to the procedural guarantees under article 6 (although this provision is not mentioned in the reservation), to the entire system of administrative penalties in the various laws (although the reservation only mentions the Procedural Code), to all penalties including fines (although the reservation clearly deals with deprivation of liberty only), and to penalties imposed after 1958 when the reservation was made. It was only afterwards, under the influence of the case-law of the Strasbourg organs, that this rigid and restrictive interpretation of the scope of application of article 6 was relaxed, such as, for example, with respect to tax evasions, which have been subjected to the jurisdiction of administrative authorities.[82] In the case of *Chorherr*,[83] for instance, the Strasbourg Court stated that the reservation applies only to measures regarding the deprivation of liberty prescribed in the law on administrative procedure which is mentioned in the reservation. In its judgment in the case of *Gradinger*[84] the Court held further that the reservation, according to its wording, only applies to article 5, and not to article 6. Referring to its judgment in the *Miltner* case[85] the Constitutional Court refused to follow this legal view citing its previous jurisdiction.[86]

According to the Strasbourg Court's case-law the term 'criminal charge' is to be interpreted as having a meaning specific to the context of the Convention, and not on the basis of its meaning in domestic criminal law. A prosecution is of a criminal nature if sanctions are imposed which are intended to be a deterrent and which consist of a fine or a custodial sentence.[87] Consequently the Austrian administrative criminal law had and has to be qualified as criminal law within the meaning of article 6. As early as 1987 and 1988 the Constitutional Court followed in principle the case-law of the Strasbourg organs concerning the interpretation of the term 'criminal

[81] See also D/4 above and E/3 below.
[82] VfSlg. 10291/1984.
[83] Judgment of 25 Aug 1993, Series A 266–B.
[84] Judgment of 23 Oct 1995, Series A 328–C.
[85] See D/5.2. below.
[86] *Inter alia*, VfSlg. 15027/1997.
[87] Case of *Öztürk v Germany*, judgment of 21 Feb 1984, Series A 73.

charge'.[88] Furthermore, the criminal nature of the Austrian administrative criminal law was affirmed in the recent cases of *Schmautzer, Umlauft, Gradinger, Palaoro, Pfarrmeier,* and *Pramstaller* by the Strasbourg Court.[89]

However, since the establishment of the Independent Administrative Tribunals (*Unabhängige Verwaltungssenate*) in 1988 the problems resulting from this legal view have been largely minimized, mainly because now independent tribunals within the scope of article 6 tend to rule on the lawfulness of imprisonment in the course of the second round of procedures. Moreover, it follows from Strasbourg's case-law that the procedural rules for the Independent Administrative Tribunals must comply with all the article 6 requirements. It remains to be seen whether and how the Austrian judiciary will follow this requirement.

5.2. Civil proceedings The case-law of the Strasbourg Court with regard to the civil law section of article 6 may be summarized as follows: the existence of 'civil rights and obligations' is recognized if the contents of the claim or complaint are of a legal pecuniary nature and refer to an infringement of rights which have legal pecuniary implications. Consequently, Strasbourg and the Constitutional Court have developed different case-laws. The Constitutional Court differentiates between the core aspects of civil law (to which alone article 6 applies), the rights and duties of individuals *inter se*, and those areas where civil rights are only affected as a consequence,[90] in which the result of the procedure must be decisive for the civil right concerned.[91] The latter includes the well-known cases of public interference in private legal circumstances which refer to the status of the individual with regard to the public. In the *Miltner* case[92] the Constitutional Court stated that it could not follow the extensive interpretation of the term 'civil rights' by the Strasbourg Court. Nevertheless, the Constitutional Court recognized that an interpretation of the Convention as a legal constitutional norm as regards its content must be in compliance with international documents on human rights, and especially with the case-law of the Strasbourg organs. This is not possible if an interpretation violates the constitutional principles of state organization. In such cases an infringement of a right guaranteed under the Convention may only be eliminated by the legislator. The Constitutional Court admitted that an extensive interpretation of the term 'civil rights' may be the result of open-ended development of law by the institutions of the Convention.

[88] See VfSlg. 11506/1987 (*Apothekerkammer* case) and VfSlg. 11917/1988.

[89] Judgments of 23 Oct 1995, Series A 328–A, 328–B, 328–C, 329–A, 329–B, 329–C.

[90] See for example VfSlg. 5100/1965.

[91] See for example VfSlg. 5102/1965, in accordance with the case of *Ringeisen*, judgment of the Court of 16 July 1971, Series A 13.

[92] VfSlg. 11500/1987.

However, such conferral of the task of developing constitutional law to an international institution may be interpreted as the elimination of the constitutional legislator, which could result in a fundamental change of the Constitution as understood in article 44 para. 3 of the Austrian Constitution, and which would moreover require a plebiscite. I believe that this decision of the Constitutional Court is not cogent, as similar problems have emerged with regard to articles 5 and 6, as well as to the Austrian reservation to article 5, and have been resolved by the establishment of the Independent Administrative Tribunals (*Unabhängige Verwaltungssenate*) in constitutional law. As these Tribunals have been increasingly endowed with legal competence as regards rights and duties under civil law, the Austrian legislator would comply with a further interpretation of 'civil rights' as implied under article 6. In order to guarantee compliance with article 6 with regard to fundamental fields of civil law, an independent tribunal must decide at least in the last instance according to the Constitutional Court. In practice, this applies to adequate compensation under the Act on Water Law (*Wasserrechtsgesetz*)[93] and to compensation for expropriation under the Act on Regional Planning (*Raumordnungsgesetz*).[94] Recently, proceedings under governmental procurement laws have been reviewed in the light of the requirements of article 6.[95] However, a licence to build a house, the withdrawal of a licence for pharmacies, and a licence for a manufacturing plant under trade law are not considered part of the fundamental field of civil law.[96]

6. *Article 8*

One focal field of the jurisdiction of the Constitutional Court with regard to article 8 is the Aliens Act, where the protection guaranteed by the Convention is interpreted more generously than by the jurisdiction of the Strasbourg organs. The 'elsewhere approach',[97] which is core to Strasbourg's jurisdiction, has not yet been considered by the Constitutional Court.

In spite of one exception, the Constitutional Court has always considered itself to interpret regulations under the Aliens Act, which it examines on the basis of article 8, in conformity with the Constitution without repealing domestic legal norms. For a long time, the Constitutional Court was of the

[93] VfSlg. 11760/1988.

[94] VfSlg. 11762/1988.

[95] VfGH of 10 June 1999, B 1809/97 and others; of 1 Dec 1999, B 2835/96; and of 28 Feb 2000, B 420/97 and others (lacking independence and impartiality of government procurement boards).

[96] VfSlg. 11500/1987 (*Miltner* case); VfSlg. 11937/1988; and VfSlg. 12384/1990.

[97] According to the case of *Gül v Switzerland*, judgment of 19 Feb 1996, Reports 1996–I, para. 38, and in the case of *Ahmut v The Netherlands*, judgment of 28 Nov 1996, Reports 1995–IV, paras. 70 and 71, art 8 cannot be considered to impose on a state a general obligation to respect the choice of residence of a foreigner and to organize a family reunion in its own territory if the foreigner is not prevented from maintaining his family life in his country of origin.

opinion that administrative bodies dealing with the former Foreign Police Act (*Fremdenpolizeigesetz*) could implement article 8 directly on condition that no pertinent legislative measures existed, and when issuing residence bans these bodies were to consider respect for private and family life as well as possibly conflicting public interests.[98] However, these considerations were not adequately followed by the implementing agencies, and the Constitutional Court in 1985 repealed those regulations of the Foreign Police Act on the issuing of residence bans, arguing non-compliance with article 8, as the legislator had not expressly stated the right to respect for private and family life in cases of expulsion.[99] The Court argued further that a measure may conflict with article 8 when interpersonal relations guaranteed under the definition of 'family life' of article 8 are disturbed. A residence ban may involve a separation from family members who continue to live in the country. In addition, a residence ban may infringe 'private life' if the non-national has been living in the country for several years and has become fully integrated. A legal norm regulating the issuing of residence bans must therefore explicitly determine the conditions for the issuing of such bans as well as taking into account the principles of balance of interests and of proportionality.

The Constitutional Court then had recourse to interpretations in conformity with the Constitution, eg when examining a regulation of the former Residence Act (*Aufenthaltsgesetz*) which postulated standard accommodation and sufficient means for subsistence as prerequisites for a residence permit.[100] Another decision was on the rejection of a request for a residence permit due to an inadmissible application from inside the country. *Per analogiam*, the Constitutional Court was able to reach a result in compliance with article 8.[101] In a further decision, it applied this case-law to non-nationals who were legally present in the country when applying for residence, but whose application was out of time because it was not lodged four weeks before the expiration of the permit.[102] In each of these cases, the Constitutional Court quashed the notice by the administrative body due to an infringement of article 8. However, one decision by the Constitutional Court rigorously contradicts the case-law of the Strasbourg organs. In this case, the Constitutional Court found that neither issuing a residence ban nor rejecting a visa application interferes with the legal sphere of the family members.[103]

In a decision dealing with article 209 of the penal code,[104] the Constitutional Court confirmed its case-law concerning the age of consent for homosexual relationships, stipulating that the age of consent for male homosexual relationships is eighteen years, and for female relationships fourteen years.

[98] See for example VfSlg. 8792/1980, and 9028, 9029/1981.
[99] VfSlg. 10737/1985.
[100] VfSlg. 14091/1995.
[101] VfSlg. 14148/1995.
[102] VfSlg. 14300/1995.
[103] VfSlg. 14863/1997.
[104] VfSlg. 12182/1989.

The Constitutional Court stated that a difference in treatment between men and women regarding homosexual acts with juveniles infringes neither the principle of non-discrimination laid down by the Austrian Constitution, nor article 8 of the Convention. It pointed out that article 209 obviously lies within the scope of application of article 8 para. 2. Therefore, it was legitimate legislation to protect the rights of others, namely to protect the undisturbed development of juveniles threatened by these criminal acts.

In a recent outstanding decision (VfGH of 14 October 1999, G 91/98 and G 116/98) the Constitutional Court confirmed the conformity of para. 3 of the Law on Reproductive Medicine with article 8 (right to privacy) and article 12 (right to found a family) of the ECHR. The Constitutional Court found that Austria's domestic legislation is correct in treating *in-vitro* fertilization differently from artificial insemination. There are several reasons for this: *in-vitro* fertilization is medically more precarious; it raises a variety of ethical questions such as the treatment of 'surplus' embryos; and it creates a situation in which two mothers have a bond with the same child. Thus, para. 3 fell within the exception of article 8 para. 2 and no violation of either this provision or article 12 was found.

7. *Article 10*

Article 10 enlarged the functional scope of the protection of freedom of opinion as compared to the domestic article 13 of the Basic Law of 1867. The receipt and the transmission of information and ideas are now also protected. This is reflected in the case-law of the Constitutional Court. Thus, freedom of opinion protects statements and manifestations in every possible form of expression, for instance orally, in writing, in print, film, theatre, etc.[105] The statement may be made by means of banners, posters, distribution of flyers, etc. Within the case-law of the Strasbourg organs commercial advertisements are also included in this broad concept although commercial advertisements may be subject to stronger restrictions than statements of a political, cultural, or ideological character.[106] However, a prohibition of all advertisements for veterinarians clearly violates article 10 and the Constitutional Court rejected the view that the Austrian Broadcasting Corporation could arbitrarily select which adverts it chose to broadcast.[107] Pursuant to the case-law of the Constitutional Court, no obligation of the state can be derived from article 10 to guarantee access to or to provide information.[108] Article 10 grants no privileged position to the media, which have the same right as everyone else to

[105] VfSlg. 12501/1990, 13127/1992, 11651/1988, 10948/1986.
[106] VfSlg. 1948/1986, 13635/1993.
[107] VfSlg. 13675/1994 and VfGH of 17 June 1999, B 1757/98.
[108] VfSlg. 11297/1987, 12838/1991.

generally accessible sources of information. However, the media have a higher demand for information, which makes a regulation providing special protection to media entities inappropriate. A regulation which restricts the publication of parliamentary proceedings to media representatives is against the Convention.[109]

Less satisfactory is the case-law of the Supreme Court and the Higher Courts regarding article 10 and the freedom of expression of journalists, as the Austrian cases show which were brought before the Court.[110] In reaction to the judgment of the Court in the case of *Oberschlick I*,[111] the Supreme Court rejected a plea of nullity in the interests of law, which was submitted by the Procurator General to have the sentencing of the successful applicant quashed. The Supreme Court argued that the former domestic decision was in conformity with Austrian law and with the case-law of the Strasbourg Court as regards freedom of expression at the time when the internal decision was delivered. Moreover the Supreme Court interpreted the value judgement given by the applicant as 'excessive', a view which was not shared by the Strasbourg Court.[112]

Generally speaking, there is considerable uncertainty in the subsequent case-law about what can be seen as a free 'value judgment' and what cannot. In this context it is worth mentioning that Austrian criminal jurisdiction—in view of the restricted competence of the Supreme Court—lacks a fully adequate human rights jurisdiction as provided for by the Constitutional Court regarding administrative law. All attempts to change this situation have so far failed.

8. *Article 11*

8.1. Freedom of assembly The application of article 11 has widened the scope of the right of assembly as compared to article 12 of the Basic Law of 1867, but has left out of account the fact that, under the case-law of the Constitutional Court, every violation of the Assembly Act of 1953 (which took immediate effect as a constitutional law) amounts to an infringement of a constitutional right. Whereas article 12 of the Basic Law 1867 only applies to Austrian citizens, article 11 of the Convention is drafted as a human right, which is why it also guarantees to foreigners the right of assembly under constitutional law. According to the newer case-law on article 11, the term 'assembly' in the Convention exceeds the meaning of the same term within the Basic Law of 1867 and the Assembly Act of 1953. Article 11 covers 'all meetings of

[109] VfSlg. 13577/1993.

[110] See E/6.3 below.

[111] Judgment of 23 May 1991, Series A 204.

[112] Judgment of the Supreme Court of 17 September 1992, 12 Os 24–25/92.

human beings which according to colloquial usage are seen as assemblies, thus every organized non-recurrent association of human beings for a joint purpose and at a determined place'.[113] According to Strasbourg case-law the Constitutional Court concluded from article 11 that the state is obliged effectively to protect legal assemblies.[114] Under the Constitutional Court's case-law, article 11 also allows spontaneous demonstrations where this is absolutely necessary to realize the right to assembly in the intended way. This is the case if a legitimate indignation can be assumed and the demonstration is in close temporal relationship to the reason for that indignation. In those cases, it is justified and not punishable that the assembly has not been registered.[115] Recently, the Constitutional Court held the complete prohibition of demonstrations during the state visit of Chinese Prime Minister Li Peng with a view to sparing him the sight of demonstrating groups of people to be a disproportionate interference and thus a violation of article 11.[116]

8.2. Freedom of association With regard to the freedom of association the Constitutional Court has generally taken up the case-law of the Strasbourg organs. For example it stated that membership of a legal interest group does not violate the right of coalition under article 11.[117]

9. *Article 1 of the 1st Protocol*

Although article 1 widened the scope of protection of property in the Austrian national legal order, the Constitutional Court basically applies—exceptions notwithstanding—the corresponding national constitutional provision of article 5 of the Basic Law of 1867. Still, the Constitutional Court has, as its case-law developed over time, applied the principle of proportionality (which is inherent in the Convention) not only to cases of deprivation of property,[118] but also to limitations of property rights.[119] Therefore, there must be evidence that a limitation of property rights is in the public interest in order to justify such infringement under the principle of proportionality.[120] But still, the Constitutional Court ignored the Strasbourg Court's case-law referring to states' obligation to compensate for expropriation.[121]

[113] VfSlg. 12501/1990 (*Hosi* case or '*Albertinaplatz*').

[114] Case of *Plattform 'Ärzte für das Leben'*, judgment of the Court of 21 June 1988, Series A 139; VfSlg. 12501/1990, basically already VfSlg. 6850/1972 and 8609/1979.

[115] VfSlg. 11651/1988.

[116] Judgment of the Constitutional Court of 10 June 1998, B 2322/97.

[117] VfSlg. 13880/1994.

[118] VfSlg. 8981/1980 ('*Rückübereignung*' = 'retransfer') and VfGH of 13 Oct 1999, G77/99 nd V 29/99 ('*Rückwidmung*' = 'rededication').

[119] VfSlg. 13659/1993.

[120] VfSlg. 14142/1995.

[121] See for example the cases of *James and Others* and *Lithgow and Others v the United Kingdom*, judgments of the Court of 21 Feb 1986 and 8 July 1986, Series A 98 and 102.

Recently the Constitutional Court changed its ruling practice rather remarkably with regard to whether a right laid down under public law is within the scope of the guarantee enshrined in article 1 of the 1st Protocol. This was in reaction to the Strasbourg Court's ruling in the case of *Gaygusuz against Austria.*[122] The Constitutional Court followed the opinion of the Strasbourg Court and qualified the right to emergency assistance as a pecuniary right under article 1. It also shared the reasons given by the Court that granting emergency assistance is a social security benefit which is linked—as a precondition—to a service in return by the beneficiary. As far as a claim laid down under public law is constituted by considerations of the beneficiary, it lies within the scope of the provision mentioned. In this decision the Constitutional Court for the first time separated the concept of property under article 1 from that pertaining to the historic interpretation of article 5 of the Basic Law of 1867. As a consequence, the Constitutional Court quashed the relevant provision of the Unemployment Insurance Act (*Arbeitslosenversicherungsgesetz*), arguing that it was not compatible with article 1 of the 1st Protocol.[123]

Also, however, the new provision which came into force in 1997 was cancelled by a ruling of the Constitutional Court,[124] which held that the new exemption clause for the general guarantee of emergency assistance (in the case of a favourable labour market situation for a certain group of unemployed people or in certain regions) was not in compliance with the prohibition of discrimination under article 14 ECHR in conjunction with article 1 of the 1st Protocol.

10. Sixth Protocol

Some cases concerned the admissibility of the expulsions of Kosovo-Albanian deserters to the Republic of Yugoslavia, where they were not threatened with torture or inhuman treatment but with capital punishment.[125] Although the expulsions would not have been lawful under paragraph 57 of the Aliens Act, the question arose whether the expulsions were also forbidden according to constitutional law (the Constitutional Court held that article 3 was not applicable). Because the prohibition of capital punishment does not apply in times of war, the Constitutional Court examined the cases in the light of article 85 of the Constitution, which provides for the abolition of the death penalty in Austria. Based on a systematic interpretation of both provisions, the Constitutional Court concluded that the Constitution

[122] Case of *Gaygusuz*, judgment of 16 Sep 1996, Reports 1996–IV.
[123] Judgment of the Constitutional Court of 11 Mar 1998, G 363/97 and others.
[124] VfGH of 9 June 1999, G 48/99 and others.
[125] See the leading case VfSlg. 13981/1994.

includes the comprehensive fundamental right of not being subjected to capital punishment and that this right has an ex-territorial effect. Thus, nobody is allowed to be expelled or extradited into a state where they risk the death penalty.[126]

E. CASES BROUGHT BEFORE THE EUROPEAN COMMISSION AND THE COURT OF HUMAN RIGHTS

1. *Introduction*

Due to the fact that the Convention is well known in Austria and was implemented on the constitutional level, many applications have been lodged against Austria. Until 30 October 1998 (the end of the mandate of the Commission and the old Court[127]) 3,276 applications against Austria were brought before the Commission, 251 applications were declared admissible, and seventy-eight were decided by judgment of the Court. In forty-five applications the Court found a violation of the Convention, in eighteen cases no violation was observed, in seven cases brought before the Court friendly settlements were reached, and eight cases were struck out of the list. Seventy-three applications were decided by the Committee of Ministers. Between 1 November 1998 and 31 March 2000 292 applications were filed before the new Court, nineteen cases were declared admissible, and eight judgments against Austria were delivered. (All data from the Court's own database.)

With regard to their content: most cases were related to articles 5 and 6 and some to articles 3, 8, 10, 11, and to article 1 of the 1st Protocol, with only a few to other provisions of the Convention. In the following the most important judgments of the Strasbourg Court condemning Austria for infringements of the Convention are considered.

2. *Article 3*

In the *Ahmed* case,[128] the applicant complained against his deportation to Somalia. The Court agreed with the application and held that the deportation would breach article 3 as long as the applicant faced a serious risk of being subjected to torture or inhuman or degrading treatment in Somalia.

In the *Ribitsch* case,[129] the Court stated that, in respect of a person deprived of liberty, any recourse to physical force which is not strictly necessary

[126] Subsequently see also VfSlg. 13995/1994.

[127] See the 11th Protocol to the ECHR.

[128] Judgment of 17 Dec 1994, Reports 1996–VI.

[129] Judgment of 4 Dec 1995, Series A 336.

because of the conduct of the detainee diminishes human dignity and is, in principle, a violation of article 3. Where there is no dispute that the applicant's injuries were sustained during his detention in police custody, the government is under an obligation to provide a plausible explanation of how the applicant's injuries were caused. The injuries in the instant case, and the insufficient explanations from the government, revealed ill-treatment of the applicant which amounted to both inhuman and degrading treatment.[130]

3. Article 5

3.1. Paragraph 1 (liberty and security of person) The *Herczegfalvy* case[131] dealt, *inter alia*, with the detention and psychiatric treatment of a person of unsound mind. Regarding article 5 para. 1 the Court, distinguishing four periods of detention, found that there had been no violation because all periods of detention came under either para. 1(c) or para. 1(e).

The subject of the *Chorherr* case[132] was the applicant's arrest and the imposition of an administrative criminal fine for causing a breach of the peace during a military parade by distributing leaflets calling for a referendum against the country's purchase of fighter aircraft. Having regard to article 5, the Court held that the arrest in issue was founded on laws covered by the Austrian reservation. Examining the validity of the reservation in the light of article 64, the Court found that the degree of generality prohibited by article 64 was not attained because the limited number of laws encompassed by the reservation constituted a well-defined and coherent body of provisions. In view of the fact that it was possible to identify the precise laws and to obtain any information regarding them, the requirement of 'a brief statement of the law concerned' was also met. As the reservation was thus valid, there was no violation of article 5.

3.2. Paragraphs 3 and 4 (trial within a reasonable time, lawfulness of detention) In the *Herczegfalvy* case,[133] having regard to article 5, para. 3, the Court stated that the length of the two periods of pre-trial detention taken into consideration did not exceed the limit of 'reasonable time'. Regarding the first period, which lasted for more than seven months, no negligence was found on the part of the authorities. Moreover, the applicant himself had contributed to the prolongation. The second period, lasting for more than six

[130] It is a depressing fact that in Austrian police custody persons deprived of their liberty are often treated in an inhuman and degrading manner; see both Reports of the European Committee for the Prevention of Torture and Inhuman or Degrading Treatment or Punishment (CPT) on its visit to Austria in May 1990 and Sep/Oct 1994.

[131] Judgment of 24 Sep 1992, Series A 242–A.

[132] Judgment of 25 Aug 1993, Series A 266–B.

[133] Judgment of 24 Sep 1992, Series A 242–A.

months, was evaluated specifically in view of the different composition of the court to which the case had been remitted. Concerning article 5, para. 4, the Court held that two of the three decisions taken in the context of the automatic periodic review of the lawfulness of the detention prescribed by the Austrian Criminal Code had not been taken at reasonable intervals, which constituted a breach of article, 5 para. 4.

The subject of the case of *B*[134] was the length of detention on remand and of criminal proceedings. As to the alleged violation of article 5, para. 3, the Court stated that the starting point of the period to be taken into consideration was the day of the applicant's arrest. Concerning the closing date the Court found that a person convicted at first instance is in the position provided for by article 5, para. 1(a) and that the period in question ended with the pronouncement of the first-instance judgment: the word 'after' in para. 1(a) did not simply mean that the detention had to follow the conviction in point of time; in addition the detention had to result from the conviction (there had to be a causal connection). In view of the fact that the applicant's detention subsequent to the pronouncement of the first instance judgment satisfied these chronological and causal conditions and that the first-instance judgment also fitted the Court's definition of the word 'conviction', the closing date was as mentioned above. Concerning the reasonableness of the length of detention, the Court stated that the persistence of suspicion was a condition *sine qua non* for the validity of the continued detention, but after a certain lapse of time, it was no longer sufficient. It was necessary to examine the grounds which persuaded the judicial authorities that the detention should be continued and to ascertain whether these authorities displayed due diligence. In this instance, they had done so. The delay of one year may appear excessive but the need to give priority to the case of an accused in detention on remand must not stand in the way of the efforts of the judges to clarify the facts in issue fully. Consequently, and in view of the fact that it had been an especially complex case, the Court stated that the length of the applicant's detention, two years and more than four months, was not unreasonable for the purposes of article 5, para. 3.

In the *Toth* case,[135] the applicant complained about the unreasonable length (more than two years) of his detention on remand and the appeal procedures reviewing the detention. The Court accepted the government's justification of the detention, as the applicant had several previous convictions and frequently changed addresses without registration, which indicated a risk of repetition of offences and a danger of absconding in case of his release. Nevertheless, it came to the conclusion that there had been a violation of

[134] Judgment of 28 Mar 1990, Series A 175.

[135] Judgment of 12 Dec 1991, Series A 224.

article 5, para. 3 because the excessive length of the proceedings could not be attributed to the high complexity of the case or to the applicant's conduct.

The cases of *Neumeister*,[136] *Stögmüller*,[137] *Matznetter*,[138] and *Ringeisen*[139] all dealt with the question of reasonable time of detention on remand and the length of the proceedings. The applicants were detained for 24, 26, 26, and 29 months respectively. The Court established the general rule that the maximum length of detention that was still compatible with article 5, para. 3 could not be generally fixed, but had to be considered in each case in relation to the complexity of the case and the existence of well founded reasons for the refusal of a release. In the cases of *Neumeister*, *Stögmüller*, and *Ringeisen*, violations of article 5, para. 3 were found, whilst in the *Matznetter* case the Court had found no such breach. *Matznetter* and *Neumeister* also claimed breaches of article 5, para. 4 relating to the principle of equality of arms, but the Court stated that there was no breach as this was a question of fair and public hearing within the meaning of article 6, para. 1, which was not applicable to the examination of requests for release where publicity was not in the interest of the accused person anyway.

4. *Article 6*

4.1. Paragraph 1 (fair hearing) In the *Kamasinski* case,[140] the Court found that provisions allowing prosecution witnesses to join criminal proceedings as 'civil parties' with a view to recovering compensation from the accused in the event of conviction were not in themselves inconsistent with the principles of a fair trial. Concerning the nullity proceedings in the *Kamasinski* case, the Court further held that it was an inherent part of the principle of 'fair hearing' in criminal proceedings that the defendant should be given the opportunity to comment on the evidence obtained in regard to disputed facts. The fact that neither applicant nor counsel was given notice of the inquiry carried out by the Supreme Court as to the degree of the interpretation provided at trial thus constituted a violation of the principle that contending parties should be heard.

4.2. Paragraph 1 (reasonable time) In the *Lechner and Hess* case,[141] the length of the civil and criminal proceedings, which started before the Regional Civil Court and ended before the Supreme Court, amounted to more than eight years and three months. The Court found that the reasonable length of the proceedings had to be assessed in the light of the particular circumstances. In the present case there had been no exceptional legal difficulties but a number of complex facts. Although the applicants took steps

[136] Judgment of 27 June 1968, Series A 8.
[137] Judgment of 10 Nov 1969, Series A 9.
[138] Judgment of 10 Nov 1969, Series A 10.
[139] Judgment of 16 July 1971, Series A 13.
[140] Judgment of 19 Dec 1989, Series A 168.
[141] Judgment of 23 Apr 1987, Series A 118.

slowing the progress of the proceedings, various delays were also attributable to some of the competent courts, which meant that the reasonable time was exceeded and, accordingly, article 6, para.1 was violated as regards the requirement of holding a trial within a reasonable time.

As to the case of *B*,[142] the Court held that the reasonable length of the proceedings, lasting from the applicant's arrest to the Supreme Court's final decision and requiring more than five years and five months, had to be assessed according to the circumstances of the case. Although the case had been quite complex, the Court found that the fact that it had taken thirty-three months just to draw up the already pronounced judgment specifically constituted a breach of article 6, para. 1.

The *Obermeier* case[143] dealt, *inter alia*, with the length of proceedings before civil courts called upon to rule on the lawfulness of the suspension and dismissal of the applicant, who had been declared disabled for the purposes of the Disabled Persons Employment Act. The Court held that the reasonable time was exceeded, as the proceedings had been instituted nine years previously and were still not concluded, which, although the contested proceedings had been somewhat complex, represented a breach of article 6, para.1.

In the cases of *Neumeister*,[144] *Matznetter*,[145] and *Ringeisen*[146] the Court stated that there was no breach of article 6, para. 1 as regards the length of the proceedings. In the *Neumeister* case the seven years of detention was justified by the extraordinary complexity of the case as well as by the fact that the lawyers and judges involved had to be given time to acquaint themselves with the case record of more than 10,000 pages. The duration of the criminal proceedings against Mr Ringeisen resulted from the complexity of the case and the innumerable requests and appeals lodged by the applicant, challenging most of the competent judges and requesting the transfer of proceedings to different court jurisdictions areas. The *Matznetter* case was also characterized by enormous complexity. Furthermore, the judges involved could justify the delays in a credible way while the investigating judges were relieved of their duty to take on new cases in order to avoid further delays.

In the *Wiesinger* case[147] and the case of *Erkner and Hofauer*,[148] the Court stated that the requirement of proceedings within a 'reasonable time' had not been fulfilled as the procedures following consolidation measures for agricultural land belonging to the applicants had taken more than nine years and sixteen and a half years respectively, and were still pending. Therefore, the Court concluded that there had been a violation of article 6, para. 1.

[142] Judgment of 28 Mar 1990, Series A 175.
[143] Judgment of 28 June 1990, Series A 179.
[144] Judgment of 27 June 1968, Series A 8.
[145] Judgment of 10 Nov 1969, Series A 10.
[146] Judgment of 16 July 1971, Series A 13.
[147] Judgment of 30 Oct 1991, Series A 213.
[148] Judgment of 23 Apr 1987, Series A 117.

In the *Poiss* case,[149] which concerned consolidation plans, a violation of article 6, para. 1 was found by the Court, which held that a period of over nineteen years was excessive in the view of the authority's special duty to act expeditiously in connection with the provisional transfer of land.

The case of *W. R.* (Judgment of 21 December 1999) concerns the length of disciplinary proceedings against a lawyer on whom a fine was imposed. Having regard to recent case-law, the Court observed that in this case the possible penalties for disciplinary offences under Austrian law included a suspension of the right to practise as a lawyer for up to one year. Thus, the applicant ran the risk of a temporary suspension of his right to practise his profession. It followed that the applicant's right to continue to practise as a lawyer was at stake in the disciplinary proceedings against him. Accordingly, article 6, para. 1 was applicable under its civil head. The Court held that the overall duration of the disciplinary proceedings of seven years and four months, at three levels of jurisdiction, could not be considered 'reasonable' within the meaning of article 6, para. 1 of the Convention.

In the case of *G. S.* (Judgment of 21 December 1999) the applicant applied for the grant of a licence to run a pharmacy, and the application was dismissed. Years after having filed an appeal with the Administration Court the applicant obtained the required licence following a private agreement with a competing pharmacist which caused the applicant to withdraw the appeal. Nevertheless the applicant lodged an application before the Strasbourg Court maintaining that the length of proceedings, in particular before the Administrative Court (which lasted more than four years and four months, with a period of total inactivity of three and a half years) was in breach of the 'reasonable time' requirement laid down in article 6, para. 1 of the Convention. Although the Court accepted the Government's argument that the proceedings were of some complexity the Court criticized the fact that the proceedings before the Administrative Court never proceeded to an examination of the merits of the case. The Court took into consideration that Austria had taken certain measures to reduce the workload of the Administrative Court. But, recalling that it is for contracting states to organize their legal systems in such a way that their courts can guarantee the right of everyone to obtain a final decision on disputes relating to civil rights and obligations within a reasonable time, the Court found the applicant's claim to be justified.

4.3. Paragraph 1 (public hearing) The *Pauger* case[150] dealt with the lack of a public hearing in the Constitutional Court in proceedings concerning the entitlement to a survivor's pension. The Court, after finding that the right in

[149] Judgment of 23 Apr 1987, Series A 117.
[150] Judgment of 28 May 1997, Reports 1997–III.

question was a civil right and that the relevant section of the Constitutional Court Act was not covered by Austria's reservation, held that the fact that the applicant, a professor of public law, had not expressly asked for a public hearing, although he had been familiar with the Constitutional Court procedure, unequivocally constituted a waiver of his right to a public hearing. Consequently there was no breach of article 6, para. 1.

In the *Bulut* case[151] the Court, dealing with the applicant's complaint that there had been no hearing in the Supreme Court, found that the applicant's grounds of appeal raised no question of fact bearing on the assessment of the applicant's guilt or innocence that would have necessitated a hearing; it only challenged the trial court's assessment of evidence. As a hearing was not necessary, there was no violation of article 6, para. 1.

Concerning the second complaint in the *Fischer* case[152] the Court, having regard to the facts that the applicant expressly requested an oral hearing in the Administrative Court, which was the first and only judicial body before which the case was brought, and that the proceedings in question were very important for the applicant's business existence, held that his right to a public hearing included an entitlement to an oral hearing. The refusal to hold such a hearing therefore amounted to a violation of article 6, para.1.

In the case of *Stallinger and Kuso*,[153] the applicants claimed that in their land consolidation proceedings before the Land Reform Boards no public hearings were held and that the Administrative Court refused to hold a hearing. The Court first examined whether the Austrian reservation in respect of article 6 was valid in this case and then came to the conclusion that national legal provisions coming into force after the reservation was made in 1958 were not covered; thus the applicants' right to a public hearing was definitely not excluded from review by the Court. As no exceptional circumstances were identified by the government that might have justified a dispensing with oral hearings, the Court found a violation of article 6, para. 1.

In the *Werner* case,[154] the applicant complained about the lack of a public hearing in proceedings concerning compensation for detention. The Court stated that there has been a violation of article 6, para. 1 and pointed out that one could not blame the applicant for not having asked for an oral hearing as the relevant provisions did not provide for such a hearing.

By comparison, in the *Zumtobel* case,[155] dealing with expropriation proceedings, the lack of a public hearing before the Administrative Court was not

[151] Judgment of 22 Feb 1996, Reports 1996–II.
[152] Judgment of 26 Apr 1995, Series A 312.
[153] Judgment of 23 Apr 1997, Reports 1997–II.
[154] Judgment of 24 Nov 1997, Reports 1997–VII.
[155] Judgment of 21 Sep 1993, Series A 268–A.

a violation of article 6, para. 1 as the applicants had not asked for a hearing and there were no questions of public interest making such a hearing necessary either.

In the case of *Ettl and Others*,[156] decisions on land consolidation were given without a public hearing, which the Court held was covered by the Austrian reservation regarding article 5.

In the *Szücs* case (Judgment of 24 Nov 1997, Reports 1997–VII) as well as in the *Werner* (Judgment of 24 Nov 1997, Reports 1997–VII) and *Rushiti* cases (Judgment of 21 March 2000, Reports 2000–I) the Court found that article 6, para. 1 of the Convention applied to the proceedings under the Compensation (Criminal Proceedings) Act (*Strafrechtliches Entschädigungsgesetz*) 1969, as they involved a determination of civil rights and obligations, and that the lack of a public hearing in these proceedings constituted violations of article 6, para. 1.

4.4. Paragraph 1 (access to independent and impartial tribunal) Some cases have concerned the question whether both the Constitutional Court and the Administrative Court can be regarded as 'tribunals' in the meaning of article 6, para. 1. In the cases of *Pfarrmeier*[157] and *Umlauft*,[158] the district authority imposed on the applicants a fine for their refusal to submit to a breath test. The applicants applied to the Administrative and the Constitutional Court. In the *Gradinger* case,[159] the applicant caused an accident while under the influence of drink. The Regional Court convicted him of causing death by negligence (article 80 of the Criminal Code). Four months later a district authority issued a sentence order for driving under the influence of drink. The Administrative Court dismissed the appeal as ill founded. The *Palaoro* case[160] dealt with administrative criminal proceedings for speeding, the *Pramstaller* case[161] with administrative criminal proceedings for carrying out works in breach of the planning permission, and the subject of the *Schmautzer* case[162] were administrative criminal proceedings for failure to wear a safety belt. In all six cases, the Constitutional Court declined to allow the appeals. As to compliance with article 6, para.1, the Court found that decisions taken by administrative authorities which do not themselves satisfy the requirements of article 6, para.1, as was the case in this instance, had to be subject to subsequent control by a 'judicial body that has full jurisdiction'. Neither the Constitutional Court nor the Administrative Court could be regarded as a

[156] Judgment of 23 Apr 1987, Series A 117.
[157] Judgment of 23 Oct 1995, Series A 329–C.
[158] Judgment of 23 Oct 1995, Series A 328–B.
[159] Judgment of 23 Oct 1995, Series A 328–C.
[160] Judgment of 23 Oct 1995, Series A 329–A, 329–B.
[161] Judgment of 23 Oct 1995, Series A 329–A.
[162] Judgment of 23 Oct 1995, Series A 328–A.

'tribunal' within the meaning of the Convention. The former could only look at the impugned proceedings from the perspective of their conformity with the Constitution and was not able to examine all the relevant facts. The latter lacked the power to quash in all respects on questions of fact and law the decision of the body below, which is one of the defining characteristics of 'a judicial body that has full jurisdiction'. It follows that the applicants did not have access to a court, so there was a violation of article 6, para. 1 in each of the six cases.

In the first set of proceedings in the *Mauer* case,[163] the Federal Police Authority had imposed a provisional penal order on the applicant, who had a taxi business, for having failed to disclose the identity of the driver of one of his taxis at a particular time. After he had declared his objections at a police station the authority instituted ordinary penal administrative proceedings and issued a penal order. The authority of appeal, whose decision was confirmed by the Administrative Court, found that the initial provisional penal order remained valid because the applicant had not effectively raised objections against it. In the second set of proceedings, the Federal Police Authority fined the applicant on the ground that a tyre on one of his taxis had too worn a tread. The Administrative Court dismissed his appeal and found that the further evidence which the applicant had wished to put forward was irrelevant. The Court found that the substantive issues had to be decided in the same way as in recent similar cases, namely *Schmautzer, Umlauft, Gradinger, Pramstaller, Palaoro, and Pfarrmeier*,[164] and that there had therefore been a violation of article 6, para. 1 in each set of proceedings. Further, the Court held that it was not necessary to rule on the allegations of violation of article 6, para. 3(c), concerning the first set, and para. 3(d), concerning the second set of proceedings.

The *Obermeier* case[165] dealt, *inter alia*, with access to courts called upon to rule on the lawfulness of the suspension and dismissal of the applicant, who had been declared disabled for the purposes of the Disabled Persons Employment Act. In Austria the dismissal of a disabled person is subject to authorization by administrative authorities, namely the Disabled Persons Board and, on appeal, the Provincial Governor, both of which enjoy discretionary power. The labour courts considered themselves bound by the administrative decisions authorizing his dismissal. They inferred that they were precluded from inquiring into the validity of the dismissal authorized by those authorities, unless it was contested because of the assessment, which fell outside the Board's competence, which had not been the case. Consequently, the administrative decisions had to meet the requirements of article 6, para. 1. In

[163] Judgment of 18 Feb 1997, Reports 1997–I.
[164] See above. [165] Judgment of 28 June 1990, Series A 179.

view of the fact that the two said authorities did not constitute independent tribunals and that the Administrative Court could only determine whether these authorities exercised their discretionary power in conformity with the law, the Court found that there was no effective review of these bodies, which constituted a violation of article 6, para. 1 as regards access to a court.

In previous cases the question had already arisen whether the Administrative Court was to be seen as an independent tribunal in the meaning of article 6. In the *Ortenberg* case,[166] the applicant complained about an infringement of her civil rights resulting from land use plans and building permits for neighbouring land, and that she did not have access to a court with full jurisdiction in order to defend her rights. The Court pointed out that, under article 6, para. 1, it was necessary that decisions of administrative authorities which do not themselves satisfy the requirements of this article should be subject to subsequent control by a judicial body with full jurisdiction. Even if the Constitutional Court was not such a body, the Court decided that this was a decision taken by an administrative authority on grounds of expediency and therefore that the review by the Administrative Court fulfilled the requirements of article 6, para. 1 in this instance. In the *Fischer* case,[167] the applicant's complaints concerned his right of access to a court in administrative proceedings to challenge the revocation of his tipping licence, which ended before the Administrative Court, as well as the complete lack of any oral hearing. As to the first complaint the Court found that there was nothing to suggest that any of the limitations on the Administrative Court's powers to examine questions of fact and to take new evidence were in issue in his case. Regard being had to the nature of the applicant's complaints and to the scope of review necessitated by such complaints, the Administrative Court's review fulfilled the requirements of article 6, para.1. Accordingly there was no violation of that Article.

As regards the first of the three individual complaints in the *Bulut* case,[168] concerning the participation in the trial of a judge who had participated in the preliminary investigation, the Court found that the mere fact that the judge had also dealt with the case at the pre-trial stage does not in itself justify fears as to his impartiality. In addition, it was not for the applicant to question the impartiality of a trial court when he had not made use of his right to challenge it. Accordingly, there was no violation of article 6, para. 1.

In the case of *Pfeifer and Plankl*[169] the applicant Pfeifer claimed that the two judges involved in his criminal proceedings should have been replaced as they had been investigating judges in the same case. The Court followed this

[166] Judgment of 25 Nov 1994, Series A 295–B.
[167] Judgment of 26 Apr 1995, Series A 312.
[168] Judgment of 22 Feb 1996, Reports 1996–II.
[169] Judgment of 25 Feb 1992, Series A 227.

argument and stated that the pertinent waiver expressed by the applicant in the absence of his lawyer was not effective: as a layman, Mr Pfeifer did not realize the implications of this act. There was accordingly a violation of article 6, para. 1 regarding the impartiality of the court.

In the *Sramek* case,[170] the applicant complained that the Regional Real Property Transactions Authority, which refused to approve her contract for the purchase of land, did not constitute an impartial and independent tribunal within the meaning of article 6, para. 1. The Court stated that the authority in question was established by law and that the civil servants acting as members were not subject to instructions while carrying out their judicial functions. Only the subordinate status of the rapporteur gave rise to legitimate doubt about his independence. As such an appearance seriously affects the confidence which courts must inspire in a democratic society, a violation of article 6, para. 1 was found by the Court.

In the *Fey* case,[171] a criminal case before a district court, the judge had undertaken certain pre-trial measures, including preliminary inquiries. The applicant contended that he had not received a fair hearing before an impartial tribunal. But the Court held that there had been no violation of article 6, para. 1 as it did not appear that the various measures the judge had taken prior to the trial were such as could have led her to reach a preconceived view of the merits. Thus, the fact of taking pre-trial decisions in a case does not justify fears as to the impartiality of a judge.

In the case of *Ettl and Others*,[172] *inter alia*, the impartiality and independence of land reform boards were questioned. The Court held that the fact that civil servants constituted a majority of members of these boards did not itself indicate a violation of article 6, para. 1. The national law provides sufficiently for the independence of the boards; hierarchical links were of no consequence. The mere fact that members were appointed on account of their special experience cannot raise doubts about the independence and impartiality of the boards.

In the case of *Stallinger and Kuso*,[173] the Court pointed out that the participation of expert members in the decisions of regional boards was not legally objectionable, and consequently found that there was no violation of article 6, para. 1 regarding the independence of the tribunal.

4.5. Paragraph 1 (public pronouncement of judgment) The *Szücs* case,[174] and the *Rushiti* and *Werner* cases,[175] all dealt with the lack of a public pronouncing

[170] Judgment of 22 Oct 1984, Series A 84.
[171] Judgment of 24 Feb 1993, Series A 255–A.
[172] Judgment of 23 Apr 1987, Series A 117.
[173] Judgment of 23 Apr 1997, Reports 1997–II.
[174] Judgment of 24 Nov 1997, Reports 1997–VII.
[175] Judgment of 24 Nov 1997, Reports 1997–VII.

of judgments in proceedings to claim compensation for detention. The Court stated that the possibility of obtaining copies of the judgment for third parties who showed a legitimate interest did not constitute the required publicity and that there was a breach of article 6, para. 1. In the *Werner* case, it was further stated that there was a breach of article 6, para. 1 due to the failure of the Court of Appeal to communicate the principal public prosecutor's observations to the applicant.

4.6. Paragraph 1 (criminal charge) Concerning the applicability of article 6, para. 1 in the cases of *Schmautzer, Umlauft, Gradinger, Palaoro, Pfarrmeier, and Pramstaller,*[176] the Court stated in all six cases that, although the offences in issue fell within the administrative sphere, they were nevertheless criminal in nature. On one hand, this was reflected in the terminology employed (the Austrian law refers to 'administrative criminal procedure') and on the other hand, in the fact that the fine imposed had been accompanied by an order for the applicants' committal to prison in the event of their defaulting on payment. Accordingly article 6 applied.

In the *Adolf* case,[177] criminal proceedings had been terminated pursuant to section 42 of the Penal Code, which is headed 'acts not meriting punishment', by a court decision the reasoning of which had been capable of being understood as involving a finding of guilt. As to the applicability of article 6, the Court held that the expressions 'criminal charge' and 'charged with a criminal offence' were to be interpreted as having an 'autonomous' meaning in the context of the Convention, and not on the basis of their meaning in domestic law. The prominent place held by the right to a fair trial favoured a 'substantive', rather than a 'formal', conception of the expression 'charge'. In particular, the applicant's situation under domestic law had to be examined in the light of article 6, namely the rights of the defence. In view of these circumstances and the fact that the District Court used the phrasings 'criminal proceedings' and 'accused', the Court stated that there was a 'criminal charge' within the meaning of the Convention. The Court held further that article 6 did not distinguish between non-punishable or unpunished criminal offences, it applied whenever a person was 'charged' with any criminal offence. Article 6 was therefore applicable in the present case.

In the *Putz* case,[178] the applicability of article 6 was in question as the Court had to find whether pecuniary penalties for disrupting court proceedings were of a 'criminal nature'. Considering the fact that most member states hold similar rules to enable proper conduct in court and given the strong dis-

[176] Judgments of 23 Oct 1995, Series A 328–A, 328–B, 328–C, 329–A, 329–B, 329–C.
[177] Judgment of 26 Mar 1982, Series A 49.
[178] Judgment of 22 Feb 1996, Reports 1996–I.

ciplinary character of such penalties the Court did not qualify them as criminal, therefore article 6 was not applicable in this case.

4.7. Paragraph 1 (principle of equality of arms) In the *Bönisch* case,[179] the applicant had been found guilty by a Regional Court of offences under the Food Act 1975 (*Lebensmittelgesetz 1975*) on the ground that his products, containing an excessive quantity of benzopyrene, had been dangerous to health. The Court, without giving a separate ruling of the alleged violation of paragraphs 3(d) and 2 of article 6, found that there was a breach of article 6, para. 1, because the expert, who had been appointed in the proceedings, was the Director of the Federal Food Control Institute, which had reported the case to the prosecuting authorities and, being enabled to play a dominant role in the proceedings, was more like a witness against the accused than a neutral and impartial auxiliary of the court, whereas the 'expert witness' of the defence was examined as a mere witness. For these reasons, the equal treatment of both parties, required by the principle of equality of arms as one of the features of the wider concept of a fair trial, had not been afforded in the proceedings.

In the *Brandstetter* case,[180] the Court dealt with three different proceedings. In the first one, the applicant, a wine merchant, had been convicted under the Wine Act (*Weingesetz*) of adulterating wine. As in the *Bönisch* case, the appointed expert was a member of the Federal Agricultural Chemical Research Institute, which initiated the prosecution, but had not been involved in the drawing up of the Institute's first report. In the Court's view the mere fact that the expert was employed by the Institute did not of itself justify doubts as to his neutrality, so that there was no ground for considering him as a witness for the prosecution. Therefore there was no breach of the principle of equality of arms within the meaning of article 6, para. 1 in conjunction with para. 3(d). As regards the proceedings on the charge of tampering with evidence, the Court found that there had been no violation of para. 1 in conjunction with para. 3(d), because, although the charge had originated in the court expert's report and the applicant's own expert was heard only as a witness, the court expert did not play a dominant role. Concerning the defamation proceedings, the Court held that the principle of equality of arms also included the fundamental right to an adversarial trial, which means, in a criminal case, that both prosecution and defence must be given an opportunity to have knowledge of, and comment on, each other's observations and evidence. The fact that the Court of Appeal had relied on submissions by the Senior Public Prosecutor, which had not been communicated to the accused, was in the Court's view a violation of article 6, para. 1.

[179] Judgment of 2 June 1986, Series A 103.

[180] Judgment of 28 Aug 1991, Series A 211.

As to the third complaint in the *Bulut* case,[181] suggesting that, after the applicant had lodged his appeal with the Supreme Court, the Attorney-General submitted observations which were not served on the defence, the Court held that it was a matter of the defence to assess whether a submission deserved a reaction. It was therefore unfair for the prosecution to make submissions to a court without the knowledge of the defence. The principle of the equality of arms was not respected, which constituted a breach of article 6, para.1.

4.8. Paragraph 2 (presumption of innocence) In the *Adolf* case,[182] criminal proceedings had been terminated by a court decision the reasoning of which may well have been understood as involving a finding of guilt. Concerning the observance of article 6, the Court found that the District Court's reasoned decision had to be read jointly with the judgment of the Supreme Court and in the light of it, which had cleared the applicant of any finding of guilt and thus the presumption of his innocence was no longer called into question. There was accordingly no breach of article 6, paras. 1, 2, or 3(d).

As to the defendant's initial reply to the indictment in the *Kamasinski* case,[183] the Court held that the option was available to him, but there was no obligation to speak, so that the presumption of innocence was not undermined.

In the *Sekanina* case,[184] the applicant, who was accused of having murdered his wife but was acquitted of the charges brought against him, had asked for compensation for his detention on remand. The request was refused. The Court argued that there was a violation of article 6, para. 2 as the voicing of suspicions regarding an accused's innocence was conceivable in the absence of any decision in the case, but not after an acquittal.

In the *Kremzow* case,[185] the Court found that the statement of the Supreme Court on the applicant's 'financial misdeeds' could not violate the presumption of innocence as the applicant had already been found guilty of murder and the statement related solely to the question of his motive for the offence.

4.9. Paragraph 3(a) (right to be informed promptly in an understandable language of the accusation) In the *Kamasinski* case,[186] the Court held that, although the applicant had received no written translation of the indictment, he had been sufficiently informed of the 'accusation' as a result of oral explanations in English.

[181] Judgment of 22 Feb 1996, Reports 1996–II.
[182] Judgment of 26 Mar 1982, Series A 49.
[183] Judgment of 19 Dec 1989, Series A 168.
[184] Judgment of 25 Aug 1993, Series A 266–A.
[185] Judgment of 21 Sep 1993, Series A 268–B.
[186] Judgment of 19 Dec 1989, Series A 168.

4.10. Paragraph 3(b) (adequate time and facilities for the preparation of the defence) As to the *Kamasinski* case,[187] the rule restricting access to court files to the defendant's lawyer, was, in the Court's view, neither in itself nor in terms of its operation incompatible with the above right.

In the *Kremzow* case,[188] the Court observed that a period of three weeks before the oral hearing in a criminal proceeding was sufficient to formulate a reply in time, so that the 'adequate time and facilities' requirement was fulfilled. Also the restriction of the right to inspect the file to the accused's lawyer is compatible with the rights of defence under article 6.

4.11. Paragraph 3(c) (right to self-defence) In the *Brandstetter* case,[189] the Court held that the applicant's conviction for defamation did not violate article 6, para. 3(c) because the concept of the right of defence would be overstrained if accused could not be prosecuted when they intentionally aroused false suspicions against a person.

In the *Kamasinski* case,[190] the Court stated that the mere appointment of a legal aid defence lawyer did not necessarily ensure compliance with article 6, para. 3(c). On the other hand the state could not be held responsible for every shortcoming of the legal aid lawyer: the national authorities were required to intervene only if his failure was brought to their attention. Accordingly, there was no infringement of the Convention. In the proceedings on appeal, the Supreme Court had decided not to authorize the applicant's attendance at the hearing, which in the applicant's view constituted unjustified differential treatment between appellants in custody, such as himself, and appellants at liberty, who were not under such a disability. The Court held that the personal attendance of the defendant did not take on the same crucial significance for an appeal hearing as it did for a trial hearing. Consequently, national authorities enjoy a margin of appreciation in assessing whether differences in otherwise similar situations justify different treatment in law. In the light of the particular circumstances, the Court held that the Supreme Court's decision did not fall outside the respondent state's margin of appreciation. There was consequently no discrimination within the meaning of article 14 in conjunction with article 6, paras. 1 and 3(c).

In the *Kremzow* case,[191] regarding attendance at the hearing of pleas of nullity, the Court found that there was no breach of article 6, para. 3(c) as such nullity proceedings before a Supreme Court are primarily concerned with questions of law. Taking into consideration that the applicant was legally represented, his presence at the proceedings was not required.

[187] Ibid. [188] Judgment of 21 Sep 1993, Series A 268–B.
[189] Judgment of 28 Aug 1991, Series A 211.
[190] Judgment of 19 Dec 1989, Series A 168.
[191] Judgment of 21 Sep 1993, Series A 268–B.

This legal opinion of the Strasbourg Court was recalled in the cases of *Prinz* and *Cooke* (both Judgments of 8 February 2000, Reports 2000–I). In the case of *Prinz* the Supreme Court examined further of its own motion (also in absence of the applicant) whether the conditions for the applicant's placement in an institution for mentally ill offenders were met. Having regard to the limited jurisdiction of the Supreme Court in the present case, and taking into account what was at stake for the applicant, a deprivation of liberty subject to a yearly review in further court proceedings, the Court found that it was not essential to the fairness of the proceedings that the applicant be present at the hearing together with his official defence counsel. The Court therefore considered that the Supreme Court was not under a positive duty of its own motion to ensure the applicant's presence at the hearing to defend himself in person.

The Court found the opposite in the case of *Cooke*, in which the applicant had been sentenced to twenty years' imprisonment for murder. The Court, having regard to the nature of the main issue before the Supreme Court, namely a new assessment of the applicant's personality and character, incuding his state of mind at the time of the offence, his motive, and his dangerousness and aggressiveness in general, and taking into account the gravity of what was at stake for the applicant, a possible increase in sentence to life imprisonment, did not consider that his case could have been properly examined without gaining a personal impression of the applicant. It was therefore essential to the fairness of the proceedings that he be present at the hearing of the appeals and afforded the opportunity to participate, together with his defence counsel. Because the applicant's official defence counsel had not requested that the applicant be summoned to the hearing of the appeals, despite the gravity of what was at stake for the applicant, the Court found that the respondent State was under a positive duty to ensure the applicant's presence in order to enable him to defend himself in person, as required by article 6, para. 3(c).

4.12. Paragraph 3(d) (attendance and examination of witnesses) In the *Unterpertinger* case,[192] the applicant claimed that he had been convicted only on the basis of evidence from his close relatives. As the statements made to the police were read out in the trial, in the absence of the witnesses, he could not have them cross-examined. The Court stated that there was a breach of article 6, para. 1 in conjunction with para. 3(d) because the Appeal Court had not assessed the material before it and had based its conviction only on the testimony in respect of which the applicant's rights of examination had been restricted. It also stated that the mere fact that the testimony was only read out in trial was not incompatible with the rights guaranteed in article 6.

[192] Judgment of 24 Nov 1986, Series A 110.

In the *Artner* case,[193] the Regional Court convicted the applicant on the basis of a witness's statements to the police and before the investigating judge, which had been read out pursuant to the Code of Criminal Procedure, after having made every effort to find the witness, who had disappeared. In view of the fact that the witness's statements did not constitute the only item of evidence on which the Regional Court based its finding, and that the applicant's own prolonged absence made any confrontation between him and the victim impossible, the Court held that the fact that it was not practicable to examine her at the hearing did not, in the circumstances of the case, infringe the rights of the defence to such an extent that it constituted a breach of article 6, paras. 1 and 3(d) taken together.

In the *Asch* case,[194] a criminal conviction had been based in part on the statements made by a witness to the police which had been read out in court after the witness, the accused's cohabitee, had withdrawn the complaint against him and refused to testify in court. The Court found that there was no violation of article 6, paras. 1 and 3(d) taken together because the contested statements had not been the only evidence on which the domestic court based its finding and the applicant had available to him other means of defence which he did not use. The fact that it was impossible to question the witness at the hearing did not violate the rights of the defence or deprive the accused of a fair trial.

In the *Windisch* case,[195] the applicant's conviction had been based to a large extent on statements by two anonymous witnesses who had only been heard, in the absence of the accused and his counsel, by the police, and not by the trial court. The Court found that, in principle, all the evidence had to be produced in the presence of the accused at a public hearing. Statements obtained at the pre-trial stage could be used as evidence provided that the rights of the defence, which require that the defendant have an adequate opportunity to challenge and question a witness against him, were respected. In view of the fact that neither the applicant nor his counsel had ever had such an opportunity and that the trial court had not been able to form its own impression of the witnesses' reliability, the use of this evidence involved such limitations on the rights of the defence that it constituted a violation of article 6, paras. 1 and 3(d) taken together.

In the *Kamasinski* case,[196] the applicant's complaint, concerning the non-attendance of witnesses at the trial, was directed, in the Court's view, in effect against decisions by the defence counsel. For the purposes of para. 3(d), the

[193] Judgment of 28 Aug 1992, Series 242–A.
[194] Judgment of 26 Apr 1991, Series A 203.
[195] Judgment of 27 Sep 1990, Series A 186.
[196] Judgment of 19 Dec 1989, Series A 168.

applicant had to be identified with the counsel. Consequently, there was no violation of the Convention.

4.13. Paragraph 3(e) (free assistance of an interpreter) As to the *Kamasinski* case,[197] the Court held that the entitlement to the free assistance of an interpreter applied not only to oral statements but also to documentary material and pre-trial proceedings, but article 6, para. 3(e) did not require written translations of all items of written evidence. The obligation of the authorities did not consist of the appointment of an interpreter only but also in controlling the effectiveness of the interpretation provided. Further, the interpretation could be consecutive and summarizing. Any differences of treatment between defendants in civil actions and defendants to civil claims in criminal proceedings were justified by the interests of proper administration of justice and did not constitute discrimination in the meaning of article 14. Concerning the nullity proceedings, the Court found that, even assuming any difference of the treatment between German-speaking and non-German-speaking defendants, it was not unreasonable to limit challenges on the ground of an inadequate interpretation to instances where the motion had been made at trial. Consequently, there was no discrimination. The Court held further that the requirements of article 13 were less strict than, and here absorbed by, those of article 6.

5. *Article 8*

The *Hoffmann* case[198] dealt with the refusal of a mother's parental rights after divorce in view of her membership of the Jehovah's Witnesses. The Supreme Court's decision compelled the applicant to give up the children to their father. In its judgment the Court did not deny that, depending on the circumstances of the case, the factors relied on by the Supreme Court (rejection of public holidays, opposition to blood transfusions, position as a social minority) could in themselves be capable of tipping the scales in favour of one parent rather than the other. However, the Supreme Court also introduced a new element, namely the Federal Act on the Religious Education of Children, which it clearly considered decisive. Therefore, the Court accepted that there was a difference in treatment on the ground of religion. Indeed, the aim pursued was a legitimate one, namely the protection of the health and rights of the children. But where the Supreme Court did not rely solely on the Federal Act on the Religious Education of Children, it weighed the facts differently from the courts below, whose reasoning was moreover supported by psychological expert opinion. Notwithstanding any possible arguments to the con-

[197] Judgment of 19 Dec 1989, Series A 168.
[198] Judgment of 23 June 1993, Series A 255–C.

trary, in the Court's view, a distinction based essentially on a difference in religion alone is not acceptable. Therefore, the Court stated that no reasonable relationship of proportionality existed between the means employed and the aim pursued, so there was a violation of article 8 in conjunction with article 14. The Court considered that it was not necessary to examine the case under article 8 alone and that no separate issue arose under article 9.

In the *Petrovic* case,[199] the applicant complained of the Austrian authorities' refusal to award him a parental leave allowance on the ground that it was only available for mothers, which constituted in the applicant's view a discrimination on the ground of sex. As to the applicability of article 14 (which in the Court's view complements the other substantive provisions of the Convention and has no independent existence) taken together with article 8 the Court held that, although the refusal to grant the applicant a parental leave allowance could not amount to a failure to respect family life, since article 8 did not impose any positive obligation on states to provide the financial assistance in question, this allowance was nonetheless intended to promote family life. By granting parental leave allowance states are able to demonstrate their respect for family life within the meaning of article 8, the allowance therefore came within the scope of that provision, so that article 14 taken together with article 8 was applicable. Concerning compliance with these articles the Court found that in principle a difference in treatment is discriminatory for the purposes of article 14 if there is not a 'reasonable relationship of proportionality between the means employed and the aim sought to be realized'. Although the fact that parental leave allowance was paid only to mothers, and not fathers, amounted to a difference in treatment on the ground of sex, and very weighty reasons would be needed for such a difference in treatment to be regarded as compatible with the Convention, the contracting states enjoy a certain margin of appreciation in assessing whether and to what extent differences in otherwise similar situations justify different treatment in law. One of the factors relevant to determining the scope of margin of appreciation could be the existence or non-existence of common ground between the laws of the contracting states. In view of the facts that at the material time there was no common standard in this field and that there still remains a very great disparity between the legal systems of the contracting states, of which only a very few grant parental leave allowance to fathers, the Austrian authorities' refusal to grant it to the applicant did not exceed the margin of appreciation allowed to them. Consequently, the difference in treatment was not discriminatory within the meaning of article 14.

[199] Judgment of 27 Mar 1998, Reports 1998–II.

6. *Article 10*

6.1. Introduction In the Court's jurisdiction in respect of Austria and the guarantee of article 10, journalistic freedom of expression and freedom of information for the media are the centre of attention. The judgments in the cases of *Lingens* and *Oberschlick I and II* on the admissibility of value judgements[200] and the case of *Informationsverein Lentia 2000 and Others* on the prohibition of monopolies of the media[201] are leading cases of Strasbourg's case-law.

6.2. Freedom of the media The case of *Informationsverein Lentia 2000 and Others*[202] dealt with the question whether the legal monopoly of the Austrian Broadcasting Corporation (*Österreichischer Rundfunk—ORF*) to impart information by radio and television was in accordance with article 10. Three of the five applicants applied for an operating licence but were dismissed. Two applicants decided not to make any application to the appropriate authorities but to turn immediately to Strasbourg. The Court concluded that the monopoly system operated in Austria was capable of contributing to the quality and balance of programmes, through the supervisory powers over the media thereby conferred on the authorities. In the circumstances of the case it is therefore consistent with the third sentence of article 10, para. 1. It remains to be determined whether it also satisfies the relevant conditions of para. 2. The Court stressed the fundamental role of freedom of expression in a democratic society, in particular where, through the media, it serves to impart information and ideas of general interest, which the public is moreover entitled to receive. Such an undertaking cannot be successfully accomplished unless it is grounded in the principle of pluralism, of which the state is the ultimate guarantor. This observation is especially valid in relation to audio-visual media, whose programmes are often broadcast very widely. Of all the means of ensuring that these values are respected, a public monopoly imposes the greatest restrictions on the freedom of expression, namely the total impossibility of broadcasting otherwise than through a national station. As a result of the technical progress made over the last decades, justification for these restrictions can no longer be found today in considerations relating to the number of frequencies and channels available and in view of the multiplication of foreign programmes aimed at Austrian audiences and the decision of the Administrative Court to recognize the lawfulness of their retransmission by cable. Likewise, it cannot be argued that there are no equivalent less restrictive solutions; it is sufficient, by way of example, to cite the practice of

[200] See 6.3 below. [201] See 6.2 below.
[202] Judgment of 24 Nov 1993, Series A 276.

certain countries which either issue licences subject to specified conditions of variable content, or make provision for forms of private participation in the activities of the respective national corporations. Finally the Government's argument that the Austrian market is too small to sustain a sufficient number of stations to avoid regroupings and the constitution of 'private monopolies' was contradicted by the experience of several European states of a comparable size to Austria, in which private and public stations coexist. Therefore, the Court considered that the monopoly was disproportionate to the aim pursued and unnecessary in a democratic society, which led to a violation of article 10.

Similarly to the case of *Informationsverein Lentia 2000 and Others*, the case of *Telesystem Radio ABC*[203] dealt with the impossibility of setting up and operating private radio stations on account of the Austrian Broadcasting Corporation's monopoly, so the Court found a violation of article 10.

6.3. Freedom of expression of journalists and politicians In the *Lingens* case,[204] the applicant, a journalist, was found guilty of defamation for having used the expressions 'the basest opportunism', 'immoral', and 'undignified' in an article in the magazine *profil*, denouncing the behaviour of the former prime minister, Mr Bruno Kreisky, concerning his political relationship to another head of a party who had served in an SS Brigade during the Second World War. The applicant was fined and the magazine confiscated, and the domestic judgment had to be published. In its judgment, the Strasbourg Court held that there had been a breach of article 10. The Court stated that a careful distinction needs to be made between facts and value judgements, because the existence of facts can be demonstrated, whereas the truth of value judgements is not susceptible to proof. As regards value judgements, the requirement to prove the truth is impossible to fulfil, and infringes the freedom of opinion itself, which is a fundamental part of the right secured by article 10. It appears that the interference with Lingen's exercise of the freedom of expression was not necessary in a democratic society for the protection of the reputation of others, and was therefore disproportionate to the legitimate aim pursued.

Following the *Lingens* case, in the case of *Oberschlick I*,[205] the applicant, a journalist and editor of the periodical *FORVM*, was convicted of defamation and sentenced to pay a fine. By publishing an article in the form of a criminal indictment, the applicant accused, *inter alia*, a politician of the misdemeanour of incitement to hatred contrary to the Criminal Code and of offences relating to Nazi activities within the meaning of the National Socialist Party Prohibition Act of 1945. The national courts also ordered the seizure of the

[203] Judgment of 27 Oct 1997, Reports 1997–VI.
[204] Judgment of 8 July 1986, Series A 103.
[205] Judgment of 23 May 1991, Series A 204.

relevant issue of the magazine in which the applicant had made the accusations. The Court stated that the freedom of expression constitutes an essential foundation of a democratic society and is a precondition for its progress and for each individual's self-fulfilment. Thus, article 10 protects not only the substance of ideas and information but also their form. The task of the press is to impart information and ideas on political issues and other matters of general interest. The freedom of the press affords the public the best means of discovering and forming an opinion on the ideas and attitudes of political leaders. The limits of acceptable criticism are wider with regard to a politician than in relation to a private individual. A politician must display greater tolerance, especially when making public statements susceptible to criticism. The requirements of protection of his reputation have to be weighed against the interests of an open discussion of political issues. The applicant's article contributed to a public debate on a political question of general importance, namely the different treatment of nationals and foreigners in the social field. It sought to draw the public's attention in a provocative manner to proposals made by a politician during an election campaign, which were likely to shock many people. The relevant court decisions required the applicant to prove the truth of his value judgements, a requirement which was impossible to fulfil and which itself infringed the freedom of expression.

The *Schwabe* case[206] concerned the conviction of a politician for defamation and for having accused another person of an offence (causing the death of a person under the influence of alcohol in a traffic accident) for which he had already served a sentence. The Court considered the impugned judicial decisions in the light of the case as a whole. The applicant contributed to a general debate on political morals between two rival Austrian parties, mentioning only incidentally a recent traffic accident for which a politician had been convicted, and compared it with an earlier accident caused by another politician under the influence of alcohol. The applicant used substantially the same words as the tribunal which pronounced the conviction in the first case. The domestic courts required the applicant to prove the truth of his comparison of the two accidents in relation to the consumption of alcohol by the two politicians concerned. The applicant described both accidents in different terms but concluded that they warranted the resignation of both politicians. The Court stated that the impugned comparison amounted to a value judgement for which no proof of truth is possible. The applicant had not exceeded the limits of freedom of expression, so article 10 was violated.

The case of *Vereinigung Demokratischer Soldaten Österreichs and Gubi*[207] concerned the freedom of information of soldiers. The first applicant, a pri-

[206] Judgment of 28 Aug 1992, Series A 242–B.
[207] Judgment of 19 Dec 1994, Series A 302.

vate association of democratic soldiers (*Vereinigung Demokratischer Soldaten Österreichs—VDSÖ*) published a monthly magazine aimed at soldiers serving in the Austrian army and entitled *Der Igel* ('The Hedgehog') which contained information and articles, often of a critical nature, on military life. The association requested to have the magazine distributed in the barracks in the same way as the only other two military magazines published by private associations, which were sent out by the army, alternately and at its own expense, with the official information bulletin distributed to all conscripts. The Minister of Defence refused this request and stated that he would not authorize the distribution of *Der Igel* in barracks. Based on the military law, all armed forces personnel have the right to receive, without any restriction, and through sources accessible to the public, information on political events. However, on military premises the only publications that could be supplied were those which identified at least to some extent with the constitutional duties of the army, did not damage its reputation, and did not lend column space to political parties. Even critical magazines would not be banned if they respected these conditions. *Der Igel* did not comply with these conditions. The Court reiterated its jurisdiction regarding the basic importance of freedom of expression and stated that the same is true when the persons concerned are servicemen, because article 10 applies to them just as it does to other persons. The second applicant, a soldier and member of *VDSÖ*, while distributing one issue of the magazine, was ordered by an officer to cease. Later on, the applicant was informed of the content of regulations of the barracks, which prohibited any distribution or despatching within the barracks of publications without the authorization of the commanding officer. The applicant complained about this ban and the order imposed on him. The complaint was rejected due to the fact that the barracks were to be regarded as the property of the Federal state, which is protected by the right to property within the meaning of article 5 of the Basic Law of 1867. The applicant's freedom of expression secured under article 13 of the Basic Law of 1867 was subject to statutory limits, such as those which stemmed from the duty of discretion and obedience laid down in the Armed Forces Act and derived from the very nature of this special relationship of subordination. The contested measures had therefore in no way interfered with the freedom in question. The applicant's appeal to the Constitutional Court was rejected on the ground that it did not raise genuine constitutional issues and had insufficient prospects of success. In the Court's opinion, none of the issues of *Der Igel* submitted in evidence recommended disobedience or violence, or even question of the usefulness of the army, but set out complaints, put forward proposals for reforms, or encouraged readers to institute legal complaints or appeal proceedings. Despite their often polemical tenor, they did not overstep the bounds of what is permissible in the context of a mere discussion of ideas, which must be tolerated in the army of a democratic State just as it must be in the society which that army serves. The refusal to distribute the magazine was disproportionate to the legitimate aim pursued. Therefore the applicants were victims of a violation of article 10.

In the case of *Prager and Oberschlick*,[208] the applicants (journalists, the latter also a publisher) were convicted for the defamation of eight judges in the article 'Danger! Harsh judges!' ('*Achtung! Scharfe Richter!*') published in the magazine *FORVM*. The article contained critcism of the judges sitting in Austrian criminal courts due to their attitude against accused persons. As sources for his article the author gave his own experience, statements of lawers and legal correspondents, and surveys carried out by university teachers. In summarizing, the author came to the conclusion that 'some Austrian criminal court judges are capable of anything; all of them are capable of a lot; there is a pattern to all this'. Both applicants were convicted of defamation and fined, and the relevant issue of the magazine was seized. The Court mentioned the pre-eminent role of the press in a state governed by the rule of law and its responsibility to impart information on the functioning of the system of justice. Because the judiciary must enjoy public confidence in carrying out its duties, it may be necessary to protect such confidence against destructive attacks that are essentially unfounded. Some of the allegations made by the author had been of an extremely serious nature. In the absence of a sufficient factual basis, he had, by implication, accused judges of having broken the law or breached their professional obligations, which could damage the reputation of those concerned and undermine public confidence in the integrity of the judiciary as a whole. This led to a lack of good faith and failure to respect the ethics of journalism. By five votes to four, the Court rejected the appeal.[209]

The case of *Oberschlick II*[210] dealt with the conviction and fining of the journalist and editor of the periodical *FORVM* (also the applicant in the case *Oberschlick I*[211]) for insulting a politician by using a swearword. On the occasion of a peace celebration, the leader of the 'Austrian Freedom Party', Mr Haider, argued that the German Army had fought for peace and freedom and that freedom of opinion reaches its limit where people lay claim to that spiritual freedom which they would never have got if others had not risked their lives so that they may now live in democracy and freedom. This speech was

[208] Judgment of 26 Apr 1995, Series A 313.

[209] This judgement was not very convincing: but see the comprehensive dissenting opinion of Judge Martens, joined by Judges Pekkanen and Makarczyk, who voted impressively in favour of freedom of opinion.

[210] Judgment of 1 July 1997, Reports 1997–IV.

[211] See above.

reproduced in full and commented on by the applicant describing Mr Haider as a '"Trottel" (idiot) rather than a Nazi' and justifying the use of this word, mainly because in his speech Mr Haider had excluded himself from enjoying any freedom of opinion. The Court found that the applicant's article could be considered polemical, but did not on that account constitute a gratuitous personal attack as he had provided an objectively understandable explanation, derived from the provocative speech of the politician concerned, for using the term complained of. The article constituted part of a political discussion provoked by that speech and amounted to an opinion truth is not susceptible of proof. Such an opinion may be excessive and offending, but the word does not seem disproportionate to the indignation intentionally aroused by Mr Haider, and article 10 protects not only the substance of ideas and information expressed but also the form in which they are conveyed. Because necessity for the interference with the exercise of the applicant's freedom of expression had not been shown, the Court considered that there was a breach of article 10.

In the *Worm* case,[212] the applicant, a journalist with the magazine *profil*, dealt with the case of Hannes Androsch, a former Vice-Chancellor and Minister of Finance, concerning charges of tax evasion. An article written by the applicant and published in *profil* led to a conviction and a fine for publishing an article considered capable of influencing the outcome of criminal proceedings. The Court stated that courts cannot operate in a vacuum, wherefore room has to be provided for the discussion of subject matters of criminal trials in specialized journals, in the general press, or among the public at large. The limits of acceptable comments are wider as regards a politician than as regards private individuals, although public figures are entitled to enjoy fair-trial guarantees on the same basis as every other person. The conviction of the applicant was not directed against his right to impart information in an objective manner about public figures trial but against the unfavourable assessment of an element of evidence at the trial. The impugned article could not be said to be incapable of warranting the conclusion as to its potential for influencing the outcome of the trial, especially upon lay judges reading this article. The interests of the applicant and the public in imparting and receiving ideas concerning matters of general concern did not outweigh considerations of the adverse consequences of diffusion of the impugned article for the authority and impartiality of the judiciary. The applicant's conviction and sentence were therefore 'necessary in a democratic society'.

In the case of *News Verlags GmbH & CoKG* (Judgment of January 2000, Reports 2000–I) the Vienna Court of Appeal in 1994 and 1995 issued

[212] Judgment of 29 Aug 1997, Reports 1997–V.

injunctions prohibiting the applicant company (a publisher and the owner of the weekly magazine *News*) from publishing pictures of B (a right-wing extremist, who was arrested on suspicion of having been involved in the 'letter-bomb campaign') in the context of criminal proceedings against him irrespective of the accompanying text. Its judgments were upheld by the Supreme Court.

In the view of the Strasbourg Court, the articles which gave rise to the injunction proceedings were written against the background of a spectacular series of letter bombs sent to politicians and other persons in the public eye in Austria and had severely injured several victims. The attacks were thus a news item of major public concern. The applicant company's articles dealt with the activities of the extreme right, and in particular with B, who had entered the public scene well before the letter-bombs were sent. Moreover, it has to be borne in mind that the offences he was suspected of, namely offences under the National Socialist's Prohibition Act (*Verbotsgesetz*) and aiding and abetting assault through letter bombs, were offences with a political background, directed against the foundations of a democratic society. It may be added that the photographs of B, with the possible exception of one wedding photograph, did not disclose any details of his private life. Thus, the Strasbourg Court did not subscribe to the Government's argument that the publications at issue encroached upon B's right to privacy.

These circumstances were taken into account by the Strasbourg Court when assessing whether the reasons adduced by the Austrian courts justifying the injunctions were 'relevant and sufficient' and whether the injunctions were 'proportionate to the legitimate aims pursued'. Recalling its case-law on the essential function of the press in a democratic society, the Court argued that the press's duty extends to reporting and commenting on court proceedings which, provided that they do not overstep the bounds set out above, contribute to their publicity and are thus perfectly consonant with the requirement under article 6, para. 1 of the Convention that hearings be public. Not only do the media have the task of imparting such information and ideas: the public also has a right to receive them. This is all the more so where, as in the present case, a party has laid himself open to public scrutiny by expressing extremist views. However, the limits of permissible comment on pending criminal proceedings may not extend to statements which are likely to prejudice, whether intentionally or not, the chances of a person receiving a fair trial or to undermine the confidence of the public in the role of the courts in the administration of justice. Thus, the fact that B had a right under article 6 para. 2 of the Convention to be presumed innocent until proven guilty is also of relevance for the balancing of competing interests which the Court must carry out.

The Court acknowledged that there may be good reasons for prohibiting the publication of a suspect's picture in itself, depending on the nature of the offence at issue and the particular circumstances of the case. A similar line of argument was followed by the Supreme Court, which stated that even the publication of a picture accompanied by a correct statement of fact could infringe the legitimate interests of the person concerned. However, no reasons to that effect were adduced by the Vienna Court of Appeal. Nor did it weigh B's interest in the protection of his picture against the public interest in its publication which, as the Government pointed out, is required under section 78 of the Copyright Act. This is all the more surprising as the publication of a suspect's picture is not generally prohibited under the Austrian Media Act.

In sum, the reasons adduced by the Vienna Court of Appeal, although 'relevant', were not 'sufficient. The Court's view was that the injunctions in no way restricted the applicant company's right to publish comments on the criminal proceedings against B. However, they restricted the applicant company's choice as to the presentation of its reports, while it was undisputed that other media were free to continue to publish B's picture throughout the criminal proceedings against him. Having regard to these circumstances and to the domestic courts' finding that it was not the pictures used by the applicant company but only their combination with the text that interfered with B's rights, the Strasbourg Court found that the absolute prohibition of the publication of B's picture went further than was necessary to protect B against defamation or against violation of the presumption of innocence. Thus, there was no proportionality between the injunctions as formulated by the Vienna Court of Appeal and the legitimate aims pursued. It followed from these considerations that the interference with the applicant company's right to freedom of expression was not 'necessary in a democratic society'. Accordingly, there was a violation of article 10 of the Convention.

In the *Wabl* case (Judgment of 21 March 2000, Reports 2000-I) in June 1988 the applicant (a Green Party politician) had participated in a campaign of protest against the stationing of interceptor fighter aeroplanes near Graz airport. Following police action, a police officer charged the applicant with having scratched his right arm, and subsequently requested that the applicant be prosecuted for having caused grievous bodily harm. In July 1988 the Graz Public Prosecutor's Office informed the applicant that the investigation proceedings against him had been discontinued. In August 1988 the newspaper *Neue Kronen-Zeitung-Steirerkrone* published an article under the title 'Styrian Green politician and member of Parliament injured civil servant/Request for him to be handed over on account of the risk of infection' and with the headline 'Police Officer claims: AIDS test for Wabl!' This article was accompanied by a photograph showing the applicant and two police officers with the subtitle 'AIDS test for the privileged member of Parliament? Wabl (centre) in an altercation with the police'.

Also in August 1988 the applicant, during a press conference, commented on the events of June 1988 and in particular on this article. He informed the press of his opinion regarding the background to the events which he considered to be 'political character assassination' (*politischer Rufmord*). When asked by a journalist how he felt about the above events, the applicant replied 'This is Nazi journalism'. This statement was quoted in the Austrian media. In the following days the company publishing the newspaper *Kronen-Zeitung* brought injunction proceedings under section 1330 of the Civil Code against the applicant. It requested that the applicant be prohibited from repeating the statement that the contents of the *Kronen-Zeitung* were 'Nazi-journalism' and to arrange for rectification.

After the plaintiff's appeal was dismissed at the first and the second instances (because the impugned statement was held to be a value judgment) in December 1993 the Austrian Supreme Court, upon the plaintiff's further appeal, reversed the Appeal Court's decision and issued an injunction against the applicant prohibiting him from repeating the statement that the article amounted to 'Nazi journalism', and from making any similar statements. The Strasbourg Court found that the Supreme Court had duly balanced the interests involved and that the detailed reasons which it gave were also 'sufficient' for the purposes of article 10, para. 2 of the Convention. In reaching this conclusion, the Court had particular regard to the special stigma which attaches to activities inspired by National Socialist ideas. (In this context it should be noted that, pursuant to constitutional provisions and legislation introduced in Austria after the Second World War, it is a criminal offence to perform such activities.) The Court considered that the article published in the *Kronen-Zeitung* was defamatory. It was also questionable whether it contributed to a debate of general concern as it contained hardly any information about the protest campaign against the stationing of interceptor fighter aeroplanes in which the applicant had participated. Thus, even bearing in mind that the applicant was a politician, who inevitably and knowingly lays himself open to close scrutiny of his every word and deed by both journalists and the public at large and must display a greater degree of tolerance, the Court found that the article at issue was an understandable ground for indignation. Nevertheless, the Court noted that the applicant did not use the expression 'Nazi journalism' as an immediate reaction but only a few days later when the *Kronen-Zeitung* published a rectification which included a statement drafted by the applicant himself. Furthermore, the applicant, as stated by the Supreme Court, could himself have brought injunction proceedings under section 1330 of the Civil Code. In this context, the Court also noted that the applicant did avail himself of the possibility of a private prosecution against the company publishing the *Kronen-Zeitung*, which resulted in the latter's conviction for defamation pursuant to the Media Act. Finally, the Court observed that the contested injunction was confined to prohibiting the applicant only from repeating the statement that the article amounted to 'Nazi journalism' or the making of similar statements. The applicant thus retained the right to voice his opinion regarding the reporting by the *Kronen-Zeitung* in other terms. Having regard to these surprising considerations, the Court found that the Supreme Court was entitled to consider that the injunction was 'necessary in a democratic society' for the protection of the reputation and rights of others. (But see the more convincing dissenting opinion of Judge Greve.)

6.4. Freedom of art The freedom of art as part of the freedom of expression was the subject of the case of the *Otto-Preminger-Institut*.[213] The applicant association announced a series of public showings, in the Catholic province Tyrol, of the film 'Council in Heaven' (*Das Liebeskonzil*) by Werner Schroeter. Based on Oskar Panniza's satirical tragedy, the film was set in the context of the writer's reconstruction of a trial and conviction for blasphemy in 1895. In the film, trivial imagery and absurdities of the Christian creed are targeted in a caricatural mode and the relationship between religious beliefs and worldly mechanisms of oppression is investigated. At the request of the Roman Catholic Church, the Public Prosecutor instituted criminal proceedings against the manager of the applicant due to the applicant's disparaging of religious doctrines. After the film had been shown at a private session in the presence of a duty judge, the Public Prosecutor made an application for its seizure. As a result, the public showings could not take place. By a subsequent judgment, the film was forfeited. The Court stated that the respect for the religious feelings of believers guaranteed in article 9 could legitimately have been thought to have been violated by provocative portrayals of objects of religious veneration. Because the Convention has to be read as a whole, the interpretation and application of article 10 must be in harmony with the logic of the Convention. The freedom of expression, one of the essential foundations of a democratic society, is applicable not only to information or ideas that are favourably received or regarded as inoffensive or as a matter of indifference, but also to those that shock, offend, or disturb the state or any sector of the population. The attendant 'duties and responsibilities' may legitimately include obligations to avoid expressions gratuitously offensive to others, and thus an infringement of their rights that may be considered necessary in certain democratic societies to sanction or even prevent improper attacks on

[213] Judgment of 20 Sep 1994, Series A 295–A.

objects of religious veneration. In seizing and forfeiting the film, the authorities acted to ensure religious peace in the Tyrol and to prevent some people feeling that their religious feelings were being attacked in an unwarranted and offensive manner. Because the margin of appreciation had not been overstepped, article 10 was not violated.

7. *Article 13*

In the case of *Plattform 'Ärzte für das Leben'*,[214] the applicant association—a group of doctors opposed to legalized abortion—claimed a violation of article 13 of the Convention for being disrupted when holding a counter-demonstration, despite the presence of a large contingent of police, and for not having a remedy against the acts of the police during the demonstration. The Court found that individuals should have a remedy in domestic law in respect of an arguable claim of a violation of provisions of the Convention. Therefore the Court examined a violation of article 11. The Court stated—concurring with the Austrian Government and the Commission—that the effective freedom of peaceful assembly cannot be reduced to a mere duty on the part of the state not to interfere. A purely negative conception would not be compatible with the object and purpose of article 11. Like article 8, article 11 sometimes requires positive measures to be taken, even in the sphere of relations between individuals, so that participants are able to hold demonstrations without the fear of physical violence by opponents of their opinion. Such a fear would be liable to deter people from openly expressing their opinions on controversial issues. In a democracy, the right to counter-demonstrate cannot extend to inhibiting the exercise of the right to demonstrate. The Court also referred to the wide discretion enjoyed by contracting states as regards the choice of means to be used for this purpose. In this area, their obligation under article 11 is an obligation regarding measures to be taken, and not regarding the results to be achieved. The Court found that there was no arguable claim of violation of article 11 and that article 13 was therefore not applicable.

8. *Article 1 of the 1st Protocol*

In the *Gaygusuz* case,[215] the Austrian authorities refused to grant emergency assistance to the applicant who had exhausted his entitlement to unemployment benefits on the ground that he did not have Austrian nationality. The applicant was lawfully resident in Austria and worked there, paying contributions to the unemployment insurance fund in the same capacity and on the

[214] Judgment of 21 June 1988, Series A 139.
[215] Judgment of 16 Sep 1996, Reports 1996–IV.

same basis as Austrian nationals, who, in the same situation, would have received emergency assistance. The Court stated unanimously that the difference in treatment had not been based on any objective and reasonable justification, so that the refusal to grant emergency assistance was a violation of article 14, which in the opinion of the Court has no independent existence but complements the other substantive provisions of the Convention and the Protocols, taken in conjunction with article 1 of the 1st Protocol.

In the *Inze* case,[216] the Court found it to be a violation of article 14 taken together with article 1 of the 1st Protocol that the illegitimate birth of the applicant deprived him in law of any possibility of taking over his mother's farm in the distribution of her estate. The farm in question was subject to a special regulation providing that farms of a certain size may not be divided in the case of hereditary succession and that one of the heirs (usually the eldest son) must take over the entire property and pay off the other heirs. The Court also stated that a difference of treatment was discriminatory if it had no objective and reasonable justification, that is, if it did not pursue a legitimate aim or if there was not a reasonable relationship of proportionality between the means employed and the aim sought to be realized. Legitimacy is not a sufficient justification for differing treatment as it does not reflect the real situation in this special case. Consequently, the Court unanimously held that there was a breach of article 14 taken together with article 1 of the 1st Protocol.

In the case of *Erkner and Hofauer*,[217] dealing with the provisional transfer of land without compensation in kind by the final decision of the relevant authorities, the Court held that article 1 of the 1st Protocol comprised three distinct rules: the first sentence of the first paragraph, the second sentence of the first paragraph, and the second paragraph. The two latter were inapplicable because the applicants had not been definitively deprived of possessions nor had the transfer been designed to restrict or control the use of land. Accordingly, the transfer had to be considered under the first sentence of the first paragraph, which demanded a proper balance between the demands of the community's general interest and the requirements of protecting the fundamental rights of the individual. The relevant considerations were, on one hand, the length of the proceedings, the impossibility of reconsidering a provisional transfer, and the impossibility of financially compensating loss sustained on account of a forced exchange of land, and on the other hand, the aim of the legislature and the allocation of land to the applicants in lieu of their own. In the present case the necessary balance was lacking, the

[216] Judgment of 28 Oct 1987, Series A 126.
[217] Judgment of 23 Apr 1987, Series A 117.

applicants had been made to bear a disproportionate burden, so there was a breach of article 1 of the 1st Protocol.

In the *Prötsch* case,[218] the applicants also complained about the length and the inadequacy of land transfer proceedings, which they claimed had resulted in decreased productivity of the compensatory parcels allocated to them, and financial damage due to the loss of yield, for which they had been unable to obtain financial compensation. The Court, considering the interference under the first sentence of the first paragraph of article 1, held, as in the case of *Erkner and Hofauer*, that there had to be a proper balance between the demands of the community's general interest and the requirements of protecting the fundamental rights of the individual. A temporary disadvantage could be justified in the general interest if it was not disproportionate to the aim pursued. As to the alleged inadequacy, the Court found that the Upper Austria Land Reform Board had twice held that the parcels allotted to the applicants had been of approximately the same value as the old ones and the agricultural performances at least as good. Concerning the length of the proceedings—the final consolidation scheme came into force six years after the transfer of the land—the Court stated that this period was not unreasonable in itself having regard to the aim of the proceedings. There was accordingly no violation of article 1 of the 1st Protocol.

In the case of *Mellacher and Others*,[219] dealing with rent reductions imposed in accordance with the law, the Court held that the measures taken did not constitute either a formal or a *de facto* expropriation but merely control of the use of property, so that the second paragraph of article 1 of the 1st Protocol applied in this instance. As to the question of compliance with the second paragraph, the Court found that the legislature must have a wide margin of discretion with regard to the implementation of social and economic policies, in particular in the field of housing. In the Court's view, the explanations given for the legislation in question could not be regarded as manifestly unreasonable, so the Court accepted that the 1981 Rent Act had a legitimate aim in the general interest. Regarding the proportionality of the interference, the Court further held that it could not be said that the measures taken to achieve the legitimate aims had been so inappropriate or disproportionate as to take them outside the State's margin of appreciation. Although the rent reductions were undoubtedly striking in their amount, they did not constitute a disproportionate burden. The fact that the original rents had been agreed upon and corresponded to the market conditions did not mean that the legislature could not reasonably decide as a matter of policy that they

[218] Judgment of 15 Nov 1996, Reports 1996–V.
[219] Judgment of 19 Dec 1989, Series A 169.

were unacceptable from the point of view of social justice. There was accordingly no violation of article 1 of the 1st Protocol.

9. *Article 4 of the 7th Protocol*

The *Gradinger* case[220] dealt, *inter alia*, with the question of whether a criminal *and* an administrative criminal sentence for the same offence, ie causing death by negligence and driving under the influence of alcohol, was in accordance with article 4 of the 7th Protocol. The Austrian 'declaration' concerning this provision was seen by the Court as a reservation which was not accepted as admissible due to the fact that the government failed to enclose the texts of the relevant laws. The intoxication of the applicant was not made outby by by the Regional Court, but the administrative authorities found that the relevant alcohol level had been attained. Indeed, the provisions in question differed as regards the designation of the offences and also as regards their nature and purpose. The offence provided for in the Road Traffic Act represented only one aspect of the offence punishable under the Criminal Code. Nevertheless, in the Court's view the impugned decisions were based on the same conduct. Therefore the Court found a violation of article 4 of the 7th Protocol.

F. REMEDIAL ACTION TAKEN BY THE GOVERNMENT IN RESPONSE TO BEING HELD IN VIOLATION OF THE CONVENTION

First of all, it must be mentioned that Austria has always punctually and fully paid its financial compensations based on judgments of the Court in accordance with article 41. In several cases existing laws were amended or new laws set into force in reaction to adverse judgments of the Court, fulfilling the obligation of states to conform with the legal view held by the Court according to article 46.[221] But whenever remedial action should have been taken to give full satisfaction to a successful applicant, problems have arisen.[222] For example, only a few cases in which a violation of the right to fair trial was found have been retried in domestic courts.[223] It does not follow from the constitutional status and the direct applicability of the Convention that

[220] Judgment of 23 Oct 1995, Series A 328–C. [221] See C above.
[222] For more details see Tretter, 'The implementation of judgements of the European Court of Human Rights in Austria', in: Barkhuysen/Emmerik/van Kempen (eds), *The Execution of Strasbourg and Geneva Human Rights Decisions in the National Legal Order*, 1999, pp. 165.
[223] In the Cases of *Unterpertinger* and *Windisch* (see 4.12 above).

judgments of the Court are directly applicable within domestic law and that, on the basis of these judgments, domestic decisions infringing the Convention have to be abolished, and proceedings have to be reopened to give full satisfaction to the successful applicant. For that purpose, specific legal provisions need to be set in force. This has recently only been done in regard to criminal, but not civil and administrative law. Given the lack of comparable legal provisions in civil and in administrative law, it is not surprising that in most cases the applicants have not obtained full redress.

In reaction to two judgments of the Court, *Oberschlick I*[224] and *Kremzow*,[225] which led to findings against Austria in 1996, a procedure was provided for in 1996 by article 363a of the amended Code of Criminal Procedure to implement judgments of the Court in domestic law. If the Court finds that a decision or order by a domestic criminal court has infringed the Convention, the Austrian Supreme Court can *ex parte* reopen the proceedings at the first or second instance, depending on the stage at which the violation of the Convention occurred. The request for reopening, afforded essentially to the person affected by the decision issued in violation of the Convention and to the Procurator General at the Supreme Court, is not subject to a time-limit.

Up to now, there has been little use of this provision. In one case, *Oberschlick II*,[226] the former domestic convictions were quashed and the proceedings reopened, but subsequently abandoned. In this case, the judgment of the Court was pronounced after the amendment of the Code of Criminal Procedure had come into force. In the cases mentioned above, *Kremzow* and *Oberschlick I*, the motions for reopening were rejected by the Supreme Court due to the fact that the judgment of the Court was delivered before the amendment of the Code of Criminal Procedure had come into force. This practice is not in accordance with the intent of the legislator, even though the wording of the provision allows both interpretations. Clarification by the legislator is needed to bring the Court's practice into line with the principle of equality.

In Austrian civil law, there are no legal provisions comparable to those of the Code of Criminal Procedure described above, so that no reopening can take place to comply with the judgment of the Court in an individual case. Only where a criminal conviction has been abolished, which was at the same time the basis for a civil law judgment, can a reopening of the latter be instituted. In view of this lack of legal protection, it is not surprising that in most

[224] Judgment of 23 May 1991, Series A 204.
[225] Judgment of 21 Sep 1993, Series A 268–B.
[226] Judgment of 1 July 1997, Reports 1997–IV.

of the civil law cases concerned, the applicants did not obtain full redress, except for financial compensation.

As in its civil law, Austrian administrative law also lacks legal provisions relating to the reopening of proceedings to assess a violation of the Convention. This legal situation has led to some unsatisfying consequences, such as in the *Gradinger* case,[227] which did not result in the annulment of the administrative decision which violated the Convention.

In general, it must said that there is little readiness in Austria to implement the judgments of the Strasbourg Court concerning the specific cases of applicants by taking the appropriate legal measures. There is more readiness to ensure by legal amendments that comparable violations of the Convention are not repeated.

G. ASSESSMENT AND PROSPECTS

The Convention has assumed a key role within the Austrian legal order. Austria was the first state to incorporate the Convention fully into its constitutional legal order, so that the Convention was granted the same legal status as the domestic bill of rights. As a result, domestic legislation as well as courts and administrative authorities are obliged to observe and implement effectively the rights and freedoms of the Convention.

The fact that public awareness of the Convention in Austria is high and that it was implemented on the constitutional level has generated a high volume of applications lodged against Austria. Most of those cases concerned articles 5 and 6, and some to articles 3, 8, 10, and 11, and to article 1 of the 1st Protocol; only a few pertained to other provisions of the Convention.

Domestic courts and administrative authorities have ruled on nearly every right or freedom of the Convention. In this context the Constitutional Court assumes a central role which has had an impact on domestic jurisdiction as well as legislation, giving the rights and freedoms of the Convention greater standing within national law. This positive influence is undercut by the fact that the Constitutional Court tends frequently to react to findings against Austria, instead of independently screening the national legal order according to the requirements of the Convention. Furthermore, it is deplorable that it acts on the premiss that a Convention right cannot go further than the parallel national fundamental right. However, the Constitutional Court has also established an autonomous and extensive jurisdiction regarding those rights

[227] Judgment of 23 Oct 1995, Series A 328–C.

of the Convention which had no equivalent in the domestic human rights order. This has allowed their content to be developed further, but has also triggered concerns pertaining to article 3 which are related to measures by police authorities, in connection with the termination of residence, and to article 8 related to the law on aliens.

It should also be noted that the principle of proportionality, which is inherent in the Convention,[228] exerts a profound influence on the jurisdiction of the Constitutional Court as well as on the legislation and the dogmatics of fundamental rights and freedoms within Austrian jurisprudence.

Many areas of Austrian legislation have continuously been influenced by the Convention itself and by the case-law of the Strasbourg organs. However, government and parliament remain reluctant to observe and fulfil the obligations of the Convention. Authorities often did no more than was absolutely necessary to observe the obligations under the Convention with regard to the relevant jurisdiction, when they should have moved to amend the questionable legislation as a whole.

There is some willingness on the part of the authorities to take the appropriate legal measures in order to implement the rulings of the Strasbourg Court with regard to the specific cases of applicants. Austria is more prepared to take action when it comes to ensuring—with the help of legal amendments—that comparable violations of the Convention are not repeated. However, this is not the case with regard to the freedom of information of television enterprises. So far government and parliament have failed to move on their obligation to permit private television enterprises in Austria.

Withdrawing the reservation concerning article 5 constitutes a particular challenge for the future. The improvement of the legal situation, above all the establishment of independent administrative tribunals, calls for action now. The structural problems arising from the assessment of the Strasbourg Court that both the Constitutional and the Administrative Court lack some requirements of a 'tribunal' in the meaning of article 6 should also be resolved in the foreseeable future.

The Convention is still inadequately established within the jurisdiction of the criminal courts. This has become evident in several findings against Austria by the Court regarding criminal proceedings, eg relating to the freedom of opinion of journalists. A solution would be to establish a mandate for

[228] See Berka, *Die Europäische Menschenrechtskonvention und die österreichische Grundrechtstradition*, Österreichische Juristen Zeitschrift 1979, pp. 365 and 428; Öhlinger, *Die Grundrechte in Österreich—ein systematischer Überblick*, Europäische Grundrechte Zeitschrift 1982, pp. 216; Holoubek, 'Die Interpretation der Grundrechte in der jüngeren Judikatur des Verfassungsgerichtshofs', in: Machacek/Pahr/Stadler (eds), *Grund- und Menschenrechte in Österreich* 1991, pp. 43; Berka, *Konkretisierung und Schranken der Grundrechte*, Zeitschrift für öffentliches Recht 1999, pp. 31.

reviewing the judicial power by the Constitutional Court, which at present is only entitled to examine decisions of administrative authorities.

At present Austria faces a formidable number of human rights problems with regard to rights and freedoms of the Convention. These include, above all, the detention and treatment practices by the police, the judicial pre-trial review process, freedom of speech in relation to the law of the media, administrative provisions and measures terminating the residence of aliens, and asylum issues. To overcome these current deficiencies in human rights protection the Convention will continue to play an essential role in the future.

6

Belgium

SILVIO MARCUS-HELMONS AND
PHILIPPE MARCUS-HELMONS

INTRODUCTION

Human rights have flourished over the centuries in Belgium, as they have in other countries of Europe. Back in the Middle Ages, a wealthy middle class of artisans and tradesmen fostered the development of the towns. The feudal lords, constantly in need of money to pay for their warfare and simply to maintain their standard of living, often had to turn to these rich burghers. In return the latter exacted growing privileges which were enshrined in a large number of charters.[1]

These freedoms enabled many towns to grow and helped the Belgian provinces prosper. So it came as no surprise that, on independence, Belgium adopted a liberal Constitution in 1831, long a model for many countries. Part II of this Constitution, 'The Belgians and their Rights', covered a large number of civil and political rights to which the people had become accustomed.

The United Nations Organization issued the Universal Declaration of Human Rights in 1948 and Belgium, naturally, subscribed to it enthusiastically.

It was with the same enthusiasm, on 4 November 1950, that Belgium signed the European Convention for the Protection of Human Rights, on the day of its adoption, but it took time to ratify and it was not until 1955 that the State was actually bound internationally by the Convention.[2]

There was no political or legal reason for the delay: this is the normal slow speed at which the Belgian Parliament approves international treaties. It is

[1] For example, the Charte de Franchise, granted by Henry I, Duke of Lotharingia and Brabant, in 1204, the so-called Albert de Cuyck Charter of 3 June 1208 confirming privileges granted to the burgers of Liège, the Peace of Fexhe (18 June 1316); the Treaty of Fexhe of 18 June 1316; the Joyeuse Entrée into the city of Louvain of Duchess Jeanne and her husband Wenceslas of Bohemia on 3 Jan 1356; the Great Privilege of Marie de Bourgogne (1477); and the Perpetual Edict of the Archdukes Albert and Isabella, 12 July 1611, etc.

[2] The act by which the Belgian Parliament agreed to the Convention dates back to 13 May 1955 (Moniteur Belge, 19 Aug 1955). So far Belgium has ratified only 6 of the 11 Protocols.

worth noting that, in the interests of winning the members' support, the parliamentary rapporteur presented the situation in two columns, one containing the Articles of the Convention and the other all the corresponding Articles from Belgian's own Constitution, laws, and decrees. The idea was to reassure Parliament that the commitment did not involve the country in any risk or responsibility and it led to Belgium ratifying the Convention with no reservations.

Although its laws are by and large in line with the Convention, this does not mean all is well in the Kingdom. As we shall see later, Belgium, like many other countries, is a regular defendant in cases brought to the European Commission and Court of Human Rights.

This, which has surprised more than one legal expert, could well be the explanation for the time it took for Belgium to accept the UN's two human rights Covenants. These were in fact adopted by the UN General Assembly on 16 December 1966, but Belgium did not sign them until 10 December 1968, ratifying them on 21 April 1983.[3]

We would stress, however, that no lawyer today would think of questioning the fact that the Convention is an integral part of Belgian law.

A. THE STATUS OF THE CONVENTION IN NATIONAL LAW

As we have just said, Belgian lawyers see the Convention as part of their law, as it stands, but this has not always been the case.

In a judgment on 14 February 1963, the Supreme Court of Appeal announced that it would only consider the legal provisions of the Convention if they were invoked via a reference to the Belgian law which enshrined them in the national legislation.[4] At that stage, some judges also maintained that the principle of the separation of powers prevented Belgian courts from assessing the extent to which national law conformed with the Convention.[5]

Fortunately, the court practice was quick to evolve. With the famous judgment of 27 May 1971, the Supreme Court of Appeal acted on the findings of the public prosecutor, Mr Ganshof van der Meersch, and established that the rule of international law took precedence over national law.[6] They only con-

[3] Moniteur Belge, 6 July 1983. For obvious reasons, Belgium did not ratify the optional Protocol relating to the International Covenant on Civil and Political Rights until early in the summer of 1994.

[4] Pas., 1963, I, p. 673 et seq.

[5] See J. Velu, 'L'application et l'interpretation de la Convention européenne des droits de l'homme dans la jurisprudence belge' (1968) *Journal des Tribunaux* 696.

[6] Pas., 1971, I, p. 886.

flict, obviously, if the international law has not been internalized by a national law. That is why the problem of a possible clash has to be tackled alongside the problem of the direct applicability of the Convention in the Belgian legal system.

Are the provisions of the European Human Rights Convention directly applicable in the Belgian legal system?

That depends on the article, obviously, because the international rule clearly has to meet certain criteria if it is to be applied directly. What is directly applicable in national law, in fact, is the:

> clear, legally complete rule of a treaty which forces the Contracting States either to refrain from acting or to take deliberate action and which can be invoked as a source of a right by people within the jurisdiction of those States or subject these people to obligations.[7]

It would be reasonable to say that this is indeed the case for many of the articles of the European Convention.

> An analysis of the terms of the Convention, in context and in the light of the aims and intentions of that agreement, shows that most of the rules in Section I and Protocols 1 and 4 can directly affect the internal laws of the States and actually do so in Belgium.[8]

> In many instances Belgian courts have admitted implicitly that the rules on the rights and freedoms laid down in Articles 2–12, 14, 15, 17 and 18 of the Convention and Articles 1 and 2 of Protocol No. 1 have direct effects in the Belgian legal system.[9]

Furthermore, the Convention even has a bearing on public policy,[10] in that it aims to establish a European public human rights order.

Indeed, on occasions the Belgian Supreme Court of Appeal has also of its own initiative raised a point related to violation of an article of the Convention. In criminal matters, for example, it has, on its own initiative, referred to the necessity to respect article 6(1)[11] and to article 5, paragraphs 1c, 3, and 4.[12]

[7] J. Velu, 'Les effets directs des instruments internationaux en matière de droits de l'homme' in *L'effet direct en droit belge des traités internationaux relatifs aux droits de l'homme* (Bruylant: University of Brussels, 1981), p. 56.

[8] J. Velu, 'Les effets directs des instruments internationaux en matière de droits de l'homme', ibid, p. 60. These lines were written in 1980 and the other Protocols enshrining the fundamental rights can be added to Protocols 1–4 here.

[9] Ibid.

[10] W. Ganshof van der Meersch, 'La Convention européenne des droits de l'homme a-t-elle, dans le cadre du droit interne, une valeur d'ordre public?' in *Les droits de l'homme en droit interne et droit international* (Bruylant: Presses Universitaires de Bruxelles, 1968), pp. 155–251.

[11] Cass., 31 May 1976, Pas., 1970, I, pp. 534 and 723.

[12] Cass., 4 Sep 1979, Pas., 1980, I, p. 3.

So with the Convention occupying such a position in Belgium's national law, it is bound to be referred to frequently.

Human rights and the Convention are often mentioned in lawyers' addresses, political speeches, and parliamentary debates. There is no time to list every parliamentary reference to human rights and the Convention here, but they are bound to come up when Parliament amends legislation after the European Court has ruled against Belgium. We shall return to this later.

Even where it is not a case of aligning Belgian law with the provisions of the Convention, MPs may well refer to human rights in general[13] or make explicit reference to the Convention and the decisions of its organs. Now that Belgium has become a federal state, human rights are a concern at both federal level[14] and in the parliamentary assemblies of the federal communities.[15]

Some people are unhappy about over-frequent references, because, although these can be beneficial, paradoxically they could also be damaging, for too much mention of human rights could make them seem too commonplace. Clearly, reference to the Convention should only be made for human rights and their greater respect.

B. HUMAN RIGHTS IN BELGIAN LAW: MAIN DECISIONS

An examination of Belgian legal decisions over the two decades following the Law of 13 May 1955, whereby the Government was able to ratify the European Convention, reveals the grudging manner and reserve with which the courts and tribunals have referred to this agreement.[16]

As we have already made clear, to begin with the Belgian Supreme Court of Appeal maintained that it could only allow a reference to the legal provisions of the Convention if this was made via the Belgian approving Act.

[13] For example, the Belgian bill of 7 February 1994 on development co-operation in relation to human rights (Moniteur Belge 13 Sep 1994).

[14] For example, the bill on the protection of privacy from telephone tapping, from listening in and from the recording of private communications and telecommunications—Parliamentary document—Sénat 843–2 (1992–1993), 1993–1994 session, report by Mr Erdman.

[15] Decree of the French-speaking Community of Belgium of 31 Mar 1994 laying down the neutrality of teaching in the Community. See Moniteur Belge 7 Feb 1994 on the evaluation of the development co-operation policy in the light of respect for human rights, Moniteur Belge, 13 Sep 1994. 18 June 1994.

[16] See G. Grimonprez and K. Lenaerts, 'La jurisprudence de la Cour de cassation belge au sujet de la Convention européenne des droits de l'homme' in *Rapports belges au XIe Congrès de l'Académie internationale de droit comparé, Caracas 1982*, vol. 2 (Anvers: Kluwer, 1985), pp. 65–88.

Various decisions taken by the courts also refused to check whether national laws were in line with the Convention.[17]

Some attempt was made to declare various provisions directly applicable in Belgian law and prevailing over the latter,[18] but nothing happened until the Supreme Court issued its judgment of 27 May 1971, the importance of which we examined earlier. Since then the articles of the Convention have been applied more and more frequently, although Belgian courts and legal practitioners continued to be slow in adapting to the idea.

A systematic list of the legal decisions that have applied the Convention is beyond the scope of this paper, so we focus below on the principal decisions which have reflected[19] the effect of the Convention on Belgian law.

The following synthesis of Belgian legal decisions is based on the main areas of law affected by the Convention.[20]

1. Criminal law

While the principle of the non-retroactivity of criminal provisions involving sentences is set out formally in article 2 of the Criminal Code and article 7, paragraph 1, of the Convention, the Supreme Court of Appeal took a decision on the laws amending time limits. In its judgment of 25 November 1981[21] the Supreme Court stated that provisions which extended the time limit did not at the same time worsen the sentence applicable at the time the offence was committed. According to the Court, time limits did not in themselves affect the substance of the law, or the nature of the sentence, since they were merely a way of allowing the threat of prosecution to lapse through the passing of a specific period of time.

Therefore legal provisions changing the time limits laid down by a previous law and applying to unlapsed offences are not in breach of article 2 of the Criminal Code nor article 7 of the European Convention.[22]

In an abortion case, the Supreme Court found that article 2 of the Convention involved protecting the life of the unborn child.[23]

The presumption of innocence enshrined in article 6, paragraph 2, of the Convention was found only to apply where the accused has pleaded guilty to

[17] J. Velu, 'L'application et l'interpretation de la Convention européenne des droits de l'homme dans la jurisprudence belge', op. cit., p. 696.

[18] For example, Civ. Bruxelles, 8 Nov 1966, Pas., 1967, III, p. 50.

[19] Some decisions have been quashed or confirmed by legal provisions.

[20] We have been inspired here by the method which P. Lambert uses in his *La Convention européenne des droits de l'homme dans la jurisprudence belge* (Brussels: Nemesis, 1987), p. 139

[21] Cass., 25 Nov 1981, Pas. 1982, I, p. 420. See also Cass., 7 May 1980, RBDC, 1981, p. 976.

[22] This approach was used recently by articles 25 et seq. of the Law of 24 Dec 1993 (Moniteur Belge, 31 Dec 1993), which raise the prescription time on various offences to five years and took effect on the date of publication, even for non-prescribed offences.

[23] Cass., 22 Dec 1992, Larcier cassation, 1992, No. 732.

the offences with which he was charged and does not prevent the judge from taking every aspect of the accused, and his legal history in particular, into account when passing judgment.[24]

Similarly, an invitation to be heard on a criminal act or freely to specify one's timetable was found to constitute neither an attack on the presumption of innocence nor an accusation seriously affecting an individual's situation and forcing the latter to take steps to organize his defence.[25]

The Supreme Court found[26] that the passing of a death sentence, and arrangements for carrying it out, by a court in a country which has such punishment, was not in itself inhuman and degrading within the meaning of article 3 of the Convention.

It also found that the right to a fair hearing, within the meaning of article 6, paragraph 1, of the Convention, implied that the accused could not be forced either to give evidence against himself or to admit guilt.[27]

The same Court also ruled as follows:

> the mere fact that the judgment pronounced in response to the defendant's objection came from the same judges as those who pronounced the judgment by default, cannot be seen as grounds for arguing that the judgment pronounced in response to the objection did not come from an independent, impartial court as defined by article 6.1 of the Convention.[28]

2. *Criminal proceedings*

The Supreme Court of Appeal and the ordinary courts and tribunals have always been absolutely consistent in their decisions and maintained that the provisions of article 6 of the Convention apply to the defence raised in court, and not to hearings before investigating authorities.[29] The Supreme Court's grounds for this are that investigating authorities are not concerned with the cogency of criminal accusations, but solely with the existence of sufficient evidence to warrant referral to a court.

However, the provisions of article 5, paragraph 1(c) (and paragraphs 3 and 4) of the Convention have to be applied if the warrant for arrest is confirmed.[30]

[24] Cass., 16 Nov 1993, Larcier cassation, 1993, No. 1128.
[25] Cass., 31 Mar 1993, Larcier cassation, 1993, No. 384.
[26] Cass., 29 Jan 1992, Larcier cassation, 1992, No. 140.
[27] Cass., 11 Mar 1992, Larcier cassation, 1992, No. 245.
[28] Cass., 2 Nov 1993, Pas., 1993, I, p. 916.
[29] For example, Cass., 22 July 1975, Pas., 1975, I p. 1071, Cass., 27 Apr 1976, Pas., 1976, I, p. 932 and Cass., 20 July 1992, Larcier cassation, 1992, No. 733.
[30] For example, Cass., 16 Mar 1964, Pas., 1964, I, p. 762, Cass., 4 Oct 1977, Pas., 1978, I, p. 144 and Cass., 15 Apr 1980, Pas., 1980, I, p. 1015.

Following the Strasbourg Court's judgment in the *De Cubber* case,[31] in which Belgium was found guilty, the Supreme Court of Appeal radically changed the tenor of its decisions by ruling that neither the investigating judge nor the magistrates who had referred a case to the criminal courts or ordered the accused to be remanded in custody[32] could be involved in trying it. Along the same lines, the Supreme Court of Appeal has acknowledged the validity of the argument in that, in terms of the relevant documents, neither the plaintiff nor the Court has been able to check whether the sessions of the courts with jurisdiction were properly composed and thus offered all the guarantees of objective impartiality, the appeal judges not having established that any of the judges had issued a referral not containing the name of the judge.[33]

Although Protocol No. 7 of the Convention stipulates in article 2 that anyone 'convicted of a criminal offence by a tribunal shall have the right to have his conviction or sentence reviewed by a higher authority', Belgium has not ratified it. So the Supreme Court of Appeal found that, since the above Protocol was not directly applicable in Belgium, article 6, paragraph 1, of the Convention did not cover both the investigating authorities and the courts.[34]

On many occasions, it has been decided that neither article 6, paragraph 1, nor any other provision of the Convention specifies what steps should be taken by the judge who finds that the 'reasonable time' has been exceeded. The consequences of exceeding the 'reasonable time' laid down in article 6 should be examined to see how they affect both the handling of the evidence and the criminal punishment of the facts.[35]

The Supreme Court of Appeal has issued many judgments about remanding defendants in custody; however, many of them lost their point when the new Preventive Custody Act came into force on 20 July 1990. We shall therefore only look at those which came after this date. The Supreme Court found that article 5, paragraph 2, of the Convention related to arrest and not to subsequent decisions about the maintenance of preventive custody.[36]

The same Court also found that it was contrary to article 5, paragraph 3, of the Convention on the 'right to trial within a reasonable time, or to release pending trial' for the Indictments Chamber to order preventive custody to be continued without responding to the submissions in which the accused set out the reasons why he felt that the said time had been exceeded.[37]

[31] Judgment of 26 Oct 1984, Series A No. 86.

[32] For example, Cass., 19 Dec 1984, J.T. 1985, p. 447, Cass., 23 Jan and 9 May 1985, Jur. Liège 1985, p. 157 and pp. 541–543, Cass., 5 Mar 1986, Rev. Dr. Pén., 1986, p. 622 and Cass., 9 Oct 1985, J.T., 1986, p. 59.

[33] Cass., 4 Feb 1997, Larcier Cassation, 1997, p. 179.

[34] Cass., 10 Feb 1988, Rev. Dr. Pén. Et crim., 1978, p. 681.

[35] Cass., 13 Oct 1993, Larcier cassation 1993, No. 965.

[36] Cass., 20 July 1992, Larcier cassation 1992, No. 733.

[37] Cass., 12 Aug 1991, Pas., 1991, I, p. 950.

In a judgment of 9 October 1991, the Supreme Court of Appeal found that neither the Preventive Custody Act of July 1990 nor even article 5, paragraph 4, of the Convention required that items in the case files be translated at the request of the detained accused before he appeared before the investigating authorities.[38]

As a departure from the confidential nature of investigations, the right to examine the case files prior to each appearance before the magistrates in the counsel chamber, for the purpose of determining whether custody is to continue, is justified on the part of the accused when this is necessary in order to enable any person deprived of his liberty to bring an appeal before the tribunal so that the latter can issue a ruling on the legality of the detention, as contemplated in article 5.4 of the Convention.[39]

Curiously, in the context of establishing an indictment, it was decided that the mere fact that Public Prosecutor should have a longer period than that required by the accused and by the latter's counsel in order to draw up the relevant defence, does not deprive the accused of the guarantee of a fair trial.[40]

Telephone conversations are included in the concepts of private life and correspondence, the observance of which is enshrined in article 8.1 of the Convention.[41] All measures adopted and taking the form of listening in to, or recording, telephone conversations must be authorized by a justified order issued by the examining magistrate, stating the serious reasons to support the view that there has been a violation for which the law permits such a measure.[42]

3. *Disciplinary regulations*

The application of article 6, paragraph 1, of the European Convention to disciplinary proceedings has brought lively developments to the decisions of the Supreme Court of Appeal.

In 1979, after long discounting the possibility of article 6 of the Convention being applied to disciplinary proceedings against civil servants,[43] veterinary surgeons,[44] doctors,[45] architects,[46] and lawyers,[47] the Supreme Court began to relax its position, stating that:

38 Cass., 9 Oct 1991, Pas., 1992, I, p. 111.
39 Arb. Court, 18 July 1991, Pas., 1991, I, p. 950.
40 Cass., combined chambers, 6 Feb 1996, Pas., 1996, I, p. 172.
41 Cass., 26 Jan 1993, Pas., 1993, I, p. 101.
42 Cass., 26 June 1996, Pas., 1996, I, p. 705.
43 EC judgment No 14066 of 17 Apr 1970.
44 Cass., 10 Mar 1972, Pas., 1972, I, p. 643.
45 For example, Cass., 3 May 1974, Pas., 1974, I, p. 910 and Cass., 10 Apr and 29 June 1979, Pas., 1979, I, pp. 973 and 1301.
46 Cass., 12 Sep 1974, Pas., 1975, I, p. 38.
47 Cass., 1 Dec 1977, Pas., 1978, I, p.362 and Cass., 8 Feb 1979, Pas., 1979, I, p. 676.

although all the provisions of Article 6, paragraph 1, of the European Convention do not apply to disciplinary proceedings, the rule which they contain, to the effect that the tribunal has to be independent and impartial, is also a general legal principle applicable to all courts.[48]

It took two judgments from the European Court of Human Rights[49] for the Court to agree, by means of judgments issued on 14 April 1983,[50] to apply article 6, paragraph 1, of the Convention and its guarantees to disciplinary proceedings.

Nevertheless, it had clear reservations: first, the dispute, or one of the subjects of dispute, had to relate to civil rights or obligations in respect of which the outcome of the disciplinary proceedings was decisive, and secondly, the body fully empowered to ensure the *de facto* and *de jure* control of the decisions of that disciplinary court had to comply with the demands of article 6, paragraph 1, of the Convention, as the Court stated in its judgment of 4 February 1993.[51]

Moreover, it was found on many occasions that compulsory membership of a professional body—a watchdog governed by public law which looks after the professional ethics, honour, and dignity of its members—and various obligations which such bodies impose on their members did not infringe the provisions of the Convention.[52]

In a case involving a magistrate who had spoken on the radio without the permission of the head of his professional organization, the Supreme Court of Appeal ruled[53] that disciplinary proceedings against members of the Bar Association were not designed to dispute civil rights and obligations within the meaning of article 6, paragraph 1, of the Convention. These proceedings were in fact concerned with rights and obligations attendant on non-contractual legal relationships, in public law, between the state and its organs. The Court also said here that article 6, paragraph 1, did not apply to pure matters of discipline if it was clear from the way in which the act complained of was described in national law, in terms of the nature of the act or the severity of the potential punishment, that there was no question of a criminal charge within the meaning of article 6(1) of the Convention.[54]

[48] Cass., 15 June 1979, Pas., 1979, I, p. 1193, Cass., 20 Sep 1979, Pas., 1980, I, p. 93, Cass., 14 Nov 1980, Pas., 1981, I, p. 317 and Cass., 30 Apr 1982, Pas., 1982, I, p. 993.

[49] Judgment of 23 June 1981, Series A No. 43 and decree of 10 Feb 1983, Series A, No. 58.

[50] Pas., 1983, I, pp. 866 and 902.

[51] Cass., 4 Feb 1993, Larcier cassation, 1993, No. 271.

[52] For example, Cass., 25 June 1974, Pas., 1974, I, p. 1114, Cass., 25 Apr 1975, Pas., 1975, I, p. 850, Cass., 31 Jan 1980, Pas., 1980, I, p. 619 and Cass., 15 Mar 1984, Pas., 1984, I, p. 836.

[53] Cass., 14 May 1987, RCJB, No 4, 1988, p. 528.

[54] A contrasting case is Cass., 15 June 1989, JT, 1990, pp. 593 & 594, in which the Court penalized the non-application of article 6(1) to disciplinary proceedings, because the offence could have been a criminal one.

When disciplinary measures are justified by a criminal judgment and an appeal against the latter is filed with the European Commission for Human Rights, the magistrate is not required to suspend the proceedings until the Commission has pronounced judgment on the appeal.[55]

In an interesting case involving a soldier and an official, and secret NATO decisions, it was ruled that a disciplinary measure introduced against someone who had refused to obey an order contrary to article 8 of the Convention, was a violation of this law and was thus illegal.[56]

4. *Civil and judicial law*

The Belgian Civil Code used to make a distinction between children born in and out of wedlock, particularly in matters of succession, and, as we know, the European Court found against Belgium for this in its *Marckx* and *Vermeire* judgments, issued on 13 June 1979 and 29 November 1991 respectively. Although the law has changed,[57] the Supreme Court of Appeal recently ruled that the old legislation applicable to cases of descent which began before the new law took effect (June 1987) was in breach of article 8, paragraphs 1 and 14, of the Convention, since it applied to cases of descent open since 13 June 1979 and it was therefore no longer possible to cut out the close family of a natural child who had died after that date.[58]

On 19 March 1992[59] the Supreme Court ruled that, in annulling a marriage in the light of properly submitted documents whereby it was able to deduce that it was a simulated union, the Court of Appeal was neither undermining the right to marry nor interfering in the private and family life of the parties (articles 8 and 12 of the Convention).

In a plenary hearing, the Supreme Court decided that the effect of the *res judicata* in criminal proceedings did not act as an obstacle to prevent one of the parties in subsequent civil proceedings from contesting the conclusions of the criminal proceedings, if it had not been party to the criminal proceedings, or if it had been unable to assert its rights.[60]

Also in a plenary hearing, the Supreme Court ruled that the guarantees enshrined in article 6 of the Convention must be observed in the performance of experts' inquiries.[61]

The monopoly, in terms of defence pleadings, granted to members of the Bar is not considered to affect the right to a fair trial (article 6.1 of the

[55] Cass., 18 Nov 1994, Rev. not., 1997, p. 180.
[56] Cons. d'Etat, 30 June 1995, Rev. Trim. Dr. H., 1996, p. 301.
[57] Law of 31 Mar 1987, Moniteur Belge 6 June 1987.
[58] Cass., 21 Oct 1993, Larcier cassation, 1993, No. 1003.
[59] Cass., 19 Mar 1992, Larcier cassation, 1992, No. 362.
[60] Cass., first ch., plen. hear., 2 Oct 1997, Larcier cassation, 1997, p. 312.
[61] Cass., 5 Apr 1996, Pas., 1996, I, p. 283.

Convention), since the Bar provides the free services of one of its members to persons unable to pay the fees of defence counsel.[62]

The right to respect for family life includes the right of each interested party to take part in judicial proceedings likely to have consequences for that party's family life.[63]

5. *Commercial, tax, and social security law*

Article 442 of the Belgian Commercial Code provides that bankruptcy may be declared on an *ex officio* basis, without the personal involvement of the bankrupt. Initially, the Supreme Court of Appeal refused to see *ex officio* bankruptcy as counter to the principle of a fair trial, because the third-party proceedings automatically enabled the bankrupt to oppose the judgment and raise a defence.[64]

In its judgment of 6 February 1987,[65] however, the Supreme Court decided that neither article 442 of the Bankruptcy Act nor any other provision allowed a debtor to be declared bankrupt at the request of a creditor, without the opportunity to be heard or to offer a defence in accordance with the general principle of the right to defence enshrined in article 6 of the Convention. The Court then extended its position on bankruptcy at the creditor's request to *ex officio* bankruptcy when it ruled that, in all but exceptionally urgent cases, the debtor should be heard in respect of his means before the *ex officio* bankruptcy declaration.[66]

With regard to tax law, the Belgian Supreme Court has always maintained that article 6, paragraph 1, of the Convention does not apply to disputes over rights and obligations in the tax field, except in cases which lead or could lead to punishment of criminal charges within the meaning of article 6.[67] However, in two judgments,[68] the Court said that some of the national legal provisions were not in breach of articles 8, 9(1), 12, and 18 of the Convention, thereby implicitly but certainly enshrining the fact that these provisions were, in principle, applicable in tax matters.

In the area of social security, the Supreme Court of Appeal[69] quashed a judgment by the Brussels Labour Tribunal whereby a worker was refused unemployment benefits because he had turned down a job on religious grounds. The Labour Tribunal, giving its decision after referral, found that

[62] Labour Court, Mons, 24 Feb 1995, Dr Quart Monde, 1996, p. 40.
[63] Arb. Court, 12 July 1996, No. 47/96, Rev. Trim. Dr. Fam. 1996, p. 604.
[64] Cass., 7 Mar 1986, Pas., I, No. 436.
[65] Cass., 6 Feb 1987, Pas., 1987, I, No. 337.
[66] Cass., 27 Apr 1989, Pas., 1989, I, No. 491.
[67] Cass., 23 Jan 1992, Larcier cassation, 1992, No. 50.
[68] Cass., 19 Nov 1981, Pas., 1982, I, p. 385 and Cass., 16 Feb 1984, Pas., 1984, I, p. 680.
[69] Cass., 12 Dec 1983, Pas., 1984, I, p. 406.

religious convictions could affect the suitability of a job, since both the Belgian Constitution and article 9 of the European Convention proclaimed freedom of thought, conscience, opinion, and religion.

6. Administrative law

The Council of State has always said that the demands of the Convention apply in its handling of administrative proceedings.

In many instances the Council of State has ruled that the provisions of article 1 of the first Protocol in no way affect the authority's right to lay down the limits of the right of ownership in the general interest and within the limits laid down by the law. Restrictions arising from a building permit,[70] a development plan,[71] or a sector plan,[72] for example, did not constitute expropriation within the meaning of the Convention.

In its decree of 12 July 1987[73] the Council of State decided that disciplinary action which might temporarily deprive someone in the civil service of various advantages which went with the job, or even of the job itself, did not constitute an attack on civil rights and obligations within the meaning of article 6, paragraph 1, of the Convention.

However serious the social and moral consequences might be, a measure which deprived a civil servant of his job, unlike one which debarred someone from the roll of his professional association, only deprived the person in question of his job and not of the right to carry out a profession.

The Council of State also found that article 6 of the Convention did not prevent an administrative authority from deciding to dispute civil rights and obligations, provided it was possible to appeal against the authority's decision before an independent and impartial tribunal. The legal protection offered by an appeal for annulment was in line with the demands of the Convention here.[74]

Finally, the Council of State decided that the European Convention on Human Rights did not guarantee the right of residence or asylum in a state to non-nationals. Under the Geneva Convention on the Status of Refugees, each state has a discretionary power to decide, on the basis of its own criteria, whether or not an applicant is a refugee.[75]

However, it was ruled that, taking into account actual circumstances, the execution of an order to deport an alien may be found to be contrary to article 8 of the Convention.[76]

[70] CS Judgment No. 16 388 of 30 Apr 1974, RACE, 1974, p. 435.
[71] CS Judgment No. 22 784 of 4 Jan 1984, RACE, 1983, p. 5.
[72] CS Judgments Nos. 22 800 and 22 801 of 4 Jan 1981, RACE, 1981, pp. 25 and 32.
[73] CS Judgment No. 31 567 of 12 July 1987, TBP, 1989, p. 608.
[74] CS Judgment No. 38 599 of 28 Jan 1992, RACE, 1992.
[75] CS Judgment No. 38 230 of 29 Nov 1991, RACE, 1991.
[76] CS Judgment Nos. 58 969 and 61 972 of 1 Apr and 25 Sep 1996.

7. Arbitration Court

Although we chose to approach Belgian jurisprudence in terms of the various branches of the law, we should still highlight the way in which the Arbitration Court—which has had the rank of constitutional court for some years now—has used the European Convention.[77]

Called on to pronounce judgment in many cases affecting the rights recognized by the Convention, since its creation in 1984, and particularly since the expansion of its jurisdiction in 1988, the Arbitration Court has always insisted on strict observance of the provisions of the Convention and of the interpretations given by the European Court of Human Rights. The present nature of this constitutional Court explains why it has incorporated the Convention and the jurisprudence of the European Court into its judgments.

Without wishing to engage in arguments about the nature of the various recourses and procedures which a constitutional court may involve, we should like to draw attention to the interesting judgment of 4 July 1991 and the previous order of 20 February 1991. Looking to article 6, paragraph 1, of the Convention, which enshrines the right to trial within a reasonable period, the Arbitration Court struck out one of the articles of the Special Arbitration Court Act of 6 January 1989, whereby proceedings before the Court were suspended on the death of one of the parties who had asked for a preliminary judgment.

With this 4 July judgment, the Court sanctioned a legal provision which was in breach of both article 14 of the Convention and two articles of the Belgian Constitution on the principle of equality.[78]

According to the jurisprudence of the European Court of Human Rights, article 6.1 of the Convention applies to a constitutional court. The latter is required to determine whether a dispute submitted to it has to do with rights and obligations of a civil nature, in accordance with article 6.1, or the validity of a charge in a criminal case brought against a party.[79]

The Arbitration Court has pronounced many judgments concerning the rights guaranteed by the Convention, and its jurisprudence has always been in accordance with that of the European Court: thus, in the areas of freedom of expression and limitations on the abuse of fundamental rights,[80] the

[77] See H. Simonart, 'La cour d'arbitrage et la Convention européenne des droits de l'homme' in *Mélanges Velu* (Brussels: Bruylant, 1990), p. 351 et seq., and J. Velu and R. Ergec, *La Convention européenne des droits de l'homme* (Bruxelles: Bruylant, 1990), p. 351 et seq.

[78] CA, 18/91, 4 July 1991 and, in particular, the order of 20 Feb 1991, which is an integral part of the judgment.

[79] Arb. Court, 17 Sep 1997, No. 55/97; 14 July 1997, Nos. 50/97, 51/97 and 52/97, CA Judgments, 1997, pp. 779, 805, 811, and 841.

[80] Arb. Court, Judgment of 12 July 1996, No. 45/96.

respect for private and family life,[81] the prohibition of torture and inhuman and degrading treatment,[82] and the right of ownership in cases of expropriation, etc.[83]

C. BELGIAN CASES BEFORE THE EUROPEAN COURT

Like other states, Belgium is a regular defendant in the organs of the European Convention on Human Rights.

We shall limit ourselves here to a brief look at the decisions of the European Court, without including the Commission's reports. There is no room for a complete study here and the Commission's main decisions have in fact led to Court proceedings.

Belgium had the unhappy privilege of being cited in the second and third cases which went before the European Court.

The *De Becker* case involved a former journalist found guilty of collaboration with the enemy during World War II. This resulted in the profession of journalist being closed to him, pursuant to one of the articles of the Criminal Code—which could be taken as denial of freedom of expression and therefore in breach of article 10 of the Convention. Since Belgian law seemed bound to be found wanting here, the Government got in first, righting the situation by removing the reprehensible article from the Criminal Code, so the Court was able to strike the case off the list.[84]

In the next case Belgium was not so lucky. Here the European Court found that an article in the Law of 2 August 1963 on the use of languages in administration was in breach of article 2 of the first Protocol, combined with article 14 of the Convention. Under this article, various children were prevented from attending French-speaking schools on the periphery of Brussels because of their parents' place of residence.[85] The Court made its first use of what was to become a common argument whereby it simply combined articles which, in isolation, were not considered to have been infringed, and thus revealed additional obligations for the states.

On 17 January 1970, in the *Delcourt* case,[86] the European Court found that involvement of the Public Prosecutor's department in the deliberations of the Supreme Court of Appeal was anomalous and even regrettable, but, in view

[81] Arb. Court, Judgment of 9 Jan 1996, No. 4/96 and 12 July 1996, No. 47/96.

[82] Arb. Court, Judgment of 24 June 1994.

[83] Arb. Court, Judgment of 22 Feb 1995, No. 51/95.

[84] Judgment of 27 Mar 1962, Series A No. 4.

[85] Judgment of 23 July 1968, Series A No. 6.

[86] Judgment of 17 Jan1970, Series A No. 11.

of the specific role of that Court, not in breach of article 6, paragraph 1 of the Convention. However, in an identical case 21 years later[87] it changed its opinion. This time, without really saying why, it decided that involvement of the Public Prosecutor's department in the deliberations of the Supreme Court judges was in conflict with article 6.[88] Once again the Court found Belgium guilty in the *Vermeulen* case,[89] and for the same reasons.

In 1971, the Court ruled that the 1891 Belgian Vagrancy Act was not in line with article 5, paragraph 4, of the Convention, because vagrants detained by the state were unable to go to court to appeal against the decisions to detain them.[90]

Some years later, a European Court judgment created a stir in Belgium. In their *Marckx* case decision,[91] the Strasbourg judges found that Belgian descent laws were in breach of the European Convention because they made a distinction between legitimate and illegitimate children, a difference which the Court maintained was no longer acceptable in 1979 because outlooks had changed.

In the *Deweer* case[92] the Court found that article 6, paragraph 1, had been infringed. The applicant had agreed to a transaction to avoid his firm being closed down following a price regulation infringement, which the Court found to be a constraint which had stood in the way of a fair trial.

The question as to whether doctors disciplined by the medical association should benefit from the guarantees provided by article 6, paragraph 1, received a positive answer from the Strasbourg Court in the *Le Compte, Van Leuven, and De Meyere* case.[93]

Although the European Court was very clear in its decision, the Belgian courts declined to espouse its interpretation, as we have already emphasized, and on 21 January 1982 the Supreme Court of Appeal, acting on the submissions of the Public Prosecutor Mr Dumon, again found that article 6 did not apply to disciplinary procedures within professional associations.[94] This ruling naturally provoked a strong, negative reaction in the legal profession.[95]

There was a similar reaction in Strasbourg when the European Court confirmed its attitude in the *Albert and Le Compte* case and insisted on article 6, paragraph 1, being applied to disciplinary procedures.[96]

[87] Judgment of 30 Oct 1991, Series A No. 214.

[88] See our critique: S. Marcus-Helmons, 'La présence du Ministère public aux déliberations de la Cour de cassation ou l'affaire Borgers' in *Mélanges Jacques Velu,* op. cit., 1992, pp. 1379–1390.

[89] *Vermeulen v Belgium*, Judgment of 20 Feb 1996, Rec. A. & D. 1996–I, p. 224.

[90] Judgment of 18 June 1971, Series A No. 12.

[91] Judgment of 13 June 1979, series A No. 31.

[92] Judgment of 27 Feb 1980, Series A No. 35.

[93] Judgment of 23 June 1981, Series A No. 43.

[94] The Court of Appeal issued two judgments of this sort on 21 Jan 1982.

[95] See, in particular, S. Marcus-Helmons, 'Observations sous cassation 21 janvier 1982', (1983) *Cahiers de droit européen* 247 et seq.

[96] Judgment of 10 Feb 1983, Series A No. 58.

Belgium was found guilty in other cases—*Van Droogenbroeck* and *Piersack*—taken to Strasbourg between these two European Court judgments.

In the *Van Droogenbroeck* case,[97] the Court found that article 5, paragraph 4, of the Convention had been infringed. This was because the applicant, deemed an habitual offender, had been sentenced to ten years' imprisonment under the Social Defence Act, and was thus detained on the orders of the Ministry of Justice, a procedure which denied him the right to have the conformity of this detention to the aims of the Social Defence Act 'decided speedily by a court', as laid down in article 5 of the Convention.

In the *Piersack* case[98] the Court found Belgium guilty of infringing article 6, paragraph 1, of the Convention because the applicant had been sentenced by a Court of Assizes, the president of which had previously been the Deputy Public Prosecutor and, as such, played a small part in the investigation of the applicant's case, thereby giving the applicant reasonable doubt as to his impartiality when presiding over the Assizes.

In 1984 the European Court found that article 6, paragraph 1, had been breached in the *De Cubber* case,[99] in which one of the three magistrates in a Criminal Court case had also acted as the investigating judge and, once again, the applicant was entitled to question the fairness of the hearing.

Another problem with professional associations cropped up in 1987, in the *H v Belgium* case, when the European Court decided that article 6(1) had been infringed because an application to re-register at the Bar had followed Bar Council proceedings which had not met the criteria required for a fair trial.[100]

Successive temporary terms of imprisonment which an applicant had suffered in accordance with the Belgian Youth Protection Act were found to be in breach of article 5, paragraphs 1 and 4, of the Convention.[101]

In the *Pauwels* case[102] the Court judgment criticized Belgian law for allowing a military official to both investigate and proceed against the applicant, a career officer. The legislation was declared to be in breach of article 5, paragraph 3, of the Convention.

In the *Lamy* case[103] Belgium was found to have infringed article 5, paragraph 4, because, when the applicant first appeared in chambers to have his arrest warrant confirmed, his lawyer had not been allowed to inspect the dossier.

[97] Judgment of 24 June 1982, Series A No. 50.
[98] Judgment of 1 Oct 1982, Series A No. 53.
[99] Judgment of 26 Oct 1984, Series A No. 86.
[100] Judgment of 30 Nov 1987, Series A No. 127.
[101] *Bouamar* case, Judgment of 29 Feb 1988, Series A No. 129.
[102] Judgment of 26 May 1988, Series A No. 135.
[103] Judgment of 30 Mar 1989, Series A No. 151.

In 1989 the European Court again concluded that Belgium had infringed article 6, paragraph 1, of the Convention because the applicant had been unable to meet the party claiming damages to discuss certain charges against him.[104]

Despite the many offences which a young Moroccan had committed throughout his youth in Belgium, the Belgian authorities' decision to send him alone back to the country of origin from which his parents had brought him at the age of two, was deemed to be in breach of article 8 of the Convention.[105]

Since Belgium still had some discrimination between illegitimate and legitimate children in its succession laws, it was found to be in breach again, in the *Vermeire* case in 1991, for infringement of article 8 of the Convention, combined with article 14,[106] as mentioned earlier. This resulted in the Belgian state being ordered to pay a very high sum on the basis of article 50 of the Convention.[107]

In *Clooth v Belgium*[108] in the same year, the national authorities were blamed for the excessive length of the provisional detention of the applicant, in breach of article 5, paragraph 3.

In the *Vidal v Belgium* case, article 6, paragraphs 1 and 3, was infringed because the applicant was not given a fair trial and was unable to have the defence witnesses heard.[109]

In June 1994 the European Court found Belgium guilty because the Bar Council had refused to allow the applicant to join the Bar Association and because that decision was taken in defiance of the guarantees provided by article 6, paragraph 1.[110] The arguments produced by the Belgian state were of a procedural nature, since the true reason, as recognized by the Court, lay in the fact that the plaintiff had already completed a full career in the Army before studying law and seeking registration with the Bar Council.

In a judgment of 20 November 1995[111] the Strasbourg Court pronounced an important judgment against Belgium. It found there had been a confiscation of property contrary to article 1 of Protocol No. 1, resulting from a law of 30 August 1988 which, without any compensation, retrospectively wiped out credits which the plaintiffs claimed against the Belgian state. These involved accidents involving large ships in the Escaut estuary, the said vessels

[104] *Bricmont* case, Judgment of 7 July 1989, Series A No. 158.
[105] *Moustaquim* case, Judgment of 18 Feb 1991, Series A No. 193.
[106] Judgment of 29 Nov 1991, Series A No. 214.
[107] *Vermeire v Belgium*, Judgment of 4 Oct 1993, Series A No. 270.
[108] Judgment of 12 Dec 1991, Series A No. 225.
[109] Judgment of 22 Apr 1992, Series A, No. 235.
[110] *De Moor* case, Judgment of 23 June 1994, Series A No. 292–A.
[111] *Pressos Compania Naviera SA et al. v Belgium*, Judgment of 20 Nov 1995, Series A No. 332.

being directed by pilots whose services were a statutory requirement imposed by the legislation in force before 17 September 1988. By way of application of article 50 of the Convention, a second judgment in the same case[112] ordered Belgium to pay several million Belgian francs to one of the plaintiff companies by way of compensation. In this connection it is interesting to note that the European judges have responded in the same way to the wiping out of a credit as they would to the violation of a right of ownership.

On 24 February 1997 the European Court ruled that there was a violation of article 10, relating to freedom of expression, on the ground that the Belgian courts had wrongly found a newspaper guilty for having reported facts about which the public had the right to be informed.[113]

Finally, in July 1998, the Strasbourg Court ruled that Belgium had failed to comply with both article 5.1 and article 6.1 in a case involving the psychiatric confinement of an individual.[114]

Belgium was found guilty in all the judgments which we have just outlined. However, in addition to the two above-mentioned judgments in which there was no conviction,[115] the country has also been involved in a dozen or so cases in which its legislation was not considered to infringe the articles of the European Convention on Human Rights.

Among the most interesting of these is the case of the Belgian National Policemen's Union,[116] in which the Court found that consultation of all unions was not mandatory under article 11 of the Convention, and the *Van Oosterwyck* case,[117] in which the Strasbourg judges found that the applicant, a transsexual, had not exhausted all the possibilities of appeal at national level.

In the *Van der Mussele* case[118] the Court found that article 4 of the Convention was not breached by the obligation for young lawyers to undergo a probationary period and in the *Mathieu-Mohin and Clerfayt* case[119] the same judges found that article 3 of the first additional Protocol, on free elections, was not breached by structures which aimed, in a very complex way, to establish linguistic peace in Belgium.

The *Muyldermans v Belgium* case was struck off the lists by the Strasbourg judges,[120] who found that the applicant had reached an agreement with the

[112] *Pressos Compania Naviera SA et al. v Belgium*, note 111 above (article 50).

[113] *De Haes and Gijsels v Belgium* case (1997) 25 EHRR 1.

[114] *Aerts v Belgium* (1998) IX Human Rights Case Digest 749.

[115] The *De Becker* Judgment of 27 Mar 1962, Series A No. 4 and the *Delcourt* Judgment of 17 Jan 1970, Series A No. 11.

[116] Judgment of 27 Oct 1975, Series A No. 19.

[117] Judgment of 6 Nov 1980, Series A No. 40.

[118] Judgment of 29 Sep 1982, Series A No. 70

[119] Judgment of 2 Mar 1987, Series A No. 113.

[120] Judgment of 23 Oct 1991, Series A No. 214.

Belgian Government and that a bill had been tabled which, once passed, would answer the Commission's criticism in this case.

In two cases in which applicants claimed that the 'reasonable time' had been exceeded, the European Court found the Belgian state wanting in its obligations under the Convention. In the first case, this was in respect of remand in custody,[121] and in the second, in respect of the length of the proceedings.[122]

Lastly, in contrast with its previous decisions, the European Court decided that article 6, paragraph 1, had not been infringed in special proceedings between the applicant and the Medical Association.[123]

On 7 August 1996 the Belgian state escaped being found guilty in a judgment which might otherwise have been pronounced on the basis of article 14, in conjunction with article 8. This case related to the expulsion of a Moroccan subject who was involved in the trafficking of large quantities of drugs; the expulsion was considered justified in light of paragraph 2 of article 8, despite the argument put forward that there had long been a family nucleus in Belgium.[124]

D. THE BELGIAN STATE'S RESPONSE TO BEING FOUND IN BREACH OF THE CONVENTION

Belgium is intent on maintaining its reputation as a state in which law prevails, and has always been careful to adopt the requisite solutions whenever the Strasbourg authorities have found it wanting in the commitments made when it joined the Convention.

The *De Becker* case is a good example. When, in the early 1960s, the problem of the former journalist (mentioned earlier) convicted for collaborating with the enemy during World War II was referred to the Court, Belgian public opinion was very concerned. The reaction in official circles and the press was particularly strong, because at that stage the European Court had only settled the *Lawless* case.[125]

At that time, it was considered to be an insult for a democratic state to be expected to defend itself before the European Court of Human Rights.

[121] *Kolompar* case, Judgment of 24 Sep 1992, Series A No. 235.

[122] *Boddaert* case, Judgment of 12 Oct 1992, Series A No. 235.

[123] *Debled* case, Judgment of 22 Sep 1994, Series A No. 292–B.

[124] *C v Belgium*, Judgment of 7 Aug 1996, Rec. A & D, 1996–III, p. 915.

[125] The three judgments in the *Lawless* case were the Judgment of 14 Nov 1960, Series A No. 1, the Judgment of 7 Apr 1961, Series A No. 2 and the Judgment of 1 July 1961, Series A No. 3.

Since it was certain that Belgium would be deemed guilty because its criminal legislation was in breach of article 10 of the Convention, on freedom of expression, the Ministry of Justice broke all records by getting both Houses of Parliament to pass a law repealing the article involved in the breach, namely article 123.6 of the Criminal Code.[126] The Government then quickly informed the European Court, two days before the first hearing. The Court found that the problem no longer existed and, since there was no reason to continue with the case on ground of public order, struck it off the lists.

By chance, Belgium was also involved in the next case referred to the Court, on various aspects of the linguistic system that prevails in Belgian education. This time the Belgian Government was unable to avoid the court case, or indeed being judged guilty, although it was in fact on only a fairly minor matter.

The reaction in Belgium was very different from that in the *De Becker* case. The question this time was a very delicate national issue: relations between the two main language communities and the new structure which the state had begun to set up with this in mind. In political circles, people were perplexed. Belgian Dutch speakers were indignant that an international court should condemn Belgian legislation which was the fruit of lengthy negotiations and a strong majority vote in Parliament. Belgian French speakers hoped for a great deal more from Strasbourg and were disappointed that, instead of rejecting all the Belgian legislation on language, the European Court decided that only one small article of that legislation violated the Convention.

We can see clearly, therefore, how difficult it is for the European Court to intervene in cases of a highly political nature. However, Belgium did its best to adhere to the judgment by passing the Law of 20 December 1970 and adding an article 6(a)[127] in the revision of the Constitution which followed the Court's judgment of 23 July 1968.

Belgium has always—albeit sometimes late in the day—stepped into line when the European Court has found it to be in breach of an article of the Convention.

Following the so-called vagrancy cases, a new law was passed on 6 August 1971, guaranteeing recourse to the courts for all vagrants detained by the Government.

Follow-up was more difficult in the *Marckx* case, where there was a judgment against the distinction made in Belgian law between legitimate and illegitimate children. Solving the problem meant reviewing the whole of the

[126] Law of 30 June 1961, Moniteur Belge, 1 July 1961.

[127] As the Belgian Constitution currently stands, this becomes article 11. It says that there shall be no discrimination in the enjoyment of the rights and freedoms granted to Belgians.

system of descent under Belgian law and amending a large number of articles in the Code, a task accomplished by the Law of 31 March 1987.[128]

The *Deweer* judgment of 27 January 1980 also acted as the impetus for a new law, the Law of 6 July 1983, amending the Economic Regulation and Price Act, whereby transactions were to be passed via a procedure which complied with the demands on hearings laid down in article 6, paragraph 1, of the Convention.

Decisions of the European Human Rights Court also led to the Belgian Remand in Custody Act of 20 July 1990.

Some of the legal practices ruled against in Strasbourg have been the spur for internal provisions designed to prevent a repetition of litigious situations.

Belgium has never shrunk from the problems of meeting its obligations. It has amended laws, on occasion, and it has altered practices. In the area of immigration, the delicate implications of which are now obvious, it respected the Court's decision.[129]

In a case involving the protection of young people and the powers of the juvenile judge[130] Belgium was faced with a problem of federal structure. The federal state, condemned in Strasbourg, was no longer competent to handle this matter, now the province of the federated units (the Regions and Communities) so the question was settled in accordance with the judgment via a decree issued by the French Community of Belgium in March 1991.

We have twice referred to the application of the provisions of article 6, paragraph 1, to disciplinary procedures in the General Medical Council, with respect to both the Pharmaceutical Council and the Bar Council. As already mentioned, the Belgian Supreme Court of Appeal did not give in immediately, but it did amend its decisions on 14 April 1983, under pressure from a new Public Prosecutor, and stepped into line with those of the European Court. Furthermore, the Law of 13 March 1985 on the publicizing of disciplinary procedures before the Medical Association and Pharmaceutical Association Councils incorporated the European Court's two *Le Compte* judgments into the national legislation.[131]

It must be pointed out that, in general terms, Belgium bows to the judgments of the European Court, and even accepts what can be unwelcome consequences!

One example of this, as mentioned above, is the involvement of the prosecuting authorities in the discussions of the Belgian Supreme Court of Appeal. Belgium's Supreme Court has a very specific function, being competent only

[128] Law amending certain legal provisions in respect of descent.
[129] *Moustaquim* case, Judgment of 18 Feb 1991, Series A No.195.
[130] *Bouamar* case, Judgment of 29 Feb 1988, Series A No.129.
[131] Judgment of 23 June 1981, Series A No.43 and Judgment of 10 Feb 1983, Series A No. 8.

in matters of law and procedure and not empowered to assess practical facts, which is why the European Court tolerated the Public Prosecutor's involvement in Supreme Court discussions the first time. However, in 1991 the European Court suddenly changed its mind, a volte-face in case-law for which there was virtually no justification.

However, the important factor here is the attitude of the Public Prosecutor, who was actually taking part in discussions in the Supreme Court, and who walked out of those discussions as soon as he heard news of the European Court's new judgment on the telephone.

However meritorious the manifestation of such respect may be, we find his gesture regrettable, for the Public Prosecutor's department has always greatly contributed to the Belgian Supreme Court's shaping of excellent case-law. It has been neither the ally nor the adversary of the parties who have appealed to the Court and it has never been more than a servant of the law.

CONCLUSIONS

Can one say that Belgium's ratification of the European Convention has affected the level of human rights protection in this country? We feel it is difficult to give a straight answer to such a blunt question.

Given that, for centuries, the Belgian provinces have had a wealthy bourgeoisie which has constantly demanded charters from its suzerains to guarantee basic freedoms, and given that the very liberal Belgian Constitution of 1831 was seen as an example in its day, it is tempting to say that the Convention has not made much difference to human rights in Belgium.

However, we believe this initial assessment should be qualified. First of all, let us remember something we stressed earlier, namely the Belgian authorities' concern to comply with the Convention whenever its organs have found the country wanting in the commitments assumed in connection with its ratification. This has improved the situation in most cases.

We do, though, have reservations in at least one case,[132] namely the withdrawal of the Public Prosecutor from the deliberations of the Supreme Court of Appeal, which represents a real loss, as we have already said. This shows that the European Court can also make mistakes.

In the vast majority of cases, however, intervention by the organs of the European Convention has had a beneficial effect on human rights in Belgium. Although Belgium respects human rights, as is the case in all truly democra-

[132] See note 70 above.

tic states, it is always a good idea to have some international monitoring of national legislation and practices.[133]

As we have said many times, our national courts, in all good faith, may well condone a situation which will then be found to be in breach of the European Convention by an international court. Lawyers from all over Europe could have a more objective view of some basic freedoms.[134] Seen from this perspective, the Convention obviously has had a positive effect on the protection of fundamental rights in all the countries which adhere to it.

But of all the benefits of the Convention, the greatest is undeniably its preventive effect.[135] The mere existence of the Convention and the states' desire to avoid too much criticism from Strasbourg have often had a restraining effect.

On at least two occasions we have seen the authorities make a real effort to head off a situation whereby an application would be made to the European Human Rights Commission—and we are not thinking here of the happy outcome of some friendly settlements, as provided for in article 28(b) of the Convention, but of problems which have been solved fairly and with proper respect for human dignity within the state itself, even before any application could be made to Strasbourg. We could probably multiply the two known cases by a factor of x to get an idea of the extent of the improvement in human rights in Belgium.

We shall end by stressing two points which we believe to be of particular importance as far as the scope of the Convention is concerned. One is a danger to be avoided and the other is a wish. The danger, we feel, lies in over-frequent, inappropriate reference to human rights in both legal proceedings and parliamentary work. The protection of fundamental rights should, as the adjective suggests, focus on freedoms which are really essential to the well-being of human dignity.

What we have in mind is not a general limitation of the application of human rights, as we shall make clear below, but the preservation of the essentials, so that if what is essential is combined with what is accessory, the whole concept is not devalued. Too many magistrates and leading figures from various circles, who cannot be suspected of base ulterior motives, claim to be tired of references to human rights being bandied about, to the point where any mention of this supreme value loses a great deal of its meaning.

[133] S. Marcus-Helmons, 'La protection des droits fondamentaux dans les perspectives internationale et fédérale' in *Québec—Communauté française de Belgique: Autonomie et spécificité dans le cadre d'un système fédéral* (Montreal: University of Sherbrooke, 1991), p. 107.

[134] Eg *Tyrer*, Judgment of 25 Apr 1978, Series A No. 26 (corporal punishment for young male delinquents on the Isle of Man).

[135] H. Rolin, 'Conclusions', in *La protection internationale des droits de l'homme dans le cadre européen* (Paris: Dalloz, 1961), p. 413.

Before referring to the European Convention, we believe that the 'users' should check whether they really are concerned about a fundamental right, and not quibbling over procedure or indulging in purely political tactics. This wish is sufficient indication of our desire to imbue the concept of human rights with extensive, dynamic value. The development of our society, the appearance of new economic factors, the development of science in every field, and other, sometimes unpredictable, factors may pose new threats to human dignity. An example of this is growing poverty, not just in the southern hemisphere, but also in the industrialized nations. Another is the ever-more frequent use of biotechnology and its indirect consequences. Yet another is the immense progress of medicine and biology and all the human sciences. Just how far can we go without threatening the basic essentials of human dignity?

It would be of value if one or two more human rights were added to those already adopted (for example on matters of social exclusion, or to prevent the abuse of biogenetics in medicine) unless we are going to rely on the extension or generalization of the teleological decisions previously taken by the European Court of Human Rights.[136] If the latter is the case, of course, there will be no proper result unless such teleological decisions are applied at both national and international level.[137]

[136] See S. Marcus-Helmons, 'De certains principles d'interpretation appliqués par les juridictions internationales' in *Liber Amicorum Professor O. De Raeymaeker* (Louvain University Press, 1977), pp. 141–162.

[137] To complete the present analysis, see also the fine work by J. Velu and R. Ergec, 'La Convention européenne . . .', op. cit., pp. 1–1145 (see n 77 above).

7

Bulgaria

ALEXANDER ARABADJIEV

A. INTRODUCTION

The European Convention for the Protection of Human Rights and Fundamental Freedoms ('ECHR' or 'the Convention') was signed by the Republic of Bulgaria on 7 May 1992, ratified, together with Protocol No. 1 thereof by the National Assembly (Parliament) on 31 July 1992, and entered into force with respect to the Republic of Bulgaria on 7 September 1992 (date of deposit of the instrument of ratification—Article 66, § 3 of the Convention).[1]

The Fourth and Seventh Protocols to the Convention were signed on 3 November 1993, and ratified on 12 October 2000.[2] The Sixth Protocol was signed on 7 May 1999 and entered into force for Bulgaria on 1 October 1999.

Pursuant to article 85, para. 1(6) of the Constitution of the Republic of Bulgaria which provides that 'the National Assembly shall ratify all international instruments concerning fundamental human rights', ratification is performed by an act of the National Assembly adopted in the form of a law.

The respective law, ie the instrument of ratification, adopted on 31 July 1992, contains a reservation in accordance with article 64 of the Convention in respect to the second provision of article 1 of the First Protocol as well as a declaration based on article 5 of the same Protocol in respect to the second provision of article 2 thereof. These read respectively as follows:

Reservation (*translation*):
The terms of the second provision of Article 1 of the Protocol shall not affect the scope or contents of Article 22, paragraph 1 of the Constitution of the Republic of Bulgaria, which states that: 'No foreign physical person or foreign legal entity shall acquire ownership over land, except through legal inheritance. Ownership thus acquired shall be duly transferred.'

[1] The Convention was promulgated (ie published in the State Gazette) on 2 Oct 1992 which, as will be seen below, concerns the issue of the Convention's incorporation into the domestic legal system and has no bearing on its entry into force.

[2] In force from 1 Feb 2001.

Declaration (*translation*):
The second provision of Article 2 of the Protocol must not be interpreted as imposing additional financial commitments on the State relating to educational establishments with a specific philosophical or religious orientation other than the commitments of the Bulgarian State provided for in the Constitution and in legislation in force in the country.[3]

Accession to the Convention coincides with membership of the Council of Europe (7 May 1992) whose Statute was ratified on 5 May 1992 and ratification of the Convention, with the adoption of declarations recognizing the right of individual petition (article 25) and the compulsory jurisdiction of the European Court of Human Rights (article 46).[4]

Both facts, whether regarded as separate or as closely connected, and in any event constituting parts of a process, could only occur as a result of political and legal developments in the country after November 1989. In terms of legal (constitutional) developments these include the June 1990 elections for a Grand National Assembly and the adoption of a new Constitution (12 July 1991—'the 1991 Constitution') by the Grand National Assembly recognizing the principles of the rule of law and declaring 'as the uppermost principle the rights, dignity and security of the individual' (Preamble of the Constitution). Prior to the changes which started in November 1989 the International Covenant on Civil and Political Rights (ICCPR) was ratified (1970) and published in the State Gazette (1976)—an act devoid of any real effect at that time as to the practical implementation of the rights and freedoms enshrined in the Covenant in view of the system then obtaining. Whereas Council of Europe membership was marked by political division of Europe throughout a period of over four decades, the collapse of the Communist system in Central and Eastern Europe and the end of the Cold War in the late eighties and early nineties added new dimensions to the all-European ambitions of this organization and the enforcement machinery created under the Convention. The radical democratic reforms carried out in Bulgaria opened the door to the Council of Europe and to the ECHR for this country. This considerable first step materializing Bulgaria's affiliation to the European structures was at the time an international recognition of the irreversibility of the democratic reforms accomplished in the country. It is also a stimulus for the successful progress thereof.

The adoption of the 1991 Constitution is in itself an act of acceptance of 'the principles of the rule of law and of the enjoyment by all persons . . . of human rights and fundamental freedoms' as required by article 3 of the

[3] All translations in the text are by the author.

[4] Unless otherwise stated all references are to the 'former' text of the Convention preceding its amendment by Protocol No. 11.

Statute of the Council of Europe. The importance of this fact (ie the adoption of the Constitution) is also highlighted in view of the situation with existing current legislation, which in its prevailing part consisted—in the period 1991–92—of laws, which preceded the Constitution and were apparently not in conformity with it.[5]

With a view to the subject of this presentation the following features of the Constitution must be underlined.

The Constitution contains a separate chapter establishing fundamental rights (and obligations) of citizens (Chapter Two).[6] On the whole, the constitutional rights catalogue embraces the major civil rights of the 'Universal Bill of Rights' and the substantive guarantees of the European Convention on Human Rights. There are common features and connections between the 'rights' provisions of the Constitution and the respective articles of the Convention. Some of these are formal; the constitutional provisions having been construed in identical form. Despite great similarities in the formulation, however, the normative scope of the Constitution's catalogue is, on the whole, wider, being at the same time an overambitious mixture of liberal and social and economical rights and, on the other hand, failing to provide for an effective review mechanism. (Pursuant to article 57, para. 3 of the Constitution non-derogable 'following a proclamation of war, martial law or a state of emergency' are the provisions establishing the right to life, the prohibition of torture or of cruel, inhuman, or degrading treatment or of forcible assimilation, the presumption of innocence, prohibition of conviction solely on the basis of a confession, the right to privacy, and the freedom of conscience, freedom of thought, and the right to freedom of religion.)

The provisions of the Constitution are directly applicable (article 5, para. 2).

Under article 5, para. 4 of the Constitution:

> any international instruments which have been ratified by the constitutionally established procedure, promulgated and come into force with respect to the Republic of Bulgaria, shall be considered part of the domestic legislation of the country. They shall supersede any domestic legislation stipulating otherwise.

The Constitution proclaims the independence of the judiciary and provides for a number of institutional guarantees in this respect (Chapter Six), 'the safeguard of the rights and legitimate interests of individuals and legal entities' being the constitutional definition of the function of the judicial branch (article 117, para. 1).

[5] Under the transitional provision of Clause 3 para. 1 of the Constitution 'the provisions of the existing laws shall be applicable insofar as they do not contravene the Constitution'.

[6] The exact title of this chapter reads 'Fundamental rights and obligations of citizens'.

The Constitution establishes a Constitutional Court (Chapter Eight), one of the functions of this Court being to:

rule on the compatibility between the Constitution and the international instruments concluded by the Republic of Bulgaria prior to their ratification,[7] and on the compatibility of domestic laws with the universally recognized norms of international law and the international instruments to which Bulgaria is a party (article 149, para. 1, subpara. 4).

As further presentation will show, it is primarily in the jurisprudence of the Constitutional Court that the ECHR and the case-law of the Convention organs have been applied. All the cases briefly reviewed below are evidence of the increasing importance attached to the European Convention on Human Rights as the codification standards of rights protection.

The importance of the Convention, however, had manifested itself already in the period of drafting the 1991 Constitution. As parliamentary journals demonstrate, the constitutional legislator was influenced by the Convention as well as by the International Covenant of Civil and Political Rights, especially while drafting the 'bill of rights' chapter. This is also the case with the Constitutional Court which referred to the Convention already in judgments of 21 April and 11 June 1992,[8] ie before its ratification, for the purposes of interpretation of the respective constitutional provisions. This is a major aspect of the influence of the Convention, which will be further discussed below. A preliminary observation is that neither the adoption of the Constitution nor the fact of becoming a party to the Convention, while both laying the foundations of a process of transformation of the legal system, can be regarded as leading to a definite situation since this process itself is still underway. On one hand, the conformity of domestic legislation with the Convention at the time of joining it may hardly be seen as certain, and even less so as permanently acquired at any particular moment. On the other hand, the 'reception' of the Convention, apart from its formal aspects and looked at with a view to the Convention's position, could only stand at the beginning of the process of legal reform both in terms of legislative transformation and transformation of attitudes, thus furthering the accomplishment of one of the

[7] This function has been exercised only once, with respect to the Framework Convention for the Protection of Minorities.

[8] The second of these judgments deals with the constitutional right to freedom of conscience, freedom of thought, and the choice of religion and of religious or atheistic views. The judgment contains a conclusion in the sense that the constitutional provision laying down the conditions upon which the state might legitimately interfere with the enjoyment of those rights nearly reproduces article 9, para. 2 of the Convention. This is a judgment delivered pursuant to the Constitutional Court's function under article 149, para. 1, subpara. 1 of the Constitution to provide binding interpretations of the Constitution.

Convention's main objectives: to influence legislative, judicial, and regulatory developments in the sphere of the protection of human rights.

B. THE STATUS OF THE CONVENTION IN NATIONAL LAW

As mentioned above, pursuant to article 5, para. 4 of the Bulgarian Constitution any international instrument which has been ratified by the constitutionally established procedure, promulgated, and entered into force with respect to the Republic of Bulgaria, shall be considered part of the domestic legislation of the country and shall supersede any domestic legislation stipulating otherwise. These constitutional requirements have been completely fulfilled with regard to the European Convention on Human Rights with the effect of the Convention's incorporation into the national legal system.

It is generally held that the Constitution provides for a direct ('automatic') incorporation of the Convention into domestic law. Without getting into theoretical analysis and discussion of the different doctrinal views as to the relationship between public international law and national law, largely discussed under the headings of 'dualism' and 'monism', it should be pointed out that the Constitution itself does not take any dogmatic position in this respect and that it is widely accepted that the Constitution, by virtue of its article 5, para. 4, ensures the direct incorporation of international conventions into the domestic legal system and the supremacy thereof over domestic legislation. As the Constitutional Court held in a judgment of 2 July 1992 on the interpretation of article 5, para. 4 of the Constitution, where an international treaty meets the requirements set out in this provision, ie that a treaty be ratified, promulgated, and come into force, it shall constitute part of the domestic legal system and legal rules contained therein shall become a source of legal rights and obligations for the subjects of domestic law. If these conditions are met, article 5, para. 4 of the Constitution provides for a further effect enshrining the paramountcy of international conventions over domestic legal rules; the international convention is given a 'supra-legislative' legal effect which allows it to supersede national laws and rules.

Set out exactly in the broad terms reproduced here, the same judgment rules also, apart from the issue of a convention's position in the hierarchy of norms in relation to 'ordinary' legislation (including delegated legislation) on the question of the relationship between an international convention and the Constitution itself. The Constitutional Court has put it in the following terms:

The norms of international treaties that have been incorporated should not, however, contravene the Constitution. This conclusion flows from the interpretation of Article 5, paras. 2 and 4 in conjunction with Article 85, para. 3 and Article 149, para. 4 of the Constitution.[9]

It follows from this ruling of the Constitutional Court that the ECHR is afforded an intermediate position within the national legal system that places it 'under' the basic law of the country and 'above' conflicting domestic laws.

The Constitutional Court later developed an even more radical approach with regard to the issue of the position of the European Convention on Human Rights in the national legal system. In a judgment of 18 February 1998 ruling on the compatibility of the Framework Convention for the Protection of National Minorities with the Constitution this Court stated, *inter alia*, the following:

The Court takes into account that in the area of human rights the norms of the ECHR possess an all-European and an all-civilization significance for the legal order of the States Parties to the ECHR and that these are norms of the European public order. The interpretation of the relevant constitutional provisions in the area of human rights should, therefore, be in conformity to the highest possible degree with the interpretation of the provisions of the ECHR. This principle of ('conformable') interpretation corresponds also to the internationally recognized by Bulgaria compulsory jurisdiction of the European Court of Human Rights on the interpretation and application of the ECHR.

This statement reflects a well established approach, adopted by the Constitutional Court, of referring to the Convention by way of 'testing' the Constitution when interpreting it by juxtaposing it to the Convention. In this respect and following this line the Constitutional Court has on a number of occasions stated that particular constitutional provisions conform with their Convention counterparts or correspond thereto, being fully in line with them or providing similarly (eg a finding to the effect that articles 39–41 of the Constitution which in their entirety enshrine the right to freedom of expression and information correspond to article 10 of the Convention and their interpretation may be carried out also by way of comparing them with that Convention article;[10] a finding that the restrictions to the right of freedom of association established in article 44, para. 2 of the Constitution correspond to those contained in article11, para. 2 of the Convention;[11] a similar finding as to article 37, para. 2 of the Constitution compared to article 9, para. 2 of the Convention.[12]

[9] Article 85, para. 3 of the Constitution reads: 'The conclusion of an international treaty requiring an amendment to the Constitution shall be preceded by the passage of such an amendment'.

[10] Judgment of 4 June 1996.

[11] In the above-mentioned judgment of 18 February 1998.

[12] Ibid.

At the same time it should be noted that the Constitutional Court has never been called upon to rule on the question of a possible incompatibility between the Constitution and the Convention. While the compatibility of the Convention with the Constitution was not called into question at the relevant time ('prior to ratification') the existence of a contradiction between them—especially in cases in which both have been invoked—may not be ruled out. A similar situation may arise in cases in which the Constitutional Court has to rule simultaneously on a challenge to the constitutionality of a law as well as on a request to establish the incompatibility of that law with the Convention. As the case-law of the Constitutional Court already referred to clearly demonstrates, and as further analysis will show, an approach combining arguments drawn from both acts and according equal significance to the constitutional and Convention provisions, both sets of norms operating in parallel and jointly, prevails at present. It may be concluded on this point, therefore, that while the supposition of a possible contradiction between the Convention and the Constitution is not inconceivable especially on the basis of a strict scrutiny of the relevant articles providing for an interference with the respective rights—such a situation is unlikely to occur as long as the Constitutional Court stands by its own opinion of 'conformable' (with the Convention) interpretation of the constitutional provisions stated in its judgment of 18 February 1998.

A further generally held view, which has not yet received adjudication on the part of the Constitutional Court, concerns the practical aspects of the direct applicability of the Convention provisions. It clearly follows from the Constitutional Court's judgment of 2 July 1992 that the Convention has a direct effect on the subjects of domestic law. It is generally maintained in the legal doctrine on the basis of a number of Constitutional Court judgments that the Court has taken the view of the Convention guarantee, or the relevant article, as being self-executing.[13] What this judgment has failed to elucidate for the purpose of furthering the implementation of international

[13] In a different part of the same judgment the Court impliedly determined the nature of provisions that may be regarded as self-executing by pointing out in relation to the Convention against Torture and Other Cruel, Inhuman, or Degrading Treatment or Punishment and with regard to international criminal law provisions that the latter have no direct effect in national law and become part of it insofar as they may serve the purpose of elucidating the meaning of criminal law norms in force in the country and create an obligation for amendments to the legislation. Significantly, in a judgment of 21 Nov 1997, when reviewing the constitutionality of an amendment to the Penal Code substantially redefining the concept of 'justifiable self-defence' the Constitutional Court seemed to regard the provision of article 2, para. 2(a) of the Convention as self-executing in the sense of being subject to direct application in the absence of a likewise provision in the Penal Code. The Court, basing itself on article 5, para. 4 of the Bulgarian Constitution, appears to have confused the issue of incorporation and self-execution with a situation in which the taking of a life by the state is justified under the Convention.

instruments in the field of human rights is the possibility of rules contained in such instruments being directly invoked as legal rules in the domestic legal system, with the legal consequence of suspending conflicting domestic laws which are rendered inapplicable. A statement to this effect, even in the form of an *obiter*, provided that the subject-matter of the case did not necessitate a separate ruling, would have well served the purpose of 'reception' of the Convention on the part of the authorities that have the duty to apply the Convention in their legislative, administrative, or judicial activities.

C. THE STATUS OF THE CONVENTION IN PARLIAMENTARY PROCEEDINGS

The low, or in any event the undoubtedly unsatisfactory degree of 'reception' of the Convention, in the sense of the extent to which the Convention is referred to or generally applied by the national authorities as a whole, is an observation made for the purposes of this chapter without, of course, it being comprehensive. Notwithstanding this general ascertainment, however, some positive events are worth noting. These demonstrate the 'programmatic' significance accorded to the Convention, the latter having been used as a source of inspiration and authority as well as having proved instrumental for certain developments.

As regards the status of the Convention in parliamentary proceedings, it is in the course of parliamentary debate that the Convention is primarily referred to. The rules adopted and followed by the Council of Ministers in the process of drafting new legislation include an expert assessment of bills as to their compatibility with international instruments to which Bulgaria is a party.

As to the legislative process as such, it is a tradition in the consecutive legislatures of the Bulgarian National Assembly (Parliament) to establish a standing committee ('permanent committee' or 'parliamentary commission') dealing with issues of human rights (the current one is operating under the title 'On Human Rights and Religious Denominations and on Complaints and Petitions of Citizens'). Following the internal rules adopted by the National Assembly, this committee is supposed to act as a 'leading committee' and play a decisive role when legislation with human rights implications is being drafted and adopted. Admittedly its function is also to carry out a general 'screening' of draft legislative acts introduced in Parliament for the purpose of identifying whether those affect or raise human rights issues and whether the relevant provisions of the Constitution and of the international treaties, including the ECHR, in this area have been complied with. The committee may exercise parliamentary control in the respective area on behalf of the National Assembly.

The following significant events may be regarded as having been directly influenced by the Convention (and judgments of the European Court of Human Rights delivered against Bulgaria).

—The adoption of a law (October 1998) introducing 'service instead of compulsory military service' for conscientious objectors (known in Bulgaria under the title 'alternative military service' which is included in the name of the act: the Substitution of Military Obligations by Alternative Service Act). Under article 3 of that law all male Bulgarian citizens subject to conscription shall be entitled to request commutation of their military obligations to alternative service ('substitution of military obligations with alternative service' in the wording of article 59 para. 2 of the Constitution pursuant to which that law was adopted) on the grounds of their constitutional rights of freedom of conscience, freedom of thought, and freedom of religion. Those who opt to substitute their military obligations with alternative civilian service have to serve twice as long as those in the regular military service.

—Introducing into the Code of Civil Procedure (December 1997) and into the Code of Criminal Procedure (February 1998) as a ground for reopening a civil or criminal case respectively and for quashing a decision that has entered into force, the finding of a violation of the Convention by a judgment of the European Court of Human Rights thus giving the judgment direct effect in the national system. It is not quite clear yet, however, how these procedural mechanisms will operate in the respective areas, the more so as a violation of the Convention is alluded to in both procedural codes as a ground for reopening a case but it is a requirement under the Code of Criminal Procedure only that the violation should have been material ('of vital significance') for deciding the case, ie for a conviction.

—Following a serious public debate and a parliamentary discussion the Council of Ministers (Government) introduced a bill aimed at regulating the issue of criminal liability of representatives of the media for insult and libel in conformity with the relevant constitutional provisions and article 10 of the Convention (February 1999). The draft is based on the idea of finding a balance between the state's obligations to guarantee the dignity and rights of the individual (by means of establishing criminal responsibility for the offences of insult and libel) as well as the right to freedom of expression. It is proposed that the punishment of 'imprisonment' for these two offences be abolished and replaced with a fine the size of which would be significantly increased amounting in some cases to considerable sums. Another important aspect of the proposed amendments removes the existing discriminatory distinction between 'publicly' and 'privately' prosecuted offences providing for *ex officio* criminal proceedings and the use of the state resources for criminal prosecution in cases of libel against a 'public official' in contrast to libel cases against 'private' persons where criminal proceedings are instituted on the initiative of the person concerned. According to the bill, criminal proceedings in the case of both offences may be instituted only after a request of the victim. Significantly, these proposals are based on a judgment of the Constitutional Court of 14 July 1998 which rejected a request to the effect, which the bill seeks, to a large extent to achieve.

—The abolition of the death penalty and its replacement by life imprisonment (on 10 December 1998, the date of the adoption of the *Universal Declaration of Human Rights*) by repealing the relevant parts of the articles of the Criminal Code providing for capital punishment, thus bringing about a situation in which Bulgaria discharged its 'obligation' under article 1 of Protocol No. 6 without being a party to that Protocol having not signed it, when the death penalty was abolished. In the course of parliamentary discussion article 2 of Protocol No. 6 was referred to in support of the idea of limiting the abolition to peacetime and making a provision for the death penalty in time of war—a proposal which was not accepted. At the same time providing for a form of life sentence which precludes commutation into a fixed term of imprisonment (or release on licence) which apparently was the 'price' paid by the champions of the abolition is open to criticism and might in itself raise issues under the Convention. There exists an awareness of the problems that may arise in the course of execution of this type of punishment (imprisonment) and those are expected to be resolved by introducing the necessary amendments to the Law on the Execution of Sentences. In any event the total abolition of capital punishment demonstrates the existence of a positive will within circles of parliamentarians who initiated it, grouped on a non-political, multi-party basis. A further and attendant effect following the abolition of the death penalty is that the death sentences of persons on whose execution the Grand National Assembly imposed a moratorium in the summer of 1990 were subsequently commuted. This put an end to a situation giving rise to issues under articles 3 and 5 of the Convention and resulting in applications to Strasbourg.

A bill adopted by the Council of Ministers in February 1999 (which passed into law in July 1999; in force as from 1 Jan 2000) on the amendment of the Code of Criminal Procedure should be added to the list of important events directly influenced by the Convention and demonstrating its status in the legislative process. The aim of bringing the Code of Criminal Procedure into conformity with the European Convention on Human Rights and the case-law of the European Court of Human Rights has been expressly stated in the reasons backing the proposed amendments adduced by the Government. The draft seeks to take into account to the highest possible extent articles 5, 6, and 8 of the Convention when regulating the issues concerning the right to liberty and security of the person (arrest and detention), *habeas corpus* proceedings, fair trial, and respect for private life, home, and correspondence in criminal proceedings.

D. LEADING HUMAN RIGHTS CASES DECIDED BY THE NATIONAL COURTS

While the question as to the current status of the Convention in parliamentary proceedings may hardly be considered as being permanent, at least for the reason that the process of general legal reform in the country is still in progress, notwithstanding the above-listed acts of Parliament (and Government) which clearly indicate the Convention 'presence' in these forms of public debate and action, it is inexplicable that the courts in the country are reluctant to apply the Convention in cases in which Convention issues have been raised before them. In the light of this last remark, which warrants further attention and discussion, it is difficult to speak of and to single out any leading human rights cases decided by the national courts.

Regard being had to the characteristics and specific functions of the Constitutional Court,[14] it is exclusively this court that has delivered significant decisions in the area of human rights and in particular on matters involving direct interpretation and application of the Convention.

In addition to what has already been noted with respect to the Constitutional Court's contribution to getting the Convention into the public sphere by referring to it prior to its ratification by Bulgaria and by establishing its status *vis-à-vis* the Constitution (see B above) this Court's case-law relating to the subject of this survey merits a more extensive presentation since it constitutes the main body of jurisprudence in the area under consideration.

In two of its judgments—the above-mentioned judgment of 18 February 1998 as well as an earlier one dated 4 June 1996—the Constitutional Court has used the case-law of the European Court of Human Rights as a source of reference when interpreting the national Constitution on the basis of a juxtaposition (or with a view to its conformity with) the Convention. The judgment of 4 June 1996 even reproduces in full a frequently reiterated statement of the European Court: 'freedom of expression constitutes one of the essential foundations of a democratic society and that the safeguards to be afforded to the press are of particular importance . . .' (as summarized in for instance the *Jerslid v Denmark* judgment of 23 September 1994, Series A no. 298, p. 23, § 31). A later judgment of the Constitutional Court ruling on the constitutionality of a law on professional association of medical practitioners (of 11 November 1998) is entirely based on a judgment of the European Court.[15] What is at issue with regard to the judgments considered under this point is that both of them stop short of explicitly stating that the case-law of the European Court itself is subject to incorporation into the domestic legal system.

[14] The Bulgarian Constitution makes no provision for an individual constitutional complaint. Under article 150, para. 1 'the Constitutional Court shall act on an initiative from not fewer than one-fifth of all Members of the National Assembly, the President, the Council of Ministers, the Supreme Court of Cassation, the Supreme Administrative Court or the Chief Prosecutor'. The Court ruled on the constitutionality of laws and their compatibility with international treaties *in abstracto* and not on allegations of an individual's rights violations.

[15] The *Le Compte, Van Leuven and De Meyere*, Judgment of 23 June 1981, Series A No. 43.

In the absence of an express statement to that effect it would be a matter of speculation to determine the case-law status regardless of the fact that in practice it is being invoked and taken account of both in the form of direct reference and as a source of argument.

As regards the Convention itself, it is referred to in Constitutional Court judgments on an equal basis with the Constitution.

In this respect the impact of the Convention and of relevant Strasbourg pronouncements is manifested by both being granted a significance of persuasive authority. The Constitutional Court has thus taken a bold attitude on the relevance of the ECHR when interpreting the Bulgarian Constitution, applying Convention standards in conjunction with constitutional rights whenever these human rights guarantees converge. This standard-setting function of the Convention in a legal order with a not yet fully developed human rights regime has proven to be of crucial importance in the process of imposing the constitutional guarantees. In a series of judgments examining the compatibility of particular statutes with the Constitution where a violation of a specific constitutional guarantee is involved the Court has adduced the corresponding Convention provision for the purpose of reinforcing and corroborating its reasoning when interpreting and applying the respective constitutional guarantee, even in cases in which compatibility with the Convention is not at issue. Provided that it is the function of this Court to examine possible norm conflicts between the European Convention on Human Rights and domestic legislation which may be exercised when the matter is referred to the Court by those authorized to approach it (article 150, para. 1 of the Constitution), the Court's tendency to rely on the Convention and base its argument on it has greatly enhanced the internal realization of the Convention and of human rights standards generally.

The underlying philosophy is that the provisions of the ECHR constitute norms of the European *public order* and that the interpretation of the constitutional provisions in the area of human rights should correspond to the interpretation of the Convention provisions containing the substantive guarantee, the latter have been accepted as standards of programmatic intent when interpreting and applying their constitutional counterparts. Thus, they have been applied even when, as mentioned above, compatibility with the Convention did not constitute part of the subject-matter of a case, serving as 'model solutions' or interpretative guidelines, a frequently applied formula being a statement to the effect that a conclusion reached on the basis of a constitutional text ensues also from the content of a respective article of the Convention.

This approach, which departs from the strict scheme of interrelation between Constitution and Convention described above, confers on the

Convention the significance of an authority of a 'higher instance' which goes beyond the usual convergence and complimentarity observed in the field of human rights guarantees at international and national levels.

A closer analysis of this level of application of the Convention on the part of the Constitutional Court in Bulgaria should, however, take account of the fact[16] that the Court is only empowered to provide binding interpretations of the Constitution and review the constitutionality and/or compatibility with the Convention *in abstracto*. In the absence of an individual constitutional complaint and lacking the function to review decisions of regular courts and administrative bodies if a violation of a specific right is alleged and complained of, it is primarily the standard-setting influence of the Convention that the Constitutional Court reflects in its judgments. This enables the Court to make general observations establishing that the Convention guarantees have been taken into consideration in the Constitution rights catalogue or the existence of great similarities in the formulation of basic rights at both levels. This is presumably also the reason for the steadily concurring pronouncements of the Court when seized with requests to rule on both the constitutionality and the conformity with the Convention of a particular law,[17] apart from the already emphasized issue of the general impact of the Convention.

The great similarities in the formulation of basic rights established by the Constitutional Court have, however, on some occasions blurred the marked differences of application, implementation, and general effect. In a judgment of 18 February 1997 dealing with judicial control over administrative acts, for example, the Court ruled unconstitutional the provisions of a particular act according to which the layoffs in the state-owned railway system were not subject to judicial control and, additionally, that the same provisions were not in conformity with article 6, para. 1 of the Convention. As to the applicability of the Convention article it may be inferred from the reasoning of the judgment that the Court limited its application by employing the notion of 'civil rights in the constitutional sense' which appears to be also the basis of the ruling on compatibility with the Constitution. Though the same result might eventually have been achieved, the restrictive approach adopted by the Court in reading article 6, para. 1 of the Convention was not based on the autonomous Convention meaning of civil rights but on the concept elaborated in its own case-law for the purposes of outlining the scope of judicial

[16] See n 15 above.

[17] When the Court is seized to rule simultaneously on the constitutionality and compatibility with the Convention of a law it is the normal practice for it to pass a judgment on both issues. On rare occasions the Court has declined to rule on the issue of compatibility with the Convention after having declared a particular provision unconstitutional with the effect of a similar finding being that the provision in question ceases to apply thus rendering the attendant subject-matter (of compatibility with the Convention) non-existent.

control over administrative acts in the sense that claims concerning constitutionally established rights only fall within that ambit of judicial determination. Neither did the Court examine the question of applicability of article 6, para. 1 of the Convention with respect to disputes concerning employment in the public sector. Given that the national legislation did not at that time[18] make the basic distinction between civil servants and employees subject to private law the Court failed to address the question, otherwise not presented before it, whether disputes relating to the termination of the career of a person employed in the public sector concerned a civil right within the meaning of article 6 of the Convention.[19] The field of application of article 6 was thus expanded and was even held to imply, in conjunction with article 13 of the Convention, the 'right to defence whenever an individual's rights or legitimate interests are violated or endangered' (article 56 of the Constitution) provided, however, that constitutionally established rights are concerned. (Article 56 of the Constitution, taken on its own, may be considered, along with the procedural safeguards contained therein, as the constitutional counterpart of article 13 of the Convention with respect to constitutionally enshrined rights.)

By contrast, on a number of occasions, when examining conformity with the Convention of particular statutes in the context of articles 9–11 of the Convention, for example, the Court has relied on a broad outline of the respective second paragraphs in which the conditions upon which the state might legitimately interfere with the enjoyment of those rights are laid down, frequently satisfying itself with a reference in a declaratory form to the Convention provision as containing an internationally established principle (judgment of 22 September 1997). This approach has led the Court to conclusions of a rather general and obviously imprecise character, such as the statement that article 10, para. 2 of the Convention explicitly provides for the preservation of 'public and state interests of a higher value' as a legitimate reason for interference with the freedom to receive information without specifying any of the public interest purposes listed in the same paragraph (judgment of 10 July 1995). This same approach has prevented the Court from carefully considering the protection of the 'reputation of an institution' as not falling within the list of justifiable interference with the freedom of expression (judgment of 9 July 1998) or from recognizing that, though being construed in identical form, article 37 of the Constitution of Bulgaria (freedom of con-

[18] The Civil Servants Act was only adopted in June 1999.

[19] In a judgment of 30 Apr 1998 where the application of article 6 of the Convention was not at issue the Constitutional Court employed the notion of 'political figure' for the purpose of determining the scope of judicial control leaving disputes over termination of careers of a certain level of civil servants considered to be 'political figures' outside the field of application of such control.

science, freedom of thought, and choice of religion and of religious or atheistic views) is not identical in its contents to its Convention counterpart (article 9) so far as justifiable interference is concerned: article 9, para. 2 of the Convention does not cover the purpose of protection of national security (judgment of 11 June 1992).

While the above observations may be correct in the light of the abstract manner in which the Constitutional Court exercises its functions of review of legislative acts, the Court not being empowered to deal with violations of specific rights (in the judgment of 9 July 1998 the Court held that the issue of the exact scope of permissible interference with the freedom of expression was to be determined on the facts of each case by the regular courts applying the law) these should not lead to an underestimation of the Court's contribution in expounding and establishing some basic rights under both the Constitution and the Convention.

Already before the Convention's entry into force with respect to Bulgaria, but heavily relying on the Convention, the Court, as mentioned above, seriously influenced the general legislative framework guaranteeing the right to freedom of thought, conscience, religion, or belief by declaring unconstitutional a number of provisions of the outdated Denominations Act (judgment of 11 June 1992).[20]

In the judgment of 4 June 1996, mentioned above, when interpreting articles 39–41 of the Constitution which, taken as a whole, correspond to article 10 of the Convention, the Constitutional Court wholly relied on the Convention and the case-law of the European Court of Human Rights making the best use of both as an 'interpretative instrument' in revealing the contents of the relevant constitutional provisions. It is in this judgment that the Court introduced the method of interpretation of the Constitution whereby the latter is compared to the Convention and took a view on the relevance of the European Court case-law (both further elaborated in the judgment of 18 February 1988, see above). This judgment which reflects the fundamental importance attached to freedom of expression, particularly freedom of the press, effectively served later as the basis for drafting and reviewing (judgment of 14 November 1996) media legislation.

Though occasionally inconsistent and imprecise (especially when referring to and applying article 6, para. 1 of the Convention) the Constitutional Court has considerably contributed to imposing and expanding judicial control over administrative acts, thus being conducive to the development of remedies in the national legal system within the meaning of article 13 of the Convention.

[20] Notwithstanding this judgment the outdated Denominations Act as well as article 133a of the Persons and Family Act considered to be discriminatory with respect to religious associations continue to be in force.

Notwithstanding the existence of this remedy, it does not always satisfy the requirement of remedial effectiveness even in cases in which the national authorities are in a position to grant a remedy. This may be partly explained by the above-noted continuing reluctance on the part of judicial and administrative authorities to apply the Convention, still giving priority to national legislation and 'insensitive' to international human rights standards incorporated into the domestic legal system. This brings us back to the issue of the practical absence of leading human rights cases decided by the regular courts. The few exceptions are:

—a case of direct application of article 6, para. 3(c) of the Convention in which the Supreme Court relying on that provision allowed free legal aid to an indigent accused in appeal proceedings although relevant provisions of the Code of Criminal Procedure did not require obligatory legal assistance;
—isolated cases of applying the 'reasonable time' guarantee in article 5, para. 3 of the Convention;
—a case of a reference to the 'access to court' aspect of article 6, para. 1 of the Convention in a situation in which a specific statutory provision barred such access;
—a reference to the Constitutional Court by the Supreme Court of the matter of constitutionality and conformity with the Convention of a provision of the Code of Criminal Procedure providing for mandatory detention on remand (repealed by Parliament in the meantime).

No comprehensive practice by the courts in applying the Convention may be shown, partly because of the inadequate qualification of judges in this respect.

An illustrative example of the manner in which the local courts react when violations of the Convention have been claimed is the decision on admissibility in the case of *Christian Association Jehovah's Witnesses v Bulgaria* (Application No. 28626/ 95, Dec.3.7.1997) where the applicant association appealed to the Supreme Court against a decision of the Council of Ministers refusing authorization for the re-registration [of the applicant association] claiming that that refusal amounted to a breach of the applicant's rights under Articles 9, 10, 11, 14, and 18 of the Convention. By a judgment of 13 March 1995 the Supreme Court dismissed the appeal, stating that:

> the restrictions on religious denominations are enunciated in the provisions of article 37 of the Constitution and article 9, para. 2 of the Convention . . . The question whether the aims declared in the [applicant association's] draft statute of association are in compliance with the exhaustive list of limitations contained in the above provisions is within the competence of the highest organ of the executive power who decides on the basis of its free assessment. The judicial control of lawfulness in such a case is limited to an examination of whether the impugned act is within the administrative organ's competence and whether it complies with the procedural and substantial legal requirements as regards its adoption.

Though undoubtedly possessing 'full jurisdiction' to examine the case on its merits, the court declined to exercise it, depriving the applicant association of a remedy provided for in the national legal system.

E. CASES BROUGHT BEFORE THE EUROPEAN COMMISSION AND COURT OF HUMAN RIGHTS

While it is not necessary that an individual obtain a favourable decision on the substance of his Convention claims, the case just cited, without drawing a general conclusion from it, is at least indicative of the extent to which the national legal system reacts to such claims and may be relied upon for protection against breaches of Convention rights. The point to be noted concerns the effectiveness of a procedure that failed to address substantive arguments as to the grounds allowing restriction on the exercise of Convention (as well as constitutional) rights.

In this particular case a friendly settlement was reached between the parties,[21] further discussed below in view of its impact on new legislation. Altogether fourteen applications lodged by individuals, groups of individuals, or non-governmental organizations have been declared admissible by the European Commission of Human Rights, this paper not covering the period after the entry into force of Protocol No. 11. No inter-state cases have been brought by or against Bulgaria. Article 31 Reports have been adopted in eight cases, a friendly settlement has been effected by the Commission in two cases, one petition has been stricken out of the Commission's list of cases, and a further three cases still find themselves in the post-admissibility stage of procedure before the Commission.

Most of the issues raised in the applications declared admissible concern complaints under articles 5 (and 6) of the Convention which form the subject-matter of the judgments holding Bulgaria to be in breach of Convention duties so these judgments are mainly discussed further on.

Up to the present Bulgaria has been found to be in breach of the Convention by the European Court of Human Rights in six cases, with four cases left by the Commission for a decision by the Committee of Ministers.

In the case of *Loukanov v Bulgaria* (judgment of 20 March 1997, *Reports of Judgments and Decisions*, 1997–II) the European Court held that there had been a violation of article 5, para. 1 of the Convention stating that:

[21] Article 28 para. 2. Report adopted on 9 Mar 1998.

[in the circumstances of the case] the Court does not find that the deprivation of the applicant's liberty during the period under consideration was 'lawful detention' effected on 'reasonable suspicion of [his] having committed an offence' (p. 544, § 45).

While this seems very much a case on its own facts, its significance can be measured exactly against the background of the circumstances which gave rise to an application to the Convention institutions and which characterize the attitude and positions of the Bulgarian authorities in the course of Strasbourg's proceedings and theirs, as well as the public's reactions in the light of the European Court's judgment. The applicant was a former minister, then Deputy Prime Minister, and in 1990 Prime Minister of Bulgaria. He was a member of the Bulgarian National Assembly at the time of the events giving rise to the case and was shot dead on 2 October 1996. Belonging to the former political elite and strongly involved in the process of transformation, the applicant was undoubtedly a popular, influential, and highly controversial figure. The criminal proceedings instituted against him, involving his detention on remand, were based on a suspicion related to his participation as a Deputy Prime Minister, between 1986 and 1990, in a number of decisions granting sums in assistance and loans to certain foreign countries.

The Government stated before the European Court of Human Rights that they were prepared to accept the Commission's opinion that there had been a violation of article 5, para. 1 of the Convention, whilst at the same time informing the Court of the views of the Prosecutor General, the authority which had ordered the applicant's detention on remand, pointing out that it was not in the Government's powers to assess the measures taken by independent judicial authorities.

On this last point the Court emphasized that:

Governments are answerable under the Convention for the acts of such authorities as they are for those of any other State agency. In all cases before the Court what is in issue is the international responsibility of the State (p. 544, § 40).

This statement of the Court is of particular importance for the comprehension on the part of the country's authorities of the manner in which the Convention operates. Equally important are the findings of the Court based on the particular circumstances of the case and on its assessment of compliance with domestic law leading to the conclusion that at the time his detention was ordered the applicant was not reasonably suspected of having sought to obtain for himself or a third party an advantage from his participation in the allocation of funds (see § 44 of the judgment on p. 544).

In a changing political environment and in the atmosphere of controversial public attitudes, however, the message contained in this statement and its relevance to the interpretation and application of domestic law and practice could not receive an adequate reaction.

Of much greater significance as to its impact on the national legal system is the second judgment delivered against Bulgaria in the case of *Assenov and Others* (judgment of 28 October 1998, to be published in *Reports of Judgments and Decisions 1998*) where Bulgaria was found to be in breach of several articles of the Convention.

Of principal importance both as regards the general situation in this country with respect of excessive use of force by law enforcement officials and as an illustration of the 'dynamic and evolutive interpretation' of the Convention by the Court is the part of the judgment related to the complaint under article 3. While the Court held that there had been no violation of article 3 based on the applicant's allegations of ill-treatment by the police, the Court further held that there had been a violation under the same article based on the failure to carry out an effective official investigation into these allegations. On the particular circumstances of the case the Court stated that:

> where an individual raises an arguable claim that he has been seriously ill-treated by the police or other such agents of the State unlawfully and in breach of Article 3, that provision, read in conjunction with the State's general duty under Article 1 of the Convention 'to secure to everyone within their jurisdiction the rights and freedoms in [the] Convention', requires by implication that there should be an effective official investigation. This obligation, as with that under Article 2, should be capable of leading to the identification and punishment of those responsible. If this were not the case, the general legal prohibition of torture and inhuman and degrading treatment and punishment, despite its fundamental importance, would be ineffective in practice and it would be possible in some cases for agents of the State to abuse the rights of those under their control with virtual impunity'(§ 102).

Referring to its findings that Mr Assenov had an arguable claim that he had been ill-treated by agents of the State and that the domestic investigation of this claim was not sufficiently thorough and effective the Court found that there had also been a violation of article 13 of the Convention.

Penetrating into a variety of issues constituting a subject of a heated discussion on the organization of criminal jurisdiction in Bulgaria, the Court held that there had been a violation of article 5, para. 3 of the Convention in that the applicant was not brought promptly before a judge or other officer authorized by law to exercise judicial power, that there had been a separate violation of article 5, para. 3 of the Convention in that the applicant was not given a trial within a reasonable time or released pending trial, and that there had been a violation of article 5, para. 4 of the Convention.

The Court noted that:

under Bulgarian law, investigators do not have the power to make legally binding decisions as to the detention and release of a suspect. Instead, any decision made by an investigator is capable of being overturned by the prosecutor, who may also withdraw a case from an investigator if dissatisfied with the latter's approach. It follows that the investigator was not sufficiently independent properly to be described as an 'officer authorized by law to exercise judicial power' within the meaning of Article 5 § 3 (§ 148 of the judgment).

With regard to prosecutors the Court stated:

in any case, since [any one of these] prosecutors could subsequently have acted against the applicant in criminal proceedings, they were not sufficiently independent or impartial for the purposes of Article 5 § 3 (§ 149).

The finding of a violation of article 5 § 4 was based on the impossibility for the applicant, during his two years of pre-trial detention, to have the continuing lawfulness of this detention determined by a court on more than one occasion, and the failure of the court to hold an oral hearing on that occasion (§ 165).

Finally and mostly affecting this country's record, the Court considered:

that the questioning of [two of the applicants] by a representative or representatives of [the authorities] led the applicants to deny in a sworn declaration that they had made any application to the Commission, amounted to a form of improper pressure in hindrance of the right of individual petition (§ 171).

The court found that there had been a violation of article 25, para. 1 of the Convention.

In the third judgment in which Bulgaria was found to be in breach of the Convention delivered in the case of *Nikolova v Bulgaria* (judgment of 25 March 1999, to be published in *Reports of Judgments and Decisions* 1999) the Court, stating that the facts of the case disclosed no material difference when compared to the judgment in *Assenov and Others v Bulgaria*, concluded that there had been a violation of article 5, para. 3 of the Convention. As to the scope and nature of the judicial review afforded to the applicant as regards her detention on remand and the attendant procedure the Court also found that these did not satisfy the requirements of article 5, para. 4 of the Convention.

The significance of this judgment is to be measured not in terms of the particular circumstances of the case that gave rise to the applicant's complaints under the Convention but in view of the Court's stance *vis-à-vis* the Government's position relying on future legislative amendments envisaged to bring the Bulgarian Code of Criminal Procedure into line with the Convention. With regard to these submissions the Court rightly observed that its task was to assess the actual circumstances of the applicant's case

(§ 52 of the judgment). For its part, the Government was correct to accept that in the light of *Assenov and Others* the current Bulgarian legislation could not be regarded as being in conformity with the Convention. By maintaining that full judicial control over any measure affecting the individual's rights during the preliminary investigations preceding criminal proceedings was to be introduced, the Government pointed at recent developments seeking to effect a necessary reform of both law and practice in response to a judgment finding Bulgaria to be in violation of the Convention.

In the case of *Velikova v Bulgaria* (Judgment of 18 May 2000) two violations of article 2 of the Convention were found: in respect of the man with whom the applicant had lived for about twelve years and in respect of the State's obligation to conduct effective investigation. In this judgment a violation of article 13 of the Convention was also found. Basing itself on the facts of the case, the Court concluded that it was beyond reasonable doubt that the victim had died as a result of injuries inflicted while he was in the hands of the police. The issue of excessive use of force by law enforcement officials thus emerged again and, with respect to the second violation of article 2, an enduring failure on the part of the authorities to conduct an effective investigation in such cases was revealed.

The Judgment of 5 October 2000 in the case of *Varbanov* points to issues which are still unresolved in domestic legislation. The applicant's compulsory confinement in a psychiatric hospital, ordered by a prosecutor for the purpose of obtaining a medical opinion to assess the need for instituting judicial proceedings with a view to his psychiatric treatment, was found to be a breach of article 5, para. 1 of the Convention on account of the fact the applicant's deprivation of liberty was not justified under subparagraph (e) of this provision and had no basis in domestic law (which, moreover, does not provide the required protection against arbitrariness as it does require the seeking of a medical opinion). In view of the fact that the prosecutor's order was subject to appeal solely to higher prosecutors, the European Court further held that the remedy required by article 5, para. 4 of the Convention was not available to the applicant.

The significance of the European Court's findings in the case of *Hasan and Chaush v Bulgaria* (Judgment of 26 October 2000) is that it exposed a failure by the authorities to remain neutral in the exercise of acts of formal registration of religious communities and changes in their leadership, which amounts to an interference with the believers' freedom to practise their religion within the meaning of article 9 of the Convention. The Court further found that the interference with the internal organization of the respective religious community and the applicants' freedom of religion were not 'prescribed by law' but were arbitrary and was based on legal provisions which allowed unfettered discretion to the executive and did not meet the required standards of clarity and foreseeability. On the other hand, in view of the Supreme Court's refusal to exercise its 'full jurisdiction' when reviewing an act of the executive, and of the repeated refusal of the Council of Ministers to comply with other judgments of this Court, a violation of article 13 of the Convention was found.

F. REMEDIAL ACTION TAKEN BY THE GOVERNMENT IN RESPONSE TO BEING HELD IN VIOLATION OF THE CONVENTION

No information about any remedial action taken by the Government in response to being held to be in violation of the Convention in so far as the individual applicants themselves are concerned may be provided.[22] Remedial action following the two cases in which friendly settlements were reached is not considered here with one exception which deserves attention—the friendly settlement reached in the above-mentioned case of *Christian Association Jehovah's Witnesses*. Since one of the issues that gave rise to the application to the Commission concerned the Council of Minister's refusal to grant authorization for court registration, this being a condition to acquire legal personality, the Bulgarian Government gave the undertaking to revoke the relevant part of the decision refusing that authorization and to register the association as a recognized religious denomination under the Denominations Act. Furthermore, the Government gave an undertaking to submit a bill to Parliament proposing the adoption of a Substitution of Military Obligations by Alternative Service Act.[23]

In a direct response to the *Assenov and Others* judgment, however, the Government adopted and introduced in Parliament a bill amending the Code of Criminal Procedure. Along with amendments aimed at a general reform of the criminal procedure the bill contains proposals immediately provoked by the *Assenov* judgment. The Council of Ministers has stated the following reasons to substantiate them:

[22] This does not concern the obligation to pay compensation and costs awarded by the Court under Article 50 of the Convention. Following the *Loukanov* judgment, by a decision of 21 Apr 1997 adopted for the purpose of its 'acceptance' and execution, the Council of Ministers ordered the Ministry of Finance to pay to the applicant's heirs within a period of one month the sums awarded in compensation for non-pecuniary damage and for legal costs and expenses. The Council of Ministers adopted a similar decision on 25 January 1999 following the *Assenov and Others* judgment.

[23] The Substitution of Military Obligations by Alternative Service Act was passed by the National Assembly following this friendly settlement though it would be speculative to maintain that the adoption of the Act was in implementation thereof.

Particular attention has been attached to the requirements of Article 5, §§ 1, 3 and 4 and Article 6 ECHR. The Code of Criminal Procedure in force makes no provision for preliminary judicial control over limitations to the right to liberty and security of the person enshrined in [the Convention]. This predetermines the unsuccessful outcome for the Republic of Bulgaria in a number of cases brought before the European Court in Strasbourg in which complaints under Article 5, § 3 have been made. The regulation of the *habeas corpus* procedure also does not comply with all the requirements established in the case-law of the European Court. Furthermore, under the legal arrangement now in force, the *habeas corpus* procedure is being applied in relation to detention on remand only. Control exercised on the part of the court does not spread to placement for examination in a psychiatric institution which is considered by the European Court and in a number of foreign judgments to be one of the most drastic breaches of the right to liberty and security of the person. It is permissible under Article 5, § 1(c) of [the Convention] under the condition that the rights of the individual are guaranteed. These are the considerations for the preliminary control exercised by a court over detention on remand, placement in a psychiatric institution for examination, and removal from office to be introduced. The institute of follow-up judicial control over breaches of individual's rights during the pre-trial stage of the proceedings has also been improved. Subject to judicial control will be also other breaches of constitutionally established rights of citizens as required by [the Convention]—house arrest, search and seizure, apprehension of correspondence. Courts will also control the public prosecutor's function to discontinue criminal proceedings. In case of a dispute between the public prosecutor and the investigative organs, on the imposition of detention on remand the issue will be referred for a final determination by a court.

These amendments to the Code of Criminal Procedure bring the legislation into full conformity with [the Convention] and articles 126 and 127 of the Constitution.

G. ASSESSMENT AND PROSPECTS

If a general assessment of the achievements of the Convention in the improvement of human rights in Bulgaria were to be made on the basis of the developments immediately provoked by the *Assenov and Others* judgment, a conclusion that the Convention has successfully served as a catalyst for legal change might easily be reached. Since a conclusion to that effect would be precipitate and incomplete, though these developments do indicate an undoubtedly positive trend, a thorough analysis should take into account the general situation in which the Convention operates in Bulgaria. The purpose of this assessment is to provide information rather than to criticize or still less to reproach. The lack of some important elements of a fully comprehensive system of Convention rights protection should be acknowledged.

The changes in the Code of Criminal Procedure pointed out above could only occur as a part of a general legal reform in the relevant area and as a direct effect of a judgment involving a determination that a national law is inconsistent with the Convention. While this latter effect may be considered typical of the manner in which the Convention exercises its influence upon national law, it is also indicative of the pace of legal reform in the area of human rights.

Even a cursory survey of current legislation would demonstrate the presence of laws which ought to be amended for the purpose of bringing them fully into line with the Convention on one hand, and the necessity of adopting new legislation so that the Treaty obligation in article 1 of the Convention are complied with, on the other. The first group could include, by way of example only, article 80 of the Ministry of the Interior Act which governs the use of firearms by police officers (with a view to article 2 of the Convention), the outdated Denomination Act (especially after the *Hasan and Chaus* judgment of the European Court), or the placement in reformatory schools of juvenile delinquents (as to its compliance with the principles of fair trial), the second should cover issues of investigation of excessive use of force by law enforcement officials (following the strong messages contained in the *Assenov* and *Velikova* judgments), the introduction of a legal aid scheme for indigent defendants and of a law consistent with the Convention regulating the exercise of the right to freedom of peaceful assembly and freedom of association.

While much more may be added to this obviously incomplete list with regard being had to the positive developments indicated (see C and F above) it should be borne in mind that Bulgaria joined the Convention at a time when the basis of its legal system did not conform to the requirements of the Convention as it was not a representative of the 'common heritage of political traditions, ideals, freedoms and the rule of law' to which the Convention Preamble refers. The implementation of an overall legal reform must very often reconcile conflicting social interests (in view of, for instance, the struggle against high criminal activity or the need for a speedy economic reform) which adversely affects even the general attitude towards the notion of human rights.

This inevitably bears upon the inconsistency and inadequacy of the process of bringing the national legal system into compliance with the Convention. It also explains why the Convention is considered as having a 'declarative' character and function, rather than being an effective instrument for the protection of human rights. The notion of national law only being directly applicable is still deeply entrenched, and this usually prevents judicial and administrative authorities from accepting that the relevant Convention provisions can be relied upon directly by them without further steps being needed by way of legislative or other state action. The sensitivity of national authorities to the developments in the Convention case-law (including the concept of 'positive obligations') leaves much to be desired, and there is still room for improvement as to establishing an effective and embracing scheme of national remedies.[24]

For some of these objectives to be achieved institutional and even constitutional reform may be required. Certain steps in this respect have already been taken with regard to the judiciary.[25] These are an indication of the existence of possible solutions in complex situations. Along with the 'programmatic' influence of the Convention on current developments by providing a statement of European human rights values and the clear signals that it sends to national authorities in its capacity of an operational system, its achievements and prospects in Bulgaria may finally be assessed—without seeking to weigh out exactly the achievements and failures—in the light of the key role which the Convention has played and is set to play in the ongoing process of Bulgaria's overall transformation. Were the latter to be carried out in the absence of this powerful instrument and its civilizing influence, the progress of reforms would undoubtedly be slowed down.

[24] The introduction of an individual constitutional complaint system and the establishment of an Ombudsman-like institution are some of the ideas under consideration in this respect.

[25] By introducing amendments to the Judiciary Act (1998).

8

CYPRUS

ANDREAS NICOLAS LOIZOU

INTRODUCTION

Cyprus is the third largest island in the Mediterranean. It lies in its north-eastern corner, where three continents—Europe, Asia, and Africa—meet. Its strategic position has through the centuries attracted many conquerors. It was under Ottoman rule from 1571 to 1878 when it was ceded to Britain in return for help in the event of an attack by Russia on certain bordering provinces. At the outbreak of the First World War, Cyprus was annexed to the British Empire and in 1925, by virtue of the Treaty of Lausanne, was formally declared a British Colony and remained so until 16 August 1960, when it was proclaimed an independent Republic.

Its Constitution was based on the provisions of the Zurich and London Agreements and the Treaty Concerning the Establishment of the Republic of Cyprus.[1] In the latter it was specifically provided that the Republic of Cyprus undertook to:

> secure to everyone within its jurisdiction human rights and fundamental freedoms comparable to those set out in section I of the European Convention for the Protection of Human Rights and Fundamental Freedoms and its Protocol.

This is one of the reasons why Part II of the Constitution, entitled 'Fundamental Rights and Liberties', is modelled on the said European Convention ('the Convention') which has largely served as the prototype for this Part,[2] but has been extended and enlarged in some respects with a number of social and economic rights added in order to meet the basic requirements of a modern society. After all, poverty, unemployment, illiteracy, lack

[1] The first Agreement was concluded between Greece and Turkey and the second between the governments of the United Kingdom, Greece and Turkey, and Representatives of the Greek Cypriot and the Turkish Cypriot communities. The third one was signed by the three aforesaid governments of the one part and the government of the Republic of Cyprus of the other. See Cmnd. 679 and Cmnd. 1093.

[2] *Christou v Christou* (1964) CLR 336.

of social security, unhealthy conditions of life, and lack of appropriate treatment of ill health all prevent and indeed deny the enjoyment of human rights.

An example of how the Constitution has been extended in comparison with the Convention is to be found in article 28 of the Constitution. The right of equality before the law, the administration, and justice, and the entitlement to equal protection and treatment are safeguarded by art. 28.1 of the Constitution. Paragraph 2 of this article provides that:

Every person shall enjoy all the rights and liberties provided for in this Constitution without any direct or indirect discrimination against any person on the ground of his community, race, religion, language, sex, political, or other convictions, national, or social descent, birth, colour, wealth social class, or on any ground whatsoever, unless there is express provision to the contrary in this Constitution.

Article 28 is so formulated that the guarantee of equal protection provided for in its first paragraph, which affords a right independent of other substantive provisions of the Constitution, is combined with a specific prohibition of discrimination in the second paragraph; that prohibition is modelled on art. 14 of the Convention which affords protection against discrimination in the enjoyment of the rights and freedoms safeguarded by the other substantive provisions of the Convention on the grounds set out above.[3] Article 14 of the Convention, however, is not autonomous. Its application is not dependent upon a finding of a violation of another article of the Convention but, as put by the European Court of Human Rights ('the Court') in the *Belgian Linguistic* case:[4]

a measure which in itself is in conformity with the requirements of the Article enshrining the right or freedom in question may, however, infringe this Article when read in conjunction with Article 14 for the reason that it is of a discriminatory nature.[5]

Needless to say, not every difference in treatment will amount to violation of this article. Instead, it must be established that other persons in analogous or relevantly similar situation enjoy preferential treatment, and that there is no reasonable or objective justification for this distinction.[6]

The rights contained in Part II of the Constitution are guaranteed for every person, but the state is not precluded, where there is express provision to that effect, as for example in art. 11.1(f) of the Constitution which speaks of 'an alien' against whom action is taken for deportation or extradition whereas

[3] See P. G. Polyviou, *The Equal Protection of the Laws* (London, Duckworth, 1979) p. 697.

[4] (Merits) Judgment of 23 July 1968, Series A No. 6 § 9.

[5] The ambit of this provision being so restricted, has necessitated the inclusion in the additional Protocols that contain new substantive rights of a provision that they shall be regarded as additional rights to the Convention.

[6] *Sheffield and Horsham v United Kingdom*, Judgment of 25 June 1998.

art. 5.1(f) of the Convention refers to 'a person' against whom such an action is taken, from regulating any matter relating to aliens in accordance with international law.[7] So the Constitution protects citizens but not aliens against banishment or exclusion from the Republic.

Whilst Cyprus was still a British Crown Colony, the United Kingdom extended the Convention to Cyprus among certain other territories for whose international relations the UK government was responsible.[8] On the basis of this undertaking by the United Kingdom, Greece filed two inter-state applications[9] against the United Kingdom regarding alleged violations of the Convention in Cyprus at that time. Both applications were declared admissible by the Commission and were pending until the conclusion of the Zurich and London Agreements in 1959. The Committee of Ministers decided in August and December of that year, on the application of the interested parties, not to take any further action on them.

The Convention was considered as having lapsed on the date Cyprus became independent, namely 16 August 1960, according to a Declaration made by the United Kingdom on 9 June 1964 and the approach of the Cypriot authorities upon independence. Cyprus had already become a member of the Council of Europe on 24 May 1961. It signed the Convention on 16 December 1961 and ratified it by Law No. 39 of 1962. The instrument of ratification was deposited with the Secretary General of the Council of Europe on 6 October 1962 and on that date the Convention came into force as regards the Republic of Cyprus. In this way the question of the applicability of the Convention to Cyprus after it became independent was resolved without issues arising as to state succession in this respect.

THE STATUS OF THE CONVENTION UNDER NATIONAL LAW

To the extent that it has been incorporated into the Constitution, the Convention has constitutional force. As a consequence, no law that violates such conventional norms is valid. Thus the superiority of the Convention is fully guaranteed.

[7] Art. 32 of the Constitution. It seems that this art. is wider than art. 16 of the Convention which provides that 'Nothing in Art. 10, 11 and 14 shall be regarded as preventing the High Contracting Parties from imposing restrictions on the political activity of aliens'.

[8] Declaration contained in a letter from the Permanent Representative dated 23 Oct 1953.

[9] Applications 176/56 and 299/57.

Apart from this position, however, under article 169(3) of the Constitution, treaties, conventions, and agreements concluded by decision of the Council of Ministers and approved by a law enacted by the House of Representatives have, from the date of their publication in the Official Gazette of the Republic, force superior to any municipal law on condition that they are applied by the other party thereto. It may be noted here that the general principle of reciprocity and the rule in art. 21(1) of the Vienna Convention on the Law of Treaties do not apply to the obligations under the Convention, which are:

> essentially of an objective character, being designed rather to protect the fundamental rights of individual human beings from infringement by the High Contracting Parties than to create subjective and reciprocal rights for the High Contracting parties themselves.[10]

In the light of this the Convention has not only been incorporated into the legal system of the Republic but has force superior to any municipal law either antecedent to or subsequent to its ratification,[11] but not to the Constitution to the extend that any of its provisions have not been incorporated into it. Moreover, the Cypriot courts invoke the case-law concerning the Convention as an aid to the interpretation of the corresponding provisions of the Constitution and the Convention. This is imperative because the international supervision envisaged by the Convention, and the commitments undertaken thereunder, may lead to a finding by the Convention organs of a violation of a provision of the Convention, even if the conduct complained of is not contrary to the Constitution.

Therefore, whenever possible from the wording of a particular provision of the Constitution, the interpretation to be given by the courts has to be such as to make that provision of the Constitution consistent with that of the Convention. The case-law of the Strasbourg organs, as we shall see, is referred to in relation to the interpretation of the Convention

A. THE STATUS OF THE CONVENTION IN PARLIAMENTARY PROCEEDINGS

Legislation has to be consonant with the provisions of the Constitution; otherwise it may be declared unconstitutional in the light of the relevant provi-

[10] *Austria v Italy*, Yearbook No. 4 p. 112 at p. 140; *France, Norway, Denmark, Sweden, the Netherlands v Turkey* (1984) DR 35 p. 143 at p. 169.

[11] This has been accepted by the Supreme Court. See, *inter alia, Christou v Christou* note 2 above; *Kantara Shipping Limited v The Republic* (1971) 3 CLR176 at p. 183; *Tsirides v The Police* (1973) 2 CLR 204 at p. 207.

sions of the Constitution concerning the exercise of judicial review of legislative enactments. With regard to the principles governing the exercise of this review, the Supreme Court has looked for guidance to the case-law of the Supreme Court of the United States of America. These principles can be found in its leading case, *The Board for the Registration of Architects and Civil Engineers v Christodoulos Kyriakides*.[12] They may be summed up as follows.

(a) A law is presumed to be constitutional until proved otherwise 'beyond reasonable doubt'.
(b) The courts are concerned only with the constitutionality of legislation and not with its motives, policy, or wisdom, or with its concurrence with natural justice, fundamental principles of government, or the spirit of the Constitution.
(c) If at all possible the courts will construe the statute so as to bring it within the law of the Constitution.
(d) The judicial power does not extend to the determination of abstract questions, that is questions of a constitutional nature, unless absolutely necessary to a decision of the case.
(e) In cases involving statutes, portions of which are valid and other portions invalid, the Courts will separate the valid from the invalid and annul only the latter unless such portions are inextricably connected.

Judicial review of legislative enactments may take place in two ways. The first is the pre-emptive or preventive control, provided for by article 140 of the Constitution, whereby the President or the Vice-President of the Republic, or the two jointly, may at any time prior to the promulgation of any law or decision of the House of Representatives refer to the Supreme Constitutional Court, now the Supreme Court, for its opinion the question whether such law or decision, or any specific provision thereof, is repugnant to or inconsistent with any provision of the Constitution, otherwise than on the ground that such law or decision, or any provision thereof, discriminates against either of the two Communities.[13]

The Supreme Court, after hearing arguments on behalf of the President and the Vice-President and on behalf of the House of Representatives, gives its opinion and if the provisions under examination are found to be repugnant to or inconsistent with the Constitution the same shall not be promulgated.

The second mode of judicial review is the repressive or remedial control. Even when the aforesaid provision of the Constitution is not invoked by the

[12] (1966) 3 CLR 640 at pp. 654, 655.

[13] A right of recourse by the President or the Vice-President of the Republic on the ground that any law or decision of the House of Representatives discriminates against either of the two Communities is provided for in art. 137 of the Constitution.

President of the Republic and a law has been promulgated, any party to any judicial proceedings, including proceedings on appeal, at any stage thereof, may, under article 144 of the Constitution, raise the question of the unconstitutionality of any law or decision, or of any provision thereof, material for the determination of any matter at issue in such proceedings. Thereupon the Court before which such issue was raised must reserve the question for the decision of the Supreme Constitutional Court and stay further proceedings until the question has been determined by that Court.

Since 1964, however, such issues of unconstitutionality of laws are determined in the first instance by the trial court concerned as questions of law.[14]

B. LEADING HUMAN RIGHTS CASES DECIDED BY THE NATIONAL COURTS

The first case to come before the Cypriot courts in which reference was made to the Convention was that of *Attorney-General of the Republic v Aphamis.*[15] In this case, which turned on an application by the Attorney-General of the Republic for the committal to prison of the applicant, a citizen of the Republic, under section 5 of the Fugitive Offenders Act 1881, with a view to extradition, a comparison was made between the word 'alien' in art. 11.2(f) of the Constitution on one hand and of the word 'person' used in art. 5(1)(f) of the Convention on the other hand. It was held that it was intended to restrict the power of arrest or detention to 'aliens', with the inevitable result that extradition also was limited to 'aliens'.

In *Christou v Christou,*[16] a maintenance case, it was held that it was correct to interpret the provisions of art. 30.3 of the Constitution, which were obviously intended to apply mainly to civil cases, as designed to ensure a fair trial in view of the particular provision made under art. 12.5 of the Constitution for criminal cases, which corresponds to art. 6(3)(d) of the Convention.[17]

In *Pilavachi and Co v International Chemical Co Ltd*[18] the registration of a judgment obtained in England against the defendants was effected in the

[14] See the Administration of Justice (Miscellaneous Provisions) Law 1964 (Law 33 of 1964) and the judgment of the Supreme Court in *Attorney-General of the Republic v Mustafa Ibrahim and Others* (1964) CLR 195, in which on the basis of the doctrine of necessity the procedure for a reference under art. 144 of the Constitution was found not to be applicable or necessary and that questions of alleged unconstitutionality are to be treated as issues of law and be subject to revision on appeal in view of the provisions of the aforesaid Law.

[15] 1 RSCC 121 at p. 125.

[16] See note 2 above.

[17] Support for this approach was drawn from the Opinion of the Commission in Application 852/60, Yearbook No. 4 p. 354.

[18] (1965) 1 CLR 97.

appropriate court in Cyprus under the Foreign Judgments (Reciprocal Enforcement) Law.[19] The defendants applied to have the registration of this judgment set aside on the ground, *inter alia,* that it would be contrary to public policy and to art. 30.2 and 3(b) of the Constitution to deprive a citizen of his right to present his case before a Cyprus court. It was held that the applicants had a reasonable opportunity of presenting their case to the English court of which they failed to avail themselves. The issue turned on the interpretation of art. 30.2 and 3(b) of the Constitution which substantially reproduces art. 6(1) of the Convention. The Court referred to and adopted the Opinion of the European Commission that:

> the right to a fair hearing guaranteed by art. 6(1) of the Convention appears to contemplate that every one who is a party to civil proceedings shall have a reasonable opportunity of presenting his case to the Court under conditions which do not place him at a disadvantage *vis-à-vis* his opponent.[20]

Kannas v The Police[21] concerned the interpretation of art. 12.5(a) of the Constitution which corresponds to art. 6(3)(a) of the Convention on the requirement of giving sufficient details of the nature and grounds of the charge. The Supreme Court said that it was pertinent to bear in mind the relevant jurisprudence of the Convention and referred to and followed the test that could be deducted from *Offner v Austria*[22] and *Nielsen v Denmark*.[23]

In the case of *Matsis v The Republic*[24] the Supreme Court expressed the view that 'civil rights and obligations', a term that can be found in both art. 30.2 of the Constitution and art. 6(1) of the Convention, does not apply to the determination of 'liability under a fiscal law, which is a branch of public law'. Support for this proposition was found in *X v Belgium* decided by the Commission on 1 October 1965.[25]

As regards a disciplinary charge against a civil servant before the Public Service Commission, the Court held that it was not a criminal charge and therefore the right 'to have a lawyer of his choice' provided in art. 6(3)(c) of the Convention, which corresponds to art. 30(3)(d) of the Constitution, did not come into play, following the relevant decisions of the Commission.[26] In

[19] Statute Laws of Cyprus, 1959, ch 10.

[20] Application 434/58, Yearbook No. 2 pp. 354, 370, 372, and Application 1092/61, Yearbook No. 5 pp. 210, 212.

[21] (1968) 2 CLR 29 at pp. 35–37.

[22] Yearbook No. 2 p. 344.

[23] Yearbook No. 4 p. 490.

[24] (1969) 3 CLR 245 at p. 270.This approach was approved by the Full Bench of the Supreme Court in *Kantara Shipping Ltd v The Republic* (1971) 3 CLR176 at p. 183, with reference to *A, B, C, and D v The Netherlands,* Yearbook No. 9 p. 268 at p. 284.

[25] Yearbook No. 8 p. 282 at p. 312.

[26] Application 423/58, Collection of Decisions of the Commission No. 1 and Application 1931/63 Yearbook No. 7 p. 212.

the case of *Lambrou v The Republic*[27] the issue was the constitutionality of Regulation 18(1) of Regulations 13/62, made by the Greek Communal Chamber, precluding appearance with an advocate of an educationalist facing disciplinary proceedings. The position, however, was changed by the repeal of the said Regulation and as far as the public service was concerned such rule was enacted by the Public Service Law of 1967, although, in spite of the absence of such provision before this law, public officers, unlike educationalists, were as a matter of practice allowed to be defended by an advocate in disciplinary proceedings before the Public Service Commission.

The issue in *Tsirides v The Police*[28] was the interpretation of art. 11.2(a) of the Constitution, which corresponds to art. 5(1)(c) of the Convention, on the meaning of the term 'reasonable suspicion' to be found in both texts. The Supreme Court referred with approval to the case of *Stögmüller v Austria*[29] and Application 1936/63[30] before the Commission, where it was said that:

> in determining what is 'a reasonable suspicion of having committed an offence' permitting the arrest or detention of a person under art. 5(1)(c), regard must be had to the circumstances of the case as they appeared at the time of the arrest and detention

The Supreme Court adopted that position.

The case of *Police v Georghiades*[31] turned on the right to privacy under arts. 15 and 17 of the Constitution and art. 8 of the Convention, and in particular on the legality and admissibility of evidence concerning what a witness had overheard by the use of an electronic listening and recording devise, regarding a conversation between the accused and another person, without the knowledge of either of them. The Supreme Court ruled that piece of evidence inadmissible. In support of this approach it made extensive references to textbooks on the Convention.[32]

In *Pitsillides and Another v The Republic*,[33] a question arose of interpretation of art. 18 of the Constitution which corresponds to art. 9 of the Convention, on freedom of thought, conscience, and religion, in relation to conscientious objectors. The Supreme Court adopted the approach of the Commission in Applications 2299/64 and 5591/72 to the effect that, as expressly recognized in art. 4(2)(3) of the Convention, which corresponds to art.10.2 and 3 of the Constitution, civilian service may be imposed on consci-

[27] (1972) 3 CLR 379 at p. 386, 387.
[28] See note 11 above.
[29] Judgment of 10 Nov 1969, Series A No. 9.
[30] Yearbook No. 7 p. 224 at p. 244.
[31] (1983) 2 CLR 33.
[32] F. Castberg, *The European Convention of Human Rights* (Leiden: Sijthoff, 1974), pp. 138, 139, F. Jacobs, *The European Convention on Human Rights* 1975, pp. 126, 127, J. Fawcett, *The Application of the European Convention on Human Rights*, 1969 p. 187 with particular reference to Application 2645/65 *Scheichelbauer v Austria*, No. 2645/65, YB (1969) DA.
[33] (1983) 2 CLR 374 at pp. 383–388.

entious objectors as a substitute for military service and that objections of conscience do not, under the Convention, entitle a person to exemption from such service. With the inclusion of the words 'in countries where they are recognized' a choice is left to the High Contracting Parties to the Convention whether or not to recognize conscientious objectors and, if so recognized, to provide some substitute service for them, such as civilian service, that may be imposed by law as a substitute for military service. On the basis of this the Court found that, in the light of the then prevailing circumstances in Cyprus, to impose the obligation to provide military service on all citizens irrespective of whether the right to religion and conscience is restricted was not unconstitutional.

Since then, however, the National Guards Laws 1964 to 1996 have been amended by Law No. 2 of 1992 by which the right of conscientious objectors to choose civilian service has been recognized. They have to submit an application to the Minister of Defence thirty days prior to the day of their enlistment. Such application is examined by a board of experts who advise the Minister. If the application is rejected there is a right of appeal to the Council of Ministers.

Cosmos Press v The Police[34] dealt with art. 19 of the Constitution and the corresponding art. 10 of the Convention on the freedom of speech and the right of expression on the question of contempt of court. The conviction in that case was set aside following the *Sunday Times* case.[35]

In the case of *National Line of Cyprus SA v The Ship 'Sunset'*[36] it was held that the inclusion of an arbitration clause in an agreement between individuals, though it may amount to partial renunciation of the right of access to a court which is defined in art. 30.2 of the Constitution and art. 6(1) of the Convention, was not contrary to the said provisions as there was nothing in the said articles that explicitly prohibits such renunciation.[37]

In *Archangelos Domain v Van Nievelt, Contian*[38] the Supreme Court considered what is sufficient reasoning of judgments in both civil and criminal proceedings within the notion of 'fair trial' under art. 30.2 of the Constitution and the corresponding art. 6(1) of the Convention. The court adopted the view of the Commission expressed in its Decision on Admissibility in Application 5460/72 that:

> if a court gives reasons, then *prima facie* the requirements of Art. 6 in this respect are satisfied, and this presumption is not upset simply because the judgment does not deal

[34] (1985) 2 CLR 73 at pp. 76–81.

[35] Judgment of 26 Apr 1979 Series A. No. 30.

[36] (1986) 1 CLR393 at pp. 402–406.

[37] The Supreme Court relied on the Report of the Commission in Application 1197/61, Yearbook No. 5 p. 88.

[38] (1988) 1 CLR 51 at p. 55.

specifically with one point considered by an applicant to be material to his case. It does not follow from Article 6 that reasons given by a court should deal specifically with all points which may have been considered by one party to be essential to his case: a party does not have an absolute right to require reasons to be given for rejecting each of his arguments.[39]

In the case of *The Republic v Piperides and Others*[40] the exemption of one of the judges of the Supreme Court was asked for on the ground that he had decided a case and delivered a judgment on the legal point that was raised in that appeal before the full bench of the Court. The Supreme Court, after reviewing a number of judgments of the European Court of Human Rights on the question of fair trial and impartiality,[41] confirmed its previous case-law to the effect that the expression of an opinion and the taking of a stand on legal issues does not constitute a ground for exemption for the same judge to take up a case between the same or different parties in which the same legal point is raised. The Supreme Court in the concluding paragraph of its judgment said that the case-law of the Cypriot courts, to which it had referred, was not contrary to or in disagreement with that of the Convention organs.

C. CASES BROUGHT BEFORE THE EUROPEAN COURT AND THE COMMISSION

Inter-state cases

Article 24 of the Convention, now renumbered by Protocol 11 as art. 33 (and with the addition of the title 'Inter-State Cases') provides that:

> Any High Contracting Party may refer to the Court any alleged breach of the provisions of the Convention [and the protocols thereto[42]] by another High Contracting Party.

This is in substance a reproduction of article 24 of the Convention before its said amendment.[43] The purpose for which such provision was included in the Convention was, as it was said in *Austria v Italy*[44] and in the Commission's decision on admissibility in *France, Norway, Denmark, Sweden and the Netherlands v Turkey ('the Turkish case')*[45] for the High Contracting

[39] Yearbook No. 16 p. 152.

[40] (1994) 3 CLR 569.

[41] *De Cubber v Belgium*, Judgment of 26 Oct 1984, Series A No. 86.

[42] The words in square brackets were added by Protocol 11.

[43] The differences from the old text are that the term Court has replaced the term Commission and that it is no longer provided that the reference is made through the Secretary General but directly to the Court.

[44] See note 10 above.

[45] See note 10 above.

Parties to realize the aims and ideals of the Council of Europe, as expressed in its Statute, and to establish a common public order of the free democracies of Europe.

As the Commission stated regarding applications brought under art. 24 of the Convention in the case of *France, Norway, etc v Turkey*:[46]

[The Convention] does not of itself envisage any direct rights or obligations between the High Contracting parties concerned, the special objective obligation, accepted by the High Contracting Parties under the Convention, being obligations towards persons within their jurisdiction, not to the other High Contracting Parties. (Dec. No. 8007/77, *Cyprus v Turkey,* D R 13, 147 = Yearbook No. 21 pp. 226, 228). As further observed, the Convention clearly indicates where, as regards a right of action under it, a question of reciprocity may arise. This is the case in Article 46, paragraph 2, concerning recognition of the Court's jurisdiction, but not in Article 24, which contains no such indication.

The government of the Republic of Cyprus submitted under art. 24 of the Convention to the Commission two applications. In the first, Application 6780/7, the applicant government stated that Turkey had on 20 July 1974 invaded Cyprus, until 30 July occupied a sizeable area in the north of the island, and on 14 August 1974 extended its occupation to about 40 per cent of the territory of the Republic. It alleged violations of arts. 1, 2, 3, 4, 5, 6, 8, 13, and 17 of the Convention, art. 1 of Protocol No. 1, and art. 14 in conjunction with the aforementioned articles. There followed Application 6950/75, in which the applicant government contended that, by acts unconnected with any military operation, Turkey had, since the introduction of the first application, committed, and continued to commit, further violations of the above articles in the occupied territory.

In its Report of 10 July 1976 concerning those two applications, the Commission, after ascertaining the facts of the case as was its duty under art. 28(1)(a) of the Convention, concluded that Turkey had violated articles 2, 3, 5, 8, 13, and 14 of the Convention and art. 1 of Protocol No. 1.

The Committee of Ministers of the Council of Europe, acting under article 32 of the Convention, as the matter was not referred to the Court because Turkey had not then accepted its compulsory jurisdiction under art. 46 of the Convention, adopted on 20 January 1979 Resolution DH (79) in respect of the first two applications. In this Resolution the Committee of Ministers referred to its decision of 21 October 1977 by which it had:

taken note of the report of the European Commission of Human Rights as well as of the memorial of the Turkish Government and found that events which occurred in Cyprus constitute violations of the Convention, had asked that measures be taken in

[46] See note 10 above.

order to put an end to such violation as might continue to occur and so that the events are not repeated.

It went on to urge the parties to resume intercommunal talk, convinced that the enduring protection of human rights in Cyprus could only be brought about through the re-establishment of peace and confidence between the two communities and that the intercommunal talks constituted the appropriate framework for reaching a solution to the dispute. It decided to urge the parties strongly to resume intercommunal talks under the auspices of the Secretary General of the United Nations and viewed that decision as completing its consideration of the case of *Cyprus against Turkey*. It then declassified the documentation on 31 August 1979.

That was the outcome of the first two applications by the highest political organ of the Council of Europe and the third organ under the Convention entrusted with the supervision of the respect of the rights safeguarded thereby.

It may be noted that by Protocol No. 11 a restructure of the whole system of judicial supervision was effected. In addition to other changes to the constitution of the Court and the Commission and their merger into one permanent Court, the participation of the Committee of Ministers was abandoned.

In the third Application (8007/77[47]) submitted to the Commission by the government of Cyprus against Turkey, the applicant government contended that, since 18 May 1976 when the Commission concluded its investigation in the aforesaid first two applications, Turkey had continued to commit breaches of articles 1, 2, 3, 4, 5, 6, 8, 13, and 17 of the Convention, of arts. 1 and 2 of Protocol No. 1 and art. 14 of the Convention in conjunction with the said articles. The respondent government raised on the admissibility of the application a number of preliminary objections requesting the Commission to declare the application inadmissible.

In its Decision of 10 July 1978 on the admissibility of the application the Commission found that the application was validly introduced by the applicant government which was entitled to represent the state of Cyprus and had standing before the Commission under art. 24 of the Convention; that Turkey's jurisdiction in the north of the Republic of Cyprus, exercised by reason of the presence of her armed forces there, which prevented the exercise of jurisdiction by the applicant government, could not be excluded on the ground that jurisdiction in that area was allegedly exercised by the 'Turkish Federated State of Cyprus'; that the application could not be rejected for non-exhaustion of domestic remedies or for non-observance of the six-month

[47] See the Report of the Commission adopted on 4 Oct 1983. 72 D R 5, made public by Resolution DH (92) 12 of 2 Apr 1992.

rule; that the application could not be declared inadmissible as being the same as the two previous applications; that the Commission was not precluded from dealing with the application by the Decision of the Committee of Ministers of 21 October 1977 concerning the two previous applications, nor could the objection that the application was abusive[48] be accepted.

On the merits the respondent government submitted that 'it maintained its views raised at the admissibility stage and that they were unable to take part in the proceedings'.

The Commission called on the parties to assist it in the performance of its task. The respondent government reiterated its view that the application in question was not lodged by a competent authority of the Republic of Cyprus in as much the Greek Cypriot administration did not have the quality of an applicant.

On 12 July there was adopted the *Interim Report of the Commission on the Present State of the Proceedings*. The Commission expressed the opinion that:

> by its refusal to participate in the Commission's examination of the merits of the present application, Turkey has so far failed to respect its obligations under Art. 28 of the Convention.[49]

It further asked the Committee of Ministers to urge the Turkish government to meet its obligations. The Committee of Ministers' Deputies decided, and accordingly informed the Commission, that having taken cognizance of the Interim Report, it 'Recalls the obligations imposed on all Contracting Parties by article 28 . . .'

The Commission then invited the respondent government once more to submit its observation on the merits but the latter maintained its previous refusal. Thereupon the Commission pursued its examination of the case and proceeded to ascertain the facts. Having done so it drew up its Report and stated its opinion under art. 31 of the Convention. Its Conclusions were as follows.[50]

On the issue of the missing persons:

> The Commission, having found it established in three cases, and having found sufficient indications in an indefinite number of cases, that the Greek Cypriots who are still missing were unlawfully deprived of their liberty, in Turkish custody in 1974, noting that Turkey has failed to account for the fate of these persons.[51]

The Commission concluded that Turkey had violated art. 5 of the Convention.

[48] Ibid. pp. 147–159, Decision on Admissibility appended to the said Report.
[49] Interim Report § 45.
[50] Report of the Commission, see note 47 above, part IV pp. 47, 48.
[51] Ibid. § 123.

As regards the displacement of persons and the separation of families the Commission concluded that:

> by her continued refusal to allow over 170,000 Greek Cypriots to return to their homes in the north of Cyprus, Turkey continued to violate Art. 8 of the Convention in all these cases.[52]

Moreover, Turkey continued to violate art. 8 of the Convention in the cases of continued separation of families resulting from Turkey's refusal to allow the return of Greek Cypriots to join their family members in the north.

The Commission further concluded that Turkey had violated art. 1 of Protocol No.1 on account of the deprivation of possessions.[53]

The Committee of Ministers at its 473rd meeting held on the 2 April 1992, almost nine years after the Commission submitted to it its Report under art. 31 of the Convention, adopted Resolution DH(92)12 by which it decided only 'to make public the above-mentioned report of the Commission' and viewed that decision as 'completing its consideration of the present case'.

Cases involving citizens' rights of petition to the Commission and the Court

The case of *Modinos v Cyprus*[54] was the first one to reach the Court. The Commission had unanimously found a violation of art. 8, the right to privacy, on the ground that the government had failed to:

> show the existence of such 'particularly serious reasons' creating a pressing social need, to maintain in force in Cyprus the prohibition by criminal law of homosexual activities between consenting male adults.

This article corresponds to art. 15 of the Constitution. The Commission and the Court proceeded on the basis that the applicant, though he had not been prosecuted nor were criminal investigations commenced, was a victim, following the same line taken in *Norris v Ireland*.[55] The Court relied on its judgment in *Dungeon v United Kingdom*,[56] though in that case there had been a criminal investigation into the applicant's activities. The Court ruled that:

> in the mere existence of the legislation itself there is involved, for all those to whom the legislation could be applied, a menace of surveillance.[57]

The *ad hoc* Judge Pikis dissented on this point, as well as on the substance, on the ground that under art. 188 all laws in force on the date of the coming into force of the Constitution should be construed and applied with modification

[52] Report of the Commission, §§ 135, 136.
[53] Ibid. § 155.
[54] Judgment of 22 Apr 1993, Series A No. 259.
[55] Judgment of 26 Oct 1988, Series A No. 142.
[56] Judgment of 22 Oct 1981, Series A No. 45.
[57] See note 54 above.

so as to bring them into conformity with the Constitution. The relevant law was part of the old Criminal Code of 1928 to which this provision of the Constitution applied and therefore if a proper case was brought before the Supreme Court article 188 of the Constitution would have been applied.

In *Chrysostomos and Papachrysostomou v Turkey*[58] the applicants participated as clergymen in a demonstration of about 1,000 Greek Cypriot women demonstrating for the refugees' right to return to their homes in the northern part of Cyprus. A religious memorial was held in a nearby church. The service was conducted by the two applicants. The demonstrators then proceeded to a derelict church situated in the buffer zone established by the United Nations Peace-Keeping Force. The demonstrators entered the buffer zone and penetrated beyond that into territory on which, the Commission found:

> the Government of the Republic of Cyprus have since 1974 been prevented from exercising their jurisdiction. The restriction is due to the presence of Turkish armed forces in northern Cyprus.[59]

The two applicants were arrested and they gave evidence that they were forced to appear before a 'court' in the North which the applicants said had no legitimate existence or jurisdiction over them. They were 'tried' on 21 July 1989 and 'sentenced' to three days' imprisonment and to a fine of one hundred Cyprus pounds or by ten days' imprisonment if the fine was not paid within twenty-four hours. The applicants were released on 30 July 1989.

The Commission conducted an inquiry and ascertained the facts. The first question that had to be resolved was whether the acts of the men who arrested the applicants were imputable to Turkey. The answer given by the Commission was in the affirmative, 'noting the overall control exercised by Turkey' in that area. The reasons the Commission advanced were, first, the fact that the application of the Convention, as it had said in its Decision on admissibility, extends beyond national frontiers of the contracting states and includes acts of state organs abroad. It went on to say that the High Contracting Parties are bound to secure the rights and freedoms defined in section I to all persons under their actual authority and responsibility, whether the authority is exercised within their territory or abroad. Authorized agents of a state, including armed forces, not only remain under its jurisdiction when abroad but also bring any other persons within the jurisdiction of that state to the extent that they exercise authority over such persons.[60] It also referred to the presence of the Turkish forces in Cyprus, and opined that they were the authorized agents of Turkey and bring any other persons in Cyprus 'within the jurisdiction' of Turkey.

[58] Applications 15299/89 and 15300/89. Report adopted on 8 July 1993.
[59] Ibid. § 98.
[60] Ibid. §§ 90 to 102.

The Commission concluded that there had been no violation of articles 3, 5(1), and 13 in respect of either applicant and no violation of art. 8 as regards the first applicant, but that there had been a violation of art. 8 as regards the second applicant.

The case was dealt with by the Committee of Ministers under article 32 of the Convention. By Decisions of its Deputies, taken at their 507th and 517th meetings, Turkey was to pay to the second applicant, as just satisfaction, 10,000 French francs in respect of non-pecuniary damage and 75,000 French francs in respect of costs and expenses. In Resolution DH (95) the Committee of Ministers ascertained that Turkey had complied with its decision and paid the amount of just satisfaction to the said applicant and authorized the publication of the Report adopted by the Commission.

There followed the case of *Loizidou v Turkey*.[61] This was an individual application by a Greek Cypriot who grew up in Kyrenia in northern Cyprus and on her marriage in 1972 moved with her husband to Nicosia. She was the owner of land and claimed that, prior to the Turkish occupation of northern Cyprus on 20 July 1974, work had commenced on one of her plots of land for the construction of flats, one of which was intended as a home for her family.

Her complaint was that she had been denied access to and lost control of her property in the north of Cyprus which was occupied by Turkish troops. She relied on art. 8 of the Convention and art. 1 of Protocol No. 1.

The Commission concluded in its Report[62] that there had been no violation of art. 3, of art. 8 as regards the applicant's private life, of art. 5(1), of art. 8 as regards the applicant's home, nor of art. 1 of Protocol No. 1 of the Convention.

The government of Cyprus brought the case before the Court under art. 48(b) on the ground that the applicant, a national of the Republic, was alleged to be a victim. Turkey raised six preliminary objections which were dealt with by the Court in its judgment of 23 March 1993 on the Preliminary Objections.[63]

The Court concluded as follows:-

(a) On whether the applicant government had *locus standi* the Court held, dismissing this objection, that it had been recognized by the international community as the government of the Republic of Cyprus and its position as the government of a High Contracting Party could not be doubted.[64]

[61] In this case three judgments have been given by the Court. The first on the preliminary objections on 23 March 1995 Series A No. 310, the second on the merits on the 18 Dec 1996 Reports 1996–VI p. 2216 and the last one on the question of compensation under art. 50 of the Convention on 28 July 1998 Reports p. 1807.

[62] Adopted on 8 July 1993. Application 15318/89.

[63] Series A No. 310.

[64] Ibid. §§ 39–41.

(b) Concerning the objection as to the alleged abuse of process the Court held that the same had not been raised before the Commission and therefore the Turkish government was estopped from raising it before the Court insofar as it applied to the applicant. To the extent that this objection was directed against the applicant government, the Court noted that the case had been referred to the Court, *inter alia,* because of concern for the rights of the applicant and other citizens in the same situation a matter that could not be considered as an abuse of process.[65]
(c) On the Turkish government's role in the proceedings the Court held that it was not within the discretion of a Contracting Party to characterize its standing in the proceedings before the Court in the manner it sees fit. The case originated as a petition under art. 25 of the Convention against Turkey in her capacity as a High Contracting Party and was referred to the Court under art. 48(b). In this way Turkey was the respondent party.[66]
(d) As to the scope of the case the Court did not find it necessary to give a ruling on the question whether it is permissible to limit a referral to the Court to some of the issues on which the Commission has stated its opinion. This arose out of the fact that the applicant government had limited itself to seeking a ruling only on the complaints under art. 1 of Protocol No. 1 and art. 8 of the Convention, insofar as they had been declared admissible by the Commission, concerning access to the applicant's property. So it proceeded on the basis that only the above complaints were before the Court.[67]

However, in a later case[68] the Court ruled that 'the compass of the case' is delimited not by the Report but by the decision on admissibility and that the Court had full jurisdiction within these limits over the case referred to it. The whole case is referred to it under art. 48 and not those parts which a party may choose to refer.
(e) As to the objections concerning *ratione loci*:
(i) On the question whether the facts alleged by the applicant are capable of falling within the jurisdiction of Turkey under art. 1 of the Convention, the Court ruled that the concept of 'jurisdiction' under art. 1 is not restricted to the national territory of a High Contracting Party, but responsibility may also arise when as a consequence of military action, whether lawful or unlawful, a Contracting Party exercises effective control of an area outside its national territory. It held that the facts alleged by the applicant were capable of falling within Turkish 'jurisdiction' within the meaning of art. 1.
(ii) On the validity of the territorial restrictions attached to Turkey's Declarations under articles 25 and 46 the Court ruled that, if articles 25 and 46 were to be interpreted as permitting restrictions other than of a temporal

[65] Ibid. §§ 42–46. [66] Ibid. §§ 47–52. [67] Ibid. §§ 53–54.
[68] *Erdagoz v Turkey*, Judgment of 22 Oct 1997, Reports 1997, p. 2300 §§ 31–36.

nature, states would be enabled to qualify their consent under the optional clauses and so severely weaken the role of the Commission and the Court and diminish the effectiveness of the Convention as a constitutional instrument of European public order. The Court stressed that although art. 46 was modelled on art. 36 of the Statute of the International Court of Justice, there existed a fundamental difference in the role and purpose of the respective tribunals.
(iii) On the validity of the Turkish Declarations under arts. 25 and 46 the Court held that the impugned restrictions could be severed from the remainder of the text, leaving intact the acceptance of the optional clauses. The territorial restrictions were held invalid but the declarations under arts. 25 and 46 contained valid acceptances of the competence of the Commission and the jurisdiction of the Court.
(f) Regarding the objection concerning *ratione temporis,* the Court decided that because of the difficult issues raised as to the correct interpretation and application of these restrictions in the Turkish Declarations under arts. 25 and 46 and the notion of continuing violations, and because of the state of the file which did not at that stage give sufficient information to enable it to decide them, these objections should be joined to the merits of the case.[69]

By its judgment on the merits[70] the Court dismissed the Turkish government's preliminary objection *ratione temporis* that the applicant's property had been irreversibly expropriated by virtue of article 159 of the 'TRNC' ('Turkish Republic of Northern Cyprus') Constitution of 7 May 1985, prior to Turkey's declaration of 22 January accepting the Court's jurisdiction. It pointed out that it was evident from international practice and from resolutions of various international bodies that the international community did not regard TRNC as a state under international law and that the Republic of Cyprus remained the sole legitimate government of Cyprus. The Court could not, therefore, attribute legal validity for the purposes of the Convention to provisions such as the aforesaid article 159 and accordingly the applicant could not be deemed to have lost her title to her property. It then concluded that the alleged violations were of continuing nature.

As regards article 1 of Protocol No. 1 the Court examined the issue of imputability and concluded from the large number of troops engaged in active duties in Northern Cyprus that the Turkish army was exercising effective overall control there which in the circumstances of the case entailed Turkey's responsibility for the policies and actions of TRNC and thus that denial to the applicant of access to her property in northern Cyprus fell within

[69] For a detailed analysis on the limitations to articles 25 and 46 declarations see D. Harris, M. O'Boyle, and C. Warbrick, *Law of the European Convention of Human Rights* (London, Butterworths, 1995) pp. 581, 583, 643, 644, and 646.

[70] *Loizidou v Turkey*, see note 61 above.

Turkey's 'jurisdiction' for the purposes of article 1 of the Convention and was imputable to Turkey and that the establishment of state responsibility did not require the examination of the lawfulness of Turkey's intervention of 1974.

With regard to the interference with the property rights the Court held that the applicant remained the legal owner of the land in question, but that since 1974 she had lost effectively all control over, and use and enjoyment of it, and in this way the continuing denial of access amounted to interference with the rights under art. 1 of Protocol No. 1. In fact the Turkish government had not sought to justify the interference and the Court did not find such complete negation of property rights justified.

On the issue of the alleged violation of art. 8 the Court found that since the applicant did not have a home this article had not been violated. It deferred its judgment on the question of compensation under art. 50 as not ready for decision at that time.

On 28 July 1998 the Court communicated to the parties its judgment on art. 50. It dismissed the claim of the respondent government that it could not be held liable in international law for the acts of the Turkish Republic of Northern Cyprus. The Court recalled its finding in paragraph 57 of its principal judgment on the merits:

> that the continuous denial of the applicant's access to her property in northern Cyprus and the ensuing loss of all control over the property is a matter which falls within Turkey's jurisdiction within the meaning of Article 1 and is thus imputable to Turkey.

In view of the above the Court ruled that the question of Turkey's responsibility under the Convention in respect of the matters complained of is *res judicata.* It then awarded to the applicant 300,000 Cyprus pounds for pecuniary damages from 1990 to the date of the judgment, and 20,000 Cyprus pounds for non-pecuniary damages for the anguish, helplessness, and frustration suffered by her. It awarded her 137,084.83 Cyprus pounds for her costs and expenses. The Court dismissed the claim of the Cypriot government for cost and expenses, recalling 'the general principle that States must bear their costs in contentious proceedings before international tribunals'. This rule has even greater application when in keeping with the special character of the Convention as an instrument of European public order: High Contracting Parties bring cases before the Convention institutions either under art. 24 or art. 48(c) 'in pursuit of the interests of the Convention community as a whole even where this coincides with the interests of their nationals'.[71]

The case of *Andronicou and Constantinou v Cyprus*[72] was referred to the Court by the Commission and by the government of Cyprus. It originated in

[71] See note 61 above, §§ 27–49 and Conclusion of the Court.
[72] Judgment of 9 Oct 1997, Reports 1997, VI p. 2059.

an application before the Commission by the father and sister of Lefteris Andronicou, deceased, and the parents of Miss Elsie Constantinou, deceased. The two deceased were thirty-three and twenty-two years old respectively. Elsie had moved into Lefteris's flat in November 1993. Her parents tried unsuccessfully to persuade her to return home. She left for England but returned and moved back into Lefteris's flat. They announced their engagement on 22 December 1993. Early in the morning the neighbours heard shouting. Eventually the police were called who at first treated it as a family quarrel. Later it was discovered that the girl was being beaten and threatened with death and that Lefteris was in possession of a shotgun, threatening to use it on anyone who entered as well as on Elsie and finally on himself.

When it was clear that Lefteris would not let the girl leave his flat in spite of prolonged negotiations by the police and the intervention of friends and relatives, the police formed the view that he was going to carry out his threats and called in a specially trained platoon of the special police force ('MAAD') to stand by for action in case the efforts for resolution of the problem by peaceful means failed.

A rescue plan was prepared and shortly before midnight the platoon silently took position around the flat and waited for the order to intervene. According to the plan lethal force would be used only if Elsie's life, or their own lives, were in danger. When the operation started and the door of the flat was opened, Lefteris shot at the first police officer who entered. The wounded officer fell back, knocking down the officer following him. Two other police officers then entered the room and started firing at Lefteris, who was using Elsie as a shield.

The Commission concluded that there had been a violation of art. 2 but no violation of art. 6 of the Convention.[73]

The Court dismissed the Government's preliminary objection of non-exhaustion of domestic remedies and that of abuse of process. It then reiterated its case-law on the principles governing the use of lethal force by security forces.[74] It pointed out that art. 2 ranks as one of the most fundamental provisions of the Convention which, in peacetime, admits of no derogation under art. 15. Its provisions must be strictly construed, particularly the exceptions set out in paragraph 2:

> which apply not only to intentional deprivation of life but also to situations where it is permitted to use force which may result, as an unintended outcome, in deprivation of life.[75]

[73] Report of the Commission adopted on 23 May 1996, appended to the judgment of the Court, note 72 above.

[74] See *McCann and Others v the United Kingdom*, Judgment of 27 Sep 1995, Series A No. 324.

[75] See note 58 above, § 171.

The force used must be no more than 'absolutely necessary' for the achievement of one of the purposes defined in subparagraphs (a), (b) and (c). It stated further:

In this respect the use of the term 'absolutely necessary' in art. 2 paragraph 2 indicates that a stricter and more compelling test of necessity must be employed than the one normally applicable when determining whether state action is 'necessary in a democratic society' under paragraph 2 of articles 8 to 11. Deprivations of life must be subjected to the most careful scrutiny, particularly where deliberate lethal force is used, taking into consideration not only the actions of the agents of the State but also all the surrounding circumstances including such matters as the planning and control of the actions under examination.[76]

The planning and control of the rescue operation, including the decision to deploy the special platoon MAAD, was examined by the Court. Its sole concern was to evaluate whether the authorities had taken appropriate care to ensure that any risk to the lives of the couple had been minimized and that they were not negligent in their choice of action. It stated that it was not appropriate to discuss with the benefit of hindsight the merits of alternative tactics or to substitute the Court's own views for those of the authorities confronted with a dilemma unprecedented in the state and the need to take decisive action to break the deadlock. In carrying out its assessment of the planning and control phase of the operation from the standpoint of art. 2 of the Convention, the Court must have particular regard to the context in which the incident occurred as well as to the way in which the situation developed over the course of the day.[77] The Court concluded that in the circumstances there was no violation of article 2 of the Convention.

The next case was that of *Mavronichis v Cyprus*.[78] The applicant had applied for a post in the public sector. When unsuccessful, he filed a recourse before the Supreme Court and the administrative act challenged by him was annulled. Under the Constitution there were grounds for arguing that the domestic law of Cyprus gave him a right to seek compensation once he had secured the annulment of the administrative act. The applicant instituted a civil action solely to obtain financial reparation. Eventually he appealed against the judgment of the court of first instance which was the competent court to deal with the matter. It took four years and two months for the registry of the Supreme Court to fix a date for the hearing of his appeal.

The first issue before the Court was that of the applicability of art. 6(1) of the Convention. Its approach was that whilst disputes relating to, *inter alia,* the recruitment of civil servants are as a general rule outside the scope of this

[76] See also *McCann*, note 74 above, §§ 147–150.
[77] See note 58 above, §§ 181 to 186.
[78] Judgment of 24 Apr 1998, Reports 1998.

article.[79] It observed that in the instant case the issue of recruitment to a public-sector post was not at the heart of the applicant's civil action, hence it concluded that art. 6(1) was applicable, as the public-law features in the civil action could not outweigh the predominantly private-law characteristics of the proceedings, the outcome of which was decisive as to whether the applicant was entitled to reparation, a purely pecuniary right.[80]

The question of compliance with art. 6(1) presented no difficulty. The Court, having regard to its settled case-law, assessed:

> the reasonableness of the length of the impugned proceedings in the light of the particular circumstances of the case, having regard to its complexity, to the conduct of the applicant and to that of the authorities including the domestic courts which heard the case at first instance and on appeal.

It found that there had been no activity for four years and two months, and that the registry of the Supreme Court had taken too long to process the appeal proceedings, which amounted to a violation of art. 6(1). It then awarded 3,000 Cyprus pounds in respect of non-pecuniary damage and 4,784 Cyprus pounds less 2,000 French francs, as costs and expenses.

D. REMEDIAL ACTION TAKEN BY THE GOVERNMENT IN RESPONSE TO BEING HELD IN VIOLATION OF THE CONVENTION

Cyprus as a High Contracting Party was found to be in violation of article 8 in the *Modinos* case, which called for the amendment of sections 171 and 173 of the Criminal Code. However, in spite of strong public opposition and opposition from the Greek Christian Orthodox Church, as well as several members of the House of Representatives who also spoke in the House objecting to the amendment of the relevant section of the Code and indeed voted against it, the law has been amended and the Government considers that it has achieved compliance with the judgment of the Court in that case.

There is no other outstanding finding of a violation which calls for any statutory amendment.

[79] See, for example, *Neigel v France*, Judgment of 17 March 1997, Reports 1997–II p. 399 § 43.
[80] See note 70 above, §§ 31–33.

E. ASSESSMENT AND PROSPECTS

On the whole there are no fundamental problems in Cyprus as to the application of the Convention and the judicial control of any alleged violations.

First, the Convention is entrenched in the Constitution and so is part of the supreme law of the land. To the extent that it is not so entrenched it still has superior force to any municipal law. The international judicial control of any alleged violation is available through the optional articles 25 and 46 of the Convention, Cyprus having recognized the competence of the Commission to receive individual petitions and the compulsory jurisdiction of the Court. This, of course, was changed by Protocol No. 11 and since 1 November 1998 the right of individual petition and the compulsory jurisdiction of the Court are no longer optional to the Contracting Parties.

Secondly, Cyprus has a strong and independent judiciary which judicially reviews the acts of the executive as regards executory administrative acts and decisions along the general principles of administrative law, which originated from the Conseil d'Etat of France and prevail in Continental Europe, as well as the judicial review of the constitutionality of legislation. These, together with an active and independent legal profession, are essential prerequisites for the defence of civil liberties.

Thirdly, the mass media, newspapers, magazines, and privately owned radio and television stations take up any complaint which comes to their attention.

Fourthly, the people enjoy a high standard of education and economic prosperity, and spare no effort to secure for themselves and their families the safeguard of their rights through any available means, including access to courts and ultimately to the international organs, freely and without any intimidation.

In other words, democracy and the rule of law are the very foundation of the Republic of Cyprus. Needless to say, democracy and human rights are interwoven. Human rights are the cornerstone of democracy, which is in turn the only constitutional structure in which human rights can be effectively acknowledged and protected.

The prospects are excellent and the safeguarding of human rights, both classical and modern, for all its inhabitants, irrespective of race, creed, religion, or colour, will undoubtedly be the solid foundations for any future development in the political field.

9

Czech Republic

DALIBOR JÍLEK AND MAHULENA HOFMANN*

THE CONSTITUTION AND HUMAN RIGHTS

The year 1989 was not the beginning of the history of the Czechoslovak state.[1] The totalitarian state which governed from 1948 collapsed during the chilly days of the Velvet Revolution.[2] Legislative space was opened for a major metamorphosis of domestic law.[3] Human rights and the rule of law became the turning point for the process of the transformation of law. Human rights suddenly ceased to be subject to the strong impact of political and ideological indoctrination and were now intended to become the quintessence of legal existence for an individual.

A state is not a mere abstract but it represents a vital aggregate of persons. The purpose of the constitution is, *inter alia*, to lay down in law the legal status of an individual as the subject of rights and duties. The Charter of Fundamental Rights and Freedoms adopted by the Federal Assembly on 9 January 1991 drew the rights of individuals to the central attention of law.[4] As far as the form is concerned, the Charter enjoyed the binding force of constitutional law and was the top of the pyramid of the legal order. Even the

* Professor Jílek is the author of this chapter down to its section on the national domestic case-law of the Constitutional Court which was written by Dr Hofmann.

[1] The National Committee in Prague declared the existence of the Czechoslovak state in 1918, establishing by a political fiction the Czechoslovak nation whose two branches were created by the Czech and Slovak communities.

[2] The decisive events came on Nov 18 and 19. The newly formed Civic Forum changed the course of events in an astonishingly short period of time. In November huge crowds of people gathered on Wenceslas Square and shouted their mandate for Václav Havel, the leading dissident, to become the President. G. H. Flanz (ed), *Constitutions of the Countries of the World*: The Czech Republic (New York, 1993) p. 79.

[3] The Constitution was amended on 29 Nov 1989 in an extraordinary session of the Federal Assembly. After a turbulent discussion the Deputies voted to delete art 4 which stated that the Communist Party was the guiding force in society and in the state. Changes were also made to arts 6 and 16. References to Marxism-Leninism were deleted. See G. H. Flanz (ed), op. cit., p. 79.

[4] The Charter of Fundamental Rights and Freedoms was promulgated on 9 Jan 1991 as Act No. 23/1991. It was published on 8 Feb in the Official Gazette and came into effect on the same day. See G. H. Flanz (ed), op cit., p. 86.

form of the constitutional law reflects the content significance of the Charter. The Federal Assembly did not pursue a monologue by means of the Charter, nor create a political proclamation, but intended to legislate a positive legal regulation.[5] The Federal Assembly not only conceived the Charter in a comprehensive sense but primarily emphasized the judicial protection of human rights. Human rights and fundamental freedoms as provided in the Charter have appeared under the protection of the Constitutional Court.

Such protection is not exclusive but is superior in significance because any ordinary court provides the protection for human rights.[6]

Even during the preparation of the draft the framers emphasized the harmony of the Charter with international treaties on human rights.[7] They were inspired, first of all, by the Universal Declaration on Human Rights of 1948 and the Convention for the Protection of Human Rights and Fundamental Freedoms of 1950. The text of the Charter should cover international commitments resulting from the European Convention on Human Rights.[8]

The immediate influence of the European Convention on Human Rights upon the content of obligations incorporated into the Charter was multiplied by the provision of section 2 of Constitutional Act No. 23/1991.[9] This provision became the first rule governing the relation between international and domestic law for the sphere of human rights in Czechoslovak history[10] and it acquired a unique character. The unique character stems from the following aspects:

- introducing incorporation into Czechoslovak constitutional law,
- eliminating a sharp caesura between international and domestic law in the sphere of human rights,
- supremacy of international treaties on human rights over ordinary laws, and
- direct effect of international obligations on human rights in the domestic legal realm.[11]

[5] See V. Pavlíček: Listina základních práv a svobod a problémy přeměny právního řádu. Právník, 1992, No.5, pp. 365–366.

[6] Ibid, p. 367.

[7] See Č. Čepelka: V čem se změní ochrana lidských práv vstupem do Rady Evropy. Právo a zákonnost, 1991, No. 4, pp. 192–193.

[8] Ibid, p. 193.

[9] Section 2 reads: 'Treaties on human rights and fundamental freedoms, ratified and promulgated by the Czech and Slovak Federal Republic, are universally binding on its territory and supersede its own laws'.

[10] J. Malenovský: Mezinárodní smlouvy o lidských právech a československé ústavní právo (pokus o doktrinární výklad § 2 ústavního zákona č. 23/1991 Sb.), Právník, 1992, No. 11, p. 931.

[11] V. Týč, Aplikace mezinárodních smluv ve vnitrostátním právu. Právník, 1993, No. 4, p. 333.

Section 2 of the Constitutional Act was a response to the *de facto* supremacy of domestic law over international law that prevailed in the totalitarian state.[12] The *de facto* supremacy of domestic law was manifested in the preference for national regulation of human rights and in the refusal to apply international treaties on human rights by which Socialist Czechoslovakia was bound. Judicial and other state authorities applied domestic provisions only. The Czechoslovak state consistently refused to accept international control of human rights.

Section 2 of Constitutional Act resulted in a number of favourable legal consequences. However, it still faced criticism. The Czechoslovak doctrine of international law referred to unbalance[13] and contradictory[14] and legislatively technical hastiness.[15] The theoretical debate concentrated especially on the relationship between international treaties on human rights and constitutional laws governing the rights of an individual. A disputation was instituted by the contribution delivered by V. Ševčík as the rapporteur of the House of Nations when discussing Constitutional Act No. 23/1991. V. Ševčík characterized the construction of the provision referring to similarity with the French constitutional model. He stated that treaties on human rights prevailed over ordinary law[16] and such international instruments had been awarded a mezzanine status between constitutional and ordinary statutes. Other authors shared the now prevailing opinion and came to the conclusion that section 2 established, in its essence, *de iure* supremacy of domestic law.[17] The opposite pole of the doctrinal spectrum included the views of Z. Valentovič, P. Vršanský, and Š. Šebesta, who interpreted the term 'the law' in an extensive manner. In their opinion, the law designates the national legal order and international treaties on human rights have priority over the domestic rules including constitutional laws adopted by the Federal Assembly and constitutional laws adopted by the Czech National Council and Slovak National Council.[18] J. Malenovsky has analysed section 2 with close attention and legal thoroughness. He achieved a trustworthy result of

[12] J. Malenovský, Mezinárodní právo veřejné. Obecna část (Brno, 1993), pp. 60–1.

[13] Z. Valentovič, P. Vršanský, Š. Šebesta, Výklad § 2 ústavního zákona č. 23/1991 Zb., ktorým sa uvadza Listina základních práv a slobod ako ústavný zákon Federálneho zhromaždenia Českej a Slovenskej Federativnej Republiky. Právny obzor, 1992, No. 5, p. 471.

[14] V. Strážnická, K výkladu § 2 ústavného zákona č. 23/Zb. 'Medzinárodne zmluvy o l'udských právách a základných slobodách, ratifikované a vyhlásené Českou a Slovenskou Federatívnou Republikou, su na jej území všeobecne záväzné a majú prednost' před zákonom, Právny obzor, 1992, No. 5, p. 476.

[15] J. Azud, Poznámka k § 2 ústavného zákona č. 23/1991 Zb., Právny obzor, 1992, No. 5, p. 479.

[16] V. Ševčík, K Listině základních práv a svobod (I.), Justičná revue, 1992, No. 3, p. 8.

[17] See J. Azud, op. cit., p. 479.

[18] See Z. Valentovič, P. Vršansky, S. Sebesta, op. cit., p. 475.

interpretation. In accordance with his interpretation it cannot be asserted that there is a relationship of superiority and inferiority between the international treaties on human rights and the constitutional statutes.[19] They enjoy identical legal force in the national legal order. In the case of incompatibility between those forms of law, the principle of *lex posterior derogat priori* is applied.[20] Such legal situations seem to be rare. The rules of behaviour may differ in the degree of detail or particularity more frequently.[21] The principle *lex specialis derogat legi generali* is applied to such cases.

Section 2 of the Constitutional Act established the complementarity of international and national protection of human rights for the sphere of substantive rules. However the Czech and Slovak Federal Republic (ČSFR) was concerned about its non-participation in the European system of human rights protection. Therefore, the ČSFR applied for admission to the Council of Europe, and after due consideration by the Committee of Ministers and Parliamentary Assembly were invited to become a member. The ČSFR complied with the material and formal legal conditions for admission on 21 February 1991 and became a member of the Council of Europe.[22] The Czechoslovak representative, at the same time as depositing the instrument of accession, signed the European Convention on Human Rights and its additional Protocols. The signature of this most significant instrument among approximately 150 treaties which have been concluded so far in the framework of the Council of Europe is considered to be an unwritten political prerequisite for membership in this organization.[23]

The bicameral Czechoslovak Parliament agreed with the ratification of the European Convention on Human Rights at the common meeting of both chambers on 21 January 1992. The President ratified this Convention in accordance with article 61, paragraph 1, letter a of Constitutional Act No. 143/1968 on the Czechoslovak Federation. The instrument of ratification was deposited with the Secretary General of the Council of Europe on 18 March 1992. The European Convention was promulgated in the Official Gazette (No. 209/1992). The ČSFR declared that it recognized the competence of the European Commission of Human Rights to receive individual petitions in accordance with article 25 of the Convention and compulsory jurisdiction of the European Court of Human Rights pursuant to article 46. The unilateral

[19] See J. Malenovský, op. cit. in note 10 above, p. 943.

[20] D. Jílek, 'Human Rights Treaties and the New Constitution', *Connecticut Journal of International Law*, 1993, No. 2, p. 411.

[21] See J. Malenovský, op. cit. note 10 above, p. 944.

[22] J. Malenovský, D. Jílek, V. David: Organizace spojených národů. Evropská společenství, Rada Evropy (Brno, 1992), pp. 152–153.

[23] J. Malenovský, K právním aspektům přijetí České Republiky do Rady Evropy, Právník, 1993, No. 10–11, p. 887.

declaration made by the ČSFR contributed to international judicial protection of human rights, and complementarity in the substantive and procedural senses was accomplished.

If the right of self-determination influenced the establishment of the Czechoslovak state, then the implementation of this collective right caused its extinction. The Slovak nation had been showing its desire for emancipation for a long time. The constitutional and political crisis arose after the elections held on 5–6 July 1992.[24] The victorious political forces were considering either the remodelling or the dissolution of the Federation.[25]

A political agreement was made that the Czech and Slovak Federal Republic should be split by 1 January 1993; this was achieved on 26 August 1992. This political decision posed the problem of how to dismember the state juristically. Several ways of doing this were suggested which did not violate the principle of constitutionality. The opposition political parties asserted the way of direct democracy: a referendum. The decisions of authorities for the representative democracy such as the Federal Assembly and both national councils should have been especially considered. There was also, for example, the possibility of concluding the agreement between the republican legislative assemblies. The practice, however, inclined towards splitting up of the Federation pursuant to the Constitutional Law of the Federal Assembly.

The Czech National Council adopted Resolution No. 103 of 24 November 1992, expressing the desire that the Czech Republic become a member of the Council of Europe after the eventual splitting up. The deputies requested the Chairman of the Council to prepare a note of the adopted resolution and to send it to the representatives of the Council of Europe.

The Federal Assembly passed the Constitutional Act No. 542/1992 concerning the dissolution of the Czech and Slovak Federal Republic. One hundred and eighty-three Deputies voted for the adoption of the Constitutional Act, thirty-eight were against it, with fifty-five abstentions. Pursuant to article l, paragraph 1 of the Constitutional Act, by 31 December 1992 the composite state ceased to exist as a legal personality. In accordance with article l, paragraph 2 the Czech Republic and Slovakia became the successor states. The provision qualifies the manner of the state extinction by *dismembratio* and the international legal personality of the ČSFR ceased to exist

[24] In the Czech Republic, Václav Klaus and the Civic Democratic Party in alliance with the Christian Democratic Party won 33.1% of the votes. In Slovakia Mečiar won an impressive victory, and could then state that his insistence on sovereignty for Slovakia had won support. See G. H. Flanz (ed), op. cit., p. 106.

[25] The Movement for Democratic Slovakia wanted a confederation in which both republics would be subjects of international law. The Civic Democratic Party favoured two fully independent states but not a confederation. See G. H. Flanz (ed), op. cit., p. 107.

on the last day of that year. Article 1 of the Constitutional Act recognized both Republics as being successor states from 1 January 1993.

A letter from the Chairman of the Czech National Council dated 27 November 1992 was sent to the President of the Committee of Ministers, to the President of Parliamentary Assembly, and to the Secretary General of the Council of Europe. The letter describes the situation in respect of the membership of the ČSFR in the Council of Europe and the position of this state as a contracting party to the European Convention on Human Rights and other international instruments. The Czech National Council declares that the Czech Republic, as one of the successor states after the dissolution of the ČSFR, desires to be a member of the Council of Europe. The content of this letter is noteworthy in that the Czech National Council assumes uninterrupted membership in this intergovernmental organization or automatic succession to membership in the Council of Europe. The Czech Republic is pledged to respect the principles of the Council of Europe and expresses its readiness to comply with the obligations arising from the Statute. It promises to be bound by the European Convention on Human Rights, its Protocols, and its Declarations, pursuant to articles 25 and 46, without any prejudice to the question of membership of the Council of Europe. As a unilateral act the letter articulates the will of the state.

On 16 December 1992 the deputies of the Czech National Council adopted the Constitution of the Czech Republic, voting by 172 votes for, 16 votes against, and 10 abstentions. The Constitution, in article 1, declares the Czech Republic to be a sovereign, unitary, and democratic state governed by law and based on respect for the rights and freedoms of man and citizen. In accordance with article 3, the Charter of Fundamental Rights and Freedoms forms a constituent part of the constitutional order of the new state. Fundamental rights and freedoms pursuant to article 4 of the primary legal instrument enjoy judicial protection. Simplified enumeration of some constitutional provisions in Chapter I of the Charter shows the harmony between the content and material conditions embodied in article 3 of the Statute. Nevertheless, a very rough comparison is made in the world of normativity and by no means in the world of fact.

The common state of Czechs and Slovaks died with the very last moment of New Year's Eve 1992. At midnight the Constitution of the Czech state came into force.[26] On the very first day of the existence of the Czech Republic the Minister for Foreign Affairs applied in writing on behalf of the government for admission to the Council of Europe. Upon the instruction of the

[26] The Constitution of the Czech Republic was published in the Official Gazette under No. 1/1993.

government, he simultaneously sent the Secretary General of the Council of Europe a letter which was a declaration of succession to international treaties.

MEMBERSHIP OF THE COUNCIL OF EUROPE AND ECHR

Implementation of the Czech Republic's accession to the European Convention on Human Rights followed a broadly similar pattern to that of the Slovak Republic (see chapter 29, especially pp. 755–760). The former state of Czechoslovakia (the Czech and Slovak Federal Republic) had already ratified the ECHR on 18 March 1992, and both the Czech Republic and Slovak Republic regarded themselves as bound by the ECHR. However, because of the ECHR's 'closed' treaty status, in order to be a contracting party to its organization and machinery, a member state must first be established as a member of the Council of Europe. Furthermore, the Committee of Ministers stressed that the Czech Republic's desired membership of the Council of Europe could not be implemented simply by way of succession to the membership of the former Czechoslovakia, and the Czech government must follow the admission procedure (see also below, Chapter 29 on Slovakia Republic).

Opinion was justified in the light of legal theory and practice. General international law has no customary rule entitling a state to succeed to rights and duties resulting from membership of an international institution by its predecessor state, nor imposing a duty upon the new state to apply in such case for admission to an international organization.[27] Neither can the lack of customary rules governing succession to international organizations be replaced by legal analogy and the application of the Vienna Convention on Succession of States in Respect of Treaties of 1978 because the statute of an international organization is understood as an international treaty *sui generis* and establishes legal relations not only between the contracting parties but also between the members and the institution. This binary structure of relations creates obstacles to the application of the Vienna Convention of 1978.

Article 3 of the Statute of the Council of Europe stipulates a trio of material conditions for the accession to the institution. Pursuant to article 4 of the Statute the state must be subjectively willing and objectively able to fulfil legal requirements. Implementing principles of the rule of law, protection of human rights and fundamental freedoms, and the existence of effective institutions in a pluralistic parliamentary democracy are not transmitted from one

[27] See V. Mikulka, Sukcese států (Praha, 1987), p. 68.

state to another in the same way as the genetic qualities inherited by a child from its parents. Such requirements must be respected in the national legal order and implemented in reality.

Formal application for admission to membership of the Council of Europe was therefore made on 27 November 1992 by the Czech Republic, which meanwhile expressed its wish to be regarded as bound by the principles of the ECHR. This was followed by the Czech government's unilateral declaration of succession to various international treaties[28] including the ECHR on 1 January 1993, which was treated by the Committee of Ministers at its meeting of Ministers' deputies on 8 January 1993 as a request for accession. On 13 January 1993 the Committee of Ministers met again to consider the situation, and proceeded to invite the Parliamentary Assembly to state its opinion on whether the Czech Republic as a successor state should be able to join the organization at the earliest opportunity. Furthermore, the Committee of Ministers stated that everything possible should be done to reduce the duration and consequences of the period separating the dissolution of the Czech and Slovak Federal Republic from the accession of the Czech Republic to the Council of Europe. The Assembly unanimously concluded that the Czech Republic was both able and willing to respect the provisions of article 3 of the Statute, to play a sincere and effective part in achieving the aims settled by the Council of Europe, and to comply with the conditions for membership as specified in article 4 of the Statute.

The next day the Committee of Ministers at its 496th meeting of the Ministers' Deputies adopted Resolution (93)32 on the invitation to the Czech Republic to become a member of the Council of Europe and the accession to the Statute. At the voting in the Committee, the representative of Liechtenstein abstained, but this did not prevent formal unanimity according to article 9, paragraph 1, letter f and article 10, paragraph 2, letter c of the internal rules (*Réglement intérieur*) of 1955.

The resolution of the Committee of Ministers on the Czech Republic's membership (as with that of the Slovak Republic) expressed the view that its government should be considered a contracting party to the ECHR with retrospective effect from 1 January 1993. No separate signature and ratification of the treaty was required, in the light of the formalities earlier conducted by

[28] The European Convention on the Equivalence of Diplomas Leading to Admission to Universities of 1953, the European Cultural Convention of 1954, the European Convention on the Equivalence of Periods of University Study of 1956, the European Convention on the Academic Recognition of University Qualification of 1959, the Protocol to the European Convention on the Equivalence of Diplomas Leading to Admission to Universities of 1964, the European Convention on Extradition of 1957, the European Convention on Mutual Assistance in Criminal Matters of 1989, the European Convention of the Transfer of Proceedings in Criminal Matters of 1972, and the Convention on the Transfer of Sentenced Persons of 1983.

the Czech and Slovak Federal Republic (ratification having taken place on 18 March 1992). The interim period between 18 March 1992 (ratification by the CSFR) and 1 January 1993 (dissolution of the CSFR, and formal accession date of the new Czech state) remained theoretically problematic, however, on whether the government could be held liable for human rights violations under the ECHR machinery committed during that interval of time. Subsequently the question appears to have been answered in the affirmative by the Strasbourg enforcement machinery, following the case of *Brazny v Slovakia*[29] in which the European Commission of Human Rights held that it possessed the competence to examine the facts of a case arising during that period.

Thus, despite the different legal interpretations which could have been adopted on the position of the successor states following the dissolution of the former Czechoslovakia, the Czech Republic has achieved uninterrupted conventional relations.

THE STATUS OF THE CONVENTION IN NATIONAL LAW

The Constitution of the Czech Republic makes use of legal heritage embodied in section 2 of the Constitutional Act No. 23/1991. Article 10 of the Constitution says that ratified and promulgated international treaties on human rights and fundamental freedoms by which the Czech Republic is bound are directly binding and take precedence over domestic law. No internal transformating act is necessary to establish their national legal force.[30]

The Constitution manifests the dualistic theory solving the relationship between international and national law. International commitments relating to human rights are transformed into national law by incorporation. No doubt incorporation ensures internal legal effects for the establishment of an international treaty[31] and an international treaty on human rights remains at the same time a formal source of international law.[32] Whilst the legal life of such a treaty is governed by international law:[33] through incorporation a treaty of this kind also becomes national law: formal monism is valid in that sphere.

[29] Discussed in chapter 29 below at pp. 759–760.

[30] See V. Pavlíček and J. Hřebejk: Ústava a ústavní řád České Republiky (Praha, 1994), vol. I., p. 57.

[31] See J. Bárta, Některé otázky přístupu k mezinárodní úmluvě a potřeby transformace do vnitrostátního práva. (Úvaha nad Vídeňskou úmluvou o občanskoprávní odpovědnosti za jaderné škody), Právník, No. 9–10, p. 797.

[32] See V. Týč, Aplikace mezinárodních smluv ve vnitrostátním právu, Právník, 1993, No. 3, p. 335.

[33] See D. Jílek, Mezinárodněprávní pohled na ustanovení článku 10 Ústavy České Republiky. Časopis pro právní vědu a praxi, 1993, No. l, p. 117.

The European Convention on Human Rights, including its protocols, belongs to the *ratione materiae* operation of article 10 of the Constitution and the formulation of international treaties on human rights and fundamental freedoms is related to these instruments. Article 10 of the Constitution requires that the above-mentioned treaties be ratified. The term 'ratification' possesses different meanings in international and in constitutional law. The expression has to be interpreted in accordance with constitutional law because the branch of domestic law explains its special content. Article 63, paragraph 1, letter b of the Constitution lays down the ratification procedure.[34]

The expression 'promulgated' is also governed by national law. For the time being, international treaties on human rights are promulgated in the Collection of International Treaties in the form of notification. The Collection of International Treaties contains a Czech translation of such instruments. In principle, the state authorities also publish the binding wording of the treaty in this Collection. The Czech translation fulfils particularly the informative function in respect of persons of national law.[35] Therefore the authorities have to take the authentic wording of international treaties into account. The promulgation in the Collection of International Treaties does not enjoy the legal effects of transformation. Pursuant to the former Official Gazette Act, the European Convention on Human Rights and additional Protocols were promulgated in the Official Gazette and *conditio sine qua non* validity was granted.

Incorporation establishes the direct effect of international treaties on human rights in the national system of law. There is a rebuttable presumption that the provision is directly binding.[36] If the judicial or other authority takes the view that a provision of the treaty on human rights is not capable of governing the legal relationship between persons of national law, ie is not self-executing, then the direct effects will be individually denied. Self-executing provisions may operate within domestic law and create expected legal effects.[37]

Scholars in the field of constitutional law rely particularly on historic interpretation.[38] They place these treaties between constitutional laws and ordinary laws and emphasize that the Constitution and particularly the Charter of Fundamental Rights and Freedoms guarantee, even in this sphere, a uniform and consistent legal order that cannot be endangered by international

[34] On parliamentary proceedings see below.

[35] See D. Jílek, op. cit. in note 33 above, p. 115.

[36] See J. Malenovský, op. cit. in note 34 above, p. 863.

[37] See D. Jílek, op. cit. in note 20 above, p. 417.

[38] J. Malenovský, Poměr mezinárodního a vnitrostátního právo obecně a v českém právu zvláště (Brno, 2000), pp. 63–7.

treaties on human rights, so that constitutional laws must take precedence over treaties.[39] These theoreticians mistakenly assume that international treaties on human rights establish a minimal standard, which cannot be extended by domestic law. The conclusion may apply to universal treaties on human rights, but not to the European Convention on Human Rights.

The textual interpretation, using the principles of logic and good faith to interpret the meanings of words, does not justify the superiority of constitutional laws over international treaties on human rights. Moreover, each rule must be analysed in its context. Article 39, paragraph 4 of the Constitution stipulates that it takes both chambers of the Parliament to pass a constitutional law; for an international treaty, according to article 10, the same applies.[40] Furthermore, pursuant to article 87 of the Constitution, the Constitutional Court of the Czech Republic decides on the abrogation of laws, other legal regulations, or their specific provisions if they contradict constitutional law or an international treaty on human rights. It should be considered, however, that the legal order of the Czech Republic may not review the constitutionality of international treaties according to article 10.

The synthesis of interpretative canons does not justify the assertion *de lege lata* that there is a relationship of superiority and inferiority between constitutional laws and international treaties on human rights. International treaties on human rights possess the same legal force as constitutional act in the national law of the Czech Republic. Such a conclusion can be fully applied to the European Convention on Human Rights and its Protocols.

THE STATUS OF THE CONVENTION IN PARLIAMENTARY PROCEEDINGS

The Constitution of the Czech Republic guarantees the principle of division of powers for negotiating treaties on human rights. The Parliament reviews the text of such a treaty and participates in the procedure of ratification. Qualified agreement by both chambers of the Parliament is required for treaties on human rights.[41] Debating the treaty according to article 10 of the Constitution in the Parliament is the only procedure which ensures harmony between the Charter of Fundamental Rights and Freedoms and such treaties

[39] See V. Pavlíček and J. Hřebejk. op. cit., p. 62.

[40] The agreement of a three-fifths majority of all Deputies and of a three-fifths majority of present Senators is required to pass a constitutional law and to approve an international treaty according to art. 10.

[41] See art 49, para 2 of the Constitution.

because the institutes of constitutionality of international treaties on human rights are not embodied in the Constitution.

International treaties on human rights belong to what are known as presidential treaties. The presidential treaties require, before ratification by the President, parliamentary agreement. If Parliament approves the international treaty in accordance with article 39, paragraph 4 of the Constitution, this determines the nature of an instrument as a treaty on human rights. The Constitutional Court is rarely able to change that qualification if it decides to abrogate laws or other regulations or their individual provisions or constitutional complaint.[42]

The government submits to the Parliament a proposal to conclude an international treaty. The explanatory report is prepared by the competent Ministry and provides an overall evaluation of the object and purpose of the treaty and its analysis in accordance with domestic law. The report also indicates the category proposed and includes the scrutiny if the agreement of the Parliament is necessary for the approval of the instrument.

The process of debating the treaty in its material and temporal context involves several stages, of which the government and the Parliament are the actors. The Parliament alone, however, determines the character of the treaty. The President cannot change such a determination. The President finalizes the process of ratifying the treaty.[43] The text and the particulars of the instrument of ratification are regulated by domestic law. The instrument of ratification is signed by the head of the state and countersigned by the Prime Minister.

The government and Parliament treated the European Convention on Human Rights as a treaty pursuant to article 10 of the Constitution. When the Parliament approved Protocol No. 11 in 1995, it expressed its agreement in accordance with article 49, paragraph 2 of the Constitution, although this instrument is mixed in content because it includes mostly organizational norms and the minority of obligations has the integral structure.

HUMAN RIGHTS CASE-LAW

The national domestic case-law of the Constitutional Court

The articles of the ECHR and judgments of the European Court of Human Rights as rules of international law have been frequently referred to and applied in the practice of the Constitutional Court. Some selected recent

[42] See art. 87 of the Constitution.
[43] See art. 63, para l, letter b of the Constitution.

examples of their influence and effect are set out as follows, grouped around the relevant Article of the ECHR.

In the decision No. 91 of 2 July 1997[44] the Constitutional Court—on its own initiative—applied article 5, paragraph 1, of the Convention. In this case, which dealt on the one hand with the differences of custody time limit provisions under the code of criminal procedure, and on the other hand with the then valid police laws, the Constitutional Court argued *inter alia* that the code of criminal procedure is compatible with the Convention and its related European jurisprudence (*Ireland v United Kingdom*,[45] *De Wilde, Ooms and Versyp v Belgium*,[46] *Engel et al. v Netherlands*,[47] *De Jong, Baljet and van den Brink v Netherlands*[48]).

Article 5, paragraph 4 of the Convention played a decisive role in judging the compatibility of a rule of the police code No. 283/1991 Slg., in its later versions, with the constitution and the Convention. This rule of the police code did not require that police decisions to arrest persons for their identification, who had entered the territory of the Czech Republic without any authorization, had to be reviewed by the courts 'within a short time limit'. The Constitutional Court based its decision of 2 June 1999[49] on the jurisprudence of the Court of Human Rights (*De Wilde, Ooms and Versyp*[50] and *De Jong, Baljet & Van den Brink*[51]), and it came to the conclusion that the challenged rule contradicted the principle of judicial protection during imprisonment.

In the decision of 24 September 1994, 'about compliance with the constitutional principles in the administrative jurisdiction',[52] the Constitutional Court cited the cases of *Fredin*,[53] *Pretto*,[54] and *Håkansson and Sturesson*[55] to justify the unconstitutionality of a civil procedure rule which made it possible to conclude the single-staged administrative court proceeding without a hearing. The Constitutional Court emphasized that if the highest administrative court is the first and only court deciding a case, a non-public hearing of that matter results in a violation of article 1 of the Convention, and it stated that judging questions of law without taking into consideration the relevant questions of fact is impossible.

[44] Pl. ÚS 2/97, Sbírka nálezů a usnesení 8 (1997–II. part), pp. 342–3.
[45] *Ireland ./.*GB, ECHR ser. A No. 25.
[46] *De Wilde, Ooms & Versyp ./.* B, ECHR ser. A No. 14.
[47] *Engel et al ./.* N., ECHR ser. A No. 22.
[48] *De Jong, Baljet & Van den Brink ./.* NL, ECHR ser. A No. 77.
[49] Decision No. 83 of 2 June 1999, Pl. ÚS 29/98, Sbírka nálezů a usnesení 14 (1999–II. Part), p. 195 ff.
[50] See n. 44 above.
[51] See n. 48 above.
[52] Decision No. 85 of 24 Sept. 1996, Pl. ÚS 18/96, Sbírka nálezů a usnesení 6 (1996–II. Part), p. 109 ff.
[53] *Fredin ./.*S, ECHR ser. A No. 283-A.
[54] *Pretto et al../.* I., ECHR ser. A no 71.
[55] *Håkansson* and *Sturesson ./.* P., ECHR ser. A No. 171.

In the decision of the plenum of 27 November 1996 in connection with the not yet completed structure of the administrative jurisdiction in the Czech Republic, the interpretation of article 6, paragraph 1 of the Convention by the Constitutional Court was not so clear:[56] in its view, article 6, paragraph 1 of the Convention does not impose the obligation on the contracting states to exclude from their laws the possibility of administrative decisions determining rights and responsibilities of natural and legal persons. According to the Court, article 6, paragraph 1 of the Convention does not require that a legal system excludes the competence of administrative organs to decide civil law matters, obligations, or criminal charges against a citizen. It stated that an inconsistency of the system of laws of the Czech Republic with article 6, paragraph 1 of the Convention can be found only in the respect that there is no existing statutory rule, which clearly establishes the right of full scrutiny of the decision of an administrative organ by a tribunal, which is independent, impartial, and meets the requirements of article 6, paragraph 1; thus, by a tribunal, which not only decides on the legality of the administrative decision but also on questions of fact (full jurisdiction). It is interesting that the Constitutional Court relied in its reasoning upon the Directive (EC) 62/95 of the European Parliament and of the Council of 13 December 1995 on the application of open network provision to voice telephony and the decision of the European Court of Human Rights in the matter *Le Compte*,[57] stating that both 'indicate the trend of the legal regulation in the Czech Republic, which tries to become member of the European institutions'. The dissenting opinion of a minority on the Court had a critical view of the conclusions of the majority vote: the impossibility to review administrative decisions, it argued, leads to a violation of article 6, paragraph 1 of the Convention.

Article 8 of the Convention was relied up as the main argument of the Constitutional Court in its decision of 21 April 1999,[58] involving an individual constitutional complaint against the decision of a district court in the criminal proceeding case *Ústí nad Labem*, in which the district court had ordered the expulsion for an indefinite period of a convicted robber with family ties in the Czech Republic. The Constitutional Court based the reasoning of its decision, which sustained the constitutional complaint, on the European jurisprudence of article 8, paragraph 2, of the Convention (*Berrehab*,[59] *Beldjoudi*[60] and *Moustaquim*[61]), reaching the conclusion that the prevention

[56] Decision No. 126 of 27 Nov. 1996, Pl. ÚS 28/95, Sbírka nálezů a usnesení 6 (1996–II. Part), p. 407.

[57] *Le Compte, Van Leuven and De Meyere ./.* B., ECHR ser. A No. 43.

[58] Decision No. 57 of 21 Apr. 1999, II. ÚS 178/98, Sbírka nálezů a usnesení 14 (1999–II. Part). p. 29.

[59] *Berrehab ./.* NL, ECHR ser. A No. 138.

[60] *Beljoudi ./.* F, ECHR ser. A No. 234-A.

[61] *Moustaquim ./.* B., ECHR ser. A No. 193.

of crime is an admissible and therefore legitimate goal of any democratic society. However, when the penalty consists of the expulsion of the perpetrator for an indefinite period of time, and the possibility of his reformation has not been examined, the measure exceeds the principle of proportionality.

Article 8, paragraph 2, of the Convention has also helped the Constitutional Court to assess the authority of the governmental information service to collect, keep, and use information of natural persons[62]. It has argued that article 8, paragraph 2, allows public authorities to intrude upon the right of privacy under clearly established statutory requirements.

In a decision of 2 June 1999—on request of the district court in *Nový Jičín*—the Constitutional Court based its reasoning on article 9, paragraph 2 of the Convention, when examining the compatibility with the constitution and the Convention of a provision of the Law on the Community Service of 1992,[63] which established a very short preclusive time limit for persons liable for military service to express their binding decision to do community service instead of military service for religious reasons; the law automatically linked the lapse of this time limit with criminal consequences. The character and extent of the limitations under article 9, paragraph 2 of the Convention, which are reflected in the jurisprudence of Strasbourg (in the case *Grandrath*),[64] and their connection with article 14 of the Convention, contributed to the result that the Constitutional Court did not declare the time limit itself but its preclusive character unconstitutional and unconventional.

In the decision of 15 May 1996[65] article 14 of the Convention was applied: the Constitutional Court argued that the requirement of an 'election deposit' under the law No. 247/95 Slg. concerning the election of the parliament does not contradict the requirement of non-discriminating elections and therefore neither violates article 14 of the Convention nor article 3 of the First Additional Protocol.

The Constitutional Court justified the decision No. 74 Pl. ÚS 5/95[66] concerning Czech nationality by arguing *inter alia* that the objective expressed in article 17 of the law No. 40/1993 Slg. to avoid double nationality (the acquisition of a foreign nationality causes the loss of the Czech nationality *ex lege*) is in accordance with modern European tendencies. It stated that differences

[62] Decision No. 28 of 10 Apr. 1996, Pl. ÚS 34/95, Sbírka nálezů a usnesení 5 (1996–I. Part), p. 233 ff.

[63] Decision No. 82 of 2 June 1999, Pl. ÚS 18/98, Sbírka nálezů a usnesení 14 (1999–II. Part), p. 181 ff.

[64] *Grandrath ./.* D., ECHR E 2299/64

[65] Decision No. 39 of 15 May 1996, Pl. ÚS 3/96, Sbírka nálezů a usnesení 5 (1996–I. Part), p. 315 ff.

[66] For questions about the Czech Republic's nationality see also decision No. 40 of 13 Sept. 1994, Pl. ÚS 9/94, Sbírka nálezů a usnesení 2 (1993, 1994–II. Part), p. 7 ff.

in the legal status of nationals and foreign nationals under a number of aspects of the valid laws are acceptable and non-discriminating. The Court argued further that the prohibition of discrimination set forth by article 14 of the Convention applies only where there is a concrete violation of another constitutional right or civil liberty. In the view of the Court, the European jurisprudence sees 'discrimination' in cases, in which a given group of people is treated worse than another, although there is no objective and sound justification for such a treatment.

According to the reasoning behind this decision, double nationality is generally undesirable in international law. The prevention of double nationality has been the subject of many bilateral agreements of the former Czechoslovakia. The Constitutional Court stated that the Council of Europe's Convention on the Reduction of Cases of Multiple Nationality and on Military Obligations in Cases of Multiple Nationality of 6 May 1963, to which the Czech Republic is not a contracting party, is also relevant, in that article 1, paragraph 1 imposes upon states that nationals, who deliberately acquire a foreign nationality, be stripped of their former nationality. Additionally, the Court argued, the principles of the draft European Convention on Nationality and on Military Obligations in Cases of Multiple Nationality[67] allow states to decide that their nationals may have only one nationality.

In the reasoning to the decision No. 76 of 14 December 1999,[68] the Constitutional Court—on its own initiative—relied upon article 34 of the Convention. In this case, the Court was required to examine whether the Ministry of Finance as a governmental organ had the capacity to file a constitutional complaint. The Constitutional Court pointed to an analogy with article 34 of the Convention, which excludes State organs from the circle of persons entitled to file an individual complaint (only 'non-governmental organizations' or 'groups of individuals' are mentioned). This served to confirm the Constitutional Court in its view that a State organ does not qualify as a legal person in the sense of the applicable provisions governing the Law on the Constitutional Court and cannot therefore act as an applicant or participant in the proceedings.

Article 4, paragraph 1, of Protocol No. 7 of the Convention has been used by the Constitutional Court in a number of decisions dealing with the repeated punishment of an individual's continuous refusal to perform military service. The Constitutional Court's decision of 18 September 1995,[69] has

[67] The draft has later been adopted as the *European Convention on Nationality* (ETS 166, 1997).

[68] Decision No. 76 of 14 Dec. 1999, Sbírka nálezů a usnesení 16 (1999–IV. Part), p. 397 ff.

[69] Decision No. 50 of 18 Aug. 1995, IV. ÚS 81/95, Sbírka nálezů a usnesení 4 (1995–II. Part), p. 47; similar also decisions I.ÚS 184/9 6, IV ÚS 82/97, I. ÚS 322/96 und I. ÚS 400/97.

been seen as fundamental, in which it reversed two decisions of general courts in the same matter because of a violation of the principle '*ne bis in idem*', as stated both in article 40, paragraph 5, of the Charter of Constitutional Rights and Civil Liberties and in article 4, paragraph 1, of the Protocol to the ECHR. In its reasoning, the Court stated that 'a court, which decides about guilt and punishment for a criminal offence, has to respect the principle, laid down in article 40, paragraph 5 of the Charter and Art. 4, paragraph 1 of Protocol No. 7 of the Convention, that nobody can be persecuted and punished more than once for the same offence: thus, the principle '*ne bis in idem*'.

Cases before the ECHR and remedial action

As at 4 November 2000, a total of four cases had been decided by the European Court of Human Rights in which one or more violations were found to exist.[70] The judgments in each of these was delivered during the course of 2000. Three of the cases, those of *Ceský* (judgment of 6 June 2000), *Punzelt* (judgment of 25 April 2000), *Barfuss* (judgment of 31 July 2000), concerned the excessive length of the applicant's detention on remand, being a violation of article 5(3). The judgment in the *Barfuss* case also found an excessive length of certain criminal proceedings, in violation of article 6(1). In response, it is expected that the Czech government will confirm publication of the judgments, and specifically draw the attention of judges to the 'special diligence' required by them in these types of cases. It is hoped that information on the average length of detentions on remand, and on the number of detentions on remand compared with the number of pending criminal cases, will be made available.

The case of *Krčmář and others* (judgment of 3 March 2000) concerned the non-respect of the applicants' right to a fair trial by the Constitutional Court, since they did not receive certain documentary evidence provided to the Court in order to influence the final decision and did not have the opportunity to comment on it, being a violation of article 6(1). In the civil proceedings at issue, the applicants were challenging the lawfulness of the expropriation in 1949 of a company which belonged to members of their family. In response, the Delegation of the Czech Republic has informed the Committee of Ministers that the judgment has now specifically been brought to the attention of all judges of the Constitutional Court, and it has been published (in Czech translation) in *Pravnyi praxe*, a journal of the Ministry of Justice which is widely distributed in legal circles.

[70] This section was added at proof stage by the editors from information prepared by the Council of Europe.

At the request of the Committee of Ministers, as expressed during its examination of the last-mentioned case, the government is preparing to supply it with examples of domestic judgments which show that the articles of the ECHR and the judgments of the European Court of Human Rights are being effectively taken into account by Czech courts when applying domestic law.

10

Denmark[1]

PETER GERMER

A. INTRODUCTION

On 13 April 1953 Denmark ratified the European Convention on Human Rights and the First Protocol. Subsequently, Protocols Nos. 2–11 have been ratified by Denmark. In ratifying Protocol No. 7 Denmark made a reservation in respect of article 2(1).

Right from the beginning Denmark recognized the competence of the European Commission of Human Rights to receive complaints from individuals under the original article 25 of the Convention as well as the compulsory jurisdiction of the European Court of Human Rights under the original article 46 of the Convention. The first Danish declarations to that effect were limited to a period of two years, but the Danish government repeatedly renewed the declarations for subsequent periods of varying length. In 1997 the Danish government renewed the declarations for an unlimited period.[2] Protocol No. 11 was ratified by Denmark in July 1996, and the Danish legislative provisions relating to this Protocol entered into force on 1 November 1998.

B. THE STATUS OF THE CONVENTION IN DANISH LAW

In general, international treaties are not directly applicable in Denmark, but the fulfilment of treaty obligations is secured in various ways. New legislation

[1] The original version of this report was submitted in January 1995. The present contribution is a revised version, submitted in October 1998. A few references to source materials have been updated in January 2001 in connection with proofreading. A complete rewriting of the report has not been possible.

[2] See Lovtidende C (the Danish Official Gazette, part C), 1997, p. 446. In addition to the declarations under the original arts 25 and 46 of the Convention, the Danish government made comprehensive statements under art 6(2) of Protocol No. 4 and the original art 7(2) of Protocol No. 7.

may be adopted before the treaty is ratified by the Danish government, creating in advance the requisite harmony between Danish law and the treaty. Furthermore, it is generally agreed that Danish laws should be interpreted so as to comply with international treaty obligations.[3] It may also be assumed that Danish administrative authorities will exercise their discretionary powers in such a way that their administrative acts conform to international treaty obligations.[4]

For nearly 40 years the European Convention on Human Rights was not directly applicable in Denmark, but by Act No. 285 of 29 April 1992 concerning the European Convention on Human Rights the Convention was incorporated into Danish law. The Act entered into force on 1 July 1992.

Section 1 of the Act of 29 April 1992 concerning the European Convention on Human Rights, which contained the basic provisions regarding incorporation, referred to the Convention and the first eight additional Protocols. The Convention as amended by Protocols Nos. 3, 5, and 8 were annexed to the Act as Appendix 1, and Protocols Nos. 1, 2, 4, 6, and 7 were annexed to the Act as Appendices Nos. 2–6.[5] Act No. 1080 of 20 December 1995 amended the Act of 29 April 1992 so as to include in section 1 additional references to Protocols Nos. 9, 10, and 11. The amendment authorized the Minister of Justice to determine the date of entry into force. Regulation No. 418 of 20 May 1996, issued by the Minister of Justice, decreed that the legislative provision concerning Protocol No. 9 should enter into force on 1 June 1996. Regulation No. 423 of 20 May 1996, issued by the Minister of Justice, inserted the provisions of Protocol No. 9 into the Danish version of the Convention, and the consolidated text of the Convention as amended by Protocols Nos. 3, 5, 8, and 9 was annexed to the Regulation as an appendix.[6] Regulation No. 749 of 19 October 1998, issued by the Minister of Justice, decreed that the legislative provision concerning Protocol No. 11 should enter into force on 1 November 1998 and updated the legislative references to the Protocols.[7] Consolidated Act No. 750 of 19 October 1998 contains an updated version of the legislative provisions.[8]

[3] See, eg C. Gulmann, J. Bernhard, and T. Lehmann, *Folkeret*, 1989, pp. 91–93.

[4] At an early stage the Danish Ministry of Justice recognized that art 8 of the European Convention on Human Rights concerning the protection of family life restricted the Ministry's discretionary powers with regard to expulsion of aliens. See eg M. Sørensen, *Statsforfatningsret*, 2nd edn, 1973, p. 278. See also S. Stenderup Jensen, *The European Convention on Human Rights in Scandinavian Law*, 1992, pp. 160–165.

[5] See Lovtidende A (the Danish Official Gazette, part A), 1992, pp. 1088–1104.

[6] See Lovtidende A, 1996, pp. 2270–2279.

[7] See Lovtidende A, 1998 , pp. 4353–4369.

[8] See Lovtidende A, 1998, pp. 4370–4371. A footnote to the Consolidated Act indicated that, for obvious reasons, the Ministry of Justice had no intention of issuing a regulation covering Protocol No. 10. See ibid, p. 4371 note 1.

Section 3 of the Act concerning the European Convention on Human Rights provides that the Act does not modify the provisions of section 962, subsection 2, of the Danish Administration of Justice Act concerning limitations with regard to certain decisions in criminal cases. The explanatory remarks which accompanied the legislative bill when it was introduced in the Folketing (the Danish Parliament) in February 1992 referred to the fact that Denmark in ratifying Protocol No. 7 made a reservation with regard to the relationship between article 2(1) of the Protocol and the provisions of the Danish Administration of Justice Act concerning criminal cases subject to police prosecution.

As the legal basis for the incorporation of the European Convention on Human Rights is an Act of Parliament, the Convention is incorporated into Danish law at the level of ordinary legislation. The Convention does not amend the Danish Constitution, and it does not have the status of constitutional law in Denmark. The Danish legislature may at any time repeal or amend the Act of 29 April 1992 concerning the European Convention on Human Rights.

C. THE STATUS OF THE CONVENTION IN PARLIAMENTARY PROCEEDINGS

Generally speaking, the European Convention on Human Rights does not play a major role in parliamentary debates in Denmark.[9] Normally, when a legislative bill is being prepared, the Legal Department of the Ministry of Justice will examine its content with a view to ascertaining whether it is in conformity with the European Convention on Human Rights. If the Legal Department finds that this is not the case, it will suggest appropriate amendments to the bill.[10] Consequently, in most cases, when a bill comes before the Parliament, there is nothing to discuss in relation to the European Convention on Human Rights. However, there have been cases where the Parliament has had occasion to consider matters relating to the Convention.

In December 1952 and March 1953, when the Folketing was discussing questions concerning Denmark's ratification of the European Convention on Human Rights, several members spoke in favour of recognizing the competence

[9] In recent years the European Convention on Human Rights has been more in vogue in Danish parliamentary debates.

[10] See eg A. Jensen, 'Incorporation of the European Convention seen from a Danish Point of View', in L. A. Rehof and C. Gulmann (eds), *Human Rights in Domestic Law and Development Assistance Policies of the Nordic Countries*, (Dordrecht: Nijhoff, 1989), pp. 161–170, at p. 167.

of the Commission to receive complaints from individuals under the original article 25 as well as the compulsory jurisdiction of the Court under the original article 46, and there seemed to be widespread enthusiasm for the Strasbourg machinery both in government circles and in Parliament.[11] However, in November 1975 the Danish government contested the jurisdiction of the European Court of Human Rights in the case of *Kjeldsen, Busk Madsen, and Pedersen*. This was criticized during a parliamentary debate on 15 January 1976.[12] That caused the government to change its position, and the following day it informed the Registrar of the European Court of Human Rights that it had decided to withdraw its preliminary objection.[13]

In 1982 the Danish Parliament adopted a bill concerning protection against dismissal relating to trade union affiliation.[14] When introducing the bill in Parliament, the Minister of Labour referred to the judgment of the European Court of Human Rights of 13 August 1981 in the *'Closed Shop'* case.[15] The Minister of Labour stated that Danish law did not fully respect those principles of freedom of association which had been proclaimed by the European Court of Human Rights, and the government, taking for granted that Denmark should respect its obligations under the European Convention on Human Rights, had therefore introduced the bill concerning protection against dismissal relating to trade union affiliation. The Minister stressed that the bill would entail no further changes in the existing rules of Danish law than those that were necessary to comply with the judgment of the European

[11] See *Rigsdagstidende 1952–53, Folketinget*, cols. 1385–1459 and cols. 3492–3497.

[12] See *Folketingstidende 1975–76, Forhandlingerne (Parliamentary Debates)*, cols. 3954–4096.

[13] See *Kjeldsen, Busk Madsen, and Pedersen*, Judgment of 7 December 1976, Series A No. 23, pp. 5–6.

[14] The bill was promulgated as Act No. 285 of 9 June 1982. In the case of *Steen Bille Frederiksen and Others v Denmark* (Application No. 12719/87) the European Commission of Human Rights found that Denmark had taken reasonable steps to comply with its obligations under art 11 of the European Convention on Human Rights by adopting this Act. The Commission declared the application inadmissible. See *European Commission of Human Rights, Decisions and Reports*, vol. 56, p. 245. An English translation of Act No. 285 of 9 June 1982 will be found ibid, at p. 242.

The Act of 9 June 1982 was amended by Act No. 347 of 29 May 1990 which added to the protection of wage-earners. The Act, as amended, provides that wage-earners who, in violation of the provisions of the Act, are dismissed because of trade union affiliation or because they do not belong to a trade union shall be reinstated in their previous positions. This applies without exception to civil servants, while there is a limited exception which applies to private employees, as the courts in special cases may award monetary compensation instead of ordering reinstatement, if reinstatement of the private employee would be manifestly unreasonable. What constitutes a dismissal 'in violation of the provisions of the Act' must be determined under the detailed provisions of sections 1–3 of the Act.

The provisions of Act No. 285 of 9 June 1982, as amended by Act No. 347 of 29 May 1990, are compiled in Consolidated Act (*lovbekendtgørelse*) No. 443 of 13 June 1990.

[15] *Young, James, and Webster v United Kingdom*, Judgment of 13 August 1981, Series A, No. 44.

Court of Human Rights.[16] During the parliamentary debates concerning the bill, the judgment of the European Court of Human Rights was heavily criticized by some of the members who opposed the bill, but a majority of the members supported the government's view that Denmark should respect the principles that had been asserted by the European Court of Human Rights in its judgment of 13 August 1981 in the '*Closed Shop*' case.[17]

In May 1989 the Folketing adopted a decision urging the Government to appoint a Commission which should be asked to study the advantages and disadvantages of incorporating the European Convention on Human Rights.[18] The Commission, appointed in August 1989, submitted a comprehensive report in 1991.[19] In February 1992 the Minister of Justice introduced a bill concerning incorporation of the Convention. The bill was adopted by the Folketing in April 1992. 107 members of the Folketing voted in favour and 7 members voted against. There was very little debate about the bill in the Folketing. The first reading was brief, and at the second and third readings nobody took the floor.[20] Only three questions were asked of the Minister of Justice.[21]

The Danish Administration of Justice Act has been amended more than once to make it conform with the case-law of the European Court of Human Rights.[22] These amendments have not given rise to heated debates in the Folketing.

D. LEADING HUMAN RIGHTS CASES DECIDED BY DANISH COURTS

Until 1 July 1992, when the European Convention on Human Rights was incorporated into Danish law, the Convention had the same status in Denmark as other international treaties. The Danish legal tradition regarding the relationship between treaties and domestic law was based on dualism, but

[16] See *Folketingstidende 1981–82, 2nd Session, Forhandlingerne*, cols. 798–799.

[17] Ibid, cols. 1423–1470, 7763–7779 and 8050–8052.

[18] See *Folketingstidende 1988–89, Annex C*, col. 1079.

[19] *Betænkning nr. 1220 om Den Europæiske Menneskerettighedskonvention og dansk ret (Official Report No. 1220 on the Incorporation of the European Convention on Human Rights—With a Summary in English)*, 1991.

[20] See *Folketingstidende 1991–92, Forhandlingerne*, cols. 7044–7053, col. 8608 and cols. 8661–8662.

[21] See J. Lundum, 'Den danske inkorporering af Den Europæiske Menneskerettigheds-konvention', *Mennesker og rettigheder*, vol. 11, 1993, pp. 274–279, at p. 275.

[22] See *op. cit.*, note 19 above, pp. 53–61. For more recent examples, see eg Act No. 390 of 14 June 1995 and Act No. 414 of 10 June 1997.

there was speculation that Danish courts had gradually become more heedful of international treaty obligations.[23] However, in a case which was decided in October 1986, the Danish Supreme Court adopted a dualist approach.

The case was brought before the courts by a group of bus drivers who had been dismissed by the public transport body for the metropolitan area of Copenhagen because of their trade union affiliation. The plaintiffs had left the large trade unions to which their colleagues belonged, and had joined a smaller trade union. This had given rise to widespread strikes and picketing. The Supreme Court held that article 11 of the European Convention on Human Rights was not directly applicable in Denmark, but the decision to dismiss the plaintiffs must be dealt with in accordance with the provisions of Act No. 285 of 9 June 1982 concerning protection against dismissal relating to trade union affiliation, which had been adopted to fulfil Denmark's obligations under article 11 of the Convention. This meant that the decision to dismiss the plaintiffs could not be annulled, but the plaintiffs were awarded compensation because their dismissal was illegal.[24]

In a case which was decided on 23 March 1992 the Supreme Court reached a different result, because Act No. 285 of 9 June 1982 had been amended by Act No. 347 of 29 May 1990 which added to the protection against dismissal.[25] The plaintiff was employed as a fireman by the municipal authorities of Copenhagen. In 1984 he resigned from the Firemen's Union, and when he rejected repeated invitations to rejoin the union his colleagues refused to co-operate with him. In 1988 the municipal authorities of Copenhagen decided to institute an administrative dismissal procedure against him, but this procedure was interrupted when the Minister of the Interior annulled the decision. In June 1990 the Supreme Court delivered a judgment setting aside the annulment decision of the Minister of the Interior whereupon the municipal authorities of Copenhagen on 20 August 1990 decided to dismiss the plaintiff. However, Act No. 347 of 29 May 1990 had now entered into force.[26] In its judgment of 23 March 1992 the Supreme Court held that the new legislative provisions applied to the decision of 20 August 1990 concerning dismissal of the plaintiff, and these provisions gave the plaintiff an unconditional right to keep his position.

[23] See eg N. Madsen, 'Domstolenes anvendelse af folkeret og EF-ret', in T. Jensen, W. E. von Eyben, and M. Koktvedgaard (eds), *Højesteret 1661–1986*, 1986, pp. 33–43, especially at pp. 34 and 43.

[24] The case is reported in *Ugeskrift for Retsvæsen*, 1986, pp. 898–916.

[25] For an account of the content of Act No. 285 of 9 June 1982 see note 14 above. The Supreme Court judgment of 23 Mar 1992 is reported in *Ugeskrift for Retsvæsen*, 1992, pp. 469–476. See also the more recent Supreme Court decisions ibid, 1999, pp. 1316–1321 and pp. 1496–1500, and ibid, 2000, pp. 1728–1736.

[26] See for an account of the content of Act No. 347 of 29 May 1990, see note 14 above.

In a case decided on 29 August 1989 the Supreme Court held that the provisions of chapter VIII of the Danish Social Assistance Act, in accordance with the pertinent case-law of the European Court of Human Rights, must be read so as to comprise questions about changing the placement of children who under an administrative decision have been involuntarily removed from their home.[27] The Supreme Court affirmed a judgment of the Western High Court which had reached its result without referring to the European Convention on Human Rights.[28]

In a case decided on 1 November 1989 the Supreme Court proved willing to comply with the requirements of the European Court of Human Rights regarding disqualification of judges in criminal cases.[29] The Supreme Court held that the relevant provisions of the Danish Administration of Justice Act must be interpreted in accordance with the principles on which the judgment of the European Court of Human Rights of 24 May 1989 in the *Hauschildt* case[30] were based. This was the first case in which the Danish Supreme Court applied the European Convention on Human Rights in an affirmative way, leading to a result that did not follow from the existing Danish law.

In a more or less comparable case decided on 21 December 1989 the Danish Supreme Court took a different stand.[31] The case raised complicated questions concerning criminal procedure. The procedure which had been followed by the lower courts was in accordance with longstanding practice of Danish courts. The Supreme Court stated that, in view of the judgment of the European Court of Human Rights in the *Hauschildt* case, it was doubtful whether this practice was compatible with article 6 of the European Convention on Human Rights. However, the Supreme Court did not quash the decision of the lower courts, stating that an interpretation to the contrary would have wide-ranging consequences for the organization of the judiciary in Denmark, and therefore it should be left to the legislature to solve the problem.

It has been suggested that, after the incorporation of the European Convention of Human Rights in 1992, the case-law of the European Commission of Human Rights and the European Court of Human Rights has become 'directly applicable' in Denmark.[32] This view is misguided. The provisions of the Convention and the Protocols may have direct effect, but the decisions of the European Commission of Human Rights and the European

[27] The Supreme Court judgment is reported in *Ugeskrift for Retsvæsen*, 1989, pp. 928–929.

[28] The judgment of the Western High Court is reported in *Ugeskrift for Retsvæsen*, 1988, p. 404.

[29] The case is reported in *Ugeskrift for Retsvæsen*, 1989, pp. 13–21.

[30] *Hauschildt* case, Judgment of 24 May 1989, Series A, No. 154.

[31] The case is reported in *Ugeskrift for Retsvæsen*, 1990, pp. 181–187.

[32] See K. L. Thylstrup, 'Kilder til Den Europæiske Menneskerettighedskonvention', (1994–95) *EU-ret & Menneskeret*, pp. 13–17, at p. 13.

Court of Human Rights are not 'directly applicable'. In the explanatory remarks accompanying the bill concerning the incorporation of the European Convention on Human Rights it was stated that the Ministry of Justice was of the opinion that the balance between the Danish legislature and the Danish courts which had been established by the case-law of the Supreme Court should not be disturbed. The Folketing should continue to determine the content of the Danish legislation, and incorporation of the Convention should not lead to increased law-making on the part of the Danish courts.[33] Similar views were expressed by a majority of the members of the parliamentary committee which scrutinized the bill in the course of the parliamentary proceedings.[34] *Travaux préparatoires* of this kind play an important role in the legal process in Denmark.

The Supreme Court referred to these *travaux* in a case concerning the disqualification of a temporary judge, decided on 18 April 1994.[35] This was a criminal case, and the temporary judge in question was allowed to sit as a judge for twenty-five days a year. At the same time she was employed by the Ministry of Justice as a civil servant working in a department which, *inter alia*, dealt with cases concerning the police and the prosecution service. The Supreme Court stated that temporary judges had been used increasingly over the course of time, but there was no sufficient basis for holding that the usual practice concerning temporary judges was in violation of the Danish Constitution. Moreover, the Supreme Court stated that the case-law of the European Commission of Human Rights and the European Court of Human Rights did not give sufficient grounds for holding that the use of temporary judges in general was in violation of article 6(1) of the European Convention on Human Rights, but the proportions and the character of the usual practice concerning temporary judges were such that it was a matter of doubt whether the system, on the whole, was compatible with the Convention. However, as there was no certain basis for determining the scope of the Convention in this respect, and as an interpretation of article 6(1) to the effect of substantially limiting the use of temporary judges would have wide-ranging consequences for the organization of the judiciary in Denmark, the Supreme Court held that it must be left to the legislature to find an overall solution.

As for the case in hand, the Supreme Court drew attention to the requirement concerning an 'appearance of independence' which, according to the case-law of the European Commission of Human Rights and the European

[33] See *Folketingstidende 1991–92, Annex A*, col. 5470.
[34] See ibid, *Annex B*, cols. 891–892.
[35] The case is reported in *Ugeskrift for Retsvæsen*, 1994, pp. 536–544.

Court of Human Rights, was an essential element of impartiality in relation to article 6(1) of the Convention.[36] In view of this requirement, the fact that the temporary judge in question had taken part in deciding the case constituted a violation of article 6(1) of the Convention, and therefore the case was remanded to the court of first instance for re-trial.[37]

In a 1993 case before the Impeachment Court the defendant, a former minister of justice, raised objections based on article 6 of the European Convention on Human Rights. Section 59 of the Danish Constitution provides that the Impeachment Court shall consist of up to fifteen Supreme Court judges and an equal number of members elected for six years by Parliament according to proportional representation. More specific rules are laid down in a legislative act concerning the Impeachment Court. In a decision of 5 January 1994 the Impeachment Court held that there could be no doubt that the Impeachment Court fulfilled the requirements of article 6(1) regarding 'a fair hearing by an independent and impartial tribunal'. Moreover, the Impeachment Court held that although the media might have covered the case to an unusual extent and to the detriment of the defendant, there was no reason to believe that the Impeachment Court would not be able to disregard that possible influence; therefore, there was no reasonable doubt that the defendant would be given a fair trial in accordance with the requirements of article 6 of the European Convention on Human Rights.[38] The decision of the Impeachment Court was rather brief, and there was no mentioning of the requirement of an 'appearance of independence' which the Supreme Court referred to in the above-mentioned judgment of 18 April 1994.

In some cases decided after the incorporation of the European Convention on Human Rights, the Supreme Court has referred to the case-law of the

[36] The Supreme Court referred, *inter alia*, to the *Belilos* case, Judgment of 29 April 1988, Series A, No. 132, § 67.

[37] The Supreme Court made it clear that the case was decided on narrow grounds. In a case decided on 8 March 1995, the Supreme Court stated that there was no basis for holding that lawyers employed as civil servants by the Ministry of Justice were prevented from acting as temporary judges in criminal cases to a wider extent than what would follow from the Supreme Court decision of 18 April 1994. The Supreme Court decision of 8 March 1995 is reported in *Ugeskrift for Retsvæsen*, 1995, pp. 428–429.

[38] The Impeachment Court also rejected an objection relating to the defendant's right to a hearing within a reasonable time. The decision is reported in *Ugeskrift for Retsvæsen*, 1994, pp. 409–419. On 6 April 1995 the Impeachment Court decided that the defendant was not legally prevented from being present at the criminal proceedings because of his alleged disability; thus was the legal position under the relevant Danish rules, and the provisions of art 6 of the European Convention on Human Rights did not warrant a different conclusion. This decision is reported in *Ugeskrift for Retsvæsen*, 1995, pp. 418–422. The final verdict of the Impeachment Court is reported in *Ugeskrift for Retsvæsen*, 1995, pp. 672–681. (The official reports of cases decided by the Impeachment Court will be found in *Rigsretstidende*). The former minister of justice lodged a complaint with the European Commission of Human Rights. (Application 28972/95). On 18 May 1999 the Commission declared the application inadmissible.

European Court of Human Rights as supporting arguments for its decisions. These supporting arguments may have weighted the scales in favour of more liberal decisions on the part of the Supreme Court.

In a case decided on 26 August 1992 the case-law of the European Court of Human Rights was mentioned in support of the Supreme Court's decision not to order the pre-trial detention of a murder suspect.[39] The case concerned a young man who under very special circumstances had shot his older brother. The death of his father had strongly affected the older brother who had turned violent and had brutalized the family, especially the mother. This became unbearable for the younger brother and caused him to shoot the older brother while he was asleep. The younger brother was charged with murder and was remanded in custody, but after a period of more than six months the Western High Court ordered his release on the ground that there was no longer sufficient reason to believe that his release would disturb public opinion.[40] The Supreme Court affirmed the decision of the Western High Court on the ground that the very special circumstances of the case and the young age of the accused must lead to the result that the need to protect public opinion from being disturbed did not give sufficient foundation for remanding the accused back into custody after he had been at large for more than two months. The Supreme Court added that the judgments of the European Court of Human Rights in the *Letellier* case and the *Kemmache* case[41] confirmed this result.

In October 1994 the Supreme Court invoked the case-law of the European Court of Human Rights as a supporting argument in a case concerning trespassing in connection with news coverage of picketing at a private residence.[42] In August 1992 the City Court of Copenhagen convicted a number of young people of trespassing and vandalism after they staged a protest action in the private garden in front of the house of a leading politician. They were demonstrating against the planned construction of a bridge between Denmark and Sweden, and they tried to underscore their point by digging in the garden. A television reporter who covered the event for a local television station was convicted of trespassing. The reporter appealed to the Eastern High Court claiming that she had passed through the garden to get to the house in order to interview the politician. Having failed to get in touch with the politician she

[39] The case is reported in *Ugeskrift for Retsvæsen*, 1992, pp. 877–878.

[40] The Western High Court reached this decision on appeal from a criminal court which had held that the accused must remain in custody. The decision of the criminal court was based on a provision of the Administration of Justice Act concerning pre-trial detention 'for the sake of the enforcement of law' ('*hensynet til retshåndhævelsen*').

[41] *Letellier* case, Judgment of 26 June 1991, Series A, No. 207, and *Kemmache* case, Judgment of 27 Nov 1991, Series A, No. 218.

[42] The case is reported in *Ugeskrift for Retsvæsen*, 1994, pp. 988–990.

stayed in the garden to cover the event. The Eastern High Court upheld the conviction, but in the Supreme Court she was acquitted.

In her pleadings before the Supreme Court the television reporter referred to the case-law of the European Court of Human Rights under article 10 of the Convention. Against this, the prosecution pointed out that all the decisions of the European Court of Human Rights which the television reporter had invoked related to content-based regulation of expression, and therefore they had no bearing on the restrictions relating to trespassing relevant in the instant case. The Supreme Court did not address itself to this issue. The Supreme Court held that the interests of privacy must be balanced against the interests of free news reporting. In such a case, where the object of the protest was related to a current political question, the interest in news coverage was weighty, and the violation by the television reporter of the right to privacy was of minor importance, particularly because her presence in the garden did not in any substantial way add to the violation committed by the protesters. The balancing of interests must therefore lead to the result that the presence of the television reporter in the garden could not be considered unjustified.[43] The Supreme Court added that this result was in harmony with the case-law of the European Court of Human Rights under article 10 of the Convention, most recently the judgment of 23 September 1994 in the case of *Jens Olaf Jersild v Denmark*.

In a case decided on 9 December 1996 the Supreme Court referred to the European Convention on Human Rights in support of its decision to dismiss libel charges against a journalist and her editor-in-chief.[44] The Eastern High Court had found the journalist and the editor-in-chief guilty of libel, but the Supreme Court reversed this decision. A dissenting judge of the Eastern High Court had referred to various mitigating circumstances, without mentioning the European Convention on Human Rights. The Supreme Court endorsed the reasons stated by the dissenting High Court judge, but at the same time the Supreme Court drew attention to the European Convention on Human Rights. The Supreme Court stated that the provisions of the Danish criminal code concerning libel must be read in the light of article 10 of the Convention. In balancing the value of free speech against the counter-value relating to protection from libel great weight should be given to the media's role of public watchdog. In making this statement the Supreme Court referred to the above-mentioned 1994 decision concerning trespassing in connection with news coverage of picketing a residence. The Danish Supreme Court seems to apply

[43] For a similar, more recent Supreme Court decision, see *Ugeskrift for Retsvæsen*, 1999, pp. 1675–1678. In two earlier cases the balancing of interests had led the Supreme Court to the opposite result, see *Ugeskrift for Retsvæsen*, 1987, pp. 934–937 and pp. 937–939.

[44] The case is reported in *Ugeskrift for Retsvæsen*, 1997, pp. 259–272.

the same yardstick to all kinds of free speech cases involving the media, and the judgment of the European Court of Human Rights in the *Jersild* case seems to have had a deep effect on the minds of the Danish Supreme Court judges.

A remarkable decision regarding the direct effect of article 6(1) of the European Convention on Human Rights was pronounced on 18 September 1998 by the Eastern High Court, acting on appeal from the City Court of Copenhagen.[45] The case concerned economic crime, and the criminal procedure related to very complex facts. Before the Eastern High Court the defence lawyers argued that the lengthy criminal proceedings constituted a violation of article 6(1) of the Convention. The Eastern High Court found that there had been no breach of article 6(1) of the Convention in relation to three of the defendants who had been found guilty of embezzlement. However, in relation to three other defendants who had only been charged with offences committed through gross negligence the lengthy criminal proceedings violated their right to a hearing within a reasonable time as guaranteed by article 6(1) of the Convention, and this was taken into account by the Eastern High Court in setting the penalty.

E. CASES BROUGHT BEFORE THE EUROPEAN COMMISSION AND THE EUROPEAN COURT OF HUMAN RIGHTS

The official report on incorporation of the European Convention on Human Rights into Danish law, published in 1991, gave a comprehensive account of the cases brought against Denmark in the European Commission of Human Rights and in the European Court of Human Rights.[46] The report stated that of more than 200 applications involving Denmark which had been registered since the first application was lodged in 1956, only ten had been declared admissible by the Commission. Two of these were resolved by friendly settlement under article 28 of the Convention, and one was referred to the Committee of Ministers which decided that there had been no violation of the Convention. The remaining seven cases were referred to the European Court

[45] The case is reported in *Ugeskrift for Retsvæsen*, 1998, pp. 1752–1754.

[46] See *op. cit.* note 19 above, pp. 82–110. The statistics covered the period from July 1956 to April 1991. For more recent statistics see N. Holst-Christensen and J. F. Kjølbro, 'Den europæiske Menneskerettighedskommissions admissibilitetspraksis i danske klagesager (1989 til 1997)', *Ugeskrift for Retsvæsen*, 1998, part B, pp. 382–395.

of Human Rights,[47] which in only one case held that there had been a violation of the Convention.[48]

In the *Jersild* case, which was decided in 1994, the European Court of Human Rights for the second time held that Denmark had violated the Convention. In the case of *A and Others v Denmark*, decided in 1996, the European Court of Human Rights for the third time held that Denmark had violated the Convention. In the case of *Kurt Nielsen v Denmark*, decided in 2000, the European Court of Human Rights for the fourth time held that Denmark had violated the Convention.

The first case in which the Court held that Denmark had violated the Convention was the *Hauschildt* case.[49] The application was lodged with the European Commission of Human Rights on 26 August 1980. On 9 October 1986 the Commission declared the application admissible regarding a complaint under article 6(1) of the Convention but rejected all other complaints. In its report of 16 July 1987 the Commission expressed the opinion, by nine votes to seven, that there had been no violation of the Convention, but the European Court of Human Rights held, by twelve votes to five, that there had been a breach of article 6(1) of the Convention.

The European Court of Human Rights was of the opinion that the mere fact that a trial judge or an appeal judge, in a system of criminal procedure like the Danish, had also made pre-trial decisions in the case, including decisions concerning detention on remand, could not in itself be held to justify fears as to his impartiality. However, in the instant case there were special circumstances which warranted a different conclusion. On several occasions before the opening of the respective trials, both the trial judge and some of the appeal judges had based their decisions that Mr Hauschildt should be detained specifically on a provision of the Danish Administration of Justice Act according to which the judge must be satisfied that there was a 'particularly confirmed suspicion' that the accused had committed the crime with which he was charged. This wording had been officially explained as meaning that the judge had to be convinced that there was 'a very high degree of clarity' on the question of guilt. Consequently, the difference between the issue which the judge had to settle when applying the precarious provision of the Administration of Justice Act and the issue he would have to settle when giving judgment at the trial became tenuous. The European Court of Human Rights was therefore of the view that, in the circumstances of the case, the impartiality of the Danish courts in question was 'capable of appearing to be open to doubt and that the applicant's fears in this respect [could] be

[47] Three of the seven cases were grouped together.
[48] See *op. cit.* note 19 above, p. 83.
[49] *Hauschildt* case, Judgment of 24 May 1989, Series A, No. 154.

considered objectively justified'. There had thus been a violation of article 6(1) of the Convention.

In the *Jersild* case[50] the European Court of Human Rights held, by twelve votes to seven, that there had been a violation of article 10 of the Convention. In May 1985 a Danish newspaper published an article describing the racist attitudes of members of a group of young people in Copenhagen. In the light of this article the editors of a Danish television programme decided to produce a documentary on the group. Mr Jersild was a reporter assigned to the television programme and he interviewed three members of the group for more than five hours, of which more than two hours were video-taped. Subsequently he edited and cut the film of the interview down to a few minutes, and this edited feature was broadcast on 21 July 1985. The Public Prosecutor instituted criminal proceedings in the City Court of Copenhagen against the three members of the group that had been interviewed, charging them with violation of a provision of the Danish Penal Code concerning racist speech. At the same time Mr Jersild was charged with aiding and abetting the three members of the group. The City Court of Copenhagen convicted the three members of the group as well as Mr Jersild. The latter appealed to the Eastern High Court which dismissed the appeal, and the Supreme Court reached the same result.

The European Court of Human Rights noted that the Danish courts had laid considerable emphasis on the fact that the applicant had himself taken the initiative of preparing the feature and that he not only knew in advance that racist statements were likely to be made during the interview but also encouraged such statements and edited the feature in such a way as to include the offensive assertions. Without his involvement the remarks would not have been disseminated to a wide circle of people and would thus not have been punishable under the provision of the Danish Penal Code concerning racist speech. The European Court of Human Rights was satisfied that these were relevant reasons for the purposes of article 10(2) of the Convention. However, in the circumstances of the instant case a majority of the Strasbourg judges found that the reasons adduced in support of the applicant's conviction were not sufficient to establish convincingly that the interference thereby occasioned with the enjoyment of his right to freedom of expression was 'necessary in a democratic society'.

In *A and Others v Denmark*,[51] a case relating to haemophiliacs who had become HIV-positive as a result of receiving contaminated blood in transfusions at Danish hospitals, the applicants complained that, in breach of article 6(1) of the Convention, their case had not been determined within a reason-

[50] *Jersild* case, Judgment of 23 September 1994, Series A, No. 298.
[51] *A and Others v Denmark*, Judgment of 8 Feb 1996, Reports 1996–I, pp. 85–122.

able time. The European Court of Human Rights held, by six votes to three, that there had been a violation of article 6(1) with respect to some of the applicants. The three dissenting judges reached the conclusion that, even bearing in mind the special diligence owed by national authorities in cases such as the case in hand, there had been no delays attributable to the state which might justify the finding that a reasonable time had been exceeded. The Court held unanimously that Denmark should pay compensation for non-pecuniary damage and meet the applicants' legal fees and expenses.

In the case of *Kurt Nielsen v Denmark*,[52] which also concerned the reasonableness of the length of proceedings, the European Court held unanimously that there had been a violation of article 6(1) of the Convention, and the Court awarded the applicant compensation for non-pecuniary damage.

F. REMEDIAL ACTION TAKEN BY THE DANISH GOVERNMENT IN RESPONSE TO BEING HELD IN VIOLATION OF THE CONVENTION

The fact that there are very few cases in which Denmark has violated the European Convention on Human Rights means that the Danish government has seldom had occasion to take remedial action. However, it is the declared intent of the Danish government that appropriate remedial action will be taken whenever Denmark is being held in violation of the Convention.

In the *Hauschildt* case the European Court of Human Rights rejected the applicant's claim for compensation. It also rejected his claim for reimbursement of costs and expenses incurred in proceedings outside Strasbourg, but for the proceedings in Strasbourg it awarded him 20,000 pounds sterling. The amount was set off against the costs which Mogens Hauschildt had been ordered to pay in connection with the criminal proceedings against him in Denmark. This arrangement was approved by a resolution adopted by the Committee of Ministers of the Council of Europe on 13 February 1991.[53] A more important consequence of the *Hauschildt* case was that the Danish Administration of Justice Act was amended so as to fulfil the requirements under article 6(1) of the Convention as expounded by the European Court of Human Rights.[54]

In the *Jersild* case[55] the applicant claimed 1,000 Danish kroner in respect of the fine imposed upon him in the criminal case in Denmark. The Danish

[52] *Kurt Nielsen* case, Judgment of 15 Feb 2000.
[53] See *op. cit.* note 19 above, p. 86.
[54] See ibid, pp. 59–61.
[55] See note 50 above.

government did not object, and the European Court of Human Rights found that the amount should be awarded. As to the alleged non-pecuniary damage, the finding of a violation in itself constituted 'adequate and just satisfaction'. The Danish government did not object to the applicant's claim for reimbursement of costs and expenses, and the European Court of Human Rights found that the applicant was entitled to recover the sums in their entirety.

Having succeeded in Strasbourg Mr Jersild brought the case before the Court of Special Complaints (*Den Særlige Klageret*), which on 24 January 1995 decided that the criminal case should be reopened. Mr Jersild was then indicted on the same charges, but this time the prosecution pleaded for his acquittal. On 4 June 1996 the Eastern High Court pronounced the final verdict, acquitting Mr Jersild.

After the decision of the European Court of Human Rights in *A and Others v Denmark* initiatives were taken to speed up judicial proceedings. The end result was a legislative act amending the Administration of Justice Act.[56]

Sometimes the Danish government seems to have adopted a pragmatic approach, preferring to pay rather than run the risk of being held in violation of the Convention. This is illustrated by the case of *S v Denmark*.

On 16 February 1990 Mr S lodged an application with the European Commission of Human Rights, and on 30 June 1993 the Commission declared the application partly admissible.[57] The applicant had been found guilty of serious crimes, and the complaint that was declared admissible by the Commission seemed, at most, to be a question of technicalities. Prior to February 1988 the Danish narcotics police had received information indicating that the applicant was in possession of two kilograms of heroin intended for sale in Denmark. On 3 February 1988 the City Court of Copenhagen sitting with one judge authorized the police to use an undercover agent in order to prevent the sale and to arrest the applicant. The authorization was made under a provision of the Danish Administration of Justice Act to that effect. On 4 February 1988 the applicant was arrested, and charged with drug trafficking. The applicant's trial commenced in November 1988 in the City Court of Copenhagen sitting with one presiding professional judge and two lay judges. The presiding judge had originally authorized the use of an undercover agent. On 29 November 1988 the City Court of Copenhagen found the applicant guilty of drug trafficking and illegal possession of firearms, and he was sentenced to three and a half years' imprisonment. The Eastern High Court rejected the applicant's request for a new trial on the ground that the fact that the presiding judge in the City Court prior to the trial had authorized

[56] Act No. 414 of 10 June 1997.

[57] Application No. 17293/90. See Council of Europe, *Yearbook of the European Convention on Human Rights 1993* (vol. 36), p. 140.

the use of an undercover agent did not disqualify him. Having considered the evidence before it, the Eastern High Court upheld the judgment of the City Court.

Before the European Commission of Human Rights the applicant complained that the City Court of Copenhagen was not an impartial tribunal within the meaning of article 6(1) of the Convention due to the fact that the presiding judge had, prior to the trial, authorized the use of an undercover agent. Following the decision on the admissibility of the application, the Commission placed itself at the disposal of the parties with a view to securing a friendly settlement. The applicant's lawyer indicated that his client would accept a settlement against the payment of 20,000 Danish kroner, which amount should not be set off against costs, plus costs and expenses relating to the proceedings before the Commission. The Danish government accepted this proposal, emphasizing that its acceptance did not imply the recognition of any legal obligation. The government declared that it would be willing to accept, as requested by the applicant, that the payment would not be set off against any claim of costs.

Seen against the background of the judgment in the *Hauschildt* case and the arrangement that was approved by the Committee of Ministers after that judgment,[58] the pragmatism of the Danish government in the case of *S v Denmark* seems to have gone too far. The easy solution is not always the right one. One can buy a lot of dope in the wholesale market for 20,000 Danish kroner.

G. ASSESSMENT AND PROSPECTS

Prior to the incorporation of the European Convention on Human Rights into Danish law, discerning lawyers pointed out that there was no need to incorporate the Convention. One high-ranking lawyer went further, stating that 'incorporation might lead to infringement of the rule of law'.[59] Since the incorporation of the Convention, criticism has ceased.

It has been said that the main object of the incorporation was to call attention to the Convention. In this respect the incorporation yielded results, since much publicity surrounded the Convention at the time of the incorporation.[60]

In recent years provisions of the European Convention on Human Rights have been invoked before the Danish courts in an increasing number of cases. The majority of those cases have raised questions concerning criminal procedure.

[58] See p. 273 above.

[59] *Loc. cit.* note 10 above, p. 170.

[60] See *loc. cit.* note 21 above, p. 279.

There can be no doubt that the Danish courts will give full effect to the European Convention on Human Rights. They are bound to do so under the Act concerning incorporation of the Convention. The judgments of the European Court of Human Rights may be taken into account by the Danish courts, but sometimes they will leave it to the legislature to determine whether a change of Danish law is called for.

One should not exaggerate the importance of the European Convention on Human Rights in Denmark. After all, there have only been four cases where the European Court of Human Rights has found that Denmark violated the Convention, and there were weighty dissenting opinions in three of these cases.[61] If human rights activists, in promoting the European Convention on Human Rights, overdo their part, they may end up creating human rights weariness instead of human rights awareness.

[61] *Hauschildt* case, Judgment of 24 May 1989, Series A No. 154, pp. 28–30; *Jersild* case, Judgment of 23 Sep 1994, Series A No. 298, pp. 29–32; *A and Others v Denmark*, Judgment of 8 Feb 1996, Reports 1996–I, pp. 111–112.

11

Estonia

RAIT MARUSTE

INTRODUCTION

For Estonia, as for the other Baltic States, the restoration of independence and real enjoyment of human rights only became possible after the withdrawal of foreign troops in the beginning of the nineties. Thus, the Estonian experience of practising democracy and international law is not the richest one. Due to the short time period the administrative and judicial practice in applying international law and pertinent scholarly analysis are relatively limited.

One of the outcomes of the half-century of annexation and separation from the natural development of human rights philosophy and law was, and to certain extent still is, a certain deviation from and devaluation of human rights categories. The totalitarian regime has politicized the idea of human rights, turned them into a slogan, and made them abstract. At the same time human rights were separated from problems of practical implementation in everyday life and legal practice. Therefore the real nature of international human rights law in domestic law, especially the status and meaning of international law in domestic jurisprudence, is relatively purely elaborated and domestic legal practitioners of the field are not very encouraged or experienced.

In the case of Estonia it should also be mentioned that the traditionally strong influence of legal positivism inherited from the first period of independence, mixed with the later Socialist normativism, still have a remarkable influence on legal thinking and interpretation.

A. THE STATUS OF THE CONVENTION IN THE HIERARCHY OF ESTONIAN LEGAL NORMS

The structure of the Estonian Constitution[1] lays emphasis on fundamental rights and freedoms. This is highlighted by the fact that the Bill of Rights chapter comes immediately after the seven general provisions of the Constitution in Chapter I. Chapter II of the Constitution, titled 'Fundamental Rights, Freedoms, and Duties' contains forty-eight Articles, more than a quarter of the total of 168 Articles of the Constitution. Thus, the scope and position of the Bill of Rights section indicates the importance of the fundamental rights and freedoms in the system of constitutional norms. It also reflects a certain historical tradition: in the Constitutions of 1920 and 1938 the relevant chapter was also the second.

The present Estonian Constitution is new and modern. It was drafted and adopted in 1992. As several other constitutions which were drafted and adopted at the end of the '80s and the beginning of the '90s, the present Estonian Constitution reflects the trend of transformation of international human rights treatise into domestic law at constitutional level.[2] As Martin Scheinin said, this kind of harmonization gives the human rights provisions an important role in the interpretation and implementation of constitutional provisions.

Many domestic and international analysts have come to the conclusion that the catalogue of rights and freedoms contained in Chapter II of the Estonian Constitution almost entirely corresponds to the rights and freedoms enshrined in the European Convention on Human Rights and other relevant international instruments. The Republic of Estonia joined the Council of Europe on 14 May 1993 by signing the Statute of the Council of Europe and the European Convention on Human Rights, together with the integrated Protocols Nos. 2, 3, 5, and 8, and the amended Protocols Nos. 1, 4, 6, 7, 9, and 10. The political decision to sign was made by the government on 7 May 1993.[3] Protocol No. 11 was signed by Estonia on 11 May 1994 and it entered into force on 1 November 1998.

Tthe Convention was ratified on 16 April 1996.

Protocol No. 6 was signed on 17 April 1998 and entered into force on 1 November of that year.

[1] See The Constitution of the Republic of Estonia. The Constitution of the Republic of Estonia Implementation Act.—Estonian legislation in translation. No 1, 1996. (Estonian Translation and Legislative Support Centre).

[2] See M. Scheinin, Rahvusvahelised inimoigused riikide siseoiguses.—Euroopa inimoiguste konventsiooni oiguslikud tagajarjed, Seminari ettekanded. Tallinn, 1996, p. 41.

[3] *Riigi Teataja* (Official Gazette) II, 1993, 15, art. 20.

The ratification procedure for international treaties and the relationship between international and domestic law are usually regulated by the basic law of the land.

The Estonian Constitution[4] contains several provisions on ratification and the status of international treaties.

According to Estonian law the ratification of international treaties is the prerogative of the Parliament (Riigikogu). Paragraph 121 of the Constitution enumerates five grounds for the Parliament to ratify treaties. These relate to those:

1) which alter state boundaries;
2) the implementation of which requires the passage, amendment, or repeal of Estonian laws;
3) by which the Republic of Estonia joins international organizations or unions;
4) by which the Republic of Estonia assumes military or proprietary obligations;
5) in which ratification is prescribed.

Article 66 para 1 of the Convention in force at that time prescribed that the 'Convention shall be ratified' and the 'ratifications shall be deposited with the Secretary General of the Council of Europe'. So this was clearly the case where the ratification comes from the treaty.

The Parliament (Riigikogu) ratified the Convention on 13 March 1996. The Ratification Act[5] entered into force according to the general procedure, that is on the tenth day after its publication in the Riigi Teataja (State Gazette).[6] The Convention therefore became legally binding in domestic law as from 11 April 1996.

According to Article 78 para 6 of the Constitution the President of the Republic signed the instruments of ratification and they were deposited with the Secretary General of the Council of Europe on 16 April 1996. Consequently, and according to Article 66, the Convention came into force at the date of the deposit of the instruments of ratification and became internationally legally binding for Estonia as from 16 April 1996.

It is also obvious that the execution of the Treaty obligations required the change of Estonian laws, by adoption, amendment, or repeal (as stipulated in Art. 121 para 2 of the Constitution). This was mainly done in the course of preparatory work for ratification, but also afterwards. Thus, one may conclude that the need to change the law could also be regarded as a ground for ratification.

The Convention allows the High Contracting Parties, when signing the Convention or when depositing their instruments of ratification, to make

[4] The present constitution, adopted by referendum on 28 June 1992, is the fourth in the history of Estonian statehood. Previous ones entered into force in 1920, 1933, and 1938.

[5] *Riigi Teataja* II 1996, 11/12, 34.

[6] *Riigi Teataja* II 1996, 11/12.

reservations. This opportunity was used by Estonian state, and Estonia made two reservations.[7]

On several later occasions the subject of the second reservation (the principle of protection of property) became an object of constitutional review by the Supreme Court.[8]

1. The status of the Convention in the hierarchy of domestic law

The first general indication concerning the relationship of international and Estonian domestic law is given in Chapter I of the Constitution (general provisions) where the second sentence of Article 3 stipulates that 'generally recognized principles and rules of international law are an inseparable part of the Estonian legal system'. In addition to this major and important provision for interpretation of Estonian Constitution and other legislation, the Constitution contains another and more concrete provision on the relationship of international treatise and domestic law. Article 123 stipulates that:

[7] **The first reservation.** The Republic of Estonia, in accordance with Article 64 of the Convention, declared that pending the adoption of amendments to the Code on Civil Procedure within one year from entry into force of the Ratification Act, she cannot ensure the right to a public hearing at the appellate court level (Ringkonnakohtus) as provided in Article 6 of the Convention, in so far as cases foreseen by Articles 292 and 298 of the Code on Civil Procedure (published in the Riigi Teataja [State Gazette] I 1993, 31/32, 538; 1994, 1, 5; 1995, 29, 358; 1996, 3, 57) may be decided through written procedure. Declaration contained in a letter from the Minister of Foreign Affairs of Estonia, dated 12 April 1996, handed to the Secretary General at the time of deposit of the instrument of ratification, on 16 April 1996.

The second reservation. The Estonian Riigikogu made a reservation according to which after regaining her independence, Estonia started large-scale economic and social reforms, which have encompassed the restoration or compensation to previous owners or their heirs property which was nationalized or otherwise unlawfully expropriated during the period of Soviet annexation; the restructuring of collectivized agriculture and privatization of state-owned property.

Estonia declared that the provisions of Article 1 of the First Protocol shall not apply to the laws on property reform which regulate the restoration or compensation of property nationalized, confiscated, requisitioned, collectivized or otherwise unlawfully expropriated during the period of Soviet annexation; the restructuring of collectivized agriculture and privatization of state-owned property. The reservation concerns the Principles of the Property Reform Act (published in *Riigi Teataja* [State Gazette] 1991, 21, 257; RT I 1994, 38, 617; 40, 653; 51, 859; 94, 1609), the Land Reform Act (RT 1991, 34, 426; RT I 1995, 10, 113), the Agricultural Reform Act (RT 1992, 10, 143; 36, 474; RT I 1994, 52, 880), the Privatization Act (RT I 1993, 45, 639; 1994, 50, 846; 79, 1329; 83, 1448; 1995, 22, 327; 54, 881; 57, 979), the Dwelling Rooms Privatization Act (RT I 1993, 23, 411; 1995, 44, 671; 57, 979; 1996, 2, 28), the Act on Evaluation and Compensation of Unlawfully Expropriated Property (RT I 1993, 30, 509; 1994, 8, 106; 51, 859; 54, 905; 1995, 29, 357), the Act on Valuation of Collectivized Property (RT I 1993, 7, 104) and their wording being in force at the moment of the Ratification Act entered into force. A brief summary of the laws mentioned in the reservation was added.

Declaration contained in a letter from the Minister of Foreign Affairs of Estonia, dated 12 April 1996, handed to the Secretary General at the time of deposit of the instrument of ratification, on 16 April 1996.

[8] See for example judgments of 12.04.95 No III–4/A-2/95 and 08.11.96 No 3–4–1–2/96.

The Republic of Estonia shall not conclude international treaties which are in conflict with the Constitution. If laws or other legislation of Estonia are in conflict with international treaties ratified by the Riigikogu, the provisions of the international treaty shall apply.

The first subparagraph of the quoted provision very clearly establishes the principle of the supremacy of the Constitution. The Constitution of the Republic of Estonia is the highest law of the land. This conclusion is also supported by the principle fixed in general provisions of the Constitution (Art. 3) which states that 'the powers of state shall be exercised solely pursuant to the Constitution and laws which are in conformity therewith'.

The highest legitimacy of the Constitution partly springs from the procedure of its adoption. The Constitution of the Republic of Estonia and The Constitution of the Republic of Estonia Implementation Act are the only laws in Estonia which were adopted directly by the people by means of a referendum.

The second subparagraph of Article 123 establishes the principle of the supremacy of international law and clarifies the meaning of that principle in the Estonian domestic legal system. Neither the Constitution nor the Convention can be regarded as ordinary statutory law. Consequently, Article 123 para 2 of the Constitution deals with ordinary legislation and clarifies that in the hierarchy of Estonian legal norms the Convention lies between Constitution and ordinary legislation.[9]

An additional argument in support of this conclusion arises from the general constitutional scheme for judicial constitutional review in Estonia. According to Articles 4(1)(5) and 6(1)(2) of the Constitutional Review Court Procedure Act and Articles 13 and 15 of the Legal Chancellor Act, the Supreme Court exercises judicial constitutional review of international treaties prior to their entrance into force. It is the exceptional competence of the Legal Chancellor to submit applications to the Constitutional Court[10] for constitutional review of international treaties. According to Article 15(2) of the Legal Chancellor Act, the Legal Chancellor shall, in case of conflict between legislation and international treaty, propose to the body which

[9] In the course of preparatory work the proposal to give to the Convention status equal to the Constitution was also made, but it did not find enough support.

[10] Estonia is a rare example of system where the constitutional review is in the jurisdiction of the ordinary supreme court (see Articles 15 and 152 of the Constitution). Article 149 para 3 stipulates that *The Supreme Court is the highest court in the state and shall review court judgements by way of cassation proceedings. The Supreme Court is also the court of constitutional review.* Article 152 para 2 stipulates that *The Supreme Court shall declare invalid any law or other legislation that is in conflict with the provisions and spirit of the Constitution.* For the purposes of constitutional review the Court has a separate panel consisting of 5 justices who are at same time members of ordinary panels—administrative, civil, or criminal. The case could also be transferred to the plenary Court.

passed the legislation to suspend the effect of the legislation for the period defined. He proposes that the body which passed the legislation conflicting with an international treaty shall suspend the effect of the legislation until it is brought into conformity with the Constitution. These provisions imply that legislation conflicting with an international treaty is automatically in conflict with the Constitution.[11] Consequently, international treaties are subject to judicial constitutional review. In fact during the period when the relevant laws have been in force (since 1993) this has never arisen in practice: no international treaty has been transferred to the Supreme Court for review of its constitutionality.

The European Convention of Human Rights and its Protocols were ratified by the Parliament by means of the adoption of The Ratification of ECHR Act. The Act contains 9 Articles and stipulates only two things: 1) to ratify the Convention and 2) to make declarations (under Articles 25 and 46). The Act says nothing about the status of the treaty in domestic law. Even the texts of ratified instruments were not annexed to the Act. It must be concluded that through the adoption of a separate law by the Parliament the object of ratification became a part of Estonian law; in other words, the Convention was incorporated into Estonian law. The non-inclusion of the texts of the ratified instruments can only be estimated as an oversight by the inexperienced new parliament.

Even for those with a different opinion about incorporation, it must be kept in mind that Article 1 of the Convention does not require that a state party incorporate the Convention into its domestic law.[12] As we know, a party may instead satisfy Article 1 by ensuring, in whatever manner it chooses, that its law and practice are such that they guarantee an individual his or her rights under the Convention.

Conclusion

The Convention was signed and ratified in the manner prescribed by the Constitution, and its constitutionality has not been challenged,[13] consequently the Convention is in full conformity with the Constitution and is an integral part of the Estonian legal system.

[11] See also P. Roosma, Constitutional Review under the 1992 Constitution, Juridica International III, 1998, p. 37.

[12] See eg *Observer and Guardian v UK* A 216 (1991), also *Law of the European Convention on Human Rights* by DJ Harris, MO Boyle, and C Warbrick, 1995, pp. 24–25.

[13] The constitutionality of the ECHR was challenged for example in Lithuania.

B. THE IMPLEMENTATION OF THE CONVENTION IN ESTONIAN JUDICIAL PRACTICE

The High Contracting Parties have the responsibility of securing for everyone within their jurisdiction the rights and freedoms defined in the Convention. Article 13 of the Convention requires that each state provide an 'effective remedy' under national law for a person who has an arguable claim under the Convention.

The above-mentioned international obligation of Estonia is supported also by constitutional and other legal provisions. Article 14 of the Constitution prescribes that 'the guarantee of rights and freedoms is the duty of the legislative, executive, and judicial powers, and of local governments'. Article 15(1) establishes that 'everyone whose rights and freedoms are violated has the right of recourse to courts'.

The Estonian constitutional legal system offers a wide range of legal guarantees for the protection of rights and freedoms. In the case of an infringement of rights and freedoms, the person is provided with legal (judicial) and administrative protection (remedies).

Judicial protection is exercised by courts of general jurisdiction, administrative courts, and via judicial constitutional review. Certain non-judicial and specified constitutional obligations for the protection of rights and freedoms are also given to the President of the Republic and the Legal Chancellor.

Remedy through courts of general jurisdiction

In the Estonian system the courts of general jurisdiction are county and city courts, appeal courts, and the Supreme Court. Courts of first and second instance act as trial courts; the Supreme Court is the court of cassation and the court for constitutional review. Courts of general jurisdiction handle civil and criminal matters.

All courts are also to fulfil the function of constitutional review. Article 15 para 1 of the Constitution guarantees to everyone the right, while his or her case is before the court, to challenge the constitutionality of any relevant law, other legislation, or action (procedure).[14] Pursuant to Article 15 para 2 the courts must observe the Constitution and declare unconstitutional any law,

[14] It is disputable whether in the course of constitutional control, the laws, other legal acts, or procedures must be subjected also to control from the international treaty obligations angle. Having in mind the position of international treaty law in Estonian domestic law described above and the constitutional obligation of the courts to guarantee rights and freedoms, the conclusion of one author is that it must *ex officio* and *proprio motu* be done by the Supreme Court. In practice the Court has been restrained from that and has avoided clear statements on that issue.

other legislation or act that violates the rights and freedoms provided by the Constitution or which is otherwise in conflict with the Constitution. If an unlawful act has caused moral and material damage to a person, he or she has the right to compensation (Article 25).[15]

1. Exercising constitutional review

The Supreme Court held on 30 September 1994 that:

> in a democratic state both the drafting of legislation and implementation of law, including interpretation of law, are to be guided by the Constitution (law) and by historically established general principles of law. In forming and developing general principles of Estonian law, principles shaped by the Council of Europe and institutions of the European Union must be taken into consideration alongside the Estonian Constitution. These principles have been derived from general principles of law of the Member States with developed legal cultures.

These general principles of law recognized in the European legal space are also valid in Estonia, the Court concluded.[16]

Despite the fact that there are no obstacles preventing national courts from regarding the provisions of the Convention as self-executing and directly applicable, the Estonian courts do not make frequent use of what is seen by them as 'foreign law'. In this sense the Estonian national practice is more inclined towards the Italian programmatic rules approach[17] rather than towards the Austrian, Swiss, or Netherlands approach to regard the provisions of the Convention as self-executing.

For example, several Supreme Court rulings are related to the general principles of democracy and the rule of law principle. In its decision of 20 December 1996 the Court held that:

> pursuant to the Constitution, the basis for the constitutional and democratic exercise of public power is that it must be founded on law and principles of separate and balanced powers, democracy, and the rule of law . . . Ambiguity of competence or an excess of authority prejudice general legal certainty and endanger both the exercise of state power, as provided for in the Constitution, and everyone's rights and freedoms . . . The executive is generally empowered to issue only *intra legem* regulations . . .[18]

The Constitution establishes that every essential decision must be made on the basis of laws and not on the basis of discretion. According to the Estonian

[15] There is also a new special law for compensation of victims of unlawful actions (inc. arrests and detention) of law enforcement institutions and officials.

[16] See Decision of the Constitutional Review Panel of the Supreme Court No. 9, Review of the Conformity of par. 25(3) of the Law of Property Act Implementation Act with the Constitution regarding the invalidation of par. 30(2) of the Peasant Act of the Estonian SSR. Decisions of the Supreme Court, Tallinn:1966, pp. 11–16.

[17] See DJ Harris, MO, Boyle, C Warbrick, note 12 above, p. 25.

[18] See *Riigi Teataja* I , 1997, 4 , 28.

system laws must be passed in accordance with the Constitution (Article 102), the government issues regulations and orders, and the ministers issue regulations and directives on the basis of and for the implementation of law (§§ 87(6) and 94(2) correspondingly). The Constitutional Review Chamber of the Supreme Court has substantiated the principle of the rule of law in this connection in several decisions. It its decision of 12 January 1994 the Court observed that:

pursuant to the principle of the rule of law as a generally recognized principle of international law and in accordance with the principle established by Article 3 of the Constitution, the fundamental rights and liberties may be restricted only in accordance with the law.

Later on, when evaluating the validity of the legal ground for the restriction of fundamental rights stemming from the Constitution (legality test) the Court ruled that:

the principle (requirement) of a legal ground for the restriction of fundamental rights and freedoms is absolute and precludes the establishment of restrictions by legislative acts of lower levels.

In the so-called *Police Operational-Technical Special Measures* case the Court ruled that:

the Constitution prohibits state agencies, local governments, and their officials from interfering with the private or family life of any person, except in the cases and pursuant to the procedure provided by law.[19]

So the Court used a restrictive interpretation of the notion 'law' and has taken the stand that fundamental rights and freedoms provided by the Constitution may be restricted only by valid legislation enacted by the Parliament, ie by a formal law.

The Supreme Court has also interpreted the extent to which the legislator may delegate authority to impose restraints on fundamental rights and freedoms. The court found that pursuant to Articles 11, 26, and 43 of the Constitution, the Parliament (Riigikogu) itself (not executive agencies) should have established in which explicit procedures operational–technical special measures can be applied, and what the possible restraints of the corresponding rights should be, instead of delegating the task to the officials of the Security Police. That function may not be delegated to the executive power, not even temporarily or on condition that it be reviewed by the court.

[19] See *Riigi Teataja* I, 1994, 8, 129–130.

2. *Exercising ordinary jurisdiction*

The Administrative Law Chamber of the Supreme Court has ruled that:

> the right of an alien to live family life in Estonia comes not only from the Aliens Act, but also from the Constitution and the European Convention on Human Rights.

It invoked Articles 8 and 12 of the Convention and made references to the cases of *Berrehab v Netherlands* (1988) and *Abdulazis, Cabales, and Balkandali v United Kingdom* (1985). The Court also stipulated that 'if the Aliens Act is not in conformity with the Constitution and the ECHR, the Constitution and the Convention need to be applied.'[20]

The Civil Chamber of the Supreme Court, examining a case concerning compensation for unlawful arrest, ruled that the only legal bases for deprivation of liberty are the Constitution, the Convention and the Criminal Procedure Code. If it is established by the court that a person has been deprived of their liberty otherwise than in conformity with those legal grounds and requirements, then that person has, according to the European Convention on Human Rights Article 5(5), the right to compensation. In another case the Civil Chamber ruled on the applicability of the reservation made by Estonia under Article 64 of the Convention concerning oral hearings, and stated that as the government had not at that time made necessary amendments to the relevant domestic law, the Convention provisions should be applied and an oral hearing should be granted to the party on the merits of the case and if the Court invoked Article 6(1) of the Convention.[21]

The Criminal Chamber of the Supreme Court, when examining an appeal on release from arrest, ruled that the requirement of Article 5(1)(c) of the Convention concerning deprivation of liberty, *inter alia*, is satisfied if there is a reasonable suspicion of someone having committed an offence and this suspicion is proved and not declaratory. The Court referred to the case of *Fox, Campell, and Hartly*.[22]

References to the Convention and to the case-law of the Human Rights Court have also been made in several other cases.

3. *Administrative law courts*

A remarkable role in granting judicial remedy in cases of violation of rights and freedoms is played by the administrative courts. Estonian administrative law courts examine two types of cases subject to two separate court procedure

[20] See case No. 3–3–1–16–97 of the Administrative Panel of the Supreme Court.
[21] See cases Nos. 3–2–1–117–97 and 3–2–1–138–97 of the Civil Panel of the Supreme Court.
[22] See case No. 3–1–1–27–97 of the Criminal Panel of the Supreme Court.

laws: 1) judicial review of administrative acts takes place in accordance with the Administrative Court Procedure Act, and 2) administrative offences (minor delicts) are dealt with under the Code of Administrative Offences. In this connection especially the important role of judicial review of administrative acts should be mentioned. This system was created in the course of judicial reforms and started to operate on 15 September 1993. Any individual legal act or action by an administrative authority or official can be challenged in an administrative court if this executive act or action violates someone's rights and freedoms. After a relevantly modest start the system has been playing extremely important role in supporting the rule of law and in the control of the executive.

All Estonian court judgments are printed and made public, but not all of them are published. Only judgments of the Supreme Court are published in a separate issue of the Official Gazette (Riigi Teataja) and in a separate annual issue. Therefore it is complicated to gain a comprehensive overview of court practice at lower levels. As far as it can be decided on the basis of cases (files) referred to the Supreme Court and of the practice of the Supreme Court itself, the courts are using ECHR provisions and case-law in motivating (reasoning) parts of their decisions. But the present author has never come across a decision where the Convention was used in resolutive (operative) part of their decision. This means that the Convention is not used as a law on the basis of which the decision was made or substantiated. Consequently, it seems that Estonian courts still do not regard the Convention as self-executing and directly applicable.

Generally, it cannot be concluded that all Estonian national courts have realized that their decisions may find their way to Strasbourg to be scrutinized there in reference to Convention standards. The process will probably be accelerated after the first Estonian cases have been tried in the Strasbourg Court.

12

Finland

ALLAN ROSAS*

INTRODUCTION

Every member state's adherence to the European Convention on Human Rights displays some country-specific features. In the case of Finland, two background factors should be emphasized. First, there is the question of Finland's foreign and treaty policy preceding its membership in the Council of Europe and ratification of the ECHR, which explains why it ratified the ECHR as late as May 1990. Secondly, the Finnish constitutional and legal system offers some distinctive features, which are relevant when considering the status and impact of the ECHR in national law.

After having achieved independence in 1917–18, Finland enacted a Constitution Act in 1919. Until a recent reform in 1995, the fundamental rights listed in chapter II of the Constitution Act were restricted to Finnish citizens. The 1919 constitutional Bill of Rights was based on the Western liberal tradition, with a strong emphasis on civil and political freedoms.[1] The

* The original manuscript for this chapter was written in February 1995. While it has not been possible to prepare a complete update, we have, with much appreciated help from Professor Martin Scheinin, Director of the Åbo Akademi Institute for Human Rights (Turku/Åbo), added some references to developments in 1995–2000. The author also wishes to thank Mr Arto Kosonen, Counselor (Finnish Ministry for Foreign Affairs) and Mr Jarmo Vuorinen, Secretary of the Committee for Constitutional Law (the Finnish Parliament) for their assistance.

[1] Political rights in the strict sense (electoral rights) are not listed in the Bill of Rights but in a separate constitutional Parliament Act of 1928. This reluctance to recognize electoral rights as true fundamental or human rights is not at all unique in the framework of Western liberal theory. This reluctance can also be seen in the controversies surrounding the inclusion of electoral rights in the ECHR (they were ultimately included in Article 3 of Protocol No. 1). See eg A. Rosas, 'Democracy and Human Rights', in: A. Rosas and J. Helgesen (eds) *Human Rights in a Changing East-West Perspective* (London: Pinter Publishers, 1990), pp. 17–57 at pp. 18–21. On the original Bill of Rights enacted in 1919 see eg M. Scheinin, 'Constitutional Law and Human Rights', in: J. Pöyhönen (ed) *An Introduction to Finnish Law* (Helsinki: Finnish Lawyers' Publishing Company, 1993), pp. 27–58 at pp. 38–45.

Bill of Rights of 1995 includes also the constitutional protection of economic, social, and cultural rights.[2]

After two wars against the Soviet Union (1939–40, 1941–44) Finland had to re-orient her foreign and security policy to accommodate the powerful Eastern neighbour. The 1947 Treaty of Peace with the Allied and Associated Powers and the bilateral Treaty of Friendship, Co-operation, and Mutual Assistance of 1948 symbolized the new era (the 'Second Republic'). On the other hand, this orientation was countered by a commitment to a Western political system and the rule of law, and a cautious move towards both universal and Western co-operation frameworks, including membership of the United Nations (1955) and the Nordic Council (1955), an association with the European Free Trade Association (1961), and membership of the Organization for Economic Co-operation and Development (1969).

In the human rights field, Finland started to adhere to most conventions concluded under the auspices of the United Nations.[3] These include the two Covenants of 1966 with the Optional Protocols to the International Covenant on Civil and Political Rights (CCPR), the 1965 Racial Discrimination Convention, the 1979 Women's Convention, the 1984 Torture Convention, and the 1989 Children's Convention.[4] Finland has also accepted the complaint systems of the CCPR, the Torture Convention, and since 1994 the Racial Discrimination Convention.[5] The Finnish record with respect to formal adherence to universal human rights treaties is thus quite good.[6]

The significance of this is underscored by the fact that, while the official doctrine is dualism, international treaties binding on Finland are normally incorporated into national law. The incorporating acts (either statutory

[2] The reform was introduced to Parliament as Government Bill No. 309/1993 and promulgated as Act No. 969/1995. An English language translation is available in *Constitutional Laws of Finland* (Helsinki 1996: Parliament of Finland, Ministry for Foreign Affairs, Ministry of Justice) as well as in M. Scheinin (ed), *International Human Rights Norms in the Nordic and Baltic Countries* (Dordrecht: Martinus Nijhoff, 1996), pp. 289–294.

[3] See eg K. Törnudd, *Finland and the International Norms of Human Rights* (Dordrecht: Martinus Nijhoff, 1986), p. 335; A. Rosas, 'The Nordic Countries and the International Protection of Human Rights', (1988), 57 *Nordic Journal of International Law*, 424–441 at p. 425; Scheinin, n. 1 above, pp. 46–48.

[4] International Convention on the Elimination of All Forms of Racial Discrimination, Convention on the Elimination of All Forms of Discrimination against Women, Convention against Torture and Other Cruel, Inhuman, or Degrading Treatment or Punishment, Convention on the Rights of the Child.

[5] Concerning the (First) Optional Protocol to the CCPR, see Finnish Treaty Series (FTS) 8/1976 and the complaints system provided for in Article 22 of the Torture Convention, FTS 60/1989. The right to submit communications under Article 14 of the Racial Discrimination Convention was recognized as late as November 1994, FTS 81/1994.

[6] For a comprehensive survey of the CSCE states' adherence to human rights conventions see L. Hannikainen, 'CSCE States' Adherence to Human Rights Conventions', in: Rosas and Helgesen, n. 1 above, pp. 334–366.

orders or statutory orders supplemented by an Act of Parliament) are statutes *in blanco*, which means that they do not repeat the wording of the treaty but merely refer to it and declare it to be part of the law of the land.[7] While legal doctrine for some time held that this may imply direct applicability (and, depending on the treaty, direct effect as well) it was, as far as human rights treaties were concerned, only in the late 1980s that courts and administrative authorities started to follow suit. The Supreme Administrative Court took the lead in a couple of decisions of 1988, that is before the final decision to join the Council of Europe had been taken.[8] Also the Parliamentary Ombudsman started to refer to international human rights treaties in his decisions.[9]

While these developments did not dispel the uneasiness of most judges and practising lawyers *vis-à-vis* the application of international human rights treaties, they at least helped to pave the way for a more open attitude towards adherence to, and application of, the ECHR. At the same time, there was a general desire in many leading circles to get Finland into the Council of Europe, mainly to reaffirm that Finland adheres to Western European values. Also critical voices were heard, mainly in leftist political circles. Legal experts were divided, some holding that adherence to and incorporation of the ECHR would lead to legislative and other improvements, while others, according to one of the leading opponents:

> referred to the principle of national sovereignty, the risk of the judiciary state, and the legitimate differences between the legal cultures of the Western European countries.[10]

While in the 1970s the Government still did not want to provoke the Soviet Union and thus to jeopardize Finnish efforts to obtain the go-ahead for economic and trade links with the West,[11] the era of perestroika and glasnost led

[7] The most comprehensive study of the status of international human rights norms in Finnish law is M. Scheinin, *Ihmisoikeudet Suomen oikeudessa* (Helsinki: Suomalainen Lakimiesyhdistys, 1991), which (pp. 349–364) includes an English Summary. See also, eg, K. Joutsamo, 'The Direct Effect of Treaty Provisions in Finnish Law', (1983) 52 *Nordic Journal of International Law*, 34–44; M. Scheinin, 'The Status of Human Rights Conventions in Finnish Law', in: A. Rosas (ed) *International Human Rights Norms in Domestic Law: Finnish and Polish Perspectives* (Helsinki: Finnish Lawyers' Publishing Company, 1990), pp. 25–43; A. Rosas, 'Human Rights Obligations: A Finnish Perspective' (1991) 1 *All-European Human Rights Yearbook*, pp. 235–247 at pp. 238–241; Scheinin n. 1 above, pp. 48–49.

[8] *KHO 1988 A 48*; *KHO 1988 A 49*. See also *KHO 1979 I 4*, where the CCPR was mentioned in a minority opinion, and Scheinin, n. 7 above, pp. 35–40.

[9] L. Lehtimaja, 'International Human Rights and Domestic Legality: Experiences of the Finnish Parliamentary Ombudsman', in: A. Rosas (ed), *International Human Rights Norms in Domestic Law: Finnish and Polish Perspectives* (Helsinki: Finnish Lawyers' Publishing Company, 1990), pp. 93–108.

[10] A. Jyränki, 'Taking Democracy Seriously—The Problem of the Control of the Constitutionality of Legislation: The Case of Finland', in: M. Sakslin (ed) *The Finnish Constitution in Transition* (Helsinki: The Finnish Society of Constitutional Law, 1991), pp. 6–16 at p. 14.

[11] The then President of the Republic Dr Urho Kekkonen is reported to have opposed in the early 1970s even Finnish participation in Council of Europe committees and ministerial

the government to apply for membership of the Council of Europe, which came about on 5 May 1989.[12] This took place without much public debate, which indicated that opposition to membership in the Council and adherence to the ECHR was waning. From the very outset, it was almost self-evident that Finland should not only sign and ratify the ECHR but also accept the system of individual petition and the jurisdiction of the Court.

This led to an intensive period of preparatory work, which was initiated in 1988. A working group co-ordinated by the Ministry for Foreign Affairs started to map out the main problems. A comprehensive survey of the relation between the ECHR and Finnish law was prepared for the Ministry of Justice by Professor Matti Pellonpää, later the Finnish member of the European Commission of Human Rights and then judge at the new Court of Human Rights which started to function on 1 November 1998.[13] His study revealed that the main problems were related to Articles 5 (liberty and security of person) and 6 (right to fair trial) of the ECHR. Legislative amendments were introduced with respect, *inter alia*, to the legislation concerning pre-trial investigations, military disciplinary punishments, the enforcement of sentences, and the status of aliens. There was a consistent effort to take into account not only the text of the ECHR but also the case-law of the Strasbourg organs.[14]

Awareness of the Strasbourg case-law was shown not only by the introduction of such legislative amendments as reducing the maximum period for pre-trial police arrest from ten or more days (under Act No. 450/1987) to four

meetings, as he was afraid that closer ties to the Council might jeopardize an envisaged free-trade agreement to be concluded between Finland and the European Economic Community. See the account provided by his then *chef de cabinet* A. Jyränki, *Kolme vuotta linnassa. Muistiinpanoja ja jälkiviisautta* (Porvoo: Werner Söderström, 1990), p. 119.

[12] The Parliamentary Assembly of the Council of Europe gave its favourable opinion at the beginning of 1989, and the Committee of Ministers subsequently, in Resolution (89)1, invited Finland to become a member of the Council of Europe, 32 *Yearbook of the European Convention on Human Rights* 1989 (1993), p. 268.

[13] M. Pellonpää, 'Euroopan neuvoston ihmisoikeussopimus Suomen näkökulmasta', *Oikeusministeriön lainvalmisteluosaston julkaisu* 21/1988 (Helsinki: Ministry of Justice, 1989).

[14] See on Finnish adherence to the ECHR and the status of the Convention in Finland generally M. Pellonpää, 'The Finnish Accession to the European Convention on Human Rights', in *The Implementation in National Law of the European Convention on Human Rights: Proceedings of the Fourth Copenhagen Conference on Human Rights* (Copenhagen: Publications from the Danish Center of Human Rights No. 11, 1989), pp. 67–71; idem, 'The Implementation of the European Convention on Human Rights in Finland', in Rosas and Helgesen (eds) n. 6 above, pp. 44–67; idem, 'Die EMRK in der finnischen Rechtsordnung', 273 *Vorträge, Reden und Berichte aus dem Europa-Institut* (Saarbrücken, 1992); idem, 'Nationaler Individualrechtsschutz und europäischer Menschenrechtsstandard in Finnland', (1993) 20 *Europäische Grundrechte*, 590–594; idem, 'La Convention européenne des droits de l'homme: Quelques réflexions comparatives entre la Finlande et la France', (1995) 47 *Revue internationale de droit comparé*, 669–679; Scheinin, n. 7 above, passim.

days (Act No. 361/1990),[15] but also by a carefully drafted reservation to Article 6, paragraph 1. According to the reservation (which was the only one formulated by Finland) it could not 'for the time being' be guaranteed that oral hearings are always held in cases before appellate and supreme general and administrative courts as well as some special courts and tribunals, insofar as existing Finnish law does not provide such a right.[16] This reservation was mainly prompted by the *Ekbatani* case, which interpreted Article 6 to require an oral hearing in a criminal case under circumstances where the defendant would under existing Finnish law not necessarily have the right to request an oral hearing in an appeal court.[17]

The Government Bill on the Convention together with its eight Protocols was submitted to Parliament in March 1990.[18] After Parliament had given its consent, and passed the necessary incorporating Act (Act No. 438/1990), the Convention and the Protocols were ratified by the President of the Republic on 4 May 1990 (FTS 19/1990). The instruments of ratification were deposited on 10 May and the Convention consequently entered into force on that date. Protocol No. 9 was ratified in December 1990 (FTS 72/1994) and Protocol No. 11 in January 1996.[19]

This commitment to the ECHR system was supplemented by acceptance of the European Social Charter and the 1987 European Convention for the Prevention of Torture and Inhuman or Degrading Treatment or Punishment. The Torture Convention was approved in December 1990 (Finnish Treaty Series FTS 17/1991) and the Social Charter in April 1991 (FTS 44/1991). It should be noted that not only the Torture Convention but also the Social Charter were incorporated through an Act of Parliament (Acts No. 463/1991, 843/1991) under circumstances which suggest that the Social Charter might be directly applicable by national courts.[20] There is no case-law to date, however, to back up this hypothesis.

[15] This amendment, of course, was designed to bring Finnish law into harmony with the case-law on Article 5, paragraph 3, as illustrated by *Eur. Court H.R., Brogan and Others*, Judgment of 29 November 1988, Series A No. 145–B.

[16] For the English text of the reservation see 33 *Yearbook of the European Convention on Human Rights* 1990 (1994), p. 9. In December 1996, the reservation was partly withdrawn: see Statutory Order No. 1067 of 18 December 1996. A further partial withdrawal took place on 29 April 1998, Statutory Order No 285 of 24 April 1998.

[17] *Ekbatani*, Judgment of 26 May 1988, Series A No. 134.

[18] Government Bill No. 22/1990.

[19] The official publication of Protocol No. 11 in the *Finnish Treaty Series* took place only as the Protocol was to enter into force, FTS 86/1998 of 23 October 1998.

[20] See A. Rosas, 'The Implementation of Economic and Social Rights: Nordic Legal Systems', in: F. Matscher (ed) *The Implementation of Economic and Social Rights: National, International and Comparative Aspects* (Kehl am Rhein: Engel, 1991), pp. 223–235 at pp. 228–229.

A. THE STATUS OF THE CONVENTION IN NATIONAL LAW

In accordance with established practice, the Act incorporating the ECHR was, together with an accompanying Statutory Order, published in the Finnish legislative series *The Statutes of Finland* (Nos. 438–439/1990) while the actual text of the Convention was published in the treaty series (FTS) only. As noted above, the incorporating acts are statutes *in blanco*, which merely refer to the treaty in question and declare its provisions to be part of the law of Finland. Thus the ECHR *is* part of Finnish law, but the content of the law is not to be found in the legislative series but in the separate FTS. This inconvenience is mitigated by the fact that the text of the Convention (together with some other human rights instruments[21]) is published in the unofficial but widely used Book of Statutes published by the Finnish Lawyers' Union.[22] This is the compilation to which judges, civil servants, and practising lawyers would normally turn.

It was from the outset considered necessary to incorporate the ECHR through an Act of Parliament, and not only by a Statutory Order issued by the President of the Republic. An Act of Parliament had been used in regard to some earlier human rights treaties, including the CCPR (but not the International Covenant on Economic, Social, and Cultural Rights, which was incorporated through a Statutory Order only). Moreover, the government proposed that the incorporating Act be adopted in a special procedure applying to constitutional amendments and derogations, which in the case of international treaties means a requirement of a two-thirds majority. In the Government Bill, this requirement was based on the ECHR control machinery, which was deemed to constitute deviations from Sections 1 and 2 of the Constitution Act relating to the sovereignty of the Republic. There is no special clause in the Constitution Act which would regulate approval of supra-national mechanisms and so mechanisms deemed to constitute serious limitations on Finnish sovereignty have been considered to be in conflict with Sections 1 and 2.

The Parliamentary Committee for Constitutional Law adhered to this interpretation but specified that the limitations of Finnish sovereignty followed, not from the powers of the European Commission of Human Rights, but from the jurisdiction and powers of the Court as well as of the Committee

[21] The CCPR, the International Covenant on Economic, Social, and Cultural Rights, the European Social Charter, the Universal Declaration of Human Rights, the Convention for the Elimination of All Forms of Discrimination Against Women, and the Convention on the Rights of the Child.

[22] See *Suomen Laki* I 1996, p. 4.

of Ministers.[23] The Committee also reaffirmed that the ECHR belongs to the category of treaties which 'contain provisions within the legislative sphere', as stated in Section 33 of the Constitution Act. This implies that Parliament must both give its consent and adopt an incorporating Act. In the hearings of experts held by the Committee[24] the view was put forward that the ECHR might not fall within the domain of parliamentary legislation, as there had been a concerted effort to bring Finnish domestic law into harmony with the Convention. According to a traditional and quite restrictive interpretation of Section 33 of the Constitution Act, the 'legislative sphere' merely referred to situations where there was a conflict between an existing Finnish statute and the treaty to be adopted and incorporated. The Committee—quite rightly, it is submitted—refuted this line of reasoning and determined that the ECHR constituted such a regulation of the legal status of individuals that it must be deemed to fall within the domain of parliamentary legislation, even if no outright conflict existed between its provisions and domestic legislation.

Does the fact that the incorporating Act was adopted by a two-thirds majority imply that the ECHR was elevated to the hierarchical level of a Basic (constitutional) Law? The answer is in the negative. The Convention did not become a Basic Law.[25] This is because it was adopted in accordance with a peculiar Finnish procedure for 'exceptions' to the Basic Laws.[26] Such constitutional 'exceptions' (or derogations), even though their *adoption* requires a qualified majority (in the case of incorporation of international treaties, a two-thirds majority) can be *repealed* by an ordinary Act of Parliament, adopted by a simple majority. This is because the derogation is construed as an inroad into the Basic Laws, which will be restored to their former glory when the Act of derogation is abolished. Thus, the Finnish Parliament could at any time repeal the Act incorporating the ECHR by a simple majority, depriving the ECHR of its current status as part of the law of the land.

Such a possibility seems to be of academic interest only. What might happen in practice is that Parliament could pass an ordinary Act relating to any subject and this Act could be in conflict with the ECHR. Moreover, it is of course possible that conflicts might be found between the ECHR and previous legislation, despite efforts to remove such discrepancies when Finland joined the Council of Europe and the Convention.

It should be noted first that according to the prevailing view the courts have not had the right to review the constitutionality of Acts of Parliament. This

[23] Opinion No. 2/1990 of the Committee for Constitutional Law.

[24] The present writer was one of the experts heard by the Committee for Constitutional Law.

[25] The Basic Laws are the Constitution Act of 1919, the Parliament Act of 1928, and two Acts of 1922 relating to the legal responsibility of the members of the Council of State (ie Cabinet Ministers).

[26] See eg Jyränki, n. 10 above , p. 8.

principle may be eroding, as there are a few cases where the Supreme Court has applied the principle of presuming the constitutionality of an Act so as to come up with an interpretation which almost goes beyond the wording of the Act, in order to achieve harmony between the Act and a provision in a Basic Law.[27] Be that as it may, the ECHR, as noted above, is not a Basic Law and the incorporating Act can, in principle, be repealed by an ordinary Act. Thus, the relationship between the ECHR (as incorporated) and (other) Acts of Parliament has been held to be governed by the normal principles governing the relation between legislative acts of the same hierarchical order, the *lex posterior* principle in particular.[28] The ECHR would thus take precedence over Acts which entered into force before the ECHR Act, while subsequent Acts would prevail over the ECHR.

This is not the whole story, however. The principle of presumption, which tells courts to presume that Parliament could not have meant to enact a law which derogates from a Basic Law, can be applied with equal or even enhanced force to the relationship between the ECHR and ordinary legislation.[29] Parliament should not be presumed to have wished to depart from the ECHR, one of the cornerstones of Finland's international commitments and a European legal and quasi-constitutional system. The fact that the incorporating Act was adopted by applying the procedure for constitutional amendments can be an additional argument in favour of a strong principle of presumption. One could thus arrive at a solution in which the only situation where a subsequent Act of Parliament supersedes the ECHR with its incorporating Act would be when Parliament clearly expressed an intention to deviate from the ECHR. Such a scenario is not likely.[30]

[27] See eg Scheinin, n. 7 above, pp. 216–220.

[28] This was also stated in the opinion of the Committee for Constitutional Law of the Parliament referred to in n. 23 above.

[29] Scheinin, n. 7 above, p. 361, refers to the tendency in the Supreme Court to apply the principle of presumption to the relation between constitutional provisions and ordinarily legislation and adds: 'The same line of argumentation could be used in relation to Acts of Parliament passed *after* the incorporation of a human rights treaty: if there is no clear indication of the legislature's intention to enact a law conflicting with the treaty, the legislature must be presumed not to have violated Finland's international obligations. Therefore provisions of the treaty may take precedence over the wording of the domestic enactment.'

[30] One can also argue, as Scheinin, n. 7 above, p. 362, has done, that 'a combination of the international obligations of the Finnish State and the constitutional position of Parliament leads to the conclusion that Parliament is legally bound by human rights treaties to which Finland is a party, irrespective of the method of their domestic implementation.'

B. THE CONVENTION IN THE LEGISLATIVE AND POLITICAL PROCESSES

Traditionally, international human rights norms have not occupied a prominent place in parliamentary proceedings nor in the legislative processes. A study on the role of human rights norms in the process of drafting legislation relating to the deprivation of liberty, which was made before Finnish adherence to the ECHR, showed a gradual increase in the number of references to international instruments in the reports of law commissions, Government Bills, and parliamentary proceedings.[31] This trend has been strengthened by the upsurge of new human rights commitments and instruments (including the OSCE political commitments[32]), the move towards a human rights approach in the Finnish 'legal culture' in general, and, of course, the membership of the Council of Europe with its human rights treaties, including the ECHR.[33]

A distinctive Finnish feature has to be stressed in this context. While the ECHR may be the single most important instrument referred to in the legislative and political process, attention has since 1990 also been paid to the CCPR, special conventions such as the Women's and Children's Conventions, and OSCE commitments. It is not uncommon that two or several instruments are invoked at the same time in legislative processes, before the courts, and so on.

Another feature worth mentioning is the input into the legislative process by expert academics and non-governmental organizations. It is standard procedure to involve professors of law and other experts in the work of governmental law commissions and working groups. The committees of the Parliament regularly conduct closed hearings with not only government civil servants but also academic experts and sometimes representatives of non-governmental organizations. There is a growing human rights community and academic research potential. In 1988 the government established an Advisory Board for International Human Rights Affairs. This Advisory Board brings together politicians, NGO representatives, academics, and civil servants and has to a certain extent been a forum for discussions not only on

[31] K. Myntti, *Mänskliga rättigheter och frihetsberövande i Finland* (Turku/Åbo: Institute for Human Rights, 1988).

[32] See M. Pentikäinen, *Human Rights Commitments within the CSCE Process: Nature, Contents and Application in Finland* (Helsinki: Publications of the Advisory Board for International Human Rights Affairs No. 3, Ministry for Foreign Affairs, 1992). The Conference on Security and Co-operation in Europe (CSCE) on 1 January 1995 became the Organization on Security and Co-operation in Europe (OSCE).

[33] See, in particular, Scheinin, n. 7 above, passim, English Summary pp. 358–363.

Finland's human rights policies in general but also on domestic implementation issues.[34]

These developments mean that human rights considerations are often brought into the discussion on legislative issues and in this way the risk of new legislation which could contravene the ECHR or other human rights treaties is diminished. Needless to say, much depends on the legislative project and circumstances at hand and human rights concerns may sometimes, at best, be of marginal relevance only.[35] It is clear that the non-governmental organizations and interest groups of relevance for human rights considerations are not as active in putting forward proposals and criticism as their counterparts in Denmark, Norway, and Sweden.

Reference was made above to the conscientious effort to review Finnish legislation when preparations were made in 1988–90 for Finland becoming a Contracting Party to the ECHR. A number of legislative amendments were introduced, sometimes invoking the ECHR alone, sometimes invoking the ECHR in conjunction with other human rights instruments, and sometimes referring in a more indirect way to the ECHR and/or other human rights instruments. The amendments included such disparate areas as criminal investigations, military discipline, the law on aliens, the protection of children, freedom of association, and freedom of assembly.[36]

An amendment to the Military Discipline Act (No. 331/1983) deserves special mention, as it illustrates the difficulties which are sometimes encountered when human rights considerations are brought into the legislative process. The original Act prohibited access to courts in the case of military arrest (confinement for a period of up to thirty days). Such a prohibition is probably in contravention not only of Article 5, paragraph 4, of the ECHR but also Article 9, paragraph 4, of the CCPR. The Finnish translation of the expression 'arrest and detention' appearing in the latter provision misleadingly pointed to criminal arrest and detention only. This mistake was observed in connection with the enactment of a new Aliens Act in 1982, but not in connection with the Military Discipline Act. Although the Parliamentary Ombudsman in 1987 asked the government to revise the Military Discipline Act as well, and scholars had pointed out the discrepancy between the Act

[34] The present writer was a member of the Advisory Board 1988–93 and in 1993–95 a permanent expert to the Board.

[35] The question of which Ministry is mainly responsible for the project may play a decisive role. There are Ministries such as those of Agriculture, Trade and Commerce, Defence, the Interior, and Transport and Communications, where human rights considerations are not expected to be among the primary sources of concern.

[36] The most important legislative amendments are listed in 32 *Yearbook of the European Convention of Human Rights* 1989 (1993), pp. 309–310; 33 *Yearbook of the European Convention on Human Rights* 1990 (1994), pp. 319–320.

and the CCPR,[37] no action was taken.[38] It was only after the Human Rights Committee acting under the CCPR in 1989 had established a violation of Article 9, paragraph 4,[39] and Finland had signed the ECHR, that a Government Bill was submitted to Parliament, proposing a right to submit a decision on military arrest for judicial review.[40]

While these amendments were usually based on Government Bills, Parliament could also sometimes initiate human-rights inspired amendments. In a Government Bill (No. 135/1989) for amendments to the Building Act, it was proposed to restrict the right to submit administrative appeals to the Supreme Administrative Court in certain matters. The Committee for Constitutional Law of the Parliament wished to enlarge the scope for administrative appeals and invoked as an additional reason Article 6, paragraph 1, of the ECHR. As the proposed amendment could in some cases have deprived a landowner from access to an (administrative) court, the Committee concluded that the amendment could 'in particular cases lead to situations which can be deemed to contravene' Article 6, paragraph 1.[41] Consequently, the Government Bill was revised on this point (Act No. 696/1990). It should be noted that the opinion of the Committee was adopted after Finland had signed the ECHR, but before ratification.

The Convention has, of course, continued to play a certain role in legislative processes since it entered into force in May 1990.[42] To mention an example, the Committee for Constitutional Law of the Parliament held in May 1994 that the proposed legislation introducing police wire-tapping and surveillance of communications in the case of certain serious crimes—taking into account that it can take place only if authorized by a court in a concrete criminal investigation—is not in violation of Article 8 of the ECHR.[43] In some

[37] See M. Pellonpää, 'Ihmisoikeussopimukset ja Suomi' (Study commissioned by a Working Group on Fundamental Rights), in Perusoikeustyöryhmän muistio, *Oikeusministeriön lainvalmisteluosaston julkaisu* 3/1982 (Helsinki: Ministry of Justice), pp. 14–17; K. Myntti, 'Det militära arreststraffet och artikel 9 i konventionen om medborgerliga och politiska rättigheter', in K. Myntti (ed) *Finländska mänskorättsperspektiv* (Turku/Åbo: Institute for Human Rights, 1987), pp. 22–43.

[38] Lehtimaja, n. 9 above, pp. 99–100; Scheinin, n. 1 above, p. 41; Scheinin, n. 7 above, p. 267. The letter addressed by the Ombudsman to the government is dated 14 May 1987 (No. 1435 DN:o 826/2/87).

[39] The case of *Vuolanne v Finland*, Communication No. 265/1987.

[40] Government Bill No. 100/1989. The Bill (pp. 1–2) refers to both the *Vuolanne* case and the signing of the ECHR. In a brief summary (p. 1) only the ECHR is invoked as a reason for the amendment. The Act was amended accordingly (No. 374/1990).

[41] See Opinion No. 14/1989 of the Committee for Constitutional Law.

[42] Some legislative reforms and amendments of relevance in this context are listed in 34 *Yearbook of the European Convention on Human Rights* 1991 (1995), p. 383.

[43] Opinion No. 8/1994 of the Committee for Constitutional Law, p. 4. It should be noted that before this legislative reform there was no legislation on wire-tapping, which was thus prohibited altogether. See also Opinion No. 15/1994 on a new Police Act, p. 2.

cases the CCPR or some special human rights convention rather than the ECHR has been the focus.[44]

Such considerations on the relation between the ECHR (or other human rights treaty) and Finnish legislation and proposed legislation are normally raised in the Committees of the Parliament. It is only rarely that specific human rights issues are brought up in plenary debates, and when this occasionally happens it is usually in the context of Finland's relations with other countries (such as China, Iraq, or Turkey) and concerning trade relations, arms exports, and the like. The frame of reference, then, is economic interests versus morality, rather than any specific provision of the ECHR or similar convention.

C. HUMAN RIGHTS CASES DECIDED BY THE NATIONAL COURTS

As noted above, the year 1988 saw two cases decided by the Supreme Administrative Court in which express reference was made to incorporated provisions of human rights conventions (but not the ECHR, which had not even been signed at the time).[45] Such references have subsequently become fairly common and the ECHR has, of course, been included in the sources.[46] It would, on the other hand, be an exaggeration to say that direct application of the ECHR has become standard procedure.

In 1990, soon after the ECHR had entered into force, the Supreme Court was asked to give opinions on the lawfulness of extraditing to the Soviet Union Soviet citizens guilty of hijacking Soviet civilian aircraft, in view of Article 3 and other provisions of the ECHR.[47] The Supreme Court found no legal obstacles for their extradition.

In some criminal cases, the Supreme Court has had occasion to refer to Article 6 in particular (and in this context also to Article 14 of the CCPR) and

[44] A pertinent example is Opinion No. 21/1994 of 11 November 1994 of the Committee for Constitutional Law of the Parliament, where it is held that a proposed amendment to the Health Insurance Act would be in contravention of Section 5 of the Constitution Act (principle of equality) and Article 26 of the CCPR (prohibition of discrimination), as it would have introduced a distinction between men and women concerning certain social benefits.

[45] See n. 8 above.

[46] 33 *Yearbook of the European Convention on Human Rights* 1990 (1994), pp. 330–332; 34 ibid. 1991 (1995), pp. 400–401; M. Scheinin, 'Finnish Judicial Decisions Involving Questions of International Law', (1993) 4 *Finnish Yearbook of International Law*, pp. 501–507; Scheinin, n. 1 above, pp. 49–52.

[47] Cases *KKO H90/219*; *KKO H90/220*; *KKO H 90/350*. In case *KKO H90/422*, the Opinion was given in 1991. See also case *KKO H90/393* concerning an extradition request by Switzerland.

in a manner which has had a bearing on the outcome of the case. For instance, a sentence based on statements made by persons whom the defendant had not had the opportunity to cross-examine in person was quashed and the case remitted to the court of first instance.[48] In another case, a defendant should not in the opinion of the Supreme Court have been found guilty of aggravated assault as the indictment mentioned ordinary assault only and the defendant had not been informed of the possibility that he could be found guilty of a more serious crime.[49] In yet another case, the Supreme Court held that a defendant, given the particular circumstances of the case, should have been granted free legal assistance even if no more serious punishment than a fine was expected.[50]

In some of its more recent judgments, the Supreme Court has made reference not only to the provisions of the Convention but also to the case-law of the European Court of Human Rights. In one such case two defendants had been found guilty and sentenced to short terms of unconditional imprisonment. Both appealed to the Court of Appeal, asking to have their sentences shortened and to receive free legal assistance. The Court of Appeal denied legal assistance. This decision was upheld by the Supreme Court which presented an analysis of the case-law of the European Court of Human Rights in relation to the right to free legal assistance under Article 6 of the Convention.[51] Such use of Strasbourg case-law is a sign of genuine interest on the part of the Supreme Court in the interpretation of individual Convention provisions. At the same time, some commentators have asked whether this line of development is a sign of a 'minimalist' or 'passive' application of the Convention, a pattern of interpretation under which only the existence of a clear precedent by the European Court of Human Rights is sufficient proof of the Convention being applicable.[52]

A case dealing with the establishment of paternity decided by the Supreme Court in 1993 deserves special mention.[53] According to a literal interpretation of an Act implementing the 1975 Paternity Act, the death of a presumptive father precluded paternity proceedings. But such a literal interpretation

[48] *KKO 1991:84*. See also 34 *Yearbook of the European Convention on Human Rights* 1991 (1995), p. 400 and Article 6, paragraph 3(d), of the ECHR. See further a judgment of the Vaasa Court of Appeal of 14 January 1992, Report no. 21 (R91/759).

[49] *KKO 1992:73*. See Article 6, paragraphs 1 and 3, of the ECHR.

[50] *KKO 1992:81*. See Article 6, paragraph 3(c), of the ECHR. See also cases *KKO 1993:19*; *KKO 1993:99a*; *KKO 1993:164*. *KKO 1993:156* is an example of a case where the Supreme Court relied on Article 14 of the CCPR but not Article 6 of the ECHR. See further the judgments of the Vaasa Court of Appeals of 26 February 1993, Report No. 461 (R 92/1240), and Eastern Finland Court of Appeals of 10 September 1993, Report No. 1736 (R 92/1291).

[51] *KKO 1995:7*. For details, see M. Scheinin, 'Incorporation and Implementation of Human Rights in Finland', in Scheinin (ed) n. 2 above, pp. 256–266.

[52] See, M. Scheinin, 'General Introduction', in Scheinin (ed) n. 2 above, pp. 17–18.

[53] *KKO 1993:58*. See also Scheinin, n. 1 above, pp. 50–52.

would, according to the majority of three Justices,[54] cause 'unjustified inequality' and thus the Act should be interpreted in the light of its *ratio legis*, which also brought the interpretation 'into harmony' with the principle illustrated by Article 7 of the Convention on the Rights of the Child and Articles 8 and 14 of the ECHR. Lehtimaja J, concurring, went further in finding a conflict between the human rights provisions and the domestic Act and stating that the relevant provision of the domestic Act was 'inapplicable', since the Acts incorporating the ECHR and the Children's Convention had been enacted later in time than the domestic Act.

While the majority thus relied on the principle of harmony through interpretation, a decision by the Consistory (Chapter) of the Turku Arch Diocese in 1991 expressly determined that a conflict existed between the Lutheran Church Act and Article 6 of the ECHR, as the former enabled the Consistory to function as a pre-trial investigator, to decide on the indictment, and to sentence the clergy to punishment.[55] The Consistory decided to apply the ECHR instead of the Church Act, which led it to pronounce itself incapable of passing judgment (as it had already conducted an investigation and decided on the indictment). Accordingly the charges against a vicar had to be dismissed.

The Vaasa Court of Appeal has decided some cases through argumentation that indicates a conflict between national law and the Convention, and establishes the priority of the Convention in such cases.[56]

As to the Supreme Administrative Court, the most common type of case has concerned aliens' issues, especially expulsion and related cases, in the light of Article 8 of the ECHR in particular.[57] Some have led to the quashing of expulsion orders or refusals to grant asylum, while in other cases the decisions of administrative authorities have been upheld. It would seem on the whole that the Supreme Administrative Court has applied Article 8 of the ECHR fairly extensively, and sometimes in a manner which may go further than existing Strasbourg case-law. In a case decided in 1994 the Court annulled a decision of the Ministry of the Interior to refuse admittance to a foreign citizen at the border.[58] The rejection of the foreign citizen, who was married to

[54] The case was decided in a Chamber consisting of five Justices, including Heinonen, President.

[55] Decision No. 1/91 of 13 March 1991.

[56] See judgment of 22 September 1994 No. 1643 in which the Vaasa Court of Appeal stated: 'The clause on the disqualification of judges in our national Code of Judicial Procedure and case-law based on that provision conflict with Article 6 of the European Convention on Human Rights and case-law based on that provision. The above-mentioned supranational norm together with the interpretation of the relevant case-law supersede national legislation and national case-law in this case.'

[57] See eg *KHO 1992 A 59*, *KHO 1992 A 63*, *KHO 1993 A 26*, *KHO 1993 A 27*, *KHO 1993 A 28*, *KHO 1993 A 29*, *KHO 1993 A 30*, *KHO* judgment of 7 September 1993 Report No. 3234, *KHO 1995 A 33*.

[58] *KHO* judgment of 20 April 1994 Report No. 1650.

a Finn, was not necessary on any of the grounds mentioned in paragraph 2 of Article 8 and consequently was in violation of Article 8, paragraph 1. In another case, the Supreme Administrative Court annulled a decision on expulsion, applying, *inter alia*, Articles 3 and 8 of the ECHR.[59]

Other cases decided by the Supreme Administrative Court include questions of property rights,[60] denial of passports,[61] and the relation between church taxes and freedom of religion. In two judgments of 30 December 1994,[62] the Supreme Administrative Court held that a publishing company owned by associations working for the complete separation of church and state and whose members did not belong to the (Lutheran) Church, has to pay taxes to the Lutheran Church in accordance with a special Act on the subject (which exempts natural persons and other religious communities but not companies from the obligation to pay taxes to the Lutheran Church). The company argued that this Act was in contravention of the CCPR and ECHR. The cases were decided mainly on the basis of Section 8 of the Constitution Act and Article 18 of the CCPR but one of them partly also on the basis of Article 9 of the ECHR (concerning the taxation for 1990, the year when the ECHR entered into force). As to the treaty provisions, the taxes which the publishing company had to pay did not, in the view of the Supreme Court, directly or indirectly violate the right to freedom of thought, conscience, and religion recognized in Article 9, paragraph 1 (or Article 18 of the CCPR).[63]

Research undertaken in 1998 on judicial decisions of the year 1997 (not exhaustive, and mainly limited to the two Supreme Courts and the Courts of Appeal) revealed more than twenty cases where the judgment refers expressly to a provision of the ECHR, in most cases Article 6. Some judgments, in addition to the ECHR, refer to the CCPR (one judgment refers to the Convention on the Rights of the Child).

Finally, it should be noted that the Parliamentary Ombudsman often refers to human rights treaties in his or her decisions on complaints submitted to the Ombudsman.[64] As in the case of the courts, these references are not limited to the ECHR but often invoke other conventions as well, such as the CCPR and the special conventions. While the Ombudsman is not a judicial body, the importance of the institution is increased by the fact that the Ombudsman,

[59] *KHO* judgment No. 1649 of 20 April 1994.

[60] *KHO 1992 A 1.*

[61] *KHO* judgments Nos. 3171 and 3172 of 19 September 1991.

[62] Reports Nos. 6822 and 6823.

[63] After an oral hearing before its plenary, the European Commission of Human Rights, on 15 April 1996, declared the case inadmissible (Appl. 20471/96) as the company, as a corporate body, could not invoke Article 9 and as its majority shareholder, the Finnish Freethinkers' League, could not claim the status of 'a victim' under the Convention.

[64] Lehtimaja, n. 9 above; Scheinin, n. 7 above, pp. 266–273. Scheinin refers to statistics, according to which during the period 1988–90 there were 26 cases where reference was made in the decision to human rights treaties.

unlike most other parliamentary ombudsmen, can bring criminal charges against all civil servants.

D. CASES BROUGHT BEFORE THE EUROPEAN COURT AND COMMISSION

Ratification of the ECHR, which was fairly widely publicized and discussed in the mass media, led to quite a number of applications under Article 25 of the ECHR. Many of them relate to events that happened before 10 May 1990 and are thus inadmissible *ratione temporis*. The subjects raised in the applications have concerned a wide range of issues and almost all the provisions of the Convention.[65]

According to statistics relating to the period 1990–94,[66] a total of 371 applications led to a provisional file. Of these, 179 were registered as applications. A total of 98 applications had been declared inadmissible. Only seven applications had been declared admissible and four led to a report on the merits by the Commission of Human Rights.

As is often the case, the applications declared inadmissible as 'manifestly ill-founded' may still contain interesting points of fact and law. Examples are the cases concerning the extradition of Soviet aircraft hijackers, which as noted above had also been considered by the Finnish Supreme Court, two cases on the alleged discrimination against conscientious objectors, who had to serve for sixteen months as compared to the eight or eleven months applicable to the length of ordinary military service, two expulsion cases, and a case on the right of a HIV-positive prisoner to respect for his private life.[67]

In 1998 six cases concerning Finland had been decided by the Court of Human Rights and four by the Committee of Ministers after a report by the Commission. As to the four cases decided by the Committee of Ministers, two

[65] See L. Berg, 'Applications against Finland before the European Commission of Human Rights: The First Three Years', (1993) 4 *Finnish Yearbook of International Law*, pp. 508–549.

[66] European Commission of Human Rights—Statistics on Applications. Provided in January 1995 by the Legal Department of the Finnish Ministry for Foreign Affairs.

[67] Berg, n. 65 above, provides an account of many cases declared inadmissible during the period 1990–93. On the hijacking cases see *Oleg Kozlov v Finland*, 69 DR, p. 321, and n. 47 above. The question of conscientious objection was addressed in the *Autio* and *Julin* cases, Applications 17086/90 and 17087/90, D.R. 72, p. 245. Neither did the Human Rights Committee acting under the CCPR find an outright violation of Article 26 of the CCPR in the similar case of *Järvinen v Finland*, Communication No. 295/1988. The expulsion cases are *Mandusche Dreshaj v Finland* and *Ibrahim Tanko v Finland*, Applications 23159/94 and 23634/94, (1994) 77–A DR, pp. 126, 133. The case concerning the HIV-positive prisoner is Application 21780/93, *T.V. v Finland*, 76–A DR 140.

concerned property rights and the right to a fair trial,[68] one negative freedom of association (the right not to belong to a political party),[69] and one various matters relating to guardianship.[70]

The six cases against Finland so far decided by the European Court of Human Rights concerned issues relating to parental custody and visiting rights,[71] the right to change one's surname,[72] the right to a fair trial,[73] the confidentiality of medical data related to an HIV-positive person,[74] and the lawfulness of arrest and detention.[75]

In the case of *Hokkanen v Finland*, the Court held unanimously that the non-enforcement of the applicant's right of access concerning his own daughter from 10 May 1990 (the date of the entry into force of the ECHR) until 21 October 1993 constituted a violation of Article 8 of the ECHR.[76] On the other hand, the Court (by six votes to three) did not find a violation with respect to the non-enforcement of the applicant's right of custody. It was unanimous in

[68] *H v Finland*, Resolution DH (96) 103, *L v Finland*, Resolution DH (96) 104, both of 22 March 1996. In these cases, Applications 18507/91 and 18595/91, the application concerned the fairness of proceedings relating to the applicants' objections to a proposed private forestry road over their land.

[69] *Komulainen v Finland*, Resolution DH (95) 397, 15 December 1995 (Application 19576/92, Report of the Commission 16 May 1995). The applicant had been held by the Supreme Administrative Court not to be able to 'represent' a political party, as required by law with respect to membership of the Health Care Board of a Municipal Health Care Federation, as he was not a member of the party in question. The party (the National Coalition Party) had declared that it had accepted that Mr Komulainen occupied one of the four seats to which the Party was entitled. The Commission and the Committee of Ministers found no violation of Article 11 as they saw no ideological reason for Mr Komulainen not joining the Party.

[70] *Ollila v Finland*, Resolution DH (96) 3, 9 February 1996 (Application 18969/92 Report of the Commission 30 June 1993). The case concerned various matters relating to guardianship, the right to life, access to court, property rights, and alleged interference by the guardian with the ward's correspondence. It was only on the last-mentioned point that the application was declared admissible and, finally, Article 8 was found to be violated. See also Berg, n. 65 above, p. 547.

[71] Application 19823/92, *TH v Finland*. This case, which was decided by the Commission on 22 October 1993, was referred to the Court by the Commission on 9 December 1993. On the Court's judgment (*Hokkanen v Finland*), see below.

[72] Application 18131/91, *S v Finland*. The case, which was decided by the Commission on 8 July 1993, was referred to the Court by the Commission on 9 September 1993. On the judgment of the Court (*Stjerna v Finland*), see below.

[73] Application 17506/90, *Erkki Kerojärvi v Finland*. The case was decided by the Commission on 11 January 1994 and it was referred to the Court by the government on 10 June 1994. Application 20772/92, *Helle v Finland*. The case was decided by the Commission on 15 October 1996 and referred by the Commission to the Court on 5 December 1996. On the judgments of the Court, see below.

[74] Application 22009/93, *Z v Finland*. The case was decided by the Commission on 2 December 1995 and it was referred to the Court by the Commission on 25 January 1996. On the judgment of the Court (*Z v Finland*), see below.

[75] Application 20972/92, *Raninen v Finland*. The case, which was decided by the Commission on 24 October 1996, was referred to the Court by the Commission on 4 December 1996 and the Finnish Government on 25 February 1997. On the judgment of the Court, see below.

[76] Judgment of 23 September 1994, Series A No. 299–A. The Commission found a violation of Article 8 by nineteen votes to two.

not finding a violation of Article 6 as far as the length of the custody proceedings was concerned. The Court was also unanimous in holding that it was not necessary to examine the applicant's complaint under Article 13 and Article 5 of Protocol No. 7. Finland was to pay to the applicant the sum of 100,000 Finnish marks (around £15,000) for non-pecuniary damage and a sum for legal fees and expenses.

This case related to a number of procedural and practical problems concerning the enforcement of a father's right of custody and visiting rights with respect to his daughter, who was living with her grandparents, the parents of her deceased mother.[77] The Finnish legal and administrative system may sometimes be slow and ineffective in dealing with cases of this nature. It was thus a rule of law-related case rather than a case on what was in the best interest of the child. The applicant tried to convince the Court of the need to examine separately the applicant's allegations under Article 13, but the Court decided unanimously to stick to its previous line of abstaining from separate consideration of Article 13 if it has found a violation of one of the more substantive Articles.[78]

The second case, decided by the Court on 25 November 1994, is *Stjerna v Finland*.[79] Mr Stjerna had asked for permission to change his surname from Stjerna to Tawaststjerna, as his ancestors had used the latter name and his current name gave rise to practical difficulties. His request was rejected by the County Administrative Board and the Supreme Administrative Court upheld the Board's decision. The European Commission of Human Rights, in its report of 8 July 1993 expressed the opinion that there had been no violation of Article 8 (by twelve votes to nine) nor of Article 14 in conjunction with Article 8 (unanimously).

The European Court unanimously concurred with the opinion of the Commission and thus found no violation of the Convention. According to the Court, the contracting states 'enjoy a wide margin of appreciation' concerning requests for a change of name. The Court was not satisfied that the use of the name Stjerna caused much more inconvenience than the proposed name. Moreover, the last ancestor who bore the name of Tawaststjerna had died more than 200 years before the applicant's request to change his name and so no significant weight could be given to the links between the applicant and his ancestors. The judgment, however, confirms that questions of name can fall under Article 8 and that this also applies to refusals to allow individ-

[77] The present author served as an adviser to the applicant's lawyer in this case.

[78] We would tend to agree with Mr *Schermers*, who in his dissenting opinion to the Commission's report held that the Commission should have examined Article 13 as well. Mr Schermers concluded that there had also been a violation of this provision, since 'no effective remedy seemed available'.

[79] Judgment of 25 November 1994, Series A No. 299–B.

uals to adopt a specific new surname (and not only to the obligations imposed upon individuals to change their names).

The Court's judgment in the case of *Kerojärvi v Finland*[80] was delivered on 19 July 1995. This case concerns the right to fair trial, including access to court and the interpretation of the phrase 'civil rights' in Article 6, paragraph 1, in relation to social protection under public law.[81] A life annuity under the 1948 Military Injuries Act was considered individual and pecuniary in nature and the entitlement was hence a 'civil right' in the meaning of Article 6 of the Convention. The Court unanimously found a violation of Article 6, paragraph 1, as certain documents related to the medical history of Mr Kerojärvi had not been communicated to him even though they had been used in the proceedings in the Insurance Court and the Supreme Court when deciding on the applicant's case.

In the case of *Z v Finland*[82] a violation of Article 8 was found. Mr X, the former husband of the applicant, was accused of multiple sexual offences in 1991 and 1992. After committing the first crimes in question, he was found to be carrying the HIV virus. In the pre-trial investigation and court proceedings use was made of medical information relating to Z, who was also HIV-positive. It was never established how the police originally came to know of Z's HIV status, so the Court did not find here a leak of confidential medical data for which the respondent state could be held responsible. No violation of Article 8 was found in relation to court decisions compelling the doctors of Ms Z to testify to her medical records, or to the prosecutor's decision to conduct a police search in the hospital treating Z for the purpose of seizing all documents related to her medical history, as these measures according to the Court fell within the 'margin of appreciation' of 'competent national authorities'. A violation of Article 8 was found, however, because the Court of Appeal had in its judgment against X made public the full name and the HIV status of Z. The Finnish government was to pay the applicant 100,000 FIM in compensation for non-pecuniary damage and to compensate her legal costs and expenses. In addition, the Court stated that the decision of the domestic court to make the case file public in the year 2002, including the full medical records of Z, would also constitute a violation of Article 8 if implemented. In making this finding of a potential violation, the Court apparently pointed to the need to amend pertinent domestic legislation prior to the year indicated.[83]

[80] Judgment of 19 July 1995, Series A No. 322.

[81] The 1948 Military Injuries Act (No. 404/1948). See also n. 73 above.

[82] *Z v Finland*, Judgment of 25 February 1997, Reports of Judgments and Decisions 1997–I, No. 31.

[83] In para. 112 of its judgment the Court stated that 'it will confine itself to the above conclusion, as it is for the State to choose the means to be used in its domestic legal system for discharging its obligations under Article 53 of the Convention'.

The Court was unanimous in finding the two violations of Article 8, in holding that it was not necessary to examine the applicant's complaints under Article 13, and on just satisfaction. The conclusion of non-violation in relation to compelling the doctors to testify and to the search and seizure of medical documents was made by eight votes to one.[84]

In the case of *Z v Finland*, the reasoning by the Court markedly differed from the report of the Commission. As described above, the Court pronounced separately on the various alleged infringements of Article 8, whereas the Commission had made a general finding of a violation of the applicant's right to respect for her private life.[85]

The case of *Helle v Finland,* concerned proceedings before an ecclesiastical body and the Supreme Administrative Court for the determination of a pecuniary dispute. It raised, *inter alia,* issues related to the interpretation of the Finnish reservation to Article 6. The Court concluded that this reservation was valid and that Finland was under no Convention obligation to ensure that an oral hearing took place before the Supreme Administrative Court. Accordingly, no violation was found with respect to the absence of an oral hearing. Neither did the Court find a violation of Article 6, paragraph 1, with respect to the fairness of the proceedings (the applicant had argued, *inter alia,* that the national courts had failed to articulate clearly the reasons for their decisions).[86]

The case of *Raninen v Finland* related to the deprivation of liberty and handcuffing of a conscientious objector. The applicant, refusing both military and civilian service, was released from prison after serving a prison sentence for earlier refusal. At the prison gate, he was arrested and handcuffed by the military police for the purpose of taking him to a military unit where he continued to refuse any service. By 20 votes to 10 the Commission concluded that there had been a violation of Article 3 as the public and unnecessary handcuffing of the applicant amounted to degrading treatment within the meaning of the said provision. The Commission was unanimous in finding a violation of Article 5, paragraph 1, as there was no lawful basis for depriving the applicant prior to his new refusal to perform military service. The Court agreed unanimously on Article 5, paragraph 1, unanimously found no violation of Article 3, and found by seven votes to two that there had been no violation of Article 8.[87]

[84] In his partly dissenting opinion, Judge De Meyer strongly opposed the application of the 'margin of appreciation' doctrine in the case.

[85] Report of the Commission, 2 December 1995, paras. 164 and 143.

[86] *Helle v Finland*, Judgment of 19 December 1997, Reports of Judgments and Decisions 1997–VIII, No. 61.

[87] *Raninen v Finland*, Judgment of 16 December 1997, Reports of Judgments and Decisions 1997–VII, No. 60.

E. REMEDIAL ACTION TAKEN BY THE GOVERNMENT

It should be recalled that the preparations for signing and ratifying the ECHR were handled in a serious manner and that a real effort was made to bring Finnish legislation as far as possible into harmony with not only the text of the ECHR but also the Strasbourg case-law. This process, of course, will not exclude the establishment of violations in the Strasbourg institutions, as all possible situations cannot possibly have been foreseen, since much will depend on administrative and legal practice rather than the legislation as such, and because the Strasbourg case-law is amenable to dynamic interpretation and change.

The first case in which the European Court of Human Rights found a violation of the Convention was the case of *Hokkanen v Finland*, referred to above. In this case the Finnish government promptly paid the compensation and the legal fees and expenses awarded in the judgment. Secondly, the government had even before the judgement initiated preparations for reform of the legislation concerning the enforcement of decisions on child custody and access rights. In November 1994, a Working Group appointed by the Ministry of Justice submitted a proposal for a new Government Bill on the subject.[88] The Government Bill was submitted to Parliament in 1995, and the new Enforcement of Decisions on Child Custody and Access Rights Act entered into force on 1 December 1996.[89] The decision-making was transferred from the County Administrative Boards to the District Courts.

To take another example, the resolution by the Committee of Ministers in the *Ollila* case took note of a rapid amendment to the Guardianship Act for the purpose of protecting the confidentiality of correspondence by the ward.[90] In the other cases decided by the Court and referred to above, no need for legislative reform arose (in two of the cases, because no violation was found).

In this connection it may be of interest to refer briefly to two cases of remedial action with regard to the CCPR. While the views of the Human Rights Committee finding a violation of the Covenant have in many cases led to remedial action being taken by the Finnish government, the *Vuolanne* and *Torres* cases,[91] where violations were found of Article 9, paragraph 4 (arrest or detention), and which have been followed by amendments to the relevant legislation, led to disagreement concerning compensation to be paid to the victims. Mr Vuolanne instituted proceedings against the Finnish state in the

[88] Press Release from the Ministry of Justice of 16 November 1994.
[89] Government Bill No. 96 of 1995, Act No. 619 of 1996.
[90] Resolution DH (96) 3, Act No. 1151 of 1995.
[91] Communications Nos. 265/1987 and 291/1988.

general courts but the Supreme Court finally decided (in a somewhat surprising judgment) that this was a case for the administrative courts.[92] Mr Torres instituted a compensation case in a regional administrative court, which granted partial compensation. On appeal, the Supreme Administrative Court raised the compensation to be paid to Mr Torres to 20,000 Finnish marks for the human rights violation suffered by him.[93]

F. ASSESSMENT AND PROSPECTS

There is no denying that ratification of the ECHR has had a clear impact on the Finnish legal system. The main achievements have related to the improvement of procedures and remedies, issues addressed in Articles 5, 6, and 13 in particular. Most of the legislative changes introduced since 1988–89 have belonged to this category. It is a telling example that when the first Finnish case to reach the European Court of Human Rights, *Hokkanen v Finland*, included issues under Article 8, the main problems involved and the violation of Article 8 established by the Court related to deficiencies in procedures (the enforcement of domestic judgements and decisions) rather than the substantive content of domestic decisions. The only Finnish reservation to the ECHR is on Article 6 (oral hearings before certain appellate courts, this reservation being considered valid by the Strasbourg Court in the *Helle* case mentioned above).

It can be surmised that there are not so many problems relating to such 'substantive' rights as freedom from torture, freedom of expression, association and assembly, and property rights. The constitutional protection of private property in particular, has a strong position in Finland and generally speaking goes further than the minimum European requirement.[94] In so far as there are problems in this area, again they can be expected to relate to the length of proceedings and other procedural matters rather than the substance of property rights as such.[95]

It would be a great exaggeration to say that Finland has not been governed by the rule of law. However, there have been a number of deficiencies, and adherence to and incorporation of the ECHR certainly has been conducive to a process of improvements. The Convention, together with other human

[92] *KKO 1993:3.*

[93] *KHO 1993 A 25.* Also Mr. Vuolanne was finally granted compensation by the Supreme Administrative Court, *KHO* judgment of 16 April 1996, Report No. 1069.

[94] Pellonpää, n. 14 above (Europäische Grundrechte), p. 593.

[95] See the cases of *H v Finland* and *L v Finland*, n. 68 above.

rights conventions such as the CCPR, contribute to a development of the Finnish legal culture towards a greater emphasis on individual rights and the role of courts, rather than state interests. It is obvious that the ECHR in particular has helped to bring about a gradual change at the level of attitudes and paradigms.[96] The recent membership of the European Union (as from 1 January 1995) is a further step in this direction. On the other hand, the specific human rights impact of EU membership has so far been of limited significance for domestic legal developments.[97]

Finally, it should be noted that a new constitutional Bill of Rights was enacted in 1995. A Government Bill was submitted to Parliament in December 1993.[98] The Bill was unanimously approved, with minor amendments, by Parliament in two compositions, finally by the new Parliament elected in the general elections of 19 March 1995. Chapter II of the Constitution Act was promulgated by the President on 17 July 1995, and the new provisions entered into force on 1 August 1995.[99] While the original Chapter II was mainly confined to civil rights and political freedoms, the new Bill includes some economic and social rights (partly of a justifiable nature) and an elaborate set of civil and political rights. Finland's international commitments in the human rights field were a conspicuous source of reference in the preparation of the Bill.[100] By direct references to 'human rights' the new constitutional provisions may be understood to establish semi-constitutional status for international human rights treaties, including the European

[96] The two Supreme Courts and some appellate courts, the Vaasa Court of Appeal in particular, have played a significant role in this process. Rintala, President of the Vaasa Court of Appeal, has described the ratification of the ECHR as a 'turning point' in Finnish legal history: E. Rintala, 'Kansainvälisten normien vaikutuksesta tuomioistuinkäytäntöön', in: A. Rosas and C. Krause (eds) *Kansainvälinen normisto Suomen oikeuselämässä* (Helsinki: Finnish Lawyers' Publishing Company, 1993), pp. 57–65 at p. 57.

[97] It will be recalled that human rights, according to the case-law of the Court of Justice of the European Communities since 1969, form part of the general principles of Community law the Court applies as an import source of Community law but, on the other hand, that this phenomenon is limited to the domain of Community law: see eg N. Neuwahl and A. Rosas (eds) *The European Union and Human Rights* (Dordrecht: Martinus Nijhoff, 1995). The cases concerning Finland decided so far by the Court of Justice have not involved human rights matters. However, at the time of writing a request for a preliminary ruling is pending which at least implicitly raises a question of property rights (although there is the issue whether the question falls within the domain of Community law), Case C-97/98 *Jägerskiöld v Gustafsson.*

[98] Government Bill No. 309/1993.

[99] Act No. 969 of 1995.

[100] See the reports of a governmental law commission, Perusoikeuskomitean mietintö, *Komiteanmietintö* 1992:3 (Helsinki: Government's Printing Office), and a working group appointed by the Ministry of Justice, Perusoikeustyöryhmän mietintö, *Oikeusministeriön lainvalmisteluosaston julkaisu* 2/1993 (Helsinki, Ministry of Justice). See also M. Scheinin and A. Rosas, 'Les libertés fondamentales figurant dans la Constitution finlandaise', (1995) 47 *Revue internationale de droit comparé*, 643–658.

Convention on Human Rights.[101] At the same time, the new Bill may—especially as far as economic and social rights are concerned—be seen as a contribution to an ongoing human rights discourse about the content and nature of our human rights.

[101] See Section 16a of the Constitution Act and Report No. 25 of 1994 by the Committee for Constitutional Law of the Parliament. The notion of 'semi-constitutional status' is used in M.Scheinin, 'Incorporation and Implementation of Human Rights in Finland', in Scheinin (ed) n. 2 above, pp. 275–276.

13

France

CATHERINE DUPRÉ*

INTRODUCTION

The impact of the European Convention on Human Rights (ECHR, or the Convention) on French law has been slowly increasing since its ratification by the French government, but it has only become particularly significant over the last ten or fifteen years. France ratified the Convention in 1974,[1] that is twenty-four years after signing it, and accepted the right of individual petition under Article 25 only in 1981.[2]

When the ECHR was first drawn up, the political and legal context meant that its acceptance was not straightforward. Numerous reasons were given for not ratifying it immediately: the Algerian War; the state monopoly on radio and television broadcasting; and Article 16 of the 1958 Constitution, which confers exceptional powers on the President of the Republic in times of crisis. Therefore, when the European Convention on Human Rights was ratified, France made several reservations and interpretative declarations that

* I wish to express my thanks to Christophe Pettiti, *avocat au barreau de Paris*, who produced a first version of the study which provided background information for the final version printed here.

[1] At the same time, France accepted the compulsory jurisdiction of the Court under Art. 46 ECHR and ratified the First and the Fourth Protocols. Act no. 73–1227 of 31 December 1973, *Journal Officiel*, 3 January 1974, published in *Dalloz* no. 74–360, 3 May 1974, *Journal Officiel*, 4 May 1974. Protocol No. 8 of 19 March 1985 was ratified by France by Act no. 88–1250 of 30 Dcember 1988, published in *Dalloz* no. 90–245, 14 March 1990, *Journal Officiel*, 21 March 1990, which entered into force on 1 January 1990. General works: G. Cohen-Jonathan, *La Convention Européenne des Droits de l'Homme*, Ed. Economica 1989; and also the recent Ph.D. thesis of S. Braconnier, *Jurisprudence de la Cour des Droits de l'Homme et droit administratif francais*, Bruylant, 1997.

[2] Declaration of 2 October 1981 granting the right of individual petition pursuant to Article 25 ECHR, *Dalloz*, no. 81–911, 9 October 1981, *Journal Officiel*, 14 October 1981. The same day, France ratified the Second Additional Protocol without reservation. See G. Cohen-Jonathan, 'La reconnaissance par la France du droit de recours individuel devant la Commission Européenne des Droits de l'Homme', *Annuaire Français de Droit International*, 1981, p. 269. The Act authorizing the ratification of Protocol no. 11 has been published in the *Journal Officiel*, 24 February 1996, p. 2992.

set out its understanding of various provisions of the ECHR, in order to restrict their use.[3] The government made reservations to Articles 5 and 6 of the ECHR to prevent their use in relation to disciplinary proceedings in the army. The government interpreted Article 10 ECHR on freedom of expression in terms that made it compatible with the state's monopoly on radio and television. This interpretative declaration was repealed in 1988 after the abolition of that monopoly.[4] The government also made a reservation to Article 15 of the ECHR so that it could not be used to question Article 16 (emergency powers) of the French Constitution.

The government also made reservations and interpretative declarations to Protocol No. 7 when it was ratified by France on 17 February 1986, in order to safeguard the specificity of certain areas of French law concerned with that Protocol. The Government interpreted Article 2 of Protocol No. 7 as meaning that the examination of a case by a 'higher court' can be limited to the implementation of law, as in the *recours en cassation*. The government made a reservation in relation to Article 2(1) of that Protocol, in order to limit its scope to those 'criminal offences' falling within the jurisdiction of the French criminal courts. Furthermore, the government issued two reservations to Article 5 of Protocol No. 7. First, the government stated that Article 5 of that Protocol could not be used to challenge the traditional rules about inheritance of family names. Secondly, the government declared that Article 5 could not block the implementation of local rules in some overseas territories (Mayotte, New Caledonia, and the Islands of Wallis and Futuna). Finally, the French government stated that, as a whole, Protocol No. 7 would apply to the whole French territory, taking into account local requirements for overseas territories, as laid down by Article 63 ECHR.

In order to assess the impact of the ECHR on French law, one has to consider its perception and use by the domestic courts. For the purpose of this chapter, only the higher courts will be considered in that respect, ie the Cour de Cassation, the Conseil d'État and the Conseil Constitutionnel.[5] The

[3] The reservations and interpretative declarations to the ECHR are published in the *Revue Française de Droit Administratif*, 1991, pp. 113–114 in an annexe to one of the first reviews of ECHR case-law, written by V. Berger, H. Labaye, and F. Sudre.

[4] *Décret* 88–75 of 13 July 1988.

[5] The Cour de Cassation is the highest court of the ordinary judiciary for civil and criminal matters. It has five chambers for civil disputes and one for criminal cases. It can sit in mixed chambers or in plenary sessions for particularly important cases. It has to maintain the unity and consistency of case-law as developed by the ordinary judiciary. It does not examine cases on their factual merits (which is the role of courts of Appeal) but decides only on the application of law. The Conseil d'État is the highest body concerned with administrative disputes. Its competences are twofold: on one hand, it acts as adviser to the government and produces *avis* (advisory opinions); on the other hand, it acts as the highest administrative court in the country. The Conseil Constitutionnel plays the role in France of a constitutional court with a very restricted jurisdiction, because it can only check the constitutionality of statutes after Parliament has reached a

approaches of the higher French courts to the ECHR have varied greatly. While the Cour de Cassation has been quick to recognize that the provisions of the Convention were directly applicable in French law in 1975 and 1976,[6] the Conseil d'État started applying the Convention only in 1990.[7] The Conseil Constitutionnel steadily refuses to check the constitutionality of a bill against the ECHR, but seems to integrate, indirectly and implicitly, some elements of the Convention with its case-law.

A. THE STATUS OF THE CONVENTION IN FRENCH LAW

The status of the Convention in French law depends on two important issues. The first is the relationship between international and domestic law under the Constitution; the second is the recognition of the direct application of the Convention by French courts.

1. *Article 55 of the Constitution and the ECHR*

Article 55 of the Constitution of 1958 provides that:

> Treaties or agreements properly ratified or approved shall, upon their publication, have an authority superior to legislation, provided always that the relevant agreement or treaty is applied by the other party.

Taking the terms of Article 55 in order, the ECHR was properly ratified and published[8] without being submitted to the preventive review of the Conseil Constitutionnel. Additional Protocols ratified by France were likewise not referred to the Conseil Constitutionnel. Protocol No. 6 is an exception to this

final agreement on the phrasing of a bill but before its promulgation (preventive review). The Conseil Constitutionnel is also the judge of procedural propriety in elections and all electoral disputes are referred to constitutional judges (Art. 59 of the 1958 Constitution).

[6] Cour de Cassation, Crim. 3 June 1975, *Respino*, *Bull. Civ.* I, no. 382, *Gazette du Palais*, 1975, 2, Sommaire, p. 234. Cour de Cassation, Crim. 30 June 1976 *Glaeser-Touvier*.

[7] Conseil d'État, Assemblée, 21 December 1990, 'Confédération Nationale des Associations Familiales Catholiques et autres', *Revue Française de Droit Administratif*, 1990, p. 1065.

[8] According to Art. 52 of the 1958 Constitution, the President of the Republic negotiates and ratifies international treaties. The introduction into domestic law of a human rights treaty does not require a constitutional statute (Art. 53 Constitution). An ordinary statute authorizing the ratification is therefore the proper procedure. However, the statute only authorizes ratification which falls within the competence of the executive. After ratification, the treaty becomes binding in domestic law only when it is published, usually by a *décret*, in the *Journal Officiel*.

After being signed and before promulgation of the statute authorizing its ratification, an international treaty can be referred to the Conseil Constitutionnel by the President of the Republic, the Prime Minister, the President of the Assembly, and the President of the Senate. After the publication of the treaty, its control by the Conseil Constitutionnel becomes impossible.

practice because it was submitted to the Conseil Constitutionnel. The constitutional judges examined this Protocol and found it to be constitutional before its publication in 1985.[9]

As a result, the ECHR and its additional Protocols should have had, in theory, from the day of their publication, a hierarchical position superior to both prior and subsequent French norms. French courts, however, proved reluctant to apply this principle.

The Conseil Constitutionnel set out its view on the status of the ECHR for the purpose of reviewing bills[10] in a famous case of 1975 in which applicants claimed that the new and much debated bill on abortion was a breach of Article 2 ECHR.[11] In that case the constitutional judges referred to the reciprocity requirement of Article 55 and set out a distinction between the 'control of constitutionality' (compatibility with the Constitution) and the 'control of conventionality' (compatibility with international treaties). The Conseil stated that whilst the former was clearly its express function, controls falling within the scope of the latter were beyond its jurisdiction. Consequently, constitutional judges refused to review the 'conventionality' of the abortion bill with reference to the ECHR, on the basis that this operation was of a different nature from its usual role of providing constitutional adjudication. Treaties, wrote the constitutional judges, are 'relative and contingent' because they depend on reciprocal application by the parties; they cannot therefore be used as a comparative standard in the same way as the Constitution. As a result the Conseil Constitutionnel did not even mention the ECHR in its ruling and found the bill to be constitutional on the sole basis of the French *Déclaration des Droits de l'Homme et du Citoyen* of 1789.[12] Having thus excluded a possible role for itself in such a case, the Conseil Constitutionnel implicitly encouraged the ordinary courts to consider whether a domestic provision is compatible with the ECHR.[13]

[9] Conseil Constitutionnel, 22 May 1985, *Revue Française de Droit Administratif,* 1993, p. 853.

[10] A 'bill' here means, following French law, a statute definitively approved by Parliament, but not yet promulgated.

[11] Conseil Constitutionnel, 15 January 1975.

[12] Considérant que, dans ces conditions, il n'appartient pas au Conseil Constitutionnel lorsqu'il est saisi en application de l'article 61 de la Constitution, d'examiner la conformité d'une loi aux stipulations d'un traité ou d'un accord imternational; considérant, en second lieu, que la loi relative à l'interruption volontaire de la grossesse respecte la liberté des personnes appelées à recourir ou à participer à une interruption de grossesse, qu'il s'agisse d'une situation de détresse ou d'un motif thérapeutique; que dès lors, elle ne porte pas atteinte au principe de la liberté posé à l'article 2 de la Déclaration des Droits de l'Homme et du Citoyen . . .

[13] Traditionally in French law the authority competent to interpret international treaties was the Ministry of Foreign Affairs. The Conseil d'État put an end to this practice in the *GISTI* case where it interpreted for the first time an international agreement (Assemblée, 'Groupement d'Information et de Soutien des Travailleurs Immigrés', 29 June 1990). On this ruling, see the note of J. F. Lachaume, 'L'interprétation par le juge administratif des conventions

The Cour de Cassation followed the invitation of the constitutional judges almost immediately. In contrast, it took far longer for the Conseil d'État to agree to interpret, first, international treaties in 1990, and six months later, the ECHR in a case on the 'morning after', or abortion pill.[14]

The requirement of reciprocal application of the ECHR by other parties was fairly soon rejected by a growing majority of authors.[15] Their reasoning is usually based on the particular nature of the ECHR in that it recognizes *objective* rights. Many authors also use Article 60 of the Vienna Convention on the Law of Treaties in order to reject the requirement of reciprocity for human rights conventions and for the ECHR in particular.

The most sensitive issue concerning Article 55 of the French Constitution proved to be the status of the ECHR in relation to French domestic statutes. Article 55 fully recognizes that international treaties have superior authority to domestic legislation. However, it took judges, especially administrative judges, a long time to accept that a provision of the ECHR should prevail over a subsequent domestic statute. Article 55 could only be fully implemented if courts ruled that a provision of an international treaty also prevailed over subsequent domestic statutes and not only over a prior legislative norm. Only in the *Nicolo* case[16] of 1989 did the Conseil d'État declare that an international treaty (the Treaty of Rome in this case) prevailed over a subsequent statutory provision. A year later, the Conseil d'État, sitting in plenary session, applied this reasoning to the ECHR.[17] In its function of advising the government, the Conseil d'État now tends to favour the ECHR.[18]

These long-awaited decisions were facilitated by growing encouragement from the *commissaires du gouvernment*[19] to rule in favour of international law. This desire was shared by the majority of academic commentators and supported by the government.

internationales', *Revue Française de Droit Administratif*, 1990, pp. 923–939. The ECHR has never been referred for interpretation by the Conseil d'État: see P. Cassia and E. Saulnier, 'Le Conseil d'État et la CEDH', *Actualité Juridique de Droit Administratif*, 1997, p. 414.

[14] Conseil d'État, Assemblée, 21 December 1990, 'Confédération nationale des associations familiales catholiques et autres', *Revue Française de Droit Administratif*, 1990, p. 1065.

[15] On the requirement of reciprocity see for instance: G. Cohen-Jonathan, *La Convention Européenne des Droits de l'Homme*, Economica, 1989, pp. 248–250, and J. Rivero, *Actualité Juridique de Droit Administratif*, 1975, p. 136.

[16] Conseil d'État, *Nicolo*, 20 October 1989.

[17] Conseil d'État, Assemblée, 21 December 1990, 'Confédération nationale des associations familiales catholiques et autres', *Revue Française de Droit Administratif*, 1990, p.1065.

[18] *Avis*, 27 Novembre 1989, 'Manifestation des convictions religieuses à l'école', *Les Grands Avis du Conseil d'État*, Dalloz, 1997, no. 33, p. 315. See also the recent study of P. Cassia and E. Saulnier, 'Le Conseil d'État et la CEDH', *Actualité Juridique de Droit Administratif*, 1997, pp. 411–420.

[19] A *commissaire du gouvernement* is a civil servant who prepares a report on each case arising before the administrative judge in the Conseil d'État and suggests an appropriate solution. This report (called *Conclusions*), however, is not systematically published with the case, but may be attached to the publication of the most important rulings in some law journals.

2. *The direct effect of the ECHR before French courts*

The direct effect of the ECHR is now generally recognized in French law.[20] Therefore, only a few provisions, in particular Article 13 ECHR and Article 3 of the First Protocol, are still thought to be too general and vague to produce a direct effect.

The Cour de Cassation has regularly mentioned the ECHR in its rulings since 1975,[21] and it has even examined *ex officio* the compatibility of French provisions with it.[22] The Conseil d'État, following its 1989 and 1990 cases, now accepts the direct effect of many ECHR provisions.[23]

The Conseil Constitutionnel, following its 1975 decision, does not use the ECHR when reviewing the constitutionality of a bill. Nevertheless, the constitutional judges are developing many values and principles reflected in the ECHR.[24] For instance, their interpretation of the principle of equality is in harmony with the meaning of Article 14 ECHR. Similarly, the constitutional case-law on freedom of expression echoes that of the Strasbourg Court: both courts now emphasize pluralism as a necessary condition for democracy.[25] Following the ECHR, the French constitutional judges have also extended criminal law principles beyond their traditional sphere.[26]

[20] In 1976, two years after ratification of the ECHR by France, P. Chambon could write that the ECHR 'only contained general statements of principles and is not directly applicable by French courts, it is directed to the legislator', *La Semaine Juridique, Juris Classeur Périodique*, 1976, II, pp. 184–26. Compare the more recent study of R. Abraham, 'Applicabilité directe de la Convention Européenne des Droits de l'Homme devant la juridiction administrative', *Revue Universelle des Droits de l'Homme*, 1991, p. 277.

[21] See the examples cited by G. Cohen-Jonathan, *La Convention Européenne des Droits de l'Homme*, Economica, 1989, p. 257–258. See also, on the implementation of ECHR criminal courts the following articles: P. Chambon, 'Application des articles 6 paragraphes 1 et 3 par la Chambre Criminelle de la Cour de Cassation', *La Semaine Juridique, Jurisclasseur Périodique*, 1994, II, p. 22197; Douce, 'La Convention Européenne des Droits de l'Homme et la jurisprudence pénale française', *Revue Trimestrielle des Droits de l'Homme*, 1990, p. 178.

[22] Cour de Cassation, *Baroum Cherif*, 5 December 1978, and *Dif and June* 1979, cited in M. A. Eissen, 'Le statut juridique interne de la Convention Européenne des Droits de l'Homme devant les juridictions pénales', in *Droits de l'Homme en France, Dix ans d'application de la Convention Europénne des Droits de l'Homme devant les juridictions française*, Ed. N. P. Engel, 1985.

[23] See on this point the article of R. Abraham (*commissaire du gouvernement*): 'L'applicabilité directe de la Convention devant la juridiction administrative', *Revue Universelle des Droits de l'Homme*, 1991, p. 277.

[24] On the convergence between French constitutional case-law and the ECHR, see 'Protection constitutionnelle et protection internationale des droits de l'homme: concurrence ou complementarité?', *Revue Française de Droit Administratif*, 1993, p. 849. See also J. F. Flauss, 'Droit constitutionnel et Convention Européenne des Droits de l'Homme, le droit constitutionnel devant les instances de contrôle de la CEDH', *Revue Française de Droit Constitutionnel*, 1996, p. 388.

[25] Conseil Constitutionnel DC 86–217 18 September 1986, *Recueil*, p. 141, and Conseil Constitutionnel DC 89–271 11 January 1990, *Recueil*, p. 21.

[26] Conseil Constitutionnel DC 82–155 30 December 1982, *Recueil*, p. 88; DC 87–237 30 December 1987, *Recueil*, p. 63, and DC 88–248 17 January 1989, *Recueil*, p. 18.

However, in its capacity as judge of the procedural propriety of elections, the Conseil Constitutionnel regularly checks the compatibility of domestic provisions with the ECHR since the case of *Elections du Val d'Oise* (21 December 1988). This ruling seemed to suggest that from then on constitutional judges would integrate the ECHR in the body of constitutional criteria (*bloc de constitutionalité*) by reference to which they assess the constitutionality of a bill.[27] In 1994, however, constitutional judges explicitly denied this eventuality. In their decision of January 1994 they declared:

> the constitutionality of a bill considered necessary by the legislative shall not be assessed by considering its conformity with the terms of a treaty or an international convention, but only by considering its conformity with requirements of a constitutional nature.[28]

B. THE STATUS OF THE CONVENTION IN PARLIAMENTARY PROCEEDINGS

The attitude to the ECHR during the law-making process has evolved from total ignorance to a general awareness. However, it is not systematically considered by MPs, nor is it included in the introductory outline of statutes (*exposé des motifs*). Indeed, recent parliamentary debates have revealed that some MPs still sometimes confuse the European Court of Human Rights with the European Court of Justice.[29] The government, on the other hand, sometimes considers the ECHR, and some ministers occasionally draw attention to the ECHR for the implementation of a law and adopt an internal document to this effect.[30]

However, the lack of open legislative references and uses of the ECHR makes it difficult to appreciate the extent of its influence on French legislation. Therefore, we can only mention here, by way of example, a few instances where the Convention was taken into consideration when legislation was drafted. These examples do not currently reflect a general tendency; rather, they seem to be exceptional occurrences.

[27] Later decisions seemed to follow this line, such as Conseil Constitutionnel, 28 July 1989, and especially 2 September 1992, Maastricht Treaty II. See E. Picard, 'Vers l'extension du bloc de la constitutionnalité au droit européen', *Revue Française de Droit Administratif*, 1993, p. 53.

[28] Conseil Constitutionnel, 21 January 1994.

[29] The Act of 8 February on the judicial organization of civil, criminal, and administrative procedure. Cited by S. Braconnier, *Jurisprudence de la Cour des Droits de l'Homme et droit administratif français*, Bruylant, 1997, p. 76.

[30] See the *circulaire* of the Minister of Interior related to procedures for the expulsion of aliens, 25 October 1991, cited by S. Braconnier, *Jurisprudence de la Cour des Droits de l'Homme et droit administratif français*, Bruylant, 1997, p. 112

In criminal matters, the Ministry of Justice attempted to gauge the scope of the provisions of the Convention and the judgments of the European Court of Human Rights when preparing the revision of the Criminal Code and Code of Criminal Procedure. The legislature was inspired by, in particular, a report written by Professor Delmas-Marty which took ample account of European law, and in particular the Convention and the decisions of the Commission and the Court of Human Rights. Likewise, the Commission set up to investigate better methods of fighting corruption drew the government's attention to the need to adopt measures to ensure that proceedings observed the 'reasonable time' principle.[31]

However, in areas such as the law of aliens,[32] despite the existence of a substantial body of European case-law and strong decisions against France,[33] Parliament has not seemed to pay more attention to the ECHR. In the Act of 1989 (modifying the Act of 1986) on the conditions of entry and residence of aliens on French territory, only very indirect references were made to the ECHR. A subsequent statute of 1993, on the control of immigration, perceived by many as being much more repressive, explicitly refers to the ECHR, but on a minor point only.[34]

Occasionally, a concern not to be condemned by the European Court also inspired French MPs to draft a statute complying with the criteria of the ECHR. This was the case with the Act of 10 June 1983 on community service (*travail d'intérêt général*) which may be imposed by the criminal courts as a criminal penalty. In order to avoid any dispute based on the ECHR, the statute provides that community service can be ordered only when the accused is present and after he has been informed of his rights.[35]

C. LEADING HUMAN RIGHTS CASES DECIDED BY THE NATIONAL COURTS

The effective implementation of the ECHR by domestic courts has long been hindered by several obstacles. After the Conseil Constitutionnel's ruling of

[31] *Le Monde*, 3 December 1994.

[32] S. Braconnier, *Jurisprudence de la Cour des Droits de l'Homme et droit administratif français*, Bruylant, 1997, pp. 98–101.

[33] The main decisions in this area are presented in section E below.

[34] On this point see the commentary of H. Labaye and F. Sudre: 'Jurisprudence de la Cour Européenne des Droits de l'Homme et droit administratif', *Revue Française de Droit Administratif*, 1997, p. 1247. This statute had been preventively reviewed by the Conseil Constitutionnel in a decision of 18 August 1993, see *Revue Française de Droit Administratif*, 1994, p. 1191.

[35] Act no. 83–466 of 10 June 1983. J. Pradel, *Les nouvelles alternatives à l'emprisonnement créées par la loi no 83–466 du 10 juin 1983, Dalloz,* 1984, 1, p. 111.

1975, ordinary judges were invited to check the compliance of domestic rules with the ECHR. The start of this process was slow and uneasy.[36] Despite the clarification of this legal point, French judges remained generally reluctant to base their reasoning on international law and on the ECHR in particular. As a result, the use of ECHR provisions in French judicial reasoning is very meagre. They are often reproduced in the case without further references, nor discussion on their current meaning according to ECHR case-law. Moreover, references to the ECHR often lead judges to conclude that French law does not breach any of its provisions. In some instances French judges seem to have become very adept at integrating the substance of the ECHR without mentioning it openly. Instead of making direct references, French judges seem to prefer elaborate judicial arguments and read the ECHR in terms of general domestic principles or traditions. For instance, following its practice in cases related to the withdrawal of a passport, the Conseil d'État persisted in referring to the French *Déclaration des Droits de l'Homme et du Citoyen* of 1789 in the case of *Fratoni* (13 April 1996). In that case the administrative judges 'discovered' the right to leave the national territory in the famous Declaration. The Conseil d'État therefore considered that Article 2, paragraph 2 of the 4th Additional Protocol to the ECHR merely confirmed and completed the Declaration of 1789.[37]

This attitude towards the Convention has long been reinforced by the fact that judges, lawyers, and litigants were ignorant of the ECHR.[38] In this respect, the acceptance of the right to an individual remedy in 1981 certainly increased the French courts' interest in the Convention and its case-law. In 1991, the *commissaire du gouvernement*, R. Abraham, still had to draw the attention of the Conseil d'État to the significance of this remedy, inviting the Conseil to verify fully the compatibility of domestic norms with the ECHR.[39]

After a period of ten to fifteen years, which French lawyers and judges needed in order to become familiar with the ECHR, French courts now refer to the ECHR in too many rulings to allow a case-by-case study here.[40]

[36] On the obstacles to the effective implementation of ECHR by French courts, see the mixed assessment of N. Pacaud who in 1985 stated that the first references to the ECHR took place in an *ambiance malsaine*, 'Statut de la Convention en Droit Privé', *Droits de l'Homme en France, Dix ans d'application de la CEDH devant les juridictions françaises*, G. Cohen-Jonathan (ed), N. P. Engel, 1985, pp. 65–67.

[37] Cited by H. Labayle and F. Sudre in their *chronique*, *Revue Française de Droit Administratif*, 1997, p. 1259.

[38] See the survey of the first ten years of the ECHR's impact on French law edited by G. Cohen-Jonathan, *Droits de l'Homme en France. Dix ans d'application de la Convention Européenne devant les juridictions françaises*, N. P.Engel, 1985.

[39] R. Abraham, 'La CEDH et les mesures d'éloignement des étrangers', *Revue Française de Droit Administatif*, 1991, p. 502.

[40] The *Actualité Juridique de Droit Administratif* and the *Revue Française de Droit Administratif* regularly publish reviews of administrative case-law involving the ECHR.

Therefore, only two areas will be singled out as being most frequently addressed by French courts:[41] the rights of aliens involving Article 8, and the use of Article 6 by French courts.[42] These two provisions also give rise to the majority of cases brought against France before the Court (as explained section E below).

1. The use of Article 8 by French courts

The Conseil d'État's attitude towards Article 8 reflects a regular pattern in its implementation of the ECHR, consisting of a long period of ignorance of ECHR provisions until several adverse European Court rulings eventually led the Conseil d'État to depart from its previous case-law. Since then, the supreme administrative judge has regularly referred to the ECHR, but in a very restrictive manner.

The 'right to lead a normal family life' has long been recognized by French administrative courts without reference to the ECHR,[43] and it was used in order to protect aliens from deportation. Yet in a case of 1980, when the Conseil d'État referred to Article 8 of the ECHR for the first time, it was to reject that right as a valid argument.[44] Eleven years later, the administrative court integrated Article 8 ECHR into its reasoning by two rulings in plenary session on the same day: *Belgacem* and *Babas*. In these two cases, the reference to Article 8 provided the administrative court with the opportunity to extend its powers to control the challenged norm beyond their traditional scope. In other words, the Conseil d'État checked the proportionality of the deportation order.[45] In *Belgacem* the Conseil d'État interpreted Article 8 in favour of the applicant, an Algerian national who had lived in France since

[41] Other ECHR provisions have led to a few cases: Art. 9, Art. 10, Art. 5(3), Art. 6(3), and Art. 1of Protocol No. 1. However, none of these provisions has led to enough cases to allow the study of the ECHR's impact on judicial reasoning in these areas. Art. 2 led to a famous decision about the abortion pill, Conseil d'État, Assemblée, 21 December 1990, 'Confédération nationale des associations familiales catholiques et autres', published and annotated in *Revue Française de Droit Administratif,* 1990, p. 1065.

[42] The Cour de Cassation referred to the ECHR twice in 1975–1976, five times between 1978 and 1981, 10 times in 1982, 20 times in 1985, and 810 times between 1980 and 1993. The references seem to decrease from 124 cases for 1992 to 61 for 1993 (figures cited by F. Ferrand, 'La Convention Européenne des Droits de l'Homme et la Cour de Cassation Française', *Revue Internationale de Droit Comparé*, 1995, p. 692). Art. 5 ECHR is also often referred to by the criminal chamber of the Cour de Cassation.

[43] Conseil d'État, Ass. 8 December 1978, GISTI, *Recueil Lebon*, p. 493.

[44] Conseil d'État, 25 July 1980, *Touami Ben Abdeslem*: the alien 'ne peut utilement se prévaloir . . . des dispositions de l'article 8 de la Convention Européenne des Droits de l'Homme et de Sauvegarde des Libertés Fondamentales . . . à l'appui de ses conclusions tendant à l'annulation de la mesure d'expulsion dont il a fait l'objet', cited by R. Abraham in *Revue Française de Droit Administratif*, 1991, p. 501.

[45] Both cases are published in *Revue Française de Droit Administratif*, 1991, p. 497, with the conclusions of the *commissaire du gouvernement*, R. Abraham.

his birth, with no ties to Algeria. In contrast, in *Babas*, the administrative judges held that the deportation was not a disproportionate infringement of the applicant's right to family life. The Conseil noted that she was pregnant with her Moroccan partner's baby on the date of the decision to expel her, and that she had been illegally staying on French territory. Since this ruling it is clear that even when the Conseil refers to Article 8, it is not to grant the applicant better protection; instead, the Conseil d'État seems to decide in favour of deportation on the grounds of public policy (*ordre public*).

In 1993 the Conseil Constitutionnel, deciding on the new immigration bill, enshrined the right to lead a family life as a fundamental constitutional right.[46] Despite this evolution, administrative case-law did not start to offer better protection of the right to family life. The *Sylla* case (23 June 1995) ruling that an alien with no remaining ties to his country of origin, could stay in France where he had come to join his relatives seemed to be exceptional.

Furthermore, despite a well established application of Article 3 to the rights of aliens by the European Court of Human Rights, the Conseil d'État still seems very cautious about following this trend. The administrative judges frequently reject claims under Article 3 in the absence of 'details and convincing evidence sufficient to raise legal obstacles to deportation'.[47]

The Cour de Cassation has readily followed the ECHR case-law on Article 8 since the landmark ruling of 24 November 1989 by the French court sitting in plenary session. By that decision the Cour de Cassation ruled that phone tapping undertaken without a court warrant was illegal. Since then, it seems that the Cour de Cassation has been more willing to implement the ECHR requirements which were incorporated into French legislation after the *Kruslin* and *Huvig* cases (24 April 1990).

In the area of transsexualism, the Cour de Cassation has acknowledged the ECHR case-law. A few months after the famous case of *B v France* in which the European Court ruled that Article 8 protects the rights of transsexuals' identity, the French court departed from its previous case-law and held in plenary session that civil registers should record the new sexual identity of transsexuals.[48]

2. *The use of Article 6, paragraph 1 by French courts*

Article 6 is very often used by French litigants to challenge the lack of a public hearing in professional disciplinary procedures. For a long time the

[46] Conseil Constitutionnel, 18 August 1993, cited *in Revue Française de Droit Administratif*, 1994, p. 1191.

[47] Cited in the *chronique* edited by H. Labayle and F. Sudre in *Revue Française de Droit Administratif*, 1997, p. 1250.

[48] Cited in: F. Ferrand, 'La Convention Européenne des Droits de l'Homme et la Cour de Cassation Française', *Revue Internationale de Droit Comparé*, 1995, p. 701.

administrative court openly denied the relevance of the ECHR to these matters.[49] The Cour de Cassation, in contrast, held in 1984 that disciplinary procedures for *avocats* should be heard publicly.[50] The *Diennet* ruling of the Conseil d'État in 1990 is symptomatic of the overt opposition of administrative courts to ECHR requirements. In *Combescure* (23 July 1993) the Conseil d'État finally acknowledged the requirement of a public hearing for disciplinary proceedings of the medical profession. This ruling, however, is not necessarily a sign of greater compliance with the ECHR, because a few months earlier the government had adopted a decree stating that disciplinary proceedings had to be held in public. A year after *Combescure*, in *Département de l'Indre* (29 July 1994), the Conseil d'État followed the European interpretation of 'civil rights and obligations', based on the importance of the financial claim involved. Thus, in that case the administrative court departed from its previous case-law and ruled that Article 6 applied to proceedings before the *Commission Centrale d'Aide Sociale*.

The real change in the Conseil d'État's attitude towards Article 6 occurred in the *Maubleu* ruling (14 February 1996)[51] after an adverse decision of the European Court in *Diennet* (26 September 1995). Typically, the Conseil d'État, citing most of Article 6, held that the contested French provisions were in conformity with this provision, because the rule requiring closed hearings was not absolute. That is, the litigant could request that his case be heard publicly unless this would reveal some state secret. Only a few months later the Conseil d'État recognized, in the *Lhermite* case, that Article 6 ECHR applied to proceedings related to disciplinary sanctions. This tendency to minimize the importance of ECHR case-law is also reflected in the advisory opinion in the case of *Ministre c/SARL Auto-Industrie Méric* (31 March 1995). In advising the government the Conseil d'État, while taking into account the ECHR *Bendenoun* case decided a few months previously, drastically limited the scope of Article 6 to judicial proceedings alone rather than following the broader interpretation of the European Court.[52]

[49] Conseil d'État, *Debout*, 27 October 1978, and Conseil d'État, *Subrini*, 11 July 1984.

[50] Cour de Cassation Civ., 1 January 1984, *Rennemann*, *Bull. Civ.*, I, no. 8, p. 6.

[51] This case is published together with the conclusions of the *commissaire de gouvernement*, in *Revue Française de Droit Administratif*, 1996, pp. 1186–1194.

[52] L. Maublanc-Fernandez and J. P. Maublanc, 'Dynamique européenne et résistances internes: propos sur l'application de l'article 6(1) de la Convention Européenne des Droits de l'Homme en matière fiscale', *Revue Française de Droit Administratif*, 1995, pp. 1181–1188.

D. CASES BROUGHT BEFORE THE EUROPEAN COMMISSION AND COURT OF HUMAN RIGHTS

Since the acceptance of Article 25 by the French government and the first case against France to be brought before the European Court (*Bozano*, 1986) the number of cases brought against France has steadily increased. French law is regularly challenged under Article 6 paragraphs 1 and 8 of the Convention on Human Rights. The following focuses on cases involving these two provisions

1. Article 6 in ECHR cases against France

Article 6, paragraph 1 is the provision most often used to contest French legislation. In this chapter, however, we consider only two important issues under Article 6, paragraph 1: the notions of 'civil rights and obligations' and 'criminal charges' on one hand, and the requirement of a hearing within a reasonable time on the other.[53]

The notions of 'civil rights and obligations' The principal criterion used by the European Court in defining the notion of 'civil rights and obligations' is that it involves a financial element. The pecuniary basis for defining this notion has led to an extension of the scope of Article 6 to include French administrative and fiscal proceedings, which under French law are not understood as involving civil rights and obligations.

In *Société Périscope* (26 March 1992) the Court considered the importance of the pecuniary claim involved and applied Article 6 to administrative compensation proceedings for a tax concession before the Conseil d'État. Furthermore, the Court considered that a joint application by a civil party to criminal proceedings fell within the scope of 'civil rights and obligations' (*Tomasi,* 27 August 1992, and *Acquaviva*, 21 November 1995). In a recent case, however, the Court used the financial criterion to exclude a similar application from the requirements of Article 6, because the applicant had not asked for damages and only wanted to find out the truth about her brother's death (*Hamer*, 7 August 1996).

Similarly, the Court used this criterion to restrict the scope of Article 6 to disputes arising between civil servants and the State. That is, the Court applied Article 6 only when the claim was essentially of a pecuniary nature, as opposed to a matter related to career development (*Neigel*, 17 March 1997). As a result, Article 6 has been held to apply to disputes involving purely economic rights (*Cazenave de la Roche*, 9 June 1998; *Le Calvez*, 29 July

[53] The remaining cases against France under Art. 6 deal mostly with the requirement of a fair hearing by an independent and impartial tribunal.

1998; *Benkessiouer*, 24 August 1998; and *Couez*, 24 August 1998). Following this line of intepretation, Article 6 does not apply to disputes primarily related to a civil servant's career. In *Huber* (29 February 1998) the Court considered that the pecuniary claim in the case was only a consequence of the dispute about the compulsory leave which the applicant had to take, and hence that Article 6 did not apply. Similarly, in *Maillard* (9 June 1998) the Court ruled that the dispute between the state and a professional serviceman was primarily related to the promotion of the applicant, therefore its pecuniary implications did not suffice for the purposes of applying Article 6.

However, the pecuniary nature of a claim was not a decisive element in characterizing disputes related to the propriety of elections before the Conseil Constitutionnel. In *Bloch* (21 December 1997) the European Court held that the dispute concerned political rights and therefore fell outside the scope of Article 6. Moreover, the Court ruled that the financial aspect of the dispute was only a consequence of the political right at stake and did not mean that this right was to be qualified as a 'civil right' under Article 6.

The notion of a 'criminal charge' In relation to this notion, the European Court has extended the requirements of Article 6 to proceedings involving administrative and fiscal penalties, which in French law are not considered as criminal charges. In *Société Sténuit* (27 February 1992) it was decided that the administrative penalty for engaging in anti-competitive behaviour in relation to a cartel operating among companies tendering for public works was a criminal charge. As a result, the challenged proceedings fell within the scope of Article 6. Likewise, in the *Malige* case (23 September 1998) the Court ruled that the deduction of points from driving licences, considered as an administrative sanction under French law, was a punishment under the ECHR. In *Bendenoun* (23 February 1994) the Court decided, explicitly and for the first time, that fiscal penalties were to be considered as a criminal charge, notwithstanding their contrary characterization in French law. In that case the Court outlined four significant issues: the rules applied to citizens *qua* tax payers, the penalties were intended as a punishment to deter re-offending, the purpose of the rule was both punishment and deterrence, and they were substantial penalties, failure to comply with which exposed the applicant to imprisonment. However, the Court held that there was no breach of Article 6, paragraph 1. Following this ruling, the Court went on to extend the applicability of Article 6 to the preliminary proceedings before the *Commission des Infractions Fiscales* in the *Miailhe* case (26 September 1996).

The requirement of a hearing within a reasonable time in proceedings In general, the European Court of Human Rights is more severe about the length of proceedings than domestic courts and usually considers that a duration of more than four or five years looks suspicious. However, the Court does not apply a rigid rule and always considers the particular circumstances of a case, including the complexity of the matter involved, the behaviour of the parties, the conduct of the authorities, and the importance of what is at stake for the applicant. The court has in most cases ruled that domestic proceedings, and French proceedings in particular, do not comply with the requirement of reasonable time, except in instances related to particularly complex cases and those where the behaviour of the parties was questionable.

As a result of the application of these criteria, a duration of seven and a half years for an action for damages against a public hospital was found to be a violation of Article 6 in *H v France* (24 October 1990), while in *Vernillo* (20 February 1991) the same delay was accepted as being a 'reasonable time'. In the latter instance involving proceedings for rescission of a contract, the Court appreciated the complexity of the case, but also pointed to the conduct of the parties. For the same reason, in *Monnet* (27 October 1997) challenging the duration of divorce proceedings, the Court did not find seven years to be unreasonable.

The complexity of a case has not always led the Court to accept long proceedings. For instance, the great complexity of proceedings involving state security offences and different jurisdictions did not prevent the Court from ruling that the period of twelve years and ten months between the applicant's arrest and his acquittal was an unreasonable delay (*Dobbertin*, 25 February 1993). Similarly, in *Beaumartin* (24 November 1994), despite the complexity of the case, requiring the interpretation of an international treaty, the Court ruled that eight years and two months was too long for expropriation proceedings. In a later case, also challenging the length of expropriation proceedings, the Court ruled that fourteen years to obtain compensation was not a reasonable time, despite the complexity of the matter (*Guillemin*, 21 February 1997). In contrast, in *Acquaviva* (21 November 1995) the Court considered the difficult circumstances of the preliminary investigation in a case of murder in Corsica and ruled that its duration of more than four years was a reasonable time.

A number of key decisions have arisen from the 'contaminated blood' scandal in France. In a series of tragic cases brought by applicants infected with the HIV virus following blood transfusions, the European Court of Human Rights emphasized the vital importance of the compensation proceedings to the applicants. As a result, the Court has ruled that these proceedings called for exceptional diligence and has repeatedly held that French law violated the ECHR. In *X v France*, (31 March 1992) the Court ruled that, given the applicant's illness (and indeed the applicant died a few days before the ruling), the administrative courts had to speed up the proceedings. In *Vallée* (26 April

1994) the European Court had to reiterate that 'four years to obtain a judgment in first-instance proceedings is too much for a case of this nature'. The same year a 'friendly settlement' was reached in a similar case and the Commission insisted that exceptional diligence was called for, despite the establishment of a compensation fund. Subsequently, the Court has unanimously ruled against France for breaching the requirement of a hearing within a reasonable time in: *Karakaya* (26 August 1994), *Bellet* (4 December 1995), *Richard and Pailot* (22 April 1998), *Henra and Leterme* (29 *April 1998), and FE v France* (30 October 1998). The *Demai* case (28 October 1994) is particularly noteworthy in that the proceedings were struck out after the French government agreed to grant the applicant the same compensation as in previous cases without waiting for the European Court's predictable ruling.

2. Article 8 in ECHR cases against France

Article 8 has given rise to what are probably the two best known cases in France: *Kruslin* and *Huvig* (24 June 1990).[54] In both cases the Court held that the French practice of telephone tapping provided neither sufficient legal certainty, nor adequate safeguards against various possible abuses. Another famous case is that of *B v France* (25 March 1992) in which the Court recognized the right of a transsexual to have her new sexual identity registered by changing her forename.

However, we focus here on the Court's interpretation of the right to family life in relation to the deportation of aliens, and in particular second-generation immigrants,[55] which reflects an important issue under French law. The position of the Court in these matters seems to have shifted from a sympathetic conception of the importance of family life to a greater compliance with principles of public security.

In the *Djeroud* case (23 January 1991) the parties reached a 'friendly settlement' in favour of the applicant, an Algerian national. He was convicted of theft, but because he had lived in France since he was one year old the Commission considered that his deportation to Algeria would violate his right to a family life. In *Beldjoudi* (26 March 1992) the Court ruled in favour of the applicant's right to family life, despite the fact that he had committed a number of offences, such as assault and battery. In this case the Court considered the facts that the applicant (of Algerian origin) had consistently shown the desire to regain his French nationality, which he had lost after a change in the relevant legislation, and that he lived and worked in France.

[54] See the studies of J. Pradel and J. F. Flauss, 'Les écoutes téléphoniques: un régime sous surveillance', *Revue Française de Droit Administratif*, 1991, pp. 83–100.

[55] Art. 8 also gave rise to several cases against France involving the practice of search and seizure by customs officers.

Moreover, the Court noted that he was married to a French woman with whom he had had no children and that the deportation would thus 'imperil the unity and the even existence of their marriage'. Putting an even stronger emphasis on the importance of family life, the Court ruled in *Nasri* (13 July 1995) that a deaf-mute Algerian convicted of gang rape was to remain in France. The Court considered that the applicant, who was heavily disabled, had little education, and knew no sign language, was best dealt with in his family. The Court decided that his family life could prevent him from lapsing into a life of crime.

A year later in *Boughanemi* (24 April 1996) the Court balanced for the first time the seriousness of the offence, living on the earnings of prostitution, and the applicant's right to family life. In that case the Court expressed doubts about the reality of the applicant's ties with his partner from whom he had separated before the birth of a child which he none the less recognized. Again, considering the gravity of the offence (rape), in *Bouchelkia* (29 January 1997) the Court ruled that France could conclude that the deportation of the applicant to his country of origin was 'necessary in a democratic society'. The Court noted that in that case the applicant was single and childless, and that he had maintained ties with Algeria. However, in *X v France* (26 September 1997) the Court considered that the applicant's family life and his lack of ties with Algeria, his country of origin, were powerful arguments against his permanent exclusion from French territory. Therefore the Court ruled that the applicant could stay in France with his wife and children, despite his drug trafficking activity. However, this reasoning did not apply to an Algerian woman dealing in heroin who had real ties in France, but who had also maintained significant links with Algeria (*Dalia*, 19 February 1998). The Court decided that the fact that she was the mother of a French child, born when she was illegally staying in France, could not prevent her deportation. The Court therefore seems to favour a restrictive interpretation of the notion of family life in cases where an applicant has maintained some ties with the country of origin.

E. REMEDIAL ACTION TAKEN BY THE GOVERNMENT IN RESPONSE TO BEING HELD IN VIOLATION OF THE CONVENTION

The European Court does not require the signatory states to amend their legislation to comply with the outcome of a particular case. In some circumstances, however, the French government understood from the ruling of the

Court that enacting a new law would be the only appropriate remedy to the violation of the ECHR, as it did in the 1990 telephone tapping cases, *Kruslin* and *Huvig*. More recently, after deciding against France for a second time on a very similar matter within a couple of years, the Court expressed the opinion that France should have done something to improve the proceedings for compensation for HIV-infected haemophiliacs (*Vallée v France*, 1994).

The French Parliament, in an attempt to pass legislation complying with the standards of the European Convention and its case-law, has adopted a set of acts on telephone tapping and fairness of proceedings.[56] Act no. 91–646 of 10 July 1991 was adopted as a direct consequence of the *Kruslin* and *Huvig* rulings for ordinary proceedings and of *Malone v United Kingdom* for administrative proceedings. The preliminary exposition of the Act clearly indicates that the legislator is following the recommendation of the European Court of Human Rights.[57]

Following numerous rulings against France for excessive length of proceedings before administrative courts, in 1995 the *loi de programme*[58] on justice set the objective of reducing proceedings to one year only. The Act proposed to achieve this aim by increasing the appointments of judges and staff for the period 1995–1999. The Act of 8 February 1995 on 'the judicial organization of civil, criminal, and administrative proceedings' can also be seen as an attempt to comply with the requirement of reasonable time in judicial proceedings.[59] The requirement of public hearings in the disciplinary procedures of professions is another example of the French legislative waiting a long time before amending its legislation, in compliance with well established case-law. The French government did not require disciplinary hearings in the medical profession to be held in public until 1993, when it amended the *Décret* of 1948 which did not require proceedings before the *Conseil de l'Ordre des Médecins* to be heard in public.

[56] S. Braconnier studies the implications of the ECHR on French legislation in his doctoral dissertation, *Jurisprudence de la Cour Européenne des Droits de l'Homme et droit administratif français*, Bruylant, Bruxelles, 1997, pp. 72–84.

[57] The beginning of the Act states that:

> The Government considers that the time has come to put an end to this serious judicial shortcoming, because the European Court has suggested it, because the French people and its representatives desire it, and because France owes it to itself to set an example in the field of the protection of the rights of Man and the Citizen (cited by S. Braconnier, n. 56 above, p. 81).

[58] A *loi de programme* is an act that brings together several estimates of expenses in order consistently to finance a governmental project.

[59] Loi no. 95–125 of 8 February 1995 relative à l'organisation des juridictions et à la procédure civile, pénale et administrative, *Journal Officiel, Lois et décrets*, 9 February, 1995, p. 2175. See 'La loi du 8 Février 1995 et la réforme du contentieux administratif', *Revue Française de Droit Administratif*, 1996, p. 2.

More rarely, the enactment of new legislation has been aimed at avoiding a foreseeable adverse judgement by the European Court. Aware of such a risk, the Conseil Constitutionnel decided to amend its internal ruling in order to conform with the requirement of public hearings when deciding on electoral matters. The amendment of the internal rules took place at the Conseil's own initiative, on June 28 1995, while the *Bloch* case was still pending before the European Court. However, in the *Bloch* case the European Court, relying on a questionable distinction between civil and electoral rights, found that the hearings related to electoral disputes before the Conseil Constitutionnel did not have to be public.

In some cases, French courts have also tended to comply 'spontaneously' with the European Convention by following its case-law. However, this is not a quick and easy process and a specific ruling against France is usually needed before this compliance occurs, as the 1996 *Maubleu* ruling of the Conseil d'État demonstrates. For instance, the 1992 case of *B v France* was followed by a ruling of the plenary assembly of the Cour de Cassation a few months later, which departed from its previous case-law in order to integrate the ruling of the European Court of Human Rights.[60]

A final point worth noting is that, in an exceptional case, academic commentators have drawn attention to a ruling of the European Court against a different state: *Procola v Luxembourg* 1995.[61] Commentators felt that that decision could have implications for French law, because *Procola* was a decision against the Conseil d'État of Luxembourg which is very similar to the French Conseil d'État. However, in their analysis of the *Procola* case, J. L. Austin and F. Sudre considered that due to the practice developed by the Conseil d'État, the *Procola* ruling did not require immediate and significant changes to the current proceedings.

F. ASSESSMENT AND PROSPECTS

The ECHR is no longer in the weak position described by N. Pacaud in 1985:

We are not very far from thinking that the ECHR is in the same position as the declarations of human rights under the Third Republic, which were considered rather as

[60] Cour de Cassation, Assemblée Plénière, 11 December 1992, *La Semaine Juridique, Jurisclasseur Périoridique*, 1993, ed. G., II, p. 21991.

[61] J. L. Autin and F. Sudre, 'La dualité fonctionnelle du Conseil d'État en question devant la Cour Européenne des Droits de l'Homme, à propos de l'arrêt Procola contre Luxembourg, 28 Septembre 1995', *Revue Française de Droit Administratif*, 1996, pp. 777–794.

philosophical declarations, the expression of natural law concepts, or as abstract maxims.[62]

The impact of the ECHR on French law is now beyond doubt, and is continuously growing. In this respect, the ECHR's influence has certainly benefited from two trends: the development of European Union law and the increasing tendency to address law in terms of fundamental and human rights. Furthermore, the acceptance of the right of individual petition has clearly been an effective incentive for both judges and the government to devote more attention to the ECHR and to use it better. It has also encouraged litigants to argue more often and more accurately on the basis of the ECHR. The ECHR is now acknowledged by all French courts, including the administrative courts, which were more reluctant to do so than ordinary courts. The European Convention is also more frequently studied and analysed by lawyers, who increasingly specialize in this area, instead of leaving it to international lawyers with only a marginal interest in it. Even if the legislator does not yet always seem to consider the ECHR in a regular and accurate way, a certain amount of optimism that the 'spirit of Strasbourg' will expand to affect more and more areas of French law is not entirely misplaced.[63]

However, some obstacles to the impact of the ECHR on French law remain. Commentators agree that the ECHR is not used as much as it could be, partly because of persistent ignorance on the part of litigants, lawyers, and judges. As a result, many areas of law could still benefit from a greater compliance with ECHR standards, such as the 'equality of arms' in administrative proceedings, or the protection of citizens by administrative judges.[64] French judges still have to learn to develop their argumentation under the ECHR. In some cases, administrative judges have followed the method of the European Court and checked the proportionality of the challenged measure, thereby increasing the extent of their traditional control. In most cases, however, the requirements of the ECHR which judges appear to have considered are not openly discussed in judicial reasoning. Due to the French practice of very concise case reports, ECHR provisions are still not given as much importance as they deserve. ECHR provisions should receive more attention and consideration than they currently receive in most cases, where they are dealt with by way of a simple reference in the introductory part, a mere quotation or a very superficial indication of the relevant case-law. Here, it is worth men-

[62] *Droits de l'Homme en France, Dix ans d'application de la CEDH devant les juridictions françaises*, 1985, p. 68.

[63] This optimistic view is expressed by S. Braconnier, *Jurisprudence de la Cour Européenne des Droits de l'Homme et Droit Administratif Francais*, Bruylant, 1997.

[64] For an analysis of the remaining obstacles to the reception of the ECHR case-law in French administrative law, see the detailed analysis of ibid, pp. 185–305.

tioning the hidden, but probably significant, influence of the European Convention and its case-law on judicial reasoning. That is to say that French courts regularly integrate the requirements and notions of the ECHR in their reading of domestic legislation, without making express reference to the Convention. This attitude makes it difficult (and maybe impossible) to appreciate the full impact of the ECHR.

The assessment of the ECHR's influence on French law really depends on the scale of time considered. In other words, bearing in mind that the French Declaration of the Rights of Man and the Citizen of 1789 became part of the body of constitutional criteria only in 1971, by virtue of an almost accidental Conseil Constitutionnel ruling, one might consider that the current role of the ECHR in French law is quite an achievement. Furthermore, ECHR rights and legal concepts, alien to the French legal tradition and culture, are now being fairly well absorbed. However, considering that the ECHR has had binding force in French law since 1974, one could be forgiven for thinking that it has taken French judges a very long time to become fully aware of its legal importance.

14

Germany

ANDREAS ZIMMERMANN

INTRODUCTION

The Federal Republic of Germany signed the European Convention on Human Rights on 11 November 1950 and ratified it on 5 December 1952.[1] On 5 July 1955, the Federal Republic of Germany made declarations under Arts. 25 and 46 of the Convention, both being valid for a period of five years. They have since been renewed periodically.[2] The scope of application of these declarations had also been extended to all additional protocols which the Federal Republic of Germany has ratified. Finally, the 11th Additional Protocol was ratified by Germany on 2 October 1995.[3] On 4 November 2000 Germany also signed the 12th Additional Protocol.

Germany has so far made no declaration under Art. 15 of the Convention.

When ratifying the Convention, the Federal Republic of Germany made a reservation that it will apply Art. 7 para. 2 of the ECHR only within the limits of Art. 103 para. 2 of the German Basic Law, which stipulates that an act

Abbreviations: AG = Amtsgericht; Bay.Vbl. = Bayrische Verwaltungsblätter; BGH = Bundesgerichtshof; BVerfGE = Bundesverfassungsgericht (Decisions); BVerwG(E) = Bundesverwaltungsgericht (Decisions); DÖV = Die öffentliche Verwaltung; EuGRZ = Europäische Grundrechtezeitschrift; FamRZ = Zeitschrift für das gesamte Familienrecht; HRLJ = Human Rights Law Journal; JZ = Juristenzeitung; LG = Landgericht; MDR = Monatsschrift für Deutsches Recht; NJW = Neue Juristische Wochenschrift; OLG = Oberlandesgericht; OVG = Oberverwaltungsgericht; VG = Verwaltungsgericht; ZaöRV = Zeitschrift für ausländisches öffentliches Recht und Völkerrecht

[1] See Bundesgesetzblatt 1954 II, 14.

[2] As to the wording of the latest declarations see Bundesgesetzblatt 1989 II, 686. These declarations were normally made for a period of five years. In 1986, however, the duration was limited to three years, see Bundesgesetzblatt 1987 II, 213. In order to justify this behaviour, the Federal Government referred to the practice of other member states, see the answer of the Federal Ministry of Justice regarding a parliamentary question, Bundestags-Drucksache 10/6746, 13.

[3] Bundesgesetzblatt 1995 II, p. 578.

may be punished only to the extent it constituted a criminal offence under the law before the act was committed.[4]

Besides the Federal Republic of Germany, the Saar territory, being an associate member of the Council of Europe, also ratified the Convention.[5] After the Saar territory was incorporated into the Federal Republic of Germany in 1957, its status as a contracting party to the European Convention on Human Rights ended. By the same token and in accordance with general international law, the Convention became applicable to this territory by virtue of its incorporation into the Federal Republic of Germany.[6]

The Federal Republic of Germany has now ratified most of the additional protocols, starting with the First Additional Protocol, which entered into force on 13 February 1957.[7] When submitting the 4th Additional Protocol for consent to the Federal Parliament in 1967, the German government specifically stated that the relevant provisions of the German Code on Civil Procedure were compatible with Art. 1 of that Protocol.[8]

[4] For critical comment as to this position see *inter alia* M. Kenntner, Der deutsche Sonderweg zum Rückwirkungsverbot: Plädoyer für die Aufgabe eines überholten Verweigerungsdogmas, 1997, *NJW* 2298 et seq.

[5] As to the membership of the Saar territory in the Council of Europe and the ratification of the European Convention on Human Rights see generally F. Münch, 'Saar Territory', in: R. Bernhardt (ed), (1990), 12 Encylopedia of Public Int. Law 334 et seq. (335). The Federal Republic of Germany did not, however, recognize the legal status of the Saar territory as it existed at the time. Thus the German government, when ratifying the Convention, declared that this joined ratification would not amount to recognition of the Saar territory, see Bundesgesetzblatt 1954 II, 14.

[6] Unpublished decision of the Commission Application 255/57 of July 20, 1957, quoted by M.-A. Eissen, 'The independence of Malta and the European Convention on Human Rights', 1965/66, BYIL 401 et seq. (404 note 5). As to the question whether the Federal Republic of Germany could be held responsible for violations of the Convention which had previously occurred in the Saar territory see Eissen, ibid, 403. As to the relevant decisions of the Commission see also Wiebringhaus, *Die Rom-Konvention für Menschenrechte in der Praxis der Strassburger Menschenrechtskommission* (1959), 141–142.

[7] Both the Second and the Third Additional Protocols had been ratified by 1 January 1969 and entered into force on 21 September 1970. The 4th Additional Protocol was ratified by Germany on 1 June 1968. The 5th Additional Protocol was ratified by 3 January 1969 and entered into force on 20 December 1971. The 6th Additional Protocol was ratified on 1 August 1989; the 7th and 8th Additional Protocol was ratified on 19 September 1989 and entered into force on 1 January 1990. Both the 9th and the 10th Additional Protocols were ratified by 7 July 1994; the first of these entered into force 1 November 1994, the 10th Additional Protocol was ratified by Germany as of 7 July 1994 but has lost its purpose since the entry into force of Protocol No. 11 on 1 November 1998 and has accordingly not entered into force.

When signing the 7th Protocol, the Federal Republic of Germany enclosed an interpretative declaration as to the scope of application of its Arts. 2, 3, and 4. The text of the declaration can be found in Information Bulletin on Legal Activities of the Directorate of Legal Affairs of the Council of Europe 22/85 at 16. See also S. Thomsen, 'Völkerrechtliche Praxis der Bundesrepublik Deutschland im Jahre 1985', 1987, *ZaöRV* 320 et seq. (336).

[8] Bundesrats-Drucksache 477/ 66, 8; for details see M. Hilf/ K. Hailbronner, 'Völkerrechtliche Praxis der Bundesrepublik Deutschland im Jahre 1966', Zeitschrift für ausländisches öffentliches Recht und Völkerrecht 1969, 31 et seq. (77). The Protocol became binding on Germany on 1 June, 1968.

In 1983 the Federal Republic of Germany also signed the 6th Additional Protocol, which was ratified in 1989.[9] During the parliamentary proceedings, the government took the view that the prohibition of the death penalty contained therein would not run counter to a deportation to a country where the person faces such punishment.[10] Accordingly, the Federal Government, when ratifying the Protocol, formally declared that the provision in question does not extend to measures such as deportation or extradition.[11]

After German reunification in 1990, the government of the Federal Republic of Germany notified the Council of Europe that, in accordance with applicable rules of international law, the obligations under the Convention would henceforth also apply to the territory of the former German Democratic Republic.[12]

A. THE STATUS OF THE CONVENTION IN NATIONAL LAW

(1) *The substantive effects of the Convention*

The European Convention on Human Rights was incorporated into German law[13] in accordance with Art. 59 para. 2 of the Basic Law, which stipulates:

[9] During the parliamentary proceedings, the Federal Minister of Justice criticized Art. 2 of the Protocol under which the parties to the Protocol may still maintain the death penalty in time of war, see C. Lerche, 'Völkerrechtliche Praxis der Bundesrepublik Deutschland im Jahre 1988', (1990), *ZaöRV* 309 et seq. (329–330).

[10] For details see M. Hahn, 'Völkerrechtliche Praxis der Bundesrepublik Deutschland im Jahre 1987', (1989), *ZaöRV* 520 et seq. (550) with further references.

[11] For the text of the declaration see A. Wilhelm, 'Völkerrechtliche Praxis der Bundesrepublik Deutschland im Jahre 1989', (1991), *ZaöRV* 683 et seq. (727–728). See also Art. 102 of the Basic Law, which contains a general prohibition of capital punishment. In the meantime, there exists under German law a general prohibition to extradite or deport, where the accused runs the risk of being executed, see Sec. 6 of the Law on International Co-operation in Criminal and Civil Matters (*Gesetz über die internationale Rechtshilfe*). As to the relevance of Art. 3 of the Convention in cases of extradition or expulsion under the municipal law of the Federal Republic of Germany, see below.

[12] See Verbal Note of the Permanent Representative of the Federal Republic of Germany to the Council of Europe dated October 2, 1990, contained in Council of Europe, JJ 2446 C of October 3, 1990.

[13] As to the status of the Convention in the internal legal order of the Federal Republic of Germany see generally M. Hilf, 'Rang der EMRK im deutschen Recht', in: E. Mahrenholz/M. Hilf/E. Klein (eds) *Entwicklung der Menschenrechte innerhalb der Staaten des Europarates* (1987), 10 et seq.; A. Drzemczewski, *European Human Rights Convention in Domestic Law—A Comparative Study* (Oxford: Clarendon Press, 1983), 106 et seq.; J. Polakiewicz/V. Jacob-Folter, 'The European Rights Convention in Domestic Law: The Impact of Strasbourg Case Law in States where Direct Effect is given to the Convention', (1991) *Human Rights Law Journal* 65 (78–81); H. Steinberger, Reference to the case-law of the organs of the ECHR before national courts. Written Communication on the courts of the Federal Republic of German to the Sixth International Colloquy about the ECHR, Sevilla 1–16 November (1985), *Human Rights Law*

Treaties which regulate the political relations of the Federation or relate to matters of federal legislation shall require the consent or participation, in the form of a federal law, of the bodies competent in any specific case for such federal legislation.[14]

Thus the Convention has been assigned the status of *Federal* law, thus automatically overriding all laws enacted by the *Länder*.[15] Both the judiciary[16] and the majority of writers[17] take the view, however, that the Convention does not have priority over nor enjoy equal rank with the Federal constitution, the Basic Law. Notwithstanding this incorporation as a treaty, several authors have nevertheless come forward with the idea that *all* guarantees contained in the European Convention on Human Rights should be considered as enshrining at the same time rules of general or at least regional public international law,[18] which, according to Art. 25 of the German constitution,[19] take precedence over all laws of both the Federation and the *Länder*. The judiciary, however, while

Journal 402 et seq.; J.A. Frowein, 'Übernationale Menschenrechtsgewährleistungen und nationale Strafgewalt', in: J. Isensee/ P. Kirchof (eds), *Handbuch des Staatsrechts*, vol. VII (1992), 731 et seq. (735–737; 741–746; 754–764).

[14] The importance of the ratification process of the European Convention on Human Rights was stressed by the fact that the bill, approving the ratification, was introduced to the Federal parliament by all political parties represented at the time, see K. Partsch, 'Die europäische Menschenrechtskonvention vor den nationalen Parlamenten', (1956/57), *ZaöRV* 93 et seq. (99).

[15] Compare Art. 31 Basic Law: 'Federal law shall override *Land* law.'

[16] See eg BVerfGE 74, 358 (370) and BVerfG NJW 1990, 274 and the manifold references listed in R. Uerpmann, *Die Europäische Menschenrechtskonvention und die deutsche Rechsprechung—Ein Beitrag zum Thema Völkerrecht und Landesrecht* (Berlin: Duncker and Humbolt, 1993), at 72, note 7.

[17] See eg Frowein, note 13 above, 736; Steinberger, note 13 above, 403; Hilf, note 13 above, 39; G. Ress, 'The ECHR and States Practices: The Legal Effect of the Judgements of the European Court of Human Rights on the Internal Law and before Domestic Courts of the Contracting States', in: I. Maier (ed), *Protection of Human Rights in Europe* (1982), 209 (255) and the further references provided by Uerpmann, note 16 above.

But see also J. Echterhölter, 'Die Europäische Menschenrechtskonvention im Rahmen der verfassungsmäßigen Ordnung', (1955), *JZ* 689 (691), who takes the view that the guarantees provided in the Convention are part of German constitutional law by virtue of Art. 1 para. 2 Basic Law, which stipulates that the German people uphold human rights as inviolable. As to arguments contradicting this thesis see R. Herzog, 'Das Verhältis der Europäischen Menschenrechtskonvention zu späteren deutschen Gesetzen', (1959), *DÖV* 44 et seq. (45).

U. Klug, 'Das Verhältnis zwischen der Europäischen Menschenrechtskonvention und dem Grundgesetz', in: H. Conrad *et al* (eds) *Gedächtnisschrift für H. Peters* (Berlin: Vahlen, 1967), 434 et seq. (439–442), would grant the Convention a rank superior even to the Constitution, arguing that only this approach serves the objectives of the European Convention on Human Rights.

[18] See the report of the Committee for Foreign Affairs of the Federal Parliament submitting the Convention to ratification, Bundestags-Drucksache 1/3338, 3–4; H. Guradze, *Die Europäische Menschenrechtskonvention, Kommentar* (Berlin: Vehlen, 1968), Einleitung § 5, III–V and most recently T. Giegerich, 'Die Verfassungsbeschwerde an der Schnitttstelle von deutschem, internationalem und suprantionalem Recht', in: C. Grabenwarter *et al* (eds), *Allgemeinheit der Grundrechte und Vielfalt der Gesellschaft* (1994), 101 (113–114) and A. Bleckmann, 'Verfassungsrang der Europäischen Menschenrechtskonvention?', (1994), *EuGRZ* 149 et seq.

[19] Art. 25 of the Basic Law stipulates: 'The general rules of public international law are an integral part of Federal law. They shall take precedence over the laws and shall directly create rights and duties for the inhabitants of the federal territory.'

recognizing that *some* provisions of the European Convention on Human Rights might in the meantime have matured into rules of customary international law,[20] has not adopted such a general view.

Notwithstanding the fact that the Convention does not enjoy equal rank with the constitution, the German Federal Constitutional Court in a landmark decision in 1987 held that the European Convention on Human Rights must nevertheless be taken into account when interpreting the basic rights provisions of the German constitution:

> In interpreting the Basic Law, the content and state of development of the Convention are also to be taken into consideration, insofar as this does not lead to a restriction or derogation of basic-rights protection under the Basic Law (. . .) For this reason, the case-law of the European Court of Human Rights also serves in this regard as an interpretational aid in defining the content and reach of the Basic's Law basic rights and principles of rule of law. Even laws—in this case, the Rules of Criminal Procedure—are to be interpreted and applied in harmony with the Federal Republic of Germany's commitments under international law, even when such laws were enacted posterior to an applicable international treaty; it cannot be assumed that the legislature, insofar as it has not clearly declared otherwise, wishes to deviate from the Federal Republic of Germany's international treaty commitments or to facilitate violation of such commitments.[21]

This means that even a German *lex posterior*, enacted after the Convention had entered into force, and running counter to a specific provision of the European Convention on Human Rights, should be interpreted, whenever possible, in line with the Convention, unless it can be demonstrated that there was a clear will of the legislature to deviate from those guarantees. This approach has recently been reiterated by the Constitutional Court of the State of Saxony as far as the guarantees of fundamental rights contained in the Constitution of the State of Saxony[22] are concerned.

Furthermore, in certain cases the Convention will also prevail over German laws under the general principle of *lex specialis derogat lege generali*, protecting specific human rights over later enacted statutes.[23] One example,

As to the effect of such rules in the internal legal order of German and their relationship to constitutional law see generally H. Steinberger, 'Allgemeine Regeln des Völkerrechts', in: J. Isensee/P. Kirchhof (eds), *Handbuch des Staatsrechts*, vol. VII (1992).

[20] See Bundesverfassungsgericht, NJW 1987, 830 as to the right of the accused to be present during the trial under Art. 6 para. 3 ECHR and Bundesverfassungsgericht *NJW* 1988, 1462 et seq. (1464) as to Art. 6 para. 3 lit. e ECHR.

[21] BVerfGE 74, 358 et seq.; English translation to be found in Decisions of the Bundesverfassungsgericht—Federal Constitutional Court—Federal Republic of Germany, vol. 1/II: International Law and the Law of the European Communities 1952–1989 (1992), 634 et seq. (638).

[22] For the text of the decision of 14 May 1996, see EuGRZ 1996, 437 et seq. (439). For details see below D.

[23] Polakiewicz/Jacob-Foltzer, note 13 above, 79. But see also the references in Uerpmann, note 16 above, 88–89, where the respective German provisions were considered to be *lex specialis*.

which became relevant for the German judiciary, can be found in the German Code on Criminal Procedure as it stood until 1964. Until this time, the Code on Criminal Procedure contained only a general clause under which suspects could be detained with no limit to the period of imprisonment. German Courts then considered Art. 5 para. 3 of the Convention and the limitations contained therein as prevailing according to the principle of *lex specialis derogat legi generali.*[24] Similar issues arose in the context of the German Law regulating judicial fees (*Gerichtskostengesetz*). Up to 1980 the law in question provided rather broadly, without specifications, which costs a person convicted of a criminal offence had to pay. In that regard Art. 6 para. 3 lit. e ECHR was considered as being *lex specialis* as to the costs of the translation of court proceedings.[25]

Besides the question of what rank the Convention enjoys in the German legal order, it is also important to note that—right from the beginning of its existence—almost all of the substantive guarantees of the Convention have been considered by the German judiciary as being directly applicable within the German legal order and thus self-executing.[26] There are, however, some exceptions as to certain specific provisions of the Convention, where it was held that they are not self-executing and thus cannot be enforced by German courts. This applies to *inter alia*, the guarantee of secret and free elections contained in Art. 3 of the 1st Additional Protocol[27] and Art. 13 of the Convention which is also not considered to be directly enforceable by German courts.[28] Furthermore, the Federal Administrative Court has also

[24] Oberlandesgericht Saarbrücken (1961), *NJW* 337; Landgericht Köln NJW 1964, 1816. The Code of Criminal Procedure was later amended accordingly, for details see below C.

[25] See LG Bonn, *Juristisches Büro 1978*, 1849 et seq. (1850); LG Frankfurt/ M. ibid, 1687 et seq. (1688); AG Gelsenkirchen (1971), *NJW* 2320 et seq. (2321). But see also OLG Hamm, Yb. ECHR 1979, 521 et seq. (523–524), which had taken the opposite position and see generally T. Vogler, Das Recht auf unentgeltliche Beiziehung eines Dolmetschers (Art. 6 para. 3 lit. e EMRK), (1979), *EuGRZ* 640 et seq. (640–641).

[26] See eg H. Golsong, 'The European Convention on Human Rights before Domestic Courts', (1962), *BYIL* 445 et seq. (449) and more recently the excellent survey of German case-law in Uerpmann, note 16 above, 44–47.

[27] W. Morvay, 'Rechtsprechung deutscher Gerichte zur Europäischen Konvention zum Schutze der Menschenrechte und Grundfreiheiten vom 4. November 1950 nebst Zusatzprotokoll vom 20. März 1952', (1961), *ZaöRV* 89 et seq. (95).

[28] BGH *NJW* 1964, 2119; BGHZ 42, 360 et seq. (363); more recently OLG Stuttgart, Die Justiz 1985, 177 et seq. (179); see also Guradze, note 17, Art. 13, Note 3.

Furthermore, according to a decision of the German Federal Constitutional Court (EuGRZ 1984, 483), a deportable alien might not obtain a stay of execution of his deportation purely due to the fact that he filed a complaint with the Commission under Art. 25 of the Convention, since the guarantee of judicial protection against acts of public authorities contained in Art. 19 para. 4 Basic Law does not include the right to seize the European Commission of Human Rights, see also Bayerisches Oberstes Landesgericht, *DÖV* 1976, 95. For the discussion of the same problem from the point of view of the Convention itself see M. Villiger, *Handbuch der Europäischen Menschenrechtskonvention (EMRK)* (1993), 118 with further references.

uttered doubts as to the self-executing character of Art. 2 para. 2 of the 1st Additional Protocol.[29]

Apart from the above-mentioned general incorporation of the Convention into the German legal order, several provisions of both Federal law and the law of the constituent *Länder* of the Federal Republic of Germany also contain specific references to the Convention. As early as 1965 Sec. 55 para. 3 of the Aliens Law stipulated that provisions contained in treaties (such as the European Convention on Human Rights) as to the status of aliens were not intended to be overruled by this statute. In view of this specific rule, German courts have, starting from 1965,[30] frequently considered Art. 3 of the Convention as barring expulsions or deportations where the individual would face torture or inhuman treatment or punishment in his or her home country.[31] The new German Aliens Law of 1990[32] now specifically stipulates in its Sec. 53 para. 4 that deportation is illegal where it would amount to a violation of the Convention.

There are also further references to the Convention in German law: while the correspondence of prisoners or inmates of hospitals for mentally ill persons might be controlled in certain cases for reasons of security, all relevant laws provide that any correspondence with the European Commission of Human Rights will in no case be subject to any form of interference.[33]

Since 1993, when the German constitution was amended to limit the influx of asylum seekers into Germany, the Basic Law itself now also contains a reference to the European Convention on Human Rights. The newly introduced Art. 16a Basic Law stipulates that the right to asylum cannot be invoked by persons who enter 'from a member state of the European Community or from a third country where the adherence to the Geneva Convention for the Protection of Refugees and the *European Convention on Human Rights* is secured'.[34] By statute, the Federal legislature has decided

In practice, notwithstanding the holding of the European Court of Human Rights in the *Cruz Varas* case (Ser. A, No. 201) the Federal Republic of Germany has generally abided by temporary measures granted by the European Commission of Human Rights under Art. 36 of their rules of procedure, see K. Rogge, 'Einstweilige Maßnahmen im Verfahren vor der Europäischen Kommission für Menschenrechte', *NJW* (1977), S. 1570 ff.

[29] BVerwGE 57, 360 et seq. (372).

[30] OVG Münster *DÖV* 1956, 381.

[31] See more recently OVG Hamburg Informationsbrief Ausländerrecht 1985, 202; see also BVerwGE 48, 299 et seq. (300–301) referring to Art. 8 ECHR.

[32] Bundesgesetzblatt 1990 I, 1354.

[33] See Sec. 29 para. 2 of the Federal Law on the Execution of Criminal Sanctions (*Strafvollzugsgesetz*), Bundesgesetzblatt 1977 I, 436; Sec. 30 para. 2 of the Regulation of Detention under Remand (*Untersuchungshaftvollzugsordnung*) of 12 February, 1953 as amended, and eg Sec. 17 para. 4 of the law of the state of Rheinland-Pfalz dealing with the execution of measures of restraint of 23 September 1986.

[34] Emphasis added. Translation by the author.

that, apart from the member states of the European Union, the Czech Republic, Norway, Poland, and Switzerland are considered to fulfil these requirements. Furthermore, by virtue of Art. 16a para. 5 Basic Law, the Federal Republic of Germany can conclude treaties regulating jurisdictional issues for the examination of asylum requests, if the contracting parties observe the duties arising from, *inter alia,* the European Convention on Human Rights, whose application in the other states parties must be ensured.

(2) The procedural effects of the Convention

As mentioned above, an individual can rely on those provisions of the European Convention on Human Rights which are considered to be directly applicable in all dealings with public authorities and courts. As to the Federal Constitutional Court, while every individual can bring before the court constitutional complaints alleging a violation of one of the fundamental rights and liberties contained in the Basic Law,[35] the Court itself has constantly held that such a complaint cannot be based directly on a violation of the Convention.[36] Such a complaint may, however, be based on a violation of a general rule of public international law[37] as enshrined in a provision of the Convention. Such a constitutional complaint can now also be based on the allegation that a specific act runs counter to the plaintiff's individual right to be granted equal protection under the law[38] by arbitrarily disregarding the Convention or misapplying it.[39]

(3) Effects of decisions of the Commission, the Committee of Ministers, and the European Court of Human Rights

Generally speaking, under German law a decision by either the Court or the Committee of Ministers does not oblige the respective tribunal to reopen its

[35] The relevant provision of the German constitution, Art. 93 para. 1 No. 4a stipulates: 'The Federal Constitutional Court shall rule on constitutional complaints which may be filed by anybody claiming that one of their basic rights (. . .) has been violated by a public authority.'

[36] BVerfGE 74, 102 et seq. (128); see also Polakiewicz/Jacob-Foltzer, note 13 above, 80.

[37] BVerfGE 23, 288 et seq. (300); 77, 170 et seq. (232 f.); (1988), *NJW* 1462 et seq. (1463); for details see Giegerich, note 18 above, 109.

[38] Art. 3 para. 1 Basic Law stipulates: 'All men shall be equal before the law.'

[39] BVerfGE 64, 135 et seq. (157) and 74, 102 et seq. (128). The Court has, however, not (yet) followed the proposition brought forward by J. A. Frowein, 'Das Bundesverfassungsgericht und die EMRK', in: *Festschrift für W. Zeidler*, vol. 2 (1987), 1763 et seq. (1768–1772) that the Convention should be considered as forming part of the constitutional order as meant by Art. 2 para. 1 of the Basic Law, which would allow constitutional complaints to be based on a violation of this article in combination with the relevant guarantee of the European Convention on Human Rights. But see Bundesverfassungsgericht, (1986) *ZaöRV* 289 with note Frowein, where the Court hinted at such an approach. The decision of 11 Nov. 1985 (1986) *ZaöRV* 46 was dismissed for other reasons.

proceedings.[40] As far as criminal proceedings are concerned, however, the German Code of Criminal Procedure now provides in its §359 No. 6[41] that once the European Court of Human Rights had determined that a criminal conviction by a German court violated the Convention, the individual concerned can request a reopening of his or her case.

Otherwise, the vast majority of German courts take the position that they are not, as such, bound by a decision of the European Court of Human Rights declaring a German norm to be incompatible with the Convention.[42] However, some writers take the view that any such decision gives an authoritative interpretation of the Convention, which in itself is binding upon the organs of the Federal Republic of Germany;[43] this view is, however, not (yet) generally shared by German courts.[44] It seems now to be settled, though, that in situations where the act which was declared to be incompatible with the Convention continues to have legal effects, any further enforcement would be illegal under Art. 53 of the Convention.[45]

On a couple of occasions, German courts have referred to friendly settlements reached between the Commission and the Federal Government according to Art. 28 lit. b of the Convention.[46] The notification of such a settlement dealing with the question of whether parole can be revoked in light of the principle of the presumption of innocence[47] was the decisive factor for a change in the jurisprudence of some courts.[48] Other courts have taken the view, however, that such settlements are not legally binding on them and that any such notification is constitutionally debatable, taking into account the principle of the independence of the judiciary.[49]

[40] See Bundesverfassungsgericht (1986), *ZaöRV* 286 with note Frowein and the further decisions cited by Uerpmann, note 16 above, 188, note 61; and see generally J. Polakiewicz, *Die Verpflichtungen der Staaten aus den Urteilen des Europäischen Gerichtshofes für Menschenrechte* (1993), *passim*.

[41] Bundesgesetzblatt 1998 I, 1802.

[42] But see also L. G. Wuppertal, Juristisches Büro 1977, 402–403, which took the view that it was directly bound by the judgment of the Court in the *Öztürk* case.

[43] Frowein, note 13 above, 743.

[44] See eg the decision of the Oberlandesgericht Hamm of 16 June 1978, quoted by Ress, note 17 above, 263: 'Even if the European Court were to take a decision favourable for the applicants and one which committed the Federal Republic of Germany (. . .) this would not result (. . .) in the annulment of the above-mentioned German norms'.

[45] BVerfG, *ZaöRV* 1986, 289 et seq. (294) with note Frowein.

[46] See generally J. A. Frowein, 'Der freundschaftliche Ausgleich im Individualbeschwerdeverfahren nach der Menschenrechtskonvention und das deutsche Recht', (1969), *JZ* 213 et seq.

[47] See Application 12748/87 and H. Ostendorf, 'Unschuldsvermutung und Bewährungswiderruf', Strafverteidiger 1990, 230 et seq.

[48] See eg OLG Schleswig, *NJW* (1991) 2303.

[49] See eg OLG Düsseldorf, *NJW* (1992) 1183.

B. THE STATUS OF THE CONVENTION IN PARLIAMENTARY PROCEEDINGS

As well as the above-mentioned provisions in specific statutes which refer specifically to the Convention, the Federal Government and individual members of Parliament have on several occasions referred to the Convention or the jurisprudence of the Strasbourg organs when submitting proposals for legislation.[50] Such references are found especially in the field of criminal law and procedure. When the Convention was submitted for parliamentary approval, an in-depth study was already being undertaken to determine whether both the German Criminal Code and the Code on Criminal Procedure could be considered compatible with the Convention.[51]

In 1964 the German Code on Criminal Procedure was amended introducing a new Sec. 33a, which granted the accused more rights to be heard.[52] In its report to the legislature, the legal committee of the Federal Parliament specifically stated that the rights contained in Art. 6 of the Convention would otherwise not be sufficiently guaranteed.[53] Furthermore, the new Sec. 121 of the Code on Criminal Procedure, which was introduced at the same time, increased the legal hurdles to extending pre-trial custody beyond six months and provided for the possibility to challenge any such decision in court. The Federal Government, when introducing this provision, expressly stated that one of its goals was to satisfy the requirements of Art. 5 para. 3 of the Convention.[54]

In 1969 the question whether an accused found not guilty due to lack of proof could be obliged to pay the costs of the proceedings was decided in favour of the individual concerned by the Federal Parliament. The legislature expressly took into account the principle of presumption of innocence contained in Art. 6 para. 2 of the Convention.[55] In 1971 the legislature granted

[50] As to legislative reforms undertaken after Germany had been held responsible of a violation of the Convention see below F.

[51] See H. H. Jescheck, 'Die Europäische Konvention zum Schutz der Menschenrechte und Grundfreiheiten', (1954) *NJW* 783 et seq. (784). For details see also K. Kühl, *Der Einfluß der Europäischen Menschenrechtskonvention auf das Strafrecht und Strafverfahrensrecht der Bundesrepublik Deutschland, Zeitschrift für die gesamte Strafrechtswissenschaft* (1988) 406 et seq. (part 1) and 601 et seq. (part 2), (609).

[52] For details see Uerpmann, note 16 above, 57.

[53] Bundestags-Drucksache IV/1020, 5.

[54] Bundestags-Drucksache IV/178, 25; as to the drafting history see A. Bleckmann, 'Völkerrechtliche Praxis der Bundesrepublik Deutschland im Jahre 1960', (1963), *ZaöRV* 175 et seq. (342). Even before this change became effective, the courts had directly enforced the guarantee contained in Art. 5 para. 3 lit. 2 ECHR, see eg OLG Saarbrücken (1961) *NJW* 377 and generally Morvay, note 27 above, 330–332. See also the comprehensive survey of Kühl, note 51 above, 31.

[55] Report of the Legal Committee of the Federal Parliament, Bundestagsdrucksache V/2600 and 2601/19; Kühl, note 51 above, 613–614.

persons who had been kept in custody without later being sentenced, the right to compensation, referring to the same provision of the Convention.[56] On several occasions Art. 6 para. 1 lit. 2 ECHR has also been referred to in parliamentary debates, when the problem of excluding the public from trials was discussed.[57]

In 1973 the Federal Government introduced a bill, the goal of which was to provide for more expeditious criminal trials. Apart from making reference to the principle of the rule of law contained in the German constitution, the reasoning was particularly based on Art. 6 para. 1 lit. 1 of the Convention.[58] In a later reform of the Code of Criminal Procedure in 1978/79, although no particular provision of the Convention was mentioned, terms and notions incorporated from the jurisprudence of the Strasbourg organs, such as the principle of 'equality of arms' were frequently referred to during the parliamentary proceedings.[59]

On different occasions, the question whether Art. 2 para. 2 lit. a ECHR must necessarily lead to a limitation of the right of self-defence as contained in Sec. 32 of the German Criminal Code was discussed in parliamentary forums.[60] In particular, the question arose, but was finally left open and has still not been settled in legal writing, whether the limitations contained in this provision also limit the right of private individuals to defend themselves.[61] Only two German courts have so far dealt with this question, both in *obiter dicta*. Both courts said that the individual's right to self-defence is limited by Art. 2 of the Convention.[62]

Finally, since 1986, under Sec. 25a of the German Traffic Code, the *owner* of a vehicle can be fined for illegal parking if the *driver* of the car cannot be found, despite the fact that the Legal Committee of the Federal Parliament had uttered doubts as to the compatibility of this norm with the presumption of innocence as contained in Art. 6 para. 2 of the Convention.[63]

[56] Bundestagsdrucksache IV/60, 5; see also Kühl, note 51 above, 614–615 and 615–619 for further references to Art. 6 para. 2 in later legislation.

[57] Kühl, note 51 above, 619–620.

[58] Bundestagsdrucksache 7/551, 36.

[59] Kühl, note 51 above, 622. See finally Sec. 231a of the German Code of Criminal Procedure, which deals with the possible continuance of the trial despite the fact that the accused has become unable to attend the trial, J. Baumann, 'Strafprozeßreform in Raten', ZRP 1975, 38 et seq. (43). This provision was later considered by the Commission as being compatible with the Convention, see EuGRZ 1978, 314.

[60] For details see Kühl, note 51 above, 624–625.

[61] As to details of the discussion see J. A. Frowein/W. Peukert, *Europäische Menschenrechskonvention, EMRK-Kommentar* (2nd edn, 1996), 35–36.

[62] Oberlandesgericht Köln, Sammlung der Rechtsprechung der Oberlandesgerichts in Strafsachen (OLGSt) § 32 StGB, 1 et seq. (3) and Bundesverwaltungsgericht, (1974) *NJW* 1343 et seq. (1344).

[63] Bundestags-Drucksache 10/5083, 25.

C. LEADING HUMAN RIGHTS CASES DECIDED BY THE NATIONAL COURTS

The German constitution contains a detailed catalogue of basic rights which largely parallel the guarantees provided for in the Convention. Thus, most of the leading human rights cases which have arisen, especially those decided by the Federal Constitutional Court, were decided solely on the basis of those guarantees. Most references to the Convention are *obiter dicta,* and only rarely form part of the *ratio decidendi.*[64] Nevertheless some important developments can be noted.[65]

1. Article 3 ECHR

From 1956 German courts have considered Art. 3 as barring deportations or expulsions, where the person concerned would face inhuman treatment or punishment[66] and have frequently referred to the pertinent decisions of the Court. In 1992 the Federal Constitutional Court held that the extradition of a member of the IRA to Great Britain does not amount to a violation of Art. 3 ECHR, one reason among others being that the United Kingdom has submitted itself to the jurisdiction of the Strasbourg organs.[67] In 1995 and 1997 the Bundesverwaltungsgericht (Federal Administrative Court) on two occasions departed from the jurisprudence of the European Court of Human Rights[68] by finding that the danger that a person might be exposed to torture or inhuman treatment or punishment emanating from non-state actors does not fall within the scope of application of Art. 3 ECHR and accordingly does not prevent the deportation of such persons.[69]

[64] See eg Hilf, note 13 above, 21 et seq.

[65] For a more detailed survey of court decisions referring to the Convention see either the annual survey in the Yearbook on the European Convention on Human Rights or the report on German jurisprudence in the field of public international law published annually in the Zeitschrift für ausländisches öffentliches Recht und Völkerrecht.

[66] See above.

[67] See the unpublished decision reported by P. Rädler, 'Deutsche Rechtsprechung in völkerrechtlichen Fragen im Jahre 1991', (1994), *ZaöRV* 471 et seq. (523).

[68] See in particular the decision in the cases of *Ahmed v Austria* and *H. R. v France.*

[69] See BVerwGE 99, 331 and BVerwGE 104, 265; for a critical analysis of these decisions see A. Zimmer, *Abschiebungsschutz durch Art. 3 EMRK im Fall nichtstaatlicher Verfolgung, Zeitschrift für Ausländerrecht* (1998), 115 et seq.; but see also H.-G. Maaßen, 'Abschiebeschutz aus Art. 3 EMRK auch bei nicht vom Staat ausgehenden Menschenrechtsverletzungen und allgemeinen dem Ausländer im Herkunftsstaat drohenden Gefahren für Leib, Leben und Gesundheit?', *ZAR* (1998), 107 et seq. For a more detailed analysis of the jurisprudence of German courts in that respect following the decisions of the Bundesverwaltungsgericht see also L. Geburtig, 'Deutsche Rechtsprechung in völkerrechtlichen Fragen 1997', (1998) *ZaöRV* (forthcoming).

In 1985 the Bundesgerichtshof held that making three prisoners occupy one small prison cell also amounts to a violation of Art. 3 ECHR.[70]

2. Article 4, paragraph 2 ECHR

The Bundesverwaltungsgericht had found in 1994[71] that a law which provided that male persons not serving in the fire brigade of their local communities must pay a specific tax did not amount to either a violation of Art. 4 para. 2 or Art. 14 of the Convention. After the decision of the European Court of Human Rights in *K Schmidt v Germany*,[72] which found to the contrary, the German Constitutional Court[73] nullified the respective laws since, in the view of the Court, they did run counter *inter alia* to the principle of equality of sexes as contained in Art. 3 para. 2 of the Basic Law.[74]

3. Article 5 ECHR

In 1990 the Bavarian Constitutional Court held that the Bavarian Police Law, which empowers the police to take into custody a person who disobeys police orders, is consistent with Art. 5 para. 1 of the Convention, since it fulfils the requirements of Art. 5 para. 1 lit. b and lit. c.[75] In the same vein, the Constitutional Court of the State of Saxony in an elaborate decision found that the provisions on police custody contained in the police law of the State of Saxony are in conformity with the requirements of Art. 5 ECHR.[76]

As mentioned above,[77] Art. 5 para. 3 of the Convention was applied by several courts to shorten the maximum possible length of pre-trial custody before the law in question was amended accordingly.

In an important decision, the Federal Supreme Court in 1993[78] acknowledged that Art. 5 para. 5 of the Convention entails a directly enforceable claim for compensation including a claim for non-pecuniary damages.

[70] OLG Frankfurt, Neue Zeitschrift für Strafrecht 1985, 572.

[71] NVwZ 1995, 390.

[72] Series A No. 291–B.

[73] Text of the decision to be found in EuGRZ 1995, 410.

[74] For a more detailed analysis see A. Bleckmann, 'Bundesverfassungsgericht versus Europäischer Gerichtshof für Menschenrechte—Innerstaatliche Rechtskraft der Urteile des EHGMR und Gleichheit von Mann und Frau, Anmerkung zu den Feuerwehrabgabe-Entscheidungen des EGMR vom 18.7.1994 und des BVerfG vom 24.1.1995', (1995), *EuGRZ* 387.

[75] For details see 1990, BayVbl. 654 (658–659) and Giegerich, note 18 above, 411.

[76] 1996, EuGRZ 473.

[77] See above at note 24 and accompanying text.

[78] (1993), MDR 740.

4. Article 6 ECHR

Even before the judgment of the European Court of Human Rights in the *König* case, German courts have generally taken the view that an infringement of the right to have a hearing within a reasonable time does not *per se* hinder further proceedings, but is a factor to be considered to mitigate the punishment.[79] In serious cases, however, according to settled jurisprudence the case must be mooted by the court.[80]

According to the Bundesverwaltungsgeright, the presumption of innocence contained in Art. 6 para. 2 does not hinder the deportation of an alien for having committed criminal offences, even where he or she has not been brought before the court for the offences in question.

5. Article 8 ECHR

Both in the 1980s and the 1990s, Art. 8 of the Convention was frequently cited in cases where the admission into Germany of family members of resident aliens was restricted.[81] *Inter alia*, the Federal Constitutional Court found in 1987 that an eight-year residence requirement before a resident alien can be joined his or her spouse is compatible with Art. 8 of the Convention.[82] More recently, the Higher Administrative Tribunal of Baden-Württemberg considered the expulsion of a Turkish citizen to be legal, even taking into account the *Moustaquim* decision of the Strasbourg Court,[83] since the plaintiff was already nine years old when he left Turkey and was still able to speak his mother tongue at the time the deportation order was made.[84]

German courts have also held that the exclusion of joint parental authority for children born out of wedlock is legal under Art. 8 of the Convention.[85]

6. Article 9 ECHR

According to the Bavarian Higher Administrative Court, the fact that a crucifix is displayed in a classroom does not violate Art. 9 of the Convention.[86]

[79] For details see Polakiewicz and Jacob-Foltzer, note 13 above, 81.

[80] See Federal Constitutional Court, (1984), *NJW* 967; (1993), *NJW* 3254 et seq. (3255) and most recently (1995), *NJW* 1277. For an example of such a situation see OLG Stuttgart, (1993), *MDR* 680 and BGH, (1996), *NJW* 2739–2740. As to the right to receive free interpretation under Art. 6 para. 3 lit. e of the Convention and its enforcement under German law, see below.

[81] See eg the decision of the Bundesverwaltungsgericht, reported by R. Kühner, 'Deutsche Rechtsprechung zu völkerrechtlichen Fragen im Jahre 1984', (1986), *ZaöRV* 89 et seq. (130).

[82] (1987) EuGRZ 449 citing the decision of the European Court of Human Rights in the *Abdulaziz* case, Judgment of 28 May 1985, Series A, No. 94.

[83] Judgment of 18 February 1991, Series A, No. 193.

[84] See Rädler, note 67 above, 530. See also BVerwG InfAuslR 1996, 393.

[85] See OLG Celle FamRZ 1994, 1057 and OLG Köln FamRZ 1993, 1243.

[86] BayVBl. 1991, 751.

The German Constitutional Court, which in last instance had to decide whether such display of a religious symbol in a public institution is allowed,[87] did not address Art. 9 ECHR but focused solely on the protection of religious freedom enshrined in Art. 4 of the German Basic Law. The Higher Administrative Court of Hessen held in 1998 (NVwZ-RR 1999, 340) that a violation of basic religious freedoms in the country of origin of an alien might bar his deportation under Art. 9 of the Convention.

The Higher Court of the Free and Hanseatic City of Hamburg took the view that the same provision does not guarantee the right of conscientious objection (NVwZ-RR 1999, 342).

D. CASES BROUGHT BEFORE THE EUROPEAN COMMISSION AND THE COURT OF HUMAN RIGHTS

1. *Inter-state complaints*

The Federal Republic of Germany has so far never been the object of an inter-state complaint, nor has Germany participated in any such procedure. The Federal Government in particular did not take part in the proceedings initiated by France, the Netherlands, Denmark, Norway, and Sweden against Turkey in 1982,[88] because it took the view that 'due to its political contacts, it had a better opportunity to improve the situation of human rights in Turkey'.[89]

2. *Proceedings before the European Commission for Human Rights*

Of the many decisions by the European Commission for Human Rights relating to Germany, only a few are here mentioned, which—although not leading to judgments of the Court—had important political implications. In 1975 and again in 1978[90] the Commission had to deal with claims that the conditions of detention of persons charged with committing terrorists acts were counter to Art. 3 of the Convention. On both occasions the allegations were found to be unfounded.[91]

[87] BVerfGE 93, 1 et seq.

[88] Applications 9940/82–9944/82 of July 1, 1982.

[89] Replies to parliamentary questions of 15 and 16 July 1982, Bundestagsdrucksache 9/1870, 2 and 6; quoted by H. H. Lindemann, 'Völkerrechtliche Praxis der Bundesrepublik Deutschland im Jahr 1982', (1984), *ZaöRV* 495 et seq. (528). Translation by the author.

[90] Application 6166/73, *Baader, Meinhof, Grundmann v FRG*, (1975) 2 D.R. 58 and Applications 7572, 7586 and 7587/76, *Ensslin, Baader, Raspe v FRG*, (1978) 14 D.R. 64 (84 et seq.).

[91] For details see also Frowein/Peukert, note 61 above, 32–33.

In 1983 the application of *Kemal Altun*, which faced extradition to Turkey and thereby might have been exposed to torture, was declared admissible by the Commission[92] and was later struck off the list after the applicant committed suicide while being held in custody.[93]

In 1996 the Commission declared several complaints alleging violation of Art. 1 of the First Additional Protocol by not restituting property expropriated in the territory of the former German Democratic Republic between 1945 and 1949 to be inadmissible *ratione personae*, *temporis*, and *materiae*.[94]

3. *Cases decided by the European Court of Human Rights involving the Federal Republic of Germany*

Important cases decided by the European Court of Human Rights involving the Federal Republic of Germany as defendant have concerned the rights contained in Arts. 3, 4, 5, 6, 8, and 10 of the Convention.

a) Article 3 ECHR In the *Klaas* case, decided in September 1993,[95] the Court, departing somewhat from its previous decision in the *Tomasi* case,[96] held that Germany had not violated Art. 3 where the applicant had suffered bruises in connection with her arrest by police officers.

b) Article 4 in conjunction with Article 14 In the case of *Schmidt v Germany*, the Court found that the duty of male citizens not serving in the local fire brigade to pay a special tax, as provided for in the laws of the States of Bavaria and Baden-Württemberg, did amount to a violation of Art. 4 para. 3 lit. d read in conjunction with Art. 14 ECHR. The respective laws were later nullified by the German Constitutional Court.[97]

c) Article 5 ECHR As in some other states parties to the Convention, the question of judicial review of decisions to place and keep a person in an institution for mentally ill persons gave rise to the complaint that Germany had violated Art. 5 para. 4 of the Convention.[98]

Neither Art. 5 para. 1 nor Art. 6 para. 1 of the Convention were considered to have been violated by the Federal Republic of Germany in the *Stocké*

[92] For the text of the decision see EuGRZ 1983, 274.

[93] Application 10308/83. See also Application 6242/73, *Brückmann v Germany*, Yearbook XVII, 458 (476), where the Commission held that an application based on Art. 3 of the Convention was admissible in a situation where the applicant faced extradition to the German Democratic Republic.

[94] Applications 19048/91, 19049/91, 19342/91, 19549/91, and 18890/91, text to be found in EuGRZ 1996, 386.

[95] *Klaas v Germany*, Judgment of 22 September 1993, Series A, No. 269. The case had been referred to the Court by both the Commission and the German government.

[96] Judgment of 27 August 1992, Series A, No. 241–A.

[97] See above.

[98] See eg *Megyeri v Germany*, Judgment of 12 May 1992, Series A, No. 237–A.

case,[99] where the applicant had been brought to Germany against his will in order to prosecute him there since this abduction, according to the Court, could not be attributed to the German authorities.

In 1997, the European Court of Human Rights found that Germany had violated Art. 5 para. 1 of the Convention by detaining an arrested person for longer than the twelve hours provided for in domestic law without presenting the applicant to a judge.[100]

In 2001 the European Court found a violation of Art. 5 para. 4 in relation to the failure to grant detainees on remand access to their criminal case files. (See *Garcia Alva v Germany*, Application 23541/94; *Lietzow v Germany*, Application 24479/94; and *Schöps v Germany*, Application 25116/94; all Judgments of 13 February 2001).

d) Article 6 ECHR In a couple of cases, the Strasbourg Court decided that Germany had violated Art. 6 of the Convention where legal proceedings had taken several years.[101] Also, the European Court of Human Rights has on several occasions found that Art. 6 para. 1 is applicable in proceedings before the German Constitutional Court,[102] but has so far not found a violation of Art. 6 para. 1 ECHR in such a case.

In 1983 the European Court of Human Rights found that Germany had violated Art. 6 para. 3 lit. c by not granting Mr Pakelli the right to free counsel in an appeal concerning a question of law (*Revision*) despite the fact that the defendant had been sentenced to imprisonment for two years and three months.[103] In 1984 the guarantee of access to translation free of cost was extended by the European Court of Human Rights to regulatory offences, deciding against the Federal Republic of Germany.[104]

In important decisions in 1999, the European Court found that Germany had not violated Art. 6 of the Convention by granting the European Space Agency immunity before German couts (*Waite and Kennedy v Germany*, Application 26083/94, and *Beer and Regan v Germany*, Application 28934/95, both Judgments of 18 February 1999).

e) Article 8 ECHR As early as 1978 the European Court of Human Rights decided that the German law which under certain conditions provides for both tapping the telephone of an individual and excluding judicial review of

[99] Judgment of 19 March 1991, Series A, No. 199. [100] *K. F. v Germany*.

[101] *König*, A 27 (administrative tribunal proceedings: more than ten years until the first decision was rendered); *Eckle*, A 51 (criminal proceedings, which took 17 years); *Deumeland*, A 100 (proceedings concerning social benefits lasting for more than ten years); *Bock*, A 150 (divorce proceedings taking more than nine years).

[102] See *Süßmann v Germany* and most recently *Probstmeier v Germany* and *Pammel v Germany*.

[103] *Pakelli v Germany*, Judgment of 25 April 1983, Series A, No. 64.

[104] For reactions in Germany on this judgment see below.

this act, is compatible with Art. 8 ECHR.[105] In 1992 Germany was held to have breached Art. 8 of the Convention due to a search warrant issued by a court against a lawyer, whose business premises were then searched by the police. According to the European Court of Human Rights, this interference with the right to privacy was not necessary in a democratic society as provided for by Art. 8 para. 2 of the Convention.[106]

In 2000 the Grand Chamber of the European Court of Human Rights found a violation of Art. 8 of the Convention when the father of a child born out of wedlock was denied any access to his son (*Elsholz v Germany*), Application 25735/94, Judgment of 13 July 2000).

f) Article 10 ECHR In a series of cases the compatibility of the German law on unfair competition was challenged by the European Commission for Human Rights as being incompatible with Art. 10 of the Convention. While the Court did indeed find a violation of Art. 10 ECHR in the *Barthold* case,[107] it reached a different result in two other more recent cases.[108] The Court stressed in that regard that the respective municipal legal order should be granted a relatively wide discretion to regulate commercial speech and unsound competition.

In a case of a teacher dismissed for being a member of the German Communist party (DKP), the Court found by 10 to 9 votes that such dismissal constituted a violation of both Arts. 10 and 11 of the Convention.[109] In particular, the European Court of Human Rights determined that the dismissal constituted a violation of the Convention since it had not been necessary in a democratic society, as provided for in Arts. 10 para. 2 and 11 para. 2 of the Convention. The case was later settled by granting the plaintiff monetary compensation. (For the German government's position on the legal implications of the judgment see BT-Drs. 13/3853).

For a recent German court decision which took that European Court judgment into account see Higher Administrative Court of Hessen, NVwZ-RR 1999, 904. But see also the decision of the Administrative Tribunal Sigmaringen, NVwZ-RR 1998, 1104, which held that the decision in question was only relevant to the dismissal of public officials, and not to their hiring.

[105] *Klass v Germany*, Judgment of 6 September 1978, Series A, No. 28.

[106] *Niemitz v Germany*, Judgment of 16 December 1992, Series A, No. 251–B.

[107] Judgment of 25 March 1985, Series A, No. 90.

[108] See *Markt intern*, Judgment of 20 November 1989, Series A, No. 165, and see most recently the case of *Jacubowski v Germany*, Judgment of 23 June 1994, Series A, No. 291, dealing with a similar factual background.

[109] *Vogt v Germany*, Judgment of 2 September 1996, Series A, No. 323. For a detailed analysis of that decision see H. Roggemann, 'Europäische Grenzen für den deutschen Staatsschutz? Zum Radikalenerlaß-Urteil des EuGMR (Fall Vogt) vom 26.9.1995', Neue Justiz 1996, 338 et seq.

E. REMEDIAL ACTION TAKEN BY THE GOVERNMENT IN RESPONSE TO BEING HELD IN VIOLATION OF THE CONVENTION

In several instances the Federal Republic of Germany has undertaken legislative reforms either after another state party to the Convention was found to be in violation of the Convention or after Germany itself had been considered by the European Court of Human Rights to have violated the Convention.

Two of the more important instances are as follows. Following the decision of the European Court of Human Rights in the *Luedicke, Belkacem, and Koc* case,[110] the German authorities immediately took legislative measures to provide the free assistance of an interpreter in criminal cases pursuant to Article 6 para. 3 lit. e of the Convention.[111] After a negative ruling against the Federal Republic of Germany in the *Ötztürk* case, which had extended the guarantee of Art. 6 para. 3 lit. e to include regulatory offences (*Ordnungswidrigkeiten*) it took several years before the Federal Government finally introduced legislation to amend the legislation.[112] This lapse of time was due to the deplorable fact that the Federal Ministry of Justice took the position that the Court might eventually reconsider its jurisprudence, thus eventually rendering such a change superfluous.[113]

F. ASSESSMENT AND PROSPECTS

In light of the above findings, the impact of the Convention on the German legal order should not be underestimated. In particular, the Federal Government and Parliament have usually tried to bring German law into conformity with the Convention in the light of the general jurisprudence of the Strasbourg organs or when the European Court of Human Rights has found the Federal Republic of Germany to have committed a violation of the Convention.

[110] Judgment of 28 November 1978, Series A, No. 29.

[111] Polakiewicz and Jacob-Foltzer, note 13 above, 79. The judgment was rendered in November 1978. The legislative reform became effective in August 1980, see Bundesgesetzblatt 1980 I, 1503.

[112] So-called *lex Ötztürk*, EuGRZ 1989, 350; see also the relevant resolutions of the Committee of Ministers taking note of this development, DH (89) 8 of 2 March 1989, ibid at 328, and DH (89) 31 of 10 November 1989.

[113] See the critical remark by Frowein, note 13 above, 757.

Despite a certain reluctance by German courts to refer to the Convention in the early years after ratification, more and more members of the judiciary are starting to take the Convention seriously. This is demonstrated *inter alia* by the fact that the number of court decisions referring to the Convention almost doubled in the eighties compared with previous decades.

In particular it has become obvious that the Federal Constitutional Court is now more ready to take the Convention into consideration when deciding human rights cases. The extent to which the jurisprudence of both the Commission and the Court can influence the internal legal order of Germany will, however, depend not only upon the theoretical relationship between both legal orders, but also on the extent to which the Strasbourg jurisprudence is systematically published in German.[114]

Furthermore, it is worth noting that the German legal order, like that of the other member states of the European Union, is increasingly either directly or indirectly determined by the law of the European Community. Since the European Commission of Human Rights has held that acts by member states enforcing decisions by community organs are not subject to the control mechanism of the Convention,[115] ratification by the European Community of the European Convention on Human Rights could, notwithstanding the negative advisory opinion of the European Court of Justice,[116] close a significant loophole in the scope of application of the Convention.[117] However, recent developments, particularly the adoption of the European Union Charter of Fundamental Rights, seem to indicate a different path.

[114] See in that regard eg the commentary by Frowein/Peukert, note 61 above, and most recently the work of M. Villiger, *Handbuch der Europäischen Menschenrechtskonvention (EMRK)* (1993).

[115] See the decision of the Commission in *M and Co v Germany*, Application 113258/87 of 9 February 1990, text to be found in (1990), *ZaöRV* 865 et seq. with note T. Giegerich, 'Luxemburg, Karlsruhe, Straßburg—Dreistufiger Grundrechtsschutz in Europa?', (1990) *ZaöRv* 836 et seq. (860 et seq.).

[116] Advisory Opinion 2/94.

[117] The German government has frequently advocated such a step, see eg the statements referred to in A. Berg, 'Völkerrechtliche Praxis der Bundesrepublik Deutschland im Jahr 1978', (1981) *ZaöRV* 589 et seq. (609–610); W. Meng, 'Völkerrechtliche Praxis der Bundesrepublik Deutschland im Jahre 1980', (1981) *ZaöRV* 508 et seq. (530–531) and most recently in P.-T. Stoll, 'Völkerrechtliche Praxis der Bundesrepublik Deutschland im Jahre 1994', (1996) *ZaöRV* p. 998 et seq. (1053–1054).

15

Greece

KRATEROS IOANNOU

INTRODUCTION[1]

The Convention, so far as its application in Greece is concerned, has a unique history. Indeed, events like those that took place in Greece between the years 1967 and 1974 did not occur in any of the other member states of the Council of Europe, at least not during their membership. Greece signed the Convention on 20 November 1950, just one year after the end of a disastrous civil war. Parliamentary approval was given by Law 2329/ 1953. Between the years 1953 and 1967 the impact of the Convention on the Greek legal order was rather insignificant, although a great part of the legislation was undoubtedly violating the Convention.[2] Neither judges nor the administrative authorities were seriously applying the Convention and questions of the international protection of human rights were not frequently debated in academic forums. In the very few cases where the Convention was referred to in Greek judgments it was only in order to discard its application *in casu*.

This situation can be attributed to a number of factors. First, to the non-acceptance by Greece at that time of the right of individual petition. Consequently, any violation of the Convention could only be internationally sanctioned through the machinery of inter-state applications. Secondly, to the rank of international treaties within the Greek legal order under the Greek Constitution of 1952. Under that Constitution, treaties did not supersede domestic legislation and in case of conflict with a legislative provision the

[1] The structure of this text is based on an outline suggested by the editor, Professor Robert Blackburn. Throughout the text the term 'Convention' is used for the European Convention for the Protection of Human Rights and Fundamental Freedoms. References are limited to only a few articles written in either English or French. It should be noted, however, that the Greek legal literature on the Convention is very rich. I am grateful to Miss Ekaterini Sgouridou, Research Assistant at the Centre of International and European Economic Law of Thessaloniki for her assistance in the preparation of the chapter.

[2] See below, C(1).

rule of priority was applied.[3] Furthermore, neither judges nor lawyers were familiar with the Convention since the international protection of human rights was not then taught in law faculties.

On 21 April 1967 the constitutional government of Greece was overthrown by a military coup. Immediately afterwards a military dictatorship was established and the most important provisions of the Greek Constitution of 1952, including practically all guarantees of human rights and individual freedoms, were suspended. However, the military rulers were careful to appear to be complying with the international obligations of Greece and on 3 May 1967 informed the Secretary General of the Council of Europe that Greece was invoking article 15 of the Convention, claiming that there existed in Greece a 'public emergency threatening the life of the nation'. However, it took several months for the military government to describe its version of this 'threat' to the Secretary General of the Council of Europe.

Irrespective of the legal situation, the everyday administrative practice under the military dictatorship was a continuous violation of practically all freedoms guaranteed by the Convention. Although the military dictatorship was tolerated, if not encouraged, on the Atlantic level, it was nonetheless causing considerable concern in many member states of the Council of Europe. This concern led to inter-state applications by Denmark, Sweden, Norway, and the Netherlands against Greece on 27 September 1967.[4] The Report adopted by the European Commission of Human Rights on 4 October 1969 found that the Greek military government had violated articles 3, 5, 6, 8, 9, 10, 11, 13, and 14 of the Convention as well as article 3 of the First Protocol and was transmitted to the Committee of Ministers of the Council of Europe.

In view of the danger of being expelled from the Council of Europe the Greek military government on 12 December 1969 deposited with the Secretary General of the Council of Europe a *note verbale* denouncing the Convention and the Statute of the Council of Europe. On the same date the Committee of Ministers adopted Resolution (69)51, by which it considered the serious violation by Greece of article 3 of the Statute and noted the withdrawal of Greece from the Council of Europe.[5]

The denunciation of the Convention was never followed by a domestic legislative act and Law 2329/1953, which had approved the Convention, was still

[3] Although the courts were construing domestic legislation on the assumption that the legislator did not intend, unless otherwise explicitly stated, to violate a treaty. See D. Evrigenis, 'Les conflits de la loi nationale avec les traites internationaux en droit hellenique', Revue Hellenique de Droit International 1965, pp. 353 et seq.

[4] For a discussion of these inter-state cases see below, E(a).

[5] See texts of the Greek *note verbale* and of the Resolution of the Committee of Ministers in *International Legal Materials* 1970, pp. 408 et seq.

formally in force. Furthermore the denunciation of the Convention was not published in the Greek Official Journal and consequently was 'unknown' to the national judges. In fact some courts referred to the Convention[6] although no court ever applied it between 1967 and 1974.

After the fall of the military dictatorship the democratic Greek government on 20 September 1974 approved the Convention for a second time by Legislative Decree 53/1974. On 28 November 1974 a new approval of the Statute of the Council of Europe took place by Legislative Decree 196/74. However, these new legislative approvals were not followed by new ratifications of the Convention and the Statute. This situation is formally irregular. Indeed, with the denunciation of 1969 Greece ceased, as from 13 June 1970, to be internationally bound by the Convention and consequently a new ratification was necessary.[7] However, this irregularity did not create any problem either on the domestic or on the international level.

So far as the Protocols to the Convention are concerned, Greece ratified the First Protocol together with the Convention. The Second, Third, and Fifth Protocols were also ratified and approved by Legislative Decree 215/1974. The Seventh Protocol was ratified on 29 October 1987 and approved by Law 1705/1987. Greece has not signed the Fourth Protocol and has signed, but not yet ratified, the Ninth and the Tenth Protocols. The other Protocols have all been ratified and approved, the Eighth by Law 1841/1989, the Eleventh by Law 2400/1996, and lately the Sixth by Law 2610/1998. The right of individual petition was recognized by Greece on 20 November 1985 for all violations after that date. The relative declaration was made for a period of three years and is normally renewed. However, Greece did not accept the right of individual petition for the freedoms guaranteed by the Seventh Protocol.

A. THE STATUS OF THE CONVENTION IN GREEK LAW

The Convention, being an international treaty, is applied in the Greek legal order under the constitutional terms and conditions for the application of treaties in general. Therefore this section deals with the general constitutional framework for the domestic application of treaties and explores the peculiarities, if any, of the application of the Convention by the Greek authorities.

[6] Eg Judgment 371/1973 of the Greek Conseil d'Etat (Full Bench).

[7] A publication of the Greek Ministry of Justice comprising the text of the Convention and of the Protocols (January 1989) notes that the first approval of March 1953 had ceased to exist by 12 June 1970, the date on which the denunciation of the Convention became effective.

The Greek Constitution, enacted on 11 June 1975 and revised on 12 March 1986 has a strong international orientation. Drafted immediately after the collapse of the military dictatorship, it is the product of an intellectual reaction against totalitarianism. Within this spiritual framework of the drafters the rules of international law were considered as the democratic rules par excellence. Moreover, the drafters of the Constitution tended, under the influence of the overall enthusiasm for democracy, to assimilate international protection of human rights with all international norms. This constitutional internationalism is reflected in a number of stipulations of the Constitution, namely article 2, para. 2 (adherence by Greece to the rules of international law), article 5, para. 2 (reference to international law in respect to acceptable exceptions in the absolute protection of life, honour, and liberty) and article 28, paras. 1, 2, and 3 (general international law and international treaties as part of the law of the land; constitutional regulation of transfers of sovereignty to international organs).

Article 28, para. 1 of the Constitution, which is of particular relevance so far as the application of the Convention is concerned, reads as follows:

> The generally accepted rules of international law, as well as international treaties, as from their approval by law and from their entering into force according to each one's own terms, shall constitute an integral part of Greek domestic law and shall prevail over any contrary provision of law. The rules of international law and international treaties shall be applied to aliens always on the condition of reciprocity.

Furthermore, article 36, para. 2 of the Constitution lists certain types of treaties for which there is a constitutional obligation for legislative approval. In practice, however, all international treaties are submitted to Parliament for approval.

The above-mentioned constitutional stipulations do not provide for the 'transformation' or any other type of conversion of treaties into domestic legislation. Treaties, within the Greek legal order, retain their character as international enactments and are applied as such. The Constitution providing that international treaties constitute an integral part of the Greek legal order is not intended to deprive treaties of any of their properties under international law. Furthermore, it is useless to attempt the framing of the constitutional regulation within the monism/dualism typology. In fact elements from both of these traditional approaches are present in the Greek Constitution, the predominant characteristic being, however, a qualified dualism so far as the application of treaties is concerned.

The legislative approval of the treaties is achieved by an act of the Parliament, which incorporates an order for the application of the treaty. In form, it contains on one hand the approval clause and on the other the text of the treaty, in both the original languages and in a Greek translation. The Parliament may not modify in any respect the text of the approved treaty but the approval bill may contain other provisions as well (eg provisions relating to the application of the treaty, the creation of relevant administrative organs etc). Furthermore, the text of the treaty as contained in the approval bill must correspond exactly to the text which is internationally valid. Consequently, any reservations (or other form of declarations etc) may be included in the order of application of the treaty only insofar as they are internationally part of the treaty. Otherwise they do not bind the authorities. Accordingly, reservations or declarations accompanying the internationally valid text of the treaty bind the domestic authorities, irrespective of their inclusion in the bill of approval.

In this respect it should be noted that Greece ratified the Seventh Protocol to the Convention without any reservation. However, when the Protocol was approved by the Parliament the text of the bill of approval (Law 1705/1987) contained the following reservation:

> It is approved under the reservation that the provision of article 2, para. 1 of the approved Protocol does not affect the provision of article 489 of the Code of Penal Procedure.

This reservation is not valid on the international level and consequently should not be applied by the domestic courts when applying the Seventh Protocol. Unfortunately, Greek courts disregard this clear legal situation and apply the reservation.[8] This fact may of course give rise to the international responsibility of Greece, although as mentioned above Greece has not recognized the right of individual petition in regard to the Seventh Protocol.

According to article 28, para. 1 of the Constitution international treaties prevail over all contrary legislative provisions. According to the same article, the rule of supremacy is subject to the following conditions: (a) the treaty in question must have been approved by law; (b) the treaty must be in force; and (c) there should be an assessment of conflict between the treaty and the legislative rule. In respect of the Convention the third of the above conditions is mainly relevant. In fact the rule of supremacy is upheld by the courts only if:

a) There exists an actual contrariety. Contrariety is present when a symbiosis of the treaty and of a legislative norm within the same field of application is logically excluded. There is no contrariety if the two norms are mutually supplementary.
b) The norm which is contrary to the treaty must also be a legislative one. In fact the exact wording of the Constitution refers to a 'contrary provision of

[8] Eg Judgment 1419/1993 of the Supreme Court (Full Bench).

law', by 'law' meaning a legislative enactment. From this wording stem some important legal consequences. First, it is clear that treaties supersede any type of legislative norm, regardless of whether it emanates from a Parliamentary enactment or from an administrative act of a legislative character. Secondly, treaties supersede both anterior and posterior legislation. Thirdly, by specifying 'law' as the normative opponent of the treaty the Constitution evidently does not uphold the priority of the treaty over the provisions of the Constitution itself.

In regard to the Convention, a conflict between one of its rules and the Constitution is in fact very unlikely to occur. Indeed, the Greek Constitution provides in articles 4–25 a list of guaranteed individual freedoms and social rights. If for a particular freedom or right the Convention provides for a more extensive protection than the constitutional one this fact cannot be characterized as 'conflict'. In a similar case the Convention applies. Indeed, the constitutional protection of human rights and individual freedoms is applied insofar as no other norm provides for wider protection.

Apart from the constitutional provisions for the protection of human rights, other stipulations of the Constitution may in extreme cases conflict with a freedom guaranteed by the Convention. Such is the case of article 16, para. 5 of the Constitution which provides that university education is to be provided exclusively by public entities (universities), and para. 8, alinea (b) of the same article which provides that 'The establishment of highest schools (universities) by private individuals is prohibited'. These rules have been construed by the Greek authorities and courts as prohibiting the functioning of 'private universities', that is of entities of private law which offer university education. In view of the extremely limited number of places in Greek public universities, each year thousands of candidates are unable to enrol in a faculty. It is the opinion of this writer that the above constitutional prohibition of private university education, in connection with the factual situation of extremely limited places in Greek public universities, is in direct conflict with article 2 of the First Protocol, which stipulates that 'No person shall be denied the right to education'.[9] It is more than likely that Greek judges will uphold the constitutional prohibition, irrespective of the fact that they will incur the international responsibility of the State.

Finally, according to the Constitution, the supremacy of treaties in regard to aliens is subject to the condition of reciprocity. However, it has been accepted by Greek constitutional doctrine that this condition is not applicable insofar as it concerns multilateral treaties guaranteeing human rights, as

[9] Although the Commission considers, without any reasoning, that this right concerns primarily elementary education [See Application 5962/72, *X v U.K* (1975) 2 DR 50] we deem that there is nothing in the Convention to support such restrictive interpretation.

is the case of the Convention. In similar cases reciprocity has been substituted by a system of collective institutional control of the obligations of other member states. Unless this interpretation prevails Greek courts would violate either the Convention (requiring reciprocity for its application to aliens) or the Constitution.

In conclusion, in the hierarchy of the Greek legal order the Convention ranks between the Constitution and all legislative enactments, irrespective of the priority rule. Furthermore, according to the Greek judicial system any violation of the Convention by any organ of the state may give rise for an action either for judicial review or for annulment of the respective administrative act. Legislation adopted in violation of the Convention may be considered, by any court, as 'unconstitutional' and consequently inapplicable *in casu*.

B. THE STATUS OF THE CONVENTION IN PARLIAMENTARY PROCEEDINGS

The Convention is very rarely invoked, if at all, during Parliamentary proceedings or debates on public policy. However, draft legislation is scrutinized on the basis of the international obligations of the country by the Scientific Service of the Parliament. This Service, headed by distinguished lawyers and law professors and staffed by prominent young lawyers, prepares a report for each draft bill. These reports, which are published, often contain references to the Convention. Otherwise, one may discern in debates scattered references to the international protection of human rights, without any documented argumentation.

Frequent reference to the Convention was made during the Parliamentary proceedings for the drafting of the Constitution of 1975. In fact, the preparatory works of the Constitution in regard to the rank of international law and international treaties within the domestic legal order referred to the rank of the Convention in domestic law as the real purpose for upgrading the rank of treaties in the new Constitution.[10]

[10] One of the most prominent Greek politicians, the late A. Kanellopoulos, who at that time was a member of the Opposition, remarked during the constitutional debates in 1975 'Our party [The Union of the Centre] wishes to transform [automatically] international law to domestic law only for the treaties of human rights' (Plenary of Parliamentary Committee for the Constitution, Meeting of 24 February 1975).

C. LEADING HUMAN RIGHTS CASES DECIDED BY THE GREEK COURTS

In order to assess the evolution of Greek case-law in respect to the application of the Convention it is necessary to distinguish three historical periods: (a) the period from September 1953 when the Convention entered into force until the military coup of April 1967; (b) the period of military rule from April 1967 to July 1974; and (c) the period starting from the new Parliamentary approval of the Convention in September 1974 until today. This distinction is necessary because each period is characterized by its own historical background. Greek courts were functioning under different constitutional, legislative, but mainly psychological conditions during each of the three periods and this fact may explain—although not justify—the attitude of the Greek judiciary to the application of the Convention.

At the outset it should be noted that the period of the military dictatorship is not suitable for any appraisal of the judicial application of the Convention. During that period, although on one occasion the Council of State reacted to the authoritarian pronouncements of the ruling Colonels, courts were as a rule unable (and in most cases unwilling) to confront the illegal regime. Furthermore, the independence of the judiciary was non-existent, as the Commission ascertained in its Report on the Greek case.[11] Finally, as we shall explain below, there did not exist in the Greek judiciary any tradition of application of the Convention, even from the days of the previous constitutional regime. In conclusion, there can be no meaningful assessment of the application of the Convention during the military dictatorship, even for the first three years (April 1967– June 1970) when the Convention was formally binding on Greece.

1. 1953–67

In order to evaluate the application—or rather the non application—of the Convention by the Greek courts during the first of the periods mentioned above (1953–67) it is necessary to explain in brief the legislative climate of that era.[12] Due to the long Greek civil war (1944–49) the Government was vested with extended legislative powers, especially in regard to penal or quasi-penal legislation. Most of the enactments adopted during the period of the civil war and immediately afterwards aimed at the restriction of guarantees of personal

[11] See below, E(1).

[12] The discussion of the Greek case-law on the Convention during that period is mostly based on the work of the eminent Greek legal scholar Ph. Vegleris in: A. Sakkoulas, *The Convention on Human Rights and the Constitution* (Athens, 1977), pp. 31 et seq.

freedom as well as restrictions on the freedom of expression and even freedom of thought. These enactments were considered to be in force even after the entry into force of the Constitution of 1952. The more characteristic legislative measures of this type were as follows: (a) The institution of 'domestic exile' (forced displacement of a person and confinement to a specific small town or village, with the obligation to report daily to the local police) as an administrative measure and without any judicial process. (b) The institution of the administrative (meaning police) control of the political attitudes of any candidate for any public post. These measures as well as many other similar ones were in direct violation of the international obligations of Greece, and Greek courts were asked on many occasions to rule on their conformity with the Convention.

During the period under consideration no judgment of a Greek court applied the Convention, in the sense that it found a specific legislative or administrative measure to be in violation of the Convention. To the contrary, the Council of State in many instances rejected the eventuality of application of the Convention on various grounds. Thus, in Judgment 1796/1954 the Council of State had to examine whether a law providing as a requirement for civil servants their adherence to the 'national ideals' was in conformity with the Convention. The court rejected the argument that this legislative measure was in violation of the Convention, without providing any reasoning. In Judgment 607/1967 the same court was confronted with the claim of the applicant that the control of his political opinions—under the disguise of the control of 'legitimate behavior'—was in violation of the freedom of expression and of thought guaranteed by the Convention. The court observed that the Convention itself in para. 2 of article 9 and para. 2 of article 10 permitted restrictions to the respective rights. However, it did not bother to examine whether the permanent exclusion of citizens from the public service on the basis of their thoughts and opinions was not in reality a 'limitation' to the respective rights but a sanction of their ideas. Furthermore, the court did not examine whether the above restrictions were necessary in a democratic society, as required by the Convention.

In the same line of reasoning the Council of State in its Judgments 575–578/1966 rejected the argument of the applicants, who served in a civil transportation company, that their forced 'civil mobilization' in order to frustrate their plan for strike was in violation of article 4, para. 2 of the Convention. The court referred to article 4, para. 3, alinea c of the Convention and considered that the forced mobilization was legitimate due to the emergency 'threatening . . . the well-being of the community'. In Judgment 239/1966 the Council of State ruled that the administrative system of licences for the establishment of a non-Christian Orthodox church did not violate article 9 of the Convention. In fact in accordance with this system the establishment of any place of worship was subject to the approval of the local Orthodox Archbishop!

A number of judgments of the Council of State dealing with the administrative institution of 'domestic exile' are particularly interesting due to the interpretative distortion by the court of article 15 of the Convention. Judgment 724/1954 first invented the argument that all administrative restrictions to the personal freedom were justified, under the Convention, in view of the provision of article 15 which, according to the court, permits derogations from the Convention in case of 'public emergency threatening the life of the nation'. The court considered as an emergency of this type the civil war (although at that time the official term was 'Communist mutiny') of 1944–49. Of course there was no civil war at the time of the above Judgment but the court considered that, since there was no official act proclaiming its termination, the public emergency legally continued to exist. Unfortunately, the court did not consider whether the procedural conditions for the application of article 15 of the Convention had been met. In fact the Greek government at that time had not communicated to the Secretary General of the Council of Europe the information required under article 15, para. 3 of the Convention. Despite strong criticism from the leading Greek constitutional lawyer of that time, A. Svolos, the invention of the article 15 argument was followed by all subsequent Judgments of the same court dealing with the administrative restrictions of personal liberty (Judgments 35/1961, 182/1961, 181/1964, and 3258/70) notwithstanding the fact that the Commission had already ruled[13] that the declaration of article 15, para. 3 of the Convention was the key element for international control by the organs of the Convention.

2. 1974–94[14]

The dramatic change in the overall political, social, and legislative climate in Greece after the fall of the dictatorship was not followed by an analogous change in the attitude of the Greek courts towards the Convention. In a period of about twenty years one can locate only an extremely limited number of judgments that apply the Convention, although even the post-dictatorship legislation is full of rules that are in direct conflict with the

[13] Application 176/56, *Greece v UK* (1958–59) II Yearbook pp.176 et seq. For this case see below, E(1).

[14] The survey of judgments referring to or applying the Convention is based on judgments which have been published in the legal periodicals. Normally all judgments of the Council of State and of the Supreme Court are published. Judgments of other courts are published only if they have general interest. One cannot exclude the possibility that a judgment concerning the Convention has not been published in a legal periodical. However, this is not very likely to have happened, especially for a judgment that applied the Convention.

Convention.[15] Of course a wide variety of judgments referred to the Convention in order to rule out its application *in casu*. A number of these 'negative' judgments led to individual petitions and to decisions and judgments by the organs of the Convention and are discussed below.[16] The reluctance of Greek judges to apply the Convention is completely unjustified. First the Ministry of Justice with a Circular Letter of 3 February 1986, following the acceptance by Greece of the right to individual petition, urged all authorities 'to be especially careful in the application of the Convention so that the cases of application of article 25 be minimal'. There is also an abundance of Greek legal literature regarding the Convention. Finally, documentation in regard to the Convention is easily accessible to all judges. Consequently, the phenomenon of extended non-application of the Convention can only be attributed to the inherent reluctance of the Greek judges to accept that an international instrument may grant wider protection to the individual than the Greek Constitution.

Anyhow, many judgments have invoked provisions of the Convention, usually in conjuction with the relevant articles of the Greek Constitution.[17] However, few judgments, devote a special chapter of their reasoning to the application of the Convention. Some of the more interesting of these are as follows.

a) Permanent Military Court of Thessaloniki 38/1987. The Court ruled that a restriction of the rights of a person under detention violates article 5, para. 3 of the Convention.
b) Permanent Military Court of Athens 692/1986 (Opinion). The Court ruled that a provision of the Military Penal Code permitting the carrying on of interrogation without the presence of a lawyer violated article 6, para. 3, of the Convention.

[15] It should be noted that the democratic regime established in July 1974 and which adopted the Constitution of 1975 did not automatically abrogate all previous legislation. Many legislative measures of the military and even the pre-military era survived. Of course article 111, para. 1 of the Constitution stipulates that all legislative measures and administrative acts of a legislative character that are in conflict with the Constitution are abrogated. However, this abrogation can only be assessed by the courts on a case-by-case basis.

[16] See below, E(2).

[17] Article 5: Supreme Court 1106–7/1996 (First Chamber), Article 6: Supreme Court 143/1996 (Full Bench)—882/1995 (Fifth Chamber)—13/1991 (opinion), Council of State 1193/1995 (Sixth Chamber)—1160/1989 (Full Bench), Article 8: Supreme Court 17/1993 (Full Bench), Article 9: Supreme Court 1061/1994 (Fifth Chamber), Council of State 3356/1995 (Fifth Chamber), Article 10: Council of State 4331/1996, Article 11: Supreme Court 1061/1994 (Fifth Chamber), Article 12 : Council of State 1647/1987, Article 13: Council of State 3162/1989 (First Chamber), Article 14: Supreme Court 1061/1994 (Third Chamber), Article 1 Protocol 1: Supreme Court 1/1996, Council of State 4575/1996 (Full Bench), Article 2 Protocol 1: Council of State 3356/1995, Article 2 Protocol 7: Supreme Court 882/1995 (Fifth Chamber).

c) Council of State 867/1988 (Full Bench). The legislation at issue concerned an old legislative rule that a member of the armed forces had to apply for authorization to get married from the military authorities. The court ruled that the right to marry under article 12 of the Convention cannot be subject to authorization from the administrative authorities as to whether the individuals concerned are fit for marriage.
d) Court of Appeal of Athens 10616/1990. The Court accepted the binding force of the judgments of the European Court of Human Rights.
e) Mixed Jury Court of Appeal of Athens 718/1991. The court ruled that due to article 6 of the Convention the legislator cannot impose any restrictions on the right of judicial protection.
f) Supreme Court 30/1991 (Second Chamber). This judgment, delivered in a case concerning the strike of the employees of the Public Electricity Company (DEH), referred to article 6, para. 1 of the Convention about the right of each party in civil proceedings to have adequate time to prepare their arguments.
g) Council of State 1545/1995 (Full Bench). The Court ruled that a restriction on leaving the country because of debts to the state and the Social Security Fund contravenes neither article 5 of the Convention nor article 1 of Protocol 1.

The dearth of judgments applying the Convention does not signify that human rights are not enforced in Greece. Courts tend to grand the protection provided by the Constitution and prefer to refer to the constitutional guarantee than to the Convention. For example, in Judgment 1802/1986 (Third Chamber) the Council of State found that legislative restrictions on the expression of views by members of the armed forces are in conflict both with article 14, para. 1 of the Constitution, guaranteeing freedom of expression, and with article 10 of the Convention. However the court annulled a disciplinary act of the military authorities, which was adopted on the basis of the above legislation, as contrary to the Constitution. This attitude is normal since the Constitution ranks higher than the Convention and the moment a court finds that a measure or act violates the highest norm it does not consider it necessary to examine the same act on the basis of another norm. However, this attitude may prove erroneous in cases where courts confirm the constitutionality of a measure or act. Indeed, in some cases Greek courts tend to consider the protection of the Convention as equivalent to the constitutional protection, which of course is not at all true. Furthermore, whereas there is no sanction for a misapplication of a constitutional norm,[18] the misapplica-

[18] The Constitution provides for the Supreme Special Court to resolve, *inter alia*, disputes on constitutionality if the Supreme Court and the Council of State adopt conflicting solutions on a constitutionality issue. These cases are very rare.

tion of the Convention may lead to international control. Therefore, the tendency of the Greek courts to disregard the Convention in case they accept the constitutionality of a particular measure is not compatible with the Convention.

During the same period there are many judgments of the Greek courts rejecting claims that a particular legislative rule violates the Convention. Irrespective of whether the final finding of similar judgments can be considered as correct or not, the fact is that, as a rule, the legal reasoning is either non-existent or very poor. Judgments refer neither to the case-law of the organs of the Convention,[19] nor to doctrinal views, and their considerations about the Convention are laconic and very short. The long list of legislative and administrative measures whose legality in regard to the Convention has been upheld by Greek courts includes (a) the institution of civil mobilization [Council of State 575/1966 (Full Bench)]; (b) the deprivation of personal liberty for tax debts (Supreme Court 1753/1983 (First Chamber); (c) the obligation for the parties to judicial review proceedings to present their case through a lawyer [Supreme Court 724/1992 and 868/1992 (Full Bench)—Council of State 993/1991 (First Chamber)—Supreme Special Court 1/1993]; and (d) the maximum term for preventive detention (Supreme Court 1320/1991–Opinion).

D. CASES BROUGHT BEFORE THE EUROPEAN COMMISSION AND THE COURT OF HUMAN RIGHTS

1. *Inter-state Cases*

Greece has twice been involved in inter-state proceedings, once as an applicant and once as a respondent.

The very first inter-state cases brought before the Commission were initiated by Greece against the United Kingdom. [Applications Nos. 176/56 of 7 May 1956 (*First Cyprus* case) and 299/57 of 17 July 1957 (*Second Cyprus* case)]. The applications concerned the situation in Cyprus, which at that time was a British colony. By mid-1955 an anticolonial wave swept the island of Cyprus and the British authorities applied very repressive measures against the revolting Cypriots. These measures, including collective punishments, whipping, and the prohibition of certain newspapers, were in direct violation

[19] In one occasion the Supreme Court referred to a Report of the Commission, dated 6 June 1991 (without the name of the case or the number of the application) in order to assess that the Convention does not, in principle, require that judicial pronouncements be reasoned: Judgment 656/1992 (Full Bench).

of the Convention. On 7 October 1955 the United Kingdom informed the Secretary General of the Council of Europe that the Convention was being disapplied on the island of Cyprus due to public emergency threatening the life of the nation. Greece, by its applications, requested the Commission to ascertain the misuse of article 15 of the Convention and to find that the UK had violated a number of rights guaranteed by the Convention.

The Commission adopted its Report on the first case on 26 September 1958. The Report remained confidential. However, in February 1959 an overall settlement of the Cypriot question was agreed in Zurich and London, and Cyprus became an independent state. In view of this evolution the Committee of Ministers adopted its Resolution (59)12 of 20 April 1959 with which it decided that there was no reason to take any further action for this case.

As to the second case the parties, in view of the Zurich settlement, requested the Commission to refrain from any further procedural action. This situation was confirmed by Resolution (59)32 of 14 December 1959 of the Committee of Ministers.

Greece was involved as defendant in the only inter-state case that had to do with a military dictatorship in a member-state of the Council of Europe. The applicants were Denmark, Norway, and Sweden who filed their applications against Greece on 20 September 1967 (Applications 3321/67, 3322/67 and 3323/67). They were joined on 27 September 1967 with the application from the Netherlands (Application 3344/67). The facts of these cases can be summarized as follows.[20]

As mentioned above, on 21 April 1967 a military dictatorship was established in Greece. The Parliament was dissolved and the Constitution was suspended as to its most important provisions. The military rule did not recognize any human rights in law. So far as administrative practice was concerned, the police and the military were acting without any legal restriction, arresting and torturing politicians and laymen who were considered to be democrats. This situation was almost immediately considered as intolerable within the various institutions of the Council of Europe, although the Greek military government had informed the Secretary General of the Council of Europe on 3 May 1967 that it was invoking article 15 of the Convention. The

[20] The most extensive presentation of the procedure before the Commission of the above cases is the one by Ph. Vegleris and A. Kiss, 'L'affaire grecque devant le Conseil de l' Europe et la Commission europeenne des droits de l' homme', in *Annuaire Français de Droit International*, 1971, pp. 890–931. In Greek see the presentation by S. Perrakis, *The international protection of human rights* (Athens, Komotini, 1984) pp. 339 et seq. See also from a political perspective D. Constas, *The Greek Case Before the Council of Europe* (Athens, 1976). A comprehensive summary of the inter-state cases against Greece, with exact references to the documents of the Commission, is provided in the Stock-Taking of the European Convention on Human Rights (The first thirty years: 1954 until 1984), Strasbourg 1984, pp. 9 et seq.

first institutional reaction in this respect was Resolution 346 of June 23 1967, of the Permanent Commission of the Parliamentary (at that time: Consultative) Assembly. The Resolution, after expressing the serious concern of the Assembly for the situation in Greece, urged governments to refer to the Commission violations of human rights by the Greek military government, in application of article 24 of the Convention.

The immediate response to the above Resolution were the four inter-State applications mentioned above. In their applications the claimant governments alleged that Greece had violated articles 5, 6, 8, 9, 10, 11, 13, and 14 of the Convention.[21] Furthermore they alleged that the invocation of article 15 of the Convention by the Greek military government was not justified. The applicants extended the scope of their application at a later stage, alleging violations of articles 3 and 7 of the Convention and 1 and 3 of the Additional Protocol.

On 24 January 1968 the Commission found the applications to be admissible as to the first package of violations, and on 31 March 1968 as to the second package. Following the admissibility stage the Commission established a Sub-Commission for the administration of evidence. The Sub-Commission received oral and written submissions from the parties and, in five sessions in 1968 and 1969, heard eighty-seven witnesses. Following a rather adventurous on-site examination in Athens the Sub-Commission adopted its Report on 4 October 1969. The Report was confirmed by the Commission, which communicated it on 18 November 1968 to the Committee of Ministers. Although the Report was confidential it was leaked to the press. This event caused the Greek military Government to react with a *note verbale* of 7 December 1969, stating that the Commission had violated almost all procedural rules and that the Report was null and not binding.

The Report of the Commission on the 'Greek case' is one of the most extensive in the Commission's history. In four volumes and after elaborate consideration of the evidence, the Commission established the violations of the Convention by the Greek military rulers. First, it did not accept the argument of the respondent government that in April 1967 Greece was threatened by a public danger such as is described in article 15 of the Convention. Furthermore, in 430 pages the Commission described the violations of article 3 of the Convention. All in all the Commission found that the military government of Greece had violated nine articles of the Convention as well as article 3 of the Additional Protocol. It did not find any violation of article 7 of the Convention nor of article 1 of the Additional Protocol.

[21] S. Perrakis, op. cit. p. 410 considers it strange that the applicants did not invoke article 17 of the Convention.

The aftermath of the Greek cases, with the withdrawal of Greece from the Council of Europe, has been described above.[22] On 18 April 1970 the Committee of Ministers adopted Resolution DH(70)1, by fifteen votes of the total seventeen member-states present. France and Cyprus did not participate in the voting. With the said Resolution the Committee of Ministers endorsed the Report of the Commission, urged the Greek government to restore rights and freedoms in Greece without delay, and decided to publish the Report. Indeed, the publication of the Report was the only meaningful sanction available to the Committee of Ministers in this case. Following the restoration of democracy in Greece and the return of Greece to the Council of Europe, the Committee of Ministers adopted on 26 November 1974 Resolution DH (74)2, by which the Committee decided to discontinue the examination of these cases.

On 10 April 1970, Denmark, Norway, and Sweden filed before the Commission a new inter-state application against Greece (Application No 4448/70). The application concerned violations of articles 3 and 6 of the Convention, during the year 1969 and the beginning of 1970, in regard to the 'trial' of an anti-dictatorship organization called 'Democratic Defence'. The applicants had reason to believe that the Greek military regime would impose the death penalty upon some of the defendants and requested the intervention of the President of the Commission with the Greek authorities in order to suspend any eventual execution.[23] However, Greece refused to participate in the proceedings before the Commission, claiming that the denunciation of the Convention absolved her from any respective obligation. The Commission on 26 May 1970 adopted an interim 'Report on the actual stage of the procedure', with which it considered the application as admissible *ratione temporis*.[24]

The lack of any procedural co-operation from the Greek authorities obliged the Commission to inform the Committee of Ministers that it could not effectively exercise its duties in regard to the application in question. In fact the Commission adopted on 5 October 1970 a rather peculiar Report, in the sense that it did not contain the elements specified in article 31, para. 1 of the Convention. The Commission asked the Committee of Ministers to take note of the Report but decided not to publish it. The Committee of Ministers considered the Report in April 1971 and, in their Statutory Report of 26 April 1971 to the Consultative Assembly, described the action taken by the

[22] See above, Introduction.

[23] The military court finally did not impose any death penalties in regard to members of the Democratic Defence.

[24] In accordance with article 65 of the Convention Greece was bound by the Convention until 13 June 1970.

Commission and stated that they had decided to take note of the Report. Following the restoration of democracy in Greece and the new approval of the Convention by the Greek Parliament, the Commission resumed its consideration of this case. On 14 July 1976 the Commission decided to comply with the request of all the parties and closed the proceedings in the case. A short Report, for information purposes, was sent to the Committee of Ministers.

2. Individual petitions

As mentioned above, Greece recognized the right of individual petition on 20 November 1985 for all violations after that date. However, neither Greek lawyers nor private citizens were much aware in Greece of this new international legal remedy. Moreover, only a few were familiar with the substantive and procedural prerequisites for an individual petition. In fact the very first individual petition against Greece (application 12185/86) was considered inadmissible by the Commission due the non-exhaustion of local remedies. The peculiarity of this case is that the applicant was himself a lawyer and a professor of law, who withdrew his appeal to the Greek Supreme Court (which would have satisfied the local remedy rule) just before filing his application with the Commission.

The nature of the overall Greek legislation, which for decades was promulgated without regard to the Convention, gave rise to hundreds of individual petitions by Greek citizens or persons under the Greek jurisdiction. A great number of them were found by the Commission to be manifestly unfounded, and a great number more were not pursued by the applicants themselves. The cases that were finally examined by the Commission on the merits and in which a violation was found refer to very important aspects of the Greek legislation.[25] By the end of the year 1994 the Commission had considered as admissible a total of 122 individual petitions against the Greek government. By July 1998 this number has already become 147. As regards the Court, by July 1998 thirty-seven cases had been adjudicated.

In two of them [*Stamoulakatos v Greece*, Application 12086/87 and *Kefalas and Others v Greece*, Application 14726/89] the Court found that it did not have jurisdiction *ratione temporis*. Some of the other thirty-five cases in which the Court found a violation of the Convention are presented in the following paragraphs. During the same time the Commission has rejected, one way or the other, more than two hundred applications.

[25] The summaries of the facts of the cases reported below are taken, sometimes verbatim, either from the summaries drafted by the Registrar of the Court or from the summaries contained in the judgments.

Cases adjudicated by the Court

Case of Philis v Greece (Judgment of 27 August 1991). The applicant, an engineer in Athens, carried on a number of projects for installations of central-heating and electro-mechanical equipment on the account of various clients. When his fees were not paid he started several actions via the Technical Chamber of Greece. In one case, however, he went directly to court. That action was dismissed on the ground that Greek legislation (Royal Decree 30/1956) provided that the Technical Chamber had sole capacity to bring claims for recovery of fees owed to engineers.

The applicant lodged with the Commission three applications (Applications 12750/87, 13780/88, and 14003/88) complaining that the above legislation violated article 6, paras. 1, 13, and 14 of the Convention and Article 1 of the Additional Protocol. In particular he maintained that he had not had a fair trial before an independent and impartial tribunal within a reasonable time; he also complained of a violation of his right of access to a court, on the ground that the Technical Chamber of Greece had been subrogated *ex officio* to his right to recover the remuneration due in respect of a number of projects which he had designed.

On 8 May 1990 the Commission adopted its Report and on 21 May 1990 it referred the case to the Court. The Commission declared admissible only the allegations concerning the right of access to a court, the length of the proceedings, and article 13 of the Convention. The Court found by eight votes to one (Judge Pettiti dissenting) that there had been a violation of the right of access to a court, guaranteed under article 6, para. 1 of the Convention and ruled that it was necessary to examine the other allegations of the applicant. The Court also unanimously awarded to the applicant 1,000,000 drachma for non-pecuniary damages and 6,800,000 drachma for expenses (in total about US$ 31,000).

Case of Hadjianastasiou v Greece (Judgment of 16 December 1992, Series A N. 252–A). The applicant, Mr. Hadjianastasiou, an aeronautical engineer and a Greek citizen, was an officer of the Greek Air Force. On 22 October 1984 he was found guilty by the Permanent (Military) Air Force Court of Athens of having disclosed military secrets, because he had communicated a study on guided missiles to a private company. The court considered that the study contained elements of a previous study which the applicant had carried out for the Air Force. The applicant appealed to the Martial Appeal Court which, following a hearing, examined *in camera* a list of questions, which it answered either 'yes' or 'no'. The judgment, read out in open court, found the applicant guilty of disclosing military secrets of minor importance and sentenced him to five months' imprisonment.

On 26 November 1985 the applicant appealed to the Greek Supreme Court on the ground of 'erroneous application and interpretation' of the relevant provisions of the Military Criminal Code. However, it was not until January 1986 that he received a copy of the record of the proceedings before the Martial Appeal Court, setting out the specific reasons for his conviction. Although the applicant submitted a testimonial specifying that he had not received the full text of the judgment sentencing him, and did so within the time limit set for an appeal in review (five days), the Greek Supreme Court declared the appeal inadmissible, finding that the grounds stated were too vague.

The applicant lodged a complaint with the Commission (Application 12945/87) on 17 December 1986, alleging violations of article 6, paras. 1 and 3(b) and article 10 of the Convention. More particularly he complained that the lack of reasons in the judgment of the Courts Martial Appeal Court and the shortness of the time-limit for appealing had prevented him from further substantiating his appeal to the Supreme Court. He maintained in addition that his conviction for the disclosure of military secrets of secondary importance had infringed his right to freedom of expression guaranteed under article 10 of the Convention. The Commission drew up a Report on 6 June 1991 in which it expressed the unanimous opinion that there had been a violation of article 6, paras. 1 and 3(b), but not of article 10 of the Convention. The case was referred to the Court on 12 July 1991.

The Court unanimously decided that his rights to defend the case against him had been subject to such restrictions that he had not had the benefit of a fair trial. However, it did not find a violation of article 10 of the Convention. The Court awarded the applicant for costs and expenses 29,260 French francs and 520,000 drachmas.

Case of Papamichalopoulos and Others v Greece (Judgment of 24 June 1993, Series A No. 260–B). By a law adopted a few months after the military dictatorship, the Greek State transferred an area of 1,165,000 square miles of beach in Attica to the Navy Fund. The transfer of the land took place on the assumption that it was public forest and consequently belonged to the state. Ten of the applicants who owned part of this land (approximately 165,000 square miles) started a series of actions before the courts to obtain the return of their land or compensation. Although on several occasions their property rights were acknowledged, until 1988 the applicants had neither acquired possession of their land nor received any compensation for its loss.

The applicants applied to the Commission on 7 November 1988 (Application 14556/89). They relied on article 1 of the Additional Protocol, alleging that their land had been unlawfully occupied by the Navy Fund since 1967 and that to date they had not been able either to resume possession or to obtain compensation. The Commission, in its Report adopted on 9 April

1992, expressed the unanimous opinion that there had been a violation of article 1 of Protocol No. 1. The Commission transferred the case to the Court on 25 May 1992.

The Court unanimously held that there had been and continued to be a breach of article 1 of Protocol No. 1. It deferred its decision on article 50 of the Convention, although the Commission suggested a just satisfaction of about 621 million drachmas (about US$ 248,000) plus expenses. It is interesting to note that the Court declared that the Greek government was estopped from pleading the applicants' lack of victim status and failure to exhaust domestic remedies, since the respective objections were not raised before the Commission.

The judgment on the award of 'just satisfaction' was eventually delivered on 31 October 1995. The Court unanimously decided that the Greek state should return to the applicants, within six months, the land in issue, including the buildings on it. Failing such restitution, it was to pay the applicants 5,551,000,000 Greek drachmas in respect of pecuniary damage. It was also to pay them 6,300,000 Greek drachmas in respect of costs and expenses. Lastly, it was to pay the experts 36,000,000 Greek drachmas in respect of the costs and fees for writing their report on the value of the land.

Case of Kokkinakis v Greece (Judgment of 25 May 1993, Series A No. 260–A). Mr Kokkinakis, a Greek citizen born into an Orthodox family, became a Jehovah's Witness in 1936. He was then arrested more than sixty times for proselytism, which according to the Greek penal legislation (Section 4 of Law No. 1363/1938), is a criminal offence. Between 1936 and 1952 he was also convicted of the same crime on several occasions. On 2 March 1986 he and his wife called at the home of Mrs Kyriakaki, in Sitia (a town in the island of Crete) and engaged in a discussion with her, attempting also to sell to her some booklets of their faith. Mrs Kyriakaki's husband, who was the cantor at a local Orthdox church, informed the police, who arrested Mr and Mrs Kokkinakis. The couple were convicted by a criminal court on 20 May, 1986. The Crete Court of Appeal acquitted the wife but upheld the conviction of Mr Kokkinakis. An appeal by Mr Kokkinakis to the Supreme Court was dismissed.

Mr Kokkinakis applied to the Commission on 22 August 1988 (Application 14307/88) claiming that his conviction for proselytism was in breach of the rights secured by articles 7, 9, and 10 of the Convention. The Commission adopted its Report on 3 December 1991 and expressed the unanimous opinion that there had been a violation of article 9 of the Convention. It rejected by a majority the allegations of the applicant that there had been a violation of articles 7 and 10 of the Convention.

In its judgment the Court held by six votes to three that there had been a violation of article 9 of the Convention (Judges Valticos, Foighel, and Loizou dissented). It found that the conviction of the applicant had not been shown as justified in the circumstances of the case by a pressing social need. Consequently, the legislative and judicial measures taken against the applicant in order to restrict his freedom to manifest his religion were not, according to the Court, necessary in a democratic society. The Court rejected the allegations of the applicant concerning violations of articles 7 and 10 of the Convention and awarded to him about US$ 12,800 for non-pecuniary damage and expenses.

Case of Larissis and Others v Greece (Judgment of February 24, 1998; (1999) 27 EHRR, 329). Together with the above case of *Kokkinakis*, the similar case of *Larissis and Others* deserves mention since it also concerns unjustified punishment for proselytizing according to section 4 of Law 1363/1938. In this second case, the applicants were at all material times officers in the Greek Air Force and followers of the Pentocostal Church. They all allegedly approached various airmen serving under them, all of whom were Orthodox Christians, and spoke to them about the teachings of the Pentecostal Church. In addition, two of the applicants attempted to convert a number of civilians. On 18 May 1992 the applicants stood trial before the Permanent Air Force Court of Athens, which dismissed their objection that section 4 of Law 1363/1938 was unconstitutional and convicted them of various offences of proselytism against airmen and civilians. They appealed and the Martial Appeal Court upheld the first judgment but reduced the length of their terms of imprisonment. Finally, the Court of Cassation dismissed their appeal on points of law, and held that section 4 did not contravene either the provisions of the Greek Constitution, which enshrine the principle of *nullem crimen sine lege certa* and the right to religious freedom, or article 9 of the Convention.

Mr Larissis, Mr Mandalarides, and Mr Sarantis applied to the Commision on 28 January 1994, and on 12 September 1996 the Commision adopted its Report expressing the opinion that there had been a violation of article 9. In its judgment the Court found no violation of article 9 in relation to the conviction of the applicants for proselytizing the airmen, but it did find such a violation in respect of the civilians. Furthermore, the Court rejected the allegations of the applicants concerning violation of articles 7 and 10. It awarded 500,000 Greek drachmas for non-pecuniary damage.

Case of Stran Greek Refinieries etc v Greece (Judgment of 9 December 1994, Series A No. 301–B). Under a contract concluded on 22 July 1972 (during the military dictatorship) between the Greek state and Mr Andreadis (a well known banker) the latter undertook to build and, through a company to be set up subsequently, to operate an oil refinery in Greece. The state, which had undertaken to acquire the land on which the refinery was to be built, ratified the contract in a decree published in the Official Gazette; but it failed to discharge its obligation.

On 14 October 1977 (after the restoration of democracy in Greece) the government terminated the contract, under Law 141/1975 which provided for the termination of preferential contracts concluded under the military regime. An arbitration which took place subsequently issued an award on 27 February 1984 against the Greek state and in favour of the Stran Company (the Company established by Andreadis in order to carry out the initial contract). The award declared the claims of Stran Company to be well founded for an amount of about US$ 18,000,000.

The state challenged the award before the courts but the courts found against the state. On 25 May 1987 when the case was pending before the Supreme Court and after the judge rapporteur had already sent to the parties his opinion, which was favourable to the applicants, the Greek Parliament passed Law 1701/1987 which provided that all clauses, including arbitration clauses, in preferential contracts concluded under the military regime were revoked and that any arbitration award was null and void. The same Law provided also that all claims arising from the termination of these contracts were statute-barred. The Supreme Court held that this Law was constitutional and set aside all previous judgments in favour of the applicants.

The applicants applied to the Commission on 20 November 1987 (Application 13427/87). They maintained that there had been a breach of article 6, para. 1 of the Convention inasmuch as they had not had a fair trial within a reasonable time. They claimed further that as a result of the length and the dilatory nature of the proceedings and of the provisions of Law 1701/1987 their right of property guaranteed under article 1 of Protocol No. 1 had been infringed. The Commission adopted its Report on 12 May 1993 and held unanimously that there had been a violation of article 6, para. 1 of the Convention and of article 1 of Protocol No. 1. The case was referred by the Commission to the Court on 12 July 1993.

A unanimous Court ruled in favour of the applicants. At the beginning the Court rejected the preliminary objection of the Greek government that the local remedies rule had not been complied with by the applicants. It held that:

> when a State relies on the exhaustion rule, it must indicate with sufficient clarity the effective remedies to which the applicants have not had recourse; in this area it is not for the Convention bodies to cure of their own motion any shortcomings or lack of precision in respondent States' arguments.

The Court further held that the provisions of article 6, para. 1 had been violated, as the enactment of Law 1701/1987 at a time when proceedings between the parties were pending constituted an unjustified interference by the state in the administration of justice. In an important consideration it held that:

The principle of the rule of law and the notion of fair trial enshrined in Article 6 preclude any interference by the legislature with the administration of justice designed to influence the judicial determination of the dispute.

The Court also found that there had been a violation of article 1 of Protocol No. 1 since the debt owed to the applicants constituted a 'possession' and that the enactment of legislation rendering it impossible for them to get satisfaction for the debt constituted an interference with this possession. The Court, while recognizing the right of the State to terminate contracts paying compensation, ruled that:

it would be unjust if every legal relationship entered into with a dictatorial regime was regarded as invalid when the ragime came to an end [and that] the unilateral termination of a contract does not take effect in relation to certain essential clauses of the contract, such as the arbitration clause.

Finally, the Court held that the applicants were entitled to reimbursement of the sums accorded by the arbitral award.

Case of the Holy Monasteries v Greece (Judgment of 9 December 1994, Series A No. 301–A). A number of Greek monasteries accumulated a considerable amount of real property, mainly through donations. According to legislation dating back to 1930, this property was administered by a Church institution, the ODEP, the members of whose board of governors were appointed by the Holy Synod (the highest organ of the Greek Orthodox Church). Law 1700/1987 changed this regime and gave exclusive representation and management rights over the monasteries' property to ODEP. However, the same Law provided that the majority of the ODEP board would be appointed by the state and that the state would automatically be the owner of the above property unless the monasteries, within a six-month period, produced either a duly registered title deed or a final court decision against the state.

The monasteries applied to the Commission in two groups. The first group applied on 16 July 1987 (Application 13092/87) and the second group on 15 May 1988 (Application 13984/88). They relied on articles 6, 9, 11, 13, and 14 of the Convention and on article 1 of Protocol No. 1. The Commission adopted its Report on 14 January 1993 and in most of the headings of the application it expressed the unanimous opinion that there had been no violation of the Convention or the Additional Protocol. In one heading the same finding was by a majority. The Commission referred the case to the Court on 7 April 1993.

The Court did not follow the Commission. It held unanimously that the 1987 Law constituted a deprivation of the peaceful enjoyment of the property of the applicants. This interference with the property rights of the applicants, although pursuing, according to the Court, a legitimate aim, could be said to be proportionate as the law did not provide for the payment of any compensation. Consequently, the Court found a violation of article 1 of Protocol No. 1 but rejected all other claims by the applicants. Finally, the Court awarded the applicants costs and expenses but reserved the question of the amount of compensation due to them.

This matter was arranged following the conclusion of a friendly settlement between the Greek government and the applicant monasteries, and the Court, by its judgment of 1 September 1997, decided to strike the case from its list.

Case of Manoussakis and Others v Greece (Judgment of 26 September 1996, Reports 1996–IV, Vol. 17). The four applicants in this case were all Jehovah's Witnesses and lived in Crete. In March 1983 they rented a hall to be used 'for all kinds of meetings, weddings, etc of Jehovah's Witnesses'. Then they applied to the Ministry of Education and Religious Affairs for permission to use the hall as a place of worship. The Ministry informed them that their application was being considered, but that procedure was never completed. Meanwhile, the applicants were prosecuted under section 1 of Law 136/1938, as amended by Law 1672/1939, on the ground that they had 'established a place of worship fer religious meetings and ceremonies without authorization from the recognized ecclesiastical authorities and the Minister of Education and Religious Affairs'. The applicants were aquitted by the Criminal Court of First Instance, but found guilty by the Criminal Appeal Court.

The four applicants addressed themselves to Strasbourg on 7 August 1991 (Application 18748/91) and the Commission expressed on 25 May 1995 the unanimous opinion that there had been a breach of article 9. The Court agreed with the Commission and awarded the applicants 4,030,100 Greek drachmas in respect of their costs and expenses.

Along with the above judgment, one has to cite the case of *Pentidis and Others v Greece* (Judgment of 9 June 1997) which deals with the same matter of using a building as a place of worship without prior authorization and which was finally struck off the list of the Court, since the applicants were granted the authorization they sought.

Case of Ahmet Sadik v Greece (Judgment of 15 November 1996, (1996) 24 EHRR 323). This case concerned an activist of the Muslim minority in Western Thrace, who was a doctor, a publisher of a Turkish-language newspaper, and a member of the Greek Parliament. Mr Sadik died on 24 July 1995 in a traffic accident near Komoniti. During his election campaign in October 1989 the applicant, being also at that time a member of the Greek Parliament, distributed leaflets containing *inter alia* references to the 'Turkish minority' of Western Thrace. He was subsequently charged wuth electoral deception, because in his leaflets he had mentioned that the candidates of the main political parties had created a climate of terror and anarchy among the Muslim population. He was further charged with 'disturbing the peace' by open or indirect incitement to violence and by provoking rifts among the population through the use of the noun 'Turk' or the adjective 'Turkish' in connection with the Muslims of Western Thrace. Mr Sadik was aquitted of electoral deception but found guilty of disturbing the peace. The Court of Appeal stated that the applicant had deliberately described the Greek Muslims of Western Thrace as 'Turks', although he knew that the 1923 Treaty of Lausanne recognized only a religious (Muslim) minority and not an ethnic (Turkish) minority. In the meantime, at the end of January 1990, violent disorder broke out on Komotini, numerous shops were damaged, and a Christian was killed by a Muslim in a hospital. Then, Mr Sadik applied to the Commission on 11 July 1991 (Application 18877/91) and the Commission expressed on 4 April 1995 the opinion that there had been a violation of article 10. The applicant, as mentioned above, was killed in the meantime, but the proceedings were continued by his heirs, widow, and children. However, the application was dismissed by the Court due to non-exhaustion of domestic remedies and because Mr Sadik had not raised before the national courts, even in substance, the complaint relating to a violation of article 10.

Case of Katikaridis and Others v Greece; Case of Tsomtsos and Others v Greece (Judgments of 15 November 1996). These cases concern two separate applications (19385/92 and 20680/92) and two indepedent judgments of the Court, but deal with very similar facts and with the same legal reasoning.

The issue at stake was in both cases the presumption created by Law 653/1977, namely that the benefit obtained from road improvements amounted to sufficient compensation. Thus it had been impossible for the applicants to obtain compensation in full for the expropriation of part of their properties fronting a major road, since it had been considered by national courts and under Law 653/1977 that they derive from the road-widening an economic benefit that would offset the property loss. The Court found that there existed a breach of article 1 of Protocol No. 1 and reserved the award of pecuniary damage in both cases.

There are other interesting cases. A group of them concerns Jehovah's Witnesses: the cases of *Valsamis* and *Efstratiou*, Judgments of 18 December 1996, were about the refusal of children of Jehovah's Witnesses to take part in school National Day Parade, and the case of *Georgiadis*, Judgment of 2 May 1997, was about a Religious Minister of Jehovah's Witnesses who refused military service and was thus imprisoned. Another remarkable judgment was delivered on 19 March 1997 in the case of *Hornsby v Greece*, referring to the right of Community citizens to set up in Greece foreign-language schools and the failure of administrative authorities to comply with judgments of the Council of State. Of the most recent ones, one should stand to the case of *Sidiropoulos and others v Greece*, where the Court concluded in its judgment of 10 July 1998 that the inhabitants of a region of a country, including Greek Makedonia, are entitled to form associations in order to promote the region's special characteristics.

Recent cases before the Court of Human Rights including the following. 1) In *Iatridis v Greece* (Application 31107/96) concerning allegations about the occupation of property by a town council without compensation for almost ten years and without a final decision on legality the Court found a violation of article 1 of Protocol No. 1 and article 13 of the Convention (judgment of 25 March 1999); 2) *Papachelas v Greece* (Application 31423/96), a case similar to the above presented ones of *Katikaridis* and *Tsomtsos* the Court found again a violation of article 1 of Protocol No. 1 and reserved the question of just satisfaction (judgment of 25 March 1999). Following a friendly settlement, the case was eventually struck out of the list (judgment of 4 April 2000).

Finally, it is noteworthy to mention the case of *Former King Constantine of Greece and eight members of his family v Greece*, which after an oral hearing on 21 April 1998 was declared admissible only for the complaint concerning the property issue. In its judgment of 23 November 2000, the Court found a violation of article 1 of Protocol No. 1 (Application 25701/94).

E. REMEDIAL ACTION

As analysed above, in several cases the Court has ruled against Greece. The Greek government has already complied with several of them, ie judgment of the Court in the *Philis* case, and with the Resolutions of the Committee of Ministers concerning the *Papaioannou* case, the *Andreadis* case and the *Kokkinakis* case. In general, Greece is taking some measures to modernize its penal legislation, taking into account the provisions of the Convention. The most characteristic of these measures is the enactment of a new Code of Military Penal Procedure.

F. ASSESSMENT AND PROSPECTS

Despite the fact that Greece has been a member of the Convention since 1950 (with an interruption in 1970–74) the impact of the Convention upon everyday legal practice is unfortunately minimal. As explained above, Greek courts tend to disregard the Convention on the erroneous assumption that constitutional protection suffices to remedy all injustices. Moreover, the Parliament is not giving the Convention the necessary consideration. Finally, the government has not made any institutional input regarding the requirements of the Convention. Some efforts to organize a special service within the Legal Service of the Ministry of Foreign Affairs, which would deal with individual applications against Greece and would consult the government on the necessary remedial action, failed when in 1992 questions regarding the Convention were assigned to the Legal Council of the State, a body of state legal counsellors. However, the members of the above Council, with a traditional national view of the obligations of the state, have proved unable to perform the role of serious advisers to the government on human rights cases. Due to this handicap the representation of the Greek government before the organs of the Convention is, to say the least, inadequate. One positive development is, however, the establishment of a Human Rights Directorate within the Ministry of Foreign Affairs.

In complete contrast to the above picture, legal discussion about the Convention is flourishing in Greece. The international protection of human rights is presently taught as a separate course in all three law faculties in Greece and in some faculties of political science. Legal periodicals frequently publish doctrinal articles about the Convention as well as commentaries and observations on the main judgments of the Court. Seminars and colloquia about the Convention are frequent and there are at least two research centres, one in Thessaloniki and one in Athens, that deal permanently with projects concerning the Convention. It is hoped that sooner or later the seeds of this activity will produce tangible results. Lawyers familiar with the Convention will, in the near future, influence governmental decision-makers, and then the Convention will play a more important role in the minds of legislators and judges in Greece.

16

Hungary

HANNA BOKOR-SZEGÖ AND MÓNIKA WELLER

INTRODUCTION

The radical political and economic transformation which took place in Hungary in 1989–90 has led to the establishment of a pluralistic democracy.

As a result of this evolution, legal order in Hungary had basically come into harmony, even prior to the ratification or the European Convention on Human Rights, with the norms of this Convention. The provisions of the Hungarian Constitution in force concerning human rights[1] are concordant with those of the European Convention. The same can be stated in respect of several Acts of fundamental importance adopted before 1990. Such are the Acts on the freedom of association,[2] on the freedom of assembly,[3] on the functioning and management of political parties,[4] and on freedom of thought, conscience, and religion.[5]

A. THE STATUS OF THE CONVENTION IN NATIONAL LAW

According to Article 7(1) of the Hungarian Constitution:

The legal system of the Republic of Hungary shall respect the generally accepted rules of international law, and shall ensure harmony between the assumed international law obligations and domestic laws.

Thus, on one hand, the Constitution recognizes the general norms of international law, while in respect of international treaties, it only ensures the basic harmony between domestic law and these treaties. It is to be added that the terms used in the above-quoted Articles of the Constitution have been

[1] General Provisions, Articles 1 and 8.
[2] Act No. II of 1989.
[3] Acts Nos. III and IV of 1989.
[4] Act No. XXXII of 1989.
[5] Act No. IV of 1990.

interpreted also by the Hungarian Constitutional Court (in its decision No. 53/1993, Item III. a–b) as the reception into Hungary of the general rules of international law. Since it is well known that there is no exhaustive catalogue of the general principles of international law in any document related to international law, the terms used in the first part of Article 7(1) of the Hungarian Constitution—just like the similar provisions contained in the constitutions of other countries—have to be considered rather as the manifestation of the country's commitment to international law. Therefore, these terms can be primarily interpreted as a guideline to Hungary's foreign policy. This opinion is confirmed by the fact that Hungarian courts do not refer directly to one or the other general norm of international law as the source of law upon which their jurisdiction has been based.

In practice, the Constitution applies the dualist doctrine in respect of international treaties. International treaties are not regarded at present as directly applicable in Hungary.

As far as the 'incorporation' of international treaties into the Hungarian legal order is concerned, the following can be stated. Article 7(2) of the Constitution declares that the process of legislation shall be regulated by an Act. However, there has been no new enactment on this subject since 1989–90. Even today, Act No. XI of 1987 is still valid, which virtually adopted the construction of Law-Decree No. 27 of 1982, as it declares in Section 16(1): 'International treaties containing general rules of conduct shall be promulgated by legal rules appropriate to their content'.

It follows clearly from this provision that an international treaty containing general rules of conduct is to be 'incorporated' individually into domestic law. This provision requires a further, more precise definition with respect to the field of human rights.

Article 8(2) of the Hungarian Constitution stipulates that:

> In the Republic of Hungary, the rules pertaining to fundamental rights and obligations shall be determined by law which, however, shall not limit the substantial contents of any fundamental right.

Hence, in conformity with the Constitution, international treaties concerning the protection of human rights have to be promulgated in the form of Acts: ie 'incorporated' into Hungarian law by individual acts. The authorities, including the courts, will not apply the international treaties directly: in each case the corresponding Hungarian domestic law will be applied.

As for the status in Hungarian law of the European Convention on Human Rights, the following applies. At its session of 30 October 1990, the Hungarian Parliament adopted a Resolution (No. 76/1990) on the signature of the European Convention on Human Rights. The Convention, together with its nine Additional Protocols, was signed by Hungary on 6 November 1990. As referred to above, the Hungarian Constitution and the Acts defining fundamental human rights and freedoms have already, since 1989–90, been harmonized in many respects with the requirements formulated in the Convention. At the same time, in the explanatory report to the Resolution, the Parliament expounded in detail that it should be assessed during the period between signature and ratification of the Convention whether the Hungarian legal order has been in full harmony with all the provisions of the Convention.

The organizational framework allowing this analysis was assured by an interdepartmental committee set up by the Minister of Justice, on Government initiative. The result of the analysis was made public *in extenso* in Nos. 6–7 of Acta Humana, the periodical of the Hungarian Centre for Human Rights, under the title 'The European Convention on Human Rights and the Hungarian Legal System'. All members of the National Assembly received and could study this volume in the course of the debate on the ratification of the Convention. On the basis of this analysis, more or less essential modifications of twelve Acts has been found necessary.

In June 1992 a Government resolution specified the laws to be enacted in order to harmonize the Hungarian legal order fully with the Convention. Such modifications were required in respect of Articles 5, 6, 8, and 13 of the Convention, as well as of Article 1 of its Protocol No. 1.

The ratification of the Convention and its Additional Protocols took place on 5 November 1992. These were promulgated by Act XXXI of 1993. Provisions contained in the Convention, Additional Protocol No. 1, and Additional Protocols Nos. 2 and 4 had to be applied in Hungary from 5 November 1992, those contained in Additional Protocol No. 6 from 1 December 1992, and those contained in the Additional Protocol No. 7 from 1 February 1993.

Upon authorization by the National Assembly, the government of the Hungarian Republic issued the following statements on the occasion of the deposition of the instrument of ratification:

The Republic of Hungary declares that for a period of five years, which will be tacitly renewed for further periods of five years, unless the Republic of Hungary withdraws its declaration before the expiration of the appropriate term:

a. It recognizes in accordance with Article 25 of the Convention, Article 6 of Protocol No. 4, and Article 7 of Protocol No. 7 the competence of the European Commission of Human Rights to receive petitions from any person, non-governmental organization, or group of individuals claiming to be the victim of a violation of the rights set forth in the Convention and its Protocols, where the facts of the alleged violation of these rights occur after the Convention and its Protocols have come into force in respect of the Republic of Hungary;

b. it recognizes in accordance with Article 46 of the Convention, Article 6 of Protocol

No. 4, and Article 7 of Protocol No. 7 as compulsory, *ipso facto* and without special agreement, on condition of reciprocity, the jurisdiction of the European Court of Human Rights in all matters concerning the interpretation and application of the Convention and its Protocols and relating to facts occurring after the Convention and its Protocols have come into force in respect of the Republic of Hungary.

The above declaration is interpreted by the government of the Republic of Hungary, that measures taken by the Hungarian Republic for the reparation of the violation of the aforesaid rights which had taken place prior to the entry into force of the Convention and its Protocols shall not be considered as facts of the alleged violation of these rights.

At the time of the ratification and in accordance with Article 64 of the Convention, the Republic of Hungary made the following reservation in respect of the right to access to courts guaranteed by Article 6(1) of the Convention:

For the time being in proceedings for regulatory offences before the administrative authorities, Hungary cannot guarantee the right to access to courts, because the current Hungarian laws do not provide such right, the decision of the administrative authorities being final.

The relevant provisions of the Hungarian law referred to above are:

—Section 4 of Act No. IV of 1972 on courts, modified several times, which provides that the courts, unless an Act stipulates otherwise, may review the legality of the decisions taken by the administrative authorities;

—An exception is contained in Section 71/A of Act No. I of 1968 on proceedings for regulatory offences, modified several times, which allows for the offender to request judicial review solely against the measures taken by the administrative authority to commute to confinements the fine the offender had been sentenced to pay; no other access to court against final decisions taken in proceedings for regulatory offences is permitted.

After ratification of the Convention, the government urged the National Assembly to elaborate and adopt, as soon as possible, the Acts on the protection of personal data and on the right to know and disseminate data of public interest, on national security, on the police, on the freedom of press, on broadcasting and television, and on public education. All these Acts have since been adopted.

With a view to rendering possible the early revocation of the reservation made by the Hungarian Republic in respect of Article 6 of the Convention, the possibility of adopting reforms of the law on regulatory offences is being studied.

B. THE IMPACT OF THE CONVENTION ON HUNGARIAN LEGISLATION

The impact of the European Convention on Human Rights on the evolution of the Hungarian legal order is proved by the fact that the contents of the new Acts touching fundamental rights do correspond to the provisions of the Convention; explicit reference to them has even been made in their Preambles. This is true of eg Act No. LXXXV of 1993 concerning the entry and immigration into and the residence in Hungary of aliens, and for Act No. LXXVI of 1993 on the rights of national and ethnic minorities. As to Act No. XXXIV of 1994 on the police, though reference is made in its Preamble to Hungary's obligations in respect of international law in general, its provisions do unequivocally reflect the obligations under the European Convention on Human Rights.

C. LEADING HUMAN RIGHTS CASES DECIDED BY THE NATIONAL COURTS

The Hungarian legal system is not a case-law system but a continental legal system where not all judgments of (higher) courts are published but only a selection of judgments intended to provide guidance on the most important questions of interpretation of laws. These judgments are not of binding force but of persuasive authority. A compilation is published monthly by the Supreme Court as 'Decisions of Courts' (*Bírósági Határozatok*; BH) which also contains summaries of judgments of the European Court of Human Rights.

Many of these judgments of higher courts (County Courts and the Supreme Court) contain references to the Convention in order to give weight to arguments based on corresponding national legislation. It is very rare that provisions of the Convention (that is the Act promulgating the text of the Convention and its Protocols) are referred to as an independent basis for decision, and the courts very rarely refer to the case-law of the Strasbourg organs. It is interesting to note that when such a reference is made in the judgment, the 'source' is specified as being the publication in the above-mentioned compilation (BH) and not with reference to the original English or French sources (eg Series A).

In this context, two cases deserve mention. The first judgment (published as BH1996.189) concerned the right to defence in case of two juvenile offenders where legal assistance was compulsory. Each of the defendants had a legal representative assigned to them by the court but one of the lawyers was substituted by the other at the first hearing, and both of them were substituted by a third at the second hearing without authorization by the court or the defendants. The appellate court held, with reference to Article 6(3)b of the Convention, that compulsory legal representation must not be interpreted formally: the mere presence of a lawyer is not sufficient, he must have enough time to prepare the defence of his client. When the legal representative assigned by the court in respect of one of the defendants is substituted by the lawyer of the other defendant (which is possible only when there is no conflict of interest between them) the court must satisfy itself that the latter is well prepared in the cases of both defendants.

The other case (BH1998.132) concerned parental rights and the placement of children after the divorce of the parents. In the divorce proceedings, upon the agreement of the parents, the two children were placed in the custody of the mother. But the father very soon filed a legal action to change the placement of the children on the ground that the mother regularly attended meetings of Jehovah's Witnesses and by so doing she neglected her children and even put their lives and health at risk. At the hearing, she failed to give a definite answer whether she would allow the children to undergo a blood transfusion in case of medical need. Evidence showed, however, that she did take proper care of her children. On the other hand, expert opinion stated that the elder boy was more attached to his father than to his mother, and that he had suffered some psychological damage (eg strong fear of death) on account of his mother's religious influence on him. Therefore the court decided that the older boy should be placed with the father while the younger remained with the mother. The Supreme Court, however, held that not only was the separation of the siblings not in their interest, but also the judgment was unlawful because it was based primarily on the mother's religious conviction and failed to take into account other relevant factors favourable to her. With reference to Articles 8 and 14 of the Convention, as well as the judgment of the European Court of Human Rights in *Hoffmann v Austria*,[6] the Supreme Court stated that the religious conviction of a parent cannot be a decisive factor in custody cases, whether in favour or to the disadvantage of the parent concerned. With reference to Article 5 of Protocol No. 7 to the Convention, the Supreme Court held that the equality of the spouses required that when there was a conflict between the religious or philosophical convictions of the parents each of them should equally be responsible to resolve this conflict in the interest of their children, and one of them (the parent belonging to the Jehovah's Witnesses denomination) could not be held exclusively responsible for the harmful effects resulting from this conflict.

[6] Judgment of 23 June 1993, Series A No. 255–C.

Besides the jurisprudence of ordinary courts, a survey of the practice of the Hungarian Constitutional Court is very interesting and allows us to state that this organ has already done much to observe the provisions of the Convention. To illustrate this statement, some of the most significant cases are next noted.

The first such decision to rouse a wide echo was the one declaring the unconstitutionality of the death penalty.[7] The judgment was delivered a few days before the Convention was actually *signed* by Hungary. In item V/4 of the comments to this decision, reference is made to, among other documents of international law relating to death penalty, Protocol No. 6 of the European Convention on Human Rights as a demonstration of European legal development towards the abolition of the death penalty, but the decision was, of course, based on arguments stemming from the text of the Constitution itself. The Constitution prohibited the arbitrary deprivation of life, and a subsequent amendment to another provision declared that the substantive content of fundamental rights must not be restricted by law. The Court held that the right to life and human dignity was a source of and a precondition for many other fundamental rights and the execution of the death penalty led to a total and irreversible destruction of these rights, and therefore it contravened the Constitution.

Constitutional Court decision No. 22 of 10 April 1992, in the period between signature and ratification, concerned the right to marry which (as opposed to the Convention) is not expressly provided for by the Constitution, but can be derived from the constitutional protection of marriage, as well as from the right to human dignity which includes the right to personal self-determination. The Court referred to Article 12 of the Convention in connection with Article 7 of the Hungarian Constitution providing that the Hungarian legal order accepts the generally recognized principles of international law. The Court stated that any restriction on the right to marry (eg the requirement of a marriage licence for members of the armed forces and services) can only be justified when it is unavoidable, absolutely necessary, and proportional.

Constitutional Court decision No. 30 of 26 May 1992 concerned the balancing of freedom of expression and the rights of others (the right to human dignity). Among Hungary's international obligations, the Court referred to the Convention (still before ratification) stating that it did not contain an obligation on the state to punish acts of incitement to hatred (as opposed to the International Covenant on Civil and Political Rights) but rather provided limits on restricting freedom of expression. The Court also referred to the

[7] Constitutional Court decision No. 23 of 31 October 1990.

practice of the European Commission on Human Rights that prohibition of communications of racial hatred constituted a justified restriction under the Convention. The Constitutional Court held that freedom of expression was particularly important in a democratic society and could be restricted only when it was proportional to the aim pursued and only by the lightest possible means of protecting the rights of others: eg, subject to the circumstances of the case, a civil law action for immaterial damages was preferable to using the criminal law. Therefore the Court decided that freedom of expression was constitutionally restricted by criminal sanctions with regard to incitement to hatred but not with regard to the use of degrading expressions in general.

In Constitutional Court decision No. 4 of 12 February 1993, in deciding on a series of issues raised by Act No. XXXII of 1991 providing for the restitution of formerly Church-owned real property, including buildings operated as state schools, the Constitutional Court relied on Article 2 of Protocol No. 1 to the Convention in order to determine the scope of the state's obligations. It held that freedom of religion and the right to education must be balanced. Referring to the judgment of the European Court of Human Rights in *Kjeldsen, Busk Madsen, and Pedersen*,[8] it stated that state schools were prohibited from providing any kind of education which could be considered as disregarding convictions of the parents (and the child). Parents have a right to choose religious education for their children but they also have the right not to be obliged to send their children to schools that provide education contrary to their convictions. The state is not obliged to establish religious (philosophically committed) schools, and 'neutral' state schools are proper alternatives to committed schools in accordance with the right to freedom of conscience. The attendance at neutral state schools, however, must not impose a disproportionate burden on those who do not want to attend religious schools. But it is only in the circumstances of each case that proportionality can be determined, and the Act was found to contain sufficient guarantees, therefore it was not declared unconstitutional.

Constitutional Court decision No. 60 of 29 November 1993 referred to two decisions of the European Commission on Human Rights[9] upholding the constitutionality of the compulsory use of safety belts in cars.

In Constitutional Court decision No. 64 of 22 December 1993, the Court declared that its conception of the protection of the right to property is the same as that of the European Convention on Human Rights, as reflected in the case-law of the European Court of Human Rights, with special reference to the judgment in *James and Others*;[10] and in Constitutional Court decision

[8] Judgment of 7 December 1976, Series A No. 23.
[9] Applications 8707/79 and 7992/77.
[10] Judgment of 21 February 1986, Series A No. 98.

No. 35 of 24 June 1994 concerning the restrictions on acquiring agricultural land property, the President of the Constitutional Court, in his concurring opinion, referred to the case-law of the Convention (including the decision of the Commission in *Szechenyi v Hungary*: see below) to the effect that the Convention does not guarantee a right to acquire property, but only protects the peaceful enjoyment of property against unreasonable or disproportionate intervention or restrictions.

Constitutional Court decision No. 22 of 16 April 1994, referring to the Judgment of the European Court of Human Rights in the case of *Le Compte, Van Leuven*, and *De Meyere* (Series A No. 43) declared that compulsory membership of a professional organization established under public law (Bar Association) did not infringe the right to freedom of association.

The Constitutional Court has referred to Article 10 of the Convention in many cases, emphasizing its fundamental importance in a democratic society (eg in decision No. 34 of 24 June 1994). In Constitutional Court decision No. 36 of 24 June 1994, the Court held that according higher protection to officials of state (including politicians and members of the Government) in terms of more severe punishment for 'insulting an authority or an official person' than for libel or slander was unconstitutional, since the European Court of Human Rights had held that the limits of acceptable expression were broader in case of politicians and public figures than that of private persons. This kind of restriction on expressing value judgments is not 'necessary' and is disproportionate.

In Constitutional Court decision No. 14 of 13 March 1995, the Court stated that the right to marriage was reserved for a man and a woman (as confirmed by the European Court of Human Rights in its judgment in *Rees*[11]) but relations of cohabitation (life partnership) of couples of the same sex merit, without discrimination, the same legal recognition and protection as a life partnership between a man and a woman. The Civil Code was changed accordingly.

Constitutional Court decision No. 58 of 15 September 1995 concerned the relationship between the right to privacy of an accused person in relation to information on his mental condition and the publicity of criminal trials. The Constitutional Court observed that, according to the jurisprudence of the Strasbourg Organs, the publicity of trials is an important guarantee both for the individual and the public, and the person concerned does not have a right to exclusion of publicity. Although the Hungarian Code of Criminal Procedure is less detailed than Article 6(1) of the Convention setting forth the grounds for exclusion of publicity, 'moral grounds' mentioned in the

[11] Judgment of 17 October 1986, Series A No. 106.

Hungarian provision may be interpreted extensively, and the Constitutional Court added that there was nothing to prevent trial courts from bearing in mind the provisions of international conventions (such as the European Convention on Human Rights) in determining whether there was a need to exclude publicity from the whole or a part of the trial in order to protect the privacy of the accused. Thereby, in fact, the Constitutional Court ruled that ordinary courts may (or even should) apply the provisions of the Convention directly.

In Constitutional Court decision No. 67 of 7 December 1995, the Court held that in the case of an objection by the defendant to sentencing without trial (penal order) when a hearing must be held, the provision that this hearing is held by the same judge who previously imposed a sentence without trial was not, in general, contrary to the impartiality of judges. The Court referred to the jurisprudence of the European Court of Human Rights on the approaches to be applied in determining the impartiality of judges, as well as to Recommendation No. R(87)18 of the Committee of Ministers encouraging the application of penal orders as a means of expediting criminal procedures. The Constitutional Court laid emphasis on the fact that, besides there being sufficient guarantees for the defendant in a case of sentencing without trial, there was another fundamental right at stake: the right to a fair trial within a reasonable time.

Finally, a decision of great importance was Constitutional Court decision No. 63 of 12 December 1997. The Court found that the lack of judicial review in cases of regulatory offences before the administrative authorities—a field covered by Hungary's reservation to the Convention—contravened various provisions of the Hungarian Constitution and set this provision (Section 71/A of Act No. I of 1968 on proceedings for regulatory offences referred to in the reservation) aside *pro futuro*, as from 31 December 1998. This provision was also found to be unconstitutional on the ground that the possibility of access to court in a case of commuting to imprisonment the fine to which the offender had been sentenced did not constitute a sufficient guarantee in terms of protection against deprivation of liberty, since the court was only entitled to revise the decision of commutation on grounds of lawfulness, not in terms of facts. Thus decisions of administrative authorities imposing fines were in fact decisions of a conditional deprivation of liberty. So the provision restricting access to courts, covered by Hungary's reservation, ceased to be in force on 1 January 1999, and a new Act on regulatory offences had to be adopted which provides for a right of access to court. The new Act entered into force on 1 March 2000 and Hungary has accordingly withdrawn its reservation to Article 6(1) of the Convention.

D. CASES BROUGHT BEFORE THE EUROPEAN COMMISSION AND COURT OF HUMAN RIGHTS

The instrument of ratification of the Convention and its nine Protocols was deposited by Hungary on 5 November 1992, the date of entry into force of the Convention with respect to Hungary. In the period between 1993 and 1997, 823 provisional files were opened (there was a peak in 1995) and about 47 per cent of them had been registered (387 applications in five years). The rate of registration has increased from 40 to 55 per cent which shows, to some extent, that potential applicants (natural or juridical persons under Hungarian jurisdiction) are increasingly aware of the requirements and possibilities of this mechanism or that they more often availed themselves of the assistance of legal counsel.

During these five years, 24 applications were referred to the Hungarian government for their comments. Until the end of 1997, 11 of these applications were declared inadmissible and 7 were pending admissibility decision. Of 6 applications declared admissible, 2 cases were ended by friendly settlement (both concerning protracted civil procedures) and 2 applications concluded by Article 31 reports of the Commission.

There are two cases which are interesting, although they have been declared inadmissible by the Commission without having been communicated to the government. Application 21344/93 by *August Szechenyi* concerned compensation for expropriation effected in or about 1945. As mentioned above, the Hungarian government made a declaration upon ratification that:

'measures taken by the Hungarian Republic for the reparation of the violation of the [rights set forth in the Convention] which had taken place prior to the entry into force of the Convention and its Protocols shall not be considered as facts of the alleged violation of these rights.

According to its content, this declaration could be considered as a reservation. The Commission, however, examined Szechenyi's application without even taking note of this declaration. The Commission held that expropriations in 1945 were instantaneous acts and did therefore not constitute continuous violations, and that the Convention did not guarantee a right to restitution or other reparation of injuries which were not in themselves violations of the Convention. Therefore we may conclude that this 'interpretative declaration' had no relevance to the interpretation of the Convention.

The Commission has also examined the Hungarian reservation to Article 6(1) concerning the limitation of access to courts with regard to regulatory offences before administrative authorities.[12] The Commission found that the

[12] Application 31506/96 by Istvánné Rékási.

reservation complied with the requirements of Article 64 para. 2 of the Convention and declared the application inadmissible.

Of the 24 applications referred to the Government, about 10 complained of the length of civil procedures: 4 of them have been declared inadmissible, 3 are pending admissibility decision, 2 have been concluded by friendly settlement, and in one case, the Commission has drawn up a report on the merits under Article 31 finding a violation of Article 6 § 1 of the Convention. There have been other applications under Article 6 concerning access to court and various aspects of fairness of criminal proceedings but they were all declared inadmissible or are still pending admissibility decision.

An application by a Bulgarian national complained under Article 5 of the length of his detention on remand and the lack of any reasonable suspicion against him.[13] He was suspected of having been involved in committing a currency offence and also the offence of receiving stolen goods. He was detained on remand for about one year and five months, then the criminal proceedings were 'offered' to the General Prosecutor of the Republic of Bulgaria under a bilateral treaty on mutual assistance. The applicant was transferred to Bulgaria but no criminal proceedings were instituted against him by the Bulgarian authorities. The Commission examined whether there was a reasonable suspicion against him justifying his arrest, and whether there were sufficient reasons justifying his continued detention on remand, and found the application manifestly ill founded.

Other applications submitted by persons of foreign nationality have concerned complaints under Article 3 of the applicants' proposed expulsion to their country of origin. The first application of this kind[14] was filed by four Somalian citizens who applied for refugee status with the UNHCR Branch Office in Budapest. Their application was refused at first. Finally, upon intervention by Amnesty International, the UNHCR requested the Hungarian government to grant provisional residence permits to the applicants. The government did so, and the applicants were placed in the Red Cross refugee home in Budapest and were granted free movement in Hungary. A few months later, however, the applicants illegally left Hungary and ceased to keep in contact with the Commission. Therefore the Commission has struck the application off its list of cases. A similar application[15] introduced by fifteen Syrian nationals was declared manifestly ill-founded. (See Application 34772/97 by *Mahmoud Mamou and Others*, admissibility decision of 20 May 1997. Further complaints made by this application under Articles 5, 8, and 13 were also declared inadmissible on 22 June 1999.)

[13] Application 22172/93 by Georgi Lukov Romanov.
[14] Application 30471/96. [15] Application 34772/97.

Further issues raised under Article 3 include the conditions of detention of a convicted disabled person in a prison hospital (see Application 23636/94 by *PM*, where the Commission found a violation in its Report of 9 September 1998) as well as treatment by the police. One of the applications (Application 26692/95 by *Gábor Bethlen*) concerning this matter has been declared inadmissible because of non-observance of the six-month time limit. The other (Application 31561/96 by *Géza Farkas*) has been found inadmissible as manifestly ill founded.

Two applications raise issues under Article 11 concerning freedom of association. The first applicant complained that participation in certain political activities and membership in political parties were prohibited for him as a police officer.[16] What gives this case special importance is that a finding of violation would have entailed the need to amend the Constitution. It also raised issues under Article 10.

The Commission found in its Report of 9 July 1998 that there was no violation of Article 11. The applicant's right to freedom of expression had been violated because the law restricting political activities lacked the required foreseeability. However, the Court found that neither provision had been violated (Judgment of 20 May 1999).

The second application concerned the refusal to register an association under a name containing a reference to a public authority.[17] The complaint under Article 11 was declared manifestly ill-founded, but the Court found a violation of Article 6 for failure to respect the principle of equality of arms in the non-contentious registration proceedings.

Finally, three applications primarily concerned Article 8. Application No. 21647/93 was made by *Géza Szegő*, a father who complained about the absence of the possibility of enforcement of his right to access to his son. The Commission confirmed that besides an obligation to refrain from arbitrary interference by public authorities, there may be positive obligations on the part of the state inherent in an effective 'respect' for family life. The obligation to take such measures, however, is not absolute: the co-operation of all concerned will always be an important ingredient, which in this case was totally lacking. The Commission found that in the circumstances of the case the authorities made reasonable efforts to enforce the applicant's right of access to his son and, having regard to the margin of appreciation enjoyed by the competent Hungarian authorities, found the application manifestly ill founded.

[16] Application 25390/94 by *László Rekvényi*.

[17] Application 32367/96, admissibility decision of 31 August 1999, Judgment of 5 October 2000.

Application 23198/94 by *László Beck* complained about the control of correspondence of prisoners under Article 8. The Commission found that the Hungarian practice was in conformity with the Convention, the occasional opening of a prisoner's letters, chosen at random, did not exceed the scope of control measures warranted by the ordinary and reasonable requirements of imprisonment. Therefore this application was declared inadmissible on the ground of being manifestly ill founded.

Similar complaints were introduced in Application 21967/93 by *Sándor Sárközi*. He complained about the conditions of his detention under Article 3, interference with his correspondence with his family under Article 8, and the lack of an effective remedy under Article 13. None of these complaints were found to disclose any violation of the Convention. In the process of the examination of the case, however, a letter addressed to the applicant by the Commission had been opened by the prison authorities before it was handed over to the applicant. The Hungarian legislation then in force prohibited any interference with letters addressed to international organizations but checking mail coming from those organs (with a view to verifying that the sender is indeed the organization indicated on the envelope) was permitted. So the measure in question was effected in accordance with the law. Unfortunately, the Commission, having noted that, under Section 36 para. 5 of the Law on the Execution of Sentences, prisoners' correspondence may be controlled by the prison authorities for reasons of security, except for letters *sent to* international organizations (§ 94 of the Report of 6 March 1997) declared in its report that the opening of the letter *sent by* the Commission was not in accordance with the law (§ 95). This little confusion might have been created by the fact that Hungarian legislation had been changed to exclude the control of letters coming from international organizations well before the Commission's report was drawn up. Fortunately, the Commission went on to examine 'for reasons of completeness' whether the other conditions under paragraph 2 of Article 8 had been satisfied and held that the opening of the Commission's letter could not be regarded as necessary in a democratic society within the meaning of paragraph 2 of Article 8 and found a violation of the Convention.

E. REMEDIAL ACTION TAKEN BY THE GOVERNMENT IN RESPONSE TO BEING HELD TO BE IN VIOLATION OF THE CONVENTION

In the above-mentioned case of *Sárközi*, the government apologized to the applicant for opening the letter from the Commission and paid 850,000

Hungarian forints as just satisfaction (including costs and expenses). When the Commission found a violation, the Hungarian legislation had already been changed to exclude the possibility of prison authorities controlling any correspondence with (that is letters both to and from) international organizations.

There have been two cases of protracted civil proceedings where friendly settlement has been reached and the government paid 600,000 and 750,000 Hungarian forints, respectively, to the applicants. Independently of these cases, reform of the Hungarian judicial system and its codes of civil and criminal procedure is under way. Some elements of the reform have already been implemented but it remains to be seen whether they will be more effective in avoiding proceedings exceeding a reasonable time. A new body has been established for the administration of the judiciary consisting of nine judges elected by courts through delegates, the Minister of Justice, the Chief Public Prosecutor, the President of the National Bar Association, and two members of the Parliament; its president is the president of the Supreme Court. This body of *self*-administration (since two-thirds of its members are judges) is the National Council of the Judiciary which shall have as its task to analyse the causes of excessively lengthy proceedings and to propose measures to prevent similar cases.

The reopening of proceedings before domestic courts following decisions by the Convention organs is a current topic in the Council of Europe. Athough there has not yet been a case in respect of Hungary where it was necessary to reopen a domestic proceeding following a finding of a violation by the Commission, the new Code on Criminal Procedure, which entered into force in 2000, provides that such decisions of international human rights organs are to be considered as 'new evidence' for the purpose of reopening a criminal case. A similar provision is likely to be included in a new Code on Civil Procedure.

F. ASSESSMENT AND PROSPECTS

Although the Convention has only been in force in Hungary for a relatively short time, it has already had a considerable impact on the Hungarian legal order.

The elaboration of a new Constitution is under way in Hungary. In the course of this process the practices pursued by the European Commission of Human Rights and by the European Court of Human Rights will certainly be analysed along with the provisions of the Convention. The same holds for the new Acts intended to regulate fundamental human rights in detail, on the basis of the provisions of the new Constitution.

17

Iceland

GUDRUN GAUKSDÓTTIR

INTRODUCTION

Iceland joined the Council of Europe on 7 March 1950 and ratified the European Convention on Human Rights on 19 June 1953. Iceland has successively ratified the Additional Protocols to the Convention.[1] In accordance with Article 25 of the Convention, Iceland has made a declaration, for an indefinite period, recognizing the competence of the Commission to receive individual complaints. It has also accepted the jurisdiction of the Court in accordance with Article 46 for a specified period. The initial declaration was given on 3 September 1958 and is renewed periodically.

The Convention played a relatively subordinate role in Icelandic law until the late 1980s. Upon ratification of the Convention it was simply assumed that Icelandic law and practice were in conformity with the Convention. By the end of the 1980s and at the beginning of the '90s several factors played a role in enhancing the status of the Convention within the Icelandic legal system which finally led to its incorporation.

The Commission and Court of Human Rights came to the conclusion in three cases that Icelandic law or practice had violated the Convention. These cases led to a shift of attitude in the legal community as to the possible role of the Convention in the protection of human rights in Iceland and awakened public awareness of its existence.

Secondly, the Supreme Court in a judgment of 9 January 1990 interpreted Icelandic law in the light of the Convention in a way that came close to overturning it. Thirdly, then existing constitutional provisions were deficient and thus the spotlight was on the Convention as to the protection of certain rights. The Institution of the Parliamentary Ombudsman was established in 1988.

[1] Iceland has ratified the protocols securing the individual additional rights: Protocol No. 1 on 19 June 1953, Protocol No. 4 on 16 November 1967, and Nos. 6 and 7 on 22 May 1987. The Protocols amending the procedural provisions of the Convention Nos. 3 and 5 were ratified on 16 November 1967 and Protocol No. 8 on 22 May 1987. Iceland ratified Protocol No. 11 on 29 June 1995. Iceland has not ratified Protocol No. 9.

The Ombudsman, exercising his power to point out deficiencies in legislation, brought to the attention of the Prime Minister and Parliament the deficiency of constitutionally protected human rights and submitted that they provided in some respects inferior protection than that provided by international human rights instruments. Lastly, developments in the other Nordic countries pointed towards the incorporation of the Convention in the respective countries.

In 1992 the Minister of Justice appointed a committee to look into the question of incorporating the Convention. The committee concluded *inter alia* that incorporation would enhance legal security in Iceland and the protection of individual rights. Further the Convention was expected to fill gaps in Icelandic law. The Convention as incorporated would enable the individual to refer to it as directly applicable law and not only as a guiding instrument for the interpretation of law. Incorporation would also facilitate adjudication and decisions by the executive. The Committee accordingly submitted a proposal for a bill of incorporation, which was later enacted by Parliament. The Convention was adopted in Icelandic law through the incorporating Act No. 62 of 1994 on the European Convention on Human Rights, which entered into force on 30 May 1994. The findings of the Committee are contained in an Explanatory Report accompanying the Act.[2]

The status of the Convention within the Icelandic legal system was thus formally altered. The Convention was no longer a subordinate source of law, and became part of the domestic legal system ranking as ordinary law. However, the standing of the Convention as a source of Icelandic law must be seen in the light of a process which has taken place particularly over the last decade. This process has primarily been conducted by the Icelandic Supreme Court, and is continuing.

A. THE STATUS OF THE CONVENTION IN NATIONAL LAW

A discussion of the European Convention as a source of Icelandic law must start with the general rules on the status of international law. Iceland has in principle been dualistic in its approach to international law, which generally implies that municipal law and international law are two distinct legal systems that exist independently of each other. Support for this dualistic

[2] The bill of law together with its explanatory report is published in the Parliamentary Reports A (Alþingistíðindi) of 1992–1993. The subsequent references to the Explanatory Report apply to its special edition.

approach has been found in specific constitutional provisions and practice.[3] The dualistic approach to international law means that it only becomes part of municipal law if it is expressly adopted as such by way of a legislative act.

In Iceland international law is a specific source of law though it is subordinate to certain other sources. However, the effect of international law as a subordinate source of law is minimized through the leading principle that Icelandic law should be interpreted so as to conform with international legal obligations. In cases where these sources of law conflict, international law must yield to the provisions of Icelandic law with which it is incompatible.[4]

Until the late 1980s the Convention was subordinate to domestic law in accordance with the principles listed above on the status of international law in general. This is reflected in the case-law of the Supreme Court and the opinions of Icelandic scholars. However, the standing of the Convention in the early '90s, before its incorporation, cannot be described as subsidiary in Icelandic law. A judgment delivered by the Supreme Court on 9 January 1990 shows a different approach to the interpretation of domestic law in the light of the Convention.[5]

The Convention introduced a new dimension into the traditional theory of sources of Icelandic law. The dualistic approach towards international law was no longer applicable to the Convention and this has caused obscurity as to its standing as a source of Icelandic law and has complicated the analysis of case-law and theory.[6]

The Convention had in this respect a special status compared to other international human rights instruments, the decisive factor being the effective supervisory system established by the Convention. This increased weight of the Convention was confirmed in a number of subsequent Supreme Court judgments. On the basis of the aforementioned judgment the opinion has been expressed that the Convention had the status of Icelandic law, albeit not formally, even before its incorporation.[7] Others have suggested that this

[3] S. M. Stefansson and R. Adalsteinsson, 'Incorporation and implementation of human rights in Iceland' in: Scheinin (ed) *International Human Rights Norms in the Nordic and Baltic Countries*, p. 169.

[4] Ibid, p. 170.

[5] Supreme Court Reports 1990, p. 2, see p. 410 below.

[6] For a detailed discussion on the standing of the Convention as a source of law in Iceland: D. Gudmundsdóttir, 'Um lögtöku Mannréttindasáttmála Evrópu og beitingu í íslenskum rétti' (1994) 44 *Tímarit lögfræðinga* p. 154 and D. Björgvinsson, 'EES samningurinn og Mannréttindasáttmáli Evrópu sem réttarheimildir í íslenskum landsrétti' (1997) 50 *Úlfljótur* p. 98.

[7] It has been maintained that this judgment entailed that the provisions of international human rights instruments which had been ratified by Iceland had become a part of domestic law and that provisions of incompatible domestic law should yield, see R. Adalsteinsson, 'Alþjóðlegir mannréttindasáttmálar og íslenskur landsréttur', (1990) 40 *Tímarit lögfræðinga* p. 22. The Committee that prepared the incorporation of the Convention stated that some of the judgments of the Supreme Court could be interpreted as implying a tendency towards the indirect implementation of the Convention through a liberal application of the principle of interpreting national law in harmony with the Convention, see the Explanatory Report, p. 83.

judgment entailed change as to the method of interpreting law but did not amend its status as a source of law.[8]

Act No. 62 of 1994 on the European Convention on Human Rights contains three articles. Article 1 enumerates the conventions covered by the Act and thus incorporated into Icelandic law, that is the Convention itself together with its Protocols. Protocol No. 11 was enacted through Act No. 25 of 1998. The Convention text itself is appended to the Act. Article 2 stipulates that the case-law of the Convention's organs is not binding according to Icelandic law. Thus the case-law is not a part of Icelandic law, only the Convention text itself. Article 3 contains provisions on the entry into force of the Act.[9]

The Convention did not obtain the status of constitutional law nor was a provision included in the Constitution as to its standing in relation to other law in general. Through incorporation the Convention became a part of ordinary law. Consequently the general principle is that provisions of previously enacted law conflicting with the Convention are obsolete as from the time of its entry into force (the principle of *lex posterior derogat legi priori*). The Convention's provisions should accordingly yield to subsequent law, as it does not rank higher than ordinary law. However, the Explanatory Report contains an interesting clause on the standing of the Convention as compared to ordinary law and constitutional law:

> Despite that the provisions of the Convention on Human Rights are not enacted as constitutional law it is not possible to assume, if this bill of law is enacted, that the provisions of the Convention shall yield to subsequently enacted law. In that connection it has to be kept in mind that the enactment of this bill inevitably will influence the interpretation of existing constitutional provisions in such away that subsequent law, possibly conflicting with the Convention, might at the same time conflict with the Constitution as interpreted in the future.[10]

It is assumed that the Convention has a special status as compared to equivalent law and the Constitution. The problem of potentially conflicting law is solved by the interpretation of constitutional law in harmony with the Convention's requirements. The Explanatory Report states that the constitutional provisions on human rights are relatively short and old. Even though the incorporation of the Convention would not amend the content of these

[8] See *inter alia* Gudmundsdóttir, n. 6 above, p. 161.

[9] One member of the Committee recommended that only the material provisions of the Convention should be incorporated. He considered that sufficient arguments had not been brought forward in support of the incorporation of the operating provisions of the Convention. It had not been shown how they would enhance the protection of individual rights: see p. 93 of the Explanatory Report. For critical remarks on this point see also G. Alfredsson, in a newspaper article 'Um lögfestingu mannréttindasamnings' (1994) 26 *Tíminn*, 26.

[10] Explanatory Report, p. 87.

provisions it could be assumed that it entails an indirect indication to interpret the Constitution widely in order to conform with the Convention requirements.[11] This approach is indicated in a Supreme Court judgment of 18 May 1995.[12] Generally speaking the Convention would be seen as a special law covering the area of human rights. This applies both to previously and subsequently enacted law.

The Explanatory Report expressed the opinion that there is a need to review the constitutional provisions on human rights. It would enhance the effectiveness of the human rights provisions covered by the Convention.[13] The Constitution was amended by Act No. 97 of 1995. The Act contains a revision of the human rights provisions contained in Chapter VII of the Constitutional Act No. 44 of 1944. The reasons for this revision according to its explanatory report were the need to increase the effectiveness of and to modernize the human rights provisions, and the intention to bring them into conformity with the international obligations of Iceland under human rights instruments. The provisions of the Convention and International Covenant on Civil and Political Rights were considered to be more comprehensive than the applicable constitutional provisions.[14]

Icelandic scholars seem to agree that the Convention ranks higher than ordinary law. This has been explained by the nature of the rights protected by the Convention as fundamental rights and because of their international background.[15] According to one commentator the incorporation of the Convention should be seen as confirmation of the existence of unwritten principles on the protection of human rights ranking as fundamental law and applied to complement the constitutional provisions. Accordingly the Convention is equal to the Constitution.[16]

The judgments of the Supreme Court reveal that the Court has extensive powers to scrutinize the conformity of law and practice with the Convention.[17]

[11] Ibid, p. 89.

[12] See p. 413 below. For comments on this case see Björgvinsson, 'Skranker for lovgivningsmyndigheten', 1998 (1–2), *Jussens Venner* pp. 90–91.

[13] Ibid, p. 88.

[14] Explanatory report to the Constitutional Act No. 97 of 1995 on the amendment of the Constitution No. 33 of 1944, Parliamentary Reports 1994–95 (Document 389), p. 2073

[15] Ibid, p. 98 and Björgvinsson, n. 6 above, pp. 89–90. See also P. Þórhallsson, 'Lögfesting Mannréttindasáttmála Evrópu' (1994) 47 *Úlfljótur*, p. 164.

[16] S. Líndal, *Inngangur ad lögfraedi, Réttarheimildir. Sett lög. Venjuréttur*. Brádabirgdaútgáfa til kennslu, 1994, p. 17.

[17] The power of the courts to review the conformity of ordinary law with the Constitution is based on a constitutional custom since express provision is lacking in the Constitution. The established principle is that ordinary law shall be interpreted in conformity with the Convention. Icelandic courts have been restrictive in their application of their power of constitutional review. For a discussion on the restrictions upon legislative power in Iceland see Björgvinsson (n. 12 above).

Despite the non-binding force of the case-law of the Convention's organs according to Article 2 of the 1994 Act the Explanatory Report assumes that the Icelandic courts and executive authorities seek guidance on the case-law in their interpretation of the Convention. The provision was enacted to secure the independence of the judiciary and executive authorities. In this connection it is stated that the courts and the executive are empowered to interpret the Convention's provisions independently. This encompasses those Convention provisions on which there is not much case-law. The report stresses that decisions on important matters would hardly be based on interpretation that did not have any basis or support in scholarly theories although the courts and executive authorities were free to do so.[18] Commentators have raised questions as to the implications of Article 2 of the 1994 Act.[19]

According to the Explanatory Report this provision serves only to emphasize that the institutions are as hitherto only empowered to decide upon whether the Icelandic state has fulfilled its international obligations according to the Convention and eventually to grant just satisfaction in case of a violation. The decisions can thus not change the validity of Icelandic legislation or judgments. The judgment of the Court of Human Rights as to just satisfaction cannot be directly enforced in Iceland.[20]

When adjudicating the conformity of national law with the Convention the Supreme Court has in a number of judgments looked for guidance to the Convention case-law. The Court seems to apply the case-law liberally in the sense that it seems to have given it a rather wide interpretation, for example in its judgments of 2 February 1990[21] and 18 May 1995.[22] How decisive the application of the Convention is depends upon which right is at stake. The Convention and its case-law have been of particular importance in areas where domestic legal protection has been inferior, eg on freedom of expression and the right to a fair trial before the Constitutional Amendment of 1995. If domestic law provides stronger protection than the Convention then the Convention automatically plays a lesser role in accordance with its subsidiary character, eg concerning property rights.

The question arises which interpretative methods should be decisive in the application of the Convention by Icelandic courts and executive authorities: traditional methods or those applied by the European Court of Human Rights. It has to be assumed in cases on which there is no case-law that

[18] Explanatory Report, pp. 87–88.

[19] See eg Gudmundsdóttir, n. 6 above, p. 167 and Alfredsson in his newspaper article, n. 9 above.

[20] Explanatory Report, p. 92.

[21] See p. 411 below.

[22] See p. 413 below.

domestic courts strive to interpret the provisions of the Convention in the light of the methods developed by the Court of Human Rights.[23] This approach is indicated *inter alia* in Supreme Court judgments of 17 October 1997 and 2 April 1998.[24]

B. THE STATUS OF THE CONVENTION IN PARLIAMENTARY PROCEEDINGS

Upon Iceland's ratification of the Convention in 1953 it seems that the legislator did not consider it necessary to amend municipal law. The Minister of Justice when discussing the parliamentary resolution empowering the ratification of the Convention in 1953 stated that the rights enumerated in the Convention were in all relevant parts expressly guaranteed to the citizens in Icelandic law, either by the Constitution or because they were such fundamental rights as to form part of the general principles of Icelandic law. No formal investigation of the conformity of existing legislation seems to have taken place.[25]

According to the Explanatory Report some attempts had been made to transform national law to bring it into conformity with the Convention but these had not been successful. Incorporation might prove more effective.[26] A short survey on the conformity of Icelandic law with the Convention was made at the request of the Committee, which prepared the proposal for the incorporating act of 1994.[27]

As submitted in the introduction to this chapter the Convention played a subordinate role in parliamentary proceedings until the late '80s. In connection with the findings of the Commission and the Court of Human Rights of violations of the Convention the Parliament enacted substantial amendments of Icelandic law. It can be assumed that since the early '90s the Parliament has taken notice of the Convention requirements when adopting legislation in the field covered by the Convention.

In relation to the finding of a violation of Article 6 of the Convention in the case of *Jon Kristinsson*[28] the Government of Iceland called for a redrafting of

[23] See Björgvinsson, n. 6 above, pp. 91–92.
[24] See p. 416 below.
[25] Ibid, p. 78.
[26] Ibid, p. 88.
[27] The survey points out several provisions of Icelandic law which could be in violation of the Convention but concludes that in general Icelandic law conforms with the Convention as interpreted by the Commission and the Court. It stresses the importance of the application and interpretation of domestic law in conformity with the Convention. See Appendix 2 to the Explanatory Report, p. 104.
[28] Judgment of 1 March 1990, Series A No. 171–B.

the legislation on the organization of the judicial system. On 19 May 1989 the Parliament adopted Act No. 92 of 1989 on the Separation of District Judicial and Administrative Powers which entered into force on 1 July 1992. Under this Act the administration of the police is entrusted to district executive agents and criminal cases are dealt with by district court judges, independently of the executive. In relation to the finding of a violation of Article 10 in the *Thorgeir Thorgeirsson* case[29] the Minister of Justice appointed a Committee to decide upon the reaction to that judgment and to look into the question of incorporating the Convention, which resulted in its incorporation. In response to the finding of a violation of Article 11 in the case of *Sigurdur Sigurjonsson*[30] the Parliament in 1995 enacted a law to bring Icelandic law into harmony with the Convention's requirements. The explanatory reports of the Code of Criminal Procedure No. 19 of 1991 and the Children's Act No. 20 of 1992 refer expressly to the Convention as regards specific points of law.

The Institution of the Parliamentary Ombudsman was established by Act No. 13 of 1987. The Ombudsman is empowered *inter alia* to bring to the attention of the Parliament and Ministers defects in legislation. In 1989 the Ombudsman brought to the attention of the Prime Minister and the Presidents of Parliament imperfect provisions on the protection of human rights in Icelandic law. The Ombudsman pointed out that the Constitution lacked some specific important human rights provisions and that many of the existing provisions were defective. The Ombudsman pointed out that Iceland was a party to important international agreements on human rights which in some respects provided more comprehensive protection. The Ombudsman continued to say that this could cause problems in the execution of laws and even entail responsibility for the Icelandic state before the supervisory institutions established by these agreements. Improvements could be made through revision of the human rights provisions of the Constitution and possibly the incorporation of these human rights agreements in whole or in part into Icelandic law.[31]

In 1989 the Ombudsman considered that a provision on disciplinary actions in prisons, Article 26 of Act No. 48 of 1988 on Prisons, could easily violate Articles 5 and 6 of the Convention.[32] This provision was subsequently amended by Act No. 3 of 1991.

A case of 1994 concerned the revocation of a permit to operate a taxi-cab according to Act 1989 on Taxi-cabs. The plaintiff's licence was an 'opera-

[29] Judgment of 25 June 1992, Series A No. 239.
[30] Judgment of 30 June 1993, Series A No. 264.
[31] The Ombudsman *Annual Report* 1988, p. 45, case No. 70/1988.
[32] *Annual Report* 1990, p. 97, case No. 170/1989.

tional licence' that is permitting the holder to operate a taxi without driving it himself. In its decision the Ombudsman referred to the judgment of the Supreme Court of 3 June 1993 which considered that the Act in question did not violate the constitutional principle of equality. The Ombudsman referred to the European Convention on Human Rights, which had been incorporated into Icelandic law through Act No. 62 of 1994. The employment rights of those who had acquired a licence to operate a taxi-cab were to be considered as possessions within Article 1 of Protocol No. 1 to the Convention, which prohibits discrimination between individuals as concerns such rights. The decision stresses that the administrative practice in cases concerning important individual rights must be clear and secure. Enacted laws should be clear and unequivocal, and legislative rules should be general, clear, and predictable and should not have retroactive effects to the disadvantage of those enjoying rights before the new legislation is enacted.[33]

The Explanatory Report does not elaborate on the role of the legislator subsequent to incorporation. It is nevertheless clear that the legislator carries the primary responsibility of guaranteeing harmony between domestic law and the Convention. That is the basis for the proper application of law by the executive and the judiciary.[34]

C. LEADING HUMAN RIGHTS CASES DECIDED BY NATIONAL COURTS

The case-law of the Supreme Court reveals that the standing of the Convention as a source of Icelandic law has undergone substantial changes since the time of ratification. The judgments delivered by the Supreme Court prior to 1990 reflect that the Convention was a subordinate source of law in Iceland. However, the approach of the Court was not consistent in every respect.

In a judgment of 25 June 1963[35] the Court held that the seizure of a British trawler, in connection with an inquiry into an offence relating to the violation of the territorial waters of Iceland, was in conformity with specific provisions of Icelandic law and Article 1 of Protocol No. 1 *in fine* to the European Convention on Human Rights. Accordingly the Convention seems to have some status as a source of Icelandic law.[36]

[33] *Annual Report* 1994, p. 41, case No. 1071/1994.

[34] As to the role of the legislator see *inter alia* Gudmundsdóttir, n. 6 above, p. 186.

[35] Supreme Court Reports (SCR) 1963, p. 461.

[36] In a case of 2 March 1970 (SCR 1970, p. 212) the Court addressed the question whether a captain could be punished for an offence against a fisheries act that he had had no part in committing. The majority of the Court convicted the captain, with one judge finding him not

In other judgments the Court has dismissed arguments based on an alleged violations of the Convention, in the first place because Icelandic law was not inconsistent with the Convention. Secondly, even if inconsistency was established it would not change the validity of enacted Icelandic law, whether ordinary or constitutional. Occasionally the Court did not state its view on the argument.

In a judgment of 18 June 1975[37] the Court considered the refusal to grant a licence to keep a dog in the city of Reykjavik to be in accordance with specific provisions in Icelandic law and regulations. In the Court's view these provisions did not infringe Article 66 of the Constitution but could not be ignored because they violated Article 8 of the European Convention:

The Convention has not acquired the status of law in Iceland and leaving that question aside the prohibition of keeping dogs in Reykjavik does not violate the same provision.

The Supreme Court judgment of 25 November 1985[38] is important as to its consequences. The case was the subject of a complaint to the European Commission on Human Rights which came to the unanimous conclusion that Article 6 had been violated. An individual complained about his conviction of a traffic offence by the district criminal court of Akureyri. A deputy judge, who at the same time was the deputy chief of police, delivered the judgment. Before the Supreme Court the plaintiff claimed the annulment of the judgment since an impartial judge had not delivered it. This, he maintained, violated Articles 2 and 61 of the Constitution and Article 6 of the Convention. The Supreme Court dismissed the claim stating that:

Under the Icelandic court system, judicial powers in district courts outside Reykjavik are vested in town and county magistrates who serve collaterally as chiefs of police. The District Criminal Court decision cannot be set aside on the ground that the deputy town magistrate of Akureyri tried the case in question. Furthermore, no specific facts have been established which would disqualify the town magistrate or his deputy.

The Supreme Court did not refer to the Convention in its reasoning but two years later, concerning a comparable point of law, in a judgment of 10 March 1987,[39] the Court came to the same conclusion but with more thorough reasoning. The Court stated that the provisions of Article 2 of the Constitution of the Republic of Iceland had not been held to stand in the way of the orga-

guilty. The judge held that the fisheries act in question did not contain express provisions on the objective criminal responsibility of the captain as concerns offences committed on board his ship. The captain could not be considered responsible for the offence on the basis of the general principles of Icelandic law as reflected in specified provisions of the Penal Code and the Code of Criminal Procedure and Article 6, paragraph 2 of the Convention.

[37] SCR 1975, p. 601.

[38] SCR 1985, p. 1290.

[39] SCR 1987, p. 356.

nization of the judicial system pronounced by law entailing that town and county magistrates also serve as chiefs of police. Article 61 of the 1944 Constitution implied that judges could have administrative powers. Then the Court stated:

The provisions of Article 6 of the European Convention on Human Rights, cf. Announcement No. 11 of 9 February 1954 has not been given the status of law in this country. They do not alter the system prescribed by law and described above. Since the appealed judgment was accordingly delivered by a competent district court judge according to Icelandic law it cannot be annulled on the basis of the argument at issue.[40]

This case was referred to the Commission of Human Rights and resulted in a friendly settlement between the parties.[41]

In a judgment of 15 December 1988[42] the issue was the obligation for taxi drivers to belong to the 'Frami' Automobile Association. On 24 October 1984 the plaintiff was granted a licence to operate a taxi-cab. He undertook to abide by the relevant Ministerial Regulation, which provided, *inter alia*, that he had to become a member of Frami. The Committee subsequently revoked his licence for taxi-cab supervision, at Frami's request, as of July 1986, in particular on the ground that he had ceased to pay his membership dues. He had previously informed Frami that he did not wish to continue being a member. The plaintiff protested against the revocation to the Ministry of Transport, which nonetheless confirmed the decision. On 1 August 1986 the police stopped him while driving and removed the plates identifying his vehicle as being for public hire. The plaintiff complained that this condition for operating a taxi violated Article 73 of the Icelandic Constitution and Article 11 of the Convention. The Supreme Court dismissed the claim that this obligation conflicted with Article 73 of the Constitution and stated that:

The appellant has not proved that there is inconsistency between Article 73 of the Constitution and the provisions of the international Conventions he refers to and which are mentioned in the district court judgment and would in any case not automatically change the constitutional provisions.

However, the Supreme Court reversed the lower court's judgment on the ground that the said obligation lacked a statutory basis. Again it is explicit in this judgment that the Convention's requirements were considered to have to yield to domestic legislation in case of conflict. The Icelandic Parliament subsequently passed a new Act on Motor Vehicles in 1989, providing expressly that membership of the relevant trade union should be a condition for the

[40] In its judgment of 9 January 1990 the Court overturned this reasoning, see p. 410 above/below.

[41] See p. 418 below.

[42] SCR 1988, p.1532.

granting of a taxi-cab licence. The plaintiff filed an application to the European Commission of Human Rights complaining about the lack of conformity of this act with the Convention.[43]

The issue of the organization of criminal justice in Iceland was again the subject of scrutiny by the Supreme Court in a case of 9 January 1990.[44] This judgment was the major turning point as to the Court's application of the Convention. The Court reviewed the conformity of domestic law with the Convention in a detailed way. It came to the conclusion despite express provisions and practice that it violated the Convention. The claim of annulment of the district criminal court judgment was, as in the cases of 1985 and 1987, based on the alleged violation of Article 6 of the Convention. The Supreme Court stated:

In Supreme Court Reports 1985 p. 1290 and 1987 p. 356 this Court held that such an arrangement was not prevented by Article 2 of the Icelandic Constitution No. 33 of 1944, viewing the fact that its Article 61 assumes that judges may hold administrative offices. Owing to historical and geographical conditions judicial as well as administrative functions have, in this country, been discharged by the same persons. This is not in harmony with the views prevailing in states whose legal conceptions are in other respects similar to those of Iceland.

The Court then discussed Article 6 of the Convention. It stated that the government, at the time of ratification, had considered Icelandic law to be in conformity with the Convention. Since that time the Commission and the Court of Human Rights had clarified many of its provisions. The Court held that the following was to be considered:

The Constitution of the Republic is based on the general principle that state authority is divided into three branches, and that judicial powers are exercised separately by judges.

The particular historical and geographical conditions underlying the arrangement of frequently committing both administrative and judicial duties to the same persons outside Reykjavik are now of less significance than previously, *inter alia* on account of better communications than in the past.

The Parliament has passed an Act relating to the separation of district administrative and judicial powers, which shall enter into effect 1 July 1992.

Iceland has undertaken the obligation according to international law to honour the European Convention on Human Rights.

The European Commission on Human Rights has unanimously concluded that the procedure described above in the case of Mr Jón Kristinsson was not in conformity with Article 6, paragraph 1 of the Human Rights Convention.

The Icelandic Government has, subsequent to the referral of the case to the European Court of Human Rights, concluded a settlement with Mr Jón Kristinsson

[43] See p. 419 below. [44] SCR 1990, p. 2.

in the manner described, and also with another person who has submitted an application relating to a similar matter.

Article 36, paragraph 7 of the Code of Civil Procedure, No 85 of 1936, provides, *inter alia* that a judge shall yield his seat if there is a danger 'that he may not be able to view the case impartially'. According to Article 15, paragraph 2 of the Code of Criminal Procedure, No. 74 of 1974, this provision is also to be applied to criminal cases.

In this case no evidence has been submitted to indicate that the judge's deputy who rendered the district court judgment held partial views. Nevertheless this Court must concur with the opinion of the European Commission on Human Rights that impartiality in the performance of judicial functions is not adequately secured when a person performs such functions while also administrating police matters.

With regard to the above quoted legal provisions they shall now be construed as having the effect that the county magistrate of Árnessysla and his deputy, who rendered the district court judgment, should have yielded their seat in this case. The judgment appealed against shall therefore be invalidated and the case remanded to the district court for renewed procedure and adjudication.

This increased role of the Convention is reflected in a judgment of 2 February 1990.[45] The case concerned an individual who had been placed in detention on remand. The decision was based on a provision of the Code of Criminal Procedure then in force that authorized such deprivation of liberty in cases when there were reasons to believe that the accused had committed an offence and that this offence was punishable with at least two years' imprisonment. Subsequently a criminal action was brought against the accused. The judge assigned to try the case was the same as had previously taken the decision to detain the accused on remand. The Supreme Court referred to the obligation of the Icelandic state to respect the Convention and to guarantee to the individual the right to a fair trial. The Court referred to the judgment of the Court of Human Rights of 24 May 1989 in the *Hauschildt* case. The Court then referred to its judgment of 9 January 1990, which is based on the obligation of Iceland to interpret Icelandic law in the light of the Convention. The Court came to the conclusion that the judge should have relinquished his seat.

A judgment of 5 November 1991[46] concerned a claim made on behalf of a fish processing factory to annul the decision of the Minister of Fisheries to confiscate an illegal fish catch on the basis of Act 32 of 1976. The plaintiff maintained that the legislator had given too extensive powers to the executive. The Court *inter alia* stated that this law did not violate Article 6, paragraph 1 of the Convention and in any case the Convention had not acquired the force of law in Iceland.

[45] SCR 1990. p. 92. Same conclusion in SCR 1990, p. 266.
[46] SCR 1991, p. 1690.

A judgment of 6 February 1992[47] concerned the procedure of a criminal case where the accused was not able to express himself in the Icelandic tongue and obtained the assistance of an interpreter. According to the Code of Criminal Procedure No. 74 of 1974 then in force the expenses resulting from the assistance of an interpreter belonged to prosecution expenses to be charged to the accused if convicted. The Supreme Court confirmed the judgment as to conviction. As to the question of the expenses occurred in relation to the assistance of an interpreter the Court considered that the provisions of the Code of Criminal Procedure had to be interpreted in conformity with Article 6, paragraph 3, point e of the Convention and accordingly the expenses should be charged to the state Treasury. The other prosecution expenses were charged to the accused.

The Supreme Court case of 5 March 1992[48] concerned defamation proceedings against a journalist as to his criticism of the activities of a civil servant, a priest and custodian of the Videy precinct. The majority of the Court considered Article 108 of the Penal Code No.19 of 1940, which deals specifically with the defamation of civil servants, applicable. The Supreme Court stated that according to general rules of interpretation Article 108 of the Penal Code should be interpreted in the light of Article 72 of the Constitution. The Court then stated:

> These provisions should also be interpreted taking into consideration the obligations which the Icelandic State has undertaken in respect of international human rights conventions protecting an individual against defamation, guaranteeing personal freedom and the freedom of expression. Here to mention is the European Convention on Human Rights, cf. Announcement No. 11 of 1954, and the United Nations International Covenant on Civil and Political Rights, cf. Announcement No. 10 of 1979.

The Court considered certain statements to be defamatory and sentenced the journalist to pay a fine.[49]

[47] SCR 1992, p. 174.

[48] SCR 1992, p. 401.

[49] This judgment was delivered subsequent to the finding of the Commission on Human Rights of a violation of Article 10 in the case of *Thorgeir Thorgeirsson*, p. 418 below. The Court of Human Rights upheld the opinion of the Commission in its judgment of 25 June 1992. Supreme Court judgment of 17 December 1992 is also of interest here. Following the publication of a newspaper article in which an advocate commented on a Probate Court judge's handling of a case the Board of the Icelandic Bar Association decided, on 14 October 1992, to admonish the lawyer on account of certain expressions in the newspaper article. The Court upheld this decision. The lawyer filed a complaint with the Commission on Human Rights and the case resulted in a friendly settlement.

It can be argued that the Supreme Court has become more cautious as to conviction in defamation cases in particular when the target is a public activity. The reasoning of the Court in a judgment of 4 December 1997 (a journalist criticizing the Prison Authority in a newspaper article) points in that direction. The Supreme Court did not refer to the Convention in its reasoning but

In a case of 28 January 1993[50] the Court held that the delay in the proceedings of a criminal case was to be ascribed the Prosecution Authority, had not been explained, and was thus reprehensible. This delay was in violation of the applicable acts of the Code of Criminal Procedure and of Article 6, paragraph 1 of the European Convention on Human Rights.[51]

A judgment of 25 February 1993[52] concerned the alleged impartiality of a district court judge. According to a police report presented to the district court judge the plaintiff denied the road traffic offence of speeding. The judge offered the plaintiff to finish the case by settlement but he refused. The prosecutor subsequently started criminal proceedings against the plaintiff who was sentenced to a fine by the same judge who had offered him the settlement. The Supreme Court considered that by offering the plaintiff the settlement the judge had taken stand as to the alleged offence, preventing him from acting as judge in the case in accordance with Article 36, point 7 of the Code of Civil Procedure 85 of 1936 then in force, cf. Article 19, paragraph 2 of the Code of Criminal Procedure No. 74 of 1974 as interpreted in the light of the European Convention on Human Rights. The judgment was invalidated.

The most significant judgment since the incorporation of the Convention into Icelandic law was delivered on 18 May 1995.[53] It concerned the conformity of the system of assigning cases to deputy judges with the Constitution

reviewed the conformity of the restriction with the Constitution. Of interest here is also the judgment of 2 April 1998 where the critical remarks were directed at the state Housing Authority.

Two other judgments in defamation cases have referred to the Convention. In a case of 19 February 1998 the plaintiff demanded that certain statements in a letter written by a former neighbour harshly criticizing him for keeping a dog in an apartment building be declared defamatory. The letter was presented to the authorities that handled a claim that the plaintiff was to be deprived of his licence to keep the dog. The Court stated that the applicable provisions of the Penal Code were lawful restrictions on the freedom of expression permitted by Article 73 of the Constitution. The restriction was also in conformity with Article 10, paragraph 2 of the European Convention on Human Rights, which is comparable to the Constitutional provision referred to. The Court partly sustained the plaintiff's claims. In a judgment of 5 February 1998 the Supreme Court upheld the conviction of an individual for providing access to pornographic photos on his homepage on the Internet. The Court considered this a legitimate restriction upon the freedom of expression in conformity with the Constitution and the Convention. See also two Supreme Court judgments delivered on 25 February 1999: case number 252/1998 (an author convicted and sentenced since he in co-operation with a medical doctor registered and published in the doctor's memoirs personal information about his former patient) and case *Bynber* 415/1998 (an executive of a beer manufacturing company charged and found to have violated the prohibition of advertising alcoholic beverages. The SC held that this prohibition violated neither the constitutional provision guaranteeing freedom of expression nor Article 10 of the ECHR.)

For a detailed discussion of the freedom of expression in Icelandic law, see H. Einarsson, *Tjáningarfrelsi og fjölmiðlar*, 1997.

[50] SCR 1993, p. 147.

[51] In a case of 23 May 1996 (SCR 1996, p. 1868) the Supreme Court found that a delay in a case with the Prosecution Authority violated the Code of Criminal Procedure and Article 6, paragraph 1 of the Convention and Article 70, paragraph 1 of the Constitution. The delay was not ascribed to the accused and had not been justified.

[52] SCR 1993, p. 355.

[53] SCR 1995, p. 1444.

and with Article 6 of the Convention. Before a district criminal court the accused had been sentenced to pay a fine for a violation of the Traffic Act. Deputy judges do not enjoy the same legal protection as ordinary judges, who are appointed for life.

The Court stated:

> The Supreme Court had already before the entry into force of Act no. 62 of 1994 on the European Convention on Human Rights established in its case-law that Icelandic law, including the Constitution, should be interpreted so as to achieve the best conformity with the Convention.

The Supreme Court referred to its earlier case-law and proceeded to discuss Article 6 of the Convention and its interpretation by the Commission and Court of Human Rights.

> The Commission and Court of Human Rights have considered that according to this provision the courts must be independent of the legislator, the executive, and the parties to a case. A court will not be considered independent within the meaning of this provision unless judges are not bound by instructions from others and their position in other respects is not insecure while they hold their office.

The Supreme Court referred to the judgment in the case of *Langborger v Sweden*. The Court then stated that the Commission and Court of Human Rights had considered the requirement of an independent court to be twofold, subject to both the subjective and the objective test.

The Supreme Court continued by stating that in this case no attempt had been made to demonstrate that the deputy judge who was assigned the case had been partial. The accused on the other hand claimed that the position of deputy judges on the whole, when considered objectively, raised doubts as to their independence from the executive. The Supreme Court held:

> When this question is decided the Court must take into consideration the legal provision and practice concerning the position of deputy judges and compare them to the demands which the defendant could make on the judicial power in a democratic society as described in the above mentioned constitutional provisions and provisions of the European Convention.
>
> It is stated in the explanatory report to Act No. 92 of 1989 that it was considered necessary to keep the offices of deputy judges in order to train lawyers in judicial work. The terms of employment cannot alone be decisive whether a deputy judge is to be considered to be so independent of the executive that he cannot carry out judicial work under the supervision, on the responsibility, and in the name of an ordinary judge. It has, however, been described above how this system has turned out in practice and that it cannot be accepted that this comprehensive judicial work of a deputy judge can be the responsibility of a district court judge. In fact they work in the same manner as ordinary judges and often are assigned with just as important cases. However, they are rarely as experienced and have not at the beginning of their career had to swear an

oath to respect the Constitution of the Republic. The Ministry of Justice is formally empowered to revoke their authorization and to dismiss them without bringing that matter before the courts. The executive can by exerting its influence and taking measures put an end to their term of office in a short time. It must thus be accepted that the position of deputy judges as it now is does not meet with the requirements of the basic norms of the Constitution on the independence of the judiciary as interpreted in the light of Article 6 paragraph 1 of the European Convention on Human Rights on independent and impartial tribunals so that they can in their own name and on their own responsibility carry out the judicial work as described in the above mentioned letter of the Ministry of Justice.

By a majority, the Supreme Court overturned the judgment.[54]

The Supreme Court case of 4 October 1995[55] addressed the competence of deputy judges to deliver decisions concerning detention on remand. The accused claimed that Article 6 of Act No. 92 of 1989 on the Separation of District Judicial and Administrative Powers, cf. Article 1 of Act No. 80/1995, did not conform with Article 67, paragraph 3 of the Constitution as amended by Act No. 97 of 1995. According to that provision a judge must decide whether the accused is to be detained on remand. The accused maintained that this provision referred to ordinary judges and not deputy judges and supported his claim by Article 6, paragraph 1 of the European Convention on Human Rights as incorporated by Act No. 69 of 1994. The Supreme Court concluded that in the light of the present position of deputy judges the system must be considered to conform with the requirements of the Constitution and the international agreements to which the Icelandic state is party. The decision of the deputy judge on the detention on remand was thus confirmed.[56]

[54] One judge considered that the system of deputy judges did not violate the Constitution or Article 6 of the Convention. He stated:

> It cannot be deduced from the case-law of the European Court of Human Rights that dismissal of judges has to be excluded. The emphasis is rather whether the power of dismissal has in fact been applied and if so how. The Minister of Justice has never made use of his power under Article 8, paragraph 4 of Law No. 92 of 1989. The position of deputy judges in relation to the executive cannot be considered as conflicting with the Convention.

The question of the competence of deputy judges was again at issue in a case of 24 May 1995 (SCR 1995, p. 1518) but this time as to their competence to deal with civil cases. The Court annulled the district civil court judgment with the same reasoning. A Supreme Court judgment of 18 June 1998 concerned a judgment of the Court delivered on 7 June 1995 invalidating a district court judgment since a deputy judge had delivered it. The defendant claimed compensation for the costs incurred because the appeal of the case to the Supreme Court did not lead to any result. The Court granted the defendant compensation based on the following reasoning:

> When deciding whether the defendant has the right to compensation for the costs that can be proved to be related to this, it must be observed that there was a question of a violation of important human rights, *inter alia* provided for in the European Convention on Human Rights. There is thus sufficient legal basis for the responsibility of the Icelandic state.

[55] SCR 1995, p. 2172.

[56] See also judgments of 13 June 1995 (SCR 1995, p. 1673), 17 December 1997, and 23 February 1998. In Supreme Court case of 3 June 1996 (SCR 1996, p. 1998) the issue was again

The Supreme Court case of 10 May 1996[57] concerned provisions in the Code of Criminal Procedure on the conditions for detention on remand and the claim of the accused that they violated Article 5 of the Convention. The Supreme Court held that:

> The interpretation is accepted in the case-law of the institutions of the Council of Europe that the wording of Article 5, paragraph 3, point c does not exclude detention on remand in the interests of an investigation if there is a reasonable suspicion of the accused having committed an offence. There is no reason to interpret the provisions of Act No. 62 of 1994 in another way.

In a Supreme Court case of 23 September 1996[58] the Court found that the registration by the Post and Telephone Office of information on the use of the defendant's mobile phone on the basis of the Code of Criminal Procedure did not violate either the Constitution or Article 8 of the Convention.

In a Supreme Court case of 3 January 1997[59] the Court sustained the argument of the parties that the district court judge had not given them adequate time to prepare their case, a right of which the defendant is guaranteed by Article 6, paragraph 3 of the Convention. This, however, was not reason enough to sustain the claim that the judge should relinquish his seat despite the reprehensible defects in conducting the case.

The Supreme Court case of 23 July 1997[60] concerned the right of an accused to acquaint himself with all the documents on which the prosecution based its case prior to the hearing of this case before the court. The Supreme Court referred to previous case-law according to which it was not considered to be a breach of the principle of equality of arms and a fair hearing if the defendant was questioned before an independent tribunal prior to his access to the case file, *inter alia* the testimony of co-accused, if this was thought necessary for justified and relevant reasons. Nothing in Article 6, paragraphs 1 or 3 of the Convention nor Article 70 of the Constitution changed this or resulted in a breach of the equality of arms if the accused was not granted the opportunity to study the case file in full prior to giving his testimony before a court and before his case has been pleaded. Defence lawyers always have the right to aquaint themselves with the case file at every stage of the proceedings and can thus take care of their client's interests.

In its judgment of 17 October 1997 the Court held that the legal requirements for extraditing a couple to the United States where they faced charges

the independence of a deputy judge in a case relating to detention on remand. The deputy judge who ordered detention on remand did that within the authority of the ordinary judge who pronounced a judgment in the case. The majority of the Court found this to be contrary to the provisions of the Code of Criminal Procedure, the Constitution, and Article 6 of the European Convention on Human Rights.

[57] SCR 1996, p. 1633.
[58] SCR 1996, p. 2553.
[59] SCR 1997, p. 11.
[60] SCR 1997, p. 2155.

of kidnapping a child were not fulfilled. The Court considered that the extradition authorities had not respected the principle of proportionality in exercising its power. The Court stated *inter alia*:

If an executive authority has a choice as to the means of achieving the purpose of a decision, it shall choose the less burdensome means that achieves the purpose in question. The more burdensome a restriction is which is caused by the decision the stronger demands must be made as to its necessity. This applies in particular to those interests of individuals which concern their freedom and inviolability and are protected in the Constitution and international human rights instruments to which Iceland is a party. The principle of proportionality applies beyond doubt to the measures taken by Icelandic executive authorities, which aim at fulfilling a request of extradition submitted by another state.

The authorities had not taken into account the rightful arguments of the defendants, which would have achieved the primary aim of the extradition to secure the defendants fair proceedings in conformity with Article 70 of the Constitution and Articles 5 and 6 of the Convention.[61]

Since its judgment of 9 January 1990 the Supreme Court has firmly established the application of the principle of interpreting domestic law in conformity with the Convention. However, the Court has applied the principle liberally and has in some cases put the Convention requirements higher than explicit provisions in domestic law. The approach of the Supreme Court is not firmly established and further developments can be expected. In a defamation case of 4 December 1997 the Court based its acquittal on Article 73 of the Constitution. In contrast to the judgment of the district court there was no reference to Article 10 of the Convention.

D. CASES BROUGHT BEFORE THE EUROPEAN COMMISSION AND COURT OF HUMAN RIGHTS

There have been no inter-state complaints against Iceland to the Commission of Human Rights. Until September 1998 fifty-nine individual applications had been registered. By the end of 2000 sixty-nine individual aplications had been registered. The Commission came to the conclusion in three cases that there had been a violation of the Convention. These cases were referred to the

[61] By a judgment of 23 June 1997 the Supreme Court overturned a district court judgment that declared the extradition to be legal. The Court held that the district court judge had not taken into consideration the main arguments of the defendants, relating, *inter alia,* to humanitarian grounds. On 7 July 1997 the district court judge delivered a new judgment in the case and found that the requirements of extradition were not fulfilled in light of Article 68 of the Constitution and Article 3 of the Convention.

Court of Human Rights. Three cases resulted in friendly settlements, one subsequent to the referral of the case to the Court and two before the Commission.[62]

The applications filed with the Commission concern a broad range of complaints. A frequently quoted case from the early years of the Commission is the 1957 case of *Gudmundur Gudmundsson*. The question arose as to the dividing line between taxation and confiscation according to Article 1 of Protocol No. 1 to the Convention. In fifteen applications it was maintained that the prohibition of keeping dogs in Reykjavík violated Article 8. A number of cases have concerned Article 6 on the right to a fair trial.

The following cases were brought before the European Court of Human Rights. The case of *Jon Kristinsson*, judgment of 1 March 1990, resulted in a friendly settlement, subsequent to a unanimous vote by the Commission on the violation of Article 6. The case concerned the conformity of the Icelandic system where investigative and judicial powers are combined with Article 6 of the Convention.[63] The Commission came to the unanimous conclusion that the system did not fulfil the requirements of Article 6 on a fair procedure before an independent tribunal. In its Report the Commission, quoting its earlier case-law, attached particular weight to the functions exercised and the internal organization in regard to the case before it. At stake is the confidence which the courts in a democratic society must inspire in the public and above all, as far as criminal proceedings are concerned, in the accused. The Commission considered that in the circumstances there were reasons to fear that the deputy in his capacity as judge did not offer sufficient guarantees of impartiality.[64]

The Court took formal note of the friendly settlement reached by the government and the applicant. The Court stated that in view of its responsibilities under Article 19 of the Convention it could disregard this settlement and proceed with the consideration of the case if a reason of public policy appeared to necessitate such a course. However, the Court, having regard to the changes in Icelandic law, the Supreme Court judgment of 9 January 1990, and the case-law of the European Court on Human Rights on the matter saw no such reason. Thus the Court decided to strike the case from the list.[65]

The second case was that of *Thorgeir Thorgeirsson* concerning the freedom of expression under Article 10, judgment of 25 June 1992. The facts can be

[62] Application 13291/87, *Einar Sverrisson v Iceland*, Report of the Commission adopted on 6 February 1990 and Application 22103/93 *Georgsson v Iceland*, Report of the Commission (Chamber) adopted on 15 April 1997.

[63] See p. 408 above.

[64] Report of the Commission of 8 March 1989.

[65] Judgment of 1 March 1990, Series A No. 171–B.

summarized as follows. From 1979 to 1983 a number of incidents occurred in Iceland involving allegations of police brutality, about ten of which were reported to the police. The last such complaint was made in the autumn of 1983 by a journalist and led to the prosecution of three members of the Reykjavík police. Two officers were acquitted and one convicted. This caused the applicant, a writer, to publish two articles in the daily newspaper about police brutality. He called for a new, more effective system of investigating accusations against the police. On account of certain passages in these articles, he was charged with the offence of defaming civil servants, contrary to Article 108 of the General Penal Code of 1940. The majority of the Supreme Court upheld his conviction and found no violation of the Constitution. The Court did not refer to the Convention in its reasoning.

The Commission came to the conclusion that Article 10 had been violated. The Court confirmed that finding.[66] The Court observed that there was no precedent in its case-law for distinguishing, as suggested by the government, between political discussion and discussion of other matters of public concern. Moreover, their submission that freedom of expression must, in order to be protected by Article 10, have been exercised in a manner consistent with democratic principles failed to take into account that this freedom could be restricted only on the conditions provided for in the second paragraph of that Article.

As regards the specific circumstances of the case the Court noted the following points. The applicant, in addition to referring to an undisputed case of police brutality, was essentially reporting what was being said by others about police brutality and was convicted partly because of his failure to justify the allegations. Insofar as he was required to establish their truth, he was faced with an unreasonable, if not impossible task. The principal purpose of the applicant's articles had not been to damage the reputation of the police but to call for independent and impartial investigation of allegations of police brutality. The articles bore on a matter of serious public concern. Bearing in mind their purpose, the language used could not be considered as excessive. The impugned measures were capable of discouraging open discussion on matters of public concern.[67]

The facts of the *Sigurdur Sigurjonsson* case concerned the negative aspect of the freedom of association. The applicant complained of a revocation of his licence to operate a taxi-cab.[68] The Commission and the Court came to the conclusion that Article 11 had been violated.

[66] The applicant complained of a violation of Article 6, but neither the Court nor the Commission found a violation of that Article.

[67] Judgment of 25 June 1992, Series A No. 239.

[68] See p. 409 above.

As to the general scope of the freedom of association the Court held that Article 11 had to be viewed as encompassing a negative right of association. As regards the concrete circumstances of the case, the Court was not convinced by the government's argument that the applicant had accepted the obligation to join Frami, or that such an obligation existed for any other reason, when he obtained his licence in 1984. Only later, when the 1989 Law entered into force, did it become clear that membership was a licence condition. He had since been compelled to remain a member and would otherwise run the risk of losing his licence. This form of compulsion, in the circumstances of the case, struck at the very substance of the right guaranteed by Article 11 and itself amounted to interference. In addition, the fact that the impugned compulsion was contrary to his own opinions also constituted an interference with his right under Article 11 as viewed in the light of Articles 9 and 10. It was not contested that the impugned membership obligation was in accordance with the law and pursued a legitimate aim.

In the Court's view, the membership obligation, being imposed by law, was a form of compulsion that, on the very face of it, had to be considered incompatible with Article 11. The Court did not doubt that Frami had a role which served the public interest and that its performance of this role was facilitated by the obligation imposed on every taxi licence holder within its area to be a member. However, the reasons adduced by the government, although they could be considered relevant, were not sufficient to show that it was necessary to compel the applicant to be a member of Frami, on pain of losing his licence and contrary to his own opinions. In particular, notwithstanding Iceland's margin of appreciation, the measures complained of were disproportionate to the legitimate aim pursued.[69]

E. REMEDIAL ACTION TAKEN BY THE GOVERNMENT IN RESPONSE TO BEING HELD IN VIOLATION OF THE CONVENTION

The reaction of the Icelandic government to the Commission's finding of a violation in the case of *Jon Kristinsson* has already been mentioned.[70] Subsequent to the referral of the case to the Court the parties entered a friendly settlement. Following the Commission's finding the Icelandic court system was fundamentally reformed by Act No. 92 of 1989 on the Separation of District Judicial and Administrative Powers which entered into force on 1 July 1992.

[69] Judgment of 30 June 1993, Series A No. 264.

[70] See p. 418 above.

Following the judgment of the Court in the case of *Thorgeir Thorgeirsson* the Minister of Justice appointed a Committee to decide upon the reactions to the finding of violation of Article 10 and to look into the question of incorporating the Convention. The Committee suggested that the Convention should be incorporated into Icelandic law and this proposal was enacted as Act No. 62 of 1994. The findings and reasoning of the Committee formed the explanatory report to the Act. According to the information submitted by the government to the Committee of Ministers the judgment was translated into Icelandic and brought to the attention of the courts and the State Prosecutor.[71]

In response to the judgment in the case of *Sigurdur Sigurjonsson* the Parliament passed Act No. 61 of 1995, which entered into force on 8 March 1995, abolishing the requirement that taxi operators in Iceland had to belong to a specified union in order to obtain a licence to conduct business.[72]

F. ASSESSMENT AND PROSPECTS

The assessment of the effects of the Convention on Icelandic law has to be seen in the light of the process which started in the late 1980s and in particular the judgment delivered by the Supreme Court on 9 January 1990. This process is still ongoing and it is hard to provide concrete answers to the different aspects of the Convention as a source of law in Iceland.

The Convention has the formal status of ordinary law. However, in practice it has been given higher ranking, somewhere between that of ordinary law and that of constitutional law. The Convention presented a new dimension to the traditional sources of law and the application of the dualistic doctrine has not been able to give satisfactory answers to these new questions. Thus Icelandic scholars have called for a rethinking of the traditional theory of legal sources in Iceland.

The Supreme Court has applied the principle of interpreting law and practice in harmony with the Convention. However, the principle has been applied liberally and the Court has changed the interpretation of domestic law, including the Constitution, to meet with the Convention's requirements. The Supreme Court has looked to and applied the case-law of the Convention organs when adjudicating the conformity of domestic law with the Convention. The Supreme Court seems to have given the case-law a rather wide interpretation, for example in its judgments of 9 February 1990 and 18 May 1995.

[71] Res. DH (92)59. [72] Res. DH (95)36.

The delicate issue of the balance between legislative and judicial power was not elaborated in the Explanatory Report to the 1994 Act. The courts have been provided with extensive power to adjudge the conformity of law and practice with the Convention. Both the Danish and the Swedish explanatory reports stressed that the consequences of incorporating the Convention into the respective country should not upset the balance established between these two branches of government. The Parliament has been responsible for assuring the conformity of enacted law with the Convention, although there is almost no documented practice prior to 1989. Since then several bills have been enacted taking into account the Convention's requirements on specific points of law. The incorporation of the Convention did not change this primary responsibility of the legislator to observe the conformity of domestic legislation with the Convention.

The approach of the Supreme Court has not yet been firmly established. This can be explained by the relatively recent active application of the Convention. The incorporation of the Convention and the 1995 Constitutional Amendment are factors that have provided new dimensions into this process. The Convention is a new source of law in Iceland and it takes time to adapt judicial practice to new reality. The preferable development is a harmonious interaction between the national courts and the European Court of Human Rights in the elaboration of human rights protection.[73]

[73] This contribution was written in October 1998 and therefore I would like to point out some relevant developments which have occurred until the end of year 2000.

On 30 May 2000 the European Court of Human Rights decided to strike two cases against Iceland out of the list as a result of friendly settlements: The former is *Siglfirdingur ehf v Iceland*. The applicant company complained *inter alia* that since it had not been able to obtain a review by a superior court of a fine imposed by the Labour Court, there had been a violation of Article 2, paragraph 1 of Protocol No. 1 to the Convention. The latter is *Sigurdardóttir v Iceland*. The applicant alleged *inter alia* that her right under Article 6, paragraph 2 to be presumed innocent until proven guilty of the commission of an offence had been violated in that the Supreme Court had rejected her claim for compensation on the ground that 'she was not deemed more likely to be innocent than guilty of the conduct with which she was charged'.

The Supreme Court of Iceland has referred to the Convention in a number of cases during this period and seems to confirm the trend of liberal interpretation of the Convention when establishing the conformity of law or practice with the Constitution and the Convention. This approach has perhaps been most notable in the area covered by the provision of the Constitution prohibiting discrimination, as reflected, *inter alia*, in the following judgments of the Supreme Court: Judgment of 4 February 1999 concerning a disabled student's access to adequate support and facilities to pursue her studies at the University of Iceland; Judgment of 6 May 1999, prohibition of amateur boxing upheld; Judgment of 18 December 2000 declaring a legal impediment for a father to institute proceedings to establish the paternity of a child unconstitutional; Judgment of 19 December 2000 declaring a law providing for reduction of disablement benefits due to the income of the other spouse unconstitutional.

18

Ireland

DONNCHA O'CONNELL

INTRODUCTION

The ECHR was adopted by the Council of Europe and signed by the Irish Minister for External Affairs on 4 November 1950. It was confirmed and ratified by the Irish Government on 25 February 1953 and laid before Dail Eireann on 29 March 1954. It had entered into force on 3 September 1953.

At the time of Ireland's ratification of the ECHR the government was pursuing a dogged anti-partition policy in the Assembly of the Council of Europe and other supranational forums. In pursuance of this policy, it sought to obstruct the business of such bodies by constantly raising the 'unfinished business' of the border between Northern Ireland and the Republic established in the treaty settlement of 1922 for the purposes of seeking to embarass the United Kingdom government. It was therefore somewhat surprising that the Irish government, without highlighting the usual anti-partitionist propaganda, embraced the internationalization of human rights protection through the ECHR in a relatively unqualified and enthusiastic manner by accepting the compulsory jurisdiction of the Commission and Court with a temporally unlimited right of individual application. The government probably had no real choice in the matter as it had patently failed to interest other European countries in the partition issue which by then had become, in the words of one Irish newspaper, 'a Strasbourg joke'.[1]

Although anti-British sentiment informed much of Irish foreign policy in the middle of the twentieth century, it was by no means an unbridled source of inspiration. Recently released Irish cabinet papers disclose an interesting attempt by the British Aeronautical Engineers' Association (AEA) to circumvent the non-acceptance by the UK government of the right of individual

[1] Blake, 'The National Archives: New Perspectives on Ireland's Approach to the International Protection of Human Rights', (February 1992), *Irish Law Times* 44.

application under the ECHR in the years immediately after its coming into force.[2]

In May 1955, the AEA requested the then Irish Minister for External Affairs to bring an inter-state application against the UK government arising out of a dispute between the association and the government. It claimed that certain legislation had been amended and/or repealed in the House of Commons in order to deny AEA members rights enshrined in the Convention but the letter was not specific as to what precise violations might be involved. Ultimately, a political decision was reached within the Irish Department of External Affairs to reject the request but only after considering all the advantages and disadvantages from an Irish perspective. The propaganda value of bringing such a case was not lost on the then Legal Adviser at the Department of External Affairs, who noted that the request raised two partition issues. First, the AEA was registered in Belfast and thus the complaint was of a violation of the ECHR in the six counties of Northern Ireland with the obvious propaganda value that that entailed. The second partition element was decidedly less advantageous from an Irish perspective. In 1954 the Irish government had resisted suggestions that an inter-state application under the Convention be made against the UK government in respect of the imprisonment for sedition of Liam Kelly, a nationalist member of the Stormont Assembly and the Irish Seanad. If the Irish government were now to support a case involving a complaint by a trade union which operated mainly in Great Britain, a dim view would be taken by the nationalist community in Northern Ireland. These were only some of the considerations given to the request by the AEA but they illustrate the importance of the anti-partition dimension of Irish foreign policy at that time.

If the Convention can be viewed as an instrument for the embarrassment of contracting states, its potential in that regard was undoubtedly realized in *Ireland v United Kingdom*[3] (which is discussed further in the chapter on United Kingdom cases). However, notwithstanding the foregoing historical considerations, it would be mistaken to think that the only Irish use for the Convention has been as a stick with which to beat its nearest neighbour. That is far from the case and, as will be seen in the following sections of this chapter, the most significant cases involving Ireland have been where the government is the respondent in cases involving the individual right of petition under Article 25 of the Convention. Some of these cases have contributed significantly to the development of the European Court's burgeoning jurisprudence while others have had little significance beyond their own facts.

[2] See generally: Doolan, 'Ireland—The Human Rights Defender of British Trade Unions?', (August 1996), *Irish Law Times*, 197–198.

[3] [1978] 2 EHRR 25, Series A No. 25.

A. THE STATUS OF THE CONVENTION IN NATIONAL LAW

There is a growing literature on the domestic status of the ECHR[4] and the generally accepted view is that, because of the dualistic nature of the Irish legal system, the Convention does not form part of domestic law. In other words, while the Convention applies *to* Ireland it does not apply *within* Ireland. There is, however, widespread acknowledgement of its increasing significance as a persuasive authority in legal proceedings before national courts.

1. The orthodoxy

The Irish Constitution of 1937 contains a number of apparent bars to domestic enforcement of the ECHR. Article 15.2 provides that:

> The sole and exclusive power of making laws for the State is hereby vested in the Oireachtas: no other legislative authority has power to make laws for the State.

Article 29.6 provides specifically that:

> No international agreement shall be part of the domestic law of the State save as may be determined by the Oireachtas.

Notwithstanding the relatively unqualified ratificiation of the Convention by the Irish government in 1953 it has never been incorporated into domestic Irish law by the Oireachtas and therefore lacks the force of municipal law in domestic legal proceedings by virtue of the foregoing constitutional provisions. This view has been repeated consistently in a number of cases.[5]

[4] See for example: Drzemczewski, *The European Human Rights Convention in Domestic Law—A Comparative Study*, (Oxford: Clarendon Press, 1983) 170–175; Whyte, 'The Application of the European Convention on Human Rights Before the Irish Courts', (1982) 31 *International and Comparative Law Quarterly*, 856–861; Jaconelli, 'The European Convention on Human Rights as Irish Municipal Law' (1987) *Irish Jurist* (new series) 13–27; Gleeson, 'The European Convention on Human Rights: Its Practical Relevance', (1993) 2 *Irish Journal of European Law*, 248–265; Connelly, 'Ireland and the European Convention on Human Rights: An Overview', in: Heffernan and Kingston (eds), *Human Rights—A European Perspective* (Dublin: Round Hall Press, 1994) 34–47; Dillon-Malone, 'Individual Remedies and the Strasbourg System in an Irish Context', ibid, 48–66; Flynn, 'The Significance of the European Convention on Human Rights in the Irish Legal Order', (1994) 1 *Irish Journal of European Law*, 4–29; O'Connell, 'Review of the Cases from the Republic of Ireland in Strasbourg Over the Last Decade', (1995) *Irish Human Rights Yearbook*, 1–14; Connelly, 'Ireland and the European Convention', in: Dickson (ed), *Human Rights and the European Convention: The Effects of the Convention on the United Kingdom and Ireland* (London: Sweet & Maxwell, 1997), 185–209; Flynn, 'Chapter 5—Ireland', in: Gearty (ed), *European Civil Liberties and the European Convention on Human Rights* (The Netherlands: Kluwer Law International, 1997) 177–215; O'Connell, 'Belt and Braces or Blinkers: The Irish Constitution and the ECHR', (2000) *Irish Human Rights Review* (Dublin: Round Hall Sweet and Maxwell, 2000) 81–101.

[5] In *The People v McKeever*, Unrep. CCA, (11 July 1992) it was stated that incorporation of the Convention was solely a matter for the Oireachtas and that the courts had no role to play in this matter.

In *Re O Laighleis*[6] the plaintiff sought to challenge his detention under the Offences Against the State (Amendment) Act 1940 as being contrary to Articles 1, 5, and 6 of the ECHR. The Supreme Court unanimously rejected the contention that the supremacy of domestic law could be displaced by any contrary international obligation contained in an international agreement such as the ECHR. According to Maguire CJ, Articles 15 and 29 of the Constitution constituted an 'insuperable obstacle to importing the provisions of the Convention'. He went on to state:

> The Oireachtas has not determined that the Convention . . . is to be part of the domestic law of the State, and accordingly this Court cannot give effect to the Convention if it be contrary to domestic law or purports to grant rights or impose obligations additional to those of domestic law
>
> . . . Nor can the Court accept the contention that the Act of 1940 is to be construed in the light of, and so as to produce conformity with, a convention entered into ten years afterwards. The intention of the Oireachtas must be sought in the conditions which existed when it became law.[7]

In the *Application of Woods*[8] the principle established *in O'Laighleis* was applied in the context of an attempt by the applicant to invoke a provision of the Universal Declaration on Human Rights.

In another case, *E v E*,[9] there was an unsuccessful attempt in the High Court to have the European Court of Human Rights decision in *Airey v Ireland*[10] applied as an analogous authority. In this case it was argued that the *O'Laighleis* principle could be distinguished on the basis that what was being sought in *E v E* was the enforcement at a domestic level of a decision of the European Court in which Ireland was the respondent state. O'Hanlon J rejected this argument and stated that if a person felt that the Irish government's response to a decision of the European Court was inadequate the appropriate course of action was for him/her to make a further application under the Convention to the Strasbourg organs. However, the basis on which the judge came to this conclusion is not entirely clear and this case is given

[6] [1960] IR 93. [7] Ibid. [8] [1970] IR 154.

[9] [1982] ILRM 497. A similar approach was adopted by the Supreme Court in a later case (*W O'R v EH* [1996] 2 IR 248) when the Court was asked in a consultative case stated from the Circuit Court whether the concept of *de facto* family ties, referred to in the European Court of Human Rights decision in *Keegan v Ireland* (1994) 18 EHRR 342, was afforded recognition under the Irish Constitution. In answering this question for the majority Hamilton CJ stated:

> The decision of the European Court is not part of the domestic law of Ireland. The family referred to in Articles 41 and 42 of the Constitution is the family based on marriage. The concept of a '*de facto*' family is unknown to the Irish Constitution. The Irish Supreme Court, however, in its decision in *JK v VW* [1990] 2 IR 437 recognised the existence of '*de facto* families' and also the fact that a natural father who lived in such a family might have extensive rights' (at 270).

[10] [1979] Series A, No. 32.

further consideration below in the context of an alternative view of the Convention's status in domestic law.

2. The ECHR as 'belt & braces'[11]

Occasionally Irish judges invoke the provisions of the Convention to bolster their reasoning in relation to a matter of Irish law. In such circumstances, it assumes no greater significance than other international human rights instruments to which Ireland is party nor indeed than such instruments to which it is not. For example, in the case of *O'Leary v Attorney General*,[12] when discussing the universal recognition of the presumption of innocence, Costello J (as he then was) at the High Court stage of the proceedings, had recourse to Article 6 of the ECHR, Article 11 of the Universal Declaration of Human Rights, Article 8(2) of the Inter-American Convention on Human Rights, and Article 7 of the African Charter of Human and Peoples' Rights. When this case was appealed to the Supreme Court[13] the decision of the trial judge was confirmed but without reference to external sources of law. In fact, O'Flaherty J, delivering the unanimous decision of the court, expressly asserted that it was unnecessary to refer to such sources.[14]

In *Heaney v Ireland*[15] a declaration was sought to the effect that section 52 of the Offences Against the State Act 1939, which permitted the drawing of adverse inferences from the silence of an accused in certain circumstances, was unconstitutional on the basis that it infringed an as yet unacknowledged constitutional right to silence.[16] Although the impugned section was upheld, Costello J (as he then was) found that the right to silence did form part of a cluster of due process rights guaranteed by Article 38 of the Irish Constitution.[17] In so doing the judge was mindful of the provisions of Article 6 of the ECHR and of the decision of the European Court of Human Rights in *Funke v France*.[18] The proportionality test used by the Court of Human Rights in that case was the appropriate test to be applied to any restrictions

[11] This phrase is taken from Flynn, 'The Significance of the European Convention on Human Rights in the Irish Legal Order' (1994) 1 *Irish Journal of European Law*, 12. See n. 4 above.

[12] [1993] 1 IR 102.

[13] 1 [1995] IR 254.

[14] Ibid, 259.

[15] [1994] 2 ILRM 420. For general comments on the use of the ECHR in this and other Irish cases see further: O'Connell, 'The Right to Silence and Access to a Lawyer: *Murray v United Kingdom*', (August 1996) *Irish Law Times*, 185–187.

[16] The existence of a common law right to silence in the form of a privilege against self-incrimination during trial and pre-trial detention was well established in Irish law—*State (McCarthy) v Lennon* [1936] IR 485. Until the *Heaney* decision the generally accepted view was that this right was not of constitutional origin: cf Kelly, *The Irish Constitution* (3rd edn) 593–4. The possibility, therefore, of challenging statutory incursions on the right to silence was slim.

[17] The decision was subsequently followed in a case involving a challenge to the incursions on the right to silence contained in sections 18 and 19 of the Criminal Justice Act 1984 (No. 22 of 1984): *Rock v Ireland* (10/11/95) High Court Unreported Decision.

[18] (1993) 16 EHRR 297.

imposed on the constitutional right to silence in this jurisdiction.[19] The proportionality test had earlier been applied in an Irish case involving a constitutional challenge to a statutorily imposed restriction on the right to earn a living following upon a conviction for certain criminal offences.[20] Again, the Supreme Court upheld Judge Costello's decision but it did so on the basis of the freedom of expression guarantee contained in Article 40 of the Irish Constitution.[21] It also applied the proportionality test to the impugned section but there is no reference in the single judgment of the Supreme Court, delivered by O'Flaherty J, to any provision of the ECHR nor to any decision of the European Court of Human Rights.

This unarticulated euroscepticism on the part of the Irish Supreme Court is further evidenced by the approach taken in an earlier case by a differently composed court. In *Finucane v McMahon*,[22] which came shortly after the decision of the European Court of Human Rights in *Soering v United Kingdom*,[23] the Irish Supreme Court unanimously found that a request for extradition could be refused where there was a probable risk that a suspect's fundamental rights would be breached or inadequately protected by the authorities in the requesting state. Although this basis for refusing extradition had been accepted by the Supreme Court in an earlier case[24] the significance of the decision in *Finucane* lies in the fact that none of the judges adverted to the European Court's decision in *Soering*, although the principle involved in

[19] An appeal against this decision was rejected by the Supreme Court in a judgment delivered on 23 July 1996. *Heaney v Ireland* [1996] 1 IR 580.

[20] *Cox v Ireland* [1992] 2 IR 503.

[21] Article 40.6.1.i of the Irish Constitution guarantees liberty for the exercise of freedom of expression (and other rights), subject to public order and morality, in the following terms:

> The right of the citizens to express freely their convictions and opinions.
>
> The education of public opinion being, however, a matter of such grave import to the common good, the State shall endeavour to ensure that organs of public opinion, such as the radio, the press, the cinema, while preserving their rightful liberty of expression, including criticism of Government policy, shall not be used to undermine public order or morality or the authority of the State.
>
> The publication or utterance of blasphemous, seditious or indecent matter is an offence which shall be punishable in accordance with law.

[22] [1990] IR 165.

[23] (1989) 11 EHRR 439.

[24] *Russell v Fanning* [1988] IR 505. In this case the then Chief Justice, Finlay CJ stated:

> I would accept that if a court, upon the hearing of an application to set aside an order for delivery under the Extradition Act 1965, were satisfied as a matter of probability that the plaintiff would, if delivered into another jurisdiction, be subjected to assault, torture or inhuman treatment, that it would, in order to protect the fundamental constitutional rights of that plaintiff, be obliged to release him from detention and to refuse to deliver him out of the jurisdiction of these courts (at 531).

He went on to find (in concurrence with the trial judge) as a matter of fact that no such probability had been established in this case.

both cases was remarkably similar. While the cases were factually distinguishable it is noteworthy that the Irish Supreme Court did not attempt to bolster its reasoning with regard to what was, after all, a newly developed basis for refusing extradition by reference to a precedent as authoritative as that established by the European Court.

Thus, it can be said with some justification that if certain High Court judges use the ECHR as belt and braces their counterparts on the Supreme Court have generally preferred to hug the ample girth of Bunreacht na hEireann with the elasticated waist of their own jurisprudence! Even on the rare occasion when judges of the Supreme Court have referred to the Convention primacy is always accorded to domestic constitutional sources.[25] The composition of the Supreme Court has changed significantly in the past two years and it remains to be seen what approach will be taken in the future.

3. *Is there a presumption of compatibility with the ECHR?*

In a number of cases the Irish courts have accorded the Convention a more elevated status as giving rise to a presumption that certain aspects of Irish law are in conformity with its provisions. This presumption has been characterized as follows:

> . . . no greater than a principle of statutory interpretation or a presumption at common law. Although it might operate to clarify or even supplement statutory words, it cannot prevail against them nor provide a remedy when statutory provisions are lacking completely. It might also be questioned whether such a presumption can operate in respect of laws enacted prior to Ireland's signature . . . and ratification.[26]

For example, in the case of *The State (DPP) v Walsh and Conneely*[27] which involved the issue of criminal contempt of court arising from the publication by *The Irish Times* of a statement of the Association for Legal Justice criticizing a decision of the Special Criminal Court it was stated, *obiter,* by Henchy J:

[25] A good example of this is the judgment of Barrington, J in *The Irish Times and Others v His Honour Judge Anthony G. Murphy and Others* [1998] 2 ILRM 161. The case arose from a judicially imposed ban on contemporaneous media reporting of evidence in a drugs trial. The Supreme Court, in a unanimous decision, quashed the order of the trial judge to impose such a ban. Four of the five judges based their decisions exclusively on domestic law but Barrington, J did have regard to Article 10 ECHR. He stated:

> It appears to me also that when the European Convention on Human Rights states that the right to freedom of expression is to include '. . . freedom to receive and impart information' it is merely making explicit something which is already implicit in Article 40.6.1 of our Constitution' (at 192–193).

[26] Dillon-Malone, 'Individual Remedies and the Strasbourg System in an Irish Context', in: Heffernan and Kingston (eds), *Human Rights—A European Perspective* (Dublin: Round Hall Press, 1994) 49, see n. 4 above.

[27] [1981] IR 412.

. . . In upholding the current position, to the extent of saying that it is for a judge and not a jury to say if the established facts constitute a major criminal contempt, I would stress that, in both the factual and legal aspects of the hearing of the charge, the elementary requirements of justice in the circumstances would have to be observed. There is a presumption that our law in this respect is in conformity with the European Convention on Human Rights, particularly Articles 5 and 10(2) thereof.[28]

In the subsequent case of *O'Domhnaill v Merrick*,[29] which involved a dispute over the application of the Statute of Limitations 1957 to a personal injuries case involving a minor, Henchy J stated that the statute was to be construed in the light of the ECHR as it was passed after Ireland's ratification and contained no contrary intention. However, he went on to qualify this statement by saying:

. . . I do not wish to express a concluded opinion on the point, as the application of the Convention in this case has not been argued.[30]

Griffin J agreed with the judgment of Henchy J without any further comment, whereas McCarthy J, in a separate opinion, stated:

. . . I accept, as a general principle, that a statute must be construed, so far as possible, so as not to be inconsistent with established rules of international law and that one should avoid a construction which will lead to a conflict between domestic and international law . . . the matter was not argued during the course of the hearing this appeal but since, as Mr Justice Henchy points out, the Convention is not part of the domestic law of the State . . . , I cannot subscribe to the view that the Statute of Limitations (passed in 1957, four years after the ratification of the Convention . . .) is to be limited by the terms of Article 6(1) of the Convention.[31]

In *Norris v Attorney General*[32] it was argued by counsel for Mr Norris that the decision of the European Court of Human Rights in *Dudgeon v United Kingdom*[33] (which arose from a complaint involving the same legislation challenged by Norris) should be treated as more than a persuasive precedent and followed by the Irish Supreme Court. She further argued that because of Ireland's ratification of the ECHR there arose a presumption that the Irish Constitution was compatible with the Convention and that in considering whether pre-1937 legislation was carried over by virtue of Article 50[34] of the Constitution and compatible therewith regard should be had to whether the laws in question were consistent with the Convention itself. Speaking for

[28] [1981] IR 412 at 440. [29] [1984] IR 151. [30] Ibid, 159. [31] Ibid, 166.
[32] [1984] IR 36. [33] (1982) 4 EHRR 149.
[34] Article 50.1 of the Irish Constitution provides:

Subject to this Constitution and to the extent to which they are not inconsistent therewith, the laws in force in Saorstat Eireann immediately prior to the date of the coming into operation of this Constitution shall continue to be of full force and effect until the same or any of them shall have been repealed or amended by enactment of the Oireachtas.

the majority,[35] O'Higgins CJ repeated the principle regarding Article 29.6 of the Irish Constitution established in *In re O'Laighleis*[36] and rejected the argument, stating:

. . . acceptance of [counsel's] submission would be contrary to the provisions of the Constitution itself and would accord to the Government the power, by an executive act, to change both the Constitution and the law. The Convention is an international agreement to which Ireland is a subscribing party. As such, however, it does not and cannot form part of our domestic law, nor affect in any way questions which arise thereunder.[37]

In his otherwise dissenting opinion Henchy J appeared to agree with the majority regarding the domestic status of the ECHR when he stated:

Notwithstanding the submission of the plaintiff's counsel to the contrary, the constitutional question that calls for resolution is unaffected by the fact that the precise statutory provisions in question in this case were held by the European Court of Human Rights in *Dudgeon v United Kingdom* to be in breach of Article 8 of the European Convention for the Protection of Human Rights and Fundamental Freedoms. That Convention, as has been held by this Court, although it has by its terms a binding force on the Government of this State as one of its signatories, forms no part of the domestic law of this State. Moreover, Article 8 of the Convention has no counterpart in our Constitution. Since the constitutionality of the impugned statutory provisions is the only issue raised in this litigation, the touchstone of constitutionality must be held to reside solely in our Constitution. That does not mean that this Court is not open to the persuasive influence that may be drawn from decisions of other courts, such as the European Court of Human Rights, which deal with problems similar or analogous to that now before us.[38]

The persuasive authority of the ECHR and of European Court of Human Rights decisions in the area of criminal contempt of court was reiterated by O'Hanlon J when, in *Desmond v Glackin*,[39] he cited with approval *dicta* of Henchy J in *State (DPP) v Walsh and Conneely*,[40] stating:

As Ireland has ratified the [European] Convention and is a party to it, and as the law of contempt of court is based [. . .] on public policy, I think it is legitimate to assume that our public policy is in accord with the Convention or at least that the provisions of the Convention can be considered when determining issues of public policy.[41]

A reaffirmation along similar lines of the persuasive authority of the Convention in matters of public policy was evident in the judgment of Budd J, at the High Court stage of *Croke v Smith and Others*,[42] in which extended

[35] The other two judges forming the majority were Finlay P, and Griffin J.

[36] See n. 6 above.

[37] Norris at 66.

[38] Ibid, 68–69. McCarthy J also dissented but he did not base his opinion on any provision of the ECHR or any decision of the European Court of Human Rights.

[39] [1992] ILRM 490.

[40] See n. 27 above.

[41] Glackin, n. 39 above, 513.

[42] Unreported High Court decision of 27 and 31 July 1995.

consideration was given to the role of the ECHR and international law (*UN Principles for the Protection of Persons with Mental Illness and the Improvement of Mental Health Care, 1991*). The mild enthusiasm of the High Court judge for the ECHR and international sources as a guide to public policy was not reflected in the Supreme Court decision in the same case.[43] The case involved consideration of the constitutionality of certain provisions of the Mental Treatment Act 1945 arising from the detention of a schizophrenic patient. The somewhat retricted interpretative role of the ECHR was expressed by Budd, J, as follows:

> . . . while this Court can look to the European Convention and the United Nations principles as being influential guidelines with regard to matters of public policy, nevertheless in the circumstances of this case in which there is a challenge to the constitutionality of . . . [legislation] . . . such Conventions may not be used as a touchstone with regard to constitutionality. This Court is at present bound to approach this issue wearing blinkers as to Conventions setting out internationally accepted norms and standards.[44]

An Alternative View of the Convention's Status

A view which has yet to find judicial or widespread academic approval[45] is that Articles 15.2 and 29.6 of the Convention do not necessarily pose an insuperable obstacle to domestic enforcement of the Convention. Article 29.3 of the Constitution provides:

> Ireland accepts the generally recognised principles of international law as its rule of conduct in its relations with other States.

According to this theory, a convention can be given indirect effect domestically when a citizen, acting as 'private attorney general',[46] seeks through legal proceedings to force the government to behave in accordance with its constitutional mandate by observing the generally recognized principles of international law. Thus, a convention, insofar as it (or parts of it) represent generally recognised principles of international law in a crystallized form, can bind the government in a domestic forum as part of its enforceable mandate under Article 29.3 of the Constitution.

The theory was first raised by Whyte[47] in an analysis of the aforementioned case, *E v E*,[48] in which he suggested that it was arguable that the principle of

[43] Unreported Supreme Court decision of 31 July 1996.

[44] High Court Decision, at 34–35.

[45] See further: Whyte, 'The Application of the European Convention on Human Rights Before the Irish Courts', (1982) *International and Comparative Law Quarterly*, 856–861, see n. 4 above .

[46] For a discussion of the concept of the 'private attorney general' see generally: Casey, *Constitutional Law in Ireland* (2nd edn, London: Sweet & Maxwell, 1992) chapter 11.

[47] See n. 45 above.

[48] See n. 9 above.

pacta sunt servanda necessitated compliance with ratified conventions before domestic as well as international tribunals and, *a fortiori*, with decisions of the appropriate authorities charged with interpretinng the provisions contained therein such as the European Commission and Court of Human Rights. He acknowledged that there were conflicting Irish decisions on this point[49] but proceeded to explain the bases on which the arguments rejecting the proposition might be challenged.

Insofar as Article 29.3 of the Constitution refers to relations with other states it could be argued that it therefore conferred no rights on individuals, rendering it impossible for a citizen to establish the requisite *locus standi* to maintain an action based on the Article. Whyte pointed out that there would be nothing to prevent a citizen seeking, through an action before the courts, to force the government to behave in accordance with its obligations under Article 29.3, at least where such compliance would directly affect their interests. It was precisely in this context that Raymond Crotty later established the requisite standing to prevent the Irish governnment from proceeding with ratification of the Single European Act. In exercising his/her rights in such a way the supremacy of domestic law over international law would not be displaced, as the citizen would merely be attempting to force the government to comply with national law as enshrined in a constitutional mandate to accept the generally recognized principles of international law.

The other reason, suggested by Whyte, for not treating Constitution Articles 15.2 and 29.6 as insuperable obstacles to domestic enforcement of the Convention is that both provisions are concerned with positive law whereas Article 29.3 could be used for the direct applicability of customary or generally recognized principles of international law. By virtue of the principle *pacta sunt servanda* it would follow that domestic tribunals would have to take cognizance of the provisions of ratified conventions.

The final argument against the Article 29.3 theory is that the language it employs is merely exhortatory in nature in that the generally recognized principles of international law are intended as no more than a 'guide' in the conduct of inter-state relations. The primary text for interpretative purposes is the Irish language text of the Constitution and although the relevent words of the Irish text of Article 29.3—*ina dtreoir*—have been judicially interpreted as meaning guide or guideline[50] it is arguable that the words could be construed as meaning direction or directive. Thus there are a number of sustainable bases on which the orthodox view of the Convention's domestic status might

[49] See for example: *Saorstat & Continental Steamships Co v de las Morenas* [1945] IR 291 which appeared to support the proposition; and *In re O'Laighleis* [1960] IR 93 and *The State (Sumers Jennings) v Furlong* [1966] IR 183 which did not.

[50] *State (Sumers Jennings) v Furlong*, ibid.

be challenged within the confines of the dualistic approach to international law.

This admittedly alternative theory may have been boosted by a recent decision of the High Court in the case of *MV Toledo: ACT Shipping (PTE) Ltd v Minister for the Marine, Ireland and the Attorney General*[51] in which Barr J held that in certain instances established principles of customary international law may become part of domestic Irish law 'provided that it is not in conflict with the Constitution or any enactment of the legislature or a rule of the common law'[52] and thus give rise to justiciable issues before the Irish courts. With reference to the necessity of reconciling this view of the meaning of Article 29.3 with the provisions of Article 15.2 he stated:

> In my opinion Article 15.2 does not inhibit the evolution of international customary law into domestic law. It relates to the 'making' of laws for the State which, it provides, is a power exclusively reserved to the Oireachtas. Customary law is not made in the sense envisaged by Article 15.2. Customary international law evolves from a practice or course of conduct which in time has become widely accepted.[53]

The High Court did not abandon the view that international treaties do not form part of domestic law unless incorporated by the Oireachtas. However, as one commentator has noted, the distinction between international treaties and customary law does not preclude the indirect application of a specific treaty provision in domestic Irish law where such a provision has generated a rule which has passed into the general body of international law and there exists the requisite *opinio juris* to establish it as a new rule of customary international law.[54]

4. Commentary

The greatest flaw in the orthodox approach adopted by the Irish judiciary is that it is based on an unduly restrictive understanding of Articles 15.2 and 29.6 of the Constitution. While both provisions point clearly to the need for legislative incorporation to maximize the domestic effect of international conventions, nothing in the Constitution prevents the judiciary from having regard to international instruments and decisions of international courts and commissions as persuasive authorities even in matters of constitutional interpretation. To that extent, the so-called belt and braces approach, favoured by

[51] [1995] 2 ILRM 30. For a commentary on this case see: Gaffney, 'The Status of International Customary Law in Irish Domestic Law: A Review of the "*Toledo*" Case', (August 1996) *Irish Law Times*, 192–196.

[52] Ibid, 43 of the judgment.

[53] Ibid, 44 of the judgment.

[54] Gaffney, n. 51 above. For a general discussion on the status of public international law in Irish constitutional law see further: Phelan, *Revolt or Revolution: The Constitutional Boundaries of the European Community*, (Dublin: Round Hall Sweet & Maxwell, 1997) chapter 26.

certain High Court judges, could be said to indicate a more faithful judicial reflection of the state's international law obligations than the comparatively 'hibernocentric' pattern of reasoning of the previous Supreme Court.

Furthermore, it is difficult, intellectually and practically, to sustain the distinction between public policy matters and constitutional issues in all cases. Insofar as the Convention appears to be more excluded from consideration of the latter this is somewhat difficult to square with the tendency in earlier constitutional jurisprudence towards relying on various 'para-constitutional' sources of law. If it is legitimate to rely on such sources—and that is, admittedly, an unsettled question[55]—why should it be illegitimate to have recourse to international human rights instruments to which this state is party when considering questions of constitutional law already informed by such nebulous concepts as natural or higher law. (This feature of Irish constitutional jurisprudence is discussed below in Section D).

It is not necessary to go to the somewhat artificial lengths of 'auto-incorporation' under Article 29.3 of the Constitution to give greater force domestically to international human rights conventions. Even on the most purposive reading of that provision (in English or Irish) the scope of aplication of the ECHR would be significantly narrowed and it is doubtful that the framers of the 1937 Constitution ever intended that it would be used to incorporate treaties though the judicial back door. In fact, a contrary intention is clearly evident from a literal reading of Article 29.6.

Notwithstanding slight inconsistencies in judicial approach it is clear that the prevailing orthodoxy—that the Convention is of no more than persuasive value in domestic proceedings—remains unpenetrated. There is, however, the possibility of a judicial *volte face* in the future if and when a court addresses the question of the status of the ECHR in EU law. In the case of *Kavanagh v Government of Ireland and Others*[56] the applicant argued that the ECHR was part of domestic law by virtue of Paragraph 2 of Article F of Title 1 of the Treaty on European Union (Maastricht Treaty). The High Court found it unnecessary to address this argument as the applicant had failed to establish

[55] See generally: Hogan, 'Constitutional Interpretation', in: Litton (ed), '*The Constitution of Ireland 1937–1987*', (Special Edition of *Administration*, Vol. 35. No. 4) (Dublin: The Institute of Public Administration, 1988); Humphreys, 'Constitutional Interpretation', (1993) 15 *Dublin University Law Journal* 59–77; Hogan, 'Unenumerated Personal Rights: Ryan's Case Re-evaluated' (1990–92) *Irish Jurist* (ns) 95–116; Humphreys, 'Interpreting Natural Rights', (1993–95) *Irish Jurist* (ns) 221–230; Quinn, 'Reflections on the Legitimacy of Judicial Activism in the Field of Constitutional Law' (1991) Winter: *Dli—The Western Law Gazette* 29–38.

[56] [1996] 1 ILRM 133 / [1997] 1 ILRM 321. The relevant *nexus* between the Irish Constitution and the Maastricht Treaty is Article 29.4.4 of the former. See further: Connelly, 'Ireland and the European Convention', in: Dickson (ed), *Human Rights and the European Convention: The Effects of the Convention on the United Kingdom and Ireland* (London: Sweet & Maxwell, 1997) n. 4 above.

the substance of his case that his trial before the Special Criminal Court amounted to a prohibited discrimination under the Irish Constitution and the ECHR. On appeal to the Supreme Court no reference was made to this argument.

B. THE STATUS OF THE CONVENTION IN PARLIAMENTARY PROCEEDINGS

There has never been a systematic survey of Irish parliamentary debates to examine, quantitively or qualitatively, the status of the ECHR in parliamentary proceedings. Thus any observations in this regard are, of necessity, impressionistic and second-hand.[57] Even if such a survey existed it would be of debatable value given the difficulty of assessing the motives of parliamentary speakers in invoking international human rights instruments to lend weight to particular debating points.

When legislation is being drafted the parliamentary draftsman's office is mindful of Irish obligations under the ECHR and the necessity of ensuring compatibility with the Convention's provisions.[58]

The Convention is also referred to by the Law Reform Commission in drafting consultation papers and reports but is not given a position of pre-eminence over other international and comparative sources of law. In fact, it is arguable that even this is of negligible significance given the extent to which many of the fine reports of the Law Reform Commission are ignored by the legislature and executive unless it is politically convenient to use them in aid of some reform. An example of this was the use to which the Commission's 1995 report, *An Examination of the Law of Bail*, was used to encourage support for the government's proposed constitutional amendment on preventive detention and bail in 1996, even though the Commission did not specifically recommend the kind of reform contained in the constitutional amendment.[59]

[57] This section draws heavily from the analysis of Flynn, n. 11 above.

[58] Donelan, 'The Role of the Parliamentary Draftsman in Preparing Legislation in Ireland' (1992) 14 *Dublin University Law Journal* (ns) 1. See generally: chapter 13, Byrne & McCutcheon, *The Irish Legal System* (3rd edn, Butterworths (Ireland), 1996).

[59] The sixteenth constitutional amendment changing Article 40 of the Constitution, which was passed by an overwhelming majority of the section of the population voting in a referendum in 1996, provides as follows:

> Provision may be made by law for the refusal of bail by a court to a person charged with a serious offence where it is reasonably considered necessary to prevent the commission of a serious offence by that person.

This amendment was further clarified by the Bail Act of 1997 (No. 16 of 1997) which has yet to be implemented.

Interestingly, the reforms contained in the amendment and subsequent legislation were more akin to the standard contained in Article 5 of the ECHR than that provided for in the Irish Constitution. As judicially interpreted, the latter was a higher standard. This points to the not insignificant danger of using international human rights instruments to (sometimes disingenuously) 'dumb-down' on domestic standards on the rare occasion when domestic standards are higher than international ones. A more recent example was the decision of the Supreme Court in *Re Article 26 of the Constitution and the Illegal Immigrants (Trafficking) Bill 1999*, unreported decision of 28 August 2000.

Occasionally, the executive will invoke the Convention and case-law thereunder as a reason for introducing legislation, even if no case has been taken against Ireland in that area. This occurred in 1992 when the then government introduced legislation to regulate telephone tapping and pointed to the necessity of such legislation by referring to the European Court of Human Right's decision in *Malone v United Kingdom*.[60] The reason for the introduction of the legislation was because of a finding of the Irish High Court that the tapping, with the permission of a previous Minister for Justice, of the telephones of a number of journalists violated their unenumerated constitutional right to privacy. A number of the senators who participated in the debate highlighted the fact that it was politically expedient for the Minister introducing the legislation to refer to an external imperative for its introduction because the real domestic origin of the legislation was politically embarassing to the government of the day.[61]

It is more common for the Convention not to be referred to at all in parliamentary debates, even where it has particular significance. For example in the parliamentary debates concerning the non-renewal of the so-called Section 31 Order, which banned broadcasts by members of certain proscribed organizations, no reference was made to the freedom of expression guarantee contained in the ECHR. This is all the more remarkable when one considers that an unsuccessful application (*Purcell v Ireland*, discussed below in Section E) had been made under the Convention challenging the compatibility of such orders therewith.

Similarly, when the Civil Legal Aid Bill was being introduced in Seanad Eireann the relevant Minister made no reference to the *Airey* case decided against Ireland by the European Court as an impetus for the proposed

[60] Judgment of 2 August 1984, Series A No. 82.

[61] In fact, so embarrassing was it to the then Cathaoirleach (Speaker) of the Seanad that the introduction of the legislation in the Upper House prompted his resignation, and ultimately led to the resignation of the then Taoiseach (Prime Minister). The Cathaoirleach had been the Minister for Justice who authorized the tapping of journalists' telephones in the early 1980s.

reform. Instead, the Pringle Committee Report of 1979 was referred to as the primary source of the legislation.

Further examples of the surprising lack of prominence of Convention-based arguments in parliamentary debate are to be found in the debates concerning the legislation introduced in the aftermath of the journalist Veronica Guerin.[62] Perhaps it is not so surprising that parliamentarians do not raise international standards in such contexts when it would be politically damaging to appear to be 'soft on crime' or, as in the case of the post-Omagh bombing legislation,[63] 'soft on terrorism'.

Ultimately, it is difficult to quibble with the conclusion drawn by Flynn when he states:

> one is left with the impression that neither the European Convention nor the decisions taken by the European Court of Human Rights under the Convention is influential in the formulation of executive policy or the shaping of legislative debate in Ireland.[64]

C. LEADING HUMAN RIGHTS CASES DECIDED BY THE NATIONAL COURTS

Certain fundamental human rights were expressly guaranteed by the Free State Constitution of 1922[65] but that Constitution did not have the status of fundamental law and was easily amenable to parliamentary amendment.

These rights were expanded and further entrenched in the 1937 Constitution, which also expressly recognized natural or higher law as a source of fundamental rights. The 1937 Constitution explicitly guarantees the following rights: the right to a trial in due course of law; equality before the law; the right to life (including the right to life of the unborn[66]); the right to person-

[62] See for example: Criminal Justice (Drug Trafficking) Act 1996 (No. 29 of 1996); Proceeds of Crime Act 1996 (No. 30 of 1996); Criminal Assets Bureau Act 1996 (No. 31 of 1996).

[63] Offences Against the State (Amendment) Act 1998 (No. 39 of 1998).

[64] See n. 11 above, at 19.

[65] See generally: Kohn, *The Constitution of the Irish Free State*, (London: Allen and Unwin, 1932). See further: Morgan (ed), *The New Irish Constitution: An Exposition and Some Arguments* (first published in 1912) (Dallas: Kennikat Press, 1971 (reissue)).

[66] The express constitutional guarantee of the right to life of the unborn was inserted by the Eighth Amendment in 1983. Article 40.3.3 of the Constitution provides:

> The State acknowledges the right to life of the unborn and, with due regard to the equal right to life of the mother, guarantees in its laws to respect, and, as far as practicable, by its laws to defend and vindicate that right.

This amendment gave rise to considerable political and legal controversy and led to further constitutional amendments. An extensive literature has emerged on the topic in Ireland. See, for example: Hesketh, *The Second Partitioning of Ireland* (Brandsma Books: 1990); Kingston and Whelan with Bacik, *Abortion and the Law* (Dublin: Round Hall Sweet & Maxwell, 1997).

hood; the right to a good name; the right to personal liberty; the right to private property and inviolability of the dwelling; the right to freedom of expression; the right to peaceful assembly; the right to form associations and unions; family rights; education rights; religious freedom.

As of September 1998, there have been nineteen attempts to amend provisions of the 1937 Constitution[67] and the holding of referendums for the purposes of constitutional amendment has given rise to considerable controversy before the courts.[68]

Because the power of judicial review is expressly conferred on the courts by Article 34.3.2 of the Constitution[69] the judiciary have had to articulate the content of the rights specified in the Constitution in order to give them life and meaning in particular cases. There have been periods of frenetic activism on the Irish Supreme Court, particularly from the 1960s to the 1980s, but there has been remarkably little analysis of this process with commentators focusing their attention on its results in particular cases.[70]

Thus, for example, in marking out a libertarian territory regarding the right to personal liberty in the context of bail applications the Supreme Court stated, in the landmark case of *The People (Attorney General) v O'Callaghan*,[71] that bail should not be refused as a form of preventive detention as to so do would be to deny a person his/her right to personal liberty and to violate the right to a trial in due course of law. This was reaffirmed in a subsequent case[72] but the position was eventually altered in a constitutional amendment passed in a referendum in 1996.[73] Essentially, the provisions of Article 5 ECHR have been incorporated into the Irish Constitution by that amendment to qualify the broad prohibition of forms of preventive detention (see discussion above in this section).

In a series of cases the Irish courts formulated what has become known as the absolute exclusionary rule of evidence as an aspect of the constitutional

[67] The process of constitutional amendment is provided for by Articles 46 and 47 of the Constitution together with referendum legislation.

[68] See, for example: *Finn v Minister for the Environment* [1983] IR 154; *Roche v Ireland* (17 June 1983) HC Unrep; *McKenna v An Taoiseach* (No. 1) [1995] 2 IR 1; *Slattery v An Taoiseach* [1993] 1 IR 286; *McKenna v An Taoiseach* (No. 2) [1996] 1 ILRM 81; *Hanafin v Minister for the Environment* [1996] 2 ILRM 161. See further: Sherlock, 'Constitutional Change, Referenda and the Courts in Ireland' (1997) Spring *Public Law*, 125–136.

[69] Article 34.3.2 of the Constitution provides:

> Save as otherwise provided by this Article, the jurisdiction of the High Court shall extend to the question of the validity of any law having regard to the provisions of this Constitution, and no such question shall be raised (whether by pleading, argument or otherwise) in any Court established under this or any other Article of this Constitution other than the High Court or the Supreme Court.

[70] Quinn, n. 55 above.

[71] [1966] IR 501.

[72] *Ryan v DPP* [1989] IR 399.

[73] See n. 59 above.

right to a trial in due course of law.[74] Thus, in *People (DPP) v Healy*,[75] it was stated by McCarthy J that:

A violation of constitutional rights is not to be excused by the ignorance of the violator no more than ignorance of the law can enure to the benefit of a person who . . . is presumed to have intended the natural and probable consequences of his conduct. If it were otherwise, there would be a premium on ignorance.[76]

In *deBurca and Anderson v Attorney General*[77] the principle of equality before the law enshrined in Article 40.1 of the Constitution was interpreted so as to strike down legislation which excused women from jury service. The constitutional jurisprudence on equality has, however, been dogged by the so-called 'human personality doctrine' which has the effect of limiting the scope of application of the principle which is, in any event, inherently limited by the text of the Constitution.[78]

In another area of specified rights, the right to life, the courts have played a highly significant, and at times controversial role. Thus, in the case of *X v Attorney General*,[79] a majority of the Supreme Court interpreted the 8th Amendment to the Constitution as permitting a pregnant girl to have an abortion where there was a real and substantial risk to her life including the risk of self-destruction. This case had been preceded by a long line of cases initiated by the Society for the Protection of the Unborn Child (SPUC) involving abortion information and pregnancy counselling.[80]

Exercising its *parens patriae* jurisdiction in relation to a ward of court nearly in a persistent vegetative state, the Supreme Court, again by a majority, found that the right to die a natural death was an aspect of the constitutionally protected right to life such that it was possible to withdraw the artificial feeding system of the ward in question and hasten her death.[81]

[74] See, for example: *People (Attorney General) v O'Brien* [1965] IR 142; *People (DPP) v Madden* [1977] IR 336; *People (DPP) v O'Loughlin* [1979] IR 85; *State (Trimbole) v Governor of Mountjoy Prison* [1985] IR 550; *People (DPP) v Shaw* [1982] IR 1; *People (DPP) v Lawless* [1985] 3 Frewen 30; *People (DPP) v Quilligan (No. 1)* [1986] IR 495; *DPP v Gaffney* [1987] IR 173; *People (DPP) v Kenny* [1990] 2 IR 110. See further: Kelly, *The Irish Constitution* (3rd edn) (Dublin: Jurist, 1980) 603–623; Charleton, 'Confessions—An Overview of the Law', (1991) Winter *Dli—The Western Law Gazette*, 39–52.

[75] [1990] 2 IR 73. [76] Ibid. [77] [1976] IR 38.

[78] See, for example: *Macauley v Minister for Posts & Telegraphs* [1966] IR 345; *East Donegal Co-operative Mart Ltd v Attorney General* [1970] IR 317; *Quinn's Supermarket v Attorney General* [1972] IR 1; *Brennan v Attorney General* [1983] ILRM 449. It should, however, be noted that there is some evidence of the erosion of this doctrine: see, for example *Cox v Ireland* [1992] 2 IR 503; *People (DPP) v Quilligan (No. 3)* [1993] 2 IR 305. See generally: Kelly, *The Irish Constitution* (3rd edn) 712–743; Casey, *Constitutional Law in Ireland* (2nd edn) chapter 13;

[79] [1992] 1 IR 1. [80] See generally: Kingston and Whelan with Bacik, n. 66 above.

[81] *In the Matter of a Ward of Court* [1995] 2 ILRM. See further: Costello, 'The Terminally Ill: The Law's Concerns', (1986) *Irish Jurist*, 35–46; Tomkin & Hanafin, 'Medical Treatment At Life's End: The Need For Legislation', 1(1) *Medico-Legal Journal of Ireland*, 3–10; Cusack, 'Re A Ward of Court: Medical Law and Medical Ethics Diverge, A Medico-Legal Analysis', (1995)

1. The doctrine of unenumerated rights

The Constitution also guarantees unwritten or unenumerated rights sourced in a higher law explicitly acknowledged by the text itself.[82] The cases in which these unenumerated rights have been declared or discovered by the Irish courts are a source of some considerable controversy among academic commentators[83] but, with one or two exceptions, the cases have attracted surprisingly little public interest.

The leading case in the establishment of a doctrine of unenumerated rights in Irish constitutional jurisprudence, and arguably Ireland's *Marbury v Madison*, was *Ryan v Attorney General*.[84] In that case, the plaintiff claimed that legislation permitting the fluoridation of drinking water violated her constitutional right to bodily integrity. Such a right was mentioned nowhere in the text of the 1937 Constitution yet Kenny J took the view that the rights contained therein were not exhaustive of the rights guaranteed by the Constitution. In making this point he referred to the use of the words 'in particular' in Article 40.3.2[85] and found that although the Constitution did impliedly protect the right to bodily integrity a violation of this right was not disclosed by the facts of the instant case. The more controversial aspect of this decision was the invocation of extra-constitutional sources such as Papal Encyclicals by the judge in elaborating on the content of the unenumerated right in question.

Having established that the rights guaranteed by the Constitution were not confined to those specified in the text the courts embarked on a process of enunciating other unspecified rights in a succession of cases. Thus, in the landmark case of *McGee v Attorney General*,[86] an unenumerated right to marital privacy was successfully invoked in a challenge to the constitutionality of legislation which effectively forbade the use of contraceptives. This was

Medico-Legal Journal of Ireland, 43–44; Tomkin and McAuley, 'Re A Ward of Court: Legal Analysis', ibid, 45–50; Iglesias, 'Ethics, Brain-Death, and the Medical Concept of the Human Being', ibid, 51–57; Kearon, 'Re A Ward of Court: Ethical Comment', ibid, 58–59; Harrington, 'Constitutional Law: Withdrawal of Treatment from an Incompetent Patient' (1995) 17 *Dublin University Law Journal* 120–135.

[82] See, for example, the wording used in Article 41 of the Constitution which recognizes the family 'as a moral institution possessing inalienable and imprescriptible rights, antecedent and superior to all positive law'.

[83] See n. 55 above. See further: *Report of the Constitution Review Group* (May 1996); Murphy and Twomey, *Ireland's Evolving Constitution* (Oxford: Hart Publishing, 1998).

[84] [1965] IR 294.

[85] Article 40.3.2 of the 1937 Constitution states:

The State shall, in particular, by its laws protect as best it may from unjust attack and, in the case of injustice done, vindicate the life, person, good name, and property rights of every citizen.

[86] [1974] IR 284.

later expressed as a right to individual privacy in *Kennedy and Arnold v Ireland*,[87] the exact parameters of which were not entirely clear.

The doctrine has also been used to establish the following rights: the right to earn a living;[88] the right to strike;[89] the right of dissociation;[90] the right to communicate;[91] the right not to be tortured or ill-treated or to have one's health endangered by the state;[92] the right of access to the courts;[93] the right to legal representation on criminal charges[94]; the right to travel;[95] the right to marry;[96] the right to procreate;[97] the right of a wife to independent domicile and to maintenance;[98] the rights of unmarried mothers in regard to their children[99]; the rights of children;[100] and the right to fair procedures in decision-making.[101]

In enunciating unenumerated constitutional rights the courts have occasionally adverted to the 'Directive Principles of Social Policy' contained in Article 45 of the Constitution[102] as a persuasive authority for their reasoning

[87] [1987] IR 587. See discussion on telephone tapping legislation above in this section on the use of the ECHR in parliamentary proceedings.

[88] *Murtagh Properties v Cleary* [1972] IR 330; *Murphy v Stewart* [1973] IR 97.

[89] *Crowley v Ireland* [1980] IR 102.

[90] *Educational Co Ltd v Fitzpatrick (No. 2)* [1961] IR 345; *Meskell v CIE* [1973] IR 121. This right arose as a corollary of the specified right of freedom of association contained in Article 40.6.1.iii of the Constitution.

[91] *The State (Murray) v Governor of Limerick Prison* [D'Arcy J, Unreported High Court, 23 August 1978]; *Attorney General v Paperlink* [1984] ILRM 343; *Kearney v Minister for Justice* [1986] IR 116.

[92] *The State (C) v Frawley* [1976] IR 365.

[93] *Macauley v Minister for Posts & Telegraphs* [1966] IR 345; *O'Brien v Manufacturing Engineering Co Ltd* [1973] IR 334.

[94] *The State (Healy) v Donoghue* [1976] IR 325.

[95] *The State (M) v Attorney General* [1979] IR 73, involving the right to travel outside the state. The right to travel within the state was recognized *obiter* in *Ryan v Attorney General* [1965] IR 294.

[96] *Ryan v Attorney General* [1965] IR 294; *McGee v Attorney* General [1974] IR 284.

[97] *Murray v Ireland* [1985] IR 532.

[98] *CM v TM* [1991] ILRM 268.

[99] *The State (Nicolau) v An Bord Uchtala* [1966] IR 567; *G v An Bord Uchtala* [1980] IR 32.

[100] *In re Article 26 and the Adoption (No. 2) Bill 1987* [1989] IR 656; *G v An Bord Uchtala* [1980] IR 32; *P.W. v A.W.* [Ellis J., Unreported High Court, 21 April 1980]; *FN (A Minor) v Minister for Education and Others* [1995] 2 ILRM 297.

[101] *In re Haughey* [1971] IR 217; *Garvey v Ireland* [1980] IR 75.

[102] Article 45 of the Constitution states:

> The principles of social policy set forth in this Article are intended for the general guidance of the Oireachtas. The application of those principles in the making of laws shall be the care of the Oireachtas exclusively, and shall not be cognisable by any Court under any of he provisions of this Constitution.
>
> 1. The State shall strive to promote the welfare of the whole people by securing and protecting as effectively as it may a social order in which justice and charity shall inform all the institutions of the national life.
>
> 2. The State shall, in particular, direct its policy towards securing:—
>
> i. That the citizens (all of whom, men and women equally, have the right to an adequate means of livelihood) may through their occupations find the means of making reasonable provision for their domestic needs.

cont./

on a given matter. These principles were intended for the guidance of the Oireachtas but were not to be directly cognizable by any court.

Other factors contributing to the development of a jurisprudence on fundamental constitutional rights are the application of fairly generous *locus standi* rules by the judiciary and the use of flexible canons of constitutional interpretation. Of overarching significance has been the use of natural or higher law as a source of constitutional rights.

D. CASES BROUGHT BEFORE THE EUROPEAN COMMISSION AND COURT OF HUMAN RIGHTS

Seven cases in which Ireland was the respondent state have been considered by the Court of Human Rights. Ireland has initiated one inter-state application, against the United Kingdom. In this section it is proposed to consider each of these individual petition cases in chronological order together with some of the Commission cases which raised interesting issues under the admissibility and other criteria. The inter-state application will only be cursorily examined as it receives extended treatment in the chapter on the United Kingdom.

1. The early years

In the years immediately after the coming into effect of the ECHR most of the applications registered against Ireland involved complaints about the

ii. That the ownership and control of the material resources of the community may be so distributed amongst private individuals and the various classes as best to subserve the common good.
iii. That, especially, the operation of free competition shall not be allowed so to develop as to result in the concentration of the ownership or control of essential commodities in a few individuals to the common detriment.
iv. That in what pertains to the the control of credit the constant and predominaant aim shall be the welfare of the people as a whole.
v. That there may be established on the land in economic security as many families as in the circumstances shaall be practicable.

3. 1. The State shall favour and, where necessary, supplement private initiative in industry and commerce.

2. The State shall endeavour to secure that private enterprise shall be so conducted as to ensure reasonable efficiency in the production and distribution of goods and as to protect the public against unjust exploitation.

4. 1. The State pledges itself to safeguard with especial care the economic interests of the weaker sections of the community, and, where necessary, to contribute to the support of the infirm, the widow, the orphan, and the aged.

2. The State shall endeavour to ensure that the strength and health of workers, men and women, and the tender age of children shall not be abused and that citizens shall not be forced by economic necessity to enter avocations unsuited to their sex, age or strength.

operation of emergency legislation enacted during the Second World War which was being used against those involved in paramilitary organizations such as the Irish Republican Army.[103] A considerable number of applications also arose from the compulsory acquisition of land by the Land Commission.[104] The Land Commission was originally established in 1881 and had the power to acquire land for distribution among small farmers to relieve congestion and to advance money for the purchase by tenants of landlords' estates. It ceased to acquire land in 1983 and provision for its dissolution was made in 1992. Complaints regarding its activities continued to give rise to applications under the Convention into the 1980s, proving that Ireland's sometimes hysterical obsession with abortion is matched only by its historical obsession with land!

The first case ever considered by the European Court of Human Rights, in 1959, was *Lawless v Ireland.*[105] The applicant had been arrested with others in a barn where the Gardai found a quantity of arms. They were each acquitted on a charge of unlawful possession of arms in the Central Criminal Court in November 1956. In May of the following year the applicant was rearrested and found to be in possession of incriminating documents for which he was sentenced to one month's imprisonment. He was acquitted on a charge of IRA membership. In July 1957 the Irish government invoked special executive powers of arrest and detention under the Offences Against the State (Amendment) Act 1940,[106] and shortly thereafter the applicant was interned without trial pursuant to that legislation. Five months later he came before the Detention Commission established under emergency legislation where he undertook not to violate the Offences Against the State Acts and was accordingly released by ministerial order. He had earlier unsuccessfully applied to the Irish High Court and on appeal to the Supreme Court for an order of *habeas corpus*.

In one of three judgments given by the Court, addressing the merits, it decided that the Irish government could not rely on Article 17 of the Convention as it was negative in scope and could not be used to deprive an applicant of his rights under Articles 5 and 6. In any event, Lawless had not sought to rely on any provision of the ECHR to justify a violation of its other provisions.

In relation to the complaints of detention without trial, based on Articles 5 and 6, the Court held that as the applicant had never been charged with a

[103] The principal pieces of legislation were the Offences Against the State Act 1939 (No. 13 of 1939) and the Offences Against the State (Amendment) Act 1940 (No. 2 of 1940).

[104] See for example: *O'N v Ireland*, Application 60/55; *K v Ireland*, Application 700/60; *S v Ireland*, Application 8151/78; *M. v Ireland*, Application 9986/82.

[105] (1979–80) 1 EHRR 1.

[106] No. 2 of 1940.

criminal offence Article 6 was irrelevant. However, it found that Lawless's detention did violate Article 5(1)(c) and 5(3) as he had not been brought before a judge on the issue of the period of detention complained of and it was therefore necessary to see whether his detention could be justified on other grounds. As his detention was preventative as opposed to punitive the Court found that it did not violate Article 7 of the Convention.

With reference to the government's defence under Article 15 of the ECHR the Court agreed that the conditions laid down for a valid derogation had been satisfied and that the form of detention without trial provided for in Irish law was necessary for dealing with the emergency situation which existed in Ireland due to the proven inadequacy of the ordinary law. The safeguards built into the 1940 Act also strengthened the government's case and there was no evidence that it had contravened other obligations under international law.

In its other judgments, the Court established important procedural rules and rules regarding the standing of applicants under the Convention.

In an application against Ireland considered by the Commission subsequent to *Lawless*, *C v Ireland*,[107] the applicant complained of his internment in February 1958 under the Offences Against the State (Amendment) Act 1940. The Commission followed the Court's finding in *Lawless* that there existed in Ireland at the relevant time an emergency situation threatening the life of the nation and that the government had derogated validly from its Convention obligations in accordance with Article 15. Thus, the complaint regarding internment without trial was rejected.

The applicant had also claimed that the government used its powers under the 1940 Act and Article 15 of the ECHR for the improper purpose of ridding itself of a political opponent. This part of the application was rejected for non-exhaustion of available domestic remedies. The appropriate domestic remedy would have been the institution of proceedings before the Detention Commission established under the 1940 Act. The Human Rights Commission was of the opinion that such proceedings before the Detention Commission did constitute an effective and sufficient means of redress as required by the non-exhaustion rule as it was satisfied that a report of the Detention Commission did bind the government. It distinguished its own earlier finding regarding the Detention Commission in *Lawless* on the ground that the applicant in that case had not questioned the *bona fides* of the Minister who made the detention order against him and had sought different redress to that sought by the applicant in the instant case.

An interesting application involving Article 11 of the Convention was considered by the Commission in *X v Ireland*.[108] The applicant was employed as

[107] Application 493/59. [108] Application 4125/69.

an electrician by the Electricity Supply Board (ESB) in 1962. He was elected shop steward for his trade union and organized an unofficial strike to protest against the failure of the union to look after the interests of the workers. In 1963 he was transferred to a power station where he was also elected trade union shop steward. Industrial relations were poor and the applicant had frequent disagreements with management. He claimed to have been offered promotion in return for resigning as shop steward. Following one particular dispute in 1964 he was made redundant but reinstated three weeks later. Soon afterwards he became ill and remained at home for a number of months.

He claimed that upon his return to work he was treated very badly by his employers by being left alone without proper facilities for long periods of time. During the course of an investigation into the placing of an order for copper wire in his name he was accused of using ESB transport for private business. Eventually, following a further transfer, he left the employment of ESB claiming that he was being given menial work and that this was likely to continue. He found new employment with another state firm but resigned in 1967 following a number of disputes. He made a number of complaints to members of the government, the Industrial Relations Commission of the ESB, and his trade union, none of which led to any satisfactory redress. Lawyers with whom he consulted refused to bring any legal action on his behalf. By way of protest he decided not to pay his car tax leading to his arrest for refusal to pay a fine resulting therefrom.

In a partial decision delivered in July 1970 the Commission rejected most of the applicant's complaints. The complaints regarding his trade union and his lawyers were incompatible *ratione personae* with the provisions of the ECHR. His allegations of victimization and of a violation of Articles 5 and 8 of the Convention were found to be manifestly ill founded and he was found not to have exhausted the domestic remedies in relation to the part of his application based on his imprisonment for non-payment of the fine for having no car tax.

The Commission referred the part of the application alleging a violation of Article 11 of the Convention by the alleged interference with the applicant in the exercise of his duties as shop steward to the government for further information. It delivered its final opinion on admissibility on 1 February 1971. Although the Commission found the remainder of the application inadmissible its decision is interesting in that as it relates to the potential responsibility of the state under Article 11 of the Convention for the activities of state-sponsored bodies or emanations of the state such as the ESB.

The government had sought to rely on a strict reading of Article 11(1) of the Convention by arguing that there had been no violation as the applicant had not been prevented from forming or joining a trade union. It also pointed to the adequate domestic constitutional and statutory protection of such rights as proof that the government had discharged its Convention obligations. The applicant responded that the right to join a trade union was useless 'unless the trade union was also entitled to a proper administration'.

Without discussing freedom of association in any detail the Commission found that Article 11 should be given a wider interpretation than that suggested by the government. It referred to the text of the Convention itself, the *travaux preparatoires*, and Article 3 of the International Labour Organization Convention of 1948. Under the latter Convention freedom of association included the right of employees' and employers' organizations 'to elect their representatives in full freedom' and 'to organize their administration'. Of particular relevance was the fact that all of the states parties to the ECHR except Turkey had ratified the ILO Convention and this connection was strengthened by the fact that the *travaux* of the ECHR indicated the affinity between Article 11 of the ECHR and Article 22(3) of the UN Covenant on Civil and Political Rights which specifically referred to the ILO Convention.

The Commission concluded that threats and inducements aimed at bringing about the relinquishment of a trade union office such as that of shop steward would, in principle, seriously restrict and impede the lawful exercise of the right of trade unions to freedom of association which Article 11 aimed to protect. However, having regard to the facts of this particular application, it found that the government had not failed to ensure that there was an effective domestic remedy for a violation of the rights protected by Article 11. The applicant had not availed himself of any of these remedies and therefore the remainder of the application was declared inadmissible.[109]

2. *The 1970s*

In *C v Ireland*,[110] which involved multiple complaints about the conditions of detention of the applicant, all of which were found by the Commission not to be substantiated, it was, however, accepted by the Commission that the constitutional remedies mentioned by the government in its submissions on the non-exhaustion of domestic remedies would have been difficult for the applicant to avail himself of due to the absence of legal aid for such remedies. As no such domestic proceedings had ever been contemplated no special circumstances could be found to exist excusing the applicant from his obligation to exhaust domestic remedies. A similar issue arose in a subsequent Irish application involving members of the travelling community (*W and W v Ireland*, discussed below).

[109] For comments on this case see: Kerr & Whyte, *Irish Trade Union Law*, 54.

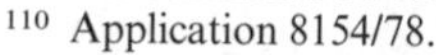

[110] Application 8154/78.

In *L and L v Ireland*[111] the applicants complained about the manner in which they had been extradited from England to Ireland; about their trial before the Special Criminal Court under the Offences Against the State Act, 1939; and about the length of their sentences and their conditions of detention. The Commissions's opinion is interesting in respect of what it says about the Special Criminal Court.[112] For the purposes of Article 6 of the Convention the Commission was satisfied that the Special Criminal Court was a tribunal established by law. The reference to Article 34 of the Irish Constitution (which deals with the courts system) in the affidavit of the Attorney General used in the extradition proceedings could not be taken to guarantee a right to trial in the ordinary courts following extradition. In any event the Convention did not guarantee an individual the right to trial in any particular domestic court. With regard to the particular proceedings in this case the Commission was satisfied that the Special Criminal Court was independent and impartial and it accepted the government's submission that Article 6 did not specify trial by jury as an essential element of a fair trial on a criminal charge.

The Commission also had to consider the nature of domestic proceedings in which another applicant had been involved in *FXM v Ireland*.[113] The applicant, who was the chairperson of a group known as The Friends of Medieval Dublin, had been involved in extremely controversial and protracted domestic litigation with the aim of preventing the destruction of a site of great historical and archaeological value in Dublin for the purposes of building civic offices. Because of his involvement in unsuccessful relator proceedings he was found to be liable for significant costs. Part of his application to the Commission involved a complaint that the domestic proceedings amounted to a denial of 'legal security of person' contrary to Article 5 of the Convention in that established legal procedures had not been adhered to. In this regard,

[111] Application 8299/78.

[112] The Special Criminal Court is provided for by Article 38.3 of the Irish Constitution which states:

> 1. Special courts may be established by law for the trial of offences in cases where it may be determined in accordance with such law that the ordinary courts are inadequate to secure the effective administration of justice, and the preservation of public peace and order.
> 2. The constitution, powers, jurisdiction and procedure of such special courts shall be prescribed by law.

The Special Criminal Court has existed for most of the period of existence of the state and has given rise to numerous legal and political controversies. See further: Hogan & Walker, *Political Violence and the Law in Ireland*, (Manchester: Manchester University Press, 1989), 227–244; Casey, *Constitutional Law in Ireland* (2nd edn), 263–266; Kelly, *The Irish Constitution* (3rd edn) 639–657; Farrell, *Irish Council for Civil Liberties Briefing Paper No. 1: The Special Criminal Court* (Dublin, 1996).

[113] Application 8569/79.

he complained of being made liable for substantial costs resulting from interlocutory proceedings in which there could be no opportunity of a full trial of the issues raised. He had not been permitted to adduce evidence which was the basis upon which he had made the undertaking as to costs. He also alleged that the Supreme Court had effectively acted as a court of first instance contrary to the Irish Constitution and to Articles 6 and 13 of the Convention.

The Commission, in its consideration of the application under Article 6, took the view that as the proceedings complained of involved the enforcement of public rights with the consent of the Attorney General it was essentially an *actio popularis*. In other words, it did not involve the determination by a court of the applicant's 'civil rights and obligations' notwithstanding the decision as to costs. Relying on the Court of Human Rights decision in *Konig v FRG*,[114] the Commission stated that:

> . . . whether or not a right is to be regarded as a civil right within the meaning of this provision [Art. 6] is to be determined by reference to the substantive context and effects of the right and not its legal classification under the domestic law of the state concerned.

At no stage had the applicant in this case claimed direct personal harm or injury to himself caused by the authorities. As the Supreme Court proceedings fell outside the scope of Article 6 of the Convention the part of the application made under Article 13 also failed.

With regard to the applicant's submission that 'security of person' under Article 5 should be interpreted as including 'legal security of person', the Commission recalled its constant jurisprudence that the term had to be read with the word 'liberty' in the first sentence of Article 5 and thus referred exclusively to physical liberty and security. The application as a whole was rejected as incompatible *ratione materiae* with the provisions of the Convention.

In *Airey v Ireland*[115] the applicant complained that due to the prohibitive cost of civil litigation and the absence of a scheme of civil legal aid in Ireland she was effectively denied access to the courts for the purposes of seeking a judicial separation from her husband contrary to Article 6(1) of the Convention. She also complained of a violation of Article 14 read with Article 6 in that the remedy of judicial separation was more readily available to the rich than to the poor and she further alleged that Ireland was in breach of Articles 8 and 13 of the Convention.

The Commission was of the opinion that there had been a breach of Article 6(1) but saw no reason to address the complaints under Articles 8, 13, and 14. The matter was referred to the Court which gave its decision in October 1979, six years after the application was first registered.

[114] (1978) Series A No. 27. [115] (1979) Series A No. 32.

The Court construed Article 6(1) as granting a right of access to the courts by relying on *Golder v United Kingdom*[116] in which it had been found that, on a purposive interpretation of the Convention, prohibitive legal costs could infringe a right of access. The government had attempted to distinguish *Golder* on the basis that it involved a complaint about a positive obstacle to access as opposed to an omission on the part of the government which was at issue in the instant case. While the Court accepted that there were factual differences between the cases it held that the Convention could be violated by act or omission and, relying on *Marckx v Belgium*,[117] that where fulfilment of a Convention obligation required positive action by a state it could not remain passive. The right of access to the courts was such a right and just because it could be classified as social and economic did not bring it outside the remit of the Convention. Article 8 entailed a positive obligation for states to ensure respect for private and family life and Mrs. Airey's inability to avail herself of the remedy of judicial separation constituted a violation of this provision.

The Court rejected the government's argument that judicial separation was an inappropriate remedy for the applicant as an individual had the right to select whatever legal remedy s/he chose to pursue. In answer to the government's submission that the applicant's right of access was not impeded as she could have appeared before the domestic courts without legal representation the Court dismissed this firmly, stating: '. . . The Convention is intended to guarantee not rights that are theoretical or illusory, but rights that are practical and effective' (para. 24). However, it did accept that there were certain remedies for which appearance before a court without legal representation would be adequate.[118]

3. *The 1980s*

The question of whether an appeal under section 29 of the Courts of Justice Act 1924[119] was an effective remedy for the purposes of the six months rule arose in *M v Ireland*.[120] A section 29 appeal was permitted in criminal cases if a point of law of exceptional public importance was raised in the case. The

[116] (1975) Series A No. 18.
[117] (1979) Series A No. 31.
[118] See further: Thornberry. 'Poverty, Litigation and Fundamental Rights—A European Perspective', (1980) 29 *International and Comparative Law Quarterly*, 250–258.
[119] Section 29 provided as follows:

> The determination by the Court of Criminal Appeal of any appeal or other matter which it has power to determine shall be final, and no appeal shall lie from that court to the Supreme Court, unless that court or the Attorney General shall certify that the decision involves a point of law of exceptional public importance and that it is desirable in the public interest that an appeal should be taken to the Supreme Court.

[120] Application 9136/80.

applicant complained of unfair criminal proceedings leading to an unfair conviction for murder. Due to various complications with prosecution witnesses during the trial the applicant was effectively tried three times for the same offence. He unsuccessfully sought leave to appeal to the Court of Criminal Appeal and failed to obtain a section 29 certificate permitting an appeal on a point of law of exceptional public importance.

The Commission rejected the application for failure to observe the six months rule. It was of the opinion that the refusal of a section 29 Certificate by the Attorney General was not an effective and sufficient final decision for the purposes of the rule for the following reasons: it was only available subject to the discretion of the Attorney General and not as of right; the application could be made at any time after refusal of leave to appeal to the Court of Criminal Appeal or dismissal of an appeal by that court; and it was not a remedy which was part of the ordinary hierarchy of judicial decisions which a person complaining of his trial, conviction, and sentence would normally be obliged to pursue.[121]

The state's responsibility for the omissions of an important national institution, the Roman Catholic Church, arose for consideration in *K v Ireland*.[122] The applicant, a Roman Catholic priest, received a letter from the Archbishop of Dublin in March 1977 withdrawing his faculties and forbidding him to celebrate mass in public in the archdiocese of Dublin. In November 1980 he consented to a High Court action which he had previously commenced against his ecclesiastical superior being struck out so as to avoid possible excommunication. He complained to the Commission of loss of livelihood without an impartial hearing with proper representation. He also complained of the non-existence of a judicial forum to hear his complaint under canon or civil law.

The Commission, referring to its constant jurisprudence regarding the addressees of the Convention, rejected the application as incompatible *ratione personae* within the meaning of Article 27(2) in that it was directed against the Roman Catholic church. With regard to the government's liability for the alleged non-availability of a judicial forum to hear his complaint the Commission pointed to the appropriateness of the common law remedy

[121] While the first and second reasons given by the Commission for not recognizing an application for a section 29 certificate as a final decision for the purposes of the six month's rule are sound. the second reason, the absence of a time limit for seeking such a certificate, at first glance seems inconsistent with the Commission's earlier decision in *Nielsen v Denmark* (Application 343/57). In that case it rejected the respondent government's submission that an appeal to a Special Court of Revision should not be considered as a final decision due to the absence of any time limits for appeal. It did, however, reserve a discretion not to consider such proceedings if there had been an abuse of the absence of a time limit.

[122] Application 9366/81.

of wrongful dismissal. The fact that the applicant had dropped his pursuit of such a remedy for fear of excommunication was not something for which the state could be held liable.

In *W and W v Ireland*[123] the applicants were members of the travelling community and members of the Association of Teachers of Travelling People. The traveller applicants had been involved in somewhat protracted domestic court proceedings regarding their occupation of unserviced sites, the property of the local authority, Bray Urban District Council. Local residents had objected to their occupation of the sites and brought proceedings for nuisance against the local authority which, in turn, sued the travellers seeking that they vacate the sites and pay compensation for the alleged nuisance. During the proceedings before the Circuit Court the travellers raised a number of constitutional points which, under the Constitution, could only be considered at first instance by the High Court. For reasons of cost and convenience the Circuit Court refused to transfer the case to the High Court and heard both cases together. Having reserved judgment in the first case (brought by the residents) until the evidence in the second one (brought by the authority) was heard the judge found in favour of the residents (awarding nominal damages of £1 and costs) and the local authority and ordered the travellers to vacate the sites.

Both cases were appealed to the High Court which affirmed the order of the Circuit Court extending it to new traveller families which had arrived on the sites but who were not original parties to the proceedings. Further proceedings ensued after the serving of the High Court order in April 1981 when more travellers occupied the sites which had been vacated by those involved in the prior proceedings.

In making an application to the Commission the applicants complained under Articles 3, 6, 8, 13, and 14 of the Convention and under Article 1 of the First Protocol thereto. They claimed that their treatment by the relevant authorities constituted inhuman and degrading treatment and that their removal from the sites was a disproportionate response to the nuisance complained of. Relying on the *East African Asian* cases,[124] they complained of differential treatment as a group based on their membership of the travelling community which was discriminatory when compared to that of homelesss families who were members of the settled community. They further complained that the procedures adopted by both the Circuit and High Courts were prejudicial to their interests and, in particular, they complained that the extension of the latter court's order to people who were not parties to the original proceedings constituted a denial of their right of access to the courts. The

[123] Application 9596/81. This case is commonly referred to as *The Bray Travellers'* case.
[124] (1973) 3 EHRR 76 Com. Rep.

effect of removal from one site with no offer of alternative accommodation had the effect of worsening the family situations of the families thereby violating their family rights and the fact that no appeal lay against the order of the High Court meant that the applicants were denied an effective remedy in Irish law. The applicants finally submitted that the disruption resulting from their being forced to move had the effect of denying their children the right to education.

In its response the government raised objections to the lack of specificity in the information regarding each of the applicants and to the legal standing of the Association of Teachers of Travelling People. It further argued that the applicants had failed to exhaust available domestic remedies by not taking declaratory proceedings based on a number of provisions of the Constitution or by seeking to avail themselves of the case stated procedure for which legal aid would have been available. In relation to the substance of the application the government argued that the applicants, in making an application under Article 8, were in effect asserting the right to a house, which was not a right guaranteed by the Convention.

Regarding the complaint of denial of the right to education, the government stated that there was no evidence to connect the High Court order to the interruptions in school attendance. It went on to defend its record in traveller education on the basis of the standard established in the *Belgian Linguistics* case.[125]

The applicants responded to the government's submission stating that it was uniquely difficult to obtain sufficiently specific information about families which were being forced to move from site to site and who were, by and large, illiterate and without access to various means of communication. Regarding the non-exhaustion point the applicants responded that there was no valid ground upon which to bring an appeal against the Circuit Court judge's decision to refuse to transfer the initial case to the High Court for the consideration of constitutional points. This had the effect of preventing them from availing themselves of what they acknowledged to be the most appropriate constitutional remedy, a declaratory action in the High Court. They further pointed out that they would not have been granted legal aid for such an action or for the case stated procedure.

The Commission, in a concise opinion, accepted the government's objections to the legal standing of the Association of Teachers of Travelling People stating that a moral interest in the welfare of their pupils was insufficient to bring them within the category of 'victim' under the Convention. It found

[125] (1968) 1 EHRR 252. This standard was said to 'vary in time and place, according to the needs and resources of a community and of the individuals'.

that domestic proceedings had not been exhausted and pointed out how it might have been possible for some of the applicants to seek a declaratory remedy. While accepting that it would have been difficult to institute such proceedings without legal aid the Commission was not satisfied that appliicants ever intended so doing. The Commission also noted that the applicants had not contended that the legal aid scheme did not extend, as a matter of law, to cover constitutional actions. It rejected the part of the application made under Article 6 regarding the alleged unfairness of domestic court procedures as manifestly ill-founded and found the entire application to be inadmissible.

Johnston v Ireland[126] essentially involved a complaint that the constitutional prohibition on *divorce a vinculo*[127] and the unequal treatment of so-called 'illegitimate children' in Irish law amounted to a violation of the Convention. The applicants argued that couples in non-marital relationships were subjected to discriminatory treatment under Irish law as were any offspring resulting from such relationships.

In December 1986, by a vote of sixteen to one, the Court confirmed the Commission's earlier opinion that the absence of divorce in Ireland, with its consequences for the first and second applicants, did not give rise to a violation of Articles 8 or 12 of the Convention. The right to marry and found a family contained in Article 12 did not by necessary implication entail a right to remarry. Notwithstanding the established practice of dynamic or evolutive interpretation of the Convention, the Court was strongly influenced by the deliberate omission of provision for a right to divorce evident from the *travaux préparatoires*. The Court also rejected the applicants' contention that they were the victims of discrimination due to the recognition of certain foreign divorces in Ireland.[128]

With respect to the first applicant's complaint under Articles 9 and 14 that his inability to live with his partner, the second applicant, other than in an extra-marital relationship was contrary to his conscience, the Court took the view that this part of the application was essentially connected with the part

[126] [1978] Series A No. 112.

[127] At the time of this application the relevant provision of the Irish Constitution (Article 41.3) read as follows:

> 1. The State pledges itself to guard with special care the institution of Marriage, on which the Family is founded, and to protect it against attack.
> 2. No law shalll be enacted providing for the grant of a dissolution of marriage.
> 3. No person whose marriage has been dissolved under the civil law of any other State but is a subsisting valid marriage under the law for the time being in force within the jurisdiction of the Government and Parliament established by this Constitution shall be capable of contracting a valid marriage within that jurisdiction during the lifetime of the other party to the marriage so dissolved.

[128] The statutory regime governing the recognition of foreign divorces in Ireland is set out in the Domicile and Recognition of Foreign Divorces Act 1986 (No. 24 of 1986).

of the application concerning the absence of divorce and was therefore not an appropriate matter for consideration under Article 9. A number of other particularized complaints were dismissed for the same reason with the Court concluding that the government was not obliged to have a special legal regime for unmarried cohabiting couples such as the first and second applicants.

In relation to the third applicant, the child of the first and second applicants, the Court held unanimously that her unequal treatment in Irish law by comparison with that of a child of validly married parents constituted a violation of Article 8 of the Convention. Although the Court did not consider the discrimination point raised under Article 14 it found that the Irish government were obliged to place the third applicant in a position legally and socially akin to that of a 'legitimate' child.

In *H v Ireland*[129] the application was found to be an abuse of the right of petition because of the efforts of the applicant to evade the criminal justice system prior to the making of the application. The applicant had been the subject of protracted extradition proceedings which culminated in a finding by the Irish Supreme Court that his extradition to the United Kingdom should proceed. Following that decision he avoided arrest and went on the run. His complaint to the Commission under Article 6 of the Convention essentially related to the length of the extradition proceedings: seven years.

The Commission agreed with the Irish government's submission that the application was an abuse of the right of petition. It noted the fact that the applicant had avoided arrest and had taken no steps to accelerate the proceedings but rather had avoided their operation. While acknowledging that occasions might arise where an applicant might, by virtue of a violation of the rights and freedoms in the Convention, be excused from compliance with the rule of law the proposed extradition of an applicant to face trial in the jurisdiction of another member state of the Council of Europe would not justify the evasion of domestic law enforcement.

K v Ireland[130] is an example of the strict application of the six months rule by the Commission in a case which might otherwise have given rise to a finding of a violation on the part of the Irish government. The applicant was on the thirty-eighth day of a hunger strike (which ended two days later) while being detained at Portlaoise Prison. He had been convicted by the Special Criminal Court in December 1978 on various charges connected with a train robbery and received two concurrent sentences of twelve years' penal servitude. He had been convicted *in absentia* as he had fled to the United States while on bail. Two co-accused were convicted in connection with the same robbery.

[129] Application 9742/82. [130] Application 10416/83.

In his application to the Commission K alleged that he had been a victim of a violation of Articles 3 and 6 of the Convention. He further submitted that as his application was being made more than six months after the final domestic decision relating to his case the rule should be waived due to special circumstances concerning his health. He tendered a psychiatrist's report and an affidavit deposed by himself in support of this submission.

In its submission to the Commission the government indicated a willingness to refrain from contesting the facts supporting an argument for special circumstances justifying a relaxation of the six months rule. It also made a number of submissions contesting the merits of the application to which the applicant responded in detail.

The Commission did not enter into a consideration of the merits of the application and rejected it for being lodged one month out of time. Referring to earlier decisions[131] it stressed that the rule was not simply to serve the interests of respondent governments in proceedings under the ECHR but also to promote legal certainty as a value in itself. The fact that the Irish government were willing to waive compliance with the rule by the applicant was irrelevant as contracting states did not have the authority to allow such a waiver. The Commission was also mindful of the fact that the applicant had lodged the application on the thirty-eighth day of a hunger strike when he would presumably have been in a worse state of health than earlier in the six-month period after the final decision of the Irish Supreme Court. It also noted that his mental state had not prevented him from pursuing a number of appeals before the Irish courts when he was reported to be suffering from post-traumatic stress disorder.

The applicant in *Norris v Ireland*[132] had challenged unsuccessfully a number of pieces of nineteenth-century legislation[133] which criminalized certain sexual acts between men (even if carried out between between consenting male adults) before the Irish courts.[134] In his application to the Commission he complained that those measures constituted an unjustifiable interference with his right to privacy under Article 8 of the Convention. The Irish government argued that the restrictions contained in the impugned legislation were necessary for 'the protection of health and morals' and that it should be

[131] For example: *X v France*, Application 9587/81.

[132] [1988] Series A No. 142.

[133] Sections 61 and 62 of the Offences Against the Person Act 1861 and section 11 of the Criminal Law (Amendment) Act 1885.

[134] *Norris v Attorney General* [1984] IR 36. For an analysis of this litigation and the issues raised by the *Norris* case see further: Connelly, 'Irish Law and the Judgment of the European Court of Human Rights in the Dudgeon Case', (1982) 4 *Dublin University Law Journal* (ns), 25; Gearty, 'Homosexuals and the Criminal Law: The Right to Privacy', (1983) 5 *Dublin University Law Journal* (ns), 264; O'Malley, 'Norris v. Ireland: An Opportunity for Law Reform', (1988) 6 *Irish Law Times*, 279. See generally: O'Malley, *Sexual Offences: Law, Policy and Punishment*, (Dublin: Round Hall Sweet & Maxwell, 1996) 139–144.

afforded a wide margin of appreciation to deal with the matter as it saw best.

The Court rejected this argument and reaffirmed the approach it had earlier adopted in the analogous case of *Dudgeon v United Kingdom*[135] stating that there was no pressing social need for the challenged law and that any justifications for it were far outweighed by its detrimental effects on individual homosexuals. Public shock or disturbance at the commission of private homosexual acts did not, in itself, warrant their criminalization.

The Court also rejected the government's challenge to the legal standing of the applicant under the Convention. The government had argued that, as the impugned law had never been enforced against the applicant, he was not a 'victim' for the purposes of Article 25, and therefore his claim was in the nature of an *actio popularis* which could not be entertained by the Court. Referring to previous judgments, including *Johnston v Ireland*, the Court stated that an applicant could be a victim for the purposes of Article 25 in the absence of enforcement of a challenged law if s/he ran the risk of being directly affected by such enforcement. Mr Norris came within this category of victim.

In *O'C v Ireland*[136] the applicant complained that the restrictions imposed on the use of his land by virtue of the listing by the Commissioners for Public Works of a promontory fort thereon as a national monument violated his rights under Article 1 of the First Protocol to the Convention read alone and read with Article 14 of the Convention. He also complained of a violation of his family rights contrary to Article 8 but this part of the application was rejected for non-exhaustion of domestic remedies.

In 1977 the applicant entered into a contract for the purchase of forty-six acres of land on which he planned to build a family residence, produce crops, and breed horses for two of his children who wished to pursue equestrian careers. The applicant was informed by the vendor of the land that it contained the remains of a listed promontory fort but he claimed that the vendor had said that the listing applied to part of the land only. It subsequently became clear that the listing affected all of the land. The Commissioners for Public Works later issued a preservation order preventing the applicant from excavating, digging, ploughing, or in any way disturbing the land in and around the fort such that the applicant could not use the land for the purpose for which it had been bought. A request for planning permission to build a house on the land was also refused on the ground, *inter alia*, that the land was subject to a preservation order.

Although there was provision under the relevant legislation for the Commissioners for Public Works to acquire compulsorily land such as that of

[135] [1981] Series A No. 45; cf *Olsson v Sweden* [1988] Series A No. 130.
[136] Application 11446/85.

the applicant it had a policy of not applying that provision. The applicant was of the view that this allowed the Comissioners all the benefits of compulsory acquisition without the obligation to pay appropriate compensation.

In considering the application the Commission, relying on earlier decisions of the Commission and Court,[137] addressed the question of whether what was involved in this case was a form of *de facto* expropriation. It reiterated its previously stated view that control over the use of property, albeit for a legitimate purpose in accordance with the general interest, would violate Article 1 of the First Protocol if it were clearly established that there was no reasonable relationship of proportionality between the interference with the individual's rights and the general interest which gave legitimacy to the aim pursued. Thus the Commission retained a limited review of the legitimacy of the aim of the legislation and a fuller review of the proportionality of an actual interference with an applicant's rights. The principal criterion for establishing whether a fair balance had been struck in cases involving control over the use of property (as opposed to cases of straightforward expropriation of property) was the use for which that property was intended by the individual owner.

Applying that test to the facts of the instant case the Commission concluded that there had been no interference with the applicant's right to peaceful enjoyment of his possessions as he was substantially on notice of the restriction on use by virtue of the listing of the promontory fort as a national monument before he purchased the land. In relation to the preservation order issued after the purchase it found that this did not amount to a control over the use of property for the purposes of Article 1 of the First Protocol.

With regard to the part of the application made under Article 14 alleging discrimination by the failure of the Commissioners for Public Works to acquire the applicant's land compulsorily and pay compensation as they did in certain other cases, the Commission stated that it lay within the margin of appreciation of state authorities to decide whether the achievement of a particular aim in the public interest should be by way of deprivation of property or the imposition of restrictions on its use. The Commission could not substitute its view for that of the state authorities. Rather, it had to confine itself to a consideration of the proportionality of the action taken with particular regard to the rights of the individual applicant. This part of the application was thus declared to be manifestly ill founded.

[137] *Lithgow and Others v UK*, Application 9006/80; *Sporrong and Lönnroth v Sweden* (1982) Series A No. 52; *Gillow v UK*, Application 9063/80.

4. The 1990s

A significant number of applications involving property disputes have been registered against Ireland.[138] *Pine Valley Developments and Others v Ireland*[139] arose from complications surrounding the grant of planning permission for development property. The first applicant, Pine Valley Developments Ltd, purchased a plot of land in 1978 in reliance on a grant of outline planning permission for industrial development. Full planning permission was originally refused by the planning authority, Dublin County Council, as the property in question was part of a proposed green belt. That decision was overturned in May 1981 on foot of an appeal brought by the first applicants. In July 1981 Pine Valley Developments sold the property to the second applicants, Healy Holdings Ltd, which was owned by the third applicant, Mr Daniel Healy.

In February 1982 the Irish Supreme Court found that the original planning permission had been granted *ultra vires* and was therefore *null ab initio* as it was contrary to the relevant planning legislation.[140] The government responded by introducing the Local Government (Planning and Development) Act 1982[141] in order retrospectively to validate such grants of planning permission irrespective of earlier legislation. The applicants in this case were of the view that the 1982 legislation did not alter their position and this view was confirmed in *dicta* of the Supreme Court. This, they submitted, gave rise to a violation of Article 1 of the First Protocol to the Convention and to discrimination when read with Article 14 of the Convention itself. They further complained that no effective remedy was available to them in Irish law contrary to Article 13 of the Convention.

The Court held as follows in relation to the various elements of the application.

1. it unanimously rejected the government's argument that the applicants could not claim to be 'victims' for the purposes of Article 25, stressing that the dissolution or insolvency of a corporate person did not extinguish the possibility of its being a victim;
2. the government could not rely on arguments it had not raised before the Commission nor could it rely on an argument which contradicted a stance it had previously and consistently adopted. It was therefore

[138] In fact, property issues gave rise to the third most numerically significant category of application against Ireland under the Convention for the first forty years after ratification: O'Connell, *Digest of Applications made Against Ireland Under the ECHR*, Unpublished research paper for the Irish Centre for the Study of Human Rights (1990).

[139] [1992] 14 EHRR 319.

[140] *Pine Valley Developments Ltd v Minister for the Environment* [1987] IR 23.

[141] No. 21 of 1982.

estopped from raising the non-exhaustion admissibility rule before the Court. In any event, a remedy which would not bear fruit in sufficient time or which did not permit total recovery of the applicants' losses was not a remedy for the purposes of Article 26. Neither was the remedy of a private action against a private party unconnected with the respondent state appropriate when the state itself had caused the loss to the applicants;

3. it was unanimously found that there had been no violation of Article 1 of the First Protocol in respect of the first applicant (Pine Valley) read alone or in conjunction with Article 14 as Pine Valley had alienated its interest in the land in question;
4. by six votes to three, it was found that there had been no violation of the First Protocol in respect of the second and third applicants (Healy Holdings Ltd and Mr Daniel Healy), but, unanimously, that there had been discriminatory treatment contrary to Article 14 read with Article 1 of the First Protocol;
5. there had been no violation of Article 13 regarding any of the three applicants;
6. the question of just satisfaction to the injured parties under Article 50 was reserved and the applicants were invited to submit written comments thereon to the Court within three months or to notify it of any agreement reached.

The *Pine Valley case* does not add significantly to the European Court's jurisprudence[142] but point no. 2 above is of practical significance in proceedings under the Convention.

The issue of abortion and the ancilliary issues of abortion information and the right to travel have exercised judicial forums in this jurisdiction since the passage of the Eighth Amendment to the Irish Constitution in 1983.[143] The issue of abortion information has also been considered by both the European Court of Justice and the European Court of Human Rights in separate cases. In *Open Door and Others v Ireland*[144] the applicants had been engaged in the provision of pregnancy counselling services to women in and around Dublin. Their application under the ECHR arose from a perpetual injunction

[142] Connelly, 'Ireland and the European Convention on Human Rights: An Overview', in: Heffernan and Kingston (eds), *Human Rights: A European Perspective*, (Dublin: Round Hall Press, 1994) 34–47, at 43.

[143] The following provision (Article 40.3.3) was inserted into the Constitution in 1983:

The State acknowledges the right to life of the unborn and, with due regard to the equal right to life of the mother, guarantees in its laws to respect, and, as far as practicable, by its laws to defend and vindicate that right.

[144] [1992] Series A No. 246.

imposed by the Irish Supreme Court restraining them from imparting information to pregnant women concerning abortion facilities outside this jurisdiction by way of non-directive counselling.[145]

The Court's decision was mainly concerned with the allegations of a violation of the freedom of expression guarantee in Article 10. It was not disputed that the injunction complained of interfered with the right to receive and impart information. The Court construed its purpose as being for the protection of morals as opposed to the prevention of crime. It did not consider whether a right to abortion was guaranteed by the Convention or whether the unborn foetus was protected by the right to life guarantee contained in Article 2 of the Convention.

While accepting that member states had a wide margin of appreciation in relation to moral issues the Court stressed that the state's discretion in such matters was not unfettered nor unreviewable. It was struck by the absolute nature of the injunction imposed in this case and, on that basis alone, it found that the restriction on freedom of expression was disproportionate to the legitimate aim it sought to achieve. The Court also noted that the restriction was ineffective as it did not prevent large numbers of Irish women from travelling abroad to obtain abortions.

The decision of the European Court of Human Rights in the *Open Door* case was by no means the end of the abortion information saga in Ireland and further domestic proceedings ensued following that decision.[146]

It is worth noting that in the considerable domestic litigation which arose as a result of the censorship of certain forms of political speech permitted by section 31 of the Broadcasting Authority Act 1960 (as amended by section 16 of the Broadcasting Authority (Amendment) Act 1976) the ECHR was never resorted to by the courts in the resolution of these cases.[147]

[145] *Attorney General (SPUC) v Open Door Counselling Ltd and Others* [1988] IR 593.

[146] See further: Kingston and Whelan with Bacik, see n. 66 above.

[147] *State (Lynch) v Cooney* [1982] IR 337; *O'Toole v RTE (No. 2)* [1993] ILRM 458; *Brandon Book Publishers Ltd v RTE* [1993] ILRM 806. These cases are discussed at 15–17 of Flynn, see n. 11 above. See generally: McGonagle, *A Textbook on Media Law*, (Dublin: Gill & Macmillam, 1996). The relevant provisions of section 31 (as amended) provide as follows:

> (1) Where the Minister is of the opinion that the broadcasting of a particular matter or any matter of a particular class would be likely to promote, or incite to crime or would tend to undermine the authority of the State, he may by order direct the Authority to refrain from broadcasting the matter or any matter of the particular class, and the Authority shall comply with the order.
>
> (2) An order under subsection (1) of this section shall remain in force for such period not exceeding twelve months as is specified in the order and the period for which the order is to remain in force may be extended or further extended by an order made by the Minister or by a resolution passed by both Houses of the Oireachtas providing for its extension: provided that the period for which an order under the said subsection (1) is extended or further extended by an order or resolution under this subsection shall not exceed a period of twelve months.

Eventually the issue gave rise to an application under the ECHR in *Purcell and Others v Ireland*.[148] The various applicants in this case complained that the effect of the section 31 Ministerial Order and guidelines issued thereunder was gravely to distort coverage of all news events, current affairs, and social developments in Northern Ireland, to deter journalists and producers from choosing to put on programmes relating to Northern Ireland issues, and to prevent journalists and producers from complying with the requirements as to balance and impartiality in programming. The applicants contended that there was a sufficient safeguard against the use of the broadcasting media to undermine the authority of the state contained in section 18 of the above-mentioned 1960 Act (as amended) which banned the broadcasting of matters:

> which may reasonably be regarded as being likely to promote, or incite to, crime or as tending to undermine the authority of the State.

The applicants complained under Article 10 of the Convention that the section 31 order constituted an unjustifiable interference with freedom of expression and seriously interfered with their right in a democratic society to impart information to the public and of the public's right to receive information without unnecessary interference by a public authority. While accepting that the order pursued a legitimate aim they complained that it lacked the requisite precision to be 'prescribed by law' within the meaning of Article 10(2). The practical effect of the order greatly exceeded the legitimate aim pursued by the government which could, in any event, be achieved under section 18 of the Act. Neither did the restrictions on freedom of speech correspond to a 'pressing social need'. The applicants further complained of violations of Article 3 of the First Protocol and of Article 14 read in conjunction with that Article and with Article 10 of the Convention. The final limb of their application was that they were denied an effective domestic remedy contrary to Article 13 because of the well established constitutionality of section 31 orders in various proceedings before the Irish courts.

The Commission, in considering the admissibility of the application, was of the opinion that the conditions set down in Article 25 of the Convention had not been satisfied insofar as two of the applicants were trade unions with an insufficient interest in the matter. However, it did find that the seventeen individual applicants, all of whom were full-time broadcasting journalists or producers of radio and television programmes, did satisfy the legal standing requirements of Article 25.

The government's submission that the applicants had failed to satisfy the requirements of Article 26 by failing to exhaust domestic remedies was

[148] Application 15404/89. The Report of the Commission is to be found in (1991) 12 *Human Rights Law Journal*, 254–261.

rejected by the Commission on the basis that any legal challenge which the applicants might launch against the impugned order was doomed as a result of an earlier decision of the Irish Supreme Court.

In considering the justifications put forward for the interference with the applicants' freedom of expression the Commission applied the usual test: was the measure complained of prescribed by law; did it pursue a legitimate aim; and were the means used necessary in a democratic society for achieving that aim. Finding the part of the application based on Article 10 to be manifestly ill founded the Commission stated:

> . . . freedom of expression constitutes one of the essential foundations of a democratic society . . . the exercise of that freedom 'carries with it duties and responsibilities' . . . the defeat of terrorism is a public interest of the first importance in a democratic society. In a situation where politically motivated violence poses a constant threat to the lives and security of the population and where the advocates of this violence seek access to the media for publicity purposes, it is particularly difficult to strike a fair balance between the requirements of protecting freedom of information and the imperatives of protecting the State and the public against armed conspiracies seeking to overthrow the democratic order which guarantees this freedom and other human rights.[149]

Thus while the restrictions complained of constituted a professional inconvenience for the applicants they did not amount to a denial of their right to freedom of expression under Article 10 of the Convention

With regard to the part of the application brought under Article 3 of the First Protocol the Commission restated the view of the Court in *Mathieu-Mohin and Clerfayt v Belgium*[150] that this provision referred to equality of treatment for the purposes of voting. Thus the complaints made under this part of the application were also manifestly ill founded as were the allegations of discrimination made under Article 14. The Commission also rejected the part of the application made under Article 13 and declared, by a majority, that the application was inadmissible.

In *X v Ireland*[151] the applicant had been involved in personal injury litigation in which photographic evidence obtained by a private investigator acting on behalf of the defendant local authority's insurer had been used against her. She claimed that this constituted a violation of her right to privacy under Article 8 of the Convention and of Article 1 of the First Protocol thereto despite the fact that her claim for damages before the domestic courts was successful.

149 Ibid.

150 (1987) Series A No. 113.

151 Application 18670/91. See further: Carolan, 'The Implications of the Right to Privacy under the European Convention on Human Rights for Irish Personal Injury Claims', (1995) 4(2) *Irish Journal of European Law* 161–173.

Due to the success of her personal injury claim the Irish government challenged her standing as a 'victim' under Article 25 of the Convention and also contended that she had failed to exhaust domestic remedies by not taking a constitutional action based on the right to privacy. The government did acknowledge that the area of privacy was only in the process of development in Irish law. By way of alternative argument, the government submitted that there had been no interference with the applicant's privacy or property rights on the basis that the defendant local authority were not responsible for the acts of its insurer which had engaged the private investigator. As parties engaged in personal injury litigation could reasonably anticipate a reduced expectation of privacy any interference with the applicant's Convention rights was, according to the government, in accordance with the law and proportionate to the protection of the interests of the defendant local authority.

In response, the applicant claimed that the payment of damages in her personal injury claim was irrelevant to her privacy claim. She further contended, on the basis of counsel's opinion obtained domestically, that she was excused from the obligation to exhaust domestic remedies in relation to the latter claim. Regarding the substantive points made by the government, the applicant argued that it could not hide behind the acts of private insurers to avoid Convention liability for interference with her right to privacy. Such interference was not, in her opinion, sufficiently prescribed by law as there were no specific statutory or common law rules regulating the activities of private investigators or protecting the right to privacy. The surveilllance carried out was draconian, unjustified, and wholly disproportionate as other methods, such as rigorous medical tests, could have been used by the defendants.

The Commission, in declaring the application inadmissible, found that the applicant had failed to exhaust domestic remedies and that there were no special circumstances absolving her of the obligation under international law so to do. It stated that:

> in a legal system which provides constitutional protection for fundamental rights, it is incumbent on the aggrieved individual to test the extent of that protection and, in a common law system, to allow the domestic courts to develop those rights by way of interpretation.[152]

The applicant in *O'H v Ireland*,[153] a British citizen born in Northern Ireland, was serving a life sentence in a Dublin prison for the murder of a young girl. He had made a number of unsuccessful applications to the Sentence Review Group[154] for release or transfer to another prison closer to

[152] Commission's Decision on Admissibility, at 7.

[153] Application 23156/94.

[154] The Sentence Review Group is a non-statutory body established in 1989 to advise the Minister for Justice, Equality, and Law reform in relation to the administration of long-term sentences. All long-term prisoners who have completed seven years of their sentence can apply to the

Northern Ireland and also failed in his efforts to obtain legal aid from the Legal Aid Board to seek judicial review of the decisions of the Group. The essence of his complaint under the Convention was that there was no parole board with the power to order release with the result that there was effectively no difference between mandatory and discretionary life sentences.

The Commisssion considered the application under Article 5 although the applicant had not pleaded any particular provision of the Convention. It found that the sentence imposed by the Irish court under section 2 of the Criminal Justice Act 1964 was punitive in nature and satisfied the requirements of Article 5(4) of the Convention. It went on to find the remainder of the application alleging discrimination on the grounds of nationality, lack of legal representation before the Sentence Review Group, delay in communicating one of the Group's decisions, and the refusal of legal aid for judicial review proceedings to be manifestly ill founded. The Commission refused to consider the part of the application complaining of a violation of the applicant's family rights by the failure to transfer him to a prison closer to Northern Ireland on the basis that he had failed to exhaust available domestic remedies.

In *H v Ireland*[155] the distinction in Irish law between the persuasive burden of proof, which always remained upon the prosecution, and the evidential burden of proof, which occasionally transferred to an accused, and the implication thereof for the presumption of innocence was found, by the Commission, not to give rise to any violation of Article 6(2) of the Convention. The applicant had been convicted under section 4 of the Explosive Substances Act, 1883 by the Special Criminal Court and sentenced to five years' penal servitude. He made an unsuccessful appeal to the Court of Criminal Appeal and subsequently challenged unsuccessfully the constitutionality of the 1883 Act before the High Court and Supreme Court.

In his application to the Commission he complained that section 4 of the 1883 Act effectively removed the presumption of innocence contrary to Article 6 of the Convention. Section 4 required the prosecution to prove beyond a reasonable doubt that an accused person knowingly had possession of explosive substances under such circumstances as to give rise to a reasonable suspicion that he did not have them in his possession for a lawful object. The various Irish courts which considered the evidence in this case were satisfied that the prosecution had established each of these elements and were mindful of surrounding evidence such as that the applicant was travelling on a false passport and subsequently attempted to evade detention.

Group to have their cases reviewed. If it declines to recommend release a date is set for further review within the next three years.

[155] Application 23456/94.

E. REMEDIAL ACTION TAKEN BY THE GOVERNMENT IN RESPONSE TO BEING HELD IN VIOLATION OF THE CONVENTION

The causal connection between the finding of a violation of the Convention and the remedial action taken by the Irish government is sometimes tenuous. It is also arguable that decisions of the Strasbourg authorities in Irish cases more frequently affect the timing of reforms in this jurisdiction than the content of such reforms.

1. Lawless

As there was no finding of a violation in *Lawless v Ireland* no remedial action was necessitated on the part of the Irish government. The 'on-off state of emergency' which provided the backdrop to that case ended in 1995 in response to the IRA ceasefire of that year.

2. Airey

In response to the decision in *Airey v Ireland* the Irish government introduced a non-statutory scheme of civil legal aid and advice in 1980 which proved to be seriously unsatisfactory. The scheme was woefully under-resourced and excluded many significant areas of law such as property, employment, and defamation disputes. Essentially, it provided a restricted family law service, and arguably did not remedy the breach of the Convention found in *Airey*.

Eventually, and not without considerable litigation in the Irish courts[156] and strenuous campaigning by various interested parties,[157] the scheme was given a statutory basis in the Civil Legal Aid Act of 1995.[158] The Law Centres established under the legislation continue to deal almost exclusively with family law litigation but there are enabling provisions in the 1995 Act to extend their remit to cover tribunal cases in areas such as employment law.

3. Johnston

The Status of Children Act of 1987,[159] which effectively abolished the legal status of illegitimacy, was introduced by the then Minister for Justice stating

[156] See for example: *Forrest v Legal Aid Board*, High Court unrep, O'Hanlon J (4th December 1992); *BS v Landy*, High Court unrep, Lardner J (10th February 1993).

[157] The Free Legal Advice Centres (FLAC) were most prominent in this regard and made a significant written submission to the Council of Europe on the legal aid crisis in Ireland. This was published in (1990) 8 *Irish Law Times* (ns) 289.

[158] No. 32 of 1995. For a critical analysis of this legislation see Phelan,'The Civil Legal Aid Bill, 1995: A Critique' (1995) *Irish Law Times* 109.

[159] No. 26 of 1987.

that it rectified the finding of a violation in *Johnston v Ireland*. It is worth noting that such a change in the law was already anticipated as a result of the *Law Reform Commission Report on Illegitimacy*[160] and the decision of the European Court of Human Rights probably just hastened its introduction.

4. Norris

The failure of the Irish government to respond to the decision of the European Court in *Norris v Ireland* for a period of five years after that decision attracted some adverse comment from both the Council of Europe and other commentators. Eventually, most forms of homosexual sexual activity between men were decriminalized by the Criminal Law (Sexual Offences) Act 1993[161] which also introduced a uniform age of sexual consent regardless of sexual orientation. Again the impetus for reform was not entirely external as the Law Reform Commission had also recommended change along the lines contained in the legislation.[162]

5. Pine Valley

Pine Valley did not necessitate any remedial legislative action by the government. The payment of compensation to the applicants was 'just satisfaction' for the purposes of the European Court's judgment as no other parties were affected by the operation of the impugned planning legislation.

6. Open Door

Although the injunction which gave rise to *Open Door v Ireland* was not immediately lifted as a result of the finding of a violation of Article 10 of the ECHR by the European Court of Human Rights a constitutional amendment was introduced which permitted the imparting of information on abortion services lawfully available in other jurisdictions. This amendment was further clarified by legislation regulating the provision of abortion information and this legislation was upheld by the Supreme Court when referred by the President under Article 26 of the Constitution.[163] It is therefore not susceptible to any constitutional challenge before the Irish courts for so long as it remains in force. It should, however, be noted that the penalties contained in the legislation for providing abortion information and advice in prohibited

[160] Law Reform Commission Report No. 4 (Dublin, 1982).

[161] No. 20 of 1993.

[162] These recommendations were contained in the Law Reform Commission's *Consultation Paper* and *Report on Child Sexual Abuse*.

[163] *In the Matter of Article 26 of the Constitution and the Regulation of Information (Services Outside the State for the Termination of Pregnancies) Bill 1995* [1995] 1 IR 1.

circumstances could give rise to future applications under Article 10 of the Convention.[164]

7. Keegan

The Adoption Act 1998[165] was introduced to remedy the breach found in *Keegan v Ireland.* Section 4 amends the 1952 Adoption Act[166] (the principal Act) by providing for elaborate consultation procedures for natural fathers in the adoption process and also sets out the circumstances when such procedures need not be followed. A previous government had attempted to introduce similar legislation but that legislation fell with the dissolution of the Dail in 1997 for general election purposes.

F. ASSESSMENT AND PROSPECTS

There has been little public debate on whether to incorporate the European Convention on Human Rights into domestic law. This may be because of the entrenchment of a 'bill of rights' in the 1937 Constitution and a sense of jurisprudential self-sufficiency evidenced in some of the case-law (discussed in Sections B and D above).

It is probably also the case that instruments such as the ECHR are hardly at the core of the collective political consciousness of the Irish public. 'European law' is frequently seen as an external amorphous concept which underpins self-serving political discourse authoritatively. It is not uncommon for it also to be used (no less authoritatively) as a counterclaim to precisely such discourse. Ignorance of European law is thus both a defence and an offence, in a manner of speaking! The relatively low number of individual applications involving Ireland as the respondent state points as much to ignorance of the Convention on the part of lawyers and litigants, coupled with an understandable reluctance to tread the apparently interminable legal road to Strasbourg, as it does to an exemplary human rights record.

To date, the most considered approach taken to the issue of incorporation is to be found in the *Report of the Constitution Review Group.*[167] The terms of reference of the CRG were:

[164] This point was raised by Deputy Liz O'Donnell in the Dail Debates on the bill: (13 March 1995) vol. 450, cols. 51–53.

[165] No. 10 of 1998.

[166] No. 25 of 1952.

[167] The CRG was established pursuant to a programme entitled 'A Government of Renewal'. This was the programme of the government which took office on 15 December 1994 and which became known as 'The Rainbow Coalition'. The CRG was chaired by the distinguished former

to review the Constitution, and in the light of this review, to establish those areas where constitutional change may be desirable or necessary, with a view to assisting the All-Party Committee on the Constitution, to be established by the Oireachtas, in its work . . .

The Group were instructed to take into account that certain issues of constitutional controversy would be the subject of separate consideration. Those issues were: Articles 2 and 3 of the Constitution dealing with national territory and related matters; divorce; the right to bail; cabinet confidentiality; and the voting rights of emigrants.

The *Report* of the CRG did not recommend direct incorporation of the ECHR into domestic law: in fact it expressly rejected this option. Rather, it opted for a form of *à la carte* incorporation whereby certain provisions of the Convention could be reflected in Irish laws where the Convention standard was higher than that already contained in domestic law. Although the CRG acknowledged, as a matter of practicality, that the only feasible form of incorporation would be by means of constitutional amendment conferring supremacy on Convention standards, it did not accept the principled arguments in favour of such an approach. Its position, which was to be applied on a section-by-section analysis of the fundamental rights provisions of the Constitution, was stated as follows:

it would be preferable to draw on the ECHR (and other international human rights instruments) where:

i) the right is not expressly protected by the Constitution;
ii) the standard of protection of such rights is superior to those guaranteed by the Constitution; or
iii) the wording of a clause of the Constitution protecting such right might be improved.[168]

Thus, for example, the freedom of expression guarantee in Article 10 of the ECHR would become the model for a re-drafted Article 40.6.1.i of the Irish Constitution.

Criticism has been levelled at the Report for its timidity in the area of social and economic rights but it is doubtful whether these shortcomings would have been addressed by a more fulsome embrace of the ECHR, which itself is more concerned with civil and political rights.[169]

civil servant and later Chancellor of the National University of Ireland, Dr T. K. Whitaker, and comprised fourteen experts drawn from different disciplines. The group met for just over one year from May 1995 until May 1996 and produced a number of reports. The report referred to throughout this chapter is the final report issued in May 1996 which is currently being considered by an All-Party Oireachtas Committee on the Constitution.

168 *Report of the CRG*, 219.

169 See generally: Morison, '"A disposition to preserve and an ability to improve": The Report of the Constitution Review Group in the Republic of Ireland', (1997) Spring *Public Law*,

The signing of the Belfast Agreement on Good Friday 1998 injected a new interest into public discussion on elevating the domestic legal status of the ECHR, largely due to the fact that a form of incorporation followed in the United Kingdom. No parallel process is yet taking place in this jurisdiction but both the Irish and British governments have committed themselves to the establishment of Human Rights Commissions whose remit will be to supervise the enforcement of human rights obligations entered into by both states.[170]

It appears at the time of writing that the Irish government is continuing to resist direct incorporation of the Convention which admittedly would present some practical difficulties. A 'softening' of this stance was, however, evident in a written response of the Minister for Foreign Affairs to a parliamentary question on 19 February 1998. Asked what steps, if any, were being taken to incorporate the UN Covenants and the ECHR into Irish law, the Minister stated:

> . . . it has been the view of successive Irish Governments that rights guaranteed under the Constitution, relevant legislation, and common law rights in Ireland, fully correspond to, and in places exceed those available through the Convention. These rights are, of course, justiciable in our domestic courts. I should point out that while we are committed to equivalence between the human rights regimes North and South, this does not mean that precisely identical mechanisms have to be in place in the two jurisdictions.
>
> However, we are prepared to examine actively proposals for incorporation if it appears that this would be necessary to ensure the equivalence we seek between human rights regimes in the North and the South. In this context, the Government has decided to ask the relevant Departments to look again at the various complex legal and practical issues, including those relating to the Constitution that would be involved in the incorporation of the European Convention *into domestic legislation*.[171]

It is undoubtedly significant that the phrase 'incorporation . . . into domestic legislation' was used by the Minister in his response. This is no more than a commitment to piecemeal incorporation of certain provisions of the Convention in ordinary legislation without displacing the supremacy of

55–65; *Re-Righting the Constitution: The Case for New Social and Economic Rights: Housing, Health, Nutrition, Adequate Standard of Living*, paper published by the Irish Commission for Justice and Peace, September 1998.

[170] Farrell, 'The Republic's Human Rights Commission: Will it be the Afterthought that Roared?', paper presented to the 'Bringing Rights Back Home' Conference organized by the Irish Council for Civil Liberties and the Committee on the Administration of Justice in Dublin on 12–13 June 1998; Dickson, 'Creating an Effective Human Rights Commission for Northern Ireland', Paper commissioned by the Standing Advisory Commission on Human Rights for Northern Ireland, May 1998.

[171] Dail Debates, vol. 487, No. 5, 19 February 1998, col. 988. Emphasis added. The Minister went on to state that the government had no plans to incorporate the UN Covenants into domestic law. The question was asked by Deputy Trevor Sargeant of the Green Party.

domestic constitutional provisions. As such, it goes no further than the approach recommended by the CRG, and arguably falls short of that standard. It is notable that the Minister made no reference to incorporation by means of constitutional amendment.

In order to mark the fiftieth anniversary of the Universal Declaration of Human Rights and to pressurize the current government to establish a Human Rights Commission the Labour Party tabled a private members' bill on 30 November 1998. The bill is not a constitutional amendment bill and proposes, *inter alia*, to incorporate the ECHR by means of ordinary legislation.

Postscript

Since this chapter was written at the end of 1998 a number of cases referred to have given rise to applications against Ireland under the Convention. Proposals for the domestic incorporation of the Convention in the Republic of Ireland have also been advanced, and legislation for the establishment of a Human Rights Commission has been enacted.

In December 2000 the European Court of Human Rights found (in the cases of *Quinn v Ireland* (Application 36887/97) and *Heaney and McGuinness v Ireland* (Application 34720/97) that section 52 of the Offences Against the State Act 1939, which made it a criminal offence to refuse to account for one's movements in the course of questioning while under arrest for certain offences, was incompatible with Article 6 of the ECHR. Pursuant to a commitment in the Belfast Agreement all of the Offences Against the State Acts are being reviewed by a Committee under the chairmanship of former Supreme Court Judge, Anthony Hederman. The Committee, which was established in 1999, has yet to publish a report. In its deliberations it will no doubt have to consider the implications of the European Court's rulings in relation to section 52 of the 1939 Act as well as the Concluding Observations of the UN Human Rights Committee, issued in July 2000, to the effect that the jurisdicton of the Special Criminal Court (established under Part V of the 1939 Act) should be brought to an end.

A friendly settlement was reached in the case of *Croke v Ireland* (Application 33267/96) which involved review of involuntary psychiatric detention. The applicant in this case had failed before the Irish Supreme Court in his attempt to challenge the relevant provisions of 1945 mental health legislation which allowed for indefinite detention of 'persons of unsound mind' without review. As part of that friendly settlement the Government pointed to the fact that a new Mental Health Bill 1999 was before the Parliament which would provide for review of such detention within a twenty-eight-day period. It is worth noting that this provision of the

Bill, which was intended to bring Ireland into line with the appropriate standard under the ECHR, was criticized as being too long by the UN Human Rights Committee in the course of Ireland's second periodic examination under the International Covenant on Civil and Political Rights in July 2000. An amendment has since been tabled by the Minister for Health and Children (at the Committee Stage of the Bill's consideration) to allow for review within twenty-eight days or a shorter period but this has been criticized as meaningless by Opposition deputies and other commentators.

At the time of writing a bill to incorporate the ECHR into domestic law is awaited. According to public statements by the Minister for Justice, Equality, and Law Reform and the Attorney General, the Bill will adopt a similar odel of interpretative incorporation as that contained in the UK Human Rights Act 1998 (which applies in Northern Ireland) and the Convention will have the force of law at sub-constitutional level.

Although the details of the legislation are not yet known it is clear that a rebuttable presumption of compatibility will apply to legislation passed after its coming into force. It will not affect pre-existing legislation. A 'double construction rule' will be used in the application of this presumption such that if two interpretations of legislation are open, one of which leads to a finding that it is compatible with the ECHR and the other to a finding that it is not, the courts will opt for the former. There will also be the added complication that legislation challenged as being incompatible with the Convention may also be subject to scrutiny as to its validity under the Irish Constitution, with the possibility of contradictory findings being made.

While the Irish Constitution and the ECHR do contain many similar guarantees there are significant differences between the two instruments and between the body of jurisprudence built up under both. In some cases it is probable that impugned legislation will be found to be consistent with the Irish Constitution but incompatible with the Convention. As the Convention is to be incorporated at a sub-constitutional level the finding of incompatibility in such cases will be of largely academic interest and applicants will still have to resort to the European Court in Strasbourg to vindicate their Convention rights fully. Had the form of incorporation now being considered been in place at the time of the *Norris* or *Keegan* cases, for example, the domestic outcome in both cases would have been no different.

The Human Rights Commission Act was passed in 2000 and the Commission which it establishes has been given extensive powers and functions. It is charged with: keeping the laws and practices of the state under review as regards adequacy and effectiveness of human rights protection; examining draft legislation and reporting on its human rights implications; consulting with national or international human rights bodies; making recommendations on measures to strengthen, protect, and uphold human rights in the state; promoting understanding and awareness of the importance of human rights in the state; conducting inquiries (with significant powers to compel witnesses and evidence); appearing before the superior courts as *amicus curiae* in proceedings which concern human rights; instituting legal proceedings; providing legal assistance in certain circumstances; and establishing and participating in a Joint Committee with the Northern Ireland Human Rights Commission.

For the purposes of its general remit the definition of human rights (contained in section 2 of the Act) allows the Commission to use the human rights protected by the Irish Constitution and those contained in all international instruments to which the state is party regardless of whether the provisions of those instruments have been incorporated into domestic law. For the purposes of the Commission's involvement in court proceedings, however, it will be confined to using those rights protected by the Irish Constitution and those contained in international instruments which have been incorporated into domestic law.

19

Italy

ENZO MERIGGIOLA

INTRODUCTION

The European Convention on Human Rights, ratified by Italy by Law No. 848 of 4 August 1955, became a domestic law, an integral part of the Italian legal system, on 26 October of the same year, after the depositing of the instrument of ratification.

The entry into effect of the Convention soon drew lawyers' attention to the development of human rights, a basic feature of the states' policy after World War II and one which raised questions about certain aspects of sovereignty and relations between nations. It also prompted a new assessment, unheard of in the years which preceded, of the value of the individual as a human being worthy of protection beyond all consideration of political opportunism.

However, the effect on government activity and judges' decisions was quite different, mainly because lawyers and judges are traditionally not very sensitive to standards laid down at international level, and it took time for the Italian legal profession to recognize that the principles laid down in the European Convention were part of our national legal heritage and directly applicable in our system.

The reasons for the difference are explained in this chapter, which outlines both the problems of applying European Convention rules in the Italian legal system and the solutions found for them in legal theory and practice.

A. EFFECT OF THE CONVENTION ON LEGAL THEORY

The first effect of the Convention was to prompt studies of the human rights doctrine, something which various authors had taken up after the war at the time of the San Francisco Conference and the Universal Declaration of Human Rights. That same year there were also major debates on the new principles laid down by the Constituent Assembly, which in 1947 created a new Constitutional Charter, officially promulgated in December.

The Constitution incorporated almost all the principles laid down in the Universal Declaration when it stated, in the introduction, that the Republic recognized and guaranteed the sanctity of man, both as an individual and as a member of the social groups to which he belongs.

Studies of the new theories mushroomed, encouraged by the unanimous belief that the traditional idea of the state as the sole guarantor of the freedom of the people had to go.

In Italy it was the new Constitution which first put human rights principles into practice. A large number of laws were gradually repealed and their place taken by other provisions, which laid down the limits of state intervention with the stated aim, as the debates in the House made clear, of pushing forward the frontiers of human rights and creating structures to monitor the way in which Parliament and the authorities used their powers.

In particular, no one in Italy doubted that the rules of the Universal Declaration were general principles which might be useful as directives or yardsticks for political behaviour in the countries which belonged to the United Nations Organization. Lawyers, on the other hand, agreed that they did not constitute a legal obligation, as such, without a legal monitoring system. But in law and in relations between the citizens and the state, the rules of the Universal Declaration were soon being referred to and quoted as a model for behaviour and for the interpretation of new rules (or old ones which the state had yet to amend), usually with a view to putting right the old ideas of the state being absolutely sovereign and the sole guardian of freedom of the people.

With the European Convention came the first national awareness of effective international protection of the individual.

The rights laid down in that Convention were no longer philosophical tenets, nor just wishes. They were reality, guaranteed by international legal machinery. Furthermore, they crystallized and gave practical shape to a whole series of aspirations and desires which, being espoused unanimously by peoples with very different histories, had become the common heritage of the countries of Western Europe.

B. THE INDIVIDUAL

When the Convention took effect, studies of it mushroomed. Lectures on human rights and the European Convention in particular were soon offered in the universities; conferences followed congresses and they all helped change the approach to problems of international law and the place of the individual in the international order.

Italian lawyers proved to be very aware of this last point, which was a popular topic of debate in universities and political circles and the subject of dozens of articles in legal journals in the 1950s.

Even after the Universal Declaration of 1948, the international community remained convinced that states alone were the subjects of the international order and the individual a legally un-assessable entity. But with the European system of human rights protection, the individual undeniably had an important part to play in international law, because he had the power to set an international guarantee system in motion.

The leading question was whether the individual's right to petition the Commission created individual rights in the international order, and whether, once the case had gone to the Commission, the individual could be considered as a party to it. The answer, in the negative, came after lengthy discussions revealed that the commitments which the states made under the Convention were objective ones, in that they aimed to protect the fundamental rights of individuals against infringement by the state rather than to create individual, reciprocal rights between the two.

Thus Italian legal theory tell into line with the opinions of writers of other European States, and of the Commission too.

However, some lawyers were tireless in pointing out that the Convention placed the individual in a position which he had never occupied before. This was clear from the simple fact that it was up to him to take the initiative for referring a case to the Commission and setting the procedural machinery in motion and that he could defend himself personally and provide proof of the infringement—a situation of undeniable legal importance.

In fact there was no real doubt that the individual could never be a party, or appear in a legal capacity before the Court. But it was also impossible for him to be considered unconnected with proceedings in which he had a direct interest—as emerged from the fact that he could give testimony.

The place of the individual developed in the light of his position as applicant to the Commission.

C. THE SPECIFIC NATURE OF HUMAN RIGHTS AND THE PRINCIPLE OF GOOD FAITH

The enthusiasm created by the success of the human rights doctrine and the entry into force of both the Convention and the UN Covenants of 1966, which were another embodiment of the principles laid down in the Universal Declaration, were such that many writers in the 1970s claimed that the principles of human rights protection, as an expression of freedom of the individual, had become the spirit to transfuse the state's every action, a world language expressing the specific demands of human life worth living. It was this which created the international law on human rights.

This was an area which had acquired characteristics quite unlike the principles of international law in general. It could be described, roughly, as the subordinate legislation of domestic systems, ideological in content and conveying the common desire of the international community to protect values which were essential to the individual as a human being with intelligence and the power of self-determination. It was non-stable, in constant evolution, and destined to help bring modern societies closer together. It was a regular component of university courses and, when put into practice, it produced solutions quite distinct from those normally suggested by classic international law.

All this was apparent in the refusal of reciprocity in the application of the rights, in the method of settling disputes, in the principle of proportional restrictions on the rights of individuals, and in the good faith in inter-state relations.

Before World War II, as we know, the notion of good faith was virtually unknown in international relations. But in the 1950s, it began to be clear that, as a basis for relations, it gave the Contracting Parties confidence and made for the success of all forms of co-operation.

Something which tends not to be mentioned in international documents is that over the past thirty years, Italian lawyers have insisted that inter-state human rights commitments be founded on mutual good faith, as one of the basics of effective, efficient protection of the rights of the individual.

D. THE INTERACTION AND CONVERGENCE OF LEGAL SYSTEMS

In the 1960s lawyers had already predicted that, once in effect, the Convention would bring about ever-greater mutual recognition of our European systems over the years—a phenomenon rightly called interaction, which is still underway in Italy, where legal journals periodically print the texts of judgments of the European Court of Human Rights, with annotations, boosting our reciprocal knowledge of national legal traditions as the years go by.

This has a remarkable effect on the gradual convergence of national laws, reflected in the reports made when bills are tabled in the House. Even the decisions of judges (particularly trial judges) sometimes echo principles held in other Contracting States and mention solutions embodied in the judgments of the Strasbourg Court, which, as we know, sometimes addresses general problems and makes statements of principle instead of settling problems raised by complainants.

In the interests of finding justification or pinpointing the extent of the coverage, the Court often runs to a comparative discussion of legal systems in the course of its investigation. This, of course, makes it easier to apply, by analogy, solutions already found in national legal systems, thereby facilitating the process of interaction I have already mentioned.

The judges' attentiveness to European Court decisions, which can be deduced from reading the judgments, when they are made public, is important, particularly since it contributes to the achievement of one of the greatest aims of the Council of Europe, that of bringing European legal systems closer together.

E. THE RANKING OF CONVENTION RULES

When the European Convention on Human Rights was ratified by the President of the Italian Republic, after an Act of Parliament had declared it applicable on the territory of the state, lawyers began to wonder where the new rules stood in the national legal system.

It was a problem to which the Constitutional Court speedily found an answer, stating several times over that the Convention ranked as an ordinary law, in the same way as any other ratified agreement, since the Ratification Act had not specified otherwise.

The principle of the Italian legal system is that international law and national law are equal systems, but they are independent and separate and they stay separate, the substance of national law being independent of its conformity with international law. The two legal systems have different sources. National law is created by the will of the state and international law by the common will of several states and. as a result, neither system can contain a mandatory rule from the other.

The state, as a subject of international law, is at the same time the creator of its internal law and bound to keep that law within the limits of its commitments. Those commitments are usually made via laws through which Parliament provides for the 'full and entire application' of the rules of the international agreement which has been signed and sealed. This is ratification, the document returned with proof of reception, ie the reproduction of international rules by internal law.

Once the rules of an agreement have been integrated into the national system they may cancel a previous law, just as they may themselves be cancelled by a subsequent law, according to the general principles of the legal system.[1] The Supreme Court of Appeal has always come into line with the decisions of the Constitutional Court[2] so the ordinary courts only make their decisions in the light of rules which have been transformed into rules of national law.

There is nothing in the Convention to say that a treaty should rank higher than an ordinary law. Automatic adjustment of the legal system is only provided for in the case of 'generally recognized' rules of international law, ie international custom and those general principles of law which all civilized nations recognize.

One school of thought, referring to Kelsen's 'General Theory of Law and State', has pointed out that the force of a treaty is founded on the idea of *pacta sunt servanda*. It is designed to be above and outside national law, a matter of general recognition in the international community for some years now. The adaptation of internal law to international law should be considered to be automatic under Article 10 of the Constitution, which refers to principles generally recognized in the community of civilized nations.

This theory has been unlucky. The Constitutional Court and the Supreme Court have thrown it out more than once.

A third and final theory says that the Convention takes precedent because of its special nature, and can therefore be considered to apply, as a general ruling, in the national legal system. In this theory, once the rules of a treaty have been transferred into the national system in accordance with the implementing order in the Ratification Act, they must be considered to be 'special' in relation to other rules, because of their 'specific' nature.

Although the Ratification Act reflects a desire to give the treaty force of law, there is no question of any subsequent law taking precedence over the treaty.

But no one is in any doubt that the rules of the Convention have to be interpreted and applied in the light of a general principle, one held in international law and enshrined in Article 2 of the Italian Constitution, which is that the legal system must recognize human rights and guarantee that they are enjoyed by the individual as an individual and as a member of the social groups to which he belongs. This is a principle by which lawyers have always abided in

[1] See Constitutional Court judgments Nos. 496/1991 and 75/1993.
[2] See judgments Nos. 15/1989 and 15483/1990.

their interpretation and application of the European Convention on Human Rights and all other human rights rulings.

F. THE APPLICATION OF THE CONVENTION IN NATIONAL LAW

Most of the first 19 Articles of the Convention, which lay down the rights guaranteed, only contain general principles of indicative value. So in the 1960s and 1970s, various courts, even the Constitutional Court, announced that the very nature of the Convention precluded direct application in the Italian courts and it was up to Parliament to institute safeguard measures to ensure the rights in question. Some decisions, in particular, suggested that the general definitions in the rules of the Convention could be interpreted in conflicting ways. And sometimes they could not even be applied to practical situations.

So any appeal to a higher court, calling for enjoyment of a right enshrined in the Convention, inevitably in general terms, was thrown out on the ground that it did not specifically state how the judgment at issue should be remedied.

However, other judgments stressed that Article 1 of the Convention bound the Contracting States to the application of the stated rights and freedoms, which meant that the national judge had as far as possible to try to guarantee the right which the Convention laid down, albeit in general terms, if necessary by reference to the interpretation of the aims or the spirit of the rule, and it was up to Parliament to make for practical application of the principle with rules governing a specific mode of behaviour. Since the Convention had been ratified, the judge had to consider its rule to be directly applicable. If this was out of the question, he had to apply the rule in the light of the interpretation given by the Strasbourg Court—in which case the rule, albeit indicative, could well help with the interpretation of the Constitutional Charter and the national laws.

So the principle was that the rules of the Convention were to be considered directly applicable and that every individual was personally entitled to enjoy the rights and freedoms guaranteed by the Convention or to appeal to a national court to have them guaranteed whenever they were denied.

It was therefore reasonable to say that the protection of rights enshrined in the Convention was direct protection and not dependent on the commitment made by the state. Furthermore, if the Convention rule was only couched in general terms, the state was committed to establishing a specific rule to achieve the degree of protection which the Convention provided.

The plenary session of the Supreme Court of Appeal confirmed these principles in its judgments of 23 November 1988[3] and 26 April 1990.[4] So, after almost thirty years of doubt, the legal profession came into line with the teachings of the Court in Strasbourg, turning its back once and for all on that heritage of a bygone age, the traditional concept of the 'closed sovereignty' of the state.

Previous judgments had claimed that the Convention worked only for High Contracting Parties and had no effect on relations between citizens, or between citizens and state. Others had maintained that national judges could not establish breaches of the Convention, because the individual only acquired the right to petition for acknowledgement of an infringement once he had exhausted all the possibilities at national level and the Convention did not therefore create personal rights for the individual in national law.

Over the past few years, lawyers have at last agreed that the guarantee system which the Convention provides is the fruit of an ideology in which all aspects of the life of peoples is merged and that it is now able to influence our interpretation of all the rules of the Italian legal system.

These noteworthy trends reflect a phenomenon which has grown up over the years, sometimes unbeknown to the legal profession, and no doubt encouraged by the general principle laid down in Article 2 of the Constitution, whereby the Republic recognizes and guarantees human rights. So the Italian legal system has attained a high degree of human rights protection.

Situations incompatible with the principles of the European Convention and the UN International Covenant are forever being denounced in legal theory and practice, while the European Court sometimes acknowledges the merits of the complainants' arguments.

It has to be admitted that the Convention is sometimes breached in even the most advanced of systems. And of course, as customs evolve, they are reflected in gradual changes in the interpretations of the Strasbourg Court, which is always anxious to strike a just balance between the protection of the general interest and the basic demands of human beings as such.

G. LEADING HUMAN RIGHTS CASES DECIDED BY THE NATIONAL COURTS

1. *Decisions of the 1960s and 1970s*

When the Convention took effect it attracted the attention of legal theorists, while practical decisions of substance and legitimacy in the 1960s and

[3] *Polo Castro*, No. 15/1989, chambers. [4] *Vierin*, No. 15483/1990.

1970s only occasionally referred to the Convention, usually to Articles 5 and 6.

There were two main reasons for the small number of decisions over this period:

1. defence lawyers were reluctant to use the possibilities offered by ratified international treaties, and
2. the provisions of the Constitution and the Italian legal system were rarely at variance with the guarantees enshrined in the Convention.

In most cases the parties saw Italian courts dismiss their claims on the ground that the Convention laid down 'abstract' principles of indicative value from which it was impossible to establish proof of infringement, a response which made it difficult for defence lawyers to come up with grounds for appeal. Almost all the cases handled had to do with rules of criminal procedure.

In civil and administrative courts, dozens of decisions were confined to stating the rules of the Convention to prove that the Italian legal system conformed to its principles.

However, one or two trial judges took the first Strasbourg judgments as a model in their interpretation of internal laws, and referred to the discretion which the Convention allowed the national Parliaments in seeking to justify the dismissal of claims.

The Civil Chambers of the Supreme Court sometimes referred to Article 8 of the Convention (on private and family life) in, say, ruling that the Public Prosecutor is entitled to take part in divorce proceedings because the state has an interest in monitoring conditions relating to the establishment or breakdown of family life.

In its turn, the Council of State decided that the authorities were empowered to investigate the family life of their staff. An employee's personal behaviour reflected on the esteem in which the authorities were held, so the law authorizing central and local authorities to investigate the private life of their employees did not conflict with the Convention.

From the 1950s to the 1970s, Italian legal journals printed almost 100 practical decisions by judges and the Constitutional Court, most of them involving comparisons of national law and the Convention and issued with a view to checking on compliance with the international rule referred to by the parties in the case.

On other occasions, the Convention was consulted for the purposes of comparison in interpreting a domestic rule.

There was a particular focus on guaranteeing the freedom of persons accused of criminal illegality during the proceedings and on the right of defence. The protection of family life was another common subject.

2. Trends in case-law in the 1980s and 1990s

In the 1980s lawyers continued to discuss the Convention and its application in the domestic system, under the influence of the political events which led Parliament to discuss new bills, in some cases amended to reflect tendencies in the Parliamentary Commission. The first major decisions were taken just as work began on the new Code of Criminal Procedure, which came into force in 1988.

On 21 March 1985 one of the chambers of the Supreme Court produced the first judgment stating that the rules of the Convention were a source of real, individual rights which the domestic system undertook to respect. A second judgment that year (13 July 1985) found that the rules of the Convention applied directly in domestic law, even if this meant interpreting existing rules or correcting previous interpretations which no longer met the demands of the new democratic society.

On 5 July 1986 the disciplinary chapter of the Bench Council said that the principle of public hearings set out in Article 6 of the Convention applied to disciplinary procedures involving magistrates, which meant that the provision of the Disciplinary Procedure Act of 1946 whereby hearings were to be held *in camera* was considered to be cancelled. A civil chamber of the Supreme Court ultimately confirmed (by judgment No. 5827/1986 and more recently by judgment No. 7662/1993) that the need for a public hearing applied to disciplinary procedures involving civil servants and state employees in general, since Article 6 had cancelled the previous rule to the opposite effect.

The Court stressed that it was important to cater for the fact that there were very good reasons for preventing publicity in the court-room in some cases.

The influence of the Strasbourg judgments on disciplinary proceedings against doctors in Belgium is obvious and all lawyers have taken note.

The new Criminal Code, which took effect in October 1988, brought in a series of rules on adversarial procedure and the establishment of a public hearing involving both accusation and defence as the essential and culminating phase in the criminal process. It also provided for cross-examination, that typical feature of the Anglo-Saxon system, during which the presiding judge only intervenes when it is unavoidable and the testimony, once taken, becomes the subject of the final discussion.

Parliament did not make the Italian adversarial procedure a pure one in which the judge has neither to move nor speak. Judges are empowered to suggest the wording of any questions, make remarks, and raise objections, so judge, public prosecutor, and defence counsel are all involved in the trial on an equal footing. The important thing is to find out the truth.

The various aspects of the accused's behaviour should be assessed. so the judge can adjust the sentence accordingly.

Lawyers have amply commented on the new system and never denied that it could well achieve the aim of a fair hearing as laid down in the Convention. In this connection, they have pointed to Strasbourg's oft-repeated principle that the Contracting State has some discretion in its application of the Convention, provided domestic law is adequate to ensure the rights laid down therein.

An investigating judge, working in the privacy of his office, has been replaced by the Public Prosecutor, who, once in possession of the *notitia criminis*, runs the enquiry with the help of the police.

At the preliminary hearing, which is always public, the parties are represented by the Public Prosecutor and defence counsel. The judge does no more than ask for clarification of documents, evidence, and expert advice, or question the accused, and immediately afterwards he decides whether to terminate the proceedings or send the accused for trial. The trial is a public hearing during which the judge helps examine the defendant and the witnesses and may, once again, step in whenever he feels it to be necessary.

When the Parliamentary Commission made its report to the Senate and the House for the discussion of the bill, it explicitly stated that the new procedure reflected the principles laid down in the Convention and the legal profession agreed, although not without producing a series of criticisms.

The Supreme Court and the basic courts interpreted the new rules in decisions which were of outstanding interest in that they touched on subjects related to the application of principles of the European Convention, often quoted explicitly.

Lastly, let us not forget the position of the Public Prosecutor, whom the new procedure has put, not on the bench alongside the judges, but next to the defence counsel. This is an example of the direct influence of the now well-known principle that prosecution and defence must be equally armed, a vital element of a fair hearing, which the case-law of the European Court has derived from Article 6 of the Convention.

This, in fact, is a formality which has very little effect on the substance of the proceedings, but demonstrates to the man in the street that those who make the laws are anxious to see all parties on an equal footing.

It has been said, rightly, that changing the Public Prospector's physical position in court has realized Strasbourg's oft-repeated principle that justice must be seen to be done, even by the person who goes into the public gallery merely to watch.

3. The presumption of innocence

Article 6 of the Convention and the Universal Declaration of Human Rights and the International Covenant on Civil and Political Rights all lay down the principle that anyone charged with an offence is to be presumed innocent until proven guilty according to law. Article 27 of the Constitution says the same.

Of course the importance of these rules has escaped neither the lawyers nor Parliament, since detention prior to the judge's decision is a serious blow to personal liberty—a drawback which, in the 1950s and 1960s at least, sometimes prompted judges to make the sentences longer so the punishment reflected the length of the preventive custody.

Preventive custody has been one of the most common subjects of discussion in Italy since the War. It is often difficult to settle down in society after a long period of such detention, although it has to be admitted that preventive custody is unavoidable if the offender is likely to continue committing crimes, run away to avoid punishment, destroy evidence, or pressurize witnesses to prevent the judge from finding out the truth.

Clearly, some offences arouse the wrath of public opinion and the provisional arrest of the guilty party may go some way to righting the wrong, and sometimes to protecting him from the vengeance of the crowd.

4. Compensation for damage caused by unfair detention and criminal unlawfulness

Under Article 5 of the Convention and Article 14 of the UN Covenant of 1966, anyone falsely arrested or illegally detained has the right to compensation. This principle was laid down in the repealed Code of Procedure—which, however, only provided for the accused to be helped if he was without means and unable to provide for his household after release.

The new international rules helped revive longstanding criticism in legal theory, and in 1960 Parliament replaced 'help' with 'compensation'. So the principle laid down in international law and in Article 24 of the Constitution (specifying the terms and arrangements of compensation for legal errors) virtually became practice where conviction and sentence were voided after a review.

Finally, the new Criminal Code established that any unfair detention entitled the detainee to compensation, except where deceit or gross negligence on the part of the accused had contributed to the miscarriage of justice. The compensation also had to be 'fair', ie in proportion to the seriousness of the error and the type of damage caused. It was of course up to the judge to assess the damage, also taking any mental suffering into account.

The progress of the law is evident and the influence of Strasbourg case-law has been recognized in the course of debates in the House, in particular following the Court judgment in *Neumeister and Brogan v United Kingdom.*

The influence of the case-law of the European Court is also apparent in the new Code, in the broadening of the content of the right to compensation for damage caused by criminal unlawfulness, whereby civil and commercial law partnerships, trade unions, state-recognized associations, committees, legal entities under public law (regional, provincial and local authorities), professional associations, etc. may take civil action before the criminal judge if they have suffered direct damage.

Under the old Code, only 'persons' had the right to bring legal proceedings. The new Code (Article 74) replaced 'persons' by 'subjects', thereby opening the way for private and public legal entities to do the same.

In fact, French and German case-law had long acknowledged that legal entities had the right to bring legal proceedings, but the change in the Italian Code was the result of the new awareness that the rights of anyone harmed by an offence had to be protected. Lawyers noted here that the right to damages for attacks on property and on the integrity and liberty of the individual had to be 'prompt and effective'.

So compensation is only adequate when damages are granted to all sufferers, even if this means compensating a group of subjects pursuing the aim of protecting professional or collective interests. Many things have contributed to the unconditional recognition of the right to damages, but it is obvious that the spotlight on the problem following entry into effect of the Convention did a lot to encourage amendments to the legislation, as the discussions of legal theory have shown.

In totalitarian systems, the state made itself the protector of interests harmed by crime and was often stubborn enough to extend that right to the protection of the interests of the citizens. In democracies, on the other hand, there is a tendency for the individual to be given a wide choice of ways of protecting his interests, although without renouncing the just cause of protecting the collective interest.

5. *Proceedings 'within a reasonable time'*

The long-windedness of civil and criminal proceedings has long been one of the worst problems of Italian justice, and one debated at length among the judiciary and in political circles. It has never been solved, because there are piles of cases on the desk of every lawyer of every rank and the number goes up rather than down. This is in fact the direct effect of the development of human relations in every field, and of the rise in crime. Criminal proceedings can go on for four or five years, and civil cases seven or eight, before a judgment settles the issue.

The Civil Code in fact provides for oral hearings and trial limitation to speed things up, but most judges are buried under hundreds of case files and quite unable to stick to the times laid down by the law or to invite the parties to file pleadings.

Criminal proceedings have speeded up over the past few years. There are more judges and the overall situation is much better, but the state is still far from being able to cope with the backlog of cases 'within a reasonable time'.

The delays in the handling of civil affairs are constantly criticized by lawyers and the general public. Dozens of Italian citizens have petitioned the European Court over the past few years because of the protracted nature of their case and the Court has almost always found the Italian State guilty of infringing the 'reasonable time' principle.

In accordance with a recent guideline from the Commission, some judgments by trial judges, well aware of the harm done when civil proceedings last too long, have censured the behaviour of parties who tried, under cover of apparently legitimate moves, to take advantage of the problems of the legal world to extend the proceedings. In such cases the party who wins has usually been put at a disadvantage by the time taken up by the manoeuvrings of the other party, and the judge has to take such behaviour into account when deciding on the amount of damages to be awarded to the winning party.

6. *Conviction* in absentia

In its judgment of 12 December 1985 (the *Colozza* case[5]), the European Court found that the Italian authorities had infringed Article 6 of the Convention, since Mr Colozza, who had failed to attend first-instance proceedings in the court in Rome because he had not received notification of the summons to appear, was told that his appeal was inadmissible because he had been late in presenting his defence, but had not had the opportunity to prove that he had had no knowledge of the proceedings. In the petition, he said that the police were aware of his address, because the local station had called him in shortly before for questioning about something else. Two months earlier the prosecuting authorities in Rome had also sent him a legal paper referring to other proceedings. Also, three public authorities had served him with a document via the relevant department in the Rome Town Hall.

In giving reasons for its judgment, the European Court stressed that the situation as it emerged from the investigation did not reflect the diligence which

[5] Series A No. 89.

the Contracting States were expected to display in ensuring the proper enjoyment of the rights enshrined in Article 6. It added that the Contracting States had considerable leeway in choosing how to enable their legal systems to comply with the demands of Article 6, although if national law authorized proceedings notwithstanding the absence of the accused, the latter, once aware of the proceedings against him, had to be able to oblige the court to hear and decide a second time, after hearing the accusations. So the resources of domestic law had to be efficient and the accused had to prove that it was not his intention to evade justice.

In 1985 a Government Commission set up to draft the text of the new Criminal Code had already started work and the Court's reasoning was taken up and echoed in rules which were in line with the stated principles. In legal theory, it was initially agreed that the accused had to be allowed to demonstrate that he had not been informed of the proceedings, or that it was not his intention to evade justice.

After examining the draft of the new Code, Parliament introduced a rule whereby a trial could be repeated where the accused had been prevented from appearing accidentally or for reasons of *force majeure*, or if, for reasons beyond his control, he had not known about the proceedings (Article 603). So the guarantee provided by Article 6 of the Convention was provided exactly as in the Court's interpretation.

7. Preventive custody

The protection of the freedom of the individual accused of committing an offence has been at the heart of discussions in legal theory and practice, under the influence of the new human rights theories.

Arrest warrants were mandatory for a series of fairly serious offences before the War, but after 1972 they were always issued at the discretion of the judge, who had to give reasons for his move. In 1984 a law established that judges could also issue warrants for non-serious offences if there was a danger of absconding or falsification of evidence, or a reasonable fear that the accused might commit further offences involving weapons or violence, or if he was known to be a member of an organized gang of criminals.

The maximum length of preventive detention was altered more than once to reflect prevailing opinions in the successive governments, until 1989, which saw the advent of a new Code of Criminal Procedure, containing rules which echoed the principles laid down in the International Covenant on Civil and Political Rights (1966) and the European Convention.

Under pressure of public opinion, which was appalled at organized crime, the terms of remand in custody, initially limited to two years, were extended by as much as six years in some cases, to prevent serious criminals from being released before the proceedings were over.

In the 1970s and 1980s dozens of cases were brought against groups of thirty to forty defendants charged with killing several people. Lengthy, complex investigations were required in cases of this sort, because organized criminals found out about the enquiries or intimidated witnesses and prevented the police from uncovering evidence of the crime.

In 1982 Parliament set up the 'Freedom Tribunal', a bench of three judges who had three days in which to rule on the lawfulness of remand in custody ordered by the Public Prosecutor or the preliminary investigating judge. The accused was entitled to appeal against the Tribunal's ruling (Article 263). Decisions were always rapid.

The Supreme Court of Appeal also took its decisions within a couple of weeks, in chambers, with the help of the Public Prosecutor and interested parties. The influence of Article 5(3) of the Convention was obvious here. The case-law of the Strasbourg Court was taken into proper consideration even in the work of the parliamentary committee responsible for shaping the new law on the Freedom Tribunal. The fact that the setting up of the Freedom Tribunal was reminiscent of the *habeas corpus* system of Anglo-Saxon law was pointed up in the course of this work.

The European Convention has had a constant, preponderant influence over ideas about the freedom of the accused during the preliminary investigations and enquiry, as it has about conviction *in absentia*, discussed above. Article 9 of the International Covenant of 1966, which offers much the same thing, is also often mentioned in legal theory and practice.

The European authorities have more than once criticized the Italian government for keeping an accused in prison before the final judgment, to which public opinion (newspapers, politicians, and lawyers) has replied that, although respect tot the individual demands that even offenders must have maximum protection of their rights, it is also clear that a society cannot tolerate a dangerous criminal, already condemned to a long term of imprisonment at the first and second instance, being released just because he has appealed in order to lengthen the period of detention. And if the defendant has to be released before the final judgment, then care must be taken to ensure he is present at the trial, which was yet another reason for laying down a set of rules to prevent the accused from evading justice.

Balancing the freedom of the individual and justice for the guilty is still one of the most difficult subjects of debate in the legal profession today. Almost every day brings its criticism, proposals, and agreement, leading to debates on television as well as at legal meetings and conferences.

8. The right of a foreigner to understand the language of the proceedings

The new Code has raised standards here too, since there is now a set of rules to help foreigners and citizens of recognized linguistic minorities understand everything written and said during the proceedings, which means that the accused is on an equal footing with everyone else involved.

Article 6(3) of the Convention has had an undeniable influence here. However, it has to be admitted that the amendments, by and large, are the inevitable result of the development of modern society, with the continuing presence of large numbers of tourists and businesspeople and almost a million immigrants from Eastern Europe, Africa, and Latin America.

Parliament's Committee on Legislation has produced special comments on Article 4 of the UN Covenant on Civil and Political Rights, which lays down similar principles.

Case-law on the new rules has emphasized that the right to the assistance of an interpreter applies to the whole of the oral and written procedure, without exception, to enable the accused to understand the import of the accusation and give him the opportunity to obtain all the clarification he wants. The interpreter is provided free. Decisions have specified, in line with the Strasbourg Court's ruling on the *Luedicke and Belkacem* case,[6] that the accused is exempt from payment even if found guilty. It addition, the right to an interpreter must be acknowledged in case the accused does not understand legal terms. He may still be entitled to an interpreter even if he can cope linguistically with shopping for bread and fruit.

Courts in Italy and other countries of Western Europe sometimes find it difficult to cope with speakers of virtually unknown African languages

The European Court looked at the foreigner's right to understand the language used in court in the case of *Brozicek v Italy*.[7] Mr Brozicek, a citizen of Federal Germany, sentenced for assault and battery and resisting the forces of order, went to the Commission alleging, *inter alia*, that he had not had any details of the case against him in his own language. In particular, both the notification (the document in which the courts inform the accused of the opening of an enquiry) and the summons to appear in court were in Italian. Since he did not understand much Italian, he had written and asked for the papers to be sent to him in his native tongue, but had had no response and so was unable to defend himself properly against the charges. The Italian court did not investigate whether he had an adequate grasp of Italian, assessed his ability as 'passable' and proceeded to make its decision in the light of the

[6] Judgment of 28 November 1978, Series A No. 29.
[7] Judgment of 19 December 1989, Series A No. 167.

outcome of the enquiry. So the Strasbourg Court found a violation of Article 6(1) of the Convention and added, *inter alia,* that the right to the assistance of an interpreter did not lapse when the foreigner had a partial grasp of the language.

H. RECENT DEVELOPMENTS

The Application of the guarantees of the Convention in the 1990s

The new Code of Criminal Procedure, which came into effect in 1988, brought in a series of rules on adversarial procedure and the introduction of a public hearing involving both accusation and defence.

The procedure is carried out in writing at the stage of preliminary investigations, and orally at the public hearing during discussion of the case, based on the use of cross-examination, that typical feature of the Anglo-Saxon system.

The judge, too, plays an active part, in that he has the power at all times to suggest the wording of questions to be put, or to raise objections in response to statements by the parties: all of this operates in the context of ensuring respect for the principle of the equal treatment of parties in the proceedings, the aim being to find out the truth.

The terms of the new Code required two years' work by a Parliamentary Commission, and contain a significant number of articles reproducing almost verbatim the principles laid down in the European Convention on Human Rights or in the UN's 1966 International Covenant on Civil and Political Rights.

The Parliamentary Commission's report, which accompanied the promulgation of the Code, confirms that it was intended to implement the principles formulated in the two international conventions.

All this was in accordance with the law whereby the government was given responsibility for drawing up a new Code, and which expressly established the following principles:

1. the participation of both prosecutor and defence on an equal footing; 2. the right of the Public Prosecutor and of the other parties to put forward evidence and submit statements at any stage in the proceedings; 3. the obligation of the judge to reach a decision, without delay, on requests submitted by the parties; 4. the right of a person accused of a criminal offence to appoint his defence lawyer and to have that lawyer present during questioning and at all times in the proceedings.

However, it was clear that the principles included in the Code required clarification in order to define their true significance in terms of their practical application.

Apart from problems to do with the direct applicability of the terms of the Convention and recognition of the accused's subjective right to respect of the guarantees on the part of the state or any other citizen, promptly resolved by the Supreme Court (as already mentioned), the courts at all levels and the Constitutional Court were quick to respond to the questions raised by the judgments, the latter in turn being a source of lengthy debate in the legal world and in the press which frequently reported criticism and approval; these reports were often of interest to the man in the street because of their impact on life in society. As from 1996, under pressure from public opinion, Parliament introduced a revision of certain articles of the Constitution relating directly to the judicial system, and indirectly to the handling of civil and criminal proceedings. Debate was rekindled and this continues on a number of matters, the independence of judges in particular, followed with great interest by the press and television which on occasions organizes discussions in which key figures from politics and the legal world take part.

To give some idea of the extent of recent developments in case-law there follows a list, albeit a partial one, summarizing certain notable decisions which demonstrate the convergence of legal theory and practice, and are indicative of the continuous progress and development made necessary by progressive adjustment to the Strasbourg case-law, to amendments of national legislation and to the demands of a changing society.

Contentious proceedings

For some time now there has been no questioning of the application of the guarantees provided by the Convention to all contentious proceedings being handled by administrative jurisdictions, the courts with powers to resolve disputes relating to tax matters, and the administrative authorities that exercise disciplinary powers.

Recently the Constitutional Court reaffirmed the general application, without exceptions, of the principles of a fair hearing, as defined in the Convention, to disciplinary proceedings involving state employees, magistrates, journalists, and those engaged in the professions, even if the law did not make explicit provision for this.[8]

[8] Judgment No. 505/1995.

The impartiality and independence of the judge

It has been affirmed that there is a need to eliminate any possible doubt concerning the impartiality of the judge who will be responsible at the hearing for deciding on the guilt of the accused, making a clear distinction between the functions exercised at the investigation stage and the functions that apply at the judgment stage. In such cases the judge's intervention is absolutely forbidden because of the danger of his being influenced by the functions performed in the first phase.[9]

This impartiality is strictly linked to the nature of the jurisdictional function, and it is not always possible to depart from this in a democratic system.

Testimony by judges and lawyers

It is not permissible for judges and magistrates from the Public Prosecutor's office to be heard as witnesses concerning facts that have been made known to them during the exercise of their duties, but this does not apply to defence counsel. Directly acquired knowledge of a case excludes any certainty that the testimony given is not influenced, even unintentionally, by what the parties or the witnesses have said or done.

The defence counsel, in contrast, performs the role of assisting a private party, and his testimony does not pose any problems from the point of view of professional ethics, such factors being outside the scope of the procedural rules. It goes without saying that, before giving testimony, the defence counsel must relinquish that position, because his position in that capacity would be incompatible with that of a defence counsel.[10]

The assistance of an interpreter

The accused is entitled to the assistance of an interpreter, free of charge, so that he may understand the import of the charges and evidence against him. To understand the reasons for his arrest, and to understand what the judge or Public Prosecutor have said or written are essential conditions if the accused is to be treated fairly. If the interpreter does not speak the accused's language well, it is the responsibility of the judge to ensure that the interpreter's intervention has been sufficient for the accused to understand the import of the charges or of the statements made by the parties.

The judge has discretionary powers of assessment in this connection and the obligation to ensure that the requirement of clear, intelligible information

[9] Constitutional Court, judgment No. 371/1996.
[10] Constitutional Court, judgment No. 215/1997.

is satisfied, taking into account the often considerable complexity of the legal language employed by the parties (Supreme Court, judgment No. 6318/1993).

Linguistic minorities

Articles 2 and 3 of the Constitution recognize that all citizens have a right to effective participation in the political, economic, and social life of the country; as a result, citizens with Slovene as their mother tongue are entitled to speak in that language when questioned by the judicial authorities and to have the assistance of an interpreter.

This safeguarding of the linguistic heritage extends to the right to receive documents from the judicial authorities translated into Slovene.

Linguistic minorities must be guaranteed the same social dignity and equality before the Courts of Justice as any other citizen of the States (Constitutional Court, judgment No. 15/1996).

Defence and self-defence

The accused may seek the assistance of a defence counsel from the moment the judge brings the accusation of a criminal offence against him until the decision on his guilt has been pronounced. Any action performed as part of the proceedings without the assistance of the defence counsel will be deemed null and void. This is an essential guarantee which disregards any personal interest of the accused, even if he refuses this defence counsel, because of the pre-eminent public interest in both parties being heard.

As a result, the accused is not permitted to renounce the right to defence counsel, and he does not have the right to refuse this assistance.

The judge has a duty to appoint a defence counsel at any point in the proceedings whenever the accused is without appropriate defence, failing which the procedural activities will be declared null and void.[11]

The principle of equality of arms

Once the proceedings are under way, the Public Prosecutor is entitled to pursue his inquiries and to add documents obtained to the case papers or to request the hearing of witnesses. This activity may be extended until the defence counsel of the private party associating with the Public Prosecutor, if there is one, has been given an opportunity to speak.

The principle of equality of arms, a prerequisite for a fair trial, is applicable to all stages in the procedure, and requires that the Public Prosecutor be

[11] Supreme Court, judgment No. 4036/1996.

regarded as 'plaintiff' in the name of society, on an equal footing with the defence counsel.[12]

Rights of the sentenced person

Measures adopted to execute criminal judgments have an effect on the personal liberty of the accused, and the latter has the right, even during the execution of those measures, to defend himself and to exercise the rights laid down by law. One of these rights is the possibility of meeting from time to time with his defence counsel and with his family.

This is a jurisdictional guarantee which stipulates that a detainee must not be prevented from having contact with the outside world; once the sentence has been served, it is this right which enables the detainee to return to normal life in society.[13]

Personal liberty during judicial proceedings

The valid reasons that, in accordance with the terms of the European Convention on Human Rights, justify provisional detention or other restrictions of personal liberty at the preliminary inquiry stage must be assessed by the judge on the basis of experience and a high degree of caution in his consideration of the elements serving as evidence.

This process of examination and assessment is a matter entrusted to the conviction and careful consideration of the judge, who must base this on suspicions that would persuade an objective person with a normal experience of life that the alleged offence has been committed.[14]

Restrictions on the adoption of minors

The rules in force which state, without scope for exceptions, that an adoptive parent must not be more than forty years older than the adopted minor violate the principles on safeguarding the family nucleus. Adoption pursues the aim of protecting the family life of the minor, and the judge may well allow adoption when the age difference is greater than forty years if he is of the view that the minor's abandoned state makes it appropriate to establish a family link if it is able to guarantee an adequate upbringing, this being an essential condition for normal life. The social interest in safeguarding such interests justifies exceeding the legal age limit.[15]

[12] Constitutional Court, judgment No. 50/1995.
[13] Constitutional Court, judgment No. 212/1997.
[14] Supreme Court, judgment No. 1885/1996.
[15] Constitutional Court, judgment No. 303/1996.

Restriction of personal liberty

A. Blood transfusions

A blood transfusion, or the use of blood derivatives, although an essential factor in treating diseases, none the less presents risks, and the consent required from the interested party under the terms of recent laws is fully justified by the requirement of respecting a person's personal liberty.

Even the judicial authority responsible for ordering a given measure during the course of the criminal inquiries does not have absolute discretionary powers, and comes up against an insurmountable obstacle when the interested party expresses a wish to the contrary.

B. Police prefects have the power to prevent people entering a sports stadium if they have been the instigators of violent scenes at sporting events. This measure is clearly a restriction of personal liberty, but one that is required by the interest of society in security and good order, to avoid the outbreak of violence.

The right to defence is sufficiently guaranteed, given that this measure requires approval from the judge who reaches his decision after hearing both the Public Prosecutor and the interested party, with the compulsory intervention of a chosen or officially appointed defence counsel.

Civil defence counsel (difensore civico)

Over a period of at least ten years the office of ombudsman, referred to in Italy as 'civil defence counsel' has spread throughout the country's administrative regions and larger towns. Legal theory has unanimously defined the ombudsman as an impartial figure between the authorities and the citizen, whose purpose is to improve the impact that public bodies have on the life of citizens, on the strength of his ability to intervene in the chain of bureaucracy. It is hoped that the defence counsel will be recognized as having the right to intervene in all contentious administrative proceedings, particularly with the aim of seeking conciliation and settling disputes which arise.

Protection of the environment

The right to appear as a private party acting in association with the Public Prosecutor in criminal proceedings instituted on the grounds of damage to the environment may be granted to those who have suffered direct damage, as well as to the associations which play an active role in protecting the environment and which demonstrate a commitment to protecting it in the common interest.

The Constitution recognizes the social importance of protecting the environment as the heritage of both the individual and the community.[16]

I. LEADING ITALIAN CASES BROUGHT BEFORE THE EUROPEAN COMMISSION AND COURT OF HUMAN RIGHTS

1. Austria v Italy[17]

In 1960, seven years after the Convention took effect, the Austrian Government, finding that an Italian court of assizes had infringed Article 6 of the Convention in a famous case against a group of young men accused of killing a customs officer, complained to the Commission. Austria said that the court had refused to hear two witnesses and had proceeded with a visit to the scene of the crime without the presence of the accused (who were in custody).

The Commission found that there had been no infringement and, for the first time, considered the scope of Article 6(2 and 3) in detail, affirming two principles which have remained fundamental to case-law ever since. Article 6(3), it said, was designed to defend total equality of treatment in respect of the accusation and the party claiming damages, but the rule did not imply that there was a right to have witnesses called endlessly. However, the court was free to decide whether a defence witness would help shed light on the truth or not, and if not to refrain from calling him.

When it came to the presumption of innocence, the Commission added that Article 6(2) was first and foremost a question of the attitude of the judge. If the Public Prosecutor and the party claiming damages used offensive language and caused an uproar during the hearing, there would be no reproach to the court unless the presiding judge failed to react and gave the impression that he shared the animosity towards the accused and believed him to be guilty in advance.

At that time legal theory and practice all over Europe had started to interpret and comment on the most important Articles of the Convention. Ideas from legal academics and the press were often echoed in the court-room and the Commission got ready to lay down the principles of its case-law, sometimes reacting to abstract and unrealistic interpretations.

Austria v Italy is an example of the difficulties which at that period faced the Commission—whose undeniable merit is that it pointed the way for the new international case-law.

[16] Supreme Court, judgment No. 9837/1996.

[17] Application 788/60 1961 Yearbook IV.

2. *The* Artico *case*[18]

The *Artico* case is also worth mentioning here. In this case, the Court first looked at whether the Commission had powers of initiative in seeking proof of facts and found that the burden of proof had to lie with the complainant, although the Commission could, if necessary, take the initiative of asking him to supply proof of the fact, since the rule that the parties controlled the course of civil proceedings was not applicable to a judgment before the Commission. This became a principle in decisions of the Court in the years which followed.

3. *The cases of* Foti, Corigliano, *and* Pretto[19]

The Court examined the scope of Article 6 of the Convention in detail in these three cases. It had already established certain basic principles in its decisions by then, but virtually every judgment was the opportunity to lay down more. In the *Foti* and *Corigliano* cases it first ruled that the guaranteed 'reasonable time' ran from the moment when official intervention had serious repercussions for the individual, which might well be when the police arrested or questioned the accused about the charges even before the judge stepped in to question him about the alleged infringement.

The idea of serious repercussions is still the starting point in Court decisions today, the moment as from which the individual must enjoy the right to a fair hearing, particularly within a 'reasonable time'. Naturally, it is left to the discretion of the judge, in his wisdom, to ascertain whether the repercussions are serious. The circumstances of the proceedings, including delays caused by the accused's behaviour or dilatoriness on the part of the judge, must also be taken into account.

These same judgments gave the Court the opportunity to confirm that the fair compensation to be granted to the injured party for the damage undergone could relate to damage both moral and material, for example, the cost of taking part in the proceedings in the Commission and the Court. At the same time, the actual recognition of the breach of the Convention established in the judgment could well constitute adequate compensation, since the decisions of the Court were read out in public, lodged at the registry where anyone could read them, and known throughout Europe.

The Court subsequently confirmed this principle on a number of occasions when the complainant produced proof of having undergone moral suffering.

[18] Judgment of 13 May 1980, Series A No. 37.

[19] *Foti* and *Corigliano* Judgment of 10 December 1982, Series A No. 56; *Pretto*, judgment of 8 December 1983, Series A No. 71.

In some states belonging to the Convention the law says that the decisions of the judges shall be published at the time they are lodged at the registry, without being read out at the hearing. This was the subject of *Pretto v Italy* in relation to judgments by the Supreme Court of Appeal. The Strasbourg Court ruled that, if decisions were lodged at the registry, anyone could find out what they contained, which achieved the aim of Article 6(1) of the Convention of having the judgment 'pronounced publicly'.

This was of course a broad interpretation of the rule, but there is no doubt that it achieved the aim of making the decision public, since in Italy anyone can go to the registry look at the judgments lodged there and obtain copies. Furthermore, the parties directly involved are duly informed within a very short time of the judgment being lodged.

In the *Pretto* judgment the Court stated, by way of justification of the principle, that the strict meaning of the term 'publicly' in Article 6 was a secondary matter and that the important thing was the aim contained in the rule, to ensure that anyone who so desired could check that the principles of a fair hearing were being respected.

At this point we should make it quite clear that all the above said relates to judgments passed in civil cases. Judgments in criminal cases are, without exception, read out in public, even in the Supreme Court. What we have to prevent is justice being done in secret, out of the public eye. The courts must inspire confidence and ensure the transparency of justice: another component of a fair hearing.

4. *The* Luberti *case*[20]

In this case the European Court decided that internment in a psychiatric hospital of a party acquitted by the Court of Assizes had to be assimilated to detention. The internee therefore had to enjoy the rights laid down in Article 5 of the Convention and the period of internment had to last only as long as was strictly necessary to provide treatment or complete a medical and psychological examination. Any delay, to be evaluated in the light of the findings, constituted a breach of Article 5(4).

The Court and the Commission have approached internment for psychiatric disorders in the same way ever since.

5. *The* Brozicek *case*[21]

We have already commented on the foreigner's right to understand the language of the court in the section on leading cases decided by the national

[20] Judgment of 23 February 1984, Series A No. 75.
[21] Judgment of 19 December 1989, Series A No. 167.

courts. All that needs to be added here is that Article 143 of the new Criminal Code, which took effect in 1989, is more or less the same as the previous rule. However, the ministerial report which accompanied the publication of the Code said that, in applying Article 143, which entitled a foreigner to the free assistance of an interpreter 'so as to understand the charges against him, follow the proceedings and defend himself . . .', Italy followed Article 6(3) of the Convention and Article 14(3) of the International Covenant on Civil and Political Rights. The terms used in this report had an inevitable effect on legal theory and practice.

Over the past few years, case-law has several times indicated that an interpreter should be provided only if the accused or his defence counsel asks for one. The judge, on the other hand, must have an interpreter where the accused is familiar with the language but does not understand the questions properly or grasp the legal terms. The same goes for witnesses.

6. 'Reasonable time'

As already mentioned, the protracted nature of civil and criminal cases has been perhaps the biggest barrier to the smooth functioning of Italian justice over the past thirty years or more. It has aroused both public opinion and the bench, on occasion, and dozens of people have complained to the Strasbourg Court, which has always agreed that Italy has indeed violated Article 6 of the Convention.

In some judgments, the mere establishment of a breach of the Convention has been said to constitute adequate and fair compensation for moral suffering, but in most cases the defendant state has had to pay what can be considerable sums for the moral and material damage incurred by the applicant while waiting to have his rights acknowledged.

In civil cases, on the other hand, the Court has said that civil proceedings in Italy are governed by the first instance, which involves giving the parties powers of initiative and force. However, this does not preclude the judges from having to meet the 'reasonable time' demands of Article 6.

Article 175 of the Italian Code, the Court has maintained, provides for the judge who prepares the trial to 'exercise all powers to ensure that the proceedings are fair and as expeditious as possible'. But there are thousands of judges each trying to work their way through 1,800 or 1,900 case files and hearings can easily be a very long time apart.

20

Lithuania

VILENAS VADAPALAS

INTRODUCTION

On 11 March 1990, when Lithuania re-established its independence, it had inherited the Soviet legal system, which was far removed from European standards of human rights. It became evident that Lithuanian legislation should be brought into conformity with such standards. The incorporation of human rights into domestic law became one of the main elements of legal reform in Lithuania.

The new Lithuanian Constitution which was adopted by referendum on 25 October 1992 created the legal basis for the incorporation of international standards of human rights and fundamental freedoms into domestic law. Chapter 2 of the Constitution (The Individual and the State) contains a list of constitutional rights and freedoms and proclaims that 'the rights and freedoms of individuals shall be inborn' (ie the rights are acquired automatically at birth, rather than being granted by the state) (Article 18). As for the international treaties of Lithuania, the Constitution is based on monistic approach and incorporates ratified international treaties into the Lithuanian legal system. Therefore, the European Convention on Human Rights (hereinafter ECHR or the Convention) is a constituent part of Lithuanian legal system.

On 14 May 1993 Lithuania signed the ECHR and the Protocols Nos. 1, 4, and 7 thereto. After a transitional period which lasted two years, on 27 April 1995 the Seimas (Parliament) ratified the Convention and Protocols Nos. 4 and 7. The First Protocol was ratified on 7 December 1995. Lithuania became a State Party to the Convention on 20 June 1995. On 24 May 1996, the First Protocol thereto took effect with regard to Lithuania.

A. THE STATUS OF THE CONVENTION IN NATIONAL LAW

1. The Lithuanian legal system and international human rights in general

The inter-relationship between Lithuanian national and international law could be characterized as monistic because the Constitution incorporates ratified international treaties into the domestic legal system (Article 138 of the Constitution, see below). However, this approach is of rather limited scope because, on one hand, the Lithuanian Constitution does not contain any provision concerning the incorporation of general international law into the Lithuanian legal system, and on the other hand, there is no constitutional provision giving international treaties priority over domestic law.

Article 135 of the Constitution which concerns main principles of Lithuanian foreign policy stipulates:

> In conducting foreign policy, the Republic of Lithuania shall pursue the universally recognized principles and norms of international law, shall strive to safeguard national security and independence as well as the basic rights, freedoms, and welfare of its citizens, and shall take part in the creation of sound international order based on law and justice.[1]

However, this disposition is devoted only to foreign policy and cannot be interpreted as giving general principles and rules of international law direct effect in domestic law.[2]

On 12 March 1991, the Supreme Council of Lithuania adopted the Decree on the accession of the Republic of Lithuania to the instruments of the International Bill of Human Rights which *inter alia* stated that the Supreme Council 'solemnly undertakes to respect the Universal Declaration of Human Rights which was adopted by the United Nations General Assembly on 10 December 1948'.

By this Decree the Supreme Council decided also to accede to the International Covenants on Human Rights and the Optional Protocol to the International Covenant on Civil and Political Rights of 1966. With regard to the Universal Declaration of Human Rights, this Decree seems to be a political declaration because there is no provision which could give *expressis*

[1] For the English text of the Constitution of the Republic of Lithuania look at: *Parliamentary Record*/Seimas of the Republic of Lithuania. 1992, Nr. 11, 2–30. It should be noted here that English versions of the texts of legal instruments reproduced in the *Parliamentary Record* are unofficial. This article does not necessarily follow these texts; the translation of relevant texts and of the extracts of the Conclusion of the Court are by the author of this chapter.

[2] See: Vilenas Vadapalas. *Der verfassungsgerechtliche Kontrolle der auswärtigen Gewalt in Litauen: Grundlagen der Verfassungsgerichtsbarkeit in Mittel- und Osteuropa*. J. A. Frowein, T. Marauhn (eds) *Beitrage zum ausländisches öffentliches Recht und Völkerrecht*, Band 130 (1998) 543.

verbis legal effect to the Universal Declaration of Human Rights in the domestic law of Lithuania. With regard to International Covenants on Human Rights and the Optional Protocol to the International Covenant on Civil and Political Rights of 1966, it should be noted that this Decree contains a formal decision of accession to the Covenants and the Optional Protocol of 1996 which were consequently incorporated into Lithuanian legal system on the basis of Article 12 of the Law on International Treaties of the Republic of Lithuania of 1991 which gives to all international treaties of Lithuania the legal effect of domestic law (see below).[3]

However, the adoption in 1992 of the Constitution which incorporates into domestic law only ratified international treaties raised a question whether the International Covenants on Human Rights and the Optional Protocol to the International Covenant on Civil and Political Rights of 1966 still have the legal force of domestic law.

The problem is that the Decree of 12 March 1991 on Lithuania's accession to the instruments of the International Bill of Human Rights does not contain a formal act of ratification of the Covenants and the Optional Protocol. Nevertheless, the answer should be positive: the Constitution could not be interpreted as depriving Lithuanian citizens of the direct effect of instruments which took effect before the Constitution entered into force. On one hand, this conclusion could find its *ratio* in the general rule of inter-temporary law which provides that legal acts should be interpreted according to the rules in force at the time of their adoption, but on the other hand, this conclusion follows from the Law on the Procedure for the Enforcement of the Constitution of the Republic of Lithuania of 1992 which stipulates:

> Article 2. Laws, other legal acts, or parts thereof which were in effect on the territory of the Republic of Lithuania prior to the adoption of the Constitution of the Republic of Lithuania, shall be effective provided that they do not contradict the Constitution and this law, and shall remain effective until they are either declared null and void or brought into conformity with the provisions of the Constitution.

Nevertheless, the question of the legal effect of international treaties to which Lithuania became a State Party still remains unresolved. The Constitutional Court in its Ruling on the compliance of Part 4, Article 7 and Article 12 of the Law of the Republic of Lithuania on International Treaties of the Republic of Lithuania with the Constitution of the Republic of Lithuania of 17 October 1995 stated:

[3] International Covenants on Human Rights and the Optional Protocol to the International Covenant on Civil and Political Rights of 1966 took effect with regard to Lithuania on 20 February 1992.

Having compared the legal scope of Article 138, para. 3 of the Constitution and Article 12 of the disputable Law, it is obvious how it differs according to the extent. Only one kind of international treaty is spoken about in Article 138 of the Constitution—those ratified by the Seimas, while in Article 12 of the disputable Law international treaties are not classified into different kinds. It is stated in said Article 12 that: 'International treaties of the Republic of Lithuania shall have the force of law on the territory of the Republic of Lithuania'.[4]

The Constitutional Court pointed out that the classification of international treaties into different kinds is an objective phenomenon which has its legal logical and constitutional reasoning. Therefore:

pursuant to the Constitution only the legislator by way of ratification may decide which statute of international law shall be the constituent part of the legal system of the Republic of Lithuania having the force of law. The Seimas shall have the right of legislation and the legislation shall not be delegated to any other institution of state power. Upon recognizing that non-ratified international treaties have the force of law, the prerogative of the Seimas to pass laws would be negated. It is also important that the treaties which must be ratified have essential significance to the further creation of the legal system. Therefore, the provision of Article 12 of the Law in dispute that 'international treaties of the Republic of Lithuania', ie also the international treaties which are not ratified by the Seimas, have the force of law, unfoundedly extends their juridical force in the system of sources of law of the Republic of Lithuania. From this standpoint the provision of Article 12 of the disputable Law that international treaties of the Republic of Lithuania 'shall have the force of law' contradicts Article 138, para. 3 of the Constitution.

2. *Legal effect of the Convention in the Lithuanian legal system*

With regard to the European Convention on Human Rights it should be emphasized that its legal effect in domestic legal system of Lithuania does not raise any major question.

The Lithuanian Constitution incorporates all ratified international treaties of Lithuania, in general, and the ECHR, in particular, into the domestic legal system. Article 138 of the Constitution stipulates *inter alia*:

International treaties which are ratified by the Seimas of the Republic of Lithuania shall be the constituent part of the legal system of the Republic of Lithuania.

The legal rank of international treaties is established by the Law on International Treaties of the Republic of Lithuania of 1991 (Article 12):

International treaties of the Republic of Lithuania shall have the force of law on the territory of the Republic of Lithuania.

[4] Valstybes zinios,1995, No. 86–1949.

The Constitutional Court of the Republic of Lithuania in its Ruling of 17 October 1995 on the compliance of Part 4, Article 7 and Article 12 of the Law of the Republic of Lithuania on international treaties of the Republic of Lithuania with the Constitution concluded:

Having compared the contents of the norms of Article 138, para. 3 of the Constitution and those of Article 12 of the disputable Law, the conclusion is to be made that according to the meaning they partly coincide, as both confirm that treaties ratified by the Seimas shall acquire the force of law.[5]

On January 24, 1995 the Constitutional Court of Lithuania delivered its *Opinion on the compliance of Articles 4, 5, 9, 14 as well as Article 2 of Protocol No. 4 of the European Convention for the Protection of Human Rights and Fundamental Freedoms with the Constitution of the Republic of Lithuania* which states:

In the third part of Article 138 it is determined:

International treaties which are ratified by the Seimas of the Republic of Lithuania shall be a constituent part of the legal system of the Republic of Lithuania.

With respect to the Convention, this constitutional provision implies that upon its ratification and enforcement the Convention will become a constituent part of the legal system of the Republic of Lithuania and shall be applied in the same way as laws of the Republic of Lithuania. The provisions of the Convention in the system of legal sources of the Republic of Lithuania are equalled to the laws, because in Article 12 of the law of 21 May 1991 'On International Agreements of the Republic of Lithuania' (Official Gazette *Valstybes Zinios* No. 16–415, 1991; No. 30–915, 1992) it is established that: 'International treaties of the Republic of Lithuania shall have the force of law on the territory of the Republic of Lithuania.'[6]

The Court reaffirmed the well known general conclusion of the European Court of Human Rights that the EHRC does not provide how States Parties are to implement internally the relevant obligations undertaken upon ratification of the Convention.[7] With regard to the means of implementation of the provisions of the ECHR the Constitutional Court has referred to Article 13[8] of the ECHR, and pointed out:

Therefore, State law enforcement bodies should directly apply the norms of the Constitution, as well as implement the provisions of the Convention. Such provisions should become a constituent part of internal law, and there should be no room for the obstacles as to their application by the courts and other law enforcement bodies.

[5] Ibid.

[6] Valstybes zinios,1995, No. 9–199.

[7] *Swedish Engine Drivers' Union* case, Judgment of 6 February 1976, Series A, No. 20.

[8] Article 13. Everyone whose rights and freedoms as set forth in this Convention are violated shall have an effective remedy before a national authority notwithstanding that the violation has been committed by persons acting in an official authority.

Besides, it should be emphasized that the Convention does not require, which would be impossible, that the norms of the internal law of a State should be identical in their wording with the content of the norms of the Convention. Besides the Convention does not strictly stipulate the means by which the rights and freedoms established by the Convention should be implemented. Here it is very important to determine the so-called margins of appreciation, ie to establish sufficiently effective legislative protection of the rights defined by the Convention. The state bodies determine such 'margins of appreciation' in the framework of jurisdiction granted to them by the Constitution.

Nevertheless, the provisions of Articvles 2, 3, 4, and 5 of the Convention mean without any doubt that the rules of the Convention should be implemented, and a breach of the rights and freedoms cannot be justified by invoking the fact that the laws of a state provide otherwise. Such an operation of the provisions of the Convention is due to the fact that a State Party to the Convention should secure the application of the rules of the Convention in its internal legal system. However, the international treaties, as well as this Convention, operate differently in different areas of legal life. Concrete means and forms of their implementation are provided for by the laws of the Republic of Lithuania. Civil law provides for the direct applicability of international treaties in the form of the resolution of their collision with the norms of the laws of the Republic of Lithuania as follows: if international treaties of the Republic of Lithuania prescribe rules other than those established by the laws of the Republic of Lithuania, the provisions of the international treaty shall apply (Article 606 of the Civil Code and Article 482 of the Code of Civil Procedure). In criminal law this method of resolution of collision of norms is not applied. In such cases the criminal laws and laws of criminal procedure of the Republic of Lithuania are directly applicable, and international treaties are directly applicable only in cases provided by such laws (Article 7–1 of the Penal Code and Articles 20, 21, 21–1, 21–2, 22, 22–1, and 22–2 of the Code of Penal Procedure). If in the case of the application of penal law there are doubts about the possibility of the enforcement of human rights provided by the Convention, the question should be resolved by means of constitutional control, asking whether or not the law contradicts the Constitution. From the other point of view, the rights provided by the Convention cannot be enforced directly without applying the internal legal instruments. In other words, if only the direct applicability of the Convention were recognized, the above-mentioned rights could not be ensured, as the Convention itself establishes neither the means of implementation of such rights in states where the Convention was ratified, nor the responsibility of the authors of breaches of rights; the necessary procedures and a special jurisdiction of the law-enforcement bodies are not established either. Here the rule *ubi jus ibi remedium* is clearly applicable: when the law establishes a right, it also provides a remedy to protect it. Such remedies in the legal system of a state are established by the laws of that state. The Convention provides for such remedies only for the cases when the dispute concerning rights guaranteed by the Convention becomes a matter of international jurisdiction.[9]

The conclusion which could be drawn according to the lines drawn by the Constitutional Court is that Article 138 of the Constitution provides for the

[9] Article 13.

incorporation of international treaties into Lithuanian legal system by the way of ratification and, in conjunction with Article 12 of the law on International Treaties, gives the ECHR the legal force of law. According to the Court:

when ratified and entered into force in Lithuania it will form a constituent part of legal system of the Republic of Lithuania and should be implemented as the laws of the Republic of Lithuania.

If this is so, it is doubtful why the Court concluded that:

in the case of the application of penal law where there are doubts about the possibility of enforcement of human rights provided by the Convention, the question should be resolved by means of constitutional control, asking whether or not the law contradicts the Constitution. From the other point of view, the rights provided for by the Convention cannot be enforced directly without applying the internal legal instruments.

The conclusion that Convention rights could not be ensured directly without applying the internal legal instruments also seems doubtful, since the Court has implicitly recognized that the Convention is applied directly in Lithuanian law and found that there was no non-conformity between the ECHR and the Constitution. The ECHR should be applied directly in all branches of Lithuanian law. Criminal law and procedure is no exception.

It seems also that direct applicability of the ECHR in Lithuanian courts follows implicitly from Article 38, para. 2 of the Law on the Courts:

In making decisions, the court shall apply such laws which do not contradict the Constitution of the Republic of Lithuania, such decrees of the Government which do not contradict the laws, and such other legal acts which do not contradict the laws and the decrees of the Government.

Notwithstanding the fact that this provision does not mention international treaties, it is established that the ECHR as a ratified treaty has legal force of law.

The Statute of the Supreme Court (Article 1, para. 3) provides: 'The Supreme Court, within its competence, deals with questions arising from international treaties.' This provision does not mean that the Supreme Court has exclusive competence to apply international treaties. On the other hand, there are some special rules concerning the application of the ECHR by the Supreme Court of Lithuania.

The Code of Civil Procedure (Article 371) stipulates:

The Senate of the Supreme Court also adjudges cases in which the Committee of Ministers of the Council of Europe or the European Court of Human Rights decided that the judgments, rulings, or orders of the courts of the Republic of Lithuania in civil cases have infringed the European Convention for the Protection of Human Rights and Fundamental Freedoms.

An analogous provision is contained in the Code of Criminal Procedure (Article 457):

The Senate of the Supreme Court also adjudges cases in which the Committee of Ministers of the Council of Europe or the European Court of Human Rights decided that the convictions and rulings made by the courts of the Republic of Lithuania in criminal cases have infringed the European Convention for the Protection of Human Rights and Fundamental Freedoms.

B. THE STATUS OF THE CONVENTION IN PARLIAMENTARY PROCEEDINGS

The statute of the Seimas (Parliament) contains special rules concerning the procedures for ensuring the compliance of draft laws and decrees of the Seimas with the standards of the ECHR and the law of the European Union.

According to Article 140 para 5–1 of the Statute of the Seimas, all draft laws and decrees should be submitted to the Seimas together with the statement by the drafters as to:

whether a draft law is in conformity with the provisions of the European Convention for the Protection of Human Rights and Fundamental Freedoms and the documents of the European Union.

Article 144, para. 5 of the Statute of the Seimas provides that parliamentary committees (legal, economic, etc) shall establish whether the draft law is in conformity with the international obligations of Lithuania (which covers, of course, conformity with the obligations deriving from the ECHR):

The committee to which a draft law has been referred for preliminary or additional consideration and which must present conclusions, shall establish (. . .) whether or not the draft is in conformity with the international obligations of the Republic of Lithuania.

On 24 February 1997, the Government decided to establish a special institution to ensure the compliance of Lithuanian draft laws and other legal acts with the law of the European Union (Decree No. 156 of the Government of 24 February 1997). The Legal Bureau under the Ministry of European Affairs was established. The main function of the Legal Bureau was to deliver legal opinions to the Seimas, the government, ministries, and departments as to whether draft laws or other legislative acts comply with European law. The competence of the Legal Bureau covered not only the compliance of draft legal acts with the EU law *stricto sensu* but also extended to the ECHR. This is based on Article F, para. 2 of the Maastricht Treaty on the European Union which incorporates the rights and freedoms guaranteed by the Convention into the law of the European Communities:

> The Union shall respect fundamental rights, as guaranteed by the European Convention for the Protection of Human Rights and Fundamental Freedoms signed in Rome on 4 November 1950 as they result from the constitutional traditions common to the Member States, as general principles of Community law.

On 30 June 1998 the Legal Bureau was reorganized and became the European Law Department under the government. The Statute of the Department (para. 2) provides *expressis verbis* that the Department is empowered to check the compliance of draft legislative acts with the requirements of EU law and the ECHR. According to the Statute of the Seimas and the Statute of the Government, all draft laws and other legislative acts shall be submitted to the Seimas and the Government together with the legal opinion of the European Law Department on the compliance of the act in question with EU law and the ECHR.

Under Article 141 of the Statute of the Seimas:

> if a draft law is submitted by Seimas members or the President of the Republic, it shall be transferred to the European Law Department under the government which shall, within 10 working days of receipt thereof, conclude whether or not this draft is in conformity with European Union law. If this is a large-scale draft, the Seimas Chancellor may extend this period, but not exceeding one month. The Seimas Chancellor shall, within 3 working days, refer the draft law together with the covering letter, and conclusions of the Legal Department and the European Law Department under the government to the Seimas.

Under Article 148 of the Statute of the Seimas, in oral presentation of the draft law or decree here should be references of the legal opinion on the draft given by the European Law Department under the Government.

C. LEADING HUMAN RIGHTS CASES DECIDED BY THE NATIONAL COURTS

It is very difficult to find decisions of Lithuanian courts which could be regarded as 'leading human rights cases'. It is interesting to note that the participants of the conference on 'Legal Reform in Lithuania and Poland and the European Convention on Human Rights' which was held on 2–3 October

1998 in Vilnius agreed with the conclusion of barrister Dr Virginijus Papirtis in his report entitled 'The ECHR and Lithuanian courts' that Lithuanian courts are more reticent to apply the ECHR than Polish courts.

Here it seems appropriate to refer to the first Lithuanian application which was declared admissible by the European Commission of Human Rights on 1 December 1997 (*Juozas Jecius v Lithuania*, Application 34578/97, see Section E below). In this case an applicant was arrested on the basis of the Law on Preventive Detention without any charge made against him and was later kept in detention without any formal decision. The applicant and his counsel have submitted several applications to the Office of Prosecutor and the domestic courts where he argued the illegality of his arrest and detention *inter alia* on the basis of Article 5 of the ECHR. However, these applications were dismissed on the basis of relevant Lithuanian domestic laws without examining the question of the legality of arrest and detention according to the Convention. It does not mean, however, that the ECHR was totally ignored in this case. The Ombudsman (the Parliamentary Controller) in his request of 21 November 1996 drew the attention of the Minister of Internal Affairs, the Prosecutor General, the Director of the Department for Correctional Institutions, and the Director of the prison to the fact that 'the applicant had been remanded in detention illegally from 14 June 1996 until 31 July 1996, Article 5 para. 1(c) of the Convention'.

It should be pointed out that the Constitutional Court of Lithuania has on many occasions based its decisions on the provisions of the ECHR. The most interesting case in this respect is the *Case concerning the compliance of Articles 4, 5, 9, 14 as well as Article 2 of Protocol No 4 of the European Convention for the Protection of Human Rights and Fundamental Freedoms with the Constitution of the Republic of Lithuania (Case No. 22/94, Opinion of the Constitutional Court of 24 January 1995).*

In the contemporary practice of the constitutional courts of European countries the question whether the European Convention on Human Rights contradicts the national constitution seems very doubtful. This question could be put in the contrary way: whether the national constitution contradicts the Convention? The way in which this case was submitted to the Constitutional Court reflects the realities of post-Communist countries, where it was very difficult to imagine how an international treaty could prevail over domestic law. One of the 'exonerating' circumstances of bringing this case to the Constitutional Court of Lithuania was the desire to ensure that the ECHR should be effectively implemented in Lithuania because in the case of its non-conformity with the Constitution it would be difficult to expect that the rights and liberties guaranteed by the ECHR could be protected by the Lithuanian authorities. As stated in the Presidential Request addressed to the Court:

Therefore, the Republic of Lithuania having ratified the European Convention for the Protection of Human Rights and Fundamental Freedoms could not fulfil its international obligations since Article 7 of the Constitution of the Republic of Lithuania stipulates that 'any law or other act which contradicts the Constitution shall be invalid'.[10]

On the basis of this assumption, the President of Lithuania addressed the Constitutional Court asking whether Articles 4, 5, 9, and 14 of the ECHR and Article 2 of Protocol No. 4 to the ECHR are consistent with the Constitution of Lithuania.

According to Article 105 of the Constitution of Lithuania the Constitutional Court is entitled to present conclusions concerning the conformity of international treaties of Lithuania with the Constitution. The Seimas (Parliament) and the President may request a conclusion from the Constitutional Court in cases concerning international treaties (Art. 106 of the Constitution). However, a final decision on the consequences of such unconformity lies within the competence of the Seimas.

The President concluded in his Request that a comparative analysis of Articles 4, 5, 9, and 14 of the ECHR and Article 2 of Protocol No. 4 to the ECHR with Articles 20, 26, 29, 32, and 48 of the Constitution shows their inconsistencies or differences in their content.

Alleged inconsistency of Article 4, para. 3a of the ECHR with Article 48 of the Constitution The President concluded that Article 4, paragraph 3a of the ECHR, which provides that 'forced or compulsory labour' shall not include (. . .) *any work required to be done in the ordinary course of detention* imposed according to the provisions of Article 5 of this Convention or *during conditional release from such detention*, is inconsistent with the provision of Article 48 of the Constitution providing that '*labour which is provided by law for persons convicted by a tribunal* shall not be deemed as forced labour either'. According to the President's Request:

The rule laid down by the Convention provides for a duty to work only in the ordinary course of detention or during conditional release from detention. Thus, the rule provided for by the Convention is shorter in its content than that of the Constitution and that allows us to conclude that Article 4 paragraph 3a of the Convention is incompatible with Article 48, part 5 of the Constitution.

The Constitutional Court pointed out that it was erroneous to interpret Article 48 of the Constitution as providing for correctional labour. This Article does not even mention any correctional works as a criminal penalty.

[10] Valstybes zinios 1995, No. 9–199.

The expression '*labour which is provided by law for persons convicted by a tribunal*' does not mean that the laws should establish a correctional labour penalty.

Making reference to the case-law of the European Court of Human Rights,[11] the Court concluded that the provisions of Article 4, paragraph 3a of the Convention did not necessarily imply a prohibition of forced labour without depriving the liberty of persons convicted of criminal offences. The Court stated that Article 4 of the ECHR links work required to be done with the requirements of Article 5 thereof, ie with the legality of detention or conditional release from detention. It is important that the work should not pass the limits of what is usually required, and the work to be done could be aimed at the reintegration of a person into society.

Therefore the Court came to the conclusion that Article 4, paragraph 3a of the Convention did not contradict the Constitution.

Alleged inconsistency of Article 5, paras. 3 and 4 of the ECHR with Article 20 of the Constitution The corresponding texts are as follows.

ECHR, Art. 5 (extract)

3. *Everyone arrested or detained* in accordance with the provisions of paragraph 1c of this Article *shall be brought promptly before a judge or other officer authorized by law to exercise judicial power* and shall be entitled to trial within a reasonable time or to release pending trial. (. . .)

4. Everyone who is deprived of his liberty by arrest or detention shall be entitled to take proceedings by which *the lawfulness of his detention shall be decided* speedily by a court and his release ordered if the detention is not lawful.

Constitution, Art. 20 (extract)

A person arrested in flagrante delicto must, within 48 hours, be brought to court for the purpose of determining, in the presence of the detainee, *the validity of the detention.*

According to the Request there are essential inconsistencies between these convention and constitutional provisions. First, Article 5, para. 3 of the ECHR established a guarantee which is broader than that of the Constitution as it states that every arrested or detained person shall be brought before a court, whereas the Constitution deals only with a person arrested *in flagrante delicto*. Secondly, Article 5, paragraph 4 of the Convention stipulates that a judge should decide on the lawfulness of the arrest, although according to the Constitution the court must determine the validity of the arrest. This difference is essential, since a lawful arrest *per se* is always valid, although a valid arrest may be unlawful. Thirdly, it is doubtful whether the term 'promptly' used in the Convention is consistent with the rule of 48 hours provided for by

[11] *Van Droogenbroeck*, Judgment of 24 June 1982, Series A, No. 50, 32–60.

the Constitution. All this allows us to conclude that the rules established by Article 5, paragraph 4 of the Convention are inconsistent with Article 20 of the Constitution both in their content and their extent.

The Court first of all noted that there was not enough in the wording of corresponding provisions of the ECHR and the Constitution to conclude that they were inconsistent. The Court found:

> . . . if the Constitution does not establish any rights, freedoms or guarantees or constructs them in different manner, it does not mean that such rights and freedoms or their enforcement could not be guaranteed in the legal system of the Republic of Lithuania. They could be and indeed are provided for in other legal instruments and are implemented in practice. Besides, they could be ensured by applying the Convention on the basis of Article 138, part 3 of the Constitution. The provisions of the Convention would not be applicable only if such provisions contradicted the Constitution.

Comparing the formulas '*to bring promptly before a judge*' and '*to bring to court within 48 hours*', the Court concluded that there was conformity. Here the Court made reference to relevant case-law of the organs of the Convention recognizing that four days in ordinary cases and five days in exceptional cases corresponded to the requirement to bring an arrested person promptly before a judge. The Court also referred to relevant Articles of the Constitutions of some States Parties to the Conventions providing the term of 48 hours (Art. 28 of the Constitution of Portugal and Art. 13 of the Constitution of Italy) and 72 hours (Art. 17 of the Constitution of Spain).

The Court further found no contradiction between the requirement that '*everyone who is arrested or detained (. . .) shall be brought before a judge*' and that providing '*a person detained in flagrante delicto must (. . .) be brought to court*'. Implemented together on the basis of Article 138 of the Constitution, both provisions substitute one another and form one legal guarantee.

Finally, the Court came to the conclusion that there is no contradiction between the provision of Article 5, para. 4 of the Convention which stipulates that a judge should decide on the *lawfulness* of the arrest, and that of Article 20 of the Constitution which requires that the court must determine the *validity* of the arrest. Both the Constitution and the Convention require that the court should decide on the lawfulness and validity of the arrest. The Court concluded:

> However one cannot interpret part 3 of Article 20 of the Constitution separating it from the whole text of this article, as well as of other provisions of the Constitution establishing guarantees of legality. Part 2 of Article mentioned above provides that: 'No person may be arbitrarily arrested or detained. No person may be deprived of freedom except on the grounds, and according to the procedures established by law.' Such provisions basically established the principle of the lawfulness of the detention

of a person as a general rule. That is why the content of the term 'validity' employed by the Article 20 is broader than the only meaning of causality of facts; it means that it covers the term of 'lawfulness'.

Therefore the Court concluded that Article 5 of the ECHR does not contradict the Constitution of Republic of Lithuania.

Alleged inconsistency of Article 9, para. 2 of the ECHR and Article 26 of the Constitution This was drawn only from differences in the wording of Article 9, para. 2 of the ECHR ('*freedom to manifest one's religion*') and Article 26 of the Constitution ('*freedom to profess and manifest his or her religion or belief*'). According to the President Article 9, paragraph 2 of the Convention allows only restrictions to a freedom to manifest religion or belief, although Article 26 of the Constitution stipulates that a freedom to profess and manifest religion or belief could be restricted.

It should be noted that the Convention, as well as the Constitution, distinguishes the freedom to profess and freedom to manifest religion or belief as two different freedoms that allows to conclude that the Convention does not provide for the possibility to restrict a freedom to profess (religion or belief—VV). Therefore the conclusion should be drawn that Article 9, paragraph 2 of the Convention by its extent contradicts part four of the Article 26 of the Constitution.

The Court found that Article 9 of the ECHR did not distinguish the right to profess and freedom to manifest religion or belief. Although the Constitution provides for the possibility to establish the limitations of freedom to profess and manifest one's religion or belief, it was only different wording. The Court pointed out that there was no possibility to restrict the freedom to profess a religion or belief because it is impossible to restrict such a moral category as a religious faith or belief. Here the court referred to the English and French texts of Article 18 of International Covenant on Civil and Political Rights where the corresponding wording '*freedom to have*' or '*la liberté d'avoir*' was used. This wording does not mean any external manifestation of religion or belief which could be subject to legal restrictions. *Lex non cogit ad impossibilia*: law does not require the impossible.

The Court concluded:

Therefore this provision of the Constitution did not entail any negative consequences with regard to freedom of religion and belief in the legal system of the Republic of Lithuania, and no law restricts freedom to profess religion or belief.

Thus, according to the Conclusion there is no contradiction between Article 9 of the ECHR and the Constitution.

Alleged inconsistency between Article 14 of the ECHR and Article 29 of the Constitution The corresponding texts are as follows:

ECHR, Art. 14

The enjoyment of the rights and freedoms set forth in this Convention shall be secured without discrimination on any ground such as sex, race, *colour*, language, religion, political or other opinion, national or social origin, *association with a national minority*, property, birth or other status.

Constitution, Art. 29 (extract)

A person may not have his rights restricted in any way, or *be granted any privileges*, on the basis of his or her sex, race, nationality, language, origin, social status, religion, convictions, or opinions.

The President on this basis concluded that:

the Convention prohibits only so-called 'negative' discrimination, although the Constitution prohibits both 'negative' and 'positive' (granting of privileges) discrimination. In addition, the Convention provides for a more extensive list of grounds of discrimination, for example: the Constitution does not mention 'colour, association with a national minority'. These two aspects allow us to conclude that Article 14 of the Convention is inconsistent to this extent with part two of Article 29 of the Constitution.

The Court concluded that positive discrimination does not mean the granting of privileges. It does not imply inequality before the law. The Constitution provides for the universally recognized specific rights inherent to some groups of people, namely to persons belonging to national minorities.

Article 29 of the Constitution stipulates that 'a person may not have his rights restricted in any way, or be granted any privileges . . .' This formula corresponds to the expression employed in Article 14 of the ECHR providing that 'the enjoyment of the rights and freedoms set forth in this Convention shall be secured without discrimination on any ground . . .' The fact that the Constitution does not mention the terms 'colour' and 'association with a national minority' is nothing more than a difference in the wording. The Court also mentioned some other differences in the wording, for example 'social origin' (Convention) and 'social status' (Constitution) as a simple difference in the wording having no implication to general principle of non-discrimination provided for in both the Convention and the Constitution.

The Court stated that Article 14 of the ECHR does not contradict the Constitution.

Inconsistency between Article 2 of Protocol No. 4 to the ECHR and Article 32 of the Constitution The corresponding texts are the following:

Protocol No. 4 to the ECHR, Art. 2 (extract)

1. *Everyone* lawfully within the territory of a State shall, within that territory, have the right to liberty of movement and freedom to choose his residence.

Constitution, Art. 32 (extract)

Citizens may move and choose their place of residence in Lithuania freely, and may leave Lithuania at their own will.

On this basis the President considered that Article 2 of Protocol No. 4 to the ECHR provides for everyone's right of liberty of movement and freedom to choose residence, whereas the Constitution limits freedom of movement only to citizens. Thus Article 2 of Protocol No. 4 is inconsistent with Article 32 of the Constitution.

The answer of the Constitutional Court on this point was also negative:

The Constitutional Court notes that Article 2 of Protocol No. 4 to the ECHR containing the rule that 'everyone lawfully within the territory of a State shall, within that territory, have the right to liberty of movement and freedom to choose his residence' consists of two interrelated constituent parts. One means the right of a person to move freely and to choose freely his residence, the second means that this right is guaranteed only to persons lawfully residing in the territory of that State. Such people could be nationals, as well as foreigners or stateless persons. The residence of a national within the territory of his State is always lawful. Article 32, part 3 of the Constitution stipulates: 'A citizen may not be prohibited from returning to Lithuania'. Although the conditions of entry or leaving the country for the foreigner or a stateless person are established by the internal law of the State. Such conditions are established by the Law of the Republic of Lithuania on the Legal Status of Foreigners in the Republic of Lithuania.[12]

Foreigners, as well as stateless persons residing lawfully in the Republic of Lithuania according to the Law mentioned above, enjoy the same rights and freedoms as citizens of the Republic of Lithuania unless the Constitution of the Republic of Lithuania, this and other laws of the Republic of Lithuania, as well as international treaties of the Republic of Lithuania provide otherwise. Therefore, the provisions of Protocol No. 4, applied in the legal system of Lithuania together with the provisions of the Law on Legal Status of Foreigners in the Republic of Lithuania, would cover each other. One practical question still to be answered is whether or not a foreigner or stateless person is lawfully in the territory of Lithuania for the purpose of full enjoyment of his right to move and freely choose his residence.

Taking into consideration all this the conclusion should be drawn that Article 2 of Protocol No. 4 of the ECHR does not contradict the Constitution of Lithuania.

It seems that all the questions put before the Constitutional Court were based on the assumption that the differences in the wording of the constitutional and conventional provisions should mean differences in content. The Constitutional Court, as shown above, rejected this approach. Therefore, some aspects of this case could be regarded as purely formalistic. However, some general remarks made by the Court in its *ratio decidendi* could be of par-

[12] For the English text of the Law on the Legal Status of Foreigners in the Republic of Lithuania see: *Parliamentary Record*/Seimas of the Republic of Lithuania. 1992, No. 5, 5–10.

ticular interest, especially the remarks concerning the legal force of international treaties in general, and of the ECHR in particular, in the Lithuanian legal system (see Section B above 'The status of the Convention in national law').

Besides, it seems that the Court found an interesting meaning of the term 'contradiction with the Constitution'. It stated:

> The provisions of the Convention could be considered inconsistent with the Constitution if:
>
> 1. the Constitution established the exhaustive and full list of the rights and freedoms, although the Convention established other rights and freedoms;
> 2. the Constitution prohibited any acts, although the Convention defined these acts as any right or freedom;
> 3. any provision of the Convention could not be applicable in the legal system of the Republic of Lithuania because it was inconsistent with any provision of the Constitution.[13]

The Court found that there was no room for such inconsistency in the sense of points 1 or 2 of this formula.

It should be emphasized that the Court's conception of conformity between the provisions of the ECHR and the Constitution is far from the formal linguistic conformity of corresponding texts. As it stated:

> the interpretation of the conformity (relationship) of the norms of the Constitution and the Convention should be essential, logical, but not identical in wording. Only the formal linguistic interpretation of human rights cannot be accepted by the very nature of human rights.

As for point 3 of the meaning of 'contradiction with the Constitution', the Court decided on this when answering the concrete points of the Request of the President of Lithuania.

In the *Case concerning the compliance of Articles 1 and 30 of the Law on Alcohol Control of the Republic of Lithuania, Articles 1, 3 and 11 of the Law on Tobacco Control of the Republic of Lithuania as well as the Resolution of the Government of the Republic of Lithuania No. 179 of 2 February 1996 on the Control of the Advertising of Alcohol with the Constitution of the Republic of Lithuania (Case No. 6/96, Ruling of the Constitutional Court of 13 February 1997)*[14] the Constitutional Court was asked to adjudge whether certain restrictions on advertising alcohol and tobacco were in compliance with the Constitution. In this case the Court referred to the criteria of legitimacy of

[13] The last point of 'inconsistency' would be more clear if the Court had used the expression 'if it precludes the applicability of any provision of the Constitution because of its inconformity with the Constitution'.

[14] Valstybes zinios,1997, No. 15–314.

restrictions on the exercise of rights according to the case-law of the ECHR organs:

Conflicts between the rights and freedoms of individuals on one hand and the interests of society on the other occasionally arise, and sometimes contradictions occur. In a democratic society such contradictions are resolved by co-ordinating different interests and seeking not to upset their balance. One way to co-ordinate interests is the restriction of the rights and freedoms of individuals. Incidentally, the European Convention for the Protection of Human Rights and Fundamental Freedoms provides for such a possibility. According to the Convention and the established practice of the European Court of Human Rights, this kind of restriction is possible, ie is regarded as justified if it meets two conditions: (1) it is legitimate, and (2) it is indispensable in a democratic society. The requirement of legitimacy indicates that restrictions must be imposed by a law that is officially published; the norms of the law are to be formulated sufficiently lucidly. Legally defining the limits of the implementation of laws, it is necessary to take account of the purpose and meaning of a corresponding right (or freedom) and the possibilities and conditions of its restriction established in the Constitution. Looking for the answer to the question whether a concrete restriction is indispensable in a democratic society, the first step is to find out the aims and purpose of the restriction, and the second is to find out whether the means of the restriction are proportionate to the legitimate aim.

In its Ruling the Constitutional Court concluded that the prohibitions of 'indirect advertisements' and the dissemination of information concerning the products, articles, and services 'not directly linked with alcoholic beverages and their consumption', as well as products, articles, and services 'not directly linked with tobacco products and their consumption', do not fit the common concept of advertisement and they groundlessly broaden it, and therefore contradict Article 25 of the Constitution which provides that freedom to express convictions, as well as to obtain and disseminate information, may not be restricted other than as established by law, when it is necessary to safeguard the health, honour, and dignity, private life, or morals of a person, or for the protection of constitutional order.

With regard to the provisions of the Government Decree of 2 February 1996 on the Control of Advertising for Alcohol which entitled the Government to establish the criteria for recognizing the content and arrangement of audio or visual information concerning alcohol and the ways of transmission thereof as advertisement for alcohol the Constitutional Court also decided that it contradicts Article 25 of the Constitution providing that freedom to express convictions, as well as to obtain and disseminate information, may not be restricted in any way other than as established by law.

In the *Case concerning the compliance of Article 16 of the Law on Civil Servants with the Constitution (Case No. 13/96, Ruling of the Constitutional*

Court of 6 May 1997)[15] the Constitutional Court was asked whether the prohibition established by this Law for a civil servant from being the owner of a personal enterprise, or full members or silent partners of a partnership, acquiring more than 10 per cent of securities of one enterprise contradicts the Constitution. The Court repeated the above-mentioned passage concerning the criteria of restrictions of rights guaranteed by the ECHR of his ruling of 13 February 1997 and referred to corresponding case-law of the European Court of Human Rights:

It was noted in the decisions of the European Court of Human Rights that the notion 'in the public interest' is inevitably broad. The Court, bearing in mind that the opportunity of choice granted to the legislator who implements social and economic policy must be broad enough, will take into consideration the decisions of the legislator in defining 'public interests' save the said decisions were unreasonably grounded. Seizure of property, when implemented for the benefit of socio-legal economic policy, may be justified by 'public interests' even when the whole society does not make direct use of the seized property (the cases *James and others v United Kingdom* (1986), *Lithgow and others v United Kingdom* (1987)). It means that the legislative power is entitled to establish limits of the public interest in particular relations, while decisions concerning the definition of the public interest and the manner its satisfaction must be realistically grounded and legitimate.

The public interest is defined in its most general sense by the provision that the 'institutions of State power shall serve the people' in Part 3 of Article 5 of the Constitution. It means that the officials of the state and local governments perform specific functions depending upon the purpose of the civil service. In order to implement these functions properly, a citizen taking office in the civil service must conform to the conditions prescribed by the laws. Under Article 9 of the Law on Civil Servants, persons who are citizens of the Republic of Lithuania, have a good command of state language, and meet other requirements as regards qualification prescribed as necessary for the office shall be employed in the civil service. The law also establishes that persons convicted of serious crimes, crimes against the civil service, as well as persons who are close relatives or are related by marriage if their service is connected with direct subordination between the relatives or with the right of one of them to control the other may not be employed in the civil service.

Part 1 of Article 16 of the Law on Civil Servants sets down special prohibitions which differ by their character from the aforementioned general requirements and prohibitions. The prohibitions consolidated in disputed Item 2 of Part 1 of Article 16 of the aforesaid law permit us to presume that the owner of a private enterprise, a full member or a silent partner of a partnership, or a person who has acquired more than 10 per cent of the securities of one enterprise and who wishes to take office in the civil service, must restrict his ownership rights. Thus by the disputed legal norm citizens are differentiated into: (1) those who do not have possessions indicated in Item 2 of Part 1 of Article 16 of the said Law and who may take office in the civil service of the Republic of Lithuania (providing they meet the other requirements of the law), and (2)

[15] Valstybes zinios,1997, No. 40–977.

those who have the possessions specified in said Item 2 of Part 1 of Article 16. The latter citizens acquire equal opportunities to take office in the civil service of the Republic of Lithuania only when they refuse the aforementioned possessions or limit them within the boundaries provided by the law.

The norm of Part 1 of Article 33 of the Constitution, whereby citizens shall have the equal opportunity to serve in a public service of the Republic of Lithuania, may not be denied by legal norms contrary to the Constitution. Meanwhile, citizens seeking to implement the right granted to them by Part 1 of Article 33 of the Constitution must, due to the prohibitions established by Item 2 of Part 1 of Article 16 (except for the prohibition of the said item to hold securities on trust) deny their other constitutional right—the right to property.

The Constitutional Court has already held in the present ruling that the prohibition prescribed in Item 2 Part 1 of Article 16 of the Law on Civil Servants stipulating that officials shall be prohibited from being the owner of a personal enterprise, or full members or silent partners of a partnership, acquiring or holding in trust more than 10 per cent of securities of one enterprise contradicts Article 23 of the Constitution.

Taking account of these circumstances and the motives set forth, as well as the fact that the Constitution is an integral and directly applicable act, the Constitutional Court has concluded that the prohibition prescribed by Item 2 Part 1 of Article 16 of the Law on Civil Servants stipulating that officials shall be prohibited from being the owner of a personal enterprise, or full members or silent partners of a partnership, acquiring more than 10 per cent of securities of one enterprise contradicts Part 1 of Article 29 and Part 1 of Article 33 of the Constitution.

D. CASES BROUGHT BEFORE THE EUROPEAN COMMISSION AND COURT OF HUMAN RIGHTS

Since the first Lithuanian provisional file was registered by the Secretariat of the European Commission of Human Rights in 1995, the number of communications and applications submitted to the Commission against Lithuania has grown substantially. In 1995 there were 2 applications, in 1996—13, in 1997—21; then in 1998 (until 1 October) 36 applications were registered. One application (*Juozas Jecius v Lithuania*, No. 34578/97) was declared admissible. There are 3 applications referred (communicated) to the Government, 23 applications are waiting for consideration by the Commission, and 46 applications were declared inadmissible or struck off the list. On 1 October 1998 the total number of provisional files was 121.

Analysis of the cases referred to the government, including the above case of *Juozas Jecius*, shows that the most controversial questions in the area of the compatibility of Lithuanian legislation with the ECHR arise from the rules and practices of criminal procedure: the lawfulness of detention, prolongation of detention, duty to bring an arrested person promptly before a judge, length of detention, the right to judicial review of the legality of detention. There were also complaints dealing with the right to examine a 'secret' witness, and confidentiality of correspondence of detained persons with the European Commission of Human Rights.

A typical category of complaints from post-Communist countries including Lithuania is the restitution of property rights. It follows from well-established case-law of the Commission that Article 1 of the First Protocol does not guarantee the right of restitution of nationalized property.[16] However, specific Lithuanian problems in this field are related to the length of the restitution procedure after the decisions to restore ownership were taken.

The case of *Juozas Jecius v Lithuania* (Application 34578/97) concerns the lawfulness of the applicant's preventive detention and of subsequent prolongations of his detention on remand, the alleged failure to bring him promptly before a judge, and the length of his detention.

The application was introduced on 30 December 1996 and registered on 24 January 1997. On 11 April 1997 the Commission decided to communicate the application to the Government of Lithuania. On 1 December 1997 the Commission declared the application admissible.

The main facts of the case are as follows.

The applicant was initially arrested on 8 February 1996 and detained until 9 June 1997 when the court at first instance acquitted him. The applicant's detention thus lasted for 16 months and 1 day.

The applicant was initially arrested under the 'preventive detention' rule without any reason or charge. According to Articles 50–1 of the Code of Criminal Procedure (in force until 30 June 1997) the Chief of the Department of Police was entitled with the authorization of the Prosecutor General or his deputy to order the arrest of a person on suspicion that this person might commit a serious offence (banditism; criminal association; terrorizing a person) with a view to preventing such an act. Within 48 hours, a judge could confirm this decision and order 'preventive detention' for no longer than two months. This decision could be taken in the absence of the arrested person. This kind of detention raises a question of its conformity under Article 5, para. 1c: whether it corresponds to 'the lawful arrest or detention of a person effected for the purpose of bringing him before the competent legal authority on reasonable suspicion of having committed an offence or when it is reasonably considered necessary to prevent his committing an offence or fleeing after having done so', In a case of 'preventive detention' the arrested person

[16] Cf. European Commission of Human Rights, Application 23131/93 *Ladislav and Aurel Brezny v Slovak Republik*, Decision on admissibility of 4 March 1996 85 DR 80–81; Application 25497/94 *Dorin Lupulet v Rumania*, Decision on admissibility of 17 May 1996 85 DR 133.

could not be brought before the competent legal authority, he is not 'informed promptly, in a language which he understands, of the reasons for his arrest and of any charge against him' (Article 5, para. 2) and moreover, there are no concrete charge against him. All this does not correspond to the usual aims and requirements of the pre-trial detention. As the Commission concluded in the report on the admissibility of application:

> In the instant case, the Commission notes that, under the then Article 50–1 of the Code of Criminal Procedure, there was no formal requirement for the domestic authorities to inform the applicant of the specific reason for his preventive detention following the order thereof. The applicant thus had no 'effective' domestic remedy available to him to obtain information as to the reasons for his preventive detention or to contest the refusal thereof.

The applicant also complained under Article 5, para. 3 that he was not 'brought promptly before a judge or other officer authorized by law'. He asserted that in the initial period of his detention from 8 February to 21 June 1996 he was not brought before a prosecutor, and that from 21 June to 14 October 1996—after the amendment to the Code of Criminal Procedure came into force and the reservation of Lithuania with respect to Article 5, para. 3 had expired—he was not brought promptly before a court or judge until the court deliberations which commenced on 14 October 1996. The Lithuanian reservation to Article 5, para. 3 of the Convention provided as follows:

> The provisions of Article 5 para. 3 of the Convention shall not affect the operation of Article 104 of the Code of Criminal Procedure of the Republic of Lithuania (amended version no. I-551, 19 July 1994) which provides that a decision to detain in custody any person suspected of having committed a crime may also, by the decision of a prosecutor, be so detained [sic]. This reservation shall be effective for one year after the Convention comes into force in respect of the Republic of Lithuania. [This reservation expired on 21 June 1996: see letter from the Permanent Representative of Lithuania, dated 19 July 1996, registered at the Secretariat General on 22 July 1996, notification JJ3634C of 30 July 1996.]

However, this reservation does not exclude the duty promptly to bring an arrested person 'before (. . .) an officer authorized by law' under Article 5, para. 3 of the ECHR, ie in case of Lithuania, before the prosecutor.

In this case the government asserted that the Lithuanian law (Article 104–1 of the Code of Criminal Procedure, in force since 21 June 1996) provides that 'the arrested person shall be brought before a judge in not more than 48 hours'. However, in the government's view, the guarantee contained in Article 5, para. 3 of the Convention applies to the initial moment of detention which, in this case, occurred before the expiry of the Lithuanian reservation in respect of Article 5, para. 3 of the Convention. The government thus argued that, since the applicant's detention on remand was ordered on 14

March 1996, he was not then nor thereafter entitled to be brought promptly before a judge or any other officer. The government also stated that there was no provision in the Law amending the Code of Criminal Procedure, under which a person, detained by an authorization of a prosecutor before 21 June 1996, had the right to be brought before a judge.

The applicant contested this interpretation of Article 5, para. 3 of the ECHR. He considered that the government could not hide behind its failure to bring him before a proper officer when he was initially arrested in order to justify their failure to bring him before a judge or any other officer thereafter.

The Commission noted that the applicant was formally brought before a judge for the first time on 14 October 1996. Until that date, he was not brought before a judge or before any other officer throughout the period of his preventive detention from 8 February 1996, or his detention on remand from 14 March 1996. Consequently, the Commission found that this part of the application raised complex questions of fact and law, including questions concerning the reservation of Lithuania to Article 5, para. 3 of the Convention, the determination of which should depend on an examination of the merits.

The applicant also claimed that he had been denied the right to trial within a reasonable time, in violation of Article 5, para. 3 of the Convention: he was initially arrested on 8 February 1996 and then detained until 9 June 1997 when the court at first instance acquitted him. The applicant's detention thus lasted for 16 months and 1 day. The Commission declared admissible this part of the application.

Under Article 5, para. 4 of the Convention the applicant complained of the refusal of the Court of Appeal and the President of the Criminal Division of the Supreme Court to examine appeals against his detention on remand.[17]

The government replied that the applicant had the right to apply to a court which would have resolved the question of the lawfulness of his detention. In the applicant's view, the Lithuanian courts, in examining his complaints, did not recognize such right as they referred solely to Article 372, para. 4 of the Code of Criminal Procedure which contradicts Article 30 of the Constitution and other relevant provisions of domestic law to which the government referred in their observations.[18]

[17] Article 5, para. 4 of the ECHR reads as follows:

Everyone who is deprived of his liberty by arrest or detention shall be entitled to take proceedings by which the lawfulness of his detention shall be decided speedily by a court and his release ordered if the detention is not lawful.

[18] Article 30 para. 1 of the Constitution reads as follows: 'Any person whose constitutional rights or freedoms are violated shall have the right to apply to court.'

Article 372 para. 4 of the Code of Criminal Procedure reads as follows: 'Decisions of courts (. . .) ordering, varying or revoking a remand measure (. . .) cannot be the subject of appeal.'

The Commission recalled that on 21 June 1996 the amendment to the Code of Criminal Procedure of Lithuania came into force, and the grounds and procedure ordering detention on remand (arrest) were changed. Even though the new system provided for detention on remand after 21 June 1996 to be ordered only by a court or judge, no new procedure was introduced for review of the detention of persons arrested prior to 21 June 1996 by a prosecutor. This was confirmed by the government in their comments on the facts of the case where they submit that after 21 June 1996 there was no possibility of reconsidering the detention authorized by a prosecutor prior to 21 June 1996. The Commission declared this part of application admissible but noted that its determination should depend on an examination of the merits.

The applicant also invoked Article 6, para. 1 of the Convention. He complained that, pursuant to Article 106 of the Code of Criminal Procedure,[19] and given the offence with which he was charged, he could have been kept in detention on remand for 10 years. This might have infringed his right to a 'hearing within a reasonable time' under Article 6, para. 1 of the ECHR.

The Commission rejected this complaint as being manifestly ill founded:

> The Commission first notes that this complaint is based on a hypothetical assumption of what might happen in the future. However, someone who only fears the risk of a future violation of the Convention in his regard cannot 'claim to be a victim' within the meaning of Article 25 of the Convention (No. 7945/77, Dec. 4.7.78, D.R. 14, p. 228). In any event, the Commission considers that the length of the criminal proceedings against the applicant did not exceed the 'reasonable time' requirement under Article 6, para. 1 of the Convention.

The applicant also invoked the right under Article 6, para. 3(b) of the Convention 'to have adequate time and facilities for the preparation of his defence'. He asserted that the above provision of the Convention had been violated because the five days from 30 May to 4 June 1996, during which the applicant was given access to the case files, were not counted towards the period of his detention. Article 226, para. 6 of the Code of Criminal Procedure of Lithuania provides in this respect:

> The period when the accused and his counsel have access to case files is not counted towards the overall term of pre-trial investigation and arrest. Where there are several accused persons, the period during which all the accused and their counsel have access to the case files is not counted towards the overall term of pre-trial investigation and arrest.

The Commission decided that this complaint related solely to a period of five days in the investigation phase of the proceedings. During that period the

[19] Article 106 of the Code of Criminal Procedure reads as follows: '(. . .) throughout the proceedings the detention on remand cannot be extended beyond two-thirds of the maximum term of the sentence of deprivation of liberty provided by law for the most serious alleged offence.'

applicant with his counsel were in fact given access to the case files, that is, facilities were granted for the preparation of his defence. Therefore, this part of the application was rejected as being manifestly ill founded.

E. REMEDIAL ACTION TAKEN BY THE GOVERNMENT IN RESPONSE TO BEING HELD IN VIOLATION OF THE CONVENTION

Since the ECHR took effect with regard to Lithuania on 20 June 1995 (and the First Protocol on 24 May 1996) there has been no remedial action because the government of Lithuania has not yet been held in violation of the Convention.

It should be noted here that Lithuanian law contains special norms providing for such remedial actions. The Law on the Compensation of Damage Caused by Illegal Acts of Prosecution and Judicial Bodies (hereinafter the Law on Compensation) of 4 November 1997 stipulates *inter alia* that compensation hould be granted on the basis of the decision of the European Court of Human Rights or the Committee of Ministers which awarded the compensation and on the basis of friendly settlement reached between the Agent of the Government and a victim of a violation (Article 4, para. 2). Under Article 5, para. 2 a victim of a violation of the ECHR shall submit via the Agent of the Government to the Ministry of Justice the decision of the European Court of Human Rights or the Committee of Ministers, as well as the friendly settlement, and ask for compensation. Article 7, para. 8 provides that the amount of compensation shall be fixed not by the tribunals of Lithuania but by the organs of the ECHR or by friendly settlement.

Article 9 of the Law on Compensation stipulates that the state budget every year shall contain provision for the compensation of damage caused to individuals by law-enforcement bodies. These financial means are at the disposal of the Ministry of Justice. In cases where the state budget does not yet provide for such compensation it shall be granted from the Reserve of the Government.

The 1998 Law on the Budget of State and Municipalities provides 5,000,000 litas (US$ 1,250,000) for the compensation of damage caused to individuals by law-enforcement bodies.

G. ASSESSMENT AND PROSPECTS

Since the re-establishment of independence in 1990, Lithuanian legislation has been substantively changed and the ECHR was effectively implemented in domestic law and practice. However, some serious problems still arise, mostly in criminal law and procedure. This is due mainly to two reasons. First, notwithstanding the fact, that the provisions of the Criminal Code and the Code of Criminal Procedure were consequently changed and amended on many occasions, the new Codes in this branch of national law were not yet adopted. Secondly, current problems of organized crime in Lithuania gave rise to the popular conviction that these problems could only be resolved by imposing more severe criminal penalties and procedures. This has led to attempts to 'Americanize' the fighting of criminality. As a result, some laws which contradicted the ECHR were adopted. The above-mentioned Law on Preventive Detention (incorporated into Article 50–1 of the Code of Criminal Procedure) could be taken as an example. This Law provided for the detention of persons suspected of being involved in organized crime without any charges against them and without bringing them before a judge or other officer, and thus contradicted Article 5, paras. 1c and 3 of the Convention. This inconsistency was the main reason for abolishing this law (on 30 June 1997) as well as the rule that the length of detention on remand can be extended to 'two-thirds of the maximum term of the sentence of deprivation of liberty provided by law for the most serious alleged offence' which contradicted Article 5, para. 3 and Article 6, para. 1 of the Convention (abolished on 11 June 1998). Therefore, even in the very sensible area of 'fighting against criminality' the Convention has had its positive impact. However, on 1 July 1997 the Law on Preventive Detention was 'substituted' by the Law on Prevention of Organized Crime which provides that in cases of suspicion of involvement in some kinds of offences a judge may order a person:

> 1) to live only in the place of his permanent residence; 2) to abstain from contacting specified persons directly, through other persons, or by technical means of communications; 3) to stay at his place of residence during certain times; 4) to abstain from visiting certain places; 5) to abstain from driving a motor vehicle; 6) to inform the police officer who supervises his control about all transactions which could exceed the amount of 2,000 litas; 7) to transfer temporarily to the police officer a firearm which this person legally possess (Article 14).[20]

Article 212–1 of the Criminal Code (as amended on 1 July 1997) provides for a criminal sanction (up to two years of deprivation of liberty) for non-respect

[20] Valstybes zinios, 1997, No. 69–1731.

of the above order in cases where a guilty person was punished already before according to the Administrative Code, but has repeatedly not complied with the order.[21] These provisions give rise to serious questions about their compliance with Article 5, para. 1 and Article 8 of the ECHR, Article 2, para. 1 of Protocol No. 4, and Article 1 of the First Protocol thereto. However, it seems that the risk of being held in violation of the ECHR will lead to the abolishment of these provisions as happened with the Law on Preventive Detention. Finally, strengthening the rule of law in the Lithuanian legal system and practice will inevitably have this effect.

[21] Valstybes zinios, 1997, No. 69–1733, Valstybes zinios,1997, No. 70.

21

Luxembourg

DEAN SPIELMANN*

A. INTRODUCTION

The Grand Duchy of Luxembourg ratified the European Human Rights Convention and its Additional Protocol on 3 September 1953 following approval by Parliament,[1] in accordance with Article 37, paragraph 1 of the Constitution.[2] The Convention came into force[3] through the deposit of this instrument of ratification—in this case the tenth. All the Additional Protocols have also been ratified by Luxembourg[4] and form part of domestic law.

* List of the main abbreviations: Ann. Dr. lux. = Annales du droit luxembourgeois (Luxembourg Law Records); Bull. dr. h. = Bulletin des droits de l'homme (Human Rights Bulletin); Bull. Laurent = Bulletin du Cercle François Laurent (Bulletin of the François Laurent Circle); C.A. = Cour d'appell (Appeal Court); Cass. = Cour de Cassation (Cassation Court); C.E. = Conseil d'Etat (Council of State); C.S.J. = Cour Supérieure de Justice (Supreme Court); F.S.Y. = Feuille de liaison de la Conférence Saint-Yves (Contact Sheet of the Saint-Yves Conference); H.R.L.J. = Human Rights Law Journal; J.L.M.B. = Revue de jurisprudence de Liège, Mons et Bruxelles (Review of Liège, Mons and Brussels Case Law); J.T. = Journal des Tribunaux (Court Gazette); Mém. = Memorial (Official Gazette); Pas. Lux. = Pasicrisie luxembourgeoise (Collection of Luxembourg Legal Judgments); R.D.P. = Revue de droit pénal et de criminologie (Criminology and Criminal Law Review); R.G.A.R. = Revue générale des assurances et des responsabilités (General Insurance and Liability Review); Rev. b. dr. const. = Revue belge de droit constitutionnel (Belgian Constitutional Law Review); Rev. trim. dr. h. = Revue trimestrielle des droits de l'homme (Quarterly Human Rights Review); T.A. = Tribunal d'Arrondissement (District Court); Yearbook = Yearbook of the European Convention on Human Rights.

[1] Act of 29 August 1953, Mém. A, 1953, 1099. For the subject as a whole, see A. Spielmann and A. Weitzel, *La Convention européenne des droits de l'homme et le droit luxembourgeois,* Brussels, Nemesis, 1991.

[2] Article 37, paragraph 1 of the Constitution states:

> The Grand Duke makes treaties. Treaties shall come into effect only after they have been approved by law and published in the manner prescribed for the publication of laws.

[3] Former Article 66 of the Convention. See A. Spielmann and A. Weitzel, n. 1 above, page 13.

[4] The Grand Duchy of Luxembourg ratified Protocols Nos. 2 and 3 on 27 October 1965. Protocol No. 4 was ratified on 2 May 1968, Protocol No. 5 on 26 June 1968, and Protocol No. 6 on 19 February 1985. Protocol No. 7 was ratified on 19 April 1989, Protocol No. 8 on 4 November 1987, and Protocol No. 9 on 9 July 1992. Protocol No. 10 was ratified on 7 February 1994 and Protocol No. 11 on 10 September 1996.

B. THE STATUS OF THE CONVENTION IN DOMESTIC LAW

The Convention and its Protocols are regarded as directly applicable. Since 1950[5] case-law has embodied the principle that directly applicable provisions of treaties take precedence over all contrary domestic legislation even where this is enacted subsequently. The earliest decisions generally cited—which embody the principle of the primacy of international treaties—are two judgments delivered by the Cour de Cassation (Court of Cassation) on 8 June 1950[6] and 14 July 1954[7] and a decision by the Conseil d'Etat (Council of State) on 28 July 1951.[8]

Through these decisions Luxembourg case-law agreed to monitor legislation from the point of view of its conformity with international treaties.[9] This is also the case with monitoring the conformity of administrative measures with international standards.[10]

Thus, in Luxembourg law, the Human Rights Convention normally takes precedence over domestic legislation even where the two conflict,[11] and

[5] For a detailed analysis see P. Kinsch, 'L'application du droit international public par les tribunaux luxembourgeois', Ann. dr. lux., 1993, pages 183 et seq.

[6] C.S.J. (cassation criminelle), 8 June 1950 (*Huberty v MP*), Pas. lux., XV, 41, to be compared, however, with Supreme Court of Justice, 7 March 1917, Pas. lux., X, 285.

[7] C.S.J. (cassation criminelle) 14 July 1954 (*Chambre des Métiers v Pagani*), Pas. lux., XVI, 150.

[8] C.E., 28 July 1951 (*Dieudonné v Administration des Contributions*), Pas. lux., XV, 263. The principle of primacy was extended to Community law by C.E. on 21 November 1984 (*Bellion*), Pas. lux., XXVI, 174.

[9] See P. Pescatore, 'L'autorité, en droit interne, des traités internationaux selon la jurisprudence luxembourgeoise', Pas. lux., XVIII, pages 97 et seq; see the same author's work, 'La prééminence des traités sur la loi interne selon la jurisprudence luxembourgeoise', J.T., 1953, pages 645 and 646 and 'Observations' under judgments of the Supreme Court of Justice, 7 March 1953 (Crim. Appeals), and of 14 July 1954 (cass.) in case *Pagani v MP and Chambres des Métiers* J.T., 1954 pages 696 et seq.; N. Wagner, 'Les réactions de la doctrine à la création du droit par les juges en droit international privé et public', in *Travaux de l'Association Henri Capitant et des amis de la culture juridique française,* Volume XXXI, 1980, pages 437 et seq., especially pages 441 and 442; A. Spielmann, 'D'un certain conformisme à un libre examen certain. (De quelques aspects de la vie juridique)', in *Mémorial 1989, La societé luxembourgeoise de 1893 a 1989 (Luxembourg society from 1839 to 1989),* Luxembourg 1989, pages 93–104, especially pages 103 et seq.; J. Polakiewicz and V. Jacob-Foltzer, 'The European Human Rights Convention in Domestic Law: The Impact of the Strasbourg Case Law in States where Direct Effect is given to the Convention', H.R.L.J., 1991, pages 126–127; for the case-law as a whole, see P. Kinsch, 'L'application du droit international public par les tribunaux luxembourgeois', Ann. dr. lux., 1993, pages 183 et seq.

[10] See in this connection P. Kinsch, 'L'application du droit international public par les tribunaux luxembourgeois', Ann. dr. lux., 1993, pages 221 et seq and the numerous references by the Judicial Committee of the Conseil d'Etat which are cited.

[11] See A. Spielmann and A. Weitzel, n. 1 above, pages 95 et seq. See also D. Spielmann, 'Le juriste luxembourgeois face au system européen de protection des droits de l'homme', F.S.Y., No. 82 (September 1992), pages 7 et seq. However, in a longstanding decision it had already been decided that Article 6 of the Convention was not directly applicable. See Trib. corr. Lux.,

judges apply it to questions which have become routine because they concern a specific international legal system.[12]

C. THE STATUS OF THE CONVENTION IN THE DRAFTING OF LAWS

The Convention and its Protocols frequently serve as a reference in the preparation of laws, as does the case-law of the European Court of Human Rights.

By way of example, a list is given below of a number of laws in the drafting of which the Convention was expressly taken into consideration.[13]

1. *Regarding criminal investigation*

—Review of criminal and correctional trials: Act of 30 April 1981:[14] amended Articles 443 to 447 of the Code of Criminal Procedure, which introduce as a ground for review a decision by the Committee of Ministers of the Council of Europe or a judgment by the European Court of Human Rights;[15]

24 October 1960 (*MP v Von Halem*) mentioned by A. Drzemczewski, *European Human Rights Convention in Domestic Law: A Comparative Study,* Oxford, Clarendon Press, 1983, page 84; Yearbook Vol. 4, 1961, 623. See also D. Spielmann, 'L'exigence du délai raisonnable des Articles 5, 3° et 6, 1° de la Convention européenne des droits de l'homme et la jurisprudence luxembourgeoise', Rev. trim. dr. h., 1991, pages 75 et seq. In the view of Patrick Kinsch, the above-mentioned decision of 24 October 1960 can be regarded as just an 'accident' which no longer corresponds to existing case-law since the European Convention is currently one of the treaties most frequently applied by the courts. See P. Kinsch, 'L'application du droit international public par les tribunaux luxembourgeois', Ann. dr. lux., 1993, page 204.

[12] The expression used by Professor Joe Verhoeven in 'Les réactions de la doctrine à la création du droit par les juges en droit international public, Belgian report, *Travaux de l'Association Henri Capitant (Proceedings of the Henri Capitant Association)*, Vol. XXXI (1980), pages 338 et seq., quoted by P. Kinsch, 'L'application du droit international public par les tribunaux luxembourgeois', Ann. dr. lux., 1993, page 185.

[13] A. Spielmann and A. Weitzel, n. 1 above, pages 153 et seq.

[14] Act of 30 April 1981 on the review of criminal and correctional trials and the compensation to be awarded to victims of miscarriages of justice (Mém. A, 1981, 755).

[15] Article 443 of the Code of Criminal Procedure, as amended by the Act of 5 July 1996 adopting Protocol No. 11 (Mém. A, 1996, 1330) states that:

> Irrespective of the court which delivered the judgment, a review may be requested on behalf of any person found to be the perpetrator of a felony or misdemeanour by a final judgment delivered in the first or last instance.
>
> [. . .]
>
> 5) when a judgment by the European Court of Human Rights pursuant to the Convention for the Protection of Human Rights and Fundamental Freedoms shows that a criminal sentence has been passed in violation of this Convention.

—Compensation in the event of inoperative detention on remand: Act of 30 December 1981;[16]
—Legislation on telephone tapping: Act of 26 November 1982:[17] Articles 88–1, 88–2, 88–3, and 88–4 of the Code of Criminal Procedure;
—Abolition of the Assize Court: Act of 17 June 1987;[18]
—Composition of courts: Act of 16 June 1989:[19] amendment of the first book of the Code of Criminal Procedure.

2. *Regarding civil law*

—Legislation governing the inheritance rights of the surviving spouse and of natural children and amending other provisions of the Civil Code concerning inheritance: Act of 26 April 1979;[20]
—Legislation reforming adoption: Act of 13 June 1989;[21]
—Legislation on the civil liability of the state and of public authorities: Act of 1 September 1988.[22]

3. *Regarding civil and commercial procedure*

—Enabling Act of 25 February 1980;[23]
—Legislation on the preparation of cases for hearing and the New Code of Civil Procedure: Act of 11 August 1996.[24]

16 Act of 30 December 1981 on compensation in the event of inoperative detention on remand (Mém. A, 1981, 2660).

17 Act of 26 November 1982 introducing Articles 88–1, 88–2, 88–3, and 88–4 into the Code of Criminal Procedure (Mém. A, 1982, 2022).

18 Act of 17 June 1987 abolishing the Assize Court and amending powers and procedure regarding the investigation and judgment of offences (Mém. A, 1987, 744).

19 Act of 16 June 1989 amending the first book of the Code of Criminal Procedure and other legal provisions, Mém. A. 1989, 774 and corrigendum (Mém. A, 1989, 1172).

20 Act of 26 April 1979 governing the inheritance rights of the surviving spouse and of natural children and amending other provisions of the Civil Code relating to inheritance (Mém. A, 1979, 743).

21 Act of 13 June 1989 reforming adoption (Mém. A, 1989, 876). See also the Act of 20 December 1993 (Mém. A, 1993, 2189).

22 Act of 1 September 1988 on the civil liability of the state and public authorities (Mém. A, 1988, 1000).

23 Act of 25 February 1980 empowering the government to regulate civil and commercial procedure (Mém. A, 1980, 197).

24 Act of 11 August 1996 on the preparation of cases for hearing in civil litigation proceedings and introducing and amending certain provisions of the Code of Civil Procedure as well as other statutory provisions (Mém. A, 1996, 1660).

4. *Regarding education*

—Legislation on moral and social training: Act of 16 November 1988.[25]

5. *Regarding disciplinary matters*

—Legislation on civil servants: Act of 14 December 1983[26] amending the Act of 16 April 1979;[27]
—Legislation on local government officers: Act of 24 December 1985;[28]
—Legislation on auditors: Act of 28 June 1984;[29]
—Legislation on consulting engineers: Act of 13 December 1989[30] ;
—Legislation on process-servers: Act of 4 December 1990;[31]
—Legislation on lawyers: Act of 10 August 1991.[32]

D. NATIONAL CASE-LAW[33]

The Convention and its Protocols are applied by the courts nearly every day. It is therefore impossible to supply a full list of decisions concerning human rights within the limits of this study. Substantial case-law excerpts are to be found in a work by Alphonse Spielmann and Albert Weitzel (*La Convention européenne des droits de l'homme et le droit luxembourgeois,* Brussels, Nemesis, 1991) and in the case-law reports published in the Council of Europe's Yearbook of the European Convention on Human Rights. Certain decisions are also reproduced in the *Pasicrisie luxembourgeoise (Collection of*

[25] Act of 16 November 1988 amending Articles 48 and 49 of the Act of 10 May 1968 on the reform of education, title VI (secondary education) and Articles 14 and 38 of the Act of 21 May 1979 concerning 1. Organization of vocational training and secondary technical education and 2. Organization of continuing vocational training (Mém. A, 1988, 1216).

[26] Act of 14 December 1983 amending the Act of 16 April 1979 laying down the general conditions of service of civil servants (Mém. A, 1983, 2262).

[27] Mém. A, 1976, 622.

[28] Act of 24 December 1985 laying down the general conditions of service of local government officers (Mém. A, 1985, 1848 and corrigendum, Mém. A, 1986, 648).

[29] Act of 28 June 1984 organizing the profession of auditor (Mém. A, 1984, 1346).

[30] Act of 13 December 1989 organizing the professions of architect and consulting engineer (Mém. A, 1989, 1626).

[31] Act of 4 December 1990 organizing process serving (Mém. A, 1990, 1248).

[32] Act of 10 August 1991 on the profession of law (Mém. A, 1991, 1110).

[33] This section is taken mainly from my contribution entitled 'Le juge luxembourgeois et la Cour européenne des droits de l'homme', in P. Tavernier (ed) *Quelle Europe pour les droits de l'homme? La Cour de Strasbourg et la realisation d'une "Union plus étroite" (35 années de jurisprudence: 1959–1994)'*, Brussels, Bruylant, 1996, pages 293 et seq., which constitutes the Luxembourg report to the colloquy organized by CREDHO (Research and Study Centre for Human Rights and Humanitarian Law) and held at the Law Faculty of Rouen on 11 and 12 May 1995.

Luxembourg Judgments) and since 1993 all decisions by the Luxembourg courts concerning the European Convention on Human Rights and other treaties relating to fundamental rights have been reproduced in the *Bulletin des droits de l'homme*.[34]

It should also be noted that an increasing number of decisions concerning fundamental rights are delivered by administrative courts, mainly the Administrative Tribunal. Excerpts from these decisions are all published in the *Pasicrisie administrative.* They mainly concern Article 8 (right to respect for private and family life in the context of immigration control), Article 13 (right to an effective remedy), and Article 1 of Protocol No. 1 (right to the peaceful enjoyment of possessions in the context of expropriation).

An analysis of the numerous orders and judgments of ordinary courts shows that the most frequently invoked rights protected by the Convention are those embodied in Article 6 (right to a fair hearing),[35] Article 8 (right to respect for private and family life),[36] Article 10 (right to freedom of expression), and Article 1 of the First Additional Protocol (peaceful enjoyment of possessions). In combination with one of the aforementioned rights, the next most frequently invoked right is that of non-discrimination, laid down in Article 14 of the Convention.[37]

The following covers only those decisions which have had the greatest impact on the development of case-law. For the purpose of examining this case-law sample, I have chosen some particularly significant fields in which the courts have broken new ground.

1. Telephone tapping

In 1980 the Cour Supérieure de Justice (Higher Justice Court) curbed the practice of telephone tapping, which was afterwards regulated by legislation.[38] In

[34] Bull. dr. h. 1 (1993), pages 99 et seq.; Bull. dr. h. 2 (1994), pages 84 et seq.; Bull dr. h. 3 (1994), pages 155 et seq.; Bull. dr. h. 4 (1995), pages 130 et seq.; Bull. dr. h. 5 (1996), pages 211 et seq.; Bull. dr. h. 6 (1996), pages 123 et seq.; Bull. dr. h. 7 (1997), pages 236 et seq.; Bull. dr. h. 8 (1998), pages 153 et seq.

[35] According to the established case-law of the Court of Cassation, Article 6 of the Convention constitutes a public policy provision. See Cass., 10 February 1994, No. 7/94, Bull. dr. h. 2 (1994), 111; Cass., 23 March 1995, No. 8/95, concl. J.-Cl. Wiwinius, Bull. dr. h. 4 (1995), 154. In these judgments the Supreme Court decided that this public policy provision 'may be invoked for the first time in appeal proceedings'. See also Appeal Court, 22 May 1992, No. 134/92.

[36] Luxembourg case-law likewise considers that Article 8 of the Convention constitutes a public policy provision. See, for example, C.A., 10 July 1992, No. 190/92.

[37] Article 14 of the Convention prohibits any discrimination in the enjoyment of the rights and freedoms set forth in the Convention and its Protocols. See the note by L. Weitzel under C.E., 7 February 1996, *Radetic*, No. 9233, Bull. dr. h. 7 (1997), 259.

[38] Act of 26 November 1982, Mém. A, 1982, 2022. See also in this connection the Commission's decision of 10 May 1985 on the admissibility of applications Nos. 10439/83, 10440/83, 10441/83, 10452/83, 10512/83, and 10513/83, published *inter alia* in A. Spielmann and A. Weitzel, n. 1 above, pages 143 et seq.; Bull. dr. h. 2 (1994), doc. No. 1.

a leading case decided on 2 April 1980[39] the Indictments Chamber excluded the result of telephone tapping from the case file. At the time such tapping was carried out on the basis of a circular from the Attorney General. The practice therefore had no legal basis, as required by paragraph 2 of Article 8 protecting private and family life. This decision, approved by international doctrine,[40] was subsequently confirmed in other judgments, particularly those of the Indictments Chamber of 10 April, 28 April, and 5 May 1980.[41]

Parliament later regulated this matter by an Act of 26 November 1982.[42]

2. *Freedom of expression and its limits*

a. The principle Referring to Article 10 of the Convention and to the judgment of 7 December 1976 of the European Court of Human Rights in the *Handyside* case,[43] the College Médical (General Medical Council), acting as a disciplinary board, found in a decision of 24 February 1982[44] that criticisms levelled primarily against the public authorities in an article by a female pharmacist were not to be regarded as contrary to professional standing and dignity and did not therefore constitute a disciplinary offence. This decision is an important contribution by a professional tribunal to freedom of expression and shows that the disciplinary board's reasoning was guided by the letter and spirit of the Convention, together with Strasbourg case-law.

b. The limits of the right to inform[45] Another field in which the Luxembourg courts have adopted a guarded approach is that concerning the limits of freedom of expression and the right to inform. Numerous decisions have been delivered in recent years in this area in connection with civil cases involving the question of journalistic responsibility. One of the most difficult problems regarding fundamental rights is to strike the right balance between freedom of expression and the right to respect for private and family life, even the presumption of innocence.[46]

Several judgments deserve particular mention.

[39] C.S.J. (Indictments Chamber), 2 April 1980, J.T., 1980, 489.

[40] See J. Messinne, 'Tendances récentes en droit penal et en procedure penale', in *Mélanges offerts à Robert Legros,* Brussels, ULB, 1985, pages 457 et seq.

[41] C.S.J. (Ind. Ch.), 10 April 1980, 28 April 1980, and 5 May 1980. See in this connection A. Spielmann, *Liberté d'expression ou censure?*, Luxembourg, 1982.

[42] Mém. A, 1982, 2022.

[43] Series A, No. 24.

[44] A. Spielmann and A. Weitzel, n. 1 above, pages 342 and 343.

[45] On the freedom of the press in relation to the protection of privacy, see M. Thewes, 'La presse et la vie privée', F.S.Y., No. 78, (April 1991), pages 5 et seq., and R.G.A.R., 1991, No. 11823.

[46] On the presumption of innocence, see the important judgment of 10 February 1995 by the European Court of Human Rights in the *Allenet de Ribemont* case (Series A No. 308) and my own comments entitled 'Procès équitable et présomption d'innocence', Rev. trim. dr. h., 1995, pages 661 et seq.

The first is a judgment by the Luxembourg district court of 13 July 1988.[47] The facts are fairly straightforward. A daily newspaper published an article describing an individual's participation in a hold-up which resulted in bloodshed and questioning the advisability of having freed the individual from pre-trial detention. It turned out, however, that the person named in the press article had not been involved in the hold-up.

Considering himself calumnied, the person concerned exercised his right of reply and sued both the publisher and the journalist involved, basing his claim particularly on domestic provisions relating to the protection of privacy, the UN Covenant on Civil and Political Rights, and Articles 1382 and 1383 of the Civil Code.[48]

In an excellent statement of reasons, the judgment weighed up the freedom of the press as guaranteed by the Constitution against the principles of liability for negligence, highlighting the established breach of the requirements of veracity and discretion.

With regard to protection of the right to privacy, the court came to a very subtly argued conclusion that respect for this right was required by the Act of 11 August 1982, by Articles 1382 et seq. of the Civil Code, and by Article 8, paragraph 1 of the European Convention on Human Rights, as well as by Article 17 of the above-mentioned United Nations Covenant.

The judgment contained further interesting arguments regarding the public nature of legal hearings and the public delivery of decisions in criminal cases, while stressing that the principle of the public nature of hearings and judgments was not designed to bring every aspect of proceedings unconditionally into the public domain or to reveal the identities of the parties.

Referring to the law on criminal records and the one governing the use of personal data, the judges expressed their opposition to all routine, unconditional publication of judicial convictions in the press. The facts themselves could be related provided the identities of the parties were concealed. Only in the case of extremely serious offences did the judges accept that the perpetrators might exceptionally be deprived of their anonymity, due regard being had to the criterion of proportionality.

The Court also laid emphasis on the state of mind of the person publishing an article. The freedom of the press ceased to apply if the author's intention was malicious.

[47] Luxembourg T.A., 13 July 1988, civ. No. 425/88.

[48] Article 1382 states: 'Every act whatever of man which causes damage to another obliges him by whose fault the damage occurred to repair it' (Zweigert and Kötz, *An Introduction to Comparative Law*, OUP 1998, trans. Tony Weir).

Article 1383 states: 'Everyone is responsible not only for the damage which he has caused by his own act but also for that which he causes by his negligence or imprudence' (ibid).

A second decision to be mentioned in this context is the Appeal Court's judgment of 13 November 1989[49] in which the scope of secrecy of judicial investigations is analysed in relation to the limits to the right to inform.

The Court examined the freedom of the press as provided for in Article 24 of the Constitution and freedom of expression as provided for by Article 10 of European Convention on Human Rights in the light of the principle of the secrecy of judicial investigations and civil liability, as well as the limits to freedom of expression laid down in paragraph 2 of Article 10 of the Convention.

The Court concluded that, in the event of violation of the principle of the secrecy of a judicial investigation, the freedom of the press and freedom of expression could no longer be invoked and the perpetrator of the violation could be held liable in civil law.

In another case involving the liability of journalists, the Court of Cassation, in a judgment of 20 March 1997,[50] rejected, an appeal based, *inter alia*, on Article 10 of the Convention. The appeal was against a judgment delivered by the Appeal Court on 30 January 1996 which had found that a journalist could not evade liability by arguing that the incriminating text he had published merely reproduced a wording already published by someone else, for by effecting such reproduction, which was his own doing, he had taken over the imputation contained in the reproduced wording and thus incurred his own liability. The Court of Cassation concurred with this argument and decided that a journalist who merely quoted an article that had already been published did not escape liability unless he expressly distanced himself from the article and its content and, from the informational point of view, there was good reason to repeat the content of the article to the public.

It should be noted that this case is the subject of an application now pending before the European Court of Human Rights.

c. The limits to the right to information In a number of judgments the Conseil d'Etat refused to endorse the argument put forward by appellants on the basis of the right to receive information in order to request authorization to set up an amateur radio station.[51] The arguments based on Article 10 of the

[49] C.S. J., 13 November 1989, No. 9637 on the case list.

[50] Pas. lux., XXX, 387. [The C.A. judgment of 30 January 1996 is published in Pas. lux., XXX, 23.

[51] This argument was also rejected by the European Commission of Human Rights. See the Commission's decision of 12 April 1996 in the *Schartz v Luxembourg* case, Bull. dr. h. 6 (1996), document No. 5.

Convention were rejected by Conseil d'Etat judgments of 12 May 1992,[52] 2 March 1994,[53] and again on 2 March 1994.[54]

3. The principle of non-discrimination

a. In inheritance matters In inheritance matters, Luxembourg case-law has adopted what is, in my view, a highly progressive approach based on the *Marckx* judgment of the European Court of Human Rights.[55]

For example, in a judgment of 10 November 1980[56] the Luxembourg District Court applied the solution adopted by the European Court of Human Rights in the *Marckx* judgment whereby the former Articles 756 et seq. of the Civil Code were declared contrary to Articles 8 and 14, taken together, of the Convention. The court concluded that the two natural children in question had the same rights to a reserved portion of a deceased's estate as though they were legitimate children. This decision was confirmed by the Appeal Court on 28 November 1983,[57] and an appeal to the Court of Cassation was rejected[58] in a judgment of 17 January 1985.[59]

b. In adoption matters In connection with adoption, mention should be made of a decision of 18 April 1986[60] by the Luxembourg District Court which, referring, in particular to Commission case-law, concluded that insofar as, in accordance with Article 354, paragraph 2 of the Civil Code, Article 349, paragraph 2 of the same Code allowed a child to be removed from the family of its natural father and mother without their consent, the latter provision was contrary to the stipulations of Article 8 of the Convention (private life) and indeed to the similar terms of Article 11, paragraph 3 of the Constitution, under which the state guarantees the natural rights of individuals and families.

[52] *Schartz* judgment No. 8600 published in excerpt form in D. Spielmann, M. Thewes, and L. Reding, *Recueil de jurisprudence administrative du Conseil d'Etat*, (1985–1995), Brussels, Bruylant, 1996.

[53] *Schartz* judgment Nos. 8826 and 8827 published in excerpt form in D. Spielmann, M. Thewes, and L. Reding, n. 52 above.

[54] *Loewen* judgment No. 8743 published in excerpt form in D. Spielmann, M. Thewes, and L. Reding, n. 52 above.

[55] European Court of Human Rights, *Marckx* case, judgment of 13 June 1979, Series A No. 31.

[56] Published in excerpt form in A. Spielmann and A. Weitzel, n. 1 above, page 303.

[57] Published in excerpt form in A. Spielmann and A. Weitzel, n. 1 above, pages 303 et seq.

[58] The Advocate-General, Robert Bendhun, reached contrary conclusions, dated 22 November 1984, which are published in A. Spielmann and A. Weitzel, n. 1 above, pages 307 et seq. He referred *inter alia* to the dissenting opinion—from which he quoted lengthy extracts—of Judge Sir Gerald Fitzmaurice which is attached to the above-mentioned *Marckx* judgment; see also, in this connection, F. Rigaux, 'La loi condamnée', J.T., 1979, pages 513 et seq.

[59] Published in excerpt form in A. Spielmann and A. Weitzel, n. 1 above, pages 320 et seq.

[60] Ibid, pages 323 et seq.

The judgment also found that in the event of a conflict between an international rule and a domestic rule the former takes precedence. In the case under consideration here, Article 349, paragraph 2 of the Civil Code concerning full adoption was excluded.[61] In a similar case, the Supreme Court of Justice, in a judgment of 21 October 1987,[62] adopted the reasoning of the aforementioned judgment.[63]

c. Regarding parental authority As regards the compatibility of the Civil Code's provisions with Articles 8 and 14 of the Convention, the first chamber of the Appeal Court—sitting as an appeal authority in cases decided by the guardianship judge—examined, in an order of 20 October 1993,[64] the compatibility with Articles 8 and 14 of the Convention, of former Article 380 of the Civil Code,[65] assigning parental authority over natural children entirely to the mother where the father and mother have recognized them.

The Appeal Court stated as follows:

> The claim that Article 380 of the Civil Code is incompatible with Articles 8 and 14 of the European Convention on Human Rights, still assuming that this claim is maintained, must be dismissed for the judicious reasons put forward by the lower court, which the Appeal Court endorses and to which should be added the relevant observation made by the representative of the Public Prosecutor's Department in his submissions, namely that even if the treaty is breached by Article 380, the spirit of this rule of international law would at the most imply a joint right of guardianship, which is not part of the claims of (the appellant), who is seeking the exclusive transfer of guardianship to himself.

However, in a judgment of 26 March 1999 (7/99: Mém. A, 1999, 1087) the Constitutional Court declared that Article 380 was inconsistent with the equality principle laid down by Article 11(2).

d. Regarding the right to peaceful enjoyment of possessions In a case concerning an application for the preferential allocation of a number of plots of

[61] The same does not apply in the case of simple adoption.

[62] A. Spielmann and A. Weitzel, n. 1 above, pages 260 et seq. and page 326.

[63] It should be noted that the subject of adoption was reformed by the Act of 13 June 1989 reforming adoption (Mém. A, 1989, 876). See also the Act of 20 December 1993 (Mém. A, 1993, 2189).

[64] Bull. dr. h. 2 (1994), 96.

[65] Former Article 380 of the Civil Code provided:

> Parental authority over the natural child is exercised by either the father or the mother, whichever has voluntarily recognised it, if it has been recognised by only one of them. If both father and mother have recognised the child, parental authority is exercised entirely by the mother. Nevertheless, the guardianship judge may, at the request of either the father or the mother or of the Public Prosecutor's Department, decide that such authority will be exercised either by the father alone or jointly by the father and mother, to whom Articles 375 to 375–2 will then apply as if the child were a legitimate child.

Article 375 the Civil Code stipulates: 'During the marriage the father and mother exercise their authority jointly.'

agricultural land forming part of the estates relinquished by the mother and father of the parties concerned, the defendant raised the question of the compatibility of the relevant provisions of the Civil Code—including Articles 832 et seq.[66]—with the right to peaceful enjoyment of possessions as guaranteed by the Protocol to the Convention.

In a judgment of 2 June 1993[67] the Luxembourg District Court, referring *expressis verbis* to the case of *Inze v Austria*,[68] concluded that Article 1 of the Protocol and Article 14 of the Convention, taken together, had not been breached, as the Luxembourg legislature had not created any discriminatory distinction but, on the contrary, had pursued a legitimate aim.[69]

4. *Immigration law and administrative courts*

The question of immigration control has given rise to an abundance of cases adjudged by the administrative courts.[70]

As already mentioned, the new administrative courts, and especially the administrative tribunal, have in recent years developed a very dense, albeit restrictive, body of case-law relating to Article 8 in the field of expulsion. All decisions are regularly published in extract form in the *Pasiscrisie administrative.*

[66] It should be noted that these provisions were amended/supplemented by the Act of 8 April 1993 relating to the organization of joint ownership and extending preferential allocation in the event of inheritance to include commercial, industrial and craft enterprises (Mém. A, 1993, 574).

[67] Luxembourg T.A., 2 June 1993, No. 483/93, Bull. dr. h. 2 (1994), 89.

[68] This case resulted in a judgment by the European Court of Human Rights of 28 October 1987, Series A No. 126.

[69] This decision is one of the few referring to Strasbourg case-law. It should be compared with the decision of the Luxembourg T.A. 29 January 1986, quoted by A. Spielmann and A. Weitzel, n. 1 above, pages 333 et seq. In that case the court referred to the judgment of 23 July 1968 of the European Court of Human Rights in the *Belgian Linguistic* case (Series A No. 6).

[70] For Conseil d'Etat case-law, see D. Spielmann, M. Thewes, and L. Reding, *Recueil de jurisprudence administrative du Conseil d'Etat* (1985–1995), Brussels, Bruylant, 1996. For the case-law of the administrative courts, see the *Pasicrisie administrative*. See, for ex., C.E., 17 July 1992, *Andrade Ferreira*, Pas. lux., XXVIII, 288. This should be compared with C.E., 13 January 1993, G.V., No. 8731, Bull. dr. h. 1 (1993), 99. Compare also with the judgment concerning the handing over to the government, with a view to expulsion, a person whose name appears in the Schengen data system and the compatibility of this measure with Article 5 of the Convention, where the Conseil d'Etat decided:

> that a measure of 'refoulement' or expulsion cannot be justified solely by reference to the fact that a person's name appears in the Schengen data system under Article 96 of the Convention implementing the Schengen Agreement, as inclusion in that system simply indicates to the other member States that the person in question is prohibited from staying in a country which is a party to the Convention. (C.E., 12 April 1995, *Galambos*, not published).

5. *Composition of courts*

a. In civil matters[71] Article 6 of the Convention lays down, *inter alia*, that a court responsible for ruling on a criminal charge or a dispute concerning civil rights and obligations must be impartial and independent.[72]

Luxembourg courts have conformed with some degree of hesitation to the requirement of this provision and to the interpretation given to it by the European Court of Human Rights in numerous cases, even though they refer only occasionally to Strasbourg case-law.

The following decisions deserve mention.

On 12 May 1989[73] the Luxembourg Industrial Relations Tribunal (Conseil de Prud'hommes) decided that its composition in the case under consideration did not comply with the provisions of Article 6 of the Convention. It declared Article 6 to be applicable to disputes amenable to labour courts. By an order of 20 March 1989, its President had released one of the parties to the case from a ban on receiving unemployment benefit on the ground that the dismissal in question appeared illegal. This fact could arouse in the mind of the defendant, who was responsible for the dismissal, a legitimate doubt about the ability of the Industrial Relations Tribunal in its current composition to judge the dispute impartially.

In a judgment of 21 May 1990[74] the Appeal Court decided that the fact that the president of the Diekirch District Court, sitting as a judge in interim proceedings, had declared an urgent application justified and had subsequently heard the case as president of the civil chamber of the same Court could have aroused a legitimate doubt in the minds of the appellants about the ability of the Diekirch District Court as thus composed to judge the case impartially.

In a judgment of 19 March 1997, however, the Appeal Court decided that the mere fact that the chamber of the district court hearing a divorce petition

[71] See also D. Spielmann, 'La notion de l'impartialité: une application de la théorie de l'apparence', F.S.Y., No. 88 (June 1996), pages 21 et seq.

[72] In a judgment of 10 February 1994, No. 7/94 (Bull. dr. h. 2 (1994), 111), the Court of Cassation stated that the challenging of a mother's right of custody, supervision, and upbringing in respect of her under-age child constitutes a civil right. The Court of Cassation also strongly reaffirmed in this judgment that Article 6 is a public policy provision which can be invoked for the first time before an appeal body. Compare with Cass., 18 March 1993, Bull. dr. h. 1 (1993), 104; C.A. 5 November 1987, No. 337/87, quoted by A. Spielmann and A. Weitzel, n. 1 above, pages 420 et seq.; C.A., 18 December 1987, ibid., pages 425 et seq.; Luxembourg, T.A. 4 March 1987; Luxembourg T.A. 12 February 1990. As regards Article 8 of the Convention and its public policy character, see C.E., 17 July 1992, *Andrade Ferreira*, Pas. lux., XXVIII, 288. As regards Article 2 of Protocol No. 7 and its public policy nature, see Cass., 14 March 1991, unpublished.

[73] Cons. Prud'hommes, Luxembourg, 12 May 1989, Pas. lux., XXVII, 344.

[74] C.A., 21 May 1990, F.S.Y., No. 77 (November 1990), 32, comments by Nothar and Spielmann; also quoted by E. Penning 'Les procédures rapides en matière civile, commerciale et le droit du travail' Bull. Laurent, 1993, No. 2, page 122. See also, as regards supervised management, the Appeal Court judgment of 10 June 1992, Pas. lux., XXVIII, 319.

was presided over by the judge who had issued an interim order between the same parties on provisional measures during the divorce proceedings was insufficient to raise objectively justified doubt in the minds of the parties about the ability of the chamber of the district court to hear the case impartially.[75]

In a judgment of 18 February 1998 the Appeal Court decided that the successive exercise by a judge in one and the same case of identical judicial functions, such as participating in a judgment by default and then in the judgment following appeal, or in an interlocutory judgment and then in the judgment on the merits, was not contrary to the requirement of objective impartiality laid down in Article 6, paragraph 1 of the Convention for the Protection of Human Rights and Fundamental Freedoms. The successive exercise of different judicial functions by a judge in the same case, or the judge's prior participation in a similar or related procedure, might possibly warrant the defendant's doubting the ability of the judge and of the court to which he belonged to reach an impartial decision. An attempt should therefore be made to see whether the functions previously exercised by the judge belonging to the court and the decision taken were liable to make the defendant fear that the judge would be reluctant to change his mind and thus, together with the court on which he sat, fail to offer adequate guarantees of impartiality. The fact that a judgment on a claim for the recovery of maintenance payments unduly paid was delivered by a panel of judges including the judge who had ordered the allocation of such payments was not contrary to the requirement of objective impartiality laid down in Article 6, paragraph 1 of the Convention for the Protection of Human Rights and Fundamental Freedoms.[76]

In a judgment of 10 June 1992[77] the Appeal Court decided that the impartiality requirement was not met by a court which rejected an application for the supervised management provided for in the Grand-Ducal Decree of 24 May 1935 after it had delegated its chamber president (who had expressed a negative opinion on the justification for the application) to report back to it on the applicant's commercial standing.

In a judgment of 27 October 1993[78] the Appeal Court held that, in the procedure for winding up companies, the fact that the duties of bankruptcy judge and president of the court of first instance were combined did not breach Article 6, paragraph 1 concerning the requirement for an impartial and independent tribunal. What was at issue was the fact that the bankruptcy judge had submitted a written report to the court and that, after the company had

[75] C.A., 19 March 1997, Pas. lux., XXX, 400.
[76] C.A., 18 February 1998, Pas. lux., XXX, 445.
[77] *Johansson and Associates* case, Pas. lux., XXVIII, 319.
[78] Judgment No. 506/93.

been put into liquidation and had intervened through its liquidators in the proceedings pending, he had submitted a further report to the court on behalf of the company. The Appeal Court noted that the bankruptcy judge had not taken up a position in these reports but had simply informed the court about the situation. The Appeal Court also said that the mere fact that the president of the chamber of the district court dealing with the case as the court of first instance had simultaneously acted as bankruptcy judge responsible for submitting the reports did not necessarily mean a lack of independence and impartiality on her part.[79]

In a judgment of 30 March 1995[80] the Court of Cassation decided that the fact that the Social Insurance Arbitration Board included a chairman and a member who had previously heard the same case and participated in a decision to reject the application concerned could awaken a legitimate doubt in the applicant's mind about the fitness of the Social Insurance Arbitration Board as thus composed to judge the case impartially.

It should further be noted that in a judgment of 12 January 1995[81] the Court of Cassation decided that judges subject to a challenge must refrain from taking part in the decision on the challenge, on pain of breaching Article 6 of the Convention.[82]

b. In criminal matters Decisions are much more numerous in criminal matters.[83] It is impossible to mention them all in this study. It should be pointed out, however, that before the introduction by the Act of 16 June 1989[84] of Article 64–1 into the administration of justice, trial courts were divided concerning the application of the 'independence and impartiality' requirements of Article 6 of the Convention.[85]

[79] Cf C.A., 20 September 1989 (*Le Foyer v Gonner*), unpublished, concerning a request for the execution of an insurance policy contracted by the bankrupt, which had been lodged by the administrator of the said bankruptcy, and C.A., 20 September 1989 (*Schleich v Schiltz*), unpublished, concerning an application for extension of bankruptcy.

[80] No. 19/95. Bull. dr. h. 4 (1995), 158. See also the conclusions of Deputy Attorney General Emile Penning.

[81] Pas. lux., XXIX, 338 and Bull. dr. h. 4 (1995), 143.

[82] The case concerned the vice-chairman of the Social Insurance Arbitration Board.

[83] An excellent overview of the case-law is supplied by Advocate-General J.-Cl. Wiwinius in his unpublished conclusions preceding the judgment of the Court of Cassation of 23 March 1995, No. 8/95, Bull. dr. h. 4 (1995) 154.

[84] Mém. A, 1989, 773. Article 64–1 states:

> The investigating judge may not validly take part in the judgment of cases he investigated. The same applies to:
> —court judges who, as members of the chamber of the district court or appeal court, previously ordered indictment to the trial court or ruled on the release of the accused;
> —officials of the Public Prosecutor's Department who are appointed as judges or advisers and who previously made, or caused to be made, submissions in the case.

[85] J.-Cl. Wiwinius, n. 83 above. For an application of Article 6, para. 1 of the Convention, see the decisions of the Sup. Court of Justice of 17 December 1985, No. 343/85, of 3 October 1986,

In two judgments of 26 February 1987[86] and 23 February 1989[87] the Court of Cassation settled the matter by opting for the setting aside of decisions on the merits by courts which had previously accepted an *indication of guilt* against the accused at the preliminary investigation stage.[88]

The Court of Cassation again confirmed this approach in a judgment of 9 March 1989[89] with respect to a judge who had previously made submissions in his capacity as deputy public prosecutor[90] to the police court dealing with the case at first instance.

As we have seen, Luxembourg case-law has proved very demanding in terms of the independence and impartiality of criminal judges.

However, in a case where the Appeal Court initially gave a decision in private, in accordance with Article 116(6) of the Code of Criminal Procedure, concerning an application for provisional release, which was also rejected because

No. 228/86, and of the Luxembourg District Court of 10 November 1986, No. 1565/86. *Contra,* C.S.J. 12 June 1986, No. 138/86, of 13 December 1988, No. 9/88, and of 3 February 1989 (regarding closure of an establishment); T.A. Diekirch, 2 May 1986, No. 173/86 and T.A. Luxembourg, 29 October 1986, No. 1472/86.

[86] Pas. lux., XXVII, 2, regarding indictment. Still regarding indictment, see the judgment of the Appeal Court of 17 December 1985 (A. Spielmann and A. Weitzel, n. 1 above, pages 349 et seq.), which established a breach of Article 6 on the basis of the judgment of the European Court of Human Rights of 1 October 1982 in the *Piersack* case (Series A No. 53) and its judgment of 26 October 1984 in the *De Cubber* case (Series A No. 86). In a subsequent judgment of the Appeal Court of 3 October 1986 (A. Spielmann and A. Weitzel, n. 1 above, pages 361 et seq.) the judges based themselves indirectly on the judgment of the European Court of Human Rights of 17 January 1970 in the *Delcourt* case (Series A No. 11) and its judgment of 10 July 1984 in the *Guincho* case (Series A No. 81) in order to establish the violation of Article 6. The question was settled by the Court of Cassation in its previously mentioned judgment of 26 February 1987.

[87] No. 5/89 crim., regarding provisional release. Compare with two judgments of the criminal chamber of the Appeal Court of 20 March 1989, No. 3/89, and 2 October 1989, No. 14/89. These judgments came, respectively, before and after the entry into force of the Act of 16 June 1989. It is interesting to note that the criminal chamber of the Appeal Court found, in its aforementioned judgment of 20 March 1989, that an objection had not been raised by the accused during the proceedings, that the accused had not doubted the impartiality of the judges, and that they had not been afraid of any prejudice towards them; it rejected the application for reference back submitted by the public prosecutor's department. In the second judgment mentioned, that of 2 October 1989, and in the light of new Article 64–1, which prohibits a judge who, as a member of the chamber, had previously decided on the release of the accused from participating in the judgment of the case, the Court decided that the judgment was invalid. This approach seems to suggest that the introduction of a domestic law provision in order to bring legislation into line with Article 6 attaches public policy status to the already existing principle.

[88] See also Cass., 23 March 1995, No. 8/95 (Bull. dr. h. 4 (1995), 154) concerning appeal judges who decided on the merits of the case after previously rejecting, in the Appeal Court chamber, an application for lifting a driving ban (imposed at first instance on the person concerned owing to 'his high alcohol level' and 'his irresponsible and highly dangerous manner of driving'), whereas the charges underlying the two appeals were the same. In this judgment the Court of Cassation found a breach of Article 6 and quashed the appeal judgment.

[89] No. 6/89 crim.

[90] The case-law of the Court of Cassation is therefore well established. See also the judgment of 23 March 1995, No. 8/95 crim., (Bull. dr. h. 4 (1995), 154) regarding the provisional driving ban.

there was a *serious indication of guilt,* at a time when it was already dealing with merits of the case, and subsequently as a trial court, with partly the same membership, the Court of Cassation did not find any breach of the accused's rights to an impartial court within the meaning of Article 6, paragraph 1.[91]

Moreover, a unique case gave rise to an Appeal Court judgment of 4 June 1996[92] establishing the existence of a breach of Article 6 as a result of a judge having had contact with a prosecution witness during the proceedings.

6. *Penalization of unreasonable delay*

Luxembourg case-law refuses to penalize non-observance of the 'reasonable time' requirement in Article 6 of the European Convention on Human Rights by declaring the procedures concerned inadmissible.[93]

Nevertheless, under a practice that may already be described as established, the 'reasonable time' requirement in Article 6, paragraph 1 of the Convention constitutes a mandatory rule which is directly applicable in domestic law and is of a public policy nature in terms of due process. Thus, by a decision of 15 July 1993[94] the Luxembourg Correctional Court, referring to established Belgian case-law under which the consequences of exceeding the reasonable time must be examined, on one hand, from the point of view of evidence, and on the other, from the point of view of the potential criminal penalty,[95] held that if cases were not of a complex nature they did not justify any delays, and it therefore found that the reasonable time laid down in Article 6, paragraph 1 of the European Convention on Human Rights had been exceeded.

The inference drawn by the court was that the penalties imposed on the defendants should be mitigated by a stay of their execution.[96]

[91] Cass., 14 March 1991, Pas. lux., XXVIII, 135. See also T.A. Luxembourg, 3 November 1993, Bull. dr. h. 2 (1994), pages 101 et seq. and comments. See also Cass., 6 January 1994, No. 2/94, Bull. dr. h. 4 (1995), 130.

[92] No. 256/96, Bull. dr. h. 6 (1996), 135 and R.D.P. 1997, 111 and case-note.

[93] C.S.J. (Indictment Chamber), 13 February 1987, (A. Spielmann and A Weitzel, n. 1 above, pages 400 et seq.) and my own study, 'L'exigence du délai raisonnable des Articles 5,3 et 6,1 de la Convention européenne des droits de l'homme et la jurisprudence luxembourgeoise', Rev. trim. dr. h., 1991, pages 77 et seq.

[94] T.A. Luxembourg, (9th crim. chamb.), 15 July 1993, Bull. dr. h. 1 (1993), 113; R.D.P., 1994, 917.

[95] Cass. b., 24 January 1990, Pas., 1990, I, 607; Cass. b., 27 May 1990, R.D.P., 1992, 998.

[96] T.A. Luxembourg, (9th crim. chamb.), 15 July 1993, Bull. dr. h. 1 (1993), 113; R.D.P., 1994, 917; along the same lines, T.A. Luxembourg, 14 March 1995, Bull. dr. h. 4 (1995), 146; C.A., 28 January 1997, No. 46/97, Bull. dr. h. 7 (1997), 269. Compare with C.A., 12 July 1994, Bull. dr. h. 3 (1994), 170, and C.A., 21 February 1995, Judgment No. 95/95 V., Bull. dr. h. 6 (1996), 127. In this judgment of 21 February 1995 the Appeal Court expressed the following view:

> For cases which the law itself regards as of limited importance, particularly by virtue of the severity of the sentences applicable and the relevant limitation period, and which are unlikely to impair the moral and physical condition of the accused, the limitation period is sufficient to determine the time-limit by which the judgment must reasonably take place.

In my view, this approach constitutes a fine example of the effectiveness which domestic courts confer on a Convention provision that has no direct penalizing force.

7. Right of appeal

Article 2 of Protocol No. 7 to the European Convention on Human Rights enshrines the right of appeal in criminal matters.

In a leading case decided on 21 December 1992, the criminal chamber of the Appeal Court of the Grand Duchy of Luxembourg held that:

> A transfer order that leads the appeal court to decide on a point of fact or law not examined at the lower level deprives the persons concerned of their right to have the matter judged, at least as regards its substantive aspect, by a higher authority.[97]

It referred the case back to the trial court after setting aside its judgment, refusing to employ the transfer order procedure provided for in Article 215 of the Code of Criminal Procedure.[98]

In the context of the right of appeal in criminal matters but with regard to persons subject to jurisdiction privilege, it is regrettable that, in its decision of 8 December 1993,[99] the European Commission on Human Rights decided

[97] Published summary of the Appeal Court (crim. ch.), 21 December 1992, J.T., 1993, 268, case-note by D. Spielmann.

[98] It should be noted that in this case the first-instance judgment was set aside on the ground of inadequate reasoning. On this point the Appeal Court expressed the following view:

> It is necessary to set aside on the ground of inadequate reasoning a decision of a trial court which limited itself to a statement of the facts without clearly indicating either the legal classification of the individual participation in the offence which is the subject of the proceedings or the ingredients of the shared guilt or complicity. (Published summary).

Regarding this case, see my note, 'Evocation et double degré de juridiction' J.T., 1993, pages 269 et seq., as well as my article 'Les mouvements de réforme de la procédure penale et la protection des droits de l'homme' R.D.P., 1993, pages 984 et seq., in particular page 992. See also C.A., 4 June 1996, Nos. 256/96, Bull. dr. h. 6 (1996), 135 and R.D.P. 1997, 111 and case-note. It would seem, however, that referring back to the first-instance court in the event of the setting aside of a judgment by the Appeal Court cannot be made a general practice. Indeed, hopes for the universalization of the solution adopted in the judgment of 21 December 1992 were soon dashed. Thus, in an unpublished judgment of 28 March 1995 (Judgment No. 146/95 V.) the Appeal Court, fifth chamber, sitting in a correctional case, annulled a judgment of the Luxembourg District Court, criminal section, of 16 November 1994, on the ground that that court had imposed an illegal sentence, and ordered the case to be brought before itself. It is true that the setting aside of a judgment on the ground of inadequate reasoning is not based on the same consideration as setting aside for the imposition of an illegal penalty. However, for reasons of legal logic and out of regard for the right of appeal, the setting aside of a first-instance judgment by an appeal court should result in reference back. Regarding the case law prior to the judgment of 21 December 1992, see A. Spielmann, 'Des récentes réformes du Code d'instruction criminelle luxembourgeois. Un bilan de six ans' R.D.P., 1993, pages 951 et seq.

[99] Application 19715/92, *X v Luxembourg*; Bull. dr. h. 1 (1993), pages 92 and 93, critical note P.K.

that an appeal on a point of law was an adequate remedy for the Convention's purposes.[100]

8. *Trial* in absentia

a. In a judgment of 31 March 1993 of the Luxembourg District Court,[101] the judges based themselves particularly on the *Colozza and Rubinat* judgment of 12 February 1985 of the European Court of Human Rights[102] in deciding that:

although this is not expressly mentioned in paragraph 1 of Article 6, the object and purpose of the Article as a whole show that a person 'charged with a criminal offence' is entitled to take part in the hearing (European Court of Human Rights, *Colozza* Judgment of 12 February 1985, Series A No. 89, page 14, paragraph 27).

The right of the individual charged to take part in the hearing in person, as stated or implied by these texts, is not, however, absolute.

On one hand, it is a general principle of judicial procedure that a defendant may not evade the jurisdiction of a competent court by simply refusing to take part in the proceedings against him and that a competent court may in such a situation deliver a judgment *in absentia* (see European Commission on Human Rights, report on the state of the procedure, 5 October 1970, '*Second Greek*' case, paragraph 18, quoted by Gerard Cohen-Jonathan, The European Convention on Human Rights, Economica, 1989, page 43, in the context of default by a state). On the other hand the impossibility of a procedure *in absentia* is liable to paralyse the conduct of criminal proceedings by leading, for example, to tampering with the evidence, the statute-barring of the offence, or a miscarriage of justice (European Court of Human Rights, *Colozza* Judgment, op. cit., page 15, paragraph 29).

The occurrence of a procedure *in absentia* is not therefore *ipso facto* contrary to the rights recognized by the texts concerned.

The rights in question are respected, first, if the person 'charged' has been informed of the proceedings initiated against him before the judgment *in absentia* was delivered, so that he was in a position to attend the hearing of the competent court which decided on those proceedings.

The rights concerned are also respected if the person charged who is sentenced *in absentia*, even if unaware of the proceedings against him, has an opportunity, once he is informed of the proceedings, to ensure that a court decides again, after hearing him, on the merits of the charge against him. (European Court of Human Rights, *Colozza* Judgment, op. cit., loc. cit.).

The Court therefore reached the conclusion that the relevant rules of Luxembourg criminal procedure met the above-mentioned criteria, as the accused was served, or given notice of, the hearing in advance of the summons

[100] Even though Article 53 of the Convention allows the Contracting Parties, at least as far as *laws* are concerned, to go further than the Convention in the protection of individual rights.
[101] No. 632/93, Bull. dr. h. 1 (1993), 106.
[102] Series A No. 89.

to appear and had the right to lodge an objection in the event of a judgment *in absentia*.[103]

b. In a judgment of 6 January 1994 the Court of Cassation ruled that the fact that the criminal chamber to which the case had been transferred owing to the accused's objection was composed of the same judges as that which had previously rejected his application for an adjournment and delivered the judgment *in absentia* against him was not such as to give rise to any legitimate distrust in the chamber's impartiality.[104]

c. With regard to automatic bankruptcy without preliminary formalities once the conditions regarding the trader are satisfied, it has been ruled that Article 6 of the Convention does not demand that it be possible to exercise the right to submit one's defence before any judicial decision. The requirement of a fair trial is thus met if the objector has an opportunity to put forward his grounds of defence under the objection procedure.[105]

9. *Application of the Convention between private individuals*[106]

Certain decisions accept, at least implicitly, that the Convention may even affect purely private relations.[107] An example is a judgment of the Luxembourg Appeal Court of 10 July 1992[108] concerning video and tape recordings made by

[103] Compare C.A., 1 October 1987, quoted by A. Spielmann and A. Weitzel, n. 1 above, pages 381 and 382 and Cass. b., 3 February 1987, Pas. 1987, I, page 646. Compare also T.A., Luxembourg, 15 July 1993, (Bull. dr. h. 1 (1993), 117) with regard to direct summons (*citation directe*).

[104] Cass., 6 January 1994, Pas. lux., XXIX, 277. Note, in the commercial field and as regards an application for the interpretation of a decision submitted to the same judges, the absence of a breach of Article 6 of the Convention, as established by the Appeal Court, 7 February 1996, Bull. dr. h. 7 (1997), 257. Compare, as regards social security, Cass., 30 March 1995, No. 19/95, Bull. dr. h. 4 (1995), 158.

[105] See T.A. Luxembourg, 23 December 1988, No. 499/88. Compare Belgian case-law, particularly Cass., 27 April 1989, Pas., 1989, I, 906. See also the new wording of Article 442, paragraph 1 of the Commercial Code, resulting from the Act of 21 July 1992 adapting the rules on bankruptcies, introducing a new definition of commercial transactions and creating the offence of misuse of company property (Mém. A, 1992, 1898). On this Act, see the study by G. Stein and J. Nies, 'Aspects nouveaux du droit de la faillite', Bull. Laurent, 1994, pages 139 et seq.

[106] Regarding this problem in Luxembourg case-law, see D. Spielmann, *L'effet potentiel de la Convention européenne des droits de l'homme entre personnes privées* Brussels, Bruylant, Nemesis, 1995, pages 44 et seq., and my article, 'L'effet potentiel entre personnes privées de la Convention européenne de sauvegarde de droits de l'homme et des libertés fondamentales' Bull dr. h. 3 (1994), pages 25 et seq., especially pages 50 et seq. See, too, my article 'Obligations positives et effet horizontal des dispositions de la Convention' in F. Sudre (ed), *L'interprétation de la Convention européenne de droits de l'homme*, Brussels, Nemesis, Bruyland, 1998, pages 133 et seq.

[107] Three trends may be observed in the case-law: decisions which expressly reject any reflex effect, those that implicitly accept such an effect, and those that explicitly accept that effect. Regarding this distinction, see L. Weitzel, note under C.A., 13 November 1996, No. 17029, Bull. dr. h. 7 (1997), page 265.

[108] Yearbook, Vol. 35, 1992, 461, quoted by L. Weitzel, Bull. dr. h. 7 (1997), page 268. See also D. Spielmann, 'Obligations positives et effet horizontal des dispositions de la Convention', in F. Sudre (ed), *L'interprétation de la Convention européenne de droits de l'homme*, Brussels, Nemesis, Bruylant, 1998, pages 133 et seq.

a private employer without the knowledge of a female employee at her work place who, as a result of these recordings, was prosecuted for 'theft by a member of the household'. The Court expressed the following view:

> The person charged rightly protests against the recordings secretly made by the management of company T in order to monitor her behaviour and institute legal proceedings, as such methods do not meet the conditions on which interference in an individual's private life is permissible under Article 8, paragraph 2 of the Convention. These methods necessarily constitute a violation of the right guaranteed by Article 8, paragraph 1.
>
> Moreover, such investigations by private individuals without any judicial supervision offer no guarantee that the recordings were made fairly or that they are complete or authentic; they therefore seriously prejudice the interests of the defence. It was in order to prevent such abuses that Parliament, in passing the Act of 26 November 1982 allowing public authorities to interfere in a person's private life, subjected any departure from the protection rule set out in Article 8 of the Convention to strict conditions.
>
> It follows from the foregoing that the evidence collected by the complainant by means of secret recordings may not be used against the defendant and must be set aside. The same applies to the examinations carried out by the officers who reported the alleged offence as well as to subsequent investigative measures based either directly or indirectly on the illicitly obtained evidence.

Regarding the press, certain courts have imposed obligations on journalists on the basis of Article 8 of the Convention, which protects private and family life.[109] These obligations may also be defined by reference to the limitations prescribed in paragraph 2 of Article 10 of the Convention.[110] Adopting a similar approach, the Luxembourg Appeal Court, in a judgment of 13 November 1989, analysed *inter alia* Article 10 of the Human Rights Convention in relation to Articles 1382 and 1383 of the Civil Code.[111]

10. Inapplicability of the guarantees of a fair trial to investigating courts

In accordance with established practice, the chambers of the Appeal Court and of the district court persist in asserting that Article 6 does not apply to investigating courts.[112]

[109] T.A. Luxembourg, 13 July 1988, Pas. lux., XXVII, 368; T.A. Luxembourg, 27 May 1992, No. 357, unpublished; see also P. Kinsch, 'L'application du droit international public par les tribunaux luxembourgeois', Ann. dr. lux., 1993, page 207; D. Spielmann, 'Le juriste luxembourgeois face au système européen de protection des droits de l'homme', F.S.Y., No. 82 (1992), pages 7 et seq., especially pages 31–32.

[110] C.A., 13 November 1989, (*Cepal SA v Paul Bever*), No. 9637. Liability in tort may thus be used as a corrective.

[111] See n. 48 above for the text of Articles 1382 and 1383.

[112] See, for example C.A. (indictments chamber), 30 January 1991, (*MP v Schreiner*). For a case in which the indictment chamber of the Appeal Court itself ruled on the merits of a criminal charge, see the judgment of 2 February 1993 (*MP v Krieps*), Bull. dr. h. 1 (1993), page 101. Compare with the order of the T.A. Luxembourg (indictments chamber), 28 April 1993, Bull. dr.

This unfortunate approach in respect of investigating courts has been endorsed by the Court of Cassation,[113] and I believe that a reversal of case-law is necessary in this field, especially as the European Court of Human Rights has ruled that in certain circumstances Article 6 of the Convention does apply to preliminary investigations in criminal matters.[114]

E. CASE-LAW OF THE EUROPEAN COMMISSION AND COURT OF HUMAN RIGHTS

The only case brought before the European Court of Human Rights against Luxembourg prior to the entry into force of Protocol No. 11 was the *Procola* case, which is commented on below.

At the time of writing this chapter (March 1999), a good twenty applications are pending before the single permanent Court.

Many of the Commission's inadmissibility decisions in respect of applications against Luxembourg are published in extract form in a work by A. Spielmann and A. Weitzel, *La Convention européenne de droits de l'homme et le droit luxembourgeois* (Brussels, Nemesis, 1991, pages 107 et seq.) and since 1993 in the *Bulletin des Droits de l'Homme*. Among these numerous decisions mention may be made of the telephone-tapping case which involved the aforementioned Act of 26 November 1982. The Commission declared the application inadmissible by a decision of 10 May 1985.[115]

h. 2 (1994), page 84. On this question, see R. Nothar and D. Spielmann, 'L'applicabilité de l'article 6.1 de la Convention européenne de sauvegarde des droits de l'homme et des libertés fondamentales aux juridictions d'instruction', Bull. Laurent, 1989, (Bulletin IV), pages 83 et seq.

[113] Cass., 17 January 1985, (*Declerck v MP*), in the field of international letters rogatory; Cass., 16 January 1986, (*Berns v MP*); Cass., 27 February 1986, (*Linden v MP*); Cass., 11 May 1989, (*Armand v MP*) Bull. Laurent, 1989, (Bulletin IV), 83, case-note Nothar and Spielmann.

[114] European Court of Human Rights, *Imbroscia v Switzerland*, judgment of 24 November 1993, Series A No. 275 and J.T., 1994, 495, obs. P. Lambert, 'L'article 6.1 de la Convention européenne des droits de l'homme et les juridictions d'instruction', *John Murray v United Kingdom*, judgment of 8 February 1996, Reports of Judgments and Decisions, 1996–I, 30; *Miailhe (No. 2) v France*, judgment of 26 September 1996, Reports of Judgments and Decisions, 1996–IV, 1319, *Tejedor García v Spain*, judgment of 16 December 1997, Reports of Judgments and Decisions, 1997–VIII, 2782. See also the Commission's case-law along the same lines. See, for example, the decision of the second chamber of 11 May 1994, Application 19219/91, *Martini and Simioni v Switzerland* (Bull. dr. h. 3 (1994), 118, note L. Weitzel). The recent case-law of the Belgian Court of Cassation follows the same lines. For the latest case-law, see Cass., 24 October 1997, J.L.M.B., 1998, 1324, obs. F. Kuty, 'Encore un arrêt encourageant . . . vers le principe de l'applicabilité de l'article 6 de la Convention européenne des droits de l'homme à la phase preparatoire du procès penal'.

[115] Applications 10439/83, 10440/83, 10441/83, 10452/83, 10512/83, and 10513/83, published *inter alia* in A. Spielmann and A. Weitzel, n. 1 above, pages 143 et seq. and in Bull. dr. h. 2 (1994), doc. No. 1.

The most important case, which gave rise to a judgment concerning Luxembourg delivered by the European Court of Human Rights, is that of *Procola*. The facts may be summarized as follows.[116]

Procola was a dairy constituted as an agricultural association under Luxembourg law. Its registered office was at Ingeldorf. Following the introduction of the milk quota system by EEC Regulations Nos. 856/84 and 857/84 of 31 March 1984, Luxembourg adopted, by a Grand-Ducal Regulation of 3 October 1984, the provisions incorporating the Community rules into domestic law. A number of ministerial orders were issued on 10 October 1984, allocating reference quantities for milk purchases to the four milk purchasers in the Grand Duchy; the quantities were based on the figures for milk collected in 1981.

Procola and two other purchasers appealed to the Judicial Committee of the Conseil d'Etat against the decisions fixing the reference quantities. Before ruling on the merits, the Judicial Committee referred a number of questions to the Court of Justice of the European Communities for a preliminary ruling.

In the light of the answers given by the Court of Justice, the Judicial Committee set aside the contested decisions on 26 February 1987, on the ground that the choice of 1981 as the reference year for calculating the quotas had led to discrimination between purchasers, contrary to the EEC Treaty. The case was referred to the State Secretary for Agriculture for a fairer apportionment of the reference quantities among the four dairies.

On 27 May 1987 the State Secretary submitted a new draft Grand-Ducal regulation on which the Conseil d'Etat expressed an opinion on 2 July. The latter proposed certain amendments and submitted a draft law giving the future regulation retroactive effect from 2 April 1984, the date on which the milk quota system had come into force in the European Community countries. After certain amendments, the draft regulation became the Grand-Ducal Regulation of 7 July 1987, and the draft law became the Act of 27 August 1987.

In pursuance of these two instruments, the State Secretary issued four min-

[116] See D. Spielmann, 'Le Conseil d'Etat luxembourgeois après l'arrêt Procola de la Cour européenne des droits de l'homme', Rev. trim. dr. h. 1996, pages 275 et seq.; M. Thewes and D. Spielmann, 'Le contentieux administratif luxembourgeois après l'arrêt Procola', Luxemburger Wort of 6, 7, 9, and 10 October 1995; M. Thewes, 'Le Conseil d'Etat luxembourgeois après l'arrêt Procola de la Cour européenne des droits de l'homme', Rev. belge dr. const., 1996, pages 69 et seq. See also the proceedings of the symposium of 13 January 1996 concerning the Conseil d'Etat and administrative courts, containing reports by P. Kinsch, G. Ravarani, D. Spielmann, M. Thewes, F. Schockweiler, and F. Delaporte, F.S.Y., No. 88 (June 1996).

isterial orders dated 21 September 1987, fixing Procola's quotas retroactively for each of the four milk-production years starting from 2 April 1984.

Procola appealed again to the Judicial Committee for the ministerial orders of 21 September 1987 to be set aside, alleging *inter alia* the unlawfulness of applying the regulation of 7 July 1987 retrospectively. The Judicial Committee dismissed the applications in a judgment of 6 July 1988.

On 22 November 1988 the appellant together with other individual appellants applied to the European Commission on Human Rights, the body which ruled on the admissibility of petitions and submitted a report, where appropriate, to the European Court.

By its admissibility decision of 1 July 1993, the Commission accepted the complaint based on Article 6 of the Convention, while excluding the individual applicants from the procedure and declaring inadmissible the complaints based on Article 7, paragraph 1 of the Convention (non-retroactivity of laws in criminal matters) and Article 1 of the Protocol to the Convention (right to peaceful enjoyment of possessions). The European Court of Human Rights delivered its judgment on 28 September 1995.[117] The most difficult question concerned the applicability of Article 6 of the Convention.

Article 6, paragraph 1 of the Convention provides as follows:

> In the determination of his civil rights and obligations or of any criminal charge against him, everyone is entitled to a fair and public hearing within a reasonable time by an independent and impartial tribunal established by law . . .

As regards the determination of a right, the government maintained that there was no dispute concerning a right, as the appeal to the Judicial Committee of the Conseil d'Etat was an 'objective' one and the application could not have led to any result affecting the applicant's financial position.

In its judgment of 28 September 1995 the Court, basing itself on its previous practice,[118] observed that before the Judicial Committee the parties had been in conflict over whether the ministerial orders fixing milk quantities could be given retroactive effect. Procola had maintained that for the years 1984–1987 no levy had been payable owing to the setting aside of the previous rules and the impossibility of making the orders retroactive, whereas the agent of the state had maintained that the orders were lawful. According to the Court, the applicant's case was sufficiently tenable as the Conseil d'Etat had conducted a detailed examination of the conflicting arguments. The Court therefore decided that there was a dispute concerning the determination of a right.

[117] Series A No. 326.

[118] See *Neves* and *Silva v Portugal*, judgments of 27 April 1989, Series A No. 153–A, page 14, para. 37, and *Editions Periscope v France*, judgment of 26 March 1992, Series A No. 234–B, page 65, para. 38.

Whether the disputed right was a civil one was also a delicate one question. The Court had no difficulty in accepting that this disputed right possessed the characteristics of a civil right, pointing out that Article 6, paragraph 1 was applicable where an action was 'pecuniary' in nature and was founded on an alleged infringement of rights which were likewise pecuniary rights, notwithstanding the origin of the dispute and the fact that the administrative courts had jurisdiction.[119]

In order to satisfy itself that the proceedings were decisive for a civil right, the Court considered it necessary to look at the proceedings as a whole. By appealing to the Conseil d'Etat, Procola had been using the only means at its disposal—an indirect one—for attempting to obtain reimbursement of the additional levies. Having regard to the close connection between the proceedings brought by Procola and the consequences their outcome might have had for one of its pecuniary rights, and for its economic activities in general, the right in question was a civil one.[120] In any event, the Court added, the payment of an additional levy to the national authorities could be construed as a deprivation of possessions within the meaning of the first paragraph of Article 1 of Protocol No. 1, and the right to peaceful enjoyment of one's possessions was undoubtedly a civil right.[121]

Having concluded that Article 6 of the Convention was applicable, the Court expressed the view that in the instant case it was not necessary to determine whether the Judicial Committee was an independent tribunal. The applicant had not put in doubt the method of appointing the Conseil d'Etat's members and the length of their terms of office or questioned that there were safeguards against extraneous pressure. On the other hand, the European Court of Human Rights did find the Conseil d'Etat lacked impartiality in the instant case and stated the following:

45. The Court notes that four members of the Conseil d'Etat carried out both advisory and judicial functions in the same case. In the context of an institution such as Luxembourg's *Conseil d'Etat* the mere fact that certain persons successively performed these two types of function in respect of the same decisions is capable of

[119] See also the previous case-law, *Editions Periscope v France*, judgment of 26 March 1992, Series A No. 234–B, page 66, para. 40, and *Beaumartin v France*, judgment of 24 November 1994, Series A No. 296–B, pages 60–61, para. 28.

[120] See in this connection also *Editions Periscope v France*, *Beaumartin v France*, n. 119 above; *Ortenberg v Austria*, judgment of 25 November 1994, No. 295–B, pages 48–49, para. 28; as well as, by implication, the *Van de Hurk v Netherlands* judgment of 19 April 1994, Series A No. 288, page 16, para. 43.

[121] The Commission had decided in its decision on admissibility of 1 July 1993 that the case came under Article 1 of Protocol No. 1, even though the conditions laid down by the second sentence of Article 1 of the Protocol were met, and had concluded in its opinion of 6 July 1994 that the appeal lodged to Conseil d'Etat did not concern a 'determination of [a] civil right' within the meaning of Article 6, para. 1 of the Convention. The decision is published in Bull. dr. h. 1 (1993), doc. No. 2, while the report is reproduced in Bull. dr. h. 3 (1994), doc. No. 3.

casting doubt on the institution's structural impartiality. In the instant case, Procola had legitimate grounds for fearing that the members of the Judicial Committee had felt bound by the opinion previously given. That doubt in itself, however slight its justification, is sufficient to vitiate the impartiality of the tribunal in question, and this makes it unnecessary for the Court to look into the other aspects of the complaint.
46. It follows that there has been a breach of Article 6 § 1.

F. THE EFFECT OF JUDGMENTS OF THE EUROPEAN COURT OF HUMAN RIGHTS

The rapid and spectacular legislative reform that has occurred since the judgment in *Procola v Luxembourg* of 28 September 1995 is noteworthy.

The European Court of Human Rights has ruled that the mere fact that certain persons successively exercise, in connection with the same decisions, advisory and judicial functions—in the present case, within the Luxembourg Conseil d'Etat—is likely to jeopardize the structural impartiality of the institution concerned.

By an Act of 27 October 1995[122] the Luxembourg Parliament amended the Act of 8 February 1961 on the organization of the Conseil d'Etat by enlarging the Judicial Committee with five substitute members, so that members would not sit in cases concerning the application of statutory provisions in respect of which they had taken part in the deliberations of the Conseil d'Etat. This interim solution was replaced by the effect of the constitutional and legislative amendment of 12 July 1996, which completely reformed administrative procedure by creating new administrative courts, namely the Administrative Tribunal and the Administrative Court.

Four separate Acts were passed on 12 July 1996, namely an Act revising Article 83 *bis* of the Constitution,[123] an Act revising Article 95 of the

[122] Mém. A, 1995, 2060. See also Resolution DH (96) 19, adopted by the Committee of Ministers on 9 February 1996 at the 556th meeting of Ministers' Deputies 'concerning the judgment of the European Court of Human Rights of 28 September 1995 in the case of *Procola against Luxembourg*', together with an appendix containing information provided by the Government of Luxembourg during the examination of the *Procola* case by the Committee of Ministers, Bull. dr. h. 7 (1997), doc No. 8. It should be noted that the Luxembourg government had introduced in May 1994—ie before the *Procola* judgment—a draft law aimed at reforming the Conseil d'Etat. On the temporary solution and its sequel, see D. Spielmann, 'Le Conseil d'Etat luxembourgeois après l'arrêt Procola de la Cour européenne des droits de l'homme', Rev. trim. dr. h., 1996, pages 275 et seq.; M. Thewes and D. Spielmann, 'Le contentieux administratif luxembourgeois après l'arrêt Procola', Luxemburger Wort of 6, 7, 9, and 10 October 1995; M. Thewes, 'Le Conseil d'Etat luxembourgeois après l'arrêt Procola de la Cour européenne des droits de l'homme', Rev. belge dr. const., 1996, pages 69 et seq.

[123] Mém. A, 1996, 1318.

Constitution,[124] an Act reforming the Conseil d'Etat,[125] and an Act amending the Act of 27 October 1995 amending the amended Act of 8 February 1961 organizing the Conseil d'Etat.[126] These four Acts were followed by an Act of 7 November 1996 organizing the administrative courts.[127]

For the effects of the European Court's judgments on case-law, reference should be made to section D above.

G. ASSESSMENT

Luxembourg case-law concerning the Convention is extremely extensive, as litigants frequently resort to arguments based on fundamental rights. The Luxembourg legislature also draws on the principles of the Convention, as proved by the non-exhaustive list given in this report. It is therefore not surprising that potential or even actual violations of the Convention and its Protocols can be rectified at national level. It is accordingly understandable that, as we have seen, the European Court has delivered only one judgment against Luxembourg; and following the adverse judgment of 28 September 1995 in the *Procola* case, the Luxembourg Parliament immediately put in hand the reforms of administrative procedure demanded by that judgment.

In my view, however, one problem has still be to settled by legislation, namely the jurisdiction privilege of higher office, whereby several categories of persons (members of the government, judges, and police officers) are deprived of their right of appeal in criminal cases, in breach of Article 2 of Protocol No. 7.[128]

[124] Mém. A, 1996, 1318.

[125] Mém. A, 1996, 1319.

[126] Mém. A, 1996, 1324.

[127] Mém. A, 1996, 2262. For an initial assessment of administrative procedure following this reform, see M. Elvinger, 'Le contentieux administratif luxembourgeois après la loi du 7 novembre 1996 "portant organisation des juridictions de l'ordre administratif"' *Mélanges dédiés à la mémoire de Fernand Schockweiler*, Bull. Laurent, 1998–IV, pp. 63 et seq.

[128] On these cases, see D. Spielmann, 'Le droit au double degré de juridiction en matière pénale dans le systeme européen de protection des droits de l'homme', Bull. Laurent, 1991 (Bulletin IV), pages 1 et seq. and the position taken by J.-M. Hengen, Bull. Laurent, 1993, (Bulletin III), pages 45 et seq. See also J. Lemmer, 'Le double degré de juridiction en matière pénale et les droits de l'homme', Bull. dr. h. 7 (1997), pages 109 et seq.

22

Malta

JOSEPH SAID PULLICINO

A. THE HISTORY OF HUMAN RIGHTS IN MALTA

With the advent of British rule in 1800, the Maltese legal system became exposed to new and perhaps more liberal ideas. The independence of the judiciary, trial by jury in criminal matters, the presumption of innocence of the accused, freedom from arrest without prompt trial (*habeas corpus*), the rule of law, and the equality of all before the law, aimed at ensuring speedy and impartial justice: in Malta these notions have their origin in the first fifty years of British rule.

On 25 March 1802 the Treaty of Amiens was signed, by virtue of which Malta was to revert to the Order of St John. When this came to the knowledge of the Congress the leaders of the people re-assembled and drew up a Declaration of the Rights of the Inhabitants of the Islands of Malta and Gozo. After declaring that the King of the United Kingdom of Great Britain and Ireland was to be considered as the Sovereign Lord of Malta, Congress provided that the King had no right to cede the islands to any new power. The Declaration, signed in Malta on 15 June 1802, affirmed that:

> Free men have a right to choose their own religion. Toleration of other religions is therefore established as a right; but no sect is permitted to molest, insult or disturb those of other religious sentiments [. . .] That no man whatsoever has any personal authority over the life, property or liberty of another. Power resides only in the law, and restraint, or punishment, can only be exercised in obedience to law.

Thus, it is evident that the representatives of the people had already envisaged the Constitution as being an inviolable charter.

On 23 October 1953 the British government, after acceding to the European Convention on Human Rights, extended its applicability to forty-two territories, including Malta, for whose international relations it was responsible at the time. However, since the Convention was not adopted as part of the municipal law of Britain it had very limited application in Malta.

Although the vicissitudes of the constitutional development of Malta were remarkable, especially in view of the fact that from 1813 to 1964 twelve Constitutions were promulgated, it was only in 1961 that another formal and written declaration of rights was provided for. Notwithstanding, in the interval other documents ensured the protection of human rights in an indirect manner. For example, the promulgation of the *Costituzione della Corte Criminale* in 1814 provided for the abolition of all forms of torture, the protection of persons who were being charged before the courts, the publicity of the trial, and the right of the accused to defend himself.

The 1961 Constitution, based on the Blood Commission's recommendations and commonly referred to as the Blood Constitution, had as its source the Nigerian Constitution of 1960, which in turn was based on the European Convention on Human Rights and on the Sierra Leone Constitution of 1961. It provided for a Bill of Rights laid down in general terms, and a mechanism for redress when a person's rights were violated or threatened with violation.[1] Article 5 of this Constitution asserted the entitlement of every person in Malta to the fundamental rights and freedoms of the individual, which rights are to be enjoyed subject to respect for the rights and freedoms of others and the public interest. The fundamental rights were described as being the right to:

(a) Life, liberty, security of the person and protection of the law;
(b) freedom of conscience, of expression and of assembly and association; and
(c) protection for the privacy of his home and other property and from deprivation of property without compensation.

On 21 September 1964 Malta acquired its independence.[2] This saw the enactment of the Malta Independence Act 1964, the instrument which legally gave independence to Malta, and the Malta Independence Order 1964, which incorporated the Independence Constitution. In the words of the then Prime Minister Borg Olivier:

[1] 'Similar provisions had in fact found their way into several other recent Commonwealth provisions': Prof. J. J. Cremona, *The Maltese Constitution and Constitutional History Since 1813*, Malta, 2nd edn, 1997, p. 69).

[2] The Malta Independence Act, 1964 provided in particular for the cessation of all responsibility of the United Kingdom government for the affairs of Malta, the abrogation of the United Kingdom Parliament's power to make laws extending to Malta as part of Maltese law, the termination of the application to Maltese legislation of the Colonial Laws Validity Act, 1865, the conferment on the Maltese Parliament of full power to make laws with extraterritorial effect and the abolition of the repugnancy rule, to give the Maltese Parliament power to make laws inconsistent with United Kingdom legislation extending to Malta, including the Independence Act itself, but subject in the latter case to the Constitution. The Constitution was envisaged as the ultimate and supreme legal principle at the apex of the nation's justice order: ibid, pp. 75–76.

The Constitution which we envisage incorporates the principle of responsible parliamentary government based on a tested democratic system. It safeguards the interests of the nation and the fundamental rights and freedoms of the individuals composing the nation. It secures the independence of such organs and authorities as must be outside political influence. It reaffirms the political sovereignty of the electorate by ensuring the holding of free elections as fixed intervals.[3]

The 1964 Constitution in Chapter IV contains an extensive and judicially enforceable bill of rights, largely based on the model of the European Convention on Human Rights. The provisions contained in the 1961 Constitution were in substance retained and also amplified. New clauses which were introduced provided for non-discrimination,[4] protection of freedom of movement, and the restriction of deportation of Maltese citizens.[5]

Other protected rights are: the right to life and security of the person, privacy of the home and other property, freedom of expression, the right to a fair trial, freedom of association and peaceful assembly, the right not to be subjected to inhuman and degrading treatment, nor to arbitrary arrest. The Constitution also provides for particular instances which legitimize derogations from the observance of these rights, for example: in the interest of public safety, public order, public morality or decency, public health, or the protection of rights and freedoms of others. Such measures have to be prescribed by law and must be 'reasonably justifiable in a democratic society.' Thus, although the Constitution acknowledged the fact that there cannot be a state of absolute liberty, it has not left the question of the limitation of such human rights entirely to the courts; it defines the scope of the limitations in each and every right, and requires that such limitations should be contained in a law or done under the authority of a law.

The Constitution also provides for the judicial enforcement of these rights. The courts are vested with the power to take cognizance of human rights cases and to grant the individuals concerned an effective remedy where it is found that their rights have been violated or are threatened. The legislator also stipulated that the Constitution is the supreme law of the land, thereby ensuring the prevalence of the Constitution over other laws.[6] Thus, unlike the Westminster Parliament, in Malta the House of Representatives is not supreme as it is subject to the Constitution. Furthermore, the amendment or repeal of the

[3] The Malta Independence Conference held in Marlborough House, London, 16 July 1963.

[4] An amendment was introduced by Act XIX of 1991 whereby protection was afforded from discrimination on grounds of sex, race, place of origin, political opinions, colour, and creed.

[5] This latter provision was inspired by the deportation from Malta during World War II of a number of Maltese citizens, without trial.

[6] Subject to the provisions of subsections (7) and (9) of section 47 and of section 66 of this Constitution, if any other law is inconsistent with this Constitution, this Constitution shall prevail and the other law shall, to the extent of the inconsistency be void (Article 6).

provisions regulating the fundamental rights and freedoms require a two-thirds majority of all members of the House of Representatives, unlike ordinary legislation.

On 19 August 1987 the European Convention on Human Rights became part of Maltese law when the European Convention Act[7] came into force. This legislation was:

> An Act to make provision for the substantive articles of the European Convention on Human Rights for the Protection of Human Rights and Fundamental Freedoms, to become and be enforceable as, part of the law of Malta.

The incorporation of the Convention in domestic law was deemed necessary as it provided for broader rights to the individual. A few months prior to the enactment of the European Convention Act, Parliament granted to all persons within the Maltese jurisdictional boundaries the right to petition the Strasbourg organs. Furthermore, it acknowledged the jurisdiction of the European Court of Human Rights for a period of five years, with effect from 1 May 1987.

The actual ratification of the European Convention on Human Rights and four of its Protocols took place on 12 December 1966 and 25 January 1967 respectively. Although Malta was a Contracting Party to the European Convention, no individual falling under the jurisdiction of Malta could invoke the provisions of the Convention either before the local authorities or before the Convention organs. According to established constitutional practice in Malta, the power to make laws is vested in Parliament, and this power is exercised by bills passed by the House of Representatives and published in the Government Gazette as Acts of Parliament, after assent by the President. Since our legal system is based on dualist principles, any international treaty cannot be said to form part of domestic law until it is incorporated in legislation. This established practice was confirmed by the enactment of the Ratification of Treaties Act in 1983[8] which provides:

> No provision of a treaty shall become, or be enforceable as part of the law of Malta except by or under an Act of Parliament.

Thus, before 1987 the rights and freedoms laid down in the European Convention on Human Rights were not enforceable in a local court.

Act XIV of 1987 stipulates that where an ordinary law is inconsistent with the Convention's protective provisions the Convention shall prevail, and such law shall, to the extent of the inconsistency, be void. Section 2 defines 'ordinary law' as 'any instrument having the force of law and any unwritten rule of law, other than the Constitution of Malta'. In a revolutionary judgment

[7] Act No. XIV of 1987. [8] Act No. V of 1983.

delivered by the Constitutional Court in the case of *Lawrence Pullicino v Commanding Officer Armed Forces of Malta nomine et al.*[9] the Court dealt with the issue whether a domestic law which is in conformity with the Constitution, but in conflict with the European Convention, is to be applied or disregarded. The point in issue was a provision in the Maltese Criminal Code which prohibited the granting of bail to persons accused of homicide. The applicant argued that this provision was in breach of the European Convention. The Constitutional Court held that a domestic law, although not contrary to the Constitution, is inapplicable if it conflicts with the provisions of the European Convention. Thus, the Constitutional Court ruled that the refusal of bail to applicant violated his fundamental rights as guaranteed under Article 5 of the European Convention.

Even prior to the enactment of Act XIV of 1987, the Constitutional Court would refer to decisions of the European Court of Human Rights and the European Commission on Human Rights. In the case of *Cecil Pace v Dom Mintoff nomine*[10] the Constitutional Court held that Article 34(3) of the Maltese Constitution,[11] which deals with the maxmimum length of time which is to elapse between the moment of arrest and passing of the verdict, corresponds to Article 5(3) of the European Convention. In passing judgment the Constitutional Court referred to various opinions delivered by the European Commission of Human Rights in this respect. Other judgments delivered by the Constitutional Court are *Emanuel Formosa v Commissioner of Police*[12] and *Vincent Ellul Sullivan et nomine v Housing Secretary.*[13]

The scope of Act XIV of 1987 was two-fold:

(1) the incorporation of the fundamental freedoms and rights as set out in Articles 3 to 18 of the Convention and Articles 1 to 3 of the First Protocol as part of Maltese law. It also provides for the supremacy of its provisions over ordinary law where the latter is inconsistent with such rights and freedoms, and

[9] 12 April 1989.

[10] 10 June 1966.

[11] Article 34(3):

Any person who is arrested or detained—(a) for the purpose of bringing him before a court in execution of the order of a court; or (b) upon reasonable suspicion of his having committed, or being about to commit, a criminal offence, and who is not released, shall be brought not later than forty-eight hours before a court; and if any person arrested or detained in such a case as is mentioned in paragraph (b) of this subsection is not tried within a reasonable time, then, without prejudice to any further proceedings which may be brought against him, he shall be released either unconditionally or upon reasonable conditions, including in particular such conditions as are reasonably necessary to ensure that he appears at a later date for trial or for proceedings preliminary to trial.

[12] 9 April 1973.

[13] 16 April 1973.

(2) to make judgments delivered by the European Court of Human Rights directly enforceable locally by the Constitutional Court of Malta.[14]

Furthermore, notwithstanding the similarity of the provisions found in the Constitution and those contained in the Convention, one should remember that the latter is an international agreement between sovereign states, binding themselves to follow certain rules in the treatment of their own nationals. Thus, it would be safe to state that the rules of interpretation are different from those relating to human rights provisions in national constitutions, in the sense that the former should be interpreted more restrictively.

Although prior to the enactment of Act XIV of 1987 the European Convention did not form part of Maltese ordinary law, throughout the years its impact was evident. Through the enactment of Act XIV of 1987, the safeguarding of rights and freedoms of individuals was extended. For example, Article 45 of the Constitution guarantees protection from discrimination on grounds of race, place of origin, political opinions, colour, creed, or sex. The grounds listed are exhaustive. On the other hand, Article 14 of the European Convention provides an illustrative list of the grounds on which discriminatory treatment would not be justified. This distinction was confirmed in the case of *Walter Cuschieri et al. v Prime Minister et al.*, decided by the Constitutional Court.[15] The Court held that the grounds of discrimination as listed in the Maltese Constitution, similar to other foreign Constitutions, are restrictive in nature. Thus, if there is any other ground or consideration for the differential treatment besides those prohibited by the particular section, the discrimination will not be unconstitutional.

Similarly, in the Maltese Constitution the right to marriage is not a fundamental right. In Act XIV of 1987, by means of which the European Convention became part of Maltese law, it is stipulated that 'men and women of marriageable age have the right to marry and found a family' (Article 12). In the case of *Raymond Gilford v Prime Minister et al.*, decided by the First Hall of the Civil Court,[16] the Court held that in 1987, for the first time, the right to marry was included as a fundamental right under Maltese law.

Another area which has broadened the spectrum of individual rights is that concerning forced labour. Article 35(1) of the Constitution provides that 'No person shall be required to perform forced labour'. On the other hand, Article 4(2) of the European Convention Act protects the individual against both forced and compulsory labour. In 1977 an amendment to the Medical Kindred Professions Ordinance[17] provided that no private clinic or hospital

[14] Judgments delivered by the European Court of Human Rights are enforced by the filing of an application in the Constitutional Court and served on the Attorney General containing a demand that the enforcement of such judgment be ordered (Article 6 of Act XIV of 1987).

[15] 30 November 1977. [16] 22 April 1997. [17] Ordinance XVII of 1901.

could employ a doctor in government service unless so authorized by the Minister of Health. This authorization was granted only if the doctor would sign a declaration that he would accept to work in government hospitals. In the case of *Walter Cuschieri v Prime Minister* decided by the Constitutional Court in the same year, applicants contended that this provision constituted an imposition of forced labour. Reference was made to decisions delivered by the European Commission where forced or compulsory labour was said to consist of work that a person is compelled to do against his will, in unjust or oppressive conditions, accompanied by unnecessary harsh treatment. However, the Court distinguished between the wording of the Constitution and the European Convention on Human Rights, and held that the phrase compulsory labour had a wider interpretation than forced labour. The Court held that the term compulsory labour was apt to describe certain forms of indirect compulsion to work. The condition being imposed on doctors was interpreted to be compulsory labour, a protection not guaranteed under the Constitution.

Although local courts have referred to Strasbourg case-law in delivering judgments dealing with human rights issues, particularly after the enactment of the European Convention Act, they are still not bound by such decisions as the doctrine of precedent does not form part of our law. Thus, in the case of *Colin J. Trundell v Minister of Foreign Affairs et al.*, decided by the Constitutional Court,[18] it was held that the right to a fair trial was also applicable in extradition proceedings. This conclusion was reached on the basis of local extradition law, which imposes on the Court a duty to inform the person who is facing extradition proceedings of his human rights, as guaranteed under the Constitution, and of the right to file an application in Court if he is of the view that his rights have been violated.

Similarly, up to 1993, although certain laws (Criminal Code, Code of Police Laws, Code of Organization and Civil Procedure, Commercial Code, and the Civil Code) could contain certain provisions which were inconsistent with the provisions laid down in the Constitution concerning human rights, they were granted immunity. However, according to Article 3(2) of the European Convention Act:

> where any ordinary law is inconsistent with the Human Rights and Fundamental Freedoms, the said . . . shall prevail, and such ordinary law, shall, to the extent of the inconsistency, be void.

In the case of *Lorry Sant v Commissioner of Police*, decided by the Civil Court, First Hall,[19] the applicant alleged that his right to a fair trial was breached as his trial was being heard by a magistrate who had carried out the

[18] 22 April 1991. [19] 15 December 1989.

preliminary investigations. Although this situation was permitted under the Criminal Code, the applicant alleged that it constituted a violation of Article 6 of the European Convention Act. The Court found in favour of the applicant and therefore ruled in favour of the provisions of the European Convention Act as against the Criminal Code. Thus, although the above-mentioned Codes were exempted from the provisions of Chapter IV of the Constitution, they could nonetheless be challenged on the basis of the Convention.

An interesting situation would be where the provisions of the European Convention Act are in conflict with the Constitution. To date no such issue has arisen before our courts, and the occurrence of such a situation seems unlikely in view of the fact that the source of our human rights provisions is the Convention itself. Notwithstanding, in 1987 the government of the day held that in cases of incompatibility and inconsistency the Constitution would prevail as the supreme law of the land. This was also the view expressed in a number of court judgments, amongst which are *Rosaria Cassar v Permanent Secretary for Housing et al.*, decided by the Civil Court, First Hall[20] and *Louis Vassallo et al. v Prime Minister nomine*, decided by the Constitutional Court.[21] Reference was made to the case of *Marbury v Madison* where it was held that:

> if a Constitution claims by its terms to limit the powers of the institutions it creates, including the legislature, its provisions must surely be regarded as of superior force to any rules or actions issuing from those institutions. To think otherwise reduces a Constitution and the business of Constitution-making to nonsense.[22]

During the parliamentary debates which preceded the enactment of Act XIV of 1987, it was argued that if a human right as expressed in the Constitution had a more limited extension than as expressed in the Convention, the latter should prevail once it became part of Maltese law. It was stressed that the principle should always be that the human rights provisions with the more extensive definition should prevail.[22]

[20] 8 February 1988.

[21] 27 February 1978.

[22] It is true that under domestic law the Constitution remains supreme in the sense that, in the case of inconsistency with the Convention provisions, it is the Constitution that prevails (sections 2 and 3 of the Act). But then whenever, after the exhaustion of domestic remedies, a case is taken to Strasbourg (Malta made the relevant declarations under articles 25 and 46 of the Convention on the 1st May 1987), the European Court of Human Rights applies of course the Convention alone, and by the same 1987 Act its judgments are in fact enforceable in Malta as if they were judgments of the Constitutional Court: Prof. J. J. Cremona, n. 1 above, p. 84.

B. THE CONSTITUTIONAL COURT AS A GUARDIAN OF HUMAN RIGHTS

An independent judiciary is an indispensable requisite of a free society under the rule of law. This implies freedom from interference by the executive or the legislature with the exercise of the judicial function.

The Civil Court, First Hall has original jurisdiction in Malta to hear and determine applications alleging the breach of an individual's fundamental human rights. However, according to Article 46(2) of the Constitution the Court may:

if it considers it desirable so to do, decline to exercise its powers under this subsection in any case where it is satisfied that adequate means of redress for the contravention alleged are or have been available to the person concerned under any other law. (Emphasis added.)

The wording is very different to that found in Article 26 of the European Convention on Human Rights, which stipulates: 'The Commission may only deal with the matter after all domestic remedies have been exhausted'.

When it is clear that the applicant has ordinary remedies at his disposal, the applicant must exhaust these remedies prior to filing a constitutional application. However, in terms of Article 46(2) of the Constitution, where the applicant has not made use of such a remedy, this does not necessarily mean that the Court is bound to decline jurisdiction to take cognizance of the case. This would be the case, for example, where the remedy available would only provide a partial remedy to the complaint of the applicant (as in the case of *Mario Vella v Joseph Bannister nomine*, decided by the Constitutional Court.[23]) It is contended that the legislator conferred such a wide discretion on the Court in the interest of the better administration of justice. In this way, applicants are precluded from filing unnecessary constitutional proceedings, while those applicants who have a genuine interest in seeking a constitutional remedy can exercise their right without being hindered by unnecessary legal obstacles.

In the case of *Joseph Arena nomine v Commissioner of Police et al.*,[24] the Constitutional Court held that there was no provision in the Constitution which expressly or implicitly required that the remedies available under ordinary legislation necessarily had to be exhausted in order for the court to exercise its constitutional jurisdiction. While it is obvious that a constitutional application is the ultimate judicial remedy, the right to a constitutional remedy is not subject to such a condition. It is not correct to argue that an aggrieved party can refer his complaint to the Constitutional Court if and

[23] 7 March 1994. [24] 16 November 1998.

until the ordinary remedies are exhausted. The Court further held that even in respect of proceedings for the safeguard of human rights under the European Convention, there may be special circumstances in which the applicant is freed from the obligation to exhaust domestic remedies even though the same may be adequate and effective. The European Commission itself held that there may exist circumstances where it is not reasonable to apply this rule in a rigid manner.

The Constitutional Court is the highest court in the hierarchical system in Malta. This Court was originally composed of the Chief Justice and four other judges. Its constitution is guaranteed by the Constitution and the relevant provisions cannot be amended without a two-thirds majority vote of all members of the House of Representatives.

The Court is entrusted with the function of securing the enjoyment of the freedoms and rights of individuals, and thus a central support for democracy. The Constitution provides for the automatic setting up of the Constitutional Court, thereby ensuring that the highest judicial organ, entrusted with the duty of ensuring the safeguarding and enforcement of the people's constitutionally protected rights, is able to function at all times. Article 95(6) of the Constitution provides that if for any reason the Constitutional Court is not constituted according to law, the three most senior judges, including where possible the Chief Justice, would automatically assume the powers and jurisdiction of the Constitutional Court without the need for any further formality or appointment. This amendment to the Constitution was introduced following a constitutional crisis in the 1970s when the Constitutional Court was suspended for a number of months.

The main argument against setting up a separate Constitutional Court is the danger of its politicization. Under Maltese law the appointment of judges who will sit in the Constitutional Court does not in any way guarantee the representation of political tendencies. This notwithstanding that it is the President of Malta who has the duty of assigning to judges the chambers of the court in which they are to serve. Upon taking office the members of the judicature are by law and custom expected to sever any political affiliations or connections.

The Constitutional Court may well be described as the guardian of the Constitution. It acts above and beyond changes which occur in the political arena. It is completely insulated from political control, including that by government, parliaments, and the pressure of political parties and interest groups.

Of its nature, the Constitutional Court is an appellate court. It hears and decides appeals from decisions of the First Hall of the Civil Court on applications for redress in respect of alleged violations of the human rights protected by the Constitution and by the European Convention on Human Rights. It also considers appeals from decisions of any court of original jurisdiction on questions as to the interpretation of the Constitution and the validity of laws. However, it also exercises an ordinary jurisdiction in determining questions as to whether a member of the House of Representatives has been validly elected, or whether any member is bound by law to cease from performing his duties as a member of the House. It has jurisdiction in deciding over the validity or otherwise of a general election which has been suspended by the Electoral Commission, for example where it is believed that illicit practices have occurred.

The procedural mechanism is regulated by the Court Practice and Procedure Rules of 1993. The application must state clearly and concisely the circumstances out of which the appeal arises, the reasons of appeal, and a prayer for the reversal or a specific variation of the decision appealed from. Time-limits and procedures for filing, service on the respondent to file a reply, and for the date of hearing or its abridgment, are also to be stipulated.[25] In almost all the cases in which the Constitutional Court must rule, there exists a previous judgment which has been delivered by another judicial organ.

Furthermore, if while proceedings are pending in any court other than the First Hall of the Civil Court or the Constitutional Court, an issue arises as to the breach of a fundamental freedom and right of any one of the parties to the proceedings, then that particular court is bound by law to refer the issue to the First Hall of the Civil Court. This referral is made as long as the issue raised is not frivolous or vexatious. The Court would be bound to order such a referral upon the satisfaction of the following conditions:

(a) proceedings are pending before a court;
(b) such proceedings are not pending before the First Hall of the Civil Court or the Constitutional Court;
(c) the issue must be raised during the proceedings;
(d) the issue must refer to an alleged breach of any one of the provisions of Articles 33 to 45 of the Constitution which regulate the fundamental freedoms and rights of individuals; and
(e) the raising of the issue must not be frivolous or vexatious.

[25] Legal Notice 35 of 1993 entitled Regulations Regarding Practices and Procedures of the Courts provides:

> The application to appeal (in the Constitutional Court) shall be made within eight working days from the date of the decision appealed from, and the respondent may file a written reply within six working days from the date of service. The Court which gave a decision subject to appeal to the Constitutional Court may in urgent cases upon demand, even by any of the parties immediately upon delivery of such decision, abridge the time for making the appeal or for filing a reply.

This interpretation has been extended by case-law to breaches of the fundamental human rights contemplated by Act XIV of 1987.

The scope of this provision is to limit the procrastination of judicial proceedings especially as regards issues which of their very nature are frivolous and vexatious. Thus, the law aims at doing away with delaying tactics.

It is pertinent to note that this procedure operates as a stay of proceedings, whereby the decision in the Constitutional proceedings will be binding upon the court referring the question, be it a court of first or second instance.

Where a referral has taken place and the court determines for example that a provision of the law is contrary to the Constitution, the legislator must remedy this unconstitutionality by enacting new legislation.[26]

C. HUMAN RIGHTS CASES DECIDED BY NATIONAL COURTS

The Constitutional Court has throughout this last decade considered several applications in which the European Convention on Human Rights has been invoked by the applicant. The following areas of law have been examined by the Constitutional Court.

1. The right to privacy

Article 8(1) of the European Convention provides that 'Everyone has the right to respect for his private and family life, his home, and his correspondence'.

In this regard Article 38 of the Constitution is more restrictive in its wording and provides that 'no person shall be subjected to the search of his person or his property or the entry by others on his premises'.

The inviolability of an individual's home is but one aspect of the wider and much more complex concept of the right to privacy. Nowadays, domestic legislation aims at safeguarding other aspects such as non-disclosure of professional secrets, and secrecy of telegraphic correspondence.

[26] Article 242 of the Code of Organization and Civil Procedure (Chapter 12 of the Laws of Malta) stipulates:

> When a court, by a judgment which has become *res judicata*, declares any provision of any law to run counter to any provision of the Constitution of Malta or to any human right or fundamental freedom set out in the First Schedule to the European Convention Act, or to be *ultra vires*, the registrar shall send a copy of the said judgment to the Speaker of the House of Representatives, who shall during the first sitting of the House following the receipt of such judgment inform the House of such receipt and lay a copy of the judgment on the table of the House.

a. The legal acknowledgement of transsexuality A number of cases have come before the local courts dealing with this aspect.

To date, only one issue relating to transsexuality has been dealt with by the local courts. This relates to the allegation of breach of respect for private life, resulting from the lack of procedure for changing the sex and name on the original birth certificate. In *Lawrence k/a Roxanne Cassar v Prime Minister*[27] the Court examined the case in the light of principles established in the case-law of the European Court. The Court considered that the decision depended on the fair balance that had to be struck between the general interest of the community and the interests of the individual. As a result, controls by the state which seek to establish the identity of the individual inevitably restrict the area of privacy of the individual. The Court concluded that the original entry in the birth certificate did not in itself amount to a breach of Article 8, as merely historical facts were recorded therein. However, it ordered an annotation in the birth certificate, to the effect that the applicant had by means of surgery acquired the female sex.

A more recent judgment was delivered by the First Hall of the Civil Court in the case of *Raymond Gilford k/a Rachel Gilford v Director of the Public Registry*.[28] The Court recognized the fact that the right to privacy consists essentially in the right to live one's own life with a minimum of interference. The Court considered that there was nothing in the law which prohibited a person from undergoing a gender re-assignment operation. Thus, should not the state provide the measures necessary so that a person could enjoy his or her newly achieved sexual identity?

The Court ordered that the birth certificate should indicate the present physical state of the applicant. However, due to the serious implications which a change in the indication of sex on a person's birth certificate may have, the Court further ordered that the Director of the Public Registry include a note on the birth certificate stating that the change was effected in terms of a judgment delivered by the Court after applicant had undergone gender re-assignment surgery. The Court argued that in certain circumstances society was entitled to be aware of the change in the birth certificate, since it could be a relevant and determining factor, for example if the applicant decided to contract marriage. It is pertinent to note that the case is still pending final judgment before the Constitutional Court.

b. The right to respect for family life In the *Martin Vella* case[29] the Constitutional Court considered the adoption of illegitimate children. According to Section 115(3) of the Civil Code[30] the adoption of a legitimate

[27] Constitutional Court, 14 July 1995. [28] 22 April 1997. [29] 22 April 1991.
[30] Chapter 16 of the Laws of Malta.

child is possible only if there is mutual consent of both parents. This does not apply to illegitimate children where the mother's consent suffices: the natural father is merely entitled to be heard by the court.

The Constitutional Court held that although applicant was objecting to the adoption of his illegitimate daughter, it considered that if the minor were adopted she would acquire the status of legitimacy. The Court emphasized that the first and paramount consideration is the welfare of the child to which other considerations must be subordinate. Although nowadays we speak of equality between legitimate and illegitimate children, the Court expressed the view that it would be preferable for a child to be brought up in a legitimate family.

It is interesting to note that the reasoning adopted by the Court reveals that it considered that in the field of fundamental human rights there are diverse situations of conflict between the fundamental rights of different persons who find themselves in conflicting relations. These conflicts have to be resolved by an examination of the hierarchy of those same rights.

Notwithstanding its decision the Court confirmed certain principles established by the European Court, including:

(i) the notion of family in terms of Article 8 is not solely confined to marriage-based relationships;
(ii) a child born out of wedlock is *ipso jure* part of that family unit from birth;
(iii) between the child and his parents there is from the very outset a bond amounting to family life even though at the time of birth the parents may no longer be cohabiting;
(iv) respect for family life requires that biological and social reality prevail over a legal presumption.

c. Entry and search by the police The entry by police and certain other public officers onto private premises is envisaged in the Criminal Code[31] and other laws such as the Customs Ordinance,[32] the Investment and Services Act,[33] and the Banking Act 1994.[34] The power of the police to enter premises is directly connected with the general duty to preserve the peace and public order, to prevent, detect, and investigate offences, to collect evidence, and to bring offenders before the judicial authorities. The abuse of such a power is regulated in the Criminal Code under the heading 'Of Abuse of Authority and of Breach of Duties pertaining to a Public Office'. Thus, it is an offence for a public officer to enter, under colour of his offices, in cases other than those allowed by, or without the formalities stipulated by, the

[31] Chapter 9 of the Laws of Malta.
[32] Chapter 37 of the Laws of Malta.
[33] Act XIV of 1994.
[34] Act XV of 1994.

law.[35] Ordinary law aims at affording effective protection to the inviolability of the home.

In the case of *Lawrence Sant v Commissioner of Police*,[36] the applicant alleged a breach of his rights as protected under Article 8 of the Convention. Police officers had effected a search in the applicant's residence, which search was recorded on film. The Constitutional Court declared that the police have no right to enter into an individual's home except for a valid reason. The Court deplored the fact that the search was carried out early in the morning and that the footage recorded during the search included also shots of intimate belongings of the applicant's wife. However, the search was in accordance with the law as:

(a) the police officer effecting the search had the authority to do so;
(b) there were reasonable indicators that a crime had been committed of which the applicant was suspected; and
(c) the police officer had fulfilled his duties of informing the applicant of his authority to carry out the search and the reasons leading to the same.

d. Recording of telephone conversations In a recent case the applicant contested the validity of a number of prison regulations concerning restrictions on correspondence and telephone conversations, amongst which was Regulation 59:

> All telephones within the prisons shall be equipped for monitoring and recording of conversations. Any Director may authorize the intentional hearing of such conversations to safeguard members of the public or to safeguard the security or safety within the prisons or to prevent the furtherance of any illegal activity.[37]

The Court considered that Article 8 of the Convention had as its main object that of protecting the individual against arbitrary interference by the public authorities in his private and family life. According to the Court, this was not an absolute right, and the state could intervene as long as it satisfied one of the conditions stipulated under Article 8(2) of the Convention. The arrest of a person after a judgment or under preventive custody implies certain restrictions to the enjoyment of his private and family life. The Court also considered that a democratic society required the striking of a balance between the legitimate interests of public order and security and that of the rehabilitation of prisoners. The Court concluded that the recording of the telephone conversation was permissible under the particular circumstances,

[35] Article 136 of the Criminal Code.

[36] Constitutional Court, 12 January 1994.

[37] Judgment delivered by the First Hall of the Civil Court on 12 April 1999, after the Court of Magistrates (Malta) as a Court of Criminal Judicature in the case *Police v Mario Camilleri* referred the issue.

as it concerned the planning of an illicit activity. Thus, the interference was justifiable and Regulation 59 was deemed to satisfy the condition of Article 8(2) of the European Convention and Article 38 of the Constitution.

2. Discrimination

Article 45 of the Constitution affords protection from discrimination on the grounds of race, place of origin, political opinions, colour, creed, or sex. This provision proclaims the principle that no law may introduce any provision that is discriminatory either of itself or in its effect, and that no person may be treated in a discriminatory manner by any person acting by virtue of any written law or in the performance of the functions of any public office or any public authority.

The following differences can be said to arise between Article 45 of the Constitution and Article 14 of the European Convention on Human Rights.

(a) The five grounds listed under the Constitution are exhaustive, whereas this is not the case for the grounds found in Article 14 of the European Convention.

(b) Whereas in terms of Article 14 one must prove some connection between the violation of one of the rights and freedoms set forth in the Convention and the violation of Article 14, this requirement is not found under Article 45 of the Constitution. In the case of *Charles Spiteri v Minister of Public Works et al.*,[38] decided by the Constitutional Court, it was held that under Article 45 of the Constitution the concept of discrimination is independent from the concept of freedom of expression as laid down in Article 41 of the Constitution. It is possible to have a violation of Article 45 without having at the same time a violation of the right protected under Article 41. This does not mean that Articles 45 and Article 41 of the Constitution cannot be breached concurrently.

a. Discrimination based on sex The European Court has expressed the principle that:

> the advancement of the equality of sexes is today a major goal in the Member States of the Council of Europe; this means that very weighty reasons would have to be put forward before a difference of treatment on the sole ground of sex could be regarded as compatible with the Convention (*Burghartz v Switzerland*, 22 February 1994. The same principle was expressed in the cases of: *Schuler-Zgraggen v Switzerland*, 24 June 1993; *Abdulaziz, Cabales, and Balkandali v United Kingdom*, 28 May 1985).

[38] 5 October 1988.

This attitude appears to have been adopted in the case of *Paul Stoner v Prime Minister*.[39] In this case the Constitutional Court went so far as to declare a provision of the Maltese Constitution protecting the right to freedom of movement as being discriminatory on the basis of sex under another provision of the Constitution. The applicants, an English citizen, and his wife, a Maltese citizen, challenged the decision of the competent authorities not to allow the applicants to live in Malta. Section 44(4)(c) of the Constitution, dealing with the right to liberty of movement, stipulates that any person who is the *wife* of a citizen of Malta and who is living with that person 'shall be deemed to be a citizen of Malta'.

The Constitutional Court held that in protecting the liberty of movement solely to women, the Constitution makes a discrimination. The complaints of the applicants were held to be justified on two grounds:

(i) if the discrimination in the protection of the freedom of movement were removed, Paul Stoner would be entitled to be deemed a citizen of Malta as of right; and
(ii) as the law stands, the applicant's wife, a Maltese citizen, was being discriminated against since she was placed at a disadvantage by marrying a foreign citizen, as compared with both foreign women who marry male Maltese citizens, and male Maltese citizens who marry foreign women.

In delivering judgment the Constitutional Court also considered that in 1987 the Maltese Parliament had approved the European Convention on Human Rights and Fundamental Freedoms. In March 1991 the government signed the UN Convention on the Elimination of all forms of Discrimination against Women. In July 1991 the Constitution was amended to provide a legal remedy to individuals who suffer sexual discrimination. Such radical changes were motivated by the principle that man and woman should enjoy equal rights.

The Constitutional Court emphasized that there was no justification for the difference in treatment, and held that the above-mentioned Article was discriminatory on the basis of sex, as it treated a foreign husband of a Maltese citizen differently from a foreign wife of a Maltese citizen.

In a judgment delivered by the First Hall of the Civil Court in the case of *Victoria Cassar v Maritime Authority* (19/10/2000), a legal notice restricting port work to men only was found to be discriminatory and to constitute a breach of the applicant's fundamental rights. Although not every differentiation of treatment constitutes discrimination where the criteria are reasonable

[39] 22 February 1996.

and objective, no such justification existed in the present case. The Court applied Article 3 of the European Convention in relation to discriminatory treatment on the basis of sex, and concluded that such treatment could be termed degrading. The case is still pending before the Constitutional Court.

b. Discrimination based on religious belief Article 40 of the Constitution of Malta stipulates that:

> all persons in Malta shall have full freedom of conscience and enjoy the free exercise of their respective mode of religious worship.

Freedom of conscience and religion is one of the foundations of a democratic society. This Article is included amongst those provisions of the Constitution which require a vote of no less than two-thirds of all member of the House of Representatives for their amendment. It appears that the right protected by Article 40 of the Constitution appertains to natural persons, churches, and other legal organizations.[40]

As in the European Convention, Maltese law does not define the terms 'conscience' and 'religion'. It would seem that these words should be interpreted according to their meaning in common usage. Furthermore, nothing contained in or done under the authority of any law is to be held inconsistent with or in contravention of Article 40 where the limitation is imposed in the interests of:

> public safety, public order, public morality or decency, public health, or the protection of the rights and freedoms of others, and except in so far as that provision or, as the case may be, the thing done under the authority thereof, is shown not to be reasonably justifiable in a democratic society.

Similarly, Article 45 provides protection against discrimination on ground of creed. The use of the word 'creed' constitutes a marked difference between the Constitution and other human rights instruments, particularly the Charter of the United Nations, the Universal Declaration of Human Rights, the Declaration on the Elimination of All Forms of Intolerance and of Discrimination based on Religion and Belief, and the European Convention on Human Rights. Although to date there is no reported case-law defining the term 'creed', it is submitted that it covers a variety of situations.

To date there has been one judgment in which the Constitutional Court found discrimination on this ground. The Archbishop of Malta sued the state following the enactment of the Devolution of Certain Church Property Act

[40] The First Hall of the Civil Court, in the case of *Mons. Giuseppe Mercieca proprio et al. v The Hon. Prime Minister nomine et al.* (24 September 1984), declared that the Roman Cahtolic Church had a right to invoke a breach of the Article 40 of the Constitution. This judgment is a declaration of principle and is applicable to other religious beliefs.

of 1983[41] and Act XI of 1983. The applicant alleged that this legislation imposed certain obligations on the Catholic Church which were not imposed on other churches or religions. The respondent state submitted that this was not the case as the Devolution of Church Property Act was aimed at ecclesiastical entities, thus including all churches and religions. However, this submission was contradicted by the applicant who stated that the reference to masses for the repose of the souls of the deceased, as well as the use of the term 'ecclesiastical', only affected the Catholic Church and, with certain limitations, the Orthodox Church in Malta. (The Devolution of Church Property Act was subsequently repealed by Act IV of 1992.)

The applicant complained, *inter alia*, of the restriction of making donations by persons professing the Roman Catholic religion for the celebration of masses for the repose of souls. The Devolution of Church Property Act stipulated that the duration of such a donation could not exceed twenty-five years. The First Hall of the Civil Court upheld the applicant's grievance and declared that this restriction was tantamount to discriminatory treatment.[42] The same conclusion was reached with respect to a provision in the law which deprived the Roman Catholic Church from acquiring rights over property by means of prescription, even though according to canon law prescription had no value unless based on good faith.

3. *Freedom of expression*

In Malta press censorship was abolished way back in 1839[43] and the Constitution proclaims the freedom of the press. This includes the right to impart opinions without being subjected to interference. The media is free to bring to the notice of the public any matter of public interest or concern. The law recognizes this by the defence of fair comment on a matter of public interest. However, this right is not free from limitations, which include legislative provisions reasonably required for the purpose of protecting the reputation, rights, and freedoms of other persons.

A number of decisions have been delivered by the Court of Appeal wherein it emphasized that people holding public office are subject to close control and scrutiny in the execution of their functions. Such control is to be performed not only by their direct rivals in the institutions of the state or other organizations, but also by public opinion, which to a large extent is formed by and expressed in the media. Freedom of expression is to be ensured even in respect of information which may be regarded as offensive, or which may shock or disturb the state or any sector of the population. Such are the demands of pluralism and tolerance, without which there can be no democratic society. Thus,

[41] Act X of 1983. [42] 24 September 1984. [43] Ordinance No. IV.

a politician should be prepared to accept even harsh criticism of his public activities and statements, and such criticism should not be understood as defamatory unless it throws a considerable degree of doubt on his personal character and good reputation. Politicians inevitably and knowingly lay themselves open to scrutiny of their words and deeds by both journalists and the public at large.

The judgments emphasized that the need to afford protection to politicians has to be weighed against the interests of open discussion of political issues. In this respect reference is made to the following judgments delivered by the Court of Appeal: *Angelo Fenech propio et nomine v Carmelo Callus et al.*;[44] *Lorry Sant v Victor Camilleri*;[45] *Richard Vella Bamber v Joe A. Vella et al.*[46]

These principles were also highlighted in a judgment delivered by the Court of Magistrates (Malta) in the criminal proceedings *Police v Olaf. A Cini*. In this case a journalist, notwithstanding a ban on publication, continued to publish articles concerning such criminal proceedings. The Court emphasized that whilst the mass media was duty-bound not to overstep the bounds imposed in the interests of the proper administration of justice, it was bound to impart information and ideas concerning matters which come before the courts just as in other areas of public interest. In delivering judgment the Court referred to various decisions of the European Court, including *Sunday Times v United Kingdom* (26 April 1979) and *Handyside v United Kingdom* (7 December 1976). Furthermore, the Court referred to the writings of Jeremy Bentham who contended that:

> Publicity is the very soul of justice. It is the keenest spur to exertion and the surest of all guards against improbity. It keeps the judge himself while trying under trial . . .[47]

Among the rights and freedoms of the individual is the right to a fair trial. The public character of judicial proceedings remains a fundamental principle of Maltese law. It is an established fact that the courts cannot operate in a vacuum. Whilst being the forum for the settlement of disputes, it does not mean that there can be no proper discussion of disputes elsewhere, whether it is in specialized journals, in the media, or amongst the public at large. However, under Maltese law the courts enjoy a general power to prohibit the publication of reports of criminal proceedings before the termination of such proceedings.[48] It is a fact that as a general rule the press in Malta is reason-

[44] 4 February 1994. [45] 14 February 1994. [46] 4 November 1994.

[47] G. Robertson and Andrew G. Nicol, *Media Law, The Rights of Journalists and Broadcasters* (2nd edn, 1990), p. 11.

[48] Article 517 of the Criminal Code provides:

> Every court of criminal justice may, by an order to be signed by the registrar and posted up at the door of the building in which the court sits, prohibit the publication, before the termination of the proceedings, of any writing, whether printed or not, in respect of the offence to

ably prudent in such matters. The courts are sometimes faced with the principle of the publicity of criminal proceedings on one hand and that of the presumption of innocence on the other.

In a judgment delivered by the Constitutional Court in the case of *Lawrence Pullicino v Prime Minister et al.*[49] the Court held that publicity is a means of guaranteeing the fairness of a trial. It helps to maintain public confidence in the administration of justice by removing any doubt as to the manner in which it is conducted. On the other hand, a virulent press campaign could prejudice the fairness of a trial by influencing public opinion. In this particular case the press had given extensive coverage, but one is to expect press comments on a trial involving a matter of public interest. The Court further expressed the view that in a trial by jury, a prejudicial comment may be countered by the judge himself during the proceedings by the statements he makes to the jury to discount such comments. This would have a neutralizing effect on such undue influence.

4. *The right to the enjoyment of one's property*

In this field it is generally held that Article 37(1) of the Constitution, which protects individuals from deprivation of property without compensation, has a wider application than the corresponding provision in the European Convention on Human Rights.[50] This view has also been confirmed by local judgments: *Oliver Siracusa nomine v Prime Minister et al.*[51] and *Alfred Balzan v Prime Minister et al.*[52]

Article 37 of the Constitution sets out four guarantees concerning the right to property:

which the proceedings refer, or of the party charged or accused; and any person who fails to comply with the order, shall for the mere default, be guilty of contempt of the authority of the court, and be liable to punishment as provided in section 686, saving always any other punishment to which the offender may be liable according to law, in respect of any other offence arising from the said writing or from its publication.

[49] 18 August 1998.

[50] Article 37 of the Constitution provides:

No property of any description shall be compulsorily taken possession of, and no interest in or right over property of any description shall be compulsorily acquired, except where provision is made by a law applicable to that taking of possession or acquisition—(a) for the payment of adequate compensation; (b) securing to any person claiming such compensation a right of access to an independent and impartial court or tribunal established by law for the purpose of determining his interest in or right over the property and the amount of any compensation to which he may be entitled, and for the purpose of obtaining payment of that compensation; and (c) securing to any party to proceedings in that court or tribunal relating to such a claim a right of appeal from its determination to the Court of Appeal in Malta.

[51] Constitutional Court, 16 November 1989.

[52] Constitutional Court, 15 January 1991.

(a) property, an interest in, or a right over property of any description may only be compulsorily taken possession of or acquired by virtue of a law;
(b) such law must provide for adequate compensation;
(c) the law must also provide for the access of the aggrieved person to an independent and impartial court or tribunal for the purpose of determining: (i) such person's interest in or right over the property which was taken possession of or acquired; (ii) the amount of compensation to which such person is entitled; and (iii) it must ensure payment of such compensation;
(d) such law must also ensure a right of appeal from any of the above determinations.

It has been argued that Article 37 of the Constitution protects the right not only to own but also to enjoy property. In the case of *Doris Spiteri v Commissioner of Police*[53] an injunction was issued prohibiting the removal of plaintiff's vending stall. The Court declared that the removal would have constituted a deprivation of applicant's right to the enjoyment of her property. This position appears to be reinforced by Article 38 of the Constitution, by which no person shall be subjected to the search of his person *or his property* or to the entry by others of his premises. However, in the case of *Dominic Mintoff et al. v Prime Minister et al.*, the First Hall of the Civil Court held that it was not clear whether the protection afforded by Article 37 of the Constitution included the deprivation of enjoyment of one's property.[54] The Court expressed the view that Article 32 of the Constitution listed as one of the fundamental rights and freedoms of the individual the right to the *enjoyment of property*. However, this Article was not enforceable in front of a court of law and was merely a declaration of principle.

It is interesting to note that the Constitution does not define property. The Civil Code in Article 307 provides that 'All things which can be the subject of private or public ownership are either movable or immovable property'.[55] However, the Constitution speaks of 'property of any description'. This would appear to include any possible asset, economic unit, or right protected by law, whether real or personal, which can be valued in money. For example, leaseholds have been deemed to constitute property capable of protection. In *Ferro v Housing Secretary*[56] this principle was confirmed by the Court. On the other hand, squatters who occupy property under no valid title cannot claim the protection of Article 37[57] of the Constitution.

[53] First Hall of the Civil Court, 20 July 1988.
[54] 11 August 1995.
[55] Chapter 16 of the Laws of Malta.
[56] Constitutional Court, 21 February 1977.
[57] *Carlo Cremona v Minister for the Development of the Infrastructure et al.* decided by the First Hall of the Civil Court in its constitutional jurisdiction on 29 November 1989.

Although the Constitution stipulates that it is the supreme law of the land (Article 6) there are certain exemptions which emanate from ordinary law. For example, Article 47(9) of the Constitution provides that 'nothing in Article 37 of this Constitution shall affect the operation of any law in force immediately before 3 March 1962 . . .' This provision came under severe criticism in 1992 during parliamentary debates concerning proposed amendments to the Housing Authority Act.[58] It was contended that the above-mentioned provision was intended only as a temporary provision. At the time the gradual removal of this provision was suggested, allowing a transitional period to amend those laws which can be seen to violate the constitutional safeguards under Article 37(1).

Notwithstanding this clear immunity, the local courts have had occasion to mitigate the effects of certain privileged laws.

It should be noted that exemptions to Article 37(1), particularly Article 47(9), have been mitigated by the enactment of Act XIV of 1987. Laws in force before 3 March 1962 must now satisfy Article 1 of Protocol No. 1. This was confirmed in the case of *Tarcisio Borg v Parliamentary Secretary for the Environment et al.* decided by the First Hall of the Civil Court.[59] The Court held that the provision that no person shall require any proof of the public purpose for the expropriation of land other than the declaration of the President of Malta,[60] was no longer applicable with the enactment of the European Convention Act. The Court held that it had to be satisfied that the expropriation of land was in the public interest. It also confirmed that the Land Acquistion (Public Purposes) Ordinance[61] could not impose limitations on Article 1 of the First Protocol.

A landmark judgment in this area of human rights was delivered by the Constitutional Court in the case *Dominic Mintoff et al. v Prime Minister et al.*[62] The applicants filed a constitutional case alleging a breach of Article 37 of the Constitution and Article 1 of the First Protocol of the European Convention. They alleged that the building of a power station a couple of metres away from their residence constituted a breach of their fundamental right to enjoy their property. The Constitutional Court emphasized that in this respect protection was to be afforded to an individual not only where there was an expropriation in the true sense of the word, but also in the absence of a formal transfer of ownership (referred to as a *de facto* expropriation). In such a case there would still be a diminution in the attributes of ownership. Although in cases of public interest the state is granted a wide

[58] Chapter 261 of the Laws of Malta.
[59] First Hall of the Civil Court, 3 May 1991.
[60] Land Acquisiton (Public Purposes) Ordinance.
[61] Chapter 88 of the Laws of Malta.
[62] 30 April 1996.

discretion on a national level, a balance had to be struck between the interests of the community and the property rights of the individual.

The Court concluded as follows:

(a) From the evidence produced, the negative effects of the power station on applicant's residence could easily have been predicted by the authorities.
(b) The authorities had originally intended to expropriate the applicants' property. However, it was later decided not to proceed with the expropriation.
(c) There was nonetheless a *de facto* expropriation as the applicants were deprived of the enjoyment their property. Since their property was not expropriated according to law they were not entitled to claim compensation under the ordinary law.
(d) Furthermore, the economic value of the property was diminished to such an extent that it was difficult to predict that the applicants' property would retain a commercial value. The applicants' quality of life was also adversely affected and they had to bear an excessive burden.
(e) Although the state enjoys a wide margin of appreciation in determining what is in the public interest, and it had every right to determine where the power station was to be built, it failed to exercise the concept of proportionality. A fair balance had to be struck between the demands of the general interests of the community and the requirements of the individual's fundamental rights.

5. *The right to a fair trial*

Even before the enactment of the Maltese Constitution of 1964, fundamental rights were guaranteed to the individual charged with a criminal offence. As rightly stated by Prof. J. J. Cremona when commenting on the Criminal Code which was promulgated in 1854:

> it is remarkable for the liberal protection afforded to the person charged or accused, while in general elaborating and consolidating the liberal principle introduced by the Constitution of the Criminal Court.[63]

This view was also expressed by the Constitutional Court in the case of *Police v Belin sive Benigno Saliba*.[64] In this respect reference is made to the following provisions of the Criminal Code:[65]

[63] *Human Rights Documentation in Malta*, 1966.
[64] 10 April 1991.
[65] Chapter 9 of the Laws of Malta.

(i) Article 454(4): where the accused does not simply answer that he is guilty, another answer, or his silence, shall be taken as a plea of not guilty. This provision is in line with the rule that the prosecution has to prove the facts alleged against the accused, and the latter on his part need not even utter a word in his own defence as he does not have to prove anything;
(ii) Article 489: during a trial, previous convictions of the accused are not to be disclosed to the jury;
(iii) Article 518: the acts and documents of the courts of criminal justice shall be accessible to the accused;
(iv) Article 519: it is the duty of the courts of criminal justice to see to the adequate defence of the parties charged or accused;
(v) Article 527: a person cannot be tried more than once on the same facts;
(vi) Article 531: sittings are to be held in open court unless if conducted in public they might be offensive to modesty, or cause scandal;
(vii) Article 570: an accused who does not have the financial means to defend himself may request that he be assisted by the Advocate for Legal Aid, who shall gratuitously undertake the defence of the accused;
(viii) Article 634: the accused may give evidence at his own request. The failure of the accused not to tender evidence shall not be made the subject of adverse comment by the prosecution;
(ix) Article 639: evidence tendered by an accomplice against the accused shall not suffice on its own, unless the evidence of the accomplice is corroborated by other circumstances;
(x) Article 646: witnesses are to be examined in court and *viva voce*.

On the other hand, a provision which has frequently come under serious criticism is section 636(b) of the Criminal Code, which provides that:

> No objection to the competence of any witness shall be admitted on the ground . . . that he was charged with the same offence in respect of which his deposition is required, when impunity was promised or granted to him by the Government for the purpose of such deposition'.

The criticism is based on the following arguments:

(i) immunity from criminal proceedings is 'promised or granted' by the Executive according to its own discretionary powers; and
(ii) it prevents the accused from producing evidence which may illustrate that the witness 'promised or granted' impunity is an incompetent witness.

The existence of courts in a legal system and the need to take care to ensure the independence of those called upon to operate within those courts is fundamental to modern society and the rule of law. It is not surprising that local courts have frequently been called upon to decide cases in the interpretation of Article 6 of the Convention, guaranteeing a fair trial.[66] The Constitutional Court has on various occasions declared that the essence of a court is its independence, and in several cases has found that there has been no bias and that the adjudicating officer was able to deliver an impartial decision

In the case of *Cecil Pace et al. v Prime Minister*[67] applicants contended that the setting up of an Appeals Board to determine certain issues under the Controlled Companies (Procedure for Liquidation) Act was a flagrant breach of Article 39(2) of the Constitution and Article 6(1) of the European Convention. The Court declared that it was evident that both documents envisaged the possibility that an individual's civil rights and obligations could be determined by a court in the true sense of the term or by any other adjudicating authority established by law, on condition that they were independent and impartial. In establishing whether the tribunal or adjudicating authority was independent, the court must have regard to the manner of appointment of its members, their term of office, and guarantees which ensure that the authority is free from extraneous pressures. Furthermore, members must enjoy security of tenure during their term of office except in grave circumstances stipulated in the law. Insofar as impartiality is concerned, this requirement is satisfied by complying with a subjective and objective test. The subjective test is based on the personal conviction of a particular member in a given case, and the objective test ascertains whether the member offered guarantees sufficient to exclude any legitimate doubt as to his impartiality.

In the case of *Antonia Bartolo proprio et nomine v Prime Minister et al.*[68] a board of inquiry was set up by the Minister of Transport following the disappearance of an aeroplane. Applicants alleged that the tribunal was not impartial and independent, and alleged a breach of their fundamental human rights as protected by Article 6(1) of the European Convention and Article 39(2) of the Constitution.[69] The Board of Inquiry was set in terms of the Civil

[66] Article 39(1) of the Maltese Constitution stipulates:

Whenever any person is charged with a criminal offence he shall, unless the charge is withdrawn, be afforded a fair hearing within a reasonable time by an independent and impartial court established by law.

[67] Constitutional Court, 3 December 1997.

[68] 29 April 1996.

[69] Article 39(2) of the Constitution provides:

Any court or other adjudicating authority prescribed by law for the determination of the existence or the extent of civil rights or obligations shall be independent and impartial; and, where proceedings for such a determination are instituted by any person before such a court or other adjudicating authority, the case shall be given a fair hearing within a reasonable time.

Aviation (Investigation of Accidents) Regulation 1956. The Constitutional Court argued that the functions of the Board of Inquiry were merely investigative. The final report could not affect any of the parties concerned, and the Minister could very well ignore the conclusions reached therein. However, the report could be relevant if the Minister decided to take certain measures on the conclusions reached, either personally or on an administrative level through one of the organs of the state. However, in such an eventuality the interested party would still be entitled at law to request the judicial review of such administrative action. This in itself was considered as a safeguard for ensuring a fair hearing in front of an impartial and independent tribunal. The same would apply if following the report criminal proceedings were instituted against any party. The report can in no way prejudice the accused who enjoys all the necessary safeguards entrenched in the Constitution, the Convention, and the Criminal Code. The Court further opined that impartiality and independence call for an absolute separation between the executive power and the judiciary. Thus, dependants of the executive should under no circumstances be granted a judicial function, even though this may merely involve the appointment of an expert to assist a court in reaching its decision. This principle was applicable notwithstanding that the appointed persons possessed technical qualifications to express an opinion in respect of the facts in issue.[70]

A particular guarantee of the independence of the judiciary is the immunity of judges and magistrates from proceedings for acts done in the exercise of their duties as adjudicators. In the case of *Lino Debono v Michael Mallia*, decided by the First Hall of the Civil Court, the applicant alleged a breach of his fundamental right to a fair hearing by the contents of a judgment delivered by the respondent magistrate.[71]

The Court noted that this was the first case where an adjudicator was personally sued for something which he had done in his capacity as magistrate. The Court argued that the Constitution aimed at protecting the independence of the judiciary in order to allow it to fulfil its duties in accordance with justice and unhindered by any possible fear. If it were possible to sue one of its members personally for anything done in the exercise of his function as adjudicator, then the judiciary could no longer be considered independent and society would suffer since justice would not be done. Thus applicant's request was dismissed.

[70] The Court referred to the judgment delivered by the European Court in the case of *Sramek v Austria*:

> a violation of Art. 6 where a member of a Court was subordinate in terms of his professional duties to one of the parties in a given suit, stating that in such circumstances, litigants may entertain a legitimate doubt about that person's independence. Such a situation seriously affects the confidence which the court must inspire in a democratic society.

[71] 4 October 1989.

So fundamental is the right to a fair trial that in a judgment delivered by the Constitutional Court in the case of *Lawrence Cuschieri v Hon. Prime Minister et al.*, the Court envisaged the possibility that the Constitutional Court could commit a breach of an individual's right to a fair hearing.[72] The Court declared that Article 6(1) of the European Convention not only contains procedural guarantees in relation to judicial procedure, but also grants a right to judicial procedure. This Article creates a substantive right for a fair trial, which must necessarily be protected in all proceedings in any court which is determining an individual's civil rights and obligations. This judgment did away with the notion that the Constitutional Court did not determine an individual's civil rights and obligations, but was only concerned with constitutional rights, in that it decides on issues as to the compatibility with the Constitution of any acts or measures by public authorities in the exercise of public power.

Similarly, in *Police v Carmelo Ellul Sullivan et al.*[73] the applicants alleged a breach of Article 79 of the Code of Organization and Civil Procedure.[74] This Article barred lawyers who were also Members of Parliament from assisting an accused in certain cases. The Court held that this provision constituted a breach of the accused's right to a fair hearing since it prevented him from choosing his own lawyer. In interpreting Article 6(1) of the European Convention, the Constitutional Court applied a wide interpretation to the words 'civil rights', and declared that constitutional rights were likewise covered by the protection of this Article. Such a deprivation would mean that the accused was not provided with a full opportunity to present his case.

An interesting issue concerned the appointment of court experts who were employed with the police force in criminal proceedings. In the case of *Nicholas Ellul v Commissioner of Police*, decided by the First Hall of the Civil Court, the applicant alleged that his fundamental right to a fair hearing had been violated by the appointment of ballistic experts who were at the same time members of the police force.[75] The prosecution was conducted by the Police Commissioner. The Court argued that the appointment of an expert by a court has the effect of changing the role of the appointed person from an *ex parte* expert to a court expert. The Court held that the appointment of such experts could not be said to respect the notion of a fair hearing since such experts were not only closely connected with the prosecution but were also its dependants. The judgment was confirmed by the Constitutional Court.

A similar conclusion was reached by the Constitutional Court in the case of *Police v Longinu Aquilina*, decided on 23 January 1993. The Court found as follows:

[72] 6 April 1995. [73] Constitutional Court, 5 April 1989.
[74] Chapter 12 of the Laws of Malta. [75] 18 March 1991.

(i) It is advisable that police officers are not appointed as experts by a magistrate at any stage of the proceedings.

(ii) The practice of an inquiring magistrate appointing police experts in order to lift fingerprints from the scene of the crime was acceptable as the same could not at that point in time be linked to any particular person.

(iii) Nor should there be an objection to the appointment of police experts merely to take the suspect's fingerprints. This merely involved a mechanical registration of fingerprints.

(iv) The appointment of an expert to effect a comparison entails more than the mere recording of fingerprints. Their findings may constitute conclusive evidence of the guilt or innocence of the suspect. It suggested that all scientific comparisons should be made by court-appointed experts who are independent from the police authorities.

In the case of *John Saliba v Attorney General et al.*[76] it was contended that the applicant could not contest the appointment of such experts, as he did not object to their appointment during the criminal proceedings. The Court held that the experts were originally appointed in 1987 when the issue concerning the legality of appointing a member of the police force as a court expert, had never been tested in the local courts. At that time no one had ever thought of contesting such appointments and applicant's right could not be prejudiced merely on the basis that at the time he had not realized that his fundamental human right to a fair hearing might have been breached by such appointment. On the other hand, the Court declared that where the accused is subsequently in a position to contest the appointment of an expert but voices no objection, he cannot claim a breach of his fundamental rights.

An interesting statement of principle was made by the Constitutional Court in the case of *Gaetano Busuttil v Prime Minister et al.*, decided on 16 November 1998. In this case the applicant alleged that Article 30(A) of the Medical Kindred Profession Ordinance[77] breached his fundamental right to a fair hearing. This provision permits the production in evidence of statements made before a magistrate and confirmed on oath. This is an exception to the general principle that witnesses should be heard *viva voce*. The Court observed that there was no reason at law why this type of evidence should be precluded. What is essential is that the accused is given an opportunity to control such evidence and to rebut it by cross-examining the witnesses who issued such declarations. A sworn statement was admissible at law like any other documentary evidence, thereby safeguarding the principle of equality of arms.

[76] Constitutional Court, 6 July 1998.

[77] Chapter 31 of the Laws of Malta.

In *Constantino Consiglio v Air Supplies and Catering Supplies Company Limited* (11/0/8/2000), the Constitutional Court held that a disciplinary board did not qualify as a tribunal as defined in Article 6 of the European Convention. The procedure was therefore not subject to the guarantees established for a fair trial, and a decision delivered by the board could not be deemed as final and conclusive. The employee was entitled by law to contest the outcome of the disciplinary proceedings by filing an appeal in terms of the procedure established in the collective agreement. Ultimately, the employee could also refer the matter to the Industrial Tribunal in terms of the Industrial Relations Act (Chapter 266 of the Laws of Malta). Notwithstanding, the Court held that the Board's refusal to grant the applicant a copy of its report placed him at a disadvantage with the respondent company. The copy of the report was required by applicants so that they could prepare the appeal proceedings following the decision, and the right to a fair trial requires compliance with the principle of equality of arms. In this respect the Court held that applicant's complaint was justified at law.

D. CASES BROUGHT BEFORE THE EUROPEAN COURT OF HUMAN RIGHTS AND THE EUROPEAN COMMISSION

Since Malta introduced the remedy of individual petition, only three cases have been brought before the European Court and decided. The first judgement was delivered in the case of *Demicoli v Malta*.[78] The case dealt with the imposition of a sanction by the House of Representatives on a journalist for breach of parliamentary privilege.

Carmel Demicoli was the editor of a satirical political periodical. Two Members of Parliament alleged breach of parliamentary privilege when an article was published in the newspaper commenting on a parliamentary session that had been transmitted live on television. They contended that the article contained insulting references to themselves. The House passed a resolution that it considered the article in question to be a breach of its privileges, and the applicant was summoned to appear before the House to answer a charge of defamation.

The applicant alleged that he had not received a fair and public hearing by an independent and impartial tribunal, and also complained of the failure to observe the presumption of innocence.

[78] 27 August 1991.

In its judgment the Court used the three criteria which it had first laid down in the judgment of *Engel and Others v the Netherlands* (8 June 1976). These were as follows:

(i) The definition of the offence in issue according to the legal system of the respondent state. However, the indication afforded by national law was not decisive for the purpose of Article 6.
(ii) The actual nature of the offence. The proceedings could not be considered to be disciplinary since they did not refer to the internal regulation and orderly functioning of the House. The offence in issue, which involved a penal sanction, was deemed to be akin to a criminal offence.
(iii) The degree of severity of the potential penalty. The applicant was facing a maximum of sixty days' imprisonment: this warranted the classification of the offence with which applicant was charged as a criminal one.

The Court reached the conclusion that the House of Representatives had undoubtedly exercised a judicial function in determining the applicant's guilt. The fact that the two Members of Parliament who had raised the issue of breach of privilege had participated throughout the proceedings sufficed to cast doubt on the impartiality of the adjudicating body and applicant's claims were justified.

In the case *TW v Malta* the applicant alleged a violation of Article 5(3) of the Convention as domestic law did not require the police to substantiate the grounds for his arrest and the magistrate could release him only if he submitted a bail application.[79] The bail application had to be notified to the Attorney General, who had one working day in which to decide whether or not to oppose the applicant's request. The bail application would be considered by a different magistrate from the one in front of whom the applicant would have appeared originally. The procedure was to allot cases by lot in order to eliminate the possibility of forum-shopping by the police.

The European Court noted that Article 5(3) of the Convention provides persons arrested or detained on suspicion of having committed a criminal offence with a guarantee against any arbitrary or unjustified deprivation of liberty. Once detention is no longer reasonable, it is essentially the object of Article 5(3) to require provisional release. The Court expressed the view that:

> this provision enjoins the judicial officer before whom the arrested person appears to review the circumstances militating for or against detention, to decide by reference to legal criteria whether there are reasons to justify detention, and to order release if there are no such reasons.

[79] 29 April 1999.

Judicial control is to be prompt, and is not to be made dependent on a previous application by the detainee. The Court stressed that the Article aims at guaranteeing the independent judicial scrutiny of deprivation of liberty. Therefore, since according to Maltese law the magistrate had no authority to order the applicant's release when the latter appeared before him for the first time, there was a breach of Article 5(3) of the Convention.[80]

In the case *Sabeur Ben Ali v Malta* (29/06/2000), the applicant complained of a violation of Article 5(3) and (4) of the European Convention (right to liberty and security). On 17 March 1995 the applicant had been arrested concerning drug-related offences. He appeared before a Magistrate on the 19 March 1995, and in terms of Article 27 of the Dangerous Drugs Ordinance was remanded in custody pending conclusion of the criminal inquiry. On conclusion of the inquiry on 4 April 1995, he was committed for trial. On 5 February 1997 the applicant was acquitted and released.

The European Court of Human Rights held that the applicant's appearance before the Magistrate on 19 April 1995 was not capable of ensuring respect for Article 5(3) of the Convention as the Magistrate could not automatically review the merits of the detention. The Court also held that it had not been shown that during his detention on remand the applicant had at his disposal a remedy for challenging the lawfulness of his detention.

An interesting case was the decision delivered by the European Court as to the admissibility of Application 45441/99 by *Lawrence Pullicino* (who had served as Police Commissioner) against Malta. A number of interesting issues were considered.

1. *Confiscation of the Applicant's notes at trial* The Court expressed the view that the right to compile notes during one's trial was one of the means for an accused to participate effectively in his trial and to facilitate the conduct of his defence. This was notwithstanding the fact that the accused was assisted by counsel during proceedings. However, different considerations applied to the use of notes during the accused's examination-in-chief or cross-examination. The presiding judge might be justified in preventing the accused from relying on written recollections while on the witness stand, thereby excluding the possibility that the evidence given had been rehearsed. Notwithstanding, before concluding that the irregularity had given rise to prejudice to the applicant's right to a fair trial, one had to examine the proceedings as a whole.

2. *Impartiality of the presiding judge* For the purposes of Article 6(1) of the European Convention, the existence of impartiality was to be assessed by means of a subjective test, that is on the basis of the personal conviction of a

[80] See also judgment delivered by the European Court of Human Rights on 29 April, 1999 in the case of *Longinu Aquilina v Malta*.

particular judge, and also according to an objective test, ascertaining whether the judge offered guarantees sufficient to exclude any legitimate doubt. The fact that the presiding judge had made pre-trial decisions could not in itself justify fears as to his impartiality. Although in the days preceding the trial the presiding judge had revoked the applicant's bail, this did not mean that before the commencement of the trial the judge had already shaped an opinion as to the credibility and honesty of the accused. Furthermore, the summing up which the judge made to the jury was balanced and in no manner unfair. Regard was also taken of the fact that at no stage did legal counsel to the accused challenge the judge presiding over the trial by jury.

3. *Prejudice suffered by the accused due to adverse media and other statements* The Court emphasized that courts could not operate in a vacuum. Although a person's guilt or innocence was to be determined by a court of law, this did not mean that there could be no prior or contemporaneous debate on criminal trials, whether in journals, newspapers, or amongst the public. The public has a right to receiving information imparted by the media. This is more so where a public figure is involved. The Court concluded that no evidence was brought forward by the applicant that the authorities had encouraged prejudicial reporting in the media, and this grievance had also been closely reviewed on appeal. Furthermore, the fact that the jury took over seven days to reach a verdict was in the Court's view a clear indication that they reached a decision according to their consciences.

On 16 November 1992 another judgment was delivered in favour of a Maltese citizen by the European Court in the case of *Joseph Brincat v Italy*. The applicant had been arrested in Italy, and contended that he had not been promptly brought before a judge or other officer authorized by law to exercise judicial power. Furthermore, it was held that the functions of investigation and prosecution must be kept separate. The public prosecutor who had taken part in the investigation and who had decided to keep the applicant in detention could not be said to have been objectively impartial as a result of the role he subsequently took on as the representative of the prosecuting authority.

A number of cases from Malta have also been considered by the European Commission. Application 16756/90 (*Connie Zammit v Malta*, decided on 12 January 1991) concerned the restrictions imposed by Maltese legislation which deprived an owner from recovering possession of his property on the expiration of a sub-emphyteusis (sub-lease). Act XXXVII of 1986 granted the occupants the right to remain in possession of the premises.

The Commission concluded that the measure adopted by the government pursued a legitimate aim in the general interest, that of protecting the interest of tenants. Notwithstanding the legislation, the applicants remained owners of their property and could thus freely dispose of it. Furthermore, they were entitled to receive rent from the occupiers. The Commission also considered the wide margin of appreciation afforded to States where the measures taken aim at regulating housing problems. The application was dismissed.

The entry and search of a home by police was in issue in Application 18420/91 (*Tonio Vella v Malta*). Police had entered the applicant's home without giving the authority for their action or any reasons. A search was conducted which produced no results. The applicant was subsequently arrested and kept in custody for forty-six hours, during which he was interrogated for one hour. During proceedings an amicable settlement was reached between the parties whereby an *ex gratia* payment was effected by government.

E. THE IMPACT OF HUMAN RIGHTS ON DOMESTIC LEGISLATION

Human rights instruments have had a bearing on the enactment of Maltese legislation. A case in point is the amendment of Article 575 of the Criminal Code.[81] Prior to the enactment of Act XXIX of 1989, persons accused of crimes intended to harm the Government or of crimes liable to the punishment of imprisonment for life could not be granted bail. The 1989 Act permitted the granting of bail in such circumstances.

Similarly, according to Article 79(2) of the Code of Organization and Civil Procedure,[82] a Member of Parliament was prevented from exercising his profession as advocate in a number of cases, for example in lawsuits where the state was a party and criminal trials where the accused was a public official. This Article was challenged in the case of *Police v Carmelo known as Charles Ellul Sullivan et al.*[83] The Constitutional Court held that since the number of lawyers who exercised their profession in lawsuits of a constitutional nature was limited in number, the said provision was in breach of the fair hearing guarantees afforded to those persons who were involved in such litigation. By means of Act XXIV of 1995 this restriction was removed.

The manner of proceeding in matters concerning contempt of court has also been revised. In its report for the review of the Code of Organization and Civil Procedure, the Commission suggested that the amendments it was proposing in this sphere of the law were aimed:

> to ensure that the law in this respect is in line with the provisions of the Constitution and the European Convention on Human Rights.[84]

[81] Chapter 9 of the Laws of Malta.
[82] Chapter 12 of the Laws of Malta.
[83] Constitutional Court.
[84] Published in November 1993.

The Commission proposed that proceedings for contempt should be instituted by the Registrar of the Court. This would do away with the problem of the apparent unfairness of Courts acting as plaintiff against the defendant. The proposed amendment also aimed to do away with the procedure of having contempt proceedings instituted and proceeded upon by the complaining party himself. This proposal was adopted by Parliament by means of Act XXIV of 1995.

Amendments have also been introduced in connection with the powers enjoyed by the state to by-pass litigation and issue executive warrants for any monetary debt due. Thus, prior to 1995 any head of a government department could recover a debt due to the department by the issue of a warrant of seizure on the debtor's property, simply by making a sworn declaration before the Registrar of Courts or a judge or magistrate of the competent court. In such circumstances an aggrieved debtor could either pay the amount under protest and then sue the authority concerned, or suffer the enforcement and institute judicial proceedings claiming compensation for damages. It was deemed that under such circumstances an individual's rights to a fair hearing as protected by the Constitution and the European Convention were being impaired as the debtor was not entitled to oppose the execution of a claim brought against him by a government department. In fact, the Constitutional Court also had the opportunity to rule on this matter. By means of Act XXIV of 1995 the debtor was granted the right to contest such claims within a stipulated time after he receives a judicial act requesting him to effect payment. This procedure aims to secure the right to a fair hearing of the individual without excessively impairing the prompt recovery of government debts.

An amendment introduced in 1995 removed the prevention of persons leaving Malta who owed debts. Although an effective precautionary measure, the basis for the objection to this procedure was its unconstitutionality in restricting an individual's freedom of movement. However, the remedy was retained in respect of vessels and the removal of minors from Malta.

Following the judgment delivered by the European Court of Human Rights in the *Charles Demicoli* case, an amendment was introduced in 1995 to the House of Representatives (Privileges and Powers) Ordinance[85] by means of Act XI. Today a breach of privilege by an individual is to be tried by the Court of Magistrates (Malta) following an order to that effect made by the Speaker of the House to the Executive Police. In this respect the Speaker's request is subject to the authority of the House of Representatives.

The publication of a White Paper on the enactment of a new Code of Police Laws gives due consideration to case-law under Article 6 of the Convention.

[85] Chapter 113 of the Laws of Malta.

Article 3 of the Professional Secrecy Act refers to privacy.[86] This Article imposes the obligation of non-disclosure on:

members of a profession regulated by the Medical and Kindred Professions Ordinance, advocates, notaries, legal procurators, accountants, auditors, employees and officers of the financial and credit institutions, trustees, officers of nominee companies or licensed nominees, persons licensed to provide investment services under the Investment Services Act 1994, stockbrokers licensed under the Malta Stock Exchange Act, insurers, insurance agents, insurance brokers, officials and employees of the State.

[86] Act XXIV of 1994.

23

The Netherlands

LEO F. ZWAAK

A. INTRODUCTION

On 31 August 1954 the Netherlands became a Party to the European Convention on Human Rights and the government recognized the compulsory jurisdiction of the European Court of Human Rights. When ratifying the Convention, however, the Netherlands did not recognize the right of individuals to lodge complaints with the European Commission on Human Rights. A declaration recognizing the right of individual petition was deposited with the Secretary General of the Council of Europe on 5 July 1960. Both declarations have been regularly renewed and since 1979 for an unlimited period. The Netherlands further ratified in 1971 the International Convention on the Elimination of All Forms of Racial Discrimination and in 1978 the International Covenant on Civil and Political Rights and its Optional Protocol and the International Covenant on Economic, Social, and Cultural Rights.

Thus the Dutch judicial organs could have gained experience of the application of human rights treaties for years. However, it is not until the 1980s that these treaties have played an important role in Dutch case-law. At the time of ratification it was thought that the European Convention would not have much influence on the Dutch legal order. During the parliamentary discussions on the approval of the European Convention, the government gave as its opinion that the Convention's effect would be negligible as domestic law already complied fully with it.[1] Before courts, it was generally assumed that the invocation of an international human rights treaty was a sign of weakness and was only adhered to when no other reasonable argument was available.

This situation has changed profoundly. Not only is every judge in the Netherlands now fully aware of the existence of the European Convention

[1] E. A. Alkema, 'The Effects of the European Convention on Human Rights and Other Human Rights Instruments on the Netherlands Legal Order', in Rick Lawson and Matthijs de Blois (eds) *The Dynamics of the Protection of Human Rights in Europe*, vol. III (Dordrecht: Nijhoff, 1994) p. 3.

(and other human rights treaties) but moreover the influence of those treaties on the Dutch legal system is considerable. Both the number of cases and the influence are still growing.

B. THE STATUS OF THE CONVENTION IN THE DUTCH LEGAL ORDER

In 1954 the relationship between the Netherlands and its overseas territories (at that time Suriname and the Dutch Antilles) had been regulated in the Charter of the Netherlands, which was revised in 1975 when Suriname became independent. This revised Charter, together with the Dutch Constitution, forms the constitutional basis of the Kingdom of the Netherlands.[2] Although the Charter is superior to the Constitution a number of matters are referred to the Constitution for further regulation. The Charter is concerned with matters such as foreign policy, defence, and nationality. The Netherlands has made a declaration under Article 56 of the European Convention and extended the application of the Convention to the Dutch Antilles and Aruba, which are autonomous regions of the Kingdom, with their own Parliaments and local governments. In 1983 the Dutch Constitution was revised mainly in respect of the chapter on fundamental rights. Apart from the traditional rights, social rights were introduced.[3]

Several authors have described the position of international treaties in the Netherlands and before its domestic courts.[4] Therefore a summary outline may will here. When giving some basic information about the domestic status of human rights treaties in the domestic legal order of the Netherlands one has to distinguish and define the following concepts: 1. the legal force of a

[2] This includes The Netherlands, the Dutch Antilles, and Aruba.

[3] See in more detail: Yvonne Klerk and Eric Janse de Jonge, 'The Netherlands' in C. A. Gearty (ed), *European Civil Liberties and the European Convention on Human Rights* (The Hague: Kluwer, 1997) pp. 108–109.

[4] Ibid, note 3; E. A. Alkema, 'The effects of the European Convention on Human Rights and Other Human Rights Instruments on the Netherlands Legal Order', in Rick Lawson and Matthijs de Blois (eds), *The Dynamics of the Protection of Human Rights in Europe*, vol. III, (Dordrecht: Nijhoff, 1994), pp. 1–15; John Vervaele, 'The Netherlands' in Mireille Dalmas-Marty (ed), *The European Convention for the Protection of Human Rights—International Protection versus National Restrictions* (Dordrecht: Nijhoff, 1992), pp. 209–225; P. van Dijk, 'Domestic Status of Human Rights Treaties and the Attitude of the Dutch judiciary—The Dutch Case' in Manfred Nowak et al. (eds), *Progress in the Spirit of Human Rights: Festschrift für Felix Ermacora* (Kehl: Engel, 1988), pp. 631–650; *idem*, 'Dutch experience with the European Convention in Domestic Law' in L. A. Rehof and C. Gulmann (eds), *Human Rights in Domestic Law and Development Assistance Policies of the Nordic Countries* (Kehl: Nijhoff, 1989), pp. 133–142.

treaty; 2. the internal effect of a treaty; 3. the direct effect of a treaty; and 4. the precedence of an international treaty over national law.[5] Human rights treaties have a very strong formal status in the legal order of the Netherlands. This is particularly true of the European Convention, but increasingly also for the self-executing provisions of other human-rights treaties. The reason is of course their internal and direct effect within the Dutch legal order and their precedence over Dutch law, including the Constitution, and the fact that the Dutch courts may, and must, review statutory law for its conformity with the (self-executing) provisions of treaties, a power which they do not have in relation to the Constitution.

2. *The legal force of a treaty*

The legal force of a treaty *vis-à-vis* a state depends on whether the treaty has entered into force, in general and for that particular state. Both are determined by ratification. The fact that a treaty has entered into force for a particular state means that this state is bound by its provisions. The character and scope of the legal obligations ensuing for the state from such a legally binding treaty, however, may vary substantially between one treaty and another, but also within one and the same treaty. This character and scope are determined by the individual provisions of the treaty as interpreted according to the general principles of treaty interpretation.

In some cases the treaty obligations have to be fulfilled completely at the moment of the entry into force of the treaty. This is the case for all obligations laid down in the European Convention.[6] In other cases states only have to fulfil the obligations progressively: for example Article 2 of the International Covenant on Economic, Social, and Cultural Rights contains the obligation for the State 'to take steps . . . to the maximum of its available resources, with a view to achieving progressively the full realization of the rights recognized in the present Covenant'. This character and scope, in their turn, determine the character and the scope of the state's discretionary powers concerning these obligations.

3. *The internal force of treaties*

The internal effect of a treaty relates to the effect given to the treaty in the domestic legal order of the state. The implementation of most treaties has certain domestic implications. This is clearly true of human rights treaties, which

[5] P. van Dijk, 'Domestic Status of Human Rights Treaties and the Attitude of the Dutch judiciary—The Dutch Case', in Manfred Nowak et al. (eds), *Progress in the Spirit of Human Rights: Festschrift für Felix Ermacora* (Kehl: Engel, 1988), pp. 633–639.

[6] See Article 1 of the European Convention.

entail the obligation on the state to ensure their internal effect in its domestic legal order. As a rule this is an obligation of result only, it being left to the state to choose the ways and means. International law has not (yet) developed any rules on the matter. There are three main ways of giving internal effect to a treaty: adoption, incorporation, and transformation. In a system of adoption the treaty provisions have legal effect *as such* in the domestic order; they keep their international character and origin, but are applied within a national legal order. At the basis of this system is the monistic view, which considers international and national law as parts of one legal order. That state's constitutional law and practice determine the system followed in a particular state.

The internal force of treaties in the legal order of the Netherlands has been expressly regulated in a monistic way in the Dutch Constitution. Article 93 of the present Constitution of 1983 provides that provisions of treaties and of decisions of international organizations the contents may be binding on everyone shall have this binding effect as from the time of publication. The words 'the contents of which may be binding on everyone' are generally understood to refer to the self-executing character, which is required for their application by Dutch courts.

4. *The direct effect of treaties*

If the provision or decision has a 'self-executing' character, no further implementation or execution measures are needed before it can be judicially enforced. Thus, in order to be invoked before a national court in the Netherlands, a provision of a treaty must fulfil the following conditions. First, the treaty must have entered into force; secondly, the Netherlands must have ratified the treaty; and thirdly, the provision or decision must be directly applicable. This does not mean, of course, that non-self-executing provisions have no internal force in the Netherlands. They are binding, as such, upon all branches of the central and local legislative and executive authorities, which also have to enforce the resulting obligations within the scope of their powers.

The rights contained in the Convention are considered self-executing by the courts and are therefore directly applicable. Only with respect to Article 6 of the ECHR insofar as it concerns the right of access to a court in situations where national law has not granted any jurisdiction to a national court and with respect to Article 13 of the ECHR has the Supreme Court taken another view.[7] The question whether a provision is self-executing must be determined by the national courts. In other words, it is for the national court to decide whether an individual can invoke a provision of a treaty before that court.

[7] Supreme Court 18 February 1986, NJ 1987, No. 62.

5. *Precedence of a treaty*

If a treaty provision is directly applicable as international law, the question arises of its legal status in relation to provisions of domestic law, which are not in conformity therewith. A treaty provision that has been incorporated or transformed into national law acquires the same status as other national law provisions of the same kind. However, in both the monistic and the dualistic situations it is clear that a treaty can ultimately be effective only if it takes precedence over domestic law. Therefore, no matter what its domestic law provides in that respect, a state is internationally responsible if the application of its domestic law results in a violation of the treaty. The State cannot invoke its internal law as a justification for this violation.

Article 94 of the Dutch Constitution provides:

> Regulations which are in force in the Kingdom of the Netherlands shall not be applied if this application is not in conformity with provisions of treaties or decisions of international organizations which are binding upon everyone.

This means that whenever the application of a regulation in a specific case will lead to a situation which conflicts with a provision of a human rights treaty, the national court is obliged not to apply that regulation in that case. In this respect it is also relevant to consider Article 120 of the Constitution, which provides that the judge cannot decide on the constitutionality of regulations and treaties. In other words, a judge may not conclude that a regulation or treaty is in violation with the Constitution.

This leads to the rather strange situation that in a specific case the court can decide whether a national regulation is in conformity with a provision of a human rights treaty. However, the court is not able to decide whether that same regulation is in conformity with a comparable or even identical provision of the Dutch Constitution. If a regulation is not in conformity with the human rights treaty, the judge is obliged not to apply that regulation in that case. However, the court is not able to nullify, repeal, or amend that regulation. The provision remains in force, but will not be applied. In one judgment the Supreme Court even affirmed the priority of the self-executing provisions of the Convention and the Sixth Protocol over conflicting treaty provisions, when it refused to allow an American serviceman to be handed over to the US authority on the grounds that he would face capital punishment.[8]

In sum, therefore, the status of human rights treaties in the Dutch legal order is very high. Treaty provisions have precedence over national regulations and even constitutional provisions. Moreover, in case of conflict, the court is obliged not to apply the national regulation.

[8] Supreme Court 30 March 1990, NJ 1991, No. 249.

C. THE STATUS OF THE CONVENTION IN PARLIAMENTARY PROCEEDINGS

Under the Dutch Constitution, Acts of Parliament should not be applied when they violate the Convention. It is the task of the legislator to amend such legislation to bring it into conformity with the Convention. An important task is, under the Dutch Constitution, given to the Council of State. This organ gives, *inter alia*, advice to the government with respect to new and amended legislation. According to Article 73 of the Dutch Constitution the Council of State or a section of the Council of State shall be consulted on bills and draft general administrative orders as well as proposals for the approval of treaties by the States General. The Council of State may put forward its own proposals with regard to legislation and administration. The government is not bound by the Council's recommendations.

Further, every Member of Parliament has the constitutional right to ask a minister or state secretary questions. This can be done in writing or orally. After the minister has replied in the first instance, and the questioner has gone on to ask further questions in the second instance, either the minister or other members of parliament may also ask each other questions. The minister is obliged to answer the questions. Written questions may be submitted at any time. After the Speaker of the Lower House has approved them, he or she passes them on to the relevant members of the cabinet (ministers and/or state secretaries). A written reply should be given to such questions within three weeks.

D. LEADING HUMAN RIGHTS CASES DECIDED BY THE NATIONAL COURTS

In a study Van Dijk stated that:

> . . . in a monistic system the courts may hamper the domestic effect of a treaty by applying very strict criteria for the self-executing character of treaty provisions or by giving self-executing provisions an interpretation which brings them into conformity with domestic law or practice.[9]

E. A. Alkema has written:

[9] Van Dijk, note 5 above, pp. 640–641.

This lack of 'European orientation' is partly due to the fact that the European organs, the Commission and the Court of Human Rights, by that time had not yet gained enough prestige.[10]

In those cases in which provisions of the Convention have been invoked in Dutch courts the conclusion reached was almost always that no violation of the provision had occurred. As Van Dijk indicated, the courts reached this result by:

—applying a comparable provision of Dutch law and, if necessary, giving it a very broad scope, while ignoring the provision of the Convention, or
—denying the self-executing character of a provision of the Convention, or
—giving to the provision of the Convention a very restrictive scope, which made it inapplicable to the case before the court, or,
—giving a broad scope to the restriction allowed for in the Convention to solve the non-conformity, or
—interpreting the provision of the Convention and the applicable domestic law in so wide a way that conflict between them is avoided.[11]

In two cases concerning Article 9 of the ECHR, on the freedom of religion, the Supreme Court found no violation. In the first case a clergyman objected to paying his contribution under the General Old Age Pensions Act because in his opinion this would be a violation of his right guaranteed in Article 9. The Supreme Court held that Article 9 did not imply that everybody had the right to review laws to ensure their compatibility with their religious beliefs.[12] In the second case the Supreme Court held Article 9 of the ECHR to be applicable. At that time the Constitution contained a prohibition on religious processions. The Supreme Court came finally to the conclusion that the prohibition fell within the ambit of the restrictions laid down in paragraph 2 of Article 9.[13]

Until 1980 the Supreme Court only once found that a provision of the Convention was not fully respected.[14] Only in one instance before 1980 did a District Court disapply a provision of national legislation because it was not

[10] 'Fundamental Human Rights and the Legal Order of the Netherlands' in H.F. van Panhuys (ed), *International Law in the Netherlands*, vol. III (Oceana: Alphen, 1980) p. 136.

[11] Van Dijk, note 5 above, pp. 640–641.

[12] Supreme Court 13 April 1960, ARB 1960, No. 567.

[13] Supreme Court 19 January 1962, NJ 1962, No. 107.

[14] Supreme Court 23 April 1974, NJ No. 272: in criminal proceedings the prosecution must be suspended as long as the suspect is not informed of the nature and cause of the accusation against him in conformity with Article 6(3)(a).

in conformity with Article 8 of the ECHR.[15] In 1980 a study on the implementation of human rights treaties in the Netherlands led to the conclusion that the role of the legislator in this implementation had been more prominent than that of the courts.[16] In the late seventies, but especially in the eighties, the attitude of several courts in the Netherlands, including the highest courts, has changed dramatically.

In 1984 the Supreme Court held that the Article of the Dutch Civil Code which provides that in the case of a divorce the court shall appoint a guardian and a supervising guardian, and which consequently implies that parental authority ends, constitutes an infringement of the right of parents to respect for their family life as laid down in Article 8 of the ECHR.[17] In the Court's view such an infringement should only be imposed upon the parents if the interests of the child so require. The Court reached its conclusion on the basis of its own interpretation of Article 8 and could not rely for that on the Strasbourg case-law. The Court showed that it was prepared to give precedence to a provision of the Convention over a provision of national law even in cases where the Convention provision as interpreted by the Strasbourg organs did not (yet) guide the Court in that direction.[18]

Matters of custody over infants, although originally intended to apply in cases of legitimate children only, have to be interpreted as applying equally to cases of illegitimate children. The Court argued that the views concerning the question whether it was justified to attach important consequences to the difference between legitimate and illegitimate children had greatly changed recently. For this the Court referred to the judgment of the European Court of Human Rights of 13 June 1979 in the *Marckx* case and the interpretation given there of Article 8 of the ECHR in conjunction with Article 14 of the ECHR.[19] On that ground it annulled a decision of the District Court taken before the *Marckx* judgment was even delivered. The Supreme Court did not find it necessary to wait for the amendment of the national law, which was in process of preparation. The decision did not overrule the statutory provision (Article 959 of the Code of Civil Procedure) but was presented as an interpretation adapted to social developments.[20]

The judgment in the *Marckx* case against Belgium[21] became very influential in the Netherlands. A series of decisions found lack of conformity between domestic law and Articles 8 and 14 of the ECHR.[22] In these cases the

[15] District Court of Maastricht, 14 November 1977, (1978) *Netherlands Yearbook of International Law*, p. 293.

[16] E. A. Alkema, note 10 above, p. 136.

[17] Supreme Court 4 May 1984, NJ 1985, No. 510.

[18] Van Dijk, note 5 above, p. 645.

[19] Supreme Court 18 January 1980, NJ 1980, No. 463

[20] E. A. Alkema, note 1 above, p. 5.

[21] Judgment of 13 June 1979, Series A No. 31.

[22] Supreme Court, 21 March 1986, Nos. 585–589.

court set conditions under which parents, in spite of the dissolution of their marriage, could continue to exercise parental authority. According to Alkema, here the court departed dramatically from its judicial role and assumed a 'quasi-legislative' task by formulating a new set of legal rules. These decisions probably went beyond that which was implied by the *Marckx* case.[23]

The Convention was also influential with respect to arrangements for parental access. A decision of the Supreme Court held that there was 'family life' in the sense of Article 8 of the ECHR between a biological father and his child.[24] Referring to the *Berrehab* case against the Netherlands,[25] the Supreme Court reconsidered this point of view and now considers that the sole fact that the father procreated the child is not sufficient to establish 'family life', and that additional factors are needed for this.[26] In 1982 the Supreme Court again interpreted a statutory provision so as to bind it into conformity with the Convention. The Supreme Court held that a provision of the Dutch Civil Code violated Article 12 of the European Convention and should therefore have been disapplied by the lower courts. This provision provided that if one parent refused permission for the marriage of an under-age child a court decision could not be a substitute for this permission. The Supreme Court took the position that such an unlimited power of veto for the parents was not compatible with the right to marry laid down in Article 12. The fact that Article 12 includes the words 'according to the national laws governing the exercise of this right' did not justify such an extensive limitation, in the view of the court.[27] Therefore, if the court finds that a refusal of permission is not reasonably motivated then the application of the domestic provision would amount to a violation of Article 12 of the ECHR. The legislator has reacted to this judgment by abolishing part of that provision.

According to the Insanity Act, a public prosecutor may in certain cases prevent a person who is detained under the Act from applying to a court for release from detention. The Supreme Court held that this provision was not in conformity with Article 5(4) of the ECHR and must therefore not be applied.[28]

Many cases in which an administrative act was found to violate a Treaty provision have concerned the requirement of a trial within a reasonable time under Article 6(1) of the ECHR. In most instances where a violation was found, the charges by the public prosecutor were declared inadmissible. The

[23] E. A. Alkema, note 1 above, p. 5.
[24] Supreme Court, 22 February 1985, NJ 1986, No. 3.
[25] Judgment of 21 June 1988, Series A No. 138.
[26] Supreme Court, 10 November 1989, No. 628.
[27] Supreme Court, 4 June 1982, NJ 1983, No. 32.
[28] Supreme Court 1 July 1983 NJ 1984, No. 161.

Dutch Supreme Court expressly indicated that this line should be followed by the courts. It held that in case of a violation of the right to a trial without unreasonable delay, the prosecution must be deemed to have been conducted so far against the fundamental principles of a fair trial that the prosecutor loses his right to continue the prosecution and his charge can no longer be received.[29] In its subsequent case-law, however, the Supreme Court stated that the consequence of exceeding the reasonable time limit is not necessarily the inadmissibility of the charge, but may instead reduce the penalty. This in itself does not remedy the fact that the trial has been unreasonably delayed, and that the ultimate determination does not therefore seem to be in conformity with the requirement of Article 6. However, this new approach by the Supreme Court could find support in the Strasbourg case-law.[30]

Dutch law lacked any provision under which judges in tax cases could be challenged until, referring to the *Hauschildt* case,[31] the Supreme Court added such a rule to Dutch law.[32]

Another example concerns the conviction of three persons on the basis of evidence given by anonymous witnesses. One of those accused, *Mr Kostovski*, brought his case before the European Commission. In its report the Commission found a violation of the Convention.[33] The two others, who were not parties to the Strasbourg proceedings, asked in summary proceedings for their release pending the examination of the case before the European Court. The victim in the case had already been extradited to Sweden. In its judgment the district court ordered the release of the two, because even though they had not complained of a violation of the Convention in the first instance, it was almost certain that the European Court would decide that conviction on the sole basis of anonymous witnesses would amount to a violation of the Convention.

In some instances the Dutch courts have applied the Convention to relations between individuals. It did so a case in which one individual interfered in the private life of another,[34] and in another case concerning the publication of a photograph of a woman embracing her fiancé in a park.[35] The Supreme Court has also applied the prohibition of racial discrimination in relations between individuals.[36]

[29] Supreme Court, 23 September 1981, NJ 1981, No. 116.

[30] see Judgment of 15 July 1982, in the *Eckle* case, Series A No. 51; report of the Commission of December 1983 in the *Neubeck* case, paras. 130–138.

[31] Judgment of 24 May 1989, Series A No. 154.

[32] Supreme Court 20 February 1991, BNB 1991/134.

[33] Report of the Commission of 12 May 1988, Series A No. 166.

[34] Supreme Court 9 January 1987, NJ 1987, No. 928.

[35] Supreme Court 1 July 1988, NJ 1988, No. 1000.

[36] Supreme Court, 22 January 1988, NJ. 1988, No. 891.

E. CASES BROUGHT BEFORE THE EUROPEAN COURT OF HUMAN RIGHTS

The case of *Engel and Others*[37] was the first case in the European Court against the Netherlands. The case concerned the conformity of Dutch military law with the European Convention. In particular the question arose whether the deprivation of liberty provided for in Dutch military law was in contravention of Article 5 of the ECHR. This Article prescribes certain procedures and gives certain guarantees in case of deprivation of liberty. According to the Court the procedure under Dutch military law violated Article 5 of the ECHR. The Court also found a breach of Article 6(1) of the ECHR in respect of the applicants because the disciplinary hearings in the presence of the parties had taken place *in camera*, in accordance with the then established practice of the Supreme Military Court in disciplinary proceedings. In 1984 the European Court of Human Rights pronounced judgment in three further cases concerning military servicemen, *De Jong, Baljet, and van den Brink,*[38] *Van der Sluijs, Zuiderveld, and Klappe*,[39] and *Duinhof and Duijf*.[40] These cases concerned the detention on remand of conscripts accused of military offences. The Court found in each case a violation of Article 5(3) of the ECHR because the hearings before the Military Court were not held 'promptly' after their arrest and the persons involved prior to the proceedings could be seen as 'officers authorized by law to exercise judicial power'. In the case of *De Jong, Baljet, and van den Brink* the Court further found a breach of Article 5(4) of the ECHR because the applicants were deprived of a 'speedy' judicial review of their detention. In the *Koster* case[41] the applicant had been brought before a military court after five days. Although the government argued that this delay had been caused by the weekend and biennially occurring manoeuvres in which the members of the military court had been participating, the Court nevertheless found a violation of Article 5(3) of the ECHR.

The *Winterwerp*[42] case also concerned Article 5 of the ECHR and deprivation of the liberty of persons of unsound mind. Article 5 prescribes that in a case of deprivation of the liberty of a person of unsound mind, the person concerned or his legal representative or his counsel may request the court at

[37] Judgment of 8 June 1976, Series A No. 22.
[38] Judgment of 22 May 1984, Series A No. 77.
[39] Judgment of 22 May 1984, Series A No. 78.
[40] Judgment of 22 May 1984, Series A No. 79
[41] Judgment of 28 November 1991, Series A No. 221.
[42] Judgment of 24 October 1979, Series A No. 33.

regular intervals to examine whether the deprivation of liberty is still necessary. Under the legislation in question the decision to refer this question to the court was decided by the public prosecutor. If the public prosecutor saw no reason to refer the matter to the court then the person involved had no direct access to a court and had to wait another year to make a new request. The Court found a violation of Article 5(4) in that the applicant's detention had been prolonged several times in procedures in which he was never present and had not been given the opportunity to argue his case. The Court also found a violation of Article 6(1) of the ECHR, because under the Lunacy Act as it was at that time any adult who was confined in a psychiatric hospital automatically lost the right to administer his or her property. According to the Court the total absence of the right to a court in the determination of civil rights as laid down by Article 6(1) of the ECHR was therefore violated. Since the Court had not found that the legislation in question was in violation of the Convention, the government ordered new guidelines. According to these a person of unsound mind is to be represented by counsel who may request the court at regular intervals to review the necessity of the deprivation of liberty. However, this did not prevent new problems. In the cases of *Van der Leer*[43] and *Wassink*[44] the Court found violations of Article 5, paragraphs 1, 2, and 4 since the applicants were not informed of the order of detention and the requirement of 'speediness' had not been fulfilled.

Other cases on Article 5 concerned the placement of persons 'at the government's disposal'. In the *Koendjbihari* case[45] a Dutch court ordered that, after serving a prison sentence, the applicant be placed 'at the government's disposal' and this led to his subsequent detention in a psychiatric hospital for treatment. Placement at the government's disposal initially lasts for two years and may be prolonged by a court for one or two years at a time at the request of the Public Prosecutor. The applicant, who considered that his detention in the hospital had become unlawful, demanded his immediate release. On the same date the Public Prosecutor requested one year's prolongation of the placement. The Court of Appeal granted this request. The applicant complained that his placement should have been terminated before the Public Prosecutor's request was made and that the court had not decided on the lawfulness of the prolongation either within the statutory time limit or speedily. In absence of any justification by the government, the Court found a failure to comply with the requirement of 'speediness' laid down in Article 5(4) of the ECHR.

[43] Judgment of 21 February 1990, Series A No. 170–A.
[44] Judgment of 27 September 1990, Series A No. 185–A.
[45] Judgment of 25 October 1990, Series A No. 185–B.

In the *Keus* case[46] the applicant after serving a prison sentence was placed 'at the government's disposal' in a psychiatric hospital for an initial period of two years. He escaped and shortly afterwards the Public Prosecutor requested the Regional Court to prolong the detention. The request was granted after hearing the Public Prosecutor and a member of the hospital staff, but neither the applicant nor his lawyer was informed of this, nor of a hearing at which the Public Prosecutor was present and following which the court granted the prolongation. The Strasbourg Court held that notwithstanding the extension of his placement at the government's disposal, the applicant retained the right protected by Article 5(4) of the ECHR to institute proceedings, on his return to the clinic, in a court to obtain a speedy decision on the lawfulness of his detention. There had been no violation of the Convention.

In the case of *Erkalo*[47] the request of the Public Prosecutor for the extension of a placement order was not received by the Regional Court until two months after the expiry of the statutory period, and so for eighty-two days the placement of the applicant had not been based on any judicial decision. The Strasbourg Court found that the detention of the applicant between the date of the expiry of the initial placement order and the date on which the Regional Court rendered its decision, from 3 July to 23 September 1993, was not compatible with the purpose of Article 5 of the ECHR, and was for that reason unlawful. Consequently, there had been a breach of Article 5(1).

The *Benthem* case[48] was a very important judgment for the Dutch legal order and concerned the application of Article 6 of the ECHR. Mr Van Benthem, a garage owner, was granted a licence for the installation of a liquid petroleum gas (LPG) storage tank. The municipal authorities granted this licence subject to fifty-six conditions, which they considered would encounter the dangers of fire and explosions. The Regional Health Inspector had written to the municipal authorities to advise them to refuse a licence. He lodged an appeal. The municipal authorities informed the applicant of the appeal and stated that since it had no suspensive effect, he could erect the installation. However, they added that if he did so, they would not be liable for any financial losses he might sustain in the event of the licence being cancelled. Subsequently the highest administrative instance, the Crown, quashed the decision to grant him a licence. Mr Van Benthem claimed that the proceedings violated Article 6 since he had no access to an independent tribunal. The Dutch government argued that Article 6 was not applicable since there was no civil right or obligation at stake. The Court considered that 'a genuine and serious' dispute as to the 'actual existence' of the right to a licence claimed by

[46] Judgment of 25 October 1990, Series A No. 185–C
[47] Judgment of 2 September 1998, Reports 1998.
[48] Judgment of 23 October 1985, Series A No. 97

the applicant arose between him and the Netherlands authorities at least after the Regional Inspector's appeal against the decision of the municipal authorities. This is shown especially by the fact that during a certain period Mr Van Benthem was able, without contravening the law, to exploit his installation by virtue of the licence granted by the latter authorities. In addition, the result of the proceedings complained of, which could—and in fact did—lead to a reversal of the decision under appeal, was directly decisive for the right at issue. The Crown thus had to determine a dispute concerning a right claimed by the applicant.

In order to determine whether the proceedings complained of were in conformity with Article 6(1), two institutions had to be considered: the Administrative Litigation Division of the Council of State and the Crown. With respect to the Administrative Litigation Division of the Council of State the Strasbourg Court observed that the Division tenders only advice. Admittedly, that advice is—as on the present occasion—followed in the great majority of cases, but this is only a practice of no binding force, from which the Crown can depart at any time. The proceedings before the Administrative Litigation Division of the Council of State thus do not constitute a 'determination by a tribunal of the matters in dispute' as is required by Article 6(1). With respect to the Crown, the Court held that unlike the Administrative Litigation Division, it is empowered to determine the dispute, but that the Convention requires more than this: the word 'tribunal' denotes 'bodies which exhibit . . . common fundamental features', of which the most important are independence and impartiality, and 'the guarantees of judicial procedure'. The Court held that the Royal Decree by which the Crown, as head of the executive, rendered its decision constituted, from the formal point of view, an administrative act and it emanated from a Minister who was responsible to Parliament therefor. Moreover, the Minister was the hierarchical superior of the Regional Inspector, who had lodged the appeal and of the Ministry's Director General, who had submitted the technical report to the Division. Finally, the Royal Decree was not susceptible to review by a judicial body as required by Article 6(1).

The case of *Oerlemans*[49] turned on whether the applicant could challenge before a court the lawfulness of an order designating his land as a protected natural site. Following the Court's judgment in the *Benthem* case, it was the view of many authorities on Netherlands law that the civil courts would be able to examine the lawfulness of any administrative decision coming within the scope of Article 6 against which an appeal lay to the Crown. The Supreme Court upheld this view and confirmed the principle in several judgments.

[49] Judgment of 27 November 1991, Series A No. 219

Accordingly under well established principles of Netherlands law which existed at the time of the Royal Decree in the present case, the applicant could have submitted his dispute to the civil courts for examination. There was thus no breach of Article 6(1).

In the *Van de Hurk* case[50] the applicant was a dairy farmer, who assumed certain financial commitments in order to extend his cowshed, bringing it into line with modern standards and increasing its capacity, enabling him to keep more dairy cattle. Under EEC Regulation No. 856/84 of 31 March 1984, implemented in the Netherlands by the Super Levy Ordinance of 18 April 1984, a dairy farmer could only produce a specified quantity of milk. A penalty, or 'additional levy', had to be paid for any surplus. The applicant was granted a reference quantity, which in his contention was insufficient for him to be able to meet his financial commitments. He claimed an extra levy-free quantity in view of the investment undertaken and the increased capacity of his cowshed. The Minister of Agriculture and Fisheries refused this. It was not disputed that the case concerned the 'determination of civil rights and obligations' so that Article 6(1) was applicable. The applicant alleged that his case had not been determined by an 'independent tribunal', since section 74 of the Industrial Appeals Act allowed the Crown—that is, the Monarch acting on the initiative and under the political responsibility of the Minister concerned—to decide that judgments of the Tribunal should not be implemented.

In the Court's opinion, the power to give a binding decision which could not be altered by a non-judicial authority to the detriment of an individual was inherent in the very notion of a 'tribunal', as was confirmed by the word 'determination'. This power could also be seen as a component of the 'independence' required by Article 6(1). The Court found that there was nothing in the information at its disposal to indicate that the mere existence of the Crown's powers under section 74 had any influence on the way the Tribunal handled and decided the cases which came before it. In particular, no significance could be attributed to the low success rate (less than 2 per cent) of appeals against decisions taken under the Ordinance on the Additional Levy. Whether or not the requirements of Article 6 had been met could not be assessed with reference to the applicant's chances of success alone, since this provision did not guarantee any particular outcome. At the material time Article 74 of the Industrial Appeals Act, which remained in force until 1 January 1994, allowed the Minister partially or completely to deprive a Tribunal judgment of its effect to the detriment of an individual. One of the basic attributes of a 'tribunal' was therefore missing. A defect of this nature might, however, be remedied by the availability of subsequent review by a

[50] Judgment of 19 April 1994. Series A No. 288.

judicial body that afforded all the guarantees required by Article 6. The Court noted that the Industrial Appeals Tribunal was not allowed to depart from the Crown's decision under section 74. To that extent the possibility of a retrial could hardly be considered an effective remedy. Moreover, although it was true that an award of compensation was possible in the event of the Crown's using its powers under section 74, compensation could not be equated with the advantages obtained under an original judgment of the Industrial Appeals Tribunal ordering a government body to take a specific decision in favour of the party seeking review. There had accordingly been a violation of Article 6(1) in that the applicant's civil rights and obligations had not been 'determined' by a 'tribunal'.

In the case of *British American Tobacco Company Ltd*[51] the applicant company argued that the Patent Office, and more particularly its Appeals Division, could not be considered to be an 'independent and impartial' tribunal. They raised several objections to the institutional structure within which the Patent Office operated and to certain aspects of its internal organization. They pointed to the fact that the members of the Patent Office were employed on the same conditions as the other civil servants of the Industrial Property Bureau. With respect to access to civil courts the Court noted that no Netherlands civil court ever held itself competent to review decisions of the Patent Office regarding patent applications. It was true that no civil proceedings directed against a decision of the Appeals Division of the Patent Office had ever resulted in a contrary ruling. In this respect the present case had to be distinguished from that of the Court's judgment in the case of *Van de Hurk v the Netherlands*, where the civil courts had held the administrative tribunal in question to afford sufficient safeguards. The finding as to the state of Netherlands law made in the Court's judgment of *Oerlemans v the Netherlands* confirmed that if, after a decision of the Appeals Division, the civil courts had found that the Appeals Division was not a 'tribunal' offering the requisite safeguards, they would as a matter of domestic law have had full jurisdiction to rule on the merits. The applicant company, however, had chosen not to submit a claim to the civil courts. It is not for the Court to prejudge the possible decision of the Netherlands civil courts or, therefore, to rule in abstract as to adequacy of the remedies available. Therefore, the Court found no violation.

In the cases of *Masson and Van Zon*[52] and *Leutscher*[53] the applicants submitted that, contrary to the requirements of Article 6(1) of the ECHR, their requests for financial compensation for the restrictions on their liberty and

[51] Judgment of 20 November 1995, Series A No. 331.
[52] Judgment of 28 September 1995, Series A No. 327–A.
[53] Judgment of 26 March 1996, Reports 1996–II, No. 6.

their requests for reimbursement of their legal costs incurred in connection with the criminal proceedings had not been dealt with in public by an impartial tribunal. The Court concluded that whether or not the impugned proceedings involved a 'dispute' for the purposes of Article 6(1), the claims asserted by the applicants did not in any event concern a 'right' which could be said to be recognized under Netherlands law. In the latter case the Court further held that Article 6(2) of the ECHR does not confer on a person 'charged with a criminal offence' a right to reimbursement of his legal costs where proceedings taken against him are discontinued, and nor does the refusal to order such reimbursement to the former accused in itself amount to a penalty or a measure that can be equated with a penalty.

In the *Feldbrugge* case[54] Article 6(1) was at stake in proceedings concerning the right to health insurance proceedings. The Court held that an analysis of the characteristics of the Netherlands system of social health insurance disclosed that the claimed entitlement comprises features of both public law and private law. Therefore it held Article 6(1) to be applicable. Mrs Feldbrugge attempted, unsuccessfully, to take her case to the full Appeals Board and subsequently to the Central Appeals Board, her action being declared inadmissible on both occasions. Under the 'permanent medical expert procedure', an objection may only be lodged with an Appeals Board against the decision of the president of the Board on one of the following four grounds: the expert knew the patient in another capacity or failed to comply with certain procedural requirements; the President's decision does not bear upon the dispute or did not follow the expert's advice. Decisions of an Appeals Board in the context of this kind of procedure are not subject to appeal before the Central Appeals Board save, as has been held in the case-law of the latter Board, in the event of non-observance of rules of a formal nature. Framed as they were in such restrictive terms, the conditions of access to the two Boards prevented Mrs Feldbrugge from challenging the merits of the decision by the President of the Appeals Board. Accordingly, the shortcoming found to exist in respect of the procedure before this judicial officer was not capable of being cured at a later stage. In conclusion, there had been a breach of Article 6(1).

The case of *Terra Woningen BV*[55] concerned the question of access to court. In a report it was found that pollution was caused by heavy metals and the local residents were informed that soil-cleaning measures were necessary. In the course of ensuing proceedings it was decided to reduce the rent of the flats. The applicant company, developers of real property who owned six

[54] Judgment of 29 May 1986, Series A No. 99.
[55] Judgment of 17 December 1996, Reports 1998–VI, No. 25.

blocks of flats nearby the place of pollution, complained that they had not had the benefit of effective judicial review in the determination of their civil rights as the District Court had considered itself bound by the Provincial's Executive finding in respect of the soil pollution and its effects on public health and the environment and had thus denied them a judicial ruling on an important part of their case. The Court held that the rent determination proceedings in question concerned a determination of the applicant company's 'civil rights and obligations'. In that respect a 'tribunal' must have jurisdiction to examine all questions of fact and laws relevant to the dispute before it. By holding that the risk of public health or environment was 'necessarily implied' by the Provincial Executive's decision, the District Court deprived itself of the jurisdiction to examine the facts which were crucial to the dispute. There had been a violation of Article 6(1) of the ECHR.

The cases of *Abdoella*[56] and *Bunkate*[57] concerned the length of criminal proceedings. The Court found violations of Article 6(1). In the first case the delays—totalling more than twenty-one months of the fifty-two which it took to deal with the case—were found to be unacceptable, especially in view of the fact that the accused was kept in detention in the meantime. In the case of *Bunkate* proceedings took as long as fifteen and a half months. In the case of *Hozee*[58] the Court did not find a violation, although in total the proceedings lasted eight years, five months, and eighteen days. The complexity was compounded by the involvement of co-suspects. There was no period of inertia on the part of the authorities. The length of this phase of the proceedings could not be considered unreasonable. In the post-investigation proceedings there were three instances involved, the District Court, the Court of Appeal, and the Supreme Court. That period also could not be said to be excessive.

In the case of *Schouten and Meldrum*[59] the length of civil proceedings was at stake. This was the first time the European Court of Human Rights had to rule on the applicability of Article 6(1) to a dispute concerning contributions under social security schemes, as distinct from entitlement to benefits under such schemes. Echoing its *Feldbrugge* judgment, the Court held that the social security legislation in question was grafted onto the contract of employment, thus forming one of the constituents of the relationship between employer and employee. Finally, the Court again drew attention to the similarity between the social security schemes and private insurance: the occupational associations used risk-covering techniques and management methods inspired by those current in the private insurance market; they also conducted

[56] Judgment of 25 November 1992, Series A No. 248–A.
[57] Judgment of 26 May 1993, Series A No. 248–B.
[58] Judgment of 22 May 1998, Reports 1998.
[59] Judgment of 9 December 1994, Series A No. 304.

their dealings in a similar way; and, more significantly, private insurance was available to cover largely the same risk as those covered by the social security schemes. The foregoing examination of the relative cogency of the features of public and private law present in the instant cases led the Court to find that the private law features were of greater significance than those of public law. On balance, the disputes in issue were accordingly to be regarded as having involved 'the determination of civil rights and obligations', and Article 6(1) was therefore applicable. The Court found that there had been a violation of Article 6(1) in both cases in that the applicants' 'civil rights and obligations' had not been determined within a 'reasonable time'.

In the *Nortier* case[60] the applicant complained under Article 6(1) that he had not received a hearing before an impartial tribunal since the judge who determined the charge against him had also acted as an investigating judge and had taken several decisions regarding his detention on remand. The Court found no violation in this case.

At the time of the judgment in the case of *Dombo Beheer*[61] the relevant legislation had been already substantially changed. During negotiations, the applicant company's managing director and the bank's branch manager acted on equal footing, both being empowered to negotiate on behalf of their respective employers. It was therefore difficult to see why they should not both have been allowed to give evidence. The applicant company was therefore placed at a substantial disadvantage *vis-à-vis* the bank. The Court held that there had been a violation of Article 6(1) of the ECHR.

In the case of *De Haan*[62] the European Court of Human Rights ruled that a judge who had presided over a Chamber of Appeals Tribunal which was called upon to decide on an objection against a decision for which he himself was responsible could not be considered objectively impartial under the guarantees of Article 6(1) of the ECHR. The judge, sitting as a single judge in the permanent medical expert procedure, had first given a decision on the merits of the individual case after examining all the evidence contained in the case file. The same judge had then presided over the Chamber of Appeals Tribunal called upon to examine the individual's objection against the same decision. This failing was not capable of being redressed at a later stage, as an appeal to the Central Appeals Tribunal was only possible on limited grounds, which did not include the grounds that an erroneous view had been taken of the medical evidence. The Tribunal was composed of a professional judge assisted by two lay judges.

[60] Judgment of 24 August 1993, Series A No. 367.
[61] Judgment of 27 October 1993, Series A No. 274.
[62] Judgment of 26 August 1997, Reports 1997–IV.

The use of anonymous witnesses was at stake in the *Kostovski* case.[63] The essence of the applicant's claim was that he had not received a fair trial (Article 6(1)) and that Article 6(3)(d) had been violated because he had not had the right to examine or have examined witnesses against him and to obtain the attendance and examination of witnesses on his behalf under the same conditions as witnesses against him. The Court recalled that in principle all the evidence had to be produced in the presence of the accused at a public hearing with a view to adverse argument. However, statements obtained at the pre-trial stage could be used as evidence, provided the rights of the defence had been respected; as a rule, those rights required that the accused be given, at some stage in the proceedings, an adequate and proper opportunity to challenge and question witnesses against him. In the Court's view that opportunity had not been afforded to him. Moreover, the Court did not consider that the procedures followed by the judicial authorities had counterbalanced the handicaps suffered by the defence. Whilst recognizing the force of the government's references to an increase in the intimidation of witnesses and the need to balance the various interests involved, the Court observed that the right to fair administration of justice could not be sacrificed to expediency. The use of anonymous statements as sufficient evidence to found a conviction, as in the present case, was a different matter from reliance on such sources at the investigation stage. The Court concluded that in the circumstances of the case Mr Kostovski could not be said to have received a fair trial. It accordingly held unanimously that there had been a violation of paragraph 3(d), in conjunction with paragraph 1 of Article 6.

The *Doorson* case[64] also concerned reliance on the evidence of anonymous witnesses, and on an incriminating statement made to the police by a named witness but retracted in open court, and on a statement made during the police investigation by a named witness whom the defence had no opportunity to question. Further the trial court had refused to hear a defence expert but heard an expert for the prosecution. In these circumstances, the handicaps under which the defence laboured were sufficiently counterbalanced by the procedures followed by the judicial authorities; even so, a conviction should not be based either solely or to a decisive extent on anonymous statements. However, that was not the case here. The evidence obtained from witnesses under conditions in which the rights of the defence cannot be secured to the extent normally required by the Convention has to be treated with extreme care. The Court was satisfied that that such care had been taken in the instant case.

[63] Judgment of 20 November 1989, Series A No. 166.
[64] Judgment of 26 March 1996, Reports 1996–II No. 6.

The Court took a different view in the case of *Van Mechelen*.[65] The Court first pointed out that balancing the interests of the defence against arguments in favour of maintaining the anonymity of witnesses raises special problems if the witnesses in question are members of the national police force, who owe a general duty of obedience to the state's executive authorities and usually have links with the prosecution. For these reasons alone their use as anonymous witnesses should be resorted to only in exceptional circumstances. In addition, it is in the nature of things that their duties, particularly in the case of arresting officers, may involve giving evidence in open court. On the other hand, the Court recognized in principle that, provided that the rights of the defence are respected, it may be legitimate for the police authorities to wish to preserve the anonymity of an agent deployed in undercover activities, for his own or his family's protection and so as not to impair his usefulness for future operations. Moreover, the only evidence relied on by the Court of Appeal which positively identified the applicants as the perpetrators of the crimes were statements of anonymous police officers. That being so the conviction of the applicants was based 'to a decisive extent' on these anonymous statements. The present case was distinguished from that of *Doorson v the Netherlands*, and the Court found that there had been a violation.

The cases of *Lala*[66] and *Pelladoah*[67] concerned convictions *in absentia*, and in particular the fact that the accuseds' lawyers were not given an opportunity to present their defences, although they were present during the trial. Under Netherlands law an accused was, as a rule, not obliged to attend his trial. In the interest of a fair and just criminal process it was, according to the Court, of capital importance that the accused should appear at his trial and be adequately defended both at first instance and on appeal. In the Court's judgment the latter interest prevails, and consequently the fact that the defendants, in spite of having been properly summoned, did not appear, could not, even in the absence of an excuse, justify depriving them of their right under Article 6(3)(c) to be defended by counsel. For the right to be defended by counsel to be practical and effective, and not merely theoretical, its exercise should not be made dependent on the fulfilment of unduly formalistic conditions. It is for the courts to ensure that a trial is fair and accordingly that the counsel who attends the trial for the apparent purpose of defending the accused in his absence, is given the opportunity to do so. The Court concluded that there had been a violation of Article 6(1).

The cases of *JJ and KDS v the Netherlands*[68] concerned plaintiffs in

[65] Judgment of 23 April 1997, Reports 1997–III, No. 36.
[66] Judgment of 22 September 1994, Series A No. 297–A.
[67] Judgment of 22 September 1994, Series A No. 297–B.
[68] Judgment of 27 March 1998, Reports 1998–II, No. 68.

taxation proceedings in the Supreme Court who were unable to reply to the advisory opinion of the Advocate-General. Regard being had by the Court to what was at stake for the applicant in the proceedings and to the nature of the advisory opinion of the Advocate-General, the fact that it was impossible for the applicants to reply to it before the Supreme Court took its decision infringed their right to adversarial proceedings. That right entails in principle the opportunity for the parties to a criminal or civil trial to have knowledge of and comment on all evidence adduced or observations filed, even by an independent member of the national legal service, with a view to influencing the court's decision. There had been a violation.

In the case of *X and Y v the Netherlands*[69] a gap in Dutch law came to light. Ms Y, a mentally handicapped sixteen-year-old had been the victim of sexual abuse. Dutch law at that time required a complaint by the actual victim in order to institute criminal proceedings against the perpetrator. Ms Y was not capable of filing such a complaint and her legal representative could no do so in her place. The Court found a violation of Article 8 of the ECHR.

In the *Berrehab* case[70] the right to family life was at stake. The applicants were Mr Berrehab, a Moroccan citizen, and his daughter who had Dutch nationality. They complained of the refusal by the Dutch authorities to grant Mr Berrehab a new residence permit after his divorce from his wife, a Dutch citizen, and of his resulting deportation from the Netherlands. The Court did not see cohabitation as a *sine qua non* of family life between parents and minor children. It has held that the relationship created between the spouses by a lawful and genuine marriage has to be regarded as family life. A child born of such a union is *ipso jure* part of that relationship; there existed family life between child and parents. The right of access was somewhat theoretical since in practice disputed measures (expulsion to Morocco) prevented the applicants from maintaining regular contacts with each other, although these were essential as the child was very young. The Court found a violation of Article 8 of the ECHR.

In the *Ahmut* case[71] the Netherlands authorities refused to grant a residence permit to a Moroccan minor which would have allowed him to live with his father, who had dual Moroccan and Netherlands nationality. The son still had strong links with the linguistic and cultural environment of his country, and still had family there. The fact that the applicants were living apart resulted from the father's decision to settle in the Netherlands rather than remain in Morocco. The father had retained his original Moroccan nationality and was not prevented from maintaining the degree of family life that he

[69] Judgment of 26 March 1985, Series A No. 91.
[70] Judgment of 21 June 1988, Series A No. 138.
[71] Judgment of 28 November 1996, Reports 1996–IV, No. 24.

himself had opted for when he moved to the Netherlands in the first place. Nor was there any obstacle to his returning to Morocco. Article 8 does not guarantee a right to choose the most suitable place to develop family life. By sending his son to a boarding school, the father had arranged for him to be cared for in Morocco. The Court saw no need to go into the question whether the son's relatives living in Morocco were willing and able to take care of him. In the circumstances of the case, there had been no failure on government's part to strike a fair balance between the applicants' interests on one hand and its own interest in controlling immigration on the other. The Court concluded that there had been no violation.

The case of *Nsona*[72] concerned the refusal by Netherlands authorities to grant one of the applicants, a nine-year-old girl, access to Netherlands territory, the removal of that applicant to Zaire, and the separation of the two applicants. The Court held that the Netherlands authorities were in principle entitled to refuse the child access to the country provided that such refusal was not inconsistent with the obligations of the respondent state under the Convention. The separation of the applicants could not be imputed to the respondent State. On the facts of the case, the way in which the removal was effected did not constitute 'inhuman or degrading' treatment as these expressions are to be understood in the context of Article 3 of the ECHR. Given that arrangements were made, although by Swissair and not by the Netherlands government, for the applicant to be met at Kinshasa Airport and that these proved adequate, there was no ground for reproaching the Netherlands government for failing to act with due diligence. There had been no violation of Article 3. The Court also found no violation of Article 8.

The case of *Kroon and Others*[73] also concerned Article 8, this time in conjunction with Article 14. Mrs Kroon had married Mr M in 1979. He subsequently disappeared and his whereabouts remain unknown. Mrs Kroon established a permanent relationship with Mr Zerrouk and their son, Samir M'Hallem-Driss, was born in October 1987. Mrs Kroon, however, remained legally married to Mr M until their marriage was dissolved in July 1988 following divorce proceedings. A request to enable Mrs Kroon to declare that Mr M was not the father of Samir and have this recognized was refused by the registrar of births, deaths, and marriages. Throughout the domestic proceedings it had been assumed by all concerned, including the registrar of births, deaths, and marriages, that the relationship in question constituted 'family life' and that Article 8 was applicable; this had also been accepted by the Netherlands courts. As it had been established that the relationship between

[72] Judgment of 28 November 1996, Reports 1996–V, No. 23.
[73] Judgment of 27 October 1994, Series A No. 297–C.

the applicants qualified as 'family life', the Court held that there was a positive obligation on the part of the competent authorities to allow complete legal family ties to be formed between Mr Zerrouk and his son Samir as expeditiously as possible. The government argued that solutions to the applicants' problems existed, so that, even assuming 'family life' to exist, the Netherlands had complied fully with any positive obligations it might have as regards the applicants. The first possible solution suggested by the government, 'step-parent adoption' (ie adoption of Samir by both Mrs Kroon and Mr Zerrouk), would make Samir the 'legitimate' child of Mr Zerrouk and Mrs Kroon. However, it would require Mrs Kroon and Mr Zerrouk to marry each other, and they did not wish to do so.

In the opinion of the Court, a solution which only allowed a father to create a legal tie with a child with whom he has a bond amounting to family life if he married the child's mother could not be regarded as compatible with the notion of 'respect for family life'. Nor did the Court accept the second possible solution suggested by the government, namely that of joint custody (for which legislation was being prepared). Even if the legislation came into force as the government anticipated, joint custody will leave the legal ties between Samir and Mrs Kroon's former husband intact and would continue to preclude the formation of such ties between Samir and Mr Zerrouk. In the Court's opinion, 'respect for family life' required that biological and social reality prevail over a legal presumption which, as in the present case, flew in the face of both established fact and the wishes of those concerned without actually benefiting anyone. Accordingly, even having regard to the margin of appreciation left to the state, the Netherlands had failed to secure for the applicants the respect for their family life to which they are entitled under the Convention. In the light of its findings under Article 8, the Court did not find it necessary to consider the issue under Article 14.

The case of *Van Raalte*[74] also concerned the question of discrimination, this time in conjunction with the right to property. The applicant had never been married and had no children. The Inspector of Direct Taxes sent the applicant an assessment of his contributions for the year 1985 under various social security schemes, including the General Child Benefits Act. The applicant filed an objection to this assessment. He based his argument on section 25(2) of the General Child Benefits Act and on the Royal Decree of 27 February 1980, by virtue of which unmarried childless women aged forty-five and older were exempted from the obligation to pay contributions under the General Child Benefits Act; in his view the prohibition of discrimination such as was contained in Article 1 of the Netherlands Constitution and Article 26

[74] Judgment of 27 February 1997, Reports 1997–I, No. 29.

of the International Covenant on Civil and Political Rights implied that this exemption should be extended to men in the same situation. The Court noted that the difference in treatment was based on gender. The exemption in question ran counter to underlying character of the scheme. While the state enjoys a certain margin of appreciation in introducing exemptions to contributory obligations, Article 14 requires in principle that these apply equally to both men and women. Just as women aged forty-five or over may give birth, some men of forty-five or younger are unable to procreate. An unmarried childless woman aged forty-five or over may become eligible for benefits under the scheme. The argument that to levy contributions from unmarried childless women aged forty-five or over would impose an unfair emotional burden applied equally to unmarried childless men or childless couples. The difference in treatment was not justified. There had been a violation of Article 14 taken together with Article 1 of Protocol No. 1.

The case of *Vereniging Weekblad Bluf!*[75] Concerned the complaint by an association which published a weekly magazine, '*Bluf!*', aimed at a readership interested in left-wing politics. The applicant association got hold of a quarterly survey of activities of the Internal Security Service, a document by then almost six years old that was classified as confidential. The newspaper was seized and withdrawn from circulation because it contained information whose secrecy was considered necessary in the interest of the state. After the newspaper was seized, the publisher printed a large number of further copies and sold them in the streets of Amsterdam, which were very crowded. Consequently, the information in question had already been widely distributed when the journal was withdrawn from circulation and had been made accessible to a large number of people, who were able in their turn to communicate it to others. Furthermore, the media had commented on the events. That being so, the protection of the information as a state secret was no longer justified and the withdrawal of the issue in question was no longer necessary to achieve the legitimate aim pursued. In short, as the measure had not been necessary in a democratic society, there had been a violation of Article 10 of the ECHR.

In the case of *Gasus Dosier- und Fördertechnik GmbH*[76] the right to property was at stake. The applicant company filed an objection against seizure by the tax authorities, but this was rejected. The Court's opinion took into account that under Netherlands law third parties whose goods were seized under the relevant legislation could use the powers conferred thereby and seek review by a tribunal under a procedure which met the requirements of Article 6(1). It therefore came to the conclusion that the requirement of

[75] Judgment of 9 February 1995, Series A No. 306–A.
[76] Judgment of 25 February 1995, Series A No. 306–B.

proportionality had been satisfied, and accordingly there had been no violation of Article 1 of Protocol No. 1.

F. REMEDIAL ACTION TAKEN BY THE GOVERNMENT IN RESPONSE TO BEING HELD IN VIOLATION OF THE CONVENTION

Under Dutch law there is no provision for reviewing or reopening a case after the European Court has found a violation of the Convention. There is provision for granting a pardon following a criminal conviction which involved a violation of the Convention. The aftermath of the case of *Van Mechelen and Others* was that since it was not possible to reopen the case the applicants were released.

While the case of *Engel and Others* was before the European Court of Human Rights, the Netherlands amended its legislation with respect to deprivation of the liberty of servicemen in order to fulfil the requirements laid down in Article 5. So by the date of the judgment no further changes were needed. As a consequence of the three judgments of 1984 in the cases of *De Jong, Baljet, and van den Brink, Van der Sluijs, Zuiderveld, and Klappe*, and *Duinhof and Duijf* the government informed the Committee of Ministers of the Council of Europe[77] that bills for revision of the administration of military justice were under revision; it took until 1 January 1991 for these bills to enter into force.

The result of the judgment in the *Winterwerp* case was not very far-reaching because the legislation in question was not found to violate the Convention, but guidelines were issued instructing the public prosecutors to deal with such questions. According to the new guidelines a person of unsound mind shall be represented by counsel who may request the court at regular intervals to review the necessity of the deprivation of liberty. While the case was pending before the Court the legislation in question had already been under review for more than ten years. The government informed the Committee of Ministers that it had introduced a revised bill to the Parliament. Provisions had been included to the effect that in all cases of involuntary admission to psychiatric hospitals, prolongations of the admission, or requests for dismissal, the patient would have the right to be heard by a court. The provision which provided for the automatic loss of the patient's power to administer his or her property had been repealed.[78] However, the

[77] Resolution DH(85)11 of 31 May 1985.

[78] Resolution DH(82)2 of 24 June 1982.

bill only entered into force on 17 January 1994 so it was not surprising that new cases had arisen in the interim, in each of which the European Court found a violation of Article 5.

At the hearings before the European Court in the case of *X and Y v the Netherlands* the Court was informed that the Dutch Ministry of Justice had prepared a bill modifying the provision on sexual offences. By the Act of 27 February 1985, the provisions of the Dutch criminal code concerning the lodging of a complaint were amended. The Act entered into force on 1 April 1985 and since then the victim's legal representative in civil matters may lodge a complaint if the victim is mentally handicapped.

To meet the requirements of the Court's judgment in the *Benthem* case the Provisional Act on Disputes before the Crown was adopted. This Act gave jurisdiction in such matters to the Administrative Litigation Division of the Council of State. Therefore, the Administrative Litigation Division acted as a 'tribunal' in the sense of Article 6(1) of the ECHR. On 1 January 1994 the General Administrative Law Act came into force, laying down new uniform rules of administrative law procedures.[79] This Act also provides a right of appeal to the Regional Court against decisions of occupational associations concerning social security contributions.[80] An appeal lies to the Central Appeals Tribunal.

Following the judgment of the European Court of Human Rights in the case of *Proccola v Luxembourg*[81] there was concern over the structural impartiality of the Dutch Council of State. In that case the Court held that a combination of an advisory role in the legislative process and a judicial role raised doubts about the impartiality of the Luxembourg Council of State acting in that capacity. As the Dutch Council of State exercises a similar combination of functions, the Netherlands Minister of Justice indicated that discussions were underway in the Netherlands as part of the restructuring of the Dutch judiciary to address this concern.

In response to the judgment in the *Feldbrugge* case the Appeals Act was amended and entered into force on 1 October 1991 in order to meet the requirements of Article 6 of the ECHR.

The *Kostovski* case gave rise to an amendment of the Code of Criminal Procedure, which resulted in a new definition of 'threatened witnesses', who may remain anonymous, and new provisions on the methods used to safeguard the rights of the accused when the testimony of such persons is used in criminal proceedings.

[79] This new Act also replaced the Industrial Appeals Act 1954, there no provisions similar Section 74 of the former Act, which gave rise to the judgment of the European Court in the *van de Hurk* case.

[80] See *Schouten and Meldrum,* Judgment of 9 December 1994, Series A No. 304.

[81] Judgment of 28 September 1995, Series A No. 326.

An amendment of the Code of Civil Proceedings was necessary as a result of the Court's judgment in the case of *Dombo Beheer BV* with respect to the law on evidence in civil proceedings. Article 190 of the Code now allows parties to give evidence on their own behalf.

Since the judgments in the cases of *Lala* and *Pelladoah* the Supreme Court has reversed its case-law to allow an accused who is absent from a hearing to which he has been summoned to be represented by counsel even if the absence is not justified.[82]

As a result of the judgment in the case of *De Haan* the Appeals Tribunals have now been abolished and replaced by administrative law divisions of the Regional Courts.

Since the judgment in the case of *De Kroon and Others*, a law of 24 December 1997, which entered into force on 1 April 1998, amended the title of the Civil Code concerning parental rights. While the presumption of paternity remains in favour of the husband of the child's mother, proceedings to contest paternity may be instituted by him, by the mother, or by the child. The biological father's paternity can then be established by his recognition of the child or by judicial proceedings.[83] To remedy the effect of the European Court judgment in the *Van Raalte* case the provision whereby single women aged forty-five and over without children were exempted from social welfare contributions under the General Child Benefits Act has been abolished.[84]

G. CONCLUDING REMARKS

As we have seen, the practical effects of human rights treaties has been less positive for the legal order of the Netherlands, especially until the end of the 1970s. In many instances Dutch courts avoided a confrontation between the Convention and Dutch law either by declaring the provision of the Convention relied upon by a party to be inapplicable, or holding it to be not directly applicable, or giving it an interpretation compatible with the applicable domestic legal provisions. This situation was partly due to a lack of familiarity among the judiciary with the content of the Convention, and in particular with the Strasbourg case-law. In the eighties the situation improved greatly, and it is still improving. Especially in legal training much more attention is paid to the international protection of human rights. On one

[82] Resolutions DH(95)240 and DH(95)241 of 19 October 1995.
[83] Resolution DH(98)148 of 11 June 1998.
[84] Resolution DH(97)353 of 11 July 1997.

hand many lawyers are now sufficiently keen on drawing their client's attention to the possibilities which human rights treaties and especially the European Convention afford in municipal proceedings. On the other hand invoking human rights treaties no longer provokes the irritation of the court or the Public Prosecutor.

The execution of European Court judgments does not create major problems in the Netherlands. Not only judgments against the Netherlands have compelled the Dutch authorities to take action: also judgments directed against other states parties have caused the Dutch legislative and executive to reconsider legislation or directives. The developments since the judgments in the *Marckx* case are discussed above. Another example is the *Brogan* case[85] in which judgment was given against the United Kingdom. This case concerned detention on remand and the right to be brought promptly before a judge or officer authorized by law to exercise judicial power to decide on the lawfulness of the deprivation of liberty. When the United Kingdom was found to be in violation, the Dutch authorities realized that the Dutch legislation also needed to be amended.[86]

Finally, some words about the European Convention in general. The impact of the Convention's mechanism is in my opinion owed mainly to the status given to the Convention in the hierarchy of domestic laws. This is mainly true of those states where the Convention has direct effect.[87] Even in states where the provisions of the Convention are not directly applicable the Convention may produce effects via the judgments of the national courts insofar as the latter give a 'reflex effect' to the Convention. This means that if the national courts cannot apply the Convention directly and are unable to refrain from applying rules of national law contrary thereto, they will interpret those rules so as to make them consistent with the Convention. This has been pointed out by A. Drzemczewski in his study on the domestic effect of the Convention, where he states for example with respect to the United Kingdom that

> the operative provisions of the decisions of the European Court of Human Rights in cases in which the United Kingdom is a party bind the authorities on the international plane under Article 53 of the Convention.[88]

[85] Judgment of 23 March 1988, Series A No. 145–B.

[86] See in this respect: Yvonne Klerk and Eric Janse de Jonge, note 3 above, pp. 119–120.

[87] G. Ress, 'The Effects of Judgments and Decisions in Domestic Law', in R. St. J. Macdonald *et al.* (eds), *The European System for the Protection of Human Rights* (Dordrecht: Nijhoff, 1993), p. 848.

[88] A. Drzemczewski, *European Human Rights Convention in Domestic Law* (Oxford: Clarendon Press, 1983), p. 316.

Another reason may be that decision-making organs and the courts of the member states are willing to effect conformity with the Convention in order to prevent any future finding by the Court or the Committee of Ministers of a violation of the Convention. In general, the domestic authorities of the parties to the Convention co-operate faithfully with the Strasbourg organs.

24

Norway

ERIK MØSE

A. INTRODUCTION

Together with representatives from eleven other states, the Norwegian Minister of Foreign Affairs, Mr Halvard Lange, signed the European Convention on Human Rights (ECHR) in the Palazzo Barberini on 4 November 1950. Norway ratified it on 15 January 1952 as the second of the signatory states, after the United Kingdom (March 1951). The Convention entered into force for Norway on 3 September 1953 when ten instruments of ratification had been deposited, cf Article 66(2).

On the basis of the Teitgen Report, submitted to the Committee of Ministers by the Parliamentary Assembly (Recommendation 38 of 8 September 1949) Norwegian representatives participated in the drafting of the Convention, first during the meetings in February and March 1950 of the Committee of Experts for Human Rights, then at the Conference of Senior Officials in June 1950 and at the sessions of the Committee of Ministers in August and November 1950. This is not the place to describe in detail the Norwegian position during the negotiations.[1] However, it is worth mentioning that the delegation belonged to the group which was in favour of a convention based on precisely defined rights and not simply an enumeration of

[1] For details, see E Møse: 'Lovavdelingen og menneskerettighetene—overblikk og tilbakeblikk' (The Department of Legislation and Human Rights—overview and retrospective view) in *Festskrift Lovavdelingen—100 år 1885–1985* (Essays in honour of the Department of Legislation), 1986, pp. 148–159, and Einar Løchen: 'Fra Ragnarokk til rettighetsforsvar: Om tilblivelsen av Den europeiske menneskerettighetskonvensjon' (From Chaos to Human Rights. The drafting of the ECHR), *Mennesker og Rettigheter*, vol. 8, 1990, pp. 31–35. Mr Løchen, then Counsellor in the Ministry of Foreign Affairs, later Supreme Court Justice, was one of the Norwegian representatives in the Expert Committee in Spring 1950 (together with Supreme Court Advocate Ole Torleif Røed) and played an important part during subsequent discussions in Oslo on draft texts submitted during Autumn 1950, together with representatives from the Department of Legislation in the Ministry of Justice. At the Conference of Senior Officials in June, the Norwegian representative was Advocate Harald Sund, later Justice in Gulating Court of Appeals.

rights.[2] Together with other delegations it also proposed that the Commission should have competence to adopt opinions on facts and on law, as well as on whether there had been a violation of the Convention.

In 1950 the Norwegian authorities were of the view that it would be unconstitutional to give a European Court jurisdiction to review decisions by the Norwegian Supreme Court in cases concerning Norwegian citizens. However, no constitutional hindrances were found when the drafters of the Convention agreed in June 1950 that the jurisdiction of the Court should be optional. There was a certain reticence concerning the wide competence of the Committee of Ministers—a political body—to make binding decisions as to whether the Convention had been violated, but in the event this did not prevent ratification.

Before ratification, Norwegian authorities in conformity with usual practice (see B.2 below) compared the requirements of the Convention with domestic law in order to find possible discrepancies which would necessitate legislative changes or reservations. Article 2 of the Constitution of 1814, which provided that 'Jesuits are not tolerated', was not considered to be in conformity with Article 9 of the Convention. When proposing to Parliament that it should give its consent to ratification, the Ministry of Justice assumed—with some reservations—in view of legal developments that the authorities were not under a duty to ensure that there were no foreign Jesuits on Norwegian territory, but that they had to take measures in cases of active propaganda or organized activities by the Order of Jesuits or by its subordinate branches.[3] By virtue of Article 64 of the Convention, Norway therefore tabled a reservation, which was later withdrawn following the abrogation of the constitutional provision after some controversy in Parliament (see C.1 below).

In a letter of 12 May 1955 to the Ministry of Foreign Affairs, the first Norwegian member of the Commission, Paal Berg, Chief Justice of the

[2] An overview of the negotiations is given in A. H. Robertson and J. G. Merrills: *Human Rights in Europe*, 1993, pp. 1–14, see in particular pp. 7–9 and 31–32 concerning the two versions based on the method of 'enumeration' and 'definition' respectively.

[3] See Stortingsproposisjon No. 93 (1951) pp. 2–3. In view of that interpretation, it is not entirely correct to describe the former Article 2 of the Constitution as an exclusion of Jesuits from Norwegian territory (see as an example Harris, O'Boyle, and Warbrick: *Law of the European Convention on Human Rights*, 1995, p. 362). It should be added that the provision had not been applied for many years. Nevertheless, it was rather peculiar and seemed to have no counterparts in other Western European countries then members of the Council of Europe. The Ministry of Foreign Affairs therefore suggested that the Ministry of Justice initiate its abolition. Løchen, above n. 1, p. 32, has described the embarrassment felt by the Norwegian representatives during the negotiations in the Committee of Experts when the Belgian delegate Beaufort, a professor of international law and a Catholic priest, expressed astonishment at the existence of such a clause in a modern democracy like Norway. Still according to Løchen, the situation in other countries was also subject to criticism based on Article 9: Turkey had a prohibition against 'obscuritisme' and Sweden against orders of monks.

Supreme Court, proposed that Norway should accept the right of individual petition under Article 25. The Ministry of Foreign Affairs and the Ministry of Justice agreed, and the declaration was deposited on 10 December 1955 (for two years), five months after the entry into force of that complaint system in accordance with Article 25(4).[4] From a Nordic perspective this was not very rapid: Sweden was the first to accept it in February 1952, and Denmark and Iceland did so in 1953 and 1955 respectively. The Norwegian declaration was subsequently renewed, from 1965 for periods of five years.

In 1958 the Ministry of Foreign Affairs recommended that Norway should accept the Court's competence under Article 46 of the Convention. The Ministry of Justice responded that in view of recent developments there were hardly any constitutional hindrances, but it recommended to suspend a final decision on the matter in order to study whether legislative measures would be required if the Court were to overturn a final criminal conviction in Norway. In this connection reference was made to the case of *Schouw-Nielsen v Denmark*.[5] It is clear that the Ministry of Justice was in doubt whether it was necessary to introduce statutory provisions enabling the reopening of final judgments at the national level. Following further initiatives, *inter alia* a letter from Chief Justice Terje Wold, who was then a member of the Strasbourg Court, Norway accepted the competence of the Court on 30 June 1964 on the basis of reciprocity and for a period of three years.[6] Since 1967 such declarations have been made for five years.

In spite of the fact that Norway has been bound by both optional clauses of the supervisory system since 1964, the number of cases before the Commission, and indeed the Court, was for many years relatively low (see E below).

Finally, it should be observed that Norway has ratified all eleven Protocols to the Convention.

B. THE STATUS OF THE CONVENTION IN NATIONAL LAW

1. Introduction

The Constitution of 1814 with subsequent amendments contains no provision on the relationship between international (customary or treaty-based) law

[4] The Ministry of Foreign Affairs proposed that Norway should submit a declaration under Article 25 in Stortingsproposisjon No. 104 (1955).

[5] No. 4311/69, Coll. 37 p. 82.

[6] Stortingsproposisjon No. 112 (1963/64). General statutory provisions enabling the reopening of final judgments because of binding decisions by international courts were introduced in 1969 (see F below).

and Norwegian law. For many years there was little case-law on the subject, and the principal source in the field was discussions in the legal doctrine. Gradually, the view emerged that Norway is a 'dualistic' country, and this has been the prevailing, but not undisputed view. It was clear, however, that the human rights conventions enjoyed a strong legal status. In 1994 this was made explicit in the Constitution of which Article 110c now reads:

It is incumbent on the Authorities of the State to respect and to ensure Human Rights.

Further Provisions concerning the Implementation of Treaties thereon shall be laid down by Statute.

Moreover, in October 1998 the Ministry of Justice submitted a bill to Parliament, according to which the ECHR and the two UN Covenants of 1966 on Civil and Political Rights (CCPR) and on Economic, Social, and Cultural Rights (CESCR) should be incorporated into Norwegian law. On 21 May 1999 Parliament adopted the Act on the Strengthening of the Status of Human Rights in Norwegian Law ('the Human Rights Act'). It entered into force immediately. It is referred to below as 'the Incorporation Act'.[7]

This double-track solution—a general constitutional provision and an Act incorporating three specific conventions—was based on proposals by a Committee which was set up in 1989 to draft legislation on the incorporation of human rights conventions into Norwegian law. Its report was submitted in 1993.[8] It was felt that such a combination of constitutional and statutory provisions would be of strong symbolic value, without highlighting some of the human rights conventions in the constitution at the expense of others. In addition the need for a certain legislative flexibility would be accommodated.

In principle, these legislative changes represent a major reform. In practice, the difference may not necessarily be significant, since human rights conventions were important sources of law also before these reforms. Be that as it may, the new provisions clarify the legal situation and strengthen the status of human rights in Norwegian law. A description of the legal development,

[7] The preparatory works of the Act are NOU 1993:18 *Lovgivning om menneskerettigheter* (Report of the Committee which drafted legislation for the incorporation of human rights conventions into Norwegian law), see text below; the bill submitted in Odelstingsproposisjon nr. 3 (1989–99); the report of the Parliamentary Legal Affairs Committee (Innst O nr. 51 1998–99); and the deliberations in Parliament, reproduced in Stortingsforhandlinger (1998–99).

[8] An English summary is given at pp. 193–199 of that report. See also the summary in Norwegian by Møse: 'Utredningen om inkorporering av menneskerettighetskonvensjoner' in *Jussens Venner* 1995 pp. 121–128 and, more extensively by the same author: 'Utredningen om inkorporeringen av menneskerettighetskonvensjoner', in Njål Høstmælingen (ed): *Gjennomføring av internasjonale menneskerettigheter i norsk rett*, 1996, pp. 15–27 (The proceedings of Torkel Opsahl's Memorial Seminar in 1995). (Professor Carsten Smith was Chairman of the Committee until his appointment as Chief Justice of the Supreme Court in 1991. The present author was Chairman from 1991–1993.)

first generally and then specifically in the field of human rights, is given below.[9] We shall then return to a further description of the constitutional and statutory provisions.

2. The legal development: overview

According to the traditional 'dualistic' view expressed in legal doctrine, Norwegian law and international law are separate, independent legal systems. International law is therefore not 'part of' Norwegian law and does not create rights or duties for individuals. When a treaty is ratified it becomes 'part of' Norwegian law either by *incorporation* (the drafting of a domestic provision which refers to the treaty) or by *transformation* (the formulation of national provisions corresponding to the international provisions). Most often used, however, is the technique of '*ascertaining legislative harmony*': a comparative study of the international requirements and existing national provisions may lead to the conclusion that no legislative amendments are necessary or, in case of a conflict, either the national provision is amended or a reservation is suibmitted when the treaty is ratified. When this method has been used, those engaged in applying the law will in principle interpret the national provisions, which have been found to be in conformity with the treaty.

Still according to the dualistic view, Norwegian law is presumed to be in conformity with international law (*the presumption principle*). If national provisions may be interpreted in several ways, but only one interpretation is in conformity with international law, then that interpretation shall be chosen. According to the traditional view, the presumption principle only applied in

[9] Numerous publications address the issue of the relationship between Norwegian law and international law or, more specifically, human rights conventions (in particular the ECHR). An overview is given in NOU 1993:18 pp. 46–78. That report contains many references, of which some will be referred to in this chapter. See also Rolv Ryssdal: 'Norwegian Problems of Compliance with the Convention and Norwegian Perspectives on Incorporation of the Convention' from 1991, published in *Aspects of Incorporation of the European Convention on Human Rights into Domestic law* (ed J. P. Gardner), 1993, pp. 31–40; Søren Stenderup Jensen: *The European Convention on Human Rights in Scandinavian Law*, 1992; Jørg Polakiewicz: 'The Implementation of the ECHR in Western Europe', in *All-European Human Rights Yearbook vol. 2*, 1992, pp. 11–52, in particular pp. 44–48, with comments from Møse: 'Incorporation of Human Rights Conventions in Norwegian Law', pp. 74–76; Carl August Fleischer: *Folkerett* (International law), 6th edn 1994, pp. 258–279 concerning the effect of international law in Norwegian law; Frode Elgesem: 'Domestic Application of The European Convention on Human Rights in English and Norwegian Law', *Nordic Journal of International Law*, 1996, pp. 183–222; Kyrre Eggen: 'Incorporation and Implementation of Human Rights in Norway', in Martin Scheinin (ed): *International Human Rights Norms in the Nordic and Baltic Countries*, 1996, pp. 203–225; *Gjennomføring av internasjonale menneskerettigheter i norsk rett* (above n. 7), with contributions by several authors in various legal fields; and Eckhoff: *Rettskildelære* (Sources of Law), 1997 (4th edn by Jan E. Helgesen) pp. 294–319.

relation to general (unwritten) international law, whereas treaties must be transformed by way of a specific decision (see above) in order to be a relevant source of law in the domestic legal order (*the principle of transformation*). However, there is now general agreement that treaties may also be used as an aid to the interpretation of Norwegian provisions (*the principle of interpretation*). Consequently, international law, including treaties, will be a relevant source of law also according to the dualistic doctrine. But if there is a clear conflict between the international and the national norm, the latter will prevail (*the principle of precedence in case of a conflict*).

This view has not been undisputed. Already in the years following World War II some authors argued that the courts should give precedence to the international norm in cases of conflict with national law. In the 1960s Professor Carsten Smith showed that Norwegian courts had to a considerable degree given international law direct effect in domestic law. The term 'principle of presumption' could be replaced by the more active expression 'principle of the effectiveness of legally binding instruments'. In his view, international law could be regarded as 'part of ' Norwegian law. A special measure of transformation was not necessary to apply international law, but it would ensure that the international norm was given the rank of the national norm which transformed it into Norwegian law. Conflicts between international and national provisions would have to be solved according to generally recognized principles in the domestic order (*lex superior*, *lex posterior*, and *lex specialis*).[10] Smith's view—which was controversial—has been supported and developed by other authors.[11]

Turning now more specifically to the status of human rights conventions, it is noteworthy that several authors have advocated the view that these conventions, in particular the ECHR, enjoy a particularly strong status in national law. In an article in 1963, Chief Justice Terje Wold argued that Norwegian courts must apply the Convention, independently of Norwegian law, and even if there is a conflicting statute. Professor Carsten Smith reached the same conclusion in his above-mentioned article in 1964. In a lecture given in the USA in 1981, Chief Justice Rolv Ryssdal expressed the view that if a conflict should arise between existing national legislation and provisions of human rights conventions, 'it could be argued that precedence should be

[10] 'Den internasjonale rettens innvirkning på den nasjonale retten' (The impact of international law on national law) and 'Folkerettens stilling ved norske domstoler' (The status of international law before the Norwegian courts) in *Tidsskrift for Rettsvitenskap* 1962 pp. 182–204 and 1964 pp. 356–374. His view is developed in subsequent publications, see eg Carsten og Lucy Smith: *Norsk rett og folkeretten* (Norwegian law and international law), 1982.

[11] See for instance Jan E. Helgesen: *Teorier om 'Folkerettens stilling i norsk rett'* (Theories about 'The status of international law in national law'), 1982.

given to the convention'.[12] Other authors have also taken the view that human rights conventions should prevail in cases of conflict[13] or have stated that at any rate the courts are under an obligation to do so if the conflict is due to an unintentional mistake (*arbeidsulykke*) on the part of the legislator, without expressing an opinion on the—so far hypothetical—situation that the legislative authorities deliberately enact rules which are not in conformity with the conventions.[14]

Leaving aside the various views expressed by authors on how to describe the status of the conventions in Norwegian law, we turn now to the case-law of the Supreme Court. It has considered many cases in which human rights conventions, particularly the ECHR, have been invoked (see D below). An important statement of principle appeared in a decision of 1984, where the Court stated that the case must, *inter alia*, be based on the consideration that:

> . . . Norwegian law must *as far as possible* be presumed to be in accordance with treaties by which Norway is bound, in this case the European Convention on Human Rights (emphasis added).

In that case (published in Norsk Retstidende—hereinafter Rt—1984 p. 1175) the Convention and relevant case-law heavily influenced the reasoning and outcome of the Supreme Court's decision. It has been seen as illustrative of that Court's open attitude towards human rights conventions. Several examples are given below (see D). On the other hand, in Rt 1997 p. 580 the Court expressed an *obiter dictum.* The case dealt with the right to strike of the workers on drilling platforms in the North Sea. In conformity with settled practice, the government had ordered compulsory arbitration of the wage dispute in view of the implications for the national economy. This practice had previously been criticized by the International Labour Organization. The Court interpreted the various human rights treaties, including the ECHR, the European Social Charter, and the relevant ILO conventions. It did not find that Norwegian law was in breach of these instruments, but added that in case of a clear conflict national law would prevail.

[12] See, respectively: Wold: 'Den europeiske menneskerettighetskonvensjon og Norge' (The ECHR and Norway) in *Legal Essays—Festskrift til Frede Castberg* (Essays in honour of Frede Castberg), 1963, pp. 353–37. (Mr Wold was a Member of the European Court of Human Rights from 1959 to 1972.) See also Smith, above n. 9, and Ryssdal: 'The Relation between the Judiciary and the Legislative and Executive Branches of the Government of Norway', *North Dakota Law Review* 1981, pp. 527 et seq., see also his article in 1991 (n. 8) p. 32. (Mr Ryssdal retired as Chief Justice of the Supreme Court in 1984 and was President of the European Court from 1985 to 1998.)

[13] For instance Helgesen (above n. 10) and Jørgen Aall: 'Menneskerettighetskonvensjonene som rettskildefaktor i intern norsk rett' (The human rights conventions as legal sources in domestic Norwegian law), *Tidsskrift for Rettsvitenskap* 1989, pp. 613–639.

[14] Trond Dolva: 'Internasjonale menneskerettighetskonvensjoner og intern norsk rett', *Tidsskrift for Rettsvitenskap* 1990 pp. 121–133. (Mr Dolva is a Supreme Court Justice and former Chairman of the Council of Europe's Steering Committee for Human Rights.)

This judgment and the implications of its *dictum* have been discussed and criticized in legal literature.[15] In the present context it is sufficient to note that the Supreme Court has never found a conflict between Norwegian law and the ECHR, and that with effect from 1999 this Convention has been incorporated and will prevail in the case of such a conflict. Further details are provided below, in section 4 on the Incorporation Act.

Irrespective of the Incorporation Act there have for many years been specific statutory provisions which incorporate international law into Norwegian law, thereby creating what has been called 'sector monism'.[16] In the field of human rights, mention should first be made of the Criminal Procedure Act of 22 May 1981. According to section 4, the Act shall apply within the limitations which are recognized in general international law or follow from treaties with other state(s). In Rt 1994 p. 610 (see D below) the Supreme Court stated that:

> . . . Norwegian courts have to apply the procedural provisions in the field of criminal law in such a way that the provisions are compatible with our treaty obligations, and [. . .] the question may arise to set aside the Norwegian provisions in case of a conflict, cf section 4 of the Criminal Procedure Act.[17]

Another example is section 4 of the Aliens Act of 24 June 1988, which provides that the Act shall be applied in conformity with international provisions binding on Norway, provided that their aim is to strengthen the status of the alien. It follows from the *travaux préparatoires* that the international provisions shall prevail in case of conflict with the Aliens Act, and this has been confirmed by the Supreme Court.[18]

Similar provisions are found in the Penal Code of 22 May 1902 (section 1, second subparagraph), the Civil Procedure Act of 13 August 1915 (section 36a), and the Act on Enforcement of Civil Claims of 26 June 1992 (sections 1–4). According to the legal doctrine, international law, including human

[15] See for instance Helgesen i *Eckhoff: Rettskildelære* (n. 9) pp. 313–319; Henning Jakhelln: 'Menneskerettigheter—nei takk?' (Human Rights—No thank you?) in *Lov og Rett 1997* pp. 577–580; Ken Uggerud: 'Internasjonale menneskerettigheter og Høyesteretts dom i Rt. 1997 p. 580—særlig om bruk av ILO-konvensjoner og Sosialpakten' in *Lov og Rett 1997* pp. 581–618 and Jens Edvin A. Skoghøy: 'Forholdet mellom internasjonale menneskerettigheter og norsk rett' in *Kritisk Juss* 1998 pp. 111–119. (Professor Skoghøy is now a member of the Supreme Court.)

[16] This expression seems to have been used for the first time by Torkel Opsahl in his study for the Committee which in 1972 submitted a report on the implementation of law-making conventions in Norwegian law, NOU 1972:16 Gjennomføring av lovkonvensjoner i norsk rett, p. 100. (Professor Opsahl was for many years a member of the European Commission of Human Rights and of the Human Rights Committee set up under the CCPR.)

[17] Similar, but less clear statements were made in Norsk Retstidende 1993 p. 112 and in a ruling of 8 June 1993.

[18] See for instance Rt 1995 p. 72 and Rt 1998 p. 1795.

rights conventions, has been incorporated into the field of application of these provisions. There is no case-law which clearly confirms this view.[19]

When assessing the status of the Convention in Norwegian law, it should also be recalled that the courts may review the constitutionality of statutory provisions (*the principle of judicial supremacy*).[20] The interpretation of written provisions of the Constitution as well as of unwritten constitutional principles may be influenced by international instruments. The human rights conventions may also have an impact in domestic law when the courts control administrative decisions (*the principle of judicial review*).[21] They have unlimited competence to review the interpretation and application of the law. In particular, encroachment by the authorities within the private sphere of the individual must have a basis in statutory provisions (*the principle of legality*). Moreover, the courts have the power to review the facts on which the decisions are based. Their competence to control the 'free discretion' of the administration is limited: a decision may be declared invalid if it is manifestly unreasonable or is based on discrimination.[22] It is important to note, however, that even in matters of pure expediency the court may decide whether the administrative assessment is in conformity with international obligations. This is obviously the case when conventions have been incorporated (in specific areas or generally) but according to the prevailing view the situation is the same when incorporation has not taken place. Reference is made to the Supreme Court's decision in the *Alta* case in 1982 (see D below) and subsequent legal developments.[23]

To sum up, it is undisputed that even human rights conventions which are not incorporated are relevant and important sources of Norwegian law. The international provisions may be applied in order to interpret statutory provisions which are ambiguous, to supplement them, and even to restrict their scope, whereas the recent *obiter dictum* suggests that national law will as a point of departure prevail in case of a clear conflict. It is somewhat misleading, therefore, to state that such conventions are 'not part of', 'do not apply

[19] In Norsk Retstidende 1994 p. 1244, the majority (3–2) raised doubts, but did not decide whether section 36a of the Civil Procedure Act shall be interpreted as an interpretation clause (see also below n. 55).

[20] The expression is borrowed from Anglo-American doctrine. The Norwegian term is *domstolenes kontroll med lovers grunnlovsmessighet*.

[21] The concept of 'judicial review' is used for instance in English law. The Norwegian phrase is *domstolenes kontroll med forvaltningen*.

[22] In addition, invalidity may result if the administration—which according to the statutory provision shall decide the case according to its free discretion—has not made a real assessment of the case, for instance because it has simply applied very precise administrative instructions, according to which there is no discretion left.

[23] Norsk Retstidende 1982 p. 241 and NOU 1993:18 pp. 68–69. See also the two Supreme Court judgments mentioned above (n. 18).

directly in', or 'have no direct effect in' Norwegian law. In order to be meaningful, such expressions need further precision.[24] But there is no doubt that the ECHR enjoys a very strong position in Norwegian law, following the introduction of constitutional and statutory provisions.

3. The new constitutional provision

Article 110c of the Constitution, cited above, demonstrates the importance of human rights conventions in legal and societal life, without highlighting some conventions at the expense of others. It includes civil and political as well as economic, social, and cultural rights. Moreover, it covers not only general conventions (such as the two UN Covenants, the ECHR, and the European Social Charter) but also conventions addressing specific areas (eg the UN conventions relating to discrimination, torture, and children).

According to the Committee report of 1993, the obligation of the authorities to respect and ensure human rights, expressed in the *first sentence*, have several functions:[25]

—The provision has a *symbolic value* and gives a signal, nationally and internationally, of the great importance which shall be accorded to human rights. It is an expression of a central value in Norwegian policy to which Parliament subscribes and on which the Norwegian society should build.

—Article 110c will be a *political guideline* and function as an incentive to take human rights conventions into account in all societal areas where they are significant.

It was assumed that the introduction of these two aspects into the Constitution was simply a codification of a principle which had already been

[24] The view that such brief catchwords may be misleading or at any rate insubstantial, has also been expressed by C. A. Fleischer in his book *Folkerett* (above n. 8), see p. 272 in the most recent edition. That author subscribes to the dualistic view. He accepts that it is also possible to say that international law is part of Norwegian law, but without the rank of statutory provisions. He argues, however, that there are certain advantages in using the traditional language (see in particular pp. 265–266). In his article of 1991 (n. 8), Ryssdal (p. 32) states 'that it does not give the full picture briefly to state that Norway is a "dualistic" country'.

[25] NOU 1993: 18 pp. 157–160. As a supplement to Article 110 c, two members of the Committee (Carsten Smith and Karl Nandrup Dahl) also proposed the following constitutional provision: 'International law, including Treaties by which Norway is bound, is Part of Norwegian Law.' The aim of this general provision was to introduce the monistic system into Norwegian constitutional law. In view of the Committee's terms of reference and composition, the other members of the Committee did not find it advisable to embark upon a study which might lead to such a proposal. It was not taken up by Parliament. The implications of the new constitutional provision are discussed by Ravlo: 'Grunnlovens § 110 c, presumsjonsprinsippet og motstridslæren' in *Jussens Venner* 1997 pp. 195–208 og Einarsen: 'Asylrettens grunnlovsvern—etter Kjuus-saken' in *Kritisk Juss*,1998, pp. 123–152.

developed in Norwegian societal life on the basis of general agreement. However, the new provision will also have legal significance in several respects:

—The first sentence lays down a *legally binding principle*. Norwegian authorities will be precluded from adopting policies in breach of the principle. It will function as a reminder to the authorities and may be invoked against them. In principle, sanctions for non-fulfilment of this legal obligation are constitutional and political responsibility (impeachment and the fall of the government).
—The reference to human rights implies that conventions in this field will be important for the *interpretation* of statutes and regulations. It should be recalled, however, that according to the well established principle of presumption, the conventions are already legal sources of considerable significance.
—The provision also establishes *limits for the administrative authorities* when they exercise their power on the basis of free discretion. Again, it should be noted that this is also considered the legal situation today, (see above).
—Finally, Article 110c will have a role to play when there is a *lacuna* in the legislation, ie when there are questions on which the legislator has not taken a position.

To sum up, in 1994 the insertion of Article 110c did not fundamentally change the situation, but it implied that the legal status of human rights was strengthened.

According to the *second sentence* of Article 110c, further provisions concerning the implementation of human rights treaties shall be laid down by statute. This is a specific reminder to the legislative authorities that they shall follow the development. One aspect of this was the Incorporation Act (see above on the double-track solution which was chosen). Moreover, it will still be an important task for the legislator to ensure that Norwegian law is in conformity with human rights. According to the committee report, the reform did not aim at shifting the balance between the legislative authorities and the judiciary.

4. The Incorporation Act

As stated above, the Incorporation Act implied that the ECHR and the two UN Covenants have been incorporated into domestic law. This is not the place to explain in detail why these conventions were chosen.[26] It is sufficient

[26] See the English summary in NOU 1993:18 (above n. 7).

to say that the ECHR and its Protocols were included as a matter of course: in principle and in practice, the Convention is already of great significance for Norway, and it is undoubtedly suitable for incorporation. Below we give a brief survey of the Act.

Section 1 provides that the purpose of the Act is to strengthen the status of human rights in Norwegian law. This is an expression of the aim of the reform: to reduce the uncertainty which has prevailed about the legal position of the human rights treaties, to increase knowledge about them, and to signal their important place in legal and societal life. The provision refers to human rights in general and thereby makes the point that conventions which are not incorporated will also still be important sources of law.

According to Section 2, the ECHR and the Covenants 'shall apply as statutory law' in Norway. It is worth noting that the Act refers to the Convention 'as amended by Protocol No. 11' and also incorporates the additional Protocols (Nos 1, 4, 6, and 7). Future protocols will have to be added to the list of instruments which are incorporated in pursuance of Section 2.[27]

An important provision is section 3 of the draft: the convention provisions concerning rights and fundamental freedoms listed in the Act *shall in case of conflict take precedence* over other statutory provisions. This provision, combined with section 1 of the Act and Article 110c of the Constitution, gives the conventions a strong status in Norwegian law.[28]

The formulation of Section 3 ('in case of conflict') does not explicitly clarify under which conditions precedence shall be given to conventions that are incorporated. As discussed below, previous case law under Section 4 of the Criminal Procedure Act required that the international norm and corresponding case-law must be sufficiently clear in order to prevail (see the discussion of Rt 1994 p. 610 under section D, Leading Human Rights Cases, below). An important question is whether this principle, developed in relation to a specific incorporation provision, also applies to the new general Incorporation Act.

This issue was clarified in a landmark decision by the Supreme Court of 23 June 2000 (Rt 2000 p. 996) concerning supplementary tax imposed as a sanction. The Court found that this was to be considered as a 'criminal charge' within the meaning of Article 6 and that the administrative proceedings had not been conducted 'within reasonable time'. Consequently, decisions to impose supplementary tax could only to a limited extent be effected against the individual.

[27] The Committee had proposed a distinction: new additional protocols would be added to the list in the Act, whereas future amending protocols would be incorporated by the Act.

[28] Odelstingsproposisjon nr. 3 (1998–99) pp. 66–71 gives further explanations concerning the interpretation of section 3.

The Supreme Court held that the question whether there is a conflict between a provision in a convention that has been incorporated and other parts of Norwegian law cannot be answered by reference to a general principle, but depends on an interpretation of the applicable provisions in the circumstances. It follows from Section 3 of the Incorporation Act that Norwegian courts must give precedence to the ECHR if the solution required by it is reasonably clear, even if this involves a deviation from well established Norwegian legislation or practice.

The Supreme Court also observed that in many instances the interpretation of the ECHR may give rise to well founded doubt. Even if Norwegian courts, in interpreting the Convention, shall use the same principles of interpretation as the European Court of Human Rights, the primary responsibility for developing the Convention lies with that Court. Norwegian courts must take into account the text of the ECHR, its purpose, and Strasbourg case-law. If there is doubt about the impact of judgments rendered by the European Court, it is important whether the decision is based on a situation which is factually and legally comparable with the situation to be determined by the Norwegian court. To the extent various interests have to be balanced against each other, Norwegian courts may—in conformity with the method used by the Strasbourg Court—also take into account traditional Norwegian priorities, in particular if the Norwegian legislator has considered the relationship to the ECHR and has found that there is no conflict between the Convention and national law.

According to the Supreme Court, Norwegian courts do not have available the same material about legislation and case-law in other European countries. When Norwegian courts in their balancing of different interests may draw on priorities that form the basis of Norwegian law, they will be able to engage in an interplay (*samspill*) with the Strasbourg Court and contribute to the development of its case-law. If Norwegian courts were as dynamic in their interpretation of the ECHR as that Court, there is the risk that they might go further than required by the ECHR. This would imply an unnecessary limitation of the powers ofthe Norwegian legislator and interfere with the balance between the legislature and the judiciary.

Based on these considerations, the Supreme Court concluded that Norwegian courts should not adopt too dynamic an approach in cases where there is doubt as to the interpretation of the ECHR.

It follows from draft section 4 that the conventions that are incorporated by statute shall be published in the Norwegian Law Gazette (Norsk Lovtidend) in an original language and in a Norwegian translation, thus ensuring that the texts of the conventions are more easily available. The importance of accessible texts has been acknowledged previously, and it is noteworthy that since 1987 the ECHR has been included in the Norwegian collection of statutes (*Norges Lover*), the principal working instrument for all lawyers in Norway. The Committee report and the bill both stress the need for disseminating information about human rights conventions and relevant case-law (see G below).

C. THE STATUS OF THE CONVENTION IN PARLIAMENTARY PROCEEDINGS

1. Constitutional revisions

The Norwegian Constitution of 17 May 1814, the oldest written constitution in force in Europe, not only has legal significance but also functions as an important national symbol. There has been a rather reticent attitude towards far-reaching reforms (often referred to as 'constitutional conservatism'), and the Constitution does not contain any modern bill of rights.[29] However, some constitutional revisions have been motivated by human rights conventions.

As stated above (see A), the government found it necessary to table a reservation to the ECHR because of the anti-Jesuit clause in Article 2 of the Constitution, and this view was accepted by Parliament when it consented to ratification of the Convention. Consequently, the Ministry of Justice in 1952 proposed to Parliament that this provision be deleted. In the debate on 1 November 1956, 111 members of Parliament were in favour of abrogation, whereas 31 voted against, and the reservation was withdrawn on 4 December 1956. The discussion focused in particular on whether it would have negative consequences to delete the anti-Jesuit clause, for instance in relation to their education of children. Several representatives referred to the Convention as one argument in favour of abolition. Among the members who wanted to keep the Constitution unchanged, some doubted whether the prohibition of Jesuits was a violation of Article 9 and whether the reservation had been necessary.[30]

The general human rights provision in Article 110c (see above B) was unanimously adopted by Parliament on 15 June 1994. All 141 members present voted in favour. There was no discussion. The member responsible for

[29] On the other hand, this has necessitated a flexible interpretation. Some Scandinavian authors have expressed this phenomenon in a consise formula: 'Rigidity in form requires flexibility in substance.'

[30] See Stortingsproposisjon Nr. 202 (1952) from the Ministry of Justice, Innstilling 224 (report from the Parliamentary Committee) and the summary records of the discussions in the plenary in 1956 (Stortingsforhandlinger pp. 2951–3018).

presenting the proposal simply made a brief introduction and recommended its adoption.

It should be added that Article 110 a concerning the obligation of the authorities to create the necessary conditions for the Sami people to ensure its language, culture, and societal life was greatly inspired by Article 27 of the CCPR when it was introduced in 1988. The ECHR played no prominent part in the drafting history of that constitutional provision, given the fact that it offers limited protection for minorities.[31]

2. Statutory provisions

For many years the Convention was not mentioned in the preparatory documents (Committee reports, bills) of statutory provisions and consequently did not play any role in parliamentary discussions on bills submitted by the relevant Ministries. Gradually, this has changed. Below we give some examples:

By an Act of 19 June 1969, a new Chapter 33 was inserted into the Civil Procedure Act, which gave the courts unlimited competence to control all aspects of administrative decisions concerning the deprivation of liberty, including matters of pure expediency. The Committee proposing this amendment invoked the Convention as an argument in favour of its proposal to give such competence to the courts and not merely to an independent Control Commission, and the Ministry of Justice subscribed to this view in the bill submitted to Parliament.[32] Another example is the Act of 13 June 1969 on Religious Communities, replacing the former Religious Dissident Act of 1891, which contained a prohibition against religious meetings behind closed doors. According to the bill leading to the 1969 Act, this was not in conformity with Article 9 of the Convention, and that provision was therefore deleted.[33]

In 1979 the death penalty in time of war and emergency situations was abolished. Human rights law did not at that juncture contain any prohibition against capital punishment, and the Convention was not expressly referred to as an argument in favour of abolition. But the bill contained an overview of relevant human rights instruments and stressed that an important aspect of the reform was to contribute to the international efforts to abolish the death penalty.[34] Subsequently, Norway had no problems in ratifying Protocol No. 6 to the Convention. On the other hand, there was disagreement in

[31] NOU 1984:18 Om samenes rettsstilling (Committee report on the legal position of the Sami People) pp. 239–242 and 250.

[32] Report of March 1967 from the Committee and odelstingsproposisjon nr. 40 (1967–68) pp. 5–6 and 12–13.

[33] Odelstingsproposisjon (1967–68) nr. 27.

[34] Odelstingsproposisjon (1978–79) nr. 45, leading to the Act of 8 June 1979.

Parliament in 1991 about whether Norway should ratify CCPR Protocol No. 2 without reservation and thereby exclude the possibility of reintroducing the death penalty in time of war (cf. Article 2) . In the event, no reservation was made.[35]

A new act on Criminal Procedure was adopted on 22 May 1981. The Committee which elaborated the draft from 1957 to 1969 did not consider the possible impact of human rights conventions. In a later article, the Chairman of that Committee explained this by referring to the fact that the Convention was less known in that period and that the case-law was limited, but he also mentioned that it did not occur to Committee members that provisions which were meticulously drafted with a focus on the legal safeguards of the individuals could be in breach of the Convention.[36] In the bills submitted to Parliament in 1984 in connection with the adoption and entry into force of that Act, some minor references were made to human rights instruments.[37] The situation was different when a Committee was set up in 1990 to consider a reform of the system of appeal in criminal cases. Its terms of reference explicitly stressed the need to take into account human rights conventions. Case-law under CCPR Article 14(5), to which Norway had tabled a reservation, as well as ECHR Article 6 and Article 2 of Protocol No. 7 played a major role during the discussions of the Committee and in the bill leading to the Act of 11 June 1993 (in force 1 August 1995) concerning the introduction of a two-instance system in all criminal cases.[38]

New provisions concerning disciplinary and police authority in the military services were drafted by a Committee which submitted its report in 1980. Due account was given to case-law under Article 6 of the Convention, for instance the *Engel* case. Disciplinary sanctions are subject to review by a Complaint Commission, and its decisions may be brought before the courts. The new Act was adopted on 20 May 1988.[39]

In its report of 1983, the Committee which drafted the new Aliens Act gave ample consideration to the implications of human rights conventions and proposed a provision which incorporated them with priority in case of con-

[35] Stortingsproposisjon (1990–91) nr. 37.

[36] Johs Andenæs: 'Den europeiske menneskerettighetskonvensjon og norsk straffeprosess' (The ECHR and Norwegian Criminal Procedure), in *Lov og Rett* 1992 pp. 375–387 (p. 376). Professor Andenæs was for several decades a prominent professor of law at the University of Oslo.

[37] Odelstingsproposisjon nr. 35 (1978–79) pp. 224–225 and odelstingsproposisjon nr. 53 (1983–84) p. 101.

[38] See NOU 1992: 28 To-instansbehandling, anke- or juryordning i straffesaker (Committee report on a system of two instances, appeal and jury in criminal cases) and odelstingsproposisjon nr. 78 (1992–93). As a consequence of the reform, Norway reduced the scope of its reservation to CCPR Article 14(5) with effect from 19 September 1995.

[39] NOU 1980: 58; odelstingsproposisjon nr. 92 (1986–87).

flict with other statutory provisions.[40] The Ministry of Justice and Parliament accepted this proposal, which was adopted as section 4 of the Act of 24 June 1988 (see B above).

Another illustrative example of the influence of the Convention is found in the report of the Committee which elaborated draft legislation on increased protection and support to victims of crime. Under Article 6(1) and (3)(d) a person charged with a criminal offence has the right to examine witnesses against him. On the other hand, an absolute right to require that the victim shall appear in court raises particular problems in relation to small children who have been subjected to sexual abuse. The report and the bill discussed methods to reconcile these conflicting interests. Another matter of concern was the possibility of prohibiting parents who are suspected, but not convicted of sexual abuse from visiting other persons or places: cf ECHR Protocol No. 4 Article 2 and CCPR Article 12. The Act was adopted on 1 July 1994.[41]

Let us end by adding two more recent examples. A bill relating to criminal responsibility and security measures contained a survey of relevant human rights provisions. The Parliamentary Committee which considered the bill became aware of an article to be published in a legal periodical in which it was argued that one of the provisions was a violation of Article 5 of the Convention. The Committee then asked the Ministry of Justice to study the matter more closely.[42] Moreover, having considered a bill on the use of force against mentally handicapped persons, in which reference was made to the Convention without further studies, the Parliamentary Committee, following critical remarks by human rights circles, asked the Ministry of Social Affairs to submit a supplementary bill which discussed whether the draft was in conformity with the Convention.[43]

It is fair to say that human rights instruments originally played a limited part in the legislative process. However, committee reports to the relevant Ministry now frequently contain reference to human rights instruments and their implications. So far, the various parliamentary Committees examining bills where reference is made to conventions will normally base their considerations on the opinion expressed therein.

[40] NOU 1983: 47 Ny fremmedlov (Committee report on New Aliens Act) pp. 174–75 and 314; odelstingsproposisjon nr. 46 (1986–87) pp. 46 and 189–190.

[41] NOU 1992: 16; Odelstingsproposisjon nr. 33 (1993–94) Chapters VII and X.

[42] Odelstingsproposisjon nr. 87 (1993–94) concerning section 13F of a draft Act on mental health care.

[43] Odelstingsproposisjon nr. 58 (1994–95) p. 13.

D. LEADING HUMAN RIGHTS CASES DECIDED BY THE NATIONAL COURTS

The ECHR was invoked before the Supreme Court for the first time in 1961 in the *Iversen* case (Rt 1961 p. 1350), which dealt with the obligation of a dentist under temporary legislation to work for a year in Northern Norway where there was a lack of dentists. The case, which was later brought before the Commission, is well known in international literature on Article 4 (forced and compulsory labour). Here it is sufficient to recall that the Supreme Court did not consider the obligation to work as a violation of Article 4, and that this was confirmed by the Commission in its decision on inadmissibility.[44] In the second dentist case (Rt 1966 p. 476) the Supreme Court followed the reasoning of the Commission when it reached the conclusion that the prolongation of the legislation was in conformity with Article 4. Only in these two cases was the Convention invoked before the Supreme Court in the 1960s.

In the 1970s the ECHR was applied in only one case (Rt 1974 p. 935) concerning a claim for compensation because security measures had been imposed. The plaintiff argued unsuccessfully that the court which had made that decision had committed procedural errors in breach of Article 6 ('fair and public hearing'). The number of cases relating to the Convention then raised sharply to seventeen in the 1980s. And the increase has continued: whereas the number of annual cases in *Norsk Retstidende* from 1990–95 was between seven and eleven, twenty to thirty cases are now not unusual.[45]

These figures relate only to judgments and decisions by the Supreme Court and its Appeals Selection Committee which have been published in *Norsk Retstidende*. They do not include, for instance, decisions where that Committee decided not to grant leave to appeal to the Supreme Court in cases where the Convention has played a significant role in the proceedings at the first or second instance.[46] Furthermore, these statistics do not reflect the

[44] No. 1468/62, YB 6 (1963) p. 278. See for instance Harris, O'Boyle, and Warbrick (above n 3) pp. 93 and 96 and van Dijk and van Hoof: *Theory and Practice of the European Convention on Human Rights*, 1990, pp. 244–246 and 249.

[45] A chronological summary of all human rights cases until August 1992 is found in NOU 1993: 18 (above n 7) pp. 51–67. A survey on an article-by-article basis is given by Dolva in *Festskrift til Jacob W. Sundberg* (Essays in honour of J. W. Sundberg), Stockholm 1993. The first edition of Muller: *Den europeiske menneskerettighetskonvensjon og Høyesterett* (1995) contained a survey of 65 Supreme Court decisions concerning the ECHR (as of May 1995), whereas the revised edition of the book (1998) contained 124 (as of October 1997).

[46] Two illustrative examples from 1990 should be mentioned. In an abortion case brought by the father of a fourteen-week-old foetus the Select Appeals Committee did not grant leave to appeal against the judgment of 17 November 1989 by Eidsivating (now Borgarting) Court of Appeals. The case was then brought before the Commission, which declared it inadmissible. See *H v Norway*, No. 17004/90, mentioned by Harris, O'Boyle, and Warbrick (above n. 3)

impact of the Convention in decisions of the first two instances which were not subject to appeal. But even if the figures do not reveal the whole picture, they clearly show the growing influence of the Convention in domestic case-law from 1980. It should be added that the ECHR has been invoked more frequently than any other human rights instrument.[47]

Turning now to some leading cases, two decisions (both briefly referred to in B above) should be mentioned at the outset, before a survey is given of decisions in some fields where the Convention has had a particular impact. In the *Alta* decision, Rt 1982 p. 241, the Supreme Court in plenary had to decide whether the government's decision to regulate the Alta waterfalls was invalid. One aspect of the case was the significance of several human rights instruments which were invoked in support of the argument that the decision was a violation of the rights of the Sami people. This argument was not accepted by the Supreme Court. The decision also contained a survey of the general principles of judicial review, in particular the point that the court cannot review the discretionary assessment of advantages and disadvantages under the relevant legislation. The Justice, expressing the view of the plenary, added:

> What I said about the limits of judicial review needs to be qualified. In the present case it has been argued that the Sami people are protected against such interferences with their interests as follow from the regulation of the Alta river by virtue of rules of international law which are binding upon Norway. The rules concerning the courts' power to review the validity of administrative acts do not prevent the Court from fully and comprehensively considering whether the expansion works violate rules of international law.

According to the prevailing view, this statement implies that even in matters of pure expediency the courts are competent to decide whether the assessment of the administrative authorities is in conformity with international obligations (see B above).

Another landmark decision is Rt 1984 p. 1175. A mentally ill person had been sentenced by the courts to security measures in pursuance of the Criminal Code. This judicial authorization included the possibility of placing him in a mental hospital. When the administrative authorities decided to do so, the question was the extent of judicial review available to him. Could he

pp. 42–43. Another example, which does not relate to the ECHR, is the Committee's decision not to allow an appeal against the judgment of the Labour Court on 13 July 1990, in which a Royal Decree to employ compulsory arbitration in connection with a strike in the oil sector was upheld even if this might not be in conformity with ILO Conventions, as interpreted by Committees within that organization.

[47] According to NOU 1993:18 (above n. 7) p. 67, the ECHR had been invoked in 51 cases as of August 1992, whereas the CCPR had been referred to in 9 cases. The figures for the Convention on the Elimination of Racial Discrimination and various ILO Conventions were 3 and 5 respectively.

make use of Chapter 33 of the Civil Procedure Act which allows the courts to review all aspects of administrative decisions, including matters of pure expediency, when a person is committed to a mental hospital? The Supreme Court first observed that neither the wording of the Mental Health Act nor its drafting history gave any direct indication as to how the problem should be solved. The decision then went on:

> The decision to be taken must accordingly take into account all relevant circumstances, in particular the consideration that domestic law must be interpreted, as far as possible, in accordance with those treaties under international law which Norway has ratified, in this instance the European Convention on Human Rights.

Taking into account the need to ensure the legal safeguards of the individual, the Supreme Court concluded that the extended judicial review available under Chapter 33 was applicable. This solution would be in conformity with Strasbourg case-law. The Court carried out a comprehensive survey of the European Court's judgments in *Winterwerp v Belgium* and *X v UK*,[48] as well as the Commission's decision in *B v UK*.[49] As stated above (B), it is the prevailing view that the decision is a particularly clear expression of the 'principle of presumption', and that the Convention heavily influenced the outcome of the case.

A great number of cases have dealt with issues of criminal procedure. In connection with the change of Chief Justice in April 1991, one of the Justices observed that the ECHR had 'become part of [the Supreme Court's] everyday life within the field of criminal procedure'.[50] Subsequent experience has confirmed and strengthened this view. This development may have several explanations. The provisions of ECHR Articles 5 and 6 are relatively precisely formulated, and section 4 of the Criminal Procedure Act has been regarded as an incorporation clause (see B above). An important reason is probably that the attention of lawyers has been drawn to the potential of the Convention in this field, first by articles in legal journals on specific items, and then by an increasing number of decisions of the Supreme Court.[51]

Most cases have dealt with the admissibility of reading out reports on statements of witnesses without the accused having the chance to examine the witnesses. On 29 March 1990 the Supreme Court made two important decisions. In the first case (Rt 1990 p. 312) the lower court had convicted a person of

[48] Series A Nos. 33 (1979) and 46 (1981). [49] Application 6870/75.

[50] A speech by Justice Christiansen, reproduced in Rt 1991 p. 466.

[51] In this context mention should be made of Jørgen Aall's articles on the implications of the ECHR in the legal journal *Lov og Rett* 1988 pp. 478–488 (the right of the accused to examine witnesses) and 1989 pp. 413–426 (whether a judge having decided on custody in remand is impartial during the main hearing). See also now more generally his book *Rettergang og menneskerettigheter* (1995) on the relationship between ECHR Article 6 and Norwegian criminal procedure.

reckless driving causing death. One witness who had been summoned to the main hearing did not appear, and the police report containing his statement was read out. The second case (Rt 1990 p. 319) dealt with the statement of an allegedly sexually abused girl under six years old. It had been recorded by the investigating judge during the police investigation. The defence counsel's request to postpone the main hearing in order to obtain a new statement from her instead of reading her former statement was rejected by the lower court, and the accused was convicted. In both cases the relevant statutory provisions were interpreted in light of Article 6(1) and (3)(d) and of the European Court's judgments in the cases of *Unterpertinger* and *Kostovski.*[52] The Supreme Court concluded that the use made of the written reports was acceptable. These landmark cases have been followed by a large number of Supreme Court decisions, and some of the proceedings of the lower courts have been quashed and referred back to the lower court because the reading out of statements was not considered to be in conformity with the statutory provisions and the Convention.

Article 5(3) concerning the right of everyone arrested to be brought 'promptly' before a judge does not normally cause difficulties in Norwegian law. Under the Criminal Procedural Act, a person charged must be brought before the court as soon as possible and whenever possible on the day after the arrest. However, periods with consecutive holidays may raise issues in relation to the Convention. In Rt 1991 p. 777, the accused had been arrested the day before the National Day, followed by a Saturday and Pentecost holidays. Consequently, six days elapsed from the arrest until he was brought before a judge. The Supreme Court stated that the statutory provision must be interpreted so as to avoid any conflict with Article 5(3) and that deprivation of liberty for a period of this length was difficult to reconcile with the requirements of the Criminal Procedure Act and the Convention.[53]

Case-law has also addressed the requirement that arrested persons shall be entitled to trial 'within a reasonable time'. In Rt 1993 p. 112, the issue was whether a person in custody charged with drug offences should be subjected to further detention. This would mean that the total time in custody before the main hearing would be nine months. According to the Supreme Court, deprivation of liberty for such a period was not in itself a violation of Article 5(3). But in spite of the fact that this provision had been invoked before the Court of Appeals, it had not explicitly considered that Article and there was

[52] Series A Nos. 110 (1986) and 166 (1989).

[53] The Supreme Court did not elaborate further on this issue, which in the circumstances had no bearing on whether the person should be released. It is of interest, however, to recall the judgment in *Brogan v UK* of 1988, in which detention for four days and six hours was considered to be a violation of Article 5(3) in a terrorist case (Series A No. 145–B).

no discussion of the criteria which are relevant according to Strasbourg case-law. Consequently, the decision of the Court of Appeals was quashed. When that Court reconsidered the issue, it solicited further information about the reasons for the delay and then maintained its original decision. This met with the approval of the Supreme Court (Rt 1993 p. 224) which noted that it had been difficult to find a period during which all the defence counsel could be present at the main hearing. The delay was therefore attributable to the way in which the accused had exercised their rights freely to defend themselves through legal assistance of their own choosing, cf. Article 6(3)(c). These decisions were followed by a very large number of cases, and in several of them the lower court's decision has been quashed. Moreover, in Rt 1998 p. 1076, the Supreme Court stressed that the courts have a duty to discuss the implications of Article 5(3) when it may be applicable even if the parties have not invoked that provision.

Many decisions have dealt with ECHR Article 6. The Supreme Court has considered the *Hauschildt* judgment on several occasions.[54] Of particular interest is a decision from 1996 (Rt 1996 p. 261). A person was convicted of grievous bodily harm and sentenced to six years' imprisonment by the Court of Appeals, composed of three professional judges (meting out the sentence) and the jury (deciding on the question of guilt). The presiding judge had previously decided together with two other judges that the accused should be remanded in custody under section 172 of the Criminal Procedure Act, which requires a high degree of probability that the accused is guilty (as in the *Hauschildt* case). At that time his offence was characterized as armed robbery, not grievous bodily harm, but according to both charges the elements of violence and harm were predominant. The Supreme Court considered that the presiding judge could not be considered as 'impartial' under section 108 of the Act on the Courts of 13 August 1915. The Court noted that on the basis of the *Hauschildt* judgment it could not be stated with certainty what the correct interpretation of Article 6(1) would be if a judge has participated only once in connection with a decision on remand in custody under section 172. Under these circumstances it was important to be clear about the composition of courts. In order to ensure public confidence in the courts, any doubts should be dispelled as regards the impartiality of judges participating in criminal cases. Consequently, section 108 should be interpreted strictly and also cover the situation when section 172 had been applied only once and irrespective of whether the judge concerned had then acted alone. Even if the

[54] Series A No. 154 (1989). That judgment was invoked in Rt 1990 p. 379 (judge having decided custody in remand should not participate in case concerning authorization of security measures) and Rt 1992 p. 538 (former decision on custody remand did not prevent judge from presiding over the hearing when the accused had pleaded guilty).

professional judge in the courts of appeals did not determine the question of guilt, the presiding judge had a central position, particularly in view of his final summing up of the evidence for the jury. The Supreme Court quashed the judgment of the Court of Appeals and referred it back.

An interesting statement of principle was made by the Supreme Court in Rt 1994 p. 610. During investigations concerning possible illegal price-fixing several persons gave statements to the administrative authorities. In the subsequent criminal case the prosecuting authorities requested that the reports containing their statements should be admitted as documentary evidence. The Supreme Court rejected this application, but allowed the reading out of the reports within the limits laid down by the general provisions of the Criminal Procedure Act. In considering the relevant human rights provisions, the Court made a general statement:

> I agree that Norwegian courts have to apply the procedural provisions in the field of criminal law in such a way that the proceedings are compatible with our treaty obligations, and that the question may arise to set aside the Norwegian provisions in case of a conflict, cf. section 4 of the Criminal Procedure Act. If a Norwegian court shall have the basis to deviate from the solution following from national procedural provisions, the deviating rule based on sources of international law must appear as sufficiently clear and precise to be given such effect. In my view, this must in particular be the case if it is a question of changing a legal situation based on clear and well established Norwegian legislation or practice. In determining whether a decision made by an international court shall be given such effect in national law, it is also of importance whether the decision is based on a situation which is factually and legally comparable with the situation to be determined by the Norwegian court.[55]

The accused invoked the principle of presumption of innocence, cf. Article 6(2), and the general principle of equality of arms, but to no avail. The main issue was whether the use of the statements would be a violation of the prohibition against self-incrimination and the right to a fair hearing, as laid down by ECHR Article 6 and CCPR Article 14(3)(g). The Supreme Court considered the implications of the *Funke* judgment by the European Court.[56] That judgment did not address the problem in the present case, where the persons had given their statements at a time when they were not charged or accused. The Strasbourg decision did not give any reason to conclude that it would be a violation of the fair hearing principle to use the summary of the previous statement as evidence in the present criminal case, and even less to assume

[55] A similar statement has been made in subsequent decisions, for instance Rt 1994 p. 1244: did a pregnant prisoner have a 'legal interest' under section 36a of the Civil Procedure Act to obtain a judgment with a concluding paragraph which explicitly stated that particular events in the past were in breach of the Convention? In the circumstances, the majority (3–2) answered the question in the negative.

[56] Series A No. 256–A (1993).

that the obligation to give statements according to legislation on illegal competition would be in breach of the Convention.

The Supreme Court's statement of principle implies that it is important to distinguish between the question of precedence between international and national law, on one hand, and the requirement that the international norm and corresponding case-law must be sufficiently clear to be given precedence, on the other. There is a connection between them: if a high level of clarity is required, there will be fewer cases in which international norms will be given priority. But in principle, it is important to maintain that these are two separate issues, and that the Supreme Court is prepared to give priority to the international norm.[57]

Before leaving the field of criminal procedure, reference should be made to two cases. In Rt 1994 p. 721 the Supreme Court assessed the implications of the judgment in *Sekanina v Austria.*[58] In the Norwegian case, a person acquitted after 191 days in custody was given compensation under section 445 of the Criminal Procedure Act (because it was considered reasonable under that provision to do so) but not under section 444 (which had certain similarities with the Austrian legislation). The Supreme Court found that Article 6(2) may be violated if the reasons of the domestic court contain doubts as to whether the acquittal was correct, or if it contains presumptions about guilt under criminal law. However, section 444 was not as such in breach of the Convention. Finally, in Rt 1996 p. 173, the Supreme Court did not accept the argument of the accused that it followed from Convention Articles 6 and 13 that a criminal case which had not been dealt with 'within a reasonable time' should be declared inadmissible. It was sufficient that the courts took the period of time into account as a mitigating circumstance when assessing the appropriate sentence. In the present case the proceedings had taken too long, but it was not necessary to decide whether there had been a violation of Article 6(1). At any rate the delay had been compensated for by the very low sentences in the case.

A very important decision was Rt 2000 p. 996 concerning supplementary taxation and the Incorporation Act. This case was considered in Section B4 above.

In several cases it has been argued that the imposition of security measures which involve deprivation of liberty would constitute inhuman treatment under Article 3 of the Convention. Until now this argument has convinced neither the Supreme Court[59] nor the European Commission. That provision

[57] This view was also expressed by Carsten Smith in *Gjennomføring av internasjonale menneskerettighet i norsk rett* (above n. 7) pp. 45–46.

[58] Series A No. 266–A (1993).

[59] Rt 1985 p. 22, 1990 p. 380, and 1991 p. 1256; Rt 1990 p. 867.

has also, so far unsuccessfully, been invoked in cases concerning expulsion.[60] Some expulsion cases have also raised issues in relation to Article 8 (see above).

An important group of cases has dealt with freedom of expression. For instance, in Rt 1990 p. 257 a newspaper was acquitted in a defamation case brought by a politician. The Supreme Court found that the statement 'With disgust they have followed the campaign of the Progress Party and [the politician] to strengthen the xenophobia amongst Norwegians' had to be accepted under Article 100 of the Constitution, which guarantees the freedom of expression. The statement related to the political arena and dealt with the plaintiff's behaviour as a politician. Referring to the *Lingens* case, the Supreme Court found that in this field the freedom of expression must weigh heavily when being balanced against the right to honour and reputation.[61] Several cases have dealt with the relationship between freedom of expression and the prohibition against racial discrimination. In the most recent decision, Rt 1997 p. 1821, the leader of a political party against immigration was convicted because of utterances of a discriminatory nature.[62]

To sum up, it is clear that the Supreme Court has played a leading role in the interpretation and application of human rights conventions. It is reason to believe that its thorough discussions of the Convention and Strasbourg case-law have influenced the attitude of the subordinate courts when confronted with such arguments. The text of the Convention and the case-law have not only been invoked by the lawyers pleading the cases, but have been applied by the Court and in many cases thoroughly discussed. On several occasions a Strasbourg solution has had a direct impact on the outcome of a Norwegian case. As a consequence of the way in which the Supreme Court has interpreted national law and the Convention, it has never found a conflict between the two sets of rules.

[60] Rt 1993 p. 1591 (claim for interim measures to stop the expulsion of Kosovo-Albanians was rejected).

[61] Series A No. 103 (1986). Article 10 has also been applied for instance in Rt 1985 p. 1421 (newspaper convicted of defamation because it had called Greenpeace 'the terrorists of environmental protection') and Rt 1993 p. 537 (five of seven defamatory statements relating to a professor's personal integrity and honesty declared null and void).

[62] See also Rt 1977 p. 114 (teacher denying the fact that Jews were exterminated—conviction), Rt 1978 p. 1072 (statement in a newspaper—acquittal) and Rt 1981 p. 1305 (leaflets against immigration—acquittal).

E. CASES BROUGHT BEFORE THE EUROPEAN COMMISSION AND COURT OF HUMAN RIGHTS

1. *Individual cases before the Commission*

As of 30 April 1996, 146 individual applications against Norway had been declared inadmissible, 8 were struck off the list, 1 case formed the basis of a friendly settlement, and 5 reports had been adopted under Article 31 of the Convention.[63] According to a survey elaborated in 1981, 50 complaints had been received by the Commission from 1955 to 1980, an average of two cases per year during that period.[64] For many years the number of complaints registered annually was well under ten, but the number increased during the 1990s.

Until 1988 all cases were declared inadmissible or struck off the list, mostly without being communicated to the government for written observations on admissibility and merits. According to the above-mentioned survey, only three cases had been communicated as of 1980. On 12 May 1988 the Commission for the first time declared admissible part of a complaint: the case of *E v Norway* was later brought before the Court (see below).[65]

The first oral hearing took place in the *Iversen* case in the 1960s (see D above). Hearings have also been carried out in the *Johansen* case, which related to deprivation of liberty under Article 5(1)(b) in connection with the obligation of a conscientious objector to perform substitute civilian service,[66] in *E v Norway* (concerning Article 3), and in the *Botten* case.[67] Several applications to the Commission which have been mentioned in legal literature were decided on the basis of a written procedure, such as the *Knudsen* case (minister of religion in the state church who was dismissed because he refused to perform duties in order to protest against abortion legislation was not a victim under Article 25),[68] *H v Norway* (potential father trying in vain to prevent abortion: see D above,) and the *Treholt* case (conditions of detention for a person convicted of espionage).[69]

[63] Source: The Commission's Secretariat.

[64] Survey elaborated by Advocate Magne Spilde and made available in November 1981 in connection with an information meeting organized by the Norwegian Bar Association and the Human Rights Directorate of the Council of Europe.

[65] Application 11701/85. By a partial decision of 7 March 1988 the Commission had declared the application inadmissible as regards Article 3 (manifestly ill founded).

[66] Application 10600/83, DR 44 (1985) p. 155.

[67] See section 3 below.

[68] van Dijk and van Hoof, p. 220; Harris, O'Boyle, and Warbrick, n. 3 above, p. 43.

[69] Application 14610/89, DR 71 (1991) p. 168; see Harris, OBoyle. and Warbrick, n. 3 above, p. 69.

The Norwegian authorities have always accepted the Commission's requests for interim measures under Rule 36 of the Rules of Procedure, which have been used in some cases of expulsion.

Only one of the seven cases which were not declared inadmissible by the Commission was decided by the Committee of Ministers: *Andreassen v Norway* related to the length of certain civil proceedings concerning the applicant's right to buy a piece of land by virtue of his allodial rights. The Commission, by ten votes to three, expressed the opinion that there had been a violation of Article 6(1). The Committee agreed with the Commission and decided that the government should pay just satisfaction.[70] The other cases in which the Commission found a violation were all brought before the Court (see below).

2. *Inter-state cases before the Commission*

Norway has been involved in three cases under Article 24 of the Convention. Proceedings were instituted against Greece by Norway together with Denmark, Sweden, and the Netherlands in 1967, and again in 1970.[71] Moreover, together with Denmark, France, the Netherlands, and Sweden, Norway filed an application in 1983 against Turkey.[72] In 1985 the parties to the last of those cases entered into a friendly settlement.

3. *Cases before the Court*

Four individual cases against Norway had been brought before the Court before Protocol No. 11 entered into force on 1 November 1998. The first judgment was delivered in 1990. In *E v Norway,* a unanimous Court, disagreeing with the unanimous Commission, found that the scope of judicial review and the courts' power to order release in cases relating to security measures was in conformity with Article 5(4). On the other hand, it agreed with the Commission that there was a violation of that provision because the proceedings concerning the lawfulness of Mr E's detention were not decided 'speedily'. The applicant's claim for just satisfaction under Article 50 was rejected. He had received free legal aid in Norway for his representation before the Convention organs, and his claim for pecuniary and non-pecuniary damage was not accepted.[73]

The second judgment, *Botten v Norway*, was given in February 1996. The Court held by seven votes to two that there had been a violation of Article 6(1) of the Convention. An officer who had been acquitted in the City Court

[70] Application 17228/90; CM Resolution DH (95) 26.
[71] Applications 3321/67 and 4448/70. [72] Application 9940—44/82.
[73] Series No. A 181–A (1990).

was convicted by the Supreme Court for neglect or carelessness in the performance of official duties without having been summoned and heard in person. He had received certain sums in legal aid for costs and expenses from the Norwegian authorities and the Council of Europe, and made no further claim under Article 50. Accordingly, the Court held unanimously that it was not necessary to make an award for costs and expenses.

In *Johansen v Norway* (August 1996) the Court found that there had been a violation of Article 8 in respect of the decision to deprive the applicant of her access and parental rights, but not as regards the taking into care of her child. Finally, in *Eriksen v Norway* (May 1997)—the same applicant as in *E v Norway*—there was no violation of Article 5. The case related to provisional detention after the expiry of an authorization to use security measures, pending examination of the appropriateness of prolonging the authorization.

The new permanent Court had its first hearing in a Norwegian case in January 1999. *Tromsø et al v Norway* dealt with the issue whether a conviction for defamation in connnection with a newpaper article on seal hunting was in breach of Article 10. The Court answered the question in the affirmative. Subsequently the new Court has found violations in two other cases concerning the relationship between defamation and freedom of expression.

F. REMEDIAL ACTION TAKEN BY THE GOVERNMENT IN RESPONSE TO BEING HELD IN VIOLATION OF THE CONVENTION

It follows from the survey given in section E above that until Protocol No. 11 entered into force the Convention organs had found violations in five Norwegian cases. None of them necessitated the amendment of statutes adopted by Parliament.

As a consequence of the Court's judgment in *E v Norway*, the Norwegian authorities issued a circular letter to all courts in Norway describing the implications of the judgment, a copy of which was enclosed. It was stressed that special expeditious measures should be taken by the courts in cases of judicial review with administrative decisions which impose security measures in the form of deprivation of liberty. The letter indicated various steps which should be taken to this effect and underlined that it is the responsibility of the head of each court to implement the necessary administrative changes to meet the time requirements set out in the Court's judgment.[74]

[74] See for further details CM Resolution DH (91) 16, adopted on 6 June 1991, and the Appendix thereto.

Following the Committee of Ministers' decision in the *Andreassen* case, the government distributed a circular to all the county governors and municipalities requesting that cases concerning proceedings for redemption of allodial rights should be given priority. Competence to take decisions in such cases was transferred from the Ministry of Agriculture to the county agricultural committees, and the Ministry is since then following up each individual case with a view to ensuring that proceedings are not unduly protracted. Of course, compensation was paid to the applicant in conformity with the decision of the Committee of Ministers.[75] A circular letter was also distributed as a consequence of the *Johansen* case. Following the *Botten* judgment the Supreme Court has made practical arrangements to enable the person charged to be present and make a statement, if necessary.

Finally, it should be mentioned that section 407 of the Civil Procedure Act and section 391 of the Criminal Procedure Act provide for the reopening of a case when the original domestic judgment is based on an interpretation of general international law or a treaty which deviates from the interpretation which an international court decides in the same case in a binding way for Norway, provided that this interpretation is presumed to lead to a different decision at the national level. These provisions are generally formulated and may be applied in relation to Strasbourg judgments against Norway. So far they have not been used.

G. ASSESSMENT AND PROSPECTS

In relation to some countries, the Convention has been described as 'the Sleeping Beauty'. Whereas this poetic description was once applicable in relation to Norway, it follows from the survey given above that the situation has changed fundamentally. The Beauty is indeed awake. In particular, the Convention has influenced legislation and judicial decisions, but it is also a framework for the administrative authorities. It is noteworthy that the Norwegian Ombudsman for the Administration has expressed an open attitude towards human rights instruments, and in some cases applied the Convention actively.[76]

[75] CM Resolution DH (95) 26, adopted on 7 April 1995, with Appendix.

[76] See statement of principle in the annual report of the Ombudsmann, 1990, p. 23. A recent example of the concrete application of the Convention was his view in a case concerning the decision of the Market Council to prohibit a television company from showing advertising films issued by the organizations in working life. The Ombudsman criticized that decision and referred *inter alia* to Article 100 of the Constitution (freedom of expression) and Article 10 of the Convention. See also Kyrre Eggen: 'Politisk reklame i kringkastingsmediene og grunnloven § 100', in *Lov og Rett* 1996 pp. 198–206.

In spite of the significant increase in case-law, the full potential of the Convention has probably still not been exploited. There is reason to believe that developments in the judicial field will continue, and there is room for improvement in the legislative and administrative area. The new human rights provisions in the Constitution and the Incorporation Act will presumably accelerate the process. But a legal reform such as 'incorporation', is one thing: real 'penetration', ie making the Convention part of everyday life in all branches of society is another. This requires increased knowledge of the ECHR.

The Committee which drafted new legislation on human rights in 1993 proposed several measures to promote human rights in Norway, of which only some can be mentioned here.[77] It found a need to improve the availability of the relevant sources of law. Moreover, it emphasized the importance for lawyers, prosecuting authorities, judges, administrative civil servants, and other persons concerned to familiarize themselves more deeply with the practice of the convention bodies. Several proposals were made in the field of information, teaching, and education. The Committee also stressed the significance of instruction about human rights in the education of police and prison officers. In the bill, the Ministry discussed such measures.[78]

Before and independently of the discussions in connection with the Incorporation Act, much had already been achieved. Human rights courses were organized for practising lawyers and judges, and relevant issues are brought up at the meetings of the prosecuting authorities. Since 1985, biennial study visits for judges to (*inter alia*) Strasbourg have been illustrative and stimulating. Students leaving university today know more about human rights than the students of years ago. For instance, basic knowledge in international human rights law has since 1992 formed part of the obligatory curriculum at the Law Faculty of the University in Oslo. In addition, students have for several years been able to choose human rights as their special subject at all law faculties, or to write a dissertation in that field. Human rights issues are also increasingly addressed in other disciplines of law, such as constitutional law and criminal procedure. It may be added that, following a Swedish initiative, representatives from law faculties in the Nordic countries are pleading a moot case concerning the ECHR every year (The Sporrong-Lönnroth competition).[79]

There is still work to be done in this area. As a result of the legal and practical measures which have been implemented and are under way, the number

[77] See NOU 1993:18 Chapter 13; pp. 198–199 of the English summary.

[78] Odelstingsproposisjon No. 3 (1989–99) chapter 9.

[79] The Swedish Professor Jacob W. Sundberg initiated and has for many years organized these competitions.

of human rights cases in Norway and subsequently in Strasbourg may increase. It is difficult to make an educated guess on possible figures, but staying with the language of fairy tales: there is little reason to believe that we will be watching the Sorcerer's Apprentice.

25

Poland

ANDREW DRZEMCZEWSKI AND
MAREK ANTONI NOWICKI

A. INTRODUCTION

In countries of the former Soviet bloc, Poland included, the ECHR was for many years a document known to a few people only. According to the official ideology of those days, it reflected an alien bourgeois concept of human rights. The Convention was quoted as an example of the hypocrisy of the West, creating formal paper guarantees but unable to stand the test of real life. Human rights, it was argued, could only find an appropriate place in the Socialist system, and only in its *Realsozialismus* version born in Soviet Russia. Others, who had never accepted the grim and hypocritical reality east of the Laba River, saw the text of the Convention and their own study of that document, if incidental, as either an expression of their honesty as researchers[1] or a manifestation of a rebellious attitude, similar to the practice of wearing bright socks or playing jazz under Stalin and even later on.

The *Realsozialismus* states were parties to a variety of international agreements on human rights protection, including the UN Covenant of Civil and Political Rights.[2] This fact, however, was of very little practical importance, especially for the citizens of those states. The documents were, in the eyes of most observers, ratified with no intention whatever of fulfilling the resultant obligations. Accession to the two UN Covenants by the Soviet Union and the other states of the Eastern Bloc, and their commitment to undertakings

[1] E.g. A. Michalska, 'Europejska Konwencja Praw Człowieka' (1978) 3 *Ruch Prawniczy, Ekonomiczny i Socjologiczny*, pp. 21–34; Z. Galicki, 'Pakty Praw Człowieka a Europejska Konwencja Praw Człowieka' (1979) 1 *Przegląd Stosunków Międzynarodowych*, pp. 35–46; J. Zajadło, 'Europejska Konwencja Praw Człowieka' (1983) December No. 123 *Chrzescijanin w Swiecie, Zeszyty O.D.i S.S.*, pp. 49–56.

This chapter is an adapted and updated version of an article published in (1993) 3 *European Human Rights Law Review* pp. 261–286.

[2] Poland ratified the Covenant without reservations on 3 March 1977: *Dziennik Ustaw* [Official Gazette] No. 38/1977, item 167); the Covenant entered into force with respect to Poland on 18 June 1977.

entered into under the so-called third basket of the CSCE Helsinki Accords, were a deception of which the West must have been aware all the time. The official propaganda and—still more—the authorities' conduct brought discredit on the ideas of international human rights protection. With time, however, certain pockets of individuals within the Eastern Bloc decided to treat seriously the obligations undertaken by their states to observe fundamental human rights: loud demands could be heard that individuals rights be respected according to the standards laid down in the Universal Declaration of Human Rights in 1948, the two UN Covenants, and various CSCE documents.

Activists of the Polish Solidarity movement, the Czech Charter 77, numerous Helsinki Watch committees, and other human rights organizations slowly but surely restored to societies of those countries confidence in the real value and importance of international documents on the protection of individual rights.

After the great political transformations in Central and Eastern Europe in 1989, when the prospect of post-Communist countries ratifying the ECHR became a reality, citizens of these countries realized that they were taking part in important events, that specific and legally binding obligations had been undertaken, and that they would be able to demand compliance with these obligations from the states themselves both at home and on the international arena. This was what they understood to be the result of the movement for democracy and human rights effected in 1989 by the great historic change symbolized by the Polish Solidarity movement and the fall of the Berlin Wall.

B. THE STATUS OF THE CONVENTION IN NATIONAL LAW

1. *Signature and ratification of the ECHR*

The ECHR was signed by Poland's Minister for Foreign Affairs, Krzysztof Skubiszewski, on 26 November 1991. Protocols Nos. 1, 4, 7, 9, and 10 were signed a little later on 14 September 1992. Protocol No. 11 was signed on 11 May 1994 and ratified on 20 May 1997; it entered into force on 1 November 1998.[3]

The Act (*Ustawa*) approving the ratification of the Convention (ie the ECHR as amended by Protocols Nos. 3, 5, and 8, together with Protocol No.

[3] See A. Drzemczewski, 'The European Human Rights Convention: A New Court of Human Rights as of November 1, 1998' (1998) 55 *Washington and Lee Law Review* pp. 1–40 (and references therein).

2) was passed on 2 October 1992 (*Ustawa* no. 427) and published in the Official Gazette [*Dziennik Ustaw*] on 24 November 1992.[4] Section 2 of the Act, which concerns only the Convention as such, provided that the Act would come into force fourteen days after its publication, namely on 8 December 1992. Lech Walesa, the President of the Republic, signed this document on 15 December 1992.

Instruments of ratification of the Convention were deposited on 19 January 1993. Protocols Nos. 1, 4, 7, 9, and 10 were signed on 14 September 1992; they were all subsequently ratified on 10 October 1994 with the exception of Protocol No. 7. Protocol No. 6 (abolition of the death penalty) remains unsigned.[5] The right of individual petition (Article 25) and the Court's jurisdiction (Article 46) were recognized from 1 May 1993, four months after ratification of the Convention and two months before publication of the text (although publication remains an essential condition for the instrument to have binding force in the domestic legal system).[6]

2. *The constitutional situation*

In the countries of Central and Eastern Europe human rights treaties did not as a general rule rank as domestic law until the changes of the late 1980s. In Poland citizens could not rely exclusively on the provisions of international conventions in support of their claims. However, they could refer to them as a secondary source of law. The Constitutional Tribunal and the Supreme Administrative Court sometimes even cited human rights treaties, if only to make their own reasoning more convincing.[7]

Until recently, the exact rank of the European Convention on Human Rights in the Polish legal order was open to a number of interpretations.

[4] *Dziennik Ustaw* no. 85, item 427, 24 November 1992, p. 1485. Protocol No. 9 entered into force on 1 February 1995 with respect to Poland.

[5] *Dziennik Ustaw* no. 61, items 284 and 285, 10 July 1993, with respect to the Convention as such. The texts of Protocols Nos. 1, 4, 2, and 9 were published in *Dziennik Ustaw* no. 36, 1994, item 175 (concerning Protocols Nos. 1 and 4), item 176 (concerning Protocol No. 2, somewhat delayed), and item 177, with regard to Protocol No. 9. The text of Prococol No. 11 was published in 1998 in *Dziennik Ustaw* no. 147, item 962.

[6] Governmental declarations made on 1 March 1993, specifying that the text would come into force subsequent to 30 April 1993: *Dziennik Ustaw* no. 61, item 286, p. 1277. The right of individual petition and the Court's compulsory jurisdiction are now, of course, both automatic by virtue of amendments to the ECHR by Protocol No. 11 thereto: new Articles 34 and 33.

For an analysis of the Convention's place in Polish law see P. Hofmański's excellent book *Konwencja Europejska a Prawo Karne* (Toruń, 1995), especially pp. 48–52 and 101–107.

[7] For an example, see the Constitutional Tribunal's decision of 3 March 1987, (1989) 15/16 *EuGRZ* p. 362. For a more in-depth analysis see K. Skubiszewski 'Völkerrecht und Landesrecht: Regelungen und Erfahrungen in Mittel- und Osteuropa' in W. Fiedler and G. Ress (eds), *Verfassungsrecht und Völkerrecht: Gedächtnischrift für W. K. Geck* (1988), pp. 777–793 and survey of case-law prior to the entry into force of the 1997 Constitution: see article by the authors, cited in footnote 1, above.

However, with the entry into force of the new Constitution of the Republic of Poland in 1997, the Convention's position is now quite clear. In its Article 9, the Constitution provides that 'the Republic of Poland abides by international law which is binding on it'. Furthermore, from Article 86 of the Constitution it follows that ratified international agreements form part and parcel of the sources of generally binding law. If international agreements concern civil liberties, rights, or duties specified in the Constitution (as, for example, with the European Convention on Human Rights) ratification may only take place with prior statutory approval. Such instruments are then promulgated in a procedure required for statutes. Article 90 of the Constitution specifies that once it has been published in the Official Gazette, a ratified international agreement constitutes part of the domestic legal order and is applicable directly, unless its application is contingent on the passing of a separate Act of Parliament. Thus, the European Convention on Human Rights enjoys priority over a statute if that statute cannot be reconciled with the Convention. It has to be stressed, however, that even before the coming into effect of the 1997 Constitution, the Convention and the case-law of its organs were already reflected in judgments of the supreme judicial instances and of the common courts. Today, all courts and state organs are constitutionally obliged to apply it. See also, in this connection, Article 188 which authorizes the Constitutional Tribunal to adjudicate upon the 'conformity of a statute with ratified international agreements whose ratification requires prior consent granted by statute'. The Constitutional Tribunal will no doubt express itself clearly on this point when given an opportunity to do so.[8]

C. THE CONVENTION AND THE LAW-MAKING PROCESS

1. Government initiatives

The process of adjusting Polish law and practice to meet the Convention's requirements started well before the actual signing of that document in 1991, and is still going on at present. This process is part of a profound and systemic reform of different branches of the law. Indeed 'Strasbourg-proofing', or verification of the compatibility of domestic law and practice with Strasbourg case-law, must be seen as an ongoing process of indefinite duration.

Although there is as yet no special procedure for reviewing the compatibility of draft legislation with the Convention during the stage of inter-department

[8] Case-law (including summaries in English) of the Constitutional Tribunal can be consulted on the Tribunal's website: http://www.trybunal.gov.pl.

adjustments, departments such as the Ministry of Foreign Affairs and the Ministry of Justice indicate, when the need arises, necessary adjustments of provisions or regulations so that draft legislation is compatible to the Convention's stipulations and with Strasbourg case-law.

In this context it is of relevance to note that Resolution No. 16/94 of 29 March 1994 of the Council of Ministers until recently imposed a duty upon different branches of the government to consult the Plenipotentiary (*Pełnomocnik*) of the Government for European Integration and Foreign Aid who, in turn, had to verify the compatibility of draft legislation with the law of the European Union. As of September 1996 this function has been given to the Office of the Commission for European Integration. The Opinion of the Offiice has to be attached to each and every government bill. If necessary, depending on the subject of the draft law or regulation, such opinions also provide an appraisal of consistency or otherwise of these drafts with Article F, paragraph 2, of the Treaty on the European Union[9] in which the Union undertook to respect the ECHR.[10] Thus, the above-mentioned Resolution of the Council of Ministers in effect provides an opportunity, for the Office of the Commission for European Integration, to give opinions, in a rather circuitous manner, as to the consistency of draft laws with the ECHR and Strasbourg case-law.[11]

2. *'Strasbourg-vetting' in Parliament*

Subsequently, at the stage of parliamentary work, the Office for Studies and Expertise of the Diet reviews a draft statute's consistency with the Convention, but only incidentally, either after having been commissioned to do so by an MP or a parliamentary commission, or on its own motion. In such cases the Office approaches recognized experts for their opinions or requests its own staff to carry out the review. The Office, however, does not review all

[9] Concluded on 7 February 1992 in Maastricht, the Treaty on the European Union entered into force on 1 November 1993. Its Article F, paragraph 2, reads as follows: 'The Union respects fundamental rights guaranteed in the European Convention on Protection of Human Rights and Fundamental Freedoms signed in Rome on 4 November 1950 and rights that follow from common constitutional traditions of member States, as the general principles of Community law'.

[10] Eg Final Opinion of 19 July 1995 on consistency of draft Penal Code, Code of Criminal Procedure, and Code of Execution of Penalties with the law of the European Union (No. 496/312/95); Final Opinion of 26 July 1995 on consistency of the draft Aliens Act with the law of the European Union (No. 542/359/95).

[11] The standpoint on this issue is, however, inconsistent: as indicated in the 'Raport z wykonania programu działań dostosowujacych polską gopodarkę i system prawny do wymagań Unii Europejskiej w 1994 r' there is no mention whatever of problems related directly to the ECHR (Bureau of the Cabinet, Office of Plenipotentiary of the Government for European Integration and Foreign Aid, Warsaw 1995).

new drafts on a regular basis. A similar practice exists with respect to the Office for Studies and Analyses of the Chancellery of the Senate.[12]

For example, the Office for Studies and Expertises of the Diet carried out a few periodic analyses of draft legislation processed by the Diet from the viewpoint of their consistency with, *inter alia*, the ECHR. In a report relating to an analysis of the period ending in May 1993, concern was expressed about inconsistency of eight draft statutes with the ECHR. For the most part, this concerned a package of draft lustration Acts.[13] In the next report, covering the period from September 1993 to September 1994, it was stated that 'the authors of the drafts . . . have greater regard to the consistency of proposed regulations with acts of international law, such as . . . the European Convention on Human Rights and Fundamental Freedoms'.[14]

In the course of parliamentary debates in both the Diet and the Senate, arguments are voiced in favour of specific solutions with reference to the European Convention and judgments of the Court of Human Rights in Strasbourg. Besides the debate concerning the ratification of the Convention itself,[15] and then its Protocols Nos. 1 and 4,[16] a few instances of the need to fulfil commitments subsequent to ratification of the ECHR can be cited. Examples are discussed in the Diet concerning a report of the Legislative Commission with regard to a judgment of the Constitutional Tribunal when it found certain provisions on the Aliens Act to be unconstitutional;[17] on the Act on protection of mental health;[18] on penal law amendments;[19] on government information on an agreement concluded by Ministers of Internal

[12] Eg in connection with the amendment of the Aliens Act (Senate document No. 182, 1995) the Office for Studies and Analyses of the Chancellery of the Senate consulted three experts. Two of the opinions stressed the need for adjustment of the discussed legal solutions with respect to the ECHR's standards.

[13] Ilościowa analiza projektów ustaw. I kadencja Sejmu RP (stan do 31.05.1993) Legal Opinions Department, Chancellery of the Diet, Office for Studies and Expertises, Report No. 48, August 1993, pp. 16–17.

[14] J. Konecka-Dobrowolska, Analiza projektów ustaw będących przedmiotem prac Sejmu II kadencji (od 19.09.1993 do 6.09.1994), October 1994, Chancellery of the Diet, Office for Studies and Expertise, Report No. 65, p. 24. The drafts were appraised on the basis of a questionnaire composed of 27 questions, prepared by the Legal Consultations Department of the Office. The appraisal on the basis of the questionnaire was made by the Department's staff.

[15] 15th session of the Diet, 21–23 May 1992 and 25th session of the Diet, 1–3 and 7 October 1992.

[16] 17th session of the Diet, 8 April 1994, see also notes 4 and 5.

[17] 10th session of the Diet, 20–21 January 1994, Shorthand Report, Warsaw 1994, pp. 66–69; eg pronouncement of Deputy T. Iwinski (pp. 68–69).

[18] See in this respect: 10th session of the Diet, 20–21 January 1994, Shorthand Report, Warsaw 1994, pp. 24–59 (I) and 26th session of the Diet, 18 August 1994, Shorthand Report, Warsaw 1994, pp. 31–44 (II). The Rapporteur of the Deputies' draft, M. Balicki, made explicit reference to the Strasbourg case-law (I p. 24; II. p. 35).

[19] 44th session of the Diet, 13 May 1993, Shorthand Report, Warsaw 1993, p. 87.

Affairs of Poland and Germany concerning readmission of aliens;[20] and in the Senate during a discussion on the amendment of the Aliens Act.[21] In some instances the Convention is not mentioned directly,[22] while in others a rigorous 'Strasbourg-vetting' process is carried out.[23]

3. *An example: the Aliens Act*

When amending, on 19 September 1991, the 1963 Aliens Act whereby administrative agencies were granted the power to impose, without judicial supervision, a variety of forms of deprivation of liberty upon persons with respect to whom an expulsion order had been made, first the Diet and then the Senate completely ignored critical comments pointing to the glaring discrepancy of some of the text's provisions with the ECHR. According to experts, the draft was patently inconsistent with Article 5 of the Convention. The Act was passed in full awareness of its inconsistency with the Convention, the signature of which was due to take place shortly afterwards (in Strasbourg on 26 November 1991). Fortunately, the Ombudsman then seized the Constitutional Tribunal to obtain a determination that the text was inconsistent with Article 87, paragraph 1, of the Constitution.[24] The Tribunal, to a great measure, shared the Ombudsman's opinion, finding the provisions inconsistent with Article 87, paragraph 1, of the Constitution, and stressed, with reference to Article 5, paragraph 4, of the ECHR that 'as far as protection of human rights is concerned, the Aliens Act amendment is a step backwards'. The Tribunal also pointed to inconsistency of this text with provisions of the International Covenant on Civil and Political Rights (Article 2, paragraph 3;

[20] 44th session of the Diet, 15 May 1993, Shorthand Report, Warsaw 1993, pp. 231ff. Deputy Minister of Internal Affairs J. Zimowski stressed that the signing of that Agreement was accompanied by awareness of commitments that follow from the Geneva Convention Relating to the Status of Refugees and the European Convention on Human Rights (p. 231).

[21] 40th session of the Senate, 2 February 1995, concerning consistency with Article 5, paragraph 4, of the Convention.

[22] Eg first reading of the new Act on the establishment of a Supreme Administrative Court (17th session of the Diet, 7 April 1994, Shorthand Report, Warsaw 1994, pp. 64–85).

[23] In his answer of 4 December 1992 (31st session of the Diet, 10–12 and 16–17 December 1992, Shorthand Report, Warsaw 1992, pp. 21–22) to a parliamentary question posed by deputy Jerzy Jaskiernia on 2 November (29th session of the Diet, 26 November 1992, Shorthand Report, Part II, Warsaw 1992, p. 6), who enquired, among other things, whether consideration is given during preparation of new penal law codes to the consequences of Poland's accession to the ECHR, the Minister of Justice replied that all the prepared draft solutions were consistent with the ECHR.

See also, in this connection, the article 'Procedura karna bliżej standardów europejskich' in newspaper *Rzeczpospolita* ('Prawo co dnia') 29 March 1995, No. 75 (4028) in which the chairman of a working party on criminal procedure (in the Commission on Reform of Penal Law), Mr J. Tylman, indicated that close scrutiny is being given the requirements set out in the Convention, as interpreted by the Strasbourg control organs.

[24] This Article guarantees the right to personal inviolability.

Article 9, paragraphs 3 and 4).[25] At its session on 21 January 1994 the Diet found the above view to be well founded.[26] Thus, as a direct result of the Tribunal's opinion, the Act of 5 January 1995 amended the Aliens Act. This step was considered to have been taken in the right direction, even if the actual extent of changes might have been broader.[27]

While proceedings relating to the Aliens Act were winding their way through Parliament, the then Vice-Prime Minister (and at the same time Minister of Justice), Mr W. Cimoszewicz, made the following statement during a General Debate on 'the state of the law':

> It is worth remembering that, with regard to obligations undertaken, [Polish] state authorities must take into account a new additional control mechanism that protects human rights . . . as guaranteed by the ECHR.[28]

Also worth stressing, in this connection, is the potentially very important role of the Plenipotentiary of the Minister of Foreign Affairs (Government Agent of the Republic of Poland before the Court of Human Rights) who can bring to the attention of the authorities 'problem areas' with respect to Convention requirements.[29] In his pronouncements, the Plenipotentiary has already had occasion to indicate apparent shortcomings of Polish law *vis-à-vis* international human rights standards.[30]

D. DOMESTIC CASE-LAW

1. The Supreme Court

Under the constitutional provisions in force,[31] the Supreme Court is the highest judicial body which reviews the decisions of all other courts: see Supreme Court Act of 20 September 1984.[32]

The Supreme Court has four divisions: the Administrative, Labour, and Social Security Division, the Criminal Division, the Civil Division, and the

[25] Judgment of the Constitutional Tribunal of 20 October 1992 (K.1/92).

[26] 10th session of the Diet, 20–21 January 1994, Shorthand Report, Warsaw 1994, pp. 66–73. (This procedure has been abolished since the coming into effect of the 1997 Constitution.)

[27] Opinions of B. Wierzbicki, M. A. Nowicki, I. Rzeplińska, and A. Rutkiewicz (Senate Document no. 182), Zeszyty Biura Studiów i Analiz Kancelarii Senatu no. 240/ 0–4/95, January 1995.

[28] 24th Session of the Diet, Shorthand Report, 1 July 1994, at p. 121.

[29] Since the Autumn of 1994 the Office of Plenipotentiary has been held by Professor Krzysztof Drzewicki, an internationally recognized human rights expert.

[30] See, for example, the 'Comments on Draft Penal Law Reform Acts' submitted to the Government (12 May 1995).

[31] See *Dziennik Ustaw* no. 84, item 426, 17 October 1992.

[32] Which consolidated the law: see *Dziennik Ustaw* (1994), no. 13, item 48, 29 January 1994.

Military Division. It does not adjudicate cases like a trial court or appellate court, but exercises supreme jurisdiction over domestic court findings. It reviews court decisions, including the Supreme Administrative Court's decisions (see below) through the process of 'extraordinary revision'; such proceedings can only be initiated by the First President of the Supreme Court, the Minister of Justice (the General Prosecutor), the Minister of Labour (in some instances), or the Ombudsman. As of 1 January 1996 the Polish Supreme Court, with the entry into force of legal provisions which substantially alter proceedings relating to criminal cases, has cassation jurisdiction[33] which replaced 'extraordinary revision'.

The second basic competence of the Supreme Court is to promulgate 'interpretations of law', which are general remarks on the correct interpretation of particular statutes and regulations so as to provide direction for the ordinary courts and other state bodies in the application of the law. 'Interpretation of the law', including any reference to the standards laid down in the ECHR, may come about either on the basis of a legal question presented before the Court in a specific case or controversial point brought before it or, in an abstract way, on the basis of a motion from the First President of the Supreme Court or from the Minister of Justice.

As a general premiss, the Supreme Court has formulated a number of practical rules concerning the relationship between the authorities and the individual, including methods of interpreting public law provisions. Among leading decisions on this matter are cases in which express reference to the ECHR has been made. For example, in a case decided on 24 June 1993, relating to uncertainty as to the meaning of a concrete legal provision, the Court specified that the interpretation to be applied in the way which best corresponds to the principles laid down in the Constitution. It then went on to say that under Article 6 of the ECHR, on excessively lengthy proceedings, can be regarded as a violation of everyone's right to have his case heard within a reasonable time by an impartial tribunal. In particular, this may concern cases where, in a period of inflation, lengthy proceedings reduce the value of compensation awarded to the party.[34]

In a judgment rendered on 26 June 1992 the Supreme Court made the following statement:

> Any uncertainty as to the limits of judicial investigation in cases concerned with the violation of the citizen's rights or interests, based on legal provisions, must be settled

[33] See *Dziennik Ustaw*, no. 89, item 443, 3 August 1995.

[34] Case III ARN 33/93, commented upon by M. Wierzbowski in (1994) 9 *PiP*, pp. 111–115. See also case I ARN 45/93 in which Article 6, ECHR was also referred to. The Court stated that international law can and must be applied directly to domestic legal relationships and does not require any act of transformation.

in accordance with the rule *in dubio pro actione*. It follows that in the case of uncertainty the principle of extension and not limitation of the Court's jurisdiction must be admitted. Confirmation of this view can also be found in Article 14 of the Covenant on Civil and Political Rights, which Poland ratified on 3 March 1977, as well as in Article 6 of the ECHR, which specifies that everyone is entitled to a fair and public hearing within a reasonable time by an impartial tribunal established by law. In its decision of 7 January 1992 (K 8/91) the Constitutional Tribunal also ruled that these provisions applied when determining the parameters of the administrative court's jurisdiction in citizens' individual cases, coming under public administration. It is therefore a principle which must govern the construction of procedural law provisions as a whole, as well as the Polish system for the protection of the citizen's rights and interests, found in law, with respect to the authorities.[35]

In a case of 11 January 1995[36] the Supreme Court specified in no uncertain terms that from the moment of Poland's ratification of the ECHR, the Strasbourg Court's case-law may, and indeed should, be used as a source of Polish law when interpreting domestic legal provisions. In this case, express reference was again made to Article 6 of the ECHR.

In a number of other cases, the Court has not hesitated to invoke other provisions of the ECHR, such as Articles 8 and 10 of the Convention and Article I of the First Protocol.[37] But probably most interesting of recent developments is a judgment rendered by the Supreme Court's Criminal Division on 29 July 1997.[38] In this case the Court, in overturning a finding of the Warsaw Appeal Court, held that the extradition of two Chinese citizens to the Chinese Peoples' Republic was unacceptable, as such action would be in violation of Articles 3 (torture, inhuman treatment, or punishment) and 6 (right to a fair trial) of the ECHR, as interpreted by the Strasbourg Court. The Supreme Court cited, *inter alia*, the *Soering*, *Cruz Varas*, *Valvarajah*, and *Ahmed* cases when determining that in the circumstances of the case the extradition of the two persons concerned would amount to a breach of Article 3 of the ECHR. It even went on to hold that Article 6 would also be violated, despite the fact

[35] Case III ARN 30/92 (our own translation from original text).

[36] Case III ARN 75/94, *OSN* Zb.U 1995/9, item 106, commented upon by A. Zieliński, (1995) 9–10 *Palestra*, pp. 202–205.

[37] Article 8, ECHR cited in Case III ARN 18/94; Article 10 (and the Strasbourg Court's case-law) in Case III ARN 23/94 of 12 May 1994; Article 1 of the First Protocol cited in Case II AZP 28/92:

> The extensive contruction of the measures relating to the population register, made by the court (even made by the Supreme Court ruling in plenary session), under the terms of which an administrative body's decisions concerning the population register could render ineffective the right of the owner or co-owner to enjoy the benefit of property, is inadmissible (Article 7 of the Polish Constitution and Article 1 of the First Protocol to the ECHR).

Article 6, ECHR, also cited in Cases III ARN 45/93 and III ARN 49/93.

[38] Case II KKN 313/97 (Mandugeqi and Jinge). See also *Human Rights of Aliens*, Council of Europe, 1985, pp. 349–427 for similar cases in other countries.

that there existed no specific Strasbourg case-law to confirm this line of reasoning.

2. The Supreme Administrative Court

In Poland private persons may appeal to the Supreme Administrative Court against administrative decisions. There exists general legislation instituting a right of administrative appeal, such a remedy being available against administrative decisions generally with exceptions explicitly provided by law, as well as certain other specific administrative acts: Article 196, paragraphs 1 to 4, of the Code of Administrative Proceedings, *Dziennik Ustaw* (1990) no. 9, item 26.

However, the powers of the Supreme Administrative Court are limited to grounds of unlawfulness. This being said, the term 'unlawfulness' is interpreted widely. It would appear from the Supreme Administrative Court's case-law that it adheres to the following principles: protection of private life against any interference by the administrative authorities; combating the 'over-administration' of private life and community life; and protection of citizens' rights against restrictions imposed by law. The Supreme Administrative Court may also interpret its own jurisdiction extensively, sometimes even in breach of the letter of the applicable law, although undoubtedly in keeping with its spirit. The Court frequently retries cases *de novo* on the merits.

In a judgment of 20 November 1990 the Supreme Administrative Court gave the following interpretation of the relationship between international law and domestic law:

> It is a generally accepted view that international treaties ratified by Poland and published in the Official Gazette require neither transformation nor incorporation and are binding *ex proprio vigore*. Moreover, in case of conflict between such treaties and domestic law, the principle of priority of international treaties over domestic law is to be applied.[39]

In a case concerning the dismissal of a police officer the Court, taking as its basis Article 14 of the International Covenant on Civil and Political Rights and Article 10 of the Universal Declaration of Human Rights, ruled as follows:

> In any case, fundamental rules of international law which are aimed at protecting human rights should be considered as directives for the interpretation of national law.[40]

[39] Case II SA 759/90 in *Orzecznictwo Sądów Polskich, OSP* 1991, No. 7–8, item 179, with a commentary by W. Masewicz.

[40] Case II SA 35/91.

This position has now been substantially reinforced by the provisions of the 1997 Constitution (as explained above).

3. *The Constitutional Tribunal*

Although the Constitutional Tribunal Act of 1985[41] did not give it a right to review the compatibility of domestic legislation with treaties ratified by Poland, Article 188 of the 1997 Constitution now authorizes it to adjudicate upon the 'conformity of a statute with ratified international agreements'.

The Constitutional Tribunal mainly gives rulings on legislation's conformity with the Constitution once such legislation has been passed and has come into force (subsequent review),[42] subject to the exception that, since 8 April 1989, the President of the Republic has had the right to refer a law to the Court, before signing it, for a decision on its compatibility with the Constitution.[43]

Legal questions with a bearing on judicial or administrative proceedings in progress may be referred to the Constitutional Tribunal where they concern the constitutionality of the proceedings or the compatibility of another law-making instrument with the Constitution or with statute law. Such questions may be raised when the outcome of the proceedings depends on the reply. In interpreting constitutional law, the Constitutional Tribunal naturally takes into consideration circumstances arising from the Republic's change of legal system since the late 1980s and the political pluralism inherent in the European Convention on Human Rights. On the basis of the principle that Poland is a 'democratic State governed by the rule of law and enforcing the principles of social justice' (Article 1 of the Constitution) the Tribunal often refers to international human rights law, generally perceiving in such law a means of clarifying the content of Polish legislation in accordance with the constitutional principle of the rule of law.

For example, in the reasons for a decision handed down on 24 October 1989 in case K 6/89, which concerned the pension scheme for miners and their families considered from the angle of equality before the law in the field of social insurance, the Constitutional Tribunal referred, *inter alia*, to the provi-

[41] Act of 29 April 1985, applicable from 1 January 1986: consolidated version published in *Dziennik Ustaw* no. 109 of 1991, item 470 as amended in 1993, *Dziennik Ustaw* no. 47, item 213, and in 1995, *Dziennik Ustaw* no. 13, item 59.

[42] *Dziennik Ustaw* no. 75, item 441.

[43] Article 27(4) of the Constitution and Article 1(1) of the Constitutional Tribunal Act.

For further information, including reference to the Tribunal's case-law prior to the adoption of the 1997 Constitution—see the Polish Constitutional Tribunal's delegation's report in *Protection constitutionnelle et protection internationale des droits de l'homme: concurrence ou complémentarité?*, (proceedings of the Ninth Conference of European Constitutional Courts, Paris, 10–13 May 1993), vol. I (French Constitutional Council, 1994), pp. 442–468.

sions of Article 3, in correlation with Article 9, of the International Covenant on Economic, Social, and Cultural Rights, requiring states parties to the Covenant to ensure equal rights for men and women, adding:

in this respect reference should be made to Article 26 of the International Covenant on Civil and Political Rights banning all discrimination.

In its Resolution of 2 March 1994, when determining that certain provisions of the Law on Radio and Television of 1992 need to be interpreted in the light of the Polish Constitution, the Tribunal stipulated that:

the freedom of expression is affirmed in international human rights treaties, in particular Article 10 of the ECHR. Poland's ratification of this Convention signifies that all state organs are tied by commitments found therein.[44]

Finally, in a request brought by the Ombudsman on 30 May 1994 before the Constitutional Tribunal,[45] by relating to the latter's competence in determining the (potential) incompatibility of duly ratified treaty norms with the Polish Constitution, the Constitutional Tribunal, in an important determination, by and large accepted the Ombudsman's analysis that:

[When looking into this issue] the Constitutional Tribunal in effect analyses the conformity of legislative changes consequent to [the ratification of international] agreements with the Constitution, in that ratification signifies, in accordance with the findings of the Supreme Court[46] . . . that [duly ratified] treaties are transformed into domestic law and possess the rank of a statute.

The Constitutional Tribunal added that not only was the above analysis correct, but that in accordance with section 33(1) of the 'Small Constitution' of 17 October 1992 (now superceded by the Constitution of 1997, discussed above), it is:

also able to determine the incompatibility of international agreements with the Constitution when a law authorizes ratification of an international agreement which possesses directly applicable (self-executing) provisions.[47]

This position has now been clearly confirmed in Article 188 of the new Constitution of 1997.[48]

[44] Sygn. akt. W 3/93 *OTK* 1994/I; item 17. (The translation is our own from pp. 157–158). For an analysis of this case see M. Wyrzykowski, *Prezegląd Sejmowy*, 2nd Year, 3(7)94, at pp. 303–311.

[45] Rzecznik Praw Obywatelskich [Commissioner for the Protection of Citizens Rights, hereinafter *RPO*], doc. *RPO*/147046/93.I of 30 May 1994.

[46] Reference here is made to a statement issued by the Supreme Court (seven judges) on 12 June 1992: Sygn. akt III CZP 48/92.

[47] *Uchwała* [Resolution] of 30 November 1994: W. 10/94 in *OTK* 1994/II, item 48, para. 2, on p. 237 (Our own translations of texts).

[48] See section B, above.

4. The role of the Ombudsman

The Polish Ombudsman, known as the Commissioner for the Protection of Citizens' Rights, first took office on 1 January 1988. This postholder has wide powers to deal with all grievances relating to political, civil, economic, social, and cultural rights and freedoms. The Polish Ombudsman, like his or her Nordic counterparts but contrary to the model followed in a number of other countries, has powers with regard to the administration of justice, that is to say, *vis-à-vis* the public bodies and all other institutions that fulfil functions on behalf of the administrative authorities.[49] The Ombudsman has the right to handle matters that come within the jurisdiction of the courts, but cannot interfere with the independence of the judiciary. This means that the Ombudsman can, for instance, draw attention to cases of unreasonable slowness in court proceedings, bring actions in the Constitutional Tribunal (see below for an example) and the Supreme Administrative Court, and lodge extraordinary appeals with the Supreme Court against final decisions against which no other appeal lies. It is also possible for the Ombudsman to require that disciplinary proceedings should be brought. No case is excluded from the Ombudsman's sphere of action, whether it concerns the prison system, home affairs, or the army, and no matter what the level of the authority complained about. The Ombudsman may take action at the request of an interested party or on his or her own initiative.[50]

Poland's first Ombudsman, Professor Ewa Łętowska, laid down the following principles, which guided her own activities and to a great extent those of her successors, Professors T. Zieliński and A. Zieliński. The Ombudsman refuses to assume the role of a lawyer, in that he does not assist parties in obtaining material benefits (such as a flat or a car). Action is only taken as a last resort when all other remedies and procedures have been exhausted. The Ombudsman essentially deals with problems of a general nature, shared by a whole category of the population, but not with matters beyond his or her reach such as housing or pollution problems (ie problems which might be handled by an Ombudsman in a 'better organized' society than Poland's).[51] The three holders of this office have assumed a key role in safeguarding citizens' rights and freedoms.

[49] Act of 15 July 1987. See the final text of the Act in *Dziennik Ustaw* no. 109, item. 471, 1991

[50] For a more detailed analysis see E. Łętowska 'The Polish Ombudsman (The Commissioner for the Protection of Human Rights), (1990) 39 *International Comparative Law Quarterly*, pp. 206–207.

[51] See E. Łętowska, 'The ombudsman in the countries of Central and Eastern Europe' in *Proceedings of the 4th Round Table with European Ombudsmen* (Lisbon, 16–17 June 1994, Council of Europe), pp. 63–73.

A few examples will show how the Ombudsman has made use of the ECHR. In an annual oral presentation before the Diet, on 28 April 1995, the Ombudsman indicated his concern about the fact that an applicant must wait on average about eight months before the Supreme Administrative Court is able to deal with his case and, perhaps of greater concern, that the steep fees which must be paid to the courts, including costs before the Supreme Administrative Court, are sometimes prohibitive. He considered this state of affairs to be in conflict with Article 6 of the ECHR. He went on to explain that the *de facto* barring of access to a court and the failure by 'a large number of courts [to respect] the duty to deal with a case within a reasonable time' are unacceptable under the Convention.[52] In another passage from the same speech, the Ombudsman indicated in no uncertain terms his concern about the probable incompatibility of Polish law, or rather the lack of appropriate law, on situations in which the freedom of speech, guaranteed by Article 10 of the ECHR, may be restricted in the interests of national security.[53]

Other areas of concern, in the eyes of the Ombudsman, were the rights of the mentally ill detained in special/psychiatric hospitals and the freedom of the media. In relation to mentally ill persons, he questioned the compatibility of a Ministerial order/decree with the requirements of Articles 5 and 6 of the ECHR and the Strasbourg case-law thereunder.[54] As regards the media, a problem appeared to exist in the implementation of a statute, dated 11 May 1995, which imposed upon Polish private TV cable companies the obligation to transmit by cable all television programmes within the purview of their catchment area, giving them no say whatsoever with regard to the contents of the programmes transmitted. This law, in the view of certain privately owned companies, was an arbitrarily imposition of state-run programmes in contravention of Article 10 of the ECHR which includes the freedom 'to receive and impart information and ideas without interference by public authority and regardless of frontiers'.[55]

More up-to-date examples of how the Polish Ombudsman takes into account the evolving Strasbourg case-law were provided by the present

[52] Information obtained from *Rzecznik Praw Obywatelskich w Parlamencie. Debata nad sprawozdaniem RPO* (1995), at pp. 59–60.

[53] Ibid, at pp. 61–62.

[54] See P. Przybysz and R. Popadyniec, 'Raport Rzecznika Praw Obywatelskich o stanie przestrzegania praw obywatelskich osób przbywających w szpitalach psychiatrycznych' (1995) Materiały, no. 26, *Biuletyn RPO*, pp. 127–159 at pp. 128, 132–133. The Ombudsman has also queried the practice of retaining parsons in 'sobering-up centres' *vis-à-vis* the requirements of Article 5 of the Convention: see J. Malec 'Informacja o stanie ochrony praw osób umieszczanych w izbach wytrzeźwień', same publication, pp. 161–209 at pp. 182–183.

[55] Complaint No. RPO/190861/95/VI of 3 August 1995 in *Informacja o pracy Rzecznika Praw Obywatelskich*, 8/95 (1995) at pp. 13–14. See also the Polish Ombudsman's report in vol. 25 of *Biuletyn RPO* (13.2.1994 to 12.2.1995), 1995, pp. 137, 143, and 197 (statistical information on pp. 45–89).

incumbent, A. Zieliński, at an Ombudsman's Round Table held in Malta in 1998.[56]

E. CASES BROUGHT BEFORE THE EUROPEAN COMMISSION AND COURT OF HUMAN RIGHTS

Poland ratified the European Convention on Human Rights on 19 January 1993; starting from 1 May that same year, the European Commission of Human Rights in Strasbourg could examine complaints of violations of the Convention by Polish authorities. Poles started applying to the Strasbourg organs much earlier. At the beginning of the nineties, even before Poland's ratification of the Convention, numerous Polish complaints had already been received: 65 in 1991, 287 in 1992, and 109 by 1 May 1993.

After Poland's accession to the Convention the number of applications grew rapidly. Suffice it to say that in 1996 there were 1,127 complaints against Poland. Polish applicants were the fourth largest group, considerably outpacing the Czech Republic, Hungary, and other Central and Eastern European countries. In 1997 there were 1,318 such applications, and about 1,280 by 31 October 1998.

In 1996 proceedings were issued before the Commission in 458 registered cases against Poland; there were 430 such cases in 1997 and a similar number by 31 October 1998. The figures place Poland among European leaders in this respect.

From the date on which the Polish government's declaration accepting the right of individual petition became operative, that is from 1 May 1993 until 31 October 1998, the Secretariat of the Commission received the total of 5,430 letters of complaint, 1,740 of which were registered. Proceedings ended with the Commission's decision refusing the application or striking it out of the list in 975 cases. Waiting to be examined are several hundred cases; after 1 November 1998 they were taken over by the new Court. In 31 cases the Commission admitted the applications for examination on the merits; 73 applications had to be communicated to the Polish government with a request for observations before a decision on their admissibility. By 31 October 1998 the Commission ended the proceedings, adopting reports under Article 31 of the Convention in 18 cases.

One case, the application of *Grzegorz Sawicki*, which concerned interference with a prisoner's correspondence, ended with a friendly settlement (the Commission issued a report under Article 28 of the Convention).

[56] See his contributions in *6th Round Table with European Ombudsmen*, held in Malta, on 7–9 October (1999).

The application of *Lechoslaw Gibas*, which concerned the length of civil proceedings, was the first Polish case in which a violation of the European Convention on Human Rights was found. This finding was expressed on 15 May 1997 by the Committee of Ministers of the Council of Europe under (former) Article 32 of the ECHR, which confirmed the Commission's opinion that the case involved a violation of Article 6, paragraph 1, of the Convention and agreed to the publication of the Commission's report on the case. The applicant is still waiting for a decision on the amount of damages to be paid by the state authorities.

However, the vast majority of applications have been turned down by the Commission. The main reason for this was that they concerned events and decisions predating 1 May 1993 or were not related in any way to the rights and freedoms guaranteed by the European Convention. Many persons complained about what they considered unjust convictions, failing to realize that the Strasbourg organs are not just another court of appeal. The Commission refused very many applications in which domestic remedies had not been exhausted, or the six-month time-limit for submission of the application had been exceeded. A considerable proportion of complaints were declared to be manifestly ill founded. With time, however, favourable changes can be observed in this respect: applications now tend to be better prepared, and ever fewer of them concern events from the distant past. Also, applicants now appear to have a better understanding of the limits of the protection offered by the Convention.

In four cases the European Court of Human Rights has delivered judgments with respect to Poland. Three of them concerned the length of proceedings in civil cases. In the case of *Bronislawa Proszak* (judgment of 16 December 1997) the Court found no violation of Article 6, paragraph 1 (by a majority of six to three votes); however, in the cases of *Janusz Podbielski* (judgment of 30 October 1998) and *Szczepan Styranowski* (judgment of 30 October 1998) the Court unanimously found violations. The case of *Belziuk* (judgment of 25 March 1998), which concerned inequality in criminal proceedings, also ended with a unanimous finding that there had been a violation of Article 6, paragraph 1. Three further cases are: *Humen* (Article 6, paragraph 1, length of civil proceedings), *Musiał* (Article 5, paragraph 4, unduly lengthy review procedure as to grounds for confinement to a psychiatric hospital), and *Janowski* (Article 10, insulting of municipal guards in Zdunska Wola) and the latter two have been decided by the European Court. After 1 November 1998 the Commission sent several other cases to the new Court.[57]

[57] *Musial*: violation found by the Court on 25 March 1999; *Janowski*: violation found by the Court on 21 January 1999. Further, in 2000 the following cases were decided: *Gladkowski* (length of civil proceedings, Article 6(1), struck out on 14 March 2000); *Baranowski* (continued detention

The cases that ended with the Strasbourg Court's judgment might suggest, to the outside observer, that most complaints against Poland concern the length of judicial proceedings. What provides better grounds for analysis, however, are those applications which have been communicated to the government, because the Commission encountered a problem that had to be clarified with the assistance of the Polish authorities. Here the proportions are different. Admittedly, cases concerning prolonged waits for court decisions are numerous; many of them, however, actually concern detention on remand (including the now historical issue of the prosecutor who was previously competent to decide about such detention), inequality of arms in proceedings on appeal against detention, and excessive length of detention. The new Code of Criminal Procedure made substantial improvements in these areas, but failed to resolve all the problems involved. For instance, waiting to be decided in Strasbourg is an interesting issue of deprivation of liberty at the 'sobering-up' stations, which is important not only for Poland but also for other states where such institutions still operate. There is also a whole group of cases pertaining to the right of respect to property, including those concerning the still unresolved issue of Polish property left behind across the River Bug, in formerly Polish and now Belarussian territory. Completing this picture are, for example, issues related to the system of registration of periodicals; ill-treatment by the police; court fees; access to cassation proceedings; and the scope of jurisdiction of the Supreme Administrative Court.

One might therefore ask why, despite the large quantity of applications, so much delay has occurred in the processing of cases concerning Poland. A

on remand, Article 5(1), and length of time taken to decide on requests for release, Article 5(4), violations found on 28 March 2000); *Witold Litwa* (detention at sobering-up centre, Article 5(1)(e), violation found on 4 April 2000); *Dewicka* (length of civil proceedings, Article 6(1), violation found on 4 April 2000); *Wojcik* (length of detention on remand, Article 5(3), and lawfulness of detention, Article 5(4), and length of criminal proceedings, Article 6(1), struck out on 23 May 2000); *Mikulski* (length of detention on remand, Article 5(3), and length of criminal proceedings, Article 6(1), and effective remedy, Article 13, friendly settlement on 6 June 2000); *Niedbala* (ordering of detention on remand by prosecutor, Article 5(3), absence of right for detainee to attend hearing of application for bail and non-communication of prosecutor's decisions, Article 5(4), and opening and delaying detainee's correspondence, Article 8, violations in all 3 instances, 4 July 2000); *Trzaska* (length of detention on remand, Article 5(3), speediness of review, Article 5(4), and length of criminal proceedings, Article 6(1), violations found on 11 July 2000); *Kazimierczak* (length of detention on remand, Article 5(3), struck out on 27 July 2000 after the death of the applicant); *Wojnowicz* (length of civil proceedings, Article 6(1), violation found on 21 September 2000); *Chojak* (ordering of detention on remand by prosecutor and length of detention on remand, Article 5(3), struck out on 12 October 2000); *Wloch* (detention in respect of acts allegedly not constituting criminal offence, Article 5(1)(c) *no* violation; lack of adversarial proceedings in review of lawfulness of detention, Article 5(4), and length of criminal proceedings, Article 6(1), violations found on 19 October 2000. Reports on the following cases can all be found on the Court's website (www.echr.coe.int); *Kudla* 26 October 2000; *Sobczyk* 26 October 2000; *Jeznach* 14 December 2000; *Malinowski* 14 December 2000; *Klinieki* 21 December 2000; *Wasilewski* 21 December 2000; and *Jablouski* 21 December 2000.

variety of reasons have contributed to this. One explanation is the following: the Secretariat of the Commission was quite simply surprised by the number of applications from Poland and failed to prepare for this in good time. Arrears in processing thus appeared; with the persisting large number of incoming cases, such arrears have been difficult to make up. It was only some two years ago, with arrival of reinforcements—new lawyers from Poland employed in the Commission and former Court's secretariats—that a concerted effort could be commenced to bring the situation under control. At the same time, the government had financial, and thus also staffing, problems organizing the Government Agent's Office. This coincided with the rapidly growing number of cases which, in the Commission's opinion, had to be discussed with the government. Also, the representatives of the applicants, taking their first steps before the Strasbourg organs, did not always act with sufficient speed. All the above factors, taken together, were bound to affect the procedure and to clog up applications in Strasbourg. However, the situation may be changing for the better, and the new Court will probably be able to examine Polish cases without such dramatic delays.

F. ASSESSMENT AND PROSPECTS

1. Dissemination of information about ECHR standards

The ECHR is not designed for politicians, state officials, and experts only. It is the property of all persons, and an important instrument of protection of their rights. In order to be effective and to be a 'living instrument', exerting the desired influence on the world around us, this instrument must be generally known. The Convention states that '[E]veryone has the right . . .' It follows from this formulation that 'everyone' should be able to learn, first, that he has certain rights, and secondly, how he can demand respect for them. Hence the immense and never-ending task of the Council of Europe, governments, NGOs, and the media: promotion of the importance of the Convention's substantive standards until they are known to everyone. It is simply not true that wide dissemination of information about the ECHR will necessarily result in an avalanche of letters to Strasbourg, which in turn will take many years to be dealt with. Reliable and responsible information will inform people what can and what cannot be gained in Strasbourg; it will explain the strict conditions of admissibility of complaints; and it will make it easier to decide whether to bring a case against a state. This was the purpose, for example, of a special booklet prepared for the Polish Ombudsman and published in several thousand copies.[58] It is now distributed to all who approach the Ombudsman intending to address a complaint to Strasbourg.

Knowledge of the Convention is necessary not only to ensure the efficient use of the Strasbourg control machinery. This particular 'appellate procedure' is but ancillary in nature. Strasbourg should remain a subsidiary procedure, after appropriate use is made of domestic (constitutionally guaranteed) procedures to protect individual rights against alleged inappropriate administrative actions or wrongful court decisions.

The problem with the promotion of the ECHR is that studying the text alone is totally insufficient; many judges and lawyers fail to realize this fact, let alone the population at large. Until recently a considerable proportion of judges were convinced that they needed no training courses on the Convention. However, to really *know* the Convention and appreciate its profound significance, one needs to read and follow, on a regular basis, the evolution of the case-law of the Strasbourg Court. It is this case-law which gives the Convention its specificity as a 'living instrument', with an ever-changing content and readjustment to present-day conditions. Yet case-law in the official languages of the Council of Europe, English and French, is not enough either. In Poland knowledge of Western languages is still poor, especially among lawyers. Thus an immediate priority is to make the case-law as widely available as possible in the Polish language.

A substantial amount of work has already been accomplished in this respect. Since 1991 a co-author of this chapter, M. A. Nowicki, publishes in the reputable daily *Rzeczpospolita*[59] extensive discussions of all judgments of the European Court of Human Rights; owing to the paper's nationwide distribution, the judgments are thereby made accessible to the general public in the whole of Poland just one day after they are rendered. That same daily also covers analyses of 'problem' articles concerning the Convention.[60] Discussion of Strasbourg Commission decisions have also appeared.[61] Yearly collections of Strasbourg Court judgments are also published as special volumes in *Bulletins* issued by the Council of Europe Centre for Information and Documentation in Warsaw,[62] which are also available on the Internet (http://www.radaeuropy.org.pl).

[58] M. A. Nowicki (ed), *Zanim napiszesz skargę—przeczytaj* (Warsaw: Office of the Commissioner for Citizens Rights, 1993), p. 28.

[59] This daily has a circulation of about 270,000 copies. Each issue has a separate yellow 4-page 'insert' 'Prawo co dnia' with news and articles on various legal questions.

[60] See, for example, the series of articles by M. A. Nowicki 'Wokól Konwencji Europejskiej', which was commenced back in 1991.

[61] The most interesting decisions of the Commission have in the past appeared in two series: 'Z wokandy Komisji' and 'Z orzecznictwa Komisji'.

[62] M. A. Nowicki, *Orzecznictwo Europejskiego Trybunału Praw Człowieka*, published regularly by the Centre, now called the Council of Europe Information Centre, in its *Bulletins*.

2. *Familiarization of the legal community with the ECHR*

A number of books on the ECHR have now appeared.[63] In addition, the legal community is able to find, with considerably more ease than even a few years ago, serious analyses of Polish law and practice relating to the rights and freedoms guaranteed in the Convention, as interpreted by its control organs.[64]

The Convention will not be a living instrument if it is not known to, and skilfully applied by, judges who have to learn the difficult art, still alien to Poland, of interpreting the law in the light of this country's international law undertakings, human rights provisions included. To ensure that this occurs, there is a need not only to make documentation (especially judgments of the Strasbourg Court) accessible and to study it thoroughly, but also to overcome the many schematic conceptions of, and approaches to the role of, a judge in democratic society. Intensive training courses, workshops, and seminars supplemented by publications specifically addressed at judges and public prosecutors are still necessary.[65]

Of course, this does not preclude the need to train others in the public service, such as policemen and persons who work in penitentiary institutions.[66] The needs are substantial, and cannot realistically be handled overnight.

An important role in the process of society's familiarization with the Convention falls to members of the Bar, who must learn to use the ECHR in their daily work. The Convention's real legal value before domestic courts depends largely on the legal practitioner and his determination and expertise in formulating appropriate arguments based on knowledge of the Convention's case-law.

3. *The work of human rights NGOs*

One cannot discuss this topic without mentioning non-governmental organizations, especially those which work in the human rights field. Chief among

[63] See list of leading books in Appendix.

[64] 82. See, *inter alia*, P. Hofmański, 'Europejskie standardy w zakresie kontroli stosowania przymusu w procesie karnym a reforma kodeksu postępowania karnego', in *Problemy kodyfikacji Prawa Karnego* (1993), pp. 451–460. For further references, see (1997) 3 *European Human Rights Law Review*, p. 282.

Regular comments on Strasbourg case-law can be found in *Palestra* as of 1992 and *Prokuratura i Prawo* as of 1995, written by A. Rzepliński.

[65] See note 63, above. The Ministry of Justice, together with the Warsaw-based Centre of Information and Documentation of the Council of Europe, organizes special seminars at regular intervals for judges and public prosecutors. The latter also runs special courses for practising lawyers.

[66] As early as 1992 the Police Training Centre in Legionowo published a Polish translation of the European Convention on Human Rights. Issues pertaining to the practical application of ECHR standards for law enforcement officials have been included in the curricula of police academies, prison staff schools, and army training programmes.

these is the Helsinki Committee in Poland, and its related Helsinki Foundation for Human Rights, which seek to play an active role as 'initiator' of complaints to Strasbourg, so helping to bring test cases to Strasbourg. Very few NGOs in Poland conduct broader-scale counselling on matters related directly to the Strasbourg procedure. One reason is, among others, a lack of qualified staff capable to render such services in a proper and responsible manner. This lack of knowledge is to some extent compounded by the fact that very few practising lawyers are sufficiently conversant with the Convention's law.

This being said, it must be recognized that NGOs do much to propagate knowledge of the Convention and its case-law: witness the very many courses, seminars, and conferences regularly organized on this topic.[67]

4. Prospects

Poles write to Strasbourg often: in 1997 they were third in number after the Italians and the French and ahead of the United Kingdom and Germany. In 1996 they held fourth place. They write to Strasbourg much more often than Czechs, Hungarians, and citizens of other countries of Central and Eastern Europe.[68] In 1997 the number of letters was greater than ever before. The only 'new' country from which many letters are received is Romania, a country which ratified the ECHR in 1994, the totals being 1,318 provisional files opened with respect to Poland and 345 with respect to Romania. Of course, the vast majority of complaints are not registered. Just over 30 per cent of correspondence concerning Poland made it through the preliminary filter in 1997 (the figure was in the region of 20 per cent in 1995): *registration* of the complaint as an application commenced formal proceedings before the (former) Commission. In the case of citizens of 'old' members of the Council of Europe, this proportion is similar—around 25 per cent. Many persons who lodge complaints from Poland mistakenly believe that all perceived harm to them can be put right in Strasbourg. People appeal against what they consider unjust convictions, failing to realize that the Strasbourg Court is not another appeal instance. Some even ask for a job, financial relief, or lodgings. This being said, there now exist number of cases in which serious issues are being

[67] For example, the now traditional sessions of the Summer School of Human Rights organized in Warsaw by the Helsinki Foundation for Human Rights in September of each year, commenced in 1990 (co-funded by and with logistical support from the Council of Europe: see (1993) 14 *Human Rights Law Journal*, p. 233) for activists from Central and Eastern Europe, as well as special courses lasting several months, held in Warsaw for future Polish teachers of human rights and civic education.

[68] For a survey see M. de Salvia 'L'état des affaires intéressant les pays d'Europe centrale et orientale devant la Commission européenne des droits de l'homme', in P. Tavernier, (ed) *Quelle Europe pour les droits de l'homme*. (1995), pp. 389–405.

addressed and with respect to which the practice of state authorities might be found to be inconsistent with Convention standards. Here, Poland is (potentially) in a situation similar to that of other 'old' democracies of Europe such as Italy, France, and the United Kingdom.

26

Portugal

JOÃO MADUREIRA

A. INTRODUCTION

Six months after the approval of its democratic Constitution, Portugal signed the European Convention on Human Rights, on 22 November 1976, the same day it was admitted as a new member state of the Council of Europe. The Convention was approved for ratification by law 65/78 of 13 October 1978 and the ratification procedure was completed in 9 November the same year.[1] In early 1979 Portugal recognized the competence of the Commission, under Articles 25 of the Convention and 6(2) of the Fourth Protocol, as well as the jurisdiction of the Court, in the light of Articles 46 of the Convention and 6(2) of the said Protocol.[2] The text then approved included the modifications introduced by Protocols Nos. 2, 3, and 5, the ratification being extended to the First and Fourth Protocols to the Convention.

Along with the deposit of the instrument of ratification, eight reservations were made,[3] concerning Articles 4(3)(b), 5, 7, and 10 of the Convention and Articles 1 and 2 of the first Additional Protocol. Seven of them were directly based on provisions of the Constitution while one arose from the ordinary law, the disciplinary code of the military forces. One of the reservations concerned the compensation due for expropriation and the possibility of excluding its application in certain cases, as foreseen by Article 82 of the Constitution. This was the only reservation that gave rise to a reaction by the international community.

On 7 February of 1979 the United Kingdom representative addressed a letter to the Secretary General of the Council of Europe reaffirming the view of its government that the:

[1] Aviso of the Ministry for Foreign Affairs, Diário da República (DR), I Série, of 2 January 1979. See Judgment of the Constitutional Court 219/89 of 25.2.89 (DR II Série of 30.6.89 p. 6476) referring to 2 January 1979 as the date of entry into force of the Convention at the domestic level.

[2] Avisos of the Ministry for Foreign Affairs, Diário da República (DR), I Série, of 31 January and 6 February 1979 respectively.

[3] See Articles 2 and 4 of Law 65/78, of 13 October.

general principles of international law require the payment of prompt, adequate and effective compensation in respect of the expropriation of foreign property.

In view of this letter, the Secretary General replied that due to the fact that the statement in the representative's letter didn't constitute a formal objection to the Portuguese reservation, it was to be

communicated for information to the governments of Member States of the Council of Europe as well as to the organs created under the Convention.

The same reaction was endorsed by the Federal Republic of Germany and France, to which the Secretary General replied in a similar form.[4] The reservation was withdrawn in 1987, together with five others.[5]

At present only two reservations are still in force: one concerning Article 5 of the Convention in the framework of the disciplinary arrest of military personnel, and the other concerning Article 7 of the Convention as to the indictment and trial of agents of the political police of the regime in place before the 1974 revolution, as a result of Article 294 of the Portuguese Constitution.

To date, Portugal has ratified Protocols Nos. 6, 8, 9, 10, and 11.[6] It is not yet bound by Protocol No. 7.

B. THE STATUS OF THE CONVENTION IN DOMESTIC LAW

In Portugal the European Convention on Human Rights is incorporated into the internal legal order and, in accordance with the prevailing school of legal thought and the Constitutional Court's case-law, it ranks above the ordinary law. However, it ranks below the Constitution.[7]

Having been incorporated into the Portuguese law,[8] the European

[4] Yearbook of the European Convention on Human Rights, no. 22, 1979, pp. 16–22. See also in Information Sheet no. 5 the reply of the Commission of the European Communities to a written question 302/78 on the reservation concerning Article 1 of the First Protocol.

[5] Law 12/87, of 7 April.

[6] Protocol 6: Resolução Assemleia da República 12/86 of 6 June and Aviso, (DR), I Série, of 8 November 1986; Protocol 8: resolução da Assembleia da República 30/86, of 10 December and Aviso (DR) I Série, of 13 April 1987; Protocol 9: Resolução Assembleia da República no. 11/94 of 7 March 1994; Protocol 10: Decreto do Presidente da República 18/94 and Resolução da Assembleia da República 16/94 of 2 April, and Aviso 303/94, of 19 October; Protocol 11: Resolução da Assembleia da República 21/97 of 3 May 1997.

[7] As regards the primacy of the international treaty law over the domestic law, see, *inter alia*, Decisions of the STJ of 11.01.77 (BMJ, no. 262, p. 195), 73325 of 18.3.86 (BMJ 355, p. 175), 76457 of 8.11.88, 73796 of 27.5.86 and as it concerns the Constitutional Court, judgment of 6.2.85 BMJ 410, p. 56 (plenary judgment).

[8] According to Article 8(2) of the Constitution 'rules provided for in international conventions duly ratified or approved shall, following their official publication apply in municipal law as long as they remain internationally binding with respect to the Portuguese State.' Once these two

Convention on Human Rights allows individuals to invoke its provisions directly before national judges. The judge must apply the Convention and it is for him/her to interpret the provisions of this instrument.

The European Convention created a legal system for the protection of human rights and fundamental freedoms to be enforced by the Convention's organs, the Commission and the Court. It is incumbent upon both organs to interpret the Convention's provisions, several of which have autonomous status, ie their extent or scope is independent of the interpretation given by each member state. By interpreting and implementing the Convention, the organs of Strasbourg ensure effective harmonization of the member states' legislation, regarded as a whole, despite the different legal systems involved, with a view to creating a true European human rights law.

The European Convention on Human Rights law is mostly a jurisprudential law, as evidenced by the great number of decisions emanating from the above-mentioned organs year after year. Such decisions are continuously disclosing new rights or enlarging the scope of existing ones in the Convention, as well as new situations to which the Convention is to be applied.

At the domestic level, the responsibility for the application of the law rests with the national courts, where the provisions of the European Convention on Human Rights are sometimes interpreted in a manner that does not take into account the interpretation adopted by the Strasbourg organs. This is mainly due to the fact that the Strasbourg case-law is as yet insufficiently known by members of the Portuguese legal profession.[9] In these circumstances, the Convention's provisions may be interpreted by the Portuguese judge in an autonomous, 'domestic' manner, with the risk that this is unlikely to coincide with the interpretation adopted by the Commission and the Court.

However, the importance accorded by national courts to the case-law of these organs may depend on other factors. For instance, it may depend on the sort of court which examines such provisions, and therefore on the Convention being acknowledged, or not, as relevant applicable law in a case pending before a given court with a special jurisdiction. For example, does the Constitutional Court have jurisdiction to consider and decide cases involving the conformity of the Portuguese law with the European Convention on

requisites are filled in, the provisions of the Conventions shall apply in domestic law as if they had been internally created, with no need to 'convert' them into law or 'transform' them into municipal law. See J. Gomes Canotilho and Vital Moreira, *Constituição da República Portuguesa Anotada*, I, p. 91.

[9] In our opinion, efforts to disseminate the case-law of the Strasbourg organs are always required in order to contribute to a correct implementation of the European Convention on Human Rights by the Contracting Parties, in particular those, like Portugal, where the Convention forms an integral part of the national legal system and is therefore directly applicable.

Human Rights? That matter falls within the jurisdiction of the ordinary courts; until today, no clear-cut jurisdiction was conferred on the Constitutional Court in this field, bearing in mind that, under the Constitution, it is vested with powers to rule solely on the conformity of laws with the constitutional provisions.[10]

Nevertheless, as regards the case-law of the Constitutional Court, even if the question has not been directly addressed in a case brought before it, it is apparent that a breach of the European Convention by a domestic law may entail a judgment of unconstitutionality on the ground of violation of the principles enshrined in the Constitution, such as *pacta sunt servanda* and the supremacy of international treaty law over domestic law.[11]

Further, it remains uncertain whether the European Convention on Human Rights should be granted a privileged status in the domestic hierarchy, in view of the particular reception recognized by Article 16(1) of the Constitution[12] and of the recognition by this provision of the rights enshrined in the international instruments on human rights, especially the European Convention on Human Rights.[13] In other words, does the Constitution confer on the Convention, and on other treaties in the field of human rights, a constitutional rank, or should the Convention at least be accepted as an autonomous and direct criterion to be used in assessing the constitutionality of internal legal provisions? So far, this question remains unresolved.[14]

C. THE STATUS OF THE CONVENTION IN PARLIAMENTARY PROCEEDINGS

It is difficult to ascertain the direct influence of the European Convention on the process of drafting new legislation. In fact, there is no evidence of recent quotations of the Convention among parliamentary debates. On the other hand, one cannot ascertain to what extent the Convention has influenced legislation proposed by the government on fundamental rights. However, there are two examples of express reference to the Convention which have to do with the Code of Criminal Procedure's provisions on free translations[15] and

[10] Constitution of the Portuguese Republic, Articles 225 and 277.

[11] Judgment 219/89 of 25.2.89, DR II Série of 30.6.89, p. 6476.

[12] According to Article 16(1) of the Constitution 'the fundamental rights embodied in the Constitution shall not exclude any other fundamental rights either in the statute or resulting from applicable rules of international law'.

[13] Judgments 99/88 and 222/90 of 20.6.90, BMJ 398, p. 225.

[14] Cardoso da Costa, *La hiérarchie des normes constitutionnelles et sa fonction dans la protection des droits fondamentaux*, RUDH, 1990, p. 269 (274).

[15] Article 92.

ways of accelerating proceedings.[16] These two examples are given detailed consideration in sections D and G below.

D. LEADING HUMAN RIGHTS CASES DECIDED BY THE NATIONAL COURTS

It is true, as stated in a Constitutional Court judgment, that:

> in the field of human rights, having regard to the density and the extension of the standard of guarantees provided by the Portuguese Constitution, there will be few situations in which a violation of the international provisions relating to basic rights will not be consumed by the violation of the fundamental rights enshrined in the Constitution, thus resulting in a question of unconstitutionality.[17]

In fact, however, references to the European Convention on Human Rights are not rare, since the Constitutional Court held that it was not prevented from taking into account:

> any contribution, as regards legal thought or case-law [relating to the application of the Convention] that could be instrumental in elucidating the nature and the scope of the provisions of the Constitution, or of those of the Universal Declaration of Human Rights.[18]

The Universal Declaration has an important role to play in the interpretation and application of the constitutional and legal provisions in the field of basic rights and freedoms, as expressly provided for in the Constitution.[19]

In view of that decision, the Constitutional Court recognized the importance of the Strasbourg case-law as a reference to be taken into account in interpreting the constitutional provisions relating to fundamental rights. Such importance is currently illustrated by the fact that the Constitutional Court acknowledges the usefulness of the Convention.[20] Should the Constitutional Court establish its own jurisdiction for assessing the compatibility of internal law with the European Convention on Human Rights,[21] then the case-law of the Strasbourg organs would surely constitute more than a useful element: rather, a basic, quasi-compulsory reference source for its rulings.

[16] Articles 108 and 109. [17] Judgment 219/89 above-mentioned (dissenting opinion).

[18] Judgment 222/90 above-mentioned.

[19] Article 16(2) of the Constitution 'The provisions of the Constitution and laws relating to fundamental rights shall be read and interpreted in harmony with the Universal Declaration of Human Rights'.

[20] See *i. a.* Judgment 124/90 of 19.4.90 BMJ 396 p. 142.

[21] See B, above.

The same is not necessarily true of the remaining courts. Their decisions often apply the provisions of the European Convention on Human Rights directly. Yet references to the text of the Convention are far more numerous than those to the Strasbourg case-law; this seems to reveal a lack of awareness of such case-law, probably by reason of its insufficient dissemination among the Portuguese judiciary and other members of the legal profession.

We can, however, bear witness to the important influence of the Strasbourg case-law on the decisions of the Constitutional Court, law courts, and administrative courts, whenever the European Convention on Human Rights is applied directly for the determination of cases submitted to them. A survey of the application of the European Convention on Human Rights by the Portuguese courts would clearly demonstrate that, of all the Convention's provisions, Article 6 (and its respective case-law) is the most frequently applied.[22]

1. Free assistance of an interpreter: the first direct application in Portugal of the Convention

By directly applying Article 6(3)(e), in the light of the consistent case-law of the European Court,[23] the Portuguese courts recognized the right of the accused to the free assistance of an interpreter in criminal proceedings.[24] Today, a provision to the same effect is contained in the Code of Criminal Procedure[25] which enshrines that specific right; but the influence of the European Court's on the effective recognition by the Portuguese courts of that right is undeniable.

2. Equality of arms: privileges of the State Counsel in civil proceedings

Several decisions relate to the equality of arms.[26] Following the entry into force of the European Convention on Human Rights in 1978, one school of legal thought maintained that provisions of the Code of Civil Procedure which allowed for some exceptions to the general rule, in relation to the role of the State Counsel when acting as a party in civil proceedings,[27] had been

[22] More than half of the decisions identified as referring to the European Convention concern Article 6.

[23] *Luedicke, Belkacem and Koç* Judgment.

[24] Supreme Court Judgment 38035 of 8.1.86, BMJ 353, p. 200.

[25] Article 92.

[26] See, on this subject, a comprehensive Annotations by Ireneu Barreto, in *Documentação e Direito Comparado* 39/40, 1989, p. 115, where several decisions are referred to.

[27] Such exceptions concern, *inter alia*, the possibility of a succession of extension of the time-limit granted by the court to the State Counsel to file its pleadings, which is not allowed to the other party, or the non-submission by the State Counsel of pleadings in reply to the originating application. This fact does not, of necessity, entail an admission of the facts, while the same does not apply to the other party.

abrogated by Article 6(1) of the Convention. This opinion was reiterated by a court judgment.[28] But nearly all courts concluded that the provisions on this issue in the Code of Civil Procedure had not been abrogated by the Convention, since the situations resulting therefrom did not infringe the principle of equality of procedural arms, as recognized by Article 6(1) of the European Convention on Human Rights.[29] It must be noted that in interpreting the above-mentioned provision those courts—with a few exceptions—did not necessarily take into account the case-law of the Strasbourg organs in this field. Instead, they interpreted this provision of the Convention in the light of Portuguese legal reality. In fact, bearing in mind the role played by the State Counsel in the representation of certain persons (the state, juveniles, and other individuals with no legal capacity) it was recognized that the granting of special treatment was justified inasmuch as:

> the law, rather than aiming at benefiting one of the parties, is designed to afford a safeguard for the rights of that party which the State Counsel has the duty to protect, since he or she cannot by himself or herself appear before the court.[30]

3. *Equality of arms:* vista *of the Public Presecutor*

The Constitutional Court[31] was also called to examine the compatibility with the principle of equality of arms under Article 664 of the Code of Criminal Procedure of 1929, according to which appeals shall be presented for assessment (*vista*) to the Public Prosecutor, before the final decision is taken by the Court. Referring to the Portuguese school of legal thought and examining this principle also in the light of Article 6 of the Convention, the Constitutional Court concluded that the role played by the Public Prosecutor in the

[28] Decisions of the Court of Appeal of Lisbon, of 26 July 1984, Colectânea de Jurisprudência, Ano IX, tomo IV, 1984, p. 103.

[29] See Attorney-General's opinion 32/83 of 7 March, Decisions of the Court of Appeal of Porto of: 7 June 1983, Colectânea de jurisprudência Ano VIII, tomo 3, p. 257; 3 November 1983, Colectânea de Jurisprudência, Ano VIII, tomo V, 1983, p. 201. Decisions of the Court of Appeal of Lisbon of 12 April, 21 June and 7 July 1988, BMJ 376, p. 644, 378, p. 779, 379, p. 631and decision of 26.4.95. Judgments of the Administrative Court 21447 in Apêncice ao Diário da República AP-DR of 30 November 1988. Judgment of the Supreme Court 71548 of 26 January 1984, BMJ pp. 333, 393. Judgment of the Constitutional Court 324/86, of 19 November 1988, DR II Série, 19 March 1987 (all mentioned in Anotações, Barreto, Ireneu, ibidem), 87062 of 9.5.95 BMJ 447, p. 441. And also Administrative Supreme Court 24151 of 5 February 1987 BMJ 364 p. 607, 6023, of 7 March and 35434 of 3.2.95.

[30] Extract of a judgment (324/86 of 19 November 1986, DR II Série, of 19 March 1987) of the Constitutional Court, which considered the special treatment justified, and clearly reflects the position of the prevailing school of legal thought. See also note 71 on this question, in the framework of the conventional provision concerning reasonable time.

[31] Judgment of the Constitutional Court 495/89 of 13 July 1989, BMJ 389 p. 265. See also Judgments of the Constitutional Court 398/89 of 18 May 1989 BMJ 387 p. 209, 496/89 of 13 July 1989 DR II Série of 1 February 1990 and 356/91 of 4 July 1991 BMJ 409 p.162.

Portuguese criminal procedure is not one of a simple party. His or her conduct must rather be guided by strict criteria of legality and objectivity. Thus the question of equality of arms was not relevant in such a framework and the Code was found not to be unconstitutional.[32]

4. Participation of the same judge in both criminal investigation and trial

More recently, and based on the Strasbourg case-law, the Constitutional Court declared unconstitutional a provision of the Code of Criminal Procedure allowing for the intervention of the same judge during the criminal investigation, and in the decision on preventive detention of the accused, and later in the judgment. The decision found Article 40 of the above-mentioned Code to be unconstitutional, and referred to the *De Cubber* and *Hauschildt* judgments of the European Court.[33]

5. Excessive length of the proceedings: liability of the state for unlawful acts pertaining to the jurisdictional function

Again with regard to Article 6(1) of the European Convention on Human Rights, an important question was brought before the Supreme Administrative Court:[34] the case involved the liability of a law court for excessively lengthy proceedings, in the framework of the state's non-contractual liability for unlawful acts pertaining to the jurisdictional function.[35] In order to ascertain the unlawful act forming the basis of the civil liability, the Supreme Administrative Court had to rely on Article 6(1) of the European Convention on Human Rights. In Portugal, provisions governing time-limits of proceedings aim at the discipline of the procedural activity, and failure to observe a time-limit is not deemed to be an unlawful act. However, a breach of Article 6(1) of the European Convention on Human Rights does constitute an unlawful act.[36] Hence, the Court relied on that provision of the Convention

[32] This is true, even if the Public Prosecutor, in the *vista*, has examined the object of appeal. However, the Public Prosecutor may not give an opinion that might in any way aggravate the position of the accused. In this event, unless the possibility of replying has been given to the accused, this would imply the violation of the principle of the contradictory: ibid Judgment 495/91.

[33] Judgment of the Constitutional Court 186/98, DR I Série A, 20.3.98. See in this line a recent decision by the European Court of Strasbourg on the role of the Attorney-General's representative in the Supreme Court (*Lobo Machado v Portugal*, of 20 February 1996).

[34] Judgment of 7 March 1989, case 26525.

[35] Pursuant to Article 22 of the Constitution, the state is jointly and severally liable in civil law with other public bodies for actions or omissions in the performance of their duties, or caused by such performance, which result in violations of rights, freedoms, and safeguards or in damage to third parties. (Also see DL 48051 on state liability).

[36] The Supreme Court of Justice, in an early decision of 8 January 1987, had superficially referred to the responsibility of the state for actions for which the court is solely responsible, entailing undue delay in the proceedings (Judgment 74663, BMJ, 363, p.436).

for the purpose of assessing the civil liability of the respondent court for the damage sustained by the applicant as a result of the excessive length of the proceedings instituted before it. In its reasoning, the Supreme Administrative Court referred not only to the wording of the said provision, but also to the case-law of the European Court of Human Rights on the reasonableness of the length of proceedings.

Later, in 1995, the Supreme Administrative Court recalled that the right to a decision within a reasonable time, according to Article 6(1) of the European Convention on Human Rights, imposes obligations on every power within the states parties to the Convention, including the judicial power. Judges should adopt all necessary measures, while bearing in mind the need to preserve the rightfulness of its decisions, in order speedily to solve conflicts before the court.[37]

6. *Re-examination of the facts in a second jurisdiction*

According to the Code of Criminal Procedure, once a case has been examined in the first instance by a collegial court, an appeal may be lodged before the Supreme Court, which is to decide solely on the legal grounds of the decision. As a rule, factual elements may not be re-examined by this Court.[38] The question raised was whether the principle of the double degree of jurisdiction was constitutionally recognized.[39] During the consideration of the recognition or not of this principle in Article 32 of the Constitution,[40] the question was also examined in the light of Article 6 of the Convention, as the infringement of this text would entail the violation of the principle *pacta sunt servanda* and, consequently, a violation of the Constitution.[41] Several later decisions confirmed the interpretation that this provision of the Convention does not provide for the right to appeal or the right to a double degree of jurisdiction.[42]

[37] Judgment of 14 December 1995, 32237, summarized in BMJ, 452, p. 473.

[38] Article 433 of Code of Criminal Procedure 1987.

[39] Before the entry into force of the new Code, this same question had been examined under the Code of Criminal Procedure of 1929 and its Article 655. See judgment of the Constitutional Court 401/91 of 30.10.91, DR I Série A of 8 January 1992.

[40] Constitutional Court reached a decision where it stated that this right is foreseen in the Constitution, ibid, 401/91.

[41] See part B.

[42] See Supreme Court 39856 of 25.1.89 BMJ 383 p. 486, 40623 of 31.1.90 BMJ 393 p. 352, 40640 of 9.5.50 BMJ 397 p. 332, 41167 of 25.10.90 BMJ 400 p. 561, 41572 of 15.5.91 BMJ 407 p. 321, and 42058 of 29.1.92 and 45690 of 9.2.94 BMJ 434 p. 451. See also Judgments of Constitutional Court 340/90 DR II Série 19.3.91, 401/91 DR II Série 8.1.92. See also, concerning Code of Criminal Procedure 1929, judgment 401/91 declaring unconstitutional Article 655 of this Code and putting an end to the divergent case-law on this issue. In certain circumstances Article 655 did not allow for factual re-examination on appeal. This situation was considered to be contrary to Article 32 of the Constitution, which enshrines the principle of double jurisdiction in criminal judgments. In civil matters, as well, the right of access to justice does not imply the

7. *The right of defence*

The importance of Article 6 of the Convention in the application of domestic law is also shown in a decision of the Supreme Court recognizing the influence of Article 6(3)(d) in the declaration of unconstitutionality of Article 439 of the Code of Criminal Procedure of 1929. Article 439 allowed for the reading in court of depositions of absent witnesses, which the accused had not been able to examine previously, and so was contrary to the right to examine the witness, enshrined in Article 6(3)(d) of the Convention.[43]

Referring to the *Artico* case, concerning Article 6(3)(c) of the Convention, the Constitutional Commission declared the unconstitutionality[44] of the provisions that imposed, in speedy criminal proceedings, the lodging of an appeal immediately after the reading of the sentence.[45] This situation violated the right of the accused to adequate time for the preparation of his defence, enshrined in Article 6(3)(b) of the Convention, which must be recognized in its substance and not in a merely formal way.

Article 6(3) of the Convention gives no absolute right to the accused to defend himself in person. The Supreme Court of Justice considered, referring to the interpretation given to the said provision by the Strasbourg organs, that states may, by law or judicial decision, require the defence to be conducted by a lawyer.[46]

8. *Access to the contents of a case file during criminal investigations*

Also based on Strasbourg case-law, the Constitutional Court more recently ruled unconstitutional the provisions which prevented the access to the case file by the accused during the criminal investigation phase in order to prepare an appeal against a decision on preventive detention taken during that phase.[47]

9. *Motivation of the decision on the facts*

Article 469 of the Code of Criminal Procedure 1929 did not allow for any declaration by judges of collegial courts on the grounds for their decision on the

existence of a double degree of jurisdiction (Judgment of the Supreme Court 163/90 of 23.5.90 BMJ 397 p. 77 and see Constitutional Court 330/91 of 2.7.91 BMJ 409 p. 45 on expropriation proceedings).

[43] Quoted in Supreme Court 37516 of 30.10.84 BMJ 340 p. 303, referring to the decision of the Constitutional Commission 146–A/81.

[44] In violation of Article 32 of the Constitution.

[45] Constitutional Court judgment 5/87, 17/86, 8/87 DR II Série of 9.2.87, 40/84 of 3.5.84 BMJ 346 p. 179.

[46] STJ 85315, of 17.10.95, BMJ 450, p. 369.

[47] The judgment refers to case *Lamy* (Serie A 153). See comment of Ireneu Barreto, in Convenção Europeia dos Direitos do Homem, Anotada, 2º edição, Coímbra Editora, pp. 51–52.

facts. Examining this provision in the light of the principles enshrined in the Constitution,[48] the Constitutional Court found that Article 6 of the Convention makes no explicit or implicit reference to the motivation of the decision on the facts. In that respect, Article 6 'is completely neutral', stated the Court.[49] Although this opinion seemed to be made by reference to the text of Article 6, no specific case-law was referred to in the decisions concerning this subject.

10. Independent Tribunal

In a case concerning the competence of a Commission created by law to assess the fiscal value of private real estate, the Supreme Court referred to Article 6 of the Convention and to the Strasbourg case-law, to examine the question of the independence of such an organ. It concluded that an organ whose members could be replaced on the basis of a free decision by the administration could not, according to Article 6, have the power to determine any civil rights or obligations.[50]

11. Application of Article 6 to proceedings concerning non-disciplinary administrative sanctions

Concerning the concept of a 'criminal charge', it is interesting to note a decision of the Administrative Supreme Court by which it declared itself incompetent to consider an appeal against a decision taken by the administration, which, according to the clearly punitive nature of the sanction, should be lodged and examined before a court with full jurisdictional power, as stated by Article 6 of the Convention, and not by a court such as the Administrative Court, which can only nullify decisions brought before it.[51] Referring to the principles resulting from Article 6 and reflected in the case-law of the European Commission and Court, the Supreme Court underlined the characteristics of an independent court.

The examples[52] above clearly show the importance attached by Portuguese

[48] I.a. Article 210.

[49] Judgment of the Constitutional Court 219/89 of 25.2.89 BMJ 384 p. 265. See also Judgments of the Constitutional Court 124/90 of 19.4.90 BMJ 296 p. 142 and Supreme Court 38609 of 29.10.86 BMJ 360 p. 494 and 40623 of 31.1.90.

[50] Supreme Court 74682 of 6.5.87 BMJ 367 p. 457.

[51] Administrative Supreme Court 27832 of 8.5.91.

[52] Others could be mentioned: the decision of the Supreme Court of Justice, concluding that four-day time-limits to lodge an appeal, in the framework of a freedom of the press criminal law proceedings, is sufficient for the preparation of the defence, according to article 6(2)(b) of the Convention (Supreme Court 37613 of 5.6.85 BMJ 348 p. 362); the possibility, in a law suit, of relegating to the enforcement phase of the proceedings the quantification of the amount that one part has to pay, is not contrary to Article 6, once in that phase the principle of the contradictory

courts to Article 6 of the Convention. Other provisions of the Convention (or case-law) have, however, occasionally been applied: there follows a quick survey.

12. Sex changes and rectification of the birth registration act

The legal implications of transsexuality, often analysed by the Strasbourg organs, have also been the subject of national court decisions. In such proceedings, reference has been made to Article 8 of the Convention and the case-law of the Commission and Court, while consideration was given to the condition of a transsexual and the inherent legal problems of someone who changes sex and wants to live his or her life according to that new condition.[53] Particular attention was paid to the right to rectify the birth certificate.

13. Conscientious objection

The Supreme Court also referred to the Convention to deny the recognition of the right to conscientious objection to military service. According to the case-law of the Commission, mentioned by the Supreme Court in its decision,[54] no such right arises under Article 9 of the Convention.[55]

14. Compulsory subscription to the Bar Association

In the light of the European Court's interpretation of Article 11 of the Convention the Supreme Court examined the question of compulsory subscription to in the Bar Association by lawyers. It stated that the obligation imposed on Portuguese lawyers to become members of the Bar Association in order to practise as an advocate lawyer was not contrary to the right to freedom of association, bearing in mind the specific nature and aims of this type of institution.[56]

is also observed (Supreme Court 81456 of 8.10.92); Article 6 (Access to Justice) and the increase of the amount of the costs of the proceedings: according to the Constitutional Court, in this question, Article 6 goes no further than the constitutional provisions (352/91 of 4.7.91 BMJ 409 p. 117). See also note 85 below.

[53] Decision of the Court of Appeal of Lisbon 16009 of 17.1.84 in Colectânea de Jusriprudência 1984, I, p. 109. See also Supreme Court 74408 of 16.11.88 BMJ 381 p. 578, decision and separate opinions, although not recognizing the applicant as transsexual.

[54] Judgment of the Supreme Court 74739 of 19.3.87.

[55] Conversely the right of medical doctors or paramedics to the conscientious objection in what concerns the fulfillment of their professional duties is foreseen in that provision, according to the interpretation given in this decision.

[56] Judgment of the Supreme Court 72732 of 23.5.85 of 23.5.85 BMJ 347 p. 227. See also, on Article 11 of the Convention, Attorney-General's opinion 40/89. See Judgment 433/87 of 4.11.87 on the free legal assistance that lawyers have to provide in the framework of the legal aid system, although in the decision no reference has been made to the Convention.

15. The condition of residence and the right to vote

The condition of residence as a prerequisite for the right to vote does not entail a violation of Article 3 of the First Additional Protocol to the Convention, the Constitutional Court concluded, referring to case-law of the European Commission.[57]

Other examples of the application of the Convention could also be mentioned.[58] The above illustrates the Convention's important role, recognized in the internal legal order. The references to the decisions of the Strasbourg organs support the idea that the interpretative approach of this instrument rests with the Commission and the Court. Domestic courts however, do not take advantage as frequently as it would be desirable of the efforts made by these organs in the innovative process of the Convention's interpretation.

As stated by a Portuguese judge, in a decision applying the European Convention on Human Rights, we should recognize that 'an orientation came into existence for every State that signed the Convention. A strong orientation that must be acceded to'.[59]

E. CASES BROUGHT BEFORE THE EUROPEAN COMMISSION AND COURT OF HUMAN RIGHTS

All Portuguese cases brought before the European Court have concerned Article 6 of the Convention, the majority of them on the question of a reasonable time for a hearing. This reality reflects, once again, the importance of this provision of the Convention in the whole set of the fundamental rights in domestic law. In each of those decisions concerning hearings within a reasonable time, the Court held the state responsible for a violation of Article 6(1), with the exception of one case, where the Portuguese government reached an agreement with the applicant while the proceedings were pending in Europe.

Let us focus now on the most innovative aspects of the interpretation of the Convention by the Court in the Portuguese cases.

The *Guincho* case,[60] the first Portuguese case to be brought before the Court, concerned a civil suit for compensation following a car accident.

[57] Judgment of the Constitutional Court 320/89 of 20.3.89.

[58] Judgment of the Supreme Court 30402 of 21.5.86 BMJ 357 p. 235, stating that the suspension of the application of the criminal sanction conditional on the payment of the compensation, is not contrary to Article 1 of the Fourth Protocol.

[59] Judgment of 3.5.82, pronounced by the Court of Cascais.

[60] Judgment of 10.7.84, Series A No. 81.

1. From declaratory to enforcement proceedings: for the purpose of Article 6 there is one single proceeding

The first question raised concerned the end of the period to be taken into consideration for the purpose of the reasonable time requirement. Should it be, as argued by the government, the final decision in the declaratory phase of the proceedings that compensation was due, or, as the Commission held, the decision in the subsequent enforcement phase, fixing the amount of the compensation?

The Court considered that the final decision is that which fixes the amount of compensation due, regardless of whether that is decided during the declaratory or the enforcement proceedings.

This position, of crucial importance in a civil procedure system such as the one in force in Portugal, was subsequently confirmed in the *Martins Moreira*[61] and *Silva Pontes*[62] cases. The Court stated, in the decision concerning the latter case:

> if the national law of a State makes provision for proceedings consisting of two stages—one when the court rules on the existence of an obligation to pay and another when it fixes the amount owed—it is reasonable to consider that, for the purposes of Article 6(1), a civil right is not 'determined' until the amount has been decided. The determination of a right entails deciding not only on the existence of that right but also on its scope or the manner in which it may be exercised, which would evidently include the calculation of the amount due.[63]

2. Domestic remedies to be exhausted in case of delay in the proceedings

The *Guincho* case also addressed the application of the previous exhaustion of domestic remedies rule, in the light of Article 26 of the Convention.

The Government had argued before the Court, on the question of the applicant's conduct, that he should have complained about the unreasonable delay before the Conselho Superior da Magistratura (High Judicial Counsel).[64]

The Court considered that even if the applicant had made such a complaint, the duration of the proceedings would not have been reduced. The most that that Court could have done was to take disciplinary measures against the magistrates or personnel responsible for the delays.[65]

The Commission, in its decision concerning admissibility,[66] had already stated that such a complaint could not be considered, strictly speaking, as a remedy. It could only be taken into consideration for the purpose of assess-

[61] Series A No. 143. [62] Series A No. 286. [63] Ibid, para. 30.

[64] This Council is an independent body, composed mainly of judicial magistrates with full power as far as the appointment, promotion, and discipline of judges are concerned.

[65] Series A No. 286, para. 34. [66] Decisions and Reports 29 p. 135.

ing the applicant's conduct when the question of reasonable time was examined.[67]

As for the administrative action for extra-contractual civil liability of the state, due to its responsibility for the delay of the judicial procedure, the Commission also considered that it could not be considered as an adequate remedy, to be exhausted according to Article 26, since it was not clear 'whether it had a chance of succeeding and whether it could have rectified speedily the situation complained of by the applicant'. Moreover, it was:

> not clear at what stage such an action could have been brought, and in particular whether it could have been brought during the proceedings or only after the judgment had become final.[68]

3. The influence of the revolutionary period in the judiciary—the theory of the 'temporary backlog' (engorgement passager)

The reasoning adopted by the Portuguese government in the *Guincho* case, according to which the proceedings had suffered from the difficult conditions resulting from the appropriateness of the judicial system to a revolutionary process such as the one endured in Portugal, did not convince the European judges. The Court referred to its case-law,[69] according to which a temporary backlog in a court causing delay in the proceedings does not entail the state's international responsibility under the Convention if prompt and adequate measures have been taken to address that situation. In this case, however, the Court concluded that the situation had a more structural nature and the measures adopted by the government seemed to be insufficient and taken at too late a stage. They surely reflected the willingness to solve the problems, but they could not, by their nature, achieve satisfactory results.[70]

In the *Baraona* case, which came before the Court, the applicant complained about the damage flowing from his arrest, based on a warrant issued in 1975, during the above-mentioned revolutionary period. To that purpose he sued the state, in the administrative court, for compensation. This procedure lasted six years and had not yet been decided by the time the European Court gave its judgment.[71] The Court, referring to the *Guincho* case and reaffirming the recognizance of the efforts made by the Portuguese people to consolidate democracy,[72] ruled that it was:

> not for the court to assess either the merits of the applicant's claim under Portuguese legislation or the influence that the revolutionary situation resulting from the events of April 1974 may have had on the application of that legislation.

[67] Ibid, para. 5.

[68] Ibid, para. 9.

[69] *Zimmermann and Steiner* case, Series A No. 66. See also the *Buchholz* case.

[70] Series A No. 81, para. 40.

[71] Judgment of 8.7.87, Series A No. 122.

[72] Ibid, para. 40.

Such questions, concluded the Court, fall within the exclusive jurisdiction of the Portuguese courts.[73]

4. Liability of the state for acts of public administration: administrative proceedings falling under Article 6

The question addressed in the *Guincho* case was whether the time taken by the administrative court to deliver a judgment was reasonable or unreasonable under Article 6(1) of the Convention. Subsequently, a very important issue was brought before the Court for consideration: the applicability of that provision to such an administrative procedure. The Court stated:

As to whether the right is a 'civil' right, the court refers to its established precedents. From these precedents it emerges among other things that the concept of 'civil rights and obligations' is not to be interpreted solely by reference to the respondent State's domestic law and that Article 6(1) applies irrespective of the status of the parties, as of the character of the legislation which governs how the dispute is to be determined and the character of the authority which is invested with jurisdiction in the matter; it is enough that the outcome of the proceedings should be 'decisive for private rights and obligations'. It is therefore not decisive that, with regard to the State's civil liability, Portuguese law distinguishes between acts of 'private administration' covered by Article 501 of the Civil Code and acts of 'public administration' dealt with in legislative decree 48051 of 1967; or that disputes concerning the latter come within the jurisdiction of the administrative courts. In any case, the Portuguese State's liability for acts of 'public administration' is based on the general principles of civil liability set out in the Civil Code, and the administrative courts follow the Code of Civil Procedure in the matter. The right to compensation asserted by the applicant is a private one, because it embodies a 'personal and property' interest and is founded on an infringement of rights of this kind, notably the right of property. The arrest warrant complained of caused Mr Baraona to flee to Brazil with his family, abandoning his house, all his property and his business, which was eventually declared insolvent.[74]

Justification concerning the complexity of the case was raised and accepted by the Court to a certain extent, but not in terms that could justify the whole delay. As to the several extensions of time requested by the State Counsel to present its reply, the Court ruled that the fact that domestic legislation allows it

does not exclude the State's responsibility for resultant delays. State Counsel could have refrained from making such applications, or the administrative court could have refused them.[75]

The third case, that of *Neves and Silva*, concerned a minority shareholder of an enterprise who complained of an arbitrary decision by the state not to

[73] Judgment of 8.7.87, Series A No. 122, para. 41. [74] Ibid, para. 44.

[75] See Judgment of the ADM 27801 of 24.4.90 BMJ 396 p. 310.

authorize the manufacture of plastic fibres. That arbitrary decision would have caused to his corporation and himself considerable damage.[76] The administrative procedure lasted thirteen years and the domestic court reached the decision that the applicant's right was statute-barred.

The main question before the European Court in this case concerned the application of Article 6 to the above-mentioned procedure. This was because, as pleaded by the government, there had been no determination of rights, in the sense of Article 6(1), since the decision of the administrative court failed to appreciate the applicant's rights and was only founded on procedural grounds. The European Court referred to its case-law:

Article 6(1) extends to 'contestations' (disputes) over (civil) 'rights' which can be said, at least on arguable grounds, to be recognized under domestic law, irrespective of whether they are also protected under the Convention.

By bringing an action before the administrative court, stated the European Court, the applicant:

claimed essentially that the fraudulent and unlawful conduct of a public official, acting from questionable motives, entailed the civil liability of the State. Various preliminary and substantive objections were raised by that State. A 'contestation' therefore arose between them. It no longer concerned the 'right' to manufacture plastic fibres, but the right to receive compensation for culpable conduct on the part of the administrative authorities . . . The Court must ascertain whether the applicant's arguments were sufficiently tenable and not whether they were well founded in terms of the Portuguese legislation. The National Commission of Inquiry expressed the opinion that the Directorate General for Industry misused its powers. For its part, the administrative court recognized that the applicant had *locus standi*; it did indeed find that the right was statute-barred, but in doing so it determined the 'contestation'. The right claimed by the applicant consisted in financial reparation for pecuniary damage. It was therefore a 'civil right', notwithstanding the origin of the dispute and the jurisdiction of the administrative courts.[77]

Accordingly, Article 6(1) was applicable to this case.

On the other hand, what the European Court had to ascertain was whether the case had been heard within a reasonable time. The fact of the applicant being a minority shareholder was immaterial in this connection.[78]

The fourth case, *Martins Moreira*, concerned the length of civil proceedings for damage resulting from a car accident.[79]

We mentioned some aspects of this case in the context of the *Guincho* case (see section 1 above). Two more questions, however, deserve to be considered.

[76] Judgment of 27.4.89, Series A No. 153.
[77] Ibid, para. 37.
[78] Ibid, para. 39.
[79] Judgment of 26.10.88, Series A No. 143.

5. The responsibility of the state extends to acts of different authorities

First, in the framework of the reasonable time concept, the State is responsible, not only for the functioning of the courts, but also for the actions and omissions of other authorities involved.

In ratifying the Convention, the Portuguese State undertook the obligation to respect it and it must, in particular, ensure that the Convention is complied with by its different authorities. In this instance, the various institutions which were prevented through inadequate facilities or an excessive work-load from complying with the requests of the Evora court were all public establishments. The fact that they were not judicial in character is immaterial in this respect. . . . In any event, the examination in question was to be effected in the context of judicial proceedings supervised by the court, which remained responsible for ensuring the speedy conduct of the trial.[80]

6. Duration of proceedings: comparing with the duration in other member states

Secondly, arguments that led to comparing the duration of the proceedings in the case under consideration with the duration of proceedings in other member states of the Council of Europe were not accepted as valid by the Court:

An argument of this nature, which is moreover not supported by precise statistics, is unconvincing. It could lead to the acceptance of unsatisfactory practices if they are sufficiently general, whereas, according to the case-law of the Court, the circumstances of each case must be taken into account and, in any event, compliance with Article 6(1) must be ensured.[81]

In the fifth case, *Oliveira Neves*,[82] concerning the length of proceedings in a labour court, the government and the applicant reached an agreement during the proceedings before the European Court.

7. The assistente *in criminal proceedings and the determination of his 'civil' right to compensation*

The sixth case, *Moreira Azevedo*,[83] concerned the duration of criminal proceedings and its effects in the compensation of the *assistente*. The issue was the application of Article 6. Since the applicant had the position of *assistente* (assistant of the prosecuting authority in the preliminary investigation) in the proceedings, the domestic court found that it could not 'determine his civil rights and obligations'.

[80] Judgment of 26.10.88, Series A No. 143, para. 60.
[81] Ibid, para. 54.
[82] Judgment of 25.5.89 Series A No. 153.
[83] Judgment of 23.10.90, Series A No. 189.

The European Court, refused to accept the position presented by the government, that the fact of being an *assistente* did not imply a request for compensation. Thus it concluded that:

> the impact on civil proceedings of the status of assistente, which attached to the applicant during the criminal proceedings, is a subject of controversy among legal writers. Clearly the applicant could have used the right available to him under Article 32 of the Code of Criminal Procedure to submit a formal claim for damages, but the Court cannot disregard the principles laid down by the Supreme Court in its 'ruling' judgment (*assento*) of 28 January 1976. In the light of these principles it appears that to intervene as an *assistente* is equivalent to filing a claim for compensation in civil proceedings.[84]

Therefore, the case concerned the determination of the right of such an *assistente*. It was also decisive to his right, and Article 6(1) was applicable to it.

8. *From the enforcement proceedings back to the declaratory proceedings*

In a judgment of 23 March 1994[85] concerning the reasonable time provision, the Court returned to this question, the same dealt with in the very first case against Portugal.

The applicant, Mr Silva Pontes, had been co-claimant in a civil lawsuit for compensation for damage resulting from a car accident caused to him and Mr Martins Moreira by a third party. The duration of these proceedings had already been considered in relation to Mr Martins Moreira in the fourth case referred to the European Court. Mr Silva Pontes, however, had not then presented the necessary complaint to the Commission. He let the declaratory stage of the proceedings be concluded, which took a period of nine years, and for the decision of the European Court concerning Mr Martins Moreira, and two years after the 'final' decision of that first stage (in fact, already in the last part of the enforcement stage) Mr Silva Pontes filed with the Commission a complaint concerning the length of the whole proceedings, covering both stages.

The government argued that the application was out of time insofar as it concerned the length of the declaratory proceedings, but the European Court, confirming its previous ruling in the *Martins Moreira* case, considered that the duration of the proceedings extended from the beginning of the declaratory stage, even though the complaint had only been presented in the last part of the enforcement stage:

> It is not for the Court to express a view on the difference of opinion among legal writers as to whether under Portuguese law enforcement proceedings are autonomous. As the Delegate of the Commission observed at the hearing, the moment at which there

[84] Ibid, para. 67. [85] Series A No. 286.

was a 'determination' of a civil right and therefore a final decision within the meaning of Article 26 has to be ascertained with reference to the Convention and not on the basis of national law.[86]

9. *Rendering the* despacho de pronúncia *and subsequently presiding over the criminal court: impartiality of the judge*

In April 1994 the European Court rendered a decision concerning *Otelo Saraiva de Carvalho*,[87] who had brought a complaint before the Commission of a breach of his right to have his case heard by an impartial tribunal, within the meaning of Article 6(1) of the Convention, in that the same judge had both issued the initial *despacho de pronúncia* (see below) and subsequently presided over the criminal court.[88] The European Court stated that:

the impartiality must be determined according to a subjective test, that is on the basis of the personal conviction of a particular judge in a given case, and also according to an objective test, that is ascertaining whether the judge offered guarantees sufficient to exclude any legitimate doubt in this respect.[89]

The personal impartiality of the judge was not disputed, so the Court continued to determine whether there were grounds which could objectively lead to a conclusion of partiality:

When it is being decided whether in a given case there is a legitimate reason to fear that a particular judge lacks impartiality, the standpoint of the accused is important but not decisive. What is decisive is whether this fear can be held to be objectively justified . . . And the fact that a judge has already taken decisions before the trial cannot in itself be regarded as justifying anxieties about his impartiality. What matters is the scope and nature of the measures taken by the judge before trial.[90]

The Court found that the *despacho de pronúncia* was not equivalent to a committal for trial, but aims to determine:

whether the file amounted to a *prima facie* case such as to justify making an individual go through the ordeal of a trial. The issues which the judge has to settle when taking this decision are consequently not the same as those which are decisive for his final judgment.[91]

[86] Series A No. 286, para. 29. The Court also took the view that 'the enforcement proceedings were not intended solely to enforce an obligation to pay a fixed amount; they also served to determine important elements of the debt itself . . . Those proceedings must therefore be regarded as second stage of the proceedings, which began on 22 December 1977. It follows that the dispute over the applicant's right to damages would only have been resolved by the final decision in the enforcement proceedings' (para. 33).

[87] Judgment of 22.4.94 Series A No. 286.

[88] Ibid, para. 28

[89] Ibid, para. 33

[90] Ibid, para. 35.

[91] Ibid, para. 37.

The Court held that there had been no breach of Article 6(1) of the Convention.[92]

10. Role of the Attorney-General's representative in the Supreme Court: not a party to the dispute, but the parties should have access to a copy of and be able to reply to Attorney-General's opinions which may influence the Court's decision

In the case of *Lobo Machado*,[93] the European Court focused on the Attorney-General's role in a Supreme Court of Justice's judgment concerning a dispute over the amount of a retirement pension of the applicant. The Strasbourg Court considered that the Attorney-General's representative in the Supreme Court was not a party to the dispute, although the law gives no indication as to how he should perform his role. The Court considered further that the opinion given by the Attorney-General's representative on the cases before the Supreme Court, while mainly focusing on the need to ensure the consistency of the case-law, is nevertheless intended to advise and accordingly influence that Court. Since the outcome of the appeal could have affected the amount of Mr Lobo Machado's retirement pension, he should have had the opportunity—in accordance with his right to adversarial proceedings—to obtain a copy of the Attorney-General's representative's opinion in his case and to reply to it before judgment was given. The European Human Rights Court concluded in its decision of 20 February 1996 that this right, as enshrined in Article 6(1):

> means in principle the opportunity for the parties to a criminal or civil trial to have knowledge of and comment on all evidence adduced, or observations filed with a view to influencing the Court's decision.

[92] By Judgment 219/89 of 25.2.89 (DR II Série 30.6.89), the Constitutional Court found that Article 365 of the Code of Criminal Procedure 1929, and other provisions allowing for the judge who rendered the *despacho de pronúncia* to decide the case was not unconstitutional (nor against Article 6 of the Convention). This was so, according to the judgment, since the *despacho de pronúncia* went no further than the bill of indictment, having thus a simple guarantee function. At most it may qualify in a different way the facts referred in the bill of indictment or describe differently, in secondary aspects, the conduct of the accused. But if, in the *despacho de pronúncia*, the judge refers to other actions of the accused that could be envisaged by the law as criminal offences different from those identified in the indictment, the *despacho de pronúncia* no longer has the function of a guarantee. In this case it will consist substantially of an accusation, and so the judge, author of the *despacho de pronúncia*, could not later decide the case (Article 32(5) of the Constitution). See also Judgment of the Supreme Court 39856 of 25.1.89 BMJ 383 p. 486 and Constitutional Court 124/90 of 19.4.90 BMJ 396 p. 142.

11. Administrative decisions affecting for a long period of time the ordinary enjoyment of the right over a land: no decision on expropriation, nor compensation granted—unbalance between the requirements of general interest and the individual right

In a judgment of 16 September 1996 the Court considered whether the rights of peaceful enjoyment of possessions of the applicants, *Mr Matos e Silva* and others, had been violated.[93] The applicants owned land which had been affected for thirteen years by a public interest declaration, a preliminary step to its expropriation in order to set up a nature reserve.

The European Court considered the difficulties faced by the applicants in gaining access to the administrative courts to appeal the decisions and concluded that, as it was conceded by the government, there had been an unreasonable delay in the proceedings. But the main focus of the judgment was Article 1 of Protocol No. 1.

While considering that the administrative decisions had not amounted to either formal or *de facto* expropriation, they were found to have had serious and harmful effects which had hindered the applicants' ordinary enjoyment of their rights for more than thirteen years, during which time virtually no progress had been made in the administrative proceedings. The long period of uncertainty, both as what would become of the possessions and as to the question of compensation, further aggravated the detrimental effects of the administrative decisions.

As a result, the Court concluded, the applicants had had to bear an individual and excessive burden which had upset the fair balance which should be struck between the requirements of the general interest and the right of peaceful enjoyment of one's possessions. Hence there had been a violation of Article 1 of Protocol No. 1.

12. Review of the decision concerning the detention of a mentally ill person

In the case of *Silva Rocha* the applicant had been prosecuted for homicide and found not to be criminally responsible on account of his mental disturbance. He was detained pursuant to a decision which the European Court found to be both a conviction by a competent court, within the meaning of Article 5(1) of the Convention, and a security measure taken in relation to a person of unsound mind, within the meaning of Article 5(1)(e) of the Convention. Both situations coexisted in this case.[94]

The Court held that the review required by Article 5(4) of the Convention was incorporated in the decision by the national court, which imposed deten-

[93] Judgment of 20.2.96. [94] Reports 1996–V.

tion for a period of three years. Only after that period could a review be required to ascertain whether the mental state of the applicant, which was the basis for the domestic decision, had improved, allowing the lifting of the measure. However, the Court noted that the legislation applied to Mr Silva Rocha (Article 93 of the Criminal Code) provided for a periodic and automatic review after two years and made it possible for the person detained to apply to the court at any moment to have the detention measure lifted.

13. *Right to effective legal assistance, not formal legal assistance*

In a judgment concerning a criminal procedure, Mr *Daud*, a foreigner who had been sentenced to imprisonment for drug trafficking and using a false passport, the European Court focused on the failure by the Portuguese Court to comply with the requirements of Article 6(3) of the Convention concerning the right to legal assistance.[95] The Court noted that the first officially assigned lawyer had not taken any steps on behalf of Mr Daud, who tried unsuccessfully to conduct his own defence. As to the second lawyer assigned after the first reported sick, the Court considered that she had not had the time she needed to study the file, visit her client in prison and prepare his defence. The time between notification of the replacement of the lawyer and the hearing had been too short for a serious, complex case in which there had been no judicial investigation and which led to a heavy sentence.

14. *Enforcement proceedings based on a notarial deed: even if there is no apparent 'contestation' (dispute) Article 6(1) applies—substantive meaning of the word 'contestation'*

The most significant part of the decision in the case of *Estima Jorge*[96] focused on whether domestic enforcement proceedings had been based, not on a previous judgment, but on another form of authority to execute: a notarial deed providing security for a specific debt. The sole object of the enforcement proceedings had been the recovery of a debt over which there was no 'contestation' (dispute).

The European Court reaffirmed that in conformity with the spirit of the Convention the word 'contestation' should not be construed too technically and that it should be given a substantive rather than a formal meaning. The Court underlined that, irrespective of whether the authority to execute took the form of a judgment or a notarial deed, Portuguese law provided that it was to be enforced through the courts and the enforcement procedure had been decisive for the effective exercise of the applicant's right. Consequently

[95] Reports 1998–II. [96] Judgment of 22.4.98.

the Court held that Article 6(1) was applicable to the proceedings which, in this particular case, had taken too long.

15. The use of agents provocateurs *or undercover agents and the fairness of the investigative process*

In the case of *Teixeira de Castro*[97] the European Court considered in substance the decision taken by a Portuguese court by which the applicant had been sentenced to jail on account of drug trafficking. The Court reviewed the investigative process led by the police and concluded that police officers acting as *agents provocateurs* had incited the commission of the offence. The Strasbourg Court concluded that their actions:

> went beyond those of undercover agents because they instigated the offence and there was nothing to suggest that without their intervention it would be committed [. . . and . . .] that intervention and its use in the impugned criminal proceedings mean that, right from the outset, the applicant was definitively deprived of a fair trial.

Many cases filed with the Commission are not forwarded to the Court.[98] Most of these concern the length of domestic proceedings and the question of reasonable time according to Article 6(1) of the Convention. It is interesting to note that there is a wide range of sorts of proceedings in these cases: civil, criminal, labour, administrative, and enforcement proceedings. The cases brought before the Court, examined above, demonstrate this.

However, none of those cases raised new legal questions before the Commission.

Reasonable time was measured in the light of the precedent case-law criteria established by the European Court. It is important, though, to underline some of the questions brought again before the Commission and its standing regarding these questions, which confirms the legal principles applied in previous Portuguese cases.

In the light of the Court's decisions in the *Guincho* and *Martins Moreira* cases, Article 6 applies to enforcement proceedings even if they are not based on a previous judgment, as in the mentioned cases, but on another document (banker's draft).[99] The Commission saw no reason to conclude differently. In this case the means offered to the debtor to oppose the debt's enforcement are even wider than in the enforcement proceedings based on a declaratory judgment. The object of these proceedings is undoubtedly the determination of civil rights and freedoms.[100]

[97] Judgment of 9.6.98.

[98] Over 50 by the end of 1998.

[99] See also the case of *Estima Jorge*, cited above.

[100] Application 14926/89, *SA v Portugal*, opinion of 10.2.93 paras. 41–42. See Judgment of the Supreme Court 81456 of 8.10.92 quoted in note 48: the possibility in a law suit of relegating to

In its opinion concerning another case[101] submitted before it, the Commission reaffirmed the previous ruling according to which in the determination of a person's civil rights and obligations, the right to a fair and public hearing within a reasonable time must be respected even if the tribunal has reached a solution without taking a decision on the substance of the case.[102]

In another case the Commission recalled the precedent case-law which held that there were no effective remedies for excessively lengthy civil proceedings in the Portuguese legal system.[103] In particular, the petition for reinitiating proceedings suspended at the applicant's request is not a legal remedy for delayed proceedings. It has more to do with the exercise of the initiative power accorded to the parties in civil proceedings, and must, as such, be examined in the context of the conduct of the applicant and its influence on the reasonable time question, in the appreciation on the merits of the application.[104]

The question of the extension of time requested by the State Counsel to reply in civil proceedings was examined not under its implications for the equality of arms[105] principle, but concerning its influence on the delay of the proceedings.[106]

The fact that the applicant had reached an agreement with the other party during proceedings in the domestic court was pleaded to justify the claim that he could no longer represent himself as a victim in the terms of the Convention. The Commission, reaffirming its precedent case-law,[107] stated that the agreement between the parties should have taken into consideration compensation for the delay of the proceedings. If it did not then the applicant could still claim to be a victim of a breach of the Convention.[108] The Committee of Ministers in this case, the first one taken before it, could not agree by the majority of two-thirds required by Article 32 of the Convention to decide the matter in the light of the Opinion submitted by the Commission. It therefore decided that it could take no further action in the case and accordingly removed this case from its

the enforcement stage of the proceedings the quantification of the amount that one part has to apply is not contrary to Article 6, since at that stage, the principle of contradiction is also observed.

[101] Application 11724/85, *Manuel Mendes Godinho e Filhos v Portugal*, opinion of 11.10.90, para. 106.

[102] See the *Neves e Silva* case, above, where a similar question was decided by the European Court.

[103] See *Oliveira Neves*, opinion of 15.12.88, Annex II. See also decision of the Commission of 6.7.82 in the *Dores e Silveira* case.

[104] Application 11498/85, *Gomes v Portugal*, decision of 10.7.89.

[105] See B above, note 27.

[106] Application 13388/87, *Ribeiro de Mello v Portugal*, opinion of 13.1.92, para. 26. See also on this question the *Baraona* case, quoted above, note 71.

[107] Opinion of 13.12.78 (*Preikhzas v Portugal*, DR 16 p. 29.

[108] Application 9346/81, *Dores e Silveira v Portugal*, Opinion of 6.7.83, paras. 90–91.

list.[109] This situation challenged the system of protection of the European human rights organs, failing to provide a solution of an individual complaint on the violation of one of the rights enshrined in the European Convention. The case paved the way to the modification of the requirement for a two-thirds majority to the simple majority, introduced by Protocol No. 10 to the European Convention.[110]

In several other cases the applicants have reached agreement with the government under the supervision of the Commission.

F. REMEDIAL ACTION TAKEN BY THE GOVERNMENT IN RESPONSE TO BEING HELD IN VIOLATION OF THE CONVENTION

What measures have been taken in Portugal in response to the above-mentioned judgments,[111] having regard to its obligations under Article 53 of the Convention to abide by the judgments of the Court?

The Committee of Ministers has declared itself satisfied that the sums awarded under Article 50 of the Convention had been paid. It has also requested, in some cases, information concerning the measures taken to prevent similar situations of undue delay in future proceedings.

Two of those cases, *Martins Moreira* and *Moreira Azevedo*, concerned, respectively, civil and criminal proceedings. In both cases the government referred to the increased the number of judges and administrative court staff involved in the case as an effective means of expediting those proceedings.[112] These measures could be envisaged as being conjunctural or formal, resulting from the normal adaptation of the judicial system to the growing needs of its users.

However, two more structural or substantive measures have been adopted as a consequence of European Court judgments. The first concerned the reform of the Forensic Medicine Institutes, which the government deemed necessary to enable a prompt response by the Institutes to requests presented before them.[113] These Institutes play an important role in some civil and crim-

[109] Resolution DH(85)7. [110] See note 6 above. [111] See part E above.

[112] See references in the appendix to the Resolution DH(89)22—Decree Law 214/88 of 17 July, Ministerial Order 537/88, of 10 August, reinforcing in terms of judges and administrative staff the Evora Court of first instance and the Court of Appeal. See also the appendix to Resolution DH(92)10, as it concerns criminal procedure—Portaria 848/83 of 23 August appointing a third judge to the Vila Nova de Famalicão Court, the creation of a Tribunal de Círculo in this judiciary district, and reinforcement of the administrative staff of that Court (Portaria 537/88 of 10 August).

[113] See appendix to Resolution DH(89)22.

inal proceedings, influencing their duration, as shown by cases brought before the European Court. The other substantive measure concerned the new procedure for expediting criminal proceedings, introduced by the Code of Criminal Proceedings of 1987, which, given its importance, deserves more detailed consideration. Article 108 of that Code provides that:

> when the time-limits set by the law for the duration of each phase of the proceedings have expired, the Public Prosecutor, the accused, the *assistente*, or the parties claiming damages may request expedition. The decision on this request is to be taken either by the Republic's General Prosecutor, if the case is under direction of the Public Prosecutor, or by the Superior Council of the Judiciary if the case was brought before a court or a judge.[114]

Article 109 of the same Code determines the procedure to be followed when dealing with a request for expedition. In particular, paragraph 5 of Article 109 states that:

> the decision taken may be either to declare the request inadmissible, as being ill founded, or because the delays found were justified; or to request further information, which must be provided within a maximum of five days; or to request that an inquiry be conducted within a period that cannot exceed fifteen days; or to suggest or determine the disciplinary sanctions, management, organizational, or rationalization measures called for by the situation.[115]

According to paragraph 6 of Article 109:

> the decision shall be immediately communicated to the court or the entity in charge of the case, as well as to the authorities who have disciplinary jurisdiction over the persons responsible for the delays found.[116]

The effectiveness of this mechanism, to be proved by the results of a decade of implementation, will certainly confer on it the nature of a domestic remedy to be exhausted within the meaning of Article 26 of the Convention.

Most of the Portuguese cases in which the European Court has found a violation of the Convention have concerned the reasonable time question. The Court awarded, in each such case, certain sums to the applicants, representing what the Court considered to be just satisfaction in each case. The government adopted the necessary measures to pay them, and where appropriate further measures were adopted in order to comply fully with the Court's decisions.

As yet there has been no decision which, for its full application, would entail the revision of a domestic judgment. It is undeniable that the revision of an internal decision may, in certain circumstances, be considered necessary

[114] Appendix to Resolution DH(92)10 of the Committee of Ministers. [115] Ibid.
[116] Ibid.

to redress the situation. Under Portuguese law, however, the revision of a court's decision is only possible on extremely strict conditions and grounds.[117] The procedure for revision involves an extraordinary remedy to be taken before the Supreme Court. Unlike the situation in other states parties to the Convention, the possibility of revising a judgment of a national court following a decision by the Strasbourg Court that it violates the Convention would in practice not have any chance of success in Portugal, given the internal legal requirements. It seems that such revision is not envisaged by the domestic provisions.

G. ASSESSMENT AND PROSPECTS

The importance which the members of the legal profession attach to the European Convention on Human Rights is undeniable. At the Constitutional level, new steps are envisaged on the question of the privileged status to be granted to the European Convention, as well as to other treaties in the field of human rights. Attention will probably also be paid to the development of the Constitutional Court's case-law on the question of its competence to examine the compatibility of domestic law with the provisions of the European Convention on Human Rights.

The delay in domestic proceedings, the issue on which the European Convention has had the largest number of applications, will surely also be reviewed. This problem is possibly due to the fact that the right to a judicial decision within a reasonable time is not, as such, among the procedural rights expressly recognized in the Constitution. The Administrative Supreme Court may also play an important role here in reaffirming its case-law, according to which the violation of Article 6 may entail the responsibility of the state for unreasonable delays in proceedings. This could lead to the recognition of a new domestic remedy, to be exhausted in accordance with Article 26 of the Convention. This could confer a new role on the Supreme Administrative Court, which would be called upon to examine cases concerning excessively lengthy proceedings before they can be referred to the European Commission.

The European Convention will continue to influence court decisions and even administrative practices in the field of human rights. It will surely have a key role in certain domains where legislation could be more restrictive, thus limiting the level of enjoyment of the individual fundamental rights. One

[117] See Articles 449 of the Code of Criminal Procedure and 771 of the Code of Civil Procedure on the conditions and grounds for revision.

domain where recent legislation is clearly restrictive, compared to the legislation previously in force in Portugal, is that concerning aliens. The Strasbourg case-law will surely play an important role in this field, particularly on admission to and departure from the national territory. The right to respect for family life and the notion of family unification, as well as racial discrimination and degrading treatment, are questions on which the European Commission and Court have pronounced far-reaching decisions in the context of the European Convention.

However, recent developments in Strasbourg case-law, which have held states responsible for violations of the European Convention by third states to which aliens were or are to be expelled, bring to light again the international responsibility which Portugal undertook by its ratification of the European Convention. Portugal, being an entry state to European Union territory, will surely be submitted to strong pressure by the number of entry requests and expulsion measures. This will test its capacity to meet the international responsibility in the field of human rights, which Portugal decisively embraced in 1978 when it ratified the European Convention on Human Rights.

27

Romania

RENATE WEBER

A. INTRODUCTION

Throughout the period from the end of World War II until December 1989 Romania was governed by a tough Communist regime. In fact, the country was absent from the great moments which marked the evolution of international human rights law. The Romanian government signed the two International Covenants on Civil and Political Rights and on Economic, Social, and Cultural Rights (UN) in 1974, and became a party to the 1975 Helsinki Final Act (CSCE), but the purpose of such gestures was only to show the Western world an openness which did not apply to Romanian society: respect for human rights within the country was non-existent. Moreover, the concept of human rights itself was absent from the study of international law: merely referring to it was considered to be a means of undermining the power of the Communist state.

Therefore, when the Communist regime was defeated, Romanian society was unprepared to cope with the concept of human rights: the new political power was very tempted to consider that once declared a democratic regime everything would be solved without much effort. Lawyers and the judiciary also had no expertise on the topic and the media was unaware of its significance. The Council of Europe, the European Convention on Human Rights, the Commission, and the Court were merely abstract words. This total lack of knowledge is one of the explanations for the slow rhythm of changes.

In fact, the European Convention was brought into discussion during the process of drafting and adopting the Constitution, since the experts consulted by the Drafting Committee included Council of Europe experts. Thus, many provisions of the European Convention were considered in the chapter on 'Fundamental Rights and Freedoms', in some instances being dealt with in even more detail. At the same time, the constitutional restrictions reflect the limits of the Constitutional Assembly in coping with this new approach, namely human rights protection. Such is the case, for example, of Article 49, on restriction of the exercise of certain rights or freedoms, which mentions all the conditions set forth by the Convention, with one notable exception: the requirement of necessity in a democratic society, a concept not easily understood at that time. Similarly, for freedom of expression additional restrictions were provided, although not consistent with any international human rights treaty: 'defamation of the country and the nation', 'instigation to class hatred', and 'incitement to territorial separatism'.

Back in 1994, when ratification of the Convention was under discussion, the debates within the Parliament were almost insignificant, in the sense that no one really questioned the Romanian legal provisions, nor the changes needed to many domestic laws, and no one pointed out that 'Romanian traditional values' would jeopardize compliance with the Convention and the Strasbourg case-law. Rather, the discussions were muted and the ratification was meant to prove Romania's willingness to become a 'civilized nation'. The European Convention was ratified with:

—one reservation to Article 5, allowing the domestic military disciplinary system to provide for disciplinary custody within the army for up to fifteen days and

—one declaration that Romania's interpretation of Article 2 of Protocol No. 1 is that it does not impose any supplementary financial obligations regarding private education, other than those accepted by its domestic legislation.

The European Convention was ratified by the Parliament by means of Law 30 of May 18 1994, published in the Official Gazette on May 31 1994.

Immediately after ratification the Human Rights Centre (within the Romanian Helsinki Committee) conducted an investigation addressed to the highest authorities in the country in order to assess how prepared they were to implement the Convention. The answers showed how theoretical the topic was perceived to be.[1] Several interviewees did not respond (the Romanian Senate, the Law Faculty in Bucharest, the Ministry of Justice, the Ministry of Foreign Affairs) while others offered plenty of theoretical details.

The Speaker of the Chamber of Deputies listed several laws adopted by the Parliament on human rights protection and stated in his answer that:

> one cannot speak about an initiative regarding the harmonization of Romanian legislation with the European Convention and its protocols since such initiatives exist in relation with each draft law or legislative proposal.[2]

[1] See 'Ancheta Centrului pentru Drepturile Omului: Efectele ratificarii Conventiei europene a drepturilor omului asupra dreptului intern român' (The Centre for Human Rights Investigation: the Impact of the European Convention on Human Rights upon the Romanian Legal System), in *Revista Română de Drepturile Omului* (the Romanian Review of Human Rights), No. 5, 1994.

[2] Ibid, p. 64.

He added that:

it is natural to wish to go beyond the minimal standards set forth by international documents [but] this will take place with some difficulties due to the economic and social conditions in Romania, as well as in the world.[3]

The answer received from the National Institute for Magistracy proved how poorly equipped it was at that time to embark upon a programme in relation with the Convention: Our Institute has no connection with international institutions on the study of the European Convention and we did not make any particular effort in this direction since our activity is broader than this specific domain [. . .] Our professors' possibilities to become acquainted with international documents are at this moment in their own hands since our documentation office is only at the beginning and due to our budgetary constraints is quite poor.[4]

Interesting details were offered by the Ministry of Interior, especially on the Law on the Police and the co-operation with human rights NGOs, but not perceiving any specific changes needed by the Romanian legislation and affecting police conduct. In its turn the Ministry of Defence mentioned several aspects in relation to the army and its activities, including a draft law for alternative civil service on religious grounds.

Detailed answers came from the Constitutional Court. Among other things, the President of the Court stated that:

observance of the Convention is not dependent on a review of the legislation, since the Convention is directly enforceable.[5]

At the same time it was stated that:

the logical relation between the European Convention and the Constitution must take into consideration how the European Convention has been interpreted by the European Court case-law. Therefore, the Constitutional Court of Romania emerges as a jurisdictional authority which has not only the right but also the obligation to base its own interpretation of the Constitution in a manner which will ensure the compatibility of domestic legislation with the Convention.[6]

It is worth noting that during the last six years the Constitutional Court has been the only jurisdictional authority which has constantly referred in its jurisprudence to the Convention and the Strasbourg case-law.

[3] Ibid, p. 65. [4] Ibid, pp. 69–70. [5] Ibid, p. 66. [6] Ibid, p. 67.

B. THE STATUS OF THE CONVENTION IN NATIONAL LAW

The Romanian Constitution was adopted by the Constitutional Assembly on 21 November, 1991 and entered into force after being confirmed by a national referendum held on December 8 1991. It has three provisions which confer on human rights treaties a special status.

Article 11 reads as follows:

(1) The Romanian State pledges to fulfil in good faith its obligations deriving from the treaties to which it is party.
(2) Treaties ratified by Parliament, according to the law, are part of national law.

Article 20 says:

(1) Constitutional provisions concerning the citizens' rights and liberties shall be interpreted and enforced in conformity with the Universal Declaration of Human Rights, with the covenants and other treaties to which Romania is party.
(2) Where any inconsistencies exist between the covenants and treaties on fundamental human rights to which Romania is party and domestic law, the international regulations shall take precedence.

Article 51 says:

The observance of the Constitution, of its supremacy and of the laws is binding.

The Romanian Constitution adopted the monist principle, according to which international legislation once ratified is included in the domestic legislation. According to Article 11(2) of the Constitution, treaties ratified by the state become part of domestic legislation, 'treaty' designating any instrument used in international practice to evince the common will of states, be it a covenant, convention, protocol, agreement, statute, final act, final document, etc. A first remark to be made in connection with this text refers to the specificity of treaties whose precedence over domestic legislation is recognized. These are exclusively human rights treaties.[7] A second remark concerns Article 20(1) which stipulates that constitutional norms relating to the rights and liberties of individuals must be interpreted in accordance with the Universal Declaration of Human Rights, and with the covenants and other treaties to which Romania is party. Some scholars have held that the Article was worded so as to express Romania's attachment to the Universal Declaration of Human Rights, a fundamental political document in the

[7] More recently, in connection with Romania's desire to join the European Union, views have been expressed on the necessity to amend the Constitution and to make all international treaties prevail over domestic legislation.

human rights field.[8] According to a second opinion, the reference to the Universal Declaration has no consequences, because the Declaration is merely a political document and not a treaty in the form provided for by international law.[9] A third opinion holds that by incorporating the Universal Declaration into the Constitution of Romania and making it compulsory for the interpretation of constitutional provisions relating to human rights, the former has acquired legal power in Romanian domestic law.[10]

The most controversial as well as the most important matter, from a practical point of view, is the precedence of international human rights regulations over domestic laws. The Constitution sets forth the pre-eminence of international law but leaves unsolved the issue of the relationship between international and constitutional legal norms. Could one hold that international regulations should take precedence even when they run counter to the Constitution? One opinion is that the Romanian authorities competent to negotiate and conclude treaties should examine the compatibility of such treaties with the Constitution and that treaties which run against the Constitution should be ratified either with reservations and declarations or after the revision of the fundamental law.[11] According to another opinion,[12] the constitutional text in Article 20 is inadequate because of its vague wording. Moreover, the provision relating to the precedence of international regulations is regarded as difficult to enforce, because the Constitutional Court may pronounce only on the constitutionality of laws, not on the compatibility of laws and international treaties.[13]

For practical reasons, it is important to explore the intention of the Constituent Assembly when Articles 11 and 20 were adopted, in order to understand the competencies of courts in connection with international treaties. Opinions are split in this field too. Some authors and practitioners

[8] Gheorghe Iancu, *Drept constituţional şi institupii politice (Constitutional Law and Political Institutions)*, Universitatea Ecologică, 1993, pp. 66–67.

[9] Dan Ciobanu and Victor Duculescu, *Drept constituţional român (Romanian Constitutional Law)*, Editura Hyperion XXI, Bucharest, 1993, pp. 87–88.

[10] Ioan Muraru and Mihai Constantinescu, *Drept parlamentar* (Parliamentary law), Gramar, 1994, p. 203. See also Genoveva Vrabie, *Organizarea politico-etatica a Romaniei* (The Romania's political organization and state structure), Virginia, 1995, p. 442.

[11] Ioan Muraru, in *Constitupia României comentată şi adnotată*, (The Romanian Constitution with annotation and comments) Regia autonomă 'Monitorul oficial', Bucharest, 1992, pp. 47–50.

[12] See Nicolae Ecobescu and Victor Duculescu, *Drept internapional public (Public International Law)*, Editura Hyperion XXI, Bucharest, 1993, p. 59. See Nicolae Ecobescu and Victor Duculescu, *Drept internapional public (Public International Law)*, Editura Hyperion XXI, Bucharest, 1993, p. 59.

[13] See also Dan Ciobanu and Victor Duculescu, note 9 above. For critical opinions on this stand see Renate Weber, 'Receptarea dreptului internapional al drepturilor omului de către sistemul juridic român' (Human rights international law in the Romanian legal system), in the *Revista Română de Drepturile Omului*, no. 12/1996.

hold that constitutional provisions moved away from the 'traditional solution of enforcing international conventions at the internal level by means of the laws adopted on their basis' and established the '"self-executing" principle, according to which these conventions may be enforced directly, with no need for the screening of the law'.[14] This is the most widely held opinion.[15] Other authors, however, hold that in the Romanian legal system the judge does not enforce international treaties directly, as happens for instance in the United States, because he is only empowered to enforce the internal laws of the state.[16]

Several practitioners have argued against such interpretation.[17] So far there is no established practice of Romanian courts other than the Constitutional Court in this field, although there has been a recent judicial dispute.[18]

It is interesting to note that this kind of discussion did not take place before the adoption of the Constitution, proving that during the drafting process these questions were not envisaged by the drafters; this seems to be a confirmation of the fact that such provisions were accepted at the suggestion of international experts and in order to please institutions such as the Council of Europe. However, Articles 11 and 20 have turned out to be among the best provisions of the Constitution, although the Romanian magistrates have difficulty understanding their meaning and the great opportunities they open for the defence of human rights.

C. THE STATUS OF THE CONVENTION IN PARLIAMENTARY PROCEEDINGS

Romania's accession to the Council of Europe was a complex and difficult process. Immediately after the overthrow of the Communist regime[19] Romania declared its openness toward international structures promoting human rights and made its accession to the Council of Europe a major goal of its foreign policy. However, several events during 1990, such as the elections held in May, particularly the electoral campaign, the inter-ethnic clashes

[14] See Ioan Muraru, Mihai Constantinescu, note 10 above, p. 203.

[15] See also Doru Cosma 'Rolul instan|elor de judecat| în aplicarea Conven|iei europene a drepturilor omului' (The role of national courts in implementing the European Convention on Human Rights), in *Revista Română de Drepturile Omului*, no. 6–7/1994.

[16] Nicolae Ecobescu and Victor Duculescu, note 12 above, p. 59. See also Dan Ciobanu and Victor Duculescu, note 13 above, p. 88.

[17] See Renate Weber 'România şi dreptul internapional al drepturilor omului' (Romania and International Human Rights Law) in Thomas Buergenthal's *Dreptul internapional al drepturilor omului (International Human Rights)*, All, Bucharest, 1996, pp. 221–228.

[18] See section D below.

[19] 22 December 1989.

which took place in March in Târgu-Mures, as well as the violent raids by coalminers in June and the lack of capacity of the Romanian legal system to cope with them, were considered by the Council of Europe as being incompatible with its Statute. Therefore all discussions on membership were postponed. In February 1991 Romania obtained special observer status and has become subject to a monitoring procedure. On 7 October 1993 Romania was accepted as a full member, but in its Opinion 176 of 28 September 1993 the Parliamentary Assembly made a series of recommendations whose achievement was considered necessary to ensure compatibility between Romania's *de facto* and its *de jure* situation with regard to the Council of Europe's standards. The recommendations concerned the independence of the judiciary, the right to property, freedom of the media, the protection of national minorities, prison conditions, decriminalization of homosexuality, etc. Special rapporteurs were designated to evaluate the follow-up process. A Report was issued in May 1994 which found some achievements but many shortcomings.[20]

Due to this difficult relationship with the Council of Europe, for several years public debates, particularly in the Parliament and the media, viewed any recommendation from the Council as interference with Romania's internal affairs. This lack of understanding of the new situation, including the issue of what a limited transfer of sovereignty implies, was shared not only by extremist parties or journalists but also by the Romanian political elite and media. It affected all Parliamentary debates on domestic human rights protection, even after ratification of the European Convention. Thus any Parliamentary debate on, for example, homosexuality, freedom of expression, or religious rights has been expressed as a struggle between 'Romania's traditional values' and the obligations 'imposed by the Council'. Not even the fact that the Convention had been ratified, thus becoming legally binding, and moreover taking precedence over Romanian domestic law on human rights, achieved a shift in this understanding.

On several occasions the European Convention was referred to in government and parliamentary debates. One must admit that, at least for the last three or four years, a significant difference has become apparent between how the government approached the Convention and Parliament's approach. Although no government programme ever mentioned human rights, during the last few years several initiatives from various ministries, particularly the Ministry of Justice, have promoted the idea of complying with the European Convention. On the contrary, whenever sensitive issues were discussed by the Parliament and they did not wish to amend a law or adopt a new law, depending on the topic,

[20] See Renate Weber, 'Memorandumul Ministerului Afacerilor Externe: Raportul Konig-Jansson', in *Revista Română de Drepturile Omului*, no. 5, 1994.

references to the Convention or the Strasbourg jurisprudence did not help. Such was the case for homosexuality, and freedom of expression, particularly on defamation of state authorities. In October 1996 a law amending the Penal Code was adopted and in spite of a wide campaign to abolish these crimes by media and human rights groups and despite all relevant European Court case-law, the two crimes remained and their sanctions were increased. In 1998 a new draft law amending the Penal Code was issued by the Ministry of Justice. It dealt with a series of new economic crimes, demanded by the courts, but it also intended to abolish homosexuality as a crime and to abolish defamation in general. While approving this initiative the government did not agree to give up the penal sanction for defamation. The Parliament discussed all the other amendments in one day, but spent several more days debating the proposed decriminalization of homosexuality and defamation. In the end it preferred to vote against the entire package of amendments than to change anything regarding those two specific crimes.

At the time of writing (March 2000) an entire package of draft laws on a substantial reform of the legal system is waiting to be submitted by the government to the Parliament. It deals with the judiciary, the prison system (among other things introducing alternative sentencing and probation), the Penal Code and the Penal Procedure Code, etc. While the Ministry of Justice stresses the necessity to comply with international and European standards on human rights, and calls particularly upon the European Convention and its related case-law, the political elite is reluctant to embark upon such a substantial reform and to justify its adoption based on the necessity of complying with international requirements and Romania's commitments. However, two topics were excluded from the amendments to the Penal Code and were to be sent to Parliament separately, making it almost certain that they would not be adopted: the articles on homosexuality and on freedom of expression (defamation and outrage against state authorities by means of defamation).

D. LEADING HUMAN RIGHTS CASES DECIDED BY THE NATIONAL COURTS

For several years only a few articles and papers were published on the impact of the European Convention on the Romanian legal system. The result has been that the vast majority of Romanian Courts still perceive the Convention to be an exotic document whose relation to domestic legislation is almost non-existent.

So far only one Romanian Court has pronounced a decision based entirely on the provisions of the European Convention on Human Rights.[21] In its Decision 59/1995 the Military Appeal Court held that:

> In the light of these constitutional provisions, the understanding of the European Convention on Human Rights and of its Additional Protocols . . . as well as of other international treaties, conventions, and covenants is governed by the principles of the direct consequence [Article 11(2) of the Constitution] and of precedence [Article 20(2) of the Constitution], to which may be added—exclusively in the field of human rights and fundamental liberties—the principle of precedence of the *optimum* legal treatment, set forth in Article 60 of the Convention [. . .] In the light of the above elements, the Court considers that the fundamental rights sanctioned by Articles 6 and 13 of the above mentioned Convention . . . are part of the positive domestic law and shall be observed and complied with as such.

Other courts have been much more reluctant to enforce the European Convention, in spite of the fact that more and more lawyers base their cases on its provisions.

The only court which has regularly referred to the European Convention and stated its direct applicability is the Constitutional Court. The domestic case-law based on the Convention encompasses some twenty cases, some of them important for the Romanian legal system.

The first decision to invoke international treaties was Decision No. 6/1993, when the Constitutional Court ruled unconstitutional the provisions of Law No. 58/1992 which stipulated different taxes for three categories of persons (taxes were increased by 30 per cent for income resulting from multiple sources). The Court invoked the provisions of Article 26 of the International Covenant on Civil and Political Rights referring to non-discrimination, Article 2, para. 2 of the International Covenant on Economic, Social, and Cultural Rights, and Article 14 of the European Convention on Human Rights.

A few months later, the Constitutional Court declared the provisions of Article 75, para. 1 of the Labour Code unconstitutional by Decision No. 59/1994. According to these provisions, complaints filed against decisions to annul employment contracts, as well as litigation relating to the reintegration of managers in their former jobs, were to be solved by an administrative body ranking higher in the hierarchy or by a collective leadership body. The Court found violations of Article 16 of the Constitution on non-discrimination and of Article 21 on free access to justice, and based its decisions on the provisions of Article 6, para. 1 of the European Convention, on the ground that the administrative bodies that annulled the contract could not represent an independent impartial tribunal, as the Convention requires.

[21] See Doru Cosma, 'Dreptul la un proces echitabil și impartial' (The right to a fair trial), in *Revista Romana de Drepturile Omului*, no. 9, 1995

One of the most notable decisions was on the unconstitutionality of Article 200, para. 1 of the Penal Code that used to punish by imprisonment homosexual acts between consenting adults (Decision No. 81/1994). The Court invoked the provisions of Article 8 of the European Convention, making reference to the case-law of the Strasbourg European Court, more precisely to the *Dudgeon*, *Norris*, and *Modinos* cases. However, this decision held that Article 200(1) was unconstitutional only insofar as it applied to homosexual acts between adults who freely consent and which do not take place in public nor generate a public scandal. The Constitutional Court did not define 'public scandal' in its decision, nor did the Parliament do so in 1996 when it amended the Penal Code according to that decision, thus giving rise to various interpretations and even abuse.

In Decision 45 of 10 March 1998 the Constitutional Court referred to Article 3 of Protocol No. 7 in a case regarding the compatibility between the constitutional provision on state responsibility for penal judicial errors and Article 504 of the Penal Procedure Code which limited this responsibility to two situations only, namely when no crime had been committed and when it was not committed by the defendant. The Court decided that Article 504 is constitutional only insofar as it does not limit state responsibility to those two cases.

In a series of decisions between 1994 and 1998, the Constitutional Court held that Article 149(3) of the Penal Procedure Code was unconstitutional. Article 149(3) provided for the possibility of holding a defendant in detention for the entire period of the trial without reviewing this detention. Since the Constitution says that a person may be held in custody for a maximum of thirty days, without defining the starting point for that period (during the investigation period or during the trial) the Constitutional Court ruled that even during the trial the judge must review the defendant's status every thirty days.

In order to understand the importance of the above decisions we must note two Articles of the Constitution which determine their place within the Romanian legal system.

Article 144 says:

The Constitutional Court shall have the following powers:
a) to adjudicate on the constitutionality of laws, before promulgation . . .
b) [. . .]
c) to decide on exceptions brought to the Courts of laws as to the unconstitutionality of laws and orders [. . .]

Article 145 reads as follows:

(1) In cases of unconstitutionality, in accordance with Article 144 paragraphs (a) and (b), the laws or orders shall be returned for reconsideration. If the law is passed again in the same formulation by a majority of at least two-thirds of the members

of each Chamber, the objection of unconstitutionality shall be removed and promulgation thereof shall be binding.

(2) Decisions of the Constitutional Court shall be binding and effective only for the future. They shall be published in the Official Gazette of Romania.

For several years some courts applied the findings and decisions of the Constitutional Court, while others ignored them, not necessarily as a desire to disobey them but rather due to their lack of information and expertise. However, more recently a real dispute has started between the Constitutional Court and the Supreme Court of Justice. In several cases, the Supreme Court of Justice has stated that the decisions of the Constitutional Court are not legally binding:

. . . the constitutional provisions do not directly address the judiciary organs which apply the ordinary law but only through the legislative body which has to comply with the Constitution and amend the ordinary laws.

The decisions of the Constitutional Court have the same status. They represent a reproach to the legislative body and this legislative body must draw its conclusions from this reproach, amending those provisions of ordinary laws that were criticized by the decisions of the Constitutional Court . . .

If we apply another rationale it means that the law enforcement judiciary organs, not having a concrete provision in the ordinary law, should refer to the constitutional text in order to reject the provisions criticized by the decisions of the Constitutional Court, which is inadmissible.

The judiciary organs enforce the ordinary law that applies and not directly the Constitution, the legislative body having the obligation to comply with the Constitution and the constitutional principles by amending the ordinary law in order to observe the Constitution (Supreme Court of Justice, Decision 1613 of 7 May 1999).

The judges who have to decide a case as a first-level court, on appeal or recourse, may not however periodically review during the trial, each thirty days, the pre-trial detention of the defendant, directly enforcing Article 25(4) of the Romanian Constitution, as has been stated by several decisions of the Constitutional Court (such as Decision No. 546 of 4 December 1997) or as it results from the motivation of other decisions of the same Court.

By doing so, they would in practice no longer be subject only to the penal procedure provisions established by law but to some *ad hoc* procedural norms set up by the Constitutional Court by means of interpretation of Article 23(4) of the Constitution which set forth the principle that the pre-trial detention of a defendant may not be longer than thirty days.

Not obeying the norms of the Penal Procedure Code, which provide for the maintaining of the pre-trial detention of the defendant, the judges wold infringe Article 123(2) of the Constitution according to which they are independent and subject only to the law.

At the same time, applying directly the provisions of the Constitution, they would make justice in the name of other normative provisions than those provided by the law, thus violating Article 123(1) of the Constitution according to which justice shall be rendered in the name of the law (Supreme Court of Justice, Decision 2531 of 17 June 1999).

According to the Romanian legal system the decisions of the Supreme Court of Justice are not binding on other courts. However, being the highest authority in the country it is very likely that many such cases will end up before it. Therefore the Romanian courts are currently split: some apply the decisions of the Constitutional Court, particularly on review of pre-trial detention by the courts each thirty days, while others do not. The result is that more than 1,000 defendants awaiting trial are still in prison (in those cases where the courts did not comply with the Constitutional Court requirement) while others have been released because the courts applied the Constitutional Court decisions. The Bucharest Court of Appeal recently issued a paper on this topic, addressed to the judges in Bucharest, clearly stating that it considers the decisions of the Constitutional Court not to be legally binding. Apart from the fact that that document in itself runs against the Constitution for the very reason that it invokes, the fact remains that for the first time the powers and competence of the Constitutional Court are being challenged.

Given that the highest court in the country holds that the Constitution is not directly enforceable, one may reconsider the status of the international treaties on human rights, the European Convention included, as well as their precedence over some constitutional provisions which, according to the Supreme Court of Justice, may not be taken into account by the courts.

The draft law amending the Penal Procedure Code, once adopted, will solve the issue of pre-trial detention but not the deeper conflict between the two courts and certainly not the status of the Constitution and international treaties on human rights.

E. CASES BROUGHT BEFORE THE EUROPEAN COMMISSION AND COURT OF HUMAN RIGHTS

No inter-state case has yet been brought against Romania. When the European Convention was ratified the Parliament also ratified the right of individual petition and a few dozen individual complaints have been registered in Strasbourg, some of them on violations which occurred before the European Convention entered into force in Romania. Many petitions relate to the right to property or access to justice. At the time of writing the European Court of Human Rights has ruled on six cases against Romania, each time finding the country to be in violation with one or several Articles of the Convention.

1. *Case of* Vasilescu v Romania *(22 May 1998)*

The applicant complained that in 1966 the militia had unlawfully seized 327 gold coins. After the change of the regime she tried to get them back and she was successful at all court levels. However, in 1994 the General Prosecutor applied, in an extraordinary procedure provided for by domestic legislation, to the Supreme Court of Justice. This appeal was allowed, and the Supreme Court of Justice ruled that according to Article 275 of the Penal Procedure Code the courts had no jurisdiction over an act issued by a prosecutor, as in the applicant's case, and that sole jurisdiction was in the hands of the local prosecutor's office.

Analysing the merits of the complaint, the European Court of Human Rights held that:

the Procurator-General's department . . . consists of officials who carry out all their duties under the authority of the Procurator-General. The Minister of Justice supervises all the members of the Procurator-General's department including the Procurator-General.

Even where, as in the instant case, State Counsel for a county exercises powers of a judicial nature, he acts as a member of the Procurator-General's department subordinated first to the Procurator-General and then to the Ministry of Justice.

The Court reiterates that only an institution that has full jurisdiction and satisfies a number of requirements, such as independence of the executive and also the parties, merits the description 'tribunal' within the meaning of Article 6(1) [of the Convention].

There has therefore been a violation of Article 6(1).

The Court also found that there had been a violation of Article 1 of Protocol No. 1, that Article 13 was absorbed by Article 6(1), and did not consider it necessary to examine the case under Article 8. The Court held the Romanian state liable to pay the applicant 60,000 French francs as pecuniary damages, 30,000 French francs as non-pecuniary damages, and 5,185 French francs in respect of costs and expenses.

2. *Case of* Petra v Romania *(23 September 1998)*

In January 1994 the applicant, who had been convicted of a crime and was detained in prison, wanted to file a complaint with the Commission on the grounds of his unfair trial. During his correspondence with the Commission it turned out that he was unable to mail any letter directly to the Commission or to his wife. Each of his letters was taken by prison staff and afterwards put in an envelope and sent by them. The Court held that:

Mr Petra did not enjoy the minimum degree of protection to which citizens are entitled under the rule of law in a democratic society. The Court therefore concludes that the interference complained of was not in accordance with the law and that there has been a violation of Article 8.

The Romanian state was obliged to pay to the applicant 10,000 French francs in respect of non-pecuniary damages.

3. *Case of* Dalban v Romania *(23 September 1999)*

The applicant was a journalist in a small town in Romania and in a series of articles he wrote about alleged frauds at a local state-owned company as well as about the behaviour of a local Senator. Brought to justice and charged with calumny, he was convicted and sentenced to three months' imprisonment and obliged to pay pecuniary damages to the plaintiffs.

Analysing the merits of the case, the Court stated:

there is no proof that the description of the events given in the articles was totally untrue and was designed to fuel a defamation campaign against GS and Senator RT Mr Dalban did not write about aspects of RT's private life, but about his behavior and attitudes in his capacity as an elected representative of the people.

The Court decided that there had been a violation of Article 10 of the Convention. The Romanian state was obliged to pay 20,000 French francs in respect of non-pecuniary damages.

4. *Case of* Brumarescu v Romania *(28 October 1999)*

The case concerned one of the most hotly debated issues in Romania, the restitution of real estate nationalized or illegally seized during the Communist regime. In 1993 Mr Brumarescu successfully asked the court to restore his right to property. After a couple of years the Procurator-General lodged an application with the Supreme Court of Justice which quashed the first judgment and dismissed the applicant's claim. The European Court found a violation of Article 6(1) for the following reasons:

In the present case the Court notes that at the material time the Procurator-General of Romania, who was not a party to the proceedings, had power under Article 330 of the Code of Civil Procedure to apply for a final judgment to be quashed. The Court notes that the exercise of that power by the Procurator-General was not subject to any time-limit, so that judgments were liable to challenge indefinitely.

The Court observes that, by allowing the application lodged under that power, the Supreme Court of Justice set at naught an entire judicial process which had ended in, to use the Supreme Court of Justice's words, a judicial decision that was 'irreversible' and thus *res judicata*, and which had moreover been executed.

In applying the provisions of Article 330 in that manner, the Supreme Court of Justice infringed the principle of legal certainty [. . .]

The Court notes that the ratio of the judgment of 1 March 1995 was that the courts had no jurisdiction whatsoever to decide civil disputes such as the action for recovery of possession in the instant case. It considers that such exclusion is in itself contrary to the right of access to a tribunal guaranteed by Article 6(1) of the Convention.

The Court also decided that there was an ongoing violation of Article 1 of Protocol No. 1 to the Convention. In its decision of 23 January 2001 on just satisfaction the Court held unanimously that Romania was to return to the applicant, within six months, the house in issue and the land on which it was situated, except for the flat and the corresponding part of the land already returned. It further held that, failing such restitution, Romania was to pay the applicant 136,205 United States dollars (USD) for pecuniary damage. It also awarded the applicant USD 15,000 for non-pecuniary damage and USD 2,450, less 3,900 French francs received by way of legal aid, for legal costs and expenses. Those sums were to be converted into Romania lei at the rate applicable on the date of settlement. (The Romanian Prime Minister, Adrian Nastase, was on his first official visit to the European Union when this decision came out. Asked for comments during a press conference, he nervously made public his surprise that the European Court had acted as a real estate agent.)

5. Case of Ignaccolo-Zenide v Romania *(25 January 2000)*

The applicant complained of a violation of Article 8, due to the fact that her right to family life was infringed by the Romanian authorities who did not enforce a Court decision placing her two daughters under her custody. The European Court concluded that there had been a violation and obliged the state to pay 100,000 French francs in respect of non-pecuniary damages and 86,000 French francs in respect of costs and expenses.

6. Case of Rotaur v Romania *(4 May 2000)*

In 1992 Rotaru, who in 1948 had been sentenced to a year's imprisonment for having expressed criticism of the Communist regime established in 1946, brought an action in which he sought to be granted the rights that Decree no. 118 of 1990 afforded persons who had been persecuted by the Communist regime. In the proceedings which followed the Ministry of the Interior submitted to the court a letter sent to it on 19 December 1990 by the Romanian Intelligence Service, which contained, among other things, information about the applicant's political activities between 1946 and 1948. According to the same letter, Mr Rotaru had been a member of the Christian Students' Association, an extreme right-wing 'legionnaire' movement, in 1937. Mr Rotaru considered that the information was false and defamatory, in particular the allegation that he had been a member of the legionnaire movement, and brought proceedings against the Romanian Intelligence Service, claiming compensation for the non-pecuniary damage. He asked for amendment or destruction of the file containing the untrue information. The claim was dismissed by the Bârlad Court of First Instance in a judgment that was upheld by the Bucharest Court of Appeal on 15 December 1994. Both courts held that they had no power to order amendment or destruction of the information and that the RIS had only been a depositary. In a letter of 6 July 1997 the Director of the Romanian Intelligence Service informed the Ministry of Justice that after further checks in their registers it appeared that the information about being a member of the 'legionnaire' movement referred not to the applicant but to another person of the same name. In the light of that letter the applicant sought review of the Court of Appeal's judgment of 15 December 1994 and claimed damages. In a decision of 25 November 1997 the Bucharest Court of Appeal quashed the judgment of 15 December 1994 and declared the information about the applicant's past membership of the 'legionnaire' movement null and void. It did not rule on the claim for damages. The European Court concluded that the applicant could claim to be a 'victim' for the purposes of Article 34 of the Convention. On Article 8 of the Convention the Court noted that the RIS's letter of 19 December 1990 contained various pieces of information about the applicant's life, in particular his studies, his political activities, and his criminal record, some of which had been gathered more than fifty years earlier. In the Court's opinion, such information, when systematically collected and stored in a file held by agents of the State, fell within the scope of 'private life' for the purposes of Article 8 § 1 of the Convention. The Court considered that both the storing of that information and the use of it, which were coupled with a refusal to allow the applicant an opportunity to refute it, had amounted to interference with his right to respect for family life as guaranteed by Article 8 § 1. If it was not to contravene Article 8, such interference had to have been 'in accordance with the law', pursue a legitimate aim under paragraph 2, and, furthermore, be necessary in a democratic society in order to achieve that aim. In that connection, the Court noted that in its judgment of 25 November 1997 the Bucharest Court of Appeal had confirmed that it was lawful for the RIS to hold the information as depositary of the archives of the former security services. That being so, the Court could conclude that the storing of information about the applicant's private life had had a basis in Romanian law. As regards the requirement of foreseeability, the Court noted that no provision of domestic law laid down any limits on the exercise of those powers. Thus, for instance, domestic law did not define the kind of information that could be recorded, the categories of people against whom surveillance measures such as gathering and keeping information could be taken, the circumstances in which such measures could be taken, or the procedure to be followed.

Similarly, the Law did not lay down limits on the age of information held or the length of time for which it could be kept. Section 45 empowered the RIS to take over for storage and use the archives that had belonged to the former intelligence services operating on Romanian territory and allowed inspection of RIS documents with the Director's consent. The Court noted that the section contained no explicit, detailed provision concerning the persons authorized to consult the files, the nature of the files, the procedure to be followed, or the use that could be made of the information thus obtained. It also noted that although section 2 of the Law empowered the relevant authorities to permit interferences necessary to prevent and counteract threats to national security, the ground allowing such interferences was not laid down with sufficient precision. The European Court also noted that the Romanian system for gathering and archiving information did not provide any safeguards, no supervision procedure being provided by Law no. 14/1992, either while the measure ordered was in force or afterwards. The Court considered that domestic law did not indicate with reasonable clarity the scope and manner of exercise of the relevant discretion conferred on the public authorities and concluded that the holding and use by the RIS of information on the applicant's private life had not been 'in accordance with the law', a fact that sufficed to constitute a violation of Article 8. The Court also concluded that the applicant had been the victim of a violation of Article 13. On Article 6 of the Convention the Court noted that the applicant's claim for compensation for non-pecuniary damages and costs was a civil one within the meaning of Article 6 § 1, and the Bucharest Court of Appeal had had jurisdiction to deal with it. The Court accordingly considered that the Court of Appeal's failure to consider the claim had infringed the applicant's right to a fair hearing within the meaning of Article 6 § 1. On Article 41 of the Convention, the Court considered that the events in question had entailed serious interference with mr Rotaru's rights and that the sum of FRF 50,000 would afford fair redress for the non-pecuniary damage sustained.

F. REMEDIAL ACTION TAKEN BY THE GOVERNMENT IN RESPONSE TO BEING HELD IN VIOLATION OF THE CONVENTION

So far only six cases against Romania have been decided by the Court; in each one Romania was held to be in violation of one or several Articles of the Convention. The remedies decided by the Court were different in each case.

Financial remedies. In *Vasilescu v Romania*, *Petra v Romania*, and *Dalban v Romania* the financial compensation decided by the Court have been paid by the Romanian state to the victims. In the case of *Ignaccolo-Zenide* Romania paid the financial compensation. In *Brumarescu* the real estate has not been returned and neither has compensation been paid.

Legislative remedies. The case of *Vasilescu* was based on the provision that a person could not complain to a court against a decision issued by a prosecutor. The current draft law amending the Penal Procedure Code contains a specific provision making such complaints possible. If adopted by the Parliament, the decision will be entirely complied with.

In the case of *Petra*, regarding the right to privacy of inmates in relation with their correspondence, the Minister of Justice issued an order immediately after the complaint was admitted by the Commission, and before it was decided by the Court. A draft Law on the Execution of Sentences, issued in 2000, specifically mentions this right, but there is very small chance of the draft being adopted by Parliament in the near future.

In the case of *Brumarescu*, a new law on the restitution of real property was adopted by the Parliament, although its implementation has raised many internal problems which are unlikely to be solved soon.

However, if one wants to evaluate the broader impact of these decisions upon the rule of law in Romania then one faces difficulties in identifying strategies for their dissemination. While the government has tried to comply as far as possible with the European Court's decisions, neither the Parliament nor the media seem to know of these cases or to understand their significance. As for the judges there are no professional training discussions of these decisions addressing the need to know, understand, and comply with them in other cases. Therefore, unless new laws are adopted, similar violations may occur in the future.

G. ASSESSMENT AND PROSPECTS

Slowly but surely the European Convention for Human Rights and the Commission and Court case-law seem to be finding their way into Romanian public life. Acknowledged as a need more by the Romanian public rather than by the legal and political elite, compliance with European standards on human rights protection will continue to be a central issue of public discussion in the years to come. However, a much more consistent effort and a more coherent approach will be necessary to have a systemic influence on the Romanian legal system.

First, Romanian lawyers should learn and write more about the Convention and its related case-law. Although various training courses have been organized over the years there is an obvious reluctance to invoke the Convention in the Romanian courts, and for the courts to base decisions on the interpretation provided by the European Court of Human Rights. It is significant that with the exception of the quarterly *Romanian Review for Human Rights* (*Revista Română de Drepturile Omului*) no legal review has embarked upon a systematic presentation of the Convention and analysis of its impact. The best known Romanian monthly legal journal *The Law* (*Dreptul*) very seldom publishes articles on human rights and the Convention, although its impact is considerable within the legal community.

Secondly, law faculties all over the country should have special courses on human rights and the European Convention. Unfortunately, this subject is taught only in a few faculties (whether public or private) sometimes as an optional subject, and generally in the last semester of the final year, thus preventing any earlier discussion on the compatibility of Romanian legal provisions with the European Convention during the study of other subjects (penal law, penal procedure law, administrative law, civil procedure law, etc.) Of course, one must admit that not enough professors in the country have the necessary expertise and understanding of the field to teach it. However, the persistence of this situation six years after the ratification of the Convention says much about the lack of interest on the part of the professors to specialize in this particular subject. It is also significant for the understanding of how human rights in general are perceived. This is even more perplexing given that for several years teams of students from Romanian faculties have achieved prizes in international human rights competitions.

In a sense Romania has been in a vicious circle: the subject is not considered sufficiently interesting to be taught to lawyers and law students because it is seldom discussed in the legal literature and there are few cases in the courts; on the other hand, as long as new generations of lawyers are not taught in this specialized field, there will be neither publications nor cases based on the Convention. The circle is already broken, but the pace of the dissemination is slow and the process will be long.

Thirdly, the media could play a role in making the Convention and its interpretation by the Court more visible. Unfortunately the Romanian media, or its vast majority, focus more on the political aspects of Romanian society, and with so many unsolved legal problems the journalists pay less attention to human rights aspects. Of course there are also exceptions, particularly on issues involving the freedom of the press, access to information, homosexuality, or national security. But the media do not always present the debates from a general human rights perspective; for example, it is not freedom of expression that is generally considered to be at stake, but merely the freedom of the press (whose importance is beyond any doubt); similarly, access to information is not perceived as a right belonging to every person, but simply as a right which the media should enjoy. On other human rights topics considered to be more sensitive, such as homosexuality, discrimination, freedom of religion, and legislation on national security, the debate within the media is even tougher. Obviously, the opinions expressed are varied, and this plurality of opinions is valuable in itself. What is needed is a presentation of the opinions expressed by the European Court over the years, proving that, from this point of view, Romania is not in a unique position and that such debates have taken place in other European countries as well. This would support public awareness of belonging to an international community where real problems are shared and discussed and similar solutions can be found and adopted.

In this respect media could play an important role by publishing decisions of the European Court of Human Rights against Romania, focusing on the changes which the Romanian government, Parliament, and judiciary must undertake.

Another social actor who should play a greater role is the NGO sector, particularly human rights associations. Over the years their involvement in human rights protection and monitoring has been of the utmost importance and their visibility has increased in recent years.

A public policy which took into account all these actors could accelerate the pace of change of Romanian society in relation to the European Convention. So far, no government and no political force has seemed interested in developing such a policy, and it seems likely that the process will take longer than was initially expected.

28

Russia

MAXIM FERSCHTMAN

A. INTRODUCTION

An examination of the impact of the European Convention on Human Rights[1] within the legal order of Russia two years after ratification inevitably has an exploratory character, leading to tentative suggestions rather than decisive conclusions. Prior to ratification, many questions had been raised about both its consequences for Russia and the future role and status of the Convention itself. Two viewpoints need to be considered with regard to this. On one hand, it was suggested that if Russia became a party to the Convention, this would mean that the legal standards developed by the European Commission and Court of Human Rights would have to be watered down.[2] Another view is that although Russia may not be fully ready to become a party to the Convention, it would do better to join anyway and use the Convention to improve its system of human rights protection.

Several arguments have been put forward in support of both views. A practical process-oriented consideration concerned Russia's size and human rights record. With 150 million inhabitants and a very weak human rights record, individual access to Strasbourg could prompt an enormous flood of complaints which would impair the Court's ability to function.[3] From a historical–contextual perspective, critics have suggested that Russia's legal culture as a former front-runner of Communist ideology is too divergent from what the Convention envisages for the two to be practically compatible.

The core of Convention ideology is to place the individual in a central position, obliging the state to protect the individual from any interference with his life, notably by the state. Russian legal culture, as it developed historically, has considered the individual as a subject of a larger community or collective.

[1] Hereinafter 'the Convention'.

[2] The Permanent Court of Human Rights, created with the adoption of Protocol 11 to the Convention, had its first session on 12 November 1998 (hereinafter 'the Court').

[3] See among others on this issue, M. Janis, 'Russia and the "Legality" of Strasbourg Law' in *European Journal of International Law*, vol. 8, No. 1, 1997, pp. 95–96.

The individual's relation to the state was considered in terms of reciprocity. In order to receive a service or a good, including basic human rights, the individual had to make a positive contribution to the state. Thus, Russia could be expected to claim a broader margin of appreciation as to the extent to which certain rights are applicable in Russia. However, this argument is inappropriate as far as the Convention is concerned. Although the Convention is acknowledged to be a dynamic instrument which takes into account the specific situation of each state, and changes to new attitudes, the state itself cannot claim a position which would contradict the spirit and the core principles of the Convention.

If the Court continues to apply the standards already developed in the Convention case-law, there is no reason to fear the 'watering down' of the those standards. Most state representatives, defending their case in Court, will argue that their actions have not constituted a violation of the Convention or that the interference was justified. If one examines issues such as the fight against crime and terrorism, and the protection of national and other public interests, one can identify clear Convention case-law that is considered to be part of the conventional law.[4] Even in those cases where there is a substantive margin of appreciation for the state, certain constraints defined in the case-law have to be respected. It will be up to Court to maintain these standards in its future work. Russia, like all the other States Parties, will have to fulfil the legal obligations that follow from the Court's judgments.

Some authors raise objections at this point. It is argued that the result of Russia's signing the Convention will be to increase the likelihood that 'European human rights law will both be disobeyed and be seen to be flouted'.[5] To support this, one could point to shortcomings in Russia in the areas of the rule of law and (experience in) human rights protection on the national level and the likely political reluctance on the part of the Council of Europe to compel Russia, when necessary, to comply with the Court's judgments.[6]

With these issues in mind, this chapter first examines the specifics of Russia's accession to the Council of Europe. Subsequently, we will look at areas of Russian legislation which have been identified as problematic from the point of view of the Convention. This chapter, for reasons of space, is limited to examining the scope of the rights protected under Articles 5 and 6 of the Convention and Article 2 of Protocol No. 4, because the level of protec-

[4] See eg *Brogan and Others*, 29.11.1988, A145–B.

[5] See Janis, p. 98.

[6] See in this respect the Committee of Ministers' monitoring, in accordance with Article 46(2) of the Convention, of the execution of the Court's judgment against Turkey in the case of *Socialist Party and Others v Turkey*, and in the *Akdivar*, *Çetin, Aksoy, Aydin* and *Mentes* cases and in the *Loizidou* case.

tion of these rights seems to show most acute divergence between Russian legal practice and the Convention.

On 28 February 1996 Russia became a member state of the Council of Europe. On that day Russia committed itself to maintaining a pluralistic and democratic political system, respecting the rule of law, and ensuring the enjoyment by all persons within their jurisdiction of human rights and fundamental freedoms.[7] Moreover, Russia's membership of the Council of Europe has been accepted under conditions set out in *Opinion 193(96)* by the Council of Europe Parliamentary Assembly which were formulated prior to accession.[8]

When examining Russia's accession to the Council of Europe it is necessary to bear in mind a number of domestic factors which played an important role at the time. Russia had experienced an unprecedented rise in its crime rate following the breakdown of Communist rule. This posed a major obstacle to the establishment of a stable legal system. An example of how solutions to the rising crime problem were pursued can be seen in the adoption of Presidential Decree 1226 of 14 June 1994, which provided for the possibility of detention of suspects for thirty days without having to bring them before a judge. This Decree contradicted the new 1993 Constitution and the Code of Criminal Procedure, but was enforced anyway.[9]

The report submitted in 1994 by the Council of Europe's Eminent Experts concluded that the Russian legal order did not adequately conform to the Council of Europe's standards. The Report stated that despite positive steps taken, the Russian legal system and practice still fell short of evolving a rule of law and human rights and a pluralistic democracy.[10]

Another issue was the war in Chechnya which started in 1994 and caused the Parliamentary Assembly to suspend Russia's application for membership. The harsh attitude of the Parliamentary Assembly was, however, quickly reversed after Russia's reassurance that it intended to settle the dispute in a

[7] Article 3 of the Statute of the Council of Europe, London, 5.5.1949. Article 4 of the Statute provides that a state which is deemed able and willing to fulfil the provisions of Article 3 of the Statute may be invited to become a member of the Council of Europe. Signing the Convention is obviously an expression of willingness to fulfil the obligation of protecting human rights. On problems encountered by the new member states of the Council of Europe in view of their accession see H. Klebes and D. Chatzivassiliou, 'Problèmes d'ordre constitutionnel dans le processus d'adhésion d'etats de l'Europe centrale et orientale au Conseil de l'Europe' *Revue universelle des droits de l'homme,* vol. 8, 1996, pp. 269–286.

[8] Adopted on 25 January 1996.

[9] The Supreme Court had ruled, however, that access to the judge if demanded by the detainee should be possible; the suspects would not be brought automatically before a judge, though. The decree was annulled on 1 July 1997.

[10] 'Conclusions of the Report on the Conformity of the Legal Order of the Russian Federation with Council of Europe Standards', p. 195.

peaceful manner.[11] Thus, a political commitment was established, but no more than that.

When the Eminent Experts Report came out, it was clear to many, despite Russia's official disagreement with the conclusions of the Report, that Russia would not be ready to accede to the Council of Europe in the short term. In the end, some argue it was the political expediency of letting Russia join the organization which served as the decisive factor in favour of prompt admission.[12] The argument presented to those who opposed Russia's accession was that prospective and new member states which 'have come from far' as far as Council of Europe standards are concerned should be accepted sooner than later, while they are still in the period of transition to democracy and the rule of law.

The above-mentioned Opinion was voted upon in the Parliamentary Assembly which approved Russia's accession to the Council of Europe on the terms specified in the Opinion.[13]

As regards the Convention, the Parliamentary Assembly noted that:

> the Russian Federation shares fully its understanding and interpretation of commitments entered into [. . .] and intends to sign the European Convention on Human Rights at the moment of accession; to ratify the Convention and Protocols Nos. 1, 2, 4, 7, and 11 within a year; to recognize, pending the entry into force of Protocol No. 11, the right of individual application to the European Commission and the compulsory jurisdiction of the European Court (Articles 25 and 46 of the Convention); and to sign within one year and ratify within three years from the time of accession Protocol No. 6 to the European Convention on Human Rights on the abolition of the death penalty in time of peace, and to put into place a moratorium on executions with effect from the day of accession.

The reason for formulating these conditions in such a way is that despite the political necessity to let Russia join the organization, most signs showed that this was in fact not yet possible with the organization's objectives. Therefore, as a sort of guarantee for Russia to proceed in the right direction, the Parliamentary Assembly put forward what can be seen as exceedingly high demands for continued membership. For instance, the condition calling for Russia to ratify the Convention within one year after its signature can be seen as excessively stringent considering that Estonia, a considerably smaller and less troubled country, was granted three years to adapt its legislation before it was ready to ratify the Convention.[14]

[11] Parliamentary Assembly Resolution 1065 (1995), *HRLJ*, vol. 17, nos. 3–6, pp. 196–197.

[12] See Janis, p. 98.

[13] See 'Council of Europe, Strasbourg: Accession of Russia, Parliamentary Assembly: Opinion No. 193 and Report by Ernst Muehleman', *Human Rights Law Journal*, vol. 17, Nos. 3–6, pp. 185–187.

[14] See *Compatibility of Estonian Law with the requirements of the European Convention on Human Rights*, Council of Europe, Directorate of Human Rights, December 1996, H (96) 20.

It was not clear why Russia was expected to ratify the Convention at such short notice. One should take into consideration that most Russian judges, who should play a central role in applying the Convention, did not have a proper opportunity to familiarize themselves with its contents and application. On the other hand, any party to the Convention must learn the ways of Convention by direct application through a continuing learning process.

Despite the counter-arguments, the Opinion of the Parliamentary Assembly was upheld by the Committee of Ministers on 14 February 1996, which invited Russia to join the organization. One should bear in mind the difference between the political demands[15] which the Parliamentary Assembly presented to Russia as a condition for its accession to the Council of Europe and the legal consequences of the Convention after its ratification.[16]

B. THE STATUS OF THE CONVENTION IN RUSSIAN LAW

In the new Russian Constitution[17] of 1993 international law has gained formal recognition in the Russian legal system. The position of international treaties in the legal order is regulated by the Law on International Treaties of 1995.

1. The Constitution

The Constitution contains the following provisions that are relevant with respect to the application of the Convention.

Article 15(4)

The commonly recognised principles and norms of international law and treaties of the Russian Federation shall be a component part of its legal system. If an international treaty of the Russian Federation stipulates other rules than those stipulated by the law, the rules of the international treaty shall apply.

[15] Many Russian officials had held that these conditions were merely recommendations for Russia from the Council of Europe. A number of Russian lawyers have written on this issue: I. Petrukhin in a comment on the Russian ratification of the Convention, *Rossiiskaia Iustitsia*, 7/98, p. 4, acknowledges that Russia has taken on concrete legal obligations to the organization which it has to fulfil.

[16] The mentioned political commitments are subject to two monitoring procedures. One procedure is exercised by the Parliamentary Assembly under order, and is public, focusing on several issues each time or a separate country. The other procedure is the confidential Committee of Ministers' monitoring, which applies to all member states, each time on one specific topic. See Council of Europe documents, Monitor/Inf (96) & (97))

[17] The Russian Constitution was adopted by a referendum on 12 December 1993 and entered into force on 25 December 1994.

Specifically concerning human rights and international law, Article 17(1) of the Constitution provides:

> The basic rights and liberties in conformity with the commonly recognised principles and norms of the international law shall be recognised and guaranteed in the Russian Federation and under this Constitution.

With regard to the adoption and ratification of treaties the Constitutional Court can be asked for an opinion as to the conformity of the respective treaty with the Constitution. In cases of non-conformity, Article 125(6) of the Constitution provides:

> Acts and their provisions deemed unconstitutional shall lose their force; international treaties of the Russian Federation may not be enforced and applied if they violate the Constitution.

At first glance it appears that the Convention is directly applicable on Russian territory upon its entry into force for Russia and that individuals can invoke its provisions directly in domestic court proceedings. The Convention has priority over ordinary laws as long as it does not contradict the Constitution. Still, the status of international treaties remains ambiguous. A closer look at the Russian legislation shows the following differentiation at various levels of normative acts.

The first is the Constitution which, as we have seen, appears to rank above all other legislation including international treaties. Russian legal scholars argue that when a treaty contradicts the Constitution the latter takes precedence.[18] However, this is sometimes interpreted in a peculiar way. Petrukhin offers the example of the 'presumption of innocence' in the Convention, arguing that it provides a lower level of protection than the Russian Constitution and would therefore be in contradiction with it. It is, however, generally accepted that international human rights treaties provide a minimum level of protection and that states can always choose to elevate the level of protection of the same right. The state's international obligation is not to fall below the level foreseen in the treaty.[19]

On a lower legislative level follow the constitutional federal laws. These laws have a 'privileged' status because they regulate issues directly referred to by the Constitution. They form, as it were, a practical elaboration of certain constitutional issues. The Constitutional Federal Law on the Constitutional Court is an example, which can be adopted and amended only by a two-thirds parliamentary majority.

[18] See Petrukhin, p. 4 and the compatibility exercise described below, carried out by the Council of Europe Directorate of Human Rights. Doc H (98) 7.

[19] See, among others, van Dijk and van Hoof.

On the next level are regular federal laws which are adopted by a simple majority. Article 15(b) of the Law on International Treaties of 1995 provides that international treaties which relate human rights and freedom are subject to ratification. Some Russian authors argue that, when formally considering the type of parliamentary ratification procedure (simple majority) international treaties seem to have a place inbetween the constitutional federal and the federal laws.[20] No real solution seems to exist to the problem which would arise if the Constitution included a provision which conflicted with an international treaty and thus took precedence over it, creating a violation of Russia's obligations under international law.

2. *Addressing international supervisory bodies*

Article 46(3) of the Constitution provides that, in conformity with the international treaties of the Russian Federation, everyone shall have the right to apply to inter-state organs concerned with the protection of human rights and liberties when all the means of legal protection available within the state have been exhausted. Russia recognized the right of individual petition under the Convention when it ratified the Convention.[21] In a judgment of 2 June 1996 the Constitutional Court decided that in accordance with Article 46(3) of the Constitution decisions of inter-state supervision bodies should be considered as new circumstances arising after a final domestic decision and as a ground for reopening the domestic proceedings.[22]

3. *Convention ratification and reservations*

The domestic ratification of the Convention took place on 30 March 1998 upon the entry into force of the law on the ratification of the Convention.[23] After a relatively quick passage through Parliament, the Duma[24] adopted the ratification law on 20 February 1998 and the Council of the Federation[25] did the same on 13 March 1998.[26] On 5 May 1998 Russia's then Minister of Foreign Affairs, Mr Primakov, officially deposited the instruments of

[20] See the compatibility exercise below.

[21] See *HRLJ*, vol. 17, Nos. 3–6, and ETS Nos. 5, 46, 117.

[22] Constitutional Court *Kulnev* decision of 4–P, 2.2.1996. See also for a more detailed comment as regards the possibility of reopening judicial proceedings after the Court's judgments, M. Ferschtman, 'Reopening of judicial procedures in Russia: the way to implement the future decisions of the Convention supervisory organs?' *in The Execution of Strasbourg and Geneva Human Rights Decisions in the National Legal Order*, ISBN 9041111522, pp. 123–135.

[23] A law enters into force when the President signs it.

[24] Directly elected First Chamber of the Russian Parliament.

[25] This chamber consists of representatives of the 89 'Subjects of the Federation', territorial administrative units.

[26] Law No. 54–f3. Published in *Rossiiskaia Gazeta* on 07.04.1998

ratification at the Council of Europe, by which means the Convention legally entered into force in respect of Russia.

The ratification document states that the Convention is only applicable to alleged violations which arose after its entry into force. Some Russian legal scholars have argued that this provision means that the actual act of violation must have taken place after the entry into force of the Convention for Russia, and so does not include judicial decisions on cases brought by individuals contesting actions which may have taken place before 5 May 1998.[27] A counter-argument supposes that a judicial decision taken by a national court upholding a Convention violation which took place prior to the entry into force of the Convention can justifiably be petitioned against before the Court. Moreover, there is considerable Convention case-law which establishes that where a domestic court decision was made subsequent to the entry into force of the Convention in the respondent state, the Commission (and the Court) are competent to examine the proceedings leading up to that decision, as the proceedings before a court are embodied in its final decision which thus incorporates any defect by which they may have been affected.[28]

In its ratification document Russia makes a number of reservations, indicating that several provisions of Russian legislation are to be exempted from the application of the Convention. The articles concerned, most of which concern arrest and detention, stem from the Code of Criminal Procedure[29] of 27 October 1960, the Disciplinary Regulations of the Armed Forces of the Russian Federation, and the Law On the Status of Servicemen. These reservations are of a temporary nature and are to stay in force only until new legislation is adopted to replace the old provisions.

When inviting Russia to become a member of the Council of Europe, the Parliamentary Assembly also imposed the condition of adopting a new code of criminal procedure. Despite repeated efforts to accomplish this, the Parliament's continuing lack of agreement on its contents has delayed adoption. The draft passed its first reading in the Duma on 6 June 1997, after which it was to be sent to parliamentary commissions for further elaboration. These commissions are yet to come to an agreement.

In its Information Report on 'Honouring of Obligations and Commitments by the Russian Federation',[30] the Monitoring Committee of the Parliamentary noted that the new CCP had still not been adopted, and that

[27] See I. Petrukhin in a comment to Russia's ratification law of the Convention, in *Rossiiskaia Iustitsia*, 7/98. p. 4.

[28] See No. 18507/91, Dec. 12.05.1994 and No. 11306/84, Dec. 16.10.86, DR 50 p. 162, No. 15963/90 19.05.1994.

[29] Hereinafter 'CCP'.

[30] Parliamentary Assembly Report, Doc. 8127, 2 June 1998.

the available drafts still showed important discrepancies with the Convention. The Report noted that:

far too much recourse is made to pre-trial detention, often even for petty crimes. A neo-inquisitional model of criminal procedure giving the bodies of criminal prosecution considerable advantages over the defence. The presumption of innocence is apparently also not upheld in all instances.

In addition, as regards the freedom of movement, the Monitoring Information Report underlined that

in many fields Russia must make further efforts to fulfil the obligations and commitments it entered into when joining the Council of Europe. Particular attention should be directed to the implementation of freedom of movement and of choice of residence.

The Information Monitoring Report stated that Russia had committed itself upon accession to guaranteeing the effective exercise of the rights enshrined in Article 27 of the Constitution[31] and in the Law on Freedom of Movement and Choice of Place of Residence, and to lifting the restriction of international travel by persons with knowledge of state secrets.

The Report continues:

the freedom of movement in the Russian Federation, though constitutionally guaranteed, is still often restricted by administrative officials practising the outlawed Soviet *propiska* (residence permit system), especially in the big cities such as Moscow and St Petersburg. The international NGO Human Rights Watch/Helsinki highlighted this illegal and unconstitutional but nevertheless widespread practice in a recent report. It reported that according to several sources, including the UNHCR, the Russian government continues to support restrictions on the freedom of movement as ostensible measures to keep public order and prevent housing discrimination. As a consequence, the administration not only enforces obsolete mandatory residence registration (with violators incurring fines, illegal beatings, or even eviction from their homes) but also resorts to the detention and forced deportation of 'vagrants and beggars' in accordance with Presidential Decree No. 1025. Human Rights Watch/Helsinki reported that in the first five months of 1997 1.3 million registration checks in private homes were effected by Moscow police alone. The enforcement of such shadowy *propiska* requirements also leaves the door wide open for abuse by law enforcement agents. [. . .] A shadow *propiska* system must not be tolerated any longer, especially in view of the Constitutional Court decision of 2 February 1998, which declared the government-issued regulations on registration unconstitutional, and thus invalid. Mr Luzhkov, Moscow's mayor, then publicly declared that he would not abide by this judgment.

The issue of residence registration as a remnant of *propiska* and its use in the light of the Convention is ambiguous. The regulation as such does not contradict Article 2 of Protocol No. 4 to the Convention. In its literal sense it

[31] Freedom of movement.

is merely a system of notification to the authorities and the subsequent registration of residence. Moreover, legislation imposing restrictions on settling in certain areas, when interests like protecting big cities against excessive migration and overcrowding are at stake, is acceptable under the Convention. However, it is the practical use of the system of residence registration which has been identified as a restriction of the right to the freedom of movement and which poses problems under Article 2 of Protocol No. 4 to the Convention.[32] It will be up to the Court to decide in individual cases whether the interference was justified.

Before examining specific cases, it is relevant to consider a special bilateral co-operation activity, the 'compatibility exercise', which was introduced by the Directorate of Human Rights of the Council of Europe when the first Central and Eastern European Countries joined the Council of Europe. The aim of this exercise was to assist future states parties to the Convention in identifying the areas where problems of conformity and/or compatibility could arise between the Convention and national legislation.[33] The focus has been far more on legislation than on domestic judicial practice. This document, also elaborated for Russia, is useful here as a basis for identifying possible problematic areas. In the following section we look at national case-law to see how domestic courts operate in the areas concerned.

The provisions of the Convention with which Russian legislation appears to show most discrepancies are Articles 5 and 6 of the Convention and Article 2 of Protocol No. 4 to the Convention.

The compatibility exercise raised the following issues with regard to Article 5 of the Convention:

1. the authority of the Prosecutor to decide upon pre-trial detention of suspects without having to bring the case before a judge;[34]
2. excessive terms of often unnecessary pre-trial detention, without a functioning system of bail;
3. potential tampering by the suspect to obstruct the investigation as a reason for pre-trial detention;
4. danger/suspicion that a person will commit a crime as a reason for pre-trial detention, and

[32] Elaborated in more detail in section C below.

[33] This document exists only in French and Russian. The references and quotes from the compatibility exercise are translated by the author.

[34] The European Court on Human Rights decided in the *Schiesser* case, 04/12/1979, Series A 34, that a prosecutor is not recognized as a judge or other officer authorized by law to exercise judicial power in the sense of Article 5(3) Convention. As far as detention during trial is concerned, the Court does decide upon that measure of prosecution. The Constitutional Court ruled in a case in 1998 that two provisions of the CCP which did not allow for appeal against such a decision were unconstitutional, case 20–P, 2.7.1998, published in *Rossiiskaia Gazeta*, N 131, 14.07.98 and *Collection of Legislation of the Russian Federation*, N 28, 13.07.98, item. 3393.

5. procedures regarding the detention of persons and establishing rules for keeping them in custody.[35]

In respect of Article 6 of the Convention the following topics were underlined:

1. there is only a small number of regions where jury trial has been introduced, whereas according to legislation certain criminal cases should only be considered by a court sitting with a jury;
2. the very broad supervisory powers of the Prosecutor's Office *vis-à-vis* the judiciary;
3. the existence of administrative procedures which can result in punishment and confiscation of property, in fact constituting criminal or civil procedures cases but not in accordance with the fair trial requirements; and
4. the fact that a number of cases are within the sole jurisdiction of the Supreme Court and thus cannot be appealed.

Russia's reservations to the Convention exempt, as could be expected, many important provisions of Russian legislation which have been identified as problematic in terms of compatibility with the Convention. In the CCP this concerns Article 11, paragraph 1 'Personal inviolability'; Article 89 'Application of preventive measures'; Article 90 'Application of a preventive measure in respect of a suspect'; Article 92 'Order and decision on the application of a preventive measure'; Article 96 'Placing in custody'; Article 96–1 'Procedure for detaining persons placed in custody', Article 96–2 'Time-limits for detaining persons placed in custody in temporary detention centres'; Article 97 'Time-limits for keeping in custody'; Article 101 'Cancellation or modification of a preventive measure; and Article 122 'Apprehension of a person suspected of committing a criminal offence'.These reservations clearly touch upon the core of Article 5(3) and (4) of the Convention which accordingly practically excludes them presently from application for Russia.

As regards the right to free movement and residence, the compatibility exercise identified that registration of residence should be carried out by the state authorities automatically after notification. However, the exceedingly high registration fees established by some regional authorities preclude most applicants, who cannot afford it, from registration. Thus residence registration risks turning into a permit system for residence, which is incompatible with the Convention.

[35] See among others Amnesty International Report—EUR 46/04/97, April 1997 Russian Federation Torture in Russia 'This Man-Made Hell' on conditions of pre-trial detention in Russia. This problem has been openly recognized by the Russian Parliamentary Delegation in the Parliamentary Assembly of the Council of Europe in its reply to the draft monitoring report NR 8217.

C. DOMESTIC LAW AND PRACTICE *VIS-À-VIS* THE CONVENTION

A number of decisions have been taken at the Supreme and Constitutional Court level which are relevant to the Convention and the aforementioned issues. Both the Constitutional Court and the Supreme Court have referred a number of times to the Convention to support the legal considerations in their judgments.[36] Here we focus on decisions after the entry into force of the Convention in respect of Russia. The scope of this chapter does not allow for a comprehensive list of cases even at the highest judicial level.

1. Article 5 of the Convention

(a) Constitutional Court In the case of *Ianchev and Others* the Constitutional Court looked into the constitutionality of provisions of the CCP which allow for the prolongation of remand in custody when the investigation has finished and the case has been given to the suspect and his counsel for information and preparation of the defence.[37]

The Court reasoned that the preventive measures served the aims mentioned in Article 55 Constitution, which sets out the conditions for restrictions of rights. The aims are to prevent the accused from going into hiding, obstructing or tampering with evidence, or committing (further) criminal activity. However, a prolongation of remand in custody is allowed only if there are sufficient grounds for this for the purpose of substantiating the evidence. The necessity for a co-accused to become familiar with the evidence collected is not a sufficient argument for a prolongation of custody. The court argued that keeping persons in custody because co-accused need to learn the facts of the case is unconstitutional. It did not pronounce on the merits of the case since in an earlier case[38] it had declared paragraph 5 of Article 97 CCP unconstitutional.

In the case of *Guralnik and Others* the Constitutional Court looked into the issue of the constitutionality of Article 331 CCP, which did not allow for suspects detained in custody to appeal against a decision to prolong custody if their case was being sent back to the prosecutor for additional investigation.

[36] A number of case-law extracts here are taken from G. P. van den Berg's 'Comments to the 1993 Constitution of the Russian Federation'. This work had not been published at the time of writing but a copy on CD-rom can be obtained from its author at the Institute of East European Law and Russian Studies, Leiden University Faculty of Law, the Netherlands.

[37] Decision No.167–O of 25.12.1998, published in *Rossiiskaia Gazeta* of 21.01.1999 and *the Collection of Legislation of the Russian Federation*, No. 1, 4.1.1999.

[38] Judgment 14–P, 13.06.1996 published in *Rossiiskaia Gazeta* of 2.7.1996 and *the Collection of Legislation of the Russian Federation*, No. 26, 24.6.1996.

The Court declared the impugned provisions unconstitutional and ruled that an appeal lodged by such a person must now be considered.

A breakthrough judgment from the point of view of the Convention was delivered by the Constitutional Court in the *Maslov* case.[39] Maslov was arrested and interrogated for sixteen hours. When he asked for access to a lawyer he was informed that in accordance with Article 47 CCP this was only possible after the formal presentation of the accusation, a *procès-verbal* of his arrest, or a decision of the appropriate law enforcement authority to apply a preventive measure against him as a suspect. The applicant was told that for the time being he was being interrogated in the capacity of a witness. Following the interrogation the applicant was formally accused from which moment he was allowed access to a defence counsel.

The Constitutional Court invoked, among others, Articles 5 and 6 of the Convention and the Court's case-law[40] ruling that the CCP provision contradicted the Constitutional provisions on protection of personal freedom and fair trial. It argued that it is the actual deprivation or limitation of freedom which should be looked at to establish when criminal procedural measures are being applied against a suspect, as opposed to when the prosecuting or investigating authorities determine that this is the case and decide to inform the suspect of it.

2. *Article 6 of the Convention*

(a) Supreme Court A case which received a lot of attention from international organizations, human rights NGOs, and other states is the case of *Nikitin*. Nikitin was charged with treason, revealing state secrets, and falsifying documents while working for the Norwegian environmental group Bellona. He was arrested in February 1996 for writing two chapters for a Bellona report on the risk of radioactive pollution from nuclear submarines in Russia's Northern Fleet. Nikitin maintained that he had used only public sources to write the report. The case brought against him by the FSB[41] and the prosecutor was partly based on secret documents. Nikitin went to trial on 20 October 1998, more than two and a half years after his first arrest and detention on remand (later changed to house arrest). In a decision of 29 October 1998 the St Petersburg City Court ruled that the prosecutor had failed to compile adequate evidence and sent the case back for further investigation. The

[39] Judgment No. 11–P, 27.6.2000.

[40] 24 May 1991 *Quaranta*, Series A No. 205, para. 27; 24 November 1993 *Imbrioscia*, Series A No. 275, para. 36; 8 February 1996 *Murray*, 1996–I, para. 66; 27 February 1980 *Deweer*, Series A No. 35, paras. 44, 46; 15 July 1982 *Eckle*, Series A No. 51, para. 73; 10 December 1982 *Foti*, Series A No. 56, para. 52.

[41] The National Security Service.

prosecutor appealed this decision to the Supreme Court on 3 November 1998 to overturn the decision to send the case back for further investigation. The ground of appeal was that the lower court had reached premature conclusions about the evidence gathered against Nikitin. Nikitin's lawyers have filed their own appeal, demanding that the charges against Nikitin be dismissed entirely and that he be allowed to travel outside the country.[42]

On 4 February 1999 the Supreme Court confirmed the City Court judgment of 29 October 1998 and the case was referred back for further investigation. On 18 July 1999 Nikitin's case was filed in the Strasbourg Court. In Bellona's working papers the following violations of the Convention were alleged: the presumption of innocence was not upheld (Article 6(2)), the case was not settled within a reasonable time (Article 6(1)), arbitrary deprivation of personal freedom (Article 5), lack of legal foundation for the accusation (Article 7), breach of the right to respect for private life (Article 8), breach of the freedom of movement (Protocol No. 4, Article 2), and lack of an effective remedy (Article 13).[43]

Finally, on 29 December 1999 Nikitin was acquitted by the St Petersburg City Court. The verdict was not appealed by the prosecutor. However, three months after the verdict the prosecutor lodged a protest (request for review) with the Supreme Court. This was rejected by the Supreme Court on 17 April 2000. On 30 May 2000 the Deputy Prosecutor General filed a new protest, this time with the Presidium of the Supreme Court, to quash the St Petersburg Court acquittal and to send the case yet again to the St Petersburg Prosecutor's office for a new investigation. On 13 September 2000 the Presidium of the Supreme Court rejected the Deputy Prosecutor's application to reopen the case, thereby apparently settling the case.

The Supreme Court Presidium of the Russian Federation found no grounds to accept the appeal due to the following reasons.

It is evident from the case files that organs of preliminary investigations really used the provisions of article 5 of the Law of the Russian Federation 'On State Secrets' of July 21, 1993, while levelling the charges against Nikitin regarding state treason in the form of espionage and disclosing information pertaining to state secrets.

However, on each of the charges, while giving reasons for the secrecy of the discussed information, the investigation organs always referred to the alterations and additions put in force by the Law of the Russian Federation 'On state secrets' in edition of 6 October 1997, the law which was adopted and came into force after the alleged action of Nikitin. This law has no retroactive

[42] *RFE/RL* 19 May, 1 July, 5 November 1998; *Jamestown* 21.

[43] Bellona Working Paper No. 2:99, by Jon Gauslaa. Available on the Bellona Internet site www.bellona.org.

force. The experts used precisely the provisions from this law while giving their conclusions about the secrecy of the information disclosed by Nikitin.

Such a formula of the accusations led to the non-concrete charges, mentioned in the verdict, and which could not be eliminated.

That is why the court of first instance and the court collegium of the Supreme Court of the Russian Federation had grounds to come to such a conclusion about illegally charging Nikitin with the above-mentioned actions basing on the alterations and additions which were adopted to the Law of the Russian Federation 'On state secrets' on 6 October 1997 (Bellona, http://www.belona.org).

The Bulletin of the Supreme Court has quoted a number of cases concerning the right to a fair trial.

In the *Utochkin* case[44] the Supreme Court ruled that the refusal to let the accused consult the case file with the assistance of his lawyer violates the right of the accused to prepare his defence.

In the *Zhigatov* case[45] the Supreme Court, after a protest by the prosecutor in a supervisory review procedure, established that the Supreme Court of the Kabardino-Balkarsaya Republic had correctly acquitted the accused after it had established that the evidence against him was obtained through the use of force by law enforcement officers.

In the *Gauftudinov* case,[46] concerning reconsideration of cases after first-instance decisions were quashed on appeal, the Supreme Court ruled that this cannot be done by the same judge who had considered the case at first instance.

In the case of *Dolev and Others*[47] the Supreme Court ruled that an opinion expressed by the judge before all the evidence was adduced at trial that the guilt of the suspects was proven breached the presumption of innocence and the required impartiality of the court.

On 18 November the Supreme Court issued an informative guideline ruling as to the length of proceedings in civil and criminal cases.[48] It established, with special reference to Article 6 of the Convention, that despite positive developments in the promptness of consideration of cases, the problem of over-lengthy proceedings remained serious. The ruling stated that in many cases the accused had been ordered by the courts to remain in custody in breach of statutory provisions. The Court explained that this was partly due to the understaffing of courts and an excessive case-load.

[44] Summary in Bulletin of the Supreme Court No. 2 of 1 February 1999, case No. 9.

[45] Summary in Bulletin of the Supreme Court No. 5 of 31 May 1999, case No. 5.

[46] Summary in Bulletin of the Supreme Court No. 6 of 28 June 1999, case No. 5.

[47] Summary in Bulletin of the Supreme Court No. 6 of 28 June 1999, case No. 15.

[48] Ruling of 18 November 1999 No. 79 published in the Bulletin of the Supreme Court No. 1 of 2000.

(b) Constitutional Court In 'supervisory review in criminal procedures case'[49] the Moscow Regional Court addressed the Constitutional Court with a question on the constitutionality of CCP provisions which allow a supervisory court (the Presidium of the Supreme Court) to overturn a final decision and all subsequent rulings and send the case back for a fresh prosecution or court examination. This was also possible after an acquittal. The Constitutional Court reasoned that an exception to the *ne bis in idem* rule is made for new facts when a reconsideration of the case is possible. Cases may also be reopened following a miscarriage of justice. However:

In other instances, final judgments of courts are not subject to revision. After a final acquittal, a second trial is not allowed, except to eliminate injustice if the position of the convicted person improves by this.

Under the Constitution, laws adopted before the Constitution entered into force apply only insofar as they do not contravene the Constitution.[50] The Regional Court established that the impugned provisions of the CCP contravene Article 14 ICCPR, and therefore the norms of international law were to be applied. The Constitutional Court, however, merely concluded that there was a gap in the law, but noted that it is not entitled to fill gaps in legal regulation, which was the preserve of the legislator, and it did not pronounce on the merits. It may also not decide whether an international act is applicable in a given case when a domestic law appears to be incompatible with it, as this is a matter for the general courts.[51]

In the case of *Arbuzova and Others* the Constitutional Court looked into fair trial requirements in the light of procedures under the Code of Administrative Violations. It concluded that the lack of provision for appeal contradicts the Constitution to the extent it does not allow for a judicial appeal against decisions of courts on administrative violations which can lead among others to detention and/or fines.[52]

A fair trial issue in the light of Article 2 of Protocol No. 7 to the Convention was raised in the *Shaglia* case.[53] The issue was that Article 325 CCP does not

[49] Decision of 3.7.1997.

[50] The Constitutional Court seems to hold that the applicable provisions of the Code do not contravene the Constitution. This does not follow from its explanations of the rules on *ne bis in idem*.

[51] *Reporter of the Constitutional Court of the Russian Federation,* 1997 No. 5, 31; see also *Reporter of the Constitutional Court of the Russian Federation,* 1998.

[52] Published in *Rossiiskaia Gazeta* No. 109, 09.06.99 and *the Collection of Legislation of the Russian Federation*, No. 23, 07.06.99. See also decision No. 8–P of 11.03.1998: the Constitutional Court decided in that case that procedures under the administrative and customs codes which can lead to confiscation of property have to be taken as judicial decisions and not the respective administrative authority, published in *Ekonomika i Zhizn*, N 12, 1998

[53] No. 21–P of 6.7.1998, Published in *Rossiiskaia Gazeta*, N 132, 15.07.98 and *the Collection of Legislation of the Russian Federation*, No 28, 13.07.98, item. 3394.

provide for an appeal against a decision in criminal cases over which the Supreme Court has first-instance jurisdiction. The Constitutional Court declared the Article concerned unconstitutional and made a recommendation to Parliament to amend the CCP accordingly.

In the *Baronin* case[54] the Constitutional Court declared Article 335(2) CCP to be unconstitutional to the extent it allows the Court of Cassation to reject the petition of a convicted person who is in custody to attend the hearing of his or her appeal, particularly since the Court of Cassation can give final judgment in the case.

In the *Smirnova* case[55] the Constitutional Court looked into the constitutionality of provisions of the CCP which enable a court, when considering a criminal case against one person, to initiate criminal proceedings against and order the arrest of another person on the basis of facts discovered during the trial. The Constitutional Court found that if a court decides to initiate new criminal proceedings it can no longer be considered impartial and independent to consider the case on its merits and ensure equality of arms.

In the case of *Aulov and Others*[56] the Constitutional Court looked into the constitutionality of the supervisory review procedure in criminal cases to the extent it allows the court carrying out the supervisory review to refuse to give information about the hearing to the convicted or acquitted person, the victim, and their representatives and not to invite them to the hearing. The supervisory review decisions had moreover worsened the position of some of the applicants. The Constitutional Court decided that the corresponding provisions of the CCP were unconstitutional and that the applicants' cases had to be reviewed with their participation.

In the *Kekhman* case[57] the issue was access to the case file of the prosecutor. The Samara Prosecutor was conducting an investigation into the lawfulness of actions by the municipal authorities against Kekhman in a housing dispute. The applicant requested access to the prosecutor's file but this was refused. His appeals to the courts also met with refusal. This was possible on the basis of Article 5(2) of the Law on the Prosecution (*Prokuratura*) which enables the prosecutor to deny access to case files. The applicant addressed the Constitutional Court for a pronouncement on the constitutionality of that provision. The Constitutional Court declared the provision unconstitutional

[54] No. 27–P of 10.12.1998, published in *Izvestiia* 12 December 1998.

[55] No. 1–P of 14 January 2000, published in *Rosiiskaia Gazeta*; No. 23, 02.02.2000 and *the Collection of Legislation of the Russian Federation* No. 5, 31.01.2000.

[56] No. 2–P of 14.2.2000, published in *Rosiiskaia Gazeta*; No. 38, 23.02.2000 and *the Collection of Legislation of the Russian Federation*, No. 8, 21.02.2000.

[57] No. 3–P of 18.2.2000, published in *Collection of Legislation of the Russian Federation* No. 14, 05.04.99.

to the extent it makes it possible to deny to an individual the right of access to information concerning his rights and obligations.

3. Article 2 of Protocol No. 4 to the Convention

(a) Constitutional Court The Constitutional Court has pronounced once on the issue of freedom of movement since the entry into force of the Convention. Important judgments on this topic, however, were delivered in 1996 and in February 1998.

The *Propiska fees in Moscow* judgment[58] concerned the Moscow Regional Government Rules requiring residence registration in Moscow City and some other localities. These rules established extremely high fees. The Constitutional Court ruled that this could paralyse the right of freedom of residence and movement (Article 27 of the Constitution). It continued that freedom of movement may be regulated and restricted, but restrictions must be enacted in a federal law. An obligation to pay a fee and to show that this has been done as a condition for registration turns the registration system into a permit system and refusal to register under this system is a sanction for not paying the fee. The Court concluded that the realization of a constitutional right may not be subject to the payment of taxes or fees, because fundamental rights are guaranteed unilaterally without fiscal or other conditions. The regional Moscow legislation was declared unconstitutional.[59]

In the case of the *Governor of Nizhegorodskiy Region*[60] the Constitutional Court addressed the constitutionality of several provisions of the Government Instructions on Residence Registration and Striking Off the Residence Register of Citizens of the Russian Federation of 1995. The Constitutional Court ruled that registration of citizens may not be subject to additional rules and conditions set by the Instructions such as time-limits for temporary residence and presentation of specific documents which are not required by the Law on the Freedom of Movement and Choice of Residence of 1993, in the absence of which residence registration may be refused. The Court concluded that the respective part of the Instructions was unconstitutional and could not be applied by executive bodies and courts.

In a decision of 3 November 1998 the Constitutional Court was asked to review the constitutionality of Krasnodar regional legislation which set limits

[58] No. 9–P, 4.4.1996 *Rossiiskaia Gazeta* 17 April 1996 and *Collection of Legislation of the Russian Federation*, 1996 No. 18, item 1909; *Reporter of the Constitutional Court of the Russian Federation* 1996 No. 2, 42; Konstitutsionnyi sud Rossiiskoi Federatsii: *Postanovleniia. Opredeleniia*. 1992–1996, Moscow 1997, p. 418.

[59] See, however, comments above. The Moscow Mayor simply did not comply but continued to apply the strict registration regime.

[60] 4–P, 2 February 1998, published in *Rossiiskaia Gazeta* No. 25, 10.02.98 and *Collection of Legislation of the Russian Federation* No. 6, 09.02.98.

on the acquisition of immovable property in default of residence registration in the region. The Constitutional Court did not pronounce on the issue, referring to the judgment of 2 February 1998 and stating that the legal constitutional position expressed there was valid also for the Krasnodar region and had to be applied accordingly.[61]

***

Looking at these cases from the perspective of the Convention generally leads to the conclusion that at the highest judicial level considerable efforts are being made to ensure proper judicial human rights protection in accordance with both national and international law. One sees an increased tendency to take international human rights instruments seriously. This is especially true of the Constitutional Court, which has made substantive reviews of the constitutionality of, in particular, criminal procedure provisions.[62] The problem with the Constitutional Court is that there is no mechanism for enforcing its judgments in concrete cases, even though there is a statutory obligation for executive bodies and courts to do so. In terms of their impact on judicial proceedings, the judgments should be seen as new (legal) circumstances which can give rise to revision of decisions of courts of general jurisdiction.[63] However, this does not occur *de jure* but depends on the discretionary powers of the organs exercising supervision, such as the General Prosecutor and the President of the Supreme Court.

In order to create a solid basis for the understanding and use of such instruments as the Convention and even the human rights provisions of the new Constitution, the Supreme Court, the Constitutional Court, and also the *Prokuratura* have to make a substantive effort to team up to create such a sound basis.

[61] Decision 116—O, published in *Rossiiskaia Gazeta* of 03.11.98.

[62] G. P. van den Berg expressed the opinion that this instrument has in fact lost its extraordinary character and seems to have become a regular remedy. However, the result of that would be that domestic remedies in Russia would not be exhausted. See the *Nikitin* case above where, after an acquittal, the prosecutor several months later was still able to launch requests for a supervisory review with the Supreme Court to reopen the case and start the proceedings all over again. See also the *Tumilovich* case in which the Strasbourg Court decided that supervisory review proceedings cannot be considered as an effective domestic remedy within the meaning of Article 35(3) of the Convention.

[63] By analogy with the Constitutional Court's reasoning in the *Kulnev* case, cited above.

D. CASES BROUGHT BEFORE THE EUROPEAN COURT ON HUMAN RIGHTS

As expected, the Court was promptly confronted with a steadily growing flow of individual applications from Russia. In 1998 the Court's statistics for Russia showed that 211 provisional files had been opened, with 51 applications formally registered, no files communicated or declared admissible, 4 applications declared inadmissible, and 118 applications pending on 1 January 1999.[64] For May 2000 the figures showed that 2,584 provisional files have been opened, 1,541 cases registered, 763 cases declared inadmissible or stuck out, and 6 cases communicated to the government. By May 2000 no Russian cases had progressed beyond admissibility proceedings.[65]

An important major admissibility decision as to what is considered an effective domestic remedy in terms of Article 35(1) of the Convention was taken in the *Tumilovich* case.[66] The European Court decided that the applicant's two applications for supervisory review which had been dismissed by the President of the Civil Chamber of the Supreme Court and by the Deputy Prosecutor General constitute extraordinary remedies, whose use depends on the discretion of the President of the Supreme Court and the (Deputy) Prosecutor General, and not on the applicant's appeal. The Court concluded that these applications and the subsequent dismissals did not therefore constitute effective remedies within the meaning of Article 35(1) of the Convention. This decision is relevant to the determination of the *ratione temporis* and the six-month time-limit of the European Court. Applications for a supervisory review which do not lead to the reopening of proceedings and review of the judicial decision which has already become final can therefore not be invoked by the respondent state as a remedy in domestic proceedings to be exhausted before addressing the Court.[67]

The Court further decided that letters from the Constitutional Court which inform applicants about its lack of the competence to deal with the complaint are also not relevant to the determination of the jurisdiction of the European Court.

[64] See Court statistics on www.echr.coe.int.

[65] Some of the summaries which will follow are taken from the case-law summaries issued by the Court.

[66] Application 47033/99.

[67] The Court based its decision among others on earlier decisions of the Commission, which had not excepted the government's arguments that the applicant had to go through the extraordinary review procedure in order to exhaust all available domestic remedies. See Application 14545/89, 9.10.1990, DR 66, p. 239 and Application 12604/86, 10.7.1991, DR 70, p. 125.

1. Articles 5, 6, and 8 of the Convention

The *Kalashnikov* case[68] concerns the arrest and detention on remand of the applicant in June 1995. The examination of the case by the City Court started in November 1996, but was adjourned in May 1997. In February 1998 the applicant was informed that the City Court would not resume consideration of his case before July 1998, given the complexity of the case and the workload of the court. Despite numerous requests by the applicant to the judicial authorities to speed up the proceedings, the case remained pending before the City Court. The applicant complained about the poor conditions of his detention and the fact that he had been unable to see either his wife or his children since his placement in detention. The case was communicated under Articles 5(3), 6(1), 3, and 8 of the Convention.

In the *Syrkin* case[69] the applicant complained of the disappearance of his son while serving in a military unit stationed in Germany. The Russian authorities conducted an investigation jointly with the German authorities which did not produce any results. The applicant invoked Article 13 in conjunction with Article 5 of the Convention in support of his complaint. The Court declared the application inadmissible as manifestly ill founded, stating that despite the fact that the investigation had not led to any positive results and had been suspended several times, overall the authorities could not be considered to have failed in their duty to take the appropriate steps to help its progress.

In the *Zhukov* case[70] the applicant had been in pre-trial detention since 1996 without a hearing of his case in first instance on the merits. The hearing of his case was postponed several times for procedural reasons and he remained in custody during the entire period. The applicant complained of excessively lengthy detention on remand; the case was communicated to the Russian government under Articles 5(3) 3 and 6(1) of the Convention.

2. Article 9 of the Convention

The *Nikishina* case[71] concerned the transfer of custody of a child from the applicant mother to the father because of the applicant's activities as a Jehovah's Witness. The domestic court which decided upon the issue based its decision, *inter alia*, upon a religious expert report by the Russian academy of Education which describes Jehovah's Witnesses as a destructive totalitarian sect. The applicant complained of breaches of Articles 8, 9, and 14 of the Convention. The case was communicated to the government.

[68] Application 47095/99.
[69] Application 44125/98, decision of 25.11.99.
[70] Application 54260/00.
[71] Application 47655/99.

In the *Pitkevich* case[72] the applicant was a member of the Living Faith Church, which belongs to the Russian Union of Evangelical Christian Churches. She was a judge at the Noyabrsk City District Court. Disciplinary proceedings were instituted against her by an association of judges before the Judiciary Qualification Panel, composed of four judges. The applicant maintained that the Panel had refused to call several witnesses in her favour. She was eventually dismissed on the grounds that she had 'damaged her reputation as a judge' and misused her office to proselytize. She appealed unsuccessfully to the Supreme Judiciary Qualification Panel of the Russian Federation. She alleged that her legal representative had not been allowed to attend the hearing. The Supreme Court rejected her other appeal, that she was not present at the hearing because the date had been changed without her being informed. The case was communicated under Articles 6(1) (access to court, fair trial), 9, 10, and 14 of the Convention.

3. *Article 11 of the Convention*

The *OVR* case concerned compulsory membership in a regional notary chamber for the applicant, who wanted to open a private notary practice. When the applicant refused to become a member of the chamber because the financial costs were too high she was deprived by a judicial decision of the right to carry on her practice. The applicant complained of the obligation to join the chamber, which she considered to be a private association, and because this obligation had not existed when she was employed at a state notary firm. The case was communicated under Article 11 alone and in conjunction with Article 14 of the Convention.

4. *Article 1 of Protocol No. 1 to the Convention*

In the *Taykov* case[73] the applicant had not received his retirement benefits for a considerable period of time. He claimed in the district and later on appeal in the regional court for his benefits. The courts rejected his claims invoking an apparent lack of funds in the regional authorities' treasury. The case was communicated by the European Court to the government and subsequently settled when the local authorities paid all monies due to the applicant.

E. ASSESSMENT AND PROSPECTS

As a first premiss, Russia's membership in the Council of Europe, by which it committed itself to the principles for which the organization stands, and

[72] Application 47936/99. [73] Application 48498/99.

Russia's ratification of the Convention are positive developments. This is true for individuals who are entitled to the protection provided under the Convention and other Council of Europe instruments.

Two years after ratification there had been no judgments of the European Court finding Russia in breach. However, this is probably only a matter of time. Most applicants to the Court are not familiar with the Convention mechanism, especially the admissibility criteria. Another factor is that domestic proceedings started after entry into force of the Convention may take a long time to be exhausted before the applicant can apply to the Court.

Looking from a domestic perspective at Russia's compliance with the requirements of human rights protection, and more importantly the legal requirements of the Convention, it is clear that this requires close attention and constant effort at implementation by those Russian authorities with the power to change the present system. Doubts have been expressed about the willingness and ability of the Russian authorities to fulfil this obligation. The recent wars in Chechnya are a clear example of an executive political decision to place state interests far above individual interests, which calls the seriousness of Russia's commitment to human rights protection as envisaged by the Convention into question.

Further, looking at human rights protection on the domestic level, an important technical obstacle is the lack of an enforcement mechanism for judgments of the Constitutional Court, which is clearly set on developing human rights protection. The Constitutional Court has until now played a positive role in protecting human rights, but its decisions are not necessarily taken into account or complied with. If the reluctance of Russia's judiciary to comply with decisions rendered by the Constitutional Court decisions is sign of anything, then certainly Russia's attitude towards the European Court's future judgments may be questioned.

The most problematic areas, identified in the compatibility exercise, have become subject to reservations from Russia. As a temporary measure, reservations may be acceptable. However, the adoption of a new Code of Criminal Procedure—one of the stumbling blocks for granting protection under Article 5 of the Convention—had still not been adopted two years after the entry into force of the Convention.[74] An additional concern is that the draft CCP does not present solutions to the incompatibilities between the Convention and present Russian law: there seems to be insufficient political will to make the necessary changes. Notably, the Prosecutor's Office possesses decision-making powers in pre-trial detention matters which is *ipso*

[74] See Petrukhin's comments to Russia's reservations to the Convention and the apparently obstructive attitude by Russia's legislature at the time he wrote his article, p. 5.

facto linked to the lack of judicial control over these decisions. One can expect Russia to claim a special exemption for justifying certain inconsistencies in the law, by referring to its excessive crime-rate and weak economic/financial position. When the CCP is adopted, however, these reservations will automatically lose their force. One may consequently expect an even greater flow of complaints on Article 5 issues to Strasbourg.

As far as the right to a fair trial is concerned, one can see a positive tendency in Russian case-law towards its enforcement. The Constitutional Court and the Supreme Court have given a number of decisions ensuring a better position for the defendant both at first instance and on appeal. At the same time, the powers of the public prosecutor still remain dominant before and during the trial.

Supervisory review remains a problematic institution. On one hand it has some elements of a third-instance hearing, but its use is completely dependant on the discretion of the prosecutor and (deputy) presidents of regional courts and the Supreme Court who can use this instrument at any time. Legal certainty is not served by this.

Freedom of movement is another area of concern, but more legislative reforms have been introduced following the Constitutional Court's judgments and decisions. Here again compliance with those judgments has been shown to be problematic.

Despite these problems and difficulties in the application of the Convention in Russia, it is important to note that Russia's signing of the Convention provides the impetus for advancing the rights of persons residing in the Russian Federation. This should remain the main stimulus for supporting Russia's reform in the area of human rights, and the Council of Europe's efforts to promote and respect those fundamental rights.

29

Slovakia

MILAN BLAŠKO

A. INTRODUCTION

1. Relevant elements of the constitutional system

The Velvet Revolution, which started in November 1989 and which led to the fall of the Communist regime in Czechoslovakia, brought about substantial political, economic, and social changes. One of the repercussions was the need to adjust the constitutional system in order to eliminate the shortcomings of the Czecho-Slovak Federation which had been established on 1 January 1969 and to redistribute the powers between the federal State and the two national republics by which Czechoslovakia was constituted. Lengthy political talks on these issues were fruitless and, after the 1992 parliamentary elections, the leaders of the political parties in power concluded an agreement that the Czech and Slovak Federal Republic would be constitutionally dissolved.

As a result, the Federal Assembly adopted Constitutional Law No. 542/1992 of 25 November 1992 providing that the Czech and Slovak Federal Republic would cease to exist upon the expiry of 31 December 1992. The Law designated the Czech Republic and the Slovak Republic as its successors, and governed the transfer of powers from the federal authorities to the successor states. It also entitled the latter, prior to 1 January 1993, to conclude, treaties both between themselves and with third States. Such treaties could, however, only enter into force after 31 December 1992.

On 17 July 1992 the newly elected Slovak National Council (the Parliament) adopted the Declaration of Sovereignty of the Slovak Republic. On 1 September 1992 it approved the Constitution of the Slovak Republic which was solemnly signed on 3 September 1992. The Constitution provides for a multi-party and multi-ethnic parliamentary democracy with separation of powers and an independent judiciary. It stipulates that the Slovak Republic is governed by the rule of law and that it is not bound by any ideology or religion. The bulk of its provisions entered into force on 1 October 1992.[1]

Part Two of the Constitution is entitled 'Fundamental Rights and Freedoms' and it governs, in separate chapters, the fundamental human rights and freedoms, political rights, the rights of national minorities and ethnic groups, economic, social, and cultural rights, the right to protection of the environment and cultural heritage, as well as the right to judicial and other legal protection.

The human rights and fundamental freedoms laid down in the Constitution cover, albeit not always in identical terms, the rights and freedoms set out in the European Convention on Human Rights and the other international instruments adopted in this area. In some cases the Constitution offers even stronger guarantees than those established under the European Convention on Human Rights. Thus under Article 17, para. 2 of the Constitution a person suspected of having committed an offence must be brought before a judge not later than twenty-four hours after his or her arrest, and the judge is obliged to hear such a person and to decide on his or her detention or release within another twenty-four hours.

Furthermore, the Constitution also guarantees human rights not included in the European Convention on Human Rights as interpreted and applied by the Convention organs. For example, Article 25, para. 2 of the Constitution provides that nobody may be forced to perform military service if it is contrary to his conscience or religious beliefs (only men are obliged to perform military service). Another example is Article 34 of the Constitution which guarantees to persons belonging to a national minority or an ethnic group, *inter alia,* the rights to create and maintain associations and educational and cultural institutions, to be educated in their language, or to use a minority language in official communications.

The aforesaid specific features of the human rights guarantees under the Constitution of the Slovak Republic are probably one of the reasons for which, in accordance with Article 11 of the Constitution:

> international treaties on human rights and fundamental freedoms ratified by the Slovak Republic and promulgated in accordance with the statutory requirements shall take precedence over national laws provided that such treaties guarantee fundamental rights and freedoms to a larger extent.

The power to protect the integrity of the constitutional principles is vested in the Constitutional Court which started functioning on 17 March 1993. It has

[1] The Constitution was promulgated in the Collection of Laws under No. 460/1992. Several of its provisions (which are enumerated in Article 156 and govern, for example, border changes, extradition of nationals, granting asylum to foreigners, and declaration of war on another state) became effective on 1 January 1993.

been conceived as an independent judicial authority separate from the system of the general courts (which are headed by the Supreme Court). The Constitutional Court is composed of ten judges appointed by the President of the Slovak Republic for seven years from a list of twenty candidates approved by the National Council of the Slovak Republic.

The principal function of the Constitutional Court is decision-making on constitutional conflicts. This power is set out in Article 125 of the Constitution.[2] The Constitutional Court is further entitled: to decide on disputes concerning the distribution of competences among the central state administration authorities; to interpret the constitutional statutes in conflicting cases; to examine complaints against decisions concerning the election of a member of the National Council of the Slovak Republic; to decide whether the elections to the latter and to local self-governing authorities have been held in conformity with the Constitution and the law; to deal with petitions challenging the results of a referendum; to decide whether a decision dissolving a political party or suspending its activities is consistent with the constitutional statutes and other laws; and to examine allegations of treason committed by the President of the Slovak Republic. Individuals can seek redress before the Constitutional Court by means of two remedies which are examined in more detail below.

2. *'Retroactive' succession of Slovakia to the Convention*

The Czech and Slovak Federal Republic ratified the Convention together with its Protocols on 18 March 1992. On the same day Czechoslovakia made declarations by which it recognized the right of individual petition and the compulsory jurisdiction of the European Court of Human Rights. These declarations were made for a period of five years and were renewable by tacit agreement unless they were withdrawn. Czechoslovakia's instrument of ratification contained a reservation pursuant to Article 64 of the Convention. It was made in respect of Articles 5 and 6 of the Convention to the effect that

[2] Article 125 of the Constitution provides:

The Constitutional Court shall have jurisdiction to decide on constitutional conflicts between:
a) laws and the Constitution including the constitutional statutes;
b) regulations passed by the government or generally binding rules passed by the Ministries or other central state administration authorities and the Constitution, constitutional statutes or other laws;
c) generally binding rules passed by local self-governing authorities and the Constitution or other laws;
d) generally binding rules passed by local self-governing authorities and the Constitution, laws or other generally binding legal rules;
e) generally binding legal rules and international treaties promulgated in accordance with the law.

those provisions should not hinder the imposition of disciplinary penitentiary measures under Section 17 of the Armed Forces Service Act 1959.[3] As a result of its dissolution, the Czech and Slovak Federal Republic ceased to be a party to the Convention on 31 December 1992.

In accordance with Article 152 of the Constitution of the Slovak Republic, the constitutional statutes, laws, and other generally binding rules passed in the Czech and Slovak Federal Republic have remained in force in Slovakia unless they contradicted its Constitution. Pursuant to Article 153 of its Constitution, the Slovak Republic has succeeded to all rights and obligations ensuing from international treaties to which the Czech and Slovak Federal Republic was a party.

The extent of the succession was to be specified either in a constitutional statute of the federal state or in an agreement between Slovakia and the Czech Republic.

Despite the will expressly manifested by the Slovak authorities to succeed to all international treaties by which its predecessor had been bound, Slovakia was prevented from succeeding to the European Convention on Human Rights directly because of the latter's 'closed' character. In fact, the Convention is only 'open to the signature of the Members of the Council of Europe'.[4] Thus, membership of the Council of Europe was a prerequisite for Slovakia to become a party to the Convention.

In a declaration adopted to this effect on 3 December 1992, the National Council of the Slovak Republic confirmed Slovakia's wish to be a member of the Council of Europe. The National Council further stated that it considered itself bound by the Convention.

In a letter of 1 January 1993 addressed to the Secretary General of the Council of Europe, the government expressed the wish that the Slovak Republic be invited to become a member of the Council of Europe and declared its readiness to respect the principles set out in Article 3 of its Statute.[5] The letter further stated that the Slovak Republic as a successor state of the Czech and Slovak Federal Republic considered itself bound, from 1 January 1993, by the multilateral international treaties to which the Czech and Slovak Federal Republic was a party at that date, including the European Convention on Human Rights, as well as by the reservations and declarations as to their provisions made by its legal predecessor.

[3] Act No. 76/1959 of the Collection of Laws.

[4] See Article 59, para. 1 (Article 66, para. 1 prior to the entry into force of Protocol No. 11) of the Convention.

[5] Pursuant to Article 3 of the Statute, every member of the organization must accept the principles of the rule of law and of the enjoyment by all persons within its jurisdiction of human rights and fundamental freedoms, and collaborate sincerely and effectively in the realization of the aim of the Council of Europe.

In its Resolution (93)4 of 13 January 1993 the Committee of Ministers noted the above facts with satisfaction and invited the Parliamentary Assembly to express its opinion on Slovakia's wish to become a member of the Council of Europe.

After the Parliamentary Assembly had expressed a favourable opinion, the Committee of Ministers resolved, by Resolution (93)33 adopted on 30 June 1993, to invite Slovakia to become a member of the Council of Europe and to accede to its Statute. In the resolution the Committee of Ministers made reference, *inter alia*, to its decision that Slovakia was to be considered, with retroactive effect from 1 January 1993, a Contracting Party to the Convention.

That decision, which represented a solution *sui generis* and which was even described as a 'curiosity' from the point of view of the law of international treaties,[6] enabled Slovakia to become a party to the Convention without having to sign and ratify it. Similarly, Slovakia has been considered bound, as of 1 January 1993, by the declarations made by the Czech and Slovak Federal Republic on 18 March 1992 in respect of what were then Articles 25 and 46 of the Convention. The aforesaid decision did not give rise to any serious problems as regards its implementation in practice.

In the case of *Brežný and Brežný v Slovakia*[7] the Commission examined the question whether the Slovak Republic was bound by the Convention for the period from 18 March 1992 (the date on which the Czech and Slovak Federal Republic ratified the Convention) to 31 December 1992 (when Czechoslovakia was dissolved). Having regard to the aforesaid statements made by the Slovak authorities at the international level, to the national legislation concerning the transfer of powers arising out of the dissolution of the Czech and Slovak Federal Republic, and to the Slovak government's express confirmation, in the course of the proceedings concerning the aforesaid application, that Slovakia was responsible for matters relating to the period from 18 March to 31 December 1992, the Commission concluded that it was competent *ratione personae* to examine the case.

Similarly, when dealing with individual cases, the Commission found that it had competence *ratione temporis* to examine facts relating to the period between 18 March and 31 December 1992. This issue has arisen mostly as regards complaints under Article 6, para. 1 of the Convention about excessively lengthy judicial proceedings. For example, in its decision on the admissibility of Application 25006/94 the Commission held (in accordance with the Government's contention) that:

[6] See J.-F. Flauss, 'Convention européenne des droits de l'homme et succession d'Etats aux traités: une curiosité, la décision du Comité des Ministres du Conseil de l'Europe en date du 30 juin 1993 concernant la République tchèque et la Slovaquie', 6 (1–2) *Revue universelle des Droits de l'Homme*, pp. 1–5.

[7] Application 23131/93, (1996) 85–B, DR p. 65.

the relevant period which it had jurisdiction to consider had not begun as from the institution of the proceedings in question in November 1991, but only as from 18 March 1992 when the former Czech and Slovak Federal Republic had ratified the Convention and had recognized the right of individual application.[8]

B. THE STATUS OF THE CONVENTION IN SLOVAK LAW

1. Conditional precedence of international treaties

International treaties on human rights were incorporated into the legal order of the former Czech and Slovak Federal Republic by virtue of Constitutional Law No. 23/1991 introducing the Charter of Fundamental Rights and Freedoms. Article 2 of the aforesaid Law stipulated that international treaties on human rights and fundamental freedoms ratified and promulgated by the Czech and Slovak Federal Republic were generally binding on its territory and had precedence over domestic laws.

The authors of the Constitution of the Slovak Republic opted for a somewhat different approach which has been described as the 'conditional precedence of international treaties' or the 'principle of precedence of the more favourable rule'.[9] As indicated above, Article 11 of the Constitution provides that the provisions of the international treaties on human rights take precedence over national laws only where such treaties guarantee wider human rights and fundamental freedoms.

The incorporation into the Slovak legal order of the human rights standards provided for by the relevant international instruments gave rise, in legal theory, to different interpretations. Some authors have considered that only the provisions of the international treaties offering stronger guarantees than the domestic law have been incorporated into the latter. However, it seems more plausible that the 'stronger guarantee' requirement set out in Article 11 of the Constitution does not concern the validity and effectiveness of an international treaty in terms of domestic law, but rather constitutes a guideline for its implementation at domestic level.[10]

There seems to be no doubt, either in theory or in practice, that the substantive provisions of the Convention have a 'supra-legislative' power in the Slovak legal order, ie they take precedence (in cases specified in Article 11 of the Constitution) over national laws and bylaws.

[8] (1997) 88–A DR pp. 34 and 40.

[9] See *Komentár k Ústave Slovenskej republiky,* 1997, pp. 69–70.

[10] See B. Repík, 'La place de la Convention Européenne des Droits de l'Homme dans l'ordre juridique interne de la République Slovaque' in *Quelle Europe pour les Droits de l'Homme?* (1996), p. 372.

Academic debate arose as regards the relationship between the provisions of the Constitution and those of the Convention. In this respect, Judge Repík rightly pointed out that nothing in the Constitution of the Slovak Republic suggested that the rules of the Convention (or other international treaties on human rights) were of a 'constitutional' or even a 'supra-constitutional' nature.[11] In fact, neither the Constitution nor the Constitutional Court Act contain guidelines as regards possible conflicts between the Constitution and the provisions of international treaties by which the Slovak Republic is bound. Such conflicts are, however, difficult to conceive since the respective provisions of the Constitution largely have as their basis the human rights set out in the relevant international instruments.

The Constitutional Court indicated a possible practical solution to such questions in a decision by which it held that, *a priori*, while interpreting a legal term (the right to free education in elementary and secondary schools in this particular case) there was nothing to prevent the application of both the Constitution and the rules of interpretation in accordance with the international law of treaties. The Constitutional Court considered that Slovakia might otherwise 'fail to respect its international undertakings'.[12]

2. *Review of the compatibility of laws by the Constitutional Court*

In practical terms, nothing prevents an individual from expressly invoking the provisions of the Convention which he or she considers have been violated in proceedings before the general courts. In fact, under Article 144, para. 2 of the Constitution, 'judges are also bound by an international treaty in cases provided for by the Constitution or the law'.

The general courts' judges are entitled, in cases where they consider that a generally binding legal rule contradicts the Convention (or any other international treaty by which the Slovak Republic is bound) to stay the proceedings and request the Constitutional Court to determine the issue in accordance with Article 125(e) of the Constitution. Article 130, para. 1 of the Constitution also allows such proceedings to be brought by a group of no less than one-fifth of the members of the National Council, or by the President of the Slovak Republic, the government, or the General Prosecutor.

If the Constitutional Court finds that a generally binding legal rule is not compatible with an international treaty by which Slovakia is bound, the relevant provisions shall cease to be operative (ie they may not be applied by the competent authorities) as from the publication of the Constitutional Court's finding in the Collection of Laws. Furthermore, the authority which issued

[11] Ibid, p. 371.

[12] PL.ÚS 5/1993, (1995) *Collection of Findings and Rulings* 1993–1994, p. 179.

the relevant rule is under the obligation to bring it, within six months from the pronouncement of the Constitutional Court's finding, into conformity with the Constitution or, as the case may be, an international treaty. If the authority concerned fails to comply with this obligation, the relevant rule shall lose its legal force upon the expiry of six months from the pronouncement of the Constitutional Court's finding.[13]

As for the practical implications of such findings, it should first be noted that if a final judgment in a criminal case which has not yet been enforced was based on a rule whose incompatibility is established by the Constitutional Court, then the fact that the rule has become inoperative is a valid reason for reopening the criminal proceedings in accordance with the relevant provisions of the Code of Criminal Procedure. Other final decisions issued in civil or administrative proceedings on the basis of a rule which later lost its effect as a result of the Constitutional Court's finding are unaffected. However, any obligations which may have been imposed by virtue of such decisions are not enforceable.[14]

3. *Constitutional protection of individual human rights*

Individuals who consider that their human rights have been violated can bring proceedings before the Constitutional Court by two means.

The first is a constitutional complaint (*ústavná st'ažnost*) pursuant to Article 127 of the Constitution which provides that:

> [t]he Constitutional Court shall decide on complaints about final decisions made by central government authorities, local government authorities and local self-governing bodies in cases concerning violations of the fundamental rights and freedoms of citizens, unless the protection of such rights falls within the jurisdiction of another court.

Procedural requirements for constitutional complaints are set out in detail in the Constitutional Court Act.[15] They comprise proceedings on admissibility, in which the compliance of the complaint with the formal requirements is examined (a complainant has to be represented by a lawyer; the complaint must be substantiated; and it may not be lodged prior to the exhaustion of other available remedies, although the Constitutional Court may in exceptional cases waive this requirement; the complaint has to be lodged within two months from the delivery of the final decision; etc.) and proceedings on the merits. The introduction of a constitutional complaint has no suspensive

[13] See Article 132, para. 1 of the Constitution and section 41a of the Constitutional Court Act.

[14] See section 41b of the Constitutional Court Act.

[15] Act No. 38/1993 on the Organization of the Constitutional Court of the Slovak Republic, on the proceedings before it and on the status of its Judges of 20 January 1993 as amended, sections 49–58.

effect on the decision complained of, but the Constitutional Court may, in certain circumstances, stay its enforcement. The Constitutional Court is entitled, if it finds a violation of the Constitution, to quash the decision in question. The Constitutional Court's opinion is binding on the authority concerned which shall in such a case deliver a new decision in the matter.

The detailed specification of the proceedings concerning constitutional complaints pursuant to Article 127 of the Constitution in the Constitutional Court Act, as well as the power of the Constitutional Court to quash decisions of state administration authorities and local self-governing bodies by which an individual's human rights were violated, mean that, *a priori,* this remedy may be considered as effective, and accordingly that this procedure should be exhausted before introducing an application under the Convention.

The second method by which an individual can bring proceedings before the Constitutional Court is a petition (*podnet*) pursuant to Article 130, para. 3 of the Constitution, which provides that:

> [t]he Constitutional Court can commence proceedings also upon the petition presented by any individual or corporation claiming that his or its rights have been violated.

Originally, the Constitutional Court Act did not govern the procedure to be followed in cases concerning a petition. A partial improvement in this respect has been achieved by enacting an amendment to the Constitutional Court Act.[16]

Unlike constitutional complaints, proceedings concerning a petition are considered to have been brought only after the Constitutional Court decides to accept the petition. The wording of Article 130, para. 3 of the Constitution implies that such a decision is within the discretion of the Constitutional Court: it is therefore questionable whether this remedy can be regarded as being 'directly accessible' within the meaning of the Convention organs' case-law.[17]

Furthermore, the Constitutional Court has consistently held that it lacks jurisdiction to examine petitions filed pursuant to Article 130, para. 3 of the Constitution when the matter requires a preliminary ruling on a constitutional conflict of rules of different legal force,[18] or when the protection of the right at issue falls within the jurisdiction of the general courts.[19]

[16] See Act No. 293/1995 of 16 November 1995. Section 31a (which was included in the Constitutional Court Act by virtue of this amendment) provides that proceedings concerning a petition admitted by the Constitutional Court shall be governed, where appropriate, by the relevant provisions concerning constitutional complaints.

[17] See eg Application 12604/86, *G v Belgium*, (1991) 70 DR 125.

[18] I. ÚS 96/93, (1995) *Collection of Findings and Rulings* 1993–1994, p. 26.

[19] See eg I. ÚS 130/93, (1995) 28 *Collection of Findings and Rulings* 1993–1994, p. 169. The jurisdiction of the general courts is set out in Article 142, para. 1 of the Constitution and includes 'civil and criminal matters as well as the review of lawfulness of decisions delivered by administrative authorities'.

The enforceability of the Constitutional Court's findings of violations of individuals' human rights in proceedings pursuant to Article 130, para. 3 of the Constitution has been open to different interpretations, but the existing case-law tends to show that the Constitutional Court's powers in this respect are rather limited and that such findings are mostly of a declaratory nature. In particular, the Constitutional Court has held that it lacks jurisdiction to interfere with proceedings before the general courts or to quash decisions of the latter even in cases where it finds that they are responsible for a violation of an individual's human rights and fundamental freedoms.[20] In these circumstances, the question arises whether a petition is an effective and sufficient remedy within the meaning of the Convention organs' case-law.[21]

The aforesaid specific features of proceedings upon petition pursuant to Article 130, para. 3 of the Constitution caused the Convention organs to opt, as explained in more detail below, for a cautious approach in determining whether such a petition represents a remedy which should be exhausted before an application can be made under the Convention.

C. THE STATUS OF THE CONVENTION IN LEGISLATIVE PROCEEDINGS

Generally speaking, it is in the interest of each Contracting State to ensure to the maximum possible extent the conformity of its legislation with its undertakings in respect of international treaties.

In Slovakia, government experts must ensure, as far as possible, that each draft law submitted for enactment by the National Council conforms to the international treaties to which Slovakia is a party. Furthermore, one of the objectives of the Institute for Approximation of Law established by the government is to promote the conformity of Slovak legislation with, *inter alia*, the Council of Europe treaties.

The Constitutional Court is not entitled to be involved in the legislative process. It cannot therefore examine the conformity of draft laws with the Constitution or with the international treaties. Nevertheless, a group of Members of Parliament who consider that enacted laws are unconstitutional can institute proceedings pursuant to Article 130, para. 1(a) of the Constitution with a view to having the issue determined by the Constitutional Court. The existing practice indicates that the Constitutional Court may in

[20] See eg I. ÚS 40/95, (1996) 44 *Collection of Findings and Rulings* 1995, No. 44/95, p. 310.
[21] See eg Application 13251/87, (1991) 68 DR p. 137.

such proceedings also have recourse to the case-law under the European Convention on Human Rights.

D. EXAMPLES OF HUMAN RIGHTS CASES DECIDED BY THE NATIONAL COURTS

As a result of the strict separation of jurisdictions between the general courts and the Constitutional Court, and given the limited power of the Constitutional Court to interfere with or review proceedings held before the general courts, the latter have in many cases delivered final decisions on issues which, in substance, fall under the Convention. However, during the period under consideration only sporadic express references were made to the provisions of the Convention in judgments delivered by the general courts.

The situation is different as regards decisions delivered by the Constitutional Court. This is not surprising given its place and role in the Slovak constitutional system. It should be noted that the Constitutional Court has most frequently applied or referred to the Convention in the context of proceedings concerning the 'conformity' of legal rules which were instituted at the request of authorities or persons empowered to do so by virtue of Article 130, para. 1(a) to (e) of the Constitution, rather than by individuals alleging a violation of their rights. An exhaustive analysis of this issue would exceed the scope of this chapter. The following overview is therefore limited to illustrating the main issues addressed by the Constitutional Court in some of the relevant cases.

In case PL. ÚS 6/94 the Constitutional Court concluded, upon a petition brought by a Higher Military Court's Chamber President, that the relevant provision of the Substitute Civilian Service Act 1992 prevented a certain group of conscripts from effectively availing themselves of their constitutional right to conscientious objection to military service under the same conditions as other conscripts in a similar position. In its finding the Constitutional Court pointed out that it had had regard also to the case-law of the 'Council of Europe's bodies' governing the prohibition of discrimination, and it expressly referred to the Committee of Ministers' Resolution in the case of *Grandrath*.[22]

In another case the Constitutional Court found, in the context of proceedings brought by forty Members of the National Council, that Act No. 370/1994 (by which the National Council had quashed earlier government

[22] (1995) *Collection of Findings and Rulings* 1993–1994, No. 5 pp. 70–74.

decisions on the denationalization of certain enterprises) was incompatible with the right to peaceful enjoyment of one's possessions as guaranteed by Article 1 of Protocol No. 1. The Constitutional Court noted that by adopting Act No. 370/1994 the National Council had exceeded its power.[23]

Proceedings in case II. ÚS 8/96 were brought upon a petition under Article 130, para. 3 of the Constitution. The petitioner was attacked near his home in Slovakia and was later found intoxicated in a car parked in an Austrian town near the Slovak border. The Austrian authorities detained the petitioner pending his extradition to Germany (which ultimately did not take place) in the context of criminal proceedings brought against him in that country. Subsequently, criminal proceedings were also brought against the petitioner in Slovakia and he unsuccessfully requested that the Slovak authorities take the necessary measures to ensure his return to Slovakia.

In its finding the Constitutional Court recalled, with reference to the judgment of the European Court of Human Rights in the case of *Drozd and Janousek v France and Spain*,[24] that the term 'jurisdiction' within the meaning of Article 1 of the Convention was not limited to the national territory of a High Contracting Party and held that the petitioner's right to enter the territory of Slovakia freely as guaranteed by Article 23, para. 4 of the Constitution and Article 12, para. 4 of the International Covenant on Civil and Political Rights, had been violated in that, during a specific period, the Ministry of Foreign Affairs had failed to take any action in response to his request that it ensure his return to Slovakia. The Constitutional Court further dismissed the petitioner's complaint about a violation of his right to respect for his family life as guaranteed by Article 8, para. 1 of the Convention on the ground that he had not raised it first before the competent Slovak authorities.[25]

In case PL. ÚS 43/95, in which proceedings had been brought at the request of the President of the Slovak Republic, the Constitutional Court found, *inter alia*, that an amendment of the Code of Civil Procedure entitling public prosecutors to participate, at the request of a general court, in proceedings in civil matters violated the principle of equality of the parties and was also contrary to the parties' right to respect for their private life as guaranteed by Article 8, para. 1 of the Convention.[26]

[23] PL. ÚS 16/95, (1996) 6 *Collection of Findings and Rulings* 1995, p. 38.
[24] Judgment of 26 June 1992,Series A No. 240.
[25] (1997) 6 *Collection of Findings and Rulings* 1996, p. 96.
[26] (1997) 7 *Collection of Findings and Rulings* 1996, p. 123.

E. CASES BROUGHT BEFORE THE EUROPEAN COMMISSION AND COURT OF HUMAN RIGHTS

Between 1 January 1993 and 31 December 2000 Slovakia was not involved in any inter-state case under the Convention. Table 29.1 is an overview of the individual applications brought against the Slovak Republic before the European Commission of Human Rights and the decisions and reports adopted on them by the latter.[27]

Table 29.1: Applications against the Slovak Republic before the European Commission

	1993	1994	1995	1996	1997	1998 (to 30 September)
Provisional files opened	36	100	83	165	160	98
Applications registered	4	36	45	80	81	65
Applications declared inadmissible or struck off the list	—	18	33	61	38	64
Applications declared admissible	—	—	—	3	4	2
Applications referred to the Slovak government	—	1	5	8	2	6
Friendly settlement reports	—	—	—	—	1	—
Reports on the merits	—	—	—	—	3	2
Reports striking a case off the list	—	—	—	—	—	—

By 1 January 2001 the above applications had given rise to six judgments (cases of *Lauko*, *Kadubec*, *Matter*, *I.S.*, *Jóri*, and *Vodeničarov*) and three resolutions by the Committee of Ministers (cases of *Savič*, *P.S.*, and *Preložnik*) finding Slovakia to be in violation of the Convention. The European Court of Human Rights further delivered four other judgments striking admissible cases out of the list on the ground that they had been settled (cases of *Bohunický*, *J.K.*, *Gaulieder*, and *Degro*).

[27] See *European Commission of Human Rights: Surveys of activities and statistics.*

Table 29.2: Applications against the Slovak Republic before the European Court of Human Rights (after the entry into force of Protocol No. 11)

	1998 (1.11.–21.12.)	1999	2000 (1.1.–31.8.)
Provisional files opened	84	227	N/A
Applications registered	5	163	178
Applications declared inadmissible or struck off	3	42	N/A
Applications referred to the Slovak government	0	14	N/A
Applications declared admissible	0	3	3
Judgments	0	2	4

1. The principal reasons for inadmissibility of applications brought against Slovakia

Table 29.1 shows that, during the initial period of the operation of the Convention system in respect of Slovakia, the majority of cases did not satisfy the admissibility requirements. Because of the relative lack of knowledge about Convention proceedings, applicants often sought redress in matters which were outside the Convention organs' jurisdiction *ratione temporis* or *ratione materiae*. In this respect, it is worth mentioning that applicants from Slovakia were rarely represented by lawyers before the Convention organs.

In a number of cases persons who considered that their human rights had been violated in proceedings before the general courts sought redress, prior to lodging an application before the Constitutional Court pursuant to Article 130, para. 3 of the Constitution. However, as indicated above, the Constitutional Court has consistently held that it lacks jurisdiction to interfere with proceedings before the general courts or to review their decisions. The Convention organs therefore could not consider the Constitutional Court's decisions rejecting a petition for lack of jurisdiction as 'final' within the meaning of what was then Article 26 of the Convention. As a result, the applicants in the majority of such cases failed to file their application within the six-month time-limit.

In the same way the Convention organs approached the cases in which the Supreme Court had rejected an appeal on points of law (*dovolanie*) on the basis that such a remedy was not available under the relevant provisions of the Code of Civil Procedure,[28] and also cases in which the applicants consid-

[28] See eg Application 29031/95, *MS v Slovakia*, Decision of 22 October 97.

ered as 'final' the decision by which their request for a complaint about a breach of the law to be lodged on their behalf was dismissed by the General Prosecutor, such a remedy being within the discretion of the latter.[29]

Finally, in a considerable number of cases against Slovakia, the Commission and the Court had to invoke their established case-law according to which a procedure directed towards reopening a case is not normally a remedy which need be exhausted and which could be taken into account for the purposes of the six-month rule.[30]

2. Assessment of the 'effectiveness' of constitutional petitions

In view of the aforementioned specific features of the petition proceedings under Article 130, para. 3 of the Constitution and the fact that the Constitutional Court's case-law in this respect was in the process of being established, the Commission examined the question whether the applicants should exhaust this remedy, as indicated above, on a case-by-case basis.

Thus the government raised the objection of non-exhaustion of domestic remedies in respect of the applicant's complaint about excessively lengthy civil proceedings which were still pending in Application 25006/94.[31] The government relied on an earlier finding by the Constitutional Court of a violation of the petitioner's constitutional rights in a similar case and argued that such a finding entitled the person concerned to claim damages under the State Liability Act.

The Commission held, however, that the decisive question in assessing the effectiveness of a remedy concerning a complaint about the length of proceedings was whether the applicant could raise this complaint before domestic courts by claiming specific redress; ie whether a remedy existed that could answer his or her complaints by providing direct and speedy, and not merely indirect, protection of the rights guaranteed in Article 6, para. 1 of the Convention. When examining the petition to the Constitutional Court from this point of view, the Commission found that the Constitutional Court could make a declaration of the excessive length of proceedings but was incapable of accelerating the proceedings which were still pending.[32] Accordingly, a petition to the Constitutional Court was not considered by the Commission as an effective remedy in cases concerning the length of pending proceedings. This approach was upheld by the new Court of Human Rights in eg

[29] See eg Application 25457/94, *Lukáčová-Kurucová v Slovakia*, Decision of 3 February 1995; Application 38855/97 *Malfatti v Slovakia*, Decision of 3 December 1997.

[30] See eg Application 30366/96, *TC v Slovakia*, Decision of 5 December 1996.

[31] *IS v Slovakia,* (1997) 88–A, DR p. 34.

[32] See also Application 25289/94, *Preložník v Slovakia*, Decision of 15 January 1997.

Remšíková v Slovakia, Application 46843/99, Decision of 7 December 2000. The Commission and the Court did not determine whether a petition could be regarded as an effective remedy as regards complaints about the length of proceedings in which a final decision has been rendered.

In its decision on the admissibility of Application 26384/95,[33] the Commission concluded that a petition to the Constitutional Court could also not be considered an effective remedy as regards complaints about the absence of a public hearing in proceedings for judicial review of the lawfulness of decisions delivered by administrative authorities.

In its aforesaid decision the Commission recalled that the formal issuing of proceedings pursuant to Article 130, para. 3 of the Constitution depended on the decision of the Constitutional Court, that the administrative court judge was entitled, in domestic law, not to hold an oral hearing, and that the Constitutional Court had earlier found that it could not interfere with proceedings before the general courts. Furthermore, the Commission held that even a possible finding by the Constitutional Court of a violation of the applicant's right to a fair and public hearing would not be capable of directly remedying the state of affairs complained of as the Constitutional Court lacked jurisdiction to quash the general courts' decisions. It therefore concluded that a petition to the Constitutional Court could not be regarded with a sufficient degree of certainty as an effective remedy in the case at issue.

3. Complaints under Article 6 of the Convention

The bulk of applications against Slovakia have concerned various aspects of the right to a fair trial enshrined in Article 6 of the Convention. This is not surprising given the scope and the 'central position' of this provision in the Convention.[34]

Most of the complaints under Article 6 were of a 'fourth-instance' nature, ie they concerned mistakes allegedly committed by Slovak courts when establishing the relevant facts of the case and assessing them from the legal point of view. The Commission and the Court, having reiterated that they had only limited power to deal with applications alleging errors of law or fact by domestic courts, confined themselves to ascertaining whether the decisions complained of were unfair or arbitrary.[35]

[33] *Šamková v Slovakia*, (1996) 86–A, DR p. 143.

[34] See *Sunday Times v United Kingdom*, Judgment of 26 April 1997, Series A No. 30, p. 34, para. 55.

[35] See eg Application 25461/94, *Seidlová v Slovakia*, Decision of 6 September 1995; Application 31904/96, *Atlas v Slovakia*, Decision of 11 September 1997; Application 26962/95, *Šulko v Slovakia*, Decision of 6 September 1995.

a. Restrictions on judicial review of certain decisions under the Minor Offences Act The first two cases in which the European Court of Human Rights found Slovakia to be in violation of the Convention concerned the impossibility of judicial review of decisions under the Minor Offences Act imposing fines not exceeding SKK 2,000.[36]

The applicants were fined by the competent local authorities pursuant to the Minor Offences Act: *I. Lauko* was fined SKK 300 on the ground that without justification he had accused his neighbours of causing a nuisance; *J. Kadubec* was fined SKK 1,000 for having disturbed boarders in a spa house and for having refused to obey police officers. The competent district offices dismissed the applicants' appeals. Since section 83(1) of the Minor Offences Act provided for review by the general courts of decisions relating to minor offences only in cases where, *inter alia,* a fine exceeding SKK 2,000 was imposed, the applicants sought redress before the Constitutional Court. However, in the case of *I. Lauko* the Constitutional Court declared itself bound by the aforesaid provision of the Minor Offences Act. The constitutional complaint by *J. Kadubec* was rejected for formal reasons. The Commission declared admissible the applicants' complaints under Articles 6, para. 1 and 13 of the Convention that their right to a fair hearing before an independent and impartial tribunal established by law had been violated in the proceedings before the competent administrative authorities and that they had had no effective remedy before a national authority in this respect. In the case of *J. Kadubec* the Commission also declared admissible the complaint under Article 6, para. 3(c) of the Convention that the applicant was not permitted to defend himself with legal assistance in the proceedings in question.[37]

The Court, like the Commission in its final reports,[38] first established, on the basis of the criteria set out in the case-law (the formal qualification of the offence under domestic law, the nature of the offence, and the nature and degree of severity of the penalty that the individual risked incurring) that Article 6, para. 1 of the Convention was applicable under its criminal head. The Court mainly relied on the nature of the minor offences for which the applicants had been fined. In particular, it noted that the legal rules infringed by the applicants were of a general character and that the penalties imposed had both a deterrent and a punitive purpose. The Court considered irrelevant the relative lack of seriousness of the penalties at stake.

Reaching the conclusion that the guarantees of Article 6, para. 1 had not been respected, the Court noted that the only bodies which had decided the

[36] See *Lauko v Slovakia* and *Kadubec v Slovakia*, Judgments of 2 September 1998.

[37] See Applications 26138/95 and 27061/95, Decision of 21 October 1996.

[38] Reports on the merits pursuant to the then Article 31 of the Convention adopted on 30 October 1997.

applicants' cases were authorities charged with carrying out local state administration under the control of the government. Since the officers of these authorities had the status of salaried employees, and in the absence of any guarantees against outside pressures and any appearance of independence, the Court concluded that those bodies could not be considered to be 'independent' of the executive.

In view of its conclusion under Article 6, para. 1 of the Convention, the Court, like the Commission, did not consider it necessary to examine the applicants' remaining complaints.

The Court awarded each of the applicants SKK 5,000 in respect of non-pecuniary damage and specific sums in respect of costs and expenses.

b. Complaints about excessively lengthy proceedings Among the cases in which the Convention organs found that there was an issue under the Convention, the problem of delays in proceedings in civil cases occurred most frequently. They found a violation of the Convention on account of excessively lengthy proceedings in five cases (cases of *Preložnik*, *P.S.*, *Matter*, *I.S.*, and *Jóri*). Two admissible cases concerning this issue (cases of *Bohunický* and *Degro*) were settled. The number of registered applications concerning this issue has considerably increased in 1999 and 2000.

c. Complaints about absence of a public hearing before administrative courts In two cases the Commission was seized with complaints concerning the absence of an oral hearing in the course of judicial review of the lawfulness of decisions delivered by administrative authorities.[39] It should be noted in this respect that section 250f of the Code of Civil Procedure entitles administrative courts[40] to deliver a judgment without a prior oral hearing in simple cases, in particular when there is no doubt that the administrative organs established the facts correctly and the point at issue is a question of law. The Commission did not examine the merits of these applications since a friendly settlement was reached in both cases on terms which are set out below.

d. Other complaints raised under Article 6 In its decision on the admissibility of Application 32110/96, the Commission found compatible with Article 6, paras. 1 and 3(d) of the Convention that criminal courts had considered statements made by the applicant's co-accused in pre-trial proceedings notwithstanding that he had later denied them and had refused to make any statements at trial. The Commission noted, in particular, that the domestic courts could consider those statements to be corroborated by other evidence

[39] Application 26384/95, *Šamková v Slovakia*, (1997) 88–A DR 67; Application 30903/96, *Poláková and Machová v Slovakia*, Decision of 3 December 1997.

[40] The administrative judiciary is governed by Part Five of the Code of Civil Procedure. It is exercised by separate chambers of the general courts.

before them and concluded that the rights of the defence had been respected.[41]

In several cases concerning dismissals from the police, the Commission reiterated that disputes relating to the recruitment, careers, and termination of service of civil servants were, as a general rule, outside the scope of Article 6, para. 1 of the Convention.[42]

Refusal to grant exemption from the obligation to pay court fees[43] and rejection of a claim for relief from hardship[44] are two examples of other issues examined by the Commission under Article 6 of the Convention.

4. Rehabilitation and restitution proceedings and the guarantees of Article 1 of Protocol No. 1

A considerable number of applications against Slovakia have concerned proceedings relating to claims for the rehabilitation, compensation, or restitution of property which had their basis in legislation enacted in Czechoslovakia after the fall of the Communist regime. For example, the purpose of the Judicial Rehabilitation Act 1990 was to quash convictions for offences pronounced between 25 February 1948 and 1 January 1990 where such convictions were incompatible with the principles of a democratic society respecting political rights and freedoms. The Extrajudicial Rehabilitation Act 1991 was aimed at redressing certain infringements of property and social rights which occurred between 1948 and 1989. The Land Ownership Act 1991 provided for the restitution of land and other agricultural property taken from its original owners under certain circumstances. This legislation did not cover all wrongs committed in the past, and it subjected the grant of redress to a number of conditions. As a result, persons who had not been able to have their claims satisfied under these laws considered that their rights had been infringed anew and many of them tried to obtain redress before the Convention organs.

In the case of *Brežný and Brežný*[45] the applicants' earlier convictions (including the consequential decision on confiscation of their property) had been quashed *ex tunc* in 1990 pursuant to the Judicial Rehabilitation Act. However, the applicants could not have their property restored as they did not reside permanently within the territory of the Slovak Republic (or, formerly, the Czech and Slovak Federal Republic) as required by the Extrajudicial Rehabilitation Act which also governed the conditions for granting redress to

[41] *Pobožny v Slovakia*, Decision of 16 April 1998.

[42] Application 30900/96, *Gallo v Slovakia*, Decision of 4 September 1996; Application 33669/96, *Perényi v Slovakia*, Decision of 14 January 1998.

[43] Application 33466/96, *Šinko v Slovakia*, Decision of 20 May 1998.

[44] Application 27552/95, *Machatová v Slovakia*, Decision of 2 July 1997.

[45] See note 7 above.

persons who had been judicially rehabilitated. Before the Commission the applicants complained, *inter alia*, of a violation of their right to peaceful enjoyment of their possessions as guaranteed by Article 1 of Protocol No. 1 and that the aforesaid permanent residence requirement was discriminatory.

The Commission found that, despite their judicial rehabilitation in 1990, the applicants' former right of ownership over the confiscated possessions was still not capable of being effectively exercised as the Judicial Rehabilitation Act expressly reserved the detailed provisions regarding redress for later legislation. For this reason, the Commission considered that when claiming the restitution of their property pursuant to the Extrajudicial Rehabilitation Act, the applicants could not be considered as owners but merely as claimants. Referring to the Convention organs' established case-law under Article 1 of Protocol No. 1, it held that the applicants' action for restitution concerned neither 'existing possessions' nor a claim which they could, at least arguably, 'legitimately expect' to have been upheld and enforced. The Commission therefore concluded that there had been no interference with the applicants' rights under Article 1 of Protocol No. 1 and declared this part of the application incompatible *ratione materiae* with the Convention. The Commission also declared inadmissible the applicants' complaint of discrimination on the ground that, given its finding under Article 1 of Protocol No. 1, Article 14 was not applicable either.

In several other cases relating to claims for compensation or restitution of property, the Commission held that the deprivation of property or another right *in rem* was in principle an instantaneous act which did not constitute a continuing 'deprivation of a right'. It therefore declared complaints of deprivation of property which occurred prior to the fall of the Communist regime in Czechoslovakia inadmissible as being incompatible *ratione temporis* with the provisions of the Convention. When addressing complaints about the dismissal of claims for restitution of such property, the Commission recalled that Article 1 of Protocol No. 1 applied only to 'existing possessions' and that it did not guarantee any right to acquire property. Such complaints were therefore dismissed as being incompatible *ratione materiae* with the Convention.[46]

In the case of *Haas and Haasová*[47] the Commission was confronted with the reverse situation. In 1989 the applicants purchased a house in good faith which had been transferred to state ownership after the original owners had left the former Czechoslovakia. They paid the purchase price as determined by an expert appointed by a public authority. In 1995 the applicants were ordered to restore the house to the original owners pursuant to the

[46] See eg Application 24506/94, *Gašparetz v Slovakia*, Decision of 28 June 1995; Application 32683/96, *Nemanová v Slovakia*, Decision of 14 January 1998.

[47] Application 34180/96, Decision of 4 March 1998.

Extrajudicial Rehabilitation Act on the ground that the house had been transferred to state ownership without any relevant legal reason and that the actual purchase price had not conformed to the price regulation then in force.

When examining the case under Article 1 of Protocol No. 1, the Commission found that the deprivation of possessions in question was provided for by the relevant provisions of the Extrajudicial Rehabilitation Act and that it had pursued a legitimate aim which was also in the public interest, namely to safeguard the lawfulness of legal transactions, to promote the principles of a democratic society, and to provide redress where wrongs had been committed as a result of disrespect of such principles. The Commission noted that the applicants had received the purchase price and had been living in the house for more than five years. It found, with reference to the wide margin of appreciation enjoyed by the contracting states in similar cases, that there had been a reasonable relationship of proportionality between the means employed and the aims sought to be realized.

Finally, it should be noted that on 1 February 2001 the European Court of Human Rights (Second Section) declared admissible the case of *Kopecký v Slovakia* (Application 44912/98) concerning the dismissal of the applicant's claim for restitution of gold and silver coins. The applicant proved that the coins had been brought to the Ministry of the Interior after they had been taken away from his late father, but the domestic courts dismissed his claim on the ground that he had failed to show where they were deposited at the moment when he filed his action.

5. *Complaints relating to deprivation of liberty*

In the case of *Matter*[48] the Commission declared admissible the applicant's complaint that his right to respect for his private life as guaranteed by Article 8 of the Convention had been violated as a result of his forcible examination in a mental hospital. It is worth mentioning in this respect that the examination was ordered after the applicant had refused to undergo an examination voluntarily in the context of proceedings brought at his own initiative with a view to determining whether legal capacity could be restored to him. In its judgment delivered on 5 July 1999 the Court (Second Section) found that the interference had been 'necessary in a democratic society' within the meaning of Article 8 § 2 of the Convention.

In its resolution adopted on 18 January 1999 the Committee of Ministers upheld the Commission's view that in the case of *Savič* (Application 28409/95) there had been a violation of Article 5, paragraph 3 of the Convention on account of the excessive length of the applicant's detention on remand. The

[48] Application 31534/96, *Matter v Slovakia*, Decision of 16 September 1997.

Committee of Ministers also found a violation of Article 5, paragraph 4 of the Convention on account of the excessive length and unfairness of certain proceedings relating to the applicant's request for release.

In the *Vodeničarov* judgment delivered on 21 December 2000 the Court confirmed the Commission's opinion that the proceedings available for the review of the applicant's detention for observation in a mental hospital (including proceedings on a petition under Article 130, para. 3 of the Constitution) did not satisfy the requirements of Article 5 § 4 of the Convention.

6. *Other issues raised before the Commission and the Court*

The use and separation of matrimonial property after the dissolution of a marriage,[49] refusal to extend visiting rights to a parent who did not have the custody of his child,[50] labour disputes, and the protection of one's good name and reputation are some of the other main issues which have been complained of in applications filed against Slovakia. In the case of *Gaulieder* (Application 36909/97) the applicant alleged a violation of Article 3 of Protocol No. 1 in that his office of a Member of Parliament had been terminated against his will. Following the settlement reached between the parties the Court struck the case out of its list by a judgment delivered on 18 May 2000. In the case of *Spišák* (Application 4373/98) the applicant also alleged a violation of Article 3 of Protocol No. 1 in that he had been prevented from exercising the office of a Member of Parliament. The case was settled at the pre-admissibility stage and struck out of the list by the Court's Decision of 7 December 2000.

F. ACTION TAKEN BY THE SLOVAK AUTHORITIES UPON APPLICATIONS INTRODUCED UNDER THE CONVENTION

As regards the cases of *Kadubec* and *Lauko,* it is worth mentioning that on 15 October 1998 the Constitutional Court found, in proceedings brought by the General Prosecutor, that Section 83(1) of the Minor Offences Act was unconstitutional and contrary to Article 6 § 1 of the Convention to the extent that it limited the judicial review of decisions on minor offences to, inter alia, fines exceeding SKK 2,000. The Constitutional Court's finding was published in the Collection of Laws on 23 October 1998. As from this date the relevant provisions of Section 83(1) of the Minor Offences Act became ineffective.

[49] See eg Application 24505/94, *Beke v Slovakia,* Decision of 19 October 1995; Application 33706/96, *EP v Slovakia,* Decision of 9 Sepetember 1998.

[50] Application 28407/95, *Olle v Slovakia,* Decision of 23 December 1996.

In the *Šamková* case the Commission adopted a report pursuant to what was then Article 28, para. 1 of the Convention noting that the parties had reached a friendly settlement on the basis of respect for human rights as defined in the Convention.[51]

In the agreement, the government undertook to provide the necessary conditions for an oral hearing of the applicant's claim. For this purpose the parties agreed that the applicant would file a petition for a retrial with the competent administrative authority which would consider the Commission's admissibility decision of 26 June 1996 to be a new fact of considerable importance justifying the commencement of new proceedings in her case.

The friendly settlement, which the parties agreed not to interpret as any admission by the government of Slovakia of any violation of the Convention, further stated that, should the applicant's case be unsuccessful at the oral hearing before the administrative authority, the competent administrative court would be ready to decide on the appeal at an oral hearing in conformity with the requirements of Article 6, para. 1 of the Convention. Furthermore, the government undertook to draw the attention of the national judicial authorities in an adequate manner to the urgent need for ensuring respect for the requirements of Article 6, para. 1 of the Convention when applying the provisions of section 250f of the Code of Civil Procedure.

A similar agreement was reached, prior to the delivery of a decision on admissibility, in Application 30903/96 concerning the same issue. The Commission therefore decided to strike the case out of its list.[52]

In Application 26079/94 the applicant company alleged violations of its right to freedom of expression, to the peaceful enjoyment of its possessions, and to a fair trial in that the Slovak authorities, through the state-owned Slovak Telecommunications, had interrupted its broadcasts. After the case had been communicated the manager of the applicant company informed the Commission that the relations between his company and its contractual partner, Slovak Radio, had been settled by agreement and that his company no longer intended to pursue its application. It was therefore struck out of the Commission's list.[53]

G. ASSESSMENT AND PROSPECTS

Generally speaking, the compatibility of a state's legal system and practice with the Convention can only be objectively assessed several years after it has

[51] Application 26384/95, (1997) 88–A DR p. 67.
[52] See note 39 above.
[53] *CDI Holding AG v Slovakia*, Decision of 16 October 1996.

become a party to the Convention. As with the other contracting states, neither the number of applications brought nor the number of cases in which a violation of the Convention was found is in itself conclusive of the human rights situation in Slovakia.

The decisions on applications against Slovakia delivered by the Convention organs during the period under consideration do not disclose any serious shortcomings. They indicate that the restrictions on judicial review of certain decisions under the Minor Offences Act, delays in proceedings resulting from the heavy workload of courts dealing with civil matters (particularly commercial disputes) and the administrative courts' power under section 250f of the Code of Civil Procedure to deliver judgment without a prior oral hearing of the case, are the principal areas in which Convention-related issues result from the domestic legal system itself rather than from erroneous implementation in individual cases.

Probably the most important achievement of the operation of the Convention system with respect to Slovakia is the fact that the rights and freedoms guaranteed by the Convention form a part of Slovakia's legal order and that the Slovak authorities are bound, both when making and when implementing the law, to ensure respect for these rights and freedoms. Furthermore, the Slovak legal system provides for the possibility of remedying alleged violations of individuals' Convention rights at the domestic level. It is true that certain improvements in this respect are conceivable, in particular as regards the effectiveness of protection of individuals' human rights in proceedings under Article 130, para. 3 of the Constitution, which has been admitted at the national level.[54]

In addition, and whatever the position may be in terms of domestic law, individuals are entitled to lodge an application under the Convention. Since Slovakia undertook to abide by the Convention organs' decisions in cases to which it may be a party, the effective protection of an individual's Convention rights is, in any event, subsidiarily ensured at the international level even in cases where redress could not be obtained before the domestic authorities.

In order to promote the operation of the Convention system on a larger scale and in a more effective manner as regards Slovakia, further dissemination of information about its functioning is desirable. Manifold activities have been organized in this respect by the Council of Europe, the UNHCR Liaison Office in Slovakia, the Ministry of Justice, and the Slovak National Centre for Human Rights. Since 1997 a bimonthly journal has been published in co-operation with the Information Centre of the Council of Europe in

[54] See the Foreword by the President of the Constitutional Court to the *Collection of Findings and Rulings 1993–1994*, pp. 5, 12.

Bratislava and the Office of the Government's Agent with a view to acquainting the Slovak public with the case-law of the Strasbourg organs.

However, the relatively high rate of inadmissible applications and the small number of cases in which applicants have been represented by practising lawyers shows that there is a need for further action in this respect. In fact, a properly presented human rights case before the national courts would have better prospects of meeting the admissibility criteria (especially as regards the requirement of exhausting domestic remedies) in the event that the case was subsequently brought to Strasbourg.

Finally, as domestic law is constantly developing and since the Convention is a living instrument to be interpreted in the light of the present-day conditions,[55] the future will show the continuing impact of the Convention system on Slovakia.[56]

[55] *Inze v Austria*, Judgment of 28 October 1987, Series A No. 126, p. 18, para. 41.

[56] On 23 February 2001 the National Council of the Slovak Republic adopted Constitutional Law No. 90/2001 introducing substantial amendments to the Constitution of Slovakia. The law provides, *inter alia*, that international treaties on human rights and fundamental freedoms which are directly applicable in Slovakia take precedence over national laws (Article 7, para. 5 of the amended Constitution). The amended Constitution (Article 127, para. 3) gives more power to the Constitutional Court in that it will be able to grant just satisfaction to persons whose fundamental rights have been violated. The respective amendments, which for time reasons could not be reflected in detail in this contribution, will enter into force on 1 July 2001 and on 1 January 2002. Further information can be found on the Constitutional Court's internet page: www.concourt.sk.

30

Slovenia

ARNE MAVČIČ

A. INTRODUCTION

The 1991 Constitution of the Republic of Slovenia guarantees wide protection against all forms of inequality and discrimination, much wider than international documents, including the European Convention for the Protection of Human Rights and Fundamental Freedoms (hereinafter 'the Convention').[1] In addition, the other rights guaranteed by provisions of the 1991 Constitution (eg the freedom to profess one's national affiliation, the right to use a minority language and script, the special rights of the Italian and Hungarian ethnic communities in Slovenia, as well as the status and special rights of Romany communities in Slovenia) are wider than the generally very narrow provisions concerning such rights in international instruments. The above-mentioned provisions of the 1991 Constitution exceed the Convention, which is silent on those matters.[2] The issue of the limitation, restriction, or

[1] See D. Tuerk, *Ustava Republike Slovenije in Europska konvencija o varstvu lovekovih provic in temeljnih svoboš in: Potencial mednarodnih standardov za doma i razvoj prava o lovekovih pravicah*, Slovenija in evropska Konvencija o lovekovih pravicah (Ljubljana, 1993), pp. 20–21.

[2] For comparative overviews of national regulations and the regulation of these matters by the Convention, see eg P. Jambrek, *Slovensko Ustavno sodišče pod okriljem evropskih standardov in mehanizmov zar varovanje človekovih pravic*, Temeljne pravice (Cankarjeva Založba, 1997) 340. On the right to life: Convention, Article 2 and Protocol No. 6; Constitution, Article 17. Prohibition of torture: Convention, Article 3; Constitution, Article 18, partially Article 21. Prohibition of slavery and forced labour: Convention, Article 4; Constitution, Article 49. Right to liberty and security: Convention, Articles 1 and 5 of Protocol No. 4; Constitution, Articles 19, 20, and 34. Right to a fair trial: Convention, Article 6 and Articles 2, 3, and 4 of Protocol No. 7; Constitution, Articles 23, 24, 27, 29, 30 and 31. Right to an effective remedy: Convention: Article 13; Constitution, Article 25. Principle of legality in criminal law: Convention, Article 7; Constitution, Article 28. Right to respect for private and family life: Convention, Article 8; Constitution, Articles 35, 36, and 37. Right to marry and equality of spouses: Convention, Article 12 and Article 5 of Protocol No. 7; Constitution, Article 53. Freedom of thought, conscience, and religion: Convention, Article 9; Constitution, Article 41. Freedom of expression: Convention, Article 10; Constitution, Article 39. Freedom of assembly and association: Convention, Article 11; Constitution, Articles 42 and 76. Protection of property: Convention, Article 1 of Protocol No. 1; Constitution, Articles 33, 67–71. Right to education and the rights of parents: Convention, Article 2 of Protocol No. 1; Constitution, Articles 54 and 57. Right to free elections: Convention, Article 3 of Protocol No. 1; Constitution, Article 43. Freedom of

temporary suspension of human rights as regulated by the 1991 Constitution is generally subject to some important conditions, eg legality, legitimacy, and urgency. By following the Strasbourg case-law, the framers of the Constitution were able to stipulate the necessary safeguards concerning urgent needs of society which allow only for a narrow margin of discretion on the part of State bodies introducing restrictions of human rights and fundamental freedoms.

The Statute of the Council of Europe came into force for Slovenia on 14 May 1993. The Convention was ratified on 31 May 1994. The Ratification of the Convention Act (in respect of ratification also of Article 25, Article 46, Protocol No. 1, and Protocols Nos. 4, 6, 7, 9, and 11) was published on 13 June 1994 (Official Gazette RS, No. 33/94) and came into force on the fifteenth day following publication. On 28 June 1994 Slovenia formally ratified the Convention in Strasbourg by depositing the appropriate instruments with the Secretary General of the Council of Europe. When ratifying the Convention Slovenia made no reservations because new legislation had been prepared following international standards and the Convention.[3] It is also interesting to note that Slovenia was the first member state to ratify Protocol No. 11. Slovenia recognized the competence of the European Commission and the jurisdiction of European Court of Human Rights under former Articles 25 and 46 of the Convention for an indeterminate period.[4] In addition, the Slovenian declarations included a restriction *ratione temporis*, to the effect that the competence of the Commission and the jurisdiction of Court are recognized only for facts arising after the entry into force of the Convention and its Protocols with respect to Slovenia on 28 June 1994.

Some decisions of the Slovenian Constitutional Court referred to the Convention even before it became formally binding for Slovenia.

Decision No. U-I-98/91 of 10 December 1992 (Official Gazette RS, No. 61/92, OdlUS I, 101) The Constitutional Court decided that statutory provisions which allowed administrative organs not to state the reasons for an individual administrative decision made on the basis of discretion and which decreed discretionary decisions in a bylaw are contrary to the legal system of the Republic of Slovenia and cannot be used according to their intention. As one of the reasons for its decision, the Court recalled that Article 13 of the ECHR ensures to everyone an effective legal remedy following the violation of his or her rights and freedoms specified therein. The Court observed that Slovenia had not yet signed and ratified the Convention, but considering its

movement: Convention, Article 2 of Protocol No. 4; Constitution, Article 32. Prohibition of expulsion of nationals: Convention, Article 3 of Protocol No. 4; Constitution, Article 47. Rights of aliens: Convention, Article 16, Article 4 of Protocol No. 4, and Article 1 of Protocol No. 7. Prohibition of discrimination: Convention, Article 14; Constitution, Article 14.

[3] Jambrek, note 2 above, pp. 338–339.

[4] See Jambrek, note 2 above, p. 348.

desire to join the Council of Europe it would necessarily have to do so, for which reason it was appropriate that Slovenian legislation be adjusted to meet the criteria of the Convention as soon as possible.

Ruling No. U-I-48/92 of 11 February 1993 (Official Gazette RS, No. 12/93, OdlUS II, 15) The Constitutional Court, taking into consideration the case-law of the European Court of Human Rights concerning Article 11 of the Convention (freedom of association), decided that obligatory association with a chamber of doctors does not constitute a limitation of the constitutional freedom of association guaranteed under Article 42 of the Slovenian Constitution.

The Constitutional Court based its decision on the case-law of the European Court of Human Rights, which, when considering mandatory membership of the *Ordre des Médecins* (medical association) of Belgium, had taken the position that the *Ordre des Médecins* was an institution of public law exercising public control over medical practice. As such, the *Ordre* could not be considered to be an 'association' in the sense of Article 11 of the Convention. Mandatory membership of the *Ordre des Médecins* does not entail any restrictions of the right ensured by Article 11 of the said Convention.[5]

Ruling No. U-I-60/92 of 17 June 1993 (OdlUS II, 54) The Constitutional Court, taking into consideration the case-law of the European Court of Human Rights concerning Article 6 of the Convention (the right to a fair trial), Article 2 of Protocol No. 7 (the right of appeal in criminal matters), and Article 13 of the Convention (the right to an effective remedy) decided that the regulation of legal remedies before the courts of associated labour was not contrary to Article 14 (equality before law), Article 15 (the exercise and restriction of rights), Article 22 (the equal protection of rights), nor Article 25 (the right to a legal remedy).

B. THE STATUS OF THE CONVENTION IN NATIONAL LAW

Slovenia is bound by constitutional provisions which require that statutes and other regulations must comply with generally accepted principles of international law and be in accordance with binding international agreements.[6] The international agreements to which Slovenia accedes take immediate

[5] Case of *Le Compte, Van Leuven, and De Meyere v Belgium*, Judgment of 23 June 1981, Series A No. 43, pp. 64–65; see V. Berger, *Case-Law of the European Court of Human Rights*, Dublin, 1991, pp. 153 *et passim*.

[6] B. Bohte, *Mednarodno varstvo temeljnih pravic, Temeljne pravice*, Ljubljana, Cankarjeva založba, 1997, 440–489; see also Jambrek, note 2 above, p. 360.

effect, which means that following ratification and publication they become part of the Slovenian domestic legal order (Article 8 of the Constitution).

Under the Constitution, the principles of international law and ratified international agreements have an important position within the hierarchy of legal acts. The Constitution makes a distinction between international agreements ratified by the National Assembly (statutes must conform with them: Article 213 of the Rules of Procedure of the National Assembly) and international agreements ratified by the government (regulations and other legislative measures must conform with them). The Constitution grants ratified international agreements the status and position of a legal source. At the request of the President of the Republic, or of the government, or of no less than one-third of the Deputies of the National Assembly, the Constitutional Court must provide an opinion on the conformity with the Constitution of an international agreement in the process of being ratified by the state. The National Assembly is bound by any such opinion of the Constitutional Court (Article 160, paragraph 2, of the Constitution; Article 70 of the Constitutional Court Act).

As a member of the United Nations and the Council of Europe, Slovenia must respect the applicable instruments which impose obligations on states.

1. The United Nations

Under Article 8 of the Constitution, the international agreements to which Slovenia accedes take immediate effect. The following UN instruments are sources of rights and freedoms in Slovenia under the Notification of Succession to the United Nations Conventions Act:

- —the Charter of the United Nations of 26 June 1945;
- —the Universal Declaration of Human Rights of 10 December 1948;
- —the International Covenant on Civil and Political Rights of 19 December 1966;
- —the International Covenant on Economic, Social, and Cultural Rights of 19 December 1966; and
- —the Optional Protocol to the International Covenant on Civil and Political Rights of 19 December 1966 (General Assembly Resolution No. 2000 A (XXI)).

2. The Council of Europe

Slovenia signed the Convention on 14 May 1993 and ratified it on 8 June 1994 (Official Gazette of the RS, International Contracts, No. 33/94).

The 1991 Slovenian Constitution treats the relationship between the ratified Convention and Slovenian national law in a monistic way. The

Convention is to be implemented directly (Article 8 of the Constitution) and all Slovenian laws and other regulations must conform with the Convention (Article 153, paragraph 2 of the Constitution). The Constitutional Court is empowered to sanction any nonconformity of a regulation and can abrogate it wholly or partially (Article 160 of the Constitution; Article 43 of the Constitutional Court Act). This means that Slovenia is among those countries where the Convention has a higher status than ordinary laws and a lower status than the Constitution.

There is no doubt that Slovenia has been inspired by the same ideals and traditions of freedom and rule of law principles as the framers of the Convention. While Slovenia is today reintroducing and developing the legal culture of human rights after almost half a century of arrears, it cannot be said that it has no tradition concerning the protection of human rights and fundamental freedoms.

The Slovenian Constitutional Court and the whole system of ordinary courts must ensure the conformity of domestic legal provisions with the provisions of the Convention. In addition, the provisions of the Convention complement national constitutional provisions. Beyond that, the case-law of the European Court of Human Rights is also directly applicable in the decision-making process of the Constitutional and other courts in Slovenia. Thus the jurisdiction of the European Court of Human Rights and Slovenian national courts overlap in several ways.

Slovenia also ratified the Revised European Social Charter on 7 May 1999. Even before this, the National Assembly referred to the European Social Charter, eg in the Resolution Concerning the Basis for the Creation of Family Policies in the Republic of Slovenia (Official Gazette RS, No. 40/93).

3. Special statutory provisions concerning the implementation of the Convention

The provisions of Articles 12 and 13 of the Constitutional Court Act are to be applied *mutatis mutandis* when proposing candidates from the Republic of Slovenia for the position of judge at the European Court of Human Rights (Article 80, paragraph 1 of the Constitutional Court Act, Official Gazette RS, No. 15/94). Candidates from the Republic of Slovenia for the position of judge at the European Court of Human Rights are to be chosen by the National Assembly by applying, *mutatis mutandis*, the provisions of Article 14 of the Constitutional Court Act (Article 80, paragraph 2 of the Constitutional Court Act).

When a final judgment or other judicial decision is modified by a decision of the Constitutional Court of the Republic of Slovenia, issued following a constitutional complaint, the court then executes such decision in accordance with the decision of the Constitutional Court (Article 112 of the Constitutional Court Act). The decisions of the European Court of Human Rights are to be directly executed by the competent courts of the Republic of Slovenia (Article 113 of the Constitutional Court Act).

4. *The European Union*

As an associated member of the European Community, Slovenia is becoming familiar with the following instruments which are not self-executing in Slovenian law:

—the Declaration of Fundamental Rights and Freedoms adopted by the European Parliament on 12 April 1989; and
—the Treaties establishing the European Communities.

C. THE STATUS OF THE CONVENTION IN PARLIAMENTARY PROCEEDINGS

Article 5 of the Convention When proposing a draft Minor Offences bill (Folder No. ESA 674 of 20 July 1992) the government, as a proponent, determined that certain administrative bodies empowered to conduct minor offences procedures are entitled to issue decisions concerning the transformation of a fine into imprisonment when the fine remains unpaid and when it is impossible to exact it even by force. Such a power for an administrative body is in contradiction with the provisions of Article 5 of the Convention. Under these provisions, administrative bodies are not empowered to decide on the deprivation of liberty. Therefore the draft bill requires that a decision to transmute a fine originally imposed by an administrative body in a minor offences procedure, can only be issued by the municipal judge for minor offences of the district in which the administrative body is located.

Article 6 of the Convention When proposing a draft Judiciary Office bill (Folder No. EPA 270 of 24 December 1993) the government, as a proponent, created a special provision which requires judges to act always in a such manner as to protect the dignity of their office and status of the judiciary. Their rights are limited by the rights of all individuals who under the provision of Article 23 of the Constitution exercise the right to judicial protection, which must be provided without undue delay or, as the Convention requires, 'within a reasonable time' (Article 6, paragraph 1).

In the draft of the Criminal Procedure bill (Folder No. EPA 287 of 9 July 1993) the government, as a proponent, proposed to recognize the right to remuneration for an individual's professional participation in a criminal procedure and to prohibit the imposition of translation costs on persons who would otherwise be entitled to reimbursement.

Both provisions constitute an adjustment to attain compatibility with the Constitution and with the provisions of Article 6 of the Convention and Article 14 of the International Covenant on Civil and Political Rights, under which a defendant has the right to an interpreter free of charge if he or she does not understand or speak the language used before the court. The exclusion of the public from a 'public' hearing is only acceptable when it is necessary for the protection of the person or the family of the defendant or victim, or when a court determines that a public hearing could affect matters of equity as foreseen in Article 6 of the Convention. It was also proposed that a judge who has conducted certain investigative activities in a pre-trial procedure must not be involved in making the final decision. This solution is in line with the case-law of the European Court on Human Rights concerning the incompatibility of the functions of investigation and the administration of justice.

Article 10 of the Convention In the draft Mass Media bill (Folder No. EPA 496 of 14 January 1994) the government, as a proponent, stated that, *inter alia*, the international instruments concerning the media which are binding on Slovenia, including the Convention, had been studied and considered. According to the draft bill, freedom of expression is the basis for the regulation of public information, a right which is guaranteed by the Constitution and by Article 10 of the Convention.

D. LEADING HUMAN RIGHTS CASES DECIDED BY THE NATIONAL COURTS

1. The national system of protection of human rights

The Slovenian constitutional order is based on the protection of human rights and freedoms (the Preamble of the Constitution). On its own territory, Slovenia protects human rights and basic freedoms (Article 5, paragraph 1 of the Constitution).

a) Judicial protection Respect for human rights and basic freedoms is ensured by judicial protection through the civil and penal law,[7] constitutional

[7] Grgič, T., Varstvo Človekovih pravic v kazenskem procesnem pravu, Pravnik, o.10/92, p. 375. Bavcon, L., Kazenskopravno varstvo človekovih pravic in temeljnih svoboščin, Temeljne

law, and administrative law. Moreover, this protection includes the right to obtain redress for the abuse of such rights and freedoms (Article 15, paragraph 4 of the Constitution).

Specialized courts have jurisdiction only in their respective field (eg employment and social courts).

b) Administrative protection If no other legal redress is provided, courts of competent jurisdiction are also empowered to decide upon the legal validity of individual activities and acts which infringe the constitutional rights of individuals (Article 157, paragraph 2 of the Constitution).

The right to judicial review of the acts and decisions of all administrative bodies and statutory authorities which affect the rights and freedoms of individuals or organizations is guaranteed (Article 120, paragraph 3 of the Constitution).

c) The Constitutional Court When Slovenia was still a federal unit of the former Yugoslav Federation, the Constitutional Court was established by the Constitution of 1963 (Official Gazette SRS, No. 10/63) within the framework of a legal system governed by the principle of the unity of powers.[8] However, in the following years the Court had mainly a formal function regarding the protection of constitutionality and legality.

The 1974 Constitution did not bring any important changes in the position and the jurisdiction of the Constitutional Court (Official Gazette SRS, No. 6/74).[9]

In 1991, Slovenia became an independent, internationally recognized state. The new Constitution of 1991 (Official Gazette RS, No. 33/91) remodeled the status and powers of the Constitutional Court. The Court's jurisdiction and proceedings were specified in detail by the new Constitutional Court Act (Official Gazette RS, No. 15/94). A new system of constitutional review was quickly adapted to the modified constitutional and legal system. Among its new powers, the Court acquired the power to abrogate an unconstitutional statute and to decide upon constitutional complaints regarding violations of human rights. The Constitutional Court is the highest forum undertaking

pravice (Ljubljana: Cankarjeva založba, 1997), pp. 406–440. Wedam-Lukič, D., Pravica do sodnega varstva 'civilnih pravic in obveznosti' (Evropska konvencija o človekovih pravicah in slovensko pravo), Temeljne pravice (Ljubljana: Cankarjeva založba, 1997), pp. 307–330.

[8] The jurisdiction of the Constitutional Court was determined in detail by the Constitutional Court Act (Official Gazette SRS, Nos. 39/63 and 1/64). Pursuant to this Act, the Court started to operate on 15 February 1964. The first Rules of Procedure of the Constitutional Court were adopted on 23 February 1965 (Official Gazette RS, No. 11/65).

[9] However, more detailed provisions on jurisdiction and procedures are contained in the Constitutional Court of the Socialist Republic of Slovenia Act (Official Gazette SRS, Nos. 39/74 and 28/76). New Rules of Procedure of the Constitutional Court were also adopted (Official Gazette SRS, No. 10/74).

judicial review, and protecting constitutionality, legality, human rights, and basic freedoms (Article 1, paragraph 1 of the Constitutional Court Act). The Slovenian model of constitutional review follows those European countries which have opted for extensive powers of constitutional review concentrated in a single court. The main powers of the Constitutional Court are set out below.

i) Abstract review (Article 160, paragraph 1 of the Constitution, Articles 22–49 of the Constitutional Court Act)
The Constitutional Court decides:

—whether statutes conform with the Constitution;
—whether statutes and other general acts conform with ratified international agreements and the general principles of international law;
—whether regulations conform with the Constitution and statutes;
—whether local government statutes conform with the Constitution and statutes; and
—whether general acts issued for the exercise of public powers conform with the Constitution, statutes, regulations, ratified international agreements, and general principles of international law.

In these matters the Constitutional Court also decides on the constitutionality and legality of procedures under which these acts were adopted (Article 21, paragraph 3 of the Constitutional Court Act).

ii) Concrete review
The Constitutional Court reviews norms when requested by regular courts, the public prosecutor, the Bank of Slovenia, or the Auditor General when an issue relating to constitutionality or legality arises during proceedings they are conducting, and by the Ombudsman with respect to individual cases (Article 156, paragraph 1 of the Constitution; Article 23, paragraph 1, subparagraphs 5 and 6 of the Constitutional Court Act).

iii) Constitutional complaints
The Constitutional Court reviews such complaints in relation to violations of human rights and basic freedoms by individual (personal) acts (Article 160, paragraph 1, subparagraph 6 of the Constitution, Articles 50–60 of the Constitutional Court Act).

d) The Ombudsman The Ombudsman is an institution for informal out-of-court protection of human rights and basic freedoms. According to the Constitution, its function is to protect human rights and basic freedoms in matters involving state bodies, local government bodies, and statutory authorities (Article 159, paragraph 1 of the Constitution). The Slovenian legal system adopted the model of a parliamentary type of ombudsman similar to the Scandinavian model. The Ombudsman is elected, on the proposal of the President of the Republic, by the National Assembly (Article 2 of the Ombudsman Act) by a two-thirds majority of all Deputies (Article 12 of the Ombudsman Act). The Ombudsman is independent and autonomous in relation to the government and Ministers and, while examining concrete matters, also in relation to the National Assembly (Article 4 of the Ombudsman Act). In his or her activities, he or she observes the provisions of the Constitution and international human rights instruments, and may apply the principle of justice and good administration (Article 3 of the Ombudsman Act).[10]

The Ombudsman is empowered to submit proposals, opinions, or recommendations to state bodies, local government bodies, and statutory authorities, who are obliged to discuss and answer within the term determined by the Ombudsman (Article 7 of the Ombudsman Act). They are also obliged to submit, at the request of the Ombudsman, all data and information within their power (regardless of the degree of confidentiality) and to facilitate the execution of inquiries (Article 6 of the Ombudsman Act). The Ombudsman may submit initiatives for amendments of statutes and other legal acts to the National Assembly and the Government (Article 45, paragraph 1 of the Constitutional Court Act), and provides his or her opinion from the viewpoint of the protection of human rights and basic freedoms on any issue dealt with by all other bodies (Article 25 of the Ombudsman Act). The Ombudsman may enter any official premises and perform an inspection, including jails and other premises where freedom of movement is limited (Article 42 of the Ombudsman Act). He or she is also authorized to discuss broader questions which are important for the protection of human rights and basic freedoms as well as for the legal protection of the citizens of the Republic of Slovenia (Article 9, paragraph 2 of the Ombudsman Act). However, the Ombudsman must not be involved in issues dealt with in judicial or other legal proceedings except in the case of unjust delay of the proceedings or obvious abuse of authority (Article 24 of the Ombudsman Act).

Proceedings before the Ombudsman are confidential and free of charge for the parties (Article 9 paragraph 3 of the Ombudsman Act). One of the basic characteristics of the Ombudsman's activities is the discretion to decide which issues he or she will consider to and which not (Article 31 of the Ombudsman

[10] See also Trpin, G., Varuh človekovih pravic in temeljnih svoboščin, Nova ustavna ureditev Slovenije, Zbornik razprav, Ljubljana, ČZP Uradni list, 1992, p. 114. See Grad, F., Kaučič, I., Ribičič, C., Kristan, I., Državna ureditev Slovenije, Ljubljana, ČZP Uradni list, 1996, p. 442. Butala, A., Varuh človekovih pravic—pristojnosti in pooblastila, Podjetje in delo, No. 5–6/95, p. 745.

Act). Anyone claiming that his or her human rights or basic freedoms have been violated by an act or action of a government body, local government body, or statutory authority may propose the initiation of such proceedings. The Ombudsman may also start proceedings on his or her own initiative (Article 9, paragraph 1 of the Ombudsman Act).

Co-operation with the Ombudsman during the execution of an inquiry is obligatory both for the body involved and for all other state bodies (Article 34 of the Ombudsman Act). All state officials must respond to the Ombudsman's request for co-operation in the inquiry and give any explanations requested (Article 36, paragraph 1 of the Ombudsman Act). He or she may summon anyone as a witness or expert to discuss the issue he or she is considering and the person summoned is obliged to respond to the summons (Article 36, paragraph 2 of the Ombudsman Act). If the Ombudsman ascertains that there has been such a violation (Article 39, paragraph 1 of the Ombudsman Act), he or she may propose a way to rectify the irregularity (Article 39, paragraph 2 of the Ombudsman Act). The Ombudsman may also propose the initiation of disciplinary measures against the employees of the bodies responsible for the irregularity (Article 39, paragraph 3 of the Ombudsman Act). The Ombudsman reports on his or her activities to the National Assembly through regular or special reports (Article 43, paragraph 1 of the Ombudsman Act). Under Article 50, paragraph 2 of the Constitutional Court Act, the Ombudsman has authority to lodge constitutional complaints before the Constitutional Court.

2. *Significant national case-law which applied or referred to the Convention*

a) *The Constitutional Court*

Cases concerning abstract control
Article 2 of the Convention
Ruling No. U-I-168/97 of 3 July 1997 (OdlUS VI, 103) Deciding upon the constitutionality of the disputed provisions of Article 201, paragraph 2, items 1, 2 and 3, of the Slovenian Criminal Procedure Act (Official Gazette RS, No. 63/94) the Constitutional Court stated that according to Article 15, paragraph 1 of the Constitution, human rights and fundamental freedoms shall be exercised directly on the basis of the Constitution. A judge may not refuse the judicial protection of constitutional rights. In the event of an arrest due to the risk of a repeat offence, it is necessary to consider not only the human rights of the person whose arrest has been ordered, but also those of others because of damage suffered by them as victims of criminal offences, if a real danger exists that their rights will be infringed. The right to personal freedom of a person charged with a criminal offence should be balanced proportionally

against equal rights, except the highest right: the inviolability of human life, which is explicitly guaranteed by Article 2 of the Convention.

Article 5, paragraph 3 of the Convention

Decision No. U-I-18/93 of 11 April 1996 (Official Gazette RS, No. 25/96, OdlUS V, 40[11]). The petitioners challenged the provisions of Article 191, paragraph 2, item 3, of the former Yugoslav Criminal Procedure Act (Official Gazette SFRY, Nos. 4/77, 14/85, 26/86, 57/89, and 3/90). They stated that the conditions for a detention order due to the risk of a repeat offence in the said provision are imprecise and abstract and as such allow the courts to use it frequently, mostly without any reasonable explanation. In the opinion of the petitioners, this detention order does not have a basis in Article 20 of the Constitution, which permits a detention order only when absolutely unavoidable for the proper course of criminal proceedings or for the protection of society. The detention order due to the risk of a repeat offence is allegedly contrary to Article 27 of the Constitution, as it permits a person's future acts and his or her guilt for offences not yet committed to be assumed during the preliminary procedure.

The Constitutional Court rejected the petitioners' claim that the Convention does not permit detention due to the risk of a repeat offence. The Convention, in Article 5, paragraph 1, item c, mentions the possibility of ordering the detention of a person 'when it is reasonably considered necessary to prevent his committing an offence or fleeing after having done so'. Numerous cases from the European Court of Human Rights show that detention due to the risk of a repeat offence is not contrary to the Convention, provided that the other conditions laid down in the Convention are met.

Article 6 of the Convention

Decision No. U-I-27/95 of 24 October 1996 (Official Gazette RS, No. 66/96, OdlUS V, 138). The petitioner claimed that the provisions of Article 177 of the Slovenian Criminal Procedure Act (Official Gazette RS, No. 63/94) were in conflict with Article 6 of the Convention and Article 2 of the Constitution, because they leave to the investigating judge and non-trial chamber the decision on the proposals of parties carrying out investigative activities. He alleged *inter alia* that the provisions of Article 6 of the Convention do not allow courts to decide or arbitrate in relation to the submission of evidence, but require them to submit evidence which is only to the benefit of the defendant.

Having carefully examined the relevant case-law of the European Commission and Court of Human Rights,[12] the Constitutional Court

[11] See also Ruling No. U-I-19/93 of 11 April 1996; Ruling No. U-I-21/93 of 11 April 1996; Ruling No. U-I-336/94 of 11 April 1996; Ruling No. U-I-293/95 of 11 April 1996; and Ruling No. U-I-154/95 of 11 April 1996: all published in the electronic database of the Constitutional Court.

[12] Dec. Adm. Com. Application 617/59, 19 December 1960; Dec. Adm. Com. Application 753/60, 5 August 1960; Dec. Adm. Com. Application 1134/61, 19 December 1961; Dec. Adm.

stressed that the right to submit evidence beneficial to a defendant was an essential element of the right to a fair trial. However, this right is not absolute. A fair trial demands that the court does exceed the evidence which is submitted by the defence, whereby the court, in the context of the requirements of the Convention for a fair trial and in accordance with national legislation, insofar as it prescribes the manner and procedure of proof, is entitled to judge whether specific evidence is crucial to the matter.

The disputed Article 177 belongs to Section XVI of the Criminal Procedure Act, which regulates the investigative procedure. During the investigation, evidence and data are collected which are required for a decision on whether to prosecute or to dismiss the procedure, and evidence which it may not be possible to repeat at the trial or whose introduction is subject to difficulties, as well as other evidence which would be useful for the proceedings, and in relation to the circumstances it would be wise to introduce (Article 167, paragraph 2). When a ruling on an investigation is handed down, an investigating judge carries out investigative activities which are suggested by the parties or which appear necessary for the successful execution of proceedings (Article 176).

The disputed Article 177 builds on the provisions of Article 176 in that it states explicitly who may propose that the investigating judge carry out individual investigative activities (the parties, and victims) and the action to be taken by a judge if he or she disagrees (he or she demands a decision of a chamber). The investigating judge generally performs the investigative activities proposed by the parties (the prosecutor and defendant(s)) and the victims. If the judge does not agree with a proposal of evidence, he or she may not dismiss the proposal but must request the decision of a non-trial chamber.

Under the 1977 Criminal Procedure Act, the public prosecutor had a specific advantage over a defendant, since the investigating judge was bound to request a ruling of a senate only if he or she did not agree with a proposal of evidence submitted by the prosecution, while the judge could decide on a proposal of evidence by the defendant or his attorney. The decision of the investigating judge was in that case informal and final. When proposing the 1994 Criminal Procedure Act amendments, it was argued that they would strengthen the adversarial character of the investigation phase, which is enshrined as a principle among the basic principles of criminal procedure (Article 16 of the Criminal Procedure Act). According to these provisions, the defendant and the prosecution should have the position of equal parties, and

Com. Application 8375/78, 16 March 1981; case of *Engel et al.*, Judgment of 8 June 1976, Series A No. 22; case of *Bricmont v Belgium*, Judgment of 7 July 1989, Series A No. 158; case of *Vidal v Belgium*, Judgment of 22 April 1992, Series A No. 235–B.

the defendant has the right to state facts and propose evidence which is to his or her benefit.

The Constitutional Court found that the legal regulations met the requirements of the Convention in relation to equality of arms of the prosecution and the defence in the investigation, in that it guarantees the submission of evidence to the defendant's benefit under the same conditions as evidence to his or her detriment.

Neither does the disputed Article 177 of the Criminal Procedure Act violate the Convention merely by the fact that it leaves the decision on the proposals of evidence of the parties to the investigating judge or a non-trial senate. Under the provisions of Article 6, paragraph 3, item d of the Convention, it is not required that a court must receive all evidence proposed by the defence. So the petitioner's interpretation of the right to have evidence considered as absolute is unjustified, since it goes beyond the guarantees which the Convention provides to a defendant. Even in completely adversarial models of criminal procedure, a judge may reject immaterial evidence, which the judge believes cannot benefit the defence simply because it is not necessary.

Of course, unrestricted arbitrary behaviour by the investigating judge or chamber is also not permissible, since the basic requirement of Article 6 of the Convention must always be met in relation to guaranteeing a fair trial. It is thus a question of whether, in addition to a general rule that procedural equality must be guaranteed between the prosecution and defence in the investigation phase, there also exists some procedural measure which could in more detail determine when an investigating judge (or external chamber) must approve a proposal of evidence from a party.

Decision No. U-I-289/95 of 4 December 1997 (Official Gazette RS, No. 5/98, OdlUS VI, 165). The petitioner claimed that the provisions of Article 344, paragraph 2 of the Slovenian Criminal Procedure Act (Official Gazette RS, No. 63/94) and Article 337, paragraph 2 of the former Yugoslav Criminal Procedure Act (Official Gazette SFRY, No. 4/77, 14/85, 74/87, 57/89, and 3/90) were in conflict with Article 6 of the Convention which guarantees a fair trial. A fair trial should entail equal possibilities for establishing the legal and material circumstances and should guarantee a hearing within a reasonable time.

The Constitutional Court held that the relevant provisions of the Constitution (not only Article 29, but also Articles 15, 22, 23, 27, 28, and 29) correspond to the concept of a 'fair trial' as defined by Article 6 of the Convention.[13] Paragraphs 2 and 3 of Article 6 of the Convention represent,

[13] The Commission has stressed that the provision of Article 6(3)(c) must be respected in the context of all the requirements of Article 6 and that in reality it is a logical link between Article 6(3)(a) and (b), that is between the right 'to be promptly . . . informed of a charge' and the right 'to have sufficient time and opportunity to prepare a defence', Dec. Adm. Com. Application 4080/69, Digest of Strasbourg Case-law relating to the ECHR, vol. 2 (Article 6), 1984, p. 772.

according to the judicial practice of the European Court of Human Rights, a specific introduction of the general principle contained in paragraph 1 of this Article. The presumption of innocence and the various rights cited as examples in paragraph 3 ('minimum rights') are a composite part of the concept of a fair trial in criminal proceedings.[14] According to the established case-law of the Court, the requirement of equality of arms in the sense of a 'fair balance' between the parties in both civil and criminal cases forms also part of this concept.[15] The European Court of Human Rights has often stressed that the intention of the Convention is not to protect rights which are theoretical or illusory, but rights which are actual and effective; this especially applies to the right of defence from the point of view of the prominent role which the right to a fair trial has in a democratic society, from which the rights of defence derive.[16]

Article 6, paragraphs 2 and 3, and Article 7 of the Convention

Decision No. U-I-67/94 of 21 March 1996 (Official Gazette RS, No. 24/96, OdlUS V, 31[17]). The Attorney General disputed the former Yugoslav Suppression of Prohibited Speculations and Economic Sabotage Act (Official Gazette DFY, No. 26/45) and the Suppression of Illegal Trade, Prohibited Speculations, and Economic Sabotage Act (Official Gazette FPRY, No. 56/46). He considered that the two statutes were neither in conformity with the then or the present constitutional system, nor with the generally accepted principles of criminal law. At the time of the decision, the two statutes were still being used by the courts while administering justice on the basis of extraordinary legal remedies concerning the legality and correctness of the sentences and procedures of the post-war period and the basis of accusations then made.

The Constitutional Court determined that, even at the time of the creation and application of the Suppression of Illegal Trade, Prohibited Speculations, and Economic Sabotage Act, the Suppression of Illegal Trade, Prohibited

[14] Case of *Deweer*, Judgment of 27 February 1980, Series A No. 56.

[15] Case of *Dombo Beheer v the Netherlands*, Judgment of 27 October 1993, Series A No. 274, p. 33.

[16] Case of *Artico*, Judgment of 13 May 1980, Series A No. 37, p. 33. As part of the right to a fair trial, guaranteed by the provisions of Article 6 as a whole, an accused person has the right to be informed not only of the basis of a charge, that is not only of the acts of which he is accused and on which the charge is based, but also the nature of the charge, namely about the legal definition of the acts and questions. Since there is a logical link between points (a) and (b) of Article 6(3), the information may consequently contain such particulars as will enable the accused to prepare his defence in conformity with them: see Dec. Adm. Com. Application 524/59, Digest of Strasbourg Case-law relating to the ECHR, vol. 2 (Article 6), 1984, p. 776.

[17] See also Ruling No. U-I-68/94 of 21 March 1996, Official Gazette RS, No. 24/96, OdlUS V, 31, associated case; Ruling No. U-I-69/94 of 21 March 1996, Official Gazette RS, No. 24/96, OdlUS V, 31, associated case; Ruling No. U-I-70/94 of 21 March 1996, Official Gazette RS, No. 24/96, OdlUS V, 31, associated case.

Speculations and Economic Sabotage Act provisions or elements had been in conflict with the basic principles of criminal law recognized by civilized nations. The Constitutional Court did not decide that the entire Suppression of Illegal Trade, Prohibited Speculations, and Economic Sabotage Act should not be applied, but prohibited the application of those elements of its provisions whose application would be in conflict with the reasons for the present decision. This applies both to provisions which are substantive in character, that is, the vague definition of punishable acts, and to the above-mentioned procedural provisions which had not ensured minimum procedural defence rights in proceedings conducted on the basis of the disputed statute. In current and future court proceedings, the use of those elements of the provisions of the Suppression of Illegal Trade, Prohibited Speculations, and Economic Sabotage Act which were already in conflict at the time of the creation and application of the same, with the above-mentioned basic principles of criminal law recognized by civilized nations, and which are also contrary to the now applicable guarantees granted in particular by provisions of Article 28, paragraph 1, Article 23, paragraph 1, Article 25, and Article 27 of the Constitution, as well as by provisions of Article 6, paragraphs 2 and 3 and Article 7, paragraph 1 of the Convention, will not be allowed.

Article 1 of Protocol No. 1 to the ECHR and Article 14 of the Convention

Decision No. U-I-23/93 of 20 March 1997 (Official Gazette RS, No. 23/97, OdlUS VI, 43). The petitioners claimed that provisions of the Slovenian Denationalization Act (Official Gazette RS, No. 27/91 and 31/93) and the former Yugoslav Nationalization Act FLRY (Official Gazette DFY, No. 64/95 and Official Gazette FLRY, No. 54/46 and 105/48) were in conflict with the provisions of Article 14 of the Convention and Article 1 of Protocol No. 1 to the Convention. Respect for property should entail not only the effective protection of property and enjoyment of the right to property, but also its return if the property is seized in an impermissible manner in conflict with Article 14 of the Convention. The petitioners alleged that the provisions violated these rights by introducing a distinction on the ground of nationality.

Article 9, paragraph 1 of the Denationalization Act stipulated that:

> physical persons . . . are rightful claimants if at the time the property was nationalized they were Yugoslav citizens, and this citizenship was recognized after 9 April 1945 by law or international agreement.

The provision thus required that a rightful claimant must have had the status of Yugoslav citizen at the time of nationalization and further that this citizenship must have been recognized after 9 May 1945 by law or international agreement. As is evident from the records of the legislative process of adopting the Denationalization Act, the intention of the legislature was as far as possible to rectify injustices committed especially in the post-War period, caused by the encroachment of the state into ownership relations in the name of the 'revolutionary transformation' of society and in the name of dealing with enemies of the old regime. In this, the legislature adopted the premise that all dispossessions of property on the basis of regulations and acts of the state and its organs in a specific period which encroached on the ownership rights of Yugoslav citizens were, as a rule, unjust unless the citizens received suitable compensation (Proposal for the issuing of the Denationalization Act from the draft law, Minutes of the Assembly RS, No. 7/91).

Denationalization was also intended to privatize that part or extent of social property which was created from the unjust nationalization of private property, so that the property is returned to the owner or his legal heirs as priority claimants in the process of the privatization of social property. The view of the National Assembly was that the Denationalization Act does not embrace property and does not encroach on ownership rights, but allows its acquisition under specified conditions from property which was formerly social property. The Denationalization Act did not annul regulations and individual decisions on the basis of which and with which nationalization was carried out in the post-War period. Those regulations encroached on ownership rights at the time that assets were nationalized. So from this point of view, the constitutional permissibility of the limitation of ownership cannot be raised, and so the disputed provisions of the Denationalization Act are not in conflict with Article 33 of the Constitution or Article 1 of Protocol No. 1 to the Convention. Similarly, they are not in conflict with Article 155 of the Constitution, which bans retroactive regulations.

Cases concerning constitutional complaints

Article 5 of the Convention

Decision No. Up-119/95 of 12 December 1996 (OdlUS, V, 73). The Constitutional Court recalled that, according to the case-law of the European Court of Human Rights, any deprivation of liberty under Article 5, paragraph 1, item c of the Convention must be terminated on the day of the delivery of the judgment.[18] After the delivery of judgment in accordance with Article 5, paragraph 1, item a, of the Convention, the guarantee of Article 5, paragraph 3, of the Convention can no longer be applied. The Court held that by a judgment in accordance with law, the commission of a criminal offence was determined, the defendant was convicted, and the penalty was imposed. The sentence is a necessary condition for prolongation of detention, while the necessary consequence of a verdict of not guilty is release from detention. According to the Constitutional Court, such an interpretation of Article 5,

[18] Eg the case of *B v Austria*, Judgment of 28 March 1990, Series A No. 175.

paragraph 3 of the Convention stems directly from the intention of the right. The reason for limiting the duration of detention to the shortest possible period is the protection of the detained person. A serious infringement of the personal freedom of the affected person which has consequences in their private life, as well as in a criminal procedure (eg the appropriate possibilities for the preparation of a defence) is therefore possible if there is a low degree of probability that the accused committed the criminal offence. The passing of judgment creates the presumption that the conviction was based on a degree of probability such that it is necessary to keep the convicted person in prison. Until the presumption is reversed, the judgment remains valid.[19]

Decision No. Up-185/95 of 24 October 1996 (OdlUS V, 186). The conclusion of the Constitutional Court that there exists a suspicion of flight must be based on concrete proven circumstances on the basis of which it is possible with a high probability to conclude that a danger of flight exists. It is not possible to keep someone in detention only on the basis of the seriousness of the criminal offence or the threat of a severe penalty. However, if these circumstances are joined to other circumstances which touch above all on the character of the person, domicile, profession, assets, family links, and all other bonds with domestic or foreign environments, together with the expectation of a possible severe penalty, the danger of flight may be confirmed or refuted. The court must ascertain whether such circumstances exist, and judge whether the danger of flight is greater than the uncertainties which an individual would have to face when fleeing. The Constitutional Court recalled that a similar view had been taken by the European Court of Human Rights on a number of occasions.[20]

Decision No. Up-155/95 of 5 December 1996 (OdlUS V, 190). The right to be tried without unnecessary delay, enshrined in Article 23, paragraph 1 of the Constitution, applies irrespective of whether the individual was deprived of their liberty during the criminal proceedings. However, it is important to consider that detention represents an interference with the constitutional right to personal freedom, regulated by Article 19 of the Constitution. So the criteria necessary to evaluate what is meant by a 'reasonable time' cannot be the same in cases where the defendant in criminal proceedings is detained as in those cases where the defendant can defend himself while at liberty. The criterion of reasonable time in the case of detention should be stricter because

[19] See also Ruling No. Up-148/95 of 20 March 1996; Ruling No. Up-205/95 of 9 April 1996; Ruling No. Up-136/96 of 19 June 1996; Ruling No. Up-140/96 of 12 July 1996; Ruling No. Up-177/96 of 12 July 1996; and Ruling No. Up-227/96 of 1 October 1996: all published in the electronic database of the Constitutional Court.

[20] Eg *Wemhoff v Germany*, Judgment of 27 June 1968, Series A No. 7; *Neumeister v Austria*, Judgment of 27 June 1968, Series A No. 8; *B v Austria*, Judgment of 28 March 1990, Series A No. 175; *Letellier v France*, Judgment of 26 June 1991, Series A No. 207.

detention means an interference with a person's liberty before a final judgment, when the presumption of innocence of the person, from Article 27 of the Constitution, still applies. In such a case state organs must act with extra care and quickly. The legislature has explicitly bound them to act in such a manner. Article 200 of the Criminal Procedure Act provides that detention last no longer than necessary, and the same Article imposes a duty of all organs that take part in criminal proceedings, and organs which offer legal aid to these organs, to proceed speedily if the defendant is detained. If competent organs do not proceed accordingly and their actions or omissions cannot be justified by the special circumstances of a concrete criminal proceeding or by the defendant's conduct, a court must terminate the interference with that person's freedom. Such an interpretation of Article 23, paragraph 1 of the Constitution is supported by the provisions of Article 5, paragraph 3 of the Convention, which provide that a detainee 'shall be entitled to trial within a reasonable time or to release pending trial'. The danger which justifies a detention order can only be shown to a degree of probability, not with certainty. It is therefore very important that courts limit detention to the shortest possible time before passing a final judgment. If state organs do not ensure this, they have to grant defendants liberty. Of course, this does not mean that in such a case the organs of the judiciary can choose in advance either to proceed speedily or to release the defendant. Public interest and the preservation of public order require the courts to punish the perpetrators of criminal offences. Thus, the courts conduct criminal proceedings in the public interest. Yet, criminal proceedings also involve a guarantee to a defendant that the state shall in those proceedings respect their human rights and fundamental freedoms as guaranteed by the Constitution. Therefore, a court is bound to evaluate, after a certain time has passed from the day when the court ordered detention, not only whether the reasons for and absolute necessity of interfering with the person's freedom still exist, but also whether the duration of the detention is still within the limits of reasonableness. The reasonable time for the duration of detention as well as for the duration of criminal proceedings can only be evaluated according to the circumstances of the particular case.

The first-instance court, when issuing the challenged ruling on 18 April 1996, should have decided solely from the viewpoint of the duration of detention whether it was permissible to await the possible joining of proceedings without violating the complainant's human rights, taking into account that almost two years had passed since the detention was ordered. The court should have evaluated whether the detention was legal according to the circumstance of the concrete case, and whether it could still be extended. In the case of a conflict between Article 397 of the Criminal Procedure Act and the constitutional right of the complainant to personal freedom, the latter should have precedence. Thus, the court should have released the defendant by applying Article 23 of the Constitution and considering the criteria of Article 5, paragraph 3 of the Convention. Nevertheless, the District Court had extended the detention, thereby violating the complainant's rights under Article 23, paragraph 1 of the Constitution. Despite explicit complaints by the defendant, the superior court did not rectify this violation in the framework of appeal proceedings.[21]

Article 6 of the Convention

Decision No. Up-277/96 of 7 November 1996 (OdlUS V, 189). The right to the due process of law under Article 23 of the Constitution entails the right of each person to have all issues relating to his rights and obligations, and any criminal charges laid against them, decided without undue delay by an independent, impartial court constituted according to statute. A similar right is also guaranteed n Article 6, paragraph 1 of the Convention. In the latter the right to a trial within 'a reasonable period of time' is guaranteed only for the adjudication of 'civil rights and obligations or criminal charges'. Article 120, paragraph 3 of the Constitution specifically guarantees the right to judicial review of acts and decisions of all administrative bodies and statutory authorities which affect the rights and legal entitlements of individuals or organizations. For the protection of the right to due process of law without undue delay, judicial protection through an administrative lawsuit against actions or omissions is available under Article 157, paragraph 2 of the Constitution. A constitutional complaint would as a rule only be allowed after the said legal remedy has been exhausted (Article 51, paragraph 1 of the Constitutional Court Act). Before that remedy is exhausted, the Constitutional Court may only decide a constitutional complaint if the alleged infringement is obvious and if the execution of the individual act would lead to irreparable consequences for the complainant (or if irreparable consequences for the complainant would result from the fact that an individual act has not been issued).

Decision No. Up-155/95 of 5 December 1996 (OdlUS V, 190). According to Article 23, paragraph 1 of the Constitution, each person is entitled to have all issues relating to his or her rights and obligations, and any criminal charges laid against him or her, decided without undue delay by an independent, impartial court, established according to statute. In criminal law, the individual against whom proceedings are instituted is entitled to expect that these proceedings will be completed by a final court decision within a reason-

[21] See also Ruling No. Up-304/96 of 10 December 1996; Ruling No. Up-4/97 of 8 April 1997; Ruling No. Up-35/97 of 8 April 1997; and Ruling No. Up-128/97 of 2 July 1997: all published in the electronic database of the Constitutional Court; Decision No. Up-327/97 of 18 December 1997 (OdlUS VI, 200).

able time. In this way, a suspect is spared the burdens of uncertainty and adverse consequences caused by prolonged criminal proceedings. Among the possible consequences, a detention order is definitely the worst. To evaluate whether a court has decided upon the charges without unnecessary delay or within a reasonable time limit, as provided by Article 6, paragraph 1 of the Convention, an appeal court has to consider all the circumstances of the case. Many factors influence the evaluation, among which are also the complainant's actions, the nature and characteristics of a particular criminal proceeding, and the activity of competent state organs.[22]

Decision No. Up-206/96 of 10 December 1996 (OdlUS V, 211). The right of appeal under Article 25 of the Constitution concerns the duty of the court to decide on an appeal, to deal with the appeal, if admissible, from the point of view of substance, and to take up a position on such statements of the appeal which could if justified be reason for the modification and/or abrogation of the disputed judgment. For the Appellate Court to consider such requests, its decision must be well founded. Accordingly, under Article 395 of the Criminal Procedure Act, the court of second instance is obliged when sufficient grounds exist to evaluate the statements of the appeal and to determine the breaches of the law considered by the court as its official duty. From Article 6 of the Convention it follows that each judgment must be based on sufficient grounds. Furthermore, in accordance with the case-law of the European Court for Human Rights, proper reasoning for a judgment is an essential element of a fair trial. The court should with appropriate clearness state the grounds which are the basis of the court's decision. In accordance with the same case-law, court practice does not correspond to a fair trial if the court simply ignores a party's allegations which could, if well founded, substantially influence the result of the proceedings. After having examined the reasoning of the disputed judgment, the Constitutional Court concluded that Article 25 of the Constitution and Article 6 of the Convention had not been violated.[23]

Decision No. Up-159/96 of 19 July 1996 (Official Gazette RS, No. 39/96, OdlUS VI, 70). The Constitutional Court determined that public order offence judges, in accordance with Article 23 of the Constitution, are to be treated as a part of the judiciary and not among the executive or administrative branches of power. This decision also means that public order offence judges are a part of the judicial branch in accordance with the principle of

[22] See also Ruling No. Up-304/96 of 10 December 1996, published in the electronic database of the Constitutional Court.

[23] Ruling No. Up-152/96 of 15 January 1997; Ruling No. Up-156/95 of 7 March 1997; Ruling No. Up-120/94 of 25 March 1997; Ruling No. Up-139/97 of 28 May 1997: all published in the electronic database of the Constitutional Court.

separation of powers (Article 3, paragraph 2 of the Constitution). Accordingly, the Constitutional Court did not consider only constitutional provisions, but also the Convention and the case-law of the European Court for Human Rights relating to the guarantees proclaimed by Articles 6 and 7 of the Convention. According to the case-law of the European Court for Human Rights, public order offence judges judge offences which rank as criminal offences in the spirit of the Convention, and which must therefore, in accordance with Article 6, paragraph 1 of the Convention, be decided by courts.[24] The decision of the Constitutional Court does not mean that the legislature cannot, in accordance with Article 23 of the Constitution and Article 6 of the Convention, regulate public order offences by new legislation or enact new regulation of powers or for the organization of bodies conducting the proceedings on public order offences. Such regulation must ensure that public order offences which rank under the terms of the Convention as criminal offences be decided by bodies which have the status of courts.[25]

Article 8, paragraph 2 of the Convention

Decision No. Up-32/94 of 13 April 1995 (OdlUS IV, 38). The provisions of Article 73 of the Basic Property Relations Act should be understood in the context of the entire institution of the protection of private property. The protection of private property is guaranteed by a state governed by the rule of law for reasons of public security and economic welfare, and to prevent disorder (Article 8, paragraph 2 of the Convention). This is why it aims mainly to protect existing and actual control over things. Upon the death of someone whose apartment has been shared with their spouse as their home, control belongs to the latter. There are no grounds for denying protection to a person who had actual power over things prior to the testator's death and subsequent to it, or even for limiting such private property with respect to its then existing content and degree. The latter would also be contrary to the general interest of the protection of an inheritance for the benefit of the heirs, this being the *ratio legis* of Article 73 of the Basic Property Relations Act from the perspective of the law of succession. This statutory provision is not in conflict with the Constitution, but in the case under consideration its application was

[24] Eg *Öztürk v Germany*, Judgment of 27 May 1983, Series A No. 73; *Lutz v Germany*, Judgment of 25 August 1987, Series A No. 123.

[25] See also Ruling No. Up-339/96 of 18 September 1997; Ruling No. Up-190/97 of 18 September 1997; Ruling No. Up-189/97 of 18 September 1997; Ruling No. Up-282/96 of 24 September 1997; and Ruling No. Up-93/96 of 22 October 1997: all published in the electronic database of the Constitutional Court; Decision No. Up-58/95 of 20 November 1997, published in OdlUS VI, 196; Ruling No. Up-201/97 of 26 November 1997, published in the electronic database of the Constitutional Court; and Decision No. Up-327/97 of 18 December 1997, published in OdlUS VI, 200; Ruling No. Up-63/94 of 5 December 1997, published in the electronic database of the Constitutional Court.

not in conformity with the statute and with the constitutional right of the complainant to privacy.

Article 13 of the Convention

Decision No. Up-134/95 of 14 March 1996 (OdlUS V, 62). In its decision No. U-I-98/91 (OdlUS I, 101) the Constitutional Court had already taken the position that the purpose of Article 25 of the Constitution, which was invoked by the complainant in her constitutional complaint, is not only to enable a person to apply for a legal remedy, but primarily effectively to protect his or her legal interests. If a regulation makes this impossible, it is incompatible with the Constitution. Such interpretation also follows from the Universal Declaration of Human Rights, which in Article 8 ensures the right of each person to an effective legal remedy against acts which violate the fundamental rights recognized by the Constitution or statute, and from the Convention, which in Article 13 guarantees to each person effective legal remedies in the event of a violation of the rights and freedoms guaranteed by it. It follows that the constitutional right to a legal remedy is effective only if the remedies can be used effectively for the protection of rights, or, according to Article 25 of the Constitution, which has wider scope than the abovementioned international instruments, also of legal interests.

b) The Supreme Court

Article 5 of the Convention

Judgment No. II Ips 393/96 of 17 July 1996. Under Article 19 of the Constitution the right to personal freedom is guaranteed to every individual. Therefore, an individual shall not be deprived of his or her freedom except in such cases and under such procedure as are determined by statute. This basic human right is also protected by international instruments such as Article 5 of the Convention, and Article 9 of the International Covenant on Civil and Political Rights. Detention in psychiatric and similar institutions is only possible when a court determines that conditions required by statute have been met. In the procedure for the prolongation of detention, the provisions concerning detention are to be applied *mutatis mutandis*. This means that in such a procedure the court evaluates all the circumstances relevant to the decision on subsequent detention.

Article 8 of the Convention

Judgment No. II Ips 494/93 of 28 October 1993. The concept of the phrase 'in the child's best interest' shall be determined by a court in the circumstances of each case. The court must consider limits determined by laws, regulating family relations in general and the rights of parents in particular. The contents of these relations indirectly influence the legal standard of children's welfare. As a general rule children should be cared for by their parents. However, connections with near relatives (eg between grandparents and grandchildren) which may be due to mutual relations also play an important role and are included in the notion of family life as protected by Article 8 of the Convention. They should be taken into account in the use of the legal standard 'in the child's best interest'.

Judgment No. U 584/94–6 of 4 October 1995. Under the provisions of the Foreigners Act (Official Gazette RS, No. 1/91) foreigners intending to reside on the territory of the Republic of Slovenia longer than determined by the same statute must prove a justifiable reason why such longer residence in the country is necessary. The Convention on Children's Rights and Article 8 of the Convention grant special protection to the family. The fact that the plaintiff lives out of wedlock with the mother of his two children is a justifiable reason according to the provisions of the Foreigners Act: the plaintiff's longer residence in the country may be necessary because the mother and both children possess citizenship of the Republic of Slovenia.

Article 14 of the Convention

Judgment No. U 1160/93–4 of 23 June 1994. The International Covenant on Civil and Political Rights (Article 26) and the Convention (Article 14) prohibit discrimination in a similar manner to Article 14 of the Constitution of the Republic of Slovenia. According to the relevant international instruments, citizenship is not a criterion which may not be used to differentiate between persons. Citizens may have certain rights (and also duties) which are not guaranteed to foreigners. The suitability or otherwise of statutory regulations under which a person whose property was nationalized is not entitled to restitution because of a change of citizenship is not within the jurisdiction of the Supreme Court.

c) The High Court

Article 5 of the Convention

Judgment No. Kp 309/94 of 19 July 1994. Detention with a view to avoiding the risk of collusion, as provided for by Article 191, paragraph 2, item 2 of the Criminal Procedure Act, is not explicitly mentioned in Article 5 of the Convention, but it is known in all legal systems of continental Europe and also in legal systems where the accusatorial procedure is predominantly applied. It has also been accepted as a basis for the imposition and prolongation of detention by the European Court for Human Rights and the European Commission for Human Rights. However, the only reasons presented by the court of first instance as grounds for its decision are so indistinct that they completely disallow proof of the existence of a reason for detention because of the risk of collusion concerning the defendants whose detention was prolonged. Therefore the Supreme Court abrogated the decision in this case and returned it to the court of first instance to decide anew.

Judgment No. Kp 132/95 of 17 May 1995. The detention of an individual at a police station for eleven hours is not a violation of Article 5, paragraph 3 of the Convention, which requires that persons deprived of liberty must be promptly brought before a judge or another official authorized by law to exercise judicial power.

Article 8 of the Convention

Judgment No. II Cp 642/94 of 20 March 1993. The collection and dissemination of data concerning an individual, the citation of their profession, their membership of different clubs, societies, associations, and other organizations, as well as facts concerning their family in the media probably interfere with the privacy of the plaintiff. Because such interference with personal rights may cause irreversible moral and material damage and because there was a proven risk that the defendant could continue with such activity, the Court considered the issuing of a temporary order (which can be valid until the final decision upon the appeal's claim) to be well founded. For such an interpretation, the Constitutional Court considered the provisions of the Convention, which the Republic of Slovenia had already signed but not ratified at the time of issuing the judgment.

E. CASES BROUGHT BEFORE THE EUROPEAN COMMISSION AND COURT OF HUMAN RIGHTS[26]

For Slovenia, 33 provisional files were opened in 1994, and roughly the same number in 1995 (33) and 1996 (34); no application was registered in 1994, but there were 7 in 1995 and 19 in 1996. On the basis of the number of communications received by the Commission (there were potential applicants' first letters, which result in the opening of a provisional file) and of applications registered, a certain overview can be made.

As of 11 March 1997, taking all files and applications together, the situation for Slovenia was as follows: provisional files: 84; applications awaiting action: 4; pending cases: 2; decided cases: 21; admissible: 0; inadmissible: 21; struck off the list: 0; friendly settlement reports: 0; report on merits: 0.

The total number of provisional files, not yet registered (which are never decided by the Commission) in the initial phase against Slovenia was 126.

[26] The following statistics are based on information provided by the Slovenian member of the European Commission of Human Rights and M. de Salvia, 'Applications Lodged against Central and East European Countries with the Human Rights Protection Organs in Strasbourg', European Sections of the International Commission of Jurists Congress, 3–5 April 1997, Offprint.

The number of cases awaiting decision by the Commission (registered, which have to be decided by the Commission) was 18.

The number of cases in the process of being decided were 2. One such case has already been accepted by the Commission as admissible and is in the process of a friendly settlement; the case concerned criminal procedure and Article 6 of the Convention.

The number of cases which have been declared inadmissible is 33.

Cases have concerned freedom of expression, the protection of property/restitution, fair trial/or proceedings without undue delay, the protection of privacy and family life, and detention. The provisions of the Convention most frequently invoked in applications before the European Commission for Human Rights were Article 1 of Protocol No. 1 and Articles 3, 5, 6, and 8 of the ECHR.

F. REMEDIAL ACTION TAKEN BY THE GOVERNMENT IN RESPONSE TO BEING FOUND IN VIOLATION OF THE CONVENTION

Two judgments of the European Court of Human Rights in 2000 where one or more violations of the Convention by Slovenia were held to exist have been the *Rehbock* and *Majaric* cases. In the *Rehbock* case,[27] the Court found that the applicant has been subjected to inhuman treatment on his arrest (violation of article 3), the domestic courts had not given a timely ruling on the lawfulness of his detention (violation of article 5(4)), and the applicant had been unable to obtain compensation for having been detained in violation of article 5(4) (violation of article 5(5)). There was also a violation of article 8, as a result of monitoring of the applicant's correspondence with the former European Commission of Human Rights, notably because of a legal lacuna which has subsequently been remedied. The general measures requested in response to the judgment have involved publication and dissemination of the judgment, and legislative changes to ensure a right of compensation in case of illegal detention of this kind.

The *Majaric* case[28] related to the excessive length (4 years, 5 months) of certain criminal proceedings brought against the applicant (violation of article 6). The relevant delays were caused by the heavy workload of the domestic courts during the economic and legislative reforms being undertaken at the time of the facts of the case. The Slovenian authorities have been requested to provide information as to whether this problem has so far been remedied, and also to publish the Court's judgment (in Slovenian).

[27] Judgment of 28 November 2000. [28] Judgment of 8 February 2000.

G. ASSESSMENT AND PROSPECTS

It was characteristic of Slovenian practice prior to 1991 concerning human rights protection (especially before the Constitutional Court) that, in comparison with Europe, it largely avoided the use of legal principles, even those explicitly included in the text of the Constitution. In common with foreign practice, however, the principle of equality greatly predominated among otherwise rarely used principles. Decisions consistently remained within the framework of legalistic (formalistic) argument and no other value references were ever allowed: the Constitutional Court respected the principle of self-restraint and stuck to the presumption of the constitutionality of statutes.

The new Constitution of the Republic of Slovenia of 1991, along with the catalogue of classical fundamental rights in combination with the newly defined powers of the Constitutional Court, paved the way for the intensification of its role in this domain. It is considered that the Constitutional Court now has sufficient space for such activity. The Slovenian Constitution contains adequate definitions of rights having the nature of legal principles and thus being sufficiently open to interpretation that they require significant further construction and implementation,[29] also taking into account the provisions of the Convention and the practice of the European Court of Human Rights.

Slovenian constitutional case-law from the period after the introduction of the 1991 Constitution comes particularly close to foreign case-law in its approach to fundamental rights. It is necessary to bear in mind that the frequency with which individual rights are invoked before the Constitutional Court mainly depends on what kind of problems appellants place before it. The Constitutional Court now appears to act as the guardian of constitutionality in that it decides not only on the conformity of general legal acts with constitutional provisions (in the sense of the abstract and specific review of general legal acts), but also on constitutional complaints of the violation of human rights and fundamental freedoms by individual acts.[30] However, it must be admitted that the new Constitution slightly limited the still broad possibilities for individuals to challenge general acts. In accordance with this principle, every individual is entitled to file a petition if he or she can prove standing. On the other hand, taking into consideration the general compatibility of the Slovenian legal system with the international law on human

[29] Citation from Pavčnik Marijan, 'Verfassungsauslegung am Beispiel der Grundrechte in der neuen slowenischen Verfassung', WGO Monatshefte für Osteuropäisches Recht, 1993 no. 6, pp. 345–356.

[30] Paragraph 1 of Article 160 and Article 162 of the Constitution.

rights, and in terms of membership in the United Nations and in the Council of Europe, the Republic of Slovenia must comply with the control mechanisms of the applicable international human rights instruments.

The core of judicial protection of human rights lies in the constitutional complaint, since:

—human rights are attributes of any democratic legal system;
—the constitutional complaint is only one of the legal remedies for protecting constitutional rights;
—the constitutional complaint is an important remedy for the protection of human rights connected with human rights themselves;[31] the Constitution guarantees the constitutional complaint, in the same way as the rights it protects; at the same time, the constitutional complaint is limited by statute in the interests of the functional capacity of the Constitutional Court.

The very existence of the constitutional complaint ensures a more effective review of violations of constitutional rights committed by government bodies, especially during the process of transforming the social and legal order.

Slovenia has reached the standard of contemporary European legal culture in which it has become normal that domestic courts are influenced by the case-law of the European Court of Human Rights, thus raising the level of human rights protection.[32] However, a legal rule and its implementation in everyday practice are two different things. Real, half-real, and often only apparent general interests of society may be extraordinarily strong, especially if they incite national socialist, ideological, or political emotions. At such a time people may forget principles which they had followed until recently, but they still demand an efficient functioning of ordinary courts. Judicial and political independence are almost the sole guarantees against the transformation of law into a tool of some or other ideological and political movement based on impatience.

[31] Ruling issued by the Slovenian Constitutional Court No. U-I-71/94 of 6 October 1994.
[32] Bavcon, L., 1997, note 7 above, pp. 436–437.

31

Spain[1]

GUILLERMO ESCOBAR ROCA

A. INTRODUCTION

On 24 November 1977, two years after the death of General Franco and at the height of the transition towards democracy (or, more specifically, when the Committee was drawing up the Preliminary Draft of the Constitution) Spain became a signatory to the European Convention on Human Rights. However, it was not until 4 October 1979[2] that it ratified the Convention, after the Spanish Constitution had been approved.

The initial ratification included ratification of Additional Protocols Nos. 3 and 5, as well as the following Declarations.

a. Spain interpreted the provision of the last sentence in the first paragraph of Article 10 of the Convention as being compatible with the rules governing the organization of radio and television broadcasting

[1] Abbreviations: Ar. = Repertorio Aranzadi de jurisprudencia = the Aranzadi Digest of Case Law; BOE = Boletín Oficial del Estado = Official State Bulletin; CE = Constitución española de 1978 = Spanish Constitution of 1978; ECHR = Convenio Europeo para la protección de los derechos humanos y las libertades fundamentales = European Convention on Human Rights and Basic Liberties, or the Convention; FJ = Fundamento Jurídico = legal consideration or ground; LOPJ = Ley Orgánica del Poder Judicial = Organic Law of the Judiciary; LOTC = Ley Orgánica del Tribunal Constitucional = Organic Law of the Constitutional Court; STC = Sentencia del Tribunal Constitucional = Constitutional Court Judgment; STS = Sentencia del Tribunal Supremo = Supreme Court Judgment; TEDH = Tribunal Europeo de Derechos Humanos = European Court of Human Rights.

[2] See BOE of 10 October 1979. According to Article 96(1) of the Spanish Constitution and Article 1(5) of the Civil Code, the date on which the ECHR came into effect was 10 October 1979, and not 4 October as one would expect from Article 66(3) of the ECHR. Given this minor difference in dates, the matter is of little practical importance. Moreover, it must be borne in mind that ratification was effected by means of Article 94(1) of the Spanish Constitution, and not by means of Article 93 of the Constitution, which according to one group of legal scholars is of particular significance: see C. Ruiz Miguel, *La ejecución de las sentencias del Tribunal Europeo de Derechos Humanos*, Madrid, 1997, pp. 132–135. We return to this matter at the end of this chapter.

in Spain,[3] and Articles 15 and 17 in the sense that they did not prevent the adoption of the measures contemplated in Articles 55 and 116 of the Spanish Constitution.[4]

b. Spain made known its intention to draw up the declaration contemplated in Article 25 of the Convention as soon as it was able to develop legislation to establish the new Constitution.[5]
c. For a period of three years from 15 October 1979, and subject to the condition of reciprocity, Spain recognized the jurisdiction of the European Court, *ipso facto* and without special agreement, for the purpose of dealing with all cases relating to the interpretation and application of the Convention arising as from 14 October 1979.[6]
d. In the exercise of the powers granted by Article 64 of the Convention, Spain reserved the right to apply:

—Articles 5 and 6, insofar as they were incompatible with the provisions contained in the Code of Military Justice,[7] relating to the rules governing the armed forces, and

—Article 11, insofar as it was incompatible with Articles 28 and 127 of the Spanish Constitution.[8]

[3] At that time radio and television were seen as a state monopoly, and this was formally established shortly afterwards in Law 4/1980, *de Estatuto de la radio y la televisión*. However, subsequent provisions (and in particular Law 10/1988, *de televisión privada*) permitted the management of these services by the private sector, generally after the necessary had been granted by the authorities.

[4] Article 55 of the Spanish Constitution regulates the general suspension of certain rights in the event of the declaration of exceptional circumstances or a state of emergency, in addition to their general suspension, subject to certain requirements, in the event of terrorist attack. The reference to Article 116 of the Spanish Constitution (on the declaration of exceptional circumstances) is deemed to be irrelevant, bearing in mind that it is directly related to Article 55(1).

[5] Spain produced this Declaration on 11 June 1981 (BOE of 30 June 1981) for a period of two years, renewed by subsequent Declarations of 7 June 1983 and 18 October 1985 (BOE of 6 December 1985), making it known that the latter 'will be automatically renewed for further five-year periods unless the intention not to do so is made known before expiry of the current period'.

[6] This declaration was renewed for successive periods of: three years on 24 September 1982 (BOE of 23 October 1982), five years on 18 October 1985 (BOE of 5 December 1985), and five years on 10 October 1990 (BOE 15 October 1990), though on the last occasion there was a clause stating: 'This declaration will be [tacitly] renewed for five-year periods [if no intention to the contrary is notified before the expiry of the current period.]' Following the entry into force of Protocol No. 11 to the ECHR, declarations under Articles 25 and 46 of the ECHR are no longer necessary.

[7] As a result of the Code of Military Justice being repealed, the reserved right was amended on 24 September 1986 (BOE of 30 September 1986), that right being retained for Articles 5 and 6 of the Convention:

> insofar as they were still compatible with the provisions found in the Rules Governing the Armed Forces, contained in Chapter II of Section III and Chapters II, III and V of Section IV of *Ley Organica* [Organic Law] 12/1985 entitled Rules Governing the Armed Forces,

which replaced the previously mentioned Code of Military Justice.

[8] The reference to Article 28 of the Constitution seems superfluous, since it does not add further limitations to those contemplated in Article 11 of the Convention. The reference to Article

The ratification of Additional Protocols, Nos. 2,[9] 6,[10] 8,[11] 1,[12] and 11,[13] came later. In relation to Protocol No. 1, Spain 'in order to avoid any uncertainty as to the application of Article 1 of the Protocol', expressed a reservation 'in the light of Article 33 of the Constitution',[14] and declared its recognition of the Commission's competence and the jurisdiction of the European Court:

> in connection with applications concerning facts subsequent to the date of deposit of the instrument of ratification of the Protocol, and in particular internal expropriation procedures set in motion subsequent to that date.

B. THE STATUS OF THE CONVENTION IN NATIONAL LAW

The European Convention on Human Rights has a similar status to other international treaties within the Spanish legal system. The latter are subject, in the first instance, to Article 93 of the Spanish Constitution, which states that:

> validly endorsed international treaties, once they have been officially published in Spain, form part of the internal regulations. Their provisions may only be repealed, amended or suspended in the manner contemplated in the treaties themselves, or in accordance with the rules of international law.

In general, the incorporation of international treaties follows the moderate monistic model implicitly adopted in Article 96(1) of the Constitution, which states that: 'validly endorsed international treaties, *once they have been officially published in Spain*, will form part of national regulations'. This system raises the question of the date on which the Convention and its Protocols come into effect, since these normally reflect the date on which the ratification instrument was submitted, whereas both Article 96(1) of the Constitution and Article 2(1) of the Spanish Civil Code take the date of publication as the relevant point. As we have seen, this does not cause any particular problems in the case of the Convention itself. However, problems do arise in the case of the Protocols as there is a significant difference between the dates of ratification and of their publication.

127 appears to be more relevant, according to which 'As long as they are in office, Judges, Magistrates and Public Prosecutors may not [. . .] belong to [. . .] unions'.

[9] Ratification instrument of 18 March 1982 (BOE of 10 May 1982).

[10] Ratification instrument of 20 December 1982 (BOE of 17 April 1986).

[11] Ratification instrument of 9 July 1989 (BOE of 11 November 1989).

[12] Ratification instrument of 2 November 1990 (BOE of 12 January 1981).

[13] Ratification instrument of 16 December 1996.

[14] This reference seems superfluous, since Article 33 does not seem to contradict anything in the Protocol.

To resolve the possible conflict between the Spanish Constitution and the Protocols regarding the date on which the latter take effect, legal doctrine favours an eclectic approach, which interprets the provisions of the Constitution in a flexible fashion.[15] Thus, it will normally be the case that ratified Protocols which have not yet been officially published in Spain do not have full effect, that is to say they cannot be invoked in general terms either between private individuals or between an individual and the public authorities. However, this does not prevent ratification having other legal effects, such as the possibility of private individuals resorting to public bodies for protection of the rights created by the Protocols. Moreover, a failure to publish a ratified Protocol could result in financial liability on the part of public bodies.[16]

When considering the relationship between international treaties and all other sources of Spanish law, a distinction must be made, as follows:

a. The relationship between international treaties and the Constitution. The precedence of the Constitution over international treaties is not disputed. We are of course excluding the aforementioned Article 96(1) of the Constitution ('validly endorsed'), in addition to Articles 95(1) of the Constitution ('The adoption of an international treaty containing provisions contrary to the Constitution will first require revision of the Constitution') and 27(2)(c) of the LOTC (Organic Law on the Constitutional Court), which regards treaties as being subject to constitutional control. Both the Constitutional Court[17] and legal theory[18] have confirmed the hierarchical superiority of the Spanish Constitution over international treaties.
b. The relationship between international treaties and general Spanish laws. The Constitution seems to indicate the precedence of international treaties over laws. Thus Article 94(1)(e) of the Constitution recognizes that a treaty may necessitate the 'amendment or repeal of a law' or require 'legislative measures for its implementation', and in accordance with Article 96(1) of the Constitution, the provisions of treaties may only be 'repealed, amended, or suspended in the manner

[15] See, for example, M. Diez de Velasco, *Instituciones de Derecho Internacional Público*, Madrid, 10th edn, 1994, pp. 222–223.

[16] See Articles 106(2) of the Constitution and 139–146 of Law 30/1992 entitled *de régimen jurídico de las Administraciones Públicas y del procedimiento administrativo*.

[17] See, in particular, the Constitutional Court Statement of 1 July 1992 on the unconstitutional nature of the European Union Treaty with regard to passive suffrage of Community citizens in municipal elections.

[18] For opposing views, see J. L. Requejo Pages, 'Consideraciones en torno a la posicion de las normas internacionales en el Ordenamiento español', *Revista Española de Derecho Constitucional*, No. 34, 1992, pp. 41 et seq.

contemplated in the treaties themselves, or on the basis of the general rules of international law'. The hierarchical superiority of treaties over laws has been recognized by the Constitutional Court[19] and the Supreme Court,[20] and is also generally accepted by legal scholars,[21] though a significant number of authors[22] defend the equal status of treaties and laws and, for that reason, support the application of the principle of competence to resolve conflicts between the two categories of regulatory provisions.

In addition to the above considerations relating to international treaties in general, we must add the fact that the European Convention on Human Rights is also governed by the provisions of Article 10(2) of the Spanish Constitution, which states that:

> The rules relating to basic human rights and liberties recognized by the Constitution will be interpreted on the basis of the Universal Declaration of Human Rights and the international treaties and agreements on the same matters ratified by Spain.

Among these 'international treaties and agreements' the European Convention on Human Rights occupies a primary position.

As a general principle, both the jurisprudence of the Constitutional Court and the majority of legal scholars[23] take the view that this constitutional rule contains only one principle for interpreting the Spanish Constitution. As a result, not only the Convention, but also the decisions of the Commission and the jurisprudence of the European Court[24] are primarily 'valuable instruments

[19] See, for example, STC [Constitutional Court Judgment] 28/1991, FJ 5.

[20] See, for example, the STSs of 30 September 1982 (Aranzadi Digest 4917), of 16 December 1985 (Aranzadi 6273), and of 22 May 1989 (Aranzadi Digest 3877).

[21] See, among others, M. Diez de Velasco, note 15 above, pp. pages 223–224; J. A. Pastor Ridruejo, *Curso de Derecho Internacional Público y Organizaciones Internacionales*, Madrid, 1992, pp. 201–202; J. D. Gonzalez Campos *et al.*, *Curso de Derecho Internacional Público*, Madrid, 1990, pp. 236, 240; I. de Otto, *Derecho constitucional, Sistema de fuentes*, Barcelona, 1989, pp. 124–126; F. Balaguer Callejon, *Fuentes del Derecho*, vol. I, Madrid, 1991, p. 84.

[22] See, for example, E. Garcia de Enterria and T. R. Fernandez, *Curso de Derecho Administrativo*, vol. I, Madrid, 1990, p. 172; E. Linde *et al.*, *El sistema europeo de protección de los derechos humanos,* Madrid, 2nd edn, 1983, pp. 173–176; J. Rodriguez-Zapata Perez, 'Derecho internacional y sistema de fuentes del Derecho', in A. Predieri and E. Garcia de Enterria, *La Constitución de 1978. Estudio sistematico*, Madrid, 1988, p. 606.

[23] See, for example, A. Mangas Martin, 'Cuestiones de Derecho internacional publico en la Constitución española de 1978', *Revista de la Facultad de Derecho de la Universidad Complutense*, No. 61, 1980, p. 150; F. Rey Martinez, 'El criterio interpretativo de los derechos fundamentales conforme a normas internacionales (Analisis del articulo 10(2) CE)', *Revista General de Derecho* No. 537, 1989, pp. 3616–3617; M. Medina Guerrero, *La vinculación negativa del legislador a los derechos fundamentales*, Madrid, 1996, pp. 16–20.

[24] This broadening of the interpretative parameter specified in Article 10(2) of the Constitution is accepted without discussion; see, for example, E. Linde *et al.*, *El sistema europeo de protección de los derechos humanos*, Madrid, 2nd edn, 1983, p. 181 and M. A. Aparicio Perez, 'La clausula interpretatia del articulo 10(2) de la Constitucion española, como clausula de integracion y apertura constitucional a los derechos fundamentales', *Jueces para la democracia*, No. 6, 1989, p. 9.

for construing the meaning and scope of rights',[25] and are not just an 'independent canon for the validity of the regulations and acts of public authorities from the viewpoint of basic rights'.[26] On the basis of this principle it seems that:

> the validity of the challenged provisions and acts must be evaluated only by reference to the constitutional rules which recognize rights and liberties [. . .], the international texts and agreements in Article 10(2) being an interpretative source which contributes to a better identification of the content of those rights.[27]

However, other judgments contradict this general principle in part, and say in effect that the determination of rights by the Convention or by the European Court is identified with the content of the constitutionally recognized rights.[28]

C. THE STATUS OF THE CONVENTION IN PARLIAMENTARY PROCEEDINGS

The Convention had a significant influence on the list of basic rights included in the Spanish Constitution and many of the precepts inevitably highlight parallels in the Convention. Article 10(2), already referred to, is clear evidence of this opening up of the Constitution to international law in general and to the Convention in particular, even though those amendments which made express reference to the latter were not finally accepted.[29]

The Convention subsequently lost influence in the political debate, and was for the most part referred to in Parliament only in the context of considering laws for the development of basic rights or legislative reforms inspired by the jurisprudence of the European Court.[30] At present its relevance in parliamentary debates, and to public opinion in general, is almost non-existent, with the exception of its impact on media coverage of court judgments against Spain, an impact which, for reasons the reader will soon appreciate, were particularly noticeable in connection with the *Castells* and *Ruiz Mateos* judgments.

[25] STC 38/1981, FJ 4. [26] STC 64/1991, FJ 4. [27] Ibid.

[28] See, for example, STC 36/1991, FJ 5 and STC 501/1995, FJ 4.

[29] On the process of drawing up Article 10(2) of the Constitution, see L. Martin-Retortillo, *La Europa de los derechos humanos*, Madrid, 1998, pp. 179–192.

[30] We refer in particular to the reform of the Law on Criminal Trials introduced by Organic Law 7/1988 in which steps were taken to separate the functions of examining magistrate and judge in criminal proceedings. See M. C. Calvo Sanchez, 'El derecho al juez imparcial en la doctrina del Tribunal Europeo de Derechos Humanos: necesidad de encomendar la instrucción y el enjuiciamiento a órganos diferentes', *La Ley*, 3 November 1989, pp. 1–6.

There has been a recent isolated case which contrasts with the previous trend. A significant impact was made on the public by a specific reference to the Convention during the course of the hearings of the Basque Parliament's Human Rights Commission, which concluded with a claim (rejected) against the Spanish government being submitted to the Commission because of that government's policy of dispersing prisoners convicted of terrorism offences. The media was unanimous in criticizing this use of the system introduced by the Convention for propaganda purposes.

D. LEADING HUMAN RIGHTS CASES DECIDED BY THE NATIONAL COURTS

Thanks to Article 10(2) of the Spanish Constitution, the influence of the European Convention on Human Rights (either directly, or through its interpretation by the Court or the Commission) on the case-law of Spanish courts has been particularly strong.[31] Among the vast number of judgments,[32] we refer only to the reception of the Convention by the Constitutional Court, since its jurisprudence has to be followed, not only by the other judicial bodies, but also by other State authorities (Articles 164(1) of the Constitution, 38(1), 40(2) of the Organic Law of the Constitutional Court, and 5.1 of the Organic Law of the Judiciary). Space here does not allow reference to the two hundred or so judgments in which the Constitutional Court has referred to the European Convention or to the jurisprudence of the European Court of Human Rights; we therefore refer only to those most relevant to the debate on the content and limitations of basic rights in our country. Thus, following the order of the Convention, we would draw attention to the following cases.[33]

1. Right to life

Constitutional Court judgment 53/1985, the draft Organic Law partially decriminalizing abortion, referred to the Commission's ruling of 13 May

[31] General descriptions of this initial influence may be found in C. Fernandez de Casadevante, *La aplicación del Convenio Europeo de Derechos Humanos en España*, Madrid, 1988, and J. Delgado Barrio, 'Proyección de las decisiones del Tribunal Europeo de Derechos Humanos en las jurisprudencia española', *Revista de Administración Pública*, No. 119, 1989, pp. 233–252.

[32] A fairly complete chronological treatment (up to 1994) of the Constitutional Court and Supreme Court judgments which refer to the European Court of Human Rights may be found in M. Martinez Alvarez, 'Las sentencias del Tribunal Europeo de Derechos Humanos', *La Ley-Union Europea*, 7 June 1996, pp. 7–8.

[33] We omit reference to rulings which do not create jurisprudence, nor do we refer to judgments whose purpose is only to confirm previous judgments, nor to special votes.

1980, which interprets Article 2 of the Convention as referring to persons already born, and therefore not to those *yet to be born*, for the purpose of determining the scope of this right.

2. Right not to be subjected to inhuman or degrading treatment

Constitutional Court Judgments 65/1986 (*FJ* 4) and 89/1987 (*FJ* 2) accepted the concept of inhuman or degrading treatment established in the *Tyrer* judgment, rejecting the arguments that penalties for the deprivation of liberty and absolute ineligibility, in the first case, and the ban on confidential communication between prisoners, in the second, belong to this category. Constitutional Court Judgment 2/1987 supported the Commission's ruling of 16 December 1981 excluding the punishment of solitary confinement from the definition of degrading treatment (*FJ* 2), and Constitutional Court Judgment 120/1990 referred to the *Ireland v United Kingdom* judgment for the purpose of completing the definition of inhuman or degrading treatment, concluding in the latter case that to force-feed prisoners on hunger strike cannot be regarded as falling within that definition (*FJ* 9).

3. Right to personal liberty

The Constitutional Court quickly adopted the position taken by the European Court case-law for the purpose of determining the duration and conditions of detention and, above all, temporary imprisonment: thus, by way of example, the *Wemhoff* judgment is referred to in Constitutional Court Judgment 41/1982 (*FJ* 5), the *Stögmüller* judgment in Constitutional Court Judgment 104/1984, and the *De Wilde*, *Ooms*, and *Versyp II* judgments in Constitutional Court Judgment 341/1993 (*FJ* 4); Constitutional Court Judgment 128/1995 made sweeping reference to many other European judgments (*FJ* 3). Constitutional Court Judgment 199/1987, on the 1984 anti-terrorist law, used Article 5(3) of the European Convention as one of the arguments in favour of the unconstitutionality of extending detention by seven days (*FJ* 8). Among others Constitutional Court Judgment 112/1988 drew on the *Winterwerp* judgment to establish the minimum conditions for the internment of aliens (*FJ* 3); Constitutional Court Judgment 144/1990 invoked Article 5(4) of the European Convention as the basis for requiring that the judicial decision on the detention of an alien pending expulsion should be motivated; and Constitutional Court Judgment 12/1994 required that a judge hearing an application for *habeas corpus* verify the material legality of administrative detention because, according to the interpretation of Articles 17(1) and (4) of the Spanish Constitution, this is an obligation imposed by Article 5(4) of the European Convention (*FJ* 6).

Moreover, Constitutional Court Judgment 21/1997 based its arguments on the *Drozd and Janousek* and *Loizidou* judgments, in the context of detention at sea, in determining obligations in line with the Convention: this will apply to all state authorities, irrespective of the territory in which they operate (*FJ* 2).

4. Procedural rights

Without question, Article 6 is the Convention provision most frequently referred to in our Constitutional Court, due both to the fact that this concept has a parallel in Article 24 of the Spanish Constitution (the Article most frequently applied in Spanish case-law in terms of basic rights) and to the fact that the wording of this concept in the Constitution is in some respects more succinct than in the Convention. We would draw attention to the following instances, among others.

a. Regarding the *categories of person* covered by these rights, Constitutional Court Judgment 99/1985 agrees with Article 6(1) of the Convention ('all persons') including aliens under this heading, and Constitutional Court Judgment 143/1995, among others, refers to the *Campbell and Fell* European judgment with regard to the inclusion of prisoners (*FJ* 2).

b. Regarding the *area of application* of these rights, Constitutional Court Judgment 140/1995 refers to the Commission's decision of 1 June 1973 to justify the constitutionality of diplomatic immunity (*FJ* 6). For its part, Constitutional Court Judgment 89/1995, among others, makes frequent reference to the Strasbourg Court case-law to justify extending procedural rights to administrative procedures involving sanctions (*FJ* 4).

c. Regarding the *right to a fair trial*, Constitutional Court Judgment 12/1981 refers to the *Delcourt* judgment to argue that this is binding on jurisdictional entities (*FJ* 3), and Constitutional Court Judgment 36/1991, regarding juvenile courts, affirms the constitutionality of different procedures for adults and juveniles, based on the *Bouamar* judgment (*FJ* 5). Constitutional Court Judgment 160/1994 refers to the *Albert-Le Compte* judgment to accord constitutional status to the right to know the proposed ruling on sanctions to be imposed in administrative proceedings (*FJ* 3).

d. Regarding the *right to a public trial*, the limits imposed on this by Article 6(1) of the Convention are employed in cases such as Constitutional Court Judgment 2/1987 as justification for not opening to the public a hearing on disciplinary, penitentiary proceedings public (*FJ* 6) or Constitutional Court Judgment 36/1991 in connection with proceedings involving minors (*FJ* 6). By contrast, the subsequent Constitutional Court Judgment 96/1987 refers to the institutional importance of the right protected in Article 6(1), making reference to the *Pretto et al.* and *Axen* judgments (*FJ* 2).

e. Regarding the *right to be tried within a reasonable period of time*, there is a wealth of jurisprudence. This dates back to Constitutional Court Judgment 24/1981 (*FJ* 5) and Judgment 5/1985 (*FJ* 6) which referred to the *Wemhoff*, *Neumeister*, and *König* cases, among others, to determine the area of application of the law and the criteria for fixing the aforementioned period. The Spanish Constitutional Court also reflects the jurisprudential development in this area, as demonstrated by, for example, the citing of the *Ruiz Mateos* judgment in Constitutional Court Judgment 186/1995 (*FJ* 4), or the *Unión Alimentaria Sanders* judgment in Constitutional Court Judgment 196/1997 (*FJ* 3). The decisions of the Commission are also taken into account; thus the *Haase* and *Buchholz* decisions are referred to in Constitutional Court Judgment 133/1988 (*FJ* 3) to limit the duration of pre-trial proceedings.

f. Regarding the *right to an independent, impartial court as laid down by law*, this is often referred to in the pronouncements of our Constitutional Court. Among others we would mention Constitutional Court Judgment 101/1984 which quotes Article 6(1) to extend the concept to civil litigation (*FJ* 2), and Constitutional Court Judgment 44/1985 (*FJ* 4), to include the impartiality of the judge in the area protected by Article 24(2) of the Spanish Constitution, making specific reference to the *Piersack* judgment. The latter judgment, and the effects of the *De Cubber* case, were referred to in Constitutional Court Judgment 145/1988, regarding the law on oral proceedings in offences involving wilful misconduct and less serious and blatant offences, in which the Constitutional Court adopted the position of the European Convention on the concept of impartiality and the need to separate the functions of examining magistrate and judge (*FFJJ* 5 and 6). Other Strasbourg Court decisions taken into account are the *Barberá et al.* judgment, referred to in Constitutional Court Judgment 199/1987, affirming that the authority of the Supreme Court in the area of terrorism does not contravene the right of the ordinary judge contemplated in Article 24(2) of the Spanish Constitution (*FJ* 6), the *Ringeisen* judgment applied in Constitutional Court Judgment 157/1993 to demonstrate that impartiality does not require two separate courts (*FJ* 2), and the *Duinhof and Duijf* judgment, to demonstrate the importance of the legislative provisions of Constitutional Judgment 204/1994 (*FJ* 2). Other judgments, such as Constitutional Court Judgment 133/1995, relate to the impartiality of the judge and the presumption of innocence (*FJ* 2).

In this field too our Constitutional Court reflects the development of the Strasbourg Court; thus in Constitutional Court Judgment 60/1995 reference is made to the *Hauschildt* and *Nortier* judgments to justify the constitutionality of the law for the reform of juvenile courts (*FJ* 4).

g. Regarding the *right to be assisted by a defence counsel chosen by the accused*, Article 6(3)(c) of the Convention is quoted by Constitutional Court

Judgment 7/1986 to show that the choice is to be made by the interested party (*FJ* 6), and by Constitutional Court Judgment 30/1989 to extend its application to cases involving administrative offences. Moreover, the extent of free legal assistance is defined in Constitutional Court Judgment 47/1987 on the basis of the *Airey* and *Pakelli* cases (*FJ* 3), and Constitutional Court Judgment 37/1988 defines the ultimate purpose of the right to a defence in the manner stated in the *Artico* judgments (*FJ* 6). Furthermore, Constitutional Court Judgment 181/1994 points out that Article 6(3)(c) of the European Convention does not distinguish between nationals (*FJ* 2) and that it includes the right to defend oneself in person (*FJ* 3).

h. Regarding the *right to be assisted by an interpreter*, relating to the defence requirement of Article 24(2) of the Constitution contemplated in Constitutional Court Judgment 5/1984 (*FJ* 2), Constitutional Court Judgment 2/1987 (*FJ* 6) indicates that this concept would only be violated if the circumstances of Article 6(3)(e) of the Convention applied, that is to say not understanding the language used in the court.

i. Regarding the *right to question witnesses*, Constitutional Court Judgment 101/1985, among others, uses Article 6(3)(d) of the Convention to determine the scope of this right to the evidence referred to in Article 24.2 of the Constitution in connection with criminal proceedings (*FJ* 2). Furthermore, Constitutional Court Judgment 64/1994 applies the *Ciulla*, *Kostovski*, and *Windisch* judgments to affirm that the anonymity of witnesses does not contravene Article 6(3)(d) of the Convention and, as a consequence, is not contrary to Article 24(2) of the Spanish Constitution (*FJ* 3). Indirect witness evidence, with the requirements laid down in the *Delta*, *Isgrò*, and *Asch* judgments, was addressed in Constitutional Court Judgment 35/1995 (*FJ* 3). Recently Constitutional Court Judgment 153/1997 referred extensively to the European Court case-law on this matter (*FJ* 5).

j. Regarding the *right of appeal in criminal matters*, not recognized in the Spanish Constitution, Constitutional Court Judgment 157/1995 adopted the position of the Protocol No. 7 to the ECHR to extend the area of application of our Article 24(2) (*FJ* 4).

k. Regarding other procedural guarantees not expressly included in Article 6 of the Convention, Constitutional Court Judgment 175/1995 drew on the *Funke* judgment to include in Article 24(2) of the Constitution a 'right to remain silent and not to incriminate oneself in any way' (*FJ* 6). Constitutional Court Judgment 91/1995, among others, has made reference to the *Ruiz Torija* and *Hiro Balani* judgments in relation to the obligation to give reasoned judgments.

5. Rights of privacy

In general terms Constitutional Court Judgment 207/1996 adopts the position of the judgments in *X and Y v the Netherlands* and *Costello* to highlight the necessity of a legal basis for restrictions on these rights (FJ 4), and Constitutional Court Judgment 199/1996 refers to the *López Ostra* judgment to show that, on some occasions, the right to an appropriate environment contemplated in Article 45 of the Constitution falls within the scope of the rights of privacy (*FJ* 2). This judgment is particularly revealing of the important influence of the Strasbourg Court jurisprudence in Spain, in that it adopts a theory which is very critical of Spanish legislation, and one which has been severely criticized in our own legal doctrine.

In specific terms, regarding the *confidentiality of communications*, Constitutional Court Judgment 85/1994 refers to the *Klass* and *Malone* judgments to establish the requirements (legality and proportionality) of the judicial provisions applying to the interception of communications (*FJ* 3), and this was picked up in Constitutional Court Judgment 49/1996, based on the *Huvig* and *Kruslin* judgments (*FJ* 3). The interests of the Treasury are used as a limit on privacy, based on the *Rieme* and *Funke* judgments, in Constitutional Court Judgment 50/1996 (*FJ* 6), relying also on the *Chappell* and *Niemietz* judgments to determine the conditions governing entry to domicile. In relation to prisoners' communications, Constitutional Court Judgment 73/1983 adopted the position of the *Golder* judgment to extend this right to communications between a prisoner and his lawyer (*FJ* 5), and Constitutional Court Judgment 175/1997 refers to the *Domenichinle* and *Calogero Diana* judgments to highlight the special nature of this type of communication (*FJ* 4).

6. Freedom of thought, conscience, and religion

First, Constitutional Court Judgment 5/1981 refers to Article 9 of the Convention to relate freedom of instruction to the religious and ideological freedoms, and to infer from this connection a broad area of application protected by the first of the aforesaid liberties (*FJ* 7). Moreover, Constitutional Court Judgment 15/1982 affirms that conscientious objection to military service is part of the right defined in Article 16(1) of the Spanish Constitution, the content of which is determined with the help of Article 9 of the European Convention: 'obliges the Member States to respect the individual liberties of religion and conscience' (*FJ* 6). By contrast, Constitutional Court Judgment 55/1996 on the penalty for refusing to perform an alternative social service rules that, as from the Commission's decisions of 5 July 1977 and 14 October

1985, this refusal is not covered by Article 9(1) of the Convention, nor by Article 16(1) of the Constitution (*FJ* 5).

7. Freedom of expression

The paramount importance of this right, for the functioning of the democratic process, is highlighted in Constitutional Court Judgment 171/1990, based on the *Handyside* and *Barthold* judgments (FJ 9). The distinction between the expression of ideas and of factual information is established in Constitutional Court Judgment 143/1991 on the basis of the *Lingens* judgment (*FJ* 3).

In the area of radio and television, Constitutional Court Judgment 206/1990, among others, makes reference to Article 10(1) of the Convention to justify the constitutionality of the public monopoly (*FJ* 6), though such subsequent rulings as Constitutional Court Judgments 31/1994 (*FJ* 6) and 127/1994 (*FJ* 6) subject this monopoly to important conditions, applying the approach developed in the *Informationsverein et al.* and *Autronic AG* judgments.

Regarding the limitations placed on freedom of expression, the *Handyside* judgment is adopted by Constitutional Court Judgment 62/1982 to include, among other things, those relating to the public interest,[34] and by Constitutional Court Judgment 176/1995 with reference to the protection of juveniles and young children (*FJ* 5); Constitutional Court Judgment 190/1992 refers to the *Castells* judgment to fix the limits of political criticism (*FJ* 4). Constitutional Court Judgment 371/1993 uses the *Engel* judgment to justify the special aspects of the freedom of expression in relation to the military (*FJ* 4), and Constitutional Court Judgment 157/1996 refers to the *Barford* judgment to justify the right of courts to control the freedom of expression of lawyers (*FJ* 3). In contrast, other decisions support a more qualified construction of the limits: thus, Constitutional Court Judgment 171/1990 is based on the *Sunday Times* judgment, with the aim of giving a more restrictive interpretation of the limitations imposed on freedom of expression (*FJ* 9), and Constitutional Court Judgment 76/1995 (which also makes reference to the concept of 'reputation' contemplated in Article 10(2) of the Convention to define the scope of the right of personal respect in Article 18(1) of the Spanish Constitution) is based on the *Lingens* judgment and seeks to argue that criticism of public authorities is legitimate.

[34] With regard to this judgment, legal doctrine has expressed the criticism that limitations not contemplated in the Constitution cover intervention affecting the content of basic rights: see, for example, L. Martin-Retortillo and I. de Otto, *Derechos fundamentales y Constitución*, Madrid, 1988, pp. 114–115.

8. *Freedom of association*

Constitutional Court Judgment 89/1989, which refers to the *Albert-Le Compete* judgments, states that the fundamental right of Article 22 of the Constitution is not violated by compulsory registration with a professional institution. Moreover, Constitutional Court Judgment 263/1994 follows the general approach of the Convention in defining the aim of the right to belong to a union (*FJ* 3).

9. *The right not to be discriminated against*

The jurisprudence of the European Court in the context of Article 14 of the Convention has been followed since the earliest judgments on Article 14 of the Constitution. Thus in Constitutional Court Judgment 21/1981 our Constitutional Court adopted the concept of the objective, reasonable justification ('material', according to Constitutional Court Judgment 9/1995, *FJ* 2) of differences of treatment, and the necessary recourse to the principle of proportionality in assessing the existence or non-existence of this justification (*FJ* 2), expressly recognizing that this construction is inspired by that adopted by the European Court. With regard to the right of union membership (in terms of equality), Constitutional Court Judgment 53/1982 makes specific reference to the *National Union of Belgian Police* and the *Swedish Train Drivers' Union* judgments for the purpose of defining the most representative union.

E. CASES BROUGHT BEFORE THE EUROPEAN COMMISSION AND COURT OF HUMAN RIGHTS

Of the total of twenty-eight claims submitted to the Commission, eleven were admitted and seventeen rejected. Most claims were based on alleged violations of rights under Article 6 of the European Convention. In addition to these, claims were frequently based on the right of equal treatment (Article 14 of the Convention) and on freedom of expression (Article 10 of the Convention).

In relation to the European Court judgments following proceedings brought against Spain, we need to distinguish between judgments finding no violation and those condemning Spain, with emphasis on the latter, and taking into account, in particular, the extent to which the Strasbourg Court has corrected decisions of the Spanish courts, and the effects that this correction may have had on its courts and on legal doctrine. As we will see below, most of the judgments implied no criticism of the legal doctrine considered in the Spanish court pronouncements, but only of the way the legislation was applied, attributable in most cases to structural inadequacies in our legal system, which has become overburdened.[35]

1. *Judgments in which Spain was absolved*

In the *Drozd and Janousek* judgment of 26 June 1992 the Court rejected the application on the grounds that the alleged violation of the rights contemplated in Article 6 of the Convention had taken place in the territory of Andorra, where the Spanish authorities did not have jurisdiction.

The *Casado Coca* judgment of 24 February 1994[36] is the most interesting of the verdicts finding no violation, in that it addresses a controversial issue of particular practical relevance, that of advertising on behalf of professionals, in this case lawyers. After pointing out that Article 10 of the Convention provides a broad interpretation of freedom of expression, as a result of which 'no distinction is to be made according to whether the type of aim pursued is profit-making or not', the Court ruled (with dissenting opinions) that advertising by lawyers is one form of exercising the right of freedom of expression, even though in this case the action taken (disciplinary sanctions imposed by the Barcelona Bar Council), apart from being laid down in legal provisions, 'was aimed at protecting the interests of the public, while ensuring respect for members of the Bar'.

In the *Van der Tang* judgment of 13 July 1995 it was held that the provisional three-year term of imprisonment to which the appellant, a foreign resident in Spain, was subjected, did not violate Article 5(3) of the Convention, as the seriousness of the crimes of which he was convicted, and the risk of his escape, were both considerable. Furthermore, the Spanish judicial authorities had not demonstrated any lack of diligence on their part in prosecuting what was in fact a very complex case (drug smuggling).

The *Gea Catalán* judgment of 10 February 1995 held that the alleged violation of the right to be informed of criminal charges was simply an error, and that the applicant could easily have found out what the charges were.

The *Salvador Torres* judgment of 24 October 1995 held that a failure to inform the aplicant of one of the aggravating facts involved in the primary

[35] With regard to these deficiencies, cf. most recently J. J. Toharia, 'La Administración de justicia en España', in J. Tusell, E. Lamo de Espinosa, and R. Pardo (publishers), *Entre dos siglos. Reflexiones sobre la democracia española*, Madrid, 1996, pp. 295–313. In 1997 the General Council of the Judiciary, a government body of Spanish judges, published a *Libro Blanco de la Justicia* [White Paper on Justice], containing a general exposition of the problem and outlining possible solutions.

[36] See L. Jimena Quesada, 'La libertad de expresión y los abogados a la luz del Convenio Europeo de Derechos Humanos', *Revista General de Derecho*, No. 600, 1994, pp. 9469–9484. An example of the effects of this judgment on legal doctrine may be found in J. L. Garcia Guerrero, 'La publicidad como vertiente de la libertad de expresión en el ordenamiento constitucional español', *Revista Española de Derecho Constitucional*, No. 50, 1997, pp. 88–92.

criminal offence (the embezzlement of public funds) did not violate the right contemplated in Article 6(3)(a) of the Convention, since the aplicant could easily have found out what the facts were.

2. The judgments in which Spain has been condemned[37]

a. Personal liberty The *Scott* judgment of 18 December 1996 took the view that the four-year term of pre-trial detention imposed on the appellant (lasting from his detention in Spain until he was handed over to the British authorities) was contrary to Article 5(3) of the Convention. In the view of the European Court, the prolonged period of pre-trial detention could not be justified simply by the alleged crimes, or in the public interest; the national authorities are under a special obligation to ensure that the prisoner is tried as quickly as possible or, in this particular case, that the extradition proceedings are conducted diligently and expeditiously. However, the *Scott* judgment does not contain any correction of the case-law of the Spanish courts, it simply criticizes their inadequate functioning.

b. Rights to a fair and public trial In the *Barberá, Messegué, and Jabardo* judgment of 6 December 1988,[38] and in the *Ruiz Mateos* judgment of 23 June 1993,[39] the Spanish courts were the direct object of the Strasbourg Court's condemnations as they were unable to blame their actions on any structural deficiencies in the administration of justice. In the first case the Court identified various irregularities (for example, the defendants were tried after a night without sleep, there was an unexpected change in the composition of the Court, the brevity of the sessions in Court, and above all the inadequate public discussion of the evidence) in the way in which the High Court had conducted the proceedings, which together adversely affected the right to a

[37] We pointed out in the preceding section the effect that these judgments have on the case-law of the Constitutional Court; of particular significance is the right to a trial within reasonable time, and the obligation to give reasoned judgments.

[38] Regarding the *Barberá* judgment see also the legal theory referred to in note 51 below, and F. Castro-Rial Garrone, 'Consideraciones a la sentencia del Tribunal Europeo de Derechos Humanos en el asunto *Barberà, Messegue y Jabardo c. España*', *Revista de Derecho procesal*, 1989, pp. 789–807, and V. Fairen Guillen, 'Sentencia del caso *Barberà, Messegue y Jabardo*. Tribunal Europeo de Derechos Humanos (24–1986–122–171–173) de 6 de Diciembre de 1988', *Revista de Derecho procesal*, No. 2, 1989, pp. 295–352.

[39] Regarding the *Ruiz Mateos* judgment see C. Escobar Hernandez, 'Sentencia del Tribunal Europeo de Derechos Humanos de 23 de junio de 1993, en el asunto *Ruiz Mateos c. Espana*', *Revista Española de Derecho Ineternacional*, Vol. XLV, 1993, pp. 578–580; A. G. Chueca Sancho, 'La sentencia dictada por el Tribunal Europeo de Derechos Humanos en el caso *Ruiz Mateos*', *Derechos y Libertades*, No. 3, 1994, pp. 553–570; V. Fairen Guillen, 'El plazo razonable y el Tribunal Europeo de Derechos Humanos (La Sentencia No. 2/1992/147/420, asunto *Ruiz Mateos c. Espana*)', *Revista de Derecho procesal*, 1994, pp. 7–43; id, *Proceso equitativo, plazo razonable y Tribunal Europeo de Derechos humanos. Variaciones sobre la sentencia de 23 de junio de 1993, Asunto* 'Ruiz Mateos v Espana', Granada, 1996.

fair, public trial. In the second case the Court pointed out that, when the interlocutory question was submitted to the Constitutional Court, the State attorney had more opportunity to discuss the applicant's arguments, and this violated the principle of equality of arms as required by Article 6(1) of the Convention.[40]

c. Right to be judged within a reasonable time In the *Unión Alimentaria Sanders* judgment of 7 July 1989 and in the *Ruiz Mateos* judgment of 23 June 1993 (mentioned above), the subject of the Court's judgment was once again the deficient functioning of the Spanish administration of justice. In the first case, the judgment criticized the tardy response to the applicant's claim, both by the judge at first instance (two years), and by the Provincial Court (*Audiencia Provincial*), eighteen months); in the second case, it was the Provincial Court (proceedings lasting eighteen months) and paradoxically the Constitutional Court (two years), the highest guarantor of our 'right to proceedings without undue delay', which were deemed to have violated the right to a trial within reasonable time.

d. The obligation to give reasoned judgments In the *Ruiz Torija* and *Hiro Balani* judgments, both of 9 December 1994, the Court developed its theory of the obligation to give reasoned judgments, implicit in its interpretation of Article 6(1) of the Convention. In both cases it criticized the judgments of the Spanish courts for not making any reference to arguments contained in the claim which were clearly different from the arguments responded to by the court: thus, in the first case the judgment addressed the basic argument on resolution of a contract, but not the question of prescription; in the second the judgment addressed the argument relating to compatibility between a brand and a commercial name, but not the question of the previous right to the brand name.

e. Rights of privacy The *López Ostra* judgment of 9 December 1994[41] has without doubt sparked the most heated debate in the realm of Spanish legal doctrine. It concerned the problem of contamination caused by a factory

[40] It would be helpful to explain briefly the circumstances of this case; these will in part explain the subsequent non-enforcement of the judgment. In 1983 the Spanish government introduced a decree law for the compulsory purchase of the company Rumasa, one of whose main shareholders was Ruiz Mateos, subsequently the appellant. Later a law was passed, replacing the original decree law. This was all declared to be constitutional in the Constitutional Court Judgments 111/1983, 166/1986, and 6/1991, although in each case the decisions were not unanimous in the Constitutional Court and were variously interpreted in the legal doctrine.

[41] Regarding the *López Ostra* judgment, see J. A. Carrillo Donaire and R. Galan Vioque, 'Hacia un derecho fundamental a un medio ambiente adecuado?', *Revista Espanola de Derecho Administrativo,* No. 86, 1995, pp. 271–285; D. Garcia San Jose, 'Derecho al medio ambiente y respeto a la vida privada y familiar', *La Ley*, 25 October 1995, pp. 1–8; F. Velasco Caballero, 'La protección del medio ambiente ante el Tribunal Europeo de Derechos Humanos', *Revista Española de Derecho Constitucional,* No. 45, pp. 305–324.

situated a few metres from the appellant's home. After establishing that the latter's complaints had not been adequately dealt with at the many different government and judicial levels at which they had been submitted, the Court ruled that there had been a violation of the right to protection of the home and of private and family life. As pointed out previously,[42] this is a solution surprising because with the laudable aim of giving a just outcome in a specific case, the right contemplated in Article 8 of the Convention is given an extremely unusual interpretation, and one that is not adequately backed up by any of the traditional methods of interpretation.

f. Freedom of expression The *Castells* judgment of 23 April 1992 took the view that the penalty imposed on Senator Castells, a member of the Basque separatist group *Herri Batasuna*, for publishing a newspaper article against the government's anti-terrorist policy constituted violation of the freedom of expression. After defining the essential function of freedom of expression as that of guaranteeing the democratic process, the Court took the view that this essential function was most clearly expressed when it involved representatives of the people making statements and when the government was the object of their criticism. As has been pointed out,[43] the judgment does, however, display a certain ambiguity: on one hand it accepts the thesis of less protection for democratic governments in the context of the publication of information or opinions against those governments; but on the other hand it reaffirms that governments may resort to criminal penalties in a case of bad faith or in the absence of justification. Because of these uncertainties the effect of this judgment on our legal doctrine and practice has been very limited.

F. REMEDIAL ACTION TAKEN BY THE GOVERNMENT IN RESPONSE TO BEING HELD IN VIOLATION OF THE CONVENTION

No regulation in the Spanish judicial framework provides specific mechanisms for executing the judgments of the European Court. Constitution Court Judgment 245/1991, relating to execution of the *Barberá* judgment, expressed views on this question, even if these were of a partial and provisional nature; but, as we will see later, these were the subject of considerable criticism.

[42] G. Escobar Roca, *La ordenación constitucional del medio ambiente*, Madrid, 1995, p. 69.
[43] P. Salvador Coderch, *El derecho de la libertad*, Madrid, 1993, p. 53.

Spanish legal doctrine has carried out a rigorous examination of the possibilities offered by the regulations for reviewing a final judgment,[44] involving the actual effectiveness of *res judicata*,[45] since, apart from very rare exceptions, the execution of a European Court judgment will make it obligatory to revise judgments of this nature. Thus there have been analyses of the procedures relating to the reopening of proceedings,[46] the *exequatur*,[47] the pardon,[48] and the nullity of proceedings,[49] concluding that, in the light of the regulations governing these instruments, none of them is currently appropriate as a basis for executing judgments by the Strasbourg Court.

Special mention must be made of the possibilities offered by appeals on the ground of unconstitutionality (*recurso de amparo*) before the Constitutional Court,[50] bearing in mind that in the Constitutional Court Judgment 245/1991[51] it appears that this remedy is only adopted to solve the problem raised in general terms. This was the judgment that resolved an appeal on the ground of unconstitutionality filed by three Spanish citizens, *Barberá*,

[44] According to Article 245(3) of the Organic Law of the Judiciary:

Enforceable judgments are those against which it is not possible to appeal, except in the case of the reconsideration of judgments or exceptional circumstances laid down by law.

[45] *Res judicata* refers to the irrevocable nature of enforceable judgments, and is a fundamental principle of Spanish procedural law, being based on Articles 9(3) (judicial security, STC 185/1990, FJ 6), 24(1) (effective judicial protection, STC 23/1994) and 117(3) (exclusive awarding of jurisdiction, understood as the *irrevocable* satisfaction of interests) of the Spanish Constitution.

[46] See D. Liñan Nogueras, 'Los efectos de las sentencias del Tribunal Europeo de Derecho Humanos en derecho español', *Revista Española de Derecho Internacional*, Vol. XXXVII, 1986, pp. 371–373; J. M. Morenilla Rodriguez, 'La ejecución de las Sentencias del Tribunal Europeo de los Derechos Humanos', *Poder Judicial*, No. 15, 1989, p. 85; C. Escobar Hernandez, 'Problemas planteados por la aplicación en el ordenamiento español de la sentencia *Bultó* (Comentario a la STC 245/1991 de la 16 de Diciembre)', *Revista de Instituciones Europeas*, Vol. 19, No. 1, 1992, pp. 154–155 and L. M. Bujosa Vadell, *Las sentencias del Tribunal Europeo de Derecho Humanos y el ordenamiento español*, Madrid, 1997, pp. 157–161.

[47] See D. Liñan Nogueras, note 46 above, pp. 367–368; A. Soria Jimenez, 'La problemática ejecución de las sentencias del Tribunal Europeo de Derechos Humanos (Analisis de la STC 245/1991. Asunto *Barberá, Messegué y Jabardo*)', *Revista Espanola de Derecho Constitucional*, No. 36, 1992, p. 328, and L. M. Bujosa Vadell, note 46 above, pp. 169–173.

[48] See J. M. Morenilla Rodriguez, note 46 above, p. 74, and C. Escobar Hernandez, note 46 above, p. 152. A certain ('residual') effectiveness of the pardon is recognized by A. Soria Jimenez, note 47 above, p. 343 and L. M. Bujosa Vadell, note 46 above, pp. 172–173.

[49] See J. M. Morenilla Rodriguez, note 46 above, page 86; C. Escobar Hernandez, note 46 above, p. 156; A. Soria Jimenez, note 47 above, p. 341 and L. M. Bujosa Vadell, note 46 above, pp. 173–184.

[50] This remedy is regulated by Articles 41–58 of the Organic Law of the Constitutional Court.

[51] Regarding Constitutional Court Judgment 245/1991, see specifically: A. Soria Jimenez, note 47 above, pp. 313–356; C. Escobar Hernandez, note 46 above, pp. 139–163; J. L. Requejo Pages, 'La articulación de las jurisdicciones internacional, constitucional y ordinaria en las defensa de los derechos fundamentales (A propósito de la STC 245/91; "Caso *Bultó*")', *Revista Espanola de Derecho Constitucional*, No. 35, 1992, pp. 179–202; A. Salado Osuna, 'Ejecución de sentencias del Tribunal de Derechos Humanos (Comentarios a la STC de 16 de Dicembre de 1991)', *La Ley*, 1992, Vol. 3, pp. 70–80.

Messegué, and Jabardo, whom the European Court held to be entitled to a fair trial, in its judgment of 6 December 1988, rejecting the position adopted by the Spanish state. These three citizens appealed after seeking execution of the European Court judgment in Spain, which was refused by the Supreme Court[52] on the basis that, according to most legal doctrine, European Court judgments were merely declaratory as this body was international, and not supra-national, in nature; it concluded that it was impossible to recognize the direct effects of such judgments until legislation was reformed. The Supreme Court therefore recommended the issuing of a pardon and the awarding of financial compensation as the only permissible solution. The three named persons appealed against the Supreme Court judgment on the ground of unconstitutionality, claiming violation of the procedural rights contemplated in Article 24(2) of the Spanish Constitution.

The Constitutional Court, in Judgment 245/1991, upheld this appeal, thereby annulling the Supreme Court judgment of 4 April 1990. In recognizing the validity of the appeal, Constitutional Court Judgment 245/1991 basically used the following arguments.

a. European Court judgments do not have any direct effect for the purpose of enforcement, but this does not rule out the possibility, in the interests of *justice in a given case*, of their having some effect under Spanish law; indeed this is required by Articles 10(2) and 96(1) of the Spanish Constitution.
b. An appeal on the ground of unconstitutionality (*recurso de amparo*) is:

> the only remedy in situations where the Constitution does not provide protection, and where those situations have been caused by procedural irregularities brought to light after a final, firm judgment has been pronounced, for which there is no provision for a procedural remedy before the ordinary courts.

However, it is clear that the Constitutional Court does not go along with this solution wholeheartedly, since it concludes by recognizing that:

> the legislative authorities ought to set up adequate procedural mechanisms whereby action can be taken on the decisions of the European Court, before the judicial authorities, in cases such as the present in which there has been a declaration of a violation of basic rights in imposing a criminal penalty that is in the process of being executed.[53]

[52] Supreme Court Judgment of 4 April 1990 (Aranzadi Digest 3157).

[53] This recommendation to the legislator is one of the main contributions of the judgment; in this connection see J. A. Carrillo Salcedo, 'España y la protección de los derechos humanos: el papel del Tribunal Europeo de Derechos Humanos y del Tribunal Constitucional español', *Archiv des Völkerrechts*, Vol. 2, 1994, p. 200.

In line with Gimeno Sendra's dissenting opinion in Constitutional Court Judgment 245/1991, legal doctrine has been very critical of the Court's approach[54] for the following reasons.

a. The judgment went against the function of an appeal on the ground of unconstitutionality, the purpose of which is to protect basic rights, not to execute European Court judgments.
b. It violated the remedy of *res judicata*, thereby jeopardizing important principles of constitutional and procedural law.
c. It relied on a broad interpretation of Article 10(2) of the Spanish Constitution, making this provision a basis for creating (and not only for interpreting) constitutional rights.

Following Constitutional Court Judgment 245/1991 the proceedings were reopened, concluding with the High Court judgment of 30 October 1993 in which the accused were absolved as a result of lack of evidence. Notwithstanding, in a new judgment (*Barberá II*) the European Court again ordered the Spanish state to pay compensation for damages to the accused persons, disregarding the opposing position adopted by the Commission, and despite the European Court's recognition of the 'importance' of Constitutional Court Judgment 245/1991. This is why *Barberá II* has been described as a:

> a real humiliation for the State, despite its having made considerable effort to recognize the execution of the European Court's judgments, even at the risk of jeopardizing very important constitutional principles.[55]

Curiously, in another case involving the execution of a European Court judgment in Spain, the Constitutional Court abandoned the principles it had adopted in its Judgment 245/1991.[56] Thus, in relation to the *Ruiz Mateos* judgment, in which the European Court ruled there had been a violation of Article 6(1) of the Convention, and pronounced judgment against the Spanish state, the Constitutional Court, through its Resolutions of 31 January 1994,[57] refused to review the case, declaring on this occasion that the appeal clearly lacked any substantial basis for a ruling on the merits, that the Constitutional Court lacked jurisdiction to revise its own decisions, and that in any case it was not under an obligation to implement European Court judgments. Despite the subsequent Resolution of the Committee of Ministers,[58] later confirmed by

[54] See, in addition to the works cited in note 51 above, L. M. Bujosa Vadell, note 47 above, pp. 192–198, and C. Ruiz Miguel, note 2 above, pp. 140–152.
[55] Ibid, p. 151.
[56] Thus, L. M. Bujosa Vadell, note 46 above, pp. 198–200, and in particular C. Ruiz Miguel, note 2 above, pp. 151–156.
[57] These texts may be consulted in C. Ruiz Miguel, note 2 above, pp. 180–183.
[58] Resolution DH (94)27 of 21 March 1994.

the Commission, we may say that in effect the *Ruiz Mateos* judgment has never been executed.

In conclusion, it cannot be said that Spanish legislation contains a clear principle, or a coherent, consolidated system, for the purpose of executing European Court judgments in Spain,[59] since, in the light of existing legislation, none of the general instruments for reviewing enforceable judgments are applicable without altering their actual meaning, and the principles proposed by the Constitutional Court in this regard are neither definitive nor accepted.

G. ASSESSMENT AND PROSPECTS

First, the influence of the European Convention on Human Rights and the jurisprudence of the European Court of Human Rights on Spanish courts in general, and on the Spanish Constitutional Court in particular, may be assessed as positive in overall terms: they were very useful in determining the content of the rights, as a minimum standard for protection, especially at a historic moment when there were no immediate precedents in Spanish case-law.[60]

The authority which the European Court now exercises over Spanish courts may be illustrated by the Constitutional Court judgment 199/1996 in which, with regard to the right to an adequate environment, reference was made to the above-quoted *López Ostra* judgment, which it appears to regard as having a binding effect—despite the fact, as we have seen, that this judgment was at variance with constitutional case-law and was fiercely criticized by some legal scholars.

In any event, most legal scholars are critical[61] of the above-mentioned jurisprudential trend, which has not yet been consolidated, of identifying the content of rights by reference to the provisions of the European Convention and pronouncements of the European Court of Human Rights; this is partly because this trend would mean a reduction of the content of the said rights, which were originally recognized only by the Constitution.

Secondly, legal scholars unanimously support introducing legislative reforms which guarantee the enforceable nature of the European Court judgments, the absence of which has in the past resulted in judgments against

[59] The execution of judgments ordering Spain to pay compensation in the form of what we might define as modest sums has not caused problems in practice (see M. Martinez Alvarez, note 32 above, p. 6), though in certain cases there remains the legal problem of the reconsideration of enforceable judgments.

[60] See, for example, E. Linde *et al.*, note 22 above, p. 202, and L. Martin-Retortillo, 'La recepción por el Tribunal Constitucional de la jurisprudencia del Tribunal Europeo de Derechos Humanos', *Revista de Administración Publica*, No. 137, 1995, pp. 7–29.

[61] The arguments are considered in the references in note 23 above.

Spain. In this sense the proposals put forward recommend the introduction of different reforms depending on the main object of the judgment, be it a law, an administrative act, or a judicial decision.[62]

Concentrating on the proposals *de lege ferenda*, aimed at fully implementing the European Court's judgments, which will normally have the effect of demanding the review of enforceable judgments pronounced by the Spanish courts, we can speak basically of two types of measures:[63]

a. the introduction of a new legal basis for review proceedings.[64] This is the position adopted by most legal scholars,[65] in whose view this modification is the one most in tune with the basic principles of Spanish procedural law; and
b. the introduction of an independent application for nullity.[66] In view of the problems of distorting the essential nature of review that the previous option would entail,[67] another group of legal scholars propose the alternative establishment of both a review[68] of the case and independent proceedings aimed at demonstrating and where applicable declaring a nullity, in addition to reopening proceedings which will continue until a proper conclusion, in accordance with the rights stated in the European Convention,[69] is reached.

Meanwhile, as a parallel initiative, there are those who also propose the adoption of a new Protocol to the Convention, with the same aim in mind,[70] which in Spain would ideally be ratified on the basis of Article 93 of the Constitution.[71]

[62] Thus, for example, C. Ruiz Miguel, note 2 above, p. 157.

[63] In general terms legal theory rightly rejects the solution based on the approval of *ad hoc* laws. See, for example, L. M. Bujosa Vadell, note 26 above, pp. 203–205.

[64] Which would require reforming Article 1796 of the Law on Civil Trials, Article 954 of the Law on Criminal Trials, Article 102 of the Law on Jurisdiction for Disputes, and Article 234 of the Law on Employment Procedures.

[65] See J. M. Morenilla Rodriguez, note 46 above, p. 86; D. Liñan Nogueras, note 46 above, pp. 371–373; J. L. Requejo Pages, note 51 above, p. 202; P. A. Fernandez Sanchez, *Las obligaciones de los Estados en el marco del Convenio Europeo de Derechos Humanos,* Madrid, 1997, p. 128, and J. Bonet I. Perez, 'El problema de la efectividad interna de las sentencias del Tribunal Europeo de Derechos Humanos', *Revista Jurídica de Cataluna*, 1993, p. 88.

[66] Which would make it necessary to reform only Article 238 of the Organic Law on the Judiciary.

[67] Pronounced by L. M. Bujosa Vadell, note 46 above, pp. 207–210.

[68] Thus A. Soria Jimenez, note 47 above, p. 350.

[69] Thus L. M. Bujosa Vadell, note 46 above, pp. 212–215.

[70] See L. M. Bujosa Vadell, note 46 above, pp. 215–217, and A. Sanchez Legido, *La reforma del mecanismo de proteccion del Convenio Europeo de Derechos Humanos*, Madrid, 1995.

[71] According to this principle:

> An organic law may be used to authorize the signing of treaties whereby powers are given to an international organization or institution to exercise the responsibilities derived from Constitution.

32

Sweden

IAIN CAMERON

A INTRODUCTION

It is not possible to analyse the function of the European Convention on Human Rights (hereinafter, the Convention) in the Swedish legal order without some knowledge of the system of constitutional rights in Sweden. Only then can one appreciate the role which it has played, and can play, in filling gaps in rights protection. Accordingly, this short introductory section gives an overview of the constitutional rights context.[1] There are three Swedish constitutional documents dealing with rights: the Freedom of the Press Act (Tryckfrihetsförordningen, TF), the Freedom of Expression Act (Yttrandefrihetsgrundlag, YGL), and the Instrument of Government (Regeringsformen, RF). The Freedom of the Press Act (1949:105)[2] and the Freedom of Expression Act (1991:1469) deal, respectively, with the printed and the electronic media. They provide *inter alia* for a special system of criminal responsibility for crimes committed by means of printed or electronic media (defamation, breaches of the Secrecy Act, etc.) and for the right to trial by jury for those accused of committing such offences. They prohibit censorship and lay down the right to communicate official information, even secret information, to the press for publication, subject to certain narrowly defined exceptions. Swedish protection of freedom of information is probably stronger than in any other European state, and forms an important part of the system of constitutional control.

[1] I deal with this issue in more detail in I. Cameron, 'The Protection of Constitutional Rights in Sweden' (1997) *Public Law* 488.

[2] References to the Swedish statute book (Svensk författningssamling, SFS) are by year followed by the relevant number. Translations of the Constitution come from the official English edition unless otherwise stated. References to a constitutional provision are by Chapter and Article number. An Article can have several paragraphs which are in turn divided into subparagraphs, thus, RF 2 kap. 1§ 1st. 1.p is translated RF 2:1, paragraph 1, subparagraph 1. References to *travaux préparatoires* are to the government commissioin of inquiry preceding legislation, Statens Offentlige Utredningar (SOU).

Other human rights are set out in Chapter 2 of the Instrument of Government (1974:152). The Instrument of Government was adopted in 1974, totally replacing the version of 1809. Chapter 2 was a late addition to the original drafts of the new Instrument of Government. The Social Democratic government of the day saw little need for constitutional protection of human rights, beyond that provided by the Freedom of the Press Act.[3] It was reluctant to do anything which could hinder its programme of legislative reforms, and considered that, in any event, the sole meaningful protection of fundamental freedoms lay in the democratic process. Originally, the majority of civil liberties (freedom of speech, assembly etc.) were formulated so as to allow restrictions by statute. These were classed as 'relative rights'. There were certain 'absolute' rights such as prohibitions of the death penalty and of retroactive criminal law which could only be altered by constitutional amendment.[4] Otherwise, there was no provision for entrenchment.

However, Chapter 2 was subsequently subjected to major amendments on three occasions, in 1976, 1979, and 1994. The first change introduced new relative rights and general substantive conditions (generally corresponding to those set out in the Convention) which have to be satisfied before relative rights can be restricted. The 1976 reform also provided that aliens present in Sweden were to enjoy, in most cases, equality of protection with Swedish citizens. The second change, in 1979 saw the introduction of a weak form of entrenchment: the 'qualified legislative procedure'. In essence this provides that a statute which restricts certain relative rights can (subject to certain minor exceptions) be delayed by a minority of MPs for a period of one year, the idea being that during this year opposition both within and without Parliament can be mobilized.[5] Another change made in 1979 was the formal recognition of the possibility for both courts and administrative agencies to review, in concrete cases, the constitutionality of statutes and subordinate legislation. A cautious practice of constitutional review had gradually developed during the early twentieth century. However, the competence of the courts to engage in this was, and is, viewed with deep suspicion by the left-wing parties, who were unwilling to confirm its existence by a constitutional provision.

[3] The Freedom of the Press Act was part of the reason why it took until 1974 for Sweden—which has always been a strong champion of human rights in other countries—to write them into its own Constitution. The Act is firmly established in the Swedish legal culture, having antecedents which date back to 1766. The opinion is still occasionally expressed that Sweden could manage quite well without Chapter 2 as long as the Freedom of the Press Act continued to apply.

[4] The provisions of the Freedom of the Press Act, and since 1991 the Freedom of Expression Act, being constitutional documents, are 'absolute rights'. Having said this, the Constitution can be amended by two votes, a simple majority sufficing for each, with an intervening general election.

[5] This is a highly simplified explanation. For more detail see Cameron, note 1 above, 497–500.

They eventually accepted it, but subject to a major limitation. This limitation stipulates that a law (*lag*) passed by Parliament or an ordinance (*förordning*) passed by the government must be 'manifestly' in breach of a constitutional provision before a court or administrative agency can refuse to apply it in the case before it (RF 11:14).[6] No such limitation applies to subordinate legislation issued by administrative agencies on delegation by the government which conflicts with higher norms. The final change made in 1979 was the reinstatement of the requirement to submit a legislative proposal involving human rights to pre-legislative scrutiny before the Law Council (*lagrådet*).[7]

The last important series of amendments to Chapter 2 was made in 1994. This added certain new (albeit weak) rights, amended and improved the protection of the right to property so as to correspond with its formulation in the Convention, and provided for a quasi-constitutional status for the Convention. This last point is dealt with in more detail in the next section.

Before doing so, however, it would be useful to conclude this section by briefly sketching out the degree of overlap between the Convention and other Swedish constitutional rights protection. Generally, it can be said that the two catalogues of rights cover very much the same ground. There are, however, a few exceptions, the most important of which are noted below.[8] First, Chapter 2 contains no general provision relating to access to a court and to the conditions of a fair trial (Article 6). Secondly, Chapter 2 has no protection of the right to privacy or to 'family life' (Article 8). It is these two areas in which the Convention has had, and is in the future likely to have, most significance in the Swedish courts. Thirdly, there is no general requirement in Chapter 2 to provide an effective remedy for the violation of a right (Article 13), a right which, it is now established, can be breached independently of a violation of a substantive right.[9] Fourthly, the provisions against racial and sexual discrimination, RF 2:15 and 2:16 respectively, are formulated differently from Article 14 of the Convention. Unlike the latter ('discrimination . . . such as. . . .') the former provisions exhaustively specify prohibited criteria for discrimination. On the other hand, RF 2:15 and 2:16 prohibit discrimination in general, in all legislation and subordinate legislation, not simply discrimination in relation

[6] The Swedish system of constitutional review is unusual in that the power of review is vested not just in courts in general (unlike, eg, the German and Italian systems where such power is vested in a specialized court) but also in administrative agencies. This can be explained partly by the quasi-independent role which administrative agencies have in the Swedish system. The formal reason for this is the independent position of agencies under the Constitution (RF 11:7). In practice, it is almost unheard of for an administrative agency to refuse to apply a law or ordinance, although there are cases where hierarchically inferior norms have not been applied.

[7] See p. 841 below.

[8] I will not go into the issue here of the narrow approach occasionally taken to the question of what is a 'restriction' of a human right: see Cameron, note 1 above, 505.

[9] See eg *Valsamis v Greece* and *Efstratiou v Greece*, 18 December 1996.

to the rights set out in Chapter 2. Fifthly, as already mentioned, Chapter 2 provides for two different systems of protection, for citizens and aliens. This can be contrasted with the standard rule in Article 1 of the Convention ('secure . . . to everyone') which is subject only to the limited qualification set out in Article 16.[10] Finally, in some areas Swedish protection goes further than the Convention, at least as it has so far been interpreted: eg RF 2:14 provides for less restrictions on the right of assembly than Article 11; RF 2:10 prohibits (subject to certain exceptions) retroactive tax legislation; RF 2:11 provides that no (alleged) offence can be tried by a Court constituted after its (alleged) commission; and TF/YGL provide much stronger protection of the freedom of information.[11]

B. THE STATUS OF THE CONVENTION IN SWEDISH LAW

1. Status before incorporation

Sweden signed the Convention on 28 November 1950. On 2 March 1951, a bill for approval of the Convention was submitted to Parliament.[12] The bill contained an extremely summary two-page comparison of the Convention provisions and Swedish law which was followed by the relevant Minister's opinion that 'a review of the Convention Articles shows that . . . there appears to be no obstacle to Sweden ratifying the Convention'.[13] The conclusion was thus that there was no need for legislation.[14] Sweden ratified the Convention on 4 February 1952. A declaration recognizing the competence of the Commission was made at the same time, although it was not until 1966 that Sweden recognized the competence of the Court to decide cases.

[10] And it should be noted that the Court interpreted this Article very restrictively in *Piermont v France*, (1996) 24 EHRR 294 Judgment of 27 April 1995, Series A No. 314.

[11] There can be specific situations in which the Convention protects freedom of information (eg *Guerra and Others v Italy*, Judgment of 19 February 1998).

[12] Prop. 1951:165.

[13] The 'analysis' of Article 6—subsequently to cause major problems for Sweden—amounted to one sentence: 'The provisions in Article 6 on legal guarantees are completely covered by the Code of Judicial Procedure': Prop. 1951: 165 sida [page, s.]12. See also H. Danelius, 'Judicial Control of the Administration—A Swedish proposal for legislative reform', in F. Matscher and H. Petzold (eds), *Protecting Human Rights: the European Dimension* (Köln, Carl Heymanns, 1988).

[14] The same conclusion was reached regarding the subsequent ratification of Additional Protocols Nos. 1, 4, 6, and 7. Apart from the fact that it was deemed to be unnecessary, another reason invoked for not converting the Convention to national law was that its drafting was alien to Swedish legal traditions and so likely to cause difficulties in interpretation (SOU 1975: 75 s. 98).

Apart from its indirect influence on the 1976 drafting reforms of Chapter 2 of the Instrument of Government, little attention was initially paid to the Convention by the Swedish Parliament, administrative agencies, or courts. In the early 1970s the Swedish courts ruled that, in the absence of legislation converting it to Swedish law, the Convention did not create direct rights capable of being invoked before national courts.[15] Following the *Sporrong and Lönnroth* case,[16] and a subsequent series of cases finding violations of Article 6 (access to a court),[17] there were a number of attempts by the centre/right political parties to incorporate the Convention. All attempts at incorporation failed due to opposition from the Social Democrats.[18]

2. The incorporation of the Convention into Swedish law

In 1991 a government commission, the Committee on Rights and Freedoms, was appointed by the new centre/right government to investigate a number of human rights questions, *inter alia* whether Sweden should incorporate the Convention. The Committee reported on this issue in 1993, recommending incorporation.[19] There were a number of reasons for this, all of them pragmatic. First, while there is no requirement in the Convention that it be incorporated, it is the best way to go about realizing the rights protected by the Convention, as it obliges Swedish courts and administrative agencies to have regard to the Convention without having to rely on their good will in applying the principle that legislation be interpreted in accordance with Treaty commitments. Secondly, it was hoped that incorporation would mean fewer issues going to Strasbourg (and fewer defeats there). Thirdly, Finland and Denmark had already incorporated the Convention and Norway and Iceland were likely to do so. Incorporation would thus bring Sweden into line with the practice of the other Nordic countries. Fourthly, and most importantly, there was the EU aspect: the Convention is part of the general principles of EC law. Sweden was, in 1993, part of the European Economic Area and thus obliged to apply EC law, albeit indirectly. Sweden was also contemplating membership of the EU. Incorporation of the Convention would avoid the awkward and inconsistent situation where Swedish courts and administrative agencies

[15] AD 1972, nr. 5 s. 75, NJA 1973, s. 423 and RÅ 1974, s. 121. Cases from the Supreme Court (*Högsta domstolen*) are cited from the semi-official Supreme Court Reports, NJA, from the Supreme Administrative Court (Regeringsrätten) from the official series, RÅ, and from the Labour Court (*Arbetsdomstolen*, AD) from the official series, AD. One of the main critics was J. Sundberg: see eg 'Om mänskliga rättigheter i Sverige' (1986) *Svensk Juristtidning* 660.

[16] Judgment of 23 September 1982, Series A No. 52.

[17] See section E below.

[18] For more detail on the incorporation debate, see I. Cameron, 'Sweden', in C. Gearty (ed) *European Civil Rights and Civil Liberties*, (The Hague, Kluwer, 1997).

[19] 'Fri- och Rättighetsfrågor, inkorporering av Europakonvention', SOU 1993:40 del B.

were obliged to have regard to the Convention when applying EC law, or national law connected to EC law, but not when applying 'pure' national law.[20] Finally, it was hoped that incorporation would also have a general pedagogical effect on Swedish political, social, and legal thinking and Swedish administration, fostering a respect for individual rights.

As already mentioned, the main opposition to incorporation has usually (although not always) come from the Social Democratic Party. The Social Democrats have feared, not without reason, that incorporation would involve a shift of power to the courts at the expense of the executive and of the democratically elected legislature. The question of incorporation was thus intimately connected to the question of the scope of the power of constitutional review. Put bluntly, the issue was which of the three organs of government was to have the final say as regards the scope of human rights, in particular the scope of the right to property. The Committee's report, and its proposal to reconcile incorporation with the weak Swedish system of constitutional review, was the result of a political compromise. As such, all the major political parties accepted it.

It was agreed that the Convention should not be given constitutional status, but rather incorporated in an ordinary law. The stated reason for this was to avoid the risk of confusion which might be caused by two parallel catalogues of rights with the same constitutional status.[21] After a short debate, this law was enacted on 5 May 1994 and entered into force on 1 January 1995.[22] The Act provides that the Convention and Protocols Nos. 1–8 shall, in their authentic texts (ie English and French) apply as Swedish law.[23] A new Swedish translation was made of the Convention because of certain problems with the old text. This was also appended to the Act, but formally it does not have the status of law, although in practice this text is used by Swedish courts and administrative agencies. The law has since been amended twice: in 1995, with the incorporation of Protocol No. 9[24] and in 1998, with the incorporation of Protocol No. 11.[25] The latter amendment resulted in a further new translation being commissioned.

[20] See p. 843 below.

[21] SOU 1993: 40 del B s. 127. The somewhat contradictory point was also made that application of the *lex posterior* principle would mean that the Convention was to be preferred to RF Chapter 2 in the case of a conflict.

[22] *Lag* (1994:1219) *om den europeiska konventionen angående skydd för de mänskliga rättigheterna och de grundläggande friheterna.*

[23] The incorporation of the whole Convention rather than only the material rights, as eg the UK has done, gives rise to interesting (and as yet unanswered) questions as to the independent effect of Article 13 and whether the 'just satisfaction' requirement in Article 41 provides the Swedish courts with the necessary procedural competence to award damages where the plaintiff's Convention rights have been breached.

[24] SFS 1995:462.

[25] SFS 1998:712.

As mentioned, the incorporation law provides that the Convention is to have the status of an ordinary statute. The problem with this was obvious: this statute could conflict with other statutes. Accordingly, a provision was added to the Constitution (RF 2:23) which lays down that 'a law or other regulation shall not be issued in conflict with Sweden's obligations under [the Convention]'. This constitutional amendment was the subject of protracted discussions between the political parties. RF 2:23 does not, as such, give the Convention constitutional status. Nor does it create a new category of laws midway between the Constitution and ordinary laws. Instead, it means that a law or other regulation which conflicts with the Convention also conflicts with the Constitution. As with all such conflicts, the normal restrictions in RF 11:14 apply on the power of the courts to engage in constitutional review.[26] This means that the courts, and administrative agencies, must refuse to apply legislation or subordinate legislation which conflicts with the Convention, although where it is a statute or a government ordinance which allegedly breaches the Convention, then the conflict must be 'manifest'. Accordingly, statutes or ordinances which do conflict with the Convention but not manifestly should thus be applied. No restriction applies to constitutional review of rules lower down in the hierarchy of norms, ie regulations promulgated by administrative agencies or local authorities. The effect of constitutional review of statutes or ordinances in the Swedish system—in the very rare cases where it has occured—is that the inferior norm is set aside only in the case at issue. It does not lapse as such. So, while a ruling determines the issue between the parties, the impugned norm continues to be formally valid.[27]

It was made abundantly clear in the *travaux préparatoires* that the rule in RF 2:23 was to be used sparingly, and as a last resort. It was stressed that the primary responsibility for ensuring that Swedish law continued to conform with the changing requirements of the Convention lay on the legislature, not the courts.[28] The courts and administrative agencies were encouraged instead to solve the problem of possible conflicts with other Swedish norms by the application of certain principles of interpretation. These were named as *lex specialis*, *lex posterior*, the principle of 'treaty conform' construction, and a rather novel varient of it proposed by the Supreme Court when commenting on the legislative proposal, namely the principle that 'human rights treaties should be given special significance in the event of a conflict with other norms'. The Convention must be understood from the case-law of the

[26] See further, Cameron, note 1 above, 502–512.

[27] Removal of the 'manifest' requirement has recently been proposed by a government commission, but for political reasons this change seems unlikely to occur in the near future.

[28] SOU 1993: 40, del B s. 126. This was also stressed in identical terms in the bill (Prop. 1993/94: 117 s. 36) and the report of the Committee on the Constitution (1993/94 KU 24, s. 17.

Commission and the Court. Although the incorporation statute itself imposes no explicit duty on the Swedish courts to pay regard to the Convention *acquis*, such a requirement is made clear in the *travaux prėparatoires* to the act of incorporation and in pronouncements from the courts themselves.[29]

However, the courts will have problems in using these principles to avoid all conceivable norm conflicts. To begin with, the effect of RF 11:14 is to rule out using the principles of *lex posterior* and *lex specialis* to solve conflicts between the Convention statute and government ordinances. Thus, although the Convention statute is constitutionally superior to an ordinance, the latter must be preferred, as long as the conflict between it and the statute is not 'manifest'. Secondly, while the principle of treaty conform construction can be assumed to exist in the legal orders of all European states, its strength and impact will vary depending upon a variety of factors, the most important of which is the judicial culture, ie how much constitutional power the judiciary wield against the Parliament and the executive. The Swedish judiciary, while independent, do not have the constitutional influence of, for example, the English or Scottish judiciary. Nor does Swedish case-law have the same impact in consitutional matters as the case-law of a strong constitutional court, such as the Bundesverfassungsgericht.[30]

There have only been two cases so far in which the issue arose as to whether another statute was 'manifestly' in conflict with the Convention.[31] No indications have been given as to how to interpret the 'manifest' requirement.[32] Logically, a provision which cannot be reconciled with the requirements of the Convention by the use of the other interpretative methods set out above must be 'manifestly' in conflict with them. On the other hand, it will invariably be Convention case-law with which a Swedish provision cannot be reconciled, not the wording of the Convention itself. The great reluctance of the Swedish courts to engage in constitutional review means that they will normally require very, very strong evidence that a statute is in breach of Convention case-law before they will refuse to apply it. It should, however, be noted that the 'manifest' requirement does not apply to norm conflicts between EC law and Swedish law. Thus, to the extent that a Swedish statute or ordinance conflicts with the Convention as part of the general principles of EC law, the Swedish courts are entitled, indeed obliged, to set the former

[29] Prop. 1993/94: 117 s. 37 and Ds 1997:25 s. 49, produced as a result of the *Holm* case (see section E below) where it is stated that ECtHR cases are a source of law to be applied by the Swedish courts. For an example of a judicial pronouncement see RH 1997:74.

[30] For a short discussion of the Swedish legal culture see Cameron, note 1 above, 502–508.

[31] RH 1995:85 and RÅ 1997 ref 65.

[32] For a fuller dicussion of this issue see I. Cameron, 'The Swedish Experience of the ECHR Since Incorporation' 48 *ICLQ* (1999).

aside. In the long run, this power and duty derived from EC law risks 'infecting' ordinary constitutional review.

C. THE STATUS OF THE CONVENTION IN PARLIAMENTARY PROCEEDINGS

It has repeatedly been stressed that the primary responsibility for ensuring compliance with the Convention lies with the legislator. It might therefore have been expected that steps would be taken to ensure that legislation, and subordinate legislation, which raises issues under the Convention is not passed without first having undergone expert scrutiny. However, no such special procedure has been instituted. On the other hand, the fact that the normal legislative process is long and open ought to enable the identification of potential breaches, at least as far as statutes are concerned. Put very briefly, the legislative process usually begins with a directive to a committee, consisting of either MPs or civil servants, to investigate the need for new legislation. Committees dealing with legal questions are often assisted by, or even led by, external experts (eg academic lawyers). After the committee has reported, an opportunity is usually given for a cross-section of interest groups (often including the law faculties) to comment upon the merits of proposals before these are laid before Parliament. The government then decides whether to propose legislation. If it does so, the relevant government department drafts a proposal. About 50 per cent of all proposals are sent to the Law Council, a group of prominent lawyers, mainly serving or retired judges from the highest courts. The Law Council comments on the technical aspects of the proposal, although it occasionally makes (guarded) criticism of the substance of it. The proposal is then submitted to Parliament as a bill and considered by the relevant parliamentary standing committee. This committee then submits a report to Parliament. The composition of this standing committee reflects the composition of Parliament as a whole so the vote in parliament seldom goes against the proposal of the committee.

This very brief description of the Swedish legislative process shows that there are several points at which critical voices can be heard. The first of these is the investigative stage. One of the standard directions to a committee is to consider in what way, if any, the changes it may propose are compatible with the Constitution. As already mentioned, the Convention does not have formal constitutional status. There is thus no general requirement for a committee to take it into account, although naturally the specific directive it receives may require it to do so. Another important stage is the scrutiny by the law faculties. A further safeguard is the Law Council. My survey of the minutes of Law Council meetings during the last four months of 1997 disclosed several proposals in which the Law Council drew the attention of the government to possible difficulties relating to the Convention. In each case the Law Council contented itself with references to the Convention itself, rather than European Court case-law. It should be noted that the Law Council has no legal assistants and its membership changes every two years: the competence of the Law Council in the field of the Convention thus depends upon the knowledge which the current individual members have of it. Thus it is by no means a total safeguard. The third and final stage at which Convention issues can be raised is in the parliamentary committee which scrutinizes the bill. Proposals relating to the Constitution are sent to the Committee of the Constitution. Other committees can also refer proposals to it for commentary. This Committee has a small legal staff which is capable of making its own investigations. Independent investigations occur rarely but a relatively recent example concerned a legislative proposal to close a nuclear power station. The political opposition *inter alia* raised the issue of the compatibility of this measure with Article 1 of Protocol No. 1, particularly whether it could be said to be 'in the public interest'.[33] The legal staff of the Committee on the Constitution, however, are not experts on the Convention.

One weakness of the Swedish system is that there is no mechanism for monitoring new Strasbourg case-law concerning other states. All the cases are copied from the Foreign Office to the Department of Justice (and both have access to new case reports published on the Internet) but no one in the Department of Justice is responsible for checking whether new cases cause problems for Swedish law. There is no centralized monitoring of ECJ case-law either. The procedural law and constitutional law units of the Department of Justice have most experience of dealing with Convention and can, hopefully, be relied upon to pick up on important Convention cases and initiate a directive to a committee to inquire into the matter. This has been known to occur, eg regarding the implications of the *Funcke* case for Swedish tax investigations.[34] The National Courts Administration Board now has a procedure for monitoring case-law developments before the Court and the ECJ and for disseminating judgments to Swedish courts. However, this is the task of a single judge, so there is still a risk that cases with important implications are missed.

[33] Prop 1996/97:22.

[34] *Funke v France*, Judgment of 25 February 1993, Series A No. 256–A, SOU 1996:116.

D. LEADING HUMAN RIGHTS CASES DECIDED BY THE NATIONAL COURTS

As indicated in section B above, the Swedish courts decided in the early 1970s that the Convention, and the judgments of the Court, were not formally binding on Swedish courts. Judicial attitudes towards the Convention began to change in the early 1980s. Milestones in this development were the European Court's judgments which found Sweden to be in breach of the Convention, particularly the *Sporrong and Lonnröth* case. While all these cases required legislative reform, rather than a simple change in judicial interpretative methods, notwithstanding their traditional deference to the legislature, the courts realized that if they continued to interpret national law totally without reference to the Convention, then there was a risk that even in other areas Swedish law would be incompatible with the Convention organs' case-law. Such cases would sooner or later end up in Strasbourg, Sweden would be found in breach of the Convention, and would thus probably be required to amend its laws. It would save a good deal of time and expense if the Swedish courts, where possible, interpreted domestic law so as to make it compatible with the Convention in the first place.

Thus, beginning in the early 1980s,[35] the higher courts began referring, first to the Convention, and then also to the Convention organs' case-law as a means of interpreting the requirements of Swedish law. The cases involved a great variety of legal issues. A few examples suffice to give a picture of this development. In *NJA 1984, s. 903*, the Supreme Court, referring to Article 6, refused to extradite a person to Italy who had been convicted there *in absentia*. In *NJA 1989, s. 131* the Supreme Court examined whether a restriction on freedom of movement of terrorist suspects (*kommunarrest*) constituted a 'deprivation of liberty' within the meaning of Article 5(4). In doing so, it referred extensively to the *Guzzardi* case.[36] Following the *Ekbatani* case in 1988, the Supreme Court and Supreme Administrative Court allowed appeals based on the fact that a party to a case in a lower court had been refused an oral hearing.[37] The Convention

[35] Even before the *Sporrong and Lönnroth* case there had been a case in which the Convention was invoked, and (at least) not dismissed as totally irrelevant. In *NJA 1981, s. 1205*, the Supreme Court in refusing to annul a clause in a contract providing for obligatory arbitration (and excluding the jurisdiction of the courts) nonetheless considered that Article 6 could be used to interpret the meaning of the Instrument of Government.

[36] *Guzzardi v Italy*, Judgment of 6 November 1980, Series A No. 39. The Supreme Court found that *kommunarrest* did not violate the Convention. The Commission came to the same conclusion in Application 14102/88, *Aygün v Sweden*, (1989) 63 DR 195.

[37] Eg NJA 1988, s. 572, NJA 1989 s. 131, NJA 1990 s. 636, RÅ 1991 not 160.Traditionally, appeal court proceedings were, although they normally involved a new trial rather than simply an appeal on a point of law, largely written in nature.Unless there were reasons for doing so, new

thus came to be used not simply passively, to confirm the reasonableness of a restriction on human rights, but actively, in that Swedish laws were being interpreted as far as possible to conform to the Convention. The Convention also began to play a role in abstract constitutional review. During the 1980s the Law Council began referring to the Convention organs' case-law in assessing the constitutionality of legislative proposals.

Of course, the principle that national law be interpreted in accordance with treaty commitments can be either a real safeguard or a mere formality depending, first, on how much time and effort the courts devote to investigating what the Convention really requires in a given case, and secondly, the status such a principle is given by the courts compared to other principles of interpretation. As regards the first point, the Supreme Court and the Supreme Administrative Court have occasionally made relatively detailed investigations of the requirements of the Convention and Court case-law. As regards the second point, as already mentioned, Swedish courts often apply the subjective/historical method of interpretation as well as the objective (textual) and teleological methods. It is still uncertain exactly how the principle of interpretation in accordance with treaty commitments should be weighed against other principles of interpretation. In *NJA 1992, s. 532*, the issue was whether a trial in which one of the chief witnesses for the prosecution was unavailable for cross-examination was 'fair' within the meaning of Article 6. The Supreme Court ruled, with detailed reference to Convention case-law, that it was not. Supreme Court Justice Lind noted in a separate opinion that the courts should prefer an interpretation of national law which conforms with the Convention even over contrary views expressed in the legislative history to the statute, doctrine, or even previous judgments of the higher Swedish courts. In Justice Lind's opinion, only the textual approach has higher status: the courts may interpret a national law in a way which conflicts with the requirements of the Convention only when it is totally clear from the wording of the national law that such a result is intended.[38] While this opinion is *obiter*, it is undoubtedly the case that the Convention, even before its incorporation in Swedish law, was finally being taken very seriously by the Swedish courts.

As regards case-law since incorporation, up to January 2001 the Convention has been a significant issue in about 100 published cases, although in a large number of these it was still of secondary importance and only cursorily examined.[39] The cases cover many different questions, in different areas of

oral hearings with witnesses and the parties were not normally held. For a discussion of the *Ekbatani* case, see section E below.

[38] For a more detailed discussion, see Cameron, note 32 above.

[39] In addition, there were a number of cases dealing with the lack of an oral hearing.

law. In family law, the issues have included standing to challenge a decision on paternity and an administrative decision fixing the place of residence of children. In criminal law, issues have included anonymous or absent witnesses, extradition of suspects on the basis of a foreign judgment pronounced *in absentia*, use of video evidence, disqualification of judges, reopening of a trial held to be unfair, and exceptional powers to investigate tax crime. In company law, issues have arisen of access to a court to challenge a decision on liquidation and the effectiveness of judicial remedies. In administrative law, issues have arisen concerning deportation, compulsory detention of mental patients, access to a court to challenge administrative decisions, and payment of church tax and tax penalties. In addition, there have been a number of cases concerning the right to an oral hearing in administrative cases. In civil procedure law, questions have arisen of capacity to sue (fair trial) and disqualification of judges. In civil law generally issues have arisen regarding the proportionality of planning and expropriation decisions and regarding standing to challenge such decisions. In employment law, issues have arisen of disqualification of judges, freedom of association, the *drittwirkung* of the Convention, and denial of access to a court by means of an arbitration clause. As already mentioned, the Swedish courts have managed to resolve potential norm conflicts without the need to engage in constitutional review. Most of these cases were politically uncontroversial. The exceptions were the employment law case dealing with negative freedom of association[40] and an expropriation case in which the Supreme Administrative Court issued a stay of execution, preventing the government from closing a nuclear power station.[41] (I have dealt with this case-law in detail elsewhere, so I will not go into it here.[42])

E. CASES BROUGHT BEFORE THE EUROPEAN COMMISSION AND COURT OF HUMAN RIGHTS

Sweden has been involved in two inter-state cases: the Greek case in 1969 and the application against Turkey in 1982. As regards individual applications,

[40] AD 1998, nr. 17. This case involved an attempt to use the Court's *dicta* in the *Gustafsson* case (see p. 849 below) against a labour union attempting to force the plaintiff into a collective, or substitute, agreement.

[41] See RÅ 1998 not 93. The government decision was later upheld in review proceedings (RÅ 1999 ref 76) and an application for reopening was denied (RÅ 1999 ref 247).

[42] See I. Cameron, 'Swedish Case Law on the ECHR Since Incorporation and the Question of Remedies', in I. Cameron and A. Simoni (eds), *Dealing with Integration*, vol. 2 (Uppsala: Iustus, 1998).

the complaints most commonly made against Sweden can be divided into five broad areas: judicial review of administrative decisions, violations of property rights, taking of children into care, procedural safeguards in civil and criminal trials, and aliens. As of January 2001, forty-nine cases had been referred to the Court for judgment and forty-five judgments delivered (four cases under Protocol No. 9 referred by applicants were not accepted by the Court). In twenty-two of the forty-five cases at least one violation was found. In fourteen cases no violation was found. Eight cases were struck off the list.[43] The most significant group of cases concerned access by an individual to a court to determine an administrative dispute (Article 6). At the time they ratified the Convention, many states, Sweden included, made the mistake of assuming that 'civil rights and obligations' referred only to the sphere of *private law*: rights and obligations between individuals.[44] In Sweden, as in the majority of Convention states, many legal disputes between the state/local government and individuals (apart from those concerning criminal law) are not settled in the ordinary courts. Unlike a number of other Convention states, however, in 1950 Sweden did not have a complete parallel system of administrative courts. Instead, the majority of disputes between an individual and an adminstrative agency, even those of a predominantly legal character, were settled by a superior adminstrative agency. The final appeal was often to the government itself. Between the 1950s and 1970s the system of administrative courts was greatly expanded. Nonetheless, there was no general right for an individual to bring an administrative dispute before a court. The jurisdiction of the administrative courts was limited to specific areas.[45]

However, the European Court of Human Rights stated as far back as 1971 that Article 6(1) was applicable to all proceedings 'the outcome of which is decisive for private rights and obligations'.[46] The Court stated that 'civil rights and obligations' was an autonomous concept. The application of the Article could not be allowed to depend on whether the national legal system classified the right in question as 'public' or 'private'. It was on the cards that the Swedish system of appeals to the government would, insofar as these concerned 'civil rights or obligations', be in violation of Article 6. The Court in the *Sporrong and Lönnroth* case did indeed find a violation of Article 6, as well

[43] One case was declared admissible in 2000 and is pending before the Court.

[44] Prop. 1951:165. See further Prop. 1990/91:176, s. 3.

[45] The rule now is that, unless otherwise provided, appeal lies to the administrative courts (Administration Law SFS 1986: 223, as amended, section 22(a)). Many exemptions exist which provide for appeal to higher administrative authorities or quasi-judicial bodies.

[46] *Ringeisen v Austria*, Judgment of 16 July 1971, Series A No. 13. See also *Golder v UK*, Judgment of 21 February 1975, Series A No. 18 in which the Court stated that Article 6(1) implied *a right of access to a tribunal* to determine one's civil rights and obligations.

as Article 1 of Protocol No. 1.[47] Nonetheless, the Swedish government of the day was reluctant to extend judicial review of administrative action. It chose to take a minimalist approach to the *Sporrong and Lönnroth* judgment and no steps were taken to correct the situation regarding access to a court.[48] Sweden paid the penalty for its legislative inaction when it lost, in quick succession, a number of cases on the issue in Strasbourg beginning in 1987. One of these cases in particular, *Pudas*, resulted in a great deal of publicity regarding the Convention.[49] These cases resulted in legislation, dealt with in the next section.

Another large group of cases have concerned the right to an oral hearing in civil and criminal appeal proceedings. The *Ekbatani* case concerned the lack of an oral hearing in proceedings before a criminal court of appeal.[50] The Court ruled that, because the court of appeal had refused Ekbatani an oral hearing and because this testimony concerned matters central to the case itself (ie Ekbatani's guilt or innocence) he had not received a 'public hearing'. The *Ekbatani* ruling has been followed and refined in a number of other cases, before both the Strasbourg and the Swedish courts. The duty to provide an oral hearing is not absolute, but depends upon the significance of the legal and factual issues which the appeal court has to determine.[51]

The *McGoff* case concerned the period for which a person suspected of a crime could be detained on the orders of a prosecutor before being brought before a court competent to order release or continued detention. The statutory provision permitting detention for fifteen days was, predictably enough, found to be in violation of Article 5(4).

[47] The remedy of 'reopening' (*resning*) a case before the Supreme Administrative Court or Supreme Court was found to be of an extraordinary nature, and thus not sufficient to satisfy the requirements of Article 6. This has been criticized by certain Swedish commentators who consider that the conditions to be satisfied before the courts will reopen a case are less onerous in practice.

[48] If further confirmation was needed of the inadequacy of Swedish law in this respect, it came with *Bentham v the Netherlands*, Judgment of 3 October, 1985, Series A No. 97. See further J. Sundberg (ed) *Laws, Rights and the European Convention on Human Rights* (Colorado: Rothman and Co, 1986) 85–98.

[49] Pudas had had his driving licence taken away by a County Administrative Board without being able to challenge this before a court. Pudas' father went on hunger strike outside the Parliament in protest against this. Other cases concerning different areas but raising the same issue were *Bodén*, Judgment of 27 October 1987, Series A No. 125, *Tre Traktörer AB*, Judgment of 7 July 1989, Series A No. 159, *Allan Jacobsson*, Judgment of 25 October 1989, Series A No. 163, *Mats Jacobsson*, Judgment of 28 June 1990 Series A No. 180A, *Skärby*, Judgment of 28 June 1990 Series A No. 180B, *Zander*, Judgment of 25 November 1993, Series A No. 279–B.

[50] Judgment of 26 May 1988, Series A No. 160.

[51] See *inter alia Helmers v Sweden*, *Fejde v Sweden*, and *Jan Åke Andersson v Sweden*, Judgments of 29 October 1991, Series A No. 212–A, 212–B, and 212–C, *Fredin v Sweden (No. 2)*, Judgment of 23 February 1994, Series A No. 283–A, *Rolf Gustafsson v Sweden*, Judgment of 1 July 1997, and *Allan Jacobsson v Sweden*, Judgment of 19 February 1998. For the national cases see section D above.

A number of cases have concerned the right to family life under Article 8. To date, custody of children has resulted in eight cases before the Court and four findings of violations.[52]

The *Leander* case concerned files held by the security police.[53] The applicant had been denied employment in the public service as a result of secret information about him (*personalkontroll*).[54] He wished to have access to this information. The Strasbourg Court found, by majority, no violation of either Article 8 or Article 13. The judges in the minority argued that there was a violation of Article 13 because there was in practice no mechanism or institution capable, either periodically or upon a specific complaint, of checking the accuracy and appropriateness of the information stored in secret files.

The applicant in the *Langborger* case complained about the composition of the Housing Court (*bostadsdomstolen*) because representatives of landlords' and tenants' associations sat as judges. Normally these representatives would 'cancel each other out' but Langborger was in dispute with both associations and the Strasbourg Court agreed with him that in the circumstances he had not received a trial by an 'impartial tribunal'.[55]

The Strasbourg Court also found a violation of the right to trial by an impartial tribunal in the *Holm* case.[56] The applicant had sued the author of a book published by a company owned by the Social Democratic party (SDP) for defamation. Being a case under the Freedom of the Press Act, it was tried by a jury. Jury members are chosen, at random, from a list provided by the political parties in the locality. Potential jury members are thus usually politically active for their respective parties. Members of the SDP happened to be in a majority on the jury and the author was acquitted.

The *MS* and *Anne-Marie Andersson* cases both concerned the transmission of confidential medical data to administrative agencies without the possibility for the individuals concerned to challenge this decision before the courts.[57] In the former case, the social welfare authorities had requested disclosure of medical records in order to check the basis of the applicant's

[52] *Olsson v Sweden*, Judgment of 24 March 1988, Series A No. 130, *Eriksson v Sweden*, Judgment of 22 June 1989, Series A No. 156, *Margareta and Roger Andersson v Sweden*, Judgment of 25 February 1992, Series A No. 226, *Rieme v Sweden*, Judgment of 22 April 1992, Series A No. 226–B, *Olsson v Sweden (No. 2)*, Judgment of 27 November 1992, Series A No. 250, *Paulsen-Medalen and Svensson v Sweden*, Judgment of 19 February 1998. *Söderbäck v Sweden*, Judgment of 28 October 1998; *Lindelöf v Sweden*, Judgment of 20 June 2000 (struck out of list, friendly settlement).

[53] Judgment of 8 July 1987, Series A No. 116

[54] See generally D. Töllborg, *Personalkontroll* (Stockholm/Lund, Symposium, 1986).

[55] *Langborger v Sweden*, Judgment of 22 June 1989, Series A No. 155.

[56] *Holm v Sweden*, Judgment of 25 November 1993, Series A No. 279–A.

[57] *MS v Sweden*, Judgment of 27 August 1997, *Anne-Marie Andersson v Sweden*, Judgment of 27 August 1997.

claim for disability payments. The Strasbourg Court found no violation of Article 8.[58] In both cases, the majority of the Court found that Article 6 was not applicable.

Finally, the case of *Torgny Gustafsson* concerned a restaurant owner who had suffered a boycott and blockade by a trade union which wanted him to sign a collective agreement. The case is interesting because it is politically controversial: trade unions in Sweden fiercely resist statutory controls on unions' resort to such measures. The Commission had considered that in taking the blockade action, the union was not representing any members employed by Gustafsson. His employees were satisfied with their pay and working conditions. The union was rather wishing, in general, to strengthen the collective bargaining system. Judicial remedies were, however, unavailable in Swedish law to prevent or minimize the effect of the boycott and blockade. The majority of the Commission ruled that, in the circumstances, the union's acts were disproportionate and the state was therefore obliged under Article 11 to make available legal remedies to Gustafsson. During the proceedings before the Court, the Swedish government (which had, following a general election, reverted to SDP control) submitted new evidence provided by the union itself, that the union had been acting to protect the interests of its members. The majority of the Court considered that Gustafsson was not being forced to join an association against his will and so went on to rule that Sweden had not violated the duty placed on it under Article 11 to take positive action to protect Gustafsson's freedom not to associate. Gustafsson later discovered that the new evidence was highly suspect, if not false, and applied for revision of the judgment. The Strasbourg Court declared his application for revision admissible, but went on to confirm its original judgment, finding that the evidence, even if false, would not have altered its finding.[59]

F. REMEDIAL ACTION TAKEN IN RESPONSE TO BEING HELD IN VIOLATION OF THE CONVENTION

The major legislative change as a result of negative judgments of the Strasbourg Court has been the introduction in 1988 of a right of judicial review of certain administrative cases decided by an adminstrative agency or the government as a final instance of appeal. The law was initially passed for

[58] Anne-Marie Andersson had not raised the Article 8 issue before the Commission.

[59] *Torgny Gustafsson v Sweden* (Revision, Admissibility), 13 October 1997, (Revision, Merits) 30 July 1998.

a trial period until 1991. It was renewed twice, and made permanent in 1996.[60] The law does not give a general right of access to a court. It applies only to cases in which there is no other available judicial remedy and in which the administrative decision imposes a burden on an individual. The intention behind the legislation was to cover the category of 'civil rights and obligations' but this term was not used because it was considered that its unfamiliarity could cause Swedish lawyers difficulties. Instead, the law refers to the areas of public activity covered by RF 8:2 and 8:3. These provide that delegation of legislative power in certain areas—particularly those involving burdens for an individual—should be approved by statute. This has the consequence that, for example, decisions to refuse permission to engage in a particular business activity are subject to review, whereas decisions to withold a benefit, such a social security payment or admission to a higher educational course, are not. It has been pointed out that the exclusion of decisions involving benefits from review is not without difficulties, particularly in view of the *Deumeland* and *Feldbrugge* cases.[61] Moreover, the scope of the provision coexists uneasily with the duty under Article 6 of the Convention on Swedish courts since incorporation to provide a right of access in cases concerning 'civil rights and obligations'. In addition to the restricted scope of the provision, decisions by certain quasi-judicial tribunals and decisions concerning matters regarded as predominently of a policy nature are excluded from review, notwithstanding the direct impact these could have in the area of 'civil rights and obligations'.[62]

Originally, all applications for review were directed to the Supreme Administrative Court. Due to the burden of work which resulted, the law was amended to provide that appeals from administrative agencies should be directed to the local administrative court of appeal, whereas the Supreme Administrative Court would retain the function of reviewing cases decided by the government. The procedure is largely written, although another amendment to the original system is to provide for oral hearings if a party requests

[60] *Lag* (1988:205) *om rättsprövning av vissa förvaltningsbeslut*. Re-enacted and amended by SFS 1991:342, SFS 1994:719, and SFS 1996:420. See generally W. Warnling-Nerep, 'Rättsprövningslagen—utgör den ett lyckat försök att anpassa Svensk rätt till Europakonventionen Art 6(1)?', in E. Nerep and W. Warnling-Nerep (eds) *Festschrift till Jacob Sundberg* (Stockholm, Juristförlaget, 1994) (hereafter Warnling-Nerep 1994).

[61] *Deumeland v Germany*, Judgment of 29 May 1986, Series A No. 100, *Feldbrugge v Netherlands*, Judgment of 29 May 1986, Series A No. 99. See further Warnling-Nerep, 1994, 134. There was also a conflict on this issue between the Supreme Court and the Supreme Administrative Court in 1994/95. For a discussion, see Cameron, note 42 above, 17–19.

[62] It is by no means clear that all of these tribunals would satisfy the requirements of Article 6. Certainly, not all of them are regarded as 'courts' in Swedish constitutional law. Warnling-Nerep 1994, 135.

this and it is not manifestly unnecessary.[63] The scope of the review—something of a novelty for Swedish law—has some similarities with the English system of judicial review. It is not limited to simply checking the strict legality of the decision but can, depending on the nature of the decision being reviewed, extend to such matters as whether the agency evaluated the facts properly and even how appropriate the decision is. Issues of 'purely political discretion' are nonetheless excluded from the court's jurisdiction.[64] The review has a cassation effect: a successful application is remitted back to the agency in question for a new decision. Reactions to the new power of review have, in general, been positive. Although a number of cases dealt with have been of a trivial character, in other cases the Supreme Administrative Court looked at both the legality and appropriateness of decisions of significance for the individual. A number of decisions have been overruled. [65] The existence of this review mechanism will, hopefully, strengthen awareness of principles of legality in administrative decision-making.

A number of amendments have been made to the Code of Judicial Procedure. Following the *McGoff* case, provision was made for a maximum period of four days' detention before being brought before a judge.[66] Following the *Ekbatani* case, appeal courts in criminal cases have been required to hold oral hearings at the request of a party unless this is manifestly unnecessary.[67] The *Holm* case led initially to an official proposal to make a constitutional amendment removing the right to jury trial in cases where the composition of the jury gives rise to doubts as to whether the trial will be fair.[68] Later, however, the government (and Parliament) took the view that the rare cases in which the composition of the jury was a problem could be dealt with by the courts applying the *Holm* case in conjunction with the above rules in the Code of Judicial Procedure dealing with disqualification of the court for lack of impartiality.[69] Following the *Langborger* case, amendments

[63] See Prop. 1995/96: 133, which stated that the situations in which an oral hearing is 'manifestly unnecessary' should be determined by reference to the Convention organs' case-law. The lack of an oral hearing in this procedure was the reason for a finding of a violation in *Fredin v Sweden (No. 2)*, Judgment of 23 February 1994, Series A No. 283–A.

[64] For a general analysis of this problem See L. Marcusson, 'Laglighets- och lämplighetsprövning—en titt i backspegeln och framåt' (1992) *Förvaltningsrättslig Tidskrift* p. 121.

[65] See Prop. 1990/91: 176, pp. 4–5. For two examples see RÅ 1990 ref 59 and the decision in case 1424–1998, note 40 above.

[66] Code of Judicial Procedure (Rättegångsbalken, RB) 24:12. For the background to the *McGoff* and *Skoogström* cases—the latter being resolved by a friendly settlement—see J. Sundberg, *Om rätt, rättskällor och rättstillämpning. Ett textpaket,* (Stockholm: Juristförlaget, 1991), 4–13.

[67] See now RB 51:13.

[68] 'Domaren i Sverige inför framtiden' SOU 1994:99 s. 315ff.

[69] RB 4:13 (Prop 97/98:43, s.129–35). These rules had previously been amended as a result of a Danish case, *Hauschildt*, Judgment of 24 May 1989, Series A No. 154.

were made to the composition of the Housing Court where a party's interests conflict with both the landlords' and tenants' associations.[70]

While the main changes have been in the area of procedural law, there have been some reforms of substantive laws. For example, the judgment in the *Sporrong and Lönnroth* case led to amendments to the Expropriation Act.[71] The *Håkansson and Sturesson* case resulted in changes to the Acquisition of Land Act.[72] On the other hand, the breaches found in child custody cases have mainly concerned the manner of implementation of Swedish legislation, rather than the laws as such, and only one legislative reform has been made as a result of these cases (on access to a court to review a decision of the social authorities, after taking a child into care, to restrict a parent's access to the child).

Even cases which Sweden has won in Strasbourg have led, directly or indirectly, to legislative changes. The criticism expressed by the minority of the Court in the *Leander* case was one of the reasons why vetting was later the subject of a number of official investigations. An independent supervisory organ monitoring the use of security information in vetting proceedings was finally established in 1996.[73] Following the case of *Cruz Varas v Sweden*[74] provision was made in the Aliens Act allowing for a stay of execution if an international body with competence to receive petitions from individuals requests this.[75]

G. ASSESSMENTS AND PROSPECTS

The Convention is already a living part of the Swedish legal system, and as regards the courts, more relevant, or at least more often invoked, than the national rights catalogue in Chapter 2 of the Instrument of Government. On the whole, the Swedish courts are faithfully attempting to take the Convention into account, even if the majority of references made are to the text of the Convention and doctrine, rather than to European Court of Human Rights case-law. It has helped in this respect that courts and administrative agencies

[70] Housing Court (Amendment) Act (SFS 1991:636). As already mentioned, the issue has also arisen in the context of national proceedings before the Labour Court.

[71] SFS 1988: 206.

[72] SFS 1991: 669.

[73] Protection of Security Act (SFS 1996.227), Ordinance with instructions for Register Board (SFS 1996:730). See further I. Cameron, *National Security and the ECHR* (Dordrecht, Kluwer, 2000) 204–212, 246–252.

[74] Judgment of 20 March 1991, Series A No. 201.

[75] Chapter 8, section 10(a). The wording of the provision thus applies not simply to the ECHR but also the UN Human Rights Committee and the UN Committee against Torture.

have had easy access to the Court's case-law. There is general Internet access to the Court's case-law after 1996. However, the fact that some judgments are now available only in French will make invocation of this case-law more difficult, because many Swedish judges do not read French. Swedish summaries of earlier Court judgments (up to 1998) are accessible in a database, but the work of summarizing was discontinued in 1999 for cost reasons. This database is, however, supplemented by regular summaries of recent case-law written by one of the leading Swedish authorities, Hans Danelius, in the main legal periodical (*Svensk juristtidning*). Admittedly, there have been deficiencies in judicial reasoning but these can probably be put down to lack of time, rather any than hostility or indifference towards the Convention. The Article of the Convention most often used is Article 6. Possible norm conflicts between the incorporated Convention and other Swedish norms have been avoided, mainly by applying the principle of treaty conform construction. There have been indications of 'increasing Europeanization' of judicial attitudes, for example less deference towards the *travaux préparatoires* in interpretation.[76] The Convention has had some influence here, although the main impact has come from EU membership. The reluctance of the Swedish courts to engage in constitutional review means that this situation is likely to continue. There may be some scope for constitutional review, particularly of ordinances, in the area of civil rights, and particularly as regards the—still unsolved—issue of access to a court (Article 6). In the future, there is unlikely to be any constitutional review on the basis of what could be called the 'civil liberties' parts of the Convention, Articles 8–11 and Article 1 of Protocol No. 1). This is because the Swedish courts, in general, consider that the courts lack legitimacy to reach a different conclusion than that of Parliament as to whether a particular restriction to a right is 'necessary in a democratic society'. This view is shared by the great majority of writers. The main protection for constitutional, and Convention, rights in Sweden will be preventive, in the form of the parliamentary process.

[76] See eg J. Nergelius, 'The impact of EC law in Swedish National Law—A Cultural Revolution' in I. Cameron and A. Simoni (eds), *Dealing with Integration, volume 2* (Uppsala: Iustus, 1998).

33

Switzerland

MARCO BORGHI

A. INTRODUCTION

When Switzerland joined the European Convention on Human Rights, it was with the same caution it has always displayed in subscribing to multilateral international commitments, particularly those setting up supranational organizations and communities. Anti-accession arguments cited neutrality, a fear of foreign judges, loss of sovereignty, and even the cost (!) of the Strasbourg institutions.[1] It was not until 6 May 1963 that Switzerland joined the Council of Europe and, with this basic condition fulfilled, the federal authorities still had to embark upon an exceptional Convention accession procedure,[2] whereby the Federal Council, despite being empowered to sign the agreement by itself, approached Parliament in December 1968 to ask its permission, failed to obtain it from one House, and only succeeded in December 1972. After the Federal Council signed and Parliament ratified, Switzerland was unable to deposit the instrument of ratification until 28 November 1974. Furthermore, the Federal Council only renewed the declaration on the 'competence of the Commission' within the meaning of Article 25 of the Convention for a period of three years. And Switzerland has still not ratified important Protocols (Nos. 1 and 4; it eventually ratified No. 2 on 17 December 1993; No. 9 on 14 December 1994; and finally Nos. 10 and 11 during the course of 1997). At the time of accession, furthermore, it expressed reservations about major provisions (Articles 5 and 6[3]) of the Convention and even one of the Protocols (No 7). But, very fortunately, our political and legal authorities have gradually lost their reticence, particularly of late, following a change of attitude which is clearly related to the new awareness (apparent

[1] Mark E. Villiger, *Handbuch der EMRK* (Schulthess, 1993) 15 *et seq*.

[2] Jean-François Aubert, *Traité de droit constitutionnel suisse No. 1320*.

[3] Concerning, in particular, detention by decision of an administrative authority and various aspects of the public nature of hearings and the reading of the judgment, the guarantee of a fair trial, and the guarantee of legal assistance and an interpreter free of charge (these two in the form of the official interpretation).

from the extraordinary number of appeals against Switzerland which the Human Right Commission has received) created in Swiss citizens and their lawyers by wide press coverage of the judgments against Switzerland and the fact that Swiss law faculties still place considerable emphasis on the Convention, as such, in the classroom. Switzerland has even been particularly active on the committee of experts working to improve human rights protection procedures.[4] More specifically, the decisions of the European Court have directly influenced amendments to various laws (see Section C below) on legal practice, whereby the Federal Council's reservation (see Section D below) and internal policy on this (see Section E below) were declared invalid.

B. THE STATUS OF THE CONVENTION IN NATIONAL LAW

Switzerland has a monistic system whereby an agreement is taken straight into the national legal system with the depositing of the instrument of ratification. Article 89(3–5) of the Constitution currently provides for the possibility of a referendum, compulsory or optional, depending on the type of treaty, but these provisions were not in effect when the Convention was adopted: the reason for the apparent contradiction in the fact that the Convention was not the subject of a referendum but some of the Protocols were.

So the Convention and the Protocols have been incorporated into the Swiss legal system, across the federation and in the cantons, but they still have their character of international laws, with major consequences when it comes to interpretation and particularly the Court's reading of the notions of autonomy.[5]

Conflicting arguments have fuelled many a legal controversy over where the Convention ranks in Switzerland. Formally speaking, according to the procedure by which legal acts are adopted in this country, it has to be said that the European Convention on Human Rights should rank below the laws, because it was only approved by a decree by the Federal Assembly and not put to a referendum, while there is an optional referendum for all federal laws. But materially speaking, given the fundamental nature of the rights which it enshrines, it ranks above the laws. This is of particular significance in Swiss constitutional law in that the Federal Tribunal has used a so-called creative

[4] At the first ministerial Conference on human rights in Vienna in 1985, it was Switzerland which first recommended the establishment of a permanent, single legal body (cf. Federal Council's *Annual Report on Switzerland's activities in the Council of Europe 1993*, January 1993, p. 563).)

[5] Mark E. Villiger, note 1 above, 96.

interpretation to derive 'unwritten constitutional rights' from the Constitution and given them the same rank and functions as the rights laid down in the Constitution, despite the fact that the obligatory referendum prescribed for all revisions of the Constitution did not take place when they were adopted. So in Swiss constitutional law, typically, the content of the rule affects its position in the hierarchy.

The Federal Tribunal, initially, wisely affirmed that the European Convention on Human Rights was 'at least of the rank of a law'[6] or 'equal to a federal law'.[7] However, it went on to emphasize that the rules which it contained were of 'constitutional rank', a legal analogy whereby anyone could claim violation of the Convention in public law proceedings in exactly the same way as of their fundamental—written and unwritten—rights. This procedural practice has recently been enshrined in an amendment to the federal legislation on the legal system.[8]

However, a major problem was posed by Article 113(3) of the Federal Constitution, which provided for the Federal Tribunal to 'apply the laws passed by the Federal Assembly and such decrees as it issues of general import' and to 'comply with the treaties which the Federal Assembly shall have ratified'. In particular, the theme of the lack of control of the constitutionality of these legal acts (contested in legislative policy in the current overhaul of the Federal Constitution) posed a serious problem, in view of the possible difference between a legal act covered by Article 113(3) and the European Convention on Human Rights (because of its dual nature as a Convention of the same status as federal legislation, but also containing 'constitutional rights') and therefore of the virtual possibility of anyone evading a national law by pointing to the right guaranteed by the Convention rather than any provision offering similar protection in the Constitution. The Federal Tribunal has usually tried to get round this by applying the principle of a standard interpretation, 'assuming' that the idea of the federal legislation is to respect the provisions of properly concluded treaties and interpreting the law in the light of this. However, this does not apply where there has been a deliberate decision to make a national rule which conflicts with international law[9] and, obviously, if the meaning of the federal law is clear, in particular following a literal interpretation, the standard interpretation cannot apply (or, in cases of interpretation *contra legem*, it is reduced to a real check on constitutionality, prohibited by Article 113(3)). So the issue of where the Convention stands in relation to federal law and the constitutionality control cannot long be evaded. Legal theory also objects to the inward-looking,

[6] ATF 101 IV 253.
[7] ATF 103 V 190.
[8] Cf. Claude Rouiller, 'L'effet dynamique de la CEDH' (1992) *Revue pénale suisse*, 233 et seq.
[9] Cf., for example, ATF 106 la 33.

side-stepping attitude[10] of the decisions of the Federal Tribunal, which has implicitly endorsed the non-application of a federal law in conflict with the Convention in various judgments, without even mentioning the problem of Article 113(3).[11]

Recently the Federal Tribunal has shown openness here, although still not entirely without ambiguity. In a major judgment of principle (1991), it made the assimilation to constitutional rights of the rights guaranteed by the Convention no more than a question of procedure and found, echoing various commentators, that the preparation for Article 113(3) had shown that this provision was designed simply to:

> settle the distribution of powers between the Federal Assembly, which is responsible for passing laws to put the Constitution into practice, and the Federal Tribunal and that nothing was said about the law of the treaties . . .

From this it derived that 'these provisions tell us nothing about the ranking of these two sources of law'.

It also pointed out that the Vienna Convention on the law of treaties, which took effect in Switzerland on 6 June 1990, expressly enshrined the principle of the predominance of international law, whereby all the implementing authorities in Switzerland had to interpret national law in line with international law.

The Tribunal stressed that:

> this does not mean an attack on the separation of powers, because all the authorities have, in their fields, to respect and apply the international law by which Switzerland is bound. Of course, the Federal Tribunal cannot repeal a federal law because it conflicts with international law. At most, it could decline to apply it in a particular case, if it is in conflict with international law and could lead to a judgment against Switzerland.[12]

This decision still reflected a degree of caution on the part of the Federal Tribunal, but it was an irreversible, timely indication of the imminence of full recognition of the superiority of the Convention over the whole Swiss legal system.

[10] Olivier Jacot-Guillarmod, 'Le juge Suisse face au droit européen—report to the Swiss Legal Association' (1993) 112 (11) *Revue de droit suisse*, 227 *et seq*. and 367 *et seq*.

[11] For example, the Federal Tribunal found the appeal of an alien, citing Article 8 of the Convention, against the official refusal to renew his residence permit to be admissible, despite the letter of the law here in the Federal Legal Organization Act (cf. the practice based on ATF 109 lb 185).

[12] ATF 117 lb 367, SJ 1994, p. 448.

C. THE STATUS OF THE CONVENTION IN PARLIAMENTARY PROCEEDINGS

First of all, the European Convention on Human Rights has an enormous influence over both federal and canton authorities. Its interest and importance are reflected in the Federal Council's annual report on Switzerland's activities in the Council of Europe and in the frequency of Convention-based judgments reported in legal journals.[13]

It had a major effect even before ratification. Legal writers say that it was a decisive force in, say, the repeal of the so-called confessional Articles of the Federal Constitution (of which Articles 51 and 52 provided, in particular, for the banning of Jesuits and new orders and convents) and an important guideline in the introduction of votes for women.[14]

The federal law amending the Civil Code provisions on loss of freedom for the purposes of assistance, passed on 6 October 1978, had the principal, if not the only aim[15] of bringing Swiss legislation into line with Article 5 of the European Convention on Human Rights and thereby enabling Switzerland to withdraw the reservations expressed on accession. (However, this positive effect has been mitigated by the unfortunate effect of the limited scope of Article 5, which is guaranteed by the right to proper therapy, which limits the effectiveness of both the federal legislation and Article 5 of the Convention).

Other federal laws have been or are being amended[16] because of European Court judgments which do not even apply to Switzerland. The example usually given here is the case in which amendments (29 March 1979) to the Military Criminal Code and the organization of the federal army's legal system and criminal procedure were made as a direct result of a Convention judgment of 8 June 1976, in *Engel v the Netherlands*, which established the principle that sentences involving strict arrest in disciplinary law in the army were only in line with Article 5 of the Convention when pronounced by a court.[17]

In 1991 a general revision of the federal legal organization provided the opportunity to amend several provisions, in particular those of the Federal

[13] There is a yearly column in the *Annuaire suisse de droit international et de droit européen* by Giorgio Malinverni and Michel Hottelier (Luzius Wildhaber until 1990).

[14] Mark E. Villiger, note 1 above, 18.

[15] Marco Borghi, *Evaluation de l'efficacité de la législation sur la privation de liberté à des fins d'assistance*, (Zurich, Pro Mente Sana, 1992) 108.

[16] Cf. Arthur Haefliger, *Die Europäische Menschenrechtskonvention und die Schweiz* (Berne, Stämpfli, 1993) 365.

[17] Appeals from Swiss soldiers (*Eggs* and *Santschi* cases) also had to be pending and the Commission, in its report, had to have found a contradiction between Swiss law and the Convention. The Committee of Ministers refused to discuss the matter because the revision of the Military Criminal Code was about to take effect (cf. EuGRZ, 1980, p. 274).

Criminal Procedure Act relating to the right of the accused to be heard on the facts which prompted arrest and the right to have a judge consider the merits of arrest and confiscation, while the Privacy Protection Act provided for monitoring by the President of the Indictments Chamber to protect people under surveillance, and subsequent reporting of the surveillance effected.[18]

But the European Convention on Human Rights has had its biggest effect on procedure in the cantons. The Confederation, above all, has reserved the right to make its own judgments on certain criminal matters which directly affect its interests, while the Federal Constitution makes procedure mainly the affair of the cantons, which operate what are often very different systems. Over a period of years, the Federal Tribunal made only a few Convention-based judgments in this area and then with restrictive interpretation, the theory being that it saw Article 6 of the Convention as having limited scope because it was anxious for maximum respect of the legislative autonomy of the cantons.[19]

The European Court has been ever-more restrictive in its decisions recently and the Federal Tribunal has shown a clear tendency to stick strictly to the Court's autonomous interpretation, in accordance, in particular, with Articles 5 and 6 of the Convention, to the point where lawyers have found that these provisions seem to be taking over as a direct source of our procedural legislation, with the Swiss criminal process changing as a result and moving ineluctably towards harmonization, if not unification.[20]

The canton Parliaments have indeed changed their codes of procedure in the light of the judgments of the European Court, usually without waiting for a judgment from the Federal Tribunal and sometimes very quickly, even via emergency decrees. For example:

—following the European Court *De Cubber* judgment (whereby it was in breach of Article 6 of the Convention for an investigating magistrate to sit as trial court judge in the same case[21]) various cantons, in which the same person had been allowed to do both jobs, were quick to amend their codes of procedure;[22]

—in the *Huber* case[23] the Court found that the current system in the canton of Zurich, whereby the same District Prosecutor could be involved

[18] Cf., in particular, Articles 47, 66(a–d) and 73 (in effect until 15 February 1992) of the Federal Criminal Procedure Act (RS 312.0).

[19] Michel Hottelier, *La CEDH dans la jurisprudence du Tribunal fédéral*, 1985, 190.

[20] Gérard Piquerez, 'Le droit à un juge indépendant et impartial garanti par les art. 56 Cst et 6(1) CEDH impose-t-il de manière absolue une séparation des fonctions judiciaires? Réflexions d'un praticien', *Semaine judiciaire*, 1989, 114 *et seq*.

[21] Judgment of 26 October 1984, Series A, No. 86. Cf. ATF 112 la 209.

[22] For example, Valais brought in the system of separating these two functions via an emergency decree (26 June 1987), provisionally amending the Criminal Code of Procedure.

[23] Judgment of 23 October 1990, Series A No. 188.

successively in both investigation and trial (and, in particular, remand the accused in custody) in the same case, was in conflict with Article 5(3) of the Convention. The judgment also produced a turn-around in the decisions of the Federal Tribunal, which stated clearly, once and for all, that Article 5(3) of the Convention was violated when a judge who had ordered an arrest subsequently worked on the prosecution in the same case.[24] Cantons which were not in line with the Court's principle had speedily to revise their legislation and overcome any opposition (in some cases this meant radically altering the role of long-standing magistrates, who sometimes put up personal resistance to the change—which could be dismissed without appeal in accordance with European Court decisions);[25]

—more generally, Strasbourg Court and Federal Tribunal decisions neutralizing Switzerland's reservations and stating the rights of the accused (see Sections D and E below) have brought major changes to important aspects of the canton laws and even the provisions of the Constitution,[26] involving such things as compliance with Article 6 of the Convention in the case of administrative offences handled by the authorities without full legal control, the right to consult case files, the right to confront the witnesses against, etc.[27]

In civil matters, the practice of the Federal Department of Justice is worth noting. After Switzerland was found guilty in the *F* case, the Head of the Department of Justice sent a letter, *inter alia*, to the committee of experts responsible for a review of family law,[28] urging them to avoid another judgment against Switzerland. The committee plans to suggest cancelling the federal provision which conflicts with Article 12 of the European Convention on Human Rights.

The Head of the Federal Department of Justice and the Police took a similar step on 26 May 1993,[29] when he wrote to the canton authorities to

[24] ATF 117, la 199.

[25] A typical example is the Ticino canton, where it was proposed to do away with the job of investigating judge, which was too dependent on the trial judge. The Court judgment made it possible to include this reform in an ongoing review which originally had not catered for it (cf. Michele Rusca, 'L'influenza della CEDU sulla riforma dell'ordinamento penale ticinese', in Marco Borghi and Guido Corti, *L'influenza della CEDU sulla legislazione federale e cantonale* (Lugano, 1991) 63.

[26] For example, Article 43 of the Constitution of the canton of Appenzell Inner-Rhoden, which did not allow trials to be made public.

[27] For example, the *Belilos* and *Weber* cases, on the Vaud canton legal system, in which, on 1 March 1989, the Vaud authorities amended the Municipal Sentence Act to include recourse to a Police Tribunal. A change in the penal procedure on 12 December 1989 introduced the right to a public hearing involving both parties and thus anticipated the Court's *Weber* judgment.

[28] Cf. ASDI, 1989, pp. 265 *et seq.*

[29] Cf. Jaac, 1992, No. 59, pp. 480 *et seq.*

recommend them to bring their legislation into line with the European Court's decisions on Article 6 of the Convention. On 17 December 1992, after a mother's appeal (accepted as a public law appeal) against the final canton decision in which the State Council of Thurgovia gave visiting rights to the father of her child, the second Civil Court of the Federal Tribunal had given a noted judgment which had a considerable effect on both the Confederation and the cantons[30] when it held that the fact that this petition could not be taken to a tribunal was a breach of Article 6(1) of the Convention. The consequences of this reached far beyond the family field, because the Federal Tribunal had had to cancel its official interpretation of Article 6(1) before it could make the ruling. The Federal Council had previously amended the official interpretation after the European Court of Human Rights' *Belilos v Switzerland* judgment (29 April 1988), saying that this judgment was a criminal matter and that the official interpretation still applied in civil cases. On 16 May 1988 it gave the Secretary-General of the Council of Europe, as depository of the Convention, confirmation and specification of Switzerland's official interpretation of Article 6(1), which was as follows:

> For the Swiss Federal Council, the guarantee of a fair trial, as laid down in Article 6 (1) of the Convention, relates, in the matter of disputed civil rights and obligations, only to the final legal check on such of the authorities' acts and decisions as affect such rights and obligations. In this statement, 'final legal check' means a legal check confined to the application of the law, such as an appellate-type control.

The Federal Council, taking account of the grounds for the judgment, and in accordance with Article 64(2) of the Convention, passed the list of provisions covered by the new official interpretation to the Council of Europe. The list contained various federal legal provisions (OJ and LPS) in addition to some 500 canton legal provisions which the canton justice departments had compiled at the invitation of the Head of the Federal Department of Justice and Police. In the judgment of 17 December 1992, the Federal Tribunal concluded that the Federal Council's official interpretation of 1988 was not a valid as a reservation, because such a reservation could only be formulated after the Convention had been ratified and that it was not valid until 1988. The Head of Department considered that the basic idea was that, since all the subjects on the list related to appeals about civil rights and obligations, none of them were excluded from the field of application of Article 6(1) of the Convention any longer. In all these cases, access had to be provided to a tribunal which met the demands of Article 6(1). An annexe to the letter contained, *inter alia*, a summary of the Court's decisions on the notion of civil rights and obligations, an autonomous notion which could not be interpreted

[30] ATF 118 la 473, EuGRZ, 1993, pp. 72 *et seq.*

merely by reference to the national law of the defendant State and which applied to various areas considered as falling within the domain of Switzerland's public law (in particular as regards regional planning, expropriation, licences to carry out an economic activity, etc.)

In Swiss law, the basic procedural issue regarding compliance with Article 6 of the Convention is the fact that, although it is agreed that Article 6(1) does not require cases of civil rights or obligations be settled by a tribunal immediately, or several tribunals complying with Article 6 of the Convention to judge the case (the theory is that one legal examination is sufficient), the Federal Tribunal alone uses procedure which is not in line with Article 6(1) if the case has not been judged by a canton tribunal. When the list of provisions covered by the Federal Council's new official interpretation was drawn up, the Confederation reserved Articles 43(2), 68, and 84 of the federal legal system (appeals or actions to set aside, where the Federal Tribunal had limited knowledge of the facts and no canton court had examined them with full powers of examination; public law appeals to the Federal Tribunal against state acts by the cantons where the canton authorities or the Federal Tribunal had only limited knowledge of the facts or the law). The Federal Council did not think the time was right for the Federal Tribunal to have full knowledge, although the MPs proposed this, and explained that 23 cantons had already set up an Administrative Tribunal and that the three others were going to have to do so, that it was important to avoid a situation in which standards of legal protection differed according to whether decisions came from an administrative authority or a tribunal, that legal protection was improved by the two-stage court process, that having power in the cantons was the only way of abiding by the principle of federalism and ensuring the cantons' sovereignty in procedural matters and lastly, that it was important to avoid overburdening the Federal Tribunal.[31]

So canton legislation was (or is being) adjusted to the above legal trends, either by the establishment of special courts, or by a general move to give powers to courts dealing with civil rights and obligations within the meaning of Article 6 of the Convention.

Lastly, it is worth noting that, for the first time, the Federal Council recently suggested altering the practice of the Federal Assembly whereby it has never declared void a popular move for partial revision of the Federal Constitution in defiance of international law. Faced with two initiatives proposing to restrict the right of asylum, the Federal Council found by reference, *inter alia*, to Articles 3 and 8 of the European Convention on Human

[31] *Bulletin official* of the States Council, 1990, 693 *et seq*., as summarized in the circular mentioned.

Rights, that no state in which law prevails may ignore those rules of international public law which are internationally considered to offer basic protection for human rights and humanitarian international law. All states in which law prevails are bound by these rules, regardless of any ratification or denunciation of treaties covered by international public law.[32]

D. LEADING HUMAN RIGHTS CASES DECIDED BY THE NATIONAL COURTS

It is impossible even to outline all the judgments issued in the application of the European Convention on Human Rights in Switzerland. A summary alone would take a whole report.[33] All the legal and administrative authorities of the Federation and the cantons, as well as the Federal Tribunal, have to apply and comply with the Convention, in accordance with the principle of the unity of the legal system, and they have met this demand rigorously, at least since the *Minelli* case, which led to the first judgment against Switzerland in 1983 (see Section E below) and was well publicized in the country.

This has been apparent in case-law, even as regards shortcomings in canton provisions (set out in Section C above) on the powers of the courts. In principle, the only possibility of adjusting Swiss law to Article 6 of the Convention is legislative reform. The courts cannot make up for shortcomings in the legislation here, because Article 6 allows for direct negative application (denying the status of tribunal to an authority taking a decision in a field covered by the rule), but it does not in theory allow a tribunal to declare itself competent if there is no law providing for such competence. However, there have been one or two attempts to do otherwise. The Supreme Court of Appeal in Vaud canton found that there was a shortcoming in the law (being amended) here and overcame it by applying, by analogy, the rules relating to opposition to prefectoral orders (whereby appeal could be made to the trial judge who looked at the case as a whole, on a *de facto* and *de jure* basis).[34] Similarly, the Administrative Tribunal of Tessin canton, also moved by the laudable aim of ensuring immediate respect for the right to be heard by a court in case of petty offences in commune affairs, gave general scope to the canton law by giving it powers in this area in exceptional cases only, interpreting it in the light of Article 6 of the Convention.[35] However, following the

32 Feuille fédérale 1994, III, 1483. Parliament subsequently supported the government proposal.
33 Cf. Tomas Poledna, *Praxis zur EMRK aus schweizerisches Sicht* (Zurich, Schulthess, 1993).
34 (1989) III *Journal des Tribunaux*, 57.
35 (1990) 9 *Rivista di diritto amministrativo ticinese*.

opinion of its legal department, highlighting, *inter alia*, the need to ensure the principle of the certainty of the law, the canton government quite rightly said that the law had to be amended.[36] The Federal Tribunal has also produced a judgment recently, giving the canton immediate responsibility for legally controlling the violation of Article 5 of the European Convention on Human Rights, independently of the revision of the canton procedural legislation which did not provide for this. However, this was an exceptional, urgent, and serious case of controlling the legality of returning someone to a psychiatric clinic.[37]

On the jurisdiction of the courts again, we should mention the new legislation on powers, on checking the legality of the rules covered by Article 113(3) of the Constitution (see Section B above). It is also important to remember the remarkable development of the Federal Tribunal's decisions relating to Switzerland's official interpretation of Article 6 of the Convention, which the European Court ruled against in the *Belilos* case. In a first judgment the Federal Tribunal said that the statement no longer covered the well-foundedness of all criminal charges and, reversing its decision,[38] found that the control exercised by the Federal Tribunal in handling a public law appeal against a decision to impose a fine was not an adequate guarantee as far as the Convention was concerned and so canton procedure, in which there was no possibility of appealing to the Council of State against traffic fines imposed by the canton automobile department, deprived the individual of the 'independent and impartial tribunal' mentioned in Article 6(1) of the Convention.[39]

In the same judgment, in a matter of civil rights and obligations, the Federal Tribunal did no more than express doubt as to the possibility of specifying the scope of an official interpretation in response to newly defined legal demands. So, faced with a case of personal relations between an unmarried father and mother, it declared it void (see Section C above).

The judgment had its effect both on legislation (see Section C above) and on the courts, because of the extension of the field of application of Article 6 of the Convention to areas which fell within public law in Switzerland. An exhaustive, detailed examination of this case-law is out of the question here, but it is worth summarizing Federal Tribunal practice, as illustrated by a recent judgment on an objection to the listing of a cinema-cum-theatre and the refusal to grant a licence to demolish the theatre itself and most of the foyer (in a tower house, built in the style of the Chicago School between 1929

[36] 'Parere del Consulente giuridico del Consiglio di Stato', *Guido Corti*, (1990) Rivista di diritto amminstrativo ticinese, 259 *et seq.*

[37] ATE 116 la 60. See also Marco Borghi, 'L'applicabilité de l'Article 6 CEDH aux contestations en matière de droit de la construction', (1991) *Droit de la construction*, Fribourg, 11 *et seq.*

[38] ATF 111 la 267.

[39] ATF 115 la 183.

[40] ATF 119 la 88.

and 1931). In this judgment[40] the Federal Tribunal said that it interpreted the notion of 'civil rights and obligations' as referred to in Article 6(1) of the Convention as broadly as the European Commission and Court of Human Rights and that this provision did not just apply to strictly private law cases, i.e. those between individuals or between an individual and the state acting as a private person, but to administrative decisions taken by an authority in the exercise of its public functions, where such decisions had a decisive effect on private rights and obligations.[41] In contrast to Swiss law, the Federal Tribunal said that federal and canton expropriation procedures,[42] the state's exercise of its legal right to a first option,[43] decisions to alter plots and mark perimeters,[44] the refusal to authorize building on a plot in an area designated for building,[45] and the adoption of a special land allocation plan designating areas required for a shooting range, approval of which entitled the competent authority to expropriate the plots in question,[46] were all cases of contestation of 'civil rights and obligations'. Then, referring to the decisions of the Court, the Federal Tribunal ultimately decided that, in the case in point, the decision by which the Council of State of Vaud canton had listed a cinema-theatre, its annexes, and its foyer was one involving the civil rights laid down in Article 6(1) of the Convention. The Federal Tribunal found that Article 6 of the Convention had been infringed, because the petitioner, who contested the *de facto* situation and the well-foundedness of the measure, had been unable to put the case to an independent, impartial tribunal.

In the field of social insurance, following a Court judgment in which Switzerland was found to be in breach of the Convention,[47] the Federal Tribunal held that disputes over benefits in all branches of social insurance under federal law were problems of civil rights and obligations within the meaning of Article 6(1) of the Convention. This therefore applied both to the canton appeal procedure and to the Federal Insurance Tribunal procedure. It left open the question of disputes over things other than insurance benefits, in particular contributions and premiums. It added that the demand for the hearing to be public had to be met, as a matter of priority, in the first court of appeal and that Article 6(1) did not oblige the social insurance judge to organize a public hearing other than in cases of outstanding public interest unless

[41] ATF 117 Ia 527/528 consid. 3c/aa, 115 Ia 68.

[42] ATF 118 Ia 227 consid. 1c, 331 *et seq.*, 115 Ia 69 consid. 2c. See also ATF 112 Ib 177/178 consid. 3a, 111 Ib 232/233.

[43] ATF 114 Ia 19.

[44] ATF 118 Ia 355/356 consid. 2a, 117 Ia 378.

[45] ATF 117 Ia 522.

[46] ATF 114 Ia 427 consid. 4c. More recently the Federal Tribunal has applied Art. 6 of the Convention to the question of the requirement to allocate certain plots in the area designated for building (cf. ATF 122 I 294).

[47] *Schuler-Zgraggen*, Judgment of 24 June 1993, Series A No. 263.

one of the parties had explicitly or tacitly requested it. Thus it denied the right to public hearings in the first and second courts here, for the dispute raised questions of a highly technical nature and the organization of a public hearing could have prevented the rapid proceedings which the law required. It also took account of the fact that the appeal, on its merits, was manifestly without foundation.[48]

In the matter of canton criminal procedure, the upheavals created by the Federal Tribunal are the fruit of many decisions, and above all of various reversals of decisions, displaying an increasing awareness of the demands of the European Convention on Human Rights. In a judgment issued in 1986,[49] for example, the Federal Tribunal went back on a previous decision[50] in which it had not excluded the possibility of the same person acting as both investigating and trial judge, in order to be completely in line with the judgments of the Court. In particular, it confirmed the importance which the *De Cubber* judgment attributed to impartiality being seen to be ensured (§ 26) and to the fact that a restrictive interpretation of Article 6(1) of the European Convention on Human Rights here was at variance with the aims of the provision (§ 30 *in fine*). This reference prompted the Federal Tribunal to take another look at its previous solution. It found that, from an institutional and functional point of view, it was unlikely that an optional challenge, even one allowed easily or without cause, was enough to bring the right to an impartial tribunal into play. This sort of arrangement would risk turning into a system of a free choice of judge.

In a subsequent judgment the Federal Tribunal dealt with a rule in a new canton law (passed following the above decision) to the effect that there were no grounds for challenging someone previously involved in the case as a registrar, so that a registrar who had taken part in the investigation could also sit in the trial court. The Federal Tribunal found that a registrar called upon to draft a judgment was expressing the wishes of the court in so doing. It was not out of the question that he might, in view of the thorough knowledge which he was bound to have of the case, have to call the attention of the judges to *de facto* and *de jure* details of great importance to the forthcoming decision during the course of the hearing, or even give them information about procedure and developments in the law. It pointed out that most Swiss judges, unlike their foreign counterparts, did not themselves draft the reasons for the judgments in which they were involved (this was the registrar's job) and that it was of decisive importance that the presence of the investigating magistrate on the bench of his immediate collaborator certainly carried a far smaller danger of confusion of functions than occurred when the investigating judge and the

[48] ATF 119 V 375. [49] ATF 112 Ia 290. [50] ATF 104 Ia 275.

trial judge were one and the same. But it was a danger which could not be warded off entirely when, as practice dictated, the registrar created a link between the investigation stage and the trial stage. This kind of thing could indeed cause the accused or even public opinion to suspect that impressions received in the course of the investigation had unfairly influenced the trial. Those are the reasons which prompted the Federal Tribunal to ban, in principle, the combination of the duties of investigating judge and trial judge.[51]

A canton court applied the same restrictive practice in a criminal law case involving minors,[52] a controversial solution[53] which failed to take account of the special functions of the judge responsible for minors and particularly of his symbolic role and duties as a go-between.[54]

In the matter of Article 5(4) of the European Convention on Human Rights and the right to self-expression in the course of the release procedure, the Federal Tribunal decided that, before the petition for release was heard, the accused was entitled to express himself on a statement by the authority responsible for the criminal proceedings. This right existed regardless of whether the authority's position involved any new arguments.[55]

In a judgment of 22 March 1989, following the reversal of a decision, the Federal Tribunal recognized the right to consult the essential items in the case file and to contest the arguments put up to justify preventive custody.[56]

Following a Strasbourg Court judgment on Switzerland,[57] the Federal Tribunal amended its decisions and recognized the right of the accused to cross-examine his opponent, in particular on the decisive question of the degree of intervention.[58]

Basically, in legal theory, European legal concepts have profoundly influenced the content of Swiss law, criminal procedure especially. We need to take a critical look at the legal formulae according to which the Convention does no more than clarify rights already recognized in our legal system and state unequivocally that the move to raise the minimum standards of the right to defence would have developed differently if we had stayed on the path lit by Articles 4 and 58 of the Constitution and our unwritten constitutional

[51] ATF 115 la 224.

[52] Judgment of 29 April 1988 of the Geneva Court of Appeal (*Semaine Judiciaire*, 1988, 465 *et seq.*).

[53] *Semaine Judiciare*, 1989, 133 *et seq.*

[54] Jean Zermatten, 'Réflexions sur les réalités de la justice des mineurs et la séparation des fonctions judiciares', (1990) 107 *RPS* 367 *et seq.*

[55] ATF 114 la 84.

[56] ATF 115 la 293 and departure from the jurisprudence publshed in *ATF 101 la 17/18*.

[57] *Lüdi*, Judgment of 15 June 1992, Series A No. 238.

[58] ATF 118 la 327. On the opponent's right to anonymity, cf. ATF 121 I 379 which recognizes the right to be heard *in camera*.

[59] Claude Rouiller, note 8 above, 234.

law.[59] This writer continues his investigation of the 'dynamic effect' of the European Convention on Human Rights with a discussion of judgment by default, automatic defence, and the right to an interpreter.

One last area in which the European Convention on Human Rights plays a major part in the Federal Tribunal's decisions is the law relating to aliens. On a number of occasions the Federal Tribunal has refused extradition, because of Article 3 of the Convention, when there has been serious reason to believe that considerations of race and political opinion could worsen the objector's situation in a criminal case in the applicant state.[60]

The same goes for the execution of a sentence of expulsion pronounced as part of a criminal judgment.[61]

Lastly, the Federal Tribunal has been constant in its belief that Article 8 of the European Convention on Human Rights allows aliens to object to any separation from their families and thereby obtain residence permits—despite the fact that it is Switzerland's policy to restrict foreign residents, in particular to ensure a proper balance between the Swiss and foreign resident population, improve the job market, and ensure the best possible employment situation.[62]

However, the Federal Tribunal[63] maintains that Article 8 of the Convention only applies where the relationship between the alien and the family member entitled to settle in Switzerland (having Swiss nationality or authorization to settle in the country) be close and genuine.[64] So it applies where an alien can prove an intact relationship with a child with the right to Swiss residency, even if that child is not under his parental authority under family law.[65]

E. CASES BROUGHT BEFORE THE EUROPEAN COMMISSION AND COURT OF HUMAN RIGHTS

Switzerland has never been involved in an inter-state case, but the Commission has received many individual claims against this country, leading to various Court judgments and pronouncements of Swiss guilt.

The *Minelli* case,[66] the first of these, caused a stir in Switzerland, creating

[60] ATF 109 lb 64. [61] ATF 116 IV 105.

[62] Cf. Article 16 of the Federal Alien Residence and Establishment Act of 26 March 1931, LSEE, RS 142.20.

[63] ATF 120 lb 1.

[64] ATF 119 lb 91 consid. 1c p. 93,, 118 lb 145 consid. 4, pp. 152/153 consid. 1c p. 157, and 116 lb 353 consid. 1b p. 355.

[65] ATF 120 Ib 1; 119 lb 81 consid. 1c p. 84, 118 lb 153 consid. 1c p. 157, 115 lb 97 consid. 2e p. 99; *Berrehab*, Judgment of 21 June 1988, Series A No. 138, p. 14, § 21.

[66] Judgment of 25 March 1983, Series A No. 62.

surprise (because of the enormous consideration in which both authorities and citizens hold their democratic system) and considerable awareness, particularly amongst practising lawyers, who then began systematically to refer to the European Convention on Human Rights, particularly in criminal cases.

Minelli also related to another aspect of criminal law (the principle of the presumption of innocence) and posed the problem of the effects of European Court judgments on canton law. The question of principle raised by the government and the applicant was how far the common Swiss practice of having legal costs and expenses paid by people who had benefited from a cancellation, discharge, acquittal, or, as in the case in point, a time limit which precluded prosecution, was compatible with Article 6(2) of the Convention. The Court ruled that the presumption of innocence was flouted if a legal decision was made about the accused which reflected the feeling that he was guilty, although guilt had not been legally established beforehand and the accused had not had the opportunity to exercise his right to a defence. It was enough for the feeling to emerge from the judgment. In its disputed decision, the court which rendered it had been convinced of the guilt of the accused, who had not had the benefit of the guarantees provided by Articles 6(1) and (3).

This did not prompt the repeal of provisions on the allocation of costs in cases of acquittal. Legal decisions on the subject abounded, stating that it was consistent with both the Constitution and the European Convention on Human Rights to have the accused pay costs in cases of acquittal or cancellation if he had clearly infringed a written or unwritten rule of behaviour in the Swiss legal system as a whole, had done so in breach of civil law (within the meaning of application by analogy of principles attendant on extra-contractual responsibility) and thus triggered or complicated the criminal procedure.[67] It was of enormous symbolic importance, particularly since it was boosted by a second judgment against Switzerland (in the *Zimmermann and Steiner* case, heard a few months later[68]), making the very first attack on the Confederation's Supreme Court and going so far as to censure its organization. The judgment found a violation of Article 6(1) (unreasonable length of proceedings: a period of three and a half years from the lodging of the appeal with the Federal Tribunal) because of a lengthy period of total inaction, only justifiable in extreme circumstances, on the part of the Tribunal. In its defence the government claimed that the Federal Tribunal was overloaded. The Court said that a state did not incur liability over a temporary hold-up if it was prompt in taking steps to overcome it, but it was another matter if the situation persisted and became structural.

[67] ATF 116 la 163. [68] Judgment of 13 July 1983, Series A No. 66.

Most of the other judgments in which Switzerland was found liable had directly or indirectly to do with the status of people accused or detained in the course of criminal proceedings.

The *Sanchez-Reisse* case[69] was on custody for the purposes of extradition and the procedure whereby the Federal Tribunal could dismiss petitions for release after a warning from the Federal Police Office. The Court found this to be a breach of Article 5(4), because of the impossibility of responding to the Federal Police Office warning and appearing in person before a court. The Court emphasized the need to ensure for the person in question the benefit of having both sides heard in some way. If the applicant had not appeared in person before the Federal Tribunal, then he should have been able to respond to the Federal Police Office in writing. The Court also pointed to the excessive time involved here: 31 days before the Federal Police Office and 46 days before the Federal Tribunal.

In the *Schönberger and Durmaz* case[70] the Court found that Article 8 of the European Convention on Human Rights had been breached by the failure to transmit a letter addressed to a preventive detainee by a lawyer acting on the instructions of the detainee's wife and because the contents of the said letter involved no danger of connivance between sender and recipient and represented no threat to the normal running of the proceedings. Given the context, the fact that the first applicant (the lawyer) had not been officially instructed by the second applicant (the detainee) was of little importance. So the condition of necessary interference in a democratic society was not fulfilled.

In the *Huber* case[71] Article 5(3) of the Convention was found to have been infringed because the same district prosecutor had been involved in both the investigation and trial of the same case. During the enquiry he had investigated whether the applicant should be charged or not, ordered her to be detained in preventive custody, and handled the case file; and fourteen months later he had been involved in the prosecution and made the charges, but not presided over the trial (although he could have done so under the canton Code of Criminal Procedure). The Court found that Article 5(3) had been breached: the Convention did not rule out the possibility of the magistrate who took the custody decision also having other functions, although his impartiality could be in doubt if he was able to be involved on the prosecution side in the subsequent criminal procedure.

The *Quaranta* case[72] concerned the refusal of the presiding judge in a regional court to appoint an official lawyer to help a detainee during the

[69] Judgment of 21 October 1986, Series A No. 107.
[70] Judgment of 20 June 1988, Series A No. 137.
[71] Judgment of 23 October 1990, Series A No. 188.
[72] Judgment of 24 May 1991, Series A No. 205.

investigation and then during the trial. Two conditions went with the right to the assistance of a lawyer. First, there had to be no 'sufficient means to pay for legal assistance' (not contested in this case) and secondly, 'the interests of justice' had to be served. In view of the seriousness of the offence and the severity of the sentence (the charge was drug dealing and drug taking and the sentence was imprisonment of up to three years), the complexity of the case, the personality of the applicant (a poor, young, foreign adult with no proper vocational training and a history of regular offending), the Court found that Article 6(3) had been infringed, because the personal appearance of the person in question before the investigating judge and then the court had not been a proper opportunity for him to plead his cause properly.

In the *S* case[73] the Court found Switzerland in breach of Article 6(3)(c) of the Convention because of impediments to free communication between the accused in preventive custody and his lawyer. In particular, the Court rejected the government's argument that there was a danger of collusion because the lawyers of various detainees intended to co-ordinate their tactics.

Lastly, in the *Lüdi* case[74] the Court found that Articles 6(1) and (3)(d) had been infringed when a detainee was sentenced on written evidence from a police officer under oath, whose job was known to the investigating judge. The refusal by both magistrate and courts to hear the witness for the prosecution, which deprived the applicant and his lawyer of all opportunity of casting doubt upon his credibility during the proceedings, was considered to be decisive. The Court found that it would in fact have been possible both to do this and to cater for the police authorities' legitimate concern to preserve the anonymity of their officer.

The Court dealt with violation of Article 6 in two more judgments: in the *Belilos* case,[75] in which there was no appeal to a court for an administrative fine, and the *Weber* case,[76] in which proceedings culminating in the sentencing of a journalist were not made adequately public. Both these judgments are very well known because of the specific extensions which they made to the field of application of Article 6 and, above all, because of the finding that Switzerland's official interpretation and reservations were invalid. In particular, the Court decided that the official interpretation had to be assimilated to a reservation and that Switzerland had infringed Article 64 of the European Convention on Human Rights in both cases, the reservation being general in character and the obligation for the state to supply 'a brief statement of the law concerned' (which Switzerland had not respected) being a

[73] Judgment of 28 November 1991, Series A No. 220.
[74] Judgment of 15 June 1992, Series A No. 238.
[75] Judgment of 29 April 1988, Series A No. 132.
[76] Judgment of 22 May 1990, Series A No. 177.

fundamental of legal certainty, constituting a basic condition and not just a token request.

The validity of the only formally surviving official interpretation of Article 6(3)(c) is a matter of controversy and legal writers are more inclined towards the negative.[77]

Other judgments concern infringement of:

—Article 10, because the Post Office, without the consent of the emitting state, refused to issue a special domestic electronics firm with a licence to use a private dish to receive uncoded television programmes for the general public from a Soviet telecommunications satellite;[78]

—Article 12, in the case of a ban on remarriage imposed, for a limited period, on the spouse said to have caused the breakdown of a previous union;[79]

—Article 14 combined with Article 8, because it was impossible for the husband to have his wife's patronymic, a family name, preceded by his own.[80] (The government had found Articles 8 and 12 to be applicable in considering Article 5 of Protocol No. 7 to be *lex specialis* and Switzerland had expressed reservations on this subject in ratifying the said Protocol. The Court stressed that Article 5 was an additional clause and could neither replace nor reduce the scope of Article 8);

—Article 14 combined with Article 6(1), essentially because of the failure to recognize sexual equality in restricting a pension to a woman, now a mother, on the assumption that she would have conformed to the everyday pattern and stayed at home to look after the child even if her health had not deteriorated;[81]

—the right to proceedings involving the due hearing of the parties, guaranteed by Article 6(1) (which, according to the Court,[82] cannot be disallowed on economic grounds or in order to speed up the proceedings);

—the presumption of innocence enshrined in Article 6(2) in the case of a financial penalty imposed on the heirs because of tax fraud committed by the deceased;[83]

—Article 5(4) because of the ineffectiveness of the applications for release due to the fact that, since the proceedings were at canton level,

[77] Cf. Claude Rouiller, note 8 above, 255.
[78] *Autronic*, Judgment of 22 May 1990, Series A No. 178.
[79] *F*, Judgment of 18 December 1987, Series A No. 128.
[80] *Burghartz*, Judgment of 22 February 1993.
[81] *Schuler-Zgraggen*, Judgment of 24 June 1993.
[82] *Nideröst-Huber v Switzerland*, Judgment of 29 August 1997.
[83] *AP, MP, and TP v Switzerland*, Judgment of 29 August 1997.

when the detainee was transferred to another canton the applications were no longer valid.[84]

Switzerland was nearly found to be in breach of the Convention in other cases, particularly when it came to freedom of expression. The Human Rights Commission concluded in its reports that Article 10 had been infringed in the cases of *Groppera*[85] (on the ban on retransmitting radio broadcasts from Italy by cable in Switzerland) and *Müller et al.*[86] (on a judgment against the exhibiting and confiscation of pictures deemed to be obscene). In the latter case the Court did not condemn the confiscation of the canvases because, making a subtle distinction in its reasoning, it ruled that the canvases had been taken for an indeterminate rather than an unlimited time and, most importantly, were returned shortly before the judgment.

Two other cases mentioned above (*Minelli* and *Weber*) also concerned freedom of information, the former indirectly and the latter directly, so it is reasonable to include this section with those (ie criminal procedure and the validity of reservations) typical of Court decisions on Switzerland.

The impact of these decisions on the Swiss legal system is described above.

F. GOVERNMENT RESPONSE TO BEING HELD IN BREACH OF THE CONVENTION

The Swiss government has promoted the revision of various federal laws in the course of its legislative activities, primarily because of a concern to come into line with the European Convention on Human Rights and developments in the decisions of the Court (see Section C above), particularly when it comes to such things as military legislation, the laws on deprivation of freedom for reasons of assistance, and the federal criminal procedure.

On the organizational front, for example, it has followed up the Court's *Zimmermann and Steiner* judgment by suggesting that Parliament increase the number of substitute federal judges and advisers at the Federal Tribunal, while the Federal Council has made explicit reference to the Court judgment in its Message.

When commenting on new legislation, the government devotes a special paragraph to constitutionality, also showing how far the bill is in conformity with the European Convention on Human Rights.

[84] *RMP v Switzerland*, Judgment of 26 September 1997.
[85] Judgment of 28 March 1990, Series A No. 173.
[86] Judgment of 24 May 1988 Series A No. 133.

A particular problem arises when the required legislative adjustment is to be made in a field which falls within the jurisdiction of the cantons. In this case the Federal Council deems it to be its responsibility to ensure compliance with the Convention in Switzerland (indeed, the main responsibility to be committed at international level is that of the Confederation). So, when the Federal Tribunal cancelled the official interpretation of 29 April 1988, the Head of the Federal Department of Justice and of the Police spoke to all the canton Governments and invited them to make the requisite legal changes as quickly as possible (see Section C above), a request to which the governments began to respond without delay.

When it comes to executing judgments, the legal possibility of cancelling administrative decisions has enabled Switzerland fully to respect Court judgments against them. For example, in the *Autronic* case (see Section E above) the holders of a radio-telecommunications concession allowing them to receive radio and television broadcasts by satellite were sent the following letter by the federal Post Office:

> You are currently the holder of a radio-communications concession authorizing you to receive the above programmes. On 21 December 1990, however, the Federal Council decided to cancel the radio-communication concessions enabling you to receive these programmes. That decision follows a judgment which the European Court of Human Rights made against Switzerland on 22 May 1990. So, as from 23 May 1990, radio and television reception concessions authorize their holder also to receive radio and television programmes broadcast by satellite. The tax on receiving and any recording of broadcasts to be collected as from 23 May 1990 will appear on your telephone bill for April.

On 21 March 1994, without waiting for the official revision of the Order, the Federal Population Office sent the canton population monitoring authorities a circular for them and their population offices, outlining the new system on the right to one's name, following the *Burghartz* judgment against Switzerland. The sole aim of the new system was to comply with the Court's decisions by making it possible for a husband to precede his wife's patronymic, the family name, with his own.

Following the judgment in the case of *F* the head of the Federal Department wrote to the presiding judges of the Federal Tribunal and the Administrative Tribunal and to the canton courts to draw their attention to the decisions of the Court and invite them to avoid any further judgments against Switzerland in that field.

When there was a question of applying federal legislation (the old law on extradition) in breach of Article 5(3) of the European Convention on Human Rights pending the entry into effect of the revised law, the Federal Tribunal declined to do so, on a *de facto* basis, following an exchange of letters between the Federal Tribunal and the Federal Council, designed, as one author put it, to find:

> a *modus vivendi* in conformity with European law, without any sterile inhibition on the question of the separation of powers, pending entry into effect [on 1 January 1983] of the Euro-compatible law on this point, ie on mutual international assistance in criminal matters.[87]

One problem not solved until recently was the implementation of European Court judgments where a Swiss court had infringed the Convention. In view of the principle *of res judicata*, the Confederation could not wipe out all the effects of the internal judgment, which officially remained in force, and tended to confine itself to granting a sum of money by way of compensation for material and non-material damage incurred. An amendment to the Federal Legal Organization Act, in force since 15 February 1992, added a new, important Article 139(a), as follows:

> 1. The request for a review of a Federal Tribunal judgment or a decision by a lower authority shall be eligible when the European Court of Human Rights or the Committee of Ministers of the Council of Europe has allowed an individual petition for infringement of the Convention for the Protection of Human Rights and Fundamental Freedoms of 4 November 1950 or of its Protocols and when compensation cannot be obtained via such review.
> 2. If the Federal Tribunal finds that a review is required, but within the competence of a lower authority, it shall send the case to that authority, which can set the review in motion.
> 3. The canton authority shall start on the review applied for, even where canton law does not provide for such a motive for review.

This provision was applied for the first time after the *Schuler-Zgraggen* case. The European Court had found that, because of the existence of this new Swiss legal procedure, the 'just satisfaction' laid down in Article 50 of the Convention was not present and it had set aside the question for later, giving the government a period of time for implementation.[88] By allowing the petition for review, the Federal Insurance Tribunal, aiming at *restititio in integrum*, to put the applicant back into the same legal situation as she would have occupied without violation, cancelled its previous judgment and granted her a full invalidity pension (backdated).

Thus, this new rule and the new trend in legal practice[89] are overcoming the

[87] Olivier Jacot-Guillarmod, note 10 above, 373.

[88] Judgment of 24 March 1994, ATF 120 V 150.

[89] Two other Federal Tribunal judgments have applied the above-mentioned Article 139 OJ in a somewhat restrictive manner; in particular the Federal Tribunal has taken the view that:

> when the European authority, assuming infringement of the principle of promptness, has itself determined the compensation it deems fair, and in particular awards compensation to the

last technical and legal impediment to Switzerland's full compliance with the decisions of the Court.

G. ASSESSMENT AND PROSPECTS

The developments outlined above demonstrate that, although Switzerland was overtly cautious when it first joined and began to apply the European Human Rights Convention, recent trends show the Swiss authorities constantly adapting to the Court's decisions. This has been effected by changes to many federal and canton laws and by the direct, widespread application of the Convention by all the administrative and legal authorities in the cantons and at federal level. Furthermore, this drive has been apparent in a particularly convincing manner, as can be seen from the Federal Tribunal judgment against Switzerland's official interpretation, from the recent adoption of the review procedure following Court judgments and, more generally, from the many reversals of Federal Tribunal decisions discussed in Section D above.

There is just one important problem left to finalize and that is the legal control of compliance with the Convention of federal laws. However, the current theory is that this is constitutional and, as already pointed out in Sections B and D above, the Federal Tribunal has not just proclaimed the fact, but even applied federal laws *contra legem* without any explicit announcements, using an interpretation in line with the Convention.

Postscript In the interval that has elapsed from the first draft of this contribution to the first update we have been comforted in this opinion. Indeed, while on one hand the acceptance of the global amendment of the federal Constitution (dated 18 December 1998) has not formally abolished the said limit,[90] we have detected some positive signs in one of the latest decisions of the Federal Tribunal which, having ascertained the insoluble discrepancy between the Convention and an article of the federal law, has enforced Article 6 of the Convention rather than the latter.[91]

applicant, the latter is no longer entitled to claim a reduced sentence on this basis in the form of a revision (ATF 123 I 329; cf. ATF 122 I 182).

[90] For example, Article 190 of the new Constitution takes up again the principle of former Articles 113 and 114. It is however necessary to point out that Article 5(4) of the new Constitution reads 'Both the Confederation and the Cantons obey international law' and Article 35(1) reads 'The fundamental rights must be implemented within the whole of the legal system'. This latter rule was applied in one of the latest judgements of the Federal Tribunal also to the rights guaranteed by the Convention, see ATF 126 II 324.

[91] The case concerned the seizure of propaganda material to safeguard national security, against which the federal law does not provide the right to appeal to a judicial authority (ATF 125 II 417).

Furthermore, to enforce the above-mentioned review procedure based on Article 139a OG, it has lately stated that a norm, *in casu* the federal law, must not be enforced any more, even if only the individual and concrete act enforcing the federal law violated the Convention. The Federal Tribunal has nonetheless specified that it considers Article 139a OG to be a *lex specialis* which, through its peculiar *ratio*, calls for the supremacy of the Convention over the contrary federal law.[92] Despite this reservation, it is undeniable that this judgement represents a further, perhaps conclusive, step towards establishing once and for all the principle of judicial control of the Federal Law. At that moment, Switzerland will have fully satisfied the obligations imposed by the Convention.

[92] Cf. ATF 124 II 480.

34

Turkey

YASEMIN ÖZDEK AND EMINE KARACAOĞLU

A. INTRODUCTION

As a member of the Council of Europe since 1949, Turkey ratified the Convention for the Protection of Human Rights and Fundamental Freedoms (ECHR), shortly after its entry into force, and Protocol No. 1 in 1954.[1] Turkey also ratified Protocols Nos. 2, 3, 4, 5, and 8 and signed Protocols Nos. 7 and 9.[2] In addition, the competence of the European Commission on Human Rights under Article 25 was recognized in 1987[3] and of the European Court of Human Rights under Article 46 in 1990.[4]

The ratification of the ECHR did not attract remarkable attention in the Turkish political life in 1954 and afterwards. In fact, the ratification policy of the government raised some doubts on whether it was aimed to guarantee and develop fundamental rights and freedoms. On the contrary, the government clearly followed the policy based on the repression of the most fundamental rights and freedoms at that time of the ratification, as indicated in the adoption of some laws of anti-democratic character.[5] With regard to the official motives for the ratification, it may be stated that it is clearly related to the integration policy of Turkey with the West. In the early '50s, in addition to

[1] The ECHR was signed on 4 November 1950; ratified by the Law No. 6366 of 10 March 1954 (see Resmi Gazete [Official Gazette, hereinafter cited as RG] No. 8662 of 19 March 1954) and deposited with the Council of Europe on 18 May 1954. Turkey attached its reservations to Article 2 of Protocol No. 1 on the right to education since Law No. 430 of 3 May 1924 prohibited the establishment of religious private schools.

[2] Protocols Nos. 2 and 3 were ratified on 25 March 1968; No. 5 was ratified on 20 December 1971; No. 8 was ratified on 19 September 1989. Protocol No. 4 has recently been ratified in 1994 (see *RG* No. 21990 of 14 July 1994); No. 7 and No. 9 were signed respectively on 14 March 1985 and 6 November 1990. Protocol No. 6 has not been signed yet. See, Council of Europe, *Chart of Signatures and Ratifications* of 1 July 1993.

[3] It was recognized on 28 January 1987 and renewed on 24 January 1990 and on 28 January 1993 for another three years see, Council of Europe's treaty website <http://Conventions.coe.int>.

[4] It was recognized on 22 January 1990 and renewed for another three years from 22 January 1993, ibid.

[5] See Rona Aybay, 'Avrupa İnsan Hakları Sözleşmesi ve Türk Pozitif Hukuku' in *İnsan Hakları Armağanı* (Ankara: BM Türk Derneği, 1978), 118.

the ratification of the ECHR, some basic laws providing permission and encouragement of foreign capital were adopted and relations between NATO, the USA, and Turkey developed. In brief, Turkey followed the policy of economic, political, and military integration with the West during this period, and ratification was a part of this policy.[6]

The ECHR did not affect the political and legal life of Turkey in the '60s either. Fundamental rights and freedoms embodied in the 1961 Constitution were more comprehensive than the ECHR, covering a wide list of social, economic, and cultural rights as well as civil and political rights. Therefore, owing to its limited content, the ECHR had not been accorded any special importance and function for the protection of human rights. It is, however, worth noting that Turkey's non-recognition of the right to individual application and the compulsory jurisdiction of the Court had prevented the ECHR from having an additional function during that period.

The ECHR took a remarkable position in the Turkish political and legal agenda shortly after the third military intervention of 12 September 1980, which was more oppressive than the 1960 and the 1971 military interventions. As a result, the foreign affairs of Turkey, especially with the West, deteriorated during the early '80s. The European countries tended to consider gross human rights violations under the military administration as an obstacle to the maintenance and development of their international relations with Turkey. In this context, some members of the Council of Europe filed an application against Turkey under Article 24 of the ECHR. On the other hand, the development of the human rights movement in Turkey accelerated towards the end of the '80s. Non-governmental organizations on human rights, whose founders and members were generally victims of violations, in particular political prisoners and torture victims, their relatives, and opposing intellectuals, also emphasized the international human rights responsibilities to the governments.

In contrast with the anti-democratic practices carried out since 12 September 1980, some significant international human rights instruments were either ratified or signed in the late '80s, with the purpose of changing the image of the bad human rights records of Turkey. In this context, for example, as a response to the allegations of human rights violations, especially accusations of systematic torture, Turkey immediately ratified the UN and the European Convention on Torture in 1988, in contrast with its traditionally slow ratification policy on international instruments. In addition, Turkey made declarations under Articles 25 and 46 of the ECHR in that period. Furthermore, in the Notice of Derogation dated 5 May 1992 made under

[6] Rona Aybay, 'Avrupa İnsan Hakları Sözleşmesi ve Türk Pozitif Hukuku' in *İnsan Hakları Armağanı* (Ankara: BM Türk Derneği, 1978), 117–119.

Article 15 of the ECHR, Turkey restricted the scope of the derogation only with respect to Article 5 of the Convention, unlike her previous more comprehensive Notices of Derogation. Turkey also took steps at the domestic level, one instance of which was the establishment of a State Ministry for Human Rights, despite the existence of serious doubts as to its function. Also, the government attempted to establish a human rights organization by Decree No. 502 in 1993.[7] However, it was annulled, since the Law authorizing the government to issue decrees was abolished by the Constitutional Court.[8] Recently, a circular letter which aims to organize a consultative department in order to provide some improvements on human rights was prepared by the Prime Ministry 'with the purpose of removing the unfair criticisms in issue at the international level'.[9]

Notwithstanding all positive steps taken either at the international or domestic level, the Turkish government still has to deal with allegations of torture, extrajudicial executions, and disappearances, in particular. As noted by the European Committee for the Prevention of Torture, existing Turkish law does not have important deficiencies with regard to torture, but action is required with regard to the practice.[10] To conclude: nowadays, despite increasing references to the concept of human rights and attempts for the establishment of human rights organizations by the Turkish government, no effective step has been taken in practice for the improvement of human rights conditions and, in fact, the purpose of preventing the systematic violations.

B. THE STATUS OF THE CONVENTION IN NATIONAL LAW

The 1924 Constitution which was in force at the time of the ratification of the Convention contained no explicit reference to the domestic status of international agreements. In the context of international agreements, Article 26 of the 1924 Constitution only provided that 'the Grand National Assembly alone exercises such functions as [. . .] concluding conventions and treaties and making peace with foreign states . . .' The main motive followed by this provision was that international agreements could be duly put into effect only by the Turkish Grand National Assembly (TGNA).[11] From the point of view

[7] *RG* No. 21690 of 6 September 1993.

[8] 6.10.1993, E.1993/39, K.1993/37 (*RG* No. 21769 of 25 November 1993).

[9] No. 1994/34 of 26 August 1994.

[10] See 'Public Statement on Turkey Before the European Committee for the Prevention of Torture' in (1993) 15 *EHRR* 309, 319.

[11] See *TBMM Zabıt Ceridesi* (Records of the Turkish Grand National Assembly) vol. 1, 1340, 213ff. See and compare, the statement of reasons of Article 65 of the 1961 Constitution, Kazım Öztürk ed., *Gerekçeli Anayasa* (Ankara: Bilgi, 1971) 128.

of the Turkish constitutional system, it may be stated that upon the Turkish ratification of the Convention, it was incorporated into domestic legal system.

Article 65 of the 1961 Constitution and Article 90 of the 1982 Constitution contained the same provisions on the status of international agreements in domestic law. Both embodied two basic principles: the first is that international agreements duly put into effect carry the force of law. Secondly, no appeal to the Constitutional Court can be made with regard to these agreements on the ground of unconstitutionality. The provisions of the 1961 and the 1982 Constitutions also embodied some constitutional procedure on duly putting international agreements into effect: ratification of international agreements should be subject to adoption by the TGNA by a law approving the ratification. In addition, Article 97 of the 1961 Constitution and Article 104 of the 1982 Constitution provided that international instruments are ratified and promulgated by the President of the Republic. After the accomplishment of this constitutional procedure, international agreements are incorporated into domestic law. Obviously, upon their ratification, international agreements constitute a part of domestic law and bind executive and judicial organs.

Related provisions of the 1961 and 1982 Constitutions have generally been interpreted as meaning that Turkish law has accepted the monist system on the relations between international law and domestic law.[12] That is to say, for Turkey international law and domestic law form a unique legal order and, accordingly, international law binds domestic law. Indeed, it follows that international law is superior to or more basic than domestic law. However, some authors have tended to consider that Turkish law has not accepted the superiority of international law.[13] In fact, there is no clear statement on the adoption of the monist system in the Turkish Constitutions. Therefore, the question of the relationship between international law and domestic law has become open to interpretation, as indicated by the different views in the Turkish law.

On the other hand, related provisions of the 1961 and 1982 Constitutions are not clear on the issue of the domestic legal hierarchy of international agreements, which is also controversial. Some have claimed that international

[12] See A. Şeref Gözübüyük, 'Avrupa İnsan Hakları Sözleşmesi ve Bireysel Başvuru Hakkı' (1987) 9 *İnsan Hakları Yıllığı*, TODAİE, 1987, 7; Süheyl Batum, *Avrupa İnsan Hakları Sözleşmesi ve Türk Anayasal Sistemine Etkileri* (Istanbul: İÜHF, 1993) 41; Mümtaz Soysal, 'Anayasaya Uygunluk Denetimi ve Uluslararası Sözleşmeler' 2 *Anayasa Yargisı* (Ankara, 1986) 15; Tekin Akıllıoğlu, 'Avrupa İnsan Hakları Sözleşmesi ve İç Hukukumuz', *AÜSBFD* 3–4 1989. 157; Mesut Gülmez, *Memurlar ve Sendikal Haklar* (Ankara: İmge, 1990) 249; Necmi Yüzbaşıoğlu, 'Avrupa İnsan Hakları Hukukunun Kiteliği ve Türk Hukuk Düzenindeki Yeri Üzerine' 11 *İnsan Hakları Merkezi Dergisi* 1, 30.

[13] See Ergun Özbudun, *Türk Anayasa Hukuku* (Ankara: Yetkin, 1986) 178; Hüseyin Pazarcı, *Uluslararası Hukuk Dersleri* I (Ankara: AÜSBF, 1985) 31.

agreements have an equal status with ordinary domestic legislation, while others consider them superior to domestic laws. The first approach interpreted the related provisions literally, which announced that international agreements have the 'force of law', arguing that the fact that judicial review of the constitutionality of international agreements has been prevented by the Constitution does not change their status.[14] According to this approach, the prevention of constitutional review of international agreements was intended to avoid the state's responsibility in international law, but not to give them a superior status over domestic laws. Consequently, it has been argued that the effects of international agreements can be amended or abolished by ordinary laws in accordance with the principle of *lex posterior*, even though the state is responsible for its disobedience to international agreements.

The second approach holds that the prevention of constitutional review of international agreements reflected their superior status over domestic laws. It has claimed that international agreements duly put into effect carry the 'force of law', as provided in the Constitution; that international agreements bind domestic law, but do not determine their status in national law.[15] In the framework of this approach, while some scholars have considered the place of international agreements as being between ordinary domestic laws and the Constitution,[16] the others have recognized their position as constitutional[17] or supra-constitutional.[18] According to the argument on the supra-constitutional position of international agreements, in the case of a contradiction between an international agreement and a domestic law, including the Constitution, the international agreement must be applied.

Undoubtedly, different interpretations of the related constitutional provisions on the status of international agreements in domestic law cause various important effects on the grounds of applicability of international agreements. In fact, the debate has practical importance because different interpretations on this issue result in different applicability levels of the ECHR. For example, in the case of a constitutional norm contrary to the Convention, while the adoption of the view that international agreements have a lower status than the Constitution would lead to the non-application of the ECHR, their adoption as supra-constitutional norms would require the ECHR to be applied. At this point, national courts gain importance in the determination of the effectiveness of the Convention.

[14] Hüseyin Pazarcı, ibid.; Ergun Özbudun, ibid.

[15] Mesut Gülmez, *op. cit.*, 249; Edip Çelik, 'Avrupa İnsan Hakları Sözleşmesinin Türk Hukukundaki Yeri ve Uygulaması', *İdare Hukuku ve İlimleri Dergisi* 1–3 1988, 50; Necmi Yüzbaşıoğlu, *op. cit.*, 34.

[16] For example, see Mümtaz Soysal, *op. cit.*, 17.

[17] Tekin Akıllıoğlu, *op. cit.*, 164.

[18] A. Şeref Gözübüyük, *op. cit.*, 7.

It is worth noting that international agreements on *human rights* have occasionally been distinguished from other international agreements, having been given a special status in the framework of the debate. It is generally accepted that the position of human rights agreements should be different from the others. Furthermore, it has been argued that some constitutional provisions which referred to international law in the context of fundamental rights and freedoms, such as Articles 15, 16, and 42 of the 1982 Constitution, required the differentiation of human rights agreements on the ground of their status in national law.[19] As a result, various approaches in the debate have agreed that human rights agreements have a special character. For example, while international agreements were accepted as having equal status with ordinary domestic laws, human rights agreements have been thought to have a different constitutional status.[20] The status of international human rights agreements has tended to be considered as an exception to the general system of the status of international agreements in domestic law.

The status of the ECHR has been interpreted in accordance with the growing importance of the concept of human rights and parallel with the development of the international law of human rights, as could be seen in the theoretical discussions of scholars, parliamentary debates, and decisions of the national courts. Furthermore, in the framework of the debate on the status of the ECHR, the view that the domestic provisions about international agreements should be interpreted as compatible with the contents of the ECHR has been supported. In this context, Article 1 of the Convention has been interpreted as obliging the contracting states to amend their domestic law according to the ECHR.[21] In addition, it has been emphasized that national judges should interpret the Convention as in accordance with the case-law of the European Commission and Court.[22]

C. THE STATUS OF THE CONVENTION IN PARLIAMENTARY PROCEEDINGS

Having examined the records of the Parliament, the number of references made to the ECHR and its Protocols, especially between 1954 and 1982, cannot be overestimated. On the other hand, the references to the ECHR have been increasing rapidly since the recognition of the individual application to the Commission in 1987. Instances of this were observed not only in draft

[19] Tekin Akıllıoğlu, *op. cit.*, 173.
[20] Hüseyin Pazarcı, *op. cit.*, 31–32.
[21] Edip Çelik, *op. cit.*, 51–52; Şeref Gözübüyük, *op. cit.*, 8.
[22] Şeref Gözübüyük, ibid.

proposals, but also in speeches delivered by members of Parliament (MP) or members of cabinet.

The first group of references made to the ECHR seem to have two purposes; first, the desire to establish good relations with Western states, and secondly, to take measures to reduce reactions against violations of human rights. The military intervention and its administration between 12 September 1980 and 7 December 1983 produced the worst relations with the Council of Europe. In this context, one MP argued that the violations of military administration and the accusations against Turkey by the international community caused troubles for the following government after the military administration, which therefore decided to take steps to reduce reactions against Turkey.[23] To this end, the ratification of some conventions such as the UN and European Conventions on Torture and the recognition of the right to individual application in 1987 might be noted in particular. It was considered that the steps taken since 1983 were welcomed by Western states, noting the withdrawal of complaints of the five states on the allegations of torture.[24] On the other hand, the existing violations of human rights in practice were considered a chronic problem of Turkey regarding the discussion created at both international and domestic levels, as noted in the general statement of reasons of the proposal for the establishment of Ministry for Human Rights. It was also asserted that the Turkish ratification of the international conventions and the dimension of the concept of human rights in the new Europe, in which Turkey wanted to take part, have led to an increase in the importance given to human rights.[25]

The second and largest group of references to the ECHR were made in the justifications for the restrictions introduced, especially in the drafting process of the 1961 and the 1982 Constitutions and the 1971 Amendments. For example, para. 3 of Article 22 of the 1961 Constitution on the restriction of the freedom of press had been stated to be in conformity with the restrictions laid down in Article 10 of the ECHR. In fact, only few of the restrictions embodied in Article 10 of the ECHR were provided in Article 22 of the Constitution.[26] However, the 1971 Amendments added some other reasons for restriction of the freedom of press, which are also found in Article 10 of the ECHR. It was explained by one MP that the remaining reasons for restriction

[23] *TBMM Tutanak Dergisi* (hereinafter cited as TBMM TD), vol. 28, 1993, 48.

[24] *TBMM TD*, vol. 3 1988, 151 (on the occasion of approval of the European Convention on Torture).

[25] *TBMM TD*, vol. 28, S.Sayısı 139, 1993.

[26] For the text and the general statement of reasons of the 1961 and the 1982 Constitutions see Müjdat Şakar (ed), *1982 Anayasası ve Önceki Anayasalar* Beta Pub., İstanbul 1990; Kazım Öztürk, *op. cit.*

were inserted within the Constitution in the light of the increasing needs of the society, and the experiences and the practices since 1961.[27]

Article 57 of the 1961 Constitution, which regulated the reasons for banning political parties on the ground of being against the state and democratic order, is another example of this group of references. The definite compatibility of this Article with the ECHR was claimed because of the fact that 'the freedom to destroy freedoms' was also not guaranteed in the Convention. In fact, Article 17 has been one of the most referred to provisions of the ECHR. In the debates on the proposal for the removal of the legislative immunity of one MP, Article 17 was interpreted as imposing a ban on the Communist Party with reference to the decision of the European Commission on Human Rights on the German Communist Party.[28]

The 1971 amendments, on the other hand, instituted more restrictions on human rights and freedoms. For example, the detention period of up to fifteen days with respect to offences falling under the jurisdiction of the Martial Courts and the State Security Courts was inserted by Article 30. It was claimed that this provision was consistent with Article 5 of the ECHR.[29]

The debates on the draft proposal of the 1982 Constitution again saw references made to the reasons for restriction. In the general statement of reasons of all rights and freedoms, the ECHR was presented as one of the main sources of the Constitution. Therefore, no specific reference was made for each provision. In the parliamentary debates, para. 7 of Article 33 of the 1982 Constitution on the possibility of the restriction of freedom of association with regard to the police force, armed forces, and administration of the state (parallel to the last para. of Article 11 of the ECHR) led to discussions between the members of the Consultative Assembly and its Constitutional Commission. Some were of the opinion that the Constitutional Commission had misinterpreted the concept of 'administration of the state' which was wrongly extended to include public servants. On the other hand, having claimed the similarity between Article 33 of the Constitution and Article 11 of the ECHR, the Chairman of the Constitutional Commission argued that although he was in favour of prohibition of this right for public servants, no prohibition was imposed, but the issue was left to the discretion of the legislative body.[30] Lastly, it is also interesting to note that the word 'vagrancy' in Article 19 of the 1982 Constitution was taken from the Convention.[31]

[27] *Millet Meclisi Tutanak Dergisi* (hereinafter cited as MM TD), vol. 17, 1971, 327.

[28] *MM TD*, vol. 21, 1967, 441. For other similar approaches see, *MM TD*, vol. 17, 1971, 280, 288; *MM TD* vol. 17, S.Sayısı 419, 1971; *MM TD*, vol. 13, 1971, *Danışma Meclisi Tutanak Dergisi* (hereinafter cited as DM TD), vol. 15, 528, *MM TD*, vol. 33, 1973, 175.

[29] *MM TD*, vol. 33, 1973, 620.

[30] *DM TD* vol. 8, 1982, 284, 322–366.

[31] Ibid., 222.

The third group of references made to the ECHR were intended to achieve support for the proposals. For example, Article 31 of the 1961 Constitution on the freedom to claim rights was said to be equivalent to Article 6 of the ECHR.[32] Moreover, having discussed whether the right to property was an individual, social, and economic right, one member of the Consultative Assembly asserted that economic and social rights are not enumerated in the ECHR, but the formulation of the right to property in the Protocol No. 1 unambiguously underlined its individual character.[33]

The last group of references to the ECHR may be considered as the most remarkable, since the proposals were intended to provide conformity with the Convention. With regard to this group of references, the provisions of the ECHR and the case-law of its supervisory bodies have been taken into consideration as guidelines. In this context, the first example is Article 30 on the security of personal liberty. It was submitted that the institution of apprehension and detention had been abused in numerous instances. Therefore, the grounds of apprehension and detention were adopted from Article 5(c) of the ECHR.[34] It was claimed that the requirement of bringing the detained or apprehended person before a judge within 24 hours was also taken from the ECHR (although the ECHR does not refer to any specific time limit, but just mentions the words 'prompt' and 'reasonable'). The same member of the National Assembly was of the opinion that since Turkey ratified the Convention, its rules had to be applied regardless of whether they were embodied in the Constitution or not and it had to be applied as the Constitution in the hierarchy of legal norms.[35] As an example of this group of references, it may be noted that 'the necessity of a democratic society' incorporated in Article 13 of the 1982 Constitution were also adopted from the ECHR. It was asserted that this concept has been well established in the international human rights agreements and in the case-law of the European Court of Human Rights since 1954.[36] In addition, the types of state of emergency due to natural disasters and serious economic crisis regulated in Article 119 of the 1982 Constitution were claimed to be incompatible with the criterion of threatening the life of the nation in Article 15 of the ECHR.[37] Another example may be given from the debates on the Law on Associations No. 2908. It was argued that

[32] Temsilciler Meclisi Tutanak Dergisi [hereinafter cited as TM TD] vol. 3, 1961, 246.
[33] Ibid., 252. [34] Ibid., 233–235. [35] Ibid., 244.
[36] *DM TD*, vol. 8, 1982, 131, 154. In fact, this criteria was not welcomed by many authors since the previously accepted criteria of essence of rights and freedoms had also been well established in the case-law of the Turkish Constitutional Court, and was difficult to restrict rights and freedoms in consideration. Also there was some doubt on whether the democratic society was the society of West or the society that was accepted in the Constitution of 1982. The speakers of the Constitutional Commission made two different statements which completely contradicted with each other. See 149, 154.
[37] Ibid., 181.

deprivation of rights and freedoms due to an abstract danger could not be justified in a democratic society, with reference to the *De Becker* case.[38]

After the adoption of the 1982 Constitution, many references to the ECHR were also made. For example, with respect to the draft amendment on Article 22 of the Passport Law No. 5682, the TGNA Commission on Human Rights was of the opinion that authorization of the administration without clarifying the reasons of restriction may lead to abuse of power, therefore the restrictions must be concrete as in the ECHR.[39] In addition, when Law No. 3842[40] was prepared, the ECHR was seriously taken into account and the case-law of the European Commission and Court were referred to with regard to the detention periods.[41] Article 23 of the Act on Martial Law No. 1402 is another example which was abolished in 1993. The main reason for the abolition, as stated in the general statement of reasons,[42] was to provide compliance with the 1982 Constitution and the ECHR, which will be explained in the context of remedies. Similarly, the abolition of Article 2 of the Act on Martial Law, which gave competence to the martial law commanders to dismiss public servants, was also claimed to provide conformity with the international instruments. The report of the TGNA Commission on Human Rights[43] directly examined the compatibility of Article 2 of the Act on Martial Law with the ECHR. First of all, the unavailability of any appeal against decisions of the commanders were found inconsistent with, *inter alia*, Article 6 of the ECHR. The Commission then considered Article 15 of the ECHR, and stated that protective measures in Article 15 had not been incorporated in Article 2 of the Act on Martial Law.

Furthermore, a government proposal dated 30 October 1994 to amend provisions of Law No. 3713 on Combating Terrorism deserves to be noted in the context of this group of references. This Law has been criticized on several grounds, as will be briefly mentioned in the section below on remedies. In the general statement of reasons of the proposal, the decisions of the European Court of Human Rights on the protective measures to be taken into account for the restrictions of rights and freedoms and the principles for public emergency as laid down in the *Greek* case (1969) were considered in detail. It was admitted that the domestic laws on the freedom of thought and expression were clearly not compatible with the international standards. Therefore, the

[38] *DM TD*, vol. 20, 1983, 263.

[39] *TBMM TD*, vol. 35, 1993, 367. In fact, an amendment on Article 22 of the Passport Law was drafted, but the TGNA Commission on Plan and Budget objected it for procedural reasons. See, *TBMM TD*, vol. 68, S.Sayısı 693, 1994.

[40] *TBMM TD*, vol. 11, S.Sayısı 83, 1992.

[41] Ibid.

[42] *TBMM TD*, vol. 50, S.Sayısı 179, 1993. See *RG* No. 21804 of 30 December 1993.

[43] Report of 15 May 191 (session 18/1).

purpose of the draft was said to be to produce compliance, particularly with the ECHR and its standards as set down by the Court and the Commission.

It is also interesting to note the ratification policy of Turkey with regard to the ECHR and its Protocols. In the reports of the related TGNA Commissions, conformity between the international human rights instruments in issue and the Turkish law has mostly been claimed, as could be seen in the process of their ratifications.[44] This policy, in fact, is consistent with the traditional ratification policy of Turkey in which instruments have been ratified provided that they were considered to be compatible with domestic laws so that Turkey was not obliged to modify its domestic law according to the human rights standards.[45] As rightly emphasized by one MP on the occasion of the approval of ratification of the Protocol No. 8 by the Parliament, the difficulty is not to ratify conventions, but to protect in practice innocent persons facing charges.[46]

On references to the ECHR, some points on the 1961 and the 1982 Constitutions should be noted. The ECHR is not one of the main sources of the 1961 Constitution. However, references to the Universal Declaration of Human Rights (UDHR) are numerous. The reason may be found in the character of the Constitution which emphasized the general concept of human rights, including social, economic, and cultural rights, but did not concentrate on conformity with the ECHR. The 1982 Constitution was largely based on the ECHR, as noted above. In addition, the similarity between many provisions, such as Articles 14, 15, 17, 19, and 38 of the Constitution and respectively Articles 17, 15, 3, 5, and 7 of the ECHR might be cited. The Constitutional Commission of the Consultative Assembly also claimed that everything concerning rights and freedoms embodied in the Constitution was adopted from the ECHR.[47] The extensive adoption of the ECHR by the 1982 Constitution was interpreted as meaning that the 1982 Constitution was prepared under the shadow of the Council of Europe in order to prevent foreseeable counteractions by the Council against military intervention.[48]

The 'successful' adoption of the Convention was, however, only in appearance, not in substance. This might be easily noticed in Article 13 which articulates the reasons for the general restriction in excessive manner on all rights and freedoms laid down in the 1982 Constitution. This article of the Constitution clearly contradicts the ECHR because no such provision can be

[44] *TBMM TD*, vol. 29/2, S.Sayısı 195, 1954; *MM TD*, vol. 18, S.Sayısı 301–302, 1967; *TBMM TD*, vol. 54, S.Sayısı 374, 1994; *TBMM TD*, vol. 25, S.Sayısı 128, 1989.

[45] Mesut Gülmez, 'Türkiye'nin İnsan Hakları Belgelerini Onaylama Politikası' 13 *İnsan Hakları Yıllığı*, TODAİE, 1991, 103–127.

[46] *TBMM TD*, vol. 25, 1989, 65.

[47] *DM TD*, vol. 8, 1982, 336.

[48] Mümtaz Soysal, 'İnsan Haklar, Açısından Temel Hak ve Özgürlüklerin Niteliği' 3 *Anayasa Yargısı*, Ankara, 1987, 42.

found in the Convention. Also, it is observed that generally the first paragraphs of the provisions on rights and freedoms in the 1982 Constitution recognize the principles, as in the ECHR, but the following paragraphs embody additional restrictions or prohibitions than the provisions of the ECHR.

On the other hand, especially having recognized the individual application in 1987, and the increase in the number of applications to the Commission in recent years, the attention of MPs and the cabinet has been attached to the Convention. In the last few years, the frequent references to the Convention can easily be observed not only in the speeches delivered, but also in the proposals. However, despite the increasing number of references to the ECHR, it is doubtful whether these may be regarded as a reflection of purely human rights considerations.

D. LEADING HUMAN RIGHTS CASES DECIDED BY THE NATIONAL COURTS

The ECHR did not draw much attention from the national courts following ratification. Until recent years Turkish courts have referred to the ECHR in only a few decisions. In the '90s, it was observed that Turkish courts have attached increasing importance to the international human rights instruments, including the ECHR. In recent decisions of the national courts, it appears that the ECHR has begun to be noticed more and more, in comparison to the early decisions. In this section some examples noteworthy from the decisions of the Constitutional Court, the Council of State (*Danıştay*), and some administrative courts are considered.

As to the status of the ECHR in domestic law, one of the previous decisions of the Constitutional Court may be interpreted as meaning that the Court, in the light of the provisions of the 1961 Constitution mentioned above, recognized the Convention as having equal status with ordinary domestic laws. In that case, the Turkish Workers' Party claimed that the ECHR nullified Articles 141(1) and 142(1) of the Turkish Penal (dated 1926), in accordance with the principle of *lex posterior*. The Constitutional Court gave no clear statement on the status of the Convention in its examination of the merits and decided that there was no contradiction between the related provisions of the Turkish Penal Code and particularly Articles 10 and 17 of the Convention.[49] The fact that the Court did not discuss the validity of the principle of *lex pos-*

[49] 26.9.1965, E.1963/173, K.1965/40 (4 *Anayasa Mahkemesi Kararlar Dergisi* [hereinafter cited as AKMD] 1967, 239ff, esp 268).

terior in terms of the Convention might be considered as an implicit acceptance of it having the status of ordinary laws.

On the other hand, the Constitutional Court has recognized the Convention as having constitutional status in its later decisions. The Court regarded the ECHR in the constitutional review: however, it generally referred to the Convention in a context which served to strengthen the meaning of the constitutional provisions, and to confirm the content of them.[50] It has generally emphasized the conformity between the constitutional provisions and the ECHR, and concluded that a domestic provision which was contrary to the Constitution was also contrary to the Convention.[51] In this context, the Court has clearly stated that the rights and freedoms set forth by the Convention were also guaranteed by the Constitution.[52] Consequently, as can be seen from these explanations, although the rule under examination was declared unconstitutional with reference to the ECHR, the Court in fact applied a domestic (constitutional) rule.

Some decisions of the Constitutional Court may be considered as direct application of the ECHR. For instance, with respect to Article 91 of the Military Penal Code, it considered whether the UDHR and the ECHR as well as the Constitution have a special provision concerning the issue. The Court consequently decided that the Article was compatible with the Constitution on the ground of the absence of a clear provision in the Constitution as well as in the UDHR and the ECHR which conflicts with that Article.[53] It may be stated that if the ECHR and/or the UDHR had had a special provision, the Court would have applied it in its examination of constitutionality.

The Constitutional Court has also referred to the Convention in the interpretation of constitutional provisions. For example, the Court referred to the second paragraph of Article 6 of the Convention in the interpretation of the concept of presumed innocence.[54] Furthermore, the Court has recently begun to take into account the case-law of the European Court of Human Rights. In a decision related to the right to defence, it referred to the cases of *Golder, Silver, Campbell, and Fell v United Kingdom* and *Can v Austria*.[55]

[50] Tekin Akıllıoğlu, *op. cit.*, 170–171.

[51] For example, 10.1.1991, E.1990/25, K.1991/1 (*RG* Nol. 21162 of 5 March 192); 3.7.1991, E.1991/6, K.1991/20 (*RG* No. 21165 of 8 March 1992); 19.12.1989, E.1989/14, K.1989/49 (*RG* No. 204492 March 1990).

[52] For example, 10.7.1992, E.1991/2, K.1992/1 (*RG* No. 21386 of 25 October 1992); 30.11.1993, E.1993/2, K.1993/3 (*RG* No. 22016 of 9 August 1994); 16.6.1994, E.1993/3, K.194/2 (*RG* No. 21976 of 30 June 1994).

[53] 24.5.1977, E.1977/19, K.1977/82 (15 *AMKD*, 1978, 388).

[54] 29.1.1980, E.1979/38, K.1980/11 (18*AMKD*, 1981, 97–98). Also, see 16.6.1992, E.1992/8, K.1992/39 (*RG* 16.6.1992, E.1992/8, K.1992/39 (*RG* No. 21367 of 6 October 1992).

[55] 16.6.1992, E.1992/8, K.1992/39 (*RG* No. 21367 of 6 October 1992).

The Constitutional Court has increasingly also taken other international human rights instruments into consideration in addition to the ECHR. In this sense, as the Court annulled an expression in Article 292 of the Turkish Civil Code which prohibited the recognition of a child born through the adultery of a married man, it concluded that the related provision was contrary to the ECHR as well as the UDHR, the European Social Charter, the Declaration on the Rights of the Child, and the Convention on the Rights of the Child.[56] Concerning the ECHR, the Court added that the Republic of Turkey had undertaken obligations upon ratification. In another decision, it clearly explained the content of the obligation, by noting that the responsibility of the state arising from international agreements to which it is a party is to ensure the conformity of domestic law with international agreements.[57] In that decision, the Court annulled Article 159 of the Turkish Civil Code which provided that a wife could only work with the permission of her husband, and concluded that the provision was contrary to the principle of equality before the law under the Constitution, referring to the UDHR, the ECHR, Protocol No. 7 of the ECHR, the Convention on the Elimination of All Forms of Discrimination Against Women, the European Social Charter, and documents of the CSCE.

The Constitutional Court has been greatly affected by the increasing importance of international human rights law. It was of the opinion that the concept of human rights is not only a domestic question, but it also has a universal content and meaning, therefore the UDHR and the ECHR cannot be ignored in the constitutionality review.[58] This comment might also be considered to reflect the moral effects of the UDHR and the ECHR on the Court. As a result, it regarded international agreements as having supra-constitutional status in a decision related to the rights of the child.[59] However, needless to say, the recognition of supra-constitutional status of international agreements requires the application of international agreements, even if they conflict with the Constitution. Nevertheless, there has not yet been a decision of the Court applying international agreements in such a case.

On the other hand, it is interesting to note that, in some decisions of the Constitutional Court, the purpose of referring to the ECHR as well as other international human rights instruments has been to justify restrictions imposed on freedoms.[60] For example, while the Court reviewed the constitu-

[56] 28.2.1991, E.1990/15, K.1991/5 (*RG* No. 21184 of 27 March 1992).

[57] 29.11.1990, E.1990/30, K.1990/31 (*RG* No. 21272 of 2 July 1992).

[58] 29.1.1990, E.1979/38, K.1980/11 (18 *AMKD*, 1981, 97). Also, see 16.6.1992, E. 1992/8, K. 1992/39 (*RG* No. 21367 of 6 October 1992).

[59] According to the statement of the Court: '[International] agreements, which we can call supra-constitutional norms, have also aimed to prevent all kinds of discrimination among children.' (See note 56 above).

[60] Rona Aybay, *op. cit.*, 23.

tionality of the death penalty, it referred to the ECHR, stating that the first paragraph of Article 2 of the Convention confirms the compatibility of the death penalty with human rights and freedoms.[61] The Court similarly held that Articles 141(1) and 142(2) of the Turkish Penal Code were in conformity with the Convention, which considered the possibility to restrict the freedom of thought and the right to form and join associations the same as the related provisions of the Turkish Penal Code. The Court added that since rights and freedoms cannot be abused in accordance with Article 17 of the Convention, the related provisions of the Turkish Penal Code cannot be considered as being contrary to the Convention.[62] Referring to the ECHR, the Court also found that the prohibition of the right to form and join trade unions for some public servants was not incompatible with the Constitution. According to the Court, Article 11 of the Convention provided a legal basis for the restriction.[63]

The Constitutional Court has referred to the ECHR in decisions concerning the dissolution of political parties. For example, when the Court decided for the dissolution of the Socialist Party, it made reference to the ECHR and documents of the CSCE, such as the Helsinki Final Act and the Charter of Paris. The Court decided that the Party aimed to destroy the integrity and indivisibility of the Turkish state with its nation and territory, since the Party supported the view of the right to self-determination of the Kurdish people and proposed a federal governmental system for the Turkish and the Kurdish people. It consequently held that the views of the Party were incompatible with the Constitution in accordance with, *inter alia*, Article 17 and the second paragraph of Article 11 of the ECHR.[64]

Similarly, the People's Labour Party,[65] the Party for Freedom and Democracy,[66] the Socialist Party of Turkey,[67] and the Party for Democracy[68] were dissolved by the Constitutional Court with references to the UDHR, the ECHR, and documents of the CSCE.[69] In its all decisions, the Court decided that these parties had acted against the principle of the integrity and indivisibility of the Turkish state with its nation and territory in the Constitution and in the Law on Political Parties No. 2820. The Court referred to the second paragraph of Article 11 and Article 17 of the ECHR, as well as to Articles 29

[61] 1.7.1963, E.1963/207, K.1963/175 (1 *AMKD*, 1971, 360).

[62] See note 49 above.

[63] 26–27.9.1967, E.1963/336, K.1967/29 (6 *AMKD*, 1975, 18).

[64] 10.7.1992, E.1991/2, K.1992/1 (*RG* No. 21386 of 25 October 1992).

[65] 14.7.1993, E.1992/1, K. 1993/1 (*RG* No. 21672 of 18 August 1993).

[66] 23.11.1993, E.1993/1, K.1993/2 (*RG* No. 21849 of 14 February 1994).

[67] 30.11.1993, E.1993/2, K.1993/3 (*RG* No. 22016 of 9 August 1994).

[68] 16.6.1994, E.1993/3, K.1994/2 (*RG* No. 21976 [*Mükerrer*] of 30 June 1994).

[69] The United Communist Party for Turkey was dissolved by the Constitutional Court with reference only to the Charter of Paris (16.7.1991, E.1990/1, K.1991/1, *RG* No. 21125 of 28 January 1992).

and 30 of the UDHR. Furthermore, it held that one MP from the People's Labour Party and 13 MPs from the Party for Democracy were to lose their seats upon the judgments.

The recent decisions of the Court on the dissolution of political parties on the ground of their opinion created serious doubts about the independence of judiciary in Turkey. The Court certainly played an important political role in these decisions.[70] It is noticeable that the application of the ECHR sometimes resulted in the restriction of freedom of thought. In this sense, the Court has referred mostly to Article 17 of the Convention. It is worth noting that Article 17 of the Convention had already been proposed by the Turkish representative in the process of preparatory work of the ECHR.[71]

In the context of leading human rights cases, the Council of State, as one of the supreme courts, also has an important role in the application of the ECHR. On the status of the ECHR, the Council of State pointed out the superior status of the Convention over domestic law and concluded that the Convention definitely bound the executive and judicial organs.[72] The Court, in recent decisions, has directly applied the provisions of the Convention. These decisions created crucial results with regard to the enjoyment of some fundamental rights and freedoms by public servants. For example, the Court referred to Article 11 of the ECHR as the legal basis of the right to form and join trade unions for public servants, although this right ha snot been clearly guaranteed by the Constitution for them.[73] Thus, in its case-law, the Court provided a legal foundation for public servants to form trade unions although they had encountered some impediments from executive authorities. In another important case, it interpreted Article 23 of the Act on Martial Law No. 1402 which provided that 'public servants who were dismissed from their jobs on the order of martial law commanders could no longer work in the public sector' as valid only during a period of martial law.[74] The Court, then, decided that a prohibition of working in the public sector for life is not compatible with Article 5 of the UDHR and Article 3 of

[70] E. Yasemin Özdek, 'The Turkish Constitutional Court and the International Human Rights Insturments', 14 *Turkish Yearbook of Human Rights*, 1992, 36.

[71] See Doc.CM/WP 1 (5O) 15, A 924, 16 March 1950, in: *Travaux Préparatoires*, vol. II, p. 488, cited in, Ömer Madra, *Avrupa İnsan Hakları Sözleşmesi ve Bireysel Başvuru Hakkı*, AÜSBF Pub., Ankara 1981, 221.

[72] 5th Chamber, 22.5.1991, E.1986/1723, K.1991/933. The Council of State also referred to the Document of the Vienna Meeting (1989) of the CSCE, under which States Parties undertook to ensure the compatibility of their domestic law with international instruments. In this context, it should be added that the Council of State directly applied the Helsinki Final Act in April 1978, which was the first example of such an implementation by a court (12th Chamber, E.1977/1349, K.1978/955; see Rona Aybay, 'Implementation of the Helsinki Final Act by a Turkish Court', XVIII *Turkish Yearbook of International Relations*, 1978, 76–79).

[73] 10th Chamber, 10.11.1992, E.1991/1262, K.1992/3911.

[74] İçt.Bir.K. 7.12.1989, E.1988/6, K.1989/4 (*RG* No. 20428 of 9 February 1990).

the ECHR. Hundreds of public servants dismissed from their jobs in the period of martial law could return to public service after the decision of the Court. In another case, the fact that a public servant dismissed from his job because he had sent a New Year card to his relatives expressing his political views, which was later published in newspapers, was found to be incompatible with the right to freedom of expression under the first paragraph of Article 10 of the ECHR.[75]

Some administrative courts have also referred to the ECHR. For example, the Administrative Court of Diyarbakır accepted the superior status of the ECHR over domestic law, expressing that the ECHR should prevail in a case of conflict between the ECHR and a domestic law.[76] In that decision, the Court stated that human rights norms have become the main feature characterizing the European public order, and that any State Party could not legislate contrary to the Convention, with reference to the case (dated 18 January 1978) of the European Court of Human Rights.

Other examples may be given from the decisions of the Administrative Court of Manisa. In one of these decisions, the Governor of Uşak claimed that a public servant could not be a member of an association under the Law on Associations No. 2908 and demanded the suspension of membership of a public servant from the Human Rights Association. On the application of the Association to the Court, it decided on a stay of execution, since the action was unlawful, with reference to Article 11 of the ECHR.[77] In another decision, the Administrative Court of Manisa, with reference to Article 11 of the ECHR, annulled the action of the Governor of Manisa who had rejected an application for the establishment of a branch of a trade union in Manisa for public servants employed in the education sector.[78]

E. CASES BROUGHT BEFORE THE EUROPEAN COMMISSION AND COURT OF HUMAN RIGHTS

1. *Inter-state applications under Article 24*

Article 24, which specifies the collective enforcement character of the ECHR,[79] provides that any state parties may lodge an application complaining of a violation of rights and freedoms embodied in the ECHR. Until the end of 1993 only 18 applications had been introduced, 8 of which were, however,

[75] 5th Chamber, 22.5.1991, E.1986/1723, K.1991/933.

[76] 12.10.1992, E.1991/565, K.1992/542.

[77] 20.5.1993, E.1993–182.

[78] 23.2.1994, E.1994/142, K.1994/128.

[79] Application 788.60, the *Pfunders* case: *Austria v Italy* (1961) IV Yearbook, 140.

lodged against Turkey. These applications may be considered in two groups; first, 3 of those were filed by Cyprus as a result of military action taken by Turkey in 1974, and the remaining applications were filed by 5 states with regard to the period of 1980–82, when military administration was in power.

The first two Cyprus cases[80] dealt with the violations of Articles 1–6, 8, 13, and 17 of the ECHR, Article 1 of Protocol No. 1, and Article 14 of the ECHR in conjunction with all the above articles. The Turkish government mainly objected to the procedural and political aspects of the applications, such as the *locus standi* of the applicant government, the Commission's competence *ratione loci*, and the applications' abusiveness.

On the first objection, the Commission referred to the United Nations documents in which the Cyprus government was recognized as a legal one and, on the second objection, to the responsibility of Turkey for the acts committed within its jurisdiction. However, Turkey did not participate in the merit examination. The Commission drafted its report[81] and transmitted it to the Committee of Ministers. In its resolution[82] the Committee of Ministers urged parties to carry on inter-communal talks under the auspices of the Secretary General of the United Nations in order to establish mutual confidence which was regarded as fundamental for the observance of human rights in Cyprus.

The third Cyprus case[83] was about continuing violations of the same Articles as put forward in the first two cases. Turkey did not participate in the merit examination again. In its report,[84] the Commission rejected the Turkish objections related to non-cooperation, by stressing the conclusive character of the admissible decisions, and the non-relevancy of the question on the recognition of the Greek Cypriot government. The non-cooperation was regarded as a failure of the obligation arising under Article 28 of the ECHR.

In its examination on merit, the Commission first dealt with the missing persons and the detention of some Greek Cypriots after the cessation of hostilities. It was of the opinion that there had been no justifiable reasons for those detentions and relatedly a deprivation of liberty. For these reasons, there had been a violation of Article 5. Of the displacement of persons, the Commission, referring to its first report, decided that the continuing violation of Article 8 constituted an exacerbating factor and as a result, a violation of Article 8 of the Convention and Article 1 of Protocol No. 1.

The Cyprus cases reflect highly intense political issues, such as the recognition of the government, and the status of the military action of Turkey under

[80] Applications 65780/74 and 6950/75 *Cyprus v Turkey* (1975) 2 DR 125–137.

[81] Report of 10 July 1976.

[82] DH (79) 1, 20 January 1979, (1979) 22 Yearbook 440.

[83] Application 8007/77 *Cyprus v Turkey*, (1979) 13 DR 85–156.

[84] Report of 4 October 1983, in 13 *Human Rights Law Journal* (*HRLJ*) 4 1992, 154–174; Resolution DH (92) 12, 2 April 1992, 13 *HRLJ* 4, 1992, 181.

international law. There has been no remedial action taken for the findings of the Commission to date and it seems that allegations on the violations of human rights with regard to Cyprus will be on the agenda, taking into account the recognition of individual applications by Turkey in 1987. However, it might be easily assumed that the solution would be political, but not a juridicial one. These cases were lodged by Cyprus as being related to the violations committed against its citizens. They also exemplify the ineffectiveness of inter-state applications and 'clearly show the limits of the international protection of human rights'.[85]

The second group of inter-state applications[86] against Turkey were lodged by five states with respect to violations of Articles 3, 5, 6, 9, 10, 11, and 15 of the ECHR between 12 September 1980 when the military administration took over the government and 1 July 1982. The applicant states complained of torture; impossibility of appeal to the Constitutional Court against the decision taken by the National Security Council; extensive application of Articles 140, 141, 142, and 146 of the Turkish Penal Code by the Martial Courts; excessive length of detention of up to 45 days without judicial control; suspension of all political and trade union activities and dissolution of political parties, and the apprehension of their leaders; the implementation of the rules of states of emergency which was not consistent with Article 15 of the Convention compared to the situation as of 1 July 1982.

The application of the five states resulted in a friendly settlement[87] in 1985. The main stress in the settlement was given to Articles 3 and 15 and the issue of amnesty. Turkey agreed to take measures on the following points: effective implementation of Article 3 and submission of the reports to the Commission on this matter; gradual repeal of the implementation of martial law in the remaining areas (the statement on this issue made by the Prime Minister was quoted) and abolition or amendment of a number of decrees, acts, etc. related to the state of emergency, and lastly a promise given on the issue of amnesty. Having considered these measures, the Commission decided to discontinue with the satisfaction of '[t]he measures taken by Turkey with a view to re-establishing an effective democracy and secure compliance with the rights and freedoms defined in the Convention'.[88]

This friendly settlement has been criticized on several grounds. As was correctly pointed out, the complaints about the violations of Articles 5, 6, 9, 10, 11, and 15 were completely disregarded and further, no specific instance of the

[85] Manfred Nowak, 'The European Convention on Human Rights and its Control System', 7 *Netherlands Quarterly of Human Rights* (NQHR) 3, 1989, p. 99.

[86] Applications 9940–9944/82, *France, Norway, Denmark, Sweden and the Netherlands v Turkey* (1984) 35 DR 143–170.

[87] (1985) 36 Yearbook, 149–161.

[88] Ibid., 157.

violation of Article 3 was given with regard to the practices of torture and degrading and inhuman treatment.[89] On the other hand, the final report of the Commission[90] gave more explanations on the issues in consideration and the measures taken, but not on the violations. Having mentioned the relating legislative framework and the compliance of those with Article 3 of the Convention, the Commission noted the number of people who were prosecuted under the offences of torture or ill-treatment, and were sentenced to several years' imprisonment. On the other hand, no evidence was found on the extention of police custody over 24 hours, but deficiencies in the protecting measures existed in practice, such deficiencies as access to a lawyer, improper application of the medical examination at the beginning and end of the police custody; the release of over 30,000 prisoners out of over 44,000 were also cited. The measures taken seemed to be welcomed by the Commission. It is very clear that the Commission did not deal with the violations in general, the process of re-establishment of democracy was, however, taken into account, regrettably raising no question on the military regime, which was claimed in Turkey to be a 'clear recognition of the military regime by the European organs'.[91] As a result, the effect of this inter-state application on the Turkish legal system has been too limited.

2. *Turkish declaration under Article 25*

The competence of the Commission under Article 25 was only recognized 33 years after Turkey's ratification of the ECHR, in January 1987.[92] The Declaration was, however, introduced together with the six conditions, as having been the first example of its kind. These conditions read as follows:

> (i) The recognition of the right of petition extends only to allegations concerning acts or omissions of public authorities in Turkey performed within the boundaries of the territory to which the Constitution of the Republic of Turkey is applicable;
>
> (ii) The circumstances and conditions under which Turkey, by virtue of Article 15 of the Convention, derogates from her obligations under the Convention in special circumstances must be interpreted, for the purposes of the competence attributed to the Commission under this Declaration, in the light of Articles 119 to 122 of the Turkish Constitution;

[89] Leo Zwaak, 'A Friendly Settlement in the European Inter-State Complaints Against Turkey: Summary and commentary', 13 SIM Newsletter 1986, 46–48.

[90] In 11 EHRR 42, 1989, 167–174.

[91] Mehmet Semih Gemalmaz, *The Institutionalization Process of the Turkish Type of Democracy: A Politico-Juridical Analysis of Human Rights*, Amaç Pub., İstanbul 1989, 29. In addition, it was regarded by the author as a political victory and the legitimation of the military regime.

[92] See notes 3 and 4 above.

(iii) The competence attributed to the Commission under this Declaration shall not comprise matters regarding the legal status of military personnel, and in particular the system of discipline in the armed forces;

(iv) For the purpose of the competence attributed to the Commission under this Declaration, the notion of 'a democratic society' in paragraph 2 of Articles 8, 9, 10, and 11 of the Convention must be understood in conformity with the principles laid down in the Turkish Constitution and in particular its Preamble and its Article 13;

(v) For the purpose of the competence attributed to the Commission under the present Declaration, Articles 33, 52 and 135 of the Constitution must be understood as being in conformity with Articles 10 and 11 of the Convention.

These conditions and the provisions of the 1982 Constitution cited in the Declaration seem to suggest the most problematic areas within the framework of the Constitution or in international sphere, such as Cyprus. With regard to the latter, therefore, the purpose of the condition restricting the Commission's competence *ratione loci* entirely within the boundaries of Turkey was to prevent applications from being filed by Cyprus.[93]

The conditions restricting the Commission's competence *ratione materae* put forward in paragraphs (ii), (iv), and (v) may be regarded as underlining the non-compliance of the mentioned Articles of the Constitution with the ECHR.

Articles 119 to 122 of the 1982 Constitution mentioned in para. (ii) of the Declaration refer to the circumstances which justify the derogation, such as natural disaster or serious economic crisis (Article 119), widespread acts of violence and serious deterioration of public order (Article 120), states of emergency (Article 121), and the application of martial law, state of war, and mobilization (Article 122). These circumstances and their detailed context indicate that every possibility for derogation has been carefully spelt out. However, it would be for the Commission to assess whether all these circumstances might be regarded as threats to the 'life of the nation' under Article 15 of the ECHR.

Paragraph (iv) of the Declaration referred to the notion of a democratic society as being understood in conformity with the Preamble and Article 13 of the Constitution, which was also briefly mentioned above. The Preamble of the Constitution had such an authoritarian character in which the Turkish state was referred to as 'sacred' and this implied the priority of the state, and then the society, over individuals, and also explicitly restricted the concept of democracy to the provisions of the 1982 Constitution.

[93] I. Cameron, 'Turkey and Article 25 of the European Convention on Human Rights', 37 *International and Comparative Law Quarterly* (*ICLQ*) 1988, 121; C. Tomuschat, 'Turkey's Declaration Under Article 25 of the European Convention on Human Rights', in Nowak *et al.* (eds) *Progress in the Spirit of Human Rights*, Engel Pub., Kehl 1988, 890.

Lastly, the references in paragraph (v) of the Declaration to Articles 33 (freedom of association), 52 (activities of trade unions), and 135 (public professional organizations) of the 1982 Constitution also underline other problematic areas. The common feature of these Articles and the rights and freedoms therein are subjected to same prohibitions, such as the prohibition of pursuing political aims, engaging in political activities, and receiving support from or giving support to political parties in order to take joint actions with each other.

The last paragraph of the Declaration was on the restriction of the Commission's competence *ratione temporis*. Its formulation sought to exclude, not only the retrospective effect which is permissible, but also the judgments delivered after the Declaration but based on facts which occurred before the date of deposit, which was not allowed under Article 25 of the ECHR either.

The standing of these conditions was interpreted differently. All authors, however, agreed that neither Article 64 nor Article 25 of the ECHR allowed a state to make any reservation except on ratification. Some,[94] including the Turkish government, were of the opinion that the conditions laid down in the Declaration should not be assumed to be reservations, but were a matter for interpretation. Others contested these arguments, defining the content of conditions as reservations in comparison to the formulation of Article 2 of the Vienna Conventions on the Law of Treaties.[95] From the latter view, the Declaration was null and void since the intention of Turkey was to be bound by the Declaration together with the conditions.[96]

The Commission had an opportunity to settle all these disputes.[97] First, the territorial limitation in para. (i) was considered. The Commission, recalling its previous decision on Article 1, stated that states parties were responsible for acts under their jurisdiction, and therefore the Northern part of Cyprus came under the jurisdiction of Turkey. Turkey renewed its Declaration in 1990 and 1992, but the limitation *ratione loci* has not been removed. It is very

[94] Şeref Gözübüyük, *op. cit.*, 24–25; Ayşe Füsun Arsava, 'Türkiye Tarafından Yapılan Bireysel Başvuruyu Kabule İlişkin Bildirinin Avrupa İnsan Hakları Sözleşmesi Işığında Değerlendirilmesi' 13 *Mali Hukuk*, 1988, 9. Both authors regarded para. (iii) of the Declaration as a reservation.

[95] Edip Çelik, 'Bireysel Başvuru ve Çekinceler' daily *Cumhuriyet*, 4 May 1987; 'Avrupa İnsan Hakları Komisyonu'na Bireysel Başvuru Hakkı ve Türkiye' *Bahri Savcı'ya Armağan*, Mülkiyeliler Vakfı Pub., Ankara 1988, 228; Münci Kapani, *İnsan Haklarının Uluslararası Boyutları* 2. ed. Bilgi Pub., Ankara 1991, 58.

[96] Edip Çelik, 'Avrupa İnsan Hakları Komisyonu'na . . .', 230; C. Tomuschat, *op. cit.*, 132.

[97] Applicatioin 15299–15300/89 *Chrysostomos et al. v Turkey*.

clear that Turkey will take no notice of any issue relating to the Cyprus problem before the Commission[98] until it is politically settled.

On the validity of the 1987 Declaration, the Commission interpreted the intention of Turkey as having been sincerely bound by the requirements of Article 25, therefore it was valid only with temporal limitation.

3. *Individual applications against Turkey*

It is true, in the case of Turkey, that the ECHR was not regarded as very effective until the recognition of the Commission's competence under Article 25. Obviously, individual applications generally underline the violations and therefore draw attention to human rights issues. As a result of the recognition of the right of individual application in 1987, the effects of the ECHR on the Turkish Parliament, government, and public opinion are becoming more significant day by day.

As at the end of 1993,[99] a total of 473 applications were registered against Turkey; 122 of these were declared inadmissible or struck off; 22 applications were admitted; 3 applications resulted in friendly settlements,[100] the Commission had drafted 6 reports on merit,[101] and only one case had been referred to the European Court on Human Rights by the applicant government.[102]

The contents of the admissible decisions concentrate mostly upon violations of Articles 3, 5, 6, and 9. The applicants have generally complained of torture and ill-treatment, the length and legality of detention, impartiality and independence of the courts, excessive length of criminal proceedings, inadequate facilities for the preparation of a defence, restrictions on freedom of expression, and freedom of association.

[98] See, The Resolution of the Committee of Ministers urging Turkey to co-operate with the Commission in the proceeding of *Chrysostomos* case, DH (91)41 of 19 December 1993, 13 *HRLJ* 4 1992, 180. The territorial limitation was also cited in the recognition of the competence of the Court dated 22 January 1990.

[99] *Survey of Activities and Statistics of European Commission on Human Rights*: 1988–1993.

[100] Application 14116–7/88 *Yağcı and Sargın v Turkey*. Report of 17 January 1991, settlement was reached during the examination of the case by the Committee of Ministers on 15 September 1993. The Turkish Government agreed to pay 1,316,700 Turkish liras. See Resolution DH (93) 59 of 14 December 1993, 6 *Human Rights Case Digest*, 1993, 280–282; Application 15202–5/89 *Gürdoğan et al. v Turkey*, Report of 20 January 1994. The government agreed to pay 300,000 FF; Application 16311–3/90 *Hazar et al. v Turkey*, Report of 10 December 1992. The government agreed to pay 115,000 FF.

[101] Application 16419–16429/90 *Sargın and Yağcı v Turkey*, Report of 30 November 1993; Application 17128/90, *Erdagöz v Turkey*, Report of 8 April 1993; Application 15318/89 *Loizidou v Turkey*, Report of 8 July 1993 (no violation); Application 15299–15300/89 *Chrysostomos and Papachrysostomou v Turkey* (information taken from the Council of Europe, Information Sheet no. 32, 1994, 66) and in 1994 also Application 16026/90 *Mansur v Turkey*, Report of 28 February 1994.

[102] Application 15318/89 *Loizidou v Turkey*, referred by Cyprus.

The Commission has examined the merits of some of these cases. For example, in the cases of *Mansur*[103] and *Sargın-Yağcı*,[104] the excessive length of detention and criminal proceedings were in consideration, which lasted between 2 and 4 years. With regard to the former case, the Commission stated that unreasonable difficulties such as improper mutual assistance between Turkey and Greece and translation problems of some documents into Turkish did not justify this length of detention. In the latter case, the arguments on the state of evidence, content of the file, the danger of absconding, and the existence of an attack on the authority of the government, as claimed by the State Security Court against the applicant's release on remand were also found groundless. In addition, the conduct of the State Security Court related to delays of approximately 20 to 30 days between each hearing was regarded as a violation of para. 1 of Article 6 of the ECHR. Another complaint before the Commission was of torture.[105] The ill-treatment of the applicant in the police custody and the existence of a medical report describing the injuries on his body were found to constitute torture.

F. REMEDIAL ACTION TAKEN BY THE GOVERNMENT IN RESPONSE TO BEING HELD IN VIOLATION OF THE CONVENTION

Although the Turkish government has become more aware of problems arising from violations of the ECHR, not many remedies have been provided for such instances. In this section the direct remedies for violations of the Convention, and then some improvements in this respect are summarized.

One remarkable remedy is the Law on Amending Certain Provisions of the Code of Criminal Procedure (CMUK) and the State Security Courts No. 3842[106] which introduced some protective measures against abuse of power. This amendment was directly based upon the principles embodied in the Convention and in the CSCE Document of the Moscow Meeting on Human Dimension, as referred to in the general statement of reasons.[107] Some of these principles are as follows: no one shall be deprived of his/her liberty without a reason prescribed by law and procedure; the reasons for apprehension and the rights of the person apprehended shall be told promptly to him/her and their relatives; apprehended and detained persons shall be brought

[103] Application 16026/90 *Mansur v Turkey*, Report of 28 February 1994.
[104] Application 16419–16429/90 *Yağcı and Sargın v Turkey*, Report of 30 November 1993.
[105] Application 17128/90 *Erdagöz v Turkey*, Report of 8 April 1994.
[106] *RG* No. 21422 of 1 December 1992.
[107] *TBMM TD*, vol. 11, S.Sayısı 83, 1992.

promptly before a judge; in the case of unlawful arrest or detention he/she shall be released immediately; apprehended or detained persons are entitled to appeal to a judge for his/her release; persons are entitled to have legal assistance and free assistance if required, and to have easy access to a lawyer; and the adoption of some measures for the prevention of unlawful testimony. All those principles have been incorporated in detail within the framework of the CMUK. In addition, it shortened maximum detention periods.

The abolition of Article 23 of the Act on Martial Law No. 1402[108] is another effective remedy. Upon the subsequent removal of martial law, Article 23 recognized the competence of the martial courts to continue their jurisdiction with regard to pending trial until the final judgment is reached. There have always been disputes about the legality and impartiality of these courts due to their composition, competence, and jurisdiction, as was put forward in the case of *Mitap and Müftüoğlu.*[109] The clear connection between Article 23 and the complaints against Turkey raised before the European Commission was pointed up in the general statement of reasons.[110] Since the martial courts having such competence were not regarded as legally qualified courts guaranteeing an impartial judge, the main purpose of this abolition was to achieve compliance with Article 6 of the ECHR.

Furthermore, Articles 141, 142 (crimes of opinion), and 163 (crime of antisecular activities) of the Turkish Penal Code were abrogated by para. 1(e) of Article 23 of the Law on Combating Terrorism No. 3713.[111] Approximately 70,000 people were charged for having violated these Articles[112] and some applications instituted against Turkey before the Commission were about these Articles.[113] On the other hand, Article 8 of the same Law is generally regarded as a different formulation of Articles 141 and 142 and envisages crimes of opinion. The present Turkish government has, in fact, drafted a proposal (dated 30 October 1994) for the amendment of some provisions of this Law, including Article 8.

The Law on Combating Terrorism also abolished the Law on Publications in Other Than the Turkish Language, which prohibited publishing in

[108] *RG* No. 21804 of 30 December 1993. In fact, the Constitutional Court declared the unconstitutionality of the Martial Courts, see 15–16.2.1972, E.1971/31, K.1972/5 (10 *AMKD*, 1972, 188–9). However, it was adopted as a constitutional rule in the Provisional Article 21 of the 1961 Constitution. The 1982 Constitution did not contain such a provision but an amendment to Article 23 by Law No. 2301 of 19 September 1980 passed at the beginning of the military regime put the abolished provision into force.

[109] Application 15530–1/89 *Mitap and Müftüoğlu v Turkey* (declared admissible).

[110] *TBMM TD*, vol. 50, S.sayısı 179, 1993.

[111] *RG* No. 20843 (mükerrer) of 12 April 1991.

[112] Bülent Tanör, *Türkiye'nin İnsan Hakları Sorunu* BDS Pub., Istanbul 1990, 111.

[113] Applications 16311–3/90 *Hazar et al. v Turkey*; 15530–1 *Mitap and Müftüoğlu v Turkey* and 14116–7/88 *Yağcı and Sargın v Turkey*.

Kurdish. In addition, the same Law enabled the conditional release of prisoners, provided in provisional Article 1. On the other hand, provisional Article 4 excluded persons who were charged with Articles 125, 146 (except last para.), 403, 404(1), 405, 406, 407, 414, 416 (last para.), and 418 of the Turkish Penal Code being released under provisional Article 1 of the Law. The Constitutional Court declared the unconstitutionality of the provisional Article 4 as being contrary to the principle of equality before the law. However, only Article 125 of the Turkish Penal Code, which deals with offences against the indivisible integrity of the state, has been found justifiable under the principles of equality.[114] It is interesting that the decision of the Constitutional Court confirmed the discrimination against prisoners sentenced under Article 125 of the Turkish Penal Code.

The amendment of Article 2 of the Act on Martial Law No. 1402[115] may also be regarded as a remedy for the thousands of people arbitrarily deprived of their jobs. This Article had provided very wide discretion for martial law commanders to dismiss or change the workplace of public servants and workers without offering any remedy against that decision, which was not necessarily based on a court judgment or a disciplinary decision. In the general statement of reasons of the amendment[116] the incompatibility between this Article and the international undertakings of Turkey was underlined, with reference to the process of the CSCE and the Charter of Paris, considering that this Article was an obstacle to integration with Europe. The report of the TGNA Commission on Human Rights, as noted above, expressed the clear incompatibility of Article 2 of the Act on Martial Law with Articles 6, 15, and 17 of the Convention.[117]

Lastly, the abrogation of Law No. 2533 on the dissolution of political parties passed in the military period by Law No. 3821[118] provided for the dissolved political parties to be entitled to have their properties back and to take part actively in political life again.

It is clear that the number of remedies against violations of the ECHR has been quite insufficient. However, the increase in the number of remedies in the last few years is considerable, which might be regarded partly as a result of the individual applications. On the other hand, since 1980 the traces of the military regime with its own laws and decrees have still been affecting the operation of Turkish democracy, under the legal protection of Provisional Article 15 of the 1982 Constitution, that is, no allegations of unconstitutionality can be made in respect of decisions or measures taken under laws or decrees

114 31.3.1992, E.1991/18, K.1992/20 (28 *AMKD* 1, 1993, 325–326).

115 Law No. 4045 of 26 October 1994, *RG* No. 22100 of 3 November 1994.

116 *TBMM TD*, vol. 68, S.Sayısı 693, 1994.

117 Report of 15 May 1991 (session 18/1).

118 *RG* No. 21273 of 3 July 1992.

enacted between 12 September 1980 and 7 December 1983. The number of laws passed during that period is over 600 and only a few have been abolished or amended. Although all political parties have long agreed to amend the mentioned Article, no steps have been taken up to date, since it turned out to be a political issue among the parties. This example clearly demonstrates that there has been no serious effective remedy so far. In sum, effective measures for human rights are needed to enable the reconstruction of the political regime in Turkey as a genuine democracy.

G. ASSESSMENT AND PROSPECTS

The ECHR was incorporated by Turkey as a part of its integration policy with the West. One of the conclusions of this study is that the growing influence of the ECHR over the Turkish legislation, administration, and judiciary might also be regarded as a corollary of that policy. The discussions throughout parliamentary proceedings since its ratification have manifested that there is no significant change in the importance attributed to the ECHR. To date, it should be underlined that the Turkish government has increasingly taken into account the Convention owing to the fact that it has generally begun to be presented as the Constitution of Europe in the prevailing process of reconstruction and regional integration.

However, the deficiencies of Turkish democracy have created some tensions in relations between Turkey and Europe, as clearly seen following the military coup in 1980. In the last three decades Turkish democracy has been broken down three times and the profound effects of the last of these are still being observed. Like the military interventions, the violations occurring in the South-Eastern region of Turkey, where the greater part of the population is ethnically Kurdish, have soured relations between the Council of Europe and Turkey. In the near future, overcoming the difficulties in relations will be subject to a democratic solution to the Kurdish question. Nevertheless, it is possible that the anti-democratic system in Turkey, which is undoubtedly a product of its economic–political structure, will continue to create human rights problems in future.

With regard to the effects of the ECHR on the prevention of violations in Turkey, it cannot be stated that it has had a notable function since Turkey's ratification. Turkey did not recognize the right of individual application until 1987, therefore the individuals of Turkey had no effective legal protection at the international level. It should be added that the only possibility of a remedy for violations before 1987 in the framework of the ECHR was by means of an inter-state application and this was not sufficiently appreciated. The complaints of the five states against Turkey in 1982 before the Commission resulted in friendly settlement, not creating the conditions for securing human rights seriously. Yet the individual applications filed against Turkey over the last few years have brought the violations to international attention and led to some steps being taken in the domestic legal framework, even if they have mostly been too little and ineffective and generally aimed to change the image of the state.

It is obvious that the importance attributed to human rights by the Turkish government, without substantial acceptance but with pragmatic reasons, is open to criticism. However, there is no doubt that nearly all states abuse human rights, as seen in many examples at international or domestic levels. Interestingly, while human rights are generalized literally, the violations are increasing all over the world. It seems that the future success of the human rights instruments, including the ECHR, will depend on whether they can help to overcome this paradoxical practice.

H. RECENT DEVELOPMENTS, 1994–1999

The most significant developments in this period with regard to the implementation and impact of the Convention in Turkey, in the context of remedies taken by the government and Parliament, Turkish parliamentary debates, and decisions of the national courts, together with the judgments of the European Court of Human Rights are described below.

1. The remedies and their parliamentary proceedings

One of the most important developments in the context of human rights law in Turkey was the amendment of the Constitution in 1995. It did not change Article 90 of the Constitution, which defined the status of international agreements as having the force of law in domestic law, so the status of the ECHR remained unaltered. The Law[119] amending the Preamble and some provisions of the Constitution has provided, *inter alia*, some improvements for fundamental rights and freedoms, especially for freedom of association, the right to belong to trade unions, and political rights. In this context, the previous bans on associations, trade unions, and public professsional organizations not pursuing political aims, engaging in political activities, receiving or giving support to political parties, or taking joint action with each other were all

[119] No. 4121 of 23 July 1995 (*RG* No. 22355 of 26 July 1995).

removed. In addition, the right to form trade unions and the right to collective negotiation for public officials were recognized. With regard to the improvement of political rights, especially the extension of the right to vote and the right to be elected should be noted. The age for the enjoyment of these electoral rights has been lowered from 21 to 18, and the same rights have been extended to Turkish citizens living abroad and prisoners on remand. Subsequently, further statutes have been adopted in order to produce conformity with the constitutional amendments.[120]

The ECHR had an impact on the Law amending the Constitution. The ECHR was referred to in both the report of the Turkish Grand National Assembly (TGNA) Justice Commission and its debates. In the report of the Commission, the restrictions imposed on the right of association for public officials were based on Article 11(2) of the ECHR.[121] The reasons for restrictions, national security, public safety, public order, the protection of morals, and the protection of the rights and freedoms of others, had not existed in the original proposal for the amendments but were included in the proposal of the Commission. They were criticized during the parliamentary debates. The inclusion of the additional reasons for restrictions taken from the ECHR was interpreted as 'abusing' the ECHR, by asserting (rightly) that it should be applied only for the purpose of extending freedoms, not for their restriction.[122] Indeed, the only reference to the ECHR in the report is the grounds for such restriction.

In addition to the constitutional amendments, the increase in the number of remedies for abuse of rights has been observed, and references to the ECHR are now made in debates in Parliament. One example is the Law shortening the length of detention without trial, recognizing the right of suspects charged with the crimes falling under the scope of the National Security Courts (NSCs) to consult a lawyer, and confining the competence of the NSCs only to offences committed against the integrity and sovereignty of the state.[123] In the report of the TGNA Justice Commission for these amendments, the conformity of the new measures with the European standards was stressed.[124] On the other hand, in parliamentary debates these amendments were deemed to be an improvement, although not yet a sufficient one, with reference to the ECHR and the decisions of the Court and Commission,

[120] See Laws Nos.: 4125 (27 October 1995), 4275 (12 June 1997), 4276 (18 June 1997), 4277 (26 June 1997), 4278 (2 July 1997), 4279 (3 July 1997), 4280 (3 July 1997), and 4274 (12 June 1997).

[121] *TBMM TD* (1995) 88, S.Sayısı: 861, 1995, 23–24.

[122] *TBMM TD* (1995) 89, 16. For the other references to the ECHR see vol. 88, 391; vol. 89, 11, 22, 25, 27, 68, 79, and 190.

[123] Law No. 4229 of 6 March 1997 (*RG* No. 22931 of 12 March 1997).

[124] *TBMM TD* (1997) 19, S.Sayısı:175.

especially with regard to the length of detention.[125] Another example in the context of remedies is the Law amending Articles 8 and 13 of the Law on Combating Terrorism.[126] With these amendments, the phrase 'regardless of the method applied, aim pursued, or opinion held' included in the prohibiton of assemblies, demonstrations, or marches aimed at the destruction of the integrity of state with its territory and nation was abolished (Article 8) and the penal sanctions for these crimes were reorganized (Article 13). In the report of the TGNA Justice Commission the purpose of these amendments was described as the abolition of the 'excessive' restrictions imposed on freedom of thought and expression and thus, the achievement of comformity with the standards laid down by the ECHR and the decisions of the Court and Commission. In this context, in addition to various other international agreements, Articles 9(2), 10(2), 15, and 17 of the ECHR were referred in this report.[127] Although the ECHR was widely taken into account, it is worth noting that these amendments did not completely abolish either Article 8 or other similar provisions in that and related laws, therefore crimes of thought still exist in Turkish law.

During the parliamentary debate on the ratification of Protocol No. 11, the ECHR and the judgments of the Strasbourg Court were also considered. It was asserted by some MPs that changes in domestic law must be enacted in order to comply with the requirements of the ECHR. However, the Court's judgments which had declared admissible some applications lodged against Turkey without the applicants having exhausted domestic remedies were criticized.[128] In order to demonstrate the opinions of the Parliament about the ECHR, we should also note the reports of the parliamentary inquiry commissions, which result from the political control of the government. It seems that these reports have not generally paid much attention to the ECHR. Nevertheless, the report on migration resulting from the evacuation of villages in the East and South-East of Turkey are an important exception. Yet it appears that the reason of this concern about the ECHR in this report originated from the judgments of the Strasbourg Court on the same issue. The report states that the evacuation of villages and the forced migration violated Articles 8 and 13 of the ECHR and Article 1 of Protocol No. 1, and refers to the case of *Menteş and Others v Turkey*.[129]

In recent years there have also been some developments which can be regarded as general remedies in the field of human rights. For example, the enjoyment of the right to belong to a trade union has become easier since

[125] *TBMM TD*, vol. 19, 1997, 413–414. For another reference to the ECHR see 477.
[126] Law No. 4126 of 27 October 1995 (*RG* No. 22448 of 30 October 1995).
[127] *TBMM TD*, vol. 95, S.Sayısı: 888, 1995, 1–3.
[128] *TBMM TD*, vol. 26, 1997, 373–6.
[129] *TBMM TD*, vol. 53, S.Sayısı: 532, 1998, 62–3.

some prohibitions and restrictions on this right were removed;[130] the security investigation applied for public officials was abolished;[131] the 'Regulation of Apprehension, Police Custody, and Interrogation' entered into force in accordance with Law No. 4229, as explained above;[132] and a Prime Minister's circular letter headed 'Respect for Human Rights, and Prevention of Torture and Ill-Treatment' was published.[133]

Furthermore, some steps have been taken by the government to organize the issue of human rights officially. In this context, the High Co-ordinating Committee for Human Rights was established, with the participation of some bureaucrats, and with the main aims of preparing, monitoring, and co-ordinating measures on this issue.[134] The draft proposals prepared by this Committee should be here noted in respect of their references to the ECHR. For instance, in the general statement of reasons in the draft proposal amending some provisions of the Turkish Penal Code and the Law on Combating Terrorism, the purpose of the amendments was described as being to provide conformity with Article 10 of the ECHR.[135] Also, the main reason given for the preparation of the draft proposal amending the Law on statutory and default interests was because of a 'human rights problem' with references to the decisions of the European Court of Human Rights which found violations of the right to property in cases concerning delayed payments of additional compensation for expropriated property.[136] In the meantime, as a remedy, the rates of the statutory and default interests were increased from 30 per cent to 50 per cent by a decision of the Council of Ministers.[137]

At the institutional level on human rights, moreover, under the supervision of the High Co-ordinating Committee for Human Rights, the National Committee for the Decade of Human Rights Education was created in order to prepare a national programme to implement the United Nations Decade of Human Rights Education.[138] Remarkably, there is an increasing interest on human rights education, which has been observed especially in the activities of certain Ministeries concerning the education of some professional groups, such as teachers, jurists, security forces, etc.[139] As an official institution on

[130] Law No. 4101 of 4 April 1994 (*RG* No. 22252 of 8 April 1995).
[131] Law No. 4045 of 26 October 1994 (*RG* No. 22100 of 3 November 1994).
[132] *RG* No. 23480 of 1 October 1998.
[133] Circular letter No. 1997/73 of 3 December 1997.
[134] Prime Minister's circular letter No. 1997/17 of 9 April 1997.
[135] See *İnsan Hakları Koordinatör Üst Kurulu'nun Çalışmaları II*, Ankara, Kasım 1998, 7ff.
[136] Ibid., 55.
[137] No. 97/9807 of 8 August 1997 (*RG* No. 23086 of 20 August 1997).
[138] See *RG* No. 23362 of 4 June 1998.
[139] See 19–20 *Turkish Yearbook of Human Rights*, TODAİE, 1997–1998, 224–5.

human rights, the TGNA Commission on Human Rights[140] has also continued to produce inquiries, statements, and draft proposals.[141]

2. The impact of the ECHR on decisions of the national courts

It seems that the courts have considered the ECHR more and more in their decisions, as has the Parliament. However, there are disagreements on the status of international agreements between the courts. The Constitutional Court has recently begun to give clearer explanations of its interpretation of international agreements, declaring that even if it did not base its review of constitutionality on the international agreements, it did have regard to them,[142] although the minority opinion was that the ECHR should be directly applied where it conflicted with restrictive national laws, in accordance with the principle of interpretation in favour of freedoms.[143] On the other hand, the High Military Administrative Court of Appeals was also of the opinion that the international agreements could not be regarded as having supranational status over the Constitution, and therefore the Constitution must be applied in a case of contradiction between international agreements and the Constitution.[144] Contrarily, Ankara Regional Administrative Court, in accordance with the previous decisions of the Council of State, mentioned in Section D above, stressed that the ECHR should be regarded as superior to the domestic law, stating that violations of international agreements cannot be justified by reference to national laws.[145]

Despite the existence of different approaches to the status of the Convention, the courts have made reference to it in their decisions. For example, the Turkish Constitutional Court has continued to refer to, in addition to other international instruments, Articles 11 and 17 of the ECHR in its decisions on dissolutions of political parties. Having found the parties' programmes or statements incompatible with the Constitution, the Court has in

[140] For the establishment of the Commission, see Law No. 3686 of 5 December 1990 (*RG* No. 20719 of 8 December 1990). In this Law, it was stated that the concept of human rights should be understood as the general notion of human rights recognized by the international agreements, including the ECHR (Article 2).

[141] See *TBMM* 'İnsan Haklarını İnceleme Komisyonu Faaliyet Raporları' 1.9.1992–30.9.1995; 1.10.1995–30.6.1997

[142] For example, 23.9.1996, E.1996/15, K.1996/34 (32/2 *AMKD*, 1997, 807). In this decision, the Constitutional Court declared the unconstitutionality of Article 441 of the Turkish Penal Code, which recognized different sentences for women and men in the crimes of adultery, by stating that it discriminated against women with reference to the Preamble and Article 14 of the ECHR, in addition to other international human rights instruments.

[143] 18.2.1997, E.1996/2 (Siyasi Parti Kapatma), K.1997/2 (33/2 *AMKD*, 1998, 758–60); 16.1.1998, E.1997/1 (Siyasi Parti Kapatma), K.1998/1 (*RG* No. 23266 of 22 February 1998, 283ff. especially 285).

[144] First Chamber, 1.4.1997, E.1997/255, K.1997/274.

[145] 24.10.1995 (Y. D. İtiraz No. 1995/2171).

the past few years dissolved the Socialist Union Party,[146] the Party for Democracy and Transformation,[147] the Labour Party,[148] and the Welfare Party.[149] In respect of the first three parties, the Court found them to be incompatible with the constitutional principle of the integrity and indivisibility of the state and its nation and territory, due to the fact that the parties supported the existence of a Kurdish nation within the territory of the Turkish Republic. As to the latter, the statements and activities of some party leaders were considered to be contrary to the principle of secularism, with reference to decisions of the European Commission of Human Rights to the effect that rights and freedoms cannot be exercised with the aim of the destruction of democracy. However, in the dissenting opinion it was claimed that there was no contradiction to the ECHR in this case, referring especially to the admissibility decisions by the Commission on the cases of the United Communist Party of Turkey (TBKP), the Socialist Party, the Peoples' Labour Party, the Party for Democracy, and the judgment of the Court on the TBKP, stressing that the Turkish Constitutional Court should have regarded these decisions in its constitutional review.[150] Among other recent decisions of national courts which referred to the ECHR, we can also cite decisions of the Council of State,[151] the Court of Cassation,[152] and İzmir Court of First Instance.[153]

3. Cases brought before the European Commission and Court of Human Rights

There was no judgment before 1995, but as at February 1999 their number had increased to 34. This fact is understandable because Turkey only recognized the right of individual application in 1987, initially for three years, and in the meantime it continued to renew its declarations pursuant to Articles 25 and 46 with the limitation of *ratione loci*,[154] and ratified Protocol No. 11.[155] In addition, in 1994 and 1997 two new inter-state applications[156] were lodged against Turkey: both are still under consideration by the Commission, and one of them (*Cyprus v Turkey*) has been found admissible.

[146] 19.7.1995, E.1993/4 (Siyasi Parti Kapatma), K.1995/1 (33/2 *AMKD*, 1998, 548ff.)
[147] 19.3.1996, E.1995/1 (Siyasi Parti Kapatma), K.1996/1 (33/2 *AMKD*, 1998, 638ff.)
[148] 14.2.1997, E.1996/1 (Siyasi Parti Kapatma), K.1997/1 (*RG* No. 23384 of 26 June 1998).
[149] 16.1.1998, E.1997/1 (Siyasi Parti Kapatma), K.1998/1 (*RG* No. 23366 of 22 February 1998).
[150] Ibid, 286ff.
[151] 10th Chamber, 7.11.1994, E.1993/2861, K.1994/5496.
[152] General Law Commission, 6.12.1995, E.1995/4–493, K.1995/1075.
[153] 18.10.1996, E.1995/1030, K.1996/844.
[154] The last declarations were renewed on 15 January 1996 under Articles 25 and 46 of the ECHR, but not published. See Yekta Güngör Özden and Bülent Serim, *İnsan Haklarına ve Temel Özgürlüklerine İlişkin Uluslararası Sözleşmeler ve Bu Sözleşmelere Yer Veren Anayasa Mahkemesi Kararları* Ankara, 1997, 488ff.
[155] See Law No. 4255 of 14 May 1997 (*RG* No. 23025 of 20 June 1997).
[156] Applications 25781/94 *Cyprus v Turkey*; 34382/97 *Denmark v Turkey*.

The most important point about judgments of the European Court of Human Rights arising from applications against Turkey is that the majority of them have found violations of the Convention. Of the 34 judgments: one resulted in a friendly settlement;[157] one was dismissed on the ground of non-exhaustion of domestic remedies;[158] one was not examined on the ground of the Court's incompetence *ratione temporis*;[159] three were found to involve no violation;[160] but the remaining 28 judgments all found violations, especially of Articles 2, 3, 5, 6, 8, 10, 11, 13, and 25 of the ECHR, and Article 1 of Protocol No. 1, and three related to Article 50.[161] The Court, in all these findings of violations, found the following facts about Turkey: lack of an effective legal remedy in the South-East region (Article 13);[162] violation of the right to life (Article 2);[163] torture and ill-treatment (Article 3);[164] violation of the right to a fair trial in the context of NSCs, excessive length of proceedings, and the violation of the right to a defence (Article 6);[165] violation of the right of personal security and liberty, especially unreasonable length of detention (Article 5);[166] violation of right of association with regard to the dissolution of political parties (Article 11);[167] violation of freedom of expression (Article 10);[168] pressure on the exercise of the right of individual application (Article 25);[169] violation of the right to property, the right to private and family life, and the right of peaceful enjoyment of possessions in the context of the deliberate burning and destruction of houses and household property by security forces in some villages of South-East Turkey, and unreasonable delays in the payments of additional compensation for expropriation, and continued denial of the applicant's access to her property in Northern Cyprus (Article 8 of the ECHR, Article 1 of Protocol No. 1).[170]

157 *Sur*, Application 137/1996/756/955, Judgment of 3 October 1997.

158 *Aytekin*, Application 102/1997/886/1098, Judgment of 23 September 1998.

159 *Yağız*, Application 62/1995/568/654, Judgment of 25 June 1996.

160 *Kalaç*, Application 61/1996/680/870, Judgment of 1 July 1997; *Erdagöz*, Application 69/1996/688/800, Judgment of 25 November 1997; *Gündem*, Application 139/1996/758/957, Judgment of 25 May 1998.

161 *Akdıvar and Others*, Application 99/1995/605/693, Judgment of 1 April 1998; *Menteş and Others*, Application 58/1996/677/867, Judgment of 24 July 1998; *Loizidou*, Application 40/1993/435/514, Judgment of 28 July 1998.

162 The cases of *Aksoy*; *Aydın*; *Ergi*; *Kaya*; *Menteş and Others*; *Selçuk and Asker*; *Tekin*; and *Yasa*.

163 The cases of *Ergi*; *Güleç*; *Kaya*; and *Yasa*.

164 The cases of *Aksoy*; *Aydın*; *Kurt*; *Selçuk and Asker*; and *Tekin*.

165 The cases of *Çıraklar*; *İncal*; *Mansur*; *Mitap and Müftüoğlu*; *Sargın and Yağcı*; and *Zana*.

166 The cases of *Aksoy*; *Demir and Others*; *Kurt*; *Mansur*; *Sakık and Others*; and *Sargın and Yağcı*.

167 The cases of the *United Communist Party of Turkey (TBKP)*; and the *Socialist Party and Others*.

168 The case of *İncal*.

169 The cases of *Akdıvar and Others*; *Ergi*; and *Kurt*.

170 The cases of *Aka*; *Akdıvar and Others*; *Akkuş*; *Loizidou*; *Menteş and Others*; and *Selçuk and Asker*.

Among the judgments, the applications which were found admissible although the applicants had not exhausted the domestic remedies have special importance, with regard to Article 26 of the Convention.[171] In this case-law, the Court based its decisions on the fact of the non-existence of effective domestic remedies in South-East Turkey. Secondly, the case of *Loizidou*[172] is worth noting, since the Court declared Turkey's limitations of *ratione loci* in her declarations on Articles 25 and 46 to be invalid, arguing that Turkey exercised jurisdiction over Northern Cyprus, and was thus responsible for the violations which occurred in that area. This case also has political implications, because it presents a jurisprudential dimension to the chronic problem of Cyprus in international law. It is highly likely that in the near future applications from Cyprus against Turkey will increase, and as a result a new crisis may arise in the relations between Turkey and the Council of Europe. Additionally, the judgments concerning the NSCs, which concluded that the structure and composition of these courts violated the impartiality and independence of the judiciary in the context of Article 6,[173] should be underlined, because more than 100,000 people were or are being tried before these courts. The organization of these courts has finally been reconsidered, owing to the trial of *Abdullah Öcalan*, who is the leader of the Workers Party of Kurdistan (PKK), and was arrested in February 1999 in Turkey. It is clear that Turkey has tried to prevent any discussion before the Council of Europe with regard to the violation of Öcalan's right to a fair trial, due to the special political importance of this case in connection with the Kurdish question. On 18 June 1999 Turkey's Grand National Assembly amended Article 143 of the Constitution and excluded military members (whether of the bench or of the prosecutor's office) from NSCs.

Although the Turkish state has taken some formal steps towards democracy, the process of reconstructing the political regime in Turkey has authoritarian characteristics. In this process, paramilitary organizations, methods, and activities have become more frequent and more efficient, which is the most dangerous trend for the future of human rights in this country. Even if the state has not accepted its connection with the paramilitary practices, this connection was apparent from the 'Susurluk accident' of November 1996,

[171] See especially *Akdıvar and Others*, Application 99/1995/605/693, Judgment of 16 September 1996; *Menteş and Others*, Application 58/1996/706/893–903, Judgment of 26 November 1997; *Selçuk and Asker*, Application 12/1997/796/998–999, Judgment of 24 April 1998; *Aksoy*, Application 100/1995/606/694, Judgment of 18 December 1996; *Kurt*, Application 15/1997/799/1002, Judgment of 25 May 1998; *Yasa*, Application 63/1997/847/1054, Judgment of 2 September 1998; and *Tekin*, Application 52/1997/836/1042 Judgment of 9 June 1998.

[172] Application 40/1993/435/514, Judgment of 23 March 1995 (preliminary objections) and Judgment of 18 December 1996 (merits).

[173] *İncal*, Application 41/1997/825/1031, Judgment of 9 June 1998; *Çıraklar*, Application 70/1997/854/1061, Judgment of 28 October 1998.

which demonstrated the links between the police forces, Parliament, and the paramilitary organizations. In this accident a police chief, an MP, and a leader of a paramilitary organization wanted by Interpol were in the same car, and two of them died. This fact supported claims of the existence of a paramilitary organization, responsible for disappearances, arbitrary executions, and kidnappings which had continued for years. It revealed the real face of the political regime. After the Susurluk accident debates about the regime increased, and the legitimacy of state practices were strongly criticized by public opinion. Subsequently, in order to provide a new framework for the regime, as a dominant factor, the Turkish Army intervened in the political process. This resulted in a meeting of the National Security Council on 28 February 1997, in which the generals dictated their new programme to the government. The consequence was a more oppressive regime, and a reorganization of the state in a more anti-democratic form. Twenty-eighth February 1997 was generally understood in Turkey to have been the date of a covert military coup. These practices demonstrate clearly that there are structural obstacles to the improvement of democracy in Turkey which in turn have reduced the efficiency of the international human rights instruments ratified by Turkey, including the ECHR. The ECHR has undoubtedly been respected especially with regard to its provisions on restrictions on freedom, as clearly seen in the parliamentary proceedings and decisions of the Constitutional Court on the dissolution of political parties, discussed above. But the history of the past fifty years in Turkey has reflected a continuing tension between the political requirements of the state in practice and the international formal norms and responsibilities to which it is a party. This tension will not be easily resolved in the near future despite the closer relations emerging between Turkey and Europe.

35

Ukraine

VICTOR POTAPENKO AND PAVLO PUSHKAR

A. INTRODUCTION

The role of law as a category of philosophy and theory, when it is filled up with real content, becomes instrumental in the community. One may argue about what law is, what realities it reflects, its origins can be viewed and interpreted in various ways, and dissenting opinions relating to the substance and mission of law may be professed. However, as soon as this issue is raised on a practical plane, regardless of one's own frame of reference, one should always endeavour to search for a common point of view, a common attitude or approach. In fact if a practising lawyer resorts to law as an instrument for resolving a specific conflict and for finding a correct solution thereof, if law shall serve as a vehicle which enables us to evaluate the actions or omissions of citizens and officials and determine whether they are lawful or wrongful, if law comes to regulate the universal scale of human behaviour, there shall be certainty at least in one aspect: which specific sources one should resort to and which sources the decisions are to be based on.

If law were understood by everyone in a different way it would lose its value and would cease to perform its fundamental function, stabilizing and regulating social relations.

Unfortunately in our country the law which was supposed to be official used to exist without being respectively applied and properly understood. In Soviet times legal nihilism was becoming more and more widespread, which resulted in the devaluation of law and legality as well as in neglecting laws or underestimating their regulatory, social role.

At the time when 'Iron Curtains' were opened and 'Berlin walls' were demolished, various legal systems came to be perceived more profoundly and different approaches to understanding law emerged. This was preceded by a complete liberation from ideological dogmas, by resorting to historical heritage. The aim to build a state governed by the rule of law has given a fresh impetus to consideration of these issues.

Nowadays, the majority of states, Ukraine among them, recognize the need to correlate the norms of domestic legislation and legislative practice with the human rights treaties, international conventions and covenants, UN Declarations and Resolutions, and other international legal instruments.

After declaring state sovereignty on 16 July 1990 and adopting the Act of the Declaration of the Independence of Ukraine on 24 August 1991, which was later confirmed by the all-Ukrainian vote on 1 December 1991, Ukraine embarked upon a course of building up its own statehood aiming at the creation of a social system and socio-political environment which would allow for the maximum degree of human rights protection and take into consideration the interests and aspirations of every individual citizen. However, the legal system that was inherited from the USSR failed to ensure the advancement of Ukraine towards a state, the state founded on the principles of the rule of law, to ensure Ukraine's transition towards market relations of a new type, towards building up a democratic, social society where a human being and his/her lawful rights and interests constitute the highest social value.

Having embarked upon the road of building up a democratic society, Ukraine recognized the universal standards and priorities of human development, and reconfirmed its commitment to the universally recognized human values, in particular those stated in the Declaration of State Sovereignty of Ukraine: 'Ukraine recognizes the priority of universal human values over the class values, the priority of the generally accepted norms of international law over the national law norms'.

Thus, from this moment on we can observe the ever growing tendency towards the enhancement of the role of international law norms, spreading their influence in the domestic sphere over economic, social, and legal activity, the political and social systems, and legal and other relations. It especially relates to the legal sphere which for the time being is the fundamental criterion for building up the state to bring it into conformity with international standards, ie a state guided by the principles of the rule of law and everyone's equality before the law.

Ukraine's accession to the Council of Europe on 9 November 1995 was another confirmation of its recognition of the democratic guidelines, its steadfast commitment to democracy based on human rights and fundamental freedoms, and to prosperity through economic liberty and social justice. However, for Ukraine's accession to the community of European states it was necessary to implement a great many changes in both the economic and social–political spheres, but primarily in implementing legal reform.

The legal reform was aimed, first and foremost, at ensuring legal stability in the state. In order to achieve that, it was imperative to adopt the Constitution of Ukraine and to introduce amendments to numerous legislative acts which require improvement. In particular, during its accession to the Council of Europe, Ukraine assumed an obligation to implement 57 organizational and legal measures, most of them of purely legislative nature.[1]

the aim of the Council of Europe is to achieve a greater unity between its Members for the purpose of safeguarding and realising the ideals and principles which are their common heritage and facilitating their economic and social progress [and as it is emphasized that:] this aim shall be pursued . . . by agreements and common action in economic, social, cultural, scientific, legal, and administrative matters and in the maintenance and further realization of human rights and fundamental freedoms.[2]

These aims also found their respective expression in the Preamble of the new Constitution of Ukraine adopted on 28 June 1996:

The Verkhovna Rada of Ukraine, on behalf of the Ukrainian people—citizens of Ukraine of all nationalities, *expressing* the sovereign will of the people, *based* on centuries-old history of Ukrainian state-building and on the right to self-determination realized by the Ukrainian nation, all the Ukrainian people, *providing for* the guarantee of human rights and freedoms and of the worthy conditions of human life, *caring for* the strengthening of civil harmony on Ukrainian soil, *striving* to develop and strengthen a democratic, social, law-based state, *aware of* our responsibility before God, our own conscience, past, present, and future generations, *guided* by the Act of Declaration of the Independence of Ukraine of 24 August 1991, approved by the national vote of 1 December 1991, adopts this Constitution: the Fundamental Law of Ukraine.[3]

The Constitution of Ukraine also enshrined the fundamental guidelines of the development of Ukrainian statehood for the future, in particular focusing on the fact that Ukraine is 'a sovereign and independent, democratic, social, law-based state' (Article 1 of the Constitution of Ukraine), that 'in Ukraine, the principle of the rule of law is recognized and effective' (Article 8 of the Constitution of Ukraine), as well as the fact that 'international treaties that are in force, agreed to be binding by the Verkhovna Rada of Ukraine, are part of the national legislation of Ukraine' (Article 9 of the Constitution of Ukraine). The provisions of Article 9 of the Constitution are of paramount legal importance for foreign policy-making, the more so under the conditions of Ukraine's enhanced activity in respect of international co-operation. This clause is a testimony of Ukraine's commitment to its international obligations and its respect for the international law norms, and it also provides more or

[1] Ukraine's Obligations before the Council of Europe. A Compilation of documents that includes: Opinion of the Council of Europe No. 190 (1995); Instructions of the President of Ukraine of 17 February 1997 No. 1–14/92; Organizational Measures approved by the Resolution of the Cabinet of Ministers of Ukraine of 20 July 1996 No 792; and Protocol of a joint session of Commissioners of 20 March 1997.

[2] Statute of the Council of Europe, 5 May 1949, London.

[3] The Constitution of Ukraine of 28 June 1996.

less detailed regulation of the status of the international law norms in Ukraine and their application.

B. THE STATUS OF THE CONVENTION IN THE NATIONAL LAW OF UKRAINE

In conformity with the legislation of Ukraine, the international treaties which Ukraine has ratified in the proper way are an integral constituent part of national legislation and are applicable by the procedure prescribed for national legislative norms.[4] In view of this, an international treaty to which Ukraine has become a party possesses the same legal force as its national laws. The procedure for ratification of an international treaty and its specificity are regulated by the legislation in respective branches of law.[5] At the same time, having adopted several normative acts in this branch, Ukraine recognized the pre-eminence of international law over national law, thus giving it a special status. Herewith the formula that was applicable as far back as Soviet times applies:

> if an international treaty prescribes other rules than those contained in the national legislation, the rules of the respective international treaty shall apply.[6]

Although the international law norms have become part of the legal system of Ukraine, thus having created a complex of legal norms, their application and implementation in Ukraine is problematic, particularly in respect of the process of the administration of justice in Ukraine.

Since the European Convention on Human Rights was signed on 9 November 1995 and ratified on 17 July 1997 (the Law on the Ratification of the Convention was adopted by the Parliament on this date, and entered into force for Ukraine on 11 September 1997) by Ukraine, it has become an integral part of Ukrainian legislation and enjoys the same status as the norms of the national law of Ukraine although its status in the national law of Ukraine is regulated by the specific features of this normative instrument and the basis thereof in Ukraine.

Thus, the European Convention is a source of law of Ukraine, but has a specific status conditioned by the following features:

[4] The Law of Ukraine 'On the Effect of International Treaties on the Territory of Ukraine' of 10 December 1991.

[5] The Law of Ukraine 'On International Treaties of Ukraine' of 22 December 1993.

[6] See 'The Civil Procedure Code of Ukraine' of 18 July 1963, Art. 428.

—it is an indivisible constituent part of the legal system of Ukraine, with the consequences ensuing therefrom;
—it prevails over national law;
—it is a self-executing norm of international law, although due to its specificity it cannot always be applied directly.

Although some legal experts express the opinion that, proceeding from the content of Article 57 of the Constitution of Ukraine which states that:

> laws and other normative legal acts that determine the rights and duties of citizens but that are not brought to the notice of the population by the procedure established by law, are not in force

the effect of the European Convention does not extend to us as it has not been made public. But this rule that 'the law shall not be binding unless it is published' applies to an individual but not to the state. At the same time this rule does not deprive an individual of his/her human rights. Moreover it does not affect the entry into force of an international treaty.

Furthermore, in pursuance of Article 20 of the Law of Ukraine 'On International Treaties of Ukraine' the international treaties that entered into force in the territory of Ukraine are subject to publication. Also, addressing the issue of the legal force of the Convention, we should take into consideration the requirements of the Vienna Convention on the Law of International Treaties of 1969 and the Vienna Convention on the Law of International Treaties between States and Organizations of 1968 which, *inter alia*, specify the methods of expressing agreement that an international treaty is binding. However, the application of the Convention may be complicated due to the absence of an official translation of the legal text.[7]

Proceeding from this, the European Convention is a source of law like other legislative acts of Ukraine, lower than the Constitution, but higher than laws and by-laws.

As far as incorporation of the Convention into the national legislation of Ukraine is concerned, two aspects should be distinguished here : first, its incorporation into the Fundamental Law, and secondly, into other normative legal acts.

As to the Constitution of Ukraine, it fully reflects the fundamental principles of the European Convention, in particular:

—Article 1: 'Ukraine is a sovereign and independent, democratic, social, law-based state', which expresses Ukraine's intentions and guidelines for its further development and advancement;

[7] Zerkalo Nedeli, 'What will Ukraine look like before the European Court?', Mirror of the Week, 31 Oct. 1998, No. 44 (213) 6.

—Article 3: 'The human being, his or her life and health, honour and dignity, inviolability and security are recognized in Ukraine as the highest social value', which reflects and expresses the principal values and priorities of the activity of the Council of Europe and the aims of the European Convention; and

—Article 21: 'All people are free and equal in their dignity and rights. Human rights and freedoms are inalienable and inviolable.'

These and other provisions of the Constitution of Ukraine have been formulated with due account of the requirements of the European Convention and are forward-looking provisions; on their basis the Constitution as the law of direct effect can be instrumental in protecting the rights and lawful interests of every individual.

Some legal writers[8] adhere to the opinion that, in compliance with Ukraine's obligations to abolish the death penalty, it is necessary to amend Article 27 of the Constitution of Ukraine, which does not exclude the death penalty as a kind of punishment. In our opinion, this is not necessary, especially since:

—the procedure for introducing amendments to the Constitution is complicated;

—the forthcoming ratification of Protocol No. 6 will resolve the issue at the respective legislative level;

—the adoption of the new Criminal Code which does not impose a death penalty will ensure the incorporation of Protocol No. 6 in the national legislation to a full extent.

As to the incorporation of the Convention and its provisions into other legislative acts of Ukraine, the following aspects reflected in the Law of Ukraine 'On the Ratification of the European Convention on Human Rights' are noteworthy.

1. *The right to liberty and personal security* (Article 5 of the European Convention). The Code of Criminal Procedure of Ukraine shall be brought into compliance with the Convention norms, in particular Articles 106 and 157 of the Code regulating the detention of a person and the procedure for a procurator's sanction for arrest, as well as paragraphs 50, 51, 52, and 53 of the Disciplinary Statute of the Armed Forces of Ukraine. In the new draft code of criminal procedure of Ukraine these issues are elaborated in detail,

[8] Otto Luchterhandt. 'On Issues of Harmonisation of the Legislation of Ukraine with the European Convention for the Protection of Human Rights and Fundamental Freedoms', *Proceedings of the Scientific-practical Conference of the Institute of Legislation of the Verkhovna Rada of Ukraine* (Kyiv, 1998).

with a view to further reduction of the scope of authority of the investigating bodies.

2. *The right to a fair and impartial trial* (Article 6 of the Convention) *and the right to an effective remedy* (Article 13 of the Convention). The aforementioned relates to the matters of bringing Articles 263 and 303 of the Criminal Procedure Code of Ukraine into line with paragraph 3(d) of Article 6 of the Convention concerning the right of a defendant 'to examine or have witnesses examined . . . and to obtain the attendance and examination of witnesses' and with regard to the right of a suspect or accused—only in the part of the right to file a petition on obtaining the attendance of witnesses and having them examined as well as conducting a cross-examination of them pursuant to Articles 43, 43(1), and 142 of the said Code.

In compliance with the provisions of the Convention that ensure the right to a fair trial within a reasonable time (Article 6) and the right to an effective remedy (Article 13), the administration of justice on the basis of the principles set forth in the Convention and incorporated in the Constitution of Ukraine will be regulated by the Law on the Judicial System of Ukraine, the Code of Civil Procedure, the Code of Criminal Procedure, the Code of Administrative Procedure and other laws that have been drafted and are being prepared for endorsement by the Parliament.

Pursuant to Article 6 of the Constitution of Ukraine courts are viewed as bodies of independent judicial power that exercise their authority within the limits established by the Constitution and in accordance with the laws of Ukraine. Article 124 of the Constitution sets forth the provision to the effect that the jurisdiction of courts extends to all legal relations that arise in the state. It also covers relations in the sphere of international law norms. Justice in Ukraine is administered exclusively by the courts. Courts as bodies of judicial power operate independently of executive and legislative bodies. The constitutional principles of the administration of justice are legality, equality before the law and the courts, the independence and irremovability of judges, the right to an effective legal remedy, the public nature and openness of a trial and its complete recording by technical aids, the right to appellate and cassational complaints against judicial decisions, the binding nature of judicial decisions and judgments, the use of a national language in the proceedings, and the participation of people's representatives in the administration of justice (people's assessors and jury courts). Judicial proceedings are heard by the Constitutional Court of Ukraine and courts of general jurisdiction (Article 125 of the Constitution of Ukraine). The provisions of this Article are basic to the establishment and further development of the court system of Ukraine and legislation on the organization and the functioning of the courts of general jurisdiction.

In general, the right of a person to a fair trial within a reasonable time by an independent and impartial tribunal established by law is regulated legislatively (but not fully, since the process of reforming the judicial system has not yet been completed). The legislative basis for regulating the activity of the courts is subject to continuing amendments and supplements, in compliance with the requirements and principles of the European Convention.

In compliance with the provisions of Article 55 of the Constitution of Ukraine:

> after exhausting all domestic legal remedies, everyone has the right to appeal for the protection of his or her rights and freedoms to the relevant international organizations of which Ukraine is a member.

3. *The right to respect for private and family life* (Article 8 of the European Convention). The provisions of Article 8 of the Convention are applicable in so far as they do not contravene paragraph 13 of Chapter XV of the Transitional Provisions of the Constitution of Ukraine and Articles 177 and 190 of the Code of Criminal Procedure of Ukraine with regard to procurator's sanctioning the search and inspection of a dwelling place.

The European Convention provides general guidelines as to human rights protection establishing the mandatory minimum level of human rights protection, first and foremost the right to life and health, liberty, personal security, and defence from prosecution. But it is the task of the national constitutional and criminal procedure legislation of each member state of the Council of Europe to regulate in detail the specific means and ways of such protection. This idea of an infallible guarantee of human rights underlies the drafts of the new legislative acts of Ukraine, and primarily the draft code of criminal procedure of Ukraine.

In conformity with the draft code of criminal procedure, courts administer justice, and through examining and resolving criminal cases courts make their contribution to the fulfilment of this task. This is consistent with Article 6 of the European Convention according to which:

> in the determination of his civil rights and obligations or of any criminal charge against him, everyone is entitled to a fair and public hearing within a reasonable time by an independent and impartial tribunal established by law.

On the basis of Article 29 of the Constitution of Ukraine the draft code of criminal procedure sets forth the decisive role of courts in securing the right of a person to liberty and personal security even during pre-trial proceedings. Decisions on the detention of a person as well as on extension of the term of detention are conferred by the draft code exclusively on the court (Article 24 of the draft code), which is in full compliance with Article 29 of the Constitution of Ukraine. Part 9 of Article 109 of the draft code gives every detained person the right to take proceedings by which the lawfulness of his detention is decided speedily by a court. Everyone detained on suspicion of having committed a criminal offence shall be brought before the procurator within twenty-four hours. The procurator interrogates the suspect, and familiarizes himself with the reasons disclosed by the case file for the detention. Having verified the lawfulness and groundedness of the detention, the procurator, within twenty-four hours, must either lodge a petition with the district (city) court at the venue of the investigation requesting to take the detained person into custody or release him. The judge within twenty-four hours of the receipt of the petition requesting to take a suspect or an accused into custody, examines it, studies the contents of the case file, hears the procurator, if necessary, and interrogates the suspect or accused. The judge then, if there are grounds therefor, pronounces a ruling on taking the suspect or accused into custody or refuses to do so if the detention was unlawful, in which case the judge orders the release of the suspect or accused. The ruling of a judge is not subject to appeal (Articles 110, 113 of the draft code of criminal procedure).

The draft code of criminal procedure also provides for supplementary non-custodial preventive measures, *inter alia*, an effective preventive measure not involving the deprivation of liberty, such as release pending trial (Article 107 of the draft) which will indisputably promote the exercise of the right of a person not to be held in custody pending trial (Article 5, paragraph 3 of the Convention).

Similarly to the current Code of Criminal Procedure, the draft code sets forth the right of a victim of unlawful arrest or detention to just satisfaction (Article 5, paragraph 5 of the Convention). According to Article 53(1) of the current Code, in the event that the case is terminated due to the absence of the fact of crime or the absence of the *corpus delicti* in the action, or if the participation of the person in the crime has not been proved, as well as in the event of an acquittal by the court, a body of inquiry, investigator, procurator, and the court are obliged to explain to the victim the procedure for the restoration of his/her violated rights and take the necessary measures to recover the damage inflicted on the victim by the unlawful conviction. These matters are regulated in detail by the Law of 1 December 1994 'On the Procedure for Recovery of the Damage Inflicted on a Citizen by Unlawful Actions of Bodies of Inquiry, Preliminary Investigation, Procuracy and Courts'. Such compensation is guaranteed to a person by Articles 56 and 62 of the Constitution of Ukraine.

Therefore, as far as the status of the European Convention in Ukrainian domestic law is concerned, the fundamental provisions of the Convention have been incorporated into the national legislation at the appropriate legislative level, though in fact there are certain problems in the direct application of the Convention. It is possible for any party in a case or their counsel, while substantiating their claims to invoke the norms of the European Convention of Human Rights and Fundamental Freedoms before the domestic courts, which frequently occurs in certain states, including Ukraine.

In general, with regard to the issue of the incorporation of the European Convention into the national legislation, the provisions of the Constitution of Ukraine comprised European standards and norms in respect of the protection of human rights and fundamental freedoms. The Constitution proclaims that in Ukraine the principle of the rule of law is recognized and effective, and the norms of the Constitution are norms of direct effect, and that the international treaties that are agreed to be binding by the Verkhovna Rada are part of the national legislation. From this it can be deduced that with the adoption of the Fundamental Law of Ukraine the main provisions of the European Convention for the Protection of Human Rights and Fundamental Freedoms enshrined therein have become norms of direct effect on the territory of Ukraine.

C. THE STATUS OF THE EUROPEAN CONVENTION IN PARLIAMENTARY PROCEEDINGS

Dealing with this matter it is necessary to address the issue of the legislative drafting in general. Legislation drafting is preceded by numerous factors, among them the general factor of resorting to numerous sources of law in the process of drafting legislation. These sources comprise: the Declaration of State Sovereignty of Ukraine, the Constitution of Ukraine, generally accepted principles and norms of international law, international treaties agreed to be binding by the Parliament of Ukraine, etc. Thus, a question arises relating to the need to applying in the process of legislative drafting the sources of law which in view of the necessity of uniformity of legislation, should have the same orientation, that is they should comply with the principles underlying the Constitution of Ukraine, which are aimed at building up an independent, democratic, law-based, social state as well as those aimed at ensuring the protection of lawful interests of citizens, human rights and fundamental freedoms. Therefore the application of the European Convention during the adoption by the Verkhovna Rada of the normative acts designated in Article 92 of the Constitution, which regulate certain social relations, might be useful for the unstable legislator, determining certain limits of the law-making, the sources that shall applicable as well as the liability of the state in the event of violation of the requirements of the European Convention and other obligations of Ukraine to the Council of Europe.

D. HUMAN RIGHTS ISSUES RESOLVED BY NATIONAL COURTS

As far as judicial practice is concerned, two aspects are distinguished here: the Constitutional Court of Ukraine and the courts of general jurisdiction, in particular the Supreme Court of Ukraine.

Decisions of the Constitutional Court are binding and not subject to appeal. The Constitutional Court resolves matters relating to the compliance of laws and other legal acts with the Constitution of Ukraine and with their official interpretation. Of paramount importance in the context of the application of the Convention are the decisions of the Constitutional Court of Ukraine in respect of citizens' petitions requesting interpretation of the Constitution and laws of Ukraine. For example, a judgment of the Constitutional Court in the case of Ms Dziuba HP concerned the right of appeal before a court against unlawful actions of an official.[9]

In his opinion in that case, the reporting Judge Skomorokha V. invoked Article 8 of the Universal Declaration of Human Rights which sets forth the right of everyone to 'an effective remedy by the competent national tribunal for acts violating the fundamental rights granted him by the constitution or by law'. This provision is fully reflected in Article 55 of the Constitution of Ukraine: 'Everyone is guaranteed the right to challenge in court the decisions, actions, or omission of bodies of state power, bodies of local self-government, officials, and officers' and is in full compliance with Article 13 of the European Convention which guarantees the right to an effective remedy before a national authority 'notwithstanding that the violation has been committed by persons acting in an official capacity'. Basing its conclusions on these and other provisions of national and international laws, the Constitutional Court ruled that Article 55 of the Constitution shall be understood in the following way:

> Everyone has the right to appeal against decisions, actions, or omission of a body of state power, body of local self-government, officials, and officers

provided that these decisions, actions, or omissions violate or are derogatory to citizens' rights and freedoms and as a result the violated right requires protection in courts.[10]

Another judgment of the Constitutional Court of 25 December 1997 was based on the constitutional petition of citizens of Ukraine requesting official

[9] (1998) 1 *Bulletin of the Constitutional Court of Ukraine*, 3–7.
[10] (1998) 1 *Bulletin of the Constitutional Court of Ukraine*, 8.

interpretation of Articles 55, 64, and 124 of the Constitution.[11] Applicants *Adamanov and Others* (21 applicants, all citizens of Zhovti Vody) claimed that their applications to courts of general jurisdiction had been dismissed and found inadmissible. The applicants claimed recovery of compensation for material and moral damage from the Cabinet of Ministers of Ukraine under the obligations for bonds of state purposeful interest-free loan of 1990. The Constitutional Court stated that:

> the refusal of the court to hear the applications of the said citizens which are in conformity with the requirements established by law is a violation of the right to an effective remedy as well as of the right to a fair trial set forth in Article 55 of the Constitution of Ukraine as one of the most important guarantees of the exercise of the constitutional and other rights and freedoms of a human being and citizen. Paragraph one of Article 55 of the Constitution of Ukraine is in compliance with the obligations undertaken by Ukraine in view of Ukraine's ratification of the International Covenant of Civil and Political Rights and the Convention for the Protection of Human Rights and Fundamental Freedoms which according to Article 9 of the Constitution 'are part of the national legislation of Ukraine'.
>
> For these reasons, the Court holds that:
>
> —everyone shall be guaranteed the right to an effective remedy and a court may not refuse to administer justice;
>
> —a refusal to accept applications or complaints for consideration is a flagrant violation of the right to a fair trial;
>
> —the jurisdiction of courts with regard to resolving disputes pertaining to law and other legal matters shall extend to all legal relations arising in the state.

The two above examples vividly illustrate the existence of two contemporary tendencies in the application of Convention provisions in the judicial procedure:

—through direct designation in the motivating part of the judgment together with the reference to the Convention;

—through the application of the norms of the Convention which have been incorporated into the national legislation.

Decisions of the Supreme Court of Ukraine are taken in the form of resolutions of plenary sessions of the Supreme Court, which constitute *a sui generis* expression of the general judicial practice of courts. They not only generalize the practice of courts but also give directions to courts concerning the application of the legislation of Ukraine.[12] A few examples will suffice for

[11] (1998) 1 *Bulletin of the Constitutional Court of Ukraine*, 34–39.

[12] According to Article 40 of the Law of Ukraine 'On the Judicial System of Ukraine' the instructions and elucidations of the Plenum of the Supreme Court of Ukraine are binding on courts, other authorities and officials that apply the law the application of which is to be interpreted.

illustration: Resolution No. 9 of the Plenum of the Supreme Court of Ukraine of 1 November 1996 'On the Application of the Constitution of Ukraine in the Administration of Justice'; Resolution No. 7 of the Plenum of the Supreme Court of Ukraine of 30 May 1997 'On the Enhancement of Judicial Protection of Human Rights and Interests of an Individual and Citizen'; Resolution No. 10 of 7 July 1995 'On Applying the Legislation Ensuring a Suspect, Accused, or Defendant the Right to a Defence' (as amended by the Resolution of the Plenum No. 12 of 3 December 1997); and other Resolutions of the Plenum of the Supreme Court, the highest judicial body of Ukraine, also focus on the main tendencies of the development of judicial practice, ie the practice of the application by courts of the legislation of Ukraine in compliance with the norms of the European Convention on Human Rights incorporated into the Constitution of Ukraine.[13] Since it is on the basis of these provisions of the Resolutions that the courts directly resolve specific cases brought before them,[14] and these Resolutions comprise the guidelines and direct recommendations to be followed by the courts, it can be clearly seen that they provide reliable guarantees for human rights protection in Ukraine.

For instance, Resolution No. 9 of the Plenum of the Supreme Court of Ukraine of 1 November 1996 'On the Application of the Constitution of Ukraine in the Administration of Justice' reaffirms that:

> the constitutional rights and freedoms of an individual and citizen are directly effective, they determine the aims and the essence of laws and other normative acts, the content and orientation of bodies of legislative and executive power, and bodies of local self-government, and are ensured by the defence on the part of bodies of justice (part 1, paragraph 1).
>
> The judicial activity shall be directed at the protection of these rights and freedoms from any encroachments through ensuring timely and conscientious consideration of concrete cases (part 2, paragraph 1). In this way these provisions reflect the spirit of the European Convention and fully comply with Article 6 thereof.[15]

Proceeding from the provision of Article 9 of the Constitution, which states that 'international treaties agreed to be binding by the Verkhovna Rada and which are in force are part of the national legislation', in resolving a dispute the court may not apply the law which regulates relations that are dealt with in a different way than the international treaty. At the same time international treaties are applicable unless they contravene the Constitution of Ukraine.

The provision of Article 55 of the Constitution of Ukraine sets forth everyone's right to appeal to a court against decisions, actions, or omissions of bodies of state power, bodies of local self-government, officials, and officers,

[13] (1998) 8 *Bulletin of Legislation and Legal Practice.*

[14] The Law 'On the Judicial System of Ukraine' of 5 June 1981.

[15] (1998) 8 *Bulletin of Legislation and Legal Practice.*

therefore courts may not refuse to accept a complaint or to examine it on the grounds of a law which is derogatory to this right.

According to Article 59 of the Constitution, everyone has the right to a defence and to legal assistance. Therefore in considering a criminal case, the court shall ensure the right of the accused to a defence as prescribed by law (Article 13 of the European Convention).

A person may only be found guilty of committing a crime when his/her guilt is proved through legal procedure and established by a court judgment. According to Article 62 of the Constitution an accusation shall not be based on assumptions or on illegally obtained evidence.

Everyone is guaranteed the inviolability of his/her dwelling place, and privacy of mail, telephone conversations, telegraphs and other correspondence. These rights are set forth in Articles 30 and 31 of the Constitution. Permits to enter a dwelling place or other property of a person, to seize correspondence, to collect it at postal and telegraph institutions, and to read information off communication channels may only be granted by a court (see Transitional Provisions paragraph 13, according to which the current procedure for arrest, holding in custody, and detention of persons suspected of committing crimes is to be preserved for five years after the Constitution enters into force).

Judging by the examples of the judgments of the Constitutional Court and resolutions of the Plenum of the Supreme Court, judicial practice testifies to the fact that in taking decisions courts are guided not only by the provisions of the legislative acts of Ukraine but also by international legal norms, both by virtue of their incorporation into the national legislation and by the direct invocation of these norms.

E. CASES BROUGHT BEFORE THE EUROPEAN COMMISSION AND COURT OF HUMAN RIGHTS

Ukraine signed the European Convention on Human Rights on 9 November 1995, and ratified the Convention and its Protocols (with the exception of Protocol No. 6) on 27 July 1997. It deposited its instruments of ratification, recognized the right to individual petitions (Article 25 of the Convention), and recognized as compulsory the jurisdiction of the Court (Article 46 of the Convention) on 11 September 1997. Since the right to individual petition was recognized three applications were registered in 1997. Seventy-four cases are known to have been registered in the first half of 1998.

So far no cases have come before the European Court of Human Rights and the Committee of Ministers of the Council of Europe, though the

European Commission of Human Rights notified the Government of Ukraine of five cases relating to the conditions of detention of prisoners on death row. Cases registered against Ukraine by the Commission numbered 77 in 1997. By 30 June 1998 two cases against Ukraine had been declared admissible by the Commission, and no Ukrainian case had come before the Court.

Although no cases against Ukraine have yet been heard by the Court, there is an ever-growing tendency to study the case-law of the European Court of Human Rights, as a practice of the judicial interpretation of the Convention for the purpose of its further application.

F. ASSESSMENT AND PROSPECTS

The scope of measures aimed at applying and implementing the European Convention on Human Rights is to a great extent dependent on the development of adequate mechanisms to ensure the observance and enforcement of its provisions. It implies that the Convention shall be applied and adhered to by all subjects of Ukraine. The most important task in the application of the Convention is to achieve a situation in which the courts invoke the norms of the Convention and substantiate court judgments by applying these norms. The requirement of paramount importance is to achieve such interaction between the Convention and the national law and legal system.[16]

One of the most important achievements in the sphere of the implementation of the Convention norms was the adoption of the Constitution of Ukraine, which created the prerequisites for building up a democratic law-based state which, for the first time in the history of our country, proclaimed that the human being and the protection of his/her life are the highest social value. Unfortunately, the adoption of the Constitution *per se* cannot achieve the intended positive results since the entire complex of measures needs to be put in place.

First of all it is imperative to adopt a number of laws laying down the main principles for the functioning of the judicial and law enforcement bodies and defining their activities more precisely. Primarily, this is being attempted with the draft 'Law on the Judicial System'[17] which is to be submitted for consideration by Parliament in the near future.

[16] Speech of Luzius Wildhaber, President of the European Court of Human Rights, at the inauguration ceremony of the New European Court of Human Rights, Strasbourg, 3 November 1998.

[17] The draft 'Law on the Judicial System' elaborated by the Institute of Legislation of the Verkhovna Rada of Ukraine, with the participation of the Supreme Court.

An essential condition for the effective judicial protection of citizens' fundamental rights and freedoms is the independence of the judiciary from the legislative and executive branches of power. The court which is independent of any public authority except the power of law stands between a citizen and the state and protects thie citizen from encroachments on his/her life, liberty, property rights, etc. In compliance with international instruments, '. . . everyone is entitled to a fair and public hearing . . . by an independent and impartial tribunal established by law'.

The experience of many countries shows that judicial power implements the protection of human rights of citizens in the most effective way. If judges are really independent and are subordinated only to law, their decisions cannot be annulled even by the head of the state.

The judicial system in Ukraine is far from perfect. It is not yet free from the traditions of the totalitarian past, when most issues were resolved by judicial bodies on the basis of instructions from the Communist Party and state officials. In order to make the courts truly independent and impartial, it is necessary to implement a great number of reforms, in particular a reform of the judicial system. The existing legislative gaps relating to the activities of courts should be also filled.

It is imperative to create a system of administrative courts in Ukraine and to adopt the Code of Administrative Procedure. It is especially topical in view of the possibility of the spread of arbitrariness of executive power and government officials and officers becoming too powerful. The creation of a system of administrative courts would extend the possibilities for the protection of human rights, by bringing the decisions of state officials within the jurisdiction of the courts, ie under judicial control.

The judicial system of Ukraine currently consists of the Constitutional Court, the courts of general jurisdiction (Article 124 of the Constitution of Ukraine), and the Supreme Court of Ukraine, which is:

> the highest judicial body in the system of courts of general jurisdiction. The respective high courts are the highest judicial bodies of specialized courts. Courts of appeal and local courts operate in accordance with the law (Article 125 of the Constitution).

In order to consider how the issue of creating a judicial system based on universally recognized principles and in compliance with world standards will be resolved by Ukraine, to produce a system for the administration of justice in the sphere of international legal norms, let us return to the draft law on the judicial system. According to Article 6 of the Constitution, courts are bodies of independent judicial power whose relations with bodies of legislative and executive power are determined by the Constitution and laws of Ukraine. In conformity with Article 124 of the Constitution, the draft provides that the jurisdiction of the courts extends to all legal relations that arise in the state and in particular to international law norms. Justice in Ukraine is administered exclusively by courts. No delegation of the functions of the courts, or appropriation of these functions by other bodies, shall be permitted, nor the creation of extraordinary or special courts. Courts as bodies of judicial power operate independently and separately from the legislative and the executive.

The constitutional principles for the administration of justice provided for in the draft law are: legality, equality before the law and the court, the independence and irremovability of judges, the right to a judicial remedy, the public nature and openness of a trial and its complete recording by technical means, the right to appellate and cassational appeal against judicial decisions, the binding nature of judicial decisions; the national language of the proceedings, and the participation of people's representatives in the administration of justice (people's assessors and jury courts).

The draft law provides for the uniformity of the judicial system of the state, and declares that all courts of Ukraine constitute a unified judicial system, that justice is administered by the Constitutional Court and courts of general jurisdiction, which constitute local, appellate courts, and by the Supreme Court of Ukraine. It also determines the main principles of organization of the judicial system as well as the procedure for the creation and liquidation of courts, and the determination of the number of judges sitting in courts.

A separate chapter of the draft law regulates the formation of state court administration in Ukraine which will have as its main objective the organization of the operation of courts and ensuring adequate conditions for the administration of justice. In the creation of an independent system for the logistics of the judicial function, the system of its budgetary financing is an important constituent. It affects the independence of judges as well as the creation of a system for judges' self-government, continuing education, and retraining, as well as their remuneration, social welfare, and social security.

Therefore we can conclude that the judicial mechanisms for human rights protection and for the implementation of international law norms in this sphere envisaged by the draft law constitute an elaborate and judicious system. However, there are drawbacks: primarily because the financial and technical support of the courts is dependent on bodies of the executive (the Ministry of Justice) which can substantially influence the mechanism of the administration of justice.

As far as financial and logistic support are concerned, according to the Law 'On the State Budget of Ukraine for 1999' the needs of the judicial system are satisfied only up to about forty per cent, which will reduce the efficiency of the judicial protection of human rights, to say nothing of the existence of judicial power *per se* in Ukraine.

As to the application of the Convention, three fundamental issues in this area must still be resolved:

—improvement of basic legislation on international legal norms in Ukraine;
—further development of the legislation regulating the activity of courts in the sphere of international law norms;
—implementation of measures with regard to studying, promoting, and disseminating the norms of European law in Ukraine.

One measure which would promote the implementation of the norms of the European Convention would be the Supreme Court passing a resolution on the Application af the European Convention in the Ukrainian justice system which could influence the application of the Convention by the courts of Ukraine. This resolution might touch upon the following issues: ascertainment of the facts of the case, legal qualification of the facts of the case, ie determination of whether they fall within the scope of the European Convention and if so of which Articles, determination of the legal characteristics of the case, the scope of their effect, especially with respect to the background of the subjects. In other words, the resolution would provide for special legal interpretation of the norms of the European Convention, establishment of the content of the norm of the European Convention, ie its international interpretation. (Here we might benefit from the practice of the European Court of Human Rights and other instruments regulating the interpretation of international law norms, in particular causal interpretation of these norms.) Courts should decide how the Convention norms should be applied to the specific circumstances, and action should be taken to ensure the implementation of those decisions.

While applying the norms of international law as part of the international legal system, the courts shall be guided by the rules of interpretation available in this system, which has a *sui generis* code of procedure: the two Vienna Conventions on the law of international treaties are gradually making their way into the practice of national courts.

Nevertheless, the analysis of judicial statistics testifies to the fact that courts of general jurisdiction operate mainly on the basis of national law, without paying much attention to international law. This approach is due to numerous reasons, including purely practical ones. National law and its norms are better suited for direct application by courts in the cases pending before them. The national law better reflects the social and political conditions and legal traditions of the country. And last but not least, national law is much more familiar to judges than international law.

Apart from these specific reasons, the more general reason is that the national legal systems in general are not sufficiently oriented at interaction with international law and particularly the application of its norms. It will suffice to recall that international law has not been properly codified. Its norms are not always explicitly worded and frequently refer to statements of intention. Many provisions express a superficial compromise, but no agreement on an explicit rule. These aspects are taken into account in the judicial practice as well.

For the further application of the European Convention it is necessary to implement a number of measures:

—its application must be regulated in a greater detail by introducing amendments and supplements to the Law 'On the Constitutional Court of Ukraine', in particular relating to its authority to hear cases on the constitutionality of international treaties;

—the courts of general jurisdiction, having gained experience of judicial practice, must elucidate and interpret the issues of the application of the European Convention by elaborating the Resolution of the Plenum of the Supreme Court of Ukraine on the implementation of the international law norms, and the norms of the European Convention in particular.

Summing up, if the judiciary know and apply the European Convention norms relating to the protection of human rights and fundamental freedoms, the courts will certainly play the most important role in raising the level of the efficient administration of justice, bringing Ukraine into line with European standards and its further integration into the European legal community.

G. CONCLUSIONS

The signature and ratification of the European Convention on Human Rights by Ukraine promoted wider knowledge and dissemination of its norms, which is vividly illustrated not only by the incorporation of the Convention into national legislation but also by the national judicial practice of the Constitutional Court and the courts of general jurisdiction. However, the process of applying and implementing the Convention needs an additional impetus, to advance the initiative on both the legislative and the law enforcement levels. This initiative should combine practical, organizational measures to be implemented very slowly. At present there is inconsistent law-making by the legislative and other powers. However, there have been positive achievements in the application and implementation of the Convention by the courts of Ukraine and allusions thereto by citizens during the defence of their rights and freedoms in the process of their exercise of the right to an effective remedy and, most important of all, the measures have aimed at the formation and proper functioning of the European system of human rights law and the interaction between national and European institutions of human rights protection.

36

The United Kingdom

ROBERT BLACKBURN

At the start of the new century the UK is undergoing a revolution in its attitudes towards human rights generally. New developments of major constitutional importance are currently or imminently being implemented that will fundamentally alter the traditional methods and procedures of the country's legal and political systems for establishing and protecting the basic rights and freedoms of its citizens and others resident within its borders. These momentous changes have been principally caused by the recent passage of the Human Rights Act 1998 which at last incorporates the European Convention on Human Rights into the domestic law of the UK. The Bill preceding the legislation was the subject of wide-ranging, lengthy debates in the House of Commons and House of Lords throughout the 1997–98 parliamentary session, and finally received the Royal Assent on 9 November 1998.[1] However, the Human Rights Act's entry into force was postponed for almost two years until 2 October 2000, to allow for the huge amount of official preparation of an administrative and educational nature, including one of the largest programmes of judicial training ever undertaken in the UK, which the government believed was necessary before the Act came into force. By a neat symmetry with the anniversary of the Convention itself, therefore, the UK became fully integrated into the Council of Europe's human rights legal system just one month prior to the half-centenary of the signing of the Convention as an international treaty by the UK and the other founding members in Rome on 4 November 1950.

This chapter provides a self-contained study of the impact of the Convention upon the domestic affairs of the UK. It is structured into six sections, beginning with (1) the history of the UK's involvement with the Convention and setting out the wider international context in which human

[1] For comprehensive documentation on the Human Rights Act 1998, including the text of the Act, the form of the original Bill prior to amendment, an explanatory commentary on the various amendments made, the White Paper (government policy) accompanying the Human Rights Bill, the parliamentary debates on the legislation, the ministerial statements on its provisions, and a wide range of other materials setting out the background to the Act, see Robert Blackburn, *Towards a Constitutional Bill of Rights for the United Kingdom* (London: Pinter, 1999).

rights have become an increasingly important component of UK domestic and foreign policy. The status and influence of the Convention in UK domestic affairs is then discussed by examining (2) the constitutional and legal framework of the UK, and the influence of the Convention in the period prior to statutory incorporation of the ECHR (completed in October 2000). Then (3) the detailed terms of the new legislation incorporating the Convention, as set out in the Human Rights Act 1998, are considered. There follows (4) an account of selected leading cases against the UK before the European Court of Human Rights, where a violation of one or more articles of the Convention was found to exist, together with the positive remedial action taken by the UK government in response. Next, (5) the role of European human rights law in parliamentary and public affairs is considered, particularly audit and scrutiny procedures for pre-empting and safeguarding against human rights violations at home. Finally, (6) an overall assessment is given of the impact of the Convention in the domestic affairs of the UK, and some related current and future developments of importance are considered.

A. UK MEMBERSHIP OF THE CONVENTION AND THE INTERNATIONAL CONTEXT

1. The UK and the drafting of the Convention, 1949–50

Immediately following the cessation of the Second World War, the UK played a leading role in promoting the formulation of international human rights treaties, both at the United Nations beginning with the Universal Declaration of Human Rights 1948, and in the work of the Council of Europe leading to the eventual agreed form of the ECHR.[2] The policy of the UK, under Clement Attlee's Labour administration in 1945–51 and powerfully supported abroad through the advocacy of former Prime Minister Sir Winston Churchill,[3] strongly endorsed a European charter of human rights which, while complementary to, would be independent from the proposed United Nations covenants.[4]

[2] See A. H. Robertson and J. G. Merrills, *Human Rights in Europe* (Manchester University Press, 3rd edn 1993); R. Beddard, *Human Rights and Europe* (Cambridge: Grotius, 3rd edn 1993); A. Lester, 'Fundamental Rights: The United Kingdom Isolated?', *Public Law* (1984) 46; G. Marson, 'The United Kingdom's Part in the Preparation of the European Convention on Human Rights' *International and Comparative Law Quarterly* (1993) 796.

[3] See Debates of the Assembly of the Council of Europe, 17 August 1949.

[4] Which were to become the International Covenant on Civil and Political Rights and the International Covenant on Economic, Social, and Cultural Rights, agreed in 1966 and entering into force in 1976.

UK government lawyers and officials were at the forefront of the Council of Europe's preparation of the detailed form and procedures of the Convention. Thus, during the negotiations in 1949–50, an important participant was Sir David Maxwell-Fyfe (later Lord Kilmuir, the Lord Chancellor) who served as Chairman of the Consultative Assembly's Legal and Administrative Questions Committee, which made the initial recommendations on the shape of the Convention submitted to the Committee of Ministers. Another participant was Sir Oscar Dowson, a retired senior legal adviser at the Home Office, who was appointed the UK's representative on the committee of experts set up by the Committee of Ministers. It was Sir Oscar Dowson who penned the wording of the rights and freedoms in Articles 2–17, taking the Universal Declaration as his starting point, which was subsequently adopted almost verbatim by the Committee of Ministers.[5]

UK ministers and officials, however, were considerably less enthusiastic than the governments of other member states about extending the terms of the Convention widely, particularly on matters relating to the enforcement of its human rights provisions. Over some important details, strong reservations or outright opposition was expressed in response to proposals put forward and widely supported within the Consultative Assembly. The effect of the UK's position on these matters was to produce a compromise in each case, and overall to contribute towards the Convention operating in its early period as a more voluntary association than some of its architects would have preferred. Most significantly, the UK government at that time did not welcome the the right of individual petition, so agreement was reached on this becoming an optional rather than a mandatory part of the Convention's enforcement machinery. A majority in the Assembly supported rights to property, education, and political freedom being included within the body of the Convention, but the UK government's resistance to this caused the Committee of Ministers to exclude those articles, and they were dealt with separately in the later 1952 optional protocol. The UK government, still responsible at that time for a large colonial administration, also voiced opposition to the automatic application of the Convention to a member state's overseas territories, and this resulted in the compromise whereby an express declaration by individual members is necessary before the

[5] The Foreign Office minister Kenneth Younger's memorandum to the Cabinet accompanying the draft Convention stated that it:

> contains a definition of the rights and limitations thereto which follows almost word for word the actual texts proposed by the United Kingdom representatives (Articles 2–17), and which is thought to be consistent with our existing law in all but a small number of comparatively trivial cases: quoted in G. Marston, note 2 above, 811.

Convention extends to overseas territories for whose international relations it is responsible.[6]

2. UK ratification of the Convention and its optional provisions, 1950–2000

The UK became the first member state to ratify the Convention, just four months after its signature in Rome. It was laid before Parliament on 23 January 1951 and the act of ratification took place on 8 March 1951.[7] The Attlee government was clear that no domestic legislation was necessary to bring the Convention into operation,[8] certainly not incorporation, and few thought it possible at that time that the UK or any of its founding members might actually be in breach of any of the terms of the Convention. Outside the Cabinet and the small group of ministers and civil servants involved in negotiating the terms of the European human rights charter, the Convention as a whole attracted negligible attention within the legal and political establishment of the UK. Only cursory references to the Convention were made in Parliament at the time,[9] with no debate at all taking place during the period while the draft treaty was laid before the Commons and Lords.

Sufficient UK government confidence in the new treaty arrangements and in the fact that it posed no threat to its domestic affairs, accompanied by a belief that the Convention was a useful foreign policy vehicle for expressing ideological solidarity and democratic values across the Western European states (particularly in contrast to the Soviet bloc regimes) encouraged the UK's active participation in matters relating to the Convention during its first two decades of existence. When following the 1951 general election the Attlee government was replaced by a Conservative administration headed by Sir Winston Churchill, the new Foreign Secretary Sir Anthony Eden proceeded to agree and sign the optional protocol dealing with the rights to property, education, and free elections on 20 March 1952, which was ratified on 3 November 1952. On 23 October 1953 the UK government lodged its formal notice with the Secretary General of the Council of Europe, as required under Article 63[10] of the Convention, expressly extending the protections of the

[6] The UK government decided shortly afterwards to extend the Convention to its overseas territories and lodged its declaration to this effect with the Secretary General of the Council of Europe on 23 October 1953. See further below regarding the Convention and the Commonwealth.

[7] In the UK ratification of treaties is an extra-parliamentary act authorized under the royal prerogative. For further comment on the future of UK parliamentary procedures with respect to human rights treaties, see page 996 below.

[8] The Attorney General told the House of Commons on 20 November 1950: 'it is not contemplated that any legislation will be necessary in order to give effect to the terms of this Convention' (col. 15).

[9] See debates on the Council of Europe: HC Deb., 13 November 1950, and HL Deb., 15 November 1950; and Marston, note 2 above, 822–24.

[10] Now Article 56, following the restructuring of the Convention's articles by Protocol No. 11.

Convention to 42 of its territories overseas. In the following decade the UK formally accepted the right of individual petition and the jurisdiction of the European Court of Human Rights, following the Labour Prime Minister Harold Wilson's agreement to recommendations from his Lord Chancellor, Lord Gardiner, and his Foreign Secretary, Michael Stewart.[11] This crucial step was completed upon ratification of Article 25 of the Convention on 14 January 1966.[12]

At the time of writing[13] the UK has ratified all other optional obligations under the Convention except for Protocol Nos. 4 and 7. A minor reservation by the UK exists with respect to the First Protocol, signed on 20 March 1952, dealing with the right to education.[14] This is the only reservation ever lodged by the UK. Under the terms of the Human Rights Act 1998 it and any future reservations must be reviewed by the government at five-yearly intervals and a report laid before each House of Parliament.[15] The most recent ratification was of Protocol No. 6 concerning the abolition of the death penalty. The Protocol was signed by Jack Straw, the Home Secretary, at Strasbourg on 27 January 1999 and ratified on 20 May 1999, following a period of consultation with the Crown Dependencies, who agreed that the ratification should extend to them, and also with the overseas territories. Progress towards ratification was expedited, unexpectedly at the time,[16] because of a successful amendment being made to the original form of the Human Rights Bill adding Protocol No. 6 to the provisions of the Convention to be incorporated into UK law.[17] Under the UK's pre-existing domestic law the death penalty for murder had already been abolished in 1965,[18] though there had subsequently been numerous unsuccessful attempts in Parliament to have it restored. The amendment to the Human Rights Bill meant that the government was obliged to legislate

[11] See Lord Lester, 'UK Acceptance of the Statutory Jurisdiction: What Went on in Whitehall in 1965', *Public Law* (1998) 237.

[12] The official decision to accept the right of individual petition was announced by Harold Wilson to the House of Commons on 7 December 1965, and ratification of Article 25 took place without any discussion of the matter in either Parliament or Cabinet. The UK declaration recognizing the competence of the Commission to receive individual petitions was initially limited to temporary periods of three years, subsequently enlarged to five-year periods.

[13] 1 March 2000.

[14] The reservation affirms the acceptance of the right to education only so far as it is compatible with the provision of efficient instruction and training and the avoidance of unreasonable public expenditure.

[15] Sections 15 and 17.

[16] The government had opposed the incorporation of Protocol No. 6 for reasoning set out in its white paper accompanying publication of the original Human Rights Bill: *Bringing Rights Home*, Cm. 3782, para. 4.13. The successful amendment was presented by Kevin McNamara MP during the Committee Stage of the Bill (HC Deb., 20 May 1998, cols. 987–1013).

[17] The original form of the Human Rights Bill was published as HL [1997–98] 38. Numerous other significant amendments were made during its parliamentary passage.

[18] Murder (Abolition of Death Penalty) Act 1965.

immediately to abolish capital punishment for all remaining offences where it applied, being treason, piracy, and some military law offences.[19]

The present Labour government has announced that it is not possible to ratify Protocol No. 4 at present because of its concern over Articles 2 (freedom of movement) and 3 (prohibition of expulsion of nationals) which might confer rights in relation to passports and a right of abode on categories of British nationals who do not at present have such rights.[20] However, the government has expressed its desire to give formal recognition to the rights contained in Protocol No. 4, and is now attempting to find a solution which would be compatible with UK domestic immigration legislation. The outcome is therefore likely to be that the UK will ratify Protocol No. 4 but will deposit with the Secretary General of the Council of Europe a reservation[21] in respect of particular provisions relating to its Articles 2 and 3. Some amending domestic legislation may also prove necessary to harmonize the UK's immigration laws with its European obligations.

Similarly, the government has made clear that it intends to ratify Protocol No. 7 as soon as is practicable. In this case, the principal reason given for the postponement is that there are inconsistencies in existing UK family law concerning the application of Article 5 and the requirement of equality between spouses, which will need to be reformed prior to ratification in order to bring domestic law into line with the Convention.[22] The divergence concerns three existing rules of UK family law. These are, first, that at common law a husband has a duty to maintain his wife, whereas a wife has no such obligation to maintain her husband; secondly, that by statute[23] where a wife gives her husband a housekeeping allowance any goods bought with it belong to the wife, whereas if a husband gives his wife a housekeeping allowance it belongs to them in equal shares (unless they agree otherwise); and thirdly, where a husband makes a payment to or puts property into his wife's name it is presumed at common law to be a gift to her, but this presumption of advancement, as it is known, does not apply vice versa in favour of a husband. The government has also referred to problems with applying Article 1(1) of

[19] The death penalty for treason and piracy was removed by section 36 of the Crime and Disorder Act 1998. Section 21(5) of the Human Rights Act 1998, which came into effect on 9 November 1998 in advance of the main provisions of the Act, replaced any liability under the Army Act 1955, the Air Force Act 1955 or the Naval Discipline Act 1957 to suffer death by imprisonment for life or any lesser punishment authorized by those Acts.

[20] Home Office, *Review of Human Rights Instruments*, March 1999.

[21] Under Article 57 of the ECHR.

[22] See HL Deb., 21 April 1998, col. WA197 for the government's statement on the inconsistent domestic law concerned. The government minister Lord Williams has told Parliament, 'We intend to legislate to amend these rules of family law as soon as a suitable opportunity occurs': HL Deb., 6 May 1998, col. WA75–6.

[23] Section 1, Married Women's Property Act 1964.

Protocol No. 7 (procedural safeguards relating to the expulsion of aliens), particularly with regard to definitional problems in UK law relating to who is to be treated as 'lawfully resident', which (similar to the case with Protocol No. 4, discussed above) may result in a reservation being expressed when ratification eventually takes place.[24]

3. *The UK's other human rights treaties and foreign policy obligations*

In common with other Council of Europe member states, the UK's commitment to human rights has a wider international dimension than the European Convention, though the enforcement machinery and jurisprudence of the Convention have proved by far the most effective and sophisticated international law system as an instrument for guaranteeing compliance. These other international commitments are of significance to the UK's membership of the Convention, since they represent political pressures and sources of obligation on the UK government which in turn influence its own participation within the Council of Europe. Furthermore, although the UK has a 'dualist' approach to treaties, meaning that on ratification treaty provisions do not automatically form part of UK law and cannot therefore be directly relied upon before the courts unless specifically incorporated into domestic law by statutory incorporation, they may nonetheless be of persuasive authority within the legal systems of the UK in enabling courts to resolve uncertainties or ambiguities in the judicial interpretation of domestic statutes and the development of the common law.[25]

Among the human rights treaties to which the UK is a party[26] are the United Nations Covenant on Civil and Political Rights and Covenant (ICCPR) and the Covenant on Economic, Social, and Cultural Rights, both of which were ratified in May 1976. Also operating under the United Nations, on particular rights and freedoms, are the Convention relating to the Status of Refugees and the Protocol thereto, ratified by the UK in March 1954 and September 1968; the Convention against Torture and other Cruel, Inhuman, or Degrading Treatment or Punishment, ratified by the UK on 8 December 1988; the Convention on the Elimination of All Forms of Racial Discrimination (ICERD), ratified by the UK in March 1969; the Convention on the Elimination of All Forms of Discrimination against Women, ratified

[24] Home Office, *Review of Human Rights Instruments*, 1999.

[25] See further below, particularly on the status of the ECHR in domestic law prior to the Human Rights Act coming into force. On monist and dualist legal systems in member states of the Council of Europe, see chapter 2 above.

[26] See Foreign and Commonwealth Office/Department of International Development, *Human Rights* (London: FCO, 1998); Lord Lester and David Pannick, *Human Rights Law and Practice* (London: Butterworths, 1999), ch. 8; Central Office of Information, *Human Rights* (London: Stationery Office, 2nd edn 1995).

by the UK on 7 April 1986; and the Convention on the Rights of the Child, ratified by the UK on 16 December 1991.[27] The UK is a signatory to the other complementary human rights instruments of the Council of Europe, including the Convention for the Prevention of Torture and Inhuman or Degrading Treatment or Punishment (UNCAT), ratified in June 1988; the Convention relating to the Status of Refugees, ratified in March 1954; and the European Social Charter, which it ratified in 1962. The UK is also an active member of the Organization for Security and Co-Operation in Europe, which since 1990 has had a broad remit for promoting human rights, democracy, and the rule of law;[28] and of the International Labour Organization which operates in the field of employment, labour relations, working conditions, and social security and which has produced a number of declarations and conventions, some of which have been ratified by the UK.[29] Most of these treaties and organizations have their own special mechanisms for promoting or enforcing their agreed international provisions, some of which are optional. At the time of writing, the UK government has still to ratify the relevant optional provisions granting the right of individual petition to its citizens or persons within its borders with respect to the ICCPR, UNCAT, and ICERD.

The election of the Labour Party into government under Tony Blair's premiership on 1 May 1997 heralded a much more pronounced and vocal emphasis being given to human rights in the UK's international affairs. Within a fortnight the new Foreign Secretary published a mission statement, speaking in terms of a new 'ethical foreign policy' and declaring that 'the Labour government will put human rights at the heart of our foreign policy'.[30] A large amount of information and presentational literature has been made public since, including documentation and detailed accounts of human rights and their place in the UK's foreign and international affairs.[31] This has been accompanied by a new government practice of producing Annual

[27] The Council of Europe has prepared a European Convention on the Exercise of Children's Rights which awaits sufficient signatures of member states to come into operation.

[28] The OSCE now has over 50 members across Europe including Russia as well as the United States and Canada. Under the Helsinki Final Act 1989 individual member countries may raise human rights concerns with other member countries and ask for information and details about particular cases. The OSCE's Charter of Paris for a New Europe agreed in 1990 emphasized member states' obligations to strengthen democracy, respect for human rights, and the rule of law, particularly regarding freedom of expression and the protection of the rights of minorities.

[29] In March 1999 the UK government announced that it would ratify ILO Convention 111 on Discrimination, and was considering ratification of ILO Convention 138 regarding Minimum Age.

[30] Robin Cook, Opening Statement by the Foreign Secretary (Press Conference on the Foreign and Commonwealth Office Mission Statement), 12 May 1997.

[31] Available over a new government internet site operated by the Human Rights Policy Department of the Foreign and Commonwealth Office: <http://hrpd.fco.gov.uk>.

Reports on its human rights work abroad.[32] On matters affecting internal affairs, such as the UK's position under international human rights instruments, information and documents are published by the Human Rights Unit of the Home Office, which has its own separate internet site. A major theme of the Blair administration generally has been proactive co-operation. Abroad, the government says:

> we shall work through international forums and bilateral relationships to spread the values of human rights, civil liberties and democracy which we demand for ourselves.

A similar approach, speaking ideologically of mutuality and the need to balance rights with responsibilities, and administratively releasing a large amount of information and documentation in the interests of transparency and accountability, can be seen in the Blair government's approach to promoting a new human rights culture within the domestic legal and political affairs of the UK accompanying the implementation of the Human Rights Act.[33]

4. The inter-relationship between the Convention and UK membership of the Commonwealth and European Union

Two other international organizations of which the UK is a member, the Commonwealth and the European Union, are of special importance to British domestic and international affairs in the field of human rights. Both have repeatedly affirmed their strong collective commitment to human rights and, in different ways, both of them have been substantially influenced by, or have interacted with, the European Convention on Human Rights. The Commonwealth[34] as an institution is a loosely knit voluntary association with no direct means of enforcing its collective agreements, most importantly for human rights, the Harare Declaration of 1991, save for expulsion.[35]

[32] The first two Reports entitled 'Human Rights' have been published jointly by the Foreign and Commonwealth Office and the Department of International Development: Report for 1998 (London: FCO, April 1998) and Report for 1999 (London: Stationery Office, Cm 4404, July 1999).

[33] See for example Jack Straw, 'Human Rights and Wrongs', *Fabian Review*, Spring 2000, 11.

[34] The Commonwealth was established by the London Declaration in April 1949. Membership is open to former colonies or dominions of the UK and the monarch of the UK takes the title of Head of the Commonwealth. It currently comprises 54 member countries who between them represent 1,700 million citizens and 30 per cent of the world's population. See *Commonwealth Yearbook* (London: Stationery Office); Central Office of Information, *Britain and the Commonwealth* (London: Stationery Office, 1992); K. C. Wheare, *The Constitutional Structure of the Commonwealth* (Oxford: Clarendon, 1960).

[35] The Harare Commonwealth Declaration 1991 agreed by Heads of Government pledged its member countries to work for democratic processes, the rule of law, and fundamental human rights, and its principles have been adopted as the criteria upon which membership of the Commonwealth depends. Subsequently a Commonwealth Action Group was established,

Collectively its influence is more informative and educative, its relevant work in this respect being conducted through a Human Rights Unit based in the Commonwealth Secretariat. Many Commonwealth countries are (or have been) UK Crown dependencies or overseas territories to which the obligations of the European Convention on Human Rights now extend (or have done so for at least part of the last half-century) following the UK's declaration of territorial application under Article 63 (as it then was) on 23 October 1953.[36]

Furthermore, numerous individual member states of the Commonwealth, on being granted independence from the UK by way of Westminster legislation or under prerogative orders of the Crown, have adopted written constitutions containing bills of rights whose drafting and interpretation has been borrowed from or been strongly influenced by the human rights articles and jurisprudence of the European Convention. In a process beginning with the framing of the Nigerian Constitution in 1959, the ECHR has been incorporated into the law of over 24 new national constitutions such as those in Jamaica, Mauritius, and the Bahamas, and it has been an important component in the drafting of constitutions in other Commonwealth states such as Cyprus, Bermuda, and Malta. In the words of one senior legal practitioner:

> The Parliament of Westminster has thus exported the fundamental rights and freedoms of the Convention to the new Commonwealth on a scale without parallel in the rest of the world.[37]

This has brought about the situation where the interpretation of those Commonwealth countries' bills of rights within their own legal systems and domestic courts has increasingly come to be influenced by the decisions and rulings of the European Court of Human Rights in Strasbourg.[38]

comprising the Foreign Secretaries of eight member states, of which the UK is one, to monitor adherence to the Harare Declaration (under whose procedures Pakistan's membership from the councils of the Commonwealth was suspended following the military coup in October 1999).

[36] 42 overseas territories were affected by this notification, with a combined population of 97 million people. Generally see Anthony Lester QC, 'Fundamental Rights: The United Kingdom Isolated?', *Public Law* (1984) 46 at 55–58.

[37] Ibid, 56.

[38] A good example is the Canadian case of *R v Keegstra* [1990] 3 SCR 697. The issue in the case was whether a Criminal Code provision prohibiting wilful promotion of hatred against identifiable groups infringed the freedom of expression article (section 2(b)) in the Canadian Charter of Rights and Freedoms, and if it did then whether such an infringement was justifiable under section 1 of the Charter. The majority of the Court (by 5–4) led by Dickson CJ referred to the European Convention on Human Rights and its case-law on freedom of expression with respect to hate propaganda, in support of its ruling that the Criminal Code provision in dispute was justifiable as being reasonably necessary in a democratic society.

It is interesting to observe in this context that a Canadian national and practising lawyer, Ronald MacDonald, has served as one of the judges of the European Court of Human Rights (nominated in the 1980s by Liechtenstein).

The European Community, of which the UK became a member on 1 January 1973, has increasingly placed human rights at the forefront of its objectives.[39] In so doing, the EC/EU has been strongly influenced by the Convention to which all of its member states have always been party. Indeed, accession to the Convention is now a precondition for EU membership.[40] This influence of the Convention in EU affairs has taken place at all levels of its organization, politically within the thinking of the European Parliament and Commission (both of whom have for many years supported the the idea that the EC should itself become a contracting party to the Convention[41]) and legally within the European Court of Justice where the Convention has been treated as forming part of the general principles of Community law.[42] Official documents of the EC/EU including its treaties[43] have regularly made express reference to the Convention, with the Treaty on European Union 1992 declaring that:

> the Union shall respect fundamental rights, as guaranteed by the European Convention for the Protection of Human Rights and Fundamental Freedoms signed in Rome on 4 November 1950.[44]

The law of the EC/EU as it has developed contains subject-matter which represents a partial body of human rights principles, and the effect of this in the

A wider significance and impact of the Convention throughout the Commonwealth can be seen as that of promoting the concept of fundamental rights itself (no doubt reinforced by its famous espousal by the United States in its constitution). Thus in recent times fundamental rights have been created as part of the constitutional law of Canada, as illustrated above (Charter of Rights and Freedoms, Schedule B, Part I, in the Constitution Act 1982, superceding its earlier 1960 Bill of Rights), New Zealand (Bill of Rights Act 1990, though its provisions are interpretative only) and South Africa (Chapter 2: Bill of Rights, in its Constitution of Republic of South Africa 1996). There is some irony in the fact that UK has so actively encouraged fundamental rights abroad over the past 50 years, yet has had such difficulty in accepting them within its own legal and political system.

A further source of Convention influence upon some Commonwealth countries has been the case-law of the UK's Judicial Committee of the Privy Council where the Commonwealth country concerned retains the Privy Council as its final court of appeal. Many such cases have involved the interpretation of national bills of rights or written constitutions and references have frequently been made by the Privy Council to the Convention for assistance in their reasoning and decisions. For example in *Pratt v Attorney-General for Jamaica* [1993] 4 All ER 826 the Privy Council held that the carrying out of a death penalty fourteen years after the passing of sentence contravened section 17(1) of the Constitution of Jamaica, being 'inhuman . . . punishment or other treatment'. In arriving at this decision, allowing the appeal from the earlier ruling of the Supreme Court of Jamaica, the Privy Council relied upon Convention case-law, particularly the case of *Soering v UK* in 1989 (on which see further below).

[39] For a fuller discussion of the EU/ECHR relationship see chapter 4 above.

[40] The membership at the time of writing (1 March 2000) comprises 15 countries.

[41] The Commission proposed EC accession to the ECHR on 4 April 1979 and on various subsequent occasions. For recent developments and discussion of possible EC/EU accession see chapter 4.

[42] See Philip Alston (ed), *The EU and Human Rights* (Oxford University Press, 1999).

[43] The Single European Act 1986 was the first EC/EU treaty to make specific reference to the ECHR (in its Preamble).

[44] Article 6.2.

UK over the period since 1973 has been to bring about significant legal advances in those areas.[45] In the absence of a constitutional bill of rights or incorporation of the Convention into domestic law, those articles in the EC/EU treaties and the regulations or directives made under them which possess a human rights dimension, such as those relating to anti-discrimination at work and the right of free movement, have helped to fill a vacuum in UK law where no fundamental rights existed.

B. THE STATUS OF THE CONVENTION IN UK DOMESTIC LAW PRIOR TO THE INCORPORATION OF THE CONVENTION, 1950–2000

1. The first two decades and the traditional UK method of protecting individual rights and freedoms

The Convention was of relative insignificance to the domestic legal and political affairs of the UK until the mid-1970s, by which time the effect of ratification of the right of individual petition (in 1966) was beginning to be felt in the earliest cases brought against the UK before the Court of Human Rights, where a violation of one or more of the Convention's articles was held to exist.[46] This lack of realization of the importance of the Convention in the UK in its first two decades was reflected in the near total absence of judicial reference to the authority, or even existence, of the Convention in the case-law of the period. The first real use of the Convention in a domestic case only came in 1973.[47] This early reluctance of the courts to refer to the Convention in their reasoning was compounded by the UK establishment's insular view

[45] For example *Commission of the European Communities v United Kingdom of Great Britain and Northern Ireland* [1982] ECR 2601 on the application of the principle 'equal pay for equal work' in Article 119 of the EC Treaty and the Equal Pay Directive 75/117, which judgment caused the UK to bring in the Equal Pay (Amendment) Regulations 1983 (SI 1983 no. 1794) permitting claims for equal pay regardless of job classification schemes; also *Dekker v VJV Centrum* [1990] ECR I-3941, [1991] IRLR 27: refusal of employment to best qualified candidate because of her pregnancy is direct discrimination contrary to the Equal Treatment Directive. See further Philip Alston (ed), *The EU and Human Rights* (Oxford University Press, 1999) and Trevor Hartley, *The Foundations of European Community Law* (Oxford: Clarendon Press, 4th edn 1998). For developments in connection with the drafting of the EU Charter of Fundamental Rights in 2000 see chapter 4.

[46] Starting with the *Golder* case in 1975 on which see further below.

[47] *R v Miah* [1974] 1 WLR 683 at 690 and see further below.

of itself in Europe, compounded by the fact that it was not until 1973 that the UK finally became a member of the European Communities.[48]

The background against which the Convention's impact in the UK should be assessed is characterized by a number of fundamental features in its traditional system of public law. First, there is no written constitution or codified body of fundamental legal principles governing the country's executive.[49] This is unlike all the 40 other member states of the Council of Europe.[50] A second, related characteristic is the omnicompetence of Parliament. An Act of the UK Parliament within the domestic operation of its legal and political systems is in legal theory absolute and unlimited. This concept, which resulted from the revolutionary settlement of 1688, has been known by lawyers since the late nineteenth century as the doctrine of parliamentary sovereignty, and it dictates that a parliamentary statute possesses an inherent right to make or unmake any law whatsoever.[51] A third major characteristic of UK public law is that there is no technical classification of constitutional law in the eyes of the courts and Parliament. In the UK there is no legal distinction between constitutional and ordinary law, in the sense that the former might ever have a higher status than and priority over the latter.[52] No domestic principles of law are held out as possessing a fundamental moral claim, on human rights or any other ground, which might have the effect of challenging or overriding the application of some other legal rule, restriction, or executive power.

An important part of the UK's inherited legal syndrome is the fact that there is no modern bill of rights, whether entrenched as higher law or otherwise,

[48] UK accession to the European Communities was doubly significant, not only because it established a concept of European law directly within the domestic legal affairs of the UK, but also because EC law served a medium through which the European Convention on Human Rights had some domestic impact within the UK (see above).

[49] On the UK method of protecting freedom see Robert Blackburn, *Towards a Constitutional Bill of Rights for the United Kingdom* (London: Pinter, 1999), chapter 1.

[50] The only liberal democracies in the world not to possess a written constitution are the UK and Israel: see S. E. Finer, V. Bogdanor, and B. Rudden (eds), *Comparing Constitutions* (Oxford University Press, 1995) and A. Blaustein and G. Glanz (eds), *Constitutions of the Countries of the World* (New York: Oceana, 1987).

[51] As enunciated by the jurist Professor Albert Dicey who committed the expression 'parliamentary sovereignty' into British legal and political vocabulary, through his magisterial lectures published as *The Law of the Constitution* (London: Macmillan, 1885; revised form 10th edn 1985):

> Parliament is, under the British constitution, an absolutely sovereign legislature . . . [it] has the right to make or unmake any law whatever . . . No person or body is recognised by the law of England as having a right to override or set aside the legislation of Parliament (10th edn, 186–188).

[52] Subject to a theoretical argument in Scottish law for an Act of the UK Parliament to be declared void as contrary to certain provisions of the Treaty of Union 1707: for discussion see S. A. de Smith and R. Brazier, *Constitutional and Administrative Law* (London: Penguin, 6th edn 1989), 73–74.

which declares the fundamental rights and freedoms of the people of the UK. There is a 1688 document known as the Bill of Rights, prior to which there was the Petition of Right in 1628, and before them both the Magna Carta enacted in successive versions in 1215, 1216, 1217, and 1225. But these documents, hugely important as they were in the past for establishing the idea of limited government and the rule of law, are today of historical significance only, and their contents, whilst fascinating historical reading, are archaic and belong to a different social order.[53]

The common law principles on which the protection of individual liberties were developed in England were, first, that individuals were free to do whatever they pleased so long as they did not infringe any general law or the enforcible rights of others; and secondly, that public authorities could only infringe the freedom of the individual if empowered to do so by a specific common law or statutory authority. As Lord Donaldson, then Master of the Rolls (senior presiding judge in the civil division of the Court of Appeal) said when giving judgment in the *Spycatcher* case:

> The starting point in our domestic law is that every citizen has a right to do what he likes, unless restrained by the common law or by statute.[54]

Safeguards for the individual have consisted of an *ad hoc* development of specific remedies to meet particular problems, the most famous of which has been habeas corpus, protecting the right of personal liberty against unlawful or arbitrary detention. Since 1950 a number of non-judicial remedies have emerged to deal with complaints about abuse of bureaucratic power, such as the office of the Parliamentary Ombudsman established in 1967. In the courts, over the past 50 years, the growth of judicial review of administrative action, and the elaboration of administrative law principles by the courts, has proved the most rapid development in the common law. Meanwhile some piecemeal equality legislation has been enacted to combat specific forms of discrimination, notably the Sex Discrimination Act and Race Relations Act under a Labour government in the 1970s, and the Disability Discrimination Act under a Conservative administration in the 1990s.

The UK government's report to the United Nations Human Rights Committee in 1989 set out its official reasons for the absence of a written constitution or a comprehensive bill of rights, explaining that:

[53] The Bill of Rights 1688, most of which is now obsolete or repealed, dealt with some matters carrying civil liberties implications, notably concerning conditions of detention, but it was otherwise a description of the constitutional settlement between Parliament and the Crown following the enforced abdication of King James II and acceptance of William and Mary on the throne. The Bill's central purpose was to curtail the actual and pretended prerogatives of the monarchy, and to safeguard the constitutional rights of Parliament, rather than the people.

[54] *Attorney-General v Guardian Newspapers* [1987] 1 WLR 1248 (CA) on which see further below.

The rights and freedoms recognised in other countries' constitutions are inherent in the British legal system and are protected by it and by Parliament unless they are removed or restricted by statute.[55]

This scheme of arrangement might be described as protecting human rights negatively since, with the exception of the discrimination legislation referred to, human rights could not be asserted positively in any court of law as actionable rights. It has meant, as the constitutional jurist Professor Sir Ivor Jennings wrote in the mid-twentieth century, that in the UK one must:

be careful in using the word 'rights'. If it is meant that they are natural rights, or if they are accepted as part of the logic of free or democratic government, the word is used in a sense different from its meaning in the phrases 'contractual right', 'right to damages'. It is a distinction between essential constitutional principles and rights actually conferred by statute law or common law.[56]

Traditionally, until 2 October 2000 when the Human Rights Act came into force, human rights and freedoms have been treated generally in the UK as a residual property, being what remains after the growing number of legal controls and infringements on human activities by public and private bodies are taken into account.

A final fundamental characteristic of UK public law is the diminutive status which its legal and political systems afford to the international treaties to which it is a party. In the great majority of states parties to the Convention, international treaties in general and the Convention in particular enjoy direct legal recognition within the judicial system of the country concerned, and are usually treated as possessing a legal status of a higher order and priority than that of their own parliamentary legislative enactments, subordinate only to their own national constitutions.[57] In such countries, therefore, where monism (as this arrangement is usually described) applies, the municipal law of a state and the public international law to which the state subscribes are treated as being directly interrelated. By contrast, the UK has a firmly established dualism in its approach to public international law, and its domestic law and international obligations are treated as being quite distinct. Politically, this is reinforced by the fact that treaty-making remains a prerogative act of the Crown and the ratification of treaties does not involve formal parliamentary consent.[58] In order for the provisions of any international treaty to have direct effect in the domestic legal system of the UK, ordinarily

[55] Third Periodic Report, 1989: for which see Robert Blackburn, *Towards a Constitutional Bill of Rights in the United Kingdom* (London: Pinter, 1999), 169–173.

[56] *The Law of the Constitution* (London: Hodder and Stoughton, 5th edn 1959) 163–165.

[57] See chapter 2 above; and F. G. Jacobs and S. Roberts (eds), *The Effect of Treaties in Domestic Law* (London: Sweet and Maxwell, 1987).

[58] For further comment on this see page 996 below.

it is necessary for an Act of the UK Parliament to be passed, specifically incorporating the provisions concerned.[59] Nonetheless there have been established situations in which reference to a treaty (including the European Convention on Human Rights) could legitimately be presented in legal argument in a court of law, in particular where some uncertainty, ambiguity, or vacuum exists within the UK's own domestic rules of law.[60]

2. The use and treatment of the Convention by domestic courts from the 1970s to the Human Rights Act

Most of the earliest cases in which mention was made of the Convention were ones where a dispute existed as to the precise meaning of a statutory provision. In construing statutory provisions whose meaning is uncertain or ambiguous, there exist legislative presumptions to which a judge may have recourse, and these include a presumption that Parliament intends to legislate in conformity with its international obligations.[61] So where a statutory provision is capable of bearing two or more meanings, the judiciary may legitimately adopt this presumption by preferring whichever meaning of the statutory provision in dispute best promotes conformity with our international obligations. However, in reality there are a large number of other legislative presumptions which may compete or conflict with one another in any given situation; and furthermore the very adoption of such legislative presumptions is usually dependent upon a purposive approach being applied by the judge concerned (as opposed to a literal approach to the textual working of the statutory provision) and his or her acceptance that some uncertainty or ambiguity does indeed exist which may itself be the subject of dispute.

The first reported case in which significant judicial use was made of the Convention[62] was *R v Miah* in 1973.[63] The court was asked to determine an

[59] With respect to the European Union, the European Communities Act 1972 delegates legislative power upon the organs of the EC to legislate with direct effect in the domestic legal system of the UK.

[60] Examples are given immediately following. Some variation in treatment of the Convention has existed between the three separately administered legal systems of England and Wales, Northern Ireland, and Scotland (see page 955 below).

[61] See Sir Rupert Cross, *Statutory Interpretation* (London: Butterworths, 3rd edn by John Bell and George Engle), especially 183–186; and Francis Bennion, *Bennion on Statute Law* (London: Longman, 3rd edn 1990) especially 156 and 248–249.

[62] There are two earlier instances of the Convention being mentioned as passing references, notably *Zoernsch v Waldock* [1964] 1 WLR 675 and *Broome v Cassell & Co* [1972] AC 1027. For a comprehensive account of English judicial references to the Convention see Murray Hunt, *Using Human Rights Law in English Courts* (Oxford: Hart Publishing, 1997). See also Nicolas Bratza, 'The Treatment and Interpretation of the European Convention on Human Rights by the English Courts', in J. P. Gardner (ed), *Aspects of Incorporation of the European Convention on Human Rights into Domestic Law* (London: BIHR/BIICL, 1991).

[63] [1974] 1 WLR 683.

unclear statutory provision contained within the Immigration Act 1971 as to whether a penal provision was to be treated as having retrospective effect. In the House of Lords appeal, Lord Reid referred to Article 7 of the Convention (which prohibits retrospective penal sanctions) and expressed the opinion that it was hardly credible that the UK government would intend to pass legislation that was in such blatant violation of its international obligations set forth in the Convention. A few years later, in *R v Secretary of State for the Home Department ex parte Phansopkar*, Sir Leslie (later Lord) Scarman in his judgment declared that it was:

> the duty of our public authorities in administering the law, including the Immigration Act 1971, and of our courts in interpreting and applying the law, including the Act, to have regard [to the Convention].[64]

Thereafter the importance of the Convention in this context of statutory interpretation gathered momentum and became firmly settled in judicial thought, and the Convention came to be regarded as a treaty of elevated and special importance. By the time of the leading case of *Brind* in 1991, Lord Bridge in the House of Lords was able to declare that it was:

> well settled that, in construing any provision in domestic legislation which is ambiguous in the sense that it is capable of a meaning which either conforms to or conflicts with the [European Convention on Human Rights], the courts will presume that Parliament intended to legislate in conformity with the Convention, not in conflict with it.[65]

There was far greater resistance, however, to the Convention having a role to play in the development and application of the common law. An early landmark case, for negative reasons, was *Malone v Metropolitan Police Commissioner* in 1978 concerning the legality of telephone tapping (which subsequently ended up before the European Court of Human Rights where the UK was found to be in violation of Article 8).[66] In the absence of any legal controls over the practice of telephone tapping, and where Parliament had deliberately abstained from introducing legislation on the subject, the then Vice-Chancellor Sir Robert Megarry explained in his judgment that it was:

> indeed difficult for the court to lay down new rules of common law or equity that will carry out the Crown's treaty obligations or discover for the first time that such rules have always existed.[67]

This case clearly displayed the incompetence of the common law to serve as the constitutional guarantor of fundamental rights and freedoms, a view

[64] [1976] 1QB 606.

[65] *R v Secretary of State for the Home Department ex parte Brind* [1991] 1 AC 696; [1991] 1 All ER 720 at 722–723.

[66] [1979] 1 Ch. 344 and see further page 977 below.

[67] At 379.

traditionally trumpeted throughout the legal establishment.[68] Above all, whereas previously the UK legal and political establishment maintained that all its domestic laws and procedures naturally conformed to the standards described in the Convention (and hence that the UK had no need to incorporate its articles into domestic law) this case was the first of its kind where a British court expressly recognized and openly stated that its decision was in breach of the Convention on Human Rights. Referring to Article 8 of the Convention which guarantees the right to respect for private life and correspondence, and to the interpretation of that Article together with the requirement for an effective remedy under Article 13 as adopted by the Court of Human Rights in the leading case of *Klass v Federal Republic of Germany*[69] the previous year, Sir Robert Megarry stated:

> It is impossible to read the judgment in the *Klass* case without it becoming abundantly clear that a system which has no legal safeguards whatever has small chance of satisfying the requirements of that court, whatever administrative provisions there may be [and that it is] impossible to see how English law could be said to satisfy the requirements of the Convention, as interpreted in the *Klass* case.[70]

A decade later, the Convention received more extensive judicial discussion in the famous *Spycatcher* litigation,[71] concerning the UK government's attempts to suppress newspaper publication of extracts from the memoirs of a retired intelligence service officer. The actual influence of the Convention on the domestic judicial decisions in *Spycatcher* was marginal at most, as with virtually all other judicial cases over this period when the Convention was mentioned.[72] The precise authority of the Convention with respect to the common law was not dealt with, and judicial references focused almost exclusively on the similarity and consistency of UK law with the Convention. Thus Lord Goff in the House of Lords observed:

> I can see no inconsistency between English law on this subject and Article 10 of the European Convention on Human Rights and Fundamental Freedoms. This is scarcely surprising since we may pride ourselves that freedom of speech has existed in this country perhaps as long, if not longer than, it has existed in any other country in the world.[73]

[68] For classic expositions see A. V. Dicey, *The Law of the Constitution* (London: Macmillan, 1885; 10th edn 1985) in his chapters on the Rule of Law; and Sir Alfred Denning, *Freedom Under the Law* (London: Stevens, 1949).

[69] 2 EHHR 214 (1978).

[70] At 379–380.

[71] *Attorney-General v Guardian Newspapers* [1987] 3 All ER 316; *Attorney-General v Guardian Newspapers (No. 2)* [1988] 3 All ER 545; *Attorney-General v Observer* [1988] 1 All ER 385.

[72] The majority of judicial references to the Convention until the 1990s were vacuous or dismissive, simply explaining how UK law conformed to the general principles contained within the Convention or else stating that the Convention was not part of UK law.

[73] *Attorney-General v Guardian Newspapers (No. 2)* [1988] 3 All ER 545 at 660.

The *Spycatcher* litigation was highly significant, however, not so much for the impact of the Convention or Strasbourg jurisprudence upon the decision in the case itself, but as a clear indication that the Convention was looming far larger than ever before in the minds of the judiciary. Previously, the Convention was mentioned only rarely in the judgments of domestic cases, between nil and 15 times each year before 1988 and usually with no more than a passing reference. But in *Spycatcher* the Convention was referred to in the judgment of the High Court of first instance, in each of the judgments of the three appellate judges in the Court of Appeal, and in the three leading judgments in the final appeal in the House of Lords. This unprecedented coverage, even if much of it was rhetorical, encouraged a far greater willingness to refer to and discuss the Convention in later cases.

The most important case in the common law's treatment of the Convention came in 1993 with *Derbyshire County Council v Times Newspapers*.[74] The legal issue in dispute was whether at common law a local authority had the legal capacity to bring an action for libel against a newspaper. It was held by the courts that a local authority could not bring libel proceedings, the underlying rationale being the public interest in protecting the perimeters of legitimate freedom of expression, particularly as applicable to a democratic institution. What was particularly significant about the case was that the Court of Appeal regarded the common law precedents on the issue as being unclear and uncertain. The Court proceeded to reach its decision by reference to Article 10 of the Convention, with Sir John Balcombe declaring that, although the Convention had not been incorporated into English law, it could be resorted to in order to help resolve uncertainties or ambiguities in English law generally: in other words, it was a principle not to be confined to the interpretation of statutes but was applicable also to the common law.[75] In his words:

> Article 10 does not establish any novel proposition under English law. Nevertheless, since it states the right to freedom of expression and the qualifications to that right in precise terms, it will be convenient to consider the question by reference to Article 10 alone. Article 10 has not been incorporated into English domestic law. Nevertheless it may be resorted to in order to help resolve some uncertainty or ambiguity in municipal law . . . In my judgment, therefore, where the law is uncertain, it must be right for the court to approach the issue before it with a predilection to ensure that our law should not involve a breach of Article 10.

On appeal, the House of Lords did not disagree with this view, though it reached the same decision in the case upon the basis of the common law being sufficiently certain.

A different category of legal principle in which the Convention might have been of earlier influence in domestic legal proceedings arose in the leading

[74] [1993] 2 WLR 449. [75] [1991] 1 QB 770 (CA) at 812–813.

case of *R v Secretary of State for the Home Department ex parte Brind*[76] in 1991, concerning a banning order on media broadcasts of any direct statement by representatives of proscribed organizations in Northern Ireland. A crucial issue raised by the applicant's lawyers[77] in the case was whether a government minister was required to take into account the principles of the Convention in exercising an administrative statutory discretion. This would require stretching legislative presumptions about statutory interpretation into a much wider field of application, and would mean that Parliament is presumed to intend that the discretionary powers it confers upon public bodies are to be exercised according to the principles of the Convention. This proposition had been argued earlier in a small number of cases, including *Fernandes v Secretary of State for the Home Department*[78] in 1981 when it had been firmly rejected by the Court of Appeal. So too in *Brind* the courts declined to go this far, regarding such a course of judicial action as being tantamount to usurping the legislative function. The Court of Appeal rejected the proposition even more firmly than the House of Lords, with Sir John Donaldson stating that it would involve imputing to Parliament:

> an intention to import the Convention into domestic law by the back door when it has quite clearly refrained from doing so by the front door.[79]

Nonetheless, the House of Lords said that where Convention rights were concerned, particularly freedom of expression, any new restrictions imposed under discretionary powers must be justified on public interest grounds. This would operate within the existing grounds or tests for reviewing discretionary decision-making, notably irrationality or *Wednesbury* reasonableness.[80] The

[76] [1991] 1 AC 696; [1991] 1 All ER 720.

[77] Anthony (later Lord) Lester QC and David Pannick (later QC) both of whom have appeared in many of the leading UK domestic cases raising Convention points of law.

[78] [1981] Imm AR 1.

[79] At page 718.

[80] *Associated Provincial Picture Houses Ltd v Wednesbury Corporation* [1948] 1 KB 223. An abuse of discretion exists where no reasonable minister could reasonably have arrived at that particular decision: for an account of judicial review principles, see H. W. R. Wade, *Administrative Law* (Oxford University Press, 7th edn 1994); S. A. de Smith, H. Woolf, and J. Jowell, *Judicial Review of Administrative Action* (London: Sweet and Maxwell, 5th edn 1995). The approach of the House of Lords in *Brind* was followed in the co-joined cases of *R v Ministry of Defence ex parte Smith, R v Same ex parte Grady, R v Admirality Board of the Defence Council ex parte Beckett, R v Same ex parte Lustig-Prean* [1996] QB 517 (which eventually went to the European Court of Human Rights: see below) dealing with the lawfulness of the discharge of four persons from the armed forces on the sole ground that they were of homosexual orientation. The Court of Appeal upheld their dismissal on the ground that the policy and decision as applied at the time could not be stigmatized as having been an irrational exercise of an administrative discretion. The court endorsed the view that it:

> may not interfere with the exercise of an administrative discretion on substantive grounds save where the court is satisfied that the decision is unreasonable in the sense that it is beyond the range of responses open to a reasonable decision-maker. But in judging whether the decision-maker has exceeded this margin of appreciation the human rights context is important. The

Brind case was viewed by many advocates of incorporation of the Convention as a major missed opportunity, but it may be regarded as having clarified the position that there would be no common law or judicial form of incorporation of the Convention, and that when incorporation occurred it would have to be effected by parliamentary enactment, which could also then specify the detailed terms upon which incorporation would take place.[81]

The judicial treatment of the Convention in the two separate legal systems of Northern Ireland and Scotland differed in some important respects from that in England and Wales over this period.[82] In Northern Ireland the general approach of the judiciary was to follow the English case-law on the subject, though it declined to apply the Convention to uncertainties in the common law in the manner indicated in the *Derbyshire County Council v Times Newspapers* case.[83] In Scotland, however, a far more restrictive view of the application of the Convention was expressed in the leading case of *Kaur v Lord Advocate*[84] in 1981, later supported by the Inner House in *Moore v Secretary of State for Scotland*[85] in 1985. This was to the effect that a Scottish court should have no regard to the Convention whatever, even as an aid to statutory interpretation in the case of uncertainties or ambiguities in legislative provisions. In Lord Ross' view, expressed in *Kaur*:[86]

> The Convention cannot be regarded in any way as part of the muncipal law of Scotland . . . A treaty is not part of the law of Scotland unless and until Parliament has passed legislation giving effect to the treaty provisions . . . With all respect to the distinguished judges in England who have said that the courts should look to [the Convention] for the purposes of interpreting a United Kingdom statute, I find such a concept extremely difficult to comprehend.

> more substantial the interference with human rights, the more the court will require by way of justification before it is satisfied that the decision is reasonable in the sense outlined above (at 554).

The court went on to remark that Article 8 of the Convention was not enforceable in the UK, and that it was not useful for the court to consider questions and proffer answers relating to any future liability under the Convention.

[81] An authoritative summary of the position immediately prior to the Human Rights Act regarding the legal principles whereby the Convention may influence domestic legal proceedings in the UK was given by Lord Bingham (then Lord Chief Justice, now senior Law Lord in the House of Lords) in his 1996 maiden parliamentary speech as a peer in the Second Chamber (HL Deb., 3 July 1996, cols. 1465–1467): Doc. 32 in Robert Blackburn, *Towards a Constitutional Bill of Rights for the United Kingdom* (London: Pinter, 1999).

[82] See Brice Dickson (ed), *Human Rights and the European Convention: The Effects of the Convention on the United Kingom and Ireland* (London: Sweet & Maxwell, 1997), especially ch. 4 on Scotland (by Jim Murdoch) and ch. 5 on Northern Ireland (by Brice Dickson); Lord Lester and David Pannick, *Human Rights Law and Practice* (London: Butterworths, 1999) especially ch. 5 on Scotland (by Lord Reed) and ch. 6 on Northern Ireland (by Brice Dickson).

[83] See above.

[84] 1981 SC 322 (Outer House).

[85] 1985 SLT 38.

[86] 1981 SC 322 at 327, 329.

Only much later in 1997, as political moves towards statutory incorporation of the Convention were becoming apparent, was this position altered and the Scottish judicial approach brought into line with that in England and Wales. In *T, Petitioner* the new Lord President, Lord Hope, expressly approved the use of the Convention as an aid to statutory interpretation, saying that:

> the drawing of a distinction between the law of Scotland and that of the rest of the United Kingdom on this matter can no longer be justified.[87]

In advance of the Human Rights Act coming into force on 2 October 2000, the Scotland Act 1998 now provides that all legislative and administrative acts of the new Scottish devolved system of government are valid only to the extent that they are compatible with the European Convention on Human Rights.[88]

3. *The pressures leading to the UK's statutory incorporation of the Convention (the Human Rights Act)*

The pressures that combined to persuade the UK government to bring forward legislation to incorporate the Convention directly into UK law are now largely of historical interest, though they may well continue to have contemporary and future relevance with respect to the degree of success or otherwise which the Human Rights Act enjoys over the early years of its existence, and also perhaps upon the development of other human rights reforms in the foreseeable future.[89]

A great deal of the early thinking and ideology in support of incorporation of the Convention was advocated and debated in the context of the desirability of a bill of rights for the UK. This feature of the UK debate over incorporation regularly bemused lawyers and politicians from other member states of Europe, whose minds (correctly) distinguished sharply between the incorporation of an international Convention and the enactment of a constitutional bill of rights as being two quite separate and distinct types of legal instrument and process.[90] However, from the 1960s onwards there was a developing view

[87] 1997 SLT 724 at 734.

[88] Sections 29 and 57.

[89] For a full study of the historical background to incorporation of the Convention (and other possible human rights reforms in the future) see the commentary and documents in Robert Blackburn, *Towards a Constitutional Bill of Rights for the United Kingdom* (London: Pinter, 1999).

[90] This observation on how the UK debate was perceived abroad was made by Professor Blackburn in his speech to the international Conference jointly organized by the British Institute of Human Rights and British Institute of International and Comparative Law in May 1991 on *Aspects of Incorporation of the European Human Rights Convention in Domestic Law*. Its accuracy was confirmed to him in the responses he received from many of those present from other member states of the Council of Europe, particularly in the discussions he had with Judge Rolv Ryssdal, then President of the European Court of Human Rights.

in the UK that its traditional unwritten constitution had become hopelessly out of date. The view was that there had arisen a powerful need for some positive legal code of basic rights and freedoms enabling individual citizens to challenge and protect themselves against administrative abuse, which had become much more likely with the huge growth in governmental size, regulation-making, and activity extending into virtually every sphere of social activity.[91] But if there was to be a bill of rights for the UK, the question arose as to the drafting and definition of the rights and freedoms it should contain. The enormous practical difficulties this presented in securing agreement across the political and ideological spectrum made it expedient that the articles of the Convention, as an established and existing civil and political rights instrument (particularly one drafted largely by UK officials in 1949–50), should be adopted for the purpose in lieu of or at least initially as the first step towards a constitutional bill of rights.[92] Consistent with this, in 1978 when a parliamentary committee was established to inquire into 'the question whether a Bill of Rights is desirable and, if so, what form it should take', after taking extensive written and oral evidence its Report recommended that a bill of rights should be adopted, with its contents based on the principles of the Convention.[93]

The international dimension of the arguments behind incorporation of the Convention only gathered strength later in the 1980s, particularly in the minds of some senior members of the judiciary[94] who proved a potent source of persuasion on government authorities and parliamentarians. One important factor driving judicial opinion on the matter related to UK membership

[91] Early exponents of this view were Anthony Lester, *Democracy and Individual Rights* (London: Fabian Tract 390, 1969); Lord Scarman, *English Law: The New Dimension* (London: Stevens, Hamlyn Lectures 1974); Michael Zander, *A Bill of Rights?* (London: Barry Rose in association with the British Institute of Human Rights, 1975); and Lord Hailsham, *Elective Dictatorship* (London: BBC, Richard Dimbleby Lecture 1976). See also Ronald Dworkin, *A Bill of Rights for Britain* (London: Chatto and Windus, 1990); Robert Blackburn, 'Legal and Political Arguments for a United Kingdom Bill of Rights', in Robert Blackburn and John Taylor (eds), *Human Rights for the 1990s* (London: Mansell, 1991); Geoffrey Robertson, *Freedom, the Individual and the Law* (London: Penguin, 7th edn 1993).

[92] This two-stage approach towards a UK bill of rights has been widely supported across the Labour and Liberal Democrat parties, and has been endorsed in their policy documents on constitutional affairs. See for example Labour Party, *A New Agenda for Democracy: Labour's Proposals for Constitutional Reform* (1993), 31.

[93] *Report of the House of Lords Select Committee on a Bill of Rights*, HL [1977–78] 176.

[94] Lord Bingham (the present senior Law Lord), Lord Browne-Wilkinson (the former senior Law Lord), Lord Slynn (a present Law Lord), and Lord Taylor (the late Lord Chief Justice) were among the most vocal supporters of statutory incorporation of the Convention in the 1990s. On the shift in judicial opinion in favour of statutory incorporation in 1980s and 1990s, see further Robert Blackburn, 'A Bill of Rights for the 21st Century', in Robert Blackburn and James Busuttil (eds), *Human Rights for the 21st Century* (London: Pinter, 1997) 25–29. For judicial speeches on the subject see extracts contained within Robert Blackburn, *Towards a Constitutional Bill of Rights for the United Kingdom* (London: Pinter, 1999).

of the EC/EU. As EC law began to establish itself directly within the UK legal system over the course of the 1970s and 1980s, appellate judges and university jurists began with increasing vigour to point to the inconsistency in the UK's position of rejecting incorporation of the Convention on one hand, while accepting the explicit recognition of human rights within the constitutional law of the EC/EU and the jurisprudence of the European Court of Justice in Luxembourg on the other. This was creating a dichotomy and two-tier system of justice in the UK legal system, as Lord Slynn, a former UK judge at the Court of Justice and now a Law Lord, described in a speech in 1992:

> Every time the European Court [of Justice] recognises a principle set out in the Convention as being part of Community law, it must be enforced in the UK courts in relation to Community law matters, but not in domestic law. So the Convention becomes in part a part of our law through the back door because we have to apply the Convention in respect of Community law matters as a part of Community law.[95]

These senior judicial figures were also well aware that this problem would become far more acute, indeed intolerable, if, as the European Commission and Parliament was proposing, the EC/EU itself acceded to the Convention as a contracting party.

An associated motivating factor behind judicial support was to remove a growing source of discomfort and professional embarrassment, caused by the increasing frequency with which UK judges were being required to hand down judgments in cases brought before them, in the almost certain knowledge that they would subsequently be condemned in the European Court of Human Rights for being in violation of the fundamental human rights set out in the Convention. The early landmark case of *Malone* in this respect has already been mentioned.[96] Similarly, Lord Browne-Wilkinson in a speech on the subject in 1995 was drawn to complain:

> I have on occasion had to reach conclusions in cases which I knew to be contrary to the Convention because I was not able to do otherwise. Why cannot we enable our courts to administer what the European Court of Human Rights does many months, many years, many hundreds of pounds later?

One of the strongest practical factors in persuading the legal and political establishment generally of the need for incorporation has been the virtual

[95] HL Deb., 26 November 1992, cols. 1095f. See also F. G. Jacobs, 'Human Rights in Europe: New Dimensions', Paul Sieghart Memorial Lecture 1992 (British Institute of Human Rights), *King's College Law Journal* (1992) 49 where Professor Jacobs (the UK Advocate General to the European Court of Justice) said of this discrepancy:

> The question may arise with increasing urgency how long these two classes of judicial review are tolerable: first class for Community law, second class for domestic law.

[96] See page 951 above.

certainty of it substantially improving the UK government's standing before the European Court of Human Rights, where the UK's record of defeats and human rights violations has been relatively high; and of reducing the number of UK cases needing to be taken to Strasbourg at all, since most of the human rights legal questions that have arisen could have been dealt with and resolved by the domestic courts.

The turning point in the party politics of the subject[97] eventually arrived with the selection of the late John Smith as leader of the Labour Party in 1992. John Smith firmly committed the Labour Party to its policy of incorporation of the Convention, giving a number of high-profile lectures on constitutional reform, where he spoke of the need for 'a new constitution for a new century' and said that 'the time has come when we should commit ourselves to a Bill of Rights'.[98] A comprehensive review of Labour policy on constitutional and human rights reform was carried out in 1992–93, with its final recommendations including statutory incorporation of the Convention as the first step towards a home-grown bill of rights.[99] This came after a long period of equivocation within the Labour Party about incorporation of the Convention,[100] matched in some respects with the thinking of the Conservative Party, some of whose members had been early exponents of a bill of rights based on the Convention. Throughout the lengthy tenure of Conservative government under Margaret Thatcher 1979–90 and John Major 1990–97, its leadership had remained firmly opposed to incorporation of the Convention,[101] although a promise to hold all-party talks on a bill of rights had featured in the Conservative election manifesto before the 1979 election. This was also despite an evidently growing level of support for incorporation among some back-bench Conservative members of Parliament, as indeed existed across all the

[97] A documentary history of the three main political parties' policies and views on incorporation of the Convention and a Bill of Rights is contained in Robert Blackburn, *Towards a Constitutional Bill of Rights for the United Kingdom* (London: Pinter, 1999) chapter 7.

[98] Leadership election statement, 1992; speech on 'A Citizens' Democracy' at Church House, Westminster, 1 March 1993.

[99] *A New Agenda for Democracy: Labour's Proposals for Constitutional Reform* (1993).

[100] A Labour Party discussion document on a statutory Charter of Human Rights had been prepared as long ago as 1976. Differing views on the subject were expressed in Labour's policy review on individual rights in 1989, and in its 1992 election manifesto promising a Charter of Rights.

[101] For example, Prime Minister Margaret Thatcher's answer to a parliamentary question as to whether she would support incorporation of the Convention was:

> No. We are committed to, and support, the principles of human rights in the European Convention on Human Rights but we believe that it is for Parliament rather than the judiciary to determine how these principles are best secured (HC Deb., 6 July 1989, cols. WA251–2).

Her successor John Major delivered a similar response (HC Deb., 15 January 1993, col. WA822).

other parties.[102] After John Smith's untimely death in 1994, Tony Blair succeeded him as Labour leader and made clear his support for the policy programme he inherited on human rights reform. The Labour Party went into the 1997 election with a specific pledge to incorporate the Convention, and once in office this acquired something of the status of a moral imperative (along with Scottish and Welsh devolution). The political decision to prepare a Human Rights Bill incorporating the Convention in the opening session of the new Parliament was taken within the first week of Tony Blair's Labour government taking office in May 1997.

C. INCORPORATION OF THE CONVENTION INTO UK DOMESTIC LAW UNDER THE TERMS OF THE HUMAN RIGHTS ACT 1998 (ENTRY INTO FORCE 2 OCTOBER 2000)

1. The purpose and effect of the Human Rights Act

On 2 October 2000 the Human Rights Act 1998 entered into force and incorporated the Convention[103] and its jurisprudence into the domestic law of the UK. The Act requires the courts to apply the Convention directly within the legal systems of the UK, and it empowers persons to bring domestic legal proceedings against public authorities for breach of their human rights in the Convention. The formal purpose of the Act as expressed in its long title is 'to give further effect' to the rights and freedoms guaranteed by the Convention.[104] It transforms the previously very limited circumstances and degree to

[102] Many private members' bills (draft legislation) designed to incorporate the Convention into UK domestic law were presented to Parliament between 1975–96, and all of them failed, although several passed through all their stages in the Second Chamber (House of Lords), with insufficient time being allowed by government whips for their consideration in the House of Commons. A Human Rights Bill 1986 (HC, 1986–87, 19) was presented in the Commons by the Conservative MP Sir Edward Gardner, which was debated on 6 February 1987. The earliest piece of draft legislation to incorporate the Convention was the Bill of Rights Bill 1975 (HC, 1974–75, 59) presented by Alan Beith MP (Liberal Party, now Liberal Democrats). Among numerous later attempts (on which see Robert Blackburn, *Towards a Constitutional Bill of Rights for the United Kingdom*, note 97 above, Doc. 39) was the Human Rights Bill 1994 (HC, 1993–94, 30) presented by Graham Allen MP (Labour) and two Human Rights Bills in 1994 (HL, 1994–95, 5) and 1996 (HL, 1996–97, 11) presented by Lord Lester QC (Liberal Democrat). See also Robert Blackburn, 'Parliamentary Opinion on a New Bill of Rights', *Political Quarterly* (1989) 469.

[103] The specific parts of the Convention which are incorporated are Articles 2–12, 14, 16–18; First Protocol Articles 1–3; Sixth Protocol Articles 1–2.

[104] Curiously, the Lord Chancellor Lord Irvine during one parliamentary debate commented that 'the Bill as such does not incorporate Convention rights into domestic law' (HL Deb., 29 January 1998, cols. 418f, which see generally for parliamentary debate thereon; and see also HL Deb., 18 November 1997, col. 478) when to the minds of virtually all other lawyers and parliamentarians in the UK and Europe this is precisely what the Human Rights Act seeks to do and

which the Convention had any relevance in domestic judicial proceedings[105] and revolutionizes the UK legal system's whole approach to the protection of civil liberties and human rights.

The legal and constitutional ramifications of incorporation of the Convention under the Human Rights Act are substantially greater than in most other member states of the Council of Europe, since the Act does not simply give statutory recognition to an international treaty, it creates positive actionable rights based on human rights grounds for the first time in its history because none previously existed under a domestic bill of rights.[106] The effect of incorporation on the legal system of Ireland, for example, will prove less far-reaching because many principles similar to those in the Convention are already contained within the Irish Constitution.[107] Within the UK, the very expression 'human rights' has until recently barely featured in the vocabulary of domestic legal and political affairs. Similarly, there was no discrete field of domestic law or legal study called by this name, whereas the trickle of juristic books, legal journals, practitioner seminars, and University courses on human rights law that existed only a few years ago has now become a torrent.[108]

Over the period 1998–99 the government, particularly its ministers of justice and home affairs, have been bracing themselves for a dramatic rise in litigation based on the new causes of action created (as well as existing ones which are facilitated) by the provisions of the Human Rights Act. An unprecedented reshuffling of senior judicial office-holders at the top of the appellate structure of the courts has taken place, with the former Lord Chief Justice, Lord Bingham, being transferred by the Lord Chancellor (and Cabinet minister) Lord Irvine, to become the senior member of the House of Lords in readiness for the complex human rights litigation anticipated to strike the courts after 2 October 2000, particularly in cases where the

achieves. The name of the Cabinet committee chaired by Lord Irvine which presided over the preparation of the Human Rights Act was termed the Ministerial Sub-Committee on Incorporation of the European Convention on Human Rights, and the Lord Chancellor's ministerial colleagues routinely refer to the legislation as incorporating the Convention (see for example Home Office, *Rights Brought Home: The Human Rights Bill,* Cm 3782, 1997, para. 1.14; Labour Party election manifesto 1997, 35; and references by the Home Secretary Jack Straw during parliamentary debates on the Human Rights Bill, for example HC Deb., 16 February 1998, cols. 769f). However, this is a matter of terminological semantics.

[105] Described in section B:2 above.

[106] See pages 947–948.

[107] See chapter 18 above.

[108] To name but a few: J. Wadham and H. Mountfield, *Blackstone's Guide to the Human Rights Act 1998* (London: Blackstone, 1999); D. Leckie and D. Pickersgill, *The 1998 Human Rights Act Explained* (London: Stationery Office, 1999); Lord Lester and D. Pannick (ed), *Human Rights Law and Practice* (London: Butterworths, 1999).

compatibility of existing primary legislation is called into dispute.[109] Consequently, the government also arranged an extensive judicial training programme over the course of 1998–99 in order to familiarize members of the judiciary and magistracy at all levels of the legal system with the Articles and jurisprudence of the Convention.[110]

2. The legal status and priority of the Convention under the Human Rights Act

Section 3 of the Human Rights Act determines the legal status of the Convention in UK domestic law, providing that:

> so far as it is possible to do so, primary legislation and subordinate legislation must be read and given effect in a way which is compatible with the Convention rights.

There is no special legislative procedure provided for in the Act governing the means by which the Human Rights Act might itself be altered or amended in the future. The Human Rights Act is therefore not an entrenched document and it does not confer upon the Convention any degree of legal priority over earlier or later domestic UK legislation. Instead, it creates a rule of interpretation or construction.[111] It is a highly potent rule of interpretation, however, and is clearly intended to be so. Thus the government white paper accompanying publication of the draft legislation stated the intention behind section 3:

> The courts will be required to interpret legislation so as to uphold the Convention rights unless the legislation itself is so clearly incompatible with the Convention that it is impossible to do so . . . This goes far beyond the present rule which enables the courts to take the Convention into account in resolving any ambiguity in a legislative provision.[112]

Section 4 of the Human Rights Act prescribes a judicial procedure that is unique in the UK constitutional tradition. This stipulates that if, after seeking to apply section 3, the court is satisfied that the provision is

[109] For comment on the implications of the Human Rights Act for the senior judiciary see page 1006 below.

[110] The training programme was provided by the Judicial Studies Board under the direction of Sir Stephen Sedley and Lord Justice Auld. For an attack on such training as being 'highly suspect, subversive of the judicial system, and likely to interfere with the course of justice' see Professor John Griffith, 'Not Getting it Right', *Guardian*, 9 April 1999.

[111] This, in the writer's view, is appropriate to the incorporation of an international treaty into UK domestic law, whereas any future indigenous bill of rights drafted as part of the UK's constitutional law should involve some degree of entrenchment suitable to its constitutional status. On this point see Robert Blackburn, *Towards a Constitutional Bill of Rights for the United Kingdom* (London: Pinter, 1999) 55–73.

[112] Home Office, *Rights Brought Home: The Human Rights Bill* (London: Stationery Office, Cm 3782, 1997) para. 2.7.

incompatible with a Convention right, then it may proceed to make a 'declaration of incompatibility'. However, essential to this mechanism is that it is a declaration of a non-legal character: it does not affect the validity, continuing operation, or enforcement of the provision in respect of which it is given, and it is not binding on the parties to the proceedings in which it is made. In many respects the declaration is analogous in its domestic effect to an adverse judgment being made against the UK by the European Court of Human Rights whose decisions are not binding or directly enforceable within the UK, depending instead for their effect on positive action being taken by the UK government to bring forward legislation to amend its domestic law so as to bring it into conformity with the Strasbourg ruling. So too, following a declaration of incompatibility by a UK court under the Human Rights Act, the government will be morally obliged to respond by considering what changes are necessary to render UK law consistent with the judicial ruling.

There is no mandatory legal duty upon the government to take remedial action, but a declaration of incompatibility 'is very likely to prompt the government and Parliament to respond', in the words of the Lord Chancellor, Lord Irvine.[113] Where a minister believes there are compelling reasons for a swift response by the government, the Human Rights Act establishes a fast-track legislative procedure for changing the law known as Remedial Orders.[114]

The existence of section 4, with its procedure for a non-legal declaration of incompatibility, serves to influence how the courts are to interpret section 3 itself. This is important because there is considerable room for flexibility and argument over the precise meaning, scope, and application of section 3, particularly concerning its words 'possible' and 'must'.[115] In the early years of the Act, the judicial response to section 3, particularly in the judgments and reasoning of the House of Lords, will be a crucial source of clearer guidelines for other courts lower down the judicial hierarchy. In developing its approach to this task, the UK judiciary will be departing significantly from their traditional common law role of ascertaining the true meaning of the statute or establishing the intention of Parliament when it enacted the statute. Instead they are now required to give preferential emphasis to whatever meaning is most compatible with the articles and jurisprudence of the Convention. They must also search for and apply whatever possible meaning prevents the

[113] HL Deb., 3 November 1997, col. 1231.

[114] Section 10.

[115] Generally see Lord Lester, 'The Art of the Possible: Interpreting Statutes under the Human Rights Act', *European Human Rights Law Review* (1998) 665.

making of a declaration of incompatibility under section 4.[116] For an authoritative opinion on this matter, one of the UK's most experienced Law Lords, Lord Steyn, has publicly said:

> Traditionally the search has been for the one true meaning of a statute. Now the search will be for a possible meaning that would prevent the need for a declaration of incompatibility. The questions will be: (1) What meanings are the words capable of yielding? (2) And, critically, can the words be made to yield a sense consistent with Convention rights? In practical effect there will be a rebuttable presumption in favour of an interpretation consistent with Convention rights. Given the inherent ambiguity of language the presumption is likely to be a strong one.[117]

An essential ingredient of the incorporation process is that, alongside the Convention articles themselves, the body of jurisprudence developed by the Strasbourg enforcement institutions is expressly made authoritative in UK domestic law as to the interpretation of the Convention's textual wording. Section 2 of the Human Rights Act stipulates that a court or tribunal when determining a question which has arisen in connection with a Convention right 'must take into account' the judgments, decisions, declarations, and advisory opinions of the European Court of Human Rights, as well as the opinions or decisions of the former Commission of Human Rights and decisions of the Committee of Ministers. A UK court or tribunal is thus under a mandatory obligation, rather than possessing a discretion, to consider these Strasbourg materials to assist in its interpretation of Convention rights and their limitations. Strasbourg decisions are to be taken into account whenever they were made or given,[118] but only 'so far as, in the opinion of the court or tribunal, it is relevant to the proceedings'. In practice, therefore, the question of relevance to the proceedings will be crucially important to the court or tribunal hearing, and for this and other reasons[119] formal rules of procedure[120] have been prepared to control the manner in which legal

[116] For criticism of a possible tension between sections 3 and 4 ('the more faithfully the courts follow the injunction to read legislation as being compatible with the Convention the less effect the Convention will have') see Geoffrey Marshall, 'Interpreting Interpretation in the Human Rights Bill', *Public Law* (1986) 167 at 170.

[117] Judicial Review Conference paper, 'Incorporation and Devolution: A Few Reflections on the Changing Scene', *European Human Rights Law Review* (1998) 153 at 155.

[118] In other words, this statutory requirement extends to Strasbourg judgments, decisions, declarations, or opinions made after the Human Rights Act as well as to ones prior to the legislation.

[119] There is considerable concern in the Lord Chancellor's Department that one effect of incorporation of the ECHR, in addition to raising the number of cases coming before the courts, will be to increase the length of case hearings due to extra points of law being dealt with founded on the Convention and Strasbourg jurisprudence.

[120] Section 2(2) provides that evidence of any judgment, decision, declaration, or opinion is to be given in proceedings in such manner as may be provided by rules of court or, in the case of proceedings before a tribunal, rules made for the purpose by the appropriate minister (by way of statutory instrument: section 20(2)).

arguments and evidence based on Strasbourg rulings are submitted by the parties in a case or their legal representatives.

It needs to be clearly understood that, whilst the requirement to take notice of Strasbourg judgments, decisions, declarations, or opinions is mandatory, UK courts and tribunals are not bound to follow them. In other words, the Strasbourg jurisprudence is highly authoritative but is not judicially binding on the decision in a domestic case. Clarifying this point during parliamentary debates on the Human Rights Bill, the Lord Chancellor Lord Irvine stated that a UK court may:

> depart from existing Strasbourg decisions and upon occasion it might well be appropriate to do so, and it is possible they might give a successful lead to Strasbourg.[121]

It is anticipated that Strasbourg decisions will normally be followed by domestic courts and tribunals,[122] and that this approach will be endorsed and elaborated upon as to its qualifications by a leading decision on the matter in the Court of Appeal or House of Lords in the next few years. Any major instances of departure, or ostensible departure, from Strasbourg decision-making are likely to reach the top domestic appellate body, the House of Lords, for a final determination of the matter together with its reasoning in support of such action. In cases where the court is considering whether to make a declaration of incompatibility, notification must be given to the government (normally represented by the Attorney General) which is then entitled to be joined as a party to the proceedings and to submit its own evidence and arguments regarding the Convention and earlier Strasbourg decisions or any other matter.[123]

[121] 'For example, it would permit the United Kingdom courts to depart from Strasbourg decisions where there has been no precise ruling on the matter', Lord Irvine went on to say: HL Deb., 18 November 1997, cols. 514–515. On a later occasion he developed the point still further, stating:

> The interpretation of the Convention rights develops over the years. Circumstances may therefore arise in which a judgment given by the European Court of Human Rights decades ago contains pronouncements which it would not be appropriate to apply to the letter in the circumstances of today in a particular set of circumstances affecting this country (HL Deb., 19 January 1998, cols. 1270–1271).

[122] 'Where it is relevant we would of course expect our courts to apply Convention jurisprudence and its principles to the cases before them' (*per* Lord Irvine, HL Deb., 18 November 1997, cols. 515).

[123] Section 5(1) Human Rights Act. Where the government (in UK law, 'the Crown') has been a party to criminal proceedings in which a declaration of incompatibility was made, it may with leave appeal to the House of Lords: section 5(4).

3. The scope of legal proceedings for breach of the Convention in the domestic courts

The Human Rights Act enables persons in the UK, for the first time, to bring legal proceedings directly against public authorities on the basis that their human rights under the Convention have been infringed. The scheme of the Act is to impose a statutory duty upon all public authorities to conduct their affairs in conformity with the standards required by the Convention. According to section 6(1), 'it is unlawful for a public authority to act in a way which is incompatible with a Convention right'. Persons aggrieved by an act or omission on the part of a public authority because it violates their fundamental human rights in the Convention can challenge the act or omission in the courts and obtain a remedy and just satisfaction.[124] However, a public authority will not be liable in such proceedings if it could not have acted in any other way because of a statutory requirement upon it, and this is clearly expressed in an Act of Parliament which the court cannot possibly interpret in a manner consistent with the Convention.[125] In such a situation, which it is hoped will be rare, the court hearing the case will proceed to consider a declaration of incompatibility under section 4, but being a non-legal ruling (as described above) this will have no effect on the outcome of the legal proceedings brought by the individual whose rights have been violated.

The category of persons who may bring legal proceedings against a public authority for breach of their human rights is restricted to those who are, or would be, a victim of the unlawful act. Proceedings should normally be brought within one year of the act complained of.[126] Where they succeed in their action, a court may award them such relief or remedy within its powers as it considers equitable in all the circumstances.[127] This victim requirement

[124] Generally see Home Office, *Rights Brought Home: The Human Rights Bill* (London: Stationery Office, Cm 3782, 1997), chapter 2: The Government's Proposals for Enforcing the Convention Rights.

[125] This proviso is expressed in section 6(2) of the Human Rights Act.

[126] Under section 7(5) a longer period may be allowed where the court or tribunal considers it equitable having regard to all the circumstances; and the one-year limitation period is subject to any shorter period applicable to the particular court proceedings being pursued, for example judicial review applications where there is a three-month limitation period (Rules of the Supreme Court, order 53; Supreme Court Act 1981, section 31).

[127] Section 9, Human Rights Act. As well as an order of the court such as a declaration or injunction, damages may be awarded but only where the court or tribunal determining the case possesses the power to award damages and the court is satisfied it is necessary to afford just satisfaction to the applicant: section 9(2) and (3). In determining the question of damages the court must take into account the principles applied by the European Court of Human Rights in relation to awards of compensation: section 9(4). The Lord Chancellor said during debate on the Human Rights Bill that, 'our aim is that people should receive damages equivalent to what they would have obtained had they taken their case to Strasbourg': HL Deb., 3 November 1997, col. 1232.

adopts the same test of standing that applies with respect to proceedings brought before the European Court of Human Rights. Furthermore, the Human Rights Act makes it clear that for the purpose of domestic legal proceedings a person is a victim of an unlawful act only if he would be a victim for the purposes of the Convention.[128] Article 34 of the Convention governs standing before the Court of Human Rights and states that 'any person, non-governmental organisation or group of individuals claiming to be the victim of a violation' may apply to it. A substantial body of Strasbourg case-law exists on the parameters of who does or does not constitute a victim, and generally it confines legal proceedings to those who are personally in need of the protection of the court (which may be actual, potential, or indirect); and it clearly excludes the possibility of an *actio popularis*, in other words proceedings by one or more citizens whose grievance is simply that a domestic law or procedure may contravene an article of the Convention.

The inclusion of a 'victim' requirement in the Human Rights Act is controversial because it is substantially narrower than the test of 'sufficient interest' which applies in ordinary common law judicial review actions which seek to challenge the acts and decisions of government and other public bodies.[129] In particular the sufficient interest test has been construed by the courts to allow public interest groups (such as the Child Poverty Action Group and the Joint Council for the Welfare of Immigrants) to bring legal proceedings in their own names on behalf of a special group of people who are, or would be, personally affected by the regulation or public act in question. By contrast, as things stand under the Human Rights Act, civil liberties pressure groups such as Liberty, Amnesty, or Justice are precluded from bringing legal proceedings themselves, though they may of course provide legal and financial assistance to someone who brings legal proceedings as a victim. Similarly, legal proceedings cannot be brought under the Human Rights Act 'victim' test by representative bodies such as trade unions or professional associations, unless that body of persons is itself the victim of the breach, as was the case in the GCHQ case where an application was received from the Council of Civil Service Unions (and six individuals), all of whose members working at a government intelligence centre in Cheltenham were without consultation

[128] See generally P. van Dijk and G. J. H. van Hoof, *Theory and Practice of the European Convention on Human Rights* (The Hague: Kluwer, 3rd edn 1998) 44–61; D. J. Harris, M. O'Boyle, and C. Warbrick, *Law of the European Convention on Human Rights* (London: Butterworths, 1995) 630–638.

[129] Supreme Court Act 1981, section 31(3); Rules of the Supreme Court, order 53 (the court may only grant leave to apply for judicial review if it 'considers that the applicant has a sufficient interest in the matter to which the application relates'). See generally Sir William Wade, *Administrative Law* (Oxford: Clarendon, 7th edn by Sir William Wade and Christopher Forsyth, 1994).

deprived as a condition of their employment of the right to belong to a trade union.[130] What aggravates this source of criticism is that no Human Rights Commission has been established which might have a role to perform in bringing test cases before the courts.[131] A further criticism of the standing test under the Human Rights Act is the sharp duality it creates within the UK legal system over legal proceedings against public bodies, since we now have:

> two streams of administrative law controls on government running side by side: a common law stream which offers plaintiffs easy access to the courts but limited grounds on which to challenge government action and a Convention stream which, while offering significantly broader grounds of review, will be substantially more difficult for a plaintiff to enter.[132]

Professor Loveland has suggested that lawyers representing clients who fall between these two tests of standing are likely to find ways of bridging the gap, by seeking *locus standi* on the basis of a common law right, and in subsequent proceedings arguing that the common law right should be construed in a way that mirrors the protections offered by the Convention.[133]

A question of major importance to the parameters of the domestic legal proceedings for breach of Convention rights surrounds the precise legal meaning of a 'public authority' (under section 6 of the Human Rights Act). Under the general scheme of the Act, the guiding test is a functional one: liability attaches to bodies who, at the time the Convention right of the victim bringing the legal proceedings is affected, are carrying out business or are in the act of performing a function of a public nature.[134] The Home Secretary explained when presenting the legislation to the House of Commons that:

> as we are dealing with public functions and with an evolving situation, we believe that the test must relate to the substance and nature of the act, not to the form and legal personality.[135]

As a minimum, liability is intended to cover those bodies in respect of whose actions the UK government are answerable to Strasbourg,[136] and where a body's activities are regarded as being of a public character for the purposes

[130] Application 11603/85, *Council of Civil Service Union v United Kingdom*, 50 DR 228; *Council of Civil Service Union v Minister for the Civil Service* [1985] AC 374.

[131] See further below. The government has not ruled out the possibility of a Human Rights Commission in the future.

[132] Ian Loveland, 'Incorporating the European Convention on Human Rights into UK Law', *Parliamentary Affairs* (1999) 112 at 121.

[133] Ibid., 122.

[134] Sub-section 6(3)(b) reads that a public authority 'includes any person certain of whose functions are functions of a public nature' which is followed by 6(5) that 'a person is not a public authority by virtue of subsection (3)(b) if the nature of the act is private'.

[135] HC Deb., 17 June 1998, col. 433.

[136] Ibid., statements of Home Secretary Jack Straw, cols. 406–408, 432–433.

of judicial review proceedings then a similar construction will normally be followed for the purposes of the Act.[137] Clear examples of public authorities, all of whose functions are public, include government departments and their executive agencies, local government, the police, immigration officers, and prisons;[138] expressly excluded by the Act are both Houses of Parliament and persons exercising any functions in connection with parliamentary proceedings.[139] The largest area of difficulty relates to the hybrid situations where a body has a mix of public and private functions, especially as in the UK over the past 20 years this type of situation has appreciably widened because of government privatization and contracting out of works formerly exercised by public sector bodies. During the passage of the Human Rights Act ministers gave examples of bodies exercising mixed functions such as train operating companies, water companies, and private security firms running prisons. So when rail and water companies are supplying their services and guaranteeing their safety they are exercising a public function, but when they are conducting commercial transactions such as the sale and purchase of the company's landholding stock those are private functions.[140]

However, a question on which there has been much analysis and conjecture is the likely impact of the Human Rights Act in the private law sphere.[141] Where private bodies, or public bodies exercising private functions, are in clear violation of a person's human rights under the Convention, they may escape liability under section 6 because they do not fall within the definition of a public authority. Yet where some other cause of action exists to enable proceedings to be brought before the court, the entire body of Convention articles and jurisprudence may then be referred to where relevant. This is on the basis that, first, all domestic statutory materials in the case must be construed for their compatibility with the Convention under section 3 (see above) and secondly, that the courts themselves are public authorities under section 6 (see above) and so must conduct their judicial work and develop UK domestic common law for compatibility with Convention principles.[142] Stated more generally, in the words of two leading UK human rights practitioners:

[137] Ibid., cols. 406–408.

[138] These bodies were specifically mentioned in the white paper accompanying publication of the Bill, Home Office, *Rights Brought Home: The Human Rights Bill* (London: Stationery Office, Cm 3782, 1997) paragraph 2.2.

[139] Section 6(3).

[140] Lord Chancellor Lord Irvine, HL Deb., 24 November 1997, col. 796.

[141] See Murray Hunt, 'The Horizontal Effect of the Human Rights Act', *Public Law* (1998) 423.

[142] The Lord Chancellor, Lord Irvine, has said that the courts

> have the duty of acting compatibly with the Convention not only in cases involving other public authorities but also in developing the common law in deciding cases between individuals (HL Deb., 24 November 1997, col. 783).

because the courts are public authorities, they have a duty to ensure that Convention rights are protected even in litigation between private parties.[143]

The overall effect of the Human Rights Act, then, in the terminology of EU law, is to allow (1) 'vertical' legal proceedings to be brought directly by individuals against state or other bodies when performing a public function, and (2) 'horizontal' legal proceedings to be brought by one private individual or company against another but indirectly through the mediation of some other originating cause of action. This wider application of the Human Rights Act is welcome because, as Professor Sir William Wade QC has commented:

> It would, indeed, be a poor sort of 'incorporation' which exempted private individuals and bodies from respecting the fundamental rights of their fellow-citizens and drove them back to Strasbourg, with all its cost in time and money—the very evil which 'incorporation' is supposed to remedy.[144]

The application of the Human Rights Act to the mass media is a controversial one, raising competing rights to be protected by the courts. On the possibility of legal proceedings being brought by victims of human rights violations under section 6, ministers have suggested that the British Broadcasting Company is subject to liability as a public authority whereas private television companies are not, and that the Press Complaints Commission is a public body but newspapers are not.[145] The press and broadcasting media receive special treatment under the Human Rights Act, regarding the legal balance between freedom of expression and the protection of personal privacy, and section 12 was added as an amendment to the original form of the Human Rights Bill following a period of intense lobbying by the media in anticipation of the courts developing a domestic law of privacy prompted by the courts' new obligations[146] to safeguard Convention rights including

[143] Lord Lester and David Pannick, *Human Rights Law and Practice* (London: Sweet & Maxwell, 1999) 31. This goes on to say that:

> The obligation of the court under section 6 will apply where the Convention has effect on the legal relationship between private parties because the state (acting through its courts) is obliged, under the Convention, to protect individuals against breaches of their rights,

and cites *inter alia Costello-Roberts v United Kingdom* (1993) 19 EHRR 112 at 132 where the European Court of Human Rights emphasized that it:

> has consistently held that the responsibility of a state is engaged if a violation of one of the rights and freedoms defined in the Convention is the result of non-observance by that state of its obligation under article 1 to secure those rights and freedoms in its domestic law to everyone within its jurisdiction . . . [T]he state cannot absolve itself from responsibility by delegating its obligations to private bodies or individuals.

[144] Sir William Wade QC, 'Human Rights and the Judiciary', *European Human Rights Law Review* (1998) 520 at 525.

[145] Home Office minister Lord Williams of Mostyn, HL Deb., 3 November 1997, cols. 1309–1310.

[146] Notably to interpret the law for conformity with the Convention under section 3 and to avoid its work as a public authority itself under section 6 violating the Convention.

Article 8. Where a court is considering whether to grant an injunction or other remedy preventing publication of material that would otherwise violate a person's rights, the court is directed to have particular regard to the importance of freedom of expression and to take into account the extent to which the material has (or is about to) become available to the public and whether it is (or would be) in the public interest for the material to be published.[147] Where an emergency injunction is applied for to prevent immediate publication by the media, the court is directed that it should only grant it if satisfied that the applicant is likely to establish at the eventual trial that publication would violate his or her rights, and if the court is satisfied that the applicant has taken all practicable steps to notify the respondent before the hearing (so as to enable them to appear before the court to make representations) or otherwise that there are compelling reasons why the respondent should not be notified.[148]

D. LEADING UK HUMAN RIGHTS CASES BEFORE THE EUROPEAN COURT OF HUMAN RIGHTS AND REMEDIAL ACTION TAKEN BY THE UK GOVERNMENT

Previous accounts[149] of the Strasbourg case-law involving the UK have tended to be chronologically narrative or grouped around the articles of the Convention, or else they have attempted to reduce the very wide and ever-growing range of subject-matter into a manageably small but artificial number of categories such as protection of minorities, conditions of punishment, or the right to a judicial decision. The study of UK cases given here is

[147] Section 12(4).

[148] Section 12(2) and (3). Another group to receive preferential treatment under the Act are Church authorities under section 13(1) which provides:

> If a court's determination of any question arising under this Act might affect the exercise by a religious organisation (itself or its members collectively) of the Convention right to freedom of thought, conscience and religion, it must have particular regard to the importance of that right.

For an argument that this section 'serves no sensible purpose' see Lord Lester and David Pannick, *Human Rights Law and Practice* (London: Sweet & Maxwell, 1999) 50–52.

[149] F. J. Hampson, 'The UK Before the European Court of Human Rights', *Yearbook of European Law* (1990) 121; A. W. Bradley, 'The UK before the Strasbourg Court 1975–1990', in W. Finnie, C. Himsworth, and N. Walker (eds), *Edinburgh Essays in Public Law* (Edinburgh University Press, 1991) 185–214; Sue Farran, *The UK Before the European Court of Human Rights: Case Law and Commentary* (London: Blackstone, 1996); C. A. Gearty (ed), *European Civil Liberties and European Convention on Human Rights* (The Hague: Martinus Hijhoff, 1997), 84–100; Brice Dickson (ed), *Human Rights and the European Convention: The Effects of the Convention on the UK and Ireland* (London: Sweet and Maxwell, 1997) chs. 3, 4, 5, 7.

illustrative and selective.[150] Its primary purpose to display, and to some extent measure, the degree of direct influence which the judgments of the

[150] A list of cases against the UK where the Strasbourg Court has found one or more violations of the Convention to exist is set out as follows, showing the applicant's name and year of judgment followed by the central human rights issue determined and the positive action taken in response by the UK government: (1) *Golder*, 1975 (interference with prisoner's correspondence: Prison (Amendment) Rules 1976, SI 1976/503), (2) *Ireland v UK*, 1978 (inhuman and degrading interrogation techniques: prime ministerial undertaking they would cease), (3) *Tyrer*, 1978 (Isle of Man corporal punishment/birching of juvenile offender: Executive Council undertaking to cease corporal punishment), (4) *Sunday Times*, 1979 (injunction restraining press reports into Thalidomide tragedy: Contempt of Court Act 1981), (5) *Young, James, and Webster*, 1981 (closed shop/compulsion to join trade union: Employment Act 1982, sections 2–14), (6) *Dudgeon*, 1981 (Northern Ireland criminality of private homosexual acts: Homosexual Offences (Northern Ireland) Order 1982, SI 1982/1536, NI 19), (7) *X (Mental Patient)*, 1981 (arbitrary detention of mentally disordered offender in hospital: Mental Health (Amendment) Act 1982, section 28 and schedule 1), (8) *Campbell and Cosans*, 1982 (corporal punishment/caning of state school children: Education No. 2 Act 1986, section 47), (9) *Silver and Others*, 1983 (interference with prisoners' correspondence: Prison (Amendment) Rules 1983, SI 1983/568), (10) *Campbell and Fell*, 1984 (restrictions on prisoners' legal representation and conduct of disciplinary proceedings: new procedural rights for prisoners including publicly funded representation), (11) *Malone*, 1984 (absence of controls over state telephone-tapping: Interception of Communications Act 1985), (12) *Abdulaziz, Cabales, and Balkandali*, 1985 (sex discrimination in immigration: Statement of Changes in Immigration Rules, laid before Parliament on 15 July 1985, HC 503), (13) *Gillow*, 1986 (Guernsey removal of pre-existing home occupation rights: damages and cessation of housing restriction), (14) *Weeks*, 1987 (arbitrary detention of mentally disordered offenders serving life sentences: government statement that Court of Appeal now unlikely to impose life sentences in similar case), (15–19, five judgments same day on similar issue) *O, H, W, B, and R* (Parental Access), 1987 (restrictions/denial of parents' access to, and independent legal review of, children compulsorily taken into state care: new code of practice and Children Act 1989, sections 22 and 34), (20) *Boyle and Rice*, 1988 (restrictions on prisoners' correspondence and visits: government apology for misapplication of rules and undertaking not to reoccur), (21) *Brogan and Others*, 1988 (special arrest and detention powers under Prevention of Terrorism Act: UK derogation from Article 5(3), ECHR), (22) *Soering*, 1989 (extradition to US state where applicant risked inhumane death row phenomenon: US government undertaking that applicant would not be charged with a capital offence), (23) *Gaskin*, 1989 (restriction on access to childhood social security records prior to Local Authority Social Services Act 1970: law on access to official information to be reformed), (24) *Granger*, 1990 (restriction on legal aid for Scottish criminal appeal: judicial practice note that courts may recommend a review of legal aid board refusal decisions), (25) *Fox, Campbell, and Hartley*, 1990 (special arrest and detention powers under 1978 Northern Ireland emergency legislation: Northern Ireland (Emergency Provisions) Act 1987, section 6, requiring reasonable suspicion before powers could be exercised, (26) *McCallum*, 1990 (interference with Scottish prisoners' correspondence: Prison (Scotland) Amendment Rules 1993, SI 1993/2227), (27) *Thynne, Wilson, and Gunnel*, 1990 (absence of judicial review of life sentence sex offenders' continued imprisonment: Criminal Justice Act 1991), (28) *Observer and Guardian*, 1991 (injunctions on press reporting of former secret serviceman's memoirs, *Spycatcher*: damages/House of Lords already refused permanent injunctions), (29) *Sunday Times*, 1991 (restrictive injunction in *Spycatcher* case extended to other newspapers: damages/House of Lords already refused permanent injunctions), (30) *Campbell*, 1992 (interference with Scottish prisoners' correspondence with lawyers and European Commission of Human Rights: administrative circular restricting any such interference to exceptional situations), (31) *Darnell*, 1993 (excessive length of time before medical disciplinary appeal proceedings: damages), (32–33, two judgments same day on similar issue) *Boner* and *Maxwell*, 1994 (refusal of legal aid for Scottish criminal appeal: Criminal Procedure (Scotland) Act 1995, section 42), (34) *Welch*, 1995 (criminal confis-

European Court of Human Rights have had upon UK domestic law and practice.

cation order under 1986 Act imposed retrospective to offence committed: confiscation order not enforced/Drug Trafficking Act 1994 and Proceeds of Crime Act 1995 ensured retrospectivity will not reoccur, (35) *McMichael*, 1995 (denial of parents' access to documents relating to children taken into state care: Children's Hearings (Scotland) Amendment Rules 1996, SI 1996/1199), (36) *Tolstoy*, 1995 (disproportionately large libel damages not 'necessary in a democratic society': Courts and Legal Services Act 1990 empowers Court of Appeal to substitute its assessment of damages for that of the jury), (37) *McCann and Others*, 1995 (SAS soldiers' shooting of suspected terrorists in Gibraltar: legal costs paid/no measures required); (38) *Murray*, 1996 (restriction on suspected terrorists' access to lawyer: UK action/execution of judgment pending), (39–40, two judgments same day on similar issue) *Hussein* and *Singh*, 1996 (arbitrary detention of persons imprisoned at Her Majesty's pleasure: Crime (Sentences) Act 1997, section 28, instituting reviews of such persons similar to discretionary life prisoners), (41) *Goodwin*, 1996 (punishment of journalist for refusing to reveal source of information: government statement that ECHR jurisprudence in some cases is taken into account in interpreting relevant legislation, (42) *Benham*, 1996 (denial of legal aid to poll tax defaulter facing sentence of imprisonment: Legal Advice and Assistance (Scope) (Amendment) Regulations 1997, SI 1997/997, providing for legal representation and extending the duty solicitor scheme in such cases), (43) *Chahal*, 1996 (deportation to India of Sikh asylum applicant: Special Immigration Appeals Commission Act 1997); (44) *Saunders*, 1996 (interference with right to silence/use by government (DTI) officials of incriminating self-statements at fraud trial: UK action/execution of judgment pending), (45) *Findlay*, 1997 (unfairness of courts martial trial process: Armed Forces Act 1996 in force from 1.4.1997 section 5 and schedule 1, section 15 and schdule 5, and section 17), (46) *Case of D*, 1997 (deportation of drug carrier with AIDS: government granted indefinite leave to stay in UK where medical treatment and care provided), (47) *Halford*, 1997 (telephone tapping: UK action/execution of judgment pending), (48) *Robins*, 1997 (excessive length of time before trial: Strasbourg judgment widely circulated to relevant bodies including Court of Appeal), (49) *Coyne*, 1997 (unfairness of courts martial trial process: Armed Forces Act 1996 in force from 1.4.1997, section 5 and schedule 1, section 15 and schedule 5, and section 17), (50) *Johnson*, 1997 (release from mental hospital: UK action/execution of judgment pending), (51) *Bowman*, 1998 (restriction on distribution of election campaign information: UK action/execution of judgment pending), (52–53, two judgments same day on similar issue) *Tinelly and Sons Ltd and Others* and *McElduff and Others*, 1998 (religious discrimination: UK action/execution of judgment pending), (54) *Case of A*, 1998 (corporal punishment: the Department of Health and the Scottish Executive have published consultation documents on how the law on reasonable chastisement of children is best reformed, UK action/execution of judgment pending), (55) *McLeod*, 1998 (police entry into home: UK action/execution of judgment pending), (56) *Osman*, 1998 (immunity of police service for negligent conduct: Home Office circular letter to police authorities advising caution in relying upon arguments of immunity in future cases, (57) *Matthews*, 1999 (restriction on Gibraltar residents' right to vote in European Parliament elections: UK action/execution of judgment pending), (58–59, two judgments same day on similar issue) *Lustig-Prean and Beckett* and *Smith and Grady*, 1999 (dismissal from armed forces for homosexuality: government statement that homosexuals no longer banned from armed forces and new code of social conduct introduced, (60) *Perks and Others*, 1999 (unfair trial for refusal to pay poll tax: UK action/execution of judgment pending), (61) *Hashman and Harrup*, 1999 (treatment of hunt saboteurs: UK action/execution of judgment pending), (62) *Thompson and Venables*, 1999 (unfair trial and arbitrary detention of juvenile offenders convicted of murder: trial judges authorized to set tariffs for juveniles sentenced to indeterminate periods of detention), (63) *Caballero*, 2000 (denial of bail/detention pending trial: Crime and Disorder Act 1998, section 56, effected in advance of judgment), (64) *McGonnell*, 2000 (Guernsey unfair trial/conflict of official work: UK action/execution of judgment pending). The list is of judgments of the European Court of Human Rights before 1 March 2000.

This influence is manifested most clearly in the remedial action taken by the UK government (where required), particularly in cases of changes to domestic primary or secondary legislation. In the UK ministerial responsibility for compliance with the judgments and decisions of the Strasbourg organs rests initially with the Foreign Secretary.[151] A designated agent for the purpose, one of the Foreign Office's legal advisers, communicates the judgment of the Strasbourg Court to the department of state concerned, together with a statement or explanation of what type of action in his opinion will be required to satisfy the judgment. Where two or more departments are affected by the Court's judgment the Cabinet Office performs a co-ordinating role operating through a committee of key officials from each department concerned.[152]

The level of impact of the Strasbourg Court's decisions, however, can be seen to have been much wider than legislative reform alone. They have been influential in prompting new departures in the development of domestic common law principle[153] and changing the criteria upon which officials conduct international relations,[154] whilst otherwise more subtly serving to shift the cultural outlook of officials and administrators of this new quasi-constitutional court over their shoulders.[155]

(1) At the time of writing a total of 102 cases have been brought against the UK by individuals leading to judgments of the European Court of Human Rights. These have taken place across a 34-year period since the right of individual petition was granted by the UK government to anyone within its juris-

[151] See statement by Lord Bassam, Home Office Minister, on the subject: HL Deb., 8 February 2000, col. WA83.

[152] Ministerial responsibility for remedial action following an adverse ruling in UK domestic courts under the Human Rights Act 1998, notably where a declaration of incompatibility might be made under section 4, is not as yet entirely clear: see ibid. Currently it is simply being emphasized that each department is responsible for ensuring that its practices, procedure, legislation, and proposals conform to the Convention's requirements: Lord Bassam, ibid, stated that 'making compatibility a matter for the centre could dilute our efforts to mainstream human rights awareness throughout Whitehall'). However, in practice some situations will require a political or senior law officer's decision, for example on whether not to accept the court's ruling and allow the case to go to Strasbourg, and this is likely to involve the Cabinet Office and/or a Ministerial Committee. Currently the Lord Chancellor, Lord Irvine, is chairman of the Cabinet ministerial sub-committee on incorporation of the Convention into UK law.

[153] As in the *Osman* case, see below.

[154] As in the *Soering* case, see below.

[155] It must be borne in mind of course that the impact of the Strasbourg enforcement machinery goes much deeper than that achieved through the formal judicial work of the European Court of Human Rights (and formerly the Commission). Unseen in official statistics are the situations where the mere threat of legal action under the Convention by an aggrieved citizen's lawyer has sometimes been enough to alter an unjustifiable or discriminatory administrative decision or impediment. Also there has been the successful work carried out under the friendly settlement procedure, brokered through the pioneering efforts of the Commission and its Secretariat. A good example of its work in the UK is the *Harman* case (Application 10038/82) which without proceeding to the Court of Human Rights led to an amendment of the law on contempt of court.

diction on 14 January 1966. By the end of the year 2000, the total number of judgments of the Court in which the UK's domestic legal or political system was held to have violated one or more articles of the Convention had reached 82.[156] In response to each adverse judgment of the Court, except for one where a derogation under Article 15 was made,[157] the UK has met its obligations (or is in the process of doing so) as required under the terms of the judgment and as supervised by the Committee of Ministers, so to give just satisfaction to the applicants and, where necessary, to take remedial action and amend domestic law or administrative procedure to bring it into conformity with the Court's ruling.[158] The issues dealt with in the UK cases before the Strasbourg Court have been broad-ranging and diverse, and cumulatively their impact upon the domestic law and practice of the UK has been pervasive. The subject-matter in the UK cases has included *inter alia* unregulated telephone-tapping practices, closed-shop trade union practices, the review of discretionary life sentences, the official birching of juvenile offenders, corporal punishment in schools, over-restrictive injunctions on freedom of expression, punishment for non-disclosure of journalistic sources of information, parental rights of access to children, access to child care records, a prisoner's right of access to a lawyer, oppressive use of incriminatory self-statements at trial, inhumane treatment of terrorist suspects, access to legal advice for fine and debt defaulters, unfair courts-martial procedures, the right to have detention orders reviewed, homosexuality in Northern Ireland, homosexuality in the armed forces, unjustifiable interference with a prisoner's correspondence, immigration rules operating in a discriminatory fashion, and extradition procedures where a risk of inhumane treatment may result.

(2) The practice of corporal punishment has been virtually terminated as a result of Strasbourg decisions on applications received from persons in the UK. The *Tyrer* case[159] in 1978 concerned the situation in the Isle of Man, a dependency of the Crown, where the practice of judicial birching of young males between 10 and 21 years of age was provided for under the Summary Jurisdiction Act 1960 (Isle of Man).[160] The victim in the case was a 15-year-old boy, who in 1972 was sentenced to three strokes of the birch by a Juvenile Court confirmed on appeal by the Manx Court of Criminal Appeal. This

[156] See chapter 1 above, Table 1.3.

[157] *Brogan, Coyle, McFaden, and Tracey v UK*, Judgment of 29 November 1988, Series A No. 145–B, on which see further below.

[158] This chapter focuses principally on leading cases which have gone to the Court of Human Rights, with some reference to cases dealt with through the decisions and opinions of the Commission of Human Rights (and the friendly settlement procedure) which have been a significant source of influence on UK affairs.

[159] *Tyrer v UK*, 25 April 1978, Series A No. 26.

[160] Judicial corporal punishment had earlier been abolished in England, Wales, and Scotland in 1948 and in Northern Ireland in 1968.

punishment was carried out at a police station in the presence of his father and a doctor where he was first made to take down his trousers and bend over a table. He complained that this constituted torture, inhuman or degrading treatment contrary to the Convention, and furthermore that it was a discriminatory practice since this type of punishment was primarily given to persons from financially and socially deprived homes. In 1976 the applicant wrote to Strasbourg to withdraw his complaint but the Commission declined to accept this since:

> the case raised questions of a general character affecting the observance of the Convention which necessitated a further examination of the issues involved.

The Court of Human Rights upheld the applicant's complaint and ruled that the practice of judicial birching was degrading treatment contrary to Article 3 (regarding it as unnecessary to deal with the Article 14 discrimination issue) and referred to the fact that judicial corporal punishment no longer existed in the great majority of member states of the Council of Europe. In response the UK authorities communicated the Court's judgment to the Isle of Man government, and expressed its opinion that this form of punishment must now be deemed to violate the Convention. The island's Chief Justice informed the judges and courts accordingly and its Executive Council gave an undertaking to stop corporal punishment.

Two complaints, joined together in the *Campbell and Cosans* case[161] in 1982, concerned corporal punishment being used as a disciplinary measure in Scottish state schools. Mrs Campbell's 9-year-old child was not actually subjected to corporal punishment but her complaint was that the school authorities refused to guarantee that he would not be. Mrs Cosans' 15-year-old son also had not actually been beaten, but he was informed he was going to be (for taking a prohibited short cut home); and subsequently because he refused to accept the punishment he was suspended from school. Mrs Campbell and Mrs Cosans submitted that the school's use of corporal punishment violated Article 3 of the Convention, and that under Protocol 1 Article 2 their rights as parents to ensure such education and teaching as was in conformity with their religious and philosophical convictions had been violated. On the particular facts of the two cases the Court found no breach of Article 3, but expressed the view that a school's threat of corporal punishment could indeed constitute torture, inhumane or degrading treatment if its anticipation in the minds of children was sufficiently real and immediate. The Court did accept, however, that there had been a breach of the parents' rights to an education for their children in conformity with their philosophical convictions, on the

[161] *Campbell and Cosans v UK*, Judgment of 25 February 1982, Series A No. 48.

basis that discipline was an integral part of an education system. The UK government's response to the *Campbell and Cosans* judgment was to include a provision in the Education (No. 2) Act 1986 abolishing corporal punishment in its state schools and in schools to which the state provided financial assistance. Shortly afterwards, prompted by further complaints relating to independent schools, including the *Costello-Roberts* case[162] in 1993, the UK extended its statutory abolition of corporal punishment to all schools, whether state, grant-maintained, or independent, in the Education Act 1996, its relevant provision now replaced by the School Standards and Framework Act 1998, section 131.

(3) A positive principle running through many of the adverse judgments against the UK has been the Court's insistence upon government according to law. This reflects the two major underlying concepts of the Convention, democracy and the rule of law, and is evident in the Convention' drafting of the scope of allowable limitations on rights.[163] Where pockets of arbitrary executive discretion have been found to exist in UK circumstances where fundamental human rights are at stake, the Court has regularly found a violation of the Convention, declaring that some sound legal framework must control the area of official activity or decision-making concerned.[164] One of the most significant events of this nature was the Strasbourg decision in the *Malone* case in 1984, an application which in the preceding domestic legal proceedings had already proved a watershed in the UK.[165] The case concerned the tapping of private telephone conversations by the police and the legal basis upon which this practice was authorized and controlled. Mr James Malone was an antiques dealer prosecuted for handling stolen goods. After two trials in 1978–79 at which the jury failed to agree a verdict he was acquitted. Mr Malone believed that his correspondence and telephone conversations had been intercepted over the period since 1971, and during his first trial the

[162] *Costello-Roberts v UK*, Judgment of 25 March 1993, Series A No. 247–C (no violation found on the particular facts but the Court elaborated on very proximate circumstances which could have breached Article 3). See also friendly settlement in *Y v UK*, Judgment of 29 October 1992, Series A No. 247–A.

[163] For example, deprivation of liberty only 'in accordance with a procedure prescribed by law' (Article 5); adjudication by an impartial body 'established by law' (Article 6); interference with privacy only 'in accordance with the law' (Article 8); restrictions on freedom of speech and expression only 'as are prescribed by law' (Articles 9 and 10); restrictions on association and assembly only as are 'prescribed by law' (Article 11).

[164] Closely associated where wide powers (of a statutory or prerogative nature) to determine a person's detention are concerned has been the Court's insistence upon legal procedures for review or appeal: see further below.

[165] As discussed above, page 951, the case was the first time in which a UK judge stated in open court that UK law was incompatible with the Convention (and that because statute had not given effect to the Convention he was powerless to redress the situation and prevent the case going to Strasbourg).

prosecution accepted that one telephone conversation had been intercepted which had been sanctioned by a warrant signed by the Home Secretary (minister for the interior). The authorities declined to disclose whether Mr Malone's mail or telephone line had otherwise been intercepted.

Mr Malone complained that the interception of his telephone conversation and the state of UK law exposed him and other residents to the risk of secret surveillance and violated his privacy as expressed in Article 8 of the Convention. Such law as existed on telephone tapping comprised an unclear mixture of various Post Office Acts and common law. and in the prior domestic proceedings the Court of Appeal held that telephone tapping was not unlawful *per se* since there was no actionable right to privacy in UK law and no right of property existed in words transmitted along telephone lines. The Court of Human Rights sitting in plenary session unanimously held that the interferences were not 'in accordance with the law' and breached the standards of the Convention. The Court ruled there was no reasonable clarity on the scope and manner of exercise of the relevant discretion conferred on public authorities and 'the minimum degree of legal protection to which citizens are entitled under the rule of law in a democratic society is lacking'.[166] As a result of the Strasbourg decision, the UK government drew up proposals for a new and comprehensive legal framework governing telephone tapping, which prohibited interceptions without a warrant, clearly defined the scope and procedure for such warrants, and created a tribunal to receive complaints, and this duly became law in 1985 as the Interception of Communications Act.

(4) The Convention has made an important contribution in UK law towards the civil rights of persons who are homosexual. In the *Dudgeon* case[167] decided in 1981, an applicant living in Belfast who was homosexual complained to Strasbourg that his right to respect for his private life under Article 8 was being unjustifiably violated by the Northern Ireland laws prohibiting and imposing criminal sanctions upon homosexual activities between consenting male

[166] Para 79. The Court followed its reasoning in the earlier German case of *Klass*, where it said:

> The rule of law implies, *inter alia*, that an interference by the executive authorities with an individual's rights should be subject to an effective control which should normally be assured by the judiciary, at least in the last resort, judicial control offering the best guarantees of independence, impartiality, and a proper procedure.

The Court in *Malone* did not find it necessary to consider whether a violation of Article 13 (right to an effective remedy) had taken place, but both the Commission and a powerful dissenting opinion by Judge Pettiti regarded an associated breach of Article 13 as essential to the substance of the case:

> The governing principle of these laws is the separation of executive and judicial powers, that is to say, not to confer on the executive the initiative and the control of the interception (*per* Judge Pettiti).

[167] *Dudgeon v UK*, Judgment of 22 October 1981, Series A No. 45.

adults. He also claimed that under Article 14 he was unjustifiably discriminated against in the enjoyment of his Convention right to a private life on the basis that as a homosexual he was subject to greater restrictions than (i) female homosexuals and (ii) male homosexuals in England and Wales where homosexual acts between consenting adults in private was not a criminal offence. In a long judgment, the Court referred to the fact that most member states of the Council of Europe did not treat homosexuality as a criminal activity, and held that interference with the applicant's right to a private life could not be justified by the UK government on the ground of any of the limitations mentioned in Article 8(2) including what was necessary in a democratic society, pressing social need, or injury to moral standards.[168] The Court awarded £3,315 costs to the applicant but no damages. As a result of the case the UK government passed the Homosexual Offences (Northern Ireland) Order 1982, which came into force on 9 December 1982, decriminalizing homosexual acts conducted in private between consenting male adults (and a similar change in the law applicable to Scotland took place).[169]

Homosexuals working for the armed forces have recently been the subject of a liberalizing judgment from the Court of Human Rights. The case of *Lustig-Prean and Beckett*,[170] on which judgment was delivered on 27 September 1999, was joined together with two similar applications, the cases of *Smith* and *Grady*. All four applicants had been dismissed from the armed forces on the sole ground of their sexual orientation, under a Ministry of Defence policy which excluded homosexuals from the services. Prior to their dismissal they were subjected to an investigation into their private lives by the military police, to whom they admitted their homosexuality. The Court of Appeal rejected their judicial review applications,[171] and they applied to Strasbourg complaining of breaches of their Convention rights under Articles 8, 14, 3, 10, and 13. The Court held that their discharge violated their right to a private life under Article 8, and made reference to the widespead and developing views and legal changes in the domestic laws of member states of the Council of Europe in favour of the admission of homosexuals into the armed forces of those states. The Court noted the lack of concrete evidence to substantiate the alleged damage to morale and operational effectiveness if homosexuals were admitted to the armed forces, and found that the views on which

[168] The Court did not examine the question of whether there had been a breach of Article 14 (non-discrimination), finding it unnecessary to do so.

[169] The restriction that then existed on homosexual activity limiting it to consenting persons who had reached the age of 21 years was held by the Court in the *Dudgeon* case not to violate Article 8 (or 14). Recent UK legislation has now reduced the age of such consent to 16.

[170] *Lustig-Prean and Beckett v UK*, Judgment of 27 September 1999: <http//www.echr.coe.int/hudoc>.

[171] *R v Ministry of Defence ex parte Smith and Others* [1996] QB 517.

the government case relied (set out in a Report commissioned on the subject) were 'founded solely upon the negative attitudes of heterosexual personnel towards those of homosexual orientation' and a 'predisposed bias'. The Court found it unnecessary to examine the complaints under Articles 10 (freedom to express their sexual identity) and 14 (non-discrimination), but held that the intrusive manner of the investigations conducted by the military police also violated Article 8. In response, the UK government on 12 January 2000 announced to Parliament that homosexuals are no longer excluded from service in the armed forces, and that a new code of social conduct had been prepared which sets out what is acceptable and unacceptable behaviour among serving personnel.[172] On 24 January 2000 it announced that over 60 offers of financial settlement had been made to persons discharged on the ground of their homosexuality.

(5) Many applications to the Court of Human Rights complaining of a breach of Convention standards in the UK have involved the fundamental rights of prisoners.[173] In the *Golder* case[174] in 1975, the first adverse ruling of the Court against the UK, the applicant was prohibited by the Home Secretary from corresponding with a solicitor for legal advice on whether to take civil proceedings against a prison officer for alleged defamatory statements which might otherwise be used prejudicially against him. He complained to the Commission that his right to respect for his correspondence and to a judicial determination of a civil right had been violated. The Court of Human Rights unanimously held that there had been a breach of Articles 8 and 6(1), adding that preventing a person from even initiating correspondence was the most far-reaching form of state interference with the right to respect for correspondence. In response, the UK government abolished the earlier requirement to petition the Home Secretary for permission to institute civil proceedings and in the Prison (Amendment) Rules 1976 created an applica-

[172] The Court had expressed its view that any difficulties arising from the change in policy towards homosexuals in the armed forces could be dealt with by the drawing up of such a code: see paras. 93–95 of the Judgment.

[173] Henry Schermers, Professor of Law at Leiden University and a former member of the Commission of Human Rights, has this interesting observation on the possible reasons for the large numbers of UK cases concerning prisons:

> Why has the treatment of prisoners in Britain given so much more reason for complaint than treatment of prisoners on the continent? One reason could be that during the War many leading personalities on the continent had been put in prison by the Nazis. The reforms of prison rules which took place after the War were therefore influenced by people who knew prison from the inside. This is why most prison regulations on the continent are rather humane. The same development did not take place in Britain. Another reason may be that at one time a part of the personnel of British prisons was recruited from the former colonial army and consisted of people who were more used to tough discipline than the social workers used in many prisons on the continent (*Legal Studies*, vol. 6 (1986) 177).

[174] *Golder v UK*, Judgment of 21 February 1975, Series A No. 18.

tion procedure for prisoners which would always be granted provided the prisoner ventilated his complaint through normal internal channels. Prison regulations were later amended again, more favourably towards prisoners, as a result of further violations of rights of access to a lawyer and censorship of prisoners' correspondence, as a result of the *Silver and Others* case[175] in 1983.

The case of *Campbell and Fell* in 1984 raised the question of disciplinary proceedings before prison tribunals (Boards of Visitors) and denial of prisoners' access to legal assistance or representation. On the facts of the case the Court found various violations in prison procedures, under Articles 6, 8, and 13 of the Convention, which related to decisions of the Board not being made public, a prisoner's inability to obtain legal assistance or representation, unjustified restriction of a prisoner's meetings and correspondence with his lawyers, and the absence of an effective domestic remedy regarding their complaints under Article 8. The applicants were awarded £13,000 in respect of their legal costs and expenses, and by way of remedial action the UK government's Prison Department amended its regulations so that publicly funded legal aid became available to prisoners facing disciplinary hearings, and decisions of Prison Boards on disciplinary cases were thereafter made public.

A prisoner's right to marry and found a family under Article 12 was raised in the *Hamer* and *Draper* cases,[176] the subject of reports by the Commission in 1979 and 1980, agreed by the Committee of Ministers the following year. In these cases two applicants complained that they were prevented from getting married whilst they were serving sentences in prison (and one of the prisoners was serving a life sentence). At that time UK law did not permit marriages in prison and the Home Secretary and prison authorities refused to allow a temporary release so that a prisoner could be married elsewhere. The Commission upheld the complaints as violations of the Convention, expressing the view that:

> the essence of the right to marry . . . is the formation of a legally binding association between a man and a woman. It is for them to decide whether or not they wish to enter such an association in circumstances where they cannot cohabit.

As a result of these cases, the UK government changed its prison procedures and passed the Marriage Act 1983 which today enables prisoners serving a determinate sentence to solemnize their marriage at their home and provides that facilities are to be made available for prisoners serving life sentences.

[175] *Silver and Others v UK*, Judgment of 25 March 1983, Series A No. 61. *Boyle and Rice v UK*, Judgment of 27 April 1988, Series A No. 131 where censorship of correspondence violated Article 8.

[176] *Hamer v UK*, No. 7114/75, 24 DR 5 (1979); *Draper v UK*, No. 8186/78, 24 DR 72 (1980).

(6) The treatment of terrorist suspects has given rise to numerous complaints against the UK before the Strasbourg authorities. In the only inter-state case[177] against the UK referred to the Court of Human Rights,[178] the Republic of Ireland complained *inter alia* of interrogation techniques introduced in Northern Ireland in 1971 which were found by the Court to be inhumane and contrary to Article 3 of the Convention. In response, the UK Prime Minister give a solemn undertaking in 1972 that the techniques of interrogation complained of would be abandoned.[179] In the *McCann* case[180] decided in 1995, the 1988 shooting of three terrorist suspects in Gibraltar by UK SAS soldiers and the military rules of engagement they were operating under were found to have violated their right to life under Article 2. The UK government paid the applicants' costs in the legal proceedings, and no further measures were required by the Court to be taken as a result of the judgment.[181] The public response of some Conservative government ministers in the UK, however, was to dispute the finding strongly.[182] The case of *Brogan*[183] in 1988 concerned the period of time for which a terrorist suspect could be held in detention. The four applicants had been held for periods of between four and six days under the Prevention of Terrorism (Temporary Provisions) Act 1983, which the Court found to be a violation of their personal liberty and rights under Article 5(3) to be brought promptly before a judge following arrest. The response of the UK government to this ruling was to insist that it was

[177] Earlier inter-state applications against the UK were brought by Greece in 1956 (No. 176/56) and 1957 (No. 299/57) concerning matters in Cyprus. The complaints alleged incompatibility of the emergency laws with the Convention and maltreatment amounting to torture. The proceedings were settled politically and the Commission's Reports on both complaints were not published.

[178] *Republic of Ireland v UK*, Judgment of 18 January 1978, Series A No. 25. The originating complaints were lodged with the Commission in 1971 and 1972.

[179] In addition new measures were taken for the better treatment of prisoners including medical examinations, procedures for investigating complaints, and stricter instructions to the security forces. The fourteen persons concerned in the case were awarded compensation of £10,000–£25,000 by the High Court of Northern Ireland.

[180] *McCann, Farrell, and Savage v UK*, Judgment of 27 September 1995, Series A No. 324.

[181] The Committee of Ministers' Deputies adopted a resolution on 20 March 1996 stating that the UK had complied with the terms of the judgment.

[182] As is often the immediate response within the domestic politics of member states to an adverse decision in Strasbourg dealing with a politically sensitive issue, the *McCann* case provoked publicly expressed dissatisfaction in the UK with the Court of Human Rights especially from within the Conservative Party. The previous year the then Prime Minister John Major had already told the House of Commons that 'We are profoundly dissatisfied with some of the court's judgments' (HC Deb., Vol. 268, Col. 488). Following the *McCann* case, it was reported in the press that the then Deputy Prime Minister Michael Heseltine had described the decision as 'incomprehensible', saying 'we will not be swayed or deterred in any way by this ludicrous decision' (*Times* and *Daily Telegraph*, 28 September 1995), and a few months later that a confidential Foreign Office memorandum was being prepared to consider how to restrict the future scope of the Court's interference in domestic matters (*Guardian*, 2 April 1996).

[183] *Brogan and Others v UK*, Judgment of 29 November 1988, Series A No. 145–B.

necessary for the special arrest and detention powers in the Act to remain in force to combat terrorism connected with the affairs of Northern Ireland. On 23 December 1988 the UK government through its permanent representative notified the Secretary General of the Council of Europe that 'a public emergency within the meaning of Article 15(1) of the Convention exists' in the UK and that it was availing itself the right of derogation conferred by Article 15(1) of the Convention 'to the extent that the exercise of these powers may be inconsistent with the obligations imposed by the Convention'.[184] This became the only UK derogation in force. Its lawfulness under the Convention (which was questioned by some at the time[185]) was confirmed by the Court of Human Rights in the subsequent case of *Brannigan and McBride*.[186] The duration of the derogation remained uncertain until the Human Rights Act imposed a maximum five-year limit upon it, effective from 2 October 2000.[187] Subsequently the derogation was formally withdrawn by the UK ambassador to Strasbourg on 19 February 2001, contemporaneously with the Terrorism Act 2000 entering into force with provisions for holding terrorist suspects in detention for beyond 48 hours only on the authority of a warrant issued by a judge.

(7) Some human rights law principles established by the Court of Human Rights as a result of litigation and complaints against the UK have acquired a continuing and wider significance across Europe generally, for the guidance and influence they offer to subsequent or newer members of the Council of Europe. These include UK cases concerning the rights of persons compulsorily detained in psychiatric institutions. It is feared that there may be, or may have been, widespread abuse of psychiatric institutions and hospitals in some parts of Europe, particularly in the former Communist Bloc states, and much has been written about such places being utilized as a means of disposing of

[184] See also, for a statement of the government's views at that time, HL Deb., 14 November 1989, cols. 307–308.

[185] See P. van Dijk and G. van Hoof, *Theory and Practice of the European Convention on Human Rights* (The Hague: Kluwer, 3rd edn 1998) 731–747 (and its earlier 1990 edition at 557–558); and F. G. Jacobs and R. C. White, *The European Convention on Human Rights* (Oxford: Clarendon, 2nd edn 1996), chapter 21.

[186] *Brannigan and McBride v UK*, Judgment of 26 May 1993, Series A No. 258–B. The complaint in this case was similar to that in the *Brogan* case, so the issue for the Court was whether the alleged breach was covered by the UK derogation.

[187] Formerly and at the time of the *Brogan* case, UK decision-making on derogation from the Convention was decided upon arbitrarily by the executive under the common law authority of the Crown prerogative requiring no formal parliamentary scrutiny, debate, or approval. Now, as from 2 October 2000, the Human Rights Act 1998 in sections 14 and 16, provides that any derogation from the Convention must be approved by both Houses of Parliament and will cease to have effect after five years, subject to the possibility of being withdrawn beforehand or being extended with the approval of both Houses of Parliament for a further five-year period.

individuals whom the state finds troublesome. The leading case of *X*[188] in 1981 concerned a convicted prisoner who was compulsorily detained indefinitely at Broadmoor, a special secure mental hospital for the criminally insane. Under the Mental Health Act 1959 the court had ordered him to be kept in Broadmoor until such time as the Home Secretary decided if and when he might be released. He was conditionally discharged in 1971 but three years later arrested and taken back to Broadmoor under warrant of the Home Secretary, following his wife complaining about him to his probation officer. His only means of challenging his detention was by way of habeas corpus proceedings, which failed.

Finding a violation of Article 5(4) of the Convention, the Court ruled that persons detained in such circumstances have the right to have the order under which they are detained reviewed at reasonable intervals. On the particular circumstances of the case, the Court did not doubt the objectivity and reliability of the medical opinion indicating that the applicant was suffering from a psychotic state. However, it emphasized that procedures for independent periodic review of detention orders were specially important in the cases of persons held in psychiatric institutions, stating that:

> a person of unsound mind compulsorily confined in a psychiatric institution for an indefinite or lengthy period is in principle entitled, at any rate where there is no automatic periodic review of a judicial character, to take proceedings at reasonable intervals before a court to put in issue the 'lawfulness' of his detention, whether that detention was ordered by a civil or criminal court or by some other authority.[189]

As a result of this case, new procedures were established in the Mental Health Act 1983 which empower persons detained to apply to a Mental Health Review Tribunal for a review of their case and possible discharge.

An earlier case settled by the Commission in 1980, *A v UK*,[190] dealt with the conditions in which psychiatric compulsory detainees should be held. The applicant, after spending periods in Broadmoor then Lincoln hospital, was released but later arrested on suspicion of starting a fire, and was compulsorily held in a secure single room in an intensive care unit at Broadmoor for about five weeks, with negligible opportunity for exercise or meeting other persons. The prisoner complained that the length of time and insanitary conditions of his solitary confinement amounted to inhuman or degrading treatment in violation of Article 3. The friendly settlement brokered by the Commission of Human Rights with the UK government brought about a major refurbishment in the intensive care unit at Broadmoor with improved

[188] *X v UK*, Judgment of 24 October 1981, Series A No. 46.
[189] See paras. 52–54.
[190] *A v UK*, case 6840/74, Report of 16 July 1980, (1980) 20 D&R 5.

accommodation and facilities, and detailed new guidelines were adopted on the regime for keeping patients in seclusion.

(8) A legal ruling of major significance to the UK's international relations beyond the Council of Europe was the *Soering* case[191] in 1989. This showed that the Court would not permit the UK (or other European member states) to co-operate in international dealings with other countries where human rights abuses awaited persons for whom they are responsible. In the case, the extradition of the applicant was sought by the United States for a murder which he and his girlfriend were alleged to have committed in Virginia when he was eighteen years old, at a time when he was suffering from mental disturbance. The state of Virginia employed the death penalty for murder and persons convicted were kept on death row for between six to eight years prior to their execution. The UK Home Secretary proceeded to sign the extradition warrant, but its implementation was suspended pending the outcome of the applicant's complaint to Strasbourg.[192] The Court of Human Rights held that the act of extradition would expose the applicant to a real risk of treatment that amounted to inhuman treatment and would therefore violate Article 3 of the Convention.[193] Responding to the ruling, the UK government informed the United States in a diplomatic note of 28 July 1989 that the extradition on murder charges for which the death penalty could be imposed was refused. When the United States agreed in a diplomatic note of 31 July 1989 that the applicant would not face capital punishment if found guilty of the charges, his extradition was allowed by the UK authorities.

(9) The *Osman* case[194] in 1998 represents a powerful source of influence over future developments in UK domestic common law. The applicants were the wife and son of a man shot dead following a series of incidents which indicated that the person who was to commit the offence posed a risk to the son, and the police were aware of the situation. Their action against the police for negligence failed in the UK courts because of their common law exclusionary

[191] *Soering v UK*, Judgment of 7 July 1989, Series A No. 161.

[192] The Commission and Court regarded the case as being of sufficient importance to speed up its normal proceedings, and the Court's decision was delivered exactly one year after the initial application was lodged and the Commission.

[193] In the court's view, having regard to the very long period of time spent on death row in such extreme conditions, with the ever-present and mounting anguish of awaiting execution of the death penalty, and to the personal circumstances of the applicant, especially his age and mental state at the time of the offence, the applicant's extradition to the United States would expose him to a real risk of treatment going beyond the threshold set by Article 3 (para. 111).

It was the death-row detention rather than capital punishment itself that could amount to inhuman treatment (paras. 100–109). The ethos of the Convention machinery clearly disapproves of the death penalty, which Protocol No. 6, Article 1 seeks to abolish, but it is provided for within the terms of Article 2(1).

[194] *Osman v UK*, Judgment of 28 October 1998: <http//www.echr.coe.int/hudoc>.

rule concerning police immunity in tort which was founded on public policy principles.[195] The Court held that the UK had breached Article 6(1) because its domestic courts applied its common law exclusionary rule disproportionately in the circumstances and this represented an unjustifiable interference with the applicant's right of access to a court. In response, on 4 March 1999 the Home Office Police Policy Directorate sent a letter to all police authorities advising police services to exercise caution before seeking to have negligence claims brought against them struck out on the legal basis of public policy immunity alone. The full implications of the Court's judgment in the *Osman* case are still being analysed by lawyers in the UK. It is almost certain to bring about a fundamental shift in the parameters and scope of the common law tort liability of public authorities generally. This will become apparent as similar or analogous cases are brought before the domestic courts over the next few years.

(10) As is discussed below,[196] the number of judgments in which the Court of Human Rights has found the UK to be in violation of the Convention has been much higher than would have been the case if the Convention had been incorporated into domestic law at an earlier stage. This has had one beneficial, if somewhat perverted, consequence in that some major landmarks in the human rights jurisprudence of the Court have been generated from issues and arguments emerging from UK cases which because of the absence of a remedy before the domestic courts have come to Strasbourg.[197] A classic instance is the case of *Young, James, and Webster*[198] in 1981, establishing the important principle that freedom of association and the right to join trade unions set out in Article 11 of the Convention means also the freedom and right of individuals not to join a trade union. The dismissal of three employees for refusing to join one of three trade unions specified in a 'closed shop' agreement with their employers, meaning that membership of one of the unions effectively became a condition of continued employment, was held by the Court to violate their human rights. The UK government accordingly amended UK law through the Employment Act 1982 so that any future dismissal from employment in such circumstances would be treated as unfair, giving rise to a legal remedy before a tribunal.

[195] The rationale is that the interests of the community as a whole are best served by a police service whose efficiency and effectiveness in the battle against crime are not jeopardized by the constant risk of exposure to tortious liability for policy and operational decisions: see para. 149 of the Court's judgment, and on the leading UK domestic law authority, *Hill v Chief Constable of West Yorkshire* [1989] AC 53.

[196] See page 999 below.

[197] F. G. Jacobs, 'Human Rights in Europe: New Dimensions', Paul Sieghart Memorial Lecture 1992 (British Institute of Human Rights), *King's College Law Journal* (1992), 49 at 51.

[198] *Young, James, and Webster v UK*, Judgment of 13 August 1981, Series A No. 44.

(11) Other major landmarks in Strasbourg jurisprudence resulting from UK cases have concerned complaints brought by newspapers to protect their freedom of expression. An important principle establishing the scope of the right to impart and receive information under Article 10 was the *Thalidomide* case[199] decided in 1979. In this case the applicant newspaper sought to publish a series of articles discussing the circumstances of the tragedy in which over 451 children were born deformed after their mothers had during pregnancy taken thalidomide as a sedative. In its first article which was published, the newspaper argued that, whether or not the company had been negligent and were legally liable in damages, they were morally obliged to make generous financial compensation to the families affected. Legal proceedings and settlement negotiations with the company were active, and in response to representations made to him by the company, the Attorney General applied to the courts for an injunction suppressing publication of the second article focusing on the question of whether the company had been negligent. The domestic courts granted the injunction on the ground that publication of the article would breach the UK *sub judice* rule prohibiting all public comment prejudicial to the outcome of legal proceedings. In its judgment, the Court of Human Rights accepted that some limitation on press freedom was necessary to preserve the independence and working of the courts, but a number of competing factors had to be taken into account in each particular case, including the right to impart and receive information of public importance and the level of likelihood of serious prejudice to the trial. On the particular circumstances of this case, the Court rejected the UK's argument that the injunctions were 'necessary in a democratic society' and held them to be an unjustified restriction on press reporting of the tragedy. Within the UK, the Strasbourg Court's ruling brought about the Contempt of Court Act 1981 which aligned domestic law with the principles expressed in the Court's judgment.

An equally famous Strasbourg ruling, again involving freedom of expression, was the *Spycatcher* case[200] in 1991. This involved a book of memoirs by Peter Wright, a former member of the British security service, which included allegations of illegal activities. The applicant newspapers complained that court injunctions obtained by the Attorney General for breach of confidence restraining their publication of extracts from Mr Wright's book violated Article 10. The Court held that during the first period of the injunction, lasting a year, there was no breach of the Convention and the suppression of the material was justified on the basis of its prejudice to the working of the

[199] *Sunday Times v UK*, Judgment of 26 April 1979, Series A No. 30.

[200] *Observer and Guardian v UK*, Judgment of 26 November 1991, Series A No. 216. See also *Sunday Times v UK*, Judgment of 26 November 1991, Series A No. 217.

security services. The injunction's validity thereafter, however, did constitute a violation of the media's right to impart information, and a new special factor supporting this reasoning was that the book had by then been published in the United States, thereby weakening the limitation on press freedom based on prejudice to the secret service. This case therefore gave emphasis to the principle of prior publication as a criterion for assessing the relevance of factors which might otherwise be conducive to imposing limitations upon freedom of expression. Once the material in dispute has become widely available, it becomes disproportionate to impose or continue restrictions upon press reporting. Within the UK judicial system, the Strasbourg Court's reasoning is now an authoritative reference for the policy grounds on which domestic courts will determine applications for injunctions against the press.

(12) Unlike the other leading cases mentioned, the more recent *McGonnell* case[201] decided in February 2000 not only concerns an individual's basic rights but has potential implications for the future constitutional structure and operation of the UK senior judiciary. The facts of the case relate to the island of Guernsey which has its own regional government and legal system operating under the Crown. In 1990 the parliament of Guernsey (the States of Deliberation) whose proceedings were then presided over by Mr Graham Dorey, Deputy Bailiff, approved a legal order (a Detailed Development Plan) governing land use on the island. The applicant sought permission from the planning authorities (the Island Development Committee) for a change of use on his land from a packing shed to a residential dwelling. This was refused on the ground that it contravened the 1990 Development Plan. The applicant proceeded to make the change to the shed anyway (for which he was convicted and fined by the Magistrates Court) and when the planning authorities threatened to carry out work to his land to remedy his breach of the planning legislation the applicant made a further application to the planning authority to allow him to continue living in the shed, which was again refused. He then appealed to the Royal Court, whose presiding judge (being the only professional judge, sitting alongside lay jurats) was the Bailiff, by that time Sir Graham Dorey, and the appeal was dismissed. The applicant complained to the European Court of Human Rights that the Royal Court had violated his right to a fair hearing by an independent and impartial tribunal under Article 6 of the Convention on the ground that the presiding judge (Sir Graham Dorey) had also been the presiding officer in the Guernsey Parliament which enacted the legislation restricting his land use. The Court of seven judges[202]

[201] *McGonnell v UK*, Judgment of 8 February 2000: <http//www.echr.coe.int/hudoc>.

[202] The case was heard by the Third Section of the Court, one of whose members was the *ad hoc* judge Sir John Laws (see note 209 below).

unanimously held that there had been a breach of Article 6.[203] At the time of writing the response of the UK government has not been communicated to the Committee of Ministers. As the decision of the Court was confined to the position of the Bailiff in Guernsey, it is most likely the communication will comprise a letter or circular from the island authorities to the effect that a new procedure providing for a substitute judge in such cases before the Royal Court will ensure no similar situation arises in the future.

The case is controversial because of its ramifications for the position of the Law Lords and the office of Lord Chancellor, who have mixed constitutional functions, as was the case with the Bailiff[204] in Guernsey. The Law Lords (or Lords of Appeal in Ordinary as they are officially styled) are members of the highest appellate court in the UK (the Judicial Committee of the House of Lords) and they are also at present automatically members of the parliamentary second chamber as a legislative body.[205] It could be argued that their independence is compromised by being both judge and law-maker and that they should therefore be disqualified from hearing cases which involve any legislative provision which they debated in Parliament or helped to prepare.

[203] The judgment reads (at para. 57):

> The Court thus considers that the mere fact that the Deputy Bailiff presided over the States of Deliberation when [the Development Plan] was adopted in 1990 is capable of casting doubt on his impartiality when he subsequently determined, as the sole judge of the law in the case, the applicant's planning appeal. The applicant therefore had legitimate grounds for fearing that the Bailiff may have been influenced by his prior participation in the adoption of [the Development Plan]. That doubt in itself, however slight its justification, is sufficient to vitiate the impartiality of the Royal Court.'

As in earlier cases against the UK where Article 6 has been in issue, the court emphasized the principle that impartiality is a question of objective appearance as well as subjective bias. The Court cited its earlier dicta in the case of *Findlay v UK,* Judgment of 25 February 1997, Reports 1997–I, where UK courts-martial procedures were held to be in violation of Article 6 that:

> in order to establish whether a tribunal can be considered as 'independent', regard must be had *inter alia* to the manner of appointment of its members and their term of office, the existence of guarantees against outside pressures and the question whether the body presents an appearance of independence (para. 73).

As a result of the *Findlay* litigation, the UK government amended its courts-martial procedures in the Armed Forces Act 1996 whereby the different functions of the convening officer are now carried out by three different bodies, the role of the confirming officer has been abolished, and a right of appeal against sentence to the Courts-Martial Appeal Court introduced.

[204] The Bailiff is appointed by the Queen and is 'the Island's chief citizen and representative'. His judicial functions include being senior judge of the Royal Court and *ex officio* the President of the Guernsey Court of Appeal. He is also President of the States of Election which *inter alia* appoint the lay members of the Royal Court who determine questions of fact and decide whether or not to allow an appeal. The Bailiff's non-judicial work includes being President of the States of Election, President of the States of Deliberation, and President of the four States Committees (the Appointments Board, the Emergency Council, the Legislation Committee, and the Rules of Procedure Committee). The person appointed has usually served beforehand as Deputy Bailiff.

[205] They are created life peers on judicial appointment under the terms of the Appellate Jurisdiction Act 1876.

The non-appearance of partiality by Law Lords is already a sensitive matter following the recent *Pinochet* litigation.[206] The Lord Chancellor is in a much worse position than the Bailiff of Guernsey under Article 6 since his office combines the functions of Cabinet Minister and senior member of the executive (usually appointed for reasons of political allegiance[207]), the head of the ministry of justice (the Lord Chancellor's Department[208]) who selects and appoints most of the judiciary, the Speaker of the parliamentary second chamber, and a judicial member of the House of Lords as the highest appellate body in cases where he chooses to sit. When asked in Parliament to respond to the *McGonnell* ruling as it affected his position, Lord Irvine, the Lord Chancellor, shrugged off the implications, saying that 'the position of the Lord Chancellor is unaffected by this decision'.[209] A spokesperson from

[206] *R v Bow Street Metropolitan Stipendiary Magistrates ex parte Pinochet Ugarte* (No. 2) [1999] 1 All ER 577 (HL) where an earlier decision of the House of Lords was invalidated on grounds of potential appearance of bias by one of the Law Lords.

[207] The present holder of the office, Lord Irvine of Lairg QC, was formerly a practising barrister and long-standing legal adviser to the Labour Party. Previous holders of the office over the past 30 years have been: between 1987–97 Lord Mackay of Clashfern, a career judge in the Scottish legal system; between June and October 1987 Lord Havers, formerly Attorney-General and a Conservative member of the House of Commons; and between 1970–74 and 1979–87 (the longest tenure this century) Lord Hailsham of Marylebone, formerly a Conservative member of the House of Commons, a Conservative peer in the House of Lords, the Chairman of the Conservative Party, and a candidate for the Conservative Party leadership.

[208] UK justice functions are not confined to the Lord Chancellor's Department and are spread across other government departments, particularly the Home Office (which for example exercises the Crown's prerogative of mercy), the Northern Ireland Office, the Welsh Office, and the Scottish Office (with certain functions devolved to the Scottish executive and parliament under the Scotland Act 1998). The legal formality is that the Queen appoints all the judges, but she always acts on the advice of the Lord Chancellor (or in the case of the top judicial officeholders including the Law Lords, Lord Chief Justice, and Master of the Rolls, on the advice of the Prime Minister who himself usually follows the recommendation of the Lord Chancellor).

[209] Parliamentary debates, HL Deb., 2 March 2000, col. 655. It is worth noting that the report on the case by the European Commission of Human Rights (20 October 1998) was taken on the basis of a significantly broader view of the institutional requirements of Article 6 than that which was subsequently adopted by the Court in its judgment (8 February 2000).

Thus whilst the Court found there had been a violation of Article 6 arising out of the Bailiff of Guernsey acting in mixed roles, it agreed with the UK government's contention that 'neither Article 6 nor any other provision of the Convention requires States to comply with any theoretical constitutional concepts as such. The question is always whether, in a given case, the requirements of the Convention are met' (para. 51). A concurring opinion by the UK judge sitting on the case, Sir John Laws, sought to narrow the implications of the decision further. He stressed that it was only the personal involvement of the Bailiff in the particular case that had given rise to the violation of Article 6. 'If it were thought arguable . . . that a violation might be shown on any wider basis, having regard to the Bailiff's multiple roles, I would express my firm dissent from any such view.' Sir John Laws (a Lord Justice of Appeal in the UK) had been nominated by the UK government to sit as an *ad hoc* judge on the case, a vacancy occurring because Sir Nicolas Bratza, the established UK judge, had previously served on the Commission when it dealt with the case.

The broader view of the Commission had been that, 'It is incompatible with the requisite appearances of independence and impartiality for a judge to have legislative and executive functions as substantial as those in the present case. The Commission finds, taking into account the

his department, however, has made it clear that from now on the Lord Chancellor will not sit in any case dealing with legislation with whose passage he was involved or where the government's interests are concerned.[210]

E. THE CONVENTION IN PARLIAMENTARY PROCEEDINGS

Until 1998 the Convention played no formal part in the proceedings of the UK Parliament. Human rights received no special attention and were not adopted in the terms of reference of any parliamentary institution or procedure of any sort, including its legislative work (where the House of Commons' detailed scrutiny of government proposals is usually carried out by standing committees) or its scrutiny of administration and policy of government departments (since 1979, conducted in more detail in the House of Commons by departmentally related select committees). For much of the period since 1950 the prevalent view among parliamentarians coincided with that of leading figures in the law, namely that the Convention merely reflected principles and practices already existing and adequately protected in the UK. The influence of the Convention in parliamentary proceedings until 1998 was entirely confined to parliamentary questions to ministers about aspects of the working of the Convention or cases before the Commission or Court and, latterly,

Bailiff's roles in the administration of Guernsey, that the fact that he has executive and legislative functions means that his independence and impartiality are capable of appearing open to doubt' (para. 61). The concurring opinion of Nicolas Bratza (as stated above, the UK Commission member at that time) supported the Commission's report, though he confined its implications to 'cases such as the present where the proceedings in which the Bailiff sits in a judicial capacity relate to the acts of decisions of the Executive'.

[210] *Guardian*, 9 February 2000; *Law Society Gazette*, 30 March 2000, 40. It is questionable whether this statement will prove a satisfactory basis for future litigation in the House of Lords, especially concerning human rights cases themselves. Later in the year the senior Law Lord, Lord Bingham of Cornhill, made a statement in the parliamentary second chamber (the House of Lords) on the principles which should guide the Law Lords with respect to their mixed legislative and judicial functions (HL Deb., 22 June 2000, col. 419). He said: 'As full members of the House of Lords the Lords of Appeal in Ordinary have a right to participate in the business of the House. However, mindful of their judicial role they consider themselves bound by two general principles when deciding whether to participate in a particular matter, or to vote: first, the Lords of Appeal in Ordinary do not think it appropriate to engage in matters where there is a strong element of party political controversy; and secondly the Lords of Appeal in Ordinary bear in mind that they might render themselves ineligible to sit judicially if they were to express an opinion on a matter which might later be relevant to an appeal to the House. The Lords of Appeal in Ordinary will continue to be guided by these broad principles. They stress that it is impossible to frame rules which cover every eventuality. In the end it must be for the judgment of each individual Lord of Appeal to decide how to conduct himself in any particular situation.'

A recent leading case on the disqualification of judges generally in the UK on grounds of bias is *Locabail (UK) Ltd v Bayfield Properties Ltd and Others* (and four other actions decided together) [2000] 1 All ER 65 (CA).

parliamentary debates about whether or not the Convention should be incorporated into UK law.[211]

However, the Human Rights Act 1998 has revolutionized the way in which government departments and parliamentary bodies take into account the Convention in carrying out their work.[212] Within government departments it is now a mandatory legal requirement for government ministers and their civil servants to examine and draw up a written report on the human rights implications of all legislation that is being prepared.[213] Section 19 of the Act[214] provides that the minister in charge of a bill in either House of Parliament must either make and publish a written statement to the effect that in his view the provisions of the bill are compatible with the Convention rights or, if he or she is unable to make such a statement, the minister must certify that the government nevertheless wishes the House to proceed with the bill. In the latter case MPs and peers will be on express notice of the implications of the legislation that is being proposed. This internal audit procedure is just part of the Labour government's declared intention to create a new awareness—or 'culture'—of human rights within and across official bureaucracies

[211] For extracts from parliamentary questions and debates on the ECHR and the form of various items of unsuccessful draft legislation to incorporate the ECHR over the period 1975 to 1996, see Robert Blackburn, *Towards a Constitutional Bill of Rights for the United Kingdom* (London: Pinter, 1999).

[212] See Robert Blackburn, 'Parliament and Human Rights', chapter XI in Dawn Oliver and Gavin Drewry (eds), *The Law and Parliament* (London: Butterworths, 1998); Robert Blackburn, 'A Human Rights Committee for the UK Parliament: The Options', *European Human Rights Law Review* (1998) 534–555; Ian Bynoe and Sarah Spencer, *Mainstreaming Human Rights in Whitehall and Westminster* (London: Institute for Public Policy Research, 1999); Justice, *Legislating for Human Rights: Developing a Human Rights Approach to Parliamentary Scrutiny* (London: Justice, 1999). For proposals earlier in the 1990s, see Liberty, *A People's Charter* (London: NCCL, 1991); David Kinley, *The European Convention on Human Rights: Compliance without Incorporation* (Aldershot: Darmouth, 1993); Michael Ryle, 'Pre-legislative Scrutiny: A Prophylactic Approach to Protection of Human Rights', *Public Law* (1994) 192; Constitution Unit, *Human Rights Legislation* (London: Constitution Unit, 1996). See further Robert Blackburn, *Towards a Constitutional Bill of Rights for the United Kingdom* (London: Pinter, 1999), chapter 5(b).

[213] Previously the theory was that government officials as a matter of course considered the implications of their work (including legislative proposals) for compatibility with UK international obligations including those under the Convention but there were considerable doubts about the rigour with which this was carried out in practice. In 1987 a new Cabinet Office circular was prepared for civil servants on Reducing the Risk of Legal Challenge, prepared in response to the huge growth in litigation in the courts against government departments. This included a section on the Convention which said:

> It should be standard practice when preparing a policy initiative for officials in individual departments, in consultation with their legal advisers, to consider the effect of existing (or expected) ECHR jurisprudence on any proposed legislative or administrative measure . . . If departments are in any doubt about the likely implications of the Convention in connection with any particular measure, they should seek *ad hoc* guidance from the Foreign and Commonwealth Office.

[214] Which came into force in 1998 in advance of the main body of the Statute.

generally. A lengthy document has been drawn up by the government[215] to form the basis upon which ministerial statements of compatibility of public bills with the Human Rights Act are made.[216]

The impact of the Human Rights Act is to extend considerably the role of parliamentary scrutiny procedures in the field of human rights affairs. The human rights articles of the Convention now figure much larger in the minds of MPs and peers as a result of their incorporation into the legal system and as a result of their attention being drawn to the Convention in the ministerial statements accompanying each government public bill. Of particular importance, however, is that under section 10 of the Human Rights Act, discussed earlier in the chapter,[217] a new legislative process is created whereby fast-track Remedial Orders may be enacted to respond swiftly to human rights violations in our existing body of primary parliamentary legislation, as determined either by a decision of the European Court of Human Rights at Strasbourg or by a declaration of incompatibility by the High Court or appellate bodies. These Remedial Orders will be affirmative statutory instruments, which are subject to a single stage of approval in each House as opposed to the three readings and committee stages applicable to a normal Bill. These Orders are authorized under the terms of the Human Rights Act to change the law in major respects which would normally be dealt with by primary Acts of Parliament, and are even empowered to amend measures of primary legislation where considered appropriate.[218]

Until the 1990s no serious thought had been given at Westminster to the creation of a parliamentary committee on human rights. No parliamentary committee had ever earlier been set up with a specific scrutiny function relating to civil liberties and human rights. Neither had any existing select committee ever incorporated any statement of human rights into its terms of reference, either of a domestic or international nature. Traditionally, this stemmed from the belief that Parliament always conducted its legislative and administrative scrutiny functions having regard to the implications of government business for the rights and freedoms of the individual, and consequently no special mechanism in either House of Parliament was necessary. In 1977 a House of Lords inquiry on incorporation of the ECHR declared itself sceptical about the utility of a special committee on human rights,

[215] The body charged with responsibility for much of the preparatory governmental work in implementing the Human Rights Act, and for monitoring and issuing guidance on the Act, has been the Human Rights Unit in the Home Office. It has generated a large amount of advisory literature and information on the Act for government departments and the public. Departmental responsibility for human rights policy formulation is shortly to be transferred from the Home Office to the Lord Chancellor's Department.

[216] *The Human Rights Act 1998 Guidance for Departments* (Home Office, 2nd edn 2000).

[217] Page 963 above.

[218] Section 10(3).

believing that such a committee was no more likely to detect a breach of human rights standards than the House as a whole would be in its general conduct of scrutinizing government bills and administrative practices.[219] Attitudes on this point began to change, however, following the *Malone* case in 1979[220] and the growing frequency with which the UK was held in violation of the Convention over the course of the next two decades.

The idea of a UK parliamentary committee on human rights emerged in the Labour Party's policy documents in 1996–97,[221] though its precise terms of reference, membership, and powers have been a source of considerable discussion and consultation. This has now been officially settled in the resolutions of both Houses of Parliament, whereby a Joint Select Committee on Human Rights has been created, which convened for its first meeting on 31 January 2001. The Committee comprises 12 members, 6 from each House, and its most specific work relates to Remedial Order legislation, described above. However, it is otherwise given a wide-ranging function to consider and report on 'matters relating to human rights in the United Kingdom (but excluding consideration of individual cases)'.[222] This allows the Committee to define its own role further and to determine the types of human rights inquiry it should prioritize.

This is important because there are a large number of human rights scrutiny functions which the Committee could usefully undertake, particularly since the government has decided, at least for the time being, not to

[219] *Report of the House of Lords Select Committee on a Bill of Rights*, HL [1977–78] 176 38.

[220] Discussed at pages 951 and 977 above.

[221] See the consultative document prepared by Jack Straw MP (then Shadow Home Secretary) and Paul Boateng (then Shadow Minister for the Lord Chancellor's Department), *Bringing Rights Home: Labour's Plans to Incorporate the European Convention on Human Rights* (Labour Party, 1996) 12; then developed in the government white paper, *Human Rights Bill: Rights Brought Home* (London: Stationery Office, Cm 3782, 1997) 14.

[222] The full terms of reference (HL Deb., 12 July 2000, cols. 233–234) are:

> To consider and report on: (a) matters relating to human rights in the United Kingdom (but excluding consideration of individual cases), (b) proposals for remedial orders, draft remedial orders and remedial orders made under Section 10 of and laid under Schedule 2 to the Human Rights Act 1998; and (c) in respect of draft remedial orders and remedial orders, whether the special attention of the House should be drawn to them on any of the grounds specified in Standing Order 73 (Lords)/151 (Commons) (Joint Committee on Statutory Instruments). To report to the House: (a) in relation to any document containing proposals laid before the House under paragraph 3 of the said Schedule 2, its recommendation whether a draft order in the same terms as the proposals should be laid before the House; or (b) in relation to any draft order laid under paragraph 2 of the said Schedule 2, its recommendation whether the draft order should be approved; and to have power to report to the House on any matter arising from its consideration of the said proposals or draft orders. To report to the House in respect of any original order laid under paragraph 4 of the said Schedule 2, its recommendation whether (a) the order should be approved in the form in which it was originally laid before Parliament; or (b) that the order should be replaced by a new order modifying the provisions of the original order; or (c) that the order should not be approved, and to have power to report to the House on any matter arising from its consideration of the said order or any replacement order.

establish an independent UK Human Rights Commission.[223] Initially, the Committee's functions are likely to be limited and are unlikely immediately to extend far into the full range of possibilities which have been canvassed in the context of the Human Rights Act and otherwise.[224] In other words, the development of human rights scrutiny procedures at Westminster will be incremental, a building-block exercise commencing with an emphasis on legislative scrutiny. Historically this is consistent with the fact that parliamentary institutions in the UK tend to prefer a process of experiment and evolution before becoming established as a permanent major innovation.

Legislation by way of Remedial Orders will clearly form a major object of inquiry for the Committee, being set out at length in its terms of reference. The provisions of the Act and parliamentary standing orders under which the Committee is established will ensure a 'scrutiny reserve', so that Remedial Orders will not be presented for parliamentary approval before each House has had the benefit of a report from the Committee. The central purpose of its work will be to ensure that the government has responded faithfully and appropriately in its drafting of the Order to the UK court's declaration of incompatibility or Strasbourg decision. But there are other categories of legislation over which the Committee could usefully extend its sphere of influence (including government bills, private members' bills, private bills, statutory instruments, and draft European law-making) whether on grounds of their compatibility with the Convention and its jurisprudence or on grounds of policy principles or good human rights practice considerations. For example, private members' bills (presented by parliamentarians who are not ministers) are not subject to statements of compatibility with the Convention in the same way as ministers, and the Committee may wish to subject selected items of such legislation to its own audit for the benefit of both Houses, analogous to the work of government departments before government bills are presented to Parliament.

Another major area in which the Committee may wish to extend its functions of scrutiny on behalf of Parliament lies in the field of international human rights treaties. The focus of this work might be twofold. A first function could be to scrutinize whether the present obligations of the UK government under

[223] See Sarah Spencer, 'A Human Rights Commission', chapter 19 in Robert Blackburn and Raymond Plant (eds), *Constitutional Reform: The Labour Government's Constitutional Reform Agenda* (London: Longman, 1999); Sarah Spencer and Ian Bynoe, *A Human Rights Commission: The Options for Britain and Northern Ireland* (London: Institute for Public Policy Research, 1998). There exists a Northern Ireland Human Rights Commission established under the Northern Ireland Act 1998, sections 68–70 and Schedule 7 (superseding the earlier Standing Advisory Committee on Human Rights).

[224] For a full study see Robert Blackburn, 'A Human Rights Committee for the UK Parliament: The Options', *European Human Rights Law Review* (1998) 534–555.

the terms of the international instruments to which it is party are being properly carried out to the satisfaction of the Westminster Parliament. This would have a wider remit than the Convention alone, and might include the International Covenant on Civil and Political Rights and the International Covenant on Economic, Social, and Cultural Rights. Recently there has been some controversy over the failure of the UK government to consult Parliament prior to carrying out its reporting obligations to the United Nations Human Rights Committee, as required under the terms of the ICCPR.[225] Similar reporting obligations are owed under a number of other international agreements to which the UK is a member, such as the International Labour Organization and the Committee on the Elimination of Discrimination against Women. New human rights scrutiny procedures might involve these draft Reports being submitted to Parliament, preceded by some form of examination and (where it is considered to be necessary) written observations by the Committee.

A second function concerns the role played by the UK Parliament in the treaty-making process. Currently, as Professor Francis Jacobs, Advocate-General at the European Court of Justice, has observed: 'by a strange anachronism, some states, notably the United Kingdom, still seem to consider that treaties are matters for governments alone'.[226] In the UK, treaties are negotiated and ratified under the extra-parliamentary common law authority of the Crown prerogative. It is the only national Parliament within the EU to lack a formal mechanism for securing parliamentary scrutiny and approval of treaties and other major foreign policy decisions. Instead, there is a voluntary government practice known as the 1924 Ponsonby rule, whereby the Foreign Office lays treaties signed by the UK before Parliament as command papers after their entry into force, and in the case of treaties requiring legal ratification a copy being placed on the Table of each House of Parliament 21 days beforehand.[227] There is a growing view that Parliament should be more closely involved in the treaty-making and treaty-amending process,[228] and the arguments for this are particularly strong with respect to human rights treaties and future amendments to the Convention itself, espe-

[225] See comments by Lord Lester, 'Taking Human Rights Seriously', chapter 4 in Robert Blackburn and James Busuttil (eds), *Human Rights for the 21st Century* (London: Pinter, 1997), especially 79–83.

[226] Quoted in parliamentary debate, HL Deb., 28 February 1996, col. 1531.

[227] See also Foreign Office, *Guidelines on Explanatory Memoranda for Treaties* (1996).

[228] Policy documents emanating from the Labour and Liberal Democrat parties have at various times proposed extending parliamentary control over a number of foreign policy matters including treaties. For example in 1993 the Labour Party argued that treaty-making (along with military involvement of UK forces overseas) was a matter requiring new formal rules for securing proper parliamentary scrutiny and approval: *A New Agenda for Democracy: Labour's Proposals for Constitutional Reform* (London: Labour Party, 1993) 33.

cially now that it has been incorporated into UK law. In 1995, for example, when Protocol No. 11 to the Convention was ratified, it was preceded by no parliamentary scrutiny or debate whatsoever. Whether or not there should now be a requirement that both Houses of Parliament signify their approval to proposed changes to the Convention or new Protocols prior to their ratification by the government, it seems appropriate for some new scrutiny reserve procedure to be developed with respect to designated international human rights instruments, among which the Convention would be first and foremost, to the effect that ratification may not take place until the draft treaty, treaty amendment, or protocol has been examined by the parliamentary committee on human rights and a report prepared for the benefit of MPs and peers beforehand.

The consultation paper on human rights reform published by the Labour Party in 1996[229] suggested that the new parliamentary Human Rights Committee could have 'a continuing responsibility to monitor the operation of the Human Rights Act'. That function might include periodic general reviews of the Act, gauging the cumulative impact of incorporation of the Convention upon the substance of UK domestic law as well as upon the administration of the courts and litigation before the Court of Human Rights at Strasbourg. The Committee might consider it worthwhile to initiate separate special inquiries into aspects of particular importance or significance to the working of the Act, such as the courts' use of their powers under section 4 to make declarations of incompatibility between statutory provisions and human rights, and questions of citizens' access to justice in the enforcement of their human rights. The Committee would no doubt seek to identify areas for improvement, where the Act was perceived by members as working less effectively than it might, and make recommendations for action.

The question of the precise workload and responsibilities of the parliamentary Committee on Human Rights is perhaps less important than ensuring that the work and functions identified as being necessary are in fact carried out by a suitable parliamentary body. In other words, a number of new parliamentary scrutiny procedures in the field of human rights are likely to emerge over the next few years, some of which have been indicated above, and what is important is that the work of the new parliamentary Committee on Human Rights dovetails with responsibilities and functions conducted by other existing or future parliamentary bodies. In particular, the role and working of the Second Chamber as a whole is now being reviewed, following the House of Lords Act 1999 removing over 600 hereditary peers from its

[229] *Bringing Rights Home: Labour's Plans to Incorporate the European Convention on Human Rights* (Labour Party, 1996).

membership, and the influential *Report of the Royal Commission on Reform of the House of Lords* in January 2000 proposed the creation of a Constitutional Committee in the House of Lords with its own Sub-Committee on Human Rights, and a new Select Committee to scrutinize all international treaties into which the government proposes to enter.[230]

The development of new human rights scrutiny procedures at Westminster over the next decade will be an important future component of Parliament's control of executive action and is to be warmly welcomed. It will help to preempt administrative practices and to minimize the risk of poorly drafted or misguided provisions reaching the statute book. Everyone agrees that the preemptive prevention of public activity and legislation likely to offend fundamental rights is preferable to relying upon the prospect of litigation under the Human Rights Act and a judicial ruling on the matter. These new developments will also, particularly in the non-legislative functions to be performed, serve to imbue the working of Parliament with a sharper sense of respect for individual rights and freedoms. Shirley Williams (the former Education Secretary in the Labour government 1974–79) put this point well during a parliamentary debate in the House of Lords on the Human Rights Bill:[231]

> Involving Parliament more in issues of human rights, giving it clear responsibilities, is not only a way of ensuring that human rights are more generally understood in the country, but also of recognising that Parliament itself could usefully discharge many functions that it is not currently asked to do. There is a great deal of talent and ability in both Houses of Parliament which remain to be tapped in the interest of trying to ensure that human rights are properly upheld.

F. ASSESSMENT AND PROSPECTS

1. *Reasons for the relatively high number of UK cases brought before the European Court of Human Rights*

A statistical assessment of all the cases brought before the European Court of Human Rights shows, in terms of numbers of cases in which a violation of the

[230] Chaired by Lord Wakeham, Cm. 4534. The Commission thought that the members of the House of Lords Sub-Committee on Human Rights could be the same peers as were members of the Joint Select Committee on Human Rights. For a view that the House of Lords should be given greater powers over constitutional and human rights affairs, see Robert Blackburn, 'The House of Lords', chapter 1 in Robert Blackburn and Raymond Plant (eds), *Constitutional Reform: The Labour Government's Constitutional Reform Agenda* (London: Longman, 1999); and Robert Blackburn, 'How Powerful Should the Second Chamber Be?', in The Constitution Unit, *The Future of the House of Lords: Conference Papers* (London: Constitution Unit, 2000) 39.

[231] HL Deb., 27 November 1997, col. 1147.

Convention was found, that the UK has the third highest total among the member states of the Council of Europe.[232] In recent years the UK has also received the third highest number of complaints brought against it by individuals. By 31 October 1998 the Commission had registered 6,118 applications of which 447 were declared admissible. This poor record has often been adversely commented upon, particularly within the UK itself.[233] It would be misleading, however, to suggest that the standard of basic human rights and the quality of freedom and tolerance in UK society are other than of a comparatively high order, and abroad throughout the period 1950–2000 the UK has continued to enjoy a favourable international reputation for the level of its protection of human rights. This is not to say that the state of human rights in the UK is without its critics.[234]

There are a number of particular national reasons which explain the relatively high numbers of complaints and findings of violations against the UK under the Convention. One is the fact that until the Human Rights Act 1998 the domestic courts in the UK were unable to apply the Convention directly themselves, so that even fairly clear cases of a breach of the Convention could not be filtered out before reaching Strasbourg. Secondly, the UK has had some special problems, notably the circumstances of Northern Ireland and its historical background, and a large number of immigration cases due to its different categories of nationality resulting from its present or former overseas territories. Thirdly, there is an unusually high level of activity among specialist organizations who are able and willing to support complaints brought under the Convention. No other country in the Council of Europe has anything near the substantial scale of this expert voluntary assistance to complainants.[235] A final factor relates to the indigenous constitutional and legal structure of the UK, particularly its lack of a written constitution or a constitutional code of fundamental rights. As Henry Schermers, a former member of the European Commission of Human Rights, has observed:

[232] See Table 1.4 in chapter 1 above.

[233] For example:

> It would help the image of Britain if those rights were brought into our law, because fewer cases would be ruled admissible by the court [at Strasbourg], to the humiliation of this country (Austin Mitchell MP, HC Deb., vol. 109, col. 1240).

[234] For example K. D. Ewing and C. A. Gearty, *Freedom under Thatcher: Civil Liberties in Modern Britain* (Oxford University Press, 1990); and Ronald Dworkin who in his pamphlet *A Bill of Rights for Britain* (Oxford University Press, 1990) argues that 'liberty is ill in Britain'.

[235] Liberty (the National Council for Civil Liberties) is the most active organization in this respect. A full list of UK bodies promoting human rights and civil liberties in this way is published by the British Institute of Human Rights at King's College London. In addition there have been a number of distinguished legal practitioners prepared to undertake *pro bono* work and offer their services free when representing victims of alleged human rights violations, including the late Peter Duffy QC, formerly lecturer in international human rights law in the University of London and governor of the British Institute of Human Rights.

[The] reason why English lawyers have been active in bringing cases to Strasbourg is a general lack of judicial control over government acts in the national legal system. There is no written constitution guaranteeing fundamental rights to individuals, English courts have no power to set aside laws which they consider contrary to human rights and their power to censure government acts is limited.[236]

2. Assessment of UK positive remedial action taken in response to Strasbourg judgments where the UK has been in violation of the Convention

In comparison with other member states of the Convention, the UK's record and standard of compliance with the judgments of the European Court of Human Rights and decisions of the Committee of Ministers is, taken as a whole, good. However, an accurate assessment of the benefit and extent of the impact made on UK law or practice as a result of the adverse Strasbourg rulings raises a number of qualifications and difficulties.

Close consideration of some of the UK cases in which the Strasbourg Court found a violation of the Convention suggests that the positive remedial action taken by the UK was in fact as limited as possible, and on occasion inadequate, despite its political acceptance by the Committee of Ministers. Thus the provisions of the Interception of Communications Act 1985, passed in response to the *Malone* judgment,[237] have been widely criticized as an inadequate guarantee against the abuse of telephone tapping as required by Strasbourg jurisprudence.[238] Applicants who complain to the tribunal established under the Act have no right to an oral hearing, nor to disclosure of documents submitted to the tribunal by the state authorities, nor to appeal from the tribunal's decision; and the tribunal's role is merely to supervise the procedure by which permission for the telephone interception was authorized, not to review the merits of whether the surveillance was a justified violation of personal privacy. Furthermore the approach of the UK government, at least until 2000, has not been to extend the implications of any single judgment into the wider aspects of the field of law concerned. Thus in response to the *Malone* case, the UK's remedial action at the time was simply to legislate for the practice of telephone-tapping alone, making no attempt to extend the principle behind the Strasbourg Court's ruling, namely, a requirement for a legal framework regulating covert state surveillance practices, to

[236] H. G. Schermers, 'Human Rights in Europe', *Legal Studies*, vol. 6 (1986) 175.

[237] See page 977 above.

[238] See John Wadham, 'Why Incorporation of the European Convention on Human Rights in Not Enough', in R. Gordon and R. Wilmot-Smith (eds), *Human Rights in the United Kingdom* (Oxford University Press, 1996) 29–30; Geoffrey Robertson, *Freedom, the Individual and the Law* (London: Penguin, 7th edn 1993) 141; Helen Fenwick, *Civil Liberties* (London: Cavendish, 2nd edn 1998), ch. 8(2), 348. See also the criticism of the Act in Parliament by Robin Cook MP on behalf of one of his constituents: HC Deb., 24 May 1990, cols. 443–450.

the host of new alternative audio and visual transmission and recording technologies.[239]

A minimalist response to adverse rulings in Strasbourg is made easier by the methods of the Court of Human Rights, which prefers to base its judicial decisions on the particular or special circumstances of the case before it. This is compounded by the perennial problem of establishing the precise parameters and binding requirements in the *ratio* of any court judgment. Making this point in a paper delivered at a British Institute of Human Rights conference,[240] Dr Robin Churchill used as an example the *Tyrer* case, mentioned above,[241] on corporal punishment.

Given that a case relates to the circumstances of a particular individual, how far is it permissible to generalise from such circumstances? Or, in other words, at what level of abstraction can the decision be read? . . . In the *Tyrer* case the Court held that the birching of a 15-year-old boy on the bare bottom as the penalty for commission of a criminal offence was 'degrading punishment' contrary to Article 3 of the Convention. From the language of the Court's judgment, it is clear that the ratio of this case is not simply that birching on the bare bottom is contrary to Article 3, but that all judicial birching of juveniles is contrary to Article 3. Probably one can go further and say that all judicial corporal punishment is contrary to Article 3, though whether one can go as far as to say that all corporal punishment is contrary to Article 3 is doubtful.

A further problem of compliance emerges from the fact that the UK is responsible for a number of separate legal systems.[242] Cases where a violation is found to exist in one jurisdiction, whether England and Wales from where most cases have arisen, or Northern Ireland, Scotland, the Channel Islands, the Isle of Man, Gibraltar or any of its other overseas territories, have not always led to reforming legislation or new administrative practice to be implemented uniformly across the whole UK, let alone throughout the dependent territories for which the UK is responsible. On the other hand, successful applications to the Commission or Court of Human Rights from residents in

[239] The absence of a statutory system to regulate the use of covert listening devices by public authorities eventually led to the case of *Khan v UK*, Judgment of 12 May 2000 (see also the domestic proceedings, *R v Khan (Sultan)* [1996] 3 All ER 289), in which the UK was again held to be in violation of Article 8 by the Court of Human Rights on similar grounds to those in *Malone*. The predictability of a violation of Article 8 being found by the Strasbourg Court in *Khan* obliged the UK government to take prior remedial action by enacting the Police Act 1997, Part III, entry into effect 1999.

[240] 'Aspects of Compliance with Findings of the Committee of Ministers and Judgments of the Court with Reference to the United Kingdom', ch. 9 in J. P. Gardner (ed), *Aspects of Incorporation of the European Convention on Human Rights into Domestic Law* (London: British Institute of International and Comparative Law & British Institute of Human Rights, 1993) 103 at 109.

[241] Page 975 above.

[242] A point also made by Dr Churchill in his valuable paper, ibid. See also Robin Churchill and James Young, 'Compliance with Judgments of the European Court of Human Rights and Decisions of the Committee of Ministers: The Experience of the United Kingdom, 1975–87', 62 *British Yearbook of International Law* (1991) 283.

one jurisdiction have sometimes spawned applications on proximate issues from another,[243] with the end result that each is brought into line with the others, representing a significant overall improvement.

The precise way in which the UK government has secured the approval of the Committee of Ministers to the action taken to fulfil its obligations arising from an adverse decision by the Court of Human Rights has on rare occasions been both unexpected and at variance with best human rights practice. The *Abdulaziz Cabales and Balkandali* case[244] in 1985 is a classic example of this. The applicants were three women from Malawi, the Philippines, and Egypt who were lawfully settled in the UK, the last a UK citizen, whose husbands from respectively Portugal, the Philippines, and Turkey were refused permission to enter or remain in the UK under new immigration rules introduced in 1980. They complained that their rights to a family life and to freedom from discrimination had been violated under Articles 8 and 14 because men lawfully resident in the UK would be entitled to be joined by their foreign wives. The Court unanimously found the effect of these immigration rules to constitute sex discrimination. The UK government duly amended the Immigration Rules on 26 August 1985, not so as to raise the position of married women to the equivalent position of men, but instead to level down the position of men so as to exclude wives joining resident husbands. Consequently neither married women nor married men could join spouses who were permanently resident in the UK, an end result that singularly failed to serve the best interests of racial minorities in the UK. Unsurprisingly, the action of the government was controversial within the UK, with some individuals hostile to the Convention greeting the result as an example of the civil liberties lobby 'shooting itself in the foot', and more sympathetic commentators describing the government's reaction as 'perverse'.[245]

The UK government has largely ignored the decisions of the European Court of Human Rights in cases against other member states. Positive action by the UK government has been confined to situations where the UK has itself been found in violation of one or more articles of the Convention, and no proactive approach has been adopted by looking for new definitional standards set by the Strasbourg Court which might be equally applicable to the UK.[246] To take just one example, the leading case of *Funke v France*,

[243] For example, the cases in each of England, Northern Ireland, and Scotland involving prisoners' correspondence and rights of access to a lawyer.

[244] *Abdulaziz, Cabales, and B Alkandali v UK*, Judgment of 28 May 1985, Series A No. 94.

[245] Francesca Klug, Keir Starmer, Stuart Weir, *The Three Pillars of Liberty* (London: Routledge, 1996) 50.

[246] This domestic attitude is widely shared by other Council of Europe countries and it is in fact rare for any state to change its law or practice following a judgment against another member state. Instances do exist, however: see ch. 3 above, especially note 42.

decided by the Strasbourg Court in 1993,[247] concerning Article 6 and the right to silence, received no special attention during the passage of the Criminal Justice and Public Order Act 1994, which provides that negative inferences may be drawn from the silence of the accused.[248] This unwillingness to act in response to rulings against other member states has been facilitated by the margin of appreciation concept[249] which, whatever its legal content, can be used in political rhetoric to deflect criticism or domestic suggestions that ethical lines drawn by the Court of Human Rights in respect of one European country might necessarily apply in others. However, since the Human Rights Act incorporated the Convention into domestic law in October 2000, UK government authorities can be expected to take a closer and more general interest in Strasbourg decisions against other member states as they arise.[250]

Yet none of the qualifications expressed above should detract from the very real, profound and beneficial impact which the Strasbourg Court rulings have had on the legal and political life of the UK, both generally in the sense of domestic acceptance of Strasbourg's external authority over the UK's historical pride and autonomy in constitutional affairs and matters of freedom, and more particularly in the steady accumulation of legislative and administrative changes which today amount to a substantial body of human rights law where no such codified law existed before.

3. Some domestic constitutional implications for the future

The Convention is accurately described as 'a law-making treaty'.[251] It empowers the Court of Human Rights to review the legislative and administrative arrangements of member states, and where they are found wanting, to require changes in the law and procedure of the national system concerned. This relationship between a judicial body and national legislature has important implications for UK domestic practice and expectations. As discussed above, no supreme court has ever existed in the UK under its unwritten constitution and the British common law has accepted the primacy of parliamentary statutes as the highest source of law. On all fundamental questions therefore, including those of an ethical and moral nature or concerning other basic human rights issues, the UK legal and political systems have proceeded

[247] Judgment of 25 February 1993, Series A No. 256–A.

[248] Subsequently challenged in Strasbourg, use of the negative inference provisions was upheld in *Murray v UK* in 1997 (judge-only trial in Northern Ireland) but not in *Condron v UK* in 2000 (jury trial in England and Wales).

[249] See pages 25 and 81.

[250] Particularly since the courts are required under s. 2 of the Human Rights Act to take into account (though not necessarily follow) the judgments of the Court of Human Rights: see pages 964–965.

[251] *Wemhoff v Germany*, Judgment of 27 June 1968, Series A No. 7.

upon the basis that Parliament has the final say, not the judiciary. The reverse side of this constitutional arrangement has been that the *responsibility* for making such decisions, for which they stand accountable to the electorate, rests firmly with the politicians in office. In UK domestic affairs a subtle shift in power and responsibility in public decision-making has started to evolve, which now looks set to become magnified as a result of incorporation of the Convention under the terms of the Human Rights Act.

To take a recent illustration, few Strasbourg cases have sharpened appreciation within the UK of the quasi-legislative function that is actually performed by the European Court of Human Rights more than that of *Lustig-Prean and Beckett*.[252] The question of whether and if so to what extent homosexuals should be allowed to serve in the armed forces had already been the subject of wide-ranging public debate in the UK, and close attention had been given to the matter by Parliament and government ministers and officials. In other words it was a matter which had been carefully thought about, not ignored. However, even though a majority of the UK population were clearly supportive of equal treatment for homosexuals, the Labour government failed to reform the discriminatory practices in the armed forces, so that progress awaited proceedings before the European Court of Human Rights. This shows the role which the Strasbourg Court has come to perform in areas where the democratic process has suffered a failure of political will to overcome prejudice or administrative obstruction. Labour government ministers who personally supported reform failed to implement the necessary changes on their own responsibility, partly one suspects because of fears about the influence of the commercially driven UK tabloid press which tends to sensationalize and exacerbate prejudice on such issues, and partly administratively (as the Court itself stated) because of the institutionalized homophobia operating within the armed forces with whom the elected government politicians had to work.

Therefore, the UK government was content for the Court of Human Rights to act as an arbitrator on the matter, so that it could avoid bringing upon itself any criticism from the armed forces or prejudiced sections of the electorate. Once the Strasbourg Court had dealt with the matter and resolved the injustice concerned, the UK government moved promptly to effect the changes required. It should also be observed that both the High Court and the Court of Appeal made plain in the prior domestic legal proceedings their view that the government was likely to lose the complaint in the *Lustig-Prean and*

[252] Page 979 above.

[253] The domestic legal proceedings are reported in *R v Ministry of Defence ex parte Smith* [1996] QB 517, and see especially the *dicta* of Simon Brown LJ at 541–542 and of Sir Thomas Bingham MR at 558–559.

Beckett case if it went before the Court of Human Rights.[253] So now, following the implementation of the Human Rights Act, the UK domestic courts will assume responsibility for deciding such public policy issues themselves. It is to be expected that other controversial and sensitive human rights policy questions will similarly be avoided by UK politicians, leaving them to be dealt with through the legal process in the domestic courts.[254]

More generally the Convention is performing a significant role in contributing to a wider process of change whereby the 'political constitution'[255] of the UK is beginning to be replaced by a more legalistic, and partly written one.[256] The present government has constantly emphasized that the Human Rights Act should be understood as forming part of a wider 'comprehensive programme of constitutional reform', as Prime Minister Tony Blair wrote in the preface to the white paper accompanying publication of the Bill.[257] The devolution legislation, in particular, is combining with the Human Rights Act to create what amounts to a network of fundamental law binding the constitutional structure of the country together.

One aspect of this is an emerging *de facto* constitutional court. The Scotland Act 1998 grants a substantial degree of legislative and executive self-government to the new Scottish Parliament and executive and establishes a mechanism whereby disputes as to its jurisdiction are to be referred to the Judicial Committee of the Privy Council, to which the Law Lords belong.[258] Furthermore, the Scotland Act makes all its legislative and executive acts

[254] On a more day-to-day level it is hoped that Members of Parliament will not abdicate any of their traditional responsibility for taking up individual grievances against official or administrative actions on behalf of their parliamentary constituents on the basis that any such grievances may now be described as being of a human rights and therefore legal nature, more suitable for citizens' advice bureaux, law centres, or legal aid solicitors' firms.

[255] See J. A. G. Griffith, 'The Political Constitution', *Modern Law Review* (1979) 1. Professor Griffith has been a leading opponent of incorporation of the ECHR into UK law: see further his book *The Politics of the Judiciary* (London: Fontana, 4th edn 1991). He was also an early advocate of creating a formal constitutional court: see his memorandum to the House of Commons Home Affairs Committee, HC [1995–96] 52–II, 260–267.

[256] The extent to which this end result was actually intended is not entirely clear. The desirability of a written constitution for the UK has not been expressly mentioned by the present Labour government since it took office in 1997 although in the 1993 Labour Party policy document, *A New Agenda for Democracy: Labour's Proposals for Constitutional Reform* (prepared at a time when Tony Blair was opposition home affairs spokesman responsible for constitutional matters), its concluding section at page 44 states:

> Though these reforms do not mean a formal written constitution, in which each aspect of government and citizens' rights is set out, they are nonetheless a significant step in that direction. Each part will require legislation which is carefully formulated and consistent with the others. We leave open the question of whether at a later stage we make progress to formal codification.

[257] *Rights Brought Home: The Human Rights Bill*, Cm. 3782 (1997).

[258] Section 33.

expressly subject to the requirements of the European Convention on Human Rights,[259] as does the Government of Wales Act 1998 in respect of its executive actions,[260] and these are constitutional questions which will go to the courts and ultimately on appeal to the Law Lords. Furthermore, the provisions of the Human Rights Act require the senior judiciary, for the first time in British constitutional history, to undertake judicial review of primary legislative Acts of Parliament. As described above,[261] section 4 of the Act provides that where a superior court is satisfied on hearing arguments from all parties to the legal proceedings that a UK statutory provision is in breach of the Convention, it may make a 'declaration of incompatibility'. The immediate consequence of such a declaration is non-legal in effect, but the significance of this unique new procedure is that the work involved, namely the examination of primary parliamentary legislation for its legitimacy in the light of a code of fundamental legal principles, is precisely the judicial function which would be exercised by a national constitutional court.

In turn, this development towards a partly written constitution and *de facto* constitutional court, drawing judges more overtly into the political arena, will focus public attention more closely than ever before upon the personalities and characteristics of the senior domestic judges, especially the Law Lords.[262] It is already widely accepted that reform of the existing judicial appointment procedures is necessary to ensure future members are drawn from a wider social and educational background.[263] More recently, these have led to the Lord Chancellor establishing an independent inquiry into judicial appointments by Sir Leonard Peach, whose recommendations in December 1999 led to the creation of an advisory Commissioner for Judicial Appointments.[264] To add to these pressures comes the recent *McGonnell* decision of the European Court of Human Rights, which has considerably strengthened the case for reorganization of the office of the Lord Chancellor and for further

[259] Sections 29(2)(d) and 57(2), Scotland Act 1998.

[260] Section 107, Government of Wales Act 1998.

[261] Page 963 above.

[262] For example the reshuffling of the Law Lords at Lord Chancellor Irvine's instigation, so that Lord Bingham took over as senior judge of the House of Lords instead of Lord Slynn (whose turn it was), started a flurry of media discussion:

> The politics of the personal is not unimportant here . . . The Human Rights Act will draw judges more into the political realm . . . The Irvine-Bingham regime—for that is what it will be, an alliance between two colleagues already very intimately acquainted—inaugurate a period of constitutional activism never before experienced by English law (Hugo Young, *Guardian*, 20 April 2000).

[263] See generally the Report of the Home Affairs Committee on Judicial Appointments Procedures, House of Commons [1995–96] 52.

[264] *Independent Scrutiny of the Appointment Processes of Judges and Queen's Counsel* (London: Lord Chancellor's Department, 1999).

restrictions on (or an end to) the Law Lords' involvement in the parliamentary second chamber.[265]

All these new directions in UK domestic affairs will be galvanized still further if the UK proceeds to adopt its own national bill of rights, a suggestion which has been made from across the political spectrum.[266] A legal code of this nature would be more elaborate in its articles and more closely attuned to the indigenous conditions of the UK,[267] whilst remaining complementary to the framework and minimum standards required by its international obligations, particularly those in the European Convention on Human Rights. On the prospects for this reform, Labour's policy documents prior to the 1997 election suggested a two-stage approach to a bill of rights.[268] They proposed that, first, the Convention should be incorporated into UK law, and then after a period in which that initial reform is successfully implemented into our domestic system, work should begin on developing a UK bill of rights:

> whilst the incorporation of the European Convention on Human Rights is a necessary first step . . . it is not a substitute for our written Bill of Rights . . . There is a good case for drafting our own Bill of Rights.[269]

The same policy documents suggested that this bill of rights should possess a measure of entrenchment and priority over ordinary Acts of Parliament in order to guarantee its provisions. Whilst Labour's 1997 election manifesto promised the Human Rights Act incorporating the Convention, it did not include a proposal for a subsequent home-grown bill of rights, concentrating

265 See page 988 above. On proposals for reform of the parliamentary second chamber and for a new Ministry of Justice, see Robert Blackburn and Raymond Plant (eds), *Constitutional Reform: The Labour Government's Constitutional Reform Agenda* (London: Longman, 1998), chapter 1: Robert Blackburn, 'The House of Lords' and chapter 16: Rodney Brazier, 'The Judiciary'. See also the large body of evidence submitted to the Royal Commission on Reform of the House of Lords (Cm 4534, 2000) together with its Report.

266 See Robert Blackburn, *Towards a Constitutional Bill of Rights for the United Kingdom* (London: Pinter, 1999), chapter 5. Leading detailed proposals have been by Institute for Public Policy Research, *A British Bill of Rights* (London: IPPR, 2nd ed. 1996); and Liberty (National Council for Civil Liberties), *A People's Charter* (London: NCCL, 1996).

267 On some 'missing rights' in the articles of the ECHR which a domestic Bill of Rights for UK society might fill, see John Wadham, Director of Liberty (National Council for Civil Liberties), in 'A British Bill of Rights', chapter 17 in Robert Blackburn and Raymond Plant (eds), *Constitutional Reform: The Labour Government's Constitutional Reform Agenda* (London: Longman, 1999) 348. They include provisions covering the right to information; the rights of immigrants, asylum seekers, and those being extradited; anti-discrimination measures; the absence of any specific rights for children; gaps in standards guaranteed for the criminal justice system and procedures for detention; and a weak provision on personal privacy not even extending to basic procedural matters covering intrusion into homes and surveillance of individuals.

268 See *A New Agenda for Democracy: Labour's Proposals for Constitutional Reform* (London: Labour Party, 1993). The constitutional reform policies of the Liberal Democrat Party are similar in this respect, as set out in their *Constitutional Declaration* (London: Liberal Democrats, 1996) and election manifesto 1997.

269 *A New Agenda for Democracy: Labour Proposals for Constitutional Reform* (London: Labour Party, 1993) 29–32.

instead on what was desirable and achievable in the short and medium term once in office. Its *Report of the Joint Consultative Committee on Constitutional Reform* in 1997, however, an agreement with the Liberal Democrat Party, expressly stated that the Human Rights Act would:

> need to be updated over time as a model for modern constitutional protection of basic human rights and responsibilities inherent in being a British citizen.[270]

In conclusion, it seems probable that a UK bill of rights will be enacted in the foreseeable future, and that whatever the government's current views on the matter may be, substantial support already exists for this next stage of reform.[271] Furthermore, the proposal is likely to gather momentum as the Human Rights Act acclimatizes the UK to the idea and practice of a positive legal code of fundamental rights in its domestic affairs.[272]

[270] Page 6.

[271] It is significant in this context that the Northern Ireland Human Rights Commission under the chairmanship of Professor Brice Dickson is currently preparing a Bill of Rights for Northern Ireland upon the basis that additional rights are required: see Northern Ireland Human Rights Commission consultation paper, *A New Bill of Rights for Northern Ireland* (Belfast, 2000).

[272] See further Robert Blackburn, *Towards a Constitutional Bill of Rights for the United Kingdom* (London: Pinter, 1999).

APPENDIX A

Speech by the Secretary General at the Commemorative Ceremony for the 50th Anniversary of the European Convention on Human Rights

Rome, 4 November 2000

Your Excellencies, Ladies and Gentlemen,

Fifty years ago today, Europe gave itself a Bill of Rights, signed here in Rome by the twelve States that made up the Council of Europe at the time.

This was an historic and unprecedented step. Two years earlier, the United Nations had adopted the Universal Declaration of Human Rights, which was to become the direct source of inspiration for the drafting of the European Convention. But the document signed here in Rome was the first text by which sovereign States agreed to be legally bound to secure to everyone within their jurisdiction a whole range of human rights and fundamental freedoms. Moreover, they agreed to set up a supranational control system in order to ensure the observance of their obligations.

Why did these European countries embark on such a daring enterprise? One does not have to look much further back in history. The Second World War and the dark days of Nazi atrocities had made it clear to everyone that one cannot rely totally on national constitutions alone to safeguard human rights. A collective guarantee was needed.

Perhaps no one has expressed this more eloquently than Pierre-Henri Teitgen, one of the great driving forces behind the creation of the Convention system. When he addressed the Consultative Assembly in September 1949 to argue the case for setting up a supranational system of human rights protection, he said (I quote):

> Many of our colleagues have pointed out that our countries are democratic and are deeply impregnated with a sense of freedom; they believe in morality and in natural law . . . Why is it necessary to build such a system? . . .
>
> Democracies do not become Nazi countries in one day. Evil progresses cunningly, with a minority operating, as it were, to remove the levers of control. One by one, freedoms are suppressed, in one sphere after another. Public opinion and the entire national conscience are asphyxiated. And then, when everything is in order, the *Führer* is installed and the evolution continues even to the oven of the crematorium.
>
> It is necessary to intervene before it is too late. A conscience must exist somewhere which will sound the alarm to the minds of a nation menaced by this progressive corruption, to warn them of the peril and to show them that they are progressing down a long road which leads far, sometimes even to Buchenwald or to Dachau. An international Court, within the Council of Europe, and a system of supervision and guarantees could be the conscience of which we all have need . . .

It is therefore fitting, on this solemn occasion, to pay tribute first of all to the wisdom and vision of all those, whether in the European Movement, the Consultative Assembly or in the Governments, who contributed to the creation of this unique system of human rights protection. In 1950, few would have expected that the pioneering work of the drafters of the Convention would lead, fifty years later, to where we are today. The Convention is now in force in forty-one countries—not counting the special position given to the Convention in Bosnia and Herzegovina under the Dayton Agreement. It constitutes an essential bill of rights for 800 million people in Europe. Well over a thousand judgments on the merits have been delivered by the old Court and the new Court together. Every week, hundreds of individuals from all parts of the continent turn their hopes to the Strasbourg Court.

But figures are only one side of the story. In fifty years' time, the Convention has grown, thanks to the development of the case law of the former Commission and the Court, and of the new Court since November 1998, into what has aptly been described as a constitutional instrument of European public order. The standards of the Convention permeate the legal systems of our member States to an extent and with an authority its founding fathers had never dreamed of. This is the result of the incredible richness of the Strasbourg case law which has given concrete content to the rights and freedoms and which today forms part and parcel of the Convention acquis. Every week, national courts in Europe apply the standards of the Convention as interpreted by the European Court of Human Rights. Innumerable are the changes of national law and practice which the Convention has brought about. I must therefore also pay tribute to the outstanding work of the former Commission, the former Court and the new Court. It is not an exaggeration to say that the law of the Convention is the common law of Europe in the field of human rights and fundamental freedoms.

I believe it is necessary to make one point very clear on the occasion of this anniversary: the Convention may have reached the age of fifty, but it is very much alive and kicking. The Court's own judicial—and perhaps more judicious—expression is that the Convention is a living instrument.

This is largely the result of the evolutive case law through which the continuing relevance of the Convention in today's world is ensured. However, let us not forget that several important protocols guaranteeing additional rights have been added to the Convention in the past decades, including Protocol No. 6 on the abolition of the death penalty. In a few hours' time, Protocol No. 12 on non-discrimination will be signed by many member States. I regard this Protocol as a landmark achievement of the Council of Europe and every signature is a clear demonstration of political will of the government concerned to combat racism and intolerance by all possible means. The same is true in respect of other kinds of discrimination. I hope and trust that the Protocol will soon obtain the number of ratifications necessary for its entry into force. But standard-setting does not stop here. Proposals for new additional protocols have been launched, including on the abolition of the death penalty in time of war.

While we rightly celebrate this fiftieth anniversary, we should not close our eyes to the many challenges that lie ahead for the Convention. The Ministerial Conference which came to a close this morning has allowed us to discuss them and to indicate pointers for the future. I will just mention three crucial issues: the future functioning of the system of individual applications given the tremendous workload of the Court; the need for increased vigilance of the Committee of Ministers in supervising the execution of judgments, and, finally, the place of the Convention in the wider European architecture, especially the question of accession by the European Union / European Community, as proposed by Finland.

The European Convention on Human Rights is a legacy which its founding fathers have given to Europe. This legacy is now in the hands of our generation. However, it is not—in the words of Protocol No. 1—a 'possession' that can be 'peacefully enjoyed'. We cannot be complacent as long as human rights continue to be violated. The full realisation of human rights and fundamental freedoms requires constant attention and efforts. The same is true for the proper functioning of the control system of the Convention.

This is not only the responsibility of the European Court of Human Rights. It is first and foremost the responsibility of the governments and the parliaments of our member States, the Committee of Ministers, the Parliamentary Assembly and the Secretary General of the Council of Europe and all others who, as national judges, as non-governmental organisations or in any other capacity, have a role to play in ensuring that the Convention rights are respected and protected across the continent. I call on all of them to exercise this responsibility to the full. The Convention exists as a collective guarantee of the individual rights of the 800 million people living in our countries. We must all do our utmost to ensure that our populations can be confident that the Convention is in good hands, now and in the future.

APPENDIX B

Resolutions and Declaration for the Future at the European Ministerial Conference, 2000

Rome, 4 November 2000

Resolution I: Institutional and Functional Arrangements for the Protection of Human Rights at National and European Level

1. The European Ministerial Conference on Human Rights ('the Conference'), meeting in Rome on the fiftieth Anniversary of the Convention for the Protection of Human Rights and Fundamental Freedoms ('the Convention'), opened for signature in Rome on 4 November 1950;

2. Noting with satisfaction the outstanding work accomplished in Europe over the last fifty years with regard to the protection and development of human rights, and stressing the unique and crucial role played in this respect by the Convention and its judicial enforcement machinery;

3. Stressing that the development of the legal protection of human rights within the framework of the Council of Europe constitutes a significant contribution towards the realisation of the aims stated in the Charter of the United Nations and of the rights stated in the Universal Declaration of Human Rights;

4. Recalling the political impetus given to the human rights work of the Council of Europe at the First and Second Summits of Heads of State and Governments of 1993 and 1997;

5. Noting, however, that there remains a need to reinforce the effective protection of human rights in domestic legal systems as well as at the European level;

6. Calling upon the member States of the Council of Europe to give new impetus to their commitments in the human rights field, essential for the security and the well-being of individuals and for the stability of the continent;

A. Improving the implementation of the Convention in member States

7. Recalling that the Convention contains common basic standards that must be implemented at national level;

8. Recalling that the status of member State of the Council of Europe implies respect for the obligations under the Convention;

9. Recalling the subsidiary nature of the control mechanism of the Convention, which presupposes that the rights guaranteed by the Convention should, first and foremost, be fully protected at national level and implemented by national authorities, in particular the courts;

10. Stressing that everyone whose rights and freedoms, as set forth in the Convention, are violated shall have the right to an effective remedy before a national authority in accordance with Article 13 of the Convention;

11. Welcoming the efforts made by member States to give full effect to the Convention in their domestic law and to conform to the judgments of the European Court of Human Rights ('the Court');

12. Welcoming in this respect the fact that the Convention has been given direct effect in the domestic legal order of almost all member States,

13. Stressing, in any case, the need to improve even further the implementation of the Convention by the member States,

14. ENCOURAGES member States to:

(i) ensure that the exercise of the rights and freedoms guaranteed by the Convention benefits from an effective remedy at national level;
(ii) undertake systematic screening of draft legislation and regulations, as well as of administrative practice, in the light of the Convention, to ensure that they are compatible with the latter's standards;
(iii) ensure that the text of the Convention is translated and widely disseminated to national authorities, notably the courts, and that the developments in the case law of the Court are sufficiently accessible in the language(s) of the country;
(iv) introduce or reinforce training in human rights for all sectors responsible for law enforcement, notably the police and the prison service, particularly with regard to the Convention and the case law of the Court;
(v) examine regularly the reservations they have made to the Convention with a view gradually to withdrawing them or limiting their scope ;
(vi) consider the ratification of Protocols to the Convention to which they are not yet Party.

B. Ensuring the effectiveness of the European Court of Human Rights

15. Paying tribute to the exceptional achievements of the Court and the former European Commission of Human Rights;

16. Concerned by the difficulties that the Court has encountered in dealing with the ever-increasing volume of applications and considering that it is the effectiveness of the Convention system which is now at issue;

17. Noting with interest the creation by the Committee of Ministers of the Council of Europe of the Liaison Committee with the European Court of Human Rights on 11 April 2000 which has the task of maintaining a dialogue between the Committee of Ministers and the Court on the future of the protection of human rights in Europe and on questions relating to the Court,

18. CALLS UPON the Committee of Ministers to:

(i) identify without delay the most urgent measures to be taken to assist the Court in fulfilling its functions;
(ii) initiate, as soon as possible, a thorough study of the different possibilities and options with a view to ensuring the effectiveness of the Court in the light of this new situation through the Liaison Committee with the European Court of Human Rights and the Steering Committee for Human Rights.

C. Improving the Committee of Ministers' supervision of the execution of Court judgments

19. Stressing the importance of the supervision of the execution of judgments for the effectiveness and credibility of the control system of the Convention;

20. Convinced of the need to exercise optimum supervision of the execution of Court judgments, which would help to avoid new violations, and to render such supervision more transparent;

21. Welcoming the adoption of Recommendation No. R (2000) 2 of the Committee of Ministers to member States on the re-examination or reopening of certain cases at domestic level following judgments of the European Court of Human Rights,

22. CALLS UPON the Committee of Ministers to:

(i) continue consideration of the ways in which this supervision can be made more effective and transparent;
(ii) pursue the revision of its Rules of Procedure concerning Article 46 of the Convention;

(iii) pursue examination of issues such as the necessity to keep applicants better informed during the supervision phase, the possible reopening or re-examination of the case, and possible responses in the event of slowness or negligence in giving effect to a judgment or even non-execution thereof;
(iv) keep the public better informed of the result of the supervision phase.

D. Improving the protection of social rights

23. Recalling the indivisibility and interdependence of all human rights;

24. Recalling the contribution of the case law of the Convention to the protection of social rights;

25. Reaffirming the importance of the European Social Charter (1961) and the Revised Social Charter (1996) and recalling that a new decisive impetus for the Charter was given by the Declaration of the second Summit of Heads of State and Government (Strasbourg, 10–11 October 1997), which called for the widest possible adherence to the Charter, and welcoming the ratifications which followed or which are being processed;

26. Welcoming the adoption of Recommendation No. R (2000) 3 of the Committee of Ministers to member States on the Right to the Satisfaction of Basic Material Needs of Persons in Situations of Extreme Hardship,

27. ENCOURAGES member States to accept the greatest possible number of provisions of the European Social Charter and Revised European Social Charter, to ratify the Protocol relating to collective complaints, to apply fully in their domestic systems those provisions of the Charter which they have accepted and to implement the above-mentioned Recommendation No. R (2000) 3;

28. INVITES the Committee of Ministers to continue consideration in order to improve the protection of social rights in Europe, including through intergovernmental co-operation and assistance.

Resolution II: Respect for Human Rights, a Key Factor for Democratic Stability and Cohesion in Europe: Current Issues

A. Improving the effectiveness of the Council of Europe's response to serious and massive violations of human rights

5. Preoccupied by situations of conflict or crisis in Europe, which pose fundamental questions of respect for human rights;

6. Recognising that terrorism in all its forms and manifestations poses a serious threat for human rights, democracy and the rule of law;

7. Noting that, notwithstanding that the Council of Europe's prime vocation is to defend human rights and that its composition is pan-European, the potential of this Organisation is not sufficiently exploited to respond to serious and massive human rights violations or to prevent such violations,

8. FIRMLY CONDEMNS all situations of serious and massive violations of human rights, including any use of torture, the systematic practice of rape and extra-judicial executions;

9. REQUESTS the appropriate bodies of the Council of Europe to assume fully their respective responsibilities, in accordance with their mandates, so that they can rapidly and effectively respond to, or prevent, such situations:

(i) The Committee of Ministers as well as the Parliamentary Assembly, each having their own political role to play whenever such violations occur in one of the member States;
(ii) the Secretary General, who can, in particular, ask any High Contracting Party to furnish explanations of the manner in which its internal law ensures the effective implementation of any of the provisions of the Convention;
(iii) the Commissioner for Human Rights who has a preventive role which he can exercise with regard to situations of crisis or conflict which could lead to serious and massive human rights violations;
(iv) the European Committee for the Prevention of Torture and Inhuman or Degrading Treatment or Punishment and those responsible for other Council of Europe bodies and mechanisms, including those monitoring member States' compliance with their commitments (the monitoring exercises), which can play a role in preventing such situations, within their respective areas of responsibility and according to their own specific means of action.

10. ENCOURAGES the Council of Europe to develop a wider range of responses to cases of failure of member States to abide by Council of Europe human rights standards;

11. CONSIDERS that it would be desirable for the Committee of Ministers to initiate consideration of the protection of human rights during armed conflicts as well as during internal disturbances and tensions, including as a result of terrorist acts, with a view to assessing the present legal situation, identifying possible gaps in the legal protection of the individual and to making proposals to fill such gaps.

B. Abolition of the death penalty, in time of war as in time of peace

12. Noting that a few member States have not yet abolished the death penalty nor ratified Protocol No. 6 to the Convention,

13. URGENTLY REQUESTS that the member States:

(i) ratify as soon as possible, if they have not yet done so, Protocol No. 6, and in the meantime, respect strictly the moratoria on executions;
(ii) refrain from extraditing or expelling individuals to countries where they run a real risk of being sentenced to death or being executed.

14. INVITES:

(i) the member States which still have the death penalty in respect of acts committed in time of war or of imminent threat of war, to consider its abolition;
(ii) the Committee of Ministers to consider the feasibility of a new additional protocol to the Convention which would exclude the possibility of maintaining the death penalty in respect of acts committed in time of war or of imminent threat of war.

C. Principles of equality and non-discrimination

15. Expressing its concern about the various threats to the principles of equality and non-discrimination, such as racism, xenophobia, anti-semitism and intolerance;

16. Recalling the Declaration and Plan of Action on combating racism, xenophobia, anti-semitism and intolerance adopted at the 1st Council of Europe Summit (Vienna, 8–9 October 1993) and the Final Declaration of the 2nd Council of Europe Summit (Strasbourg, 10–11 October 1997), which stress the need to combat racism, xenophobia, anti-semitism and intolerance;

17. Endorsing the general conclusions and the Political Declaration of the European Conference 'All different, all equal: from theory to practice' held in Strasbourg, 11–13 October 2000 (European Contribution to the World Conference against Racism, Racial Discrimination, Xenophobia and Related Intolerance);

18. Deploring, in particular, the recurrent instances of discrimination against migrants, refugees, stateless persons and asylum-seekers on grounds of their national, ethnic or cultural origin, their language, or religion, whether they belong to national minorities or not, and referring notably to the situation of Roma/Gypsies;

19. Expressing also its concern about the continuing inequalities affecting women and welcoming the work carried out by the Council of Europe in order to overcome them;

20. Endorsing also Recommendation No. R (2000) 11 of the Committee of Ministers to member States on action against trafficking in human beings for the purpose of sexual exploitation,

21. ENCOURAGES member States to reaffirm their commitment to promoting the principle of equal dignity for all as the very foundation of human rights;

22. STRESSES the adoption by the Committee of Ministers, of Protocol No. 12 to the Convention, which introduces a general prohibition of discrimination;

23. INVITES the States Parties to the Convention to consider signing Protocol No. 12 and beginning the ratification process with a view to its early entry into force;

24. ENCOURAGES member States to consider further legal, policy and other measures at the national level prohibiting incitement to hatred and discrimination;

25. INVITES the member States that have not yet done so to consider or reconsider the possibility of becoming a Party to the Framework Convention for the Protection of National Minorities (1995) and the States Parties to co-operate fully with the monitoring mechanism set up by this Convention;

26. INVITES member States to reinforce their co-operation in the framework of the Council of Europe concerning equality of women and men, with a view to:

(i) promoting increased participation of women in particular in decision-making and the balanced representation of women and men in all fields of society;
(ii) combating all forms of violence against women and particularly trafficking in women and young girls;
(iii) envisaging new initiatives in order to eliminate inequalities between women and men.

27. INVITES member States to implement the recommendations drawn up by the European Commission against Racism and Intolerance (ECRI).

D. Human rights and technological developments

28. Aware of the benefits of technological developments, but also of the possible abuses to which they could give rise, and which could threaten human dignity;

29. Welcoming the Convention for the protection of human rights and dignity of the human being with regard to the application of biology and medicine (1997) and its additional Protocol on the prohibition of cloning of human beings (1998),

30. ENCOURAGES member states that have not yet signed and ratified the above-mentioned Convention and protocol, to consider doing so;

31. SUPPORTS the activities of the Council of Europe with a view to providing for

further protection in fields such as organ transplantation, biomedical research and human genetics and the protection of the human embryo and foetus;

32. ENCOURAGES the Council of Europe to:

(i) study appropriate measures in order that other technological developments, such as in the fields of the environment and applied biotechnologies concerning products destined for human consumption, respect the quality of life and the requirements of human rights;
(ii) protect the confidentiality of private communications including those using the Internet;
(iii) pursue its work against uses of the Internet which threaten human rights, such as activities concerning child pornography, trafficking of women, racism and extremist movements.

E. Human rights and civil society

33. Reaffirming the importance of human rights education and awareness-raising and stressing that these are effective ways of preventing negative attitudes towards others and of promoting a culture of peace, tolerance and solidarity in society;

34. Recalling that such education can raise awareness of the responsibility of each individual to respect the human rights and dignity of others;

35. Stressing the importance of human rights education for the legal profession;

36. Recognising the important contribution that Ombudsmen, national human rights institutions and NGOs make to the promotion and protection of human rights and welcoming their co-operation with the Council of Europe;

37. Recalling that ensuring transparency within public administrations and guaranteeing the right of access of the public to official information are requirements of a pluralistic democratic society;

38. Recalling the fundamental importance of freedom of expression and information, as guaranteed by Article 10 of the Convention and the relevant case law of the Court, in regard to the objectives of pluralistic democracy and the protection of human rights, which are at the core of the Council of Europe action, and noting that this freedom and the freedom of the media are often among the first to be affected when massive human rights violations are committed,

39. WELCOMES the contribution of NGOs to the preparation of this Conference and the important role they play in civil society, in particular through raising awareness of human rights issues;

40. INVITES member States to take all appropriate measures with a view to developing and promoting education and awareness of human rights in all sectors of society, in particular with regard to the legal profession;

41. REQUESTS the Committee of Ministers to examine possibilities for creating a focal point within the Secretariat of the Council of Europe in order to consolidate the co-operation with Ombudsmen and national human rights institutions of the member States;

42. ENCOURAGES member States which have not yet done so to consider the possibility of establishing Ombudsmen and national human rights institutions of the member States in accordance with the relevant Recommendations of the Committee of Ministers and to ensure that there are institutions which are able to intervene in the fight against racism and intolerance;

43. WELCOMES the ongoing drafting work within the Council of Europe concerning principles which could constitute a minimum basis for access to official information,

taking into account the new environment created by information and communication technology;
44. STRESSES the necessity of guaranteeing, also in situations of conflict and tension, the freedom and independence of the media, so that they are able to inform the public without being exposed to threats, attacks or arbitrary sanctions;
45. UNDERLINES the importance of the contribution of the media to the achievement of the objectives set out by this Conference, in particular through awareness-raising of the public to human rights questions.

Declaration: The European Convention on Human Rights at Fifty—What Future for the Protection of Human Rights in Europe?

Recalling that the inherent dignity of every human being is the basis of human rights;

Reaffirming the central role of the Council of Europe in the promotion and protection of human rights in Europe and the eminent position of the Convention, with its unique system of control, as a concrete realisation of the Universal Declaration of Human Rights with regard to civil and political rights;

Emphasising the impact of the Convention and the case law of the European Court of Human Rights ('the Court') on the States Parties, and the resulting unification in Europe and welcoming the significant progress achieved in this respect across our Continent and notably, through the enlargement of the Council of Europe after 1989, in new member States;

Stressing that the Committee of Ministers' function of supervising the execution of Court judgments is absolutely essential for the effectiveness and credibility of the control system of the Convention;

Expressing willingness to strengthen further the human rights mechanisms of the Council of Europe, and in particular the control mechanism set up by the Convention, to enable them to continue to perform their function of protecting human rights in Europe;

Welcoming the commitment of other international organisations to the advancement of human rights on the continent;

Welcoming the increasing attention given to human rights within the European Union, as expressed recently through the elaboration of a Charter of Fundamental Rights,

PAYS TRIBUTE to the real progress in human rights protection made in the past fifty years;

DEPLORES the fact that, nevertheless, massive violations of the most fundamental human rights still persist in the world, including in our continent, and calls upon States to put them to an end immediately;

RECALLS that it falls in the first place to the member States to ensure that human rights are respected, in full implementation of their international commitments;

CALLS UPON all member States, to this end, to ensure constantly that their law and practice conform to the Convention and to execute the judgments of the Court;

BELIEVES that it is indispensable, having regard to the ever-increasing number of applications, that urgent measures be taken to assist the Court in carrying out its functions and that an in-depth reflection be started as soon as possible on the various possibilities and options with a view to ensuring the effectiveness of the Court in the light of this new situation;

STRESSES the need for synergy and complementarity between the Council of Europe and other institutions, particularly the United Nations, the OSCE and the European

Union, each acting in co-operation with the others and within its own field of competence.

STRESSES also the need, in regard to the European Union Charter of Fundamental Rights, to find means to avoid a situation in which there are competing and potentially conflicting systems of human rights protection, with the risk of weakening the overall protection of human rights in Europe;

EXPRESSES THE WISH that the Council of Europe bring together all European States and CALLS ON the latter to make the necessary progress in the fields of democracy, the rule of law and human rights, in order to achieve a greater unity in those key fields for the stability of the continent;

REAFFIRMS that the Convention must continue to play a central role as a constitutional instrument of European public order on which the democratic stability of the Continent depends.

SELECT BIBLIOGRAPHY

The bibliography is of selected works on national human rights law and the domestic effect of membership of the ECHR in the member states.[1]

GENERAL/COMPARATIVE WORKS

Delmas-Marty, Mireille and Chodkiewitz, C. (eds), *The European Convention for the Protection of Human Rights: International Protection versus National Restrictions* (Dordrecht: Nijhoff, 1992)

Drzemczewski, Andrew, *European Human Rights Convention in Domestic Law* (Oxford University Press, 1983, reprinted 1997)

Gardner, J. P. (ed), *Aspects of Incorporation of the European Convention on Human Rights* (London: British Institute of International and Comparative Law/British Institute of Human Rights, 1993)

Gearty, C. A. (ed), *European Civil Liberties and the European Convention on Human Rights* (The Hague: Kluwer, 1997)

Polakiewicz, Jörg, 'The Implementation of the European Convention on Human Rights in Western Europe: A Survey of National Law and Practice', and 'The Implementation of the European Convention on Human Rights in Western Europe: An Evaluation', 2 *All-European Human Rights Yearbook* (Kehl: Engel, 1992)

—— and Jacob-Foltzer, V., 'The European Human Rights Convention in Domestic Law: The Impact of Strasbourg Case-Law in States where Direct Effect is given to the Convention', 12 *Human Rights Law Journal* (1991)

AUSTRIA

Berka, Walter, 'Die Europäische Menschenrechtskonvention und die Österreichische Grundrechtstradition', *Österreichische Juristen Zeitschrift* (1979)

Ermacora, Felix; Nowak, Manfred; and Tretter, Hannes (eds), *Die Europäische Menschenrechtskonvention in der Rechtsprechung der Österreichischen Höchstgerichte* (Wien: Braumüller, 1983)

Machacek, Rudolf; Pahr, Willibald; and Stadler, Gerhard (eds), *Grund- und Menschenrechte in Österreich*, vols. I–III (Kehl-Strasbourg-Arlington: Engel, 1991, 1992, 1997)

[1] General works on the ECHR and its case-law are not included: but see Part I above and the leading publications cited therein, especially at pages 8–9, footnote 8.

Morawa, Alexander and Schreuer, Christoph, 'The Role of Domestic Courts in the Enforcement of International Human Rights: A View From Austria', in Benedetto Conforti and Francesco Francioni (eds), *Enforcing International Human Rights in Domestic Courts* (The Hague: Nijhoff, 1997)

Okresek, Wolf, 'Die Auswirkungen der Judikatur der Straßburger Menschenrechtsorgane auf die Österreichische Rechtsordnung', in: Heinrich Neisser (ed), *Menschenrechte als politischer Auftrag* (Vienna: Verlag Medien und Recht, 1993)

——'Der Einfluss der EMRK und der Judikatur der Straßburger Konventionsorgane auf die Österreichische Rechtsordnung', *Österreichisches Institut für Menschenrechte* (ed), Newsletter 1997

Tretter, Hannes, 'The implementation of judgements of the European Court of Human Rights in Austria', in: Tom Barkhuysen/Michiel van Emmerik/Piet Hein van Kempen (eds), *The Execution of Strasbourg and Geneva Human Rights Decisions in the National Legal Order* (The Hague-Boston-London: Nijhoff, 1999)

BELGIUM

Lambert, Pierre, *La Convention européenne des droits de l'homme dans la jurisprudence belge* (Bruxelles: Nemesis 1987)

Velu, Jacques, *La mise en œuvre interne de la Convention européenne des droits de l'homme* (Bruxelles: Barreau de Bruxelles, 1994)

——and Ergec, Rusen, *La Convention européenne des droits de l'homme* (Bruxelles: Bruylant, 1990)

BULGARIA

Cankov, Vasil, *Mestnoto upravlenie na Republika Balgarija: organizacionno-praven aspekt* (Sofija: Vasil Cankov, 1999)

Colakov, Radomir, *Das Recht der Rundfunkunternehmen in Bulgarien/Radomir Tscholakov* (ARGE Rundfunkrecht in den Reformstaaten, Wirtschaftsuniversität Wien) (Wien: ARGE Rundfunkrecht in den Reformstaaten, 2000)

Massias, Jean-Pierre, *Droit constitutionnel des Etats d'Europe de l'Est* (Paris: Pr. Univ. de France, 1999)

CYPRUS

Louizou, A. N., *The Constitution of the Republic of Cyprus* (Nicosia, 2001)

Nedjati, Zaim M., *Human Rights and Fundamental Freedoms* (Nicosia, 1972)

Tornaritis, C., 'The Operation of the European Convention for the Protection of Human Rights in the Republic of Cyprus', *Cyprus Law Review* (1983), 455

CZECH REPUBLIC

Čapek, J., *Evropský soud a Evropská komise pro lidská práva: přehled judikatury a nejzávažnějších případů: vzory podání* (Prague: Linde, 1995)

——*Právnický slovník evropské ochrany lidských práv* (Prague: Orac, 1998)

Čepelka, Č.; Jílek, D.; and Šturma, P., *Azyl a uprchlictví v mezinárodním právu* (Brno: Masaryk University, 1997)

Jílek, D., *Odpověď mezinárodního práva na hromadné uprchlictví* (Brno: Masaryk University, 1996)

Knapčoková, L., *Základní zásady soudního procesu obsažené v Evropské úmluvě o lidských právech a v judikatuře Evropského soudu pro lidská práva* (Prague: Charles University, 1999)

Komárková, B., *Lidská práva* (Herspice: Eman, 1997)

——*Původ a význam lidských práv* (Prague: Státní pedagogické nakladatelství, 1990)

Malenovský, J., *Poměr mezinárodního a vnitrostátního práva: obecně a v českém právu zvláště* (Brno: Doplněk, 2000)

Pavlíček, V., *Ústava a ústavní řád České republiky: komentář: 2 díl, Práva a svobody: text Listiny v plném znění, komentář, literatura, judikatura, důvodová zpráva, zpravodajská zpráva, ústavní zákon o bezpečnosti České republiky, mezinárodní smlouvy, prováděcí zákony* (Prague: Linde, 1999)

Šturma, P., *Úvod do evropského práva ochrany lidských práv* (Prague, Charles University, 1994)

——Mezinárodní a evropské kontrolní mechanismy v oblasti lidských práv (Prague: C. H. Beck, 1999)

DENMARK

Gulmann, Claus; Nielsen, Lars Nordskov; and Rehof, Lars Adam (eds), *Menneskerettigheder: Viden og handling* (1987)

Jensen, A., 'Incorporation of the European Convention seen from a Danish Point of View' in Lars Adam Rehof and Claus Gulman (eds), *Human Rights in Domestic Law and Development Assistance Policies of the Nordic Countries* (1989)

Jensen, Søren Stenderup, *The European Convention on Human Rights in Scandinavian Law: A Case Law Study* (1992)

Kjærum, Morten; Slavensky, Klaus; and Vedsted-Hansen, Jens (eds), *Grundloven og menneskerettigheder i et dansk og europæisk perspektiv* (1997)

Kofod Olsen, B., 'Denmark', in M. Scheinin (ed), *International Human Rights Norms in the Nordic and Baltic Countries* (The Hague: Kluwer, 1996), 227

Lorenzen, Peer; Rehof, Lars Adam; and Trier, Tyge, *Den Europæiske Menneskeretskonvention med kommentarer* (1994)

——; ——; and ——*Den Europæiske Menneskeretskonvention: Dokumentarbind* (1995)

Rehof, Lars Adam and Trier, Tyge, *Menneskeret* (1990)

Sørensen, Max, *Den internationale beskyttelse af menneskerettighederne* (1967)

Werlauff, Erik, *Fælleseuropæisk procesret: Europaretlige krav til dansk retspleje* (1997)

ESTONIA

Juridica International, *The Protection of Personal Rights and Freedoms* (1999)
Maruste, Rait, 'Status of the European Convention on Human Rights in the Estonian Legal System', in P. Mahoney/F. Matscher/H. Petzold/L. Wildhaber (eds), *Protecting Human Rights: The European Perspective* (Köln: Heymanns, 2000)
——*Pohiseadus ja selle jarelevalve* (1997)
——and Schneider, H., 'Constitutional Review in Estonia: Its Principal Scheme, Practice and Evaluation' in *Constitutional Reform and International Law in Central and Eastern Europe* (The Hague: Kluwer, 1998)
Merusk, K. and Narits, R., *Eesti konstitutsioonioigusest* (1988)
Neljas, A., 'Estonia', in M. Scheinin (ed), *International Human Rights Norms in the Nordic and Baltic Countries* (The Hague: Kluwer, 1996)
Trifunovska, Snezana (ed), *Minorities in Europe: Croatia, Estonia and Slovakia* (The Hague: TMC Asser Press, 1999)

FINLAND

Rosas, Allan, *International Human Rights in Domestic Law: Finnish and Polish perspectives* (Helsinki: Finnish Lawyers' Publication Company, 1990)
Scheinin, M., 'Finland', in M. Scheinin (ed), *International Human Rights Norms in the Nordic and Baltic Countries* (The Hague: Kluwer, 1996), 257
Törnudd, K., *Finland and the International Norms of Human Rights* (Dordrecht: Nijhoff, 1986)

FRANCE

Arnoux, I., *Les droits de l'être humain sur son corps* (Presses Universitaires de Bordeaux, 1995)
Braconnier, S., *Jurisprudence de la Cour européene des droits de l'homme et droit administratif français* (Bruxelles: Bruylant, 1997)
Cohen-Jonathan, G., *La Convention Européenne des Droits de l'Homme* (Paris: Economica, 1989)
——*et al.*, *Droits de l'homme en France: Dix ans d'application de la Convention européenne des droits de l'homme devant les juridictions françaises* (Kehl: Engel, 1985)
Decaux, E. 'A Report on the Role of French Judges in the Enforcement of International Human Rights' in Conforti and Francioni (eds) *Enforcing International Human Rights in Domestic Courts* (The Hague: Nijhoff, 1997)
La France et la Convention Européenne de Sauvegarde des Droits de l'Homme et des Libertés Fondamentales, XXV anniversaire de la ratification de la Convention (Paris, Special Issue of 'Europe', October 1999)
Gauchet, M., *La révolution des droits de l'homme* (Paris: Gallimard, 1989)

Heyman-Doat, A., *Libertés publiques et droits de l'homme* (4th edn, Paris: PUF, 1997)
Koering-Joulin, R. and Wachsman, P., 'France', in M. Delmas-Marty and C. Chodkiewitz (eds), *The European Convention on Human Rights: International Protection versus National Restrictions* (Dordrecht: Nijhoff, 1992)
Lebreton, G., *Libertés publiques et droits de l'homme* (Paris: Armand Colin, 3rd edn 1997)
Morange, J., *Droits de l'homme et libertés publiques* (4th edn, Paris: PUF, 1997)
Rivero, J., *Les libertés publiques 2: Le régime des principales libertés* (6th edn, Paris: PUF, 1996)
——*Le Conseil Constitutionnel et les libertés* (2nd edn, Paris: PUAM 1987)
Robert, J., *Droits de l'homme et libertés fondamentales* (6th edn, Paris: Montchrestiens 1995)
Steiner, Eva, 'France', in C. A. Gearty (ed) *European Civil Liberties and the European Convention of Human Rights* (The Hague: Kluwer, 1997)

GERMANY

Dronsch, G., *Der Rang der Europäischen Menschenrechtskonvention im deutschen Normensystem* (Quakenbrück: Kleinert 1964)
Frowein, J. A., 'The Federal Republic of Germany' in M. Delmas-Marty/ C. Chodkiewitz (eds), *The European Convention for the Protection of Human Rights: International Protection versus National Restrictions* (Dordrecht: Nijhoff 1992)
Kleeberger, W., *Die Stellung der Rechte der Europäischen Menschenrechtskonvention in der Rechtsordnung der Bundesrepublik Deutschland: Versuch einer Neubestimmung* (München: VVF 1992)
Polakiewicz, J., *Die Verpflichtungen der Staaten aus den Urteilen des Europaischen Gerichtshofs für Menschenrechte* (Berlin: Springer-Verlag 1993)
Riedl, E., 'Assertion and Protection of Human Rights in International Treaties and their Impact on the Basic Law' in C. Starck (ed), *Rights, Institutions and Impact of International Law according to the German Law* (Baden-Baden: Nomos 1987)
Simma, B.; Khan, D.; Zöckler, M.; and Geiger. R., 'The role of German courts in the enforcement of international human rights' law' in Conforti and Francioni (eds) *Enforcing International Human Rights in Domestic Courts* (The Hague: Nijhoff, 1997)
Steinberger, H., 'Reference to the case law of the organs of the European Convention on Human Rights before national courts', 6 *Human Rights Law Journal* (1985)
Stenger, C., *Gegebener und gebotener Einfluß der Europäischen Menschenrechtskonvention auf die Rechtsprechung der bundesdeutschen Strafgerichte* (Pfaffenweiler: Centaurus-Verl.-Ges. 1991)
Uerpmann, R., *Die Europäische Menschenrechtskonvention und die deutsche Rechtsprechung* (Berlin: Duncker und Humblot, 1993)
Voss, E., 'Germany' in C. A. Gearty (ed), *European Civil Liberties and the European Convention of Human Rights* (The Hague: Kluwer, 1997)

GREECE

Briolas, D., 'L'application de la Convention européenne des droits de l'homme dans l'ordre juridique des Etats contractants: Théorie et pratique helléniques', in Iliopoulos-Strangas, Julia (ed), *La protection des droits de l'homme dans le cadre européen* (Baden-Baden: Nomos 1993)

Constas, D., *The Greek Case before the Council of Europe* (Athens, 1976)

Evrigenis, D., 'Les Conflits de la Loi Nationale avec les Traités Internationaux en Droit Hellenique', *Revue Hellenique de Droit International* (1965)

Iliopoulos-Strangas, Julia, *Execution of the Judgments of the European Court of Human Rights* (Athens: Sakkoulas 1996) (in Greek)

Karagiannopoulos, F., 'The applicability of Article 6 of the ECHR in disputes between civil servants and the State', 48 *Nomiko Vima* (2000) (in Greek)

Kroustalakis, E., 'L'application de la Convention européenne des droits de l'homme dans l'ordre juridique des Etats contractants: Théorie et pratique helléniques', in Iliopoulos-Strangas, Julia (ed), *La protection des droits de l'homme dans le cadre européen* (Baden-Baden: Nomos 1993)

——'The European Convention on Human Rights: A Tool for Renewing the Courts' Jurisprudence', 48 *Nomiko Vima* (2000) (in Greek)

Milonas, Ippokratis, 'The significance of the case-law on the right to a fair trial under Article 6 of the ECHR for the Greek criminal procedure', 49 *Poinika Chronika* (1999) (in Greek)

Mpesila-Makride, Elisabet, *To Dikaioma tes Anaphoras Stis Arches Kai Ho Synegoros tu Polite* (2nd edn, Athens: Sakkoulas, 2000)

Pazartzis, Photini, 'Le statut des minorités en Grèce', 38 *Annuaire français de droit international* (1992)

Rozakis, Christos, 'The International Protection of Minorities in Greece', in Featherstone, Kevin and Ifantis, Kostas (eds), *Greece in a Changing Europe: Between European Integration and Balkan Disintegration* (Manchester University Press, 1996)

Spinellis, D., 'Conclusions from the Case-Law of the European Court of Human Rights for the Criminal Law', *Poinika Chronika* (1998) (in Greek)

Stavros, Stephanos, 'Human Rights in Greece', 17 *Journal of Modern Greek Studies* (1999)

Vegleris, Phédon, *The Convention on Human Rights and the Constitution* (Athens: Sakkoulas 1977) (in Greek)

HUNGARY

Bán, Tamás, 'The impact of the European Convention on Human Rights on Hungarian Legal Development', 1 *Európajogi tanulmányok* (1993)

Bán, T. and Bárd, K., 'The European Convention on Human Rights and the Hungarian Legal System', 6 and 7 *Acta Humana* (1992)

Bárd, Tamás and Bárd, Károly, 'The European Convention on Human Rights and the Hungarian Legal System', 6 and 7 *Acta Humana* (1992)

Blutman, L., 'The European Convention on Human Rights in the Hungarian Legal Order', 1 *Európa Fórum* (1992)
Bokor-Szegö, Hanna, 'Rights protected by the European Convention on Human Rights and obligations of states', 5 *Acta Humana* (1991)
Council of Europe Directorate of Human Rights, *Compatibility of Hungarian Law with the European Convention on Human Rights: preparatory work prior to ratification* (Council of Europe, 1995)
Grád, András, 'Hungarian family law and requirements of the European Convention on Human Rights', 7 *Társadalmi Szemle* (1997)
Kardos, Gábor, 'Prohibition of discrimination under the European Convention on Human Rights and in the jurisprudence of the European Court and Commission of Human Rights', 1 *Jogtudományi Közlöny* (1992)
Mavi, Viktor, 'The Right to Personal Liberty and Security in the European Convention on Human Rights', 10 *Acta Humana* (1993)
Takács, Albert, 'Dilemmas of constitutionalism in the decisions of the Hungarian Constitutional Court', 3 and 4 *Acta Juridica Academiae Scientiarum Hungaricae* (1991)
Weller, Mónika, 'The right to education in international law', 17 *Acta Humana* (1994)

ICELAND

Björgvinsson, D., 'EES-samningurinn og Mannréttindasáttmáli Evrópu sem réttarheimildir í íslenskum landsrétti', 1 *Úlfljótur* (1997)
Einarsson, H., *Tjáningarfrelsi og fjölmidlar* (Reykjavík: Reykjaprent 1997)
Gudmundsdóttir, D., 'Um lögtöku Mannréttindasáttmála Evrópu og beitingu í íslenskum rétti' in 3 *Tímarit lögðrædinga* 1994
Schram, G. G., *Stjórnskipunarréttur* (Reykjavík: Háskólaútgáfan 1997)
Stefansson, S. M. and Adalsteinsson, R., 'Incorporation and implementation of human rights in Iceland' in Scheinin (ed) *International Human Rights Norms in the Nordic and Baltic Countries* (The Hague: Kluwer, 1996)
Thórhallsson, P., 'Lögfesting Mannréttindasáttmála Evrópu' in 3 *Úlfljótur* 1994
Tómasson, E., *Réttlát málsmedferd fyrir dómi: Íslensk lög og lagaframkvæmd í ljósi 1. og 3. mgr. 6. gr. Mannréttindasáttmála Evrópu* (Reykjavík: Orator, 1999)

IRELAND

Connelly, Alpha, 'Ireland and the European Convention on Human Rights: An Overview' in Heffernan, Liz and Kingston, James (eds), *Human Rights: A European Perspective* (Dublin: Round Hall Press 1994)
Dickson, Brice (ed), *Human Rights and the European Convention: The Effects of the Convention on the United Kingdom and Ireland* (London: Sweet and Maxwell, 1997)
Dillon-Malone, Patrick, 'Individual Remedies and the Strasbourg System in an Irish Context' in Liz Heffernan and James Kingston (eds) *Human Rights: A European Perspective* (Dublin: Round Hall Press 1994)

Driscoll, Dennis, *Irish Human Rights Review 2000* (Dublin: Round Hall Sweet and Maxwell, 2000)

Flynn, Leo, 'Ireland', in C. A. Gearty (ed), *European Civil Liberties and the European Convention on Human Rights* (The Hague: Kluwer, 1997)

——'The significance of the European Convention on Human Rights in the Irish legal Order' 1 *Irish Journal of European Law* (1994)

Hogan, Gerard and Whyte, Gerry (eds) *The Irish Constitution* (Dublin: Butterworths, 1994)

Murphy, Tim and Twomey, Patrick, *Ireland's Evolving Constitution* (Oxford: Hart Publishing 1998)

ITALY

Bernardi, A. and Palazzo, F., 'Italy' in M. Delmas-Marty and C. Chodkiewitz (eds), *The European Convention for the Protection of Human Rights: International Protection versus National Restrictions* (Dordrecht: Nijhoff 1992)

Bultrini, Antonio, 'La convenzione europea dei diritti dell'uomo: considerazioni introduttive', 5 *Il Corriere Giuridico* (1999)

Cataldi, G., 'Convenzione europea dei diritti dell'uomo e ordinamento italiano: Un tentativo di bilancio', 11 *Rivista internazionale dei dirritti dell'uomo* (1998)

Chiavario, M., 'Cultura italiana del processo penale e Convenzione europea dei diritti dell'uomo: Frammenti di appunti e spunti per une microstoria', 3 *Rivista internazionale dei diritti dell'uomo* (1990)

de Stefani, Paolo, *Il diritto internazionale dei diritti umani* (Padova: ed Cedam, 1994)

Documenti Giustizia, Special issue: 1–2 'L'Italia e la Convenzione Europea dei Diritti dell'Uomo' (2000)

Facchin, R., *L'Interpretazione Giudiziaria della Convenzione Europea dei Dirriti dell'Uomo: Guida alla Giurisprudenza della Corte, 1960–87* (Padova: Casa Editrice Dott. Antonion Milani, 1988)

Leonardi, D. A., 'Italy' in C. A. Gearty (ed) *European Civil Liberties and the European Convention on Human Rights* (The Hague: Kluwer, 1997)

Raimondi, Guido, 'Effetti del diritto della Convenzione e delle pronunce della Corte europea dei diritti dell'uomo', 11 *Rivista internazionale dei diritti dell'uomo* (1998)

Rinoldi, D., 'La CEDU nell'applicazione giurisprudenziale in Italia: In margine ad un recente raccolta di decisione', 21 *Diritto Comunitario e degli Scambi Internazionali* (1982)

Scovazzi, T. 'The application by Italian courts of human rights treaty law' in Conforti and Francioni (eds) *Enforcing International Human Rights in Domestic Courts* (The Hague: Nijhoff, 1997)

Valabrega, V. M., *L'applicazione della Convenzione europea dei diritti nella giurisprudenza penale della cassazione tra il 1980 e il 1995* (Milano: Universita degli studi di Milano, 1996)

LITHUANIA

Council of Europe, *Compatibility of Lithuanian Law with the European Convention of Human Rights* (Strasbourg: Council of Europe, 1997)
Kuirs, P., 'Lietuva ir Europos imogaus teisiu teismas', 3 and 4 *Justitia* (1996)
Vadapalas, V., 'Lithuania', in M. Scheinin (ed), *International Human Rights Norms in the Nordic and Baltic Countries* (The Hague: Kluwer, 1996)

LUXEMBOURG

Spielmann, Alphonse and Spielmann, Dean, 'Luxembourg', in Wijngaert, Christine van Den *et al.* (eds), *Criminal procedure systems in the European Community* (London, Brussels, Dublin, Edinburgh: Butterworths, 1993)
—— and ——'Indépendance et impartialité des juridictions dans la jurisprudence luxembourgeoise', in Busuttil, Salvino (ed), *Mainly Human Right: Studies in honour of John Cremona, Fondation Internationale* (Malte: Valletta, 1999)
—— and Weitzel, Albert, *La Convention européene de droits de l'homme et le droit luxembourgeois* (Brussels: Nemesis, 1991)
Spielmann, Dean, *L'effet potentiel de la Convention européenne des droits de l'homme entre personnes privées* (Brussels: Nemesis-Bruylant, 1995)
——'Le juge luxembourgeois et la Cour Européenne des Droits de l'Homme', in Tavernier, Paul (ed), *Quelle Europe pour les droits de l'homme? La Cour de Strasbourg et la réalisation d'une 'Union plus étroite' (35 annees de jurisprudence: 1959–1994)* (Brussels: Bruylant, 1996)
——'Obligations positives et effet horizontal des dispositions de la Convention', in Sudre, Frederic (ed), *L'interprétation de la Convention européenne des droits de l'homme* (Brussels: Nemesis-Bruylant, 1998)
——Thewes, Marc; and Reding, Luc, *Recueil de la jurisprudence administrative du Conseil d'Etat luxembourgeois* (Brussels: Bruylant, 1996)

MALTA

Agius, C, 'Significant Landmarks in the History of the Development of Human Rights and Fundamental Freedoms in Malta', in *Human Rights and Prevention* (Foundation for International Studies, 1993)
Cremona, J. J., 'The European Convention on Human Rights as Part of Maltese Law', in *Judicial Protection of Human Rights at the National and International Level*, Vol. II (Milano: Giuffre, 1991)
——*An Outline of the Constitutional Development of Malta under British Rule* (Malta University Press, 1963)
——*The Maltese Constitution and Constitutional History since 1813* (Publishers' Enterprises Group, 1977)

——*Selected Papers 1946–1989* (Publishers' Enterprises Group, 1990)
——*Malta and Britain the Early Constitutions* (Publishers' Enterprises Group, 1996)
Farrugia, M. A., 'Sexual Discrimination: Recent Judicial Developments and Their Effects in Maltese Law', in *MediterraneanJournal of Human Rights* (Publishers' Enterprises Group, 1997)
Harding, H., *Maltese Legal History under British Rule 1801–1836* (Progress Press, 1968)
Mifsud, Bonnici G., 'The Presumption of Innocence: An Essay on the Jurisprudence on this Human Right', in *MediterraneanJournal of Human Rights* (Publishers' Enterprises Group, 1997)
Pullicino, J. Said, 'Right to Fair Trial, Malta', in *Questionnaire for the Unidem Seminar of Brno on the Right of a Fair Trial* (Venice Commission for Democracy through Law, 1999)
——*Relations between the Constitutional Court and the Supreme Court from the Viewpoint of Malta* (Report presented to the Venice Commission for Democracy through Law, 1997)

THE NETHERLANDS

Alkema, E. A., 'The Effects of the European Convention on Human Rights and other Human Rights Instruments on the Netherlands Legal Order', in Lawson, R. and de Blois, M., (eds) *The Dynamics of the Protection of Human Rights in Europe* (Dordecht: Nijhoff 1994)
van Dijk, P., 'Dutch Experience with the European Convention in Domestic Law' in Rehof and Gulman (eds) *Domestic Law and Development Assistance Policies of the Nordic Countries* (Dordrecht: Nijhoff 1989)
——'Domestic Status of Human Rights Treaties and the Attitude of the Judiciary: The Dutch Case', in Nowak, Steurer, and Tretter (eds), *Progress in the Spirit of Human Rights, Festschrift für Felix Ermacora* (1988)
Klerk, Y. and de Jonge, J., 'The Netherlands' in C. A. Gearty (ed), *European Civil Liberties and the European Convention on Human Rights* (The Hague: Kluwer, 1997)

NORWAY

Andenaes, J., *Statsforfatningen i Norge* (Oslo: Tanum, 1998)
Dolva, T., 'Internasjonale menneskerettigheter og intern norsk rett', *Tidsskrift for Retsvitenskap* (1990)
Eckhoff, T., *Rettskildeloere*, edited by J. E. Helgesen (Oslo: Tanum, 2000)
Eggen, K., 'Norway', in Scheinin, M. (ed), *International Human Rights Norms in the Nordic and Baltic Countries* (The Hague: Kluwer, 1996)
Elgesem, F., 'Domestic Application of the European Convention on Human Rights in English and Norwegian Law', *Nordic Journal of International Law* (1996)
Fleischer, C. A., *Folkerett* (Oslo: Universitetsforlaget, 2000)

Helgesen, J. E., *Teorier om 'Folkerettens stilling i norsk rett'* (Oslo: 1982)
NOU, 18 Lovgivning om menneskerettigheter (Report of the Committee which drafted legislation in incorporation, with English summary) (1993)
Smith, C. and Smit, L., *Norsk rett og folkeretten* (Oslo: 1982)

POLAND

Drzemczewski, A. and Nowicki, A., 'The Impact of the ECHR in Poland: A Stocktaking after Three Years', *European Human Rights Law Review* (1996)
Gronowska, B., *Wolność i bezpieczeństwo osobiste w sprawach karnych w świetle standardów Rady Europy* (Torun: University of Torun, 1996)
Hofmánski, P., *Kowencja Europejska i Prawo Karne* (Torun: TNOik, 1995)
Jasudowicz, T. and Mik, C., *O prawach człowieka: W podwójna rocznicę paktów* (Torun: TNOik, 1995)
Machinkska, H. (ed), Special edition of *Binletyn* 3, 2000, Council of Europe Information Centre, Warsaw, 'Wybór orzecznictwa organów Europeajskiej Konwencji Praw Człowieka w Sprawach Polskich' (Warsaw, 2000)
Nowicki, M., *Europejska Kowencja Praw Człowieka: Wybór Orzecznictwo* (2nd edn, C. H. Beck, 1998)
——*Kamienie Milowe: Orzecznictwo Europejskiego Trybunału Praw Człowieka* (Warsaw: Council of Europe Information and Documentation Centre, 1997)
Redelbach, A., *Europejska Konwecja Praw Człowieka w Polskim Wymiarze Sprawiedliwosci* (Warsaw, 1997)

PORTUGAL

Cabral Barreto, Ireneu, *A Convenção Europeia dos Direitos do Homem* (2nd edn, Coimbra: Livraria Almedina, 1999)
Cardoso da Costa, J. M., 'La hiérarchie des normes constitutionnelles et sa fonction dans la protection des droits fondamentaux', 2 *Revue Universelle des Droits de l'Homme* (1990)
Duarte, Maria Luísa, 'A Convenção Europeia dos Direitos do Homem: uma nova etapa (Protocolo No. 11)', in *Organizações internacionais* (Lisbon: Fundação Calouste Gulbenkian, 1999)
Eiras, Agostinho Henriques, *Revisão Constitucional e lei do Tribunal Constitucional: Constituição da República Portuguesa; Lei do Tribunal Constitucional* (Lisbon: Rei dos Livros, 1998).
Gomes Canotilho, José Joaquim (ed), *Direitos Humanos, Estrangeiros, Comunidades Migrantes e Minorias* (Oeiras: Celta Editora, 2000)
Miranda, Jorge, *Direitos Fundamentais: Introdução Geral; apontamentos das aulas* (Lisbon: 1999)
Morais Pires, Maria José, *As Reservas à Convenção Europeia dos Direitos do Homem* (Coimbra: Livraria Almedina 1997)

Moura Ramos, Rui, 'Aplicação da Convenção Europeia dos Direitos do Homem: Sua posição face ao ordenamento jurídico', 5 *Documentação e Direito Comparado* (1981), also published in *Da comunidade internacional e do seu Direito* (Coimbra: Coimbra Editora 1996)

Silva, Maria Manuela Dias Marques Magalhaes, *Noções de Direito Constitucional e Ciência Política* (Lisbon: Rei dos Livros, 2000).

Sousa, Marcelo Rebelo de, *Constituição da República Portuguesa : comentada; introdução teórica e histórica, anotações, doutrina e jurisprudência, lei do Tribunal Constitucional* (Lisbon: Lex, 2000)

ROMANIA

Andrei, Constantin, 'Dreptul la aparare in lumina Conventiei europene a drepturilor omului', 3 *Revista de drept penal* (1998)

Buergenthal, Thomas, *Dreptul International al Drepturilor Omului* (especially chapter on Romanian law by Renate Weber) (All, 1996)

Cosma, Doru, 'Receptarea Conventiei Europene a Drepturilor Omului in dreptul intern roman', 5 *Revista Romana de Drepturile Omului* (1994)

——'Rolul instantelor judecatoresti romane in aplicarea Conventiei europene a drepturilor omului', 6 and 7 *Revista Romana de Drepturile Omului* (1994)

——'Dreptul la un proces echitabil si impartial: Conventia Europeana in instantele de judecata din Romania', 9 *Revista Romana de Drepturile Omului* (1995)

——'Hotarirea Curtii Constitutionale nr. 1/1996, accesul la justitie si exigentele art. 6 CEDO', 13 *Revista Romana de Drepturile Omului* (1996)

——'Interpretarea Conventiei europene a drepturilor omului', 16 *Revista Romana de Drepturile Omului* (1998)

Cosmovici, Paul-Mircea, 'Jurisprudence de la Cour Européenne des Droits de l'Homme concernant la protection du droit de propriété et certain considérations sur le droit roumain', 1 *Revue Roumaine des Science Juridiques* (1993)

Duculescu, Victor, *Protectia juridica a drepturilor omului: mijloace interne si internationale* (Lumina Lex, 1994)

Macovei, Monica (ed) *Libertatea de exprimare: decizii ale Curtii Europene a Drepturilor Omului*, supliment al *Revistei Romane de Drepturile Omului* (1996)

——(ed) *Hotariri ale Curtii Europene a Drepturilor Omului* (selectie, Polirom, 2000)

Mateut, Gheorghita, 'Durata arestarii preventive a invinuitului sau inculpatului in lumina Constitutiei si a Conventiei Europene', 3 *Dreptul* (1996)

Popescu, Liviu-Corneliu, 'Consecintele ratificarii de Romania a Conventiei europene a drepturilor omului asupra sanctiunii disciplinare cu arest aplicate militarilor', 8 *Revista Romana de Drepturile Omului* (1995)

Predescu, Ovidiu, *Conventia europeana a drepturilor omului si implicatiile ei asupra dreptului penal roman* (Lumina Lex, 1998)

Sandru, Cristina, 'Interceptarea convorbirilor telefonice in jurisprudenta organelor de la Strasbourg', 6 and 7 *Revista Romana de Drepturile Omului* (1994)

Tanasescu, Simina, 'Rapports entre la Constitution et la Convention européenne por la sauvegarde des droits de l'homme et des libertés fondamentales', 1 *Revue Roumaine des Sciences Juridiques* (1996)

Tuculeanu, Alexandru, 'Despre calitatea de magistrat a procurorului si dreptul acestuia de a dispune arestarea preventiva in lumina Conventiei europene a drepturilor omului', 2 *Dreptul* (1999)

Weber, Renate, 'Siguranta nationala si drepturile omului in Romania', 6 and 7 *Revista Romana Drepturile Omului* (1994)

RUSSIA

Alexeieva, L. B., *Praktika primeneniya st.6 Evropeiskoi Konventsii o zashite prav cheloveka i osnovnykh svobod Evropeiskim Sudom po pravam cheloveka. Pravo na spravedlivoie pravosudiye i dostup k mekhanizmam sudebnoi zashity* (Interpretation of Art. 6 of the ECHR by the European Court of Human Rights. Right to fair trial and access to the mechanisms of judicial protection) (Moscow: Rudomino, 2000)

——, Jouinov, V. and Loukachouk, I., *Mezhdunarodnije normy o pravakh cheloveka i primenenie ikh sudami Rossiyskoi Federatsii* (International Norms on Human Rights and their Application by the Courts of the Russian Federation) (Moscow: Prava cheloveka, 1996)

Bowring, B., 'Russia's Accession to the Council of Europe and Human Rights: Four Years On', *European Human Rights Law Review* (2000), 362

Council of Europe (Directorate of Human Rights), *The Compatibility of Russian Federation Law with the Requirements of the European Convention on Human Rights*, H(98)7 (available in French and Russian) (Strasbourg: Council of Europe, 1998)

Glotov, S. A., *Pravo Sovieta Evropy i Rossiya* (The Law of the Council of Europe and Russia) (Krasnodar: Sovetskaya Kuban, 1996)

Gorchkova, S. A., 'Derogatsia po Evropeiskoi Konventsii i Rossia' (Reservations to the ECHR and Russia), *Moscow Journal of International Law* (1999), No. 6

Janis, M., 'Russia and the Legality of Strasbourg Law', Vol. 8(1) *European Journal of International Law* (1997), 95

Muehlman, E., 'Conclusions of the Report on the Conformity of the Legal Order of the Russian Federation with Council of Europe Standards', 17 *Human Rights Law Journal* (1996), 195

Petrukhin, I., 'Ogovorki i Zayavleniya RF pri Ratifikatsii Yevropeiskpoi Konventsii o Zashchite Prav Cheloveka i Osnovnikh Svobod' (Reservations and Declarations of the Russian Federation in Ratifying the ECHR), 10 *Rossiskii Byulleten po Pravam Cheloveka*, 65–69

Toumanov, Vladimir A., 'Le fonctionnement de la Cour constitutionnelle de Russie dans le contexte de l'adhésion du pays au Conseil de l'Europe', in Mahoney P., Matscher, F., Petzold, H. and Wildhaber, L. (eds), *Protecting Human Rights: The European Perspective* (Köln: Heymanns, 2000), 1437–1442

Van den Berg, G. P., *Comments to the 1993 Constitution of the Russian Federation* (Institute of East European Law and Russian Studies, Leiden University: CD-rom)

Yakovlev, Veniamin F., 'La Cour européenne des droits de l'homme et les juridictions arbitrales de la Russie', in Mahoney, P., Matscher, F., Petzold H. and Wildhaber, L. (eds), *Protecting Human Rights: The European Perspective* (Köln: Heymanns, 2000), 1547–1552

SLOVAKIA

Čič, M., 'Interaction between the European Convention on Human Rights and the protection of human rights and fundamental freedoms in the legal system of the Slovak Republic', in P. Mahoney/F. Matscher/H. Petzold/L.Wildhaber (eds), *Protecting Human Rights: The European Perspective* (Köln: Heymanns, 2000)

——*et al.*, *Komentár k Ústave Slovenskej republiky* (Martin: Matica Slovenská, 1997)

Kresák, P. *et al.*, *Rozhodovacia činnosť Ústavného súdu Slovenskej republiky 1993–1997* (Bratislava: COLPI and Kalligram 1999)

Massias, Jean-Pierre, *Droit constitutionnel des Etats d'Europe de l'Est* (Paris: Pr. Univ. de France, 1999)

Repík, Bohumil, *Ľudské práva v súdnom konaní* (Bratislava: MANZ, 1999)

Trifunovska, Snezana (ed), *Minorities in Europe: Croatia, Estonia and Slovakia* (The Hague: TMC Asser Press, 1999)

SLOVENIA

Bavcon, L., *Kazenskopravno varstvo človekovih pravic in temeljnih svoboščin*, Temeljne pravice (Ljubljana: Cankarjeva založba, 1997)

Bohte, B., *Mednarodno varstvo temeljnih pravic*, Temeljne pravice (Ljubljana: Cankarjeva založba, 1997)

Butala, A., *Varuh človekovih pravic: pristojnosti in pooblastila*, Podjetje in delo, Nos. 5–6 (1995)

Grad, F., I. *et al.*, Kristan, *Državna ureditev Slovenije* (Ljubljana: ČZP Uradni List, 1996)

Grgič, T., *Varstvo človekovih pravic v kazenskem procesnem pravu*, Pravnik, No. 10 (1992)

Jambrek, P., *Slovensko Ustavno sodišče pod okriljem evropskih standardov in mehanizmov za varovanje človekovih pravic*, Temeljne pravice (Cankarjeva založba, 1997)

Mavčič, A., *The Constitutional Court of the Republic of Slovenia* (Ljubljana: Constitutional Court of Slovenia, 1995)

——*Slovenian Constitutional Review, Its Position in the World and Its Role in the Transition to a New Democratic System* (Ljubljana: Založba Nova Revija, 1995)

——*Constitutional Law of Slovenia* (The Hague: Kluwer, 1998)

——'A Strasbourgi Birosag Esetjoganak Hatasa a Szloven Alkotmanybirosag Itelkezesere', *Fundamentum (az emberi jogok folyoirata)*, No. 2000/4, 21

——and Harutyunyan, G., *The Constitutional Review and its Development in the Modern World (A Comparative Constitutional Analysis)* (Hayagitak: Yerevan, 1999)

Trpin, G., *Varuh človekovih pravic in temeljnih svoboščin*, Nova ustavna ureditev Slovenije, Zbornik razprav (Ljubljana: ČZP Uradni List, 1992)

Tuerk, D., *Ustava Republike Slovenije in Evropska konvencija o varstvu človekovih pravic in temeljnih svoboščin: Potencial mednarodnih standardov za domači razvoj prava o človekovih pravicah*, Slovenija in evropska Konvencija o človekovih pravicah (Ljubljana, 1993)

Wedam-Lukić, D., Pravica do sodnega varstva 'civilnih pravic in obveznosti' (Evropska konvencija o človekovih pravicah in slovensko pravo) (Temeljne pravice) (Ljubljana: Cankarjeva založba, 1997)

SPAIN

Bonet I Perez, J., 'El problema de la efectividad interna de las sentencias del Tribunal Europeo de Derechos Humanos', *Revista Jurídica de Cataluña* (1993)

Bujosa Vadell, L. M., *Las sentencias del Tribunal Europeo de Derechos Humanos y el ordenamiento español* (Madrid, 1997)

Carrillo Salcedo, J. A. 'España y la protección de los derechos humanos: el papel del Tribunal Europeo de Derechos Humanos y del Tribunal Constitucional español', 32 *Archiv des Völkerrechts* (1994)

Delgado Barrio, J., 'Proyección de las decisiones del Tribunal Europeo de Derechos Humanos en la jurisprudencia española', 119 *Revista de Administración Pública* (1989)

Fernandez de Casadevante, C., *La aplicación del Convenio Europeo de Derechos Humanos en España* (Madrid, 1988)

Fernandez Sanchez, P. A., *Las obligaciones de los Estados en el marco del Convenio Europeo de Derechos Humanos* (Madrid, 1997)

Linde, E. *et al.*, *El sistema europeo de protección de los derechos humanos* (2nd edn, Madrid: 1983)

Liñan Nogueras, D., 'Los efectos de las sentencias del Tribunal Europeo de Derechos Humanos en Derecho español', 37 *Revista Española de Derecho Internacional* (1985)

Martinez Alvarez, M., 'Las sentencias del Tribunal Europeo de Derechos Humanos', *La Ley-Unión Europea* (7 de junio de 1996)

Martin-Retortillo, L., 'La recepción por el Tribunal Constitucional de la jurisprudencia del Tribunal Europeo de Derechos Humanos', 137 *Revista de Administración Pública* (1995)

Morenilla Rodriguez, J. M., 'La ejecución de las Sentencias del Tribunal Europeo de los Derechos Humanos', 15 *Poder Judicial* (1989)

Requejo Pages, J. L., 'La articulación de las jurisdicciones internacional, constitucional y ordinaria en la defensa de los derechos fundamentales', 35 *Revista Española de Derecho Constitucional* (1992)

Ruiz Miguel, C., *La ejecución de las sentencias del Tribunal Europeo de Derechos Humanos* (Madrid, 1997)

Sanchez Legido, A., *La reforma del mecanismo de protección del Convenio Europeo de Derechos Humanos* (Madrid, 1995)

SWEDEN

Bernitz, U., 'The Incorporation of the ECHR into Swedish Law: A Half Measure', *German Yearbook of International Law* (1995)
Cameron, I., 'Sweden', in C. A. Gearty (ed), *European Civil Liberties and the European Convention on Human Rights* (The Hague: Kluwer, 1997)
——'Protection of Constitutional Rights in Sweden', *Public Law* (1997)
——'The Swedish Experience of the ECHR Since Incorporation' 48 *International Comparative Law Quarterly* (1999)
——'A survey of ECHR case law and the question of remedies', in I. Cameron and A. Simoni (eds), *Dealing with Integration* vol. 2 (Uppsala: Iustus, 1998)
Danelius, H. 'Judicial Control of the Administration: A Swedish Proposal for Legislative Reform' in Matscher and Petzold (eds), *Protecting Human Rights: The European Dimension* (Köln: Heymanns, 1988)
——'The Incorporation of the European Convention on Human Rights into Swedish Law', in Mahoney, P.; Matscher, F.; Petzold, H.; and Wildhaber, L. (eds), *Protecting Human Rights: The European Perspective* (2000)
Melander, G., 'Sweden', in Scheinin, M. (ed), *International Human Rights Norms in the Nordic and Baltic Countries* (The Hague: Kluwer, 1996)

SWITZERLAND

Borghi, Marco and Corti, Guido, *L'influenza della CEDU sulla legislazione federale e cantonale* (Lugano: Commissione per la formazione permanente dei giuristi, 1991)
Haefliger, Arthur and Schürmann, Frank, *Die Europäische Menschenrechtkonvention und die Schweiz* (Bern: Stämpfli, 1999)
Hottelier, M., *La Convention européenne des Droits de l'Homme dans la jurisprudence du Tribunal fédéral* (Lausanne, 1985)
Müller, Jörg Paul, 'Wandel des Souveränitätsbegriffs im Lichte der Grundrechte: Dargestellt am Beispiel der Einwirkungen des internationalen Menschenrechtsschutzes auf die schweizerische Rechtsordnung', in Rhinow, R.; Breitenmoser, S.; and Ehrenzeller B. (eds), *Fragen des internationalen und nationalen Menschenrechtsschutzes* (Basel: Helbing and Lichtenhahn, 1997)
——*Grundrechte in der Schweiz: Im Rahmen der Bundesverfassung von 1999, der Uno-Pakte und der EMRK* (Bern: Stämpfli, 1999)
Poledna, Tomas, *Praxis zur EMRK aus schweizerisches Sicht* (Zürich: Schulthess Polygraphischer, 1993)
Villiger, Mark E., *Handbuch der Europäischen Menschenrechtskonvention (EMRK): Unter besonderer Berücksichtigung der schweizerischen Rechtslage* (Zurich: Schulthess Polygraphischer, 1999)
Wildhaber, L., *Die Schweiz und die Europäische Menschenrechtskonvention im Rahmen neuerer Entwicklungen* (Saarbrücken: Europa-Institut der Universität des Saarlandes)

TURKEY

Akıllıoğlu, Tekin and İnsan Hakları I: *Kavram, Kaynaklar ve Koruma Sistemleri* (Ankara: AÜSBF İnsan Hakları Merkezi Yayınları, 1995)

Akın, İlhan, *Temel Hak ve Özgürlükler* (İstanbul: İÜHF Yayınları, 1971)

Batum, Süheyl, *Avrupa İnsan Hakları Sözleşmesi ve Türk Anayasal Sistemine Etkileri* (İstanbul: İstanbul Üniversitesi Yayınları, 1993)

Gölcüklü, Feyyaz and Gözübüyük, Şeref, *Avrupa İnsan Hakları Sözleşmesi ve Uygulaması* (Ankara: Turhan Kitabevi, 1994)

Kaboğlu, İbrahim Ö., *Özgürlükler Hukuku: İnsan Haklarının Hukuksal Yapısı* (İstanbul: Afa Yayınları, 1993)

Kapani, Münci, *İnsan Haklarının Uluslararası Boyutları* (Ankara: Bilgi Yayınları, 1987)

Kuçuradi, İoanna and Peker, Bülent (eds), *50 Yıllık Deneyimlerin Işığında Türkiye'de ve Dünyada İnsan Hakları* (Ankara: Türkiye Felsefe Kurumu Yayınları, 1999)

Madra, Ömer, *Avrupa İnsan Hakları Sözleşmesi ve Bireysel Başvuru Hakkı* (Ankara: AÜSBF Yayınları, 1981)

Özdek, Yasemin, *İnsan Hakkı Olarak Çevre Hakkı* (Ankara: TODAİE Yayınları, 1993)

Savcı, Bahri, *Yaşam Hakkı ve Boyutları* (Ankara: AÜSBF Yayınları, 1980)

Tanör, Bülent, *Türkiye'nin İnsan Hakları Sorunu* (İstanbul: BDS Yayınları, 1990)

Yüzbaşıoğlu, Necmi, *Türk Anayasa Yargısında Anayasallık Bloku* (İstanbul: İÜHF Yayınları, 1993)

UKRAINE

Luchterhandt, Otto, 'On issues of Harmonisation of the Legislation of the Ukraine with the European Convention for the Protection of Human Rights and Fundamental Freedoms' *Proceedings of the Scientific—practical Conference of the Institute of Legislation of the Verkhona Rada of the Ukraine* (Kiev, 1998)

Marmazov, V. and Piliayev, I., *Council of Europe: Political and Legal Mechanisms of Integration* (Kiev: Yurydychna Knyga, 2000)

——and——, *Ukraine in the Political and Legal Jurisdiction of the Council of Europe. Experience and Problems* (Kiev: Venturi, 1999)

Ukrainian Legal Foundation, *Bulletin of the Information and Documentation Centre of the Council of Europe in Ukraine* (Council of Europe, 1998–2000)

UNITED KINGDOM

Blackburn, Robert, *Towards a Constitutional Bill of Rights for the United Kingdom* (London: Pinter, 1999)

——and Busuttil, James (eds), *Human Rights for the 21st Century* (London: Pinter, 1997)

——and Plant, Raymond (eds), *Constitutional Reform: The Labour Government's Constitutional Reform Agenda*, Part IV: Justice and Human Rights (London: Longman, 1999)

Bradley, A. W. and Ewing, K. D., *Constitutional and Administrative Law*, Part III: The Citizen and the State (12th edn, London: Longman, 1997)

Clayton, R., Tomlinson, H. and George, C., *The Law of Human Rights* (Oxford University Press, 2000)

Dickson, Brice (ed), *Human Rights and the European Convention: The Effects of the Convention on the UK and Ireland* (London: Sweet and Maxwell, 1997)

Emmerson, Ben and Simor, Jessica, *Human Rights Practice* (London: Sweet & Maxwell, 2000)

Feldman, David, *Civil Liberties and Human Rights in England and Wales* (2nd edn, Oxford University Press, 2001)

Gearty, C. A., 'The United Kingdom', in Gearty (ed), *European Civil Liberties and the European Convention on Human Rights* (The Hague: Kluwer 1997)

Grosz, S., Beatson, J. and Duffy, P., *Human Rights: The 1998 Act and the European Convention* (London: Sweet and Maxwell, 1999)

Hunt, Murray, *Using Human Rights Law in English Courts* (Oxford: Hart Publishing, 1997)

Klug, F., Starmer, K. and Weir, S., *The Three Pillars of Liberty* (London: Routledge, 1996)

Lester, Lord and Pannick, David, *Human Rights Law and Practice* (London: Butterworths, 1999)

Wadham, John and Mountfield, Helen, *The Human Rights Act 1998* (London: Blackstone Press, 1999)

INDEX

Austria
  abortion
    admissibility of 117
    demonstration against 158
  administrative authorities with judicial character, establishment of 109
  administrative justice 38
  administrative law, legal protection in 109–10
  administrative tribunals, establishment of 110
  aliens, protection of 123–4
  army, disciplinary measures 108
  art, freedom of 157
  assembly, freedom of 126–7
  association, freedom of 127
  asylum provisions 115
  Austrian Broadcasting Corporation, abolition of monopoly 115–16
  broadcasting licences 116
  capital punishment, abolition 128
  children, religious education of 146
  civil proceedings
    re-opening 164
    rights in 122–3
  Constitution 103
  Constitutional Court
    establishment of 103
    European Convention on Human Rights, rulings on 163
    jurisdiction 104, 106, 163
  Council of Europe, membership of 104
  Court of Human Rights judgments, implementation of 162, 164
  criminal and administrative criminal sentence, imposition of 161
  criminal proceedings
    administrative 121–2
    attendance and examination of witnesses 144–6
    compensation 111
    counsel, surveillance of conversations with 112
    criminal charge, meaning 121
    detention, lawfulness of 130–2
    detention on remand 111
    equality of arms 111, 113
    judgments by Court of Human Rights, amendments relating to 112
    legal aid 111
    plea of nullity, preparation of 113
    public hearings 112
    re-opening 162
    trial within reasonable time, right to 130–3
  data protection, right to 113–14
  demonstration, right of 158
  deportation, case-law on 108, 129
  deprivation of liberty
    case-law 119–20
    physical force, recourse to 129–30
  detention, lawfulness of 130–2
  disabled person, dismissal of 137
  domestic fundamental rights
    Basic Law 103
    bill of rights 103
    Constitution, in 103
    General Rights of nationals 103
  emergency assistance
    refusal of 158–9
    right to 128
  European Commission and Court of Human Rights, cases before 129–61
  European Convention on Human Rights
    amendments of law in respect of 107
    constitutional law, as 105
    domestic courts and administrative authorities, reliance by 163
    individual complaints, acceptance of competence 105
    jurisdiction of criminal courts, within 164
    key role of 163
    literature on 106
    national law, status in 105–6
    Parliamentary proceedings, status in 107–16
    proportionality, principle of 164
    public awareness 163
    ratification of 38, 104
    reservations 104
    violations, remedial action relating to 161–3
  expression, freedom of
    art 157
    Court of Human Rights, cases in 148–58
    defamation, and 149–53
    injunctions, justification of 154
    journalists, of 126, 149–57
    media, of 148–9
    politicians, of 149–57
    publication of picture of suspect, prohibition 155

Austria (*cont.*):
fair trial, right to 109–10
accusation, right to be informed in understandable language of 142
administrative decisions, judicial control of 138
attendance and examination of witnesses 144–6
Court of Human Rights, cases in 132–46
criminal charge, nature of 140
equality of arms, principle of 111, 113, 141
independent and impartial tribunal, access to 136–9
innocence, presumption of 142
interpreter, free assistance of 146
national case-law on 121–3
preparation of defence, right to adequate time and facilities for 143
public pronouncement of judgments 139–40
self-defence, right to 143–4
trial within reasonable time, right to 130–3
violations 161
family, right to found 125
financial compensations, payment of 161
financial offences, proceedings for 113
foreigners, respect for private and family life of 114–15, 124
homosexual relationship, age of consent 124–5
human rights problems 165
illegitimate children, discrimination against 116, 159
information, access to 125–6
land, transfer of
compensation, without 159
length and inadequacy of proceedings 160
liberty and security of person, cases on 130
media, freedom of 148–9
national courts, human rights cases in 117–29
Nazi regime in 103
opinion, freedom to express 125, 158
personal freedom, protection of 108–9
private and family life, right to respect for
Court of Human Rights, cases in 146–7
foreigners, respect for private and family life of 114–15, 124
membership of Jehovah's Witnesses, refusal of parental rights for 146
national case-law on 123–5
parental leave allowance, refusal of 147
property, protection of
Court of Human Rights, cases in 158–61
national case-law on 127–8
rent reduction, imposition of 160
residence, measures terminating 119
security police, tasks and powers of 108
self-defence, right to 143–4
Strasbourg judgments, enforcement of 67–8
telecommunications secrecy, protection of 115
torture or degrading and inhuman treatment
national case-law on 118–19
police custody, injuries in 129–30
trial within reasonable time, right to 130–6
unlawful associations 116
veterinarians, prohibition of advertisements 125
victims, witnesses, suspects and convicted persons, personality protection for 114
weapons, life-threatening use of 118

Belgium
Arbitration Court, decisions in 179
bankruptcy, human rights 177
capital punishment 172
Constitution 167
criminal proceedings
decisions on 172–4
reasonable time, right to trial in 173, 185
translation of documents 174
disciplinary regulations 174–6, 181
education, linguistic system 180, 186
European Convention on Human Rights
breach, responses to 185–8
direct application of 169
national law, status in 39, 168–70
preventive effect 189
ratification of 167–8
rights and freedoms, application of 46
expression, freedom of 184, 186
fair hearing, right to 172
federal structure, problem of 187
human rights decisions 170–80
administrative law 178
Arbitration Court, in 179
civil and judicial law 176
commercial, tax and social security law 177
criminal law 171–2
criminal proceedings 172–4
disciplinary regulations 174–6
European Court, before 180–5
human rights protection in 188–90
illegitimate children, status of 59, 176, 181, 183

innocence, presumption of 171
property, confiscation of 183
tax law, disputes in 177
UN human rights covenants, adoption of 168
Universal Declaration of Human Rights, subscription to 167
vagrancy cases 181, 186
Bulgaria
Constitution
Convention, relationship with 195–7, 202
drafting 194
features of 193
international treaties, relationship with 195–6
interpretation of 205
new, adoption of 192
Constitutional Court
basic rights, formulation of 203–4
case-law of European Court, use as source of reference 201
characteristics and specific function of 201
conformity of statutes with Convention, examination of 204–5
Constitution, interpretation of 205
Convention, authority of 202
Denominations Act, judgment on unconstitutionality of 205
establishment of 194
interpretation of Convention by 203
position of ECHR, approach to 196
Council of Europe, membership of 192
criminal jurisdiction, organization of 209–10
criminal procedure, legislative amendments 210–13
educational provision 192
European Commission and Court of Human Rights, cases before 207–12
European Convention on Human Rights
assessment of achievements 213–15
breaches, findings of 207
Constitution, relationship with 195–7, 202
declarative character and function 214
direct applicability 197
direct incorporation of 195
influence of 194
national law, status in 41, 195–8
norms of European ordre public, as 202
Parliamentary proceedings, status in 198–200
Protocols, ratification 191
ratification 191
reservation 191
violations
reaction of local courts 206
remedial action relating to 212–13
expression, justifiable interference with freedom of 204–5
fundamental rights of citizens 193
human rights, parliamentary commission on 198–200
International Covenant on Civil and Political Rights, ratification of 192
law enforcement officials, excessive use of force by 209
liberty, deprivation of 208–11
national courts, human rights cases in 200–7
ownership of land 191
police, allegation of ill-treatment by 209
political and legal developments in 192
religious communities, registration of 211

Central and Eastern Europe
European Convention on Human Rights
rights and freedoms, application of 46
status of 40–2
Congress of Europe 1948 3
Council of Europe
Austria, membership of 104
Bulgaria, membership of 192
Committee of Ministers
execution of judgments, supervision of 63, 76
judicial capacity, acting in 19
merits of case, competence to determine 19
Czech Republic, membership of 246–9
enlargement, effect of 77
European Convention on Human Rights see European Convention on Human Rights
Finland, membership of 291–2
founding aims 3–8
founding members 4
human rights secretariat 24
human rights violations
enforcement proceedings, emphasis on 11
expulsion for 11
human rights work 4
Iceland, membership of 399
inter-governmental co-operation 4
Member States, judicial appointments in 86
non-judicial human rights work 78–9
origins of 3
political realities, sensitivity to 24
Romania, membership of 716–17
Russia, membership of 733–4

Council of Europe (*cont.*):
  Slovakia, membership of 758–9
  Slovenia, membership of 782
  Statute
    Preamble 4
    signature 4
  Switzerland, membership of 855
  Turkey, membership of 879
  Ukraine, membership of 916–17
Council of Europe Commissioner for Human Rights
  creation of post 78
  role of 78–9
Cyprus
  access to court, effect of arbitration clause 225
  aliens, liberty of 222
  annulment of administrative act, right to compensation on 237–8
  civil right and obligations 223
  conscientious objectors, civilian service imposed on 224–5
  Constitution
    basis of 217
    extension of 218–19
    fundamental rights in 218
  disciplinary proceedings 223–4
  European Commission and Court of Human Rights, cases before 226–38
  European Convention on Human Rights
    assessment of achievements 239
    Constitution modelled on 217
    independence, lapse on 219
    legislation, conformity of 220–2
    national law, status in 39, 219–20
    Parliamentary proceedings, status in 220–2
    ratification 219
    violations: allegations of 219; remedial action relating to 238
  fair trial, right to 222–6, 238
  foreign judgments, registration of 223
  Greece, cases against 367–8
  individual right of petition, cases relating to 230
  invasion by Turkey, cases relating to
    applications 227
    displacement of persons 230
    families, separation of 230
    intercommunal talks 228
    missing persons, issue of 229
    property, right to 232–4
    standing 228–9, 232–3
  legislation, judicial review of 220–2
  life, right to 236–7
  national courts, human rights cases in 222–6
  privacy, right to 224, 230
  property, right to 232–4
  speech, freedom of 225
  thought, conscience, and religion, freedom of 224
  trial by court in North, jurisdiction 231–2
  Turkey, cases against 896, 913
Czechoslovakia
  dissolution 245, 248
  European Convention on Human Rights, ratification of 244
Czech Republic
  administrative jurisdiction, constitutional principles in 253–4
  Charter of Fundamental Rights and Freedoms
    form of 241–2
    international human rights treaties, harmony with 242
  Constitution
    adoption of 248
    international and national law, relationship of 249
    legal heritage, making use of 249
    purpose of 241
  Constitutional Court
    domestic case-law of 252–7
    fair trial before 257
  Council of Europe, membership of 246–9
  creation of 245
  domestic law, de facto supremacy of 243
  double nationality, undesirability of 256
  election deposit, requirement of 255
  European Convention on Human Rights
    incorporation 250
    influence of 242
    membership 246–9
    national law, status in 41, 249–51
    Parliamentary proceedings, status in 251–2
    ratification 244
  European Court of Human Rights, cases before 257
  expulsion from 254
  government information service, information collected and used by 255
  government organ, complaint filed by 256
  history of 241
  international and national protection of human rights, complementarity of 244
  international law, doctrine of 243
  military service
    alternative to 255
    refusal to serve 256
  police code, compatibility with ECHR 253
  presidential treaties 252

self-determination 245
treaties
conclusion of 252
constitutional laws, relationship with 251
presidential 252
ratification 251

Denmark
criminal proceedings
compensation, claim for 273–5
Convention invoked in 275
economic crime, lengthy proceedings relating to 270
length of 273
European Commission and Court of Human Rights
cases before 270–3
directly applicable, case-law not being 265–6
European Commission of Human Rights, recognition of competence 259
European Convention on Human Rights
assessment 275–6
importance of 276
incorporation into law 260–1, 263
national law, status in 42, 44, 259–61
Parliamentary proceedings, status in 261–3
ratification 259
violations, remedial action relating to 273–5
fair trial, right to 272–3
free speech, right to 269
human rights cases in 263–70
judges
disqualification of 265
impartially, appearance of 266–7
Impeachment Court, of 267
pre-trial decisions and impartiality 271
temporary, disqualification of 266–7
murder suspect, pre-trial detention of 268
picketing at private residence, issues 268–9
privacy, right to 268–9
racist speech, prohibition 272
removal of children from home 265
trade union affiliation, dismissal due to
cases on 264
protection against 262
treaty obligations, securing 259–60

Estonia
administrative law courts, role of 286–7
Constitution
adoption of 278
structure of 278
supremacy of 281
constitutional review, exercise of 284–5
courts of general jurisdiction, remedies in 283
European Convention on Human Rights
domestic law, status in 41, 280–2
hierarchy of legal norms, status in 278–82
judicial practice, implementation in 283–7
ratification 278, 282
reservations 280
family life, right to 286
independence, restoration of 277
international law, supremacy of 281
judgments, publication of 287
legal positivism in 277
treaties, ratification and status of 279
European Commission on Human Rights
admissibility, examination into 16
applications to 16
conciliatory approach 5
full-time Court, superseded by 15
individual applications, number of 16
legal review work 16
European Communities, *see* European Union
European Convention on Human Rights
achievements, scale and nature of 5
body of law in 51
case-law, impact of 51
civil and political rights 10
criticisms of 80
domestic law
conflict with 35
incorporation in 28
domestic law and administrative practices, conformity of 11
dynamic nature of 29
enforcement machinery 11, 15–21
enforcement, national authorities securing 34
European Union, relationship with 83, 89–100; *see also* European Union
factors in work of 5
former control mechanism 22
fundamental purpose of 29
fundamental rights and freedoms of national constitutions, position with regard to 46–9
general rights or freedoms in 8
growing scope of 24
human rights and freedoms protected by 79–81
incorporation
compliance with judgments, ensuring 35
effective remedy, provision for 33
implementation by 35

European Convention on Human
Rights (*cont.*):
incorporation (*cont.*):
obligation, issue of 31–3
preference for 32
interpretation, approach to 29–30
landmarks for 6–8
legislation incompatible with, amendment of 62–4
national law, superior to 31–2
new control mechanism 23
new member state, impact on 50
non-discrimination protocol 80
popular support, importance of 21
Preamble 5
property and education rights 10
protocols 8–10
reporting requirements 24
rights and freedoms
domestic law, application in 49–53
internal application 32
means for ensuring effective enjoyment, choosing 33
municipal courts, role of 50–2
subjective, grant of 34
Secretary General, speech on 50th anniversary of, 1009–11
signatures and ratifications, table of 12–14
special features, impact on domestic implementation 33–6
status in Member States
Constitution, as part of 38
constitutional provisions 36
directly applicable international law with superiority over domestic legal order, as 37
directly applicable law with superiority over domestic legislation, as 39–42
European Union, of 36–7
formal internal legal validity, without 45–6
lex posterior rule 43
overview 36–46
statutory law, as 42–5
variations in 36
subsidiary nature of 28
supervisory and enforcement machinery, effect of Protocol No. 11 15
treaty under international law, as
obligation to incorporate provisions into domestic law, not entailing 31–3
special features, impact on domestic implementation 33–6
traditional view 31–3
Universal Declaration of Human Rights, drawing on 9
updating 81
violations
continuing, cessation of 57–60
fair trial provisions, of 71
immediate abrogation or suspension of statutes, problems of 59
obligations resulting from 57
reparations 60–2
wide statements of principle in 50–1
wider human rights movement, emergence from 5
European Court of Human Rights
applications to 15
number of 77
authority of 83
Chambers 16–17
Committees 17
composition of 83
compulsory jurisdiction 5
decisions, no competence to annul etc 56
documents, public access to 17
ECJ, harmonization with 83
former
full-time Court, superseded by 15
plenary session, in 16
former control mechanism 22
friendly settlements 17
special procedure for 21, 23–4
general statements, no provision for 27
Grand Chamber 17
cases before 82–3
questions referred to 17–18
relinquishment of jurisdiction to 17
human rights violations, number of 26
individual applications
agreement to 11
major part of workload, as 15
numbers of 20
preactive role in 24
inter-state applications 11
internal administration problems of countries, taking into account 25
interpretation rules, development of 5
judges
appointment of 84–8
independence 18–19
nationality 18
nomination 84–7
number of 18
qualifications 18
re-election of 18
responsibilities of 84
judgments
burden of proof, shifting 75
compliance, evaluation of 73–6
consequences, obligation to comply with 56
declaratory part, legal consequences of 56

domestic courts, enforceability before 66–72
execution: problems of 74; supervision of 63, 76
finding of violation, obligations resulting from 57
general measures, implementation of 73–4
immediate legal effect 56
just satisfaction, payment of 64–5
legislation incompatible with Convention, amendment of 62–4
number of 77
obligations of result 57
precedent value of 72–3
reasoned, to be 17
jurisdiction, extent of 17
jurisprudence of 29
consistency 81–3
legal method 25–30
local discretion, sanctioning 25
margin of appreciation, doctrine of 25, 27
application, criticism of 81
divergent attitudes 82
necessary in a democratic society, application of test 82
merger with Commission 15
new control mechanism 23
organic process and dialogue, facilitating 28–9
plenary 19
precedent, doctrine of 27
President 19
pressure on 77
principles established by, impact of 983
public oral hearings 17
reactive work of 27
reference to 16
revised articles governing 17
rights protected by, universal nature of 97
rulings, lack of direct effect 98
Section Presidents 19
statutory provisions, no competence to annul, etc 56
structure and operation of 17
subsidiary nature of Convention, emphasis on 28
Vice-Presidents 19
European Court of Justice
European Court of Human Rights, harmonization with 83
European Ministerial Conference on Human Rights
resolutions and declaration 1012–19
European Parliament
fundamental rights, political declarations 91–3
European Social Charter
signature 10
European Union
charter of fundamental rights
ad hoc convention 95
compatibility with ECHR 98
ECHR, relationship with 95–6
features of 94
final version 100
nature of 94
preparation of 95
Community law, supremacy of 90
ECHR, relationship with
accession, proposal for 96–7
compatibility of measures with 83, 97
influence of 89
Treaty on European Union, reference in 90–1
foreign and defence affairs, relevance of human rights 93
fundamental rights, political declarations 91–3
human rights values, framework of 89
legal personality, absence of 98–9

fair trial
guarantees, violation of 71
Finland
Acts of Parliament, review of constitutionality 295
administrative appeals 299
Advisory Board for International Human Rights Affairs 297
aliens' issues, cases concerning 302
Bill of Rights 289, 311
compensation, payment of 309
Constitution Act 289
Council of Europe, membership of 291–2
European Commission and Court of Human Rights, cases before 304–8
European Convention on Human Rights
assessment 310–12
background factors 289
Finnish law, relationship with 292
Government Bill on 293
impact of 310
incorporation into law 294–6
legislation, review of 298
legislative and political processes, in 297–300
legislative processes, role in 299
national law, status in 42, 44–5, 294–6
reservation 293
violations, remedial action relating to 309
European Court, reference to case-law of 301

Finland (*cont.*):
European Social Charter, acceptance of 293
extradition of Soviet citizens from 300
fair trial, right to 300–2, 307–8
foreign and security policy 290
human rights cases decided in 300–4
human rights community 297
human rights conventions, adherence to 290
international treaties, incorporation into law 290–1
legal assistance, right to 301
liberty, deprivation of 308
military discipline provisions 298
parental custody, issues of 305–6
Parliamentary Ombudsman, reference to human rights treaties by 303
passports, denial of 303
paternity, establishment of 301–2
pre-trial police arrest, period of 292
private and family life, right to respect for 302, 307–8
property rights, questions of 303
religion, freedom of 303
surname, right to change 306
Torture Convention, acceptance of 293
France
abortion legislation 316–17
aliens, rights of 322–3
constitutionality of bills, review of 318
European Commission and Court of Human Rights, cases before 325–9
European Convention on Human Rights
assessment 331–3
bills, review of 316
direct effect 318–19
domestic statutes, status in relation to 317
impact of 313, 332
judicial reasoning, use in 321
national law, status in 39, 315–19
Parliamentary proceedings, status in 319–20
perception and use by domestic courts 314–15
ratification of 313
reciprocal application 317
reservations 314
rights and freedoms, application of 46
spontaneous compliance with 331
violations, remedial action relating to 329–31
fair trial, right to
administrative courts, length of proceedings before 330
civil rights and obligations, notion of 325–6
contaminated blood scandal, in case of 327–8
criminal charge, notion of 326
electoral matters, in 331
hearing within reasonable time, requirement of 326–8
professional disciplinary procedures, lack of public hearing in 323–4
human rights cases in national courts 320–4
private and family life, right to respect for
aliens, rights of 322–3, 328–9
seriousness of offence, balancing 329
telephone tapping, practice of 328, 330
Strasbourg judgments, enforcement of 67–8
treaties, authority of 315–17

Georgia
European Convention on Human Rights, status in national law of 41
Germany
asylum seekers, limitation of 341–2
Code on Criminal Procedure, amendment of 344
death penalty, prohibition 337
European Commission and Court of Human Rights, cases before 349–53
European Convention on Human Rights
assessment 353–4
basic rights provisions of Constitution, relationship with 339
decisions under, effects of 343
declarations 335
federal law, references in 341
impact of 353–4
incorporation into law 338
inter-State complaints 349
legal order, rank in 340
national law, status in 42–3, 338–44
Parliamentary proceedings, status in 344–6
procedural effects 342
ratification of 335–6
reservation 335
reunification, after 337
rights and freedoms, application of 46–7
Saar territory, ratification by 336
substantive effects 338–42
violations, remedial action relating to 353
6th Protocol, ratification of 337
expression, freedom of 352

fair trial, right to
European Space Agency, grant of immunity to 351
expeditious, aim of 345
free counsel, right to 351
reasonable time, hearing within 348, 351
forced labour, prohibition 347, 350
human rights cases in national courts 346–9
inhuman or degrading treatment, prohibition
bruises suffered in course of arrest 350
deportation and expulsion, person facing 346
terrorist acts, detention of suspects 350
innocence, presumption of 345–6, 348
later enacted statutes, human rights protected over 340
lex posterior, interpretation of 339
liberty and security, right to 347, 350–1
private and family life, right to respect for 348, 352
property, protection of 350
res judicata of Strasbourg judgments, requirement to respect 66
reunification 337
self-defence, right of 345
Strasbourg judgments, enforcement of 67–8
telephone tapping, conditions for 352
thought, conscience, and religion, freedom of 349
Greece
Constitution
Convention, effect of conflict with 360
international orientation 358
debt, impossibility of satisfaction for 377
European Commission and Court of Human Rights, cases before
adjudications 392–80
Cyprus, relating to 367–8
individual petitions 371–80
inter-state cases 367–71
military dictatorship, concerning 368–71
European Convention on Human Rights
assessment 380–1
Constitution, effect of conflict with 360
democratic government, approval by 357
impact of 380–1
individual petition, right of 355, 357, 371–80
insignificant impact of 355
legal discussion 381
military government, denunciation by 356
national law, status in 39, 357–61
Parliamentary proceedings, status in 361
Protocols, ratification of 357, 359
reservations 359
violations, remedial action relating to 380
fair trial, right to
access to court 372
appeal, short time-limit for 373
defence, right of 373
Military Criminal Code, under 372–3
reasonable time, within 376
foreign language schools, right to set up 379
human rights cases in national courts
assessment of 362
post-military government 364–7
pre-military government 362–4
Jehovah's Witnesses
military service, refusal of 379
national Day parade, refusal of permission to take part in 379
place of worship, refusal of permission for 378
proselytizing, convictions for 374
secret information file concerning 380
military dictatorship 356, 368–71
Muslim minority, activities of 378–80
preferential contracts under military regime, termination of 376
property, right to
compensation for loss 373–4, 379
debt, impossibility of satisfaction for 377
former king, of 380
monasteries, of 377–8
occupation without compensation 380
proselytizing, convictions for 374–5
regions, associations promoting characteristics of 380
religion, freedom of 374–5, 378
rules of international law, application of 358
treaties
aliens, supremacy in regard to 360–1
application of 357
incorporation into law 358–9
supremacy, rule of 359–60

Hungary
aliens, applications submitted by 394
association, freedom of 395
Constitution, preparation of 397
Constitutional Court, practice of 389
continental legal system in 387
convicted disabled person, detention of 395
death penalty, unconstitutionality of 389

Hungary (*cont.*):
European Commission and Court of Human Rights, cases before 393–6
European Convention on Human Rights
assessment 397
higher court judgments, reference in 387
legislation, impact on 387
national law, status in 41, 383–6
ratification of 383, 385–6
rights and freedoms, application of 49
signature 385
violations, remedial action relating to 396–7
expression, freedom of
balance with other rights 389–90
officials of state, protection of 391
freedom of religion and right to education, balancing 390
human rights cases in national courts 387–92
juvenile offenders, right to defence 387–8
liberty, right to 394
marry, right to 389, 391
parental rights after divorce 388
political and economic transformation 383
prisoners, control of correspondence of 396
privacy, right to 391
private and family life, right to respect for 395–6
professional organization, compulsory membership of 391
property, protection of
agricultural land, restrictions on purchasing 390–1
expropriation, compensation for 393
racial hatred, prohibition of communications on 390
refugee status, application for 394
regulatory offences
access to courts 393
judicial review, absence of 392
safety belts, compulsory use of 390
sentencing without trial, objection to 392
treaties
application of 383–4
human rights, promulgation of 384
incorporation 384

Iceland
association, freedom of 419–20
civil servants, defamation of 412
Council of Europe, membership of 399
criminal justice, organization of 410
detention on remand, conditions of 416
European Commission and Court of Human Rights, cases before 417–20
European Convention on Human Rights
assessment 421–2
consistency of law with 408
constitutional law, status of 402–3
incorporation into law 402: committee to investigate 400
increased role of 411
legal system, status in 400
national law, status in 42, 44, 400–5
Parliamentary proceedings, status in 405–7
ratification 399
source of law, as 407
subordinate role of 399
Supreme Court, scrutiny by 403–4
transformation of national law to conform with 405
violations, remedial action relating to 420–1
expression, freedom of 418–19
extradition, proportionality 416–17
fair trial, right to
conformity of law 410–11
delay in proceedings 413
impartial judge, lack of 408, 413–15
independence of judges 414
interpreter, assistance of 412
investigative and judicial powers, combination of 418
legislation, redrafting 405–6
illegal fish catch, confiscation of 411
international law, status of rules of 400–1
national courts, human rights cases in 407–17
Parliamentary Ombudsman
constitutionally protected human rights, pointing out deficiencies of 400
institution of 399, 406
prisons, disciplinary actions in 406
taxation and confiscation, line between 418
taxi-cabs, permit to operate
revocation 406–7, 419
trade union, requirement to join 409–10, 419–20
international law
implementation, issue of 32
international tribunals
judgments, dualist understanding of effects of 55–6
Ireland
abortion cases 440, 460–1, 467
abuse of right of petition 455
adoption, role of natural father 468
anti-partition policy 423
association, freedom of 446–7

bail applications, right to personal liberty raised in 439
bill of rights 468
compulsory acquisition of land 444
conditions of detention, complaints concerning 447
Constitution
amendment, attempts to 439
apparent bars to enforcement of Convention 425, 432
Convention compared 472
human rights in 438
relations with other states, reference to 433
social policy, directive principles 442
courts, access to 450
criminal cases, appeal on point of law in 450–1, 455–6
criminal contempt of court 429, 431
customary international law as part of domestic law 434
Detention Commission, proceedings before 445
detention without trial 444–5
divorce, prohibition of 454–5
domestic proceedings, nature of 448
emergency legislation, cases concerning 443–4
equality before the law, principle of 440
European Commission and Court of Human Rights, cases before 443–65
European Convention on Human Rights
apparent bars to enforcement 425, 432
assessment 468–73
belt and braces, as 427–9
executive, invoked by 437
incorporation, approach to 468–72
individual petition, right of 423–4
national law, status in 45–6, 425–36
Parliamentary proceedings, status in 436–8
presumption of compatibility with 429–34
public policy, persuasive authority in matters of 431–2
ratification 423
use of 424
violations, remedial action relating to 466–8
evidence, exclusionary rule of 439–40
extradition, complaints concerning 448
fair trial, right to 448–9
foreign policy 423
Good Friday Agreement 470
homosexual acts, criminalization 456–7, 467
Human Rights Commission 472–3
human rights conventions, autoincorporation 435
illegitimacy, abolition of status 466
inhuman and degrading treatment, travellers alleging 452–3
innocence, presumption of 465
international conventions, judiciary having regard to 434
internment 444–5
judicial review 439
legal aid 437, 466
life, right to 440
marital privacy, right to 441–2
marriage, right to 454–5
national courts, human rights cases in 438–43
offences against the state 471
peaceful enjoyment of possessions, right to 458
persuasive and evidential burdens of proof, distinction between 465
political speech, censorship of 461–3
prisoner, application for transfer by 464–5
privacy, right to 463–4
property disputes, applications involving 459
psychiatric detention, review of 471
public rights, enforcement of 449
restrictions on use of land, complaint concerning 457–8
Roman Catholic Church, responsibility of state for 451
silence of accused, adverse inferences drawn from 427
Special Criminal Court, status of 448
supremacy of national law, displacement of 426
telephone tapping 437
travellers, constitutional matters raised by 452–4
ultra vires planning permissions, effect of grant 459–60
unenumerated rights, doctrine of 441–3
voting, equality of treatment for 463
Italy
administrative jurisdictions, contentious proceedings handled by 493
adoption, rules for 496
arrest warrants, issue of 489
civil defence counsel 496
Code of Criminal Procedure 484, 489
Constitution
Universal Declaration of Human Rights, principles of 476
criminal proceedings
nature of 484–5
Public Prosecutor, role of 485

Italy (*cont.*):
criminal unlawfulness, compensation for damage 486–7
environment, protection of 496
European Commission and Court of Human Rights, cases before 498–501
European Convention on Human Rights
abstract principles in 483
guarantees, application of 492–3
individual right to petition 477
interpretation and application of 480
legal theory, effect on 475–6
national law, status in 42–3, 481–2
precedence 480
ratification 475
real, individual rights, as source of 484
rights and freedoms, application of 46
rules, ranking 479–81
studies of 476–7
fair trial, right to
burden of proof 499
compensation, grant of 499
conviction in absentia 488–9
decisions, publication of 500
defence, right to 495
equality of arms, principle of 495
interpreter, assistance of 494
judges and lawyers, testimony of 494
judges, impartiality and independence of 494
language of proceedings, right of foreigner to understand 491, 500–1
personal liberty during 496
reasonable time, within 487–8, 499, 501
sentenced person, rights of 496
treatment, equality of 498
Freedom Tribunal 490
good faith, notion of 477–8
human rights doctrine, studies of 475
innocence, presumption of 486
interaction and convergence of legal systems 478–9
legal system, principles of 479
linguistic minorities, rights of 495
national courts, human rights cases in 482–92
personal liberty, restriction of
blood transfusions, consent to 496
sports stadia, at 496
preventive custody, use of 489–90
private and family life of employees, investigation of 483
psychiatric hospital, rights on detention in 500
unfair detention, compensation for damage 486–7

just satisfaction
meaning 64
payment of 64–5

Liechtenstein
European Convention on Human Rights, status in national law of 42
Lithuania
alcohol and tobacco, advertizing 519–20
civil servants, restrictions on 520–2
Constitution
compatibility of Convention with 512–22
human rights standards, incorporation of 503
correctional labour, requirement of 513–14
criminal procedure, rules and practices of 522–7
damage by law-enforcement bodies, compensation for 527
discrimination, freedom from 517
European Commission and Court of Human Rights, cases before 522–7
European Convention on Human Rights
assessment 528
legal effect of 506–10
national constitution, contradicting 512–22
national law, status in 42, 45, 504–10
Parliamentary proceedings, status in 510–11
ratification 503
rights, ensuring 509
violations, remedial action relating to 527
fair trial, right to
defence, preparation of 526
detention on remand 526
reasonable time, within 525
human rights instruments, accession to 504–5
human rights standards 503
independence 503
lawfulness of detention, determining 514–16
legal system 504–6
liberty of movement, right to 517–18
national and international law, relationship of 504
national courts, human rights cases in 511–22
preventive detention 523–5
preventive detention, laws on 512
religion, freedom of 516
treaties, legal effect of 505–6

Luxembourg
administrative courts, decisions concerning fundamental rights in 536, 542
adoption law 540
appeal, right of 548
courts, composition of
civil matters, in 543–5
criminal matters, in 545–7
criminal investigation, law on 533–4
European Commission and Court of Human Rights, cases before 552–6
European Convention on Human Rights
assessment 557
domestic law, status in 39, 532
drafting of laws, status in 533–5
precedence 532
private individuals, application between 550–1
ratification 531
European Court of Human Rights judgments, effect of 556–7
expression, freedom of
journalists, liability of' 539
principle 537
right to inform, limits of 537–9
right to information, limits of 539
fair trial, right to
courts, composition of 543–7
impartiality of judges 555–6
in absentia 549–50
investigating courts, inapplicability of guarantees to 552
milk quotas, in relation to 553–5
unreasonable delay 547
immigration law 542
judicial investigations, scope of secrecy of 539
milk quota system 553–5
national courts, human rights cases in 535–52
non-discrimination, principle of
adoption matters, in 540
inheritance matters, in 540
parental authority as to 541
peaceful enjoyment of possessions 541–2
peaceful enjoyment of possessions 541–2
privacy, right to 538
private and family life, right to respect for 551
Strasbourg judgments, enforcement of 67–8
telephone tapping cases 536–7
trial in absentia 549–50

Macedonia
European Convention on Human Rights, status in national law of 41

Malta
bail application, requirement of 589
conscience and religion, freedom of 576
Constitution
basis of 560
Blood 560
European Convention Act in conflict with 566
House of representative subject to 561
Independence 560–1
number of 560
protected rights 561, 564
Constitutional Court
appellate court, as 568–9
European Court of Human Rights, reference to decisions of 563
guardian of human rights, as 567–70
highest court, as 568
procedure 569
right to fair trial, breach of 586
contempt of court proceedings 592
debts, leaving with 593
deprivation of liberty, safeguards 589
discrimination, protection from
constitutional provisions 574
religious belief, based on 576–7
sex, based on 574–6
doctrine of precedent, absence of 565
domestic legislation, impact of human rights on 592–4
European Commission and Court of Human Rights, cases before 588–92
European Convention on Human Rights
extension of applicability to 559
impact of 564
inconsistency of law with 562–3, 565
incorporation of 562–4
individual petition, right of 588
national law, status in 40
ratification 562
executive warrants, issue of 593
expression, freedom of 577–9
fair trial, right to
adverse media statements, prejudice due to 591
civil rights and obligations, determining 584
Constitutional Court, breach by 586
court experts, appointment of 586–7
Criminal Code, provisions of 582–3
disciplinary proceedings 588
fair trial, right to 588–9
impartiality 584–5, 590–1
judges and magistrates, immunity of 585
judges, impartiality of 565–6
judicial proceedings, public character of 578–9

Malta (*cont.*):
  fair trial, right to (*cont.*):
    notes, right to compile 590
    witness, immunity granted to 583–4
    witness statements, admission of 587
  family life, right to respect for 571–2
  forced labour, protection from 564–5
  history of human rights in 559–66
  illegitimate children, adoption of 571–2
  independence 560
  legal system 559
  liberty and security, right to 590
  marriage, right to 564
  national courts, human rights cases in 570–88
  Order of St John, reversion to 559
  parliamentary privilege, breach of 588–9
  police, entry and search by 572–3, 592
  privacy, right to 570–4
  professions, obligation of secrecy 594
  property, right to enjoyment of 579–82
  Strasbourg judgments, enforcement of 67–8
  telephone conversations, prison regulation on recording 573
  transsexuality, legal acknowledgement of 571
margin of appreciation
  doctrine of 25, 27
Moldova
  European Convention on Human Rights, status in national law of 41

Netherlands
  Administrative Litigation Division, proceedings before 608, 621
  complaint by victim of abuse, requirement of 616, 621
  Council of State, impartiality of 621
  custody of children 602
  directly applicable international law in 37
  discrimination, prohibition 618–19
  divorce, parental authority on 602
  European Convention on Human Rights
    impact of 622–4
    individual petition, right of 595
    legal order, status in 596–9
    military law, conformity of 605
    Parliamentary proceedings, status in 600
    ratification 595
    relations between individuals, application to 604
    violations, remedial action relating to 620–2
  European Court of Human Rights, cases before 605–20
  expression, freedom of 619
  fair trial, right to
    conviction in absentia 615
    court, access to 611–12
    dispute, nature of 611
    health insurance proceedings, right to 611
    impartiality of judge 613
    independent tribunal, access to 607–8
    investigating judge, tribunal acting as 613
    length of proceedings 612–13
    Patent Office, impartiality of 610
    reasonable time, in 604
    taxation proceedings 615–16
    tribunal, attributes of 609–10
    witnesses, anonymous 604, 614–15, 621
  family life, right to 616–18
  human rights instruments ratified by 595
  mental patients, detention of 603, 605–7, 620
  military law, deprivation of liberty in 605, 620
  milk quotas 609
  national courts, human rights cases in 600–4
  overseas territories, relationship with 596
  parental access, arrangements for 603
  placement of prisoners 606–7
  property, right to
    discrimination 618
    seizure by tax authorities 619
  protected natural site, land designated as 608
  religion, freedom of 601
  res judicata of Strasbourg judgments, requirement to respect 66
  tax cases, challenge to 604
  treaties
    direct effect 598
    human rights 595–7
    internal force 597–8
    legal force 597
    precedence 599
  witnesses, anonymous 604, 614–15, 621
North Atlantic Treaty Organization
  military association 4
Norway
  aliens, statutory provisions 640
  Constitution
    international and national law, no provision on 627–8
    role of 628
  criminal procedure
    issues of 644
    judge, requirement to bring arrested people before promptly 645
    statutory provisions 640

witness statements, use of 644–5, 647
criminal responsibility and security measures, human rights provisions 641
death penalty 639
deprivation of liberty, security measures constituting 648
European Commission and Court of Human Rights, cases before 650–2
European Convention on Human Rights
assessment 653–5
domestic law, comparison with 626
full potential, failure to exploit 654
individual petition, right of 627
interpretation, doubt as to 637
national law, status in 40, 627–38
Parliamentary proceedings, status in 638–41
ratification 625, 627
reservation to 626, 638
violations, remedial action relating to 652–3
European Court of Human Rights
interplay with 637
jurisdiction, acceptance of 627
jurisdiction, views on 626
expression, freedom of 649
fair trial, right to
impartiality 646
procedural errors in breach of 642
reasonable time, within 645–6, 648
forced labour 642
human rights conventions
case-law on 631
constitutional provision 634–5
implementation 635
incorporation into law 628
publication 637
sources of Norwegian law, as 633
status in national law of 630–1
statutory law, application as 636
human rights legislation 654
innocence, presumption of 647
judicial review, principle of 633
judicial supremacy, principle of 633
legality, principle of 633
mentally ill person, security measures 643–4
military services, disciplinary proceedings 640
national courts, human rights cases before 642–9
religious meetings behind closed doors, prohibition 639
Sami people, rights of 643
sector monism 632
Strasbourg judgments, enforcement of 67–8
supplementary tax, imposition of 636
treaties
incorporation into law 629, 635–8
legislative harmony, ascertaining 629
presumption principle 629–30
transformation 629
victims of crimes, protection and support 641
wage disputes, compulsory arbitration 631
Parliamentary Assembly
appointment of judges, role in 84–8
Poland
authorities and individual, relationship between 665
civil proceedings, length of 673–4
Constitutional Tribunal 668–9
criminal proceedings, inequality in 673
European Commission and Court of Human Rights, cases before 672–5
European Convention on Human Rights
assessment 675–9
compatibility with legislation 660–3
individual petition, right of 672
law-making process, and 660–4
legal community, familiarizing with 677
national law, status in 42, 658–60
Ombudsman, use by 671
prospects 678
ratification 658–9, 672
rights and freedoms, application of 49
standards, dissemination of information concerning 675–6
Supreme Court, invoked by 666
expression, freedom of 669
expulsion of aliens 663–4
human rights treaties
constitutional situation 659–60
party to 657–8
mentally ill persons, detention of 671
national courts, human rights cases in 664–72
non-governmental organizations, work of 677–8
Ombudsman
Convention, making use of 671
jurisdiction, matters within 670
office of 670
prisoners, correspondence of 672
property, right to 674
social insurance, equality in 668
Strasbourg judgments, enforcement of 67–8
Supreme Administrative Court 667
Supreme Court 664–6

Portugal
agents provocateurs, use of 704
Bar Association, compulsory subscription to 692
conscientious objection, right of 692
Constitutional Court
case-law of 684
Strasbourg case-law, recognition of 685–6
court's decision, revision of 708
European Commission and Court of Human Rights, cases before 693–706
European Convention on Human Rights
assessment 708–9
domestic law, status in 39, 682–4
incorporation of 682–3
legal profession, attitude of 708
Parliamentary proceedings, status in 684
ratification 681
reservations 681–2
rights and freedoms, application of 46
violations, remedial action relating to 706–8
fair trial, right to
acts of different authorities, State responsibility extending to 698
administrative court, access to 702
administrative proceedings, application to 696–7
agents provocateurs, use of 704
assistente, compensation of 698–9
Attorney-General, role and opinion of 701
case file, access to 690
civil proceedings, excessively lengthy 705
criminal investigation and trial, participation of same judge in 688
decision on facts, motivation of 690–1
declaratory stage of proceedings, length of 699
defence, right of 690
delay in proceedings, exhaustion of domestic remedies in case of 694
duration of proceedings, comparison of 698
effective legal assistance, right to 703
equality of arms 686–8
excessive length of proceedings 688–9
expediting proceedings, measures for 706–7
independence of tribunal 691
interpreter, free assistance of 686
investigative process, fairness of 704
judge, impartiality of 700
jurisdictional function, unlawful acts relating to 688–9
no apparent contestation, where 703
non-disciplinary administrative sanctions, application of provision to 691
public administration, liability of state for acts of 696–7
second jurisdiction, re-examination of facts in 689
single proceeding for purpose of 694
temporary backlog, effect of 695
foreign property, expropriation of 682
mentally ill person, detention of 702
national courts, human rights cases in 685–93
possessions, peaceful enjoyment of 702
residence, conditions of 693
transsexuality, legal implications of 692
vote, right to 693
psychiatric institutions
rights of persons detained in 983–4

reparation
internationally wrongful act, for 60–2; *see also* restitutio in integrum
re-opening of cases 67
restitutio in integrum
monetary compensation, alternative of 61
municipal law of respondent state, possible under 61
partial 60
principle, application of 61
scope of 60
Romania
act issued by prosecutor, jurisdiction over 724
Communist regime 711
Constitution
Convention, discussion during drafting of 711
fundamental rights in 711–12
monist principle 714
pre-eminence of international law, setting out 715
Constitutional Court
Convention, reference to 719
decisions, lack of binding effect 721
powers of 720–1
Council of Europe, membership of 716–17
custody decision, enforcement of 726
European Commission and Court of Human Rights, cases before 722–6
European Convention on Human Rights
assessment 728–9
implementation, investigation into 712
legal training on 728
legislation, harmonization of 712–13
media, role of 729

national law, status in 41, 714–16
Parliamentary proceedings, status in 716–18
ratification 712
reservations 712
violations, remedial action relating to 727
expression, freedom of 725
homosexuality, punishment of 720
human rights instruments
domestic laws, precedence over 715
party to 711
legal system, reform of 718
national courts, human rights cases in 718–22
optimum legal treatment, principle of precedence 719
penal judicial errors, state responsibility of 720
prisoners, correspondence of 725
property, right to 725–6
Supreme Court of Justice, decisions of 722
treaties
courts, competence of 715–16
decisions invoking 719
domestic legislation, as part of 714
Universal Declaration of Human Rights, status of 714–15
Russia
arrest and detention on remand, cases on 751
Chechnya, war in 733
code of criminal procedure, requirement to reform 738, 753
Constitution
application of Convention, provisions relevant to 735
basic rights and liberties 736
priority of 736
constitutional federal laws 736
Council of Europe, membership of 733–4
crime rate, rise in 733
detention, conditions for 742
European Convention on Human Rights
assessment 752–4
compatibility exercise 740
domestic law and practice 742–9
ideology, core of 731
impact of 731
individual petition, right of 737
national law, status in 41, 735–41
priority of 736
ratification 734–5, 737–8
reservations 738, 741, 753
standards, application of 732
violations arising after entry into force, application to 738
European Court of Human Rights, cases before 750–2
fair trial, right to
appeal, provision for 746
case file, access to 745, 747
Constitutional Court, consideration of measures by 746–8
decisions on 743–8, 754
further investigations, case referred for 743–5
opinion expressed by judge before all evidence adduced 745
proceedings, length of 745
reconsideration of case after quashing on appeal, impartiality of judge 745
supervisory court, powers of 746–7
use of force, evidence obtained by 745
individual, relationship with state 732
innocence, presumption of 736
international supervisory bodies, addressing 737
Jehovah's Witness, custody of child of 751
judge, proselytizing by 752
liberty and security, right to 740–3
movement, freedom of 739, 741, 748, 754
regional notary chamber, compulsory membership 752
regular federal laws 737
residence registration 739, 741, 748
retirement benefits, right to 752

Slovakia
applications against, inadmissibility of 768–9
conscientious objection to military service 765
Constitution
approval of 755
Convention, relationship with 761
fundamental rights and freedoms 756
human rights guarantees 756
Constitutional Court
compatibility of laws, review of 761–2
complaints, procedural requirements for 762–3
decisions of 765
findings, enforcement of 764
petition to 763
role of 756–7
constitutional petitions, effectiveness of 769–70
constitutional system, elements of 755–7
Council of Europe, membership of 758–9
creation of 755
Czechoslovakia, dissolution 245
Declaration of Sovereignty 755

Slovakia (*cont.*):
deprivation of liberty, complaints concerning 775–6
European Commission and Court of Human Rights, cases before 767–76
European Convention on Human Rights
applications under, action by authorities on 776–7
assessment 777–9
Constitution, relationship with 761
individual petition, right of 757
legislative proceedings, status in 764
national law, status in 41, 760–4
operation of system, achievement of 778
retroactive ratification of 757–60
succession to 758
fair trial, right to
cases concerning 770–3
excessively lengthy proceedings 772
minor offences, judicial review of decisions 771–2
public hearing before administrative courts, absence of 772
good name and reputation, protection of 776
individual human rights, constitutional protection of 762–4
labour disputes 776
matrimonial property, use and separation of 776
Member of Parliament, exercising office of 776
national courts, human rights cases in 765–6
parental rights 776
possessions, right to peaceful enjoyment of 766
property, rehabilitation and restitution proceedings 773–5
territory, right to enter 766
treaties, conditional precedence 760–1
Velvet Revolution 755
Slovenia
administrative decisions, reasons for 782
association, freedom of 783
children, welfare of 803
collusion, detention to avoid 804
Constitution
Convention, exceeding 781–2
human rights and fundamental freedoms exercised on basis of 791
inequality and discrimination, protection against 781
Constitutional Court
abstract review by 789, 791–7
concrete review by 789
constitutional complaints to 789, 797–803, 807–8
Convention, decisions referring to 782–3
establishment of 788
status and powers of 788
Council of Europe, membership of 782
courts of associated labour, regulation of legal remedies before 783
data, effect of collection of 805
denationalization 796–7
detention, duration of 797–800
discrimination, prohibition of 804
effective legal remedy, right to 803
European Commission and Court of Human Rights, cases before 805–6
European Convention on Human Rights
assessment 806–8
constitutional Court decisions referring to 782–3
implementation 785–6
national law, status in 783–6
Parliamentary proceedings, status in 786–7
ratification 782, 784
violations, remedial action relating to 806
European Social Charter, ratification of 785
European Union, instruments of 786
expression, freedom of 787
fair trial, right to
appeal, decision on 801
defence, rights of 795
delay, without 798–801
economic sabotage, prohibition of 795–6
equality of arms 794
evidence, submission of 792–4
illegal trade, suppression of 795–6
investigative process 792–4
prohibited speculation, prohibition of 795–6
reasons for decisions 801
statutory provisions 786–7
innocence, presumption of 795
international law and treaties, importance of 784
legal interests, protection of 803
liberty and security, right to 792
liberty, deprivation of 786, 797–8
life, right to 792
national courts, human rights cases in 787–805
Ombudsman
co-operation with 791
election 790
function 789

powers of 790
proceedings before 790
personal freedom, guarantee of 803
property, protection of 796–7, 802
protection of human rights, national system
administrative 788
basis of 787
Constitutional Court 788–9
judicial 787
Ombudsman 789–91
public order offence judges, nature of 801–2
repeat offence, detention due to risk of 792
residence, right to 804
United Nations treaties, effect of 784
Spain
association, freedom of 822
Constitution, interpretation 812–14
Constitutional Court, appeals before 827–9
discrimination, prohibition 822
European Commission and Court of Human Rights, cases before 822–6
European Convention on Human Rights
assessment 830–1
Constitutional provisions governing 813
national law, status in 39, 811–14
Parliamentary proceedings, status in 814–15
ratification 809–11
rights and freedoms, application of 46, 48
violations, remedial action relating to 826–30
expression, freedom of 821, 826
fair trial, right to
defence counsel, right to 818–19
independent, impartial court, by 818
interpreter, assistance by 819
public trial, right to 817
reasonable period of time, within 818, 825
reasoned judgments, requirement of 825
scope of 817, 824
witnesses, right to question 819
final judgments, review of 827
inhuman or degrading punishment, right not to be subjected to 816
life, right to 815
national courts, human rights cases in 815–22
personal liberty, right to 816, 824
prisoners convicted of terrorism offence, dispersal of 815
privacy, rights of 820, 825–6
procedural rights
appeals 819
area of application 817
fair trial, right to 817–19, 824
persons covered by 817
professionals, advertizing by 823
Strasbourg judgments, enforcement of
domestic proceedings, re-opening, 68–9
res judicata, requirement to respect 66
thought, conscience, and religion, right to 820
treaties
incorporation 811
sources of law, relationship with 812–13
status in national law of 811
state responsibility
general principles, application of 56
Sweden
Code of Judicial Procedure, amendments to 851
confidential medical data, use of 848
constitutional rights, system of
amendment 835
breach of provisions 835
constitutional documents 833
Convention, overlap with 835–6
Instrument of Government 834
relative rights 834
detention, length of 847
European Commission and Court of Human Rights, cases before 845–9
European Convention on Human Rights
administrative law issues 845
assessment 852–3
constitutional rights protection, overlap with 835–6
family law issues 845
incorporation into law 837–41
individual applications under 845–6
interpretation of national law, reference in 843
national law, status in 42, 44, 836–41
norm conflicts, avoidance of 840
ordinary statute, status of 839
Parliamentary proceedings, status in 841–2
ratification 836
statutes in conflict with 840
violations, remedial action relating to 849–52
fair trial, right to
oral hearing, right to 847
scope of 846
family life, right to 848
Housing Court 848
judicial review of administrative action 847, 849–51

Sweden (*cont.*):
liberty, deprivation of 843
national courts, human rights cases in 843–5
security information, use of 852
Strasbourg case-law, lack of system for monitoring 842
substantive laws, reforms of 852
Supreme Administrative court, cases before 850
trade union, blockade by 849
Switzerland
administrative decisions, cancellation of 875
aliens, law on 869
cantons, criminal procedure of 860–1, 867
constitutionality of legislation 874–5
Council of Europe, membership of 855
criminal procedure 859–60
discrimination, prohibition of 873
European Commission and Court of Human Rights, cases before 869–74
European Convention on Human Rights
assessment 877–8
breach, government response to 874–7
federal laws, amendment of 859
national law, status in 856–8
Parliamentary proceedings, status in 859–64
ranking of 856–8
ratification 855
rights and freedoms, application of 46, 48
Swiss court, infringement by 876
European Court judgments, effect on canton law 870
expression, freedom of 873–4
extradition, detention for 871
fair trial, right to
acquittal, costs on 870
administrative fine, no right to appeal in case of 872
areas outside public law, application to 865
case file, consultation of 868
civil rights and obligations, scope of 862–3, 866
cross-examination by accused, right of 868
final legal check 862
impartiality 867–8, 871
lawyer, assistance of 871–2
official interpretation 865
petty offences, right to be heard 864
procedural issue 863
public law appeals 865
public, proceedings in 872
social insurance disputes 866
Swiss law, adjustment of 864
family law, review of 861–2
Federal Constitution, partial revision in defiance of international law 863
federal legal organization, revision of 859
information, freedom of 874
innocence, presumption of 870, 873
loss of freedom for purposes of assistance 859
marry, right to 873
name, right to 873, 875
national court, human rights cases in 864–9
prisoner's correspondence, rights as to 871–2
property, right to 866
res judicata of Strasbourg judgments, requirement to respect 66
review procedure in 72
social insurance disputes 866
Strasbourg judgments, enforcement of 67–8

Turkey
abuse of rights, remedies for 907
administrative courts, reference to Convention by 895
association, law of 887
Constitution
amendment 906–7
Convention as source of 886, 889
Constitutional Court
constitutional provisions, interpretation of 891
Convention, recognition of status of 891
direct applications of Convention 891–4
international human rights instruments, taking into consideration 892
interpretation of decisions 890
restrictions on freedoms, justification of 892–3
Council of Europe, membership of 879
Council of State, application of Convention by 894
criminal proceedings, length of 902
death penalty 893
democracy, steps towards 913
detention, length of 886, 902
domestic remedies, lack of 913
European Commission and Court of Human Rights, cases before 895–902
European Commission on Human Rights, recognition of competence of 898–901, 911–14

European Convention on Human Rights
adoption, success of 889
assessment 905–6
changes in domestic law in accordance with 908
Constitution, as source of 886, 889
Cyprus cases 896, 913
decisions of national courts, impact on 910–11
derogations 880–1
guidelines, provisions as 887
individual application, right of 890
individual applications 901–2, 911
inter-state applications 895–8
national law, status in 881–4, 890–1
Parliamentary proceedings, status in 884–90
political and legal life, not affecting 880
ratification 879, 889
references to 884–7
violations, remedial action relating to 902–5
fundamental rights and freedoms, repression of 879
High Co-ordinating Committee for Human Rights 909
human rights, remedies 908–9
international treaties
constitutional review 883
domestic status of 881–3, 906
human rights instruments, special status of 884
international human rights instruments, ratification of signature of 880
Kurdish nation, existence of 911
Kurdish, publications in 903–4
martial courts, jurisdiction 903
military administration, government taken over by 897–8
military interventions 880
monist system 882
National Committee for the Decade of Human Rights Education 909
national courts, human rights cases in 890–5
paramilitary practices 914
passport law 888
personal liberty, security of 887
political parties, banning 886
political parties, dissolution of 893–4, 904
press, restriction of freedom of 885
property, right to 887
public servants, dismissal of 888, 894, 904
rights, freedom to claim 887
State Ministry for Human Rights 881
state, administration of 886
states of emergency 887
Strasbourg judgments, enforcement of 69–71
terrorism, combating 888, 908
trade unions, right to form and join 894

Ukraine
administration of justice 931
administrative courts 930–1
appeal, right of 927
Constitution
administration of justice, application in 927
adoption of 916, 929
application of 932
Convention principles, reflecting 919–20
Preamble 917
statehood, development of 917
Constitutional Court, decisions of 925
Council of Europe, membership of 916–17
death penalty 920
defence, right to 928
dwelling place, inviolability of 928
effective remedy, right to 926
European Commission and Court of Human Rights, cases before 928
European Convention on Human Rights
application of 932–3
assessment 929–33
national law, status in 43, 45, 918–24
norms, dissemination of 933
Parliamentary proceedings, status in 924
positive achievements 933
ratification 918
fair trial, right to 921–2
foreign policy-making 917
human rights protection, judicial mechanism 931
independence 916
international law
correlation of domestic legislation with 916
norms, enhancement of role of 916
treaties, publication of 919
judicial system 930–1
judiciary, independence of 930
legal assistance, right to 928
legislation drafting 924
liberty and personal security, right to 920, 922–3
minimum levels of human rights protection 922
national courts, human rights issues before 925–8
official law in 915
private and family life, right to respect for 922

Ukraine (*cont.*):
rule of law 915
Supreme Court, decisions of 926–7
United Kingdom
armed forces, homosexuals in 979–80, 1004
bill of rights
absence of 947–8
pressure for 957
proposal for 1007–8
civil servants, right to join trade union 967–8
common law, development of 951–2
Commonwealth, membership of 943–4
constitutional and ordinary law 947
constitutional court 1005–6
corporal punishment 975–7
domestic courts, absence of remedy before 986
European Convention on Human Rights
assessment 998–1008
domestic constitutional implications 1003–8
domestic courts, use and treatment by 950–6
domestic law, status in 42, 946–60, 962–5
drafting of 936–8
government departments and parliamentary bodies, requirement to observe 992
impact, background to 947
incorporation into law 935, 960–71
judicial support for 957–8
jurisprudence, authoritative nature of 964–5
law-making treaty, as 1003
legal proceedings for breach of 966–71
legal status of 962–5
membership of Commonwealth and European Union, inter-relationship with 943–6
Northern Ireland, treatment in 955
optional provisions 939–41
Parliamentary proceedings, in 991–8
public authority acting incompatibly with 966
ratification 938–41
requirement for government to act according to law 977
reservations 940
Scotland, treatment in 955–6
Spycatcher litigation, discussion in 952–3, 987
statutory incorporation, pressures leading to 956–60
violations, remedial action 974, 1000–3
European Court of Human Rights
cases before 971–91
record before 959, 998–1000
European Union, membership of 945–6
expression, freedom of 954
extradition to face human rights abuses, prohibition 985
foreign policy obligations 941–3
Guernsey, fair trial in 988–9
homosexuals, civil rights of 978–80
House of Lords, review of 997
Human Rights Act
Convention, legal status and priority of 962–5
declaration of incompatibility 963–4
entry into force 960
government departments and parliamentary bodies, requirement to observe Convention 992
locus standi under 968
mass media, application to 970
overall effect of 970
passing of 935
private law sphere, impact in 969
purpose and effect of 960–2
remedies 970–1
victim requirement 967
Human Rights Commission 995–6
human rights reform, consultation paper on 997
human rights treaties 941–3
human rights work, Annual Reports 942
human rights, attitude to 935
individual liberties, protection of 948
individual rights and freedoms, protection of 946–50
international human rights treaties, scrutiny of 995–6
international treaties, status of 949
Labour Party, election of 942
Law Lords, impartiality of 990
local authority, action for libel by 953
newspapers, freedom of expression 987
Northern Ireland, ban on media broadcasts by proscribed organizations 954
parliamentary committee on human rights 993–7
parliamentary scrutiny procedures 993
penal provisions, retrospective 951
police, action for negligence against 985–6
political constitution, replacement of 1005
prisoners, rights of 980–1
psychiatric institutions, rights of persons detained in 983–4
public authority, meaning 968–9
public law system 947
Scottish Parliament 1005

separate legal systems in 1001
telephone tapping 977–8
terrorist suspects, treatment of 982–3
treaty-making process, role of Parliament in 996–7
Wales, government of 1005
written constitution, absence of 948–9
Universal Declaration of Human Rights
ECHR drawing on 9